Ethics: Essential Readings in Moral Theory

Edited by

George Sher

Routledge
Taylor & Francis Group

NEW YORK AND LONDON

First published 2012
by Routledge
711 Third Avenue, New York, NY 10017

Simultaneously published in the UK and ROW
by Routledge
2 Park Square, Milton Park, Abingdon, Oxon OX14 4RN

Routledge is an imprint of the Taylor & Francis Group, an informa business

British Library Cataloguing in Publication Data
A catalogue record for this book is available from the British Library

Library of Congress Cataloging in Publication Data
Ethics : essential readings/edited by George Sher.
p. cm.
Includes bibliographical references and index.
1. Ethics.   I. Sher, George.
BJ1012.E8939 2011
170—dc23

2011031812

ISBN: 978-0-415-78230-2 (hbk)
ISBN: 978-0-415-78231-9 (pbk)

Typeset in Joanna and Bell Gothic
by RefineCatch Limited, Bungay, Suffolk, UK

Printed and bound in the United States of America by Sheridan Books, Inc. (a Sheridan Group Company).

Contents

viii Contents

Permissions

The editor and publishers wish to thank the following for permission to use copyrighted material:

Part 1: Why be Moral?

1. Selection from Plato, *Republic*, trans. G.M.A.Grube, Hackett, 1974, pp. 30–34. Reprinted by permission of Hackett Publishing Company, Inc. All rights reserved.

2. From Feinberg. *Reason and Responsibility*, 4E. © 1978 Wadsworth, a part of Cengage Learning, Inc. Reproduced by permission. www.cengage.com/permissions

5. Selection from Christine Korsgaard, *The Sources of Normativity*, Cambridge UP, 1996, pp. 7–10, 100–105, 120–126, 140–143. © Cambridge University Press 1996, reproduced with permission.

7. Russ Shafer-Landau, "Moral Rationalism," from Russ Shafer-Landau, ed., *Ethical Theory: An Anthology*, Blackwell, 2007, pp. 174–182. Copyright © 2007 Blackwell. Reproduced with permission of Blackwell Publishing Ltd.

Part 2: The Meaning of Moral Language

9. Selections from G.E. Moore, *Principia Ethica*, Cambridge UP, reprinted 1962, p. 5–17. © G. E. Moore, published by Cambridge University Press, reproduced with permission.

10. Selections from A.J. Ayer, *Language, Truth, and Logic*, Dover, no date, pp. 102–113, reproduced with permission.

11. *RULING PASSIONS* by Blackburn (1998) 5700w from pp.48–51, 59–62, 68–73. By permission of Oxford University Press.

12. *MORAL REALISM: A DEFENCE* by Shafer-Landau (2003) 3850w from pp.23–30. By permission of Oxford University Press.

13. Plato, "Euthyphro", from *The Trial and Death of Socrates*, trans. G.M.A. Grube, Hackett, 1975. Reprinted by permission of Hackett Publishing Company, Inc. All rights reserved.

14. "A New Divine Command Theory," Robert Merrihew Adams, *Journal of Religious Ethics*, 7, 2 (Spring 1979). © 1979 Blackwell. Reproduced with permission of Blackwell Publishing Ltd.

Part 3: Morality, Objectivity, and Knowledge

15. Selection from James Rachels, *The Elements of Moral Philosophy*, Random House, 1986, pp. 12–24. © The Mc-Graw Hill Companies, inc, reproduced with permission.

16. *NATURE OF MORALITY* by Harman (1977) pp.3–10 © 1977 by Oxford University Press, Inc. By permission of Oxford University Press, Inc.

17. *Morality, reason, and truth: new essays on the foundations of ethics* by Copp, David. Copyright 1984 Reproduced with permission of ROWMAN & LITTLEFIELD PUBLISHING GROUP, INC. in the format Textbook via Copyright Clearance Center.

18. *ETHICS: INVENTING RIGHT AND WRONG* by J. L. Mackie (Pelican Books, 1977). Copyright © J. L. Mackie, 1977. Reproduced by permission of Penguin Books Ltd.

19. *VIEW FROM NOWHERE* by Nagel (1986) pp.138–156, 162–163 © 1986 by Thomas Nagel. By permission of Oxford University Press, Inc.

20. *MORAL SKEPTICISMS* by Sinnott-Armstrong (2006) 10200w from pp.7–15, 73–81. By permission of Oxford University Press, Inc.

21. George Sher, "But I Could Be Wrong," *Social Philosophy and Policy*, 18, 2 (2001), pp. 64–78. © Social Philosophy and Policy Foundation, published by Cambridge University Press, reproduced with permission.

Part 4: Normative Ethics: Consequentialism

23. Selections from Bernard Williams (coauthor J.J.C. Smart), *Utilitarianism: For and Against*, Cambridge UP, 1973, pp. 110–119. © Cambridge University Press 1973, reproduced with permission.

24. Reprinted by permission of the publisher from A *THEORY OF JUSTICE* by John Rawls, pp. 11–16, 17–21, 22–27, 60–65, 108, 110–111, 152–153, 154–156, 251–257, Cambridge, Mass.: The Belknap Press of Harvard University Press, Copyright © 1971, 1999 by the President and Fellows of Harvard College.

25. Peter Railton, "Alienation, Consequentialism, and the Demands of Morality," *Philosophy and Public Affairs*, 13, 2 (Spring 1984), pp. 134–160 (abridged). © 1984 John Wiley and Sons, Inc. Reproduced with permission of Blackwell Publishing Ltd.

26. Brad Hooker, "Rule-Consequentialism," from Hugh LaFollette, ed., *The Blackwell Guide to Ethical Theory* (Blackwell 2000), pp. 183–204. © 2000 Blackwell. Reproduced with permission of Blackwell Publishing Ltd.

27. "Scalar Morality," Alastair Norcross, in James Dreier, ed., *Contemporary Debates in Moral Theory*, © 2006 Blackwell. Reproduced with permission of Blackwell Publishing Ltd.

28. John Taurek, "Should the Numbers Count?" *Philosophy and Public Affairs* 6, 4 (Summer 1977), pp. 293–295 and 297–310. Reproduced with permission of Blackwell Publishing Ltd.

Part 5: Normative Ethics: Deontology

29. BECK, L.W.; KANT, IMMANUEL, *FOUNDATIONS OF THE METAPHYSICS OF MORALS* & *WHAT IS ENLIGHTENMENT*, 1st Edition, © 1959. Reprinted by permission of Pearson Education, Inc., Upper Saddle River, NJ.

30. David Velleman, "Reading Kant's groundwork," unpublished. Reproduced with permission of the author.

31. Christine Korsgaard, "The Right to Lie: Kant on Dealing with Evil," *Philosophy and Public Affairs*, 15, 4 (Fall 1986), pp. 325–349. © 1986 John Wiley and Sons, Inc. Reproduced with permission of Blackwell Publishing Ltd.

32. *ETHIC* edited by Singer (1994) Chp. "Maria Von Herber's Challenge to Kant" pp.281–293. By permission of Oxford University Press, Inc.

33. Reprinted by permission of the publisher from *A THEORY OF JUSTICE* by John Rawls, pp. 11–16, 17–21, 22–27, 60–65, 108, 110–111, 152–153, 154–156, 251–257, Cambridge, Mass.: The Belknap Press of Harvard University Press, Copyright © 1971, 1999 by the President and Fellows of Harvard College.

34. Thomas Scanlon, "Contractualism and Utilitarianism," from Amartya Sen and Bernard Williams, eds., *Utilitarianism and Beyond* (Cambridge UP, 1982), pp. 103–128. © Maison des Sciences de l'Homme and Cambridge University Press 1982, reproduced with permission.

35. *RIGHT AND GOOD* by Ross (1965) 6100w from pp.17–47. By permission of Oxford University Press, Inc.

36. *ETHICS WITHOUT PRINCIPLES* by Dancy (2004) pp. 73–79, 81–83, 85–88. By permission of Oxford University Press, Inc.

Part 6: Virtue and Character

37. Selection from Aristotle, "Nicomachean Ethics", from *The Ethics of Aristotle*, trans. J. A.K. Thomson, Routledge, material excerpted from the text between p. 41 and p. 171

38. Martha Nussbaum, "Non-Relative Virtues: An Aristotelian Account," *Midwest Studies in Philosophy* XIII (U. of Notre Dame Press), 1988, pp. 32–53. Reprinted with permission from Notre Dame University Press.

39. *VIRTUE, VICE, VALUE* by Hurka (2001) 10000w from pp.3–23. © 2000 by Thomas Micael Hurka. By permission of Oxford University Press, Inc.

40. *BEYOND GOOD AND EVIL: PRELUDE TO A PHILOSOPHY OF THE FUTURE* by Friedrich Nietzsche, translated by R. J. Hollingdale (Penguin Classics, 1973). © R. J. Hollingdale, 1973. Reproduced by permission of Penguin Books Ltd. / From *THE BIRTH OF TRAGEDY AND THE GENEALOGY OF MORALS* by Friedrich Nietzsche, translated by Francis Golffing, copyright © 1956 by Doubleday, a division of Random House, Inc. Used by permission of Doubleday, a division of Random House, Inc.

Part 7: Value and Well-being

Part 8: Responsibility and Moral Psychology

57. Thomas Nagel, "Moral Luck," *Proceedings of the Aristoleian Society*, supplementary vol. I. (1976). Reprinted by courtesy of the Editor of the Aristotelian Society: © 1976.

58. Shaun Nichols and Joshua Knobe, "Moral Responsibility and Determinism: The Cognitive Science of Folk Intuitions," *Nous* XLI, 4 (December 2007), pp. 663–685. Reproduced with permission of John Wiley and Sons.

59. Sinnott-Armstrong, Walter, ed., *Moral Psychology, Volume 3: The Neuroscience of Morality: Emotion, Brain Disorders, and Development*, pp. 12,550 word excerpt from pages 35–36, 40–66, © 2007 Massachusetts Institute of Technology, by permission of The MIT Press.

Part 9: Applications

60. Judith Jarvis Thompson, "A Defense of Abortion," *Philosophy and Public Affairs*, 1, 1 (Fall 1971), pp. 47–66. © 1971 John Wiley and Sons, Inc. Reproduced with permission of Blackwell Publishing Ltd.

61. George Sher, "Subsidized Abortion: Moral Rights and Moral Compromise," *Philosophy and Public Affairs*, 10, 4 (Fall 1981), pp. 361–372, Reproduced with permission of Blackwell Publishing Ltd.

62. Peter Singer, "Famine, Affluence, and Morality," *Philosophy and Public Affairs* 1, 3 (Spring 1972), pp. 229–243. © 1972 John Wiley and Sons, Inc. Reproduced with permission of Blackwell Publishing Ltd.

63. Richard Miller, "Beneficence, Duty, and Distance," *Philosophy and Public Affairs*, 32, 4 (Fall 2004), pp. 357–366 and 370–383. Reproduced with permission from John Wiley and Sons.

64. R. M. Hare, "What Is Wrong With Slavery", *Philosophy and Public Affairs*, 8, 2 (Winter 1979), pp. 103–121. © 1979 John Wiley and Sons, Inc. Reproduced with permission of Blackwell Publishing Ltd.

65. Onora O'Neill, "Between Consenting Adults", *Philosophy and Public Affairs*, 14, 3 (Summer 1985), pp. 252–277. Reproduced with permission of Blackwell Publishing Ltd.

66. Thomas Nagel, "Death," in Thomas Nagel, *Mortal Questions*, Cambridge 1979, pp. 1–10 (4700 words). © Cambridge University Press 1979, reproduced with permission.

Every effort has been made to contact copyright holders for their permission to reprint material in this book. The publishers would be grateful to hear from any copyright holder who is not here acknowledged and will undertake to rectify any errors or omissions in future editions of this book.

Preface

Some fifteen years ago, I edited the second edition of an anthology titled *Moral Philosophy: Selected Readings*. My aim in that book was to bring together as much as possible of the best available work in ethics – work that runs the gamut from the abstruse questions of meta-ethics to the urgent problems of applied ethics. I was proud of the book when it appeared, and I remain proud of it today. However, much excellent work has appeared in the intervening years, and I have been thinking for some time about what an updated version of the book might look like. The current volume answers that question.

Not surprisingly, the volume's selections represent a variety of positions that have emerged, and a variety of authors whose work has come to prominence or achieved more of it over the last fifteen years. These include, but are far from exhausted by, Christine Korsgaard's work on normativity, Thomas Scanlon's contractualism, Jonathan Dancy's particularism, Alastair Norcross's scalar consequentialism, Thomas Hurka's perfectionism, and the recent trend of drawing on empirical findings as it is exemplified by John Doris, Shaun Nichols and Joshua Knobe, and Joshua Greene.

In the course of deciding which selections to include, I have had to consider a number of different factors, and it may be helpful to make some of these explicit. One obviously important question was which topics and authors have figured importantly in the recent literature. Two others were, first, the sheer quality of the work as I saw it, and, second the quality of the writing and the work's accessibility to students. However, a further and less obvious consideration, which also loomed large for me, was simply whether I found a selection fun to read. Although there certainly were trade-offs among these considerations, I am pleased to report that that there was more confluence, and less conflict, than I might have predicted.

Acknowledgments

While putting the book together, I have benefited from the assistance and advice of a number of people. In making the selections and assembling the manuscript, I was ably assisted by Krisina Zuniga, Benjamin Mayo, and Michael Barkasi. In the review stage, I received helpful comments from Chris Heathwood at University of Colorado at Boulder, Bruce Hauptli at Florida International University, and Kenneth Shockley at the University of Buffalo. At all stages, I have received help, advice, and encouragement from Tony Bruce, the philosophy acquisitions editor at Routledge, and from Jill D'Urso, Development Editor. They have both been a joy to work with, and I am delighted to acknowledge them here.

SECTION I

Why be moral?

INTRODUCTION TO SECTION I

M ORALITY REQUIRES, AMONG other things, that we keep our promises and treat others fairly. At least on the surface, acting in these ways is not always in our interest; for we can often gain advantages by breaking promises or being unfair. Why, in such cases, should we be moral?

Plato raises this question starkly in Chapter 1. He tells the story of a shepherd who finds a ring that makes him invisible. While wearing the ring, the shepherd commits adultery with the king's wife, kills the king with her help, and takes over the kingdom. Plato also asks us to compare the prosperity that a bad man with a reputation for virtue would enjoy with the misery that a good man with a reputation for vice would suffer. His point is that in these cases and many others, wrongdoing appears to pay. When it does, why not act wrongly?

To ask why we should do something is to ask what reason we have to do it. Thus, in asking "Why be moral?", we are asking whether we always have reason to conform to morality's demands. Many philosophers believe that only what can actually motivate a person can be a reason for him. Some also believe that people are motivated only by self-interest. If both claims are true, then the only way to show that we always have reason to act morally is to show that acting morally is always really in our interest.

The view that we are motivated only by self-interest is known as *psychological egoism.* Thomas Hobbes endorses a version of this view in Chapter 3, and it is discussed in some detail by Joel Feinberg in Chapter 2. As Feinberg points out, psychological egoists disagree both about what self-interest is and about why it alone can provide us with motivation. As Feinberg also points out, there are powerful objections to all forms of psychological egoism. If Feinberg is right about this, then someone who wishes to establish that we always have reason to act morally does not have to show that acting morally is always really in our interest. Still, even if other explanations of why we should act morally are possible, we may still think that this one holds the most promise.

One philosopher who argues that acting morally is always in our interest is Hobbes. In Hobbes's view, we would *not* have reason to be moral if we did not live under a government; for in a state of nature, "every man has a right to every thing." However, when we do enjoy the security of government, we can best advance our interests by adhering consistently to a familiar set of rules. These are the moral rules which assert, among other things, that we should keep our agreements, avoid needless cruelty, and in general treat others as we want them to treat us. In arguing that we always have reason to obey such rules, Hobbes is not denying that we can sometimes gain advantages by breaking them. Instead, he contends that success in gaining such advantages is sufficiently uncertain, and the penalty for failure sufficiently high, that it is never rational to take the chance.

By arguing in this way, Hobbes tries to show that being moral is in each person's interest. However, even if Hobbes is wrong about this, morality may still be in each person's interest in another sense. As long as each person gains more when others comply with morality's rules than he loses by complying himself, each person may do better if everyone (including himself) complies than if no one does. Even if true, this would not mean that it is always in each person's interest to obey the rules of morality himself. However, as David Gauthier notes in Chapter 4, it would mean that if everyone broke the rules whenever it was in his interest, the resulting situation would be worse for everyone. Even if immorality is individually rational, it therefore may be collectively irrational.

Of the chapters discussed so far, each bears on the question of whether we have self-interested reasons to be moral. But even if we lack such reasons, we may have reasons to be moral that are *not* grounded in self-interest. This view is defended by Christine Korsgaard, who argues in Chapter 5 that our reasons for being moral are rooted in our agency. Korsgaard points out that as deliberating agents, we cannot avoid trying to ascertain what we have reason to do, and that in seeking such reasons, we are inevitably thrown back on our views of who we are. Whenever we think of ourselves as a parent, a member of a profession, or simply a human being, we find that there are some things which our "practical identity" requires of us and others it will not allow us to do. Moreover, when we realize that everyone else has the same need to assume and act on a practical identity – when we see that this is a reflection of our shared humanity – we also realize that the reasons of other people are as important as our own. It is because morality treats every person's reasons as equally important that we have reason to obey its rules.

By tracing our reasons to act morally to the humanity we share with others, Korsgaard elaborates a line of argument that was famously advanced by Immanuel Kant. (For Kant's own version of the argument, see Chapter 29.) However, according to Philippa Foot (Chapter 6), the Kantian approach fails. Foot contends that there is nothing inconsistent or irrational about attaching weight to one's own concerns but not to the concerns of others. She argues, as well, that no other explanation of why everyone ought to act morally is likely to fare any better. Instead of seeking such an explanation, we should frankly acknowledge that only people who *want* to act morally have reason to do the right thing.

In taking this position, Foot is not maintaining that all reasons to act morally are self-interested. As she herself stresses, many people have non-self-interested desires to relieve the suffering of others and to deal justly with them. However, Foot does share with most self-interest theorists the conviction that not everyone has reason to be moral. Although many view morality as binding on all persons – in Kantian terms, many believe that its demands are categorical rather than hypothetical – Foot views this belief as an illusion. She argues that when we feel the pull of morality's demands, it is because we are already committed to morality.

In the section's final chapter, Russ Shafer-Landau takes issue with Foot's position. He argues in Chapter 7 that morality is intrinsically reason-giving – that is, that we necessarily have reason to do whatever it requires. To establish this claim, he considers, and argues against, a number of prominent objections to it. Of these objections, one

appeals to the familiar premise that all reasons must be capable of providing us with motivation; another takes as its starting point the equally familiar claim only self-interest can provide us with reasons; and yet a third questions the very possibility of an intrinsically reason-giving fact. In each case, Shafer-Landau maintains that the objection under discussion is not decisive. Although there are indeed problems with the view that we always have reason to act morally, these are no greater than the problems that confront the claim that we always have reason to form our beliefs on the basis of evidence.

Plato

THE RING OF GYGES

WHEN I HAD said this I thought I had done with the discussion, but evidently this was only a prelude. Glaucon on this occasion too showed that boldness which is characteristic of him, and refused to accept Thrasymachus' abandoning the argument. He said: Do you, Socrates, want to appear to have persuaded us, or do you want truly to convince us that it is better in every way to be just than unjust?

I would certainly wish to convince you truly, I said, if I could.

Well, he said, you are certainly not attaining your wish. Tell me, do you think there is a kind of good which we welcome not because we desire its consequences but for its own sake: joy, for example, and all the harmless pleasures which have no further consequences beyond the joy which one finds in them?

Certainly, said I, I think there is such a good.

Further, there is the good which we welcome for its own sake and also for its consequences, knowledge for example and sight and health. Such things we somehow welcome on both counts.

Yes, said I.

Are you also aware of a third kind, he asked, such as physical training, being treated when ill, the practice of medicine, and other ways of making money? We should say that these are wearisome but beneficial to us; we should not want them for their own sake, but because of the rewards and other benefits which result from them.

There is certainly such a third kind, I said, but why do you ask?

Under which of these headings do you put justice? he asked.

I would myself put it in the finest class, I said, that which is to be welcomed both for itself and for its consequences by any man who is to be blessed with happiness.

That is not the opinion of the many, he said; they would put it in the wearisome class, to be pursued for the rewards and popularity which come from a good reputation, but to be avoided in itself as being difficult.

I know that is the general opinion, I said. Justice has now for some time been objected to by Thrasymachus on this score while injustice was extolled, but it seems I am a slow learner.

Come then, he said, listen to me also to see whether you are still of the same opinion, for I think that Thrasymachus gave up before he had to, charmed by you as by a snake charmer. I am not yet satisfied by the demonstration on either side. I am eager to hear the nature of each, of justice and injustice, and what effect its presence has upon the soul. I want to leave out of account the rewards and consequences of each. So, if you agree, I will do the following: I will renew the argument of Thrasymachus; I will first state what people consider the nature and origin of justice; secondly, that all who practise it do so unwillingly as being something necessary but not good; thirdly, that they have good reason to

do so, for, according to what people say, the life of the unjust man is much better than that of the just.

It is not that I think so, Socrates, but I am perplexed and my ears are deafened listening to Thrasymachus and innumerable other speakers; I have never heard from anyone the sort of defence of justice that I want to hear, proving that it is better than injustice. I want to hear it praised for itself, and I think I am most likely to hear this from you. Therefore I am going to speak at length in praise of the unjust life and in doing so I will show you the way I want to hear you denouncing injustice and praising justice. See whether you want to hear what I suggest.

I want it more than anything else, I said. Indeed, what subject would a man of sense talk and hear about more often with enjoyment?

Splendid, he said, then listen while I deal with the first subject I mentioned: the nature and origin of justice.

They say that to do wrong is naturally good, to be wronged is bad, but the suffering of injury so far exceeds in badness the good of inflicting it that when men have done wrong to each other and suffered it, and have had a taste of both, those who are unable to avoid the latter and practise the former decide that it is profitable to come to an agreement with each other neither to inflict injury nor to suffer it. As a result they begin to make laws and covenants, and the law's command they call lawful and just. This, they say, is the origin and essence of justice; it stands between the best and the worst, the best being to do wrong without paying the penalty and the worst to be wronged without the power of revenge. The just then is a mean between two extremes; it is welcomed and honoured because of men's lack of the power to do wrong. The man who has that power, the real man, would not make a compact with anyone not to inflict injury or suffer it. For him that would be madness. This then, Socrates, is, according to their argument, the nature and origin of justice.

Even those who practise justice do so against their will because they lack the power to do wrong. This we could realize very clearly if we imagined ourselves granting to both the just and the unjust the freedom to do whatever they liked. We could then follow both of them and observe where their desires led them, and we would catch the just man redhanded travelling the same road as the unjust. The reason is the desire for undue gain which every organism by nature pursues as a good, but the law forcibly sidetracks him to honour equality. The freedom I just mentioned would most easily occur if these men had the power which they say the ancestor of the Lydian Gyges possessed. The story is that he was a shepherd in the service of the ruler of Lydia. There was a violent rainstorm and an earthquake which broke open the ground and created a chasm at the place where he was tending sheep. Seeing this and marvelling, he went down into it. He saw, besides many other wonders of which we are told, a hollow bronze horse. There were window-like openings in it; he climbed through them and caught sight of a corpse which seemed of more than human stature, wearing nothing but a ring of gold on its finger. This ring the shepherd put on and came out. He arrived at the usual monthly meeting which reported to the king on the state of the flocks, wearing the ring. As he was sitting among the others he happened to twist the hoop of the ring towards himself, to the inside of his hand, and as he did this he became invisible to those sitting near him and they went on talking as if he had gone. He marvelled at this and, fingering the ring, he turned the hoop outward again and became visible. Perceiving this he tested whether the ring had this power and so it happened: if he turned the hoop inwards he became invisible, but was visible when he turned it outwards. When he realized this, he at once arranged to become one of the messengers to the king. He went, committed adultery with the king's wife, attacked the king with her help, killed him, and took over the kingdom.

Now if there were two such rings, one worn by the just man, the other by the unjust, no one, as these people think, would be so incorruptible that he would stay on the path of justice or bring himself to keep away from other people's property and not touch it, when he could with impunity take whatever he wanted from the market, go into houses and have sexual relations with anyone he wanted, kill anyone, free all those he wished from prison, and do the other things which would make him like a god among men. His actions would be in no way different from those of the other and they would both follow the same path. This, some would say, is a great proof that no one is just willingly[1] but under compulsion, so that justice is not one's private good, since wherever either thought he could do wrong with impunity he would do so. Every man believes that injustice is much more profitable to himself than justice, and any exponent of this argument will say that he is right. The man who did not wish to do wrong with that opportunity, and did not touch other people's property, would be thought by those who knew it to be very foolish and miserable. They would praise him in public, thus deceiving one another, for fear of being wronged. So much for my second topic.

As for the choice between the lives we are discussing, we shall be able to make a correct judgment about it only if we put the most just man and the most unjust man face to face; otherwise we cannot do so. By face to face I mean this: let us grant to the unjust the fullest degree of injustice and to the just the fullest justice, each being perfect in his own pursuit. First, the unjust man will act as clever craftsmen do—a top navigator for example or physician distinguishes what his craft can do and what it cannot; the former he will undertake, the latter he will pass by, and when he slips he can put things right. So the unjust man's correct attempts at wrongdoing must remain secret; the one who is caught must be considered a poor performer, for the extreme of injustice is to have a reputation for justice, and our perfectly unjust man must be granted perfection in injustice. We must not take this from him, but we must allow that, while committing the greatest crimes, he has provided himself with the greatest reputation for justice; if he makes a slip he must be able to put it right; he must be a sufficiently persuasive speaker if some wrongdoing of his is made public; he must be able to use force, where force is needed, with the help of his courage, his strength, and the friends and wealth with which he has provided himself.

Having described such a man, let us now in our argument put beside him the just man, simple as he is and noble, who, as Aeschylus put it,[2] does not wish to appear just but to be so. We must take away his reputation, for a reputation for justice would bring him honour and rewards, and it would then not be clear whether he is what he is for justice's sake or for the sake of rewards and honour. We must strip him of everything except justice and make him the complete opposite of the other. Though he does no wrong, he must have the greatest reputation for wrongdoing so that he may be tested for justice by not weakening under ill repute and its consequences. Let him go his incorruptible way until death with a reputation for injustice throughout his life, just though he is, so that our two men may reach the extremes, one of justice, the other of injustice, and let them be judged as to which of the two is the happier.

Whew! My dear Glaucon, I said, what a mighty scouring you have given those two characters, as if they were statues in a competition.

I do the best I can, he replied. The two being such as I have described, there should be no difficulty in following the argument through as to what kind of life awaits each of them, but it must be said. And if what I say sounds rather boorish, Socrates, realize that it is not I who speak, but those who praise injustice as preferable to justice. They will say that the just man in these circumstances will be whipped, stretched on the rack, imprisoned, have his eyes burnt out,

and, after suffering every kind of evil, he will be impaled and realize that one should not want to be just but to appear so. Indeed, Aeschylus' words are far more correctly applied to the unjust than to the just, for we shall be told that the unjust man pursues a course which is based on truth and not on appearances; he does not want to appear but to be unjust:

> He harvests in his heart a deep furrow
> from which good counsels grow.

He rules his city because of his reputation for justice, he marries into any family he wants to, he gives his children in marriage to anyone he wishes, he has contractual and other associations with anyone he may desire, and, beside all these advantages, he benefits in the pursuit of gain because he does not scruple to practise injustice. In any contest, public or private, he is the winner, getting the better of his enemies and accumulating wealth; he benefits his friends and does harm to his enemies. To the gods he offers grand sacrifices and gifts which will satisfy them, he can serve the gods much better than the just man, and also such men as he wants to, with the result that he is likely to be dearer to the gods. This is what they say, Socrates, that both from gods and men the unjust man secures a better life than the just.

After Glaucon has thus spoken I again had it in mind to say something in reply, but his brother Adeimantus intervened: You surely do not think that enough has been said from this point of view, Socrates?

Why not? said I.

The most important thing, that should have been said, has not been said, he replied.

Well then, I said, let brother stand by brother. If Glaucon has omitted something, you come to his help. Yet what he has said is sufficient to throw me and to make me incapable of coming to the help of justice.

Nonsense, he said. Hear what more I have to say, for we should also go fully into the arguments opposite to those he mentioned, those which praise justice and censure injustice, so that what I take to be Glaucon's intention may be clearer. When fathers speak to their sons, they say one must be just—and so do all who care for them, but they do not praise justice itself, only the high reputations it leads to, in order that the son, thought to be just, shall enjoy those public offices, marriages, and the rest which Glaucon mentioned, as they belong to the just man because of his high repute; they lay even greater emphasis on the results of reputation. They add popularity granted by the gods, and mention abundant blessings which, they say, the gods grant to the pious. So too the noble Hesiod and Homer declare,[3] the one that for the just the gods make "the oak trees bear acorns at the top and bees in the middle and their fleecy sheep are heavy with their burden of wool" and many other blessings of like nature. The other says similar things:

> (like the fame) of a goodly king who, in his
> piety,
> upholds justice; for him the black earth
> bears wheat
> and barley and the trees are heavy with fruit;
> his
> sheep bear lambs continually and the sea
> provides its fish.

Musaeus[4] and his son grant from the gods more robust pleasures to the just. Their words lead the just to the underworld, and, seating them at table, provide them with a banquet of the saints, crown them with wreaths, and make them spend all their time drinking, as if they thought that the finest reward of virtue was perpetual drunkenness. Others stretch the rewards of virtue from the gods even further, for they say that the children and the children's children and the posterity of the pious man who keeps his oaths will survive into the future. Thus, and in other such ways, do they praise justice. The impious and unjust they bury in mud in the

underworld, they force them to carry water in a sieve, they bring them into disrepute while still living, and they attribute to them all the punishments which Glaucon enumerated in the case of the just with a reputation for injustice, but they have nothing else to say. This then is the way people praise and blame justice and injustice.

Besides this, Socrates, look at another kind of argument which is spoken in private, and also by the poets, concerning justice and injustice. All go on repeating with one voice that justice and moderation are beautiful, but certainly difficult and burdensome, while incontinence and injustice are sweet and easy, and shameful only by repute and by law. They add that unjust deeds are for the most part more profitable than just ones. They freely declare, both in private and in public, that the wicked who have wealth and other forms of power are happy. They honour them but pay neither honour nor attention to the weak and the poor, though they agree that these are better men than the others.

What men say about the gods and virtue is the most amazing of all, namely that the gods too inflict misfortunes and a miserable life upon many good men, and the opposite fate upon their opposites. Begging priests and prophets frequent the doors of the rich and persuade them that they possess a god-given power to remedy by sacrifices and incantations at pleasant festivals any crime that the rich man or one of his ancestors may have committed. Moreover, if one wishes to harass some enemy, then at little expense he will be able to harm the just and the unjust alike, for by means of spells and enchantments they can persuade the gods to serve them. They bring the poets as witnesses to all this, some harping on the easiness of vice, that

Vice is easy to choose in abundance, the
    path is
smooth and it dwells very near, but sweat is
    placed by
the gods on the way to virtue,

and a path which is long, rough, and steep;[5] others quote Homer as a witness that the gods can be influenced by men, for he too said:[6]

the gods themselves can be swayed by
    prayer, for
supplicant men can turn them from their
    purpose by
sacrifices and gentle prayers, by libations and
    burnt offerings
whenever anyone has transgressed and
    sinned.

They offer in proof a mass of writings by Musaeus and Orpheus, offspring, as they say, of Selene and the Muses. In accordance with these they perform their ritual and persuade not only individuals but whole cities that, both for the living and for the dead, there are absolutions and purifications for sin by means of sacrifices and pleasurable, playful rituals. These they call initiations which free from punishment yonder, where a dreadful fate awaits the uninitiated.

When all such sayings about the attitudes of men and gods toward virtue and vice are so often repeated, what effect, my dear Socrates, do we think they have upon the minds of our youth? One who is naturally talented and able, like a bee flitting from flower to flower gathering honey, to flit over these sayings and to gather from them an impression of what kind of man he should be and of how best to travel along the road of life, would surely repeat to himself the saying of Pindar: should I by justice or by crooked deceit scale this high wall and thus live my life fenced off from other men? The advantages said to be mine if I am just are of no use, I am told, unless I also appear so; while the troubles and penalties are obvious. The unjust man, on the other hand, who has secured for himself a reputation for justice, lives, they tell me, the life of a god. Therefore, since appearance, as the wise men tell me, forcibly overwhelms truth and controls happiness, this is altogether the way I should live. I should build around me a

façade that gives the illusion of justice to those who approach me and keep behind this the greedy and crafty fox of the wise Archilochus.[7]

"But surely" someone objects, "it is not easy for vice to remain hidden always." We shall reply that nothing is easy which is of great import. Nevertheless, this is the way we must go if we are to be happy, and follow along the lines of all we have been told. To protect our secret we shall form sworn conspiratorial societies and political clubs. Besides, there are teachers of persuasion who make one clever in dealing with assemblies and with the courts. This will enable us to use persuasion here and force there, so that we can secure our own advantage without penalty.

"But one cannot force the gods nor have secrets from them." Well, if either they do not exist or do not concern themselves with human affairs, why should we worry about secrecy? If they do exist and do concern themselves, we have heard about them and know them from no other source than our laws and our genealogising poets, and these are the very men who tell us that the gods can be persuaded and influenced by gentle prayers and by offerings. We should believe both or neither. If we believe them, we should do wrong and then offer sacrifices from the proceeds. If we are just, we shall not be punished by the gods but we shall lose the profits of injustice. If we are unjust we shall get the benefit of sins and transgressions, and afterwards persuade the gods by prayer and escape without punishment. "But in Hades we will pay the penalty for the crimes committed here, either ourselves or our children's children." "My friend," the young man will reply as he does his reckoning, "mystery rites have great potency, and so have the gods of absolution, as the greatest cities tell us, and the children of the gods who have become poets and prophets tell us that this is so."

For what reason then should we still choose justice rather than the greatest injustice? If we practise the latter with specious decorum we shall do well at the hands of gods and of men; we shall live and die as we intend, for so both the many and the eminent tell us. From all that has been said, Socrates, what possibility is there that any man of power, be it the power of mind or of wealth, of body or of birth, will be willing to honour justice and not laugh aloud when he hears it praised? And surely any man who can show that what we have said is untrue and has full knowledge that justice is best, will be full of forgiveness, and not of anger, for the unjust. He knows that only a man of godlike character whom injustice disgusts, or one who has superior knowledge, avoids injustice, and that no other man is willingly just, but through cowardice or old age or some other weakness objects to injustice, because he cannot practise it. That this is so is obvious, for the first of these men to acquire power is the first to do wrong as much as he is able.

The only reason for all this talk, Socrates, which led to Glaucon's speech and mine, is to say to you: Socrates, you strange man, not one of all of you who profess to praise justice, beginning with the heroes of old, whose words are left to us, to the present day—not one has ever blamed injustice or praised justice in any other way than by mentioning the reputations, honours, and rewards which follow justice. No one has ever adequately described, either in poetry or in private conversation, what the very presence of justice or injustice in his soul does to a man even if it remains hidden from gods and men; one is the greatest evil the soul can contain, while the other, justice, is the greatest good. If you had treated the subject in this way and had persuaded us from youth, we should then not be watching one another to see we do no wrong, but every man would be his own best guardian and he would be afraid lest, by doing wrong, he live with the greatest evil.

Thrasymachus or anyone else might say what we have said, and perhaps more in discussing justice and injustice. I believe they would be vulgarly distorting the effect of each. To be quite

frank with you, it is because I am eager to hear the opposite from you that I speak with all the emphasis I can muster. So do not merely give us a theoretical proof that justice is better than injustice, but tell us how each, in and by itself, affects a man, the one for good, the other for evil. Follow Glaucon's advice and do not take reputations into account, for if you do not deprive them of true reputation and attach false reputations to them, we shall say that you are not praising justice but the reputation for it, or blaming injustice but the appearance of it, that you are encouraging one to be unjust in secret, and that you agree with Thrasymachus that the just is another's good, the advantage of the stronger, while the unjust is one's own advantage and profit, though not the advantage of the weaker.

Since you have agreed that justice is one of the greatest goods, those which are worthy of attainment for their consequences, but much more for their own sake—sight, hearing, knowledge, health, and all other goods which are creative by what they are and not by what they seem—do praise justice in this regard: in what way does its very possession benefit a man and injustice harm him? Leave rewards and reputations for others to praise.

For others would satisfy me if they praised justice and blamed injustice in this way, extolling the rewards of the one and denigrating those of the other, but from you, unless you tell me to, I will not accept it, because you have spent your whole life investigating this and nothing else. Do not, therefore, give us a merely theoretical proof that justice is better than injustice, but tell us what effect each has in and by itself, the one for good, the other for evil, whether or not it be hidden from gods and men.

I had always admired the character of Glaucon and Adeimantus, and on this occasion I was quite delighted with them as I listened and I said: You are the sons of a great man, and Glaucon's lover began his elegy well when he wrote, celebrating the repute you gained at the battle of Megara:

Sons of Ariston, godlike offspring of a
    famous man.

That seems well deserved, my friends; you must be divinely inspired if you are not convinced that injustice is better than justice, and yet can speak on its behalf as you have done. And I do believe that you are really unconvinced by your own words. I base this belief on my knowledge of the way you live, for, if I had only your words to go by, I would not trust you. The more I trust you, however, the more I am at a loss what to do. I do not see how I can be of help; I feel myself incapable. I see a proof of this in the fact that I thought what I said to Thrasymachus showed that justice is better than injustice, but you refuse to accept this as adequate. On the other hand I do not see how I can refuse my help, for I fear it is even impious to be present when justice is being charged and to fail to come to her help as long as there is breath in one's body and one is still able to speak. So the best course is to give her any assistance I can.

Notes

1 This of course directly contradicts the famous Socratic paradox that no one is willingly bad and that people do wrong because they have not the knowledge to do right, which is virtue.—TRANS.

2 In *Seven Against Thebes*, 592–94, it is said of Amphiaraus that "he did not wish to appear but to be the best," and it continues with the words quoted below: "He harbours in his heart a deep furrow, from which good counsels grow."—TRANS.

3 The two quotations which immediately follow are from Hesiod's *Works and Days*, 232–33, and Homer, *Odyssey*, 19, 109.—TRANS.

4 Musaeus was a legendary poet closely connected with the mystery religion of Orphism.—TRANS.

5 Hesiod, *Works and Days*, 287–89.—TRANS.

6 Homer, *Iliad*, 9, 497–501.—TRANS.

7 I.e. the fox mentioned by Archilochus. The fable in question is not extant.—TRANS.

Joel Feinberg

PSYCHOLOGICAL EGOISM

The theory

1. "Psychological egoism" is the name given to a theory widely held by ordinary men, and at one time almost universally accepted by political economists, philosophers, and psychologists, according to which all human actions when properly understood can be seen to be motivated by selfish desires. More precisely, psychological egoism is the doctrine that the only thing anyone is capable of desiring or pursuing ultimately (as an end in itself) is his *own* self-interest. No psychological egoist denies that men sometimes do desire things other than their own welfare—the happiness of other people, for example; but all psychological egoists insist that men are capable of desiring the happiness of others only when they take it to be a *means* to their own happiness. In short, purely altruistic and benevolent actions and desires do not exist; but people sometimes appear to be acting unselfishly and disinterestedly when they take the interests of others to be means to the promotion of their own self-interest.

2. This theory is called *psychological* egoism to indicate that it is not a theory about what *ought* to be the case, but rather about what, as a matter of fact, *is* the case. That is, the theory claims to be a description of psychological facts, not a prescription of ethical ideals. It asserts, however, not merely that all men do as a contingent matter of fact "put their own interests first," but also that

they are capable of nothing else, human nature being what it is. Universal selfishness is not just an accident or a coincidence on this view; rather, it is an unavoidable consequence of psychological laws.

The theory is to be distinguished from another doctrine, so-called "ethical egoism," according to which all men *ought* to pursue their own well-being. This doctrine, being a prescription of what *ought* to be the case, makes no claim to be a psychological theory of human motives; hence the word "ethical" appears in its name to distinguish it from *psychological* egoism.

3. There are a number of types of motives and desires which might reasonably be called "egoistic" or "selfish," and corresponding to each of them is a possible version of psychological egoism. Perhaps the most common version of the theory is that apparently held by Jeremy Bentham.[1] According to this version, all persons have only one ultimate motive in all their voluntary behavior and that motive is a selfish one; more specifically, it is one particular kind of selfish motive—namely, a desire for one's own *pleasure*. According to this version of the theory, "the only kind of ultimate desire is the desire to get or to prolong pleasant experiences, and to avoid or to cut short unpleasant experiences for oneself."[2] This form of psychological egoism is often given the cumbersome name—*psychological egoistic hedonism*.

Prima facie reasons in support of the theory

4. Psychological egoism has seemed plausible to many people for a variety of reasons, of which the following are typical.

a. "Every action of mine is prompted by motives or desires or impulses which are *my* motives and not somebody else's. This fact might be expressed by saying that whenever I act I am always pursuing my own ends or trying to satisfy my own desires. And from this we might pass on to—'I am always pursuing something for myself or seeking my own satisfaction.' Here is what seems like a proper description of a man acting selfishly, and if the description applies to all actions of all men, then it follows that all men in all their actions are selfish."[3]

b. It is a truism that when a person gets what he wants he characteristically feels pleasure. This has suggested to many people that what we really want in every case is our own pleasure, and that we pursue other things only as a means.

c. *Self-Deception.* Often we deceive ourselves into thinking that we desire something fine or noble when what we really want is to be thought well of by others or to be able to congratulate ourselves, or to be able to enjoy the pleasures of a good conscience. It is a well-known fact that people tend to conceal their true motives from themselves by camouflaging them with words like "virtue," "duty," etc. Since we are so often misled concerning both, our own real motives and the real motives of others, is it not reasonable to suspect that we might *always* be deceived when we think motives disinterested and altruistic? . . .

d. *Moral education.* Morality, good manners, decency, and other virtues must be teachable. Psychological egoists often notice that moral education and the inculcation of manners usually utilize what Bentham calls the "sanctions of pleasure and pain." Children are made to acquire the civilizing virtues only by the method of enticing rewards and painful punishments. Much the same is true of the history of the race. People in general have been inclined to behave well only when it is made plain to them that there is "something in it for them." Is it not then highly probable that just such a mechanism of human motivation as Bentham describes must be presupposed by our methods of moral education?

Critique of psychological egoism: confusions in the arguments

5. *Non-Empirical Character of the Arguments.* If the arguments of the psychological egoist consisted for the most part of carefully acquired empirical evidence (well-documented reports of controlled experiments, surveys, interviews, laboratory data, and so on), then the critical philosopher would have no business carping at them. After all, since psychological egoism purports to be a scientific theory of human motives, it is the concern of the experimental psychologist, not the philosopher, to accept or reject it. But as a matter of fact, empirical evidence of the required sort is seldom presented in support of psychological egoism. Psychologists, on the whole, shy away from generalizations about human motives which are so sweeping and so vaguely formulated that they are virtually incapable of scientific testing. It is usually the "armchair scientist" who holds the theory of universal selfishness, and his usual arguments are either based simply on his "impressions" or else are largely of a nonempirical sort. The latter are often shot full of a very subtle kind of logical confusion, and this makes their criticism a matter of special interest to the analytic philosopher.

6. The psychological egoist's first argument (see 4a) is a good example of logical confusion. It

begins with a truism—namely, that all of my motives and desires are *my* motives and desires and not someone else's. (Who would deny this?) But from this simple tautology nothing whatever concerning the nature of my motives or the objective of my desires can possibly follow. The fallacy of this argument consists in its violation of the general logical rule that analytic statements (tautologies)[*] cannot entail synthetic (factual) ones.[†] That every voluntary act is prompted by the agent's own motives is a tautology; hence, it cannot be equivalent to "A person is always seeking something for himself" or "All of a person's motives are selfish," which are synthetic. What the egoist must prove is not merely:

(i)   Every voluntary action is prompted by a motive of the agent's own.

but rather:

(ii)   Every voluntary action is prompted by a motive of a quite particular kind, viz. a selfish one.

Statement (i) is obviously true, but it cannot all by itself give any logical support to statement (ii).

The source of the confusion in this argument is readily apparent. It is not the genesis of an action or the *origin* or its motives which makes it a "selfish" one, but rather the "purpose" of the act or the *objective* of its motives; *not where the motive comes from* (in voluntary actions it always comes from the agent) but *what it aims at* determines whether or not it is selfish. There is surely a valid distinction between voluntary behavior, in which the agent's action is motivated by purposes of his own, and *selfish* behavior in which the agent's motives are of one exclusive sort. The egoist's argument assimilates all voluntary action into the class of selfish action, by requiring, in effect, that an unselfish action be one which is not really motivated at all.

• • •

7. But if argument 4a fails to prove its point, argument 4b does no better. From the fact that all our successful actions (those in which we get what we were after) are accompanied or followed by pleasure it does not follow, as the egoist claims, that the *objective* of every action is to get pleasure for oneself. To begin with, the premise of the argument is not, strictly speaking, even true. Fulfillment of desire (simply getting what one was after) is no guarantee of satisfaction (pleasant feelings of gratification in the mind of the agent). Sometimes when we get what we want we *also* get, as a kind of extra dividend, a warm, glowing feeling of contentment; but often, far too often, we get no dividend at all, or, even worse, the bitter taste of ashes. Indeed, it has been said that the characteristic psychological problem of our time is the *dissatisfaction* that attends the fulfillment of our very most powerful desires.

Even if we grant, however, for the sake of argument, that getting what one wants *usually* yields satisfaction, the egoist's conclusion does not follow. We can concede that we normally get pleasure (in the sense of satisfaction) when our desires are satisfied, *no matter what our desires are for*; but it does not follow from this roughly accurate generalization that the only thing we ever desire is our own satisfaction. Pleasure may well be the usual accompaniment of all actions in which the agent gets what he wants; but to infer from this that what the agent always wants is his own pleasure is like arguing, in William James's example,[4] that because an ocean liner constantly consumes coal on its trans-Atlantic passage that therefore the *purpose* of its voyage is to consume coal. The immediate inference from even constant accompaniment to purpose (or motive) is always a *non sequitur*.

Perhaps there is a sense of "satisfaction" (desire fulfillment) such that it is certainly and

---

[*]   Traditionally, analytic statements have been taken to be statements that are true by virtue of the meanings of words, and hence convey no information about the world.

[†]   Traditionally, statements that do convey information about the world.

universally true that we get satisfaction whenever we get what we want. But satisfaction in this sense is simply the "coming into existence of that which is desired." Hence, to say that desire fulfillment always yields "satisfaction" in this sense is to say no more than that we always get what we want when we get what we want, which is to utter a tautology like "a rose is a rose." It can no more entail a synthetic truth in psychology (like the egoistic thesis) than "a rose is a rose" can entail significant information in botany.

8. *Disinterested Benevolence*. The fallacy in argument 4b then consists, as Garvin puts it, "in the supposition that the apparently unselfish desire to benefit others is transformed into a selfish one by the fact that we derive pleasure from carrying it out."[5] Not only is this argument fallacious; it also provides us with a suggestion of a counterargument to show that its conclusion (psychological egoistic hedonism) is false. Not only is the presence of pleasure (satisfaction) as a by-product of an action no proof that the action was selfish; in some special cases it provides rather conclusive proof that the action was *unselfish*. For in those special cases the fact that we get pleasure from a particular action *presupposes that we desired something else*—something other than our own pleasure—as an end in itself and not merely as a means to our own pleasant state of mind.

This way of turning the egoistic hedonist's argument back on him can be illustrated by taking a typical egoist argument, one attributed (perhaps apocryphally) to Abraham Lincoln, and then examining it closely:

Mr. Lincoln once remarked to a fellow-passenger on an old-time mud-coach that all men were prompted by selfishness in doing good. His fellow-passenger was antagonizing this position when they were passing over a corduroy bridge that spanned a slough. As they crossed this bridge they espied an old razor-backed sow on the bank making a terrible noise because her pigs had got into the slough and were in danger of drowning.

As the old coach began to climb the hill, Mr. Lincoln called out, "Driver, can't you stop just a moment?" Then Mr. Lincoln jumped out, ran back and lifted the little pigs out of the mud and water and placed them on the bank. When he returned, his companion remarked: "Now Abe, where does selfishness come in on this little episode?" "Why, bless your soul Ed, that was the very essence of selfishness. I should have had no peace of mind all day had I gone on and left that suffering old sow worrying over those pigs. I did it to get peace of mind, don't you see?"[6]

If Lincoln had cared not a whit for the welfare of the little pigs and their "suffering" mother, but only for his own "peace of mind," it would be difficult to explain how he could have derived pleasure from helping them. The very fact that he did feel satisfaction as a result of helping the pigs presupposes that he had a preexisting desire for something other than his own happiness. Then when *that* desire was satisfied, Lincoln of course derived pleasure. The *object* of Lincoln's desire was not pleasure; rather pleasure was the *consequence* of his preexisting desire for something else. If Lincoln had been wholly indifferent to the plight of the little pigs as he claimed, how could he possibly have derived any pleasure from helping them? He could not have achieved peace of mind from rescuing the pigs, had he not a prior concern—on which his peace of mind depended—for the welfare of the pigs for its own sake.

In general, the psychological hedonist analyzes apparent benevolence into a desire for "benevolent pleasure." No doubt the benevolent man does get pleasure from his benevolence, but in most cases, this is only because he has previously desired the good of some person, or animal, or mankind at large. Where there is no such desire, benevolent conduct is not generally found to give pleasure to the agent.

9. *Malevolence*. Difficult cases for the psychological egoist include not only instances of

disinterested benevolence, but also cases of "disinterested malevolence." Indeed, malice and hatred are generally no more "selfish" than benevolence. Both are motives likely to cause an agent to sacrifice his own interests—in the case of benevolence, in order to help someone else, in the case of malevolence in order to harm someone else. The selfish man is concerned ultimately only with his own pleasure, happiness, or power; the benevolent man is often equally concerned with the happiness of others; to the malevolent man, the injury of another is often an end in itself—an end to be pursued sometimes with no thought for his own interests. There is reason to think that men have as often sacrificed themselves to injure or kill others as to help or to save others, and with as much "heroism" in the one case as in the other. The unselfish nature of malevolence was first noticed by the Anglican Bishop and moral philosopher Joseph Butler (1692–1752), who regretted that men are no more selfish than they are.[7]

10. *Lack of Evidence for Universal Self-Deception.* The more cynical sort of psychological egoist who is impressed by the widespread phenomenon of self-deception (see 4c) cannot be so quickly disposed of, for he has committed no *logical* mistakes. We can only argue that the acknowledged frequency of self-deception is insufficient evidence for his universal generalization. His argument is not fallacious, but inconclusive.

No one but the agent himself can ever be certain what conscious motives really prompted his action, and where motives are disreputable, even the agent may not admit to himself the true nature of his desires. Thus, for every apparent case of altruistic behavior, the psychological egoist can argue, with some plausibility, that the true motivation *might* be selfish, appearance to the contrary. Philanthropic acts are really motivated by the desire to receive gratitude; acts of self-sacrifice, when truly understood, are seen to be motivated by the desire to feel self-esteem; and so on. We must concede to the egoist that all apparent altruism might be deceptive in this way; but such a sweeping generalization requires considerable empirical evidence, and such evidence is not presently available.

11. *The "Paradox of Hedonism" and Its Consequences for Education.* The psychological egoistic Hedonist (e.g., Jeremy Bentham) has the simplest possible theory of human motivation. According to this variety of egoistic theory, all human motives without exception can be reduced to one—namely, the desire for one's own pleasure. But this theory, despite its attractive simplicity, or perhaps because of it, involves one immediately in a paradox. Astute observers of human affairs from the time of the ancient Greeks have often noticed that pleasure, happiness, and satisfaction are states of mind which stand in a very peculiar relation to desire. An exclusive desire for happiness is the surest way to prevent happiness from coming into being. Happiness has a way of "sneaking up" on persons when they are preoccupied with other things; but when persons deliberately and single-mindedly set off in pursuit of happiness, it vanishes utterly from sight and cannot be captured. This is the famous "paradox of hedonism": the single-minded pursuit of happiness is necessarily self-defeating, for *the way to get happiness is to forget it*; then perhaps it will come to you. If you aim exclusively at pleasure itself, with no concern for the things that bring pleasure, then pleasure will never come. To derive satisfaction, one must ordinarily first desire something other than satisfaction, and then find the means to get what one desires.

To feel the full force of the paradox of hedonism the reader should conduct an experiment in his imagination. Imagine a person (let's call him "Jones") who is, first of all, devoid of intellectual curiosity. He has no desire to acquire any kind of knowledge for its own sake, and thus is utterly indifferent to questions of science, mathematics, and philosophy. Imagine further that the beauties of nature leave Jones cold: he is unimpressed by the autumn foliage, the snow-capped mountains, and the rolling oceans. Long walks in the country on spring mornings and

skiing forays in the winter are to him equally a bore. Moreover, let us suppose that Jones can find no appeal in art. Novels are dull, poetry a pain, paintings nonsense and music just noise. Suppose further that Jones has neither the participant's nor the spectator's passion for baseball, football, tennis, or any other sport. Swimming to him is a cruel aquatic form of calisthenics, the sun only a cause of sunburn. Dancing is coeducational idiocy, conversation a waste of time, the other sex an unappealing mystery. Politics is a fraud, religion mere superstition; and the misery of millions of underprivileged human beings is nothing to be concerned with or excited about. Suppose finally that Jones has no talent for any kind of handicraft, industry, or commerce, and that he does not regret that fact.

What then is Jones interested in? He must desire something. To be sure, he does. Jones has an overwhelming passion for, a complete preoccupation with, his own happiness. The one exclusive desire of his life is *to be happy*. It takes little imagination at this point to see that Jones's one desire is bound to be frustrated. People who—like Jones—most hotly pursue their own happiness are the least likely to find it. Happy people are those who successfully pursue such things as aesthetic or religious experience, self-expression, service to others, victory in competitions, knowledge, power, and so on. If none of these things in themselves and for their own sakes mean anything to a person, if they are valued at all then only as a means to one's own pleasant states of mind—then that pleasure can never come. The way to achieve happiness is to pursue something else.

Almost all people at one time or another in their lives feel pleasure. Some people (though perhaps not many) really do live lives which are on the whole happy. But if pleasure and happiness presuppose desires for something other than pleasure and happiness, then the existence of pleasure and happiness in the experience of some people proves that those people have strong desires for something other than their own happiness—egoistic hedonism to the contrary.

The implications of the "paradox of hedonism" for educational theory should be obvious. The parents least likely to raise a happy child are those who, even with the best intentions, train their child to seek happiness directly. How often have we heard parents say:

> I don't care if my child does not become an intellectual, or a football star, or a great artist. I just want him to be a plain average sort of person. Happiness does not require great ambitions and great frustrations; it's not worth it to suffer and become neurotic for the sake of science, art, or do-goodism. I just want my child to be happy.

This can be a dangerous mistake, for it is the child (and the adult for that matter) without "outer-directed" interests who is the most likely to be unhappy. The pure egoist would be the most wretched of persons.

The educator might well beware of "life adjustment" as the conscious goal of the educational process for similar reasons. "Life adjustment" can be achieved only as a by-product of other pursuits. A whole curriculum of "life adjustment courses" unsupplemented by courses designed to incite an interest in things other than life adjustment would be tragically self-defeating.

As for moral education, it is probably true that punishment and reward are indispensable means of inculcation. But if the child comes to believe that the *sole* reasons for being moral are that he will escape the pain of punishment thereby and/or that he will gain the pleasure of a good reputation, then what is to prevent him from doing the immoral thing whenever he is sure that he will not be found out? While punishment and reward then are important tools for the moral educator, they obviously have their limitations. Beware of the man who does the moral thing only out of fear of pain or love of pleasure. He is not likely to be wholly

trustworthy. Moral education is truly successful when it produces persons who are willing to do the right thing *simply because it is right*, and not merely because it is popular or safe.

12. *Pleasure as Sensation.* One final argument against psychological hedonism should suffice to put that form of the egoistic psychology to rest once and for all. The egoistic hedonist claims that all desires can be reduced to the single desire for one's own *pleasure*. Now the word "pleasure" is ambiguous. On the one hand, it can stand for a certain indefinable, but very familiar and specific kind of sensation, or more accurately, a property of sensations; and it is generally, if not exclusively, associated with the senses. For example, certain taste sensations such as sweetness, thermal sensations of the sort derived from a hot bath or the feel of the August sun while one lies on a sandy beach, erotic sensations, olfactory sensations (say) of the fragrance of flowers or perfume, and tactual and kinesthetic sensations from a good massage, are all pleasant in this sense. Let us call this sense of "pleasure," which is the converse of "physical pain," pleasure$_1$.

On the other hand, the word "pleasure" is often used simply as a synonym for "satisfaction" (in the sense of gratification, not mere desire fulfillment). In this sense, the existence of pleasure presupposes the prior existence of desire. Knowledge, religious experience, aesthetic expression, and other so-called "spiritual activities" often give pleasure in this sense. In fact, as we have seen, we tend to get pleasure in this sense whenever we get what we desire, no matter what we desire. The masochist even derives pleasure (in the sense of "satisfaction") from his own physically painful sensations. Let us call the sense of "pleasure" which means "satisfaction"—pleasure$_2$.

Now we can evaluate the psychological hedonist's claim that the sole human motive is a desire for one's own pleasure, bearing in mind (as he often does not) the ambiguity of the word "pleasure." First, let us take the hedonist to

be saying that it is the desire for pleasure$_1$ (pleasant sensation) which is the sole ultimate desire of all people and the sole desire capable of providing a motive for action. Now I have little doubt that all (or most) people desire their own pleasure, *sometimes*. But even this familiar kind of desire occurs, I think, rather rarely. When I am hungry, I often desire to eat, or, more specifically, to eat this piece of steak and these potatoes. Much less often do I desire to eat certain morsels simply for the sake of the pleasant gustatory sensations they might cause. I have, on the other hand, been motivated in the latter way when I have gone to especially exotic (and expensive) French or Chinese restaurants; but normally, pleasant gastronomic sensations are simply a happy consequence or by-product of my eating, not the antecedently desired objective of my eating. There are, of course, others who take gustatory sensations far more seriously: the *gourmet* who eats only to savor the textures and flavors of fine foods, and the wine fancier who "collects" the exquisitely subtle and very pleasant tastes of rare old wines. Such men are truly absorbed in their taste sensations when they eat and drink, and there may even be some (rich) persons whose desire for such sensations is the sole motive for eating and drinking. It should take little argument, however, to convince the reader that such persons are extremely rare.

Similarly, I usually derive pleasure from taking a hot bath, and on occasion (though not very often) I even decide to bathe simply for the sake of such sensations. Even if this is equally true of everyone, however, it hardly provides grounds for inferring that *no one ever* bathes for *any* other motive. It should be empirically obvious that we sometimes bathe simply in order to get clean, or to please others, or simply from habit.

The view then that we are never after anything in our actions but our own pleasure—that all men are complete "gourmets" of one sort or another—is not only morally cynical; it is also

contrary to common sense and everyday experience. In fact, the view that pleasant sensations play such an enormous role in human affairs is so patently false, on the available evidence, that we must conclude that the psychological hedonist has the other sense of "pleasure"—satisfaction—in mind when he states his thesis. If, on the other hand, he really does try to reduce the apparent multitude of human motives to the one desire for pleasant sensations, then the abundance of historical counter-examples justifies our rejection out of hand of his thesis. It surely seems incredible that the Christian martyrs were ardently pursuing their own pleasure when they marched off to face the lions, or that what the Russian soldiers at Stalingrad "really" wanted when they doused themselves with gasoline, ignited themselves, and then threw the flaming torches of their own bodies on German tanks, was simply the experience of pleasant physical sensations.

13. *Pleasure as Satisfaction.* Let us consider now the other interpretation of the hedonist's thesis, that according to which it is one's own pleasure$_2$ (satisfaction) and not merely pleasure$_1$ (pleasant sensation) which is the sole ultimate objective of all voluntary behavior. In one respect, the "satisfaction thesis" is even less plausible than the "physical sensation thesis"; for the latter at least is a genuine empirical hypothesis, testable in experience, though contrary to the facts which experience discloses. The former, however, is so confused that it cannot even be completely stated without paradox. It is, so to speak, defeated in its own formulation. Any attempted explication of the theory that all men at all times desire only their own satisfaction leads to an *infinite regress* in the following way:

"All men desire only satisfaction."
"Satisfaction of what?"
"Satisfaction of their desires."
"Their desires for what?"
"Their desires for satisfaction."
"Satisfaction of what?"

"Their desires."
"For what?"
"For satisfaction."—etc., *ad infinitum*.

In short, psychological hedonism interpreted in this way attributes to all people as their sole motive a wholly vacuous and infinitely self-defeating desire. The source of this absurdity is in the notion that satisfaction can, so to speak, feed on itself, and perform the miracle of perpetual self-regeneration in the absence of desires for anything other than itself.

To summarize the argument of sections 11 and 12: The word "pleasure" is ambiguous. Pleasure$_1$ means a certain indefinable characteristic of physical sensation. Pleasure$_2$ refers to the feeling of satisfaction that often comes when one gets what one desires whatever be the nature of that which one desires. Now, if the hedonist means pleasure$_1$ when he says that one's own pleasure is the ultimate objective of all of one's behavior, then his view is not supported by the facts. On the other hand, if he means pleasure$_2$, then his theory cannot even be clearly formulated, since it leads to the following infinite regress: "I desire only satisfaction of my desire for satisfaction of my desire for satisfaction. . .etc., *ad infinitum*." I conclude then that psychological hedonism (the most common form of psychological egoism), however interpreted, is untenable.

Notes

1 See his *Introduction to the Principles of Morals and Legislation* (1789), Chap. I, first paragraph: "Nature has placed mankind under the governance of two sovereign masters, *pain* and *pleasure*. It is for them alone to point out what we ought to do, as well as to determine what we shall do. . . . They govern us in all we do, in all we say, in all we think: every effort we can make to throw off our subjection will serve but to demonstrate and confirm it."

2 C. D. Broad, *Ethics and the History of Philosophy* (New York: The Humanities Press, 1952), Essay 10—"Egoism as a Theory of Human Motives," p. 218. This essay is highly recommended.

3   Austin Duncan-Jones, *Butler's Moral Philosophy* (London: Penguin Books, 1952), p. 96. Duncan-Jones goes on to reject this argument. See p. 512f.

4   *The Principles of Psychology* (New York: Henry Holt, 1890), Vol. II, p. 558.

5   Lucius Garvin, *A Modern Introduction to Ethics* (Boston: Houghton Mifflin, 1953), p. 39.

6   Quoted from the *Springfield* (Illinois) *Monitor*, by F. C. Sharp in his *Ethics* (New York: Appleton-Century, 1928), p. 75.

7   See his *Fifteen Sermons on Human Nature Preached at the Rolls Chapel* (1726), especially the first and eleventh.

Thomas Hobbes

MORALITY AND SELF-INTEREST

Of the natural condition of mankind as concerning their felicity and misery

NATURE HATH MADE men so equal, in the faculties of the body, and mind; as that though there be found one man sometimes manifestly stronger in body, or of quicker mind than another; yet when all is reckoned together, the difference between man, and man, is not so considerable, as that one man can thereupon claim to himself any benefit, to which another may not pretend, as well as he. For as to the strength of body, the weakest has strength enough to kill the strongest, either by secret machination, or by confederacy with others, that are in the same danger with himself.

And as to the faculties of the mind, setting aside the arts grounded upon words, and especially that skill of proceeding upon general, and infallible rules, called science; which very few have, and but in few things; as being not a native faculty, born with us; nor attained, as prudence, while we look after somewhat else, I find yet a greater equality amongst men, than that of strength. For prudence, is but experience; which equal time, equally bestows on all men, in those things they equally apply themselves unto. That which may perhaps make such equality incredible, is but a vain conceit of one's own wisdom, which almost all men think they have in a greater degree, than the vulgar; that is, than all men but

themselves, and a few others, whom by fame, or for concurring with themselves, they approve. For such is the nature of men, that howsoever they may acknowledge many others to be more witty, or more eloquent, or more learned; yet they will hardly believe there be many so wise as themselves; for they see their own wit at hand, and other men's at a distance. But this proveth rather that men are in that point equal, than unequal. For there is not ordinarily a greater sign of the equal distribution of any thing, than that every man is contented with his share.

From this equality of ability, ariseth equality of hope in the attaining of our ends. And therefore if any two men desire the same thing, which nevertheless they cannot both enjoy, they become enemies; and in the way to their end, which is principally their own conservation, and sometimes their delectation only, endeavour to destroy, or subdue one another. And from hence it comes to pass, that where an invader hath no more to fear, than another man's single power; if one plant, sow, build, or possess a convenient seat, others may probably be expected to come prepared with forces united, to dispossess, and deprive him, not only of the fruit of his labour, but also of his life, or liberty. And the invader again is in the like danger of another.

And from this diffidence of one another, there is no way for any man to secure himself, so reasonable, as anticipation; that is, by force, or wiles, to master the persons of all men he can,

so long, till he see no other power great enough to endanger him: and this is no more than his own conservation requireth, and is generally allowed. Also because there be some, that taking pleasure in contemplating their own power in the acts of conquest, which they pursue farther than their security requires; if others, that otherwise would be glad to be at ease within modest bounds, should not by invasion increase their power, they would not be able, long time, by standing only on their defence, to subsist. And by consequence, such augmentation of dominion over men being necessary to a man's conservation, it ought to be allowed him.

Again, men have no pleasure, but on the contrary a great deal of grief, in keeping company, where there is no power able to over-awe them all. For every man looketh that his companion should value him, at the same rate he sets upon himself: and upon all signs of contempt, or undervaluing, naturally endeavours, as far as he dares, (which amongst them that have no common power to keep them in quiet, is far enough to make them destroy each other), to extort a greater value from his contemners, by damage; and from others, by the example.

So that in the nature of man, we find three principal causes of quarrel. First, competition; secondly, diffidence; thirdly, glory.

The first, maketh men invade for gain; the second, for safety; and the third, for reputation. The first use violence, to make themselves masters of other men's persons, wives, children, and cattle; the second, to defend them; the third, for trifles, as a word, a smile, a different opinion, and any other sign of undervalue, either direct in their persons, or by reflection in their kindred, their friends, their nation, their profession, or their name.

Hereby it is manifest, that during the time men live without a common power to keep them all in awe, they are in that condition which is called war; and such a war, as is of every man, against every man. For WAR, consisteth not in battle only, or the act of fighting; but in a tract of time, wherein the will to contend by battle is sufficiently known: and therefore the notion of time, is to be considered in the nature of war; as it is in the nature of weather. For as the nature of foul weather, lieth not in a shower or two of rain; but in an inclination thereto of many days together: so the nature of war, consisteth not in actual fighting; but in the known disposition thereto, during all the time there is no assurance to the contrary. All other time is PEACE.

Whatsoever therefore is consequent to a time of war, where every man is enemy to every man; the same is consequent to the time, wherein men live without other security, than what their own strength, and their own invention shall furnish them withal. In such condition, there is no place for industry; because the fruit thereof is uncertain: and consequently no culture of the earth; no navigation, nor use of the commodities that may be imported by sea; no commodious building; no instruments of moving, and removing, such things as require much force; no knowledge of the face of the earth; no account of time; no arts; no letters; no society; and which is worst of all, continual fear, and danger of violent death; and the life of man, solitary, poor, nasty, brutish, and short.

It may seem strange to some man, that has not well weighed these things; that nature should thus dissociate, and render men apt to invade, and destroy one another: and he may therefore, not trusting to this inference, made from the passions, desire perhaps to have the same confirmed by experience. Let him therefore consider with himself, when taking a journey, he arms himself, and seeks to go well accompanied; when going to sleep, he locks his doors; when even in his house he locks his chests; and this when he knows there be laws, and public officers, armed, to revenge all injuries shall be done him; what opinion he has of his fellow-subjects, when he rides armed; of his fellow citizens, when he locks his doors; and of his children, and servants, when he locks his

chests. Does he not there as much accuse mankind by his actions, as I do by my words? But neither of us accuse man's nature in it. The desires, and other passions of man, are in themselves no sin. No more are the actions, that proceed from those passions, till they know a law that forbids them: which till laws be made they cannot know: nor can any law be made, till they have agreed upon the person that shall make it.

It may peradventure be thought, there was never such a time, nor condition of war as this; and I believe it was never generally so, over all the world: but there are many places, where they live so now. For the savage people in many places of America, except the government of small families, the concord whereof dependeth on natural lust, have no government at all; and live at this day in that brutish manner, as I said before. Howsoever, it may be perceived what manner of life there would be, where there were no common power to fear, by the manner of life, which men that have formerly lived under a peaceful government, use to degenerate into, in a civil war.

But though there had never been any time, wherein particular men were in a condition of war one against another; yet in all times, kings, and persons of sovereign authority, because of their independency, are in continual jealousies, and in the state and posture of gladiators; having their weapons pointing, and their eyes fixed on one another; that is, their forts, garrisons, and guns upon the frontiers of their kingdoms; and continual spies upon their neighbours; which is a posture of war. But because they uphold thereby, the industry of their subjects; there does not follow from it, that misery, which accompanies the liberty of particular men.

To this war of every man, against every man, this also is consequent; that nothing can be unjust. The notions of right and wrong, justice and injustice have there no place. Where there is no common power, there is no law: where no law, no injustice. Force, and fraud, are in war the

two cardinal virtues. Justice, and injustice are none of the faculties neither of the body, nor mind. If they were, they might be in a man that were alone in the world, as well as his senses, and passions. They are qualities, that relate to men in society, not in solitude. It is consequent also to the same condition, that there be no propriety, no dominion, no *mine* and *thine* distinct; but only that to be every man's, that he can get: and for so long, as he can keep it. And thus much for the ill condition, which man by mere nature is actually placed in; though with a possibility to come out of it, consisting partly in the passions, partly in his reason.

The passions that incline men to peace, are fear of death; desire of such things as are necessary to commodious living; and a hope by their industry to obtain them. And reason suggesteth convenient articles of peace, upon which men may be drawn to agreement. These articles, are they, which otherwise are called the Laws of Nature: whereof I shall speak more particularly, in the two following chapters.

Of the first and second natural laws, and of contracts

THE RIGHT OF NATURE, which writers commonly call *jus naturale*, is the liberty each man hath, to use his own power, as he will himself, for the preservation of his own nature; that is to say, of his own life; and consequently, of doing any thing, which in his own judgment, and reason, he shall conceive to be the aptest means thereunto.

By LIBERTY, is understood, according to the proper signification of the word, the absence of external impediments: which impediments, may oft take away part of a man's power to do what he would; but cannot hinder him from using the power left him, according as his judgment, and reason shall dictate to him.

A LAW OF NATURE, *lex naturalis*, is a precept or general rule, found out by reason, by which a man is forbidden to do that, which is destructive

of his life, or taketh away the means of preserving the same; and to omit that, by which he thinketh it may be best preserved. For though they that speak of this subject, use to confound jus, and lex, right and law: yet they ought to be distinguished; because RIGHT, consisteth in liberty to do, or to forbear: whereas LAW, determineth, and bindeth to one of them: so that law, and right, differ as much, as obligation, and liberty; which in one and the same matter are inconsistent.

And because the condition of man, as hath been declared in the precedent chapter, is a condition of war of every one against every one; in which case every one is governed by his own reason; and there is nothing he can make use of, that may not be a help unto him, in preserving his life against his enemies; it followeth, that in such a condition, every man has a right to every thing; even to one another's body. And therefore, as long as this natural right of every man to every thing endureth, there can be no security to any man, how strong or wise soever he be, of living out the time, which nature ordinarily alloweth men to live. And consequently it is a precept, or general rule of reason, *that every man, ought to endeavour peace, as far as he has hope of obtaining it; and when he cannot obtain it, that he may seek, and use, all helps, and advantages of war.* The first branch of which rule, containeth the first, and fundamental law of nature; which is, *to seek peace, and follow it.* The second, the sum of the right of nature; which is, *by all means we can, to defend ourselves.*

From this fundamental law of nature, by which men are commanded to endeavour peace, is derived this second law; *that a man be willing, when others are so too, as far-forth, as for peace, and defence of himself he shall think it necessary, to lay down this right to all things; and be contented with so much liberty against other men, as he would allow other men against himself.* For as long as every man holdeth this right, of doing any thing he liketh; so long are all men in the condition of war. But if other men will not lay down their right, as well as he; then there is no reason for any one, to divest himself of his: for that were to expose himself to prey, which no

man is bound to, rather than to dispose himself to peace. This is that law of the Gospel; *whatsoever you require that others should do to you, that do ye to them.* And that law of all men, *quod tibi fieri non vis, alteri ne feceris.*

To lay down a man's right to any thing, is to divest himself of the liberty, of hindering another of the benefit of his own right to the same. For he that renounceth, or passeth away his right, giveth not to any other man a right which he had not before; because there is nothing to which every man had not right by nature: but only standeth out of his way, that he may enjoy his own original right, without hindrance from him; not without hindrance from another. So that the effect which redoundeth to one man, by another man's defect of right, is but so much diminution of impediments to the use of his own right original.

Right is laid aside, either by simply renouncing it; or by transferring it to another. By simply RENOUNCING; when he cares not to whom the benefit thereof redoundeth. By TRANSFERRING; when he intendeth the benefit thereof to some certain person, or persons. And when a man hath in either manner abandoned, or granted away his right; then he is said to be OBLIGED, or BOUND, not to hinder those, to whom such right is granted, or abandoned, from the benefit of it: and that he ought, and it is his DUTY, not to make void that voluntary act of his own: and that such hindrance is INJUSTICE, and INJURY, as being *sine jure;* the right being before renounced, or transferred. So that injury, or injustice, in the controversies of the world, is somewhat like to that, which in the disputations of scholars is called absurdity. For as it is there called an absurdity, to contradict what one maintained in the beginning: so in the world, it is called injustice, and injury, voluntarily to undo that, which from the beginning he had voluntarily done. The way by which a man either simply renounceth, or transferreth his right, is a declaration, or signification, by some voluntary and sufficient sign, or signs, that he doth so

renounce, or transfer; or hath so renounced, or transferred the same, to him that accepteth it. And these signs are either words only, or actions only; or, as it happeneth most often, both words, and actions. And the same are the BONDS, by which men are bound, and obliged: bonds, that have their strength, not from their own nature, for nothing is more easily broken than a man's word, but from fear of some evil consequence upon the rupture.

Whensoever a man transferreth his right, or renounceth it; it is either in consideration of some right reciprocally transferred to himself; or for some other good he hopeth for thereby. For it is a voluntary act: and of the voluntary acts of every man, the object is some *good to himself*. And therefore there be some rights, which no man can be understood by any words, or other signs, to have abandoned, or transferred. As first a man cannot lay down the right of resisting them, that assault him by force, to take away his life; because he cannot be understood to aim thereby, at any good to himself. The same may be said of wounds, and chains, and imprisonment; both because there is no benefit consequent to such patience; as there is to the patience of suffering another to be wounded, or imprisoned: as also because a man cannot tell, when he seeth men proceed against him by violence, whether they intend his death or not. And lastly the motive, and end for which this renouncing, and transferring of right is introduced, is nothing else but the security of a man's person, in his life, and in the means of so preserving life, as not to be weary of it. And therefore if a man by words, or other signs, seem to despoil himself of the end, for which those signs were intended; he is not to be understood as if he meant it, or that it was his will; but that he was ignorant of how such words and actions were to be interpreted.

The mutual transferring of right, is that which men call CONTRACT.

There is difference between transferring of right to the thing; and transferring, or tradition, that is delivery of the thing itself. For the thing may be delivered together with the translation of the right; as in buying and selling with ready-money; or exchange of goods, or lands: and it may be delivered some time after.

Again, one of the contractors, may deliver the thing contracted for on his part, and leave the other to perform his part at some determinate time after, and in the mean time be trusted; and then the contract on his part, is called PACT, or COVENANT: or both parts may contract now, to perform hereafter: in which cases, he that is to perform in time to come, being trusted, his performance is called *keeping of promise*, or faith; and the failing of performance, if it be voluntary, *violation of faith*.

• • •

If a covenant be made, wherein neither of the parties perform presently, but trust one another; in the condition of mere nature, which is a condition of war of every man against every man, upon any reasonable suspicion, it is void: but if there be a common power set over them both, with right and force sufficient to compel performance, it is not void. For he that performeth first, has no assurance the other will perform after; because the bonds of words are too weak to bridle men's ambition, avarice, anger, and other passions, without the fear of some coercive power; which in the condition of mere nature, where all men are equal, and judges of the justness of their own fears, cannot possibly be supposed. And therefore he which performeth first, does but betray himself to his enemy; contrary to the right, he can never abandon, of defending his life, and means of living.

But in a civil estate, where there is a power set up to constrain those that would otherwise violate their faith, that fear is no more reasonable; and for that cause, he which by the covenant is to perform first, is obliged so to do.

The cause of fear, which maketh such a covenant invalid, must be always something arising after the covenant made; as some new

fact, or other sign of the will not to perform: else it cannot make the covenant void. For that which could not hinder a man from promising, ought not to be admitted as a hindrance of performing.

• • •

A covenant not to defend myself from force, by force, is always void. For, as I have showed before, no man can transfer, or lay down his right to save himself from death, wounds, and imprisonment, the avoiding whereof is the only end of laying down any right; and therefore the promise of not resisting force, in no covenant transferreth any right; nor is obliging. For though a man may covenant thus, *unless I do so, or so, kill me;* he cannot covenant thus, *unless I do so, or so, I will not resist you, when you come to kill me.* For man by nature chooseth the lesser evil, which is danger of death in resisting; rather than the greater, which is certain and present death in not resisting. And this is granted to be true by all men, in that they lead criminals to execution, and prison, with armed men, notwithstanding that such criminals have consented to the law, by which they are condemned.

Of other laws of nature

From that law of nature, by which we are obliged to transfer to another, such rights, as being retained, hinder the peace of mankind, there followeth a third; which is this, *that men perform their covenants made:* without which, covenants are in vain, and but empty words; and the right of all men to all things remaining, we are still in the condition of war.

And in this law of nature, consisteth the fountain and original of JUSTICE. For where no covenant hath preceded, there hath no right been transferred, and every man has right to every thing; and consequently, no action can be unjust. But when a covenant is made, then to break it is *unjust:* and the definition of INJUSTICE, is no other than *the not performance of covenant.* And whatsoever is not unjust, is *just.*

But because covenants of mutual trust, where there is a fear of not performance on either part, as hath been said in the former chapter, are invalid; though the original of justice be the making of covenants; yet injustice actually there can be none, till the cause of such fear be taken away; which while men are in the natural condition of war, cannot be done. Therefore before the names of just, and unjust can have place, there must be some coercive power, to compel men equally to the performance of their covenants, by the terror of some punishment, greater than the benefit they expect by the breach of their covenant; and to make good that propriety, which by mutual contract men acquire, in recompense of the universal right they abandon: and such power there is none before the erection of a commonwealth. And this is also to be gathered out of the ordinary definition of justice in the Schools: for they say, that *justice is the constant will of giving to every man his own.* And therefore where there is no *own,* that is no propriety, there is no injustice; and where there is no coercive power erected, that is, where there is no commonwealth, there is no propriety; all men having right to all things: therefore where there is no commonwealth, there nothing is unjust. So that the nature of justice, consisteth in keeping of valid covenants: but the validity of covenants begins not but with the constitution of a civil power, sufficient to compel men to keep them: and then it is also that propriety begins.

• • •

Whatsoever is done to a man, conformable to his own will signified to the doer, is no injury to him. For if he that doeth it, hath not passed away his original right to do what he please, by some antecedent covenant, there is no breach of covenant; and therefore no injury done him. And if he have; then his will to have it done being signified, is a release of that covenant: and so again there is no injury done him.

Justice of actions, is by writers divided into *commutative,* and *distributive:* and the former they

say consisteth in proportion arithmetical; the latter in proportion geometrical. Commutative therefore, they place in the equality of value of the things contracted for; and distributive, in the distribution of equal benefit, to men of equal merit. As if it were injustice to sell dearer than we buy; or to give more to a man than he merits. The value of all things contracted for, is measured by the appetite of the contractors: and therefore the just value, is that which they be contented to give. And merit (besides that which is by covenant, where the performance on one part, meriteth the performance on the other part, and falls under justice commutative, not distributive) is not due to justice; but is rewarded of grace only. And therefore this distinction, in the sense wherein it useth to be expounded, is not right. To speak properly, commutative justice, is the justice, of a contractor; that is, a performance of covenant, in buying, and selling; hiring, and letting to hire; lending, and borrowing; exchanging, bartering, and other acts of contract.

And distributive justice, the justice of an arbitrator; that is to say, the act of defining what is just. Wherein, being trusted by them that make him arbitrator, if he perform his trust, he is said to distribute to every man his own: and this is indeed just distribution, and may be called, though improperly, distributive justice; but more properly equity; which also is a law of nature, as shall be shown in due place.

As justice dependeth on antecedent covenant; so does GRATITUDE depend on antecedent grace; that is to say, antecedent free gift: and is the fourth law of nature; which may be conceived in this form, *that a man which receiveth benefit from another of mere grace, endeavour that he which giveth it, have no reasonable cause to repent him of his good will.* For no man giveth, but with intention of good to himself; because gift is voluntary; and of all voluntary acts, the object is to every man his own good; of which if men see they shall be frustrated, there will be no beginning of benevolence, or trust; nor consequently of mutual help; nor of reconciliation of one man to

another; of war; which is contrary to the first and fundamental law of nature, which commandeth men to *seek peace.* The breach of this law, is called ingratitude; and hath the same relation to grace, that injustice hath to obligation by covenant.

A fifth law of nature, is COMPLAISANCE; that is to say, *that every man strive to accommodate himself to the rest.* For the understanding whereof, we may consider, that there is in men's aptness to society, a diversity of nature, rising from their diversity of affections; not unlike to that we see in stones brought together for building of an edifice. For as that stone which by the asperity, and irregularity of figure, takes more room from others, than itself fills; and for the hardness, cannot be easily made plain, and thereby hindereth the building, is by the builders cast away as unprofitable, and troublesome: so also, a man that by asperity of nature, will strive to retain those things which to himself are superfluous, and to others necessary; and for the stubbornness of his passions, cannot be corrected, is to be left, or cast out of society, as cumbersome thereunto. For seeing every man, not only by right, but also by necessity of nature, is supposed to endeavour all he can, to obtain that which is necessary for his conservation; he that shall oppose himself against it, for things superfluous, is guilty of the war that thereupon is to follow; and therefore doth that, which is contrary to the fundamental law of nature, which commandeth *to seek peace.* The observers of this law, may be called SOCIABLE, the Latins call them *commodi;* the contrary, *stubborn, insociable, forward, intractable.*

A sixth law of nature, is this, *that upon caution of the future time, a man ought to pardon the offences past of them that repenting, desire it.* For PARDON, is nothing but granting of peace; which though granted to them that persevere in their hostility, be not peace, but fear; yet not granted to them that give caution of the future time, is sign of an aversion to peace; and therefore contrary to the law of nature.

A seventh is, *that in revenges, that is, retribution of evil for evil, men look not at the greatness of the evil*

past, but *the greatness of the good to follow.* Whereby we are forbidden to inflict punishment with any other design, than for correction of the offender, or direction of others. For this law is consequent to the next before it, that commandeth pardon, upon security of the future time. Besides, revenge without respect to the example, and profit to come, is a triumph, or glorying in the hurt of another, tending to no end; for the end is always somewhat to come; and glorying to no end, is vain-glory, and contrary to reason, and to hurt without reason, tendeth to the introduction of war; which is against the law of nature; and is commonly styled by the name of *cruelty.*

• • •

And because, though men be never so willing to observe these laws, there may nevertheless arise questions concerning a man's action; first, whether it were done, or not done; secondly, if done, whether against the law, or not against the law; the former whereof, is called a question *of fact*; the latter a question *of right*, therefore unless the parties to the question, covenant mutually to stand to the sentence of another, they are as far from peace as ever. This other to whose sentence they submit is called an ARBITRATOR. And therefore it is of the law of nature, *that they that are at controversy, submit their right to the judgment of an arbitrator.*

And seeing every man is presumed to do all things in order to his own benefit, no man is a fit arbitrator in his own cause; and if he were never so fit; yet equity allowing to each party equal benefit, if one be admitted to be judge, the other is to be admitted also; and so the controversy, that is, the cause of war, remains, against the law of nature.

For the same reason no man in any cause ought to be received for arbitrator, to whom greater profit, or honour, or pleasure apparently ariseth out of the victory of one party, than of the other: for he hath taken, though an unavoidable bribe, yet a bribe; and no man can be obliged to trust him. And thus also the

controversy, and the condition of war remaineth, contrary to the law of nature.

And in a controversy of *fact*, the judge being to give no more credit to one, than to the other, if there be no other arguments, must give credit to a third; or to a third and fourth; or more: for else the question is undecided, and left to force, contrary to the law of nature.

These are the laws of nature, dictating peace, for a means of the conservation of men in multitudes; and which only concern the doctrine of civil society. There be other things tending to the destruction of particular men; as drunkenness, and all other parts of intemperance; which may therefore also be reckoned amongst those things which the law of nature hath forbidden; but are not necessary to be mentioned, nor are pertinent enough to this place.

And though this may seem too subtle a deduction of the laws of nature, to be taken notice of by all men; whereof the most part are too busy in getting food, and the rest too negligent to understand; yet to leave all men inexcusable they have been contracted into one easy sum, intelligible even to the meanest capacity; and that is, *Do not that to another, which thou wouldest not have done to thyself*; which sheweth him, that he had no more to do in learning the laws of nature, but, when weighing the actions of other men with his own, they seem too heavy, to put them into the other part of the balance, and his own into their place, that his own passions, and self-love, may add nothing to the weight; and then there is none of these laws of nature that will not appear unto him very reasonable.

The laws of nature oblige *in foro interno*; that is to say, they bind to a desire they should take place: but *in foro externo*; this is, to the putting them in act, not always. For he that should be modest, and tractable, and perform all he promises, in such time, and place, where no man else should do so, should but make himself a prey to others, and procure his own certain ruin, contrary to the ground of all laws of nature, which tend to nature's preservation. And again,

he that having sufficient security, that others shall observe the same laws towards him, observes them not himself, seeketh not peace, but war; and consequently the destruction of his nature by violence.

And whatsoever laws bind in *foro interno*, may be broken, not only by a fact contrary to the law, but also by a fact according to it, in case a man think it contrary. For though his action in this case, be according to the law; yet his purpose was against the law; which, where the obligation is in *foro interno*, is a breach.

The laws of nature are immutable and eternal; for injustice, ingratitude, arrogance, pride, iniquity, acception of persons, and the rest, can never be made lawful. For it can never be that war shall preserve life, and peace destroy it.

The same laws, because they oblige only to a desire, and endeavour, I mean an unfeigned and constant endeavour, are easy to be observed. For in that they require nothing but endeavour, he that endeavoureth their performance, fulfilleth them; and he that fulfilleth the law, is just.

And the science of them, is the true and only moral philosophy. For moral philosophy is nothing else but the science of what is *good*, and *evil*, in the conversation, and society of mankind. *Good*, and *evil*, are names that signify our appetites, and aversions; which in different tempers, customs, and doctrines of men, are different: and divers men, differ not only in their judgment, on the senses of what is pleasant, and unpleasant to the taste, smell, hearing, touch, and sight; but also of what is conformable, or disagreeable to reason, in the actions of common life. Nay, the same man, in divers times, differs from himself; and one time praiseth, that is, calleth good, what another time he dispraiseth, and calleth evil: from whence arise disputes, controversies, and at last war. And therefore so long a man is in the condition of mere nature, which is a condition of war, as private appetite is the measure of good, and evil: and consequently all men agree on this, that peace is good, and therefore also the way, or means of peace, which,

as I have shewed before, are *justice, gratitude, modesty, equity, mercy,* and the rest of the laws of nature, are good; that is to say; *moral virtues;* and their contrary *vices,* evil. Now the science of virtue and vice, is moral philosophy; and therefore the true doctrine of the laws of nature, is the true moral philosophy. But the writers of moral philosophy, though they acknowledge the same virtues and vices; yet not seeing wherein consisted their goodness; nor that they come to be praised, as the means of peaceable, sociable, and comfortable living, place them in a mediocrity of passions: as if not the cause, but the degree of daring, made fortitude; or not the cause, but the quantity of a gift, made liberality.

These dictates of reason, men used to call by the names of laws, but improperly: for they are but conclusions, or theorems concerning what conduceth to the conservation and defence of themselves; whereas law, properly, is the word of him, that by right hath command over others. But yet if we consider the same theorems, as delivered in the word of God, that by right commandeth all things; then are they properly called laws.

Of the causes, generation, and definition of a commonwealth

The final cause, end, or design of men, who naturally love liberty, and dominion over others, in the introduction of that restraint upon themselves, in which we see them live in commonwealths, is the foresight of their own preservation, and of a more contented life thereby; that is to say, of getting themselves out from that miserable condition of war, which is necessarily consequent, as hath been shown (chapter 13) [see original reading], to the natural passions of men, when there is no visible power to keep them in awe, and tie them by fear of punishment to the performance of their covenants, and observation of those laws of nature set down in the fourteenth and fifteenth chapters.

For the laws of nature, as *justice, equity, modesty, mercy,* and, in sum, *doing to others, as we would be done*

to, of themselves, without the terror of some power, to cause them to be observed, are contrary to our natural passions, that carry us to partiality, pride, revenge, and the like. And covenants, without the sword, are but words, and of no strength to secure a man at all. Therefore notwithstanding the laws of nature (which every one hath then kept, when he has the will to keep them, when he can do it safely) if there be no power erected, or not great enough for our security; every man will, and may lawfully rely on his own strength and art, for caution against all other men. And in all places, where men have lived by small families, to rob and spoil one another, has been a trade, and so far from being reputed against the law of nature, that the greater spoils they gained, the greater was their honour; and men observed no other laws therein, but the laws of honour; that is, to abstain from cruelty, leaving to men their lives, and instruments of husbandry. And as small families did then; so now do cities and kingdoms which are but greater families, for their own security, enlarge their dominions, upon all pretences of danger, and fear of invasion, or assistance that may be given to invaders, and endeavour as much as they can, to subdue, or weaken their neighbours, by open force, and secret arts, for want of other caution, justly; and are remembered for it in after ages with honour.

• • •

It is true, that certain living creatures, as bees, and ants, live sociably one with another, which are therefore by Aristotle numbered amongst political creatures; and yet have no other direction, than their particular judgments and appetites; nor speech, whereby one of them can signify to another, what he thinks expedient for the common benefit: and therefore some man may perhaps desire to know, why mankind cannot do the same. To which I answer,

First, that men are continually in competition for honour and dignity, which these creatures are not; and consequently amongst men there ariseth on that ground, envy and hatred, and finally war; but amongst these not so.

Secondly, that amongst these creatures, the common good differeth not from the private; and being by nature inclined to their private, they procure thereby the common benefit. But man, whose joy consisteth in comparing himself with other men, can relish nothing but what is eminent.

Thirdly, that these creatures, having not, as man, the use of reason, do not see, nor think they see any fault, in the administration of their common business; whereas amongst men, there are very many, that think themselves wiser, and abler to govern the public, better than the rest; and these strive to reform and innovate, one this way, another that way; and thereby bring it into distraction and civil war.

Fourthly, that these creatures, though they have some use of voice, in making known to one another their desires, and other affections; yet they want that art of words, by which some men can represent to others, that which is good, in the likeness of evil; and evil, in the likeness of good; and augment, or diminish the apparent greatness of good and evil; discontenting men, and troubling their peace at their pleasure.

Fifthly, irrational creatures cannot distinguish between *injury*, and *damage*; and therefore as long as they be at ease, they are not offended with their fellows: whereas man is then most troublesome, when he is most at ease: for then it is that he loves to shew his wisdom, and control the actions of them that govern the commonwealth.

Lastly, the agreement of these creatures is natural; that of men, is by covenant only, which is artificial: and therefore it is no wonder if there be somewhat else required, besides covenant, to make their agreement constant and lasting; which is a common power, to keep them in awe, and to direct their actions to the common benefit.

The only way to erect such a common power, as may be able to defend them from the invasion of foreigners, and the injuries of one another,

and thereby to secure them in such sort, as that by their own industry, and by the fruits of the earth, they may nourish themselves and live contentedly; is, to confer all their power and strength upon one man, or upon one assembly of men, that may reduce all their wills, by plurality of voices, unto one will: which is as much as to say, to appoint one man, or assembly of men, to bear their person; and every one to own, and acknowledge himself to be author of whatsoever he that so beareth their person, shall act, or cause to be acted, in those things which concern the common peace and safety; and therein to submit their wills, every one to his will, and their judgments, to his judgment. This is more than consent, or concord; it is a real unity of them all, in one and the same person, made by covenant of every man with every man, in such manner, as if every man should say to every man, *I authorize and give up my right of governing myself, to this man, or to this assembly of men, on this condition, that thou give up thy right to him, and authorize all his actions in like manner.* This done, the multitude so united in one person, is called a COMMONWEALTH, in Latin CIVITAS. This is the generation of that great LEVIATHAN, or rather, to speak more reverently, of that *mortal god*, to which we owe under the *immortal God*, our peace and defence. For by this authority, given him by every particular man in the commonwealth, he hath the use of so much power and strength conferred on him, that by terror thereof, he is enabled to form the wills of them all, to peace at home, and mutual aid against their enemies abroad. And in him consisteth the essence of the commonwealth; which, to define it, is *one person, of whose acts a great multitude, by mutual covenants one with another, have made themselves every one the author, to the end he may use the strength and means of them all, as he shall think expedient, for their peace and common defence.*

And he that carrieth this person is called SOVEREIGN, and said to have *sovereign power*; and every one besides, his SUBJECT.

David Gauthier

MORALITY AND ADVANTAGE

I

H UME ASKS, rhetorically, "What theory of
morals can ever serve any useful purpose,
unless it can show, by a particular detail, that all
the duties which it recommends, are also the
true interest of each individual?"[1] But there are
many to whom this question does not seem
rhetorical. Why, they ask, do we speak the
language of morality, impressing upon our
fellows their duties and obligations, urging
them with appeals to what is right and good, if
we could speak to the same effect in the language
of prudence, appealing to considerations of
interest and advantage? When the poet, Ogden
Nash, is moved by the muse to cry out:

> O Duty,
> Why hast thou not the visage of a sweetie or
> a cutie?[2]

we do not anticipate the reply:

> O Poet,
> I really am a cutie and I think you ought to
> know it.

The belief that duty cannot be reduced to
interest, or that morality may require the agent
to subordinate all considerations of advantage, is
one which has withstood the assaults of
contrary-minded philosophers from Plato to the
present. Indeed, were it not for the conviction
that only interest and advantage can motivate
human actions, it would be difficult to understand philosophers contending so vigorously for
the identity, or at least compatibility, of morality
with prudence.

Yet if morality is not true prudence it would be
wrong to suppose that those philosophers who
have sought some connection between morality
and advantage have been merely misguided. For it
is a truism that we should all expect to be worse
off if men were to substitute prudence, even of
the most enlightened kind, for morality in all of
their deliberations. And this truism demands not
only some connection between morality and
advantage, but a seemingly paradoxical connection. For if we should all expect to suffer, were
men to be prudent instead of moral, then morality
must contribute to advantage in a unique way, a
way in which prudence—following reasons of
advantage—cannot.

Thomas Hobbes is perhaps the first philosopher who tried to develop this seemingly paradoxical connection between morality and
advantage. But since he could not admit that a
man might ever reasonably subordinate considerations of advantage to the dictates of obligation, he was led to deny the possibility of real
conflict between morality and prudence. So his
argument fails to clarify the distinction between
the view that claims of obligation reduce to
considerations of interest and the view that

claims of obligation promote advantage in a way in which considerations of interest cannot.

More recently, Kurt Baier has argued that "being moral is following rules designed to overrule self-interest whenever it is in the interest of everyone alike that everyone should set aside his interest."[3] Since prudence is following rules of (enlightened) self-interest, Baier is arguing that morality is designed to overrule prudence when it is to everyone's advantage that it do so—or, in other words, that morality contributes to advantage in a way in which prudence cannot.[4]

Baier does not actually demonstrate that morality contributes to advantage in this unique and seemingly paradoxical way. Indeed, he does not ask how it is possible that morality should do this. It is this possibility which I propose to demonstrate.

II

Let us examine the following proposition, which will be referred to as "the thesis": *Morality is a system of principles such that it is advantageous for everyone if everyone accepts and acts on it, yet acting on the system of principles requires that some persons perform disadvantageous acts.*[5]

What I wish to show is that this thesis *could be true*, that morality could possess those characteristics attributed to it by the thesis. I shall not try to show that the thesis is true—indeed, I shall argue in Section V that it presents at best an inadequate conception of morality. But it is plausible to suppose that a modified form of the thesis states a necessary, although not a sufficient, condition for a moral system.

Two phrases in the thesis require elucidation. The first is "advantageous for everyone." I use this phrase to mean that *each* person will do better if the system is accepted and acted on than if *either* no system is accepted and acted on *or* a system is accepted and acted on which is similar, save that it never requires any person to perform disadvantageous acts.

Clearly, then, the claim that it is advantageous for everyone to accept and act on the system is a very strong one; it may be so strong that no system of principles which might be generally adopted could meet it. But I shall consider in Section V one among the possible ways of weakening the claim.

The second phrase requiring elucidation is "disadvantageous acts." I use this phrase to refer to acts which, in the context of their performance, would be less advantageous to the performer than some other act open to him in the same context. The phrase does not refer to acts which merely impose on the performer some short-term disadvantage that is recouped or outweighed in the long run. Rather it refers to acts which impose a disadvantage that is never recouped. It follows that the performer may say to himself, when confronted with the requirement to perform such an act, that it would be better for him not to perform it.

It is essential to note that the thesis, as elucidated, does not maintain that morality is advantageous for everyone in the sense that each person will do *best* if the system of principles is accepted and acted on. Each person will do better than if no system is adopted, or than if the one particular alternative mentioned above is adopted, but not than if any alternative is adopted.

Indeed, for each person required by the system to perform some disadvantageous act, it is easy to specify a better alternative—namely, the system modified so that it does not require him to perform any act disadvantageous to himself. Of course, there is no reason to expect such an alternative to be better than the moral system for everyone, or in fact for anyone other than the person granted the special exemption.

A second point to note is that each person must gain more from the disadvantageous acts performed by others than he loses from the disadvantageous acts performed by himself. If this were not the case, then some person would do better if a system were adopted exactly like

the moral system save that it never requires *any* person to perform disadvantageous acts. This is ruled out by the force of "advantageous for everyone."

This point may be clarified by an example. Suppose that the system contains exactly one principle. Everyone is always to tell the truth. It follows from the thesis that each person gains more from those occasions on which others tell the truth, even though it is disadvantageous to them to do so, than he loses from those occasions on which he tells the truth even though it is disadvantageous to him to do so.

Now this is not to say that each person gains by telling others the truth in order to ensure that in return they tell him the truth. Such gains would merely be the result of accepting certain short-term disadvantages (those associated with truth-telling) in order to reap long-term benefits (those associated with being told the truth). Rather, what is required by the thesis is that those disadvantages which a person incurs in telling the truth, when he can expect neither short-term nor long-term benefits to accrue to him from truth-telling, are outweighed by those advantages he receives when others tell him the truth when they can expect no benefits to accrue to them from truth-telling.

The principle enjoins truth-telling in those cases in which whether one tells the truth or not will have no effect on whether others tell the truth. Such cases include those in which others have no way of knowing whether or not they are being told the truth. The thesis requires that the disadvantages one incurs in telling the truth in these cases are less than the advantages one receives in being told the truth by others in parallel cases; and the thesis requires that this holds for everyone.

Thus we see that although the disadvantages imposed by the system on any person are less than the advantages secured him through the imposition of disadvantages on others, yet the disadvantages are real in that incurring them is *unrelated* to receiving the advantages. The

argument of long-term prudence, that I ought to incur some immediate disadvantage *so that* I shall receive compensating advantages later on, is entirely inapplicable here.

III

It will be useful to examine in some detail an example of a system which possesses those characteristics ascribed by the thesis to morality. This example, abstracted from the field of international relations, will enable us more clearly to distinguish, first, conduct based on immediate interest; second, conduct which is truly prudent; and third, conduct which promotes mutual advantage but is not prudent.

A and *B* are two nations with substantially opposed interests, who find themselves engaged in an arms race against each other. Both possess the latest in weaponry, so that each recognizes that the actual outbreak of full scale war between them would be mutually disastrous. This recognition leads *A* and *B* to agree that each would be better off if they were mutually disarming instead of mutually arming. For mutual disarmament would preserve the balance of power between them while reducing the risk of war.

Hence *A* and *B* enter into a disarmament pact. The pact is advantageous for both if both accept and act on it, although clearly it is not advantageous for either to act on it if the other does not.

Let *A* be considering whether or not to adhere to the pact in some particular situation, whether or not actually to perform some act of disarmament. *A* will quite likely consider the act to have disadvantageous consequences. *A* expects to benefit, not by its own acts of disarmament, but by *B*'s acts. Hence if *A* were to reason simply in terms of immediate interest, *A* might well decide to violate the pact.

But *A*'s decision need be neither prudent nor reasonable. For suppose first that *B* is able to determine whether or not *A* adheres to the pact. If *A* violates, then *B* will detect the violation and will then consider what to do in the light of *A*'s

behavior. It is not to B's advantage to disarm alone; B expects to gain, not by its own acts of disarmament, but by A's acts. Hence A's violation, if known to B, leads naturally to B's counterviolation. If this continues, the effect of the pact is entirely undone, and A and B return to their mutually disadvantageous arms race. A, foreseeing this when considering whether or not to adhere to the pact in the given situation, must therefore conclude that the truly prudent course of action is to adhere.

Now suppose that B is unable to determine whether or not A adheres to the pact in the particular situation under consideration. If A judges adherence to be in itself disadvantageous, then it will decide, both on the basis of immediate interest and on the basis of prudence, to violate the pact. Since A's decision is unknown to B, it cannot affect whether or not B adheres to the pact, and so the advantage gained by A's violation is not outweighed by any consequent loss.

Therefore, if A and B are prudent they will adhere to their disarmament pact whenever violation would be detectable by the other, and violate the pact whenever violation would not be detectable by the other. In other words, they will adhere openly and violate secretly. The disarmament pact between A and B thus possesses two of the characteristics ascribed by the thesis to morality. First, accepting the pact and acting on it is more advantageous for each than making no pact at all. Second, in so far as the pact stipulates that each must disarm even when disarming is undetectable by the other, it requires each to perform disadvantageous acts—acts which run counter to considerations of prudence.

One further condition must be met if the disarmament pact is to possess those characteristics ascribed by the thesis to a system of morality. It must be the case that the requirement that each party perform disadvantageous acts be essential to the advantage conferred by the pact; or, to put the matter in the way in which we expressed it earlier, both A and B must do better to adhere to this pact than to a pact

which is similar save that it requires no disadvantageous acts. In terms of the example, A and B must do better to adhere to the pact than to a pact which stipulates that each must disarm only when disarming is detectable by the other.

We may plausibly suppose this condition to be met. Although A will gain by secretly retaining arms itself, it will lose by B's similar acts, and its losses may well outweigh its gains. B may equally lose more by A's secret violations than it gains by its own. So, despite the fact that prudence requires each to violate secretly, each may well do better if both adhere secretly than if both violate secretly. Supposing this to be the case, the disarmament pact is formally analogous to a moral system, as characterized by the thesis. That is, acceptance of and adherence to the pact by A and B is more advantageous for each, either than making no pact at all or than acceptance of and adherence to a pact requiring only open disarmament, and the pact requires each to perform acts of secret disarmament which are disadvantageous.

Some elementary notation, adapted for our purposes from the mathematical theory of games, may make the example even more perspicuous. Given a disarmament pact between A and B, each may pursue two pure strategies— adherence and violation. There are, then, four possible combinations of strategies, each determining a particular outcome. These outcomes can be ranked preferentially for each nation; we shall let the numerals 1 to 4 represent the ranking from first to fourth preference. Thus we construct a simple matrix,[6] in which A's preferences are stated first:

		B adheres	B violates
A	adheres	2,2	4,1
	violates	1,4	3,3

The matrix does not itself show that agreement is advantageous to both, for it gives only the rankings of outcomes given the agreement.

But it is plausible to assume that *A* and *B* would rank mutual violation on a par with no agreement. If we assume this, we can then indicate the value to each of making and adhering to the pact by reference to the matrix.

The matrix shows immediately that adherence to the pact is not the most advantageous possibility for either, since each prefers the outcome, if it alone violates, to the outcome of mutual adherence. It shows also that each gains less from its own violations than it loses from the other's, since each ranks mutual adherence above mutual violation.

Let us now use the matrix to show that, as we argued previously, public adherence to the pact is prudent and mutually advantageous, whereas private adherence is not prudent although mutually advantageous. Consider first the case when adherence—and so violation—are open and public.

If adherence and violation are open, then each knows the strategy chosen by the other, and can adjust its own strategy in the light of this knowledge—or, in other words, the strategies are interdependent. Suppose that each initially chooses the strategy of adherence. *A* notices that if it switches to violation it gains—moving from 2 to 1 in terms of preference ranking. Hence immediate interest dictates such a switch. But it notices further that if it switches, then B can also be expected to switch—moving from 4 to 3 on its preference scale. The eventual outcome would be stable, in that neither could benefit from switching from violation back to adherence. But the eventual outcome would represent not a gain for *A* but a loss—moving from 2 to 3 on its preference scale. Hence prudence dictates no change from the strategy of adherence. This adherence is mutually advantageous; *A* and *B* are in precisely similar positions in terms of their pact.

Consider now the case when adherence and violation are secret and private. Neither nation knows the strategy chosen by the other, so the two strategies are independent. Suppose *A* is

trying to decide which strategy to follow. It does not know B's choice. But it notices that if B adheres, then it pays *A* to violate, attaining 1 rather than 2 in terms of preference ranking. If B violates, then again it pays *A* to violate, attaining 3 rather than 4 on its preference scale. Hence, no matter which strategy B chooses, *A* will do better to violate, and so prudence dictates violation.

B of course reasons in just the same way. Hence each is moved by considerations of prudence to violate the pact, and the outcome assigns each rank 3 on its preference scale. This outcome is mutually disadvantageous to *A* and *B*, since mutual adherence would assign each rank 2 on its preference scale.

If *A* and *B* are both capable only of rational prudence, they find themselves at an impasse. The advantage of mutual adherence to the agreement when violations would be secret is not available to them, since neither can find it in his own overall interest not to violate secretly. Hence, strictly prudent nations cannot reap the maximum advantage possible from a pact of the type under examination.

Of course, what *A* and *B* will no doubt endeavor to do is eliminate the possibility of secret violations of their pact. Indeed, barring additional complications, each must find it to his advantage to make it possible for the other to detect his own violations. In other words, each must find it advantageous to ensure that their choice of strategies is interdependent, so that the pact will always be prudent for each to keep. But it may not be possible for them to ensure this, and to the extent that they cannot, prudence will prevent them from maximizing mutual advantage.

IV

We may now return to the connection of morality with advantage. Morality, if it is a system of principles of the type characterized in the thesis, requires that some persons perform acts genuinely disadvantageous to themselves, as

a means to greater mutual advantage. Our example shows sufficiently that such a system is possible, and indicates more precisely its character. In particular, by an argument strictly parallel to that which we have pursued, we may show that men who are merely prudent will not perform the required disadvantageous acts. But in so violating the principles of morality, they will disadvantage themselves. Each will lose more by the violations of others than he will gain by his own violations.

Now this conclusion would be unsurprising if it were only that no man can gain if he alone is moral rather than prudent. Obviously such a man loses, for he adheres to moral principles to his own disadvantage, while others violate them also to his disadvantage. The benefit of the moral system is not one which any individual can secure for himself, since each man gains from the sacrifices of others.

What is surprising in our conclusion is that no man can ever gain if he is moral. Not only does he not gain by being moral if others are prudent, but he also does not gain by being moral if others are moral. For although he now receives the advantage of others' adherence to moral principles, he reaps the disadvantage of his own adherence. As long as his own adherence to morality is independent of what others do (and this is required to distinguish morality from prudence), he must do better to be prudent.

If all men are moral, all will do better than if all are prudent. But any one man will always do better if he is prudent than if he is moral. There is no real paradox in supposing that morality is advantageous, even though it requires the performance of disadvantageous acts.

On the supposition that morality has the characteristics ascribed to it by the thesis, is it possible to answer the question "Why should we be moral?" where "we" is taken distributively, so that the question is a compendious way of asking, for each person, "Why should I be moral?" More simply, is it possible to answer the question "Why should I be moral?"

I take it that this question, if asked seriously, demands a reason for being moral other than moral reasons themselves. It demands that moral reasons be shown to be reasons for acting by a noncircular argument. Those who would answer it, like Baier, endeavor to do so by the introduction of considerations of advantage.

Two such considerations have emerged from our discussion. The first is that if all are moral, all will do better than if all are prudent. This will serve to answer the question "Why should we be moral?" if this question is interpreted rather as "Why should we all be moral—rather than all being something else?" If we must all be the same, then each person has a reason—a prudential reason—to prefer that we all be moral.

But, so interpreted, "Why should we be moral?" is not a compendious way of asking, for each person, "Why should I be moral?" Of course, if everyone is to be whatever I am, then I should be moral. But a general answer to the question "Why should I be moral?" cannot presuppose this.

The second consideration is that any individual always does better to be prudent rather than moral, provided his choice does not determine other choices. But in so far as this answers the question "Why should I be moral?" it leads to the conclusion "I should not be moral." One feels that this is not the answer which is wanted.

We may put the matter otherwise. The individual who needs a reason for being moral which is not itself a moral reason cannot have it. There is nothing surprising about this; it would be much more surprising if such reasons could be found. For it is more than apparently paradoxical to suppose that considerations of advantage could ever of themselves justify accepting a real disadvantage.

V

I suggested in Section II that the thesis, in modified form, might provide a necessary, although not a sufficient, condition for a moral system. I

want now to consider how one might characterize the man who would qualify as moral according to the thesis—I shall call him the "moral" man—and then ask what would be lacking from this characterization, in terms of some of our commonplace moral views.

The rationally prudent man is incapable of moral behavior, in even the limited sense defined by the thesis. What difference must there be between the prudent man and the "moral" man? Most simply, the "moral" man is the prudent but trustworthy man. I treat trustworthiness as the capacity which enables its possessor to adhere, and to judge that he ought to adhere, to a commitment which he has made, without regard to considerations of advantage.

The prudent but trustworthy man does not possess this capacity completely. He is capable of trustworthy behavior only in so far as he regards his commitment as advantageous. Thus he differs from the prudent man just in the relevant respect; he accepts arguments of the form "If it is advantageous for me to agree[7] to do x, and I do agree to do x, then I ought to do x, whether or not it then proves advantageous for me to do x."

Suppose that A and B, the parties to the disarmament pact, are prudent but trustworthy. A, considering whether or not secretly to violate the agreement, reasons that its advantage in making and keeping the agreement, provided B does so as well, is greater than its advantage in not making it. If it can assume that B reasons in the same way, then it is in a position to conclude that it ought not to violate the pact. Although violation would be advantageous, consideration of this advantage is ruled out by A's trustworthiness, given the advantage in agreeing to the pact.

The prudent but trustworthy man meets the requirements implicitly imposed by the thesis for the "moral" man. But how far does this "moral" man display two characteristics commonly associated with morality—first, a willingness to make sacrifices, and second, a concern with fairness?

Whenever a man ignores his own advantage for reasons other than those of greater advantage,

he may be said to make some sacrifice. The "moral" man, in being trustworthy, is thus required to make certain sacrifices. But these are extremely limited. And—not surprisingly, given the general direction of our argument—it is quite possible that they limit the advantages which the "moral" man can secure.

Once more let us turn to our example. A and B have entered into a disarmament agreement and, being prudent but trustworthy, are faithfully carrying it out. The government of A is now informed by its scientists, however, that they have developed an effective missile defense, which will render A invulnerable to attack by any of the weapons actually or potentially at B's disposal, barring unforeseen technological developments. Furthermore, this defense can be installed secretly. The government is now called upon to decide whether to violate its agreement with B, install the new defense, and, with the arms it has retained through its violation, establish its dominance over B.

A is in a type of situation quite different from that previously considered. For it is not just that A will do better by secretly violating its agreement. A reasons not only that it will do better to violate no matter what B does, but that it will do better if both violate than if both continue to adhere to the pact. A is now in a position to gain from abandoning the agreement; it no longer finds mutual adherence advantageous.

We may represent this new situation in another matrix:

		B adheres	B violates
A	adheres	3,2	4,1
	violates	1,4	2,3

We assume again that the ranking of mutual violation is the same as that of no agreement. Now had this situation obtained at the outset, no agreement would have been made, for A would have had no reason to enter into a disarmament pact. And of course had A expected this

situation to come about, no agreement—or only a temporary agreement—would have been made; *A* would no doubt have risked the short-term dangers of the continuing arms race in the hope of securing the long-run benefit of predominance over *B* once its missile defense was completed. On the contrary, *A* expected to benefit from the agreement, but now finds that, because of its unexpected development of a missile defense, the agreement is not in fact advantageous to it.

The prudent but trustworthy man is willing to carry out his agreements, and judges that he ought to carry them out, in so far as he considers them advantageous. *A* is prudent but trustworthy. But is *A* willing to carry out its agreement to disarm, now that it no longer considers the agreement advantageous?

If *A* adheres to its agreement in this situation, it makes a sacrifice greater than any advantage it receives from the similar sacrifices of others. It makes a sacrifice greater in kind than any which can be required by a mutually advantageous agreement. It must, then, possess a capacity for trustworthy behavior greater than that ascribed to the merely prudent but trustworthy man (or nation). This capacity need not be unlimited; it need not extend to a willingness to adhere to any commitment no matter what sacrifice is involved. But it must involve a willingness to adhere to a commitment made in the expectation of advantage, should that expectation be disappointed.

I shall call the man (or nation) who is willing to adhere, and judges that he ought to adhere, to his prudentially undertaken agreements even if they prove disadvantageous to him, the trustworthy man. It is likely that there are advantages available to trustworthy men which are not available to merely prudent but trustworthy men. For there may be situations in which men can make agreements which each expects to be advantageous to him, provided he can count on the others' adhering to it whether or not their expectation of advantage is realized. But each

can count on this only if all have the capacity to adhere to commitments regardless of whether the commitment actually proves advantageous. Hence, only trustworthy men who know each other to be such will be able rationally to enter into, and so to benefit from, such agreements.

Baier's view of morality departs from that stated in the thesis in that it requires trustworthy, and not merely prudent but trustworthy, men. Baier admits that "a person might do better for himself by following enlightened self-interest rather than morality."[8] This admission seems to require that morality be a system of principles which each person may expect, initially, to be advantageous to him, if adopted and adhered to by everyone, but not a system which actually is advantageous to everyone.

Our commonplace moral views do, I think, support the view that the moral man must be trustworthy. Hence, we have established one modification required in the thesis, if it is to provide a more adequate set of conditions for a moral system.

But there is a much more basic respect in which the "moral" man falls short of our expectations. He is willing to temper his singleminded pursuit of advantage only by accepting the obligation to adhere to prudentially undertaken commitments. He has no real concern for the advantage of others, which would lead him to modify his pursuit of advantage when it conflicted with the similar pursuits of others. Unless he expects to gain, he is unwilling to accept restrictions on the pursuit of advantage which are intended to equalize the opportunities open to all. In other words, he has no concern with fairness.

We tend to think of the moral man as one who does not seek his own well-being by means which would deny equal well-being to his fellows. This marks him off clearly from the "moral" man, who differs from the prudent man only in that he can overcome the apparent paradox of prudence and obtain those advantages which are available only to those who can

display real restraint in their pursuit of advantage.

Thus a system of principles might meet the conditions laid down in the thesis without taking any account of considerations of fairness. Such a system would contain principles for ensuring increased advantage (or expectation of advantage) to everyone, but no further principle need be present to determine the distribution of this increase.

It is possible that there are systems of principles which, if adopted and adhered to, provide advantages which strictly prudent men, however rational, cannot attain. These advantages are a function of the sacrifices which the principles impose on their adherents.

Morality may be such a system. If it is, this would explain our expectation that we should all be worse off were we to substitute prudence for morality in our deliberations. But to characterize morality as a system of principles advantageous to all is not to answer the question "Why should I be moral?" nor is it to provide for those considerations of fairness which are equally essential to our moral understanding.

Notes

1 David Hume, *An Enquiry Concerning the Principles of Morals*, sec. ix, pt. ii.
2 Ogden Nash, "Kind of an Ode to Duty."
3 Kurt Baier, *The Moral Point of View: A Rational Basis of Ethics* (Ithaca, 1958), p. 314.
4 That this, and only this, is what he is entitled to claim may not be clear to Baier, for he supposes his account of morality to answer the question "Why should we be moral?" interpreting "we" distributively. This, as I shall argue in Sec. IV, is quite mistaken.
5 The thesis is not intended to state Baier's view of morality. I shall suggest in Sec. V that Baier's view would require substituting "everyone can expect to benefit" for "it is advantageous to everyone." The thesis is stronger and easier to discuss.
6 Those familiar with the theory of games will recognize the matrix as a variant of the Prisoner's Dilemma. In a more formal treatment, it would be appropriate to develop the relation between morality and advantage by reference to the Prisoner's Dilemma. This would require reconstructing the disarmament pact and the moral system as proper games. Here I wish only to suggest the bearing of game theory on our enterprise.
7 The word "agree" requires elucidation. It is essential not to confuse an advantage in agreeing to do x with an advantage in saying that one will do x. If it is advantageous for me to agree to do x, then there is some set of actions open to me which includes both saying that I will do x and doing x, and which is more advantageous to me than any set of actions open to me which does not include saying that I will do x. On the other hand, if it is advantageous for me to say that I will do x, then there is some set of actions open to me which includes saying that I will do x, and which is more advantageous to me than any set which does not include saying that I will do x. But this set need not include doing x.
8 Baier, op. cit., p. 314.

Christine Korsgaard

THE AUTHORITY OF NORMS

D O NOT MERELY show us by argument that justice is superior to injustice, but make clear to us what each in and of itself does to its possessor, whereby the one is evil and the other good.

Plato[1]

Introduction

1.1.1

In 1625, in his book *On the Law of War and Peace*, Hugo Grotius asserted that human beings would have obligations 'even if we should concede that which cannot be conceded without the utmost wickedness, that there is no God, or that the affairs of men are of no concern to Him'.[2] But two of his followers, Thomas Hobbes and Samuel Pufendorf, thought that Grotius was wrong.[3] However socially useful moral conduct might be, they argued, it is not really *obligatory* unless some sovereign authority, backed by the power of sanctions, lays it down as the law. Others in turn disagreed with them, and so the argument began.

Ever since then, modern moral philosophers have been engaged in a debate about the 'foundations' of morality. We need to be shown, it is often urged, that morality is 'real' or 'objective'. The early rationalists, Samuel Clarke and Richard Price, thought that they knew exactly what they meant by this.[4] Hobbes had said

that there is no right or wrong in the state of nature, and to them, this meant that rightness is mere invention or convention, not something real.[5] Hobbes meant that individuals are not obligated to obey the laws of social cooperation in the absence of a sovereign who can impose them on everyone.[6] But the rationalists took him to mean what Bernard Mandeville had later ironically asserted: that virtue is just an invention of politicians, used to keep their human cattle in line.[7]

But what exactly is the problem with that? Showing that something is an invention is not a way of showing that it is not real. Moral standards exist, one might reply, in the only way standards of conduct *can* exist: people believe in such standards and therefore regulate their conduct in accordance with them. Nor are these facts difficult to explain. We all know in a general way how and why we were taught to follow moral rules, and that it would be impossible for us to get on together if we didn't do something along these lines. We are social animals, so probably the whole thing has a biological basis. So what's missing here, that makes us seek a philosophical 'foundation'?

The answer lies in the fact that ethical standards are *normative*. They do not merely *describe* a way in which we in fact regulate our conduct. They make *claims* on us; they command, oblige, recommend, or guide. Or at least, when we

invoke them, we make claims on one another.[8] When I say that an action is right I am saying that you ought to *do* it; when I say that something is good I am recommending it as worthy of your choice. The same is true of the other concepts for which we seek philosophical foundations. Concepts like knowledge, beauty, and meaning, as well as virtue and justice, all have a normative dimension, for they tell us what to think, what to like, what to say, what to do, and what to be. And it is the force of these normative claims – the right of these concepts to give laws to us – that we want to understand.

And in ethics, the question can become urgent, for the day will come, for most of us, when what morality commands, obliges, or recommends is *hard*: that we share decisions with people whose intelligence or integrity don't inspire our confidence; that we assume grave responsibilities to which we feel inadequate; that we sacrifice our lives, or voluntarily relinquish what makes them sweet. And then the question – *why?* – will press, and rightly so. Why should I be moral? This is not, as H. A. Prichard supposed, a misguided request for a demonstration that morality is in our interest (although that may be one answer to the question).[9] It is a call for philosophy, the examination of life. Even those who are convinced that 'it is right' must be in itself a sufficient reason for action may request an account of rightness which this conviction will survive. The trouble with a view like Mandeville's is not that it is not a reasonable explanation of how moral practices came about, but rather that our commitment to these practices would not survive our belief that it was true.[10] Why give up your heart's desire, just because some politician wants to keep you in line? When we seek a philosophical foundation for morality we are not looking merely for an explanation of moral practices. We are asking what *justifies* the claims that morality makes on us. This is what I am calling 'the normative question'.

•   •   •

The solution

3.3.1

Those who think that the human mind is internally luminous and transparent to itself think that the term 'self-consciousness' is appropriate because what we get in human consciousness is a direct encounter with the self. Those who think that the human mind has a reflective structure use the term too, but for a different reason. The reflective structure of the mind is a source of 'self-consciousness' because it forces us to have a *conception* of ourselves. As Kant argued, this is a fact about what it is *like* to be reflectively conscious and it does not prove the existence of a metaphysical self. From a third-person point of view, outside of the deliberative standpoint, it may look as if what happens when someone makes a choice is that the strongest of his conflicting desires wins. But that isn't the way it is *for you* when you deliberate. When you deliberate, it is as if there were something over and above all of your desires, something which is *you*, and which *chooses* which desire to act on. This means that the principle or law by which you determine your actions is one that you regard as being expressive of *yourself*. To identify with such a principle or way of choosing is to be, in St Paul's famous phrase, a law to yourself.[11]

An agent might think of herself as a Citizen of the Kingdom of Ends. Or she might think of herself as someone's friend or lover, or as a member of a family or an ethnic group or a nation. She might think of herself as the steward of her own interests, and then she will be an egoist. Or she might think of herself as the slave of her passions, and then she will be a wanton. And how she thinks of herself will determine whether it is the law of the Kingdom of Ends, or the law of some smaller group, or the law of egoism, or the law of the wanton that will be the law that she is to herself.

The conception of one's identity in question here is not a theoretical one, a view about what

as a matter of inescapable scientific fact you are. It is better understood as a description under which you value yourself, a description under which you find your life to be worth living and your actions to be worth undertaking. So I will call this a conception of your practical identity. Practical identity is a complex matter and for the average person there will be a jumble of such conceptions. You are a human being, a woman or a man, an adherent of a certain religion, a member of an ethnic group, a member of a certain profession, someone's lover or friend, and so on. And all of these identities give rise to reasons and obligations. Your reasons express your identity, your nature; your obligations spring from what that identity forbids.

Our ordinary ways of talking about obligation reflect this connection to identity. A century ago a European could admonish another to civilized behaviour by telling him to act like a Christian. It is still true in many quarters that courage is urged on males by the injunction 'be a man!' Duties more obviously connected with social roles are of course enforced in this way. 'A psychiatrist doesn't violate the confidence of her patients.' No 'ought' is needed here because the normativity is built right into the role. But it isn't only in the case of roles that the idea of obligation invokes the conception of practical identity. Consider the astonishing but familiar 'I couldn't live with myself if I did that.' Clearly there are two selves here, me and the one I must live with and so must not fail. Or consider the protest against obligation ignored: 'Just who do you think you are?'

The connection is also present in the concept of integrity. Etymologically, integrity is oneness, integration is what makes something one. To be a thing, one thing, a unity, an entity; to be anything at all: in the metaphysical sense, that is what it means to have integrity. But we use the term for someone who lives up to his own standards. And that is because we think that living up to them is what makes him one, and so what makes him a person at all.

It is the conceptions of ourselves that are most important to us that give rise to unconditional obligations. For to violate them is to lose your integrity and so your identity, and to no longer be who you are. That is, it is to no longer be able to think of yourself under the description under which you value yourself and find your life to be worth living and your actions to be worth undertaking. It is to be for all practical purposes dead or worse than dead. When an action cannot be performed without loss of some fundamental part of one's identity, and an agent could just as well be dead, then the obligation not to do it is unconditional and complete. If reasons arise from reflective endorsement, then obligation arises from reflective *rejection*.

3.3.2

Actually, all obligation is unconditional in the sense that I have just described. An obligation always takes the form of a reaction against a threat of a loss of identity. But there are two important complications, and both spring from the complexity of human identity. One is that some parts of our identity are easily shed, and, where they come into conflict with more fundamental parts of our identity, they should be shed. The cases I have in mind are standard: a good soldier obeys orders, but a good human being doesn't massacre the innocent. The other complication, more troublesome, is that you can stop being yourself for a bit and still get back home, and in cases where a small violation combines with a large temptation, this has a destabilizing effect on the obligation. You may know that if you always did this sort of thing your identity would disintegrate, like that of Plato's tyrant in *Republic* IX, but you also know that you can do it just this once without any such result. Kant points out that when we violate the laws of the Kingdom of Ends we must be making exceptions of ourselves, because we cannot coherently will their universal violation.[12] In one sense, a commitment to your

own identity – that is, to your integrity – is supposed to solve that problem. But as we have just seen, the problem reiterates within the commitment to your own integrity. The problem here does not come from the fragility of identity, but rather from its stability. It can take a few knocks, and we know it. The agent I am talking about now violates the law that she is to herself, making an exception of the moment or the case, which she knows she can get away with.

This is why it is best if we love our values as well as having them. But lest you think that I am about to make the same mistake of which I have accused Hume, let me admit that I think this argument establishes an authentic limit to the *depth* of obligation.[13] Obligation is always unconditional, but it is only when it concerns really important matters that it is *deep*. Of course, since we can see that the shallowness of obligation could give rise to problems, we must commit ourselves to a kind of second-order integrity, a commitment to not letting these problems get out of hand. We cannot make an exception 'just this once' every time, or we will lose our identities after all. But the problem will reiterate within that commitment, and so on up the line.

That, by the way, is why even people with the most excellent characters can *occasionally* knowingly do wrong.

3.3.3

To get back to the point. The question how exactly an agent *should* conceive her practical identity, the question which law she should be to herself, is not settled by the arguments I have given. So moral obligation is not yet on the table. To that extent the argument so far is formal, and in one sense empty.

But in another sense it is not empty at all. What we have established is this. The reflective structure of human consciousness requires that you identify yourself with some law or principle which will govern your choices. It requires you to be a law to yourself. And that is the source of

normativity.[14] So the argument shows just what Kant said that it did: that our autonomy is the source of obligation.

It will help to put the point in Joseph Butler's terms, the distinction between power and authority. We do not always do what upon reflection we would do or even what upon reflection we have already decided to do. Reflection does not have irresistible power over us. But when we do reflect we cannot but think that we ought to do what on reflection we conclude we have reason to do. And when we don't do that we punish ourselves, by guilt and regret and repentance and remorse.[15] We might say that the acting self concedes to the thinking self its right to government. And the thinking self, in turn, tries to govern as well as it can.[16] So the reflective structure of human consciousness establishes a relation here, a relation which we have to ourselves.[17] And it is a relation not of mere power but rather of *authority*. And *that* is the authority that is the source of obligation.

Notice that this means that voluntarism is true after all. The source of obligation is a legislator. The realist objection – that we need to explain why we must obey that legislator – has been answered, for this is a legislator whose authority is beyond question and does not need to be established. It is the authority of your own mind and will. So Pufendorf and Hobbes were right. It is not the bare fact that it would be a good idea to perform a certain action that obligates us to perform it. It is the fact that we *command ourselves* to do what we find it would be a good idea to do.

•   •   •

3.4.7

So we may begin by accepting something like the communitarian's point. It is necessary to have *some* conception of your practical identity, for without it you cannot have reasons to act. We endorse or reject our impulses by determining whether they are consistent with the ways in which we identify

ourselves. Yet most of the self-conceptions which govern us are contingent. You are born into a certain family and community, perhaps even into a certain profession or craft. You find a vocation, or ally yourself with a movement. You fall in love and make friends. You are a mother of some particular children, a citizen of a particular country, an adherent of a particular religion, because of the way your life has fallen out. And you act accordingly – caring for your children because they are your children, fighting for your country because you are its citizen, refusing to fight because you are a Quaker, and so on.

Because these conceptions are contingent, one or another of them may be shed. You may cease to think of yourself as a mother or a citizen or a Quaker, or, where the facts make that impossible, the conception may cease to have practical force: you may stop caring whether you live up to the demands of a particular role. This can happen in a variety of ways: it is the stuff of drama, and perfectly familiar to us all. Conflicts that arise between identities, if sufficiently pervasive or severe, may force you to give one of them up: loyalty to your country and its cause may turn you against a pacifist religion, or the reverse. Circumstances may cause you to call the practical importance of an identity into question: falling in love with a Montague may make you think that being a Capulet does not matter after all. Rational reflection may bring you to discard a way of thinking of your practical identity as silly or jejune.[18]

What is not contingent is that you must be governed by *some* conception of your practical identity. For unless you are committed to some conception of your practical identity, you will lose your grip on yourself as having any reason to do one thing rather than another – and with it, your grip on yourself as having any reason to live and act at all. But *this* reason for conforming to your particular practical identities is not a reason that *springs from* one of those particular practical identities. It is a reason that springs from your humanity itself, from your identity

simply as *a human being*, a reflective animal who needs reasons to act and to live. And so it is a reason you have only if you treat your humanity as a practical, normative, form of identity, that is, if you value yourself as a human being.

But to value yourself just as a human being is to have moral identity, as the Enlightenment understood it. So this puts you in moral territory. Or at least, it does so if valuing humanity in your own person rationally requires valuing it in the persons of others. There's an objection to that idea, which I will take up in the next lecture [see original reading]. For now, I will assume that valuing ourselves as human beings involves valuing others that way as well, and carries with it moral obligations.

If this is right, our identity as moral beings – as people who value themselves as human beings – stands behind our more particular practical identities. It is because we are human that we must act in the light of practical conceptions of our identity, and this means that their importance is partly derived from the importance of being human. We must conform to them not merely for the reasons that caused us to adopt them in the first place, but because being human requires it. You may give up one of your contingent practical roles. But so long as you remain committed to a role, and yet fail to meet the obligations it generates, you fail yourself as a human being, as well as failing in that role. And if you fail in all of your roles – if you live at random, without integrity or principle, then you will lose your grip on yourself as one who has any reason to live and to act at all.

Most of the time, our reasons for action spring from our more contingent and local identities. But part of the normative force of those reasons springs from the value we place on ourselves as human beings who need such identities. In this way all value depends on the value of humanity; other forms of practical identity matter in part because humanity requires them. Moral identity and the obligations it carries with it are therefore inescapable

and pervasive. Not every form of practical identity is contingent or relative after all: moral identity is necessary.

3.4.8

This is just a fancy new model of an argument that first appeared in a much simpler form, Kant's argument for his Formula of Humanity.[19] The form of relativism with which Kant began was the most elementary one we encounter – the relativism of value to human desires and interests. He started from the fact that when we make a choice we must regard its object as good. His point is the one I have been making – that being human we must endorse our impulses before we can act on them. He asked what it is that makes these objects good, and, rejecting one form of realism, he decided that the goodness was not in the objects themselves. Were it not for our desires and inclinations – and for the various physiological, psychological, and social conditions which gave rise to those desires and inclinations – we would not find their objects good. Kant saw that we take things to be important because they are important to us – and he concluded that we must therefore take ourselves to be important. In this way, the value of humanity itself is implicit in every human choice. If complete normative scepticism is to be avoided – if there is such a thing as a reason for action – then humanity, as the source of all reasons and values, must be valued for its own sake.

3.4.9

The point I want to make now is the same. In this lecture I have offered an account of the source of normativity. I have argued that human consciousness has a reflective structure that sets us normative problems. It is because of this that we require reasons for action, a conception of the right and the good. To act from such a conception is in turn to have a practical conception of your identity, a conception under which you value yourself and find your life to be worth living and your actions to be worth undertaking. That conception is normative for you and in certain cases it can obligate you, for if you do not allow yourself to be governed by any conception of your identity then you will have no reason to act and to live. So a human being is an animal who needs a practical conception of her own identity, a conception of who she is which is normative for her.

But you are a human being and so if you believe my argument you can now see that that is your identity. You are an animal of the sort I have just described. And that is not merely a contingent conception of your identity, which you have constructed or chosen for yourself, or could conceivably reject. It is simply the truth. It is because we are such animals that our practical identities are normative for us, and, once you see this, you must take this more fundamental identity, being such an animal, to be normative as well. You must value your own humanity if you are to value anything at all.

Why? Because now that you see that your need to have a normative conception of yourself comes from your human identity, you can query the importance of that identity. Your humanity requires you to conform to some of your practical identities, and you can question this requirement as you do any other. Does it really matter whether we act as our humanity requires, whether we find some ways of identifying ourselves and stand by them? But in this case you have no option but to say yes. Since you are human you must take something to be normative, that is, some conception of practical identity must be normative for you. If you had no normative conception of your identity, you could have no reasons for action, and because your consciousness is reflective, you could then not act at all. Since you cannot act without reasons and your humanity is the source of your reasons, you must value your own humanity if you are to act at all.

It follows from this argument that human beings are valuable. Enlightenment morality is true.

3.4.10

The argument I have just given is a transcendental argument. I might bring that out more clearly by putting it this way: rational action exists, so we know it is possible. How is it possible? And then by the course of reflections in which we have just engaged, I show you that rational action is possible only if human beings find their own humanity to be valuable. But rational action is possible, and we are the human beings in question. Therefore we find ourselves to be valuable. Therefore, of course, we are valuable.

You might want to protest against that last step. How do we get from the fact that we find ourselves to be valuable to the conclusion that we are valuable? When we look at the argument this way, its structure seems to be like that of Mill's argument, which proved that if there were any utilitarians, they would find their morality to be normative, and invited us to think that therefore utilitarianism is normative.

But my argument, unlike Mill's, will not fail to find its target. For Mill's readers were not already utilitarians, or did not acknowledge themselves to be so, but you are already human beings, and do acknowledge yourself to be so.

And there's a good reason why the argument must take this form after all. Value, like freedom, is only directly accessible from within the standpoint of reflective consciousness. And I am now talking about it externally, for I am describing the nature of the consciousness that gives rise to the perception of value. From this external, third-person perspective, all we can say is that when we are in the first-person perspective we find ourselves to be valuable, rather than simply that we are valuable. There is nothing surprising in this. Trying to actually see the value of humanity from the third-person perspective is like trying to see the colours someone sees by cracking open his skull. From outside, all we can say is why he sees them.[20]

Suppose you are now tempted once more to say that this shows that value is unreal just as colour is unreal. We do not need to posit the existence of colours to give scientific explanations of why we see them. Then the answer will be the same as before. The Scientific World View is no substitute for human life. If you think colours are unreal, go and look at a painting by Bellini or Olitski, and you will change your mind. If you think reasons and values are unreal, go and make a choice, and you will change your mind.

Morality, personal relationships, and conflict

3.5.1

The argument I have just given is, as I said a moment ago, a transcendental argument. What it is really intended to show is this: that if you value anything at all, or, if you acknowledge the existence of any practical reasons, then you must value your humanity as an end in itself. Or, I might put it, if you are to have any practical identity at all, you must acknowledge yourself to have moral identity – human identity conceived as a form of normative practical identity – as well. And this identity like any other carries with it obligations.

I take this argument to show that any reflective agent can be led to acknowledge that she has moral obligations. What makes morality special is that it springs from a form of identity which cannot be rejected unless we are prepared to reject practical normativity, or the existence of practical reasons, altogether – a possibility about which I will say more in the next lecture [see original reading]. Our other practical identities depend for their normativity on the normativity of our human identity – on our own endorsement of our human need to be governed by

such identities – and cannot withstand reflective scrutiny without it. We must value ourselves as human.

But I do not take the argument to show that all obligations are moral, or that moral obligations always trump others. In fact the argument requires – and our nature requires – that we do have some more local and contingent identities, which provide us with most of our reasons to live and to act. Moral identity does not swamp other forms of identity: no one is simply a moral agent and nothing more. Bernard Williams is right when he says that if morality demanded that of us, it would be incoherent.[21] But it would be wrong to conclude that therefore either moral obligation, or our other obligations, can't be unconditional. To conclude that would not be to affirm the possibility of conflict, but rather to remove its sting. Conflicting obligations can both be unconditional; that's just one of the ways in which human life is hard.

To clarify the point, we should distinguish between two kinds of conflict. One may have a practical identity that is in and of itself contradictory to the value of humanity – say, the identity of an assassin. Or, one may have a practical identity that is not by its nature contrary to moral value, but that leads to a conflict with it in this or that case. The first kind of identity, and the conflicts it generates, is, I think, ruled out by the course of reflection I have tried to describe. In so far as the importance of having a practical identity comes from the value of humanity, it does not make sense to identify oneself in ways that are inconsistent with the value of humanity. But the second kind of conflict cannot be ruled out in this way. Conflict between the specific demands of morality and those of some more contingent form of identity may still exist.

4.2.8

When we experience a desire or an impulse, we consider whether to treat it as a reason, whether to make it our maxim to act on it. We may or may not, though in ordinary cases, we will, so long as there is no reason why not. In that sense, our ordinary impulses have standing with us, an automatic right at least to be heard.

So the first point here is that the reasons of others have something like the same standing with us as our own desires and impulses do.[22] We do not seem to need a reason to take the reasons of others into account. We seem to need a reason not to. Certainly we do things because others want us to, ask us to, tell us to, all the time. We give each other the time and directions, open doors and step aside, warn each other of imminent perils large and small. We respond with the alacrity of obedient soldiers to telephones and doorbell and cries for help. You could say that it is because we want to be cooperative, but that is like saying that you understand my words because you want to be cooperative. It ignores the same essential point, which is that it is so hard not to.

Now the egoist may reply that this does not establish that other people's reasons are reasons for me. I am merely describing a deep psychological fact – that human beings are very susceptible to one another's pressure. We tend to cave in to the demands of others. But nothing I have said so far shows that we really have to treat the demands of others as *reasons*.

4.2.9

Doesn't it? Consider an exchange of reasons. A student comes to your office door and says: 'I need to talk to you. Are you free now?' and you say 'No, I've got to finish this letter right now, and then I've got to go home. Could you possibly come around tomorrow, say about three?' And your student says 'Yes, that will be fine. I'll see you tomorrow at three then.'

What is happening here? On my view, the two of you are reasoning together, to arrive at a decision, a single shared decision, about what to do. And I take that to be the natural view. But if

egoism is true, and reasons cannot be shared, then that is not what is happening. Instead, each of you backs into the privacy of his practical consciousness, reviews his own reasons, comes up with a decision, and then re-emerges to announce the result to each other. And the process stops when the results happen to coincide, and the agents know it, because of the announcements they have made to each other.

Now consider an exchange of ideas, of meanings, rather than an exchange of practical reasons. Here we do not find these two possibilities. If meanings could not be shared, there would be no point in announcing the results of one's private thinking to anybody else. If they can be shared, then it is in principle possible to think the issues through together, and that is what people do when they talk. But if we have to grant that meanings can be shared, why not grant that practical reasons can be shared too?

The egoist may reply that I am leaving out an option. The student/teacher relation is a personal one. People who enter into particular personal relationships have special reasons to take each other's reasons into account. So the exchange I've just described takes place against a background agreement that the parties involved will take each other's reasons into account. The egoist is someone who acts on his own reasons, not someone who has no concern for others. So you and your student reason together because you have tacitly agreed to, but this does not show that this is what usually happens.

But the objection re-emerges within this framework. How are we to understand this personal relationship? If reasons are still private then it goes like this: each of you has a private reason to take the reasons of the other into account. A personal relationship is then an interest in one another's interests. I've already explained, in lecture 3 [see original reading], why I think this isn't right. But in any case this wouldn't change the shape of the deliberation – you still back into your private deliberative spaces and then re-emerge to announce the results. This only

shows why you think there's a point in the exercise at all, why you hope to reach a convergence.

But if you are really reasoning together, if you have joined your wills to arrive at a single shared decision – well, then that can happen, can't it? And why shouldn't it be what usually happens? Why shouldn't language force us to reason practically together, in just the same way that it forces us to think together?

4.2.10

Now how do we get from here to moral obligation? This is where Thomas Nagel's argument, from *The Possibility of Altruism*, comes into its own.

Suppose that we are strangers and that you are tormenting me, and suppose that I call upon you to *stop*. I say: 'How would you like it if someone did that to you?' And now you cannot proceed as you did before. Oh, you can proceed all right, but not just as you did before. For I have obligated you to stop.

How does the obligation come about? Just the way Nagel says that it does. I invite you to consider how you would like it if someone did that to you. You realize that you would not merely dislike it, you would resent it. You would think that the other has a reason to stop, more, that he has an obligation to stop. And that obligation would spring from your own objection to what he does to you. You make yourself an end for others; you make yourself a law to them. But if you are a law to others in so far as you are just human, just *someone*, then the humanity of others is also a law to you. *By making you think these thoughts*, I force you to acknowledge the value of *my* humanity, and I obligate you to act in a way that respects it.

There is an appeal to consistency in this argument; it is meant to remind you of what the value of humanity requires. But it is not what makes you take my reasons into account, or bridges the gap between your reasons and mine, for there is no gap to bridge. Of course it's true that, as Nagel observes, the argument would not

go through if you failed to see yourself, to identify yourself, as just someone, a person, one person among others who are equally real. The argument invites you to change places with the other, and you could not do that if you failed to see what you and the other have in common. Suppose you could say 'someone doing that to *me*, why that would be terrible! But then I am *me*, after all.' Then the argument would fail of its effect, it would not find a foothold in you. But the argument never really fails in *that* way.

For it to fail in that way, I would have to hear your words as mere noise, not as intelligible speech. And it is impossible to hear the words of a language you know as mere noise. In hearing your words as *words*, I acknowledge that you are *someone*. In acknowledging that I can hear them, I acknowledge that I am *someone*. If I listen to the argument at all, I have already admitted that each of us is *someone*.

Nagel characterized the egoist as a practical solipsist and of course he was right. And no form of solipsism is an option for us. You can no more take the reasons of another to be mere pressure than you can take the language of another to be mere noise.

Notes

1 Plato, *Republic* II, 367b, p. 613.

2 Grotius, *On the Law of War and Peace*. Schneewind 1, p. 92. I owe a great debt to Jerome Schneewind for drawing my attention to this stretch of the historical debate, and especially for encouraging me to read Pufendorf.

3 See Hobbes, especially *Leviathan* (1651), and Pufendorf, *On the Law of Nature and Of Nations* (1672) and *On the Duty of Man and Citizen According to Natural Law* (1673). More detailed references will be given in the discussion that follows.

4 See Clarke, *A Discourse Concerning the Unchangeable Obligations of Natural Religion, and the Truth and Certainty of the Christian Revelation. The Boyle Lectures* 1705; and Price, *A Review of the Principal Questions in Morals* (1758). More detailed references will be given in the discussion that follows.

5 Hobbes, *Leviathan*, 1.13, p. 90.

6 Hobbes, *Leviathan*, 1.15, p. 110.

7 See Mandeville, *The Fable of the Bees: or, Private Vices, Public Benefits*, especially the section 'An Enquiry into the Origin of Moral Virtue', pp. 41–57. Mandeville himself denied that he meant either that virtue is unreal or that it is not worth having. See for instance 'A Vindication of the Book', pp. 384ff.; and also *An Enquiry into the Origin of Honor*, in Schneewind II, pp. 396–98.

8 For this thought see Kant, *Critique of Judgment*, especially part 1, division 1, book 1, 'The Analytic of the Beautiful'. Kant argues that when we judge something beautiful we not only take pleasure in it, but demand that everyone do so.

9 Prichard, 'Does Moral Philosophy Rest on a Mistake?' and 'Duty and Interest'. Prichard's argument is discussed in detail below.

10 Actually, as Hume and Hutcheson both argued, there are also problems about the explanatory adequacy of Mandeville's view. Neither Hume nor Hutcheson names Mandeville, but that he is their target is clear. Mandeville had suggested that politicians create the desire to be virtuous by praising virtue, and so by appealing to our pride. Hume and Hutcheson's answer is that if there were not a basis in human nature for the pleasure we take in being praised for our character and actions, the ideal of virtue could neither be made intelligible to nor motivate us. Politicians might turn the ideal of virtue to their own use but could not conceivably have invented it from whole cloth and foisted it upon animals whose only conception of the good is getting what they want. For Hume's discussion see the *Enquiry Concerning the Principles of Morals*, p. 214. For Hutcheson's see the *Inquiry Concerning the Original of our Ideas of Beauty and Virtue*, in Raphael 1, p. 291.

11 Romans 2:14. This paragraph is lifted with modifications from my 'Personal Identity and the Unity of Agency: a Kantian Response to Parfit', 111. I believe there are resources in this line of thought for dealing with the problem of personal identity, and some of them are explored in that paper.

12 Kant, *Foundations of the Metaphysics of Morals*, p. 424; in Beck's translation, p. 42.

13 I mean the objection at the end of lecture 2. Hume forgot that knowing that our hatred of injustice

was based on general rules would have a destabilizing effect on the obligation always to be just.

14   What I am saying here is that the categorical imperative is the general principle of normativity in the practical sphere. In 'Reason and Politics in the Kantian Enterprise', Onora O'Neill argues that the categorical imperative is the supreme principle of reason in general, which in my language means it is the supreme principle of normativity in general. It will become apparent in the course of this lecture and the next that I agree with that, although of course the idea is not completely defended here.

15   In lecture 4, 4.3.8, I present a further account of these moral emotions and how they are related to autonomy.

16   The distinction between the thinking self and the acting self is very close to Kant's distinction between *Wille* (will) and *Willkür* (choice). See *The Metaphysics of Morals*, pp. 213–14; in Gregor's translation, pp. 41–43.

17   In *The Metaphysics of Morals*, Kant says that all duties must be grounded in duties to the self, and yet that duties to the self are only intelligible if there are two aspects to the self. He calls them 'homo noumenon' and 'homo phenomenon' (pp. 417–18; in Gregor's translation, pp. 214–15). Notice the strange alternation of one and two here: duties must arise within one, rather than between two, and yet for them to arise that one must be two. The idea of the reflective character of human consciousness, together with the thesis that obligation springs from autonomy, explains why it has to be this way.

18   I have not mentioned giving up a practical conception of your identity (or deciding that you aren't free to give one up) for moral reasons here. This is not because I don't think that happens, of course, but because this argument is supposed to explain why moral identity has a special status. Until that conclusion is established, conflict between morality and other forms of identity just counts as one case of conflict between identities.

19   Kant, *Foundations of the Metaphysics of Morals*, pp. 427–28; in Beck's translation, pp. 45–47. I am here summarizing the interpretation of this argument I give in 'Kant's Formula of Humanity'.

20   This is why Prichard, in 'Does Moral Philosophy Rest on a Mistake?', says that when we fall into doubt about whether we have obligations the remedy is to place or imagine ourselves in a situation where we are really obligated (pp. 16–17). The normative force of reasons, obligations, and values, is a force that is felt by a deliberating agent and is imperceptible from outside of the deliberative perspective.

21   See Williams, 'Persons, Character, and Morality' and 'Moral Luck'.

22   I thank Ulrike Heuer for supplying this comparison.

References

Clarke, Samuel. *A Discourse Concerning the Unchangeable Obligations of Natural Religion, and the Truth and Certainty of the Christian Revelation: the Boyle Lectures 1705.* I have quoted from both J. B. Schneewind, *Moral Philosophy from Montaigne to Kant*, and D. D. Raphael, *British Moralists 1650–1800*.

Grotius, Hugo. *De juri belli ac pacis* (*On the Law of War and Peace*, 1625). Translated by Francis W. Kelsey. Oxford: Oxford University Press, 1925. I have quoted from J. B. Schneewind, *Moral Philosophy from Montaigne to Kant*.

Hobbes, Thomas. *Leviathan* (1651). Edited by Richard Tuck. Cambridge: Cambridge University Press, 1991.

Hume, David. *Enquiry Concerning the Principles of Morals* (1751), in *David Hume: Enquiries Concerning Human Understanding and Concerning the Principles of Morals*. 3rd edition edited by L. A. Selby-Bigge and P. H. Nidditch. Oxford: Clarendon Press, 1975.

Hutcheson, Francis. *Inquiry Concerning the Original of our Ideas of Beauty and Virtue* (1725). I have quoted from D. D. Raphael, *British Moralists 1650–1800*; except on one occasion when I have quoted a passage not in Raphael from L. A. Selby-Bigge, *The British Moralists*. Oxford: Clarendon Press, 1897; printed by The Library of Liberal Arts, 1964.

Kant, Immanuel. *Grundlegung zur Metaphysick der Sitten* (*Foundations of the Metaphysics of Morals*, 1785). Translated by Lewis White Beck. New York: Macmillan Library of Liberals Arts, 1959.

—— *Kants gesammelte Schriften*, The Prussian Academy Edition. Twenty-eight volumes. Berlin: Walter de Gruyter & Company, 1902–. The page numbers found in the margins of most translations refer to this edition. When I have cited Kant, I have therefore referred to these page numbers. The English

translations quoted or cited are listed in separate bibliographical entries for the works in question.

— *Metaphysik der Sitten* (*The Metaphysics of Morals*, 1797). Translated by Mary Gregor. Cambridge: Cambridge University Press, 1991.

Korsgaard, Christine M. 'Personal Identity and the Unity of Agency: a Kantian Response to Parfit'. *Philosophy and Public Affairs* 18 (Spring 1989): 101–32. Forthcoming in Korsgaard, *Creating the Kingdom of Ends*, chapter 13. New York: Cambridge University Press, 1995.

Mandeville, Bernard. *An Enquiry into the Origin of Honor* (1732). I have quoted from J. B. Schneewind, *Moral Philosophy from Montaigne to Kant*.

— *The Fable of the Bees: or, Private Vices, Public Benefits* (1714). Edited by F. B. Kaye. Indianapolis: Liberty Classics, 1988. This edition is a reprint of a 1924 edition published by Oxford University Press.

Nagel, Thomas. *The Possibility of Altruism*. Princeton: Princeton University Press, 1970.

O'Neill, Onora. 'Reason and Politics in the Kantian Enterprise', in *Constructions of Reason: Explorations of Kant's Practical Philosophy*. Cambridge: Cambridge University Press, 1989.

Plato. *The Collected Dialogues*. Edited by Edith Hamilton and Huntington Cairns. Princeton: Princeton University Press, 1961.

Price, Richard. *A Review of the Principal Questions in Morals* (1758). Edited by D. D. Raphael. Oxford: Clarendon Press, 1948. I have also cited the selections in Schneewind, *Moral Philosophy from Montaigne to Kant*, and Raphael, *British Moralists 1650–1800*.

Prichard, H. A. 'Does Moral Philosophy Rest on a Mistake?' (*Mind* 21 (1912)) and 'Duty and Interest' (Oxford: Clarendon Press, 1929). Reprinted in *Moral Obligation and Duty and Interest. Essays and Lectures by H. A. Prichard*. Edited by W. D. Ross and J. O. Urmson. Oxford: Oxford University Press, 1968.

Pufendorf, Samuel. *On The Law of Nature and of Nations* (1672). Translated by C. H. Oldfather and W. A. Oldfather. Oxford: Oxford University Press, 1934. I have quoted from J. B. Schneewind, *Moral Philosophy from Montaigne to Kant*.

— *On the Duty of Man and Citizen According to Natural Law* (1673). Edited by James Tully and translated by Michael Silverthorne. Cambridge: Cambridge University Press, 1991.

Raphael, D. D., editor. *British Moralists 1650–1800*. Two volumes. Indianapolis: Hackett Publishing Company, 1991. Reprint of an edition published in Oxford: Oxford University Press, 1969. Where I have quoted from this anthology rather than original sources I have cited it as Raphael I and Raphael II.

Schneewind, J. B., editor. *Moral Philosophy from Montaigne to Kant*. Two volumes. Cambridge: Cambridge University Press, 1990. Where I have quoted from this anthology rather than original sources I have cited it as Schneewind I and Schneewind II.

Williams, Bernard. *Moral Luck*. Cambridge: Cambridge University Press, 1981.

Philippa Foot

MORALITY AS A SYSTEM OF HYPOTHETICAL IMPERATIVES

THERE ARE many difficulties and obscurities in Kant's moral philosophy, and few contemporary moralists will try to defend it all. Many, for instance, agree in rejecting Kant's derivation of duties from the mere form of the law expressed in terms of a universally legislative will. Nevertheless, it is generally supposed, even by those who would not dream of calling themselves his followers, that Kant established one thing beyond doubt—namely, the necessity of distinguishing moral judgements from hypothetical imperatives. That moral judgements cannot be hypothetical imperatives has come to seem an unquestionable truth. It will be argued here that it is not.

In discussing so thoroughly Kantian a notion as that of the hypothetical imperative, one naturally begins by asking what Kant himself meant by a hypothetical imperative, and it may be useful to say a little about the idea of an imperative as this appears in Kant's works. In writing about imperatives Kant seems to be thinking at least as much of statements about what ought to be or should be done, as of injunctions expressed in the imperative mood. He even describes as an imperative the assertion that it would be 'good to do or refrain from doing something'[1] and explains that for a will that 'does not always do something simply because it is presented to it as a good thing to do' this has the force of a command of reason. We may therefore think of Kant's imperatives as statements to the effect that something ought to be done or that it would be good to do it.

The distinction between hypothetical imperatives and categorical imperatives, which plays so important a part in Kant's ethics, appears in characteristic form in the following passages from the *Foundations of the Metaphysics of Morals*:

All imperatives command either hypothetically or categorically. The former present the practical necessity of a possible action as a means to achieving something else which one desires (or which one may possibly desire). The categorical imperative would be one which presented an action as of itself objectively necessary, without regard to any other end.[2]

If the action is good only as a means to something else, the imperative is hypothetical; but if it is thought of as good in itself, and hence as necessary in a will which of itself conforms to reason as the principle of this will, the imperative is categorical.[3]

The hypothetical imperative, as Kant defines it, 'says only that the action is good to some purpose' and the purpose, he explains, may be possible or actual. Among imperatives related to actual purposes Kant mentions rules of prudence, since he believes that all men necessarily desire their own happiness. Without committing ourselves to

this view it will be useful to follow Kant in classing together as 'hypothetical imperatives' those telling a man what he ought to do because (or if) he wants something and those telling him what he ought to do on grounds of self-interest. Common opinion agrees with Kant in insisting that a moral man must accept a rule of duty whatever his interests or desires.

Having given a rough description of the class of Kantian hypothetical imperatives it may be useful to point to the heterogeneity within it. Sometimes what a man should do depends on his passing inclination, as when he wants his coffee hot and should warm the jug. Sometimes it depends on some long-term project, when the feelings and inclinations of the moment are irrelevant. If one wants to be a respectable philosopher one should get up in the mornings and do some work, though just at that moment when one should do it the thought of being a respectable philosopher leaves one cold. It is true nevertheless to say of one, at that moment, that one wants to be a respectable philosopher, and this can be the foundation of a desire-dependent hypothetical imperative. The term 'desire' as used in the original account of the hypothetical imperative was meant as a grammatically convenient substitute for 'want', and was not meant to carry any implication of inclination rather than long-term aim or project. Even the word 'project', taken strictly, introduces undesirable restrictions. If someone is devoted to his family or his country or to any cause, there are certain things he wants, which may then be the basis of hypothetical imperatives, without either inclinations or projects being quite what is in question. Hypothetical imperatives should already be appearing as extremely diverse; a further important distinction is between those that concern an individual and those that concern a group. The desires on which a hypothetical imperative is dependent may be those of one man, or may be taken for granted as belonging to a number of people engaged in some common project or sharing common aims.

Is Kant right to say that moral judgements are categorical, not hypothetical, imperatives? It may seem that he is, for we find in our language two different uses of words such as 'should' and 'ought', apparently corresponding to Kant's hypothetical and categorical imperatives, and we find moral judgements on the 'categorical' side. Suppose, for instance, we have advised a traveller that he should take a certain train, believing him to be journeying to his home. If we find that he has decided to go elsewhere, we will most likely have to take back what we said: the 'should' will now be unsupported and in need of support. Similarly, we must be prepared to withdraw our statement about what he should do if we find that the right relation does not hold between the action and the end—that it is either no way of getting what he wants (or doing what he wants to do) or not the most eligible among possible means. The use of 'should' and 'ought' in moral contexts is, however, quite different. When we say that a man should do something and intend a moral judgement we do not have to back up what we say by considerations about his interests or his desires; if no such connexion can be found the 'should' need not be withdrawn. It follows that the agent cannot rebut an assertion about what, morally speaking, he should do by showing that the action is not ancillary to his interests or desires. Without such a connexion the 'should' does not stand unsupported and in need of support; the support that it requires is of another kind.

There is, then, one clear difference between moral judgements and the class of 'hypothetical imperatives' so far discussed. In the latter 'should' is 'used hypothetically', in the sense defined, and if Kant were merely drawing attention to this piece of linguistic usage his point would easily be proved. But obviously Kant meant more than this; in describing moral judgements as non-hypothetical—that is, categorical imperatives—he is ascribing to them a special dignity and necessity which this usage

cannot give. Modern philosophers follow Kant in talking, for example, about the 'unconditional requirement' expressed in moral judgements. These, they say, tell us what we have to do whatever our interests or desires, and by their inescapability they are distinguished from hypothetical imperatives.

The problem is to find proof for this further feature of moral judgements. If anyone fails to see the gap that has to be filled it will be useful to point out to him that we find 'should' used non-hypothetically in some non-moral statements to which no one attributes the special dignity and necessity conveyed by the description 'categorical imperative'. For instance, we find this non-hypothetical use of 'should' in sentences enunciating rules of etiquette, as, for example, that an invitation in the third person should be answered in the third person, where the rule does not *fail to apply* to someone who has his own good reasons for ignoring this piece of nonsense, or who simply does not care about what, from the point of view of etiquette, he should do. Similarly, there is a non-hypothetical use of 'should' in contexts where something like a club rule is in question. The club secretary who has told a member that he should not bring ladies into the smoking-room does not say, 'Sorry, I was mistaken' when informed that this member is resigning tomorrow and cares nothing about his reputation in the club. Lacking a connexion with the agent's desires or interests, this 'should' does not stand 'unsupported and in need of support'; it requires only the backing of the rule. This use of 'should' is therefore 'non-hypothetical' in the sense defined.

It follows that if a hypothetical use of 'should' gave a hypothetical imperative, and a non-hypothetical use of 'should' a categorical imperative, then 'should' statements based on rules of etiquette, or rules of a club would be categorical imperatives. Since this would not be accepted by defenders of the categorical imperative in ethics, who would insist that these other 'should' statements give hypothetical

imperatives, they must be using this expression in some other sense. We must therefore ask what they mean when they say that 'You should answer . . . in the third person' is a hypothetical imperative. Very roughly the idea seems to be that one may reasonably ask why anyone should bother about what should (from the point of view of etiquette) be done, and that such considerations deserve no notice unless reason is shown. So although people give as their reason for doing something the fact that it is required by etiquette, we do not take this consideration as *in itself giving us reason to act*. Considerations of etiquette do not have any automatic reason-giving force, and a man might be right if he denied that he had reason to do 'what's done'.

This seems to take us to the heart of the matter, for, by contrast, it is supposed that moral considerations necessarily give reasons for acting to any man. The difficulty is, of course, to defend this proposition which is more often repeated than explained. Unless it is said, implausibly, that all 'should' or 'ought' statements give reasons for acting, which leaves the old problem of assigning a special categorical status to moral judgement, we must be told what it is that makes the moral 'should' relevantly different from the 'shoulds' appearing in normative statements of other kinds.[4] Attempts have sometimes been made to show that some kind of irrationality is involved in ignoring the 'should' of morality: in saying 'Immoral—so what?' as one says 'Not *comme il faut*—so what?' But as far as I can see these have all rested on some illegitimate assumption, as, for instance, of thinking that the amoral man, who agrees that some piece of conduct is immoral but takes no notice of that, is inconsistently disregarding a rule of conduct that he has accepted; or again of thinking it inconsistent to desire that others will not do to one what one proposes to do to them. The fact is that the man who rejects morality because he sees no reason to obey its rules can be convicted of villainy but not of inconsistency. Nor will his action necessarily be irrational.

Irrational actions are those in which a man in some way defeats his own purposes, doing what is calculated to be disadvantageous or to frustrate his ends. Immorality does not *necessarily* involve any such thing.

It is obvious that the normative character of moral judgement does not guarantee its reason-giving force. Moral judgements are normative, but so are judgements of manners, statements of club rules, and many others. Why should the first provide reasons for acting as the others do not? In every case it is because there is a background of teaching that the non-hypothetical 'should' can be used. The behaviour is required, not simply recommended, but the question remains as to why we should do what we are required to do. It is true that moral rules are often enforced much more strictly than the rules of etiquette, and our reluctance to press the non-hypothetical 'should' of etiquette may be one reason why we think of the rules of etiquette as hypothetical imperatives. But are we then to say that there is nothing behind the idea that moral judgements are categorical imperatives but the relative stringency of our moral teaching? I believe that this may have more to do with the matter than the defenders of the categorical imperative would like to admit. For if we look at the kind of thing that is said in its defence we may find ourselves puzzled about what the words can even mean unless we connect them with the feelings that this stringent teaching implants. People talk, for instance, about the 'binding force' of morality, but it is not clear what this means if not that we *feel* ourselves unable to escape. Indeed the 'inescapability' of moral requirements is often cited when they are being contrasted with hypothetical imperatives. No one, it is said, escapes the requirements of ethics by having or not having particular interests or desires. Taken in one way this only reiterates the contrast between the 'should' of morality and the hypothetical 'should', and once more places morality alongside of etiquette. Both are inescapable in that behaviour does not cease to offend against either morality or etiquette because the agent is indifferent to their purposes and to the disapproval he will incur by flouting them. But morality is supposed to be inescapable in some special way and this may turn out to be merely the reflection of the way morality is taught. Of course, we must try other ways of expressing the fugitive thought. It may be said, for instance, that moral judgements have a kind of necessity since they tell us what we 'must do' or 'have to do' whatever our interests and desires. The sense of this is, again, obscure. Sometimes when we use such expressions we are referring to physical or mental compulsion. (A man has to go along if he is pulled by strong men and he has to give in if tortured beyond endurance.) But it is only in the absence of such conditions that moral judgements apply. Another and more common sense of the words is found in sentences such as 'I caught a bad cold and had to stay in bed' where a penalty for acting otherwise is in the offing. The necessity of acting morally is not, however, supposed to depend on such penalties. Another range of examples, not necessarily having to do with penalties, if found where there is an unquestioned acceptance of some project or role, as when a nurse tells us that she has to make her rounds at a certain time, or we say that we have to run for a certain train. But these too are irrelevant in the present context, since the acceptance condition can always be revoked.

No doubt it will be suggested that it is in some other sense of the words 'have to' or 'must' that one has to or must do what morality demands. But why should one insist that there must be such a sense when it proves so difficult to say what it is? Suppose that what we take for a puzzling thought were really no thought at all but only the reflection of our *feelings* about morality? Perhaps it makes no sense to say that we 'have to' submit to the moral law, or that morality is 'inescapable' in some special way. For just as one may feel as if one is falling without believing that one is moving downward, so one

may feel as if one has to do what is morally required without believing oneself to be under physical or psychological compulsion, or about to incur a penalty if one does not comply. No one thinks that if the word 'falling' is used in a statement reporting one's sensations it must be used in a special sense. But this kind of mistake may be involved in looking for the special sense in which one 'has to' do what morality demands. There is no difficulty about the idea that we feel we *have to* behave morally, and given the psychological conditions of the learning of moral behaviour it is natural that we should have such feelings. What we cannot do is quote them in support of the doctrine of the categorical imperative. It seems, then, that in so far as it is backed up by statements to the effect that the moral law *is* inescapable, or that we *do* have to do what is morally required of us, it is uncertain whether the doctrine of the categorical imperative even makes sense.

The conclusion we should draw is that moral judgements have no better claim to be categorical imperatives than do statements about matters of etiquette. People may indeed follow either morality or etiquette without asking why they should do so, but equally well they may not. They may ask for reasons and may reasonably refuse to follow either if reasons are not to be found.

It will be said that this way of viewing moral considerations must be totally destructive of morality, because no one could ever act morally unless he accepted such considerations as in themselves sufficient reason for action. Actions that are truly moral must be done 'for their own sake', 'because they are right', and not for some ulterior purpose. This argument we must examine with care, for the doctrine of the categorical imperative has owed much to its persuasion.

Is there anything to be said for the thesis that a truly moral man acts 'out of respect for the moral law' or that he does what is morally right because it is morally right? That such

propositions are not prima facie absurd depends on the fact that moral judgement concerns itself with a man's reasons for acting as well as with what he does. Law and etiquette require only that certain things are done or left undone, but no one is counted as charitable if he gives alms 'for the praise of men', and one who is honest only because it pays him to be honest does not have the virtue of honesty. This kind of consideration was crucial in shaping Kant's moral philosophy. He many times contrasts acting out of respect for the moral law with acting from an ulterior motive, and what is more from one that is self-interested. In the early *Lectures on Ethics* he gave the principle of truth-telling under a system of hypothetical imperatives as that of not lying *if it harms one to lie*. In the *Metaphysics of Morals* he says that ethics cannot start from the ends which a man may propose to himself, since these are all 'selfish'.[5] In the *Critique of Practical Reason* he argues explicitly that when acting not out of respect for moral law but 'on a material maxim' men do what they do for the sake of pleasure or happiness.

> All material practical principles are, as such, of one and the same kind and belong under the general principle of self love or one's own happiness.[6]

Kant, in fact, was a psychological hedonist* in respect of all actions except those done for the sake of the moral law, and this faulty theory of human nature was one of the things preventing him from seeing that moral virtue might be compatible with the rejection of the categorical imperative.

If we put this theory of human action aside, and allow as ends the things that seem to be ends, the picture changes. It will surely be allowed that quite apart from thoughts of duty a

---

* One who believes that actions are performed to gain pleasure or avoid pain.

man may care about the suffering of others, having a sense of identification with them, and wanting to help if he can. Of course he must want not the reputation of charity, nor even a gratifying rôle helping others, but, quite simply, their good. If this is what he does care about, then he will be attached to the end proper to the virtue of charity and a comparison with someone acting from an ulterior motive (even a respectable ulterior motive) is out of place. Nor will the conformity of his action to the rule of charity be merely contingent. Honest action may happen to further a man's career; charitable actions do not *happen* to further the good of others.[7]

Can a man accepting only hypothetical imperatives possess other virtues besides that of charity? Could he be just or honest? This problem is more complex because there is no end related to such virtues as the good of others is related to charity. But what reason could there be for refusing to call a man a just man if he acted justly because he loved truth and liberty, and wanted every man to be treated with a certain respect? And why should the truly honest man not follow honesty for the sake of the good that honest dealing brings to men? Of course, the usual difficulties can be raised about the rare case in which no good is foreseen from an individual act of honesty. But it is not evident that a man's desires could not give him reason to act honestly even here. He wants to live openly and in good faith with his neighbours; it is not all the same to him to lie and conceal.

If one wants to know whether there could be a truly moral man who accepted moral principles as hypothetical rules of conduct, as many people accept rules of etiquette as hypothetical rules of conduct, one must consider the right kind of example. A man who demanded that morality should be brought under the heading of self-interest would not be a good candidate, nor would anyone who was ready to be charitable or honest only so long as he felt inclined. A cause such as justice makes strenuous demands, but this is not peculiar to morality, and men are prepared to toil to achieve many ends not endorsed by morality. That they are prepared to fight so hard for moral ends—for example, for liberty and justice—depends on the fact that these are the kinds of ends that arouse devotion. To sacrifice a great deal for the sake of etiquette one would need to be under the spell of the emphatic 'ought'. One could hardly be devoted to behaving *comme il faut*.

In spite of all that has been urged in favour of the hypothetical imperative in ethics, I am sure that many people will be unconvinced and will argue that one element essential to moral virtue is still missing. This missing feature is the recognition of a *duty* to adopt those ends which we have attributed to the moral man. We have said that he *does* care about others, and about causes such as liberty and justice; that it is on this account that he will accept a system of morality. But what if he never cared about such things, or what if he ceased to care? Is it not the case that he *ought* to care? This is exactly what Kant would say, for though at times he sounds as if he thought that morality is not concerned with ends, at others he insists that the adoption of ends such as the happiness of others is itself dictated by morality.[8] How is this proposition to be regarded by one who rejects all talk about the binding force of the moral law? He will agree that a moral man has moral ends and cannot be indifferent to matters such as suffering and injustice. Further, he will recognise in the statement that one *ought* to care about these things a correct application of the non-hypothetical moral 'ought' by which society is apt to voice its demands. He will not, however, take the fact that he ought to have certain ends as in itself reason to adopt them. If he himself is a moral man then he cares about such things, but not 'because he ought'. If he is an amoral man he may deny that he has any reason to trouble his head over this or any other moral demand. Of course he may be mistaken, and his life as well as others' lives may be most sadly spoiled by his selfishness. But this is not what is urged by those who think they can close the matter by an

emphatic use of 'ought'. My argument is that they are relying on an illusion, as if trying to give the moral 'ought' a magic force.[9]

This conclusion may, as I said, appear dangerous and subversive of morality. We are apt to panic at the thought that we ourselves, or other people, might stop caring about the things we do care about, and we feel that the categorical imperative gives us some control over the situation. But it is interesting that the people of Leningrad were not struck by the thought that only the *contingent* fact that other citizens shared their loyalty and devotion to the city stood between them and the Germans during the terrible years of the siege. Perhaps we should be less troubled than we are by fear of defection from the moral cause; perhaps we should even have less reason to fear it if people thought of themselves as volunteers banded together to fight for liberty and justice and against inhumanity and oppression. It is often felt, even if obscurely, that there is an element of deception in the official line about morality. And while some have been persuaded by talk about the authority of the moral law, others have turned away with a sense of distrust.

Notes

1 *Foundations of the Metaphysics of Morals*, Sec. II, trans. by L. W. Beck.
2 Ibid.
3 Ibid.
4 To say that moral considerations are *called* reasons is blatantly to ignore the problem.

In the case of etiquette or club rules it is obvious that the non-hypothetical use of 'should' has resulted in the loss of the usual connexion between what one should do and what one has reason to do. Someone who objects that in the moral case a man cannot be justified in restricting his practical reasoning in this way, since every moral 'should' give reasons for acting, must face the following dilemma. Either it is possible to create reasons for acting simply by putting together any silly rules and introducing a non-hypothetical 'should', or else the non-hypothetical 'should' does not necessarily imply reasons for acting. If it does not necessarily imply reasons for acting we may ask why it is supposed to do so in the case of morality. Why cannot the indifferent amoral man say that for him 'should$_m$' gives no reason for acting, treating 'should$_m$' as most of us treat 'should$_e$'? Those who insist that 'should$_m$' is categorical in this second 'reason-giving' sense do not seem to realise that they never prove this to be so. They sometimes say that moral considerations 'just do' give reasons for acting, without explaining why some devotee of etiquette could not say the same about the rules of etiquette.

5 Pt. II, Introduction, sec. II.
6 Immanuel Kant, *Critique of Practical Reason*, trans. L. W. Beck, p. 133.
7 It is not, of course, necessary that charitable actions should *succeed* in helping others; but when they do so they do not *happen* to do so, since that is necessarily their aim. (Footnote added, 1977.)
8 See e.g., *The Metaphysics of Morals*, pt. II, sec. 30.
9 See G. E. M. Anscombe, 'Modern Moral Philosophy', *Philosophy* (1958). My view is different from Miss Anscombe's, but I have learned from her.

Russ Shafer-Landau

MORAL RATIONALISM

ORAL RATIONALISM is the view that moral obligations entail reasons for action: necessarily, if one has a moral obligation to do something, then one has a reason to do it. I think that rationalism is more plausible than most people have thought. After briefly sketching some positive considerations on its behalf, I want to focus on trying to disarm what I think are the four most serious criticisms of it. I'll conclude by trying to draw some general lessons about how difficult it is to justify claims about the ultimate sources of normativity.

Suppose someone does an act because she thinks it right – she acts from the motive of duty, and, let us suppose, in this case she is on target about what duty requires. What justifies her in performing such an act? If someone correctly cites an action's rightness as her reason for performing it, we don't ordinarily question the legitimacy or conceptual coherence of her doing so. But if the rightness of an act itself was no reason at all for performing it, then we would have to do just that. It could never be the case that the rightness of an act was what justified or legitimated its performance, made its performance appropriate under the circumstances. For legitimacy, appropriateness, and justification are all normative notions, and their proper application depends crucially on the existence of reasons. If the rightness of an act was itself no reason to perform it, then even the *prima facie* justification of virtuous conduct would always

be contingent on a showing that it (say) serves self-interest or satisfies the agent's desires. Almost no one believes this. This implies that an action's rightness constitutes a good justifying reason for performing it.

We can support this view by considering immoral acts as well. When we deem someone's behavior morally unjustified, we imply that he has violated a standard of appropriate conduct. Suppose such standards did not by themselves supply reasons for action. Then we'd be forced to allow that though some actions are unjustified, immoral, improper, illegitimate, or inappropriate, there nevertheless may be no reason at all to avoid them. But this seems wrong – not only conceptually confused, but also gravely unfair. It seems a conceptual error to cite a standard as a guide to conduct and a basis for evaluation – to say, for instance, that S ought to have kept her promise, and was wrong for having failed to keep her promise – and yet claim that there was no reason at all for S to have kept her promise. And it seems unfair to criticize violations of such standards while admitting that an agent responsible for offensive conduct may have had no reason to do otherwise. The fairness and appropriateness of moral evaluation rest on an agent's attentiveness to reasons. An agent who correctly claims to have ignored no reasons for action cannot be held to have violated any moral standard. This plausible thought is true only if moral rationalism is true.

We are left, therefore, with the choice of either endorsing moral rationalism, or endorsing the idea that proper moral evaluation of an agent has nothing to do with the agent's attentiveness to reasons. Those who take the latter option must shoulder the burden of explaining just what (other than reasons) could serve as the basis for moral assessment, and just how this basis will manage to avoid the apparent unfairness of criticizing agents for conduct they had no reason to avoid.

I think that the considerations just offered provide some presumptive argument for the truth of moral rationalism. We can strengthen the case if we are able defuse the strongest arguments against it. Let me proceed directly to this task.

The first of the critical arguments is what I shall call *The Reasons Internalist Argument*:

1.   Reasons Internalism is true: reasons must be capable of motivating those for whom they are reasons.
2.   Desires are required for motivation.
3.   Moral obligations apply to agents independently of their desires.
4.   Therefore moral rationalism is false.

According to this argument, what reasons we have depends on our motivational capacity, which in turn depends on our desires. What moral obligations we have does not depend on our desires. Therefore we may entirely lack reason to fulfill our moral obligations. Therefore moral rationalism is false.

Here I want to consider only the merits of the first premise of this argument. According to those who favor reasons internalism, a reason must be capable of motivating in the sense that there is some rational relation that obtains between the putative reason and one's existing motivations; there must be, as Bernard Williams (1981: 104–5) puts it, a "sound deliberative route" from one's "subjective motivational set" to the belief or action for which there is a putative reason. So if internalism is true, then one's reasons are restricted to those results attainable from rationally deliberating from one's existing motivations. I believe that this restriction is spurious, and that internalism is, therefore, false.

Consider a person so misanthropic, so heedless of others' regard, so bent on cruelty, that nothing in his present set of motives would prevent him from committing the worst kind of horrors. He cannot, in the relevant sense, be moved to forbear from such behavior. But why should this unfortunate fact force us to revise our standards for appropriate conduct? Nothing we say to him will convince him to modify his behavior. But is this intransigence a basis for holding him to different standards, or isn't it rather a justification for convicting him of a kind of blindness? It is natural to say that people have reason to refrain from behavior that is fiendish, callous, brutal, arrogant or craven. We don't withdraw such evaluations just because their targets fail (or would, after deliberation, fail) to find them compelling.

Internalists are in a difficult position here. If internalism is true, then the absence of a sound deliberative link from one's motivations to Φ-ing means that there is no reason to Φ. Now if blame requires failure to adhere to good reasons, and the absence of this motivational link entails an absence of reasons, then agents are morally blameless if avoidance of evil bears no such link to their motivations. The worst of the lot – hatemongers and misanthropes, the Streichers or the Himmlers of the world – would thereby be immune from blame. And hence, presumably, from punishment, since proper punishment is predicated on blameworthiness.

The argument can be put more straightforwardly as follows:

1.   If internalism is true, then one has no reason to Φ if Φ-ing is rationally unrelated to one's existing motivations.
2.   If one has no reason to Φ, then one can't be justly blamed or punished for not Φ-ing.

3.   Therefore if internalism is true, then one can't be justly blamed or punished for not Φ-ing, if Φ-ing is rationally unrelated to one's existing motivations.

4.   Some agents *are* justly blamed or punished for their evil deeds, even though avoidance of such conduct was rationally unrelated to their motivations.

5.   Therefore internalism is false.

Those who dislike the conclusion have just two premises to choose from, since the first premise is a conceptual truth. The second premise is strong. It ties blameworthiness (and suitability for punishment) to the existence of reasons. To reject the second premise is to insist that agents may be blameworthy despite lacking any reason to refrain from their unseemly conduct. Such a stand commits one to the view that one could be properly blameworthy for Φ-ing even though one had no reason not to Φ; blameable for Φ-ing, though no consideration at all inclined against Φ-ing. I think that is a very strange view. For we rightly suppose that whenever someone is blameworthy, there is in principle some explanation of this fact, some feature in virtue of which an agent is blameworthy. That feature must embody a failing. And this failure is best understood as a failure to appreciate or adhere to considerations that favor or oppose some attitude, choice, or action. But such considerations are just what reasons are. So rejecting the second premise leaves one with an unrecognizable view of the conditions under which agents are properly subject to blame.

The last option is to reject the fourth premise. In this context, it helps if we focus again on various malefactors, say, on the disciplined immoralist, or the single-minded, principled fanatic. Those who reject the fourth premise must say of such agents that they ought to be immune from blame and punishment. Yet if anyone merits such assessments, surely those committed to evil do. As far as I can tell, the only way to justify withholding censure from such wrongdoers is to withhold it from everyone,

and argue against the existence of any moral responsibility. Perhaps, in the final analysis, no one is properly liable to blame or punishment. There are well-known arguments to this conclusion, which almost no one believes. Nevertheless, this is an option for the internalist.

So internalists are faced with the choice of withholding blame from the very worst that humanity has to offer, or embracing an unpalatable view of blameworthiness that severs its connection with sensitivity and adherence to reasons. Externalism easily avoids this dilemma, and that is good reason to prefer it to internalism. Since that is so, we are justified in rejecting the first premise of the reasons internalist argument, and so the argument itself.

Call a second antirationalist argument *The Rational Egoist Argument*:

1.   Rational Egoism is true.

2.   Ethical Egoism is false.

3.   Therefore Moral Rationalism is false.

Both premises have broad appeal. Rational egoism is the thesis that one has a reason to Φ if and only if Φ-ing will promote one's interests. Ethical egoism is the view that one is morally obligated to Φ if and only if Φ-ing will promote one's self-interest. The denial of ethical egoism entails that adherence to moral requirements may sometimes fail to promote one's self-interest. The endorsement of rational egoism entails that one lacks reason to perform actions that fail in this way. Therefore, the combination of these views entails that one may be morally obligated to Φ even though one lacks a reason to Φ. Therefore this combination entails that moral rationalism is false.

Here I just want to assume that ethical egoism is false; in other words, that premise (2) is true. Since I reject the conclusion, and the argument is valid, I will take issue with the first premise – the endorsement of rational egoism.

It may be that promotion of self-interest always supplies a good reason for action. But

why believe that this is the only kind of good reason there is? Most of us firmly hold judgments that imply the falsity of this thesis. If I see someone distractedly crossing the street, about to be run over, I have reason to yell out and warn her. If I see a gang of youths corner a young woman, taunt her and begin to drag her into a dark alley, I have reason to notify the police, immediately intervene, and call for the assistance of others to help. If I spot a seriously dehydrated hiker while in the backwoods, I have reason to offer up my canteen. Of course we can imagine situations where, all things considered, I have most reason not to perform these actions. Nevertheless, such cases certainly appear to provide at least defeasible reason for action, even though our interests are not served, and may only be hindered, by rendering such aid.

The appeal to our deeply-held beliefs about what reasons we have can be supplemented by two arguments designed to undermine rational egoism. The first relies on the importance of autonomy. Autonomous choices for desired or valued ends at least sometimes supply reasons for action, even when such choices are known by the agent not to enhance (or perhaps only to damage) his self-interest. If a soldier decides to sacrifice himself for his comrades, then he has some reason to take the means necessary to saving their lives, even though such actions are condemned from the rational egoist standpoint. If less dramatically, a person autonomously decides to bestow an anonymous charitable donation sufficiently large to do herself some harm, she nevertheless has some reason to carry through with her resolution. Reasons here, as in the soldier case, may also stem from the needs of those the agent is trying to help. But that isn't necessary to make the relevant point. All that is needed is a recognition that autonomous choices do sometimes supply reasons for action, even though such choices fail to promote the agent's own interests.

There are only two ways to dispute this anti-egoist conclusion. The first is simply to deny the

independent value of autonomy, and claim that one's welfare alone is all that should matter to an agent. Autonomous choice may in some cases supply reasons, but only derivatively — only because and to the extent that acting on such a choice promotes one's own welfare. As far as I am aware, however, there is no good argument for this conclusion — no sound argument that shows that autonomy is only derivatively valuable in this way.

The alternative is to allow for the independent importance of autonomy, but to claim that autonomous choice and self-interest can never conflict, because autonomous choice invariably promotes self-interest: one has reason to Φ if and only if Φ-ing promotes one's self interest, and, necessarily, Φ-ing promotes one's self-interest if one autonomously chooses to Φ. But why think this? Why think it impossible for an agent to know that an action will damage his interests but to autonomously choose to do it anyway? It certainly seems possible that agents may, with relevantly full information and a minimum of external pressure, choose to perform actions that they believe will damage their interests. Surely the burden is on one who claims that in every such case the agent must either mistake his interests, be ignorant of relevant facts, or somehow be subject to far greater external pressure than was initially imagined.

A second argument against rational egoism takes its inspiration from an argument against a strong form of ethical egoism, which claims that acts are right if and only if, *and because*, they promote one's self-interest. The strongest criticism of ethical egoism is its inability to justify its policy of preferential treatment. In effect, ethical egoism sanctions a policy in which each person gets to elevate his or her interests over all others. Such a policy is a departure from the default ethical position in which equals should receive equal treatment. In response to the charge that ethical egoism licenses discriminatory treatment (because it sanctions treating the welfare of others as less important than one's own, without

justifying this preference), egoists have two replies. The first is to accept that their theory is a policy of unequal treatment, but to deny that this is damaging, by citing a relevant feature that justifies such unequal treatment. The second is to argue that ethical egoism is not a policy of preferential treatment, but is perfectly egalitarian.

The second reply doesn't work. It says that egoism is egalitarian because it confers on every person the same privileges. *Everyone* gets to treat her interests as more important than anyone else's. But this is not enough to insulate the egoist from charges of undue preference. That everyone gets to treat others abominably does not justify such treatment. Ethical egoism is egalitarian in one sense – everyone gets the same moral privileges. But it is inegalitarian in another – it allows one person to give herself complete priority over another for no reason other than the fact that she is the author of the action.

The other reply admits that ethical egoism is a policy of unequal treatment, but seeks to justify this policy by citing a relevant difference that justifies the inequality. Not all discrimination is bad – some students, for instance, deservedly get As, others Bs, and so on. So long as one can cite a relevant difference that justifies the differential treatment, such treatment is completely above-board. Now suppose that you've worked very hard to earn what you have. Suppose also that I correctly judge that I would benefit by taking your goods by force. In that case, I am not only allowed to do so, but morally must do so. I am treating myself and you differently. What licenses such treatment? I'd be better off if I took your things. But you'd be better off if I didn't. Why am I allowed to give the nod to my own interests? That I would benefit does not explain why I am allowed (or required) to give my own interests priority over yours, since you would benefit (or at least avoid harm) were I to refrain from the forcible taking.

There is a stronger and a weaker criticism of ethical egoism at work here. The stronger criticism, leveled by utilitarians, says that the fact that an act will promote one's own interests supplies no basis whatever for priority. The weaker criticism claims that this fact does give some reason for priority in some contexts, but that this priority is defeasible and is in fact often defeated by such things as other persons' deserts, needs and interests. We need only the weaker claim to establish the anti-egoist point. We could go so far as to concede that it is just a brute fact that one is morally allowed to give some priority to oneself, while still demanding justification for the egoist's claim that such priority is the only morally relevant consideration there is.

It strikes me that the rational egoist faces precisely the same objections. We might allow that it is simply a brute fact that there is always reason to promote one's self-interest. But we need an argument for thinking that this is the only reason there could possibly be. Such a claim isn't self-evident, and it conflicts with some of our other very deeply held beliefs. The rational egoist claims that the only consideration that can support or justify an action is its conduciveness to self-interest. But why don't the like interests, needs, wants and autonomous choices of others also constitute a basis for rationalizing action that serves them? They are different from one's own interests, etc., in only one respect: that they are not one's own. Even if we concede (as many do not) that this difference makes some difference, why does it make *all* the difference? It seems instead simply to be an assertion of an unjustified policy of preferential treatment. What is it about oneself that gives one license in every situation to give one's own concerns priority over others? That everyone has such license does not justify it. It isn't clear what could.

Rational egoism conflicts with many firm convictions we have about cases. It cannot accommodate a suitable role for autonomy in supplying reasons for action. And rational egoism forces us away from a default position of equality, in ways that are structurally similar to those of ethical egoism, and yet fails to justify

the policy of preferential treatment that it is committed to.

If in the end rational egoism is unsupported, then the Rational Egoist Argument fails to supply good grounds for rejecting moral rationalism. Consider, then, *The Analogical Argument*, clearly inspired by an important article by Philippa Foot (1972). Requirements of law and etiquette apply to individuals regardless of their desires to comply. Yet these requirements do not entail reasons for action – one might be perfectly rational or reasonable to reject their strictures. Foot's claim is that the same goes for morality. Just because its edicts apply to agents regardless of their desires or interests – they are categorical in this regard – doesn't mean that moral obligations necessarily supply agents with reasons to behave morally. As an argument from analogy, this can't be absolutely watertight, but it can shift the burden of proof to the rationalist, who, in the face of this argument, must take either of two options.

The first is to argue that the demands of law and etiquette are in fact intrinsically reason-giving. The alternative is allow that they are not, but to point up a relevant disanalogy between moral requirements and those of law and etiquette.

The first path seems problematic. While it is true, as anyone who reads Miss Manners will know, that most rules of etiquette have a moral basis, no one would deny that certain of these rules, such as that dictating where to lay the fish knife on a table setting, are morally arbitrary. Such rules apply even to those who haven't any desire or interest in obeying them. But such rules don't generate reasons for conformity all by themselves – they generate reasons, when they do, only because the rules are coextensive with moral requirements, or because adhering to the rules will advance some other interest one may have. If in a given context properly laying the fish knife serves no moral ends, and serves no personal ones, either, then it is difficult to see what reason one could have for concern about its placement.

So there are requirements that are categorical in one sense without being categorical in another: such requirements apply to individuals regardless of their desires, but do not necessarily supply such individuals with any reason for action. It is incumbent on the moral rationalist to explain this.

The explanation, I believe, invokes the idea of jurisdiction. A jurisdiction comprises a set of standards that dictate behavior for a defined set of members. (The set may be defined territorially, as in the law, or may be defined by voluntary allegiance, as with a charitable association or bridge club, etc. Discussion of the different sources of membership is important for other contexts, especially political philosophy, but don't much matter here.) The rules of etiquette, or those of a board game, do not necessarily supply reasons for action, because they are not necessarily applicable; they are inapplicable to all who find themselves outside the relevant jurisdictions. A variety of factors can explain one's extra-jurisdictional status. An accident of birth explains why I am not subject to the civil statutes of Ethiopia. An autonomous choice explains why the code of the Benevolent Protective Order of Elks does not apply to me. The choices of others explain why I am not bound to uphold the duties of a Prime Minister or President. For these reasons, and others, the strictures of the relevant domain (law, etiquette, fraternal societies, etc.) may fail to apply in a given case. And if such standards fail to apply to one's actions, then *a fortiori* they will fail to supply one with reasons for action.

In this sense, the scope of the relevant rules is limited. The limit is explained by the *conventional origin* of such rules. For any given convention, whether it be focused on law, etiquette or play, one may lack reason to adhere to its rules because one is not a party to the convention. The requirements of law, etiquette, and games are all circumscribed. For any requirements of conventional origin, it is always in principle possible to find oneself outside of the jurisdiction. The

reasons generated by conventional rules are therefore reasons that exist only contingently.

Morality is different. Its scope is pervasive. Every action is morally evaluable – even if the pronouncement is simply one of permissibility. There is no exiting the "morality game." One may renounce morality, may act without regard to the moral status of one's conduct, may in fact act with the intention of behaving immorally, but all such dissociative strategies do not free one from susceptibility to moral assessment. This distinguishes moral requirements from those in the law, etiquette or games.

What explains this special character of moral assessment? I think it must be the claim that morality is objective, in the sense of being correct independently of whether anyone thinks so. We don't create the principles that generate moral requirements. The principles are not constituted by and do not apply to us in virtue of conventional agreements. Moral requirements are inescapable because they are not of our own making.

This does not explain why moral rationalism is true. The pervasive scope of moral evaluation does not explain why moral facts are necessarily reason-giving. But it does serve as the basis for resisting the Analogical Argument, because a relevant disanalogy among kinds of desire-independent requirements has been identified. Not every categorical requirement is necessarily reason-giving, because some such requirements are conventional in origin, and so supply reasons only contingently. Morality's content is not conventionally fixed, and so we lack this basis for thinking that it supplies reasons only contingently.

This reply assumes that moral requirements are not conventional. If morality is conventional, then the Analogical Argument, so far as I can see, is sound, and we should reject moral rationalism. But to assume that morality is conventional at this stage is just to beg the question against the moral rationalist, by supposing that his favored reply to the Analogical Argument

cannot work. By contrast, there is nothing question-begging *at this stage* about assuming the truth of moral objectivism, since objectivism by itself is neutral with respect to the merits of rationalism – indeed, many moral objectivists reject moral rationalism. There are independent grounds for doubting moral objectivism, of course – all of which, in the end, I think can be answered – but I cannot do that here. (I make an effort in Shafer-Landau, 2003.)

Consider then a final argument that I will call *The Argument from Extrinsic Reasons*:

1. If moral rationalism is true, then moral facts are intrinsically reason-giving.
2. There are no intrinsically reason-giving facts.
3. Therefore moral rationalism is false.

I think that premise (2) is false, and will spend my time here trying to show it so. I also think, perhaps surprisingly, that the first premise may be false. But I won't go into that here. Antirationalists will say that all reasons derive from an agent's perspective. For consider the alternative: if reasons exist regardless of one's desires or interests, then where do they come from? (And how can we know them?) What, other than an agent's own perspective, could serve as a source of normative authority? To insist that a set of facts could contain within themselves normative authority for agents, regardless of their outlooks on life, seems obscurantist, and appears to have the effect of prematurely cutting off any helpful explanation of normativity.

If this is obscurantist, I think we have no choice but to embrace the mysteries. I think there must be some intrinsically normative entities. To see this, consider the parallels between conditions of epistemic and moral assessment. We say that agents have reasons to believe the truth, and to conform their reasoning to truth-preserving schemas, even if believing the truth is not conducive to the goals they set themselves.

Suppose someone accepts the truth of a conditional and its antecedent, but denies that she has any reason to accept the consequent. It's not just that she may have (possibly overriding) reasons which oppose making such an inference. Someone might correctly believe that all passengers aboard a downed airliner have been killed, while knowing that her brother was among them, and yet resist drawing the terrible conclusion. Practical considerations, such as sustaining emotional stability, may militate against believing the truth, and may, for anything said thus far, be so strong as to outweigh it in given instances. But the sister who holds out hope against all evidence, and contrary to the logical implications of her own beliefs, is in some real sense acting against reason. Indeed, she is, in one sense, behaving irrationally, though also in a way that is fully understandable. She is acting contrary to sufficiently good reasons – reasons that are there to tell her, and anyone in her epistemic situation that she ought to believe something that she cannot bring herself to believe.

To say such a thing commits one to the existence of what I shall call *nonperspectival* or *intrinsic* reasons. I believe that there is intrinsic reason to think that two and two are four – the fact itself provides one with reason to believe it. One needn't show that such belief is somehow related to one's adopted goals in order to justify believing such a thing. If, unusually, success at basic mathematics was entirely unrelated to one's preferred activities, one would still have good reason to think that two and two were four, not five or three.

The basic idea here is that certain things can be intrinsically normative – reason-giving independently of the instrumental, final or unconditional value actually attached to things by agents. The opposing view insists that all reasons stem entirely from an agent's own contingent commitments. Antirationalists might allow for the existence of objective values, but would insist that whatever reason-giving force such values have is entirely dependent on the agent's

own investment. There are no reasons at all apart from a particular agent's perspective.

The rationalist insists that the reasons generated from within these perspectives can be assessed and can in cases collude with, or compete against, reasons that are nonperspectival. The epistemic rationalist claims that certain (kinds of) reasons for belief are like this. We behave in an epistemically appropriate fashion when our practices track these reasons, which are not all of our own making. There is reason to believe that the earth is roughly round, that two and two are four, and that the consequent follows from a conditional and its antecedent. We don't make these reasons up; most perspectives recognize such reasons, but their existence does not depend on the perspective one takes to the world. Those perspectives that fail to recognize these reasons are missing something.

There are clear parallels with moral rationalism. The moral rationalist says that certain kinds of facts – moral facts – necessarily supply us with reasons for action, as well as reasons for belief. Everyone has a reason to regard genocide as evil, because it is true that genocide is evil. And everyone has reason not to participate in genocide, because it is a fact that we are obligated to refrain from such participation. Or, to take the usual example, no worse for being usual: we have reason to alleviate another person's excruciating pain, if we can do so effectively at very little cost to ourselves. There are considerations in such cases that *justify* alleviating such pain, even if doing so is neither desired for its own sake, nor instrumental to one's desires. Those who overcome their indifference and manage to offer assistance in such cases are acting appropriately, or more than appropriately. Their actions are proper, legitimate and justified. They wouldn't be, were there no reason at all to undertake them. Such reasons may be defeasible, but they apply to us even in the absence of any instrumental relation to one's goals.

Here is the crucial failure of antirationalism. In its effort to cast doubt on the possibility of

intrinsic reasons, it must commit itself to the view that what reasons we have – for belief and for action – depend entirely on one's outlook. If they weren't dependent in this way, then they would be nonperspectival – there would be intrinsic reasons after all. Yet once we meet the conditions of an antirationalist theory, we see that any such theory is hoist by its own petard. For by its own lights such a view has nothing in itself to recommend it to anyone not already convinced of its merits. If antirationalism is true, then all reasons are contingent on one's perspective. Importantly, no perspective is superior to another (except as judged so from within a given perspective, which perspective is itself in no way rationally or epistemically superior to another). For if any perspective were nonperspectivally superior, this would mean that agents would have, regardless of their perspective, more reason to endorse the superior outlook. And this is just what is disallowed by antirationalism. So antirationalism succumbs to the kind of argument that undermines a global relativism.

All of this still leaves us short of an account of why moral facts *are* intrinsically reason-giving – thus far we've attempted to display the attractions of rationalism, and have tried to undermine the anti-rationalist arguments, but haven't offered any concrete explanation of *why* moral facts supply reasons (for action or evaluation). One possibility is to explain the normativity of moral facts by positing a necessary connection between them and other kinds of intrinsically reason-giving considerations. For instance, one might claim that all moral obligations entailed a reason for action, because, necessarily, fulfilling a moral obligation made one better off, and one always has reason to make oneself better off. I am not optimistic about any such strategy. But if this explanatory route is barred, what other route is available?

The worry here is the same as that which besets accounts of candidate intrinsic values. We ordinarily explain the value of something by showing its relation to something else acknowledged to be intrinsically valuable. But when one's candidate intrinsic values are themselves questioned, this strategy must fail. Suppose one claims that any situation in which an innocent child is maimed solely to produce pleasure for his tormentor is bad, in itself. Isn't this true? But there's very little one can say to someone who doesn't believe this. The intrinsic moral rationalist is in much the same boat when defending the normativity of moral facts. According to her, there is no more fundamental kind of normative consideration from which moral facts can derive their reason-giving force. But just as the inability to cite a more fundamental consideration doesn't necessarily undermine the claim about intrinsic value, so too it needn't undermine the claim about normativity. One must recognize the limits of normative explanation.

That said, rationalists must concede that their favored theory does not enjoy the same degree of endorsement as the verdict we reach in the example in which a child is maimed. But this shouldn't be seen as a stumbling block to acceptance of rationalism. Moral rationalism is a much more complicated, less obvious and less immediately appealing view than the one expressed in the example. Further, the parallel with defending claims of intrinsic value should alert us to the difficulty of justification in these contexts. Justification here is a matter of defusing arguments designed to undermine the relevant view, and adducing some non-conclusive considerations that favor it. In case such a strategy is thought by its nature to be too weak to establish the requisite degree of justification, we need to remind ourselves that this is all that can be hoped for even for those theories of practical reasons whose allegiance is much broader than moral rationalism. The brute inexplicability of the normativity of moral facts is not different in kind from that which besets other, familiar theories of practical reasons.

Consider both rational egoism and instrumentalism. Proponents of these theories claim,

respectively, that self-interest or desire satisfaction are the sole kind of intrinsically reason-giving consideration. When they defend their favored claims, they do so by trying to reply to criticisms and offer probative evidence far short of demonstrable proof as positive support for their views. Indeed, on the assumption that self-interest is not identical with or best measured exclusively by desire-satisfaction, at least one of these popular theories must be false. The relevant point here is that strategies for defending any such view – any candidate for intrinsically normative consideration – are similar across the board. The rational egoist will not be able to point to a kind of normative consideration more fundamental than self-interest, to which the reason-giving force of self-interest is of necessity related. The instrumentalist is likewise handicapped when trying to establish the intrinsic normativity of desire-satisfaction. This kind of explanatory failure is not itself an argument against any one of these theories. In response to the charge that intrinsic moral rationalists are unable to explain the normativity of moral facts, rationalists should be prepared to point to partners in crime. They needn't look very far.

If I am right, one always has reason to do as morality says. Whether this is the best possible reason – whether moral considerations are invariably overriding – is another matter. One can't settle that issue without having in hand a theory of normative ethics, an inventory of kinds of non-moral reasons, and a method for measuring their relative strength. We don't need to undertake such extensive investigations to establish the more circumscribed claim of moral rationalism's plausibility.

I have tried to show that moral rationalism can survive the strongest arguments designed to undermine it. The Reasons Internalist Argument, the Rational Egoist Argument, the Analogical Argument and the Argument from Extrinsic Reasons do not, in the end, point up insuperable difficulties for the rationalist. There are strong considerations to do with the conceptual coherence and the fairness of moral evaluation that support moral rationalism. And rationalism's insistence on the irreducibly normative character of moral facts should not be an impediment to its acceptance. Any problem that may arise in this context is one shared by any competing theory which aims to identify an intrinsically normative kind of consideration.

References

Foot, Philippa. 1972. "Morality as a System of Hypothetical Imperatives," *Philosophical Review* (82), pp. 306–15.

Shafer-Landau, Russ. 2003. *Moral Realism: A Defence.* Oxford University Press.

Williams, Bernard. 1981. "Internal and External Reasons," as reprinted in his *Moral Luck*, Cambridge University Press 1985.

The meaning of moral language

INTRODUCTION TO SECTION II

MORAL UTTERANCES resemble statements of fact in some but not all respects. On the one hand, a moral sentence such as "lying is wrong" has the same grammatical structure as the factual "gold is heavy." In addition, both sentences appear to express thoughts that most of us believe. However, on the other hand, whereas "gold is heavy" is made true by a fact in the world, it is harder to see what might determine the truth of a sentence like "lying is wrong." It is also harder to see how we can come to know that such sentences *are* true. Furthermore, someone who sincerely asserts that lying is wrong will typically be disposed not to lie, whereas sincere assertions of "gold is heavy" are not typically associated with any particular type of behavior.

Philosophers disagree about what to make of these similarities and differences. Some, impressed by the similarities, maintain that just as a sentence like "gold is heavy" can be either true or false, so too can sentences like "lying is wrong" and "suffering is bad." Others, taking their cue from the differences, deny that "lying is wrong" and "suffering is bad" are even candidates for truth or falsity. Instead of trying to describe reality, these sentences are said to serve some different function: they either express the attitudes of those who utter them or seek to influence the attitudes and actions of others. Because philosophers who hold the first view take moral assertions to have cognitive content while those who hold the second do not, their positions are known, respectively, as *cognitivism* and *noncognitivism*.

In Chapter 8, excerpted from David Hume's classic *Treatise of Human Nature*, Hume develops a complex position which contains elements of both views. He maintains that our moral commitments move us to act, but that reason by itself can never provide us with motivation. In his well-known words, "reason is, and ought only to be, a slave of the passions." From these premises, Hume concludes that morality cannot be grounded in reason, but must instead have its origins in our feelings: "when you pronounce any action or character to be vicious, you mean nothing, but that from the constitution of your nature you have a feeling or sentiment of blame from the contemplation of it." Because Hume holds that those who make moral pronouncements are not describing the world, but rather projecting their feelings onto it, his position has clear affinities with noncognitivism. However, Hume also insists that moral terms must have some kind of stable meaning, and that this compels us to abstract away from any variations in our feelings that are due exclusively to the peculiarities of our situation or perspective. Thus, although Hume takes moral discourse to be rooted in sentiment, his specification of the relevant sentiments has an important objective dimension.

Unlike Hume, G. E. Moore (Chapter 9) is a straightforward cognitivist. Moore's question is not whether ethical utterances can be true, but rather what makes them

true when they are true. Moore maintains that when we call an action right or a state of affairs good, we attribute to it a property that differs from any in the natural world. Although philosophers sometimes try to define goodness in terms of natural properties – they sometimes hold, for example, that calling something good just means it is productive of pleasure – Moore argues that all such definitions fail. He argues that if "good" meant "productive of pleasure," then the informative sentence "everything that produces pleasure is good" would be equivalent to the uninformative "everything that produce pleasure produce pleasure." He argues, as well, that for any natural property N, it is possible for someone to acknowledge that something has N while still wondering whether that thing is good. For these and other reasons, Moore concludes that all attempts to define goodness in terms of natural properties commit the error that he calls *the naturalistic fallacy*.

A. J. Ayer (Chapter 10) accepts Moore's claim that "good" and "right" cannot be defined in naturalistic terms, but uses it to draw a different conclusion. According to Ayer, every meaningful sentence is either true by definition or else verifiable through sense observation. Thus, because moral sentences pass neither test, Ayer concludes that they lack cognitive meaning. In his view, a sentence like "pleasure is good" does not attribute an undefinable property – goodness – to pleasure, but merely expresses a positive feeling *toward* pleasure. Because he compares calling something good or bad to expressing one's emotions by booing or cheering, Ayer's version of noncognitivism is known as *the emotive theory*. Along similar lines, but far more subtly, Simon Blackburn argues in Chapter 11 that ethical utterances can express the evaluative attitudes that inform a whole range of important human activities. By embracing expressivism, Blackburn suggests, we can make sense not only of what is involved in believing that something is good or right, but also of what is involved in such further activities as wondering about this, denying it, and making inferences from it.

Russ Shafer-Landau disagrees. He argues in Chapter 12 that the most straightforward way to understand what people are doing when they disagree about right and wrong is to take their dispute at face value – that is, as a dispute about which moral claims are true. He also argues that by maintaining that moral utterances can be true, we can most easily avoid the famous objection to expressivism that Blackburn calls "Frege's Abyss." In one of its versions, the difficulty is that if "What John did is wrong" merely expresses disapproval of what John did, then the words "what John did is wrong" cannot mean the same thing when uttered by themselves and as part of the larger sentence "If John stole the book then what John did is wrong"; for when uttered as part of the larger sentence, the words need *not* express disapproval of what John did. By contrast, cognitivism does offer a natural explanation of how the words can mean the same thing in both contexts. Because of this, and because cognitivism provides equally straightforward answers to such further questions as how there can be moral error and what we are doing when we deliberate, Shafer-Landau concludes that it is the better theory.

These debates over the meaning of moral language intersect in an interesting way with an important question about morality and religion. Many believe what makes an act right is just the fact that God approves of it or commands us to perform it. However, against this theory – the *divine command theory* – others advance an

objection that is often associated with Plato. In Chapter 13, Plato examines the claim that a pious act can be defined as one that is loved by the gods. That definition, he notes, would make it impossible to say that the gods love the things they do *because* they are pious. Inspired by Plato's observation, many argue that if acts like theft and murder are only wrong because God forbids them, then God cannot forbid such acts *because* they are wrong. Because this would imply that God's commands are arbitrary, and because it is unclear how arbitrary commands could have authority, these philosophers conclude that we should reject the divine command theory.

In Chapter 14, Robert Merrihew Adams draws on contemporary work in the philosophy of language to reply to this objection. As Adams interprets it, the divine command theory is a hypothesis about moral terms like "right" and "wrong." The data it seeks to explain are the things that "every competent user of 'wrong' must know" – for example, that what is wrong is independent of what we happen to believe, that acts like torturing children for fun are wrong, and that the wrongness of such acts is part of what makes us believe they are wrong. The explanation of these phenomena, Adams suggests, is that "ethical wrongness is (i.e., is identical with) the property of being contrary to the commands of a loving God." This claim, he argues, is not a definition, but, nevertheless, is necessarily true if true at all. Moreover, because the claim makes essential reference to a *loving* God, it avoids the implication that it would be wrong to disobey God even if He commanded us to act cruelly. Because Adams holds that God's commands are rooted in love, he may have the resources to avoid the objection that they are arbitrary and therefore lacking in authority.

David Hume

MORALITY AND NATURAL SENTIMENT

Of the influencing motives of the will

NOTHING IS more usual in philosophy, and even in common life, than to talk of the combat of passion and reason, to give the preference to reason, and assert that men are only so far virtuous as they conform themselves to its dictates. Every rational creature, it is said, is obliged to regulate his actions by reason; and if any other motive or principle challenge the direction of his conduct, he ought to oppose it till it be entirely subdued or at least brought to a conformity with that superior principle. On this method of thinking the greatest part of moral philosophy, ancient and modern, seems to be founded; nor is there an ampler field as well for metaphysical arguments as popular declamations than this supposed pre-eminence of reason above passion. The eternity, invariableness, and divine origin of the former have been displayed to the best advantage; the blindness, inconstancy, and deceitfulness of the latter have been as strongly insisted on. In order to show the fallacy of all this philosophy, I shall endeavor to prove, first, that reason alone can never be a motive to any action of the will; and, secondly, that it can never oppose passion in the direction of the will.

The understanding exerts itself after two different ways, as it judges from demonstration or probability; as it regards the abstract relations of our ideas, or those relations of objects of which experience only gives us information. I believe it scarce will be asserted that the first species of reasoning alone is ever the cause of any action. As its proper province is the world of ideas, and as the will always places us in that of realities, demonstration and volition seem upon that account to be totally removed from each other. Mathematics, indeed, are useful in all mechanical operations, and arithmetic in almost every art and profession: but it is not of themselves they have any influence. Mechanics are the art of regulating the motions of bodies *to some designed end* or *purpose*; and the reason why we employ arithmetic in fixing the proportions of numbers is only that we may discover the proportions of their influence and operation. A merchant is desirous of knowing the sum total of his accounts with any person: why? but that he may learn what sum will have the same *effects* in paying his debt, and going to market, as all the particular articles taken together. Abstract or demonstrative reasoning, therefore, never influences any of our actions, but only as it directs our judgment concerning causes and effects; which leads us to the second operation of the understanding.

It is obvious that when we have the prospect of pain or pleasure from any object, we feel a consequent emotion of aversion or propensity, and are carried to avoid or embrace what will give us this uneasiness or satisfaction. It is also obvious that this emotion rests not here, but,

making us cast our view on every side, comprehends whatever objects are connected with its original one by the relation of cause and effect. Here then reasoning takes place to discover this relation; and according as our reasoning varies, our actions receive a subsequent variation. But it is evident in this case that the impulse arises not from reason, but is only directed by it. It is from the prospect of pain or pleasure that the aversion or propensity arises towards any object: and these emotions extend themselves to the causes and effects of that object, as they are pointed out to us by reason and experience. It can never in the least concern us to know that such objects are causes, and such others effects, if both the causes and effects be indifferent to us. Where the objects themselves do not affect us, their connection can never give them any influence; and it is plain that, as reason is nothing but the discovery of this connection, it cannot be by its means that the objects are able to affect us.

Since reason alone can never produce any action or give rise to volition, I infer that the same faculty is as incapable of preventing volition or of disputing the preference with any passion or emotion. This consequence is necessary. It is impossible reason could have the latter effect of preventing volition, but by giving an impulse in a contrary direction to our passions; and that impulse, had it operated alone, would have been ample to produce volition. Nothing can oppose or retard the impulse of passion but a contrary impulse; and if this contrary impulse ever arises from reason, that latter faculty must have an original influence on the will and must be able to cause as well as hinder any act of volition. But if reason has no original influence, it is impossible it can withstand any principle which has such an efficacy, or ever keep the mind in suspense a moment. Thus it appears that the principle which opposes our passion cannot be the same with reason, and is only called so in an improper sense. We speak not strictly and philosophically when we talk of the combat of passion and of reason. Reason is, and ought only to be,

the slave of the passions, and can never pretend to any other office than to serve and obey them. As this opinion may appear somewhat extraordinary, it may not be improper to confirm it by some other considerations.

A passion is an original existence or, if you will, modification of existence, and contains not any representative quality which renders it a copy of any other existence or modification. When I am angry, I am actually possessed with the passion, and in that emotion have no more a reference to any other object than when I am thirsty, or sick, or more than five feet high. It is impossible, therefore, that this passion can be opposed by, or be contradictory to, truth and reason; since this contradiction consists in the disagreement of ideas, considered as copies, with those objects which they represent.

What may at first occur on this head is that as nothing can be contrary to truth or reason, except what has a reference to it, and as the judgments of our understanding only have this reference, it must follow that passions can be contrary to reason only so far as they are *accompanied* with some judgment or opinion. According to this principle, which is so obvious and natural, it is only in two senses that any affection can be called unreasonable. First, when a passion, such as hope or fear, grief or joy, despair or security, is founded on the supposition of the existence of objects which really do not exist. Secondly, when, in exerting any passion in action, we choose means sufficient for the designed end, and deceive ourselves in our judgment of causes and effects. Where a passion is neither founded on false suppositions, nor chooses means insufficient for the end, the understanding can neither justify nor condemn it. It is not contrary to reason to prefer the destruction of the whole world to the scratching of my finger. It is not contrary to reason for me to choose my total ruin to prevent the least uneasiness of an Indian, or person wholly unknown to me. It is as little contrary to reason to prefer even my own acknowledged lesser

good to my greater, and have a more ardent affection for the former than the latter. A trivial good may, from certain circumstances, produce a desire superior to what arises from the greatest and most valuable enjoyment; nor is there anything more extraordinary in this than in mechanics to see one pound weight raise up a hundred by the advantage of its situation. In short, a passion must be accompanied with some false judgment in order to its being unreasonable; and even then it is not the passion, properly speaking, which is unreasonable, but the judgment.

• • •

Moral distinctions not derived from reason

• • •

Those who affirm that virtue is nothing but a conformity to reason; that there are eternal fitnesses and unfitnesses of things which are the same to every rational being that considers them; that the immutable measure of right and wrong impose an obligation, not only on human creatures, but also on the Deity himself: all these systems concur in the opinion that morality, like truth, is discerned merely by ideas, and by their juxtaposition and comparison. In order, therefore, to judge of these systems, we need only consider whether it be possible from reason alone to distinguish betwixt moral good and evil, or whether there must concur some other principles to enable us to make that distinction.

If morality had naturally no influence on human passions and actions, it were in vain to take such pains to inculcate it; and nothing would be more fruitless than that multitude of rules and precepts with which all moralists abound. Philosophy is commonly divided into *speculative* and *practical*; and as morality is always comprehended under the latter division, it is supposed to influence our passions and actions, and to go beyond the calm and indolent judgments of the understanding. And this is confirmed by common experience, which informs us that men are often governed by their duties, and are deterred from some actions by the opinion of injustice, and impelled to others by that of obligation.

Since morals, therefore, have an influence on the actions and affections, it follows that they cannot be derived from reason, and that because reason alone, as we have already proved, can never have any such influence. Morals excite passions, and produce or prevent actions. Reason of itself is utterly impotent in this particular. The rules of morality, therefore, are not conclusions of our reason.

No one, I believe, will deny the justness of this inference; nor is there any other means of evading it than by denying that principle on which it is founded. As long as it is allowed that reason has no influence on our passions and actions, it is in vain to pretend that morality is discovered only by a deduction of reason. An active principle can never be founded on an inactive; and if reason be inactive in itself, it must remain so in all its shapes and appearances, whether it exerts itself in natural or moral subjects, whether it considers the powers of external bodies or the actions of rational beings.

It would be tedious to repeat all the arguments by which I have proved that reason is perfectly inert and can never either prevent or produce any action or affection. It will be easy to recollect what has been said upon that subject. I shall only recall on this occasion one of these arguments, which I shall endeavour to render still more conclusive and more applicable to the present subject.

Reason is the discovery of truth or falsehood. Truth or falsehood consists in an agreement or disagreement either to the *real* relations of ideas, or to *real* existence and matter of fact. Whatever, therefore, is not susceptible of this agreement or disagreement is incapable of being true or false, and can never be an object of our reason. Now, it is evident our passions, volitions, and actions, are not susceptible of any such agreement or

disagreement; being original facts and realities, complete in themselves, and implying no reference to other passions, volitions, and actions. It is impossible, therefore, they can be pronounced either true or false, and be either contrary or conformable to reason.

This argument is of double advantage to our present purpose. For it proves *directly* that actions do not derive their merit from a conformity to reason, nor their blame from a contrariety to it; and it proves the same truth more *indirectly*, by showing us that as reason can never immediately prevent or produce any action by contradicting or approving of it, it cannot be the source of moral good and evil, which are found to have that influence. Actions may be laudable or blamable, but they cannot be reasonable or unreasonable: laudable or blamable, therefore, are not the same with reasonable or unreasonable. The merit and demerit of actions frequently contradict, and sometimes control our natural propensities. But reason has no such influence. Moral distinctions, therefore, are not the offspring of reason. Reason is wholly inactive, and can never be the source of so active a principle as conscience, or a sense of morals.

• • •

But, to be more particular, and to show that those eternal immutable fitnesses and unfitnesses of things cannot be defended by sound philosophy, we may weigh the following considerations.

If the thought and understanding were alone capable of fixing the boundaries of right and wrong, the character of virtuous and vicious either must lie in some relations of objects, or must be a matter of fact which is discovered by our reasoning. This consequence is evident. As the operations of human understanding divide themselves into two kinds—the comparing of ideas and the inferring of matter of fact—were virtue discovered by the understanding, it must be an object of one of these operations; nor is there any third operation of the understanding which can discover it. There has been an opinion

very industriously propagated by certain philosophers that morality is susceptible of demonstration; and though no one has ever been able to advance a single step in those demonstrations, yet it is taken for granted that this science may be brought to an equal certainty with geometry or algebra. Upon this supposition vice and virtue must consist in some relations, since it is allowed on all hands that no matter of fact is capable of being demonstrated. Let us therefore begin with examining this hypothesis and endeavour, if possible, to fix those moral qualities which have been so long the objects of our fruitless researches, point out distinctly the relations which constitute morality or obligation, that we may know wherein they consist, and after what manner we must judge of them.

If you assert that vice and virtue consist in relations susceptible of certainty and demonstration, you must confine yourself to those four relations which alone admit of that degree of evidence; and in that case you run into absurdities from which you will never be able to extricate yourself. For as you make the very essence of morality to lie in the relations and as there is no one of these relations but what is applicable not only to an irrational but also to an inanimate object, it follows that even such objects must be susceptible of merit or demerit. *Resemblance, contrariety, degrees in quality,* and *proportions in quantity and number;* all these relations belong as properly to matter as to our actions, passions, and volitions. It is unquestionable, therefore, that morality lies not in any of these relations, nor in the sense of it in their discovery.[1]

Should it be asserted that the sense of morality consists in the discovery of some relation distinct from these, and that our enumeration was not complete when we comprehended all demonstrable relations under four general heads; to this I know not what to reply, till some one be so good as to point out to me this new relation. It is impossible to refute a system which has never yet been explained. In such a manner of fighting in the dark, a man loses his blows in the air and

often places them where the enemy is not present.

• • •

Nor does this reasoning only prove that morality consists not in any relations that are the objects of science; but, if examined, will prove with equal certainty that it consists not in any *matter of fact* which can be discovered by the understanding. This is the *second* part of our argument; and if it can be made evident, we may conclude that morality is not an object of reason. But can there be any difficulty in proving that vice and virtue are not matters of fact whose existence we can infer by reason? Take any action allowed to be vicious—wilful murder, for instance. Examine it in all lights, and see if you can find that matter of fact or real existence which you call *vice*. In whichever way you take it, you find only certain passions, motives, volitions, and thoughts. There is no other matter of fact in the case. The vice entirely escapes you, as long as you consider the object. You never can find it till you turn your reflection into your own breast and find a sentiment of disapprobation which arises in you towards this action. Here is a matter of fact; but it is the object of feeling, not of reason. It lies in yourself, not in the object. So that when you pronounce any action or character to be vicious, you mean nothing, but that from the constitution of your nature you have a feeling or sentiment of blame from the contemplation of it. Vice and virtue, therefore, may be compared to sounds, colours, heat, and cold, which, according to modern philosophy, are not qualities in objects but perceptions in the mind: and this discovery in morals, like that other in physics, is to be regarded as a considerable advancement of the speculative sciences; though, like that too, it has little or no influence on practice. Nothing can be more real, or concern us more, than our own sentiments of pleasure and uneasiness; and if these be favourable to virtue, and unfavourable to vice, no more can be requisite to the regulation of our conduct and behaviour.

I cannot forbear adding to these reasonings an observation which may, perhaps, be found of some importance. In every system of morality which I have hitherto met with, I have always remarked that the author proceeds for some time in the ordinary way of reasoning, and establishes the being of a god, or makes observations concerning human affairs; when of a sudden I am surprised to find that instead of the usual copulations of propositions *is* and *is not*, I meet with no proposition that is not connected with an *ought* or an *ought not*. This change is imperceptible, but is, however, of the last consequence. For as this *ought* or *ought not* expresses some new relation or affirmation, it is necessary that it should be observed and explained; and at the same time that a reason should be given for what seems altogether inconceivable, how this new relation can be a deduction from others which are entirely different from it. But as authors do not commonly use this precaution, I shall presume to recommend it to the readers; and am persuaded that this small attention would subvert all the vulgar systems of morality and let us see that the distinction of vice and virtue is not founded merely on the relations of objects, nor is perceived by reason.

Moral distinctions derived from a moral sense

Thus the course of the argument leads us to conclude that since vice and virtue are not discoverable merely by reason, or the comparison of ideas, it must be by means of some impression or sentiment they occasion, that we are able to mark the difference betwixt them. Our decisions concerning moral rectitude and depravity are evidently perceptions; and as all perceptions are either impressions or ideas, the exclusion of the one is a convincing argument for the other. Morality, therefore, is more properly felt than judged of; though this feeling or sentiment is commonly so soft and gentle that we are apt to confound it with an idea, according

to our common custom of taking all things for the same which have any near resemblance to each other.

The next question is of what nature are these impressions, and after what manner do they operate upon us? Here we cannot remain long in suspense, but must pronounce the impression arising from virtue to be agreeable, and that proceeding from vice to be uneasy. Every moment's experience must convince us of this. There is no spectacle so fair and beautiful as a noble and generous action; nor any which gives us more abhorrence than one that is cruel and treacherous. No enjoyment equals the satisfaction we receive from the company of those we love and esteem; as the greatest of all punishments is to be obliged to pass our lives with those we hate or contemn. A very play or romance may afford us instances of this pleasure which virtue conveys to us; and pain which arises from vice.

Now, since the distinguishing impressions by which moral good or evil is known are nothing but *particular* pains or pleasures, it follows that in all inquiries concerning these moral distinctions it will be sufficient to show the principles which make us feel a satisfaction or uneasiness from the survey of any character, in order to satisfy us why the character is laudable or blamable. An action, or sentiment, or character, is virtuous or vicious; why? because its view causes a pleasure or uneasiness of a particular kind. In giving a reason, therefore, for the pleasure or uneasiness, we sufficiently explain the vice or virtue. To have the sense of virtue is nothing but to *feel* a satisfaction of a particular kind from the contemplation of a character. The very *feeling* constitutes our praise or admiration. We go no further; nor do we inquire into the cause of the satisfaction. We do not infer a character to be virtuous because it pleases; but in feeling that it pleases after such a particular manner we in effect feel that it is virtuous. The case is the same as in our judgments concerning all kinds of beauty, and tastes, and sensations. Our approbation is implied in the immediate pleasure they convey to us.

I have objected to the system which establishes eternal rational measures of right and wrong, that it is impossible to show in the actions of reasonable creatures any relations which are not found in external objects; and therefore, if morality always attended these relations, it were possible for inanimate matter to become virtuous or vicious. Now it may, in like manner, be objected to the present system, that if virtue and vice be determined by pleasure and pain, these qualities must in every case arise from the sensations; and consequently any object, whether animate or inanimate, rational or irrational, might become morally good or evil, provided it can excite a satisfaction or uneasiness. But though this objection seems to be the very same, it has by no means the same force in the one case as in the other. For, first, it is evident that under the term *pleasure* we comprehend sensations which are very different from each other, and which have only such a distant resemblance as is requisite to make them be expressed by the same abstract term. A good composition of music and a bottle of good wine equally produce pleasure; and, what is more, their goodness is determined merely by the pleasure. But shall we say, upon that account, that the wine is harmonious, or the music of a good flavour? In like manner, an inanimate object and the character or sentiments of any person may, both of them, give satisfaction; but, as the satisfaction is different, this keeps our sentiments concerning them from being confounded, and makes us ascribe virtue to the one and not to the other. Nor is every sentiment of pleasure or pain, which arises from characters and actions, of that *peculiar* kind which makes us praise or condemn. The good qualities of an enemy are hurtful to us, but may still command our esteem and respect. It is only when a character is considered in general, without reference to our particular interest, that it causes such a feeling or sentiment as denominates it morally good or evil. It is true, those sentiments from interest and morals are apt to be confounded,

and naturally run into one another. It seldom happens that we do not think an enemy vicious, and can distinguish betwixt his opposition to our interest and real villainy or baseness. But this hinders not but that the sentiments are in themselves distinct, and a man of temper and judgment may preserve himself from these illusions. In like manner, though it is certain a musical voice is nothing but one that naturally gives a particular kind of pleasure, yet it is difficult for a man to be sensible that the voice of an enemy is agreeable, or to allow it to be musical. But a person of a fine ear, who has the command of himself, can separate these feelings and give praise to what deserves it.

Secondly, we may call to remembrance the preceding system of the passions, in order to remark a still more considerable difference among our pains and pleasures. Pride and humility, love and hatred, are excited when there is anything presented to us that both bears a relation to the object of the passion and produces a separate sensation related to the sensation of the passion. Now, virtue and vice are attended with these circumstances. They must necessarily be placed either in ourselves or others, and excite either pleasure or uneasiness; and therefore must give rise to one of these four passions, which clearly distinguishes them from the pleasure and pain arising from inanimate objects that often bear no relation to us; and this is, perhaps, the most considerable effect that virtue and vice have upon the human mind.

It may now be asked in general concerning this pain or pleasure that distinguishes moral good and evil, from what principle is it derived, and whence does it arise in the human mind? To this I reply, first, that it is absurd to imagine that, in every particular instance, these sentiments are produced by an original quality and primary constitution. For as the number of our duties is in a manner infinite, it is impossible that our original instincts should extend to each of them, and from our very first infancy impress on the human mind all that multitude of precepts which are contained in the completest system of ethics. Such a method of proceeding is not conformable to the usual maxims by which nature is conducted, where a few principles produce all that variety we observe in the universe, and everything is carried on in the easiest and most simple manner. It is necessary, therefore, to abridge these primary impulses and find some more general principles upon which all our notions of morals are founded.

But, in the second place, should it be asked, whether we ought to search for these principles in nature, or whether we must look for them in some other origin? I would reply that our answer to this question depends upon the definition of the word nature, than which there is none more ambiguous and equivocal. If nature be opposed to miracles, not only the distinction betwixt vice and virtue is natural, but also every event which has ever happened in the world, excepting those miracles on which our religion is founded. In saying, then, that the sentiments of vice and virtue are natural in this sense, we make no very extraordinary discovery.

But nature may also be opposed to rare and unusual; and in this sense of the word, which is the common one, there may often arise disputes concerning what is natural or unnatural; and one may in general affirm that we are not possessed of any very precise standard by which these disputes can be decided. Frequent and rare depend upon the number of examples we have observed; and as this number may gradually increase or diminish, it will be impossible to fix any exact boundaries betwixt them. We may only affirm on this head that if ever there was anything which could be called natural in this sense, the sentiments of morality certainly may; since there never was any nation of the world, nor any single person in any nation, who was utterly deprived of them, and who never, in any instance, showed the least approbation or dislike of manners. These sentiments are so rooted in our constitution and temper that, without entirely confounding the human mind by

disease or madness, it is impossible to extirpate and destroy them.

But *nature* may also be opposed to artifice as well as to what is rare and unusual; and in this sense it may be disputed whether the notions of virtue be natural or not. We readily forget that the designs, and projects, and views of men are principles as necessary in their operation as heat and cold, moist and dry; but, taking them to be free and entirely our own, it is usual for us to set them in opposition to the other principles of nature. Should it therefore be demanded whether the sense of virtue be natural or artificial, I am of opinion that it is impossible for me at present to give any precise answer to this question. Perhaps it will appear afterwards that our sense of some virtues is artificial, and that of others natural. The discussion of this question will be more proper, when we enter upon an exact detail of each particular vice and virtue.[2]

Meanwhile, it may not be amiss to observe from these definitions of *natural* and *unnatural* that nothing can be more unphilosophical than those systems which assert that virtue is the same with what is natural, and vice with what is unnatural. For in the first sense of the word "nature," as opposed to miracles, both vice and virtue are equally natural; and in the second sense, as opposed to what is unusual, perhaps virtue will be found to be the most unnatural. At least it must be owned that heroic virtue, being as unusual, is as little natural as the most brutal barbarity. As to the third sense of the word, it is certain that both vice and virtue are equally artificial and out of nature. For, however it may be disputed whether the notion of a merit or demerit in certain actions be natural or artificial, it is evident that the actions themselves are artificial, and performed with a certain design and intention; otherwise they could never be ranked under any of these denominations. It is impossible, therefore, that the character of natural and unnatural can ever, in any sense, mark the boundaries of vice and virtue.

Thus we are still brought back to our first position that virtue is distinguished by the pleasure, and vice by the pain, that any action, sentiment, or character, gives us by the mere view and contemplation. This decision is very commodious; because it reduces us to this simple question, *why any action or sentiment, upon the general view or survey, gives a certain satisfaction or uneasiness*, in order to show the origin of its moral rectitude or depravity, without looking for any incomprehensible relations and qualities which never did exist in nature, nor even in our imagination, by any clear and distinct conception? I flatter myself I have executed a great part of my present design by a state of the question which appears to me so free from ambiguity and obscurity.

Of the origin of justice and property

We now proceed to examine two questions, viz., *concerning the manner in which the rules of justice are established by the artifice of men; and concerning the reasons which determine us to attribute to the observance or neglect of these rules a moral beauty and deformity*. These questions will appear afterwards to be distinct. We shall begin with the former.

• • •

There are three different species of goods which we are possessed of: the internal satisfaction of our minds, the external advantages of our body, and the enjoyment of such possessions as we have acquired by our industry and good fortune. We are perfectly secure in the enjoyment of the first. The second may be ravished from us, but can be of no advantage to him who deprives us of them. The last only are both exposed to the violence of others, and may be transferred without suffering any loss or alteration; while at the same time there is not a sufficient quantity of them to supply every one's desires and necessities. As the improvement, therefore, of these goods is the chief advantage of society, so the *instability* of their possession, along with their *scarcity*, is the chief impediment.

In vain should we expect to find in uncultivated nature a remedy to this inconvenience; or hope for any inartificial principle of the human mind which might control those partial affections, and make us overcome the temptations arising from our circumstances. The idea of justice can never serve to this purpose, or be taken for a natural principle capable of inspiring men with an equitable conduct towards each other. That virtue, as it is now understood, would never have been dreamed of among rude and savage men. For the notion of injury or injustice implies an immorality or vice committed against some other person. And as every immorality is derived from some defect or unsoundness of the passions, and as this defect must be judged of, in a great measure, from the ordinary course of nature in the constitution of the mind, it will be easy to know whether we be guilty of any immorality with regard to others, by considering the natural and usual force of those several affections which are directed towards them. Now, it appears that in the original frame of our mind our strongest attention is confined to ourselves; our next is extended to our relations and acquaintance; and it is only the weakest which reaches to strangers and indifferent persons. This partiality, then, and unequal affection must not only have an influence on our behaviour and conduct in society, but even on our ideas of vice and virtue; so as to make us regard any remarkable transgression of such a degree of partiality, either by too great an enlargement or contraction of the affections, as vicious and immoral. This we may observe in our common judgments concerning actions, where we blame a person who either centers all his affections in his family, or is so regardless of them as, in any opposition of interest, to give the preference to a stranger or mere chance acquaintance. From all which it follows that our natural uncultivated ideas of morality, instead of providing a remedy for the partiality of our affections, do rather conform themselves to that partiality and give it an additional force and influence.

The remedy, then, is not derived from nature but from artifice; or, more properly speaking, nature provides a remedy in the judgment and understanding for what is irregular and incommodious in the affections. For when men, from their early education in society, have become sensible of the infinite advantages that result from it, and have besides acquired a new affection to company and conversation, and when they have observed that the principal disturbance in society arises from those goods which we call external, and from their looseness and easy transition from one person to another, they must seek for a remedy by putting these goods as far as possible on the same footing with the fixed and constant advantages of the mind and body. This can be done after no other manner than by a convention entered into by all the members of the society to bestow stability on the possession of those external goods, and leave every one in the peaceable enjoyment of what he may acquire by his fortune and industry. By this means every one knows what he may safely possess; and the passions are restrained in their partial and contradictory motions. Nor is such a restraint contrary to these passions; for if so, it could never be entered into nor maintained; but it is only contrary to their heedless and impetuous movement. Instead of departing from our own interest, or from that of our nearest friends, by abstaining from the possessions of others, we cannot better consult both these interests than by such a convention; because it is by that means we maintain society, which is so necessary to their well-being and subsistence as well as to our own.

This convention is not of the nature of a promise; for even promises themselves, as we shall see afterwards, arise from human conventions. It is only a general sense of common interest; which sense all the members of the society express to one another, and which induces them to regulate their conduct by certain rules. I observe that it will be for my interest to leave another in the possession of his goods, provided

he will act in the same manner with regard to me. He is sensible of a like interest in the regulation of his conduct. When this common sense of interest is mutually expressed and is known to both, it produces a suitable resolution and behaviour. And this may properly enough be called a convention or agreement betwixt us, though without the interposition of a promise; since the actions of each of us have a reference to those of the other, and are performed upon the supposition that something is to be performed on the other part. Two men who pull the oars of a boat do it by an agreement or convention, though they have never given promises to each other. Nor is the rule concerning the stability of possessions the less derived from human conventions, that it arises gradually, and acquires force by a slow progression and by our repeated experience of the inconveniences of transgressing it. On the contrary, this experience assures us still more that the sense of interest has become common to all our fellows, and gives us a confidence of the future regularity of their conduct; and it is only on the expectation of this that our moderation and abstinence are founded. In like manner are languages gradually established by human conventions, without any promise. In like manner do gold and silver become the common measures of exchange, and are esteemed sufficient payment for what is of a hundred times their value.

After this convention concerning abstinence from the possessions of others is entered into, and every one has acquired a stability in his possessions, there immediately arise the ideas of justice and injustice; as also those of *property, right,* and *obligation*. The latter are altogether unintelligible without first understanding the former. Our property is nothing but those goods whose constant possession is established by the laws of society—that is, by the laws of justice. Those, therefore, who make use of the words *property*, or *right*, or *obligation*, before they have explained the origin of justice, or even make use of them in that explication, are guilty of a very gross fallacy, and can never reason upon any solid foundation. A man's property is some object related to him. This relation is not natural but moral, and founded on justice. It is very preposterous, therefore, to imagine that we can have any idea of property without fully comprehending the nature of justice, and showing its origin in the artifice and contrivance of men. The origin of justice explains that of property. The same artifice gives rise to both. As our first and most natural sentiment of morals is founded on the nature of our passions, and gives the preference to ourselves and friends above strangers, it is impossible there can be naturally any such thing as fixed right or property, while the opposite passions of men impel them in contrary directions, and are not restrained by any convention or agreement.

• • •

. . . I have already observed that justice takes its rise from human conventions, and that these are intended as a remedy to some inconveniences which proceed from the concurrence of certain *qualities* of the human mind with the *situation* of external objects. The qualities of the mind are *selfishness* and *limited generosity*; and the situation of external objects is their *easy change*, joined to their *scarcity* in comparison of the wants and desires of men. But however philosophers may have been bewildered in those speculations, poets have been guided more infallibly by a certain taste or common instinct which, in most kinds of reasoning, goes further than any of that art and philosophy with which we have been yet acquainted. They easily perceived, if every man had a tender regard for another, or if nature supplied abundantly all our wants and desires, that the jealousy of interest, which justice supposes, could no longer have place; nor would there be any occasion for those distinctions and limits of property and possession which at present are in use among mankind. Increase to a sufficient degree the benevolence of men, or the bounty of nature, and you render justice useless by supplying its place with much

nobler virtues and more valuable blessings. The selfishness of men is animated by the few possessions we have in proportion to our wants; and it is to restrain this selfishness that men have been obliged to separate themselves from the community, and to distinguish betwixt their own goods and those of others.

Nor need we have recourse to the fictions of poets to learn this, but, beside the reason of the thing, may discover the same truth by common experience and observation. It is easy to remark that a cordial affection renders all things common among friends, and that married people in particular mutually lose their property and are unacquainted with the *mine* and *thine*, which are so necessary and yet cause such disturbance in human society. The same effect arises from any alteration in the circumstances of mankind; as when there is such a plenty of anything as satisfies all the desires of men; in which case the distinction of property is entirely lost, and everything remains in common. This we may observe with regard to air and water, though the most valuable of all external objects; and may easily conclude that if men were supplied with everything in the same abundance, or if *every one* had the same affection and tender regard for *every one* as for himself, justice and injustice would be equally unknown among mankind.

• • •

. . . Though the rules of justice are established merely by interest, their connection with interest is somewhat singular, and is different from what may be observed on other occasions. A single act of justice is frequently contrary to *public interest*; and were it to stand alone, without being followed by other acts, may in itself be very prejudicial to society. When a man of merit, of a beneficent disposition, restores a great fortune to a miser or a seditious bigot, he has acted justly and laudably; but the public is a real sufferer. Nor is every single act of justice, considered apart, more conducive to private interest than to public; and it is easily conceived how a

man may impoverish himself by a single instance of integrity, and have reason to wish that, with regard to that single act, the laws of justice were for a moment suspended in the universe. But however single acts of justice may be contrary either to public or private interest, it is certain that the whole plan or scheme is highly conducive, or indeed absolutely requisite, both to the support of society and the well-being of every individual. It is impossible to separate the good from the ill. Property must be stable, and must be fixed by general rules. Though in one instance the public be a sufferer, this momentary ill is amply compensated by the steady prosecution of the rule and by the peace and order which it establishes in society. And even every individual person must find himself a gainer on balancing the account; since without justice society must immediately dissolve, and every one must fall into that savage and solitary condition which is infinitely worse than the worst situation that can possibly be supposed in society. When, therefore, men have had experience enough to observe that, whatever may be the consequence of any single act of justice performed by a single person, yet the whole system of actions concurred in by the whole society is infinitely advantageous to the whole and to every part, it is not long before justice and property take place. Every member of society is sensible of this interest; every one expresses this sense to his fellows along with the resolution he has taken of squaring his actions by it, on condition that others will do the same. No more is requisite to induce any one of them to perform an act of justice, who has the first opportunity. This becomes an example to others; and thus justice establishes itself by a kind of convention or agreement, that is, by a sense of interest, supposed to be common to all, and where every single act is performed in expectation that others are to perform the like. Without such a convention no one would ever have dreamed that there was such a virtue as justice, or have been induced to conform his actions to it. Taking any single

act, my justice may be pernicious in every respect; and it is only upon the supposition that others are to imitate my example that I can be induced to embrace that virtue; since nothing but this combination can render justice advantageous, or afford me any motives to conform myself to its rules.

We come now to the *second* question we proposed, viz., *Why we annex the idea of virtue to justice, and of vice to injustice*. This question will not detain us long after the principles which we have already established. All we can say of it at present will be dispatched in a few words; and for further satisfaction the reader must wait till we come to the third part of this book. The *natural* obligation to justice, viz., interest, has been fully explained; but as to the *moral* obligation, or the sentiment of right and wrong, it will first be requisite to examine the natural virtues before we can give a full and satisfactory account of it.

After men have found by experience that their selfishness and confined generosity, acting at their liberty, totally incapacitate them for society, and at the same time have observed that society is necessary to the satisfaction of those very passions, they are naturally induced to lay themselves under the restraint of such rules as may render their commerce more safe and commodious. To the imposition, then, and observance of these rules, both in general and in every particular instance, they are at first induced only by a regard to interest; and this motive, on the first formation of society, is sufficiently strong and forcible. But when society has become numerous and has increased to a tribe or nation, this interest is more remote; nor do men so readily perceive that disorder and confusion follow upon every breach of these rules, as in a more narrow and contracted society. But though in our own actions we may frequently lose sight of that interest which we have in maintaining order, and may follow a lesser and more present interest, we never fail to observe the prejudice we receive either mediately or immediately from the injustice of others, as not being in that case either blinded by passion or

biassed by any contrary temptation. Nay, when the injustice is so distant from us as no way to affect our interest, it still displeases us, because we consider it as prejudicial to human society and pernicious to every one that approaches the person guilty of it. We partake of their uneasiness by *sympathy*; and as everything which gives uneasiness in human actions, upon the general survey, is called *vice*, and whatever produces satisfaction, in the same manner, is denominated *virtue*, this is the reason why the sense of moral good and evil follows upon justice and injustice. And though this sense in the present case be derived only from contemplating the actions of others, yet we fail not to extend it even to our own actions. The *general rule* reaches beyond those instances from which it arose; while at the same time we naturally *sympathize* with others in the sentiments they entertain of us.

•   •   •

Of the origin of the natural virtues and vices

We come now to the examination of such virtues and vices as are entirely natural, and have no dependence on the artifice and contrivance of men. The examination of these will conclude this system of morals.

•   •   •

We have already observed that moral distinctions depend entirely on certain peculiar sentiments of pain and pleasure, and that whatever mental quality in ourselves or others gives us a satisfaction by the survey or reflection is of course virtuous; as everything of this nature that gives uneasiness is vicious. Now, since every quality in ourselves or others which gives pleasure always causes pride or love, as every one that produces uneasiness excites humility or hatred, it follows that these two particulars are to be considered as equivalent with regard to our mental qualities; *virtue* and the power of producing love or pride; *vice* and the power of producing humility or hatred. In every case,

therefore, we must judge of the one by the other, and may pronounce any *quality* of the mind virtuous which causes love or pride, and any one vicious which causes hatred or humility.

If any *action* be either virtuous or vicious, it is only as a sign of some quality or character. It must depend upon durable principles of the mind which extend over the whole conduct and enter into the personal character. Actions themselves, not proceeding from any constant principle, have no influence on love or hatred, pride or humility; and consequently are never considered in morality.

This reflection is self-evident and deserves to be attended to as being of the utmost importance in the present subject. We are never to consider any single action in our inquiries concerning the origin of morals, but only the quality or character from which the action proceeded. These alone are *durable* enough to affect our sentiments concerning the person. Actions are indeed better indications of a character than words, or even wishes and sentiments; but it is only so far as they are such indications that they are attended with love or hatred, praise or blame.

To discover the true origin of morals, and of that love or hatred which arises from mental qualities, we must take the matter pretty deep and compare some principles which have been already examined and explained.

We may begin with considering anew the nature and force of *sympathy*. The minds of all men are similar in their feelings and operations; nor can any one be actuated by any affection of which all others are not in some degree susceptible. As in strings equally wound up the motion of one communicates itself to the rest, so all the affections readily pass from one person to another, and beget correspondent movements in every human creature. When I see the *effects* of passion in the voice and gesture of any person, my mind immediately passes from these effects to their causes, and forms such a lively idea of the passion as is presently converted into the passion itself. In like manner, when I perceive the *causes* of any emotion, my mind is conveyed to the effects, and is actuated with a like emotion. Were I present at any of the more terrible operations of surgery, it is certain that, even before it begun, the preparation of the instruments, the laying of the bandages in order, the heating of the irons, with all the signs of anxiety and concern in the patient and assistants, would have a great effect upon my mind, and excite the strongest sentiments of pity and terror. No passion of another discovers itself immediately to the mind. We are only sensible of its causes or effects. From *these* we infer the passion; and consequently, *these* give rise to our sympathy.

• • •

No virtue is more esteemed than justice, and no vice more detested than injustice; nor are there any qualities which go further to the fixing the character, either as amiable or odious. Now, justice is a moral virtue, merely because it has that tendency to the good of mankind, and indeed is nothing but an artificial invention to that purpose. The same may be said of allegiance, of the laws of nations, of modesty, and of good manners. All these are mere human contrivances for the interest of society. And since there is a very strong sentiment of morals, which in all nations and all ages has attended them, we must allow that the reflecting on the tendency of characters and mental qualities is sufficient to give us the sentiments of approbation and blame. Now, as the means to an end can only be agreeable where the end is agreeable, and as the good of society, where our own interest is not concerned or that of our friends, pleases only by sympathy, it follows that sympathy is the source of the esteem which we pay to all the artificial virtues.

Thus it appears that *sympathy* is a very powerful principle in human nature, that it has a great influence on our taste of beauty, and that it produces our sentiment of morals in all the artificial virtues. From thence we may presume that it also gives rise to many of the other virtues,

and that qualities acquire our approbation because of their tendency to the good of mankind. This presumption must become a certainty, when we find that most of those qualities which we *naturally* approve of have actually that tendency and render a man a proper member of society; while the qualities which we *naturally* disapprove of have a contrary tendency and render any intercourse with the person dangerous or disagreeable. For having found that such tendencies have force enough to produce the strongest sentiment of morals, we can never reasonably, in these cases, look for any other cause of approbation or blame; it being an inviolable maxim in philosophy that where any particular cause is sufficient for an effect, we ought to rest satisfied with it, and ought not to multiply causes without necessity. We have happily attained experiments in the artificial virtues, where the tendency of qualities to the good of society is the *sole* cause of our approbation, without any suspicion of the concurrence of another principle. From thence we learn the force of that principle. And where that principle may take place, and the quality approved of is really beneficial to society a true philosopher will never require any other principle to account for the strongest approbation and esteem.

That many of the natural virtues have this tendency to the good of society, no one can doubt of. Meekness, beneficence, charity, generosity, clemency, moderation, equity, bear the greatest figure among the moral qualities, and are commonly denominated the *social* virtues, to mark their tendency to the good of society.

• • •

The only difference betwixt the natural virtues and justice lies in this, that the good which results from the former rises from every single act, and is the object of some natural passion; whereas a single act of justice, considered in itself, may often be contrary to the public good; and it is only the concurrence of mankind in a general scheme or system of action which is advantageous. When I relieve persons in distress, my natural humanity is my motive, and so far as my succour extends, so far have I promoted the happiness of my fellow creatures. But if we examine all the questions that come before any tribunal of justice, we shall find that, considering each case apart, it would as often be an instance of humanity to decide contrary to the laws of justice as conformable to them. Judges take from a poor man to give to a rich; they bestow on the dissolute the labour of the industrious; and put into the hands of the vicious the means of harming both themselves and others. The whole scheme, however, of law and justice is advantageous to the society; and it was with a view to this advantage that men, by their voluntary conventions, established it. After it is once established by these conventions, it is *naturally* attended with a strong sentiment of morals which can proceed from nothing but our sympathy with the interests of society. We need no other explication of that esteem which attends such of the natural virtues as have a tendency to the public good.

• • •

Before I proceed further, I must observe two remarkable circumstances in this affair which may seem objections to the present system. The first may be thus explained. When any quality or character has a tendency to the good of mankind, we are pleased with it and approve of it because it presents the lively idea of pleasure; which idea affects us by sympathy, and is itself a kind of pleasure. But as this sympathy is very variable, it may be thought that our sentiments of morals must admit of all the same variations. We sympathize more with persons contiguous to us than with persons remote from us; with our acquaintance, than with strangers; with our countrymen, than with foreigners. But notwithstanding this variation of our sympathy, we give the same approbation to the same moral qualities in China as in England. They appear equally virtuous and recommend themselves equally to the esteem of a judicious spectator. The sympathy varies

without a variation in our esteem. Our esteem, therefore, proceeds not from sympathy.

To this I answer, the approbation of moral qualities most certainly is not derived from reason or any comparison of ideas; but proceeds entirely from a moral taste and from certain sentiments of pleasure or disgust which arise upon the contemplation and view of particular qualities or characters. Now, it is evident that those sentiments, whencever they are derived, must vary according to the distance or contiguity of the objects; nor can I feel the same lively pleasure from the virtues of a person who lived in Greece two thousand years ago that I feel from the virtues of a familiar friend and acquaintance. Yet I do not say that I esteem the one more than the other; and therefore, if the variation of the sentiment without a variation of the esteem be an objection, it must have equal force against every other system, as against that of sympathy. But to consider the matter aright, it has no force at all; and it is the easiest matter in the world to account for it. Our situation with regard both to persons and things is in continual fluctuation; and a man that lies at a distance from us may in a little time become a familiar acquaintance. Besides, every particular man has a peculiar position with regard to others; and it is impossible we could ever converse together on any reasonable terms, were each of us to consider characters and persons only as they appear from his peculiar point of view. In order, therefore, to prevent those continual *contradictions* and arrive at a more *stable* judgment of things, we fix on some *steady* and *general* points of view, and always in our thoughts, place ourselves in them, whatever may be our present situation. In like manner, external beauty is determined merely by pleasure; and it is evident a beautiful countenance cannot give so much pleasure when seen at a distance of twenty paces as when it is brought nearer us. We say not, however, that it appears to us less beautiful; because we know what effect it will have in such a position, and by that reflection we correct its momentary appearance.

In general, all sentiments of blame or praise are variable, according to our situation of nearness or remoteness with regard to the person blamed or praised, and according to the present disposition of our mind. But these variations we regard not in our general decisions, but still apply the terms expressive of our liking or dislike in the same manner as if we remained in one point of view. Experience soon teaches us this method of correcting our sentiments, or at least of correcting our language, where the sentiments are more stubborn and unalterable. Our servant, if diligent and faithful, may excite stronger sentiments of love and kindness than Marcus Brutus, as represented in history; but we say not upon that account that the former character is more laudable than the latter. We know that, were we to approach equally near to that renowned patriarch, he would command a much higher degree of affection and admiration. Such corrections are common with regard to all the senses; and, indeed, it were impossible we could ever make use of language or communicate our sentiments to one another, did we not correct the momentary appearances of things and overlook our present situation.

• • •

. . . When we form our judgments of persons merely from the tendency of their characters to our own benefit, or to that of our friends, we find so many contradictions to our sentiments in society and conversation, and such an uncertainty from the incessant changes of our situation, that we seek some other standard of merit and demerit which may not admit of so great variation. Being thus loosened from our first station, we cannot afterwards fix ourselves so commodiously by any means as by a sympathy with those who have any commerce with the person we consider. This is far from being as lively as when our own interest is concerned, or that of our particular friends; nor has it such an influence on our love and hatred; but being equally conformable to our calm and general principles, it is said to have

an equal authority over our reason, and to command our judgment and opinion. We blame equally a bad action which we read of in history, with one performed in our neighbourhood the other day; the meaning of which is that we know from reflection that the former action would excite as strong sentiments of disapprobation as the latter, were it placed in the same position.

I now proceed to the *second* remarkable circumstance which I propose to take notice of. Where a person is possessed of a character that in its natural tendency is beneficial to society, we esteem him virtuous, and are delighted with the view of his character, even though particular accidents prevent its operation and incapacitate him from being serviceable to his friends and country. Virtue in rags is still virtue; and the love which it procures attends a man into a dungeon or desert, where the virtue can no longer be exerted in action and is lost to all the world. Now, this may be esteemed an objection to the present system. Sympathy interests us in the good of mankind; and if sympathy were the source of our esteem for virtue, that sentiment of approbation could only take place where the virtue actually attained its end and was beneficial to mankind. Where it fails of its end, it is only an imperfect means and, therefore, can never acquire any merit from that end. The goodness of an end can bestow a merit on such means alone as are complete and actually produce the end.

To this we may reply that, where any object, in all its parts, is fitted to attain any agreeable end, it naturally gives us pleasure and is esteemed beautiful, even though some external circumstances be wanting to render it altogether effectual. It is sufficient if everything be complete in the object itself. A house that is contrived with great judgment for all the commodities of life pleases us upon that account, though perhaps we are sensible that no one will ever dwell in it. A fertile soil and a happy climate delight us by a reflection on the happiness which they would afford the inhabitants, though at present the country be desert and uninhabited. A man whose limbs and shape promise strength and activity is esteemed handsome, though condemned to perpetual imprisonment. The imagination has a set of passions belonging to it upon which our sentiments of beauty much depend. These passions are moved by degrees of liveliness and strength, which are inferior to *belief*, and independent of the real existence of their objects. Where a character is in every respect fitted to be beneficial to society, the imagination passes easily from the cause to the effect, without considering that there are still some circumstances wanting to render the cause a complete one. *General rules* create a species of probability which sometimes influences the judgment, and always the imagination.

It is true, when the cause is complete and a good disposition is attended with good fortune which renders it really beneficial to society, it gives a stronger pleasure to the spectator, and is attended with a more lively sympathy. We are more affected by it; and yet we do not say that it is more virtuous, or that we esteem it more. We know that an alteration of fortune may render the benevolent disposition entirely impotent; and therefore we separate as much as possible the fortune from the disposition. The case is the same as when we correct the different sentiments of virtue which proceed from its different distances from ourselves. The passions do not always follow our corrections; but these corrections serve sufficiently to regulate our abstract notions, and are alone regarded when we pronounce in general concerning the degrees of vice and virtue.

Notes

1   As a proof how confused our way of thinking on this subject commonly is, we may observe that those who assert that morality is demonstrable do not say that morality lies in the relations, and that the relations are distinguishable by reason. They

only say that reason can discover such an action in such relations to be virtuous, and such another vicious. It seems they thought it sufficient if they could bring the word "relation" into the proposition, without troubling themselves whether it was to the purpose or not. But here, I think, is plain argument. Demonstrative reason discovers only relations. But that reason, according to this hypothesis, discovers also vice and virtue. These moral qualities, therefore, must be relations. When we blame any action, in any situation, the whole complicated object of action and situation must form certain relations, wherein the essence of vice consists. This hypothesis is not otherwise intelligible. For what does reason discover, when it pronounces any action vicious? Does it discover a relation or a matter of fact? These questions are decisive, and must not be eluded.

2   In the following discourse, *natural* is also opposed sometimes to *civil*, sometimes to *moral*. The opposition will always discover the sense in which it is taken.

G. E. Moore

GOODNESS AS SIMPLE AND INDEFINABLE

THAT WHICH is meant by 'good' is, in fact, except its converse 'bad,' the *only* simple object of thought which is peculiar to Ethics. Its definition is, therefore, the most essential point in the definition of Ethics; and moreover a mistake with regard to it entails a far larger number of erroneous ethical judgments than any other. Unless this first question be fully understood, and its true answer clearly recognised, the rest of Ethics is as good as useless from the point of view of systematic knowledge. True ethical judgments, of the two kinds last dealt with, may indeed be made by those who do not know the answer to this question as well as by those who do; and it goes without saying that the two classes of people may lead equally good lives. But it is extremely unlikely that the *most general* ethical judgments will be equally valid, in the absence of a true answer to this question: I shall presently try to shew that the gravest errors have been largely due to beliefs in a false answer. And, in any case, it is impossible that, till the answer to this question be known, any one should know *what is the evidence* for any ethical judgment whatsoever. But the main object of Ethics, as a systematic science, is to give correct *reasons* for thinking that this or that is good; and, unless this question be answered, such reasons cannot be given. Even, therefore, apart from the fact that a false answer leads to false conclusions, the present enquiry is a most necessary and important part of the science of Ethics.

6. What, then, is good? How is good to be defined? Now, it may be thought that this is a verbal question. A definition does indeed often mean the expressing of one word's meaning in other words. But this is not the sort of definition I am asking for. Such a definition can, never be of ultimate importance in any study except lexicography. If I wanted that kind of definition I should have to consider in the first place how people generally used the word 'good'; but my business is not with its proper usage, as established by custom. I should, indeed, be foolish, if I tried to use it for something which it did not usually denote: if, for instance, I were to announce that, whenever I used the word 'good,' I must be understood to be thinking of that object which is usually denoted by the word 'table.' I shall, therefore, use the word in the sense in which I think it is ordinarily used; but at the same time I am not anxious to discuss whether I am right in thinking that it is so used. My business is solely with that object or idea, which I hold, rightly or wrongly, that the word is generally used to stand for. What I want to discover is the nature of that object or idea, and about this I am extremely anxious to arrive at an agreement.

But, if we understand the question in this sense, my answer to it may seem a very disappointing one. If I am asked 'What is good?' my answer is that good is good, and that is the end of the matter. Or if I am asked 'How is good to be

defined?' my answer is that it cannot be defined, and that is all I have to say about it. But disappointing as these answers may appear, they are of the very last importance. To readers who are familiar with philosophic terminology, I can express their importance by saying that they amount to this: That propositions about the good are all of them synthetic and never analytic; and that is plainly no trivial matter. And the same thing may be expressed more popularly, by saying that, if I am right, then nobody can foist upon us such an axiom as that 'Pleasure is the only good' or that 'The good is the desired' on the pretence that this is 'the very meaning of the word.'

7. Let us, then, consider this position. My point is that 'good' is a simple notion, just as 'yellow' is a simple notion; that, just as you cannot, by any manner of means, explain to any one who does not already know it, what yellow is, so you cannot explain what good is. Definitions of the kind that I was asking for, definitions which describe the real nature of the object or notion denoted by a word, and which do not merely tell us what the word is used to mean, are only possible when the object or notion in question is something complex. You can give a definition of a horse, because a horse has many different properties and qualities, all of which you can enumerate. But when you have enumerated them all, when you have reduced a horse to his simplest terms, then you can no longer define those terms. They are simply something which you think of or perceive, and to any one who cannot think of or perceive them, you can never, by any definition, make their nature known. It may perhaps be objected to this that we are able to describe to others, objects which they have never seen or thought of. We can, for instance, make a man understand what a chimaera is, although he has never heard of one or seen one. You can tell him that it is an animal with a lioness's head and body, with a goat's head growing from the middle of its back, and with a snake in place of a tail. But here the object which you are

describing is a complex object; it is entirely composed of parts, with which we are all perfectly familiar—a snake, a goat, a lioness; and we know, too, the manner in which those parts are to be put together, because we know what is meant by the middle of a lioness's back, and where her tail is wont to grow. And so it is with all objects, not previously known, which we are able to define: they are all complex; all composed of parts, which may themselves, in the first instance, be capable of similar definition, but which must in the end be reducible to simplest parts, which can no longer be defined. But yellow and good, we say, are not complex: they are notions of that simple kind, out of which definitions are composed and with which the power of further defining ceases.

8. When we say, as Webster says, 'The definition of horse is "A hoofed quadruped of the genus Equus,"' we may, in fact, mean three different things. (1) We may mean merely: 'When I say "horse," you are to understand that I am talking about a hoofed quadruped of the genus Equus.' This might be called the arbitrary verbal definition: and I do not mean that good is indefinable in that sense. (2) We may mean, as Webster ought to mean: 'When most English people say "horse," they mean a hoofed quadruped of the genus Equus.' This may be called the verbal definition proper, and I do not say that good is indefinable in this sense either; for it is certainly possible to discover how people use a word: otherwise, we could never have known that 'good' may be translated by 'gut' in German and by 'bon' in French. But (3) we may, when we define horse, mean something much more important. We may mean that a certain object, which we all of us know, is composed in a certain manner: that it has four legs, a head, a heart, a liver, etc., etc., all of them arranged in definite relations to one another. It is in this sense that I deny good to be definable. I say that it is not composed of any parts, which we can substitute for it in our minds when we are thinking of it. We might think just as clearly and

correctly about a horse, if we thought of all its parts and their arrangement instead of thinking of the whole; we could, I say, think how a horse differed from a donkey just as well, just as truly, in this way, as now we do, not only so easily; but there is nothing whatsoever which we could so substitute for good; and that is what I mean, when I say that good is indefinable.

9. But I am afraid I have still not removed the chief difficulty which may prevent acceptance of the proposition that good is indefinable. I do not mean to say that the good, that which is good, is thus indefinable; if I did think so, I should not be writing on Ethics, for my main object is to help towards discovering that definition. It is just because I think there will be less risk of error in our search for a definition of 'the good,' that I am now insisting that good is indefinable. I must try to explain the difference between these two. I suppose it may be granted that 'good' is an adjective. Well 'the good, that which is good,' must therefore be the substantive to which the adjective 'good' will apply: it must be the whole of that to which the adjective will apply, and the adjective must *always* truly apply to it. But if it is that to which the adjective will apply, it must be something different from that adjective itself; and the whole of that something different, whatever it is, will be our definition of *the good*. Now it may be that this something will have other adjectives, beside 'good,' that will apply to it. It may be full of pleasure, for example: it may be intelligent: and if these two adjectives are really part of its definition, then it will certainly be true, that pleasure and intelligence are good. And many people appear to think that, if we say 'Pleasure and intelligence are good,' or if we say 'Only pleasure and intelligence are good,' we are defining 'good.' Well, I cannot deny that propositions of this nature may sometimes be called definitions; I do not know well enough how the word is generally used to decide upon this point. I only wish it to be understood that that is not what I mean when I say there is no possible definition of good, and that I shall not mean this if I use the word again. I do most fully believe that some true proposition of the form 'Intelligence is good and intelligence alone is good' can be found; if none could be found, our definition of the good would be impossible. As it is, I believe the good to be definable; and yet I still say that good itself is indefinable.

10. 'Good,' then, if we mean by it that quality which we assert to belong to a thing, when we say that the thing is good, is incapable of any definition, in the most important sense of that word. The most important sense of 'definition' is that in which a definition states what are the parts which invariably compose a certain whole; and in this sense 'good' has no definition because it is simple and has no parts. It is one of those innumerable objects of thought which are themselves incapable of definition, because they are the ultimate terms by reference to which whatever is capable of definition must be defined. That there must be an indefinite number of such terms is obvious, on reflection; since we cannot define anything except by an analysis, which, when carried as far as it will go, refers us to something, which is simply different from anything else, and which by that ultimate difference explains the peculiarity of the whole which we are defining: for every whole contains some parts which are common to other wholes also. There is, therefore, no intrinsic difficulty in the contention that 'good' denotes a simple and indefinable quality. There are many other instances of such qualities.

Consider yellow, for example. We may try to define it, by describing its physical equivalent; we may state what kind of light-vibrations must stimulate the normal eye, in order that we may perceive it. But a moment's reflection is sufficient to shew that those light-vibrations are not themselves what we mean by yellow. They are not what we perceive. Indeed we should never have been able to discover their existence, unless we had first been struck by the patent difference of quality between the different colours. The most we can be entitled to say of those

vibrations is that they are what corresponds in space to the yellow which we actually perceive.

Yet a mistake of this simple kind has commonly been made about 'good.' It may be true that all things which are good are *also* something else, just as it is true that all things which are yellow produce a certain kind of vibration in the light. And it is a fact, that Ethics aims at discovering what are those other properties belonging to all things which are good. But far too many philosophers have thought that when they named those other properties they were actually defining good; that these properties, in fact, were simply not 'other,' but absolutely and entirely the same with goodness. This view I propose to call the 'naturalistic fallacy' and of it I shall now endeavour to dispose.

11. Let us consider what it is such philosophers say. And first it is to be noticed that they do not agree among themselves. They not only say that they are right as to what good is, but they endeavour to prove that other people who say that it is something else, are wrong. One, for instance, will affirm that good is pleasure, another, perhaps, that good is that which is desired; and each of these will argue eagerly to prove that the other is wrong. But how is that possible? One of them says that good is nothing but the object of desire, and at the same time tries to prove that it is not pleasure. But from his first assertion, that good just means the object of desire, one of two things must follow as regards his proof:

(1) He may be trying to prove that the object of desire is not pleasure. But, if this be all, where is his Ethics? The position he is maintaining is merely a psychological one. Desire is something which occurs in our minds, and pleasure is something else which so occurs; and our would-be ethical philosopher is merely holding that the latter is not the object of the former. But what has that to do with the question in dispute? His opponent held the ethical proposition that pleasure was the good, and although he should prove a million times over the psychological

proposition that pleasure is not the object of desire, he is no nearer proving his opponent to be wrong. The position is like this. One man says a triangle is a circle: another replies 'A triangle is a straight line, and I will prove to you that I am right: for' (this is the only argument) 'a straight line is not a circle.' 'That is quite true,' the other may reply; 'but nevertheless a triangle is a circle, and you have said nothing whatever to prove the contrary. What is proved is that one of us is wrong, for we agree that a triangle cannot be both a straight line and a circle: but which is wrong, there can be no earthly means of proving, since you define triangle as straight line and I define it as circle.'—Well, that is one alternative which any naturalistic Ethics has to face; if good is *defined* as something else, it is then impossible either to prove that any other definition is wrong or even to deny such definition.

(2) The other alternative will scarcely be more welcome. It is that the discussion is after all a verbal one. When A says 'Good means pleasant' and B says 'Good means desired,' they may merely wish to assert that most people have used the word for what is pleasant and for what is desired respectively. And this is quite an interesting subject for discussion: only it is not a whit more an ethical discussion than the last was. Nor do I think that any exponent of naturalistic Ethics would be willing to allow that this was all he meant. They are all so anxious to persuade us that what they call the good is what we really ought to do. 'Do, pray, act so, because the word "good" is generally used to denote actions of this nature': such, on this view, would be the substance of their teaching. And in so far as they tell us how we ought to act, their teaching is truly ethical, as they mean it to be. But how perfectly absurd is the reason they would give for it! 'You are to do this, because most people use a certain word to denote conduct such as this.' 'You are to say the thing which is not, because most people call it lying.' That is an argument just as good!—My dear sirs, what we want to know from you as ethical teachers, is

not how people use a word; it is not even, what kind of actions they approve, which the use of this word 'good' may certainly imply: what we want to know is simply what *is* good. We may indeed agree that what most people do think good, is actually so; we shall at all events be glad to know their opinions: but when we say their opinions about what *is* good, we do mean what we say; we do not care whether they call that thing which they mean 'horse' or 'table' or 'chair', 'gut' or 'bon' or 'ἀγαθός'; we want to know what it is that they so call. When they say 'Pleasure is good', we cannot believe that they merely mean 'Pleasure is pleasure' and nothing more than that.

12. Suppose a man says 'I am pleased'; and suppose that is not a lie or a mistake but the truth. Well, if it is true, what does that mean? It means that his mind, a certain definite mind, distinguished by certain definite marks from all others, has at this moment a certain definite feeling called pleasure. 'Pleased' *means* nothing but having pleasure, and though we may be more pleased or less pleased, and even, we may admit for the present, have one or another kind of pleasure; yet in so far as it is pleasure we have, whether there be more or less of it, and whether it be of one kind or another, what we have is one definite thing, absolutely indefinable, some one thing that is the same in all the various degrees and all the various kinds of it that there may be. We may be able to say how it is related to other things: that, for example, it is in the mind, that it causes desire, that we are conscious of it, etc., etc. We can, I say, describe its relations to other things, but define it we can *not*. And if anybody tried to define pleasure for us as being any other natural object; if anybody were to say, for instance, that pleasure *means* the sensation of red, and were to proceed to deduce from that that pleasure is a colour, we should be entitled to laugh at him and to distrust his future statements about pleasure. Well, that would be the same fallacy which I have called the naturalistic fallacy. That 'pleased' does not mean 'having the

sensation of red,' or anything else whatever, does not prevent us from understanding what it does mean. It is enough for us to know that 'pleased' does mean 'having the sensation of pleasure,' and though pleasure is absolutely indefinable, though pleasure is pleasure and nothing else whatever, yet we feel no difficulty in saying that we are pleased. The reason is, of course, that when I say 'I am pleased,' I do *not* mean that 'I' am the same thing as 'having pleasure.' And similarly no difficulty need be found in my saying that 'pleasure is good' and yet not meaning that 'pleasure' is the same thing as 'good,' that pleasure *means* good, and that good *means* pleasure. If I were to imagine that when I said 'I am pleased,' I meant that I was exactly the same thing as 'pleased,' I should not indeed call that a naturalistic fallacy, although it would be the same fallacy as I have called naturalistic with reference to Ethics. The reason of this is obvious enough. When a man confuses two natural objects with one another, defining the one by the other, if for instance, he confuses himself, who is one natural object, with 'pleased' or with 'pleasure' which are others, then there is no reason to call the fallacy naturalistic. But if he confuses 'good,' which is not in the same sense a natural object, with any natural object whatever, then there is a reason for calling that a naturalistic fallacy; its being made with regard to 'good' marks it as something quite specific, and this specific mistake deserves a name because it is so common. As for the reasons why good is not to be considered a natural object, they may be reserved for discussion in another place. But, for the present, it is sufficient to notice this: Even if it were a natural object, that would not alter the nature of the fallacy nor diminish its importance one whit. All that I have said about it would remain quite equally true: only the name which I have called it would not be so appropriate as I think it is. And I do not care about the name: what I do care about is the fallacy. It does not matter what we call it, provided we recognise it when we meet with it.

It is to be met with in almost every book on Ethics; and yet it is not recognised: and that is why it is necessary to multiply illustrations of it, and convenient to give it a name. It is a very simple fallacy indeed. When we say that an orange is yellow, we do not think our statement binds us to hold that 'orange' means nothing else than 'yellow,' or that nothing can be yellow but an orange. Supposing the orange is also sweet! Does that bind us to say that 'sweet' is exactly the same thing as 'yellow,' that 'sweet' must be defined as 'yellow'? And supposing it be recognised that 'yellow' just means 'yellow' and nothing else whatever, does that make it any more difficult to hold that oranges are yellow? Most certainly it does not: on the contrary, it would be absolutely meaningless to say that oranges were yellow, unless yellow did in the end mean just 'yellow' and nothing else whatever—unless it was absolutely indefinable. We should not get any very clear notion about things, which are yellow—we should not get very far with our science, if we were bound to hold that everything which was yellow, *meant* exactly the same thing as yellow. We should find we had to hold that an orange was exactly the same thing as a stool, a piece of paper, a lemon, anything you like. We could prove any number of absurdities; but should we be the nearer to the truth? Why, then, should it be different with 'good'? Why, if good is good and indefinable, should I be held to deny that pleasure is good? Is there any difficulty in holding both to be true at once? On the contrary, there is no meaning in saying that pleasure is good, unless good is something different from pleasure. It is absolutely useless, as far as Ethics is concerned, to prove, as Mr Spencer tries to do, that increase of pleasure coincides with increase of life, unless good *means* something different from either life or pleasure. He might just as well try to prove that an orange is yellow by shewing that it always is wrapped up in paper.

13. In fact, if it is not the case that 'good' denotes something simple and indefinable, only two alternatives are possible: either it is a complex, a given whole, about the correct analysis of which there may be disagreement; or else it means nothing at all, and there is no such subject as Ethics. In general, however, ethical philosophers have attempted to define good, without recognising what such an attempt must mean. They actually use arguments which involve one or both of the absurdities considered in §11. We are, therefore, justified in concluding that the attempt to define good is chiefly due to want of clearness as to the possible nature of definition. There are, in fact, only two serious alternatives to be considered, in order to establish the conclusion that 'good' does denote a simple and indefinable notion. It might possibly denote a complex, as 'horse' does; or it might have no meaning at all. Neither of these possibilities has, however, been clearly conceived and seriously maintained, as such, by those who presume to define good; and both may be dismissed by a simple appeal to facts.

(1) The hypothesis that disagreement about the meaning of good is disagreement with regard to the correct analysis of a given whole, may be most plainly seen to be incorrect by consideration of the fact that, whatever definition be offered, it may be always asked, with significance, of the complex so defined, whether it is itself good. To take, for instance, one of the more plausible, because one of the more complicated, of such proposed definitions, it may easily be thought, at first sight, that to be good may mean to be that which we desire to desire. Thus if we apply this definition to a particular instance and say 'When we think that A is good, we are thinking that A is one of the things which we desire to desire,' our proposition may seem quite plausible. But, if we carry the investigation further, and ask ourselves 'Is it good to desire to desire A?' it is apparent, on a little reflection, that this question is itself as intelligible, as the original question 'Is A good?'—that we are, in fact, now asking for exactly the same information about the desire to desire A, for which we

formerly asked with regard to A itself. But it is also apparent that the meaning of this second question cannot be correctly analysed into 'Is the desire to desire A one of the things which we desire to desire?': we have not before our minds anything so complicated as the question 'Do we desire to desire to desire to desire A?' Moreover any one can easily convince himself by inspection that the predicate of this proposition—'good'—is positively different from the notion of 'desiring to desire' which enters into its subject: 'That we should desire to desire A is good' is not merely equivalent to 'That A should be good is good.' It may indeed be true that what we desire to desire is always also good; perhaps, even the converse may be true: but it is very doubtful whether this is the case, and the mere fact that we understand very well what is meant by doubting it, shews clearly that we have two different notions before our minds.

(2) And the same consideration is sufficient to dismiss the hypothesis that 'good' has no meaning whatsoever. It is very natural to make the mistake of supposing that what is universally true is of such a nature that its negation would be self-contradictory; the importance which has been assigned to analytic propositions in the history of philosophy shews how easy such a mistake is. And thus it is very easy to conclude that what seems to be a universal ethical principle is in fact an identical proposition; that, if, for example, whatever is called 'good' seems to be pleasant, the proposition 'Pleasure is the good' does not assert a connection between two different notions, but involves only one, that of pleasure, which is easily recognised as. a distinct entity. But whoever will attentively consider with himself what is actually before his mind when he asks the question 'Is pleasure (or whatever it may be) after all good?' can easily satisfy himself that he is not merely wondering whether pleasure is pleasant. And if he will try this experiment with each suggested definition in succession, he may become expert enough to recognise that in every case he has before his mind a unique object, with regard to the connection of which with any other object, a distinct question may be asked. Every one does in fact understand the question 'Is this good?' When he thinks of it, his state of mind is different from what it would be, were he asked 'Is this pleasant, or desired, or approved?' It has a distinct meaning for him, even though he may not recognise in what respect it is distinct. Whenever he thinks of 'intrinsic value,' or 'intrinsic worth,' or says that a thing 'ought to exist,' he has before his mind the unique object—the unique property of things—which I mean by 'good.' Everybody is constantly aware of this notion, although he may never become aware at all that it is different from other notions of which he is also aware. But, for correct ethical reasoning, it is extremely important that he should become aware of this fact; and, as soon as the nature of the problem is clearly understood, there should be little difficulty in advancing so far in analysis.

Chapter 10

A. J. Ayer

THE EMOTIVE THEORY OF ETHICS

THERE IS still one objection to be met before we can claim to have justified our view that all synthetic propositions are empirical hypotheses. This objection is based on the common supposition that our speculative knowledge is of two distinct kinds—that which relates to questions of empirical fact, and that which relates to questions of value. It will be said that "statements of value" are genuine synthetic propositions, but that they cannot with any show of justice be represented as hypotheses, which are used to predict the course of our sensations; and, accordingly, that the existence of ethics and aesthetics as branches of speculative knowledge presents an insuperable objection to our radical empiricist thesis.

In face of this objection, it is our business to give an account of "judgments of value" which is both satisfactory in itself and consistent with our general empiricist principles. We shall set ourselves to show that in so far as statements of value are significant, they are ordinary "scientific" statements, and that in so far as they are not scientific, they are not in the literal sense significant, but are simply expressions of emotion which can be neither true nor false. In maintaining this view, we may confine ourselves for the present to the case of ethical statements. What is said about them will be found to apply, *mutatis mutandis*, to the case of aesthetic statements also.

The ordinary system of ethics, as elaborated in the works of ethical philosophers, is very far from being a homogeneous whole. Not only is it apt to contain pieces of metaphysics, and analyses of non-ethical concepts: its actual ethical contents are themselves of very different kinds. We may divide them, indeed, into four main classes. There are, first of all, propositions which express definitions of ethical terms, or judgements about the legitimacy or possibility of certain definitions. Secondly, there are propositions describing the phenomena of moral experience, and their causes. Thirdly, there are exhortations to moral virtue. And, lastly, there are actual ethical judgements. It is unfortunately the case that the distinction between these four classes, plain as it is, is commonly ignored by ethical philosophers; with the result that it is often very difficult to tell from their works what it is that they are seeking to discover or prove.

In fact, it is easy to see that only the first of our four classes, namely that which comprises the propositions relating to the definitions of ethical terms, can be said to constitute ethical philosophy. The propositions which describe the phenomena of moral experience, and their causes, must be assigned to the science of psychology, or sociology. The exhortations to moral virtue are not propositions at all, but ejaculations or commands which are designed to provoke the reader to action of a certain sort. Accordingly, they do not belong to any branch of philosophy or science. As for the expressions of ethical judgements, we have not yet determined

how they should be classified. But inasmuch as they are certainly neither definitions nor comments upon definitions, nor quotations, we may say decisively that they do not belong to ethical philosophy. A strictly philosophical treatise on ethics should therefore make no ethical pronouncements. But it should, by giving an analysis of ethical terms, show what is the category to which all such pronouncements belong. And this is what we are now about to do.

A question which is often discussed by ethical philosophers is whether it is possible to find definitions which would reduce all ethical terms to one or two fundamental terms. But this question, though it undeniably belongs to ethical philosophy, is not relevant to our present enquiry. We are not now concerned to discover which term, within the sphere of ethical terms, is to be taken as fundamental; whether, for example, "good" can be defined in terms of "right" or "right" in terms of "good," or both in terms of "value." What we are interested in is the possibility of reducing the whole sphere of ethical terms to non-ethical terms. We are enquiring whether statements of ethical value can be translated into statements of empirical fact.

That they can be so translated is the contention of those ethical philosophers who are commonly called subjectivists, and of those who are known as utilitarians. For the utilitarian defines the rightness of actions, and the goodness of ends, in terms of the pleasure, or happiness, or satisfaction, to which they give rise; the subjectivist, in terms of the feelings of approval which a certain person, or group of people, has towards them. Each of these types of definition makes moral judgements into a sub-class of psychological or sociological judgements; and for this reason they are very attractive to us. For, if either was correct, it would follow that ethical assertions were not genetically different from the factual assertions which are ordinarily contrasted with them; and the account which we have already given of empirical hypotheses would apply to them also.

Nevertheless we shall not adopt either a subjectivist or a utilitarian analysis of ethical terms. We reject the subjectivist view that to call an action right, or a thing good, is to say that it is generally approved of, because it is not self-contradictory to assert that some actions which are generally approved of are not right, or that some things which are generally approved of are not good. And we reject the alternative subjectivist view that a man who asserts that a certain action is right, or that a certain thing is good, is saying that he himself approves of it, on the ground that a man who confessed that he sometimes approved of what was bad or wrong would not be contradicting himself. And a similar argument is fatal to utilitarianism. We cannot agree that to call an action right is to say that of all the actions possible in the circumstances it would cause, or be likely to cause, the greatest happiness, or the greatest balance of pleasure over pain, or the greatest balance of satisfied over unsatisfied desire, because we find that it is not self-contradictory to say that it is sometimes wrong to perform the action which would actually or probably cause the greatest happiness, or the greatest balance of pleasure over pain, or of satisfied over unsatisfied desire. And since it is not self-contradictory to say that some pleasant things are not good, or that some bad things are desired, it cannot be the case that the sentence "x is good" is equivalent to "x is pleasant," or to "x is desired." And to every other variant of utilitarianism with which I am acquainted the same objection can be made. And therefore we should, I think, conclude that the validity of ethical judgements is not determined by the felicific tendencies of actions, any more than by the nature of people's feelings; but that it must be regarded as "absolute" or "intrinsic," and not empirically calculable.

If we say this, we are not, of course, denying that it is possible to invent a language in which all ethical symbols are definable in non-ethical terms, or even that it is desirable to invent such a language and adopt it in place of our own;

what we are denying is that the suggested reduction of ethical to non-ethical statements is consistent with the conventions of our actual language. That is, we reject utilitarianism and subjectivism, not as proposals to replace our existing ethical notions by new ones, but as analyses of our existing ethical notions. Our contention is simply that, in our language, sentences which contain normative ethical symbols are not equivalent to sentences which express psychological propositions, or indeed empirical propositions of any kind.

It is advisable here to make it plain that it is only normative ethical symbols, and not descriptive ethical symbols, that are held by us to be indefinable in factual terms. There is a danger of confusing these two types of symbols, because they are commonly constituted by signs of the same sensible form. Thus a complex sign of the form "x is wrong" may constitute a sentence which expresses a moral judgement concerning a certain type of conduct, or it may constitute a sentence which states that a certain type of conduct is repugnant to the moral sense of a particular society. In the latter case, the symbol "wrong" is a descriptive ethical symbol, and the sentence in which it occurs expresses an ordinary sociological proposition; in the former case, the symbol "wrong" is a normative ethical symbol, and the sentence in which it occurs does not, we maintain, express an empirical proposition at all. It is only with normative ethics that we are at present concerned; so that whenever ethical symbols are used in the course of this argument without qualification, they are always to be interpreted as symbols of the normative type.

In admitting that normative ethical concepts are irreducible to empirical concepts, we seem to be leaving the way clear for the "absolutist" view of ethics—that is, the view that statements of value are not controlled by observation, as ordinary empirical propositions are, but only by a mysterious "intellectual intuition." A feature of this theory, which is seldom recognized by its advocates, is that it makes statements of value unverifiable. For it is notorious that what seems intuitively certain to one person may seem doubtful, or even false, to another. So that unless it is possible to provide some criterion by which one may decide between conflicting intuitions, a mere appeal to intuition is worthless as a test of a proposition's validity. But in the case of moral judgements, no such criterion can be given. Some moralists claim to settle the matter by saying that they "know" that their own moral judgements are correct. But such an assertion is of purely psychological interest, and has not the slightest tendency to prove the validity of any moral judgement. For dissentient moralists may equally well "know" that their ethical views are correct. And, as far as subjective certainty goes, there will be nothing to choose between them. When such differences of opinion arise in connection with an ordinary empirical proposition, one may attempt to resolve them by referring to, or actually carrying out, some relevant empirical test. But with regard to ethical statements, there is, on the "absolutist" or "intuitionist" theory, no relevant empirical test. We are therefore justified in saying that on this theory ethical statements are held to be unverifiable. They are, of course, also held to be genuine synthetic propositions.

Considering the use which we have made of the principle that a synthetic proposition is significant only if it is empirically verifiable, it is clear that the acceptance of an "absolutist" theory of ethics would undermine the whole of our main argument. And as we have already rejected the "naturalistic" theories which are commonly supposed to provide the only alternative to "absolutism" in ethics, we seem to have reached a difficult position. We shall meet the difficulty by showing that the correct treatment of ethical statements is afforded by a third theory, which is wholly compatible with our radical empiricism.

We begin by admitting that the fundamental ethical concepts are unanalysable, inasmuch as

there is no criterion by which one can test the validity of the judgements in which they occur. So far we are in agreement with the absolutists. But, unlike the absolutists, we are able to give an explanation of this fact about ethical concepts. We say that the reason why they are unanalysable is that they are mere pseudo-concepts. The presence of an ethical symbol in a proposition adds nothing to its factual content. Thus if I say to someone, "You acted wrongly in stealing that money," I am not stating anything more than if I had simply said, "You stole that money." In addition that this action is wrong I am not making any further statement about it. I am simply evincing my moral disapproval of it. It is as if I had said, "You stole that money," in a peculiar tone of horror, or written it with the addition of some special exclamation marks. The tone, or the exclamation marks, adds nothing to the literal meaning of the sentence. It merely serves to show that the expression of it is attended by certain feelings in the speaker.

If now I generalise my previous statement and say, "Stealing money is wrong," I produce a sentence which has no factual meaning—that is, expresses no proposition which can be either true or false. It is as if I had written "Stealing money!!"—where the shape and thickness of the exclamation marks show, by a suitable convention, that a special sort of moral disapproval is the feeling which is being expressed. It is clear that there is nothing said here which can be true or false. Another man may disagree with me about the wrongness of stealing, in the sense that he may not have the same feelings about stealing as I have, and he may quarrel with me on account of my moral sentiments. But he cannot, strictly speaking, contradict me. For in saying that a certain type of action is right or wrong, I am not making any factual statement, not even a statement about my own state of mind. I am merely expressing certain moral sentiments. And the man who is ostensibly contradicting me is merely expressing his moral sentiments. So that there is plainly no sense in

asking which of us is in the right. For neither of us is asserting a genuine proposition.

What we have just been saying about the symbol "wrong" applies to all normative ethical symbols. Sometimes they occur in sentences which record ordinary empirical facts besides expressing ethical feeling about those facts: sometimes they occur in sentences which simply express ethical feeling about a certain type of action, or situation, without making any statement of fact. But in every case in which one would commonly be said to be making an ethical judgement, the function of the relevant ethical word is purely "emotive." It is used to express feeling about certain objects, but not to make any assertion about them.

It is worth mentioning that ethical terms do not serve only to express feeling. They are calculated also to arouse feeling, and so to stimulate action. Indeed some of them are used in such a way as to give the sentences in which they occur the effect of commands. Thus the sentence "It is your duty to tell the truth" may be regarded both as the expression of a certain sort of ethical feeling about truthfulness and as the expression of the command "Tell the truth." The sentence "You ought to tell the truth" also involves the command "Tell the truth," but here the tone of the command is less emphatic. In the sentence "It is good to tell the truth" the command has become little more than a suggestion. And thus the "meaning" of the word "good," in its ethical usage, is differentiated from that of the word "duty" or the word "ought." In fact we may define the meaning of the various ethical words in terms both of the different feelings they are ordinarily taken to express, and also the different responses which they are calculated to provoke.

We can now see why it is impossible to find a criterion for determining the validity of ethical judgements. It is not because they have an "absolute" validity which is mysteriously independent of ordinary sense-experience, but because they have no objective validity whatsoever. If a sentence makes no statement at all, there is

obviously no sense in asking whether what it says is true or false. And we have seen that sentences which simply express moral judgements do not say anything. They are pure expressions of feeling and as such do not come under the category of truth and falsehood. They are unverifiable for the same reason as a cry of pain or a word of command is unverifiable—because they do not express genuine propositions.

Thus, although our theory of ethics might fairly be said to be radically subjectivist, it differs in a very important respect from the orthodox subjectivist theory. For the orthodox subjectivist does not deny, as we do, that the sentences of a moralizer express genuine propositions. All he denies is that they express propositions of a unique non-empirical character. His own view is that they express propositions about the speaker's feelings. If this were so, ethical judgements clearly would be capable of being true or false. They would be true if the speaker had the relevant feelings, and false if he had not. And this is a matter which is, in principle, empirically verifiable. Furthermore they could be significantly contradicted. For if I say, "Tolerance is a virtue," and someone answers, "You don't approve of it," he would, on the ordinary subjectivist theory, be contradicting me. On our theory, he would not be contradicting me, because, in saying that tolerance was a virtue, I should not be making any statement about my own feelings or about anything else. I should simply be evincing my feelings, which is not at all the same thing as saying that I have them.

The distinction between the expression of feeling and the assertion of feeling is complicated by the fact that the assertion that one has a certain feeling often accompanies the expression of that feeling, and is then, indeed, a factor in the expression of that feeling. Thus I may simultaneously express boredom and say that I am bored, and in that case my utterance of the words, "I am bored," is one of the circumstances which make it true to say that I am expressing or evincing boredom. But I can express boredom without actually saying that I am bored. I can express it by my tone and gestures, while making a statement about something wholly unconnected with it, or by an ejaculation, or without uttering any words at all. So that even if the assertion that one has a certain feeling always involves the expression of that feeling, the expression of a feeling assuredly does not always involve the assertion that one has it. And this is the important point to grasp in considering the distinction between our theory and the ordinary subjectivist theory. For whereas the subjectivist holds that ethical statements actually assert the existence of certain feelings, we hold that ethical statements are expressions and excitants of feeling which do not necessarily involve any assertions.

We have already remarked that the main objection to the ordinary subjectivist theory is that the validity of ethical judgements is not determined by the nature of their author's feelings. And this is an objection which our theory escapes. For it does not imply that the existence of any feelings is a necessary and sufficient condition of the validity of an ethical judgement. It implies, on the contrary, that ethical judgements have no validity.

There is, however, a celebrated argument against subjectivist theories which our theory does not escape. It has been pointed out by Moore that if ethical statements were simply statements about the speaker's feelings, it would be impossible to argue about questions of value. To take a typical example: if a man said that thrift was a virtue, and another replied that it was a vice, they would not, on this theory, be disputing with one another. One would be saying that he approved of thrift, and the other that *he* didn't; and there is no reason why both these statements should not be true. Now Moore held it to be obvious that we do dispute about questions of value, and accordingly concluded that the particular form of subjectivism which he was discussing was false.

It is plain that the conclusion that it is impossible to dispute about questions of value follows

from our theory also. For as we hold that such sentences as "Thrift is a virtue" and "Thrift is a vice" do not express propositions at all, we clearly cannot hold that they express incompatible propositions. We must therefore admit that if Moore's argument really refutes the ordinary subjectivist theory, it also refutes ours. But, in fact, we deny that it does refute even the ordinary subjectivist theory. For we hold that one really never does dispute about questions of value.

This may seem, at first sight, to be a very paradoxical assertion. For we certainly do engage in disputes which are ordinarily regarded as disputes about questions of value. But, in all such cases, we find, if we consider the matter closely, that the dispute is not really about a question of value, but about a question of fact. When someone disagrees with us about the moral value of a certain action or type of action, we do admittedly resort to argument in order to win him over to our way of thinking. But we do not attempt to show by our arguments that he has the "wrong" ethical feeling towards a situation whose nature he has correctly apprehended. What we attempt to show is that he is mistaken about the facts of the case. We argue that he has misconceived the agent's motive: or that he has misjudged the effects of the action, or its probable effects in view of the agent's knowledge; or that he has failed to take into account the special circumstances in which the agent was placed. Or else we employ more general arguments about the effects which actions of a certain type tend to produce, or the qualities which are usually manifested in their performance. We do this in the hope that we have only to get our opponent to agree with us about the nature of the empirical facts for him to adopt the same moral attitude towards them as we do. And as the people with whom we argue have generally received the same moral education as ourselves, and live in the same social order, our expectation is usually justified. But if our opponent happens to have undergone a different process of moral "conditioning" from ourselves, so that, even when he

acknowledges all the facts, he still disagrees with us about the moral value of the actions under discussion, then we abandon the attempt to convince him by argument. We say that it is impossible to argue with him because he has a distorted or undeveloped moral sense; which signifies merely that he employs a different set of values from our own. We feel that our own system of values is superior, and therefore speak in such derogatory terms of his. But we cannot bring forward any arguments to show that our system is superior. For our judgement that it is so is itself a judgement of value, and accordingly outside the scope of argument. It is because argument fails us when we come to deal with pure questions of value, as distinct from questions of fact, that we finally resort to mere abuse.

In short, we find that argument is possible on moral questions only if some system of values is presupposed. If our opponent concurs with us in expressing moral disapproval of all actions of a given type t, then we may get him to condemn a particular action A, by bringing forward arguments to show that A is of type t. For the question whether A does or does not belong to that type is a plain question of fact. Given that a man has certain moral principles, we argue that he must, in order to be consistent, react morally to certain things in a certain way. What we do not and cannot argue about is the validity of these moral principles. We merely praise or condemn them in the light of our own feelings.

If anyone doubts the accuracy of this account of moral disputes, let him try to construct even an imaginary argument on a question of value which does not reduce itself to an argument about a question of logic or about an empirical matter of fact. I am confident that he will not succeed in producing a single example. And if that is the case, he must allow that its involving the impossibility of purely ethical arguments is not, as Moore thought, a ground of objection to our theory, but rather a point of favour of it.

Having upheld our theory against the only criticism which appeared to threaten it, we may

now use it to define the nature of all ethical enquiries. We find that ethical philosophy consists simply in saying that ethical concepts are pseudo-concepts and therefore unanalysable. The further task of describing the different feelings that the different ethical terms are used to express, and the different reactions that they customarily provoke, is a task for the psychologist. There cannot be such a thing as ethical science, if by ethical science one means the elaboration of a "true" system of morals. For we have seen that, as ethical judgements are mere expressions of feeling, there can be no way of determining the validity of any ethical system, and, indeed, no sense in asking whether any such system is true. All that one may legitimately enquire in this connection is, What are the moral habits of a given person or group of people, and what causes them to have precisely those habits and feelings? And this enquiry falls wholly within the scope of the existing social sciences.

It appears, then, that ethics, as a branch of knowledge, is nothing more than a department of psychology and sociology. And in case anyone thinks that we are overlooking the existence of casuistry, we may remark that casuistry is not a science, but is a purely analytical investigation of the structure of a given moral system. In other words, it is an exercise in formal logic.

When one comes to pursue the psychological enquiries which constitute ethical science, one is immediately enabled to account for the Kantian and hedonistic theories of morals. For one finds that one of the chief causes of moral behaviour is fear, both conscious and unconscious, of a god's displeasure, and fear of the enmity of society. And this, indeed, is the reason why moral precepts present themselves to some people as "categorical" commands. And one finds, also, that the moral code of a society is partly determined by the beliefs of that society concerning the conditions of its own happiness—or, in other words, that a society tends to encourage or discourage a given type of conduct by the use of moral sanctions according as it appears to promote or detract from the contentment of the society as a whole. And this is the reason why altruism is recommended in most moral codes and egotism condemned. It is from the observation of this connection between morality and happiness that hedonistic or eudaemonistic theories of morals ultimately spring, just as the moral theory of Kant is based on the fact, previously explained, that moral precepts have for some people the force of inexorable commands. As each of these theories ignores the fact which lies at the root of the other, both may be criticized as being one-sided; but this is not the main objection to either of them. Their essential defect is that they treat propositions which refer to the causes and attributes of our ethical feelings as if they were definitions of ethical concepts. And thus they fail to recognize that ethical concepts are pseudo-concepts and consequently indefinable.

Chapter 11

Simon Blackburn

EXPRESSIVISM

WE ARE ALL OF US born in moral stupidity, taking the world as an udder to feed our supreme selves: Dorothea had early begun to emerge from that stupidity, but yet it had been easier to her to imagine how she would devote herself to Mr Casaubon, and become wise and strong in his strength and wisdom, than to conceive with that distinctness which is no longer reflection but feeling—an idea wrought back to the directness of sense, like the solidity of objects—that he had an equivalent centre of self, whence the lights and shadows must always fall with a certain difference.

George Eliot, *Middlemarch*, ch. XXI

1. In the beginning was the deed

The natural world is the world revealed by the senses, and described by the natural sciences: physics, chemistry, and notably biology, including evolutionary theory. However we think of it, ethics seems to fit badly into that world. Neither the senses nor the sciences seem to be good detectors of obligations, duties, or the order of value of things. As everyone knows, nature is heartless; the universe runs as much in accordance with its own laws when it brings suffering and ruin, as on the occasions when it brings peace and prosperity. Human beings too run as much in accordance with their own mixed and fallen natures when they do each.

Iago is just as natural as Mother Theresa, and on a head-count perhaps more so. It may once have been a consolation, but it is so no longer, to think that the order of the universe is an ethical order. It is not, and even if it were, we would have no access to what the order is.

To be a naturalist is to see human beings as frail complexes of perishable tissue, and so part of the natural order. It is thus to refuse unexplained appeals to mind or spirit, and unexplained appeals to knowledge of a Platonic order of Forms or Norms; it is above all to refuse any appeal to a supernatural order. After that, the degrees of austerity that naturalism imposes can be variously interpreted: some philosophers are more relaxed than others about reconciling the world as we know it, 'the manifest image', with the world as science tells us it is, 'the scientific image'. But we nearly all want to be naturalists and we all want a theory of ethics. So the problem is one of finding room for ethics, or of placing ethics within the disenchanted, non-ethical order which we inhabit, and of which we are a part.

'Finding room' means understanding how we think ethically, and why it offends against nothing in the rest of our world-view for us to do so. It does not necessarily mean 'reducing' ethics to something else. Reductionism here, as elsewhere in philosophy, implies seeing one thing as if it were another. Fastidious philosophers are rightly suspicious of it: as Moore

famously said, quoting Butler, 'everything is what it is and not another thing'.[1] Nevertheless, the reconciliation of the normative and the natural must be carried out somehow, so if we are not reductionists we must find some other strategy.

I said in the first chapter [see original reading] that ethics was more a matter of knowing how (to behave), or knowing whom (to defer to, or punish, or admire), or knowing when (to act, or withdraw), than a matter of knowing *that* something is the case. Ethical knowledge, unlike knowledge of physics or history, can be quite inarticulate, and a novelist can paint a subject's ethics without ever showing them saying anything ethical. Whereas you could not paint a subject's knowledge of physics or history without showing them saying things belonging to those disciplines. If ethics is not in fact inarticulate, this is because we need to discuss how to behave and whom to admire, and to pass on the solutions to such problems that we find. Ethical sentences are the focus of these transactions.

The theory I want to defend is one that gives a story about the way in which ethical thought functions. Valuing something, it says, is not to be understood as *describing* it in certain terms, any more than hoping for or desiring something are describing it in particular terms. Rather, the state of mind of one who values something is distinctive, but nevertheless it is itself a natural, and naturally describable, state. Once we find ethics here, we understand the essential phenomenon, which is that of people valuing things. When they value things, they express themselves in terms of what is good, bad, obligatory, right, justifiable, and so on. When they wonder what to value, they express themselves as not being sure what is good or justifiable; when they achieve a certain kind of confidence, they say they know what to value, or what is valuable. The ethical proposition gets its identity as a focus for practical thought, as people communicate their certainties, insistences, and doubts about what to value.

This strategy—that of expressivism—leaves ethical properties and propositions alone with their own specific identities. They are the counters in our transactions with our values, just as a piece of money is a counter in financial transactions. To understand the value of a piece of money it is no good staring at it. It is necessary to understand the processes of human economic behaviour. You need to approach the token not with a microscope and a scalpel, but with an eye for large patterns of human interactions. Similarly, to understand the ethical proposition, it is no good looking for a 'concept' or 'truth condition'. We need the same eye for whole processes of human action and interaction. We need synthesis, not analysis.

So the expressivist thinks we can say interestingly what is involved for a subject S to think that X is good. It is for S to value it, and this can be explained in natural terms. Nature itself may be heartless and free of desires, but amongst the creatures it has thrown up are some which are not heartless, and not free of desires. We understand our values by understanding ourselves as valuing, and this we can do. If you go on to ask this strategist what it is for something to *be* good, the response is that this is not the subject of this theoretical concern—that is, not the subject of concern for those of us who, while naturalists, want a theory of ethics. Either the question illegitimately insists that trying to analyse the ethical proposition is the only possible strategy, which is not true. Or it must be heard in an ethical tone of voice. To answer it then would be to go inside the domain of ethics, and start expressing our standards. In this sense we may discuss whether promoting human flourishing, or manifesting respect for nature, or for liberty and equality, are good. But this kind of discussion is not furthering the project of explaining ethics in natural terms. It is taking ethical thought for granted, and trying to express and systematize our actual values.

Expressivism denies that when we assert values, we talk about our own states of mind, in

actual or potential circumstances. It says that we *voice* our states of mind, but denies that we thereby describe them.[2] Similarly, if we are sincere when we say that 'the time is midnight' we voice our belief, but we do not describe ourselves as having a belief. Our having the belief is not what makes it true that the time is midnight. It is only what makes us sincere when we say it.

Wittgenstein said, after Goethe, that in the beginning was the deed: im *Anfang war die Tat*. Words are themselves deeds ('words can be hard to say'). That is, it is only through understanding the *activities* associated with particular linguistic transactions that we understand the words used in conducting them. Amongst the activities involved in ethics are these: valuing, grading, forbidding, permitting, forming resolves, backing off, communicating emotion such as anger or resentment, embarrassment or shame, voicing attitudes such as admiration, or disdain or contempt, or even disgust, querying conduct, pressing attack, warding it off. When I say that these are involved in ethics, I mean what I have already adverted to, that by describing the contours of a character in terms of doings like these, a narrator can tell us all that is important about the character's ethics, regardless of the words said.

Should all these activities be herded together as 'expressing ethical beliefs'? It is hard to see how that could be useful to do so. It would be labelling at a level of abstraction that makes the interesting detail invisible. A philosopher might carelessly regard this as harmless: perhaps he sees it as simply revealing the 'depth grammar' or 'logical form' behind the rather ragged surface of linguistic behaviour. But it is not harmless. When we voice our ethics we have a distinct conversational dynamics. People are badgered. Reproaches are made and rejected. Prescriptions are issued and enforced. Resentments arise and are soothed. Emotions are tugged. The smooth clothing of statements proposed as true or denied as false disguises the living body beneath.

The expressivist task is to reveal that clothing for what it is—but that is not to say that we should always try to do without it.

• • •

3. States of mind: Satan and Othello

Let us now concentrate on what we regard as a person's values. Expressivism requires a naturalistic story of the state of mind of valuing something. We then go on from that to give an account of the procedures of valuation that we adopt; the modes of expression that are appropriate; and finally the logic and theory of meaning of our typical expression of values. We have already seen that we locate a person's values in the light of a number of manifestations: what they say, what they do, what they regret in themselves, what they encourage in others, what they forbid or what they insist upon. Sometimes these elements pull together, and we have no doubt what someone values. Sometimes they do not harmonize all that well, and suggest various interpretations. Someone may sincerely believe that something is best, but not do it. There may be states of loathing of ethics, or of desire to be bad, or of maliciousness or waywardness, as well as despair or lethargy (what Aquinas called *accidie*), all of which can interfere with a simple attempt to read anyone's values straight back from their choices. Nobody lives up to their better selves all the time; some people only do it very little of the time.

There are interestingly different, although related, ways of interpreting a lot of such cases. If a person fails to live up to their professed values enough of the time, we start to doubt whether the professions are sincere, or, if they are at least sincere, we may wonder about self-deception. One class of cases is the simple 'inverted commas' type of case, where an agent pays lip-service to a value that they do not really hold, either through hypocrisy or self-deception. This is no problem: a person says that

an action other than the one he intends is the 'good' action, and means only that it is what the others call 'good' (there is a specific sneering intonation that is typically used when we so speak). Another very different class of case is where something is given an evaluative label through *inertia*, even after the usual connection between valuation and motivation has been severed. For example, we deem a wine good in light of the pleasure we take in tasting it. This is the typical or basic case. But if, for some reason, we have lost our taste for wine and take no pleasure in tasting any, we could still call some wine good if we know that it once merited the label. This has an obvious point: it serves the public function of grading the wine, or encouraging others to try for the pleasure. A third class of case I would like to distinguish is different, although related. Here evaluative words have also 'gone dead' and retain a use only to specify the class of things meeting the standards that apply. Consider this conversation from Jane Austen's *Emma*:

'Mr. Dixon, you say, is not, strictly speaking, handsome.'
'Handsome! Oh! no—far from it—certainly plain. I told you he was plain.'
'My Dear, you said that Miss Campbell would not allow him to be plain, and that you yourself—'
'Oh! as for me, my judgment is worth nothing. Where I have a regard, I always think a person well-looking. But I have what I believed the general opinion, when I called him plain.'

Here Jane Fairfax, the second speaker, does not put inverted commas around 'the general opinion', yet the word 'plain' is applied in accordance with it, rather than as an expression of her own judgement. The use is in a certain sense deferential to normal opinion. But, of course, the valuation still lies in the background. It provides the reason why Mr Dixon is called plain even if, in the mouth of Jane Fairfax, it expresses no aesthetic attitude of her own. Jane is part of the social practice of rating people on their looks. If she is spectacularly out of line with the others, she will be criticized by them for misleading them, and this is what she seeks to avoid in the conversation.

Other cases are more interesting, because a person's own values are involved, yet there is only a shaky or perverted connection with motivation. On occasion, clearly, a person can act, knowingly and intentionally, against her values: she may have desires that overcome her scruples, or just knowingly succumb to temptation. Doing wrong even has its own allure. But if the values are really there, we will expect them to manifest themselves somewhere else: in regret or remorse, or in guilt or shame. Yet even that may be too simple, and some philosophers ('externalists') have suggested that there can be agents in whom a pure cognizance of ethics has no practical effect: they know what is good to do, and simply do not care. Perhaps it is only good people who care to do what they know to be good. Perhaps there are bad people who know what it is good to do and then deliberately direct their wills the other way. Thus in Book IV of *Paradise Lost* Satan describes his motivation for bringing about the Fall with the chilling resolution 'Evil be thou my Good' (l. 110). For Satan, the judgement that something is evil acts as an attraction. And the fact that this possibility makes sense casts some doubt on the very close identification I have been urging between ethics and practical, motivating states of mind. If externalists are right, perhaps we have to see ethics more in terms of awareness of fact, with it then being up to us whether we care about the perceived fact one way or another. Philosophers resisting this ('internalists') have to say how they interpret the persistent, careless person who sees what is good, and doesn't care, or who, like Satan, sees what is good, but goes the other way.

My own judgement on this debate is that externalists can win individual battles. They can

certainly point to possible psychologies about which the right thing to say is that the agent knows what it is good or right to do, and then deliberately and knowingly does something else. And they can point to psychologies like that of Satan, in which it can become a reason for doing something precisely that it is known to be evil. But internalists win the war for all that, in the sense that these cases are necessarily parasitic, and what they are parasitic upon is a background connection between ethics and motivation. They are cases in which things are out of joint, but the fact of a joint being out presupposes a normal or typical state in which it is not out.

To understand this, it is useful to think of another analogy. Consider the complex of dispositions involved in being in love with someone. This typically includes taking pleasure in their company, wanting above all to be with them, wanting to give them pleasure and take pleasure from them, and so on. Nevertheless there are cases in which one person is in love with another, but wants not to see them (it would be too painful), or even wants to hurt them (jealous revenge). These cases are necessarily parasitic upon the normal in the sense that they require a background of the normal dispositions, which have then been wrenched out of order, giving rise to jealousy or the desire for revenge: love coexisting with hatred. But it would be absurd to conclude that being in love with someone is therefore a purely cognitive state, having no necessary connection with emotion or attitude.

We can approach the issue by another ethical illustration, here a public act rather than a private attitude. What is it to forbid something? To issue an injunction against it—but what is that? We might talk of communicating an intention to invoke sanctions or to become in one way or another set against anyone who disobeys the injunction. Surely 'forbidding' inhabits that neighbourhood. But can't you forbid someone from doing something, while all the time

intending to forgive them if they do it? The case skates perilously close to pretence, or play-acting. But we might allow it: parents, for example, seem to tell their children what not to do, but without any apparent intention of doing much about it when they are disobeyed. If we allow it, we should say that the case exists, but is parasitic on a more robust social connection between forbidding and the disposition to sanction. The link is put out of joint by half-hearted parents, but it exists as the background to their activities, and is necessary to make those activities possible. Once more, it would be wrong to conclude that there is no necessary connection between an act of forbidding and an intention to invoke a sanction. That has to be the typical case that any others exploit.

• • •

4. The ethical proposition and Frege's abyss

So what at last is said when we say that something is good or right? Following Moore, we do not expect to identify the content in other terms. We can now say, however, what is done when we say such things. We avow a practical state. 'Avowal' here means that we express this state, make it public, or communicate it.[3] We intend coordination with similar avowals or potential avowals from others, and this is the point of the communication. When this coordination is achieved, an intended direction is given to our joint practical lives and choices. Saying that something is good when we do not really value it is either deceiving others about our state, or is the result of self-deception. But because we have to accommodate the flexible, many-layered nature of our minds, we may sincerely say that something is good when we are not, unhappily, motivated to pursue it, provided one of the diagnoses sketched in the previous section [see original reading] applies.

If I permit smoking in my house, but you

forbid it in yours, we do not necessarily disagree about anything. Similarly, some evaluations are happily relativized: the weather is good from the farmer's point of view, but bad from the tourist's point of view, or good in so far as it helps the crops, bad in so far as it spoils the holiday. But with much ethics there is no scope for this coexistence. If I am minded to permit smoking in our house, and my wife is minded to forbid it, we do disagree. Only one of these practical attitudes can be implemented, and I am for one, and she is for the other. When we discuss ethics with each other, we are typically talking about 'our' house, or in other words practical issues on which we want to coordinate, or have to coordinate. In that case difference of attitude means disagreement, just as surely as difference of belief does. If the case is like that of separate houses we can sometimes 'agree to differ', and drop the conversation. But sometimes, even if we do not have to coordinate our actions, we cannot agree to differ, for serious enough differences cannot be tolerated. I return to this when we discuss relativism, but meanwhile the point remains that the typical, default, position is that difference in attitude is treated as disagreement.

Ethical avowals, like decisions and verdicts, require grounds. If I grade one paper higher than another, I must be prepared to indicate some relevant difference between them. We acknowledge the need to point to something that grounds our judgement, in virtue of which one is better than the other. But, as we shall see in the next chapter [see original reading], discussing Cornell realism, no complete theory of ethics can simply point to the grounding properties, and suppose that evaluations are given their meaning by their relationship to them. We need first to understand the evaluative stance.

Expressivism claims that the ethical proposition is something that we synthesize for a purpose. Its role is to act as a focus for practical thought. So what is it to believe that something is good, wonder whether it is good, to deny that it is good, to be undecided, or to know that it is good? In basic or typical cases:

believing that X is good or right is roughly having an appropriately favourable valuation of X;

wondering whether X is good or right is wondering what to do/what to admire or value;

denying that X is good or right is rejecting a favourable attitude to X;

being undecided is not knowing what to do/what to admire, etc.;

being certain that X is good or right is having a settled attitude/rejecting the possibility that improvement could result in change;

knowing that X is good is knowing to choose X/admire X, etc.

Here the practical states on the right-hand side are voiced and discussed in terms of attitudes to the saying or thought on the left. This is what I mean by saying that the moral proposition is designed or invented or emerges naturally as the focus for our practical transactions. And in the previous section [see original reading] we established the natural credentials of the states on the right and their intricate connections with other attitudes and emotions.

The reason expressivism in ethics has to be correct is that if we supposed that belief, denial, and so on were simply discussions of a way the world is, we would still face the open question. Even if that belief were settled, there would still be issues of what importance to give it, what to do, and all the rest. For we have no conception of a 'truth condition' or fact of which mere apprehension by itself determines practical issues. For any fact, there is a question of what to do about it. But evaluative discussion just is discussion of what to do about things.

However, many writers have insisted on a 'Fregean abyss' separating expressions of attitude from expressions of belief. They point out that evaluative commitments are expressed in

ordinary indicatives, and that this enables them to occur in indefinitely many 'indirect' contexts. We not only say that X is good, but that either X is good or Y is, or that if X is good such-and-such. Some think that this puts a weighty, or even insupportable, burden on expressivism. For all the expressivist has given us is an account of what is done when a moral sentence is put forward in an assertoric context: an attitude is voiced. What then happens when it is put forward in an indirect context, such as 'if X is good, then Y is good too' and no attitude to X or Y is voiced?

It is worth asking how other parts of language answer this problem. Suppose I say that the sentence 'Bears hibernate' expresses a belief. Well, it only does so when the sentence is put forward in an assertoric context. So what happens when it is put forward in an indirect context, such as 'If bears hibernate, they wake up hungry'? For here no belief in bears hibernating is expressed. The standard answer is to introduce a proposition or thought, regarded as a constant factor in both the assertoric and the indirect context. When we say bears hibernate, we express or assert the proposition, and represent ourselves as believing it; when we say 'If bears hibernate . . .' we introduce the proposition in a different way, conditionally, or as a supposition. Frege thought that in this second kind of context we refer to the thought that we assert in the assertoric context.

If this is allowed to solve the problem for ordinary beliefs, it might simply be taken over by the expressivist. In the Fregean story a 'proposition' or 'thought' is simply introduced as the common element between contexts: something capable of being believed but equally capable of being merely supposed or entertained. So why not say the same about an 'attitude'? It can be avowed, or it can be put forward without avowal, as a *topic* for discussion, or as an alternative. Just as we want to know the implications of a proposition or a thought, so we want to know the implications of attitude. What implies it, what is it right to hold if it is to be adopted?

If we want to know in other terms what is going on when we so put forward an attitude, we must look to the function of the indirect contexts in question. The key idea here is one of a functional structure of commitments that is isomorphic with or mirrored by the propositional structure that we use to express them. Thus someone may be what I called 'tied to a tree': in a state in which he or she can only endorse some combination of attitude and belief. Suppose I hold that either John is to blame, or he didn't do the deed. Then I am in a state in which if one side is closed off to me, I am to switch to the other—or withdraw the commitment. And this is what I express by saying 'Either John is to blame, or he didn't do the deed', or equally, 'If John did the deed, he is to blame'. By advancing disjunctions and conditionals we avow these more complex dispositional states. Taking advantage of the theory of interpretation sketched above, we can regard the state in question not just in functional terms, but also in normative terms. By using the disjunction I am presenting myself in a way that will deserve reproach and bewilderment if, without explanation, I go on to suppose both that John did the deed and is blameless. This makes no sense, unless I have changed my mind about something.

There has been some scepticism about whether this approach can deliver the mighty 'musts' of logic.[4] But we now see that it can do so perfectly well. Consider the example made famous by Geach, of inference according to the pattern of modus ponens. Someone saying each of 'p' and 'If p then q' has the premises of a modus ponens whose conclusion is q. He is logically committed to q, if he is committed to the premises. To put it another way, if anyone represented themselves as holding the combination of 'p' and 'If p then q' and 'not-q' we would not know what to make of them. Logical breakdown means failure of understanding. Is this result secured, on my approach, for an evaluative antecedent, p? Yes, because the person represents

themselves as tied to a tree of possible combinations of belief and attitude, but at the same time represents themselves as holding a combination that the tree excludes. So what is given at one moment is taken away at the next, and we can make no intelligible interpretation of them.

We can put the point another way. A mental state, I have said, is identified by what it 'makes sense' to hold in combination with it. To avow a mental state is therefore partly to express acceptance of certain norms. To avow anything of the form 'If p then q' is to commit oneself to the combination 'Either not-p, or q' and to be tied to that combination is to disavow the combination of p with not-q. Holding both together is therefore unintelligible. Logic is our way of codifying and keeping track of intelligible combinations of commitment.

We might usefully compare the situation to that in the theory of probability. The basic psychological reality as we contemplate the chances, for instance in a horse race, may be one of vague differences of confidence, reflected as dispositions to bet (under idealized circumstances) at various prices, or within various ranges of prices. If we choose to voice these confidences, for instance by saying that Eclipse has no better than an evens chance, or that 100 to 12 sounds a fair price on Sunrise, then we enter a more structured normative space. We only make sense if the chances we assign to the different horses in the field obey well-known classical rules of probability, and those rules dictate inferences. For instance, in a two-horse race, if we think one horse has a better than evens chance, then we must infer that the other has not. Our dispositions to bet at different prices only make sense if they can be represented as beliefs in probabilities, satisfying those laws. Working in terms of 'belief in classical probabilities' does not, then, necessarily reflect a prior commitment to the metaphysical hypothesis that there are such things, as it were hovering above and around horse races. More economically, it simply shows us working through the implications of various dispositions to accept and reject betting prices. The 'probability proposition' is a focus for our thoughts about where to put our money. And expressing ourselves in terms of probabilities imposes a necessary logic.

Similarly, if we start with a set of beliefs and attitudes, we can put them into a structured normative space by representing them as beliefs in the ethical proposition. Accepting conditionals and disjunctions shows us working out the implications of various combinations of attitude, or combinations of attitude and belief. We crossed Frege's abyss by creating the ethical proposition, and it is there in order to generate public discourse about which actions to insist upon or forbid, and which attitudes to hold or reject.

Notes

1 G. E. Moore, *Principia Ethica*, epigraph.
2 Huw Price, 'Truth and the Nature of Assertion', *Mind*, 96 (1987), 202–20.
3 We are not prepared to avow all the norms that influence us. Gibbard makes the useful distinction here between accepting a norm, which includes preparedness to avow it, versus being in the grip of a norm, which means being subject to its sway, perhaps unwillingly or guiltily, as in the case of a not-quite-liberated racist or sexist, who knows how he ought to be, but does not quite measure up in his snap emotional reactions (*Wise Choices, Apt Feelings*, 58–61).
4 Bob Hale, 'The Compleat Projectivist', *Philosophical Quarterly*, 36 (1986), 65–84. Related work includes G. F. Schueler, 'Modus Ponens and Moral Realism', *Ethics*, 98 (1988), 492–500; M. H. Brighouse, 'Blackburn's Projectivism—An Objection', *Philosophical Studies*, 59 (1990), 225; Nick Zangwill, 'Moral Modus Ponens', *Ratio*, 5 (1992), 177–93; Mark van Roojen, 'Expressivism and Irrationality', *Philosophical Review*, 105 (1996), 311–35.

References

Brighouse, M. H. 'Blackburn's Projectivism—An Objection', *Philosophical Studies*, 59 (1990), 225.

Gibbard, Allan, 'A Natural Property Humanly Signified', forthcoming.

—— 'Morality and Thick Concepts', *Proceedings of the Aristotelian Society*, supp. vol. 66 (1992), 267–83.

—— *Wise Choices, Apt Feelings: A Theory of Normative Judgment*. Cambridge, Mass.: Harvard University Press, 1990.

Hale, Bob. 'The Compleat Projectivist', *Philosophical Quarterly*, 36 (1986), 65–84.

Moore, G. E. *Principia Ethica*. Cambridge: Cambridge University Press, 1903.

Price, Huw. 'Truth and the Nature of Assertion', *Mind*, 96 (1987), 202–20.

Schueler, G. F. 'Modus Ponens and Moral Realism', *Ethics*, 98 (1988), 492–500.

van Roojen, Mark. 'Expressivism and Irrationality', *Philosophical Review*, 105 (1996), 311–35.

Zangwill, Nick. 'Moral Modus Ponens', *Ratio*, 5 (1992), 177–93.

Chapter 12

Russ Shafer-Landau

A CRITIQUE OF NON-COGNITIVISM

Cognitivism and truth talk

ONLY COGNITIVISM straightforwardly preserves ordinary talk of moral truth. We appear to take at face value such locutions as 'it is true that infanticide is wrong'. We allow for the possibility of moral mistake and often characterize it as a case in which a person speaks falsely, or has a false belief. When we experience moral perplexity, we often see ourselves as engaged in a search for the truth about who is in the right, or where our obligations lie. We can well explain the point and persistence of moral disagreement by attributing to agents the presupposition that there is a right answer awaiting discovery. Were they convinced that there was no truth of the matter, most interlocutors would see their continued disagreement as pointless; as pointless as, say, entering an intractable debate about whether red or orange was *really* the most beautiful colour.

Relatedly, we believe that moral argument can take the logical form of other kinds of argument. We think of sentential operators in moral sentences as truth-functional. The law of excluded middle holds as strictly for moral discourse as for non-moral discourse. We recognize the validity of modus ponens inferences that incorporate moral claims as premises. We freely use the logical connectives in making and evaluating moral claims. We standardly assess moral arguments as valid or invalid, sound or

unsound. This indicates at least a tacit assumption that truth-preservation is an arm of moral argument. Cognitivists have ready, straightforward analyses of such a view of moral argument. Non-cognitivists don't.

In particular, non-cognitivists have always foundered on what Blackburn has called 'Frege's Abyss' (though for Blackburn, it is more of a divot than anything to get worried about). The problem, first noted in the contemporary literature by Geach (1960, 1965), is how expressivists can make sense of sameness of meaning in asserted and unasserted contexts. This they must do if they are to preserve the possibility of logical validity, or at least credibly explain away the appearances of validity and soundness in moral argument. The trouble arises if we note, first, that much moral argument employs assertions, negations, disjunctions, and conditionals, and then note that, by non-cognitivist lights, the meaning of a moral sentence depends on the accompanying attitude that receives expression therein. Since one's attitude changes if one asserts a claim, negates it, cites it as a disjunct, or embeds it in the antecedent of a conditional, then the meaning of the relevant phrase ought to change as well. But it surely doesn't, and can't, if the possibility of logical moral argument is to be preserved. A minor cottage industry has grown up around this problem. It has yielded some ingenious solutions, but there is good reason to doubt the success of any one of them.[1]

Cognitivists assume that moral predicates are meaningful and can be used to describe the subjects they are predicated of. We use the indicative mood when issuing moral judgements. We assert that practices, character traits, or states are vicious, morally attractive, or deserving; we state that motives or actions exemplify such things as goodness, generosity, benevolence. When using evaluative language, most people would find it perfectly natural to characterize their doings as instances of describing things as good or bad, or as attributing to things certain qualities—goodness or badness. Moral talk is shot through with description, attribution, and predication. This makes perfect sense if cognitivism is true. The non-cognitivist story cannot be nearly as natural or simple.

Consider a very simple example that reveals the comparative advantages here. Suppose someone tells me that virtue deserves reward. The cognitivist glosses the claim by saying that there is such a thing as virtue, and desert, and reward. The sentence means just what it says, and is true just in case virtue and reward are related as it says they are. But for expressivists, when we say that virtue deserves reward, we aren't describing a thing (virtue), and saying of it that it has some property (that of deserving reward). There is no such thing; there is no such property. So we must be evincing a non-descriptive attitude. What would that be?

There are two problems with expressivist efforts to provide an answer. First, expressivists will have difficulty translating the general formula 'X deserves y.' We must, at the least, be evincing an attitude of approval when contemplating the state of affairs in which X gets y. But surely there's more involved than that. For we can register such approval in any number of other cases where desert isn't involved. 'Wouldn't it be nice were X to get y'; 'it's good that X has y', etc. It isn't clear how expressivists are going to analyse the attitude that receives expression in desert claims, as opposed to the various other claims that register our approvals. Second, even

if expressivists can distinguish desert claims from others, they don't believe in virtue. 'Virtue', like other ethical terms, denotes nothing; it never refers. So not only are we asked to find a suitable candidate for the special kind of approval that gets expressed in desert claims; we have nothing, really, that serves as the object of such approvals. Perhaps expressivists can provide a plausible translation of this simple claim. But surely cognitivists have the upper hand here. They don't require a paraphrase to begin with.

The first problem, just discussed, is really a particular instance of a quite general difficulty, that of accounting for the rich diversity of moral predicates. If expressivism is true, the essence of any moral statement is the expression of a fundamentally non-representational attitude towards some natural state of affairs. If, as it seems, we convey and mean something slightly different when we say of an action that it is virtuous, right, mandatory, supererogatory, kind, beneficent, admirable, conscientious, attractive, desirable, laudable, saintly, or fine, then non-cognitivists must explain this by citing a different attitude that receives expression in each case. But our attitudes don't seem nearly as diverse or fine-grained as the predicates we standardly deploy in moral assessment.[2] Cognitivists straightforwardly account for these differences by referring to different meanings, contents, or properties that are exemplified when these different assessments are true. Expressivists must either deny that these predicates signify different assessments, or identify a different attitude for each predicate. Neither route seems very promising.

Cognitivism also has some appeal when dealing with issues of moral motivation. If moral judgements are moral beliefs, capable of truth or falsity; and if moral beliefs, like other beliefs, do not necessarily motivate those who hold them; then it is at least conceptually possible that an agent issue sincere moral judgements and yet fail to be motivated. And this does seem a conceptual possibility: we can imagine

agents who, through debilitating mental or physical illness, or an enervating lassitude, or an antipathy to morality, are left utterly cold by the moral judgements they take to be true. Non-cognitivism, by contrast, takes moral judgement to essentially involve the expression of attitudes that are motivating. So any judgement that fails to motivate, according to non-cognitivism, cannot possibly be a moral judgement. The counter-intuitive consequences of this position are discussed at length in Chapter 6 [see original reading].

Moral error

Cognitivism preserves our talk of moral belief and the possibility of moral knowledge. To say of someone that he believes certain actions to be wrong, or others to be good, is to say nothing strange, but something we all understand. To turn some such beliefs into knowledge is recognized by most to be at least a possibility. Despite reluctance that stems from egalitarian impulses, we often talk of some being morally wiser than others, and typically abandon our reluctance when pressed with concrete comparisons. And even if we are sceptical about the number of situations in which people or societies have registered moral improvement, we are less dubious about moral regression, and either idea presupposes the possibility of mistake in moral beliefs and outlooks.

Some contemporary non-cognitivists want to allow for the possibility of moral error. But this isn't meant to signify the possibility of falsehood. On their view, moral error isn't a matter of saying or believing what's false. Instead, error might be diagnosed in one of two ways. First, it might essentially involve a kind of incoherence. Second, it might involve a failure to satisfy some other standard meant to govern attitude formation.

The first diagnosis identifies moral error with the case in which one holds attitudes that are inconsistent with one another. Practical attitudes are inconsistent if they counsel actions that are not jointly realizable. But why think of this as any kind of error? If I am committed to norms that govern my work behaviour, and also committed to being a good parent, why am I making some kind of *mistake* if my domestic commitments require that I sacrifice my work ethic? And even if attitudinal conflict is what moral mistake consists in, which of the conflicting attitudes should be singled out as the faulty one? Presumably that attitude which conflicts with the relevant highest-order attitude that I hold. But what if there is conflict within my highest-order attitudes? What if they are incomplete, or specified at such a level of generality as to fail to arbitrate in particular cases? Then all we can say is that there is a mistake, but we will lack the resources for identifying the culprit. This isn't merely an epistemological problem. In the absence of a determinate highest-order attitude that can adjudicate attitudinal conflict, the non-cognitivist must say that there is no particular mistaken attitude. So any case of attitudinal conflict involves a mistake, and yet in some cases, there may be no attitude that is itself mistaken, so no determinate answer as to which should be modified or abandoned.

This isn't a contradictory view, but the cognitivist has a more palatable account of the nature of moral mistake. When attitudes conflict—and, for the cognitivist, the relevant attitudes are moral beliefs—at least one is false. This is exactly what we want to say when we charge someone with moral error. Consider: even if we grant that a conflict of *non-cognitive* attitudes must involve mistake, is this really the central error we are trying to identify when convicting someone like Himmler or Mao of gross immoralities? Indeed, the attitudes of such fanatics needn't involve any internal conflict at all. And this seems a serious shortcoming for the non-cognitivist analysis of moral error, since we do think that people can be morally mistaken even if they've built themselves a perfectly coherent set of attitudes. For

such attitudes might be pitched in precisely the wrong direction.

Non-cognitivists might instead claim that moral error involves commitments that would be excluded from a set of best possible attitudes. Not just any incoherence will mark error; and coherence is not sufficient to guarantee freedom from moral mistake. So we can set aside the worries just mentioned. But which criteria must be satisfied to secure us from error? Reducing moral error is a matter of registering improvement in one's sensibility—one's more or less integrated set of attitudes. Yet plausible candidates for measuring such improvement are themselves normative conditions. At a minimum, attitudes are improved to the extent that they are formed against consideration of relevant information, free of bias, apportioning a due or proper weight to each individual's interests. But the notions of relevance, bias, and propriety are normative. There is no reason to be confident that we can understand the concept of a sensibility's improvement, or that of a set of *best* possible attitudes, without relying on other normative concepts. And so there is no reason to think that we can make sense of moral error without importing some normative constraints. If, as non-cognitivists claim, there really aren't any such things, then there really isn't any such thing as moral error or improvement. Alternatively, if these constraints, being normative, are really nothing other than an expression of a non-cognitivist's own commitments, then we might wonder why they have earned the right to serve as standards of evaluation for anyone else.

Understanding normative questions

We commonly ask ourselves what we should do (or think or feel) in a given situation. For non-cognitivists, there isn't anything we should do, really. Doing different things will bring about different consequences, but no result is such that one *ought* to do it, since no result—no state of affairs in the world—could possess value or be obligatory. Value and obligation are normative notions that never refer. There is no such thing as normativity; we live in a value-free world, the world as science describes it. But then what is going on when we ask ourselves, in any given case, how we ought to proceed?

The expressivist analysis, presumably, will be that we are asking what the results would be were we to take certain courses of action, and then asking ourselves what attitude we would have toward the results. But that cannot be all; we weren't asking a descriptive question, but a normative one. We may be puzzled not about whether we would respond in a certain way, but whether it would be fitting or appropriate to do so.

For expressivists, the answer to that question will not be given by the truth about what has value, since there is no such truth. Instead, the answer must be rendered in terms of our other attitudes. But how is the answer to be delivered? Any response will invoke a normative constraint on attitude formation—it will tell us how our other attitudes *ought* to be used in shaping the ones under scrutiny. For if it only tells us how our attitudes actually influence other attitudes, then it isn't answering our question. We want to know whether the influence exerted is legitimate.

Let us suppose that non-cognitivists will avow the importance of consistency among attitudes. So knowing how to act will be a matter of determining the attitudes one has toward the act and its results, and then selecting that act about which we have attitudes that best cohere with our other attitudes. Assume for now that we can understand the notion of 'best cohering' in a wholly non-normative way. Still, we can always ask why we ought to select just those attitudes that best cohere with our other ones. The answer here, too, must refer to some function of our actual attitudes. We *ought* to value coherence because we *do* value what coherence makes possible, i.e. we have a favourable attitude toward

how things go when we exemplify coherence in attitude. But of course we can always ask why we should have these further attitudes toward the things that coherence makes possible, and so on.

This picture generates three problems. The first is that the series of replies to these questions about our attitudes never addresses our fundamental concern: the appropriateness of the attitudes we have. Each question in the series is answered by reference to our existing attitudes; yet each question represents another variation on the one that keeps getting deferred, namely: are our existing attitudes fit to be the primary source of evaluation? Since evaluative attitudes are, for the cognitivist, just beliefs, cognitivists will assess the fitness of the relevant attitudes by reference to whether they are true. Of course this isn't an easy matter—we have already seen the challenge to cognitivist epistemology, and will try to answer it in Part V [see original reading]—but it has the benefit of at least squarely addressing our normative concerns. The non-cognitivist, by contrast, continually refashions the question of what we ought to do so that its answer can be given just by an introspective psychological enquiry. But asking and answering normative questions does not seem to be the same thing as asking and assuring ourselves about the implications of our existing mental states.

This leads directly to a second, related problem. Suppose that we have traced the replies to our normative questions back to an attitude that is foundational: we can cite no further, more general attitude that justifies it, though many other attitudes are justified by being derivable from it. The reason we value coherence, for instance, is that when we exemplify it we tend to secure our own aims. As a general matter, we want to secure our aims. Why? We just do. If we repeat the question, we will get a causal story, which is entirely beside the point in this context. We aren't seeking an aetiology of the want, but a justification of it.

The problem for non-cognitivism is that when we reach a point of citing a 'brute' desire—a want or liking that is self-standing,

whose warrant derives from no other pro-attitude—then we have identified something that lacks a justifying reason, and so is arbitrary. For it certainly isn't self-justifying—that concept hasn't much credence in a non-cognitivist picture. Yet basing evaluation ultimately on attitudes that are arbitrary is problematic. The arbitrariness isn't problematic because recognition of it will sap one's energy or cripple one's determination.[3] It is problematic because it infects all justificatory efforts. If our evaluative attitudes rely for their justification on attitudes which themselves lack justification, then the whole network is corrupt.[4] And the cognitivist is in better shape here, because her ultimate moral commitments can avoid arbitrariness if they are *true*, and if she believes them because they are true. Many such commitments will fail to meet these two conditions, and this will have similarly serious consequences for the resulting network of moral attitudes. But if the cognitivist (who is not also an error theorist) is correct, then we can at least aspire to avoid arbitrariness, and some of us will succeed.

Notes

1 For attempts to solve the problem, see Gibbard 1990: 83–102; Blackburn 1988, 1993b, 1996: 84–85, 1998: 68–77; Stoljar 1993: 91–97. For criticisms of their efforts, see Schueler 1988; Hale 1993; van Roojen 1996; Unwin 1999. Some critics see potential for solving the Frege–Geach worry, but at the cost of the non-cognitivism that is at the heart of these expressivist theories: see Sinnott-Armstrong 1993: 299–301; Wedgwood 1997; Dreier 1999. The cumulative force of these critical papers entails a dilemma: either remain an unreconstructed non-cognitivist, in which case the Frege–Geach problem impedes hopes for logical moral argumentation, or solve that problem, but only by introducing modifications that transform the expressivism into a version of cognitivism.

2 The best argument to this conclusion that I know of is given by Judith Jarvis Thomson in chapter 7 of Harman and Thomson 1996.

3   Wiggins (1976) levelled this charge against non-cognitivism. See Blackburn 1987 and Timmons 1999: ch. 4 for replies. At best, Wiggins's charge reveals the upsetting pragmatic implications of wholeheartedly embracing non-cognitivism. But even if Wiggins's take on our psychological propensities is correct, this would not show that non-cognitivism is false (though it would be further evidence that our moral practice proceeds as if it were). Compare the predictions of dismay and lassitude that would eventuate were most of us to embrace hard determinism. The dire consequences of such an embrace would not refute determinism, though such consequences would give us some (non-epistemic) reason to stop believing it.

4   The best effort to resist this conclusion is given by Timmons (1999: ch. 5), who argues that unjustified beliefs may nevertheless confer positive justification on other beliefs. Whatever plausibility such a claim has depends on his contextualist thesis that these 'unjustified justifiers' can, in other contexts, receive justification. In what follows, I try to show that non-cognitivists lack the resources for escaping from the arbitrariness worry. Here is a preview: to do the work required of them, these unjustified justifiers must receive justification in some context. The relevant contexts are two: either a philosophical one, in which we refrain from substantive ethical engagement, or a morally engaged one, in which we advocate some first-order moral views. According to non-cognitivists, there can be no such thing as genuine justification of normative views in philosophical contexts. But (I claim) any non-cognitivist justification that arises in engaged moral contexts will entail a form of self-intimating relativism. So the introduction of a contextualist epistemology will not save the non-cognitivist from arbitrariness worries.

References

Blackburn, Simon (1987). 'How to be an Ethical Anti-Realist', in Blackburn 1993a.

—— (1988). 'Attitudes and Contents', *Ethics*, 98: 501–17.

—— (1993a). *Essays in Quasi-Realism*. Oxford: Oxford University Press.

—— (1993b). 'Realism, Quasi or Queasy?', in Haldane and Wright 1993.

—— (1996). 'Securing the Nots', in Sinnott-Armstrong and Timmons 1996.

—— (1998). *Ruling Passions*. Oxford: Oxford University Press.

Dreier, James (1999). 'Transforming Expressivism', *Nous*, 33: 558–72.

—— (2002). 'The Expressivist Circle', *Philosophy and Phenomenological Research*, 65: 136–44.

Geach, Peter (1960). 'Ascriptivism', *Philosophical Review*, 69: 221–25.

—— (1965). 'Assertion', *Philosophical Review*, 74: 449–65.

Gibbard, Allan (1990). *Wise Choices and Apt Feelings*. Cambridge, Mass.: Harvard University Press.

Hale, Bob (1993). 'Can There be a Logic of Attitudes?', in Haldane and Wright 1993.

Harman, Gilbert and Thomson, Judith Jarvis (1996). *Moral Relativism and Moral Objectivity*. Oxford: Basil Blackwell.

Schueler, George (1988). '*Modus Ponens* and Moral Realism', *Ethics*, 98: 492–500.

—— (1995). *Desire*. Cambridge, Mass.: MIT Press.

Sinnott-Armstrong, Walter (1993). 'Some Problems for Gibbard's Norm-Expressivism', *Philosophical Studies*, 69: 297–313.

Stoljar, Daniel (1993). 'Emotivism and Truth Conditions', *Philosophical Studies*, 70: 81–101.

Timmons, Mark (1999). *Morality without Foundations*. Oxford: Oxford University Press.

Umwin, Nicholas (1999). 'Quasi-Realism, Negation, and the Frege–Geach Problem', *Philosophical Quarterly*, 49: 337–52.

Van Roojen, Mark (1996). 'Expressivism and Irrationality', *Philosophical Review*, 105: 311–35.

Wedgwood, Ralph (1997). 'Non-cognitivism, Truth and Logic', *Philosophical Studies*, 86: 73–91.

Wiggins, David (1976). 'Truth, Invention and the Meaning of Life', *Proceedings of the British Academy*, 62: 331–78.

Chapter 13

Plato

EUTHYPHRO

EUTHYPHRO: What's new, Socrates, to make you leave your usual haunts in the Lyceum and spend your time here by the king-archon's court. Surely you are not prosecuting any one before the king archon as I am?

SOCRATES: The Athenians do not call this a prosecution but an indictment, Euthyphro.

E: What is this you say? Someone must have indicted you, for you are not going to tell me that you have indicted someone else.

S: No indeed.

E: But someone else has indicted you?

S: Quite so.

E: Who is he?

S: I do not really know myself, Euthyphro. He is apparently young and unknown. They call him Meletus, I believe. He belongs to the Pitthean deme, if you know anyone from that deme called Meletus, with long hair, not much of a beard, and a rather acquiline nose.

E: I don't know him, Socrates. What charge does he bring against you?

S: What charge? A not ignoble one I think, for it is no small thing for a young man to have knowledge of such an important subject. He says he knows how our young men are corrupted and who corrupts them. He is likely to be wise, and when he sees my ignorance corrupting his contemporaries, he proceeds to accuse me to the city as to their mother. I think he is the only one of our public men to start out the right way, for it is right to care first that the young should be as good as possible, just as a good farmer is likely to take care of the young plants first, and of the others later. So, too, Meletus first gets rid of us who corrupt the growth of the young, as he says, and then afterwards he will obviously take care of the older and become a source of great blessings for the city, as seems likely to happen to one who started out this way.

E: I could wish this were true, Socrates, but I fear the opposite may happen. He seems to me to start out by harming the very heart of the city by attempting to wrong you. Tell me, what does he say you do to corrupt the young?

S: Strange things, to hear him tell it, for he says that I am a maker of gods, that I create new gods while not believing in the old gods, and he has indicted me for this very reason, as he puts it.

E: I understand, Socrates. This is because you say that the divine sign keeps coming to you. So he has written this indictment against you as one who makes innovations in religious matters, and he comes to court to slander you, knowing that such things are easily misrepresented to the crowd. The same is true in my case. Whenever I speak of divine matters in the assembly and foretell the future, they laugh me down as if I were crazy; and yet I have foretold nothing that did not

happen. Nevertheless, they envy all of us who do this. One need not give them any thought, but carry on just the same.

s: My dear Euthyphro, to be laughed at does not matter perhaps, for the Athenians do not mind anyone they think clever, as long as he does not teach his own wisdom, but if they think that he makes others to be like himself they get angry, whether through envy, as you say, or for some other reason.

E: I have certainly no desire to test their feelings toward me in this matter.

s: Perhaps you seem to make yourself but rarely available, and not to be willing to teach your own wisdom, but my liking for people makes them think that I pour out to anybody anything I have to say, not only without charging a fee but appearing glad to reward anyone who is willing to listen. If then they were intending to laugh at me, as you say they laugh at you, there would be nothing unpleasant in their spending their time in court laughing and jesting, but if they are going to be serious, the outcome is not clear except to you prophets.

E: Perhaps it will come to nothing, Socrates, and you will fight your case as you think best, as I think I will mine.

s: What is your case, Euthyphro? Are you the defendant or the prosecutor?

E: The prosecutor.

s: Whom do you prosecute?

E: One whom I am thought crazy to prosecute.

s: Are you pursuing someone who will easily escape you?

E: Far from it, for he is quite old.

s: Who is it?

E: My father.

s: My dear sir! Your own father?

E: Certainly.

s: What is the charge? What is the case about?

E: Murder, Socrates.

s: Good heavens! Certainly, Euthyphro, most men would not know how they could do this and be right. It is not the part of anyone to do this, but of one who is far advanced in wisdom.

E: Yes by Zeus, Socrates, that is so.

s: Is then the man your father killed one of your relatives? Or is that obvious, for you would not prosecute your father for the murder of a stranger.

E: It is ridiculous, Socrates, for you to think that it makes any difference whether the victim is a stranger or a relative. One should only watch whether the killer acted justly or not; if he acted justly, let him go, but if not, one should prosecute, even if the killer shares your hearth and table. The pollution is the same if you knowingly keep company with such a man and do not cleanse yourself and him by bringing him to justice. The victim was a dependant of mine, and when we were farming in Naxos he was a servant of ours. He killed one of our household slaves in drunken anger, so my father bound him hand and foot and threw him in a ditch, and then sent a man here to enquire from the priest what should be done. During that time he gave no thought or care to the bound man, as being a killer, and it was no matter if he died, which he did. Hunger and cold and his bonds caused his death before the messenger came back from the seer. Both my father and my other relatives are angry that I am prosecuting my father for murder on behalf of a murderer, as he did not even kill him. They say that such a victim does not deserve a thought and that it is impious for a son to prosecute his father for murder. But their ideas of the divine attitude to piety and impiety are wrong, Socrates.

s: Whereas, by Zeus, Euthyphro, you think that your knowledge of the divine, and of piety and impiety, is so accurate that, when those things happened as you say, you have no fear of having acted impiously in bringing your father to trial?

E: I should be of no use, Socrates, and Euthyphro would not be superior to the majority of men, if I did not have accurate knowledge of all such things.

S: It is indeed most important, my admirable Euthyphro, that I should become your pupil, and as regards this indictment challenge Meletus about these very things and say to him: that in the past too I considered knowledge about the divine to be most important, and that now that he says that I improvise and innovate about the gods I have become your pupil. I would say to him: "If, Meletus, you agree that Euthyphro is wise in these matters, consider me, too, to have the right beliefs and do not bring me to trial. If you do not think so, then prosecute that teacher of mine for corrupting the older men, me and his own father, by teaching me and by exhorting and punishing him." If he is not convinced, does not discharge me, or indicts you instead of me, I shall repeat the same challenge in court.

E: Yes by Zeus, Socrates, and, if he should try to indict me, I think I would find his weak spots and the talk in court would be about him rather than about me.

S: It is because I realize this that I am eager to become your pupil, my dear friend. I know that other people as well as this Meletus do not even seem to notice you, whereas he sees me so sharply and clearly that he indicts me for ungodliness. So tell me now, by Zeus, what you just now maintained you clearly knew: what kind of thing do you say that godliness and ungodliness are, both as regards murder and other things; or is the pious not the same and alike in every action, and the impious the opposite of all that is pious and like itself, and everything is to be impious presents us with one form or appearance in so far as it is impious.

E: Most certainly, Socrates.

S: Tell me then, what is the pious, and what the impious, do you say?

E: I say that the pious is to do what I am doing now, to prosecute the wrongdoer, be it about murder or temple robbery or anything else, whether the wrongdoer is your father or your mother or anyone else; not to prosecute is impious. And observe, Socrates, that I can quote the law as a great proof that this is so. I have already said to others that such actions are right, not to favour the ungodly, whoever they are. These people themselves believe that Zeus is the best and most just of the gods, yet they agree that he bound his father because he unjustly swallowed his sons, and that he in turn castrated his father for similar reasons. But they are angry with me because I am prosecuting my father for his wrongdoing. They contradict themselves in what they say about the gods and about me.

S: Indeed, Euthyphro, this is the reason why I am a defendant in the case, because I find it hard to accept things like that being said about the gods, and it is likely to be the reason why I shall be told I do wrong. Now, however, if you, who have full knowledge of such things, share their opinions, then we must agree with them, too, it would seem. For what are we to say, we who agree that we ourselves have no knowledge? Tell me, by the god of friendship, do you really believe these things are true?

E: Yes, Socrates, and so are even more surprising things, of which the majority has no knowledge.

S: And do you believe that there really is war among the gods, and terrible enmities and battles, and other such things as are told by the poets, and other sacred stories such as are embroidered by good writers and by representations of which the robe of the goddess is adorned when it is carried up to the Acropolis? Are we to say these things are true, Euthyphro?

E: Not only these, Socrates, but, as I was saying just now, I will, if you wish, relate many other things about the gods which I know will amaze you.

S: I should not be surprised, but you will tell me these at leisure some other time. For now, try to tell me more clearly what I was asking just now, for, my friend, you did not teach

me adequately when I asked you what the pious was, but you told me that what you are doing now, to prosecute your father for murder, is pious.

E: And I told the truth, Socrates.

S: Perhaps. You agree, however, that there are many other pious actions.

E: There are.

S: Bear in mind then that I did not bid you tell me one or two of the many pious actions but that form itself that makes all pious actions pious, for you agreed that all impious actions are impious and all pious actions pious through one form, or don't you remember?

E: I do.

S: Tell me then what form itself is, so that I may look upon it, and using it as a model, say that any action of yours or another's that is of that kind is pious, and if it is not that it is not.

E: If that is how you want it, Socrates, that is how I will tell you.

S: That is what I want.

E: Well then, what is dear to the gods is pious, what is not is impious.

S: Splendid, Euthyphro! You have now answered in the way I wanted. Whether your answer is true I do not know yet, but you will obviously show me that what you say is true.

E: Certainly.

S: Come then, let us examine what we mean. An action or a man dear to the gods is pious, but an action or a man hated by the gods is impious. They are not the same, but opposites, the pious and the impious. Is that not so?

E: It is indeed.

S: And that seems to be a good statement?

E: I think so, Socrates.

S: We have also stated that the gods are in a state of discord, that they are at odds with each other, Euthyphro, and that they are at enmity with each other. That too has been said.

E: It has.

S: What are the subjects of difference that cause hatred and anger? Let us look at it this way. If you and I were to differ about numbers as to which is the greater, would this difference make us enemies and angry with each other, or would we proceed to count and soon resolve our difference about this?

E: We would certainly do so.

S: Again, if we differed about the larger and the smaller, we would turn to measurement and soon cease to differ.

E: That is so.

S: And about the heavier and the lighter, we would resort to weighing and be reconciled.

E: Of course.

S: What subject of difference would make us angry and hostile to each other if we were unable to come to a decision? Perhaps you do not have an answer ready, but examine as I tell you whether these subjects are the just and the unjust, the beautiful and the ugly, the good and the bad. Are these not the subjects of difference about which, when we are unable to come to a satisfactory decision, you and I and other men become hostile to each other whenever we do.

E: That is the difference, Socrates, about those subjects.

S: What about the gods, Euthyphro? If indeed they have differences, will it not be about these same subjects?

E: It certainly must be so.

S: Then according to your argument, my good Euthyphro, different gods consider different things to be just, beautiful, ugly, good and bad, for they would not be at odds with one another unless they differed about these subjects, would they?

E: You are right.

S: And they like what each of them considers beautiful, good, and just, and hate the opposites of these?

E: Certainly.

S: But you say that the same things are considered just by some gods and unjust by others, and as they dispute about these things they are at odds and at war with each other. Is that not so?

E: It is.

S: The same things then are loved by the gods and hated by the gods, both god-loved and god-hated.

E: It seems likely,

S: And the same things would be both pious and impious, according to this argument?

E: I'm afraid so.

S: So you did not answer my question, you surprising man. I did not ask you what same thing is both pious and impious, and it appears that what is loved by the gods is also hated by them. So it is in no way surprising if your present action, namely punishing your father, may be pleasing to Zeus but displeasing to Kronos and Ouranos, pleasing to Hephaestus but displeasing to Hera, and so with any other gods who differ from each other on this subject.

E: I think, Socrates, that on this subject no gods would differ from one another, that whoever has killed anyone unjustly should pay the penalty.

S: Well now, Euthyphro, have you ever heard any man maintaining that one who has killed or done anything else unjustly should not pay the penalty?

E: They never cease to dispute on this subject, both elsewhere and in the courts, for when they have committed many wrongs they do and say anything to avoid the penalty.

S: Do they agree they have done wrong, Euthyphro, and in spite of so agreeing do they nevertheless say they should not be punished?

E: No, they do not agree on that point.

S: So they do not say or do anything. For they do not venture to say this, or dispute that they must not pay the penalty if they have done wrong, but I think they deny doing wrong. Is that not so?

E: That is true.

S: Then they do not dispute that the wrongdoer must be punished, but they may disagree as to who the wrongdoer is, what he did and when.

E: You are right.

S: Do not the gods have the same experience, if indeed they are at odds with each other about the just and the unjust, as your argument maintains? Some assert that they wrong one another, while others deny it, but no one among gods or men ventures to say that the wrongdoer must not be punished.

E: Yes, that is true, Socrates, as to the main point.

S: And those who disagree, whether men or gods, dispute about each action, if indeed the gods disagree. Some say it is done justly, others unjustly. Is that not so?

E: Yes indeed.

S: Come now, my dear Euthyphro, tell me, too, that I may become wiser, what proof you have that all the gods consider that man to have been killed unjustly who became a murderer while in your service, was bound by the master of his victim, and died in his bonds before the one who bound him found out from the seers what was to be done with him, and that it is right for a son to denounce and to prosecute his father on behalf of such a man. Come, try to show me a clear sign that all the gods definitely believe this action to be right. If you can give me adequate proof of this, I shall never cease to extol your wisdom.

E: This is perhaps no light task, Socrates, though I could show you very clearly.

S: I understand that you think me more dull-witted than the jury, as you will obviously show them that these actions were unjust and that all the gods hate such actions.

E: I will show it to them clearly, Socrates, if only they will listen to me.

S: They will listen if they think you show them well. But this thought came to me as I was speaking, and I am examining it, saying to myself: "If Euthyphro shows me conclusively that all the gods consider such a death unjust, to what greater extent have I learned from him the nature of piety and impiety? This action would then, it seems, be hated by the gods, but the pious and the impious were not thereby now

defined, for what is hated by the gods has also been shown to be loved by them." So I will not insist on this point; let us assume, if you wish, that all the gods consider this unjust and that they all hate it. However, is this the correction we are making in our discussion, that what all the gods hate is impious, and what they all love is pious, and that what some gods love and others hate is neither or both? Is that how you now wish us to define piety and impiety?

E: What prevents us from doing so, Socrates?

S: For my part nothing, Euthyphro, but you look whether on your part this proposal will enable you to teach me most easily what you promised.

E: I would certainly say that the pious is what all the gods love, and the opposite, which all the gods hate, is the impious.

S: Then let us again examine whether that is a sound statement, or do we let it pass, and if one of us, or someone else, merely says that this is so, do we accept that it is so? Or should we examine what the speaker means?

E: We must examine it, but I certainly think that this is now a fine statement.

S: We shall soon know better whether it is. Consider this: Is the pious loved by the gods because it is pious, or is it pious because it is loved by the gods?

E: I don't know what you mean, Socrates.

S: I shall try to explain more clearly; we speak of something being carried and something carrying, of something being led and something leading, of something being seen and something seeing, and you understand that these things are all different from one another and how they differ?

E: I think I do.

S: So there is something being loved and something loving, and the loving is a different thing.

E: Of course.

S: Tell me then whether that which is (said to be) being carried is being carried because someone carries it or for some other reason.

E: No, that is the reason.

S: And that which is being led is so because someone leads it, and that which is being seen because someone sees it?

E: Certainly.

S: It is not seen by someone because it is being seen but on the contrary it is being seen because someone sees it, nor is it because it is being led that someone leads it but because someone leads it that it is being led; nor does someone carry an object because it is being carried, but it is being carried because someone carries it. Is what I want to say clear, Euthyphro? I want to say this, namely, that if anything comes to be, or is affected, it does not come to be because it is coming to be, but it is coming to be because it comes to be; nor is it affected because it is being affected but because something affects it. Or do you not agree?

E: I do.

S: What is being loved is either something that comes to be or something that is affected by something?

E: Certainly.

S: So it is in the same case as the things just mentioned; it is not loved by those who love it because it is being loved, but it is being loved because they love it?

E: Necessarily.

S: What then do we say about the pious, Euthyphro? Surely that is loved by all the gods, according to what you say?

E: Yes.

S: Is it loved because it is pious, or for some other reason?

E: For no other reason.

S: It is loved then because it is pious, but it is not pious because it is loved.

E: Apparently.

S: And because it is loved by the gods it is being loved and is dear to the gods?

E: Of course.

S: The god-beloved is then not the same as the pious, Euthyphro, nor the pious the same as

the god-beloved, as you say it is, but one differs from the other.

E: How so, Socrates?

S: Because we agree that the pious is beloved for the reason that it is pious, but it is not pious because it is loved. Is that not so?

E: Yes.

S: And that the god-beloved, on the other hand, is so because it is loved by the gods, by the very fact of being loved, but it is not loved because it is god-beloved.

E: True.

S: But if the god-beloved and the pious were the same, my dear Euthyphro, and the pious were loved because it was pious, then the god-beloved would be loved because it was god-beloved, and if the god-beloved was god-beloved because it was loved by the gods, then the pious would also be pious because it was loved by the gods; but now you see that they are in opposite cases as being altogether different from each other: the one is of a nature to be loved because it is loved, the other is loved because it is of a nature to be loved. I'm afraid, Euthyphro, that when you were asked what piety is, you did not wish to make its nature clear to me, but you told me an affect or quality of it, that the pious has the quality of being loved by all the gods, but you have not yet told me what the pious is. Now, if you will, do not hide things from me. but tell me again from the beginning what piety is, whether loved by the gods or having some other quality—we shall not quarrel about that—but be keen to tell me what the pious and the impious are.

E: But Socrates, I have no way of telling you what I have in mind, for whatever proposition we put forward goes around and refuses to stay put where we establish it.

S: Your statements, Euthyphro, seem to belong to my ancestor, Daedalus. If I were stating them and putting them forward, you would perhaps be making fun of me and say that because of my kinship with him my

conclusions in discussion run away and will not stay where one puts them. As these propositions are yours, however, we need some other jest, for they will not stay put for you, as you say yourself.

E: I think the same jest will do for our discussion, Socrates, for I am not the one who makes them go round and not remain in the same place; it is you who are the Daedalus; for as far as I am concerned they would remain as they were.

S: It looks as if I was cleverer than Daedalus in using my skill, my friend, in so far as he could only cause to move the things he made himself, but I can make other people's move as well as my own. And the smartest part of my skill is that I am clever without wanting to be, for I would rather have my arguments remain unmoved than possess the wealth of Tantalus as well as the cleverness of Daedalus. But enough of this. Since I think you are making unnecessary difficulties, I am as eager as you are to find a way to teach me about piety, and do not give up before you do. See whether you think all that is pious is of necessity just.

E: I think so.

S: And is then all that is just pious? Or is all that is pious just, but not all that is just pious, but some of it is and some is not?

E: I do not follow what you are saying, Socrates.

S: Yet you are younger than I by as much as you are wiser. As I say, you are making difficulties because of your wealth of wisdom. Pull yourself together, my dear sir, what I am saying is not difficult to grasp. I am saying the opposite of what the poet said who wrote:

> You do not wish to name Zeus, who had done it, and who made all things grow, for where there is fear there is also shame.

I disagree with the poet. Shall I tell you why?

E: Please do.

s: I do not think that "where there is fear there is also shame," for I think that many people who fear disease and poverty and many other such things feel fear, but are not ashamed of the things they fear. Do you not think so?

E: I do indeed.

s: But where there is shame there is also fear. Does anyone feel shame at something who is not also afraid at the same time of a reputation for wickedness?

E: He is certainly afraid.

s: It is then not right to say "where there is fear there is also shame," but that where there is shame there is also fear, for fear covers a larger area than shame. Shame is a part of fear just as odd is a part of number, with the result that it is not true that where there is number there is also oddness, but that where there is oddness there is also number. Do you follow me?

E: Surely.

s: This is the kind of thing I was asking before, whether where there is piety there is also justice, but where there is justice there is not always piety, for the pious is a part of justice. Shall we say that, or do you think otherwise?

E: No, but like that, for what you say appears to be right.

s: See what comes next; if the pious is a part of the just, we must, it seems, find out what part of the just it is. Now if you asked me something of what we mentioned just now, such as what part of number is the even, and what number that is, I would say it is the number that is divisible into two equal, not unequal, parts. Or do you not think so?

E: I do.

s: Try in this way to tell me what part of the just the pious is, in order to tell Meletus not to wrong us any more and not to indict me for ungodliness, since I have learned from you sufficiently what is godly and pious and what is not.

E: I think, Socrates, that the godly and pious is the part of the just that is concerned with the care of the gods, while that concerned with the care of men is the remaining part of justice.

s: You seem to me to put that very well, but I still need a bit of information. I do not know yet what you mean by care, for you do not mean it in the sense as the care of other things, as, for example, not everyone knows how to care for horses, but the horse breeder does.

E: Yes, I do mean it that way.

s: So horse breeding is care of horses.

E: Yes.

s: Nor does everyone know how to care for dogs, but the hunter does.

E: That is so.

s: So hunting is the care of dogs.

E: Yes.

s: And cattle raising is the care of cattle.

E: Quite so.

s: While piety and godliness is the care of the gods, Euthyphro. Is that what you mean?

E: It is.

s: Now care in each case has the same effect; it aims at the good and the benefit of the object cared for, as you can see that horses cared for by horse breeders are benefited and become better. Or do you not think so?

E: I do.

s: So dogs are benefited by dog breeding, cattle by cattle raising, and so with all the others. Or do you think that care aims to harm the object of its care?

E: By Zeus, no.

s: It aims to benefit the object of its care.

E: Of course.

s: Is piety then, which is the care of the gods, also to benefit the gods and make them better? Would you agree that when you do something pious you make some one of the gods better?

E: By Zeus, no.

s: Nor do I think that this is what you mean—far from it—but that is why I asked you what you meant by the care of gods, because I did not believe you meant this kind of care.

E: Quite right, Socrates, that is not the kind of care I mean.

s: Very well, but what kind of care of the gods would piety be?

E: The kind of care, Socrates, that slaves take of their masters.

s: I understand. It is likely to be the service of the gods.

E: Quite so.

s: Could you tell me to the achievement of what goal service to doctors tends? Is it not, do you think, to achieving health?

E: I think so.

s: What about service to shipbuilders? To what achievement is it directed?

E: Clearly, Socrates, to the building of a ship.

s: And service to housebuilders to the building of a house?

E: Yes.

s: Tell me then, my good sir, to the achievement of what aim does service to the gods tend? You obviously know since you say that you, of all men, have the best knowledge of the divine.

E: And I am telling the truth, Socrates.

s: Tell me then, by Zeus, what is that excellent aim that the gods achieve, using us as their servants?

E: Many fine things, Socrates.

s: So do generals, my friend. Nevertheless you could tell me their main concern, which is to achieve victory in war, is it not?

E: Of course.

s: The farmers too, I think, achieve many fine things, but the main point of their efforts is to produce food from the earth.

E: Quite so.

s: Well then, how would you sum up the many fine things that the gods achieve?

E: I told you a short while ago, Socrates, that it is a considerable task to acquire any precise knowledge of these things, but, to put it simply, I say that if a man knows how to say and do what is pleasing to the gods at prayer and sacrifice, those are pious actions such as preserve both private houses and public affairs of state. The opposite of these pleasing

actions are impious and overturn and destroy everything.

s: You could tell me in far fewer words, if you were willing, the sum of what I asked, Euthyphro, but you are not keen to teach me, that is clear. You were on the point of doing so, but you turned away. If you had given that answer, I should now have acquired from you sufficient knowledge of the nature of piety. As it is, the lover of inquiry must follow it wherever it may lead him. Once more then, what do you say that piety and the pious are, and also impiety? Are they a knowledge of how to sacrifice and pray?

E: They are.

s: To sacrifice is to make a gift to the gods, whereas to pray is to beg from the gods?

E: Definitely, Socrates.

s: It would follow from this statement that piety would be a knowledge of how to give to, and beg from, the gods.

E: You understood what I said very well, Socrates.

s: That is because I am so desirous of your wisdom, and I concentrate my mind on it, so that no word of yours may fall to the ground. But tell me, what is this service to the gods? You say it is to beg from them and to give to them?

E: I do.

s: And to beg correctly would be to ask from them things that we need?

E: What else?

s: And to give correctly is to give them what they need from us, for it would not be skillful to bring gifts to anyone that are in no way needed.

E: True, Socrates.

s: Piety would then be a sort of trading skill between gods and men?

E: Trading yes, if you prefer to call it that.

s: I prefer nothing, unless it is true. But tell me, what benefit do the gods derive from the gifts they receive from us? What they give us is obvious to all. There is for us no good that we do not receive from them, but how are

they benefited by what they receive from us? Or do we have such an advantage over them in the trade that we receive all our blessings from them and they receive nothing from us?

E: Do you suppose, Socrates, that the gods are benefited by what they receive from us?

S: What could those gifts from us to the gods be, Euthyphro?

E: What else, you think, than honour, reverence, and what I mentioned before, gratitude.

S: The pious is then, Euthyphro, pleasing to the gods, but not beneficial or dear to them?

E: I think it is of all things most dear to them.

S: So the pious is once again what is dear to the gods.

E: Most certainly.

S: When you say this, will you be surprised if your arguments seem to move about instead of staying put? And will you accuse me of being Daedalus who makes them move, though you are yourself much more skillful than Daedalus and make them go round in a circle? Or do you not realize that our argument has moved around and come again to the same place? You surely remember that earlier the pious and the god-beloved were shown not to be the same but different from each other. Or do you not remember?

E: I do.

S: Do you then not realize that when you say now that that what is dear to the gods is the pious? Is this not the same as the god-beloved? Or is it not?

E: It certainly is.

S: Either we were wrong when we agreed before, or, if we were right then, we are wrong now.

E: That seems to be so.

S: So we must investigate again from the beginning what piety is, as I shall not willingly give up before I learn this. Do not think me unworthy, but concentrate your attention and tell the truth. For you know it, if any man does, and I must not let you go, like Proteus, before you tell me. If you had no clear knowledge of piety and impiety you would never have ventured to prosecute your old father for murder on behalf of a servant. For fear of the gods you would have been afraid to take the risk lest you should not be acting rightly, and would have been ashamed before men, but now I know well that you believe you have clear knowledge of piety and impiety. So tell me, my good Euthyphro, and do not hide what you believe.

E: Some other time, Socrates, for I am in a hurry now, and it is time for me to go.

S: What a thing to do, my friend! By going you have cast me down from a great hope I had, that I would learn from you the nature of the pious and the impious and so escape Meletus' indictment by showing that I had acquired wisdom in divine matters from Euthyphro, and my ignorance would no longer cause me to be careless and inventive about such things, and that I would be better for the rest of my life.

Chapter 14

Robert Merrihew Adams

A NEW DIVINE COMMAND THEORY

I N A RECENT issue of *The Journal of Religious Ethics*, Jeffrey Stout (1978) has written about an earlier paper of mine (Adams, 1973) urging development and modification of the very point on which, as it happens, my own metaethical views have changed most. My thoughts have been moving in a rather different direction from his, however.[1] For that reason, and because of his paper's interesting and perceptive linkage of metaethical issues with the most fundamental questions in the theory of meaning, I would like to respond to him.

I. My old position

My modified divine command theory was proposed as a partial analysis of the *meaning* of '(ethically) wrong.' Recognizing that it would be most implausible as an analysis of the sense in which the expression is used by many speakers (for instance, by atheists), I proposed the theory only as an analysis of the meaning of 'wrong' in the discourse of some Jewish and Christian believers. In the theory that I now prefer, as we shall see, the identification of wrongness with contrariety to God's commands is neither presented as a meaning analysis nor relativized to a group of believers. According to the old theory, however, it is part of the meaning of '(ethically) wrong' for at least some believers that

(1) (for any action X) X is ethically wrong if and only if X is contrary to God's commands,

but also that

(2) 'X is wrong' normally expresses opposition or certain other negative attitudes toward X.

The meaning of 'wrong' seems to be overdetermined by (1) and (2). Conflicts could arise. Suppose God commanded me to practice cruelty for its own sake. (More precisely, suppose he commanded me to make it my chief end in life to inflict suffering on other human beings, for no other reason than that he commanded it.) I cannot summon up the relevant sort of opposition or negative attitude toward disobedience to such a command, and I will not say that it would be wrong to disobey it.

Such conflicts within the religious ethical belief system are prevented by various background beliefs, which are *presupposed* by (1). Particularly important is the belief that

(3) God is loving, and therefore does not and will not command such things as (e.g.) the practice of cruelty for its own sake.

But (3) is contingent. It is allowed by the theory to be logically possible for God to command cruelty for its own sake, although the believer is confident he will not do such a thing. Were the believer to come to think (3) false, however, I suggested that his concept of ethical wrongness would "break down." It would not function as it now does,

because he would not be prepared to use it to say that any action is wrong (Adams, 1973:322–24). Because of the interplay and tension of the various considerations involved in it, this picture of the meaning of '(ethically) wrong' is (as I acknowledged) somewhat "untidy." But its untidiness should not obscure the fact that I meant it quite definitely to follow from the theory that the following are necessary truths:

(4) If X is wrong, then X is contrary to the commands of God.

(5) If X is obligatory, then X is required by the commands of God.

(6) If X is ethically permitted, then X is permitted by the commands of God.

(7) If there is not a loving God, then nothing is ethically wrong or obligatory or permitted.

These four theses are still taken to be necessary truths in my present divine command theory.

• • •

III. The separation of necessity and natures from analyticity and concepts

An important group of recent papers (especially Donnellan, 1966 and 1972; Kripke, 1972; and Putnam, 1975:196–290)[2] has made a persuasive case for a view that there are necessary truths that are neither analytic nor knowable *a priori*. Among these are truths about the nature of many properties. And I am now inclined to believe that the truth about the nature of ethical wrongness is of this sort.

A case of individual identity or non-identity provides a first example of a truth that is necessary but empirical. In the Gospels according to Mark (2:14) and Luke (5:27–29) there is a story about a tax collector named 'Levi,' who left his business to follow Jesus. There is a tradition, supported by the relevant texts in Matthew (9:9 and 10:3) and by some important manuscripts

of Mark (2:14), that this man was the Matthew who appears in the lists of the twelve apostles. This belief is naturally expressed by saying that Levi was Matthew, or that Levi and Matthew were the same man. But perhaps they were not; none of us really knows.

Suppose they were in fact two different men. That is a truth that is in principle knowable, but only empirically knowable. It is certainly not an analytic truth, which could be discovered by analyzing our concepts of Levi and Matthew. But there is a compelling argument for believing it to be necessary truth if it is true at all. For suppose it were a contingent truth. Then the actual world, w_1, would be one in which Matthew the apostle and Levi the tax collector are not identical, but a world, w_2, in which they would be identical would also be possible. Since identity is a transitive relation, however, and since Levi in w_1, is identical with Levi in w_2, and Levi in w_2 is identical with Matthew in w_2, and Matthew in w_2 with Matthew in w_1, it follows that Levi in w_1 is identical with Matthew in w_1. Thus the hypothesis that the non-identity of Matthew and Levi is contingent leads to a contradiction. This argument is not completely uncontroversial in its assumptions about trans-world identity, but it seems to me to be correct. A similar argument can be given for holding that if Levi and Matthew were in fact identical, that is a necessary truth, although it is not *a priori*.

It should be emphasized that 'possible' is not being used in its *epistemic* sense here. Both worlds in which Matthew and Levi are identical and worlds in which they are distinct are epistemically possible; that is, either sort may be actual for all we know. But whichever sort is actual, the other sort lacks broadly logical possibility, or "metaphysical possibility" as it is often called by those who hold the views I am exploring here.

Another interesting feature of this example is that there is a property which our understanding of the meaning of 'Matthew' and 'Levi' in this context tells us Matthew and Levi must have had

if they (or he) existed, but which is a property that they (or he) possessed contingently. By 'Matthew' we mean the individual who stands in a certain historical relation (not yet spelled out in a very detailed way by philosophers of language) to the use of 'Matthew' (on certain occasions known to us) as a name of a man believed to have been one of the disciples of Jesus. It is epistemically possible that Matthew was named 'Levi' and not 'Matthew,' or that he was not one of the twelve apostles but got counted as one by mistake. But no one who does not stand in an appropriate historical relation to the relevant uses of 'Matthew' counts as Matthew; that is what is settled by the meaning with which we use 'Matthew.' Standing in this relation to these uses of 'Matthew' is surely a contingent property of Matthew, however. Matthew could have existed in a world in which he was never called 'Matthew' during or after his life, or in a world in which Jesus never had any disciples and the relevant uses of 'Matthew' never occurred.

Similar considerations apply to theories about the natures of properties or of kinds of things. Hilary Putnam uses the theory that the nature of water is to be H_2O as an example in arguing that such theories, if true, are commonly necessary truths but not *a priori* (see also Kripke, 1972:314–31). (As it happens, this example was given a somewhat different treatment, hereby superseded, in Adams, 1973:345.)

Suppose a vessel from outer space landed, carrying a group of intelligent creatures that brought with them, and drank, a transparent, colorless, odorless, tasteless liquid that dissolved sugar and salt and other things that normally dissolve in water. Even if we non-chemists could not distinguish it from water, we might intelligibly (and prudently) ask whether this substance really is water. Our question would be answered, in the negative, by a laboratory analysis showing that the beverage from outer space was not H_2O but a different liquid whose long and complicated chemical formula may be abbreviated as XYZ (see Putnam, 1975:223).

Why is it right to say that this XYZ would not be water? I take it to be Putnam's view that it is not an analytic truth that water is H_2O. What is true analytically, by virtue of what every competent user of the word 'water' must know about its meaning, is rather that if most of the stuff that we (our linguistic community) have been calling 'water' is of a single nature, water is liquid that is of the same nature as *that*.

This view enables Putnam to maintain against Quine that substantial change and development in scientific theories is possible without change in meaning (although he agrees with Quine "that meaning change and theory change cannot be sharply separated," and that *some* possible changes in scientific theory would change the meaning of crucial terms—see Putnam 1975:255f.). "Thus, the fact that an English speaker in 1750 might have called XYZ 'water,' while he or his successors would not have called XYZ water in 1800 or 1850 does not mean that the 'meaning' of 'water' changed for the average speaker in the interval" (Putnam, 1975:225). This claim is plausible. Had the visitors from outer space arrived with their clear, tasteless liquid in England in 1750, the English of that time might wisely have wondered whether the stuff was really water, even if it satisfied all the tests they yet knew for being water. And the correct answer to their question too would have been negative, if the liquid was XYZ and not H_2O.

Although it is not an *a priori* but an empirical truth that water is H_2O, Putnam thinks it is metaphysically necessary. Suppose there is a possible world, w_3, in which there is no H_2O but XYZ fills the ecological and cultural role that belongs to H_2O in the actual world. XYZ looks, tastes, etc. like H_2O, and is even called 'water' by English speakers in w_3. In such a case, Putnam (1975:231) maintains, the XYZ in w_3 is *not* water, for in order to be water a liquid in *any* possible world must be the same liquid (must have the same nature, I would say) as the stuff that we actually call 'water'—which is H_2O. We may say, on this view, that the property of being water is the property

of being H$_2$O, so that nothing could have the one property without having the other, or lack one without lacking the other.

It should also be noted that on this view the property ascribed to water by the description that expresses the *concept of water*, or what every competent user of 'water' knows, is not a property that belongs to water necessarily. The description is 'liquid of the same nature as most of the stuff that we have been calling "water."' But it is only contingent that water is called 'water.' Water could perfectly well have existed if no one had given it a name at all, or if the English had called it 'yoof.'

This view of the relation between the nature of water and the meaning of 'water' seems to me plausible. And if we think it is correct, that will enhance the plausibility of an analogous treatment of the nature of right and wrong. But even if Putnam's claims about 'water' are mistaken, we certainly *could* use an expression as he says we use 'water,' and it would be worth considering whether 'right' and 'wrong' are used in something like that way.

IV. The nature of wrongness and the meaning of 'wrong'

I do not think that every competent user of 'wrong' in its ethical sense must know what the nature of wrongness is. The word is used—with the same meaning, I would now say—by people who have different views, or none at all, about the nature of wrongness. As I remarked in my earlier paper, "There is probably much less agreement about the most basic issues in moral theory than there is about many ethical issues of less generality" (Adams, 1973:343). That people can use an expression to signify an ethical property, knowing it is a property they seek (or shun, as the case may be), but not knowing what its nature is, was realized by Plato when he characterized the good as

That which every soul pursues, doing everything for the sake of it, divining that it is

something, but perplexed and unable to grasp adequately what it is or to have such a stable belief as about other things (*Republic* 505D-E).

What every competent user of 'wrong' must know about wrongness is first of all, that wrongness is a property of actions (perhaps also of intentions and of various attitudes, but certainly of actions); and second that people are generally opposed to actions they regard as wrong, and count wrongness as a reason (often a conclusive reason) for opposing an action. In addition I think the competent user must have some opinion about what actions have this property, and some fairly settled disposition as to what he will count as reasons for and against regarding an action as wrong. There is an important measure of agreement among competent users in these opinions and dispositions—not complete agreement, nor universal agreement on some points and disagreement on others, but overlapping agreements of one person with another on some points and with still others on other points. "To call an action 'wrong' is, among other things, to classify it with certain other actions," as having a common property, "and there is considerable agreement . . . as to what actions those are" (Adams, 1973:344). Torturing children for fun is one of them in virtually everyone's opinion.

Analysis of the concept or understanding with which the word 'wrong' is used is not sufficient to determine what wrongness is. What it can tell us about the nature of wrongness, I think, is that wrongness will be the property of actions (if there is one) that best fills the role assigned to wrongness by the concept. My theory is that contrariety to the command of a loving God is that property; but we will come to that in section V. Meanwhile I will try to say something about what is involved in being the property that *best* fills the relevant role, though I do not claim to be giving an adequate set of individually necessary and jointly sufficient conditions.

(i) We normally speak of actions being right and wrong as of facts that obtain objectively, independently of whether we think they do. 'Wrong' has the syntax of an ordinary predicate, and we worry that we may be mistaken in our ethical judgments. This feature of ethical concepts gives emotivism and prescriptivism in metaethics much of their initial implausibility. If possible, therefore, the property to be identified with ethical wrongness should be one that actions have or lack objectively.

(ii) The property that is wrongness should belong to those types of action that are thought to be wrong—or at least it should belong to an important central group of them. It would be unreasonable to expect a theory of the nature of wrongness to yield results that agree perfectly with pre-theoretical opinion. One of the purposes a metaethical theory may serve is to give guidance in revising one's particular ethical opinions. But there is a limit to how far those opinions may be revised without changing the subject entirely; and we are bound to take it as a major test of the acceptability of a theory of the nature of wrongness that it should in some sense account for the wrongness of a major portion of the types of action we have believed to be wrong.

(iii) Wrongness should be a property that not only belongs to the most important types of action that are thought to be wrong, but also plays a causal role (or a role as object of perception) in their coming to be regarded as wrong. It should not be connected in a merely fortuitous way with our classification of actions as wrong and not wrong.[3]

(iv) Understanding the nature of wrongness should give one more rather than less reason to oppose wrong actions as such. Even if it were discovered (as it surely will not be) that there is a certain sensory pleasure produced by all and only wrong actions, it would be absurd to say that wrongness is the property of producing that pleasure. For the property of producing such a pleasure, in itself, gives us no reason whatever to oppose an action that has the property.

(v) The best theory about the nature of wrongness should satisfy other intuitions about wrongness as far as possible. One intuition that is rather widely held and is relevant to theological metaethics is that rightness and wrongness are determined by a law or standard that has a sanctity that is greater than that of any merely human will or institution.

We are left, on this view, with a concept of wrongness that has both objective and subjective aspects. The best theory of the nature of wrongness, I think, will be one that identifies wrongness with some property that actions have or lack objectively. But we do not have a fully objective procedure for determining which theory of the nature of wrongness is the best, and therefore which property is wrongness.

For example, the property that is wrongness should belong to the most important types of action that are believed to be wrong. But the concept possessed by every competent user of 'wrong' does not dictate exactly which types of action those are. A sufficiently eccentric classification of types of action as right or wrong would not fit the concept. But there is still room for much difference of opinion. In testing theories of the nature of wrongness by their implications about what types of action are wrong, I will be guided by my own classification of types of action as right and wrong, and by my own sense of which parts of the classification are most important.

Similarly, in considering whether identifying wrongness with a given property, P, makes

wrongness more or less of a reason for opposing an action, I will decide partly on the basis of how P weighs with me. And in general I think that this much is right about prescriptivist intuitions in metaethics: to identify a property with ethical wrongness is in part to assign it a certain complex role in my life (and, for my part, in the life of society); in deciding to do that I will (quite reasonably) be influenced by what attracts and repels me personally. But it does not follow that the theory I should choose is not one that identifies wrongness with a property that actions would have or lack regardless of how I felt about them.

V. A new divine command theory

The account I have given of the concept of wrongness that every competent user of 'wrong' must have is consistent with many different theories about the nature of wrongness—for example, with the view that wrongness is the property of failing to maximize human happiness, and with a Marxist theory that wrongness is the property of being contrary to the objective interests of the progressive class or classes. But given typical Christian beliefs about God, it seems to me most plausible to identify wrongness with the property of being contrary to the commands of loving God. (i) This is a property that actions have or lack objectively, regardless of whether we think they do. (I assume the theory can be filled out with a satisfactory account of what love consists in here.) (ii) The property of being contrary to the commands of a loving God is certainly believed by Christians to belong to all and only wrong actions. (iii) It also plays a causal role in our classification of actions as wrong, in so far as God has created our moral faculties to reflect his commands. (iv) Because of what is believed about God's actions, purposes, character, and power, he inspires such devotion and/or fear that contrariness to his commands is seen as a supremely weighty reason for opposing an action. Indeed, (v) God's

commands constitute a law or standard that seems to believers to have sanctity that is not possessed by any merely human will or institution.

My new divine command theory of the nature of ethical wrongness, then, is that ethical wrongness *is* (i.e., is identical with) the property of being contrary to the commands of a loving God. I regard this as a metaphysically necessary, but not an analytic or *a priori* truth. Because it is not conceptual analysis, this claim is not relative to a religious sub-community of the larger linguistic community. It purports to be the correct theory of the nature of the ethical wrongness that *everybody* (or almost everybody) is talking about.

Further explanation is in order, first about the notion of a divine *command*, and second about the *necessity* that is claimed here. On the first point I can only indicate here the character of the explanation that is needed; for it amounts to nothing less than a theory of revelation. Theists sometimes speak of wrong action as action contrary to the "will" of God, but that way of speaking ignores some important distinctions. One is the distinction between the absolute will of God (his "good pleasure") and his revealed will. Any Christian theology will grant that God in his godly pleasure sometimes decides, for reasons that may be mysterious to us, not to do everything he could to prevent a wrong action. According to some theologies nothing at all can happen contrary to God's good pleasure. It is difficult, therefore, to suppose that all wrong actions are unqualified, contrary to God's will in the sense of his good pleasure. It is God's *revealed* will—not what he wants or plans to have happen, but what he has told us to do—that is thought to determine the rightness and wrongness of human actions. Roman Catholic theology has made a further distinction, within God's revealed will, between his commands, which it would be wrong not to follow, and "counsels (of perfection)," which it would be better to follow but not wrong not to follow. It is best,

therefore, in our metaethical theory, to say that wrongness is contrariety to God's *commands*; and commands must have been issued, promulgated, or somehow revealed.

The notion of the issuance of a divine command requires a theory of revelation for its adequate development. The first such theory that comes to mind may be a Biblical literalism that takes divine commands to be just what is written in the Bible as commanded by God. But there will also be Roman Catholic theories involving the *magisterium* of the Church, a Quaker theory about "the inner light," theories about "general revelation" through the moral feelings and intuitions of unbelievers as well as believers—and other theories as well. To develop these theories and choose among them is far too large a task for the present essay.

The thesis that wrongness is (identical with) contrariety to a loving God's commands must be *metaphysically necessary* if it is true. That is, it cannot be false in any possible world if it is true in the actual world. For if it were false in some possible world, then wrongness would be non-identical with contrariety to God's commands in the actual world as well, by the transivity of identity, just as Matthew and Levi must be non-identical in all worlds if they are non-identical in any.

This argument establishes the metaphysical necessity of property identities in general; and that leads me to identify wrongness with contrariety to the commands of a *loving* God, rather than simply with contrariety to the commands of God. Most theists believe that both of those properties are in fact possessed by all and only wrong actions. But if wrongness is simply contrariety to the commands of God, it is necessarily so, which implies that it would be wrong to disobey God even if he were so unloving as to command the practice of cruelty for its own sake. That consequence is unacceptable. I am not prepared to adopt the negative attitude toward possible disobedience in that situation that would be involved in identifying wrongness simply with contrariety to God's commands.

The loving character of the God who issues them seems to me therefore to be a metaethically relevant feature of divine commands. (I assume that in deciding what property is wrongness, and therefore would be wrongness in all possible worlds, we are to rely on our own actual moral feelings and convictions, rather than on those that we or others would have in other possible worlds.)

If it is necessary that ethical wrongness is contrariety to a loving God's commands, it follows that no actions would be ethically wrong if there were not a loving God. This consequence will seem (at least initially) implausible to many, but I will try to dispel as much as I can of the air of paradox. It should be emphasized, first of all, that my theory does not imply what would ordinarily be meant by saying that no actions *are* ethically wrong if there *is* no loving God. If there is no loving God, then the theological part of my theory is false; but the more general part presented in section IV above, implies that in that case ethical wrongness is the property with which it is identified by the best remaining alternative theory.

Similarly, if there is in fact a loving God, and if ethical wrongness is the property of being contrary to the commands of a loving God, there is still, I suppose, a possible world, w_4, in which there would not be a loving God but there would be people to whom w_4 would seem much as the actual world seems to us, and who would use the world 'wrong' much as we use it. We may say that they would associate it with the same *concept* as we do although the property it would signify in their mouths is not wrongness. The actions they call 'wrong' would not be wrong—that is, they would not have the property that actually is wrongness (the property of being contrary to the commands of a loving God). But that is not to say that they would be mistaken whenever they predicated 'is wrong' of an action. For 'wrong' in their speech would signify the property (if any) that is assigned to it by the metaethical theory that would be the best

in relation to an accurate knowledge of their situation in w_4. We can even say that they would believe, as we do, that cruelty is wrong, if by that we mean, not that the property they would ascribe to cruelty by calling it 'wrong' is the same as the property that we so ascribe, but that the subjective psychological state that they would express by the ascription is that same that we express.

Readers who think that I have not sufficiently dispelled the air of paradox may wish to consider a slightly different divine command theory, according to which it is a contingent truth that contrariety to God's commands constitutes the nature of wrongness. Instead of saying that wrongness is the property that in the actual world best fills a certain role, we could say that wrongness is the property of having whatever property best fills that role in whatever possible world is in question. On the latter view it would be reasonable to say that the property that best fills the role constitutes the nature of wrongness, but that the nature of wrongness may differ in different possible worlds. The theist could still hold that the nature of wrongness in the actual world is constituted by contrariety to the commands of God (or of a loving God—it does not make as much difference which we say, on this view, since the theist believes God is loving in the actual world anyway). But it might be constituted by other properties in some other possible worlds. This theory does not imply that no action would be wrong if there were no loving God; and that may still seem to be an advantage. On the other hand I think there is also an air of paradox about the idea that wrongness may have different natures in different possible worlds; and if a loving God does issue commands, actual wrongness has a very different character from anything that could occur in a world without a loving God.

The difference between this alternative theory and the one I have endorsed should not be exaggerated. On both theories the nature of wrongness is actually constituted by contrariety to the commands of (a loving) God. And on both theories there may be other possible worlds in which other properties best fill the role by which contrariety to a loving God's commands is linked in the actual world to our concept of wrongness.

Notes

1 The metaethical position to be presented here was briefly indicated in Adams (1979). Though not all the arguments given there in favor of the theory are repeated here, the position is much more fully expounded in the present essay.

2 I have selected from these papers points that are relevant to my theory. I do not claim to give a comprehensive account of their aims and contents. I am also indebted here to David Kaplan and Bernard Kobes, for discussion and for the opportunity of reading unpublished papers of theirs.

3 Cf. Putnam (1975:290): "I would apply a generally causal account of reference also to moral terms . . ." I do not know how similar the metaethical views at which Putnam hints are to those that are developed in section IV of the present paper.

4 I follow Putnam in this use of 'concept.' I have avoided committing myself as to whether English speakers in w_4 would use 'wrong' with the same *meaning* as we do. See Putnam, 1975:234 [original note citation missing in text].

References

Adams, Robert Merrihew

1973 "A modified divine command theory of ethical wrongness." Pp. 318–47 in Gene Outka and John P. Reeder, Jr. (eds.), *Religion and Morality*. Garden City: Anchor.

1979 "Moral arguments for theistic belief." In C. F. Delaney (ed.), *Rationality and Religious Belief*. Notre Dame, In: University of Notre Dame Press.

Donnellan, Keith

1966 "Reference and definite descriptions." *The Philosophical Review* 75:281–304.

1972 "Proper names and identifying descriptions." Pp. 356–79 in Donald Davidson and Gilbert Harman

(eds.), *The Semantics of Natural Languages*. Dordrecht and Boston: Reidel.

Kripke, Paul A.

1972 "Naming and necessity." Pp. 253–355 and 763–69 in Donald Davidson and Gilbert Harman (eds.), *The Semantics of Natural Languages*. Dordrecht and Boston: Reidel.

Putnam, Hilary

1975 *Mind, Language and Reality: Philosophical Papers*, Vol. 2. Cambridge: Cambridge University Press.

Quine, Willard Van Orman

1963 *From a Logical Point of View: 9 Logico-Philosophical Essays*, 2nd ed. New York and Evanston: Harper Torchbooks.

1966 *The Ways of Paradox and Other Essays*. New York: Random House.

Stout, Jeffrey L.

1978 "Metaethics and the death of meaning: Adams' tantalizing closing." *The Journal of Religious Ethics* (Spring) 6:1–18.

Morality, objectivity, and knowledge

INTRODUCTION TO SECTION III

ARE THERE OBJECTIVE moral truths? According to noncognitivism, discussed in the chapters in Section II, the answer must be "no" because sentences like "lying is wrong" can be neither true nor false. But even if we reject noncognitivism, as many do, numerous questions will remain. It is one thing to say that moral discourse seeks to express truths, and quite another to say that it succeeds.

There are, moreover, powerful reasons for doubt. One obvious problem is that different societies notoriously disagree about *which* acts are right or wrong. Another is that moral facts do not fit comfortably with the naturalistic world view of science. Yet another problem, related but distinct, is that if moral facts do exist, it is hard to see how we can know them.

The implications of the fact that different societies adhere to different moral codes are discussed by James Rachels in Chapter 15. According to many, the proper way to respond to this fact is to adopt *cultural relativism,* the view that there are no universal moral truths and that the right thing to do is simply whatever one's society approves or commands. But Rachels argues that this does not follow. Perhaps most obviously, the fact that different societies (or individuals) disagree does not rule out the possibility that one is right and the other wrong. In addition, the fact that two societies disagree about the rightness of a given type of act may not indicate disagreement at a deeper level. Instead, it may mean only that differences in their circumstances call for different applications of the same basic principles. A further difficulty with cultural relativism is that if one accepts it, one cannot consistently criticize even societies whose institutions or traditions are abhorrent – for example, societies that practice slavery or are viciously antisemitic. For further discussion of issues related to cultural relativism, the reader may wish to consult Chapters 17, 18, and 21.

When we accept a scientific claim – for example, that certain microorganisms cause disease – we do so on the grounds that it explains some phenomenon in the world. This raises the question of whether any moral claims play a similar explanatory role. In Chapter 16, Gilbert Harman argues that none do. Whereas a physicist's observation of a vapor trail in a cloud chamber is best explained by the supposition that a proton has caused the vapor trail, we can explain a moralist's belief that a child who sets fire to a cat is acting wrongly without assuming that the child's act really is wrong. Here the best explanation is that the moralist has been brought up to believe that inflicting needless pain is wrong, and that this belief, together with his observation that the child is inflicting needless pain, leads him to regard the child's act as wrong. Because this explanation appeals to no moral facts, and would work just as well if there were none, Harman concludes that "[c]onceived as an explanatory theory, morality, unlike science, seems to be cut off from observation." In a similar spirit, J. L. Mackie argues in Chapter 18 that unlike other facts, moral facts would

have to have the odd property of being intrinsically action-guiding. As Mackie himself puts it, we must suppose that any objective good "has to-be-pursuedness somehow built into it." Because he finds the existence of such facts implausible (and also to account for the cross-cultural disagreement discussed by Rachels in Chapter 15), Mackie concludes that our moral assertions, though cognitively meaningful, are all false. To explain why we wrongly think there are objective values, he cites a number of factors that he sees as encouraging this mistake. In citing these factors, Mackie embraces, but also goes beyond, Hume's appeal to the mind's "propensity to spread itself on external objects" (Chapter 8).

Can these attacks on moral objectivity be answered? According to Nicholas Sturgeon and Thomas Nagel (Chapters 17 and 19), they can. In Chapter 17, Sturgeon takes issue with Harman's claim that moral facts have less explanatory value than scientific facts. As Sturgeon points out (and as Harman would agree), we cannot even describe the phenomena that science seeks to explain – for example, the physicist's observing a vapor trail in a cloud chamber – without assuming the truth of parts of various scientific theories. Thus, to assess Harman's claim that moral facts have less explanatory value than scientific facts, we must similarly allow ourselves to draw on aspects of the relevant *moral* theory. Because our moral theory implies that the child's setting the cat on fire is wrong, and because that act causes us to believe that the child has acted wrongly, Sturgeon argues that the fact that the child's act is wrong *does* contribute to the explanation of our belief. To the objection that the act's wrongness does not contribute to the explanation because our moral upbringing would cause us to hold the same belief even if the child performed the same act but it was not wrong, Sturgeon replies that according to our moral theory, needlessly cruel acts are *necessarily* wrong. Because of this, setting a cat on fire but not acting wrongly is not a real possibility. Given the parallels that he finds between ethics and science, Sturgeon concludes that any argument that tells against the explanatory significance of moral facts will tell equally strongly against the explanatory significance of physical facts.

Despite their disagreements, Harman, Sturgeon, and Mackie all agree that if morality is to be objective, then the world must contain moral facts. But Thomas Nagel (Chapter 19) rejects this picture of moral objectivity. In Nagel's view, the objectivity of ethics depends not on what sorts of facts the world contains, but rather on what sorts of reasons we have to act. As he writes in response to Mackie, "[t]he view that values are real is not the view that they are real occult values or properties, but that . . . our claims about value and about what people have reason to do may be true or false independently of our beliefs and inclinations." Although Nagel acknowledges the possibility that none of our desires are sources of reasons, he believes that some in fact are, and that we can discover this by scrutinizing them from an external perspective. For example, the fact that someone wants his headache to stop can be seen to give him and everyone else a reason to relieve his pain.

Whatever account of moral objectivity we accept, it must allow us to be mistaken about our moral beliefs. Moreover, according to many, even a true moral belief will not amount to knowledge if the believer does not have good reasons to hold it. This raises the question of whether we ever *do* have good reasons to hold our moral beliefs.

The view that we do not, and that we therefore cannot have moral knowledge, is known as *moral skepticism*, and it is discussed by Walter Sinnott-Armstrong in Chapter 20. Because many (though not all) of the considerations that raise questions about moral knowledge also apply in other areas, Sinnott-Armstrong couches much of his discussion in general terms. He distinguishes between two major forms of skepticism, *Academic skepticism*, which asserts that no one has any knowledge, and *Pyrrhonian skepticism*, which simply suspends belief about whether anyone has any knowledge. He also carefully analyzes two of the most important arguments for Academic skepticism as they pertain to moral knowledge.

When skeptics challenge the possibility of moral knowledge, their challenges generally apply to others as well as themselves. There is, however, another sort of challenge that is best raised from the first-person perspective. As George Sher points out in Chapter 21, each of us knows that he would have different moral beliefs if he had been raised in a different culture or had a different upbringing; and each of us knows, as well, that many of those who disagree with him are just as smart and thoughtful as he is. Given these facts, why should anyone suppose that he is right and the others are wrong? Yet if a person has no reason to believe that he is right and the others are wrong, then why should he base his actions on his moral judgments rather than theirs? According to Sher, the strongest version of this challenge is one that draws both on the fact that one's moral beliefs are contingent on one's upbringing and on the fact that one holds many controversial beliefs. Sher argues, as well, that the best way to meet the challenge is not to try to show that one's moral judgments are better-supported than those of others, but rather to recognize that being a practical agent just *is* acting on one's own best judgments.

Chapter 15

James Rachels

THE CHALLENGE OF CULTURAL RELATIVISM

"M ORALITY DIFFERS in every society, and is
a convenient term for socially approved
habits."

Ruth Benedict, *Patterns of Culture* (1934)

How different cultures have different moral codes

Darius, a king of ancient Persia, was intrigued by the variety of cultures he encountered in his travels. He had found, for example, that the Callatians (a tribe of Indians) customarily ate the bodies of their dead fathers. The Greeks, of course, did not do that—the Greeks practiced cremation and regarded the funeral pyre as the natural and fitting way to dispose of the dead. Darius thought that a sophisticated understanding of the world must include an appreciation of such differences between cultures. One day, to teach this lesson, he summoned some Greeks who happened to be present at his court and asked them what they would take to eat the bodies of their dead fathers. They were shocked, as Darius knew they would be, and replied that no amount of money would persuade them to do such a thing. Then Darius called in some Callatians, and while the Greeks listened asked them what they would take to burn their dead fathers' bodies. The Callatians were horrified and told Darius not even to mention such a dreadful thing.

This story, recounted by Herodotus in his *History*, illustrates a recurring theme in the literature of social science: different cultures have different moral codes. What is thought right within one group may be utterly abhorrent to the members of another group, and vice versa. Should we eat the bodies of the dead or burn them? If you were a Greek, one answer would seem obviously correct; but if you were a Callatian, the opposite would seem equally certain.

It is easy to give additional examples of the same kind. Consider the Eskimos. They are a remote and inaccessible people. Numbering only about 25,000, they live in small, isolated settlements scattered mostly along the northern fringes of North America and Greenland. Until the beginning of this century, the outside world knew little about them. Then explorers began to bring back strange tales.

Eskimo customs turned out to be very different from our own. The men often had more than one wife, and they would share their wives with guests, lending them for the night as a sign of hospitality. Moreover, within a community, a dominant male might demand—and get—regular sexual access to other men's wives. The women, however, were free to break these arrangements simply by leaving their husbands and taking up with new partners—free, that is, so long as their former husbands chose not to make trouble. All in all, the Eskimo practice was a volatile scheme that bore little resemblance to what we call marriage.

But it was not only their marriage and sexual practices that were different. The Eskimos also seemed to have less regard for human life. Infanticide, for example, was common. Knud Rasmussen, one of the most famous early explorers, reported that he met one woman who had borne twenty children but had killed ten of them at birth. Female babies, he found, were especially liable to be destroyed, and this was permitted simply at the parents' discretion, with no social stigma attached to it. Old people also, when they became too feeble to contribute to the family, were left out in the snow to die. So there seemed to be, in this society, remarkably little respect for life.

To the general public, these were disturbing revelations. Our own way of living seems so natural and right that for many of us it is hard to conceive of others living so differently. And when we do hear of such things, we tend immediately to categorize those other peoples as "backward" or "primitive." But to anthropologists and sociologists, there was nothing particularly surprising about the Eskimos. Since the time of Herodotus, enlightened observers have been accustomed to the idea that conceptions of right and wrong differ from culture to culture. If we assume that our ideas of right and wrong will be shared by all peoples at all times, we are merely naive.

Cultural Relativism

To many thinkers, this observation—"Different cultures have different moral codes"—has seemed to be the key to understanding morality. The idea of universal truth in ethics, they say, is a myth. The customs of different societies are all that exist. These customs cannot be said to be "correct" or "incorrect," for that implies we have an independent standard of right and wrong by which they may be judged. But there is no such independent standard; every standard is culture-bound. The great pioneering sociologist William Graham Sumner, writing in 1906, put the point like this:

The "right" way is the way which the ancestors used and which has been handed down. The tradition is its own warrant. It is not held subject to verification by experience. The notion of right is in the folkways. It is not outside of them, of independent origin, and brought to test them. In the folkways, whatever is, is right. This is because they are traditional, and therefore contain in themselves the authority of the ancestral ghosts. When we come to the folkways we are at the end of our analysis.

This line of thought has probably persuaded more people to be skeptical about ethics than any other single thing. *Cultural Relativism*, as it has been called, challenges our ordinary belief in the objectivity and universality of moral truth. It says, in effect, that there is no such thing as universal truth in ethics; there are only the various cultural codes, and nothing more. Moreover, our own code has no special status; it is merely one among many.

As we shall see, this basic idea is really a compound of several different thoughts. It is important to separate the various elements of the theory because, on analysis, some parts of the theory turn out to be correct, whereas others seem to be mistaken. As a beginning, we may distinguish the following claims, all of which have been made by cultural relativists:

1. Different societies have different moral codes.
2. There is no objective standard that can be used to judge one societal code better than another.
3. The moral code of our own society has no special status; it is merely one among many.
4. There is no "universal truth" in ethics—that is, there are no moral truths that hold for all peoples at all times.
5. The moral code of a society determines what is right within that society; that is, if the moral code of a society says that a

certain action is right, then that action *is* right, at least within that society.
6. It is mere arrogance for us to try to judge the conduct of other peoples. We should adopt an attitude of tolerance toward the practices of other cultures.

Although it may seem that these six propositions go naturally together, they are independent of one another, in the sense that some of them might be true even if others are false. In what follows, we will try to identify what is correct in Cultural Relativism, but we will also be concerned to expose what is mistaken about it.

The cultural differences argument

Cultural Relavitism is a theory about the nature of morality. At first blush it seems quite plausible. However, like all such theories, it may be evaluated by subjecting it to rational analysis; and when we analyze Cultural Relativism we find that it is not so plausible as it first appears to be.

The first thing we need to notice is that at the heart of Cultural Relativism there is a certain *form of argument*. The strategy used by cultural relativists is to argue from facts about the differences between cultural outlooks to a conclusion about the status of morality. Thus we are invited to accept this reasoning:

(1) The Greeks believed it was wrong to eat the dead, whereas the Callatians believed it was right to eat the dead.
(2) Therefore, eating the dead is neither objectively right nor objectively wrong. It is merely a matter of opinion, which varies from culture to culture.

Or, alternatively:

(1) The Eskimos see nothing wrong with infanticide, whereas Americans believe infanticide is immoral.

(2) Therefore, infanticide is neither objectively right nor objectively wrong. It is merely a matter of opinion, which varies from culture to culture.

Clearly, these arguments are variations of one fundamental idea. They are both special cases of a more general argument, which says:

(1) Different cultures have different moral codes.
(2) Therefore, there is no objective "truth" in morality. Right and wrong are only matters of opinion, and opinions vary from culture to culture.

We may call this the *Cultural Differences Argument*. To many people, it is very persuasive. But from a logical point of view, is it a *sound* argument?

It is not sound. The trouble is that the conclusion does not really follow from the premise—that is, even if the premise is true, the conclusion still might be false. The premise concerns what people *believe*: in some societies, people believe one thing; in other societies, people believe differently. The conclusion, however, concerns *what really is the case*. The trouble is that this sort of conclusion does not follow logically from this sort of premise.

Consider again the example of the Greeks and Callatians. The Greeks believed it was wrong to eat the dead; the Callatians believed it was right. Does it follow, *from the mere fact that they disagreed*, that there is no objective truth in the matter? No, it does not follow; for it *could* be that the practice was objectively right (or wrong) and that one or the other of them was simply mistaken.

To make the point clearer, consider a very different matter. In some societies, people believe the earth is flat. In other societies, such as our own, people believe the earth is (roughly) spherical. Does it follow, *from the mere fact that they disagree*, that there is no "objective truth" in geography? Of course not; we would never draw

such a conclusion because we realize that, in their beliefs about the world, the members of some societies might simply be wrong. There is no reason to think that if the world is round everyone must know it. Similarly, there is no reason to think that if there is moral truth everyone must know it. The fundamental mistake in the Cultural Differences Argument is that it attempts to derive a substantive conclusion about a subject (morality) from the mere fact that people disagree about it.

It is important to understand the nature of the point that is being made here. We are *not* saying (not yet, anyway) that the conclusion of the argument is false. Insofar as anything being said here is concerned, it is still an open question whether the conclusion is true. We *are* making a purely logical point and saying that the conclusion does not *follow* from the premise. This is important, because in order to determine whether the conclusion is true, we need arguments in its support. Cultural Relativism proposes this argument, but unfortunately the argument turns out to be fallacious. So it proves nothing.

The consequences of taking Cultural Relativism seriously

Even if the Cultural Differences Argument is invalid, Cultural Relativism might still be true. What would it be like if it were true?

In the passage quoted above, William Graham Sumner summarizes the essence of Cultural Relativism. He says that there is no measure of right and wrong other than the standards of one's society: "The notion of right is in the folkways. It is not outside of them, of independent origin, and brought to test them. In the folkways, whatever is, is right."

Suppose we took this seriously. What would be some of the consequences?

1. *We could no longer say that the customs of other societies are morally inferior to our own.* This, of course, is one of the main points stressed by Cultural Relativism. We would have to stop condemning other societies merely because they are "different." So long as we concentrate on certain examples, such as the funerary practices of the Greeks and Callatians, this may seem to be a sophisticated, enlightened attitude.

However, we would also be stopped from criticizing other, less benign practices. Suppose a society waged war on its neighbors for the purpose of taking slaves. Or suppose a society was violently anti-Semitic and its leaders set out to destroy the Jews. Cultural Relativism would preclude us from saying that either of these practices was wrong. We would not even be able to say that a society tolerant of Jews is *better* than the anti-Semitic society, for that would imply some sort of transcultural standard of comparison. The failure to condemn *these* practices does not seem "enlightened"; on the contrary, slavery and anti-Semitism seem wrong *wherever* they occur. Nevertheless, if we took Cultural Relativism seriously, we would have to admit that these social practices also are immune from criticism.

2. *We could decide whether actions are right or wrong just by consulting the standards of our society.* Cultural Relativism suggests a simple test for determining what is right and what is wrong: all one has to do is ask whether the action is in accordance with the code of one's society. Suppose a resident of South Africa is wondering whether his country's [former] policy of *apartheid*—rigid racial segregation—is morally correct. All he has to do is ask whether this policy conforms to his society's moral code. If it does, there is nothing to worry about, at least from a moral point of view.

This implication of Cultural Relativism is disturbing because few of us think that our society's code is perfect—we can think of ways it might be improved. Yet Cultural Relativism would not only forbid us from criticizing the codes of *other* societies; it would stop us from criticizing our *own*. After all, if right and wrong are relative to culture, this must be true for our own culture just as much as for others.

3. *The idea of moral progress is called into doubt.* Usually, we think that at least some changes in our society have been for the better. (Some, of course, may have been changes for the worse.) Consider this example: Throughout most of Western history the place of women in society was very narrowly circumscribed. They could not own property; they could not vote or hold political office; with a few exceptions, they were not permitted to have paying jobs; and generally they were under the almost absolute control of their husbands. Recently much of this has changed, and most people think of it as progress.

If Cultural Relativism is correct, can we legitimately think of this as progress? Progress means replacing a way of doing things with a *better* way. But by what standard do we judge the new ways as better? If the old ways were in accordance with the social standards of their time, then Cultural Relativism would say it is a mistake to judge them by the standards of a different time. Eighteenth-century society was, in effect, a different society from the one we have now. To say that we have made progress implies a judgment that present-day society is better, and that is just the sort of transcultural judgment that, according to Cultural Relativism, is impermissible.

Our idea of social *reform* will also have to be reconsidered. A reformer such as Martin Luther King, Jr., seeks to change his society for the better. Within the constraints imposed by Cultural Relativism, there is one way this might be done. If a society is not living up to its own ideals, the reformer may be regarded as acting for the best: the ideals of the society are the standard by which we judge his or her proposals as worthwhile. But the "reformer" may not challenge the ideals themselves, for those ideals are by definition correct. According to Cultural Relativism, then, the idea of social reform makes sense only in this very limited way.

These three consequences of Cultural Relativism have led many thinkers to reject it as implausible on its face. It does make sense, they say, to condemn some practices, such as slavery and anti-Semitism, wherever they occur. It makes sense to think that our own society has made some moral progress, while admitting that it is still imperfect and in need of reform. Because Cultural Relativism says that these judgments make no sense, the argument goes, it cannot be right.

Why there is less disagreement than it seems

The original impetus for Cultural Relativism comes from the observation that cultures differ dramatically in their views of right and wrong. But just how much do they differ? It is true that there are differences. However, it is easy to overestimate the extent of those differences. Often, when we examine what *seems* to be a dramatic difference, we find that the cultures do not differ nearly as much as it appears.

Consider a culture in which people believe it is wrong to eat cows. This may even be a poor culture, in which there is not enough food; still, the cows are not to be touched. Such a society would *appear* to have values very different from our own. But does it? We have not yet asked why these people will not eat cows. Suppose it is because they believe that after death the souls of humans inhabit the bodies of animals, especially cows, so that a cow may be someone's grandmother. Now do we want to say that their values are different from ours? No; the difference lies elsewhere. The difference is in our belief systems, not in our values. We agree that we shouldn't eat Grandma; we simply disagree about whether the cow is (or could be) Grandma.

The general point is this. Many factors work together to produce the customs of a society. The society's values are only one of them. Other matters, such as the religious and factual beliefs held by its members and the physical circumstances in which they must live, are also important. We cannot conclude, then, merely because customs differ, that there is a disagreement about

values. The difference in customs may be attributable to some other aspect of social life. Thus there may be less disagreement about values than there appears to be.

Consider the Eskimos again. They often kill perfectly normal infants, especially girls. We do not approve of this at all; a parent who did this in our society would be locked up. Thus there appears to be a great difference in the values of our two cultures. But suppose we ask *why* the Eskimos do this. The explanation is not that they have less affection for their children or less respect for human life. An Eskimo family will always protect its babies if conditions permit. But they live in a harsh environment, where food is often in short supply. A fundamental postulate of Eskimo thought is: "Life is hard, and the margin of safety small." A family may want to nourish its babies but be unable to do so.

As in many "primitive" societies, Eskimo mothers will nurse their infants over a much longer period of time than mothers in our culture. The child will take nourishment from its mother's breast for four years, perhaps even longer. So even in the best of times there are limits to the number of infants that one mother can sustain. Moreover, the Eskimos are a nomadic people—unable to farm, they must move about in search of food. Infants must be carried, and a mother can carry only one baby in her parka as she travels and goes about her outdoor work. Other family members can help, but this is not always possible.

Infant girls are more readily disposed of because, first, in this society the males are the primary food providers—they are the hunters, according to the traditional division of labor—and it is obviously important to maintain a sufficient number of food gatherers. But there is an important second reason as well. Because the hunters suffer a high casualty rate, the adult men who die prematurely far outnumber the women who die early. Thus if male and female infants survived in equal numbers, the female adult population would greatly outnumber the male

adult population. Examining the available statistics, one writer concluded that "were it not for female infanticide . . . there would be approximately one-and-a-half times as many females in the average Eskimo local group as there are food-producing males."

So among the Eskimos, infanticide does not signal a fundamentally different attitude toward children. Instead, it is a recognition that drastic measures are sometimes needed to ensure the family's survival. Even then, however, killing the baby is not the first option considered. Adoption is common; childless couples are especially happy to take a more fertile couple's "surplus." Killing is only the last resort. I emphasize this in order to show that the raw data of the anthropologists can be misleading; it can make the differences in values between cultures appear greater than they are. The Eskimos' values are not all that different from our values. It is only that life forces upon them choices that we do not have to make.

How all cultures have some values in common

It should not be surprising that, despite appearances, the Eskimos are protective of their children. How could it be otherwise? How could a group survive that did *not* value its young? This suggests a certain argument, one which shows that all cultural groups must be protective of their infants:

(1) Human infants are helpless and cannot survive if they are not given extensive care for a period of years.

(2) Therefore, if a group did not care for its young, the young would not survive, and the older members of the group would not be replaced. After a while the group would die out.

(3) Therefore, any cultural group that continues to exist must care for its young. Infants that are *not* cared for must be the exception rather than the rule.

Similar reasoning shows that other values must be more or less universal. Imagine what it would be like for a society to place no value at all on truth telling. When one person spoke to another, there would be no presumption at all that he was telling the truth—for he could just as easily be speaking falsely. Within that society, there would be no reason to pay attention to what anyone says. (I ask you what time it is, and you say "Four o'clock." But there is no presumption that you are speaking truly; you could just as easily have said the first thing that came into your head. So I have no reason to pay attention to your answer—in fact, there was no point in my asking you in the first place!) Communication would then be extremely difficult, if not impossible. And because complex societies cannot exist without regular communication among their members, society would become impossible. It follows that in any complex society there *must* be a presumption in favor of truthfulness. There may of course be exceptions to this rule: there may be situations in which it is thought to be permissible to lie. Nevertheless, these will be exceptions to a rule that is in force in the society.

Let me give one further example of the same type. Could a society exist in which there was no prohibition on murder? What would this be like? Suppose people were free to kill other people at will, and no one thought there was anything wrong with it. In such a "society," no one could feel secure. Everyone would have to be constantly on guard. People who wanted to survive would have to avoid other people as much as possible. This would inevitably result in individuals trying to become as self-sufficient as possible—after all, associating with others would be dangerous. Society on any large scale would collapse. Of course, people might band together in smaller groups with others that they *could* trust not to harm them. But notice what this means: they would be forming smaller societies that *did* acknowledge a rule against murder. The prohibition of murder, then, is a necessary feature of all societies.

There is a general theoretical point here, namely, that *there are some moral rules that all societies will have in common, because those rules are necessary for society to exist.* The rules against lying and murder are two examples. And in fact, we do find these rules in force in all viable cultures. Cultures may differ in what they regard as legitimate exceptions to the rules, but this disagreement exists against a background of agreement on the larger issues. Therefore, it is a mistake to overestimate the amount of difference between cultures. Not *every* moral rule can vary from society to society.

What can be learned from Cultural Relativism

At the outset, I said that we were going to identify both what is right and what is wrong in Cultural Relativism. Thus far I have mentioned only its mistakes: I have said that it rests on an invalid argument, that it has consequences that make it implausible on its face, and that the extent of cultural disagreement is far less than it implies. This all adds up to a pretty thorough repudiation of the theory. Nevertheless, it is still a very appealing idea, and the reader may have the feeling that all this is a little unfair. The theory *must* have something going for it, or else why has it been so influential? In fact, I think there is something right about Cultural Relativism, and now I want to say what that is. There are two lessons we should learn from the theory, even if we ultimately reject it.

1. Cultural Relativism warns us, quite rightly, about the danger of assuming that all our preferences are based on some absolute rational standard. They are not. Many (but not all) of our practices are merely peculiar to our society, and it is easy to lose sight of that fact. In reminding us of it, the theory does a service.

Funerary practices are one example. The Callatians, according to Herodotus, were "men who eat their fathers"—a shocking idea, to us at least. But eating the flesh of the dead could be understood as a sign of respect. It could be taken

as a symbolic act that says: We wish this person's spirit to dwell within us. Perhaps this was the understanding of the Callatians. On such a way of thinking, burying the dead could be seen as an act of rejection, and burning the corpse as positively scornful. If this is hard to imagine, then we may need to have our imaginations stretched. Of course we may feel a visceral repugnance at the idea of eating human flesh in any circumstances. But what of it? This repugnance may be, as the relativists say, only a matter of what is customary in our particular society.

There are many other matters that we tend to think of in terms of objective right and wrong, but that are really nothing more than social conventions. Should women cover their breasts? A publicly exposed breast is scandalous in our society, whereas in other cultures it is unremarkable. Objectively speaking, it is neither right nor wrong—there is no objective reason why either custom is better. Cultural Relativism begins with the valuable insight that many of our practices are like this—they are only cultural products. Then it goes wrong by concluding that, because *some* practices are like this, *all* must be.

2. The second lesson has to do with keeping an open mind. In the course of growing up, each of us has acquired some strong feelings: we have learned to think of some types of conduct as acceptable, and others we have learned to regard as simply unacceptable. Occasionally, we may find those feelings challenged. We may encounter someone who claims that our feelings are mistaken. For example, we may have been taught that homosexuality is immoral, and we may feel quite uncomfortable around gay people and see them as alien and "different." Now someone suggests that this may be a mere prejudice; that there is nothing evil about homosexuality; that gay people are just people, like anyone else, who happen, through no choice of their own, to be attracted to others of the same sex. But because we feel so strongly about the

matter, we may find it hard to take this seriously. Even after we listen to the arguments, we may still have the unshakable feeling that homosexuals *must*, somehow, be an unsavory lot.

Cultural Relativism, by stressing that our moral views can reflect the prejudices of our society, provides an antidote for this kind of dogmatism. When he tells the story of the Greeks and Callatians, Herodotus adds:

> For if anyone, no matter who, were given the opportunity of choosing from amongst all the nations of the world the set of beliefs which he thought best, he would inevitably, after careful consideration of their relative merits, choose that of his own country. Everyone without exception believes his own native customs, and the religion he was brought up in, to be the best.

Realizing this can result in our having more open minds. We can come to understand that our feelings are not necessarily perceptions of the truth—they may be nothing more than the result of cultural conditioning. Thus when we hear it suggested that some element of our social code is not really the best and we find ourselves instinctively resisting the suggestion, we might stop and remember this. Then we may be more open to discovering the truth, whatever that might be.

We can understand the appeal of Cultural Relativism, then, even though the theory has serious shortcomings. It is an attractive theory because it is based on a genuine insight—that many of the practices and attitudes we think so natural are really only cultural products. Moreover, keeping this insight firmly in view is important if we want to avoid arrogance and have open minds. These are important points, not to be taken lightly. But we can accept these points without going on to accept the whole theory.

Chapter 16

Gilbert Harman

ETHICS AND OBSERVATION

The basic issue

CAN MORAL principles be tested and confirmed in the way scientific principles can? Consider the principle that, if you are given a choice between five people alive and one dead or five people dead and one alive, you should always choose to have five people alive and one dead rather than the other way round. We can easily imagine examples that appear to confirm this principle. Here is one:

> You are a doctor in a hospital's emergency room when six accident victims are brought in. All six are in danger of dying but one is much worse off than the others. You can just barely save that person if you devote all of your resources to him and let the others die. Alternatively, you can save the other five if you are willing to ignore the most seriously injured person.

It would seem that in this case you, the doctor, would be right to save the five and let the other person die. So this example, taken by itself, confirms the principle under consideration. Next, consider the following case.

> You have five patients in the hospital who are dying, each in need of a separate organ. One needs a kidney, another a lung, a third a heart, and so forth. You can save all five if you take a single healthy person and remove his heart, lungs, kidneys, and so forth, to distribute to these five patients. Just such a healthy person is in room 306. He is in the hospital for routine tests. Having seen his test results, you know that he is perfectly healthy and of the right tissue compatibility. If you do nothing, he will survive without incident; the other patients will die, however. The other five patients can be saved only if the person in Room 306 is cut up and his organs distributed. In that case, there would be one dead but five saved.

The principle in question tells us that you should cut up the patient in Room 306. But in this case, surely you must not sacrifice this innocent bystander, even to save the five other patients. Here a moral principle has been tested and disconfirmed in what may seem to be a surprising way.

This, of course, was a "thought experiment." We did not really compare a hypothesis with the world. We compared an explicit principle with our feelings about certain imagined examples. In the same way, a physicist performs thought experiments in order to compare explicit hypotheses with his "sense" of what should happen in certain situations, a "sense" that he has acquired as a result of his long working familiarity with current theory. But scientific hypotheses can also be tested in real experiments, out in the world.

Can moral principles be tested in the same way, out in the world? You can observe someone do something, but can you ever perceive the rightness or wrongness of what he does? If you round a corner and see a group of young hoodlums pour gasoline on a cat and ignite it, you do not need to *conclude* that what they are doing is wrong; you do not need to figure anything out; you can *see* that it is wrong. But is your reaction due to the actual wrongness of what you see or is it simply a reflection of your moral "sense," a "sense" that you have acquired perhaps as a result of your moral upbringing?

Observation

The issue is complicated. There are no pure observations. Observations are always "theory laden." What you perceive depends to some extent on the theory you hold, consciously or unconsciously. You see some children pour gasoline on a cat and ignite it. To really see that, you have to possess a great deal of knowledge, know about a considerable number of objects, know about people: that people pass through the life stages infant, baby, child, adolescent, adult. You must know what flesh and blood animals are, and in particular, cats. You must have some idea of life. You must know what gasoline is, what burning is, and much more. In one sense, what you "see" is a pattern of light on your retina, a shifting array of splotches, although, even that is theory, and you could never adequately describe what you see in that sense. In another sense, you see what you do because of the theories you hold. Change those theories and you would see something else, given the same pattern of light.

Similarly, if you hold a moral view, whether it is held consciously or unconsciously, you will be able to perceive rightness or wrongness, goodness or badness, justice or injustice. There is no difference in this respect between moral propositions and other theoretical propositions. If there is a difference, it must be found elsewhere.

Observation depends on theory because perception involves forming a belief as a fairly direct result of observing something; you can form a belief only if you understand the relevant concepts and a concept is what it is by virtue of its role in some theory or system of beliefs. To recognize a child as a child is to employ, consciously or unconsciously, a concept that is defined by its place in a framework of the stages of human life. Similarly, burning is an empty concept apart from its theoretical connections to the concepts of heat, destruction, smoke, and fire.

Moral concepts—Right and Wrong, Good and Bad, Justice and Injustice—also have a place in your theory or system of beliefs and are the concepts they are because of their context. If we say that observation has occurred whenever an opinion is a direct result of perception, we must allow that there is moral observation, because such an opinion can be a moral opinion as easily as any other sort. In this sense, observation may be used to confirm or disconfirm moral theories. The observational opinions that, in this sense, you find yourself with can be in either agreement or conflict with your consciously explicit moral principles. When they are in conflict, you must choose between your explicit theory and observation. In ethics, as in science, you sometimes opt for theory, and say that you made an error in observation or were biased or whatever, or you sometimes opt for observation, and modify your theory.

In other words, in both science and ethics, general principles are invoked to explain particular cases and, therefore, in both science and ethics, the general principles you accept can be tested by appealing to particular judgments that certain things are right or wrong, just or unjust, and so forth; and these judgments are analogous to direct perceptual judgments about facts.

Observational evidence

Nevertheless, observation plays a role in science that it does not seem to play in ethics. The

difference is that you need to make assumptions about certain physical facts to explain the occurrence of the observations that support a scientific theory, but you do not seem to need to make assumptions about any moral facts to explain the occurrence of the so-called moral observations I have been talking about. In the moral case, it would seem that you need only make assumptions about the psychology or moral sensibility of the person making the moral observation. In the scientific case, theory is tested against the world.

The point is subtle but important. Consider a physicist making an observation to test a scientific theory. Seeing a vapor trail in a cloud chamber, he thinks, "There goes a proton." Let us suppose that this is an observation in the relevant sense, namely, an immediate judgment made in response to the situation without any conscious reasoning having taken place. Let us also suppose that his observation confirms his theory, a theory that helps give meaning to the very term "proton" as it occurs in his observational judgment. Such a confirmation rests on inferring an explanation. He can count his making the observation as confirming evidence for his theory only to the extent that it is reasonable to explain his making the observation by assuming that, not only is he in a certain psychological "set," given the theory he accepts and his beliefs about the experimental apparatus, but furthermore, there really was a proton going through the cloud chamber, causing the vapor trail, which he saw as a proton. (This is evidence for the theory to the extent that the theory can explain the proton's being there better than competing theories can.) But, if his having made that observation could have been equally well explained by his psychological set alone, without the need for any assumption about a proton, then the observation would not have been evidence for the existence of that proton and therefore would not have been evidence for the theory. His making the observation supports the theory only because, in order to explain his

making the observation, it is reasonable to assume something about the world over and above the assumptions made about the observer's psychology. In particular, it is reasonable to assume that there was a proton going through the cloud chamber, causing the vapor trail.

Compare this case with one in which you make a moral judgment immediately and without conscious reasoning, say, that the children are wrong to set the cat on fire or that the doctor would be wrong to cut up one healthy patient to save five dying patients. In order to explain your making the first of these judgments, it would be reasonable to assume, perhaps, that the children really are pouring gasoline on a cat and you are seeing them do it. But, in neither case is there any obvious reason to assume anything about "moral facts," such as that it really is wrong to set the cat on fire or to cut up the patient in Room 306. Indeed, an assumption about moral facts would seem to be totally irrelevant to the explanation of your making the judgment you make. It would seem that all we need assume is that you have certain more or less well articulated moral principles that are reflected in the judgments you make, based on your moral sensibility. It seems to be completely irrelevant to our explanation whether your intuitive immediate judgment is true or false.

The observation of an event can provide observational evidence for or against a scientific theory in the sense that the truth of that observation can be relevant to a reasonable explanation of why that observation was made. A moral observation does not seem, in the same sense, to be observational evidence for or against any moral theory, since the truth or falsity of the moral observation seems to be completely irrelevant to any reasonable explanation of why that observation was made. The fact that an observation of an event was made at the time it was made is evidence not only about the observer but also about the physical facts. The fact that you made a particular moral observation when

you did does not seem to be evidence about moral facts, only evidence about you and your moral sensibility. Facts about protons can affect what you observe, since a proton passing through the cloud chamber can cause a vapor trail that reflects light to your eye in a way that, given your scientific training and psychological set, leads you to judge that what you see is a proton. But there does not seem to be any way in which the actual rightness or wrongness of a given situation can have any effect on your perceptual apparatus. In this respect, ethics seems to differ from science.

In considering whether moral principles can help explain observations, it is therefore important to note an ambiguity in the word "observation." You see the children set the cat on fire and immediately think, "That's wrong." In one sense, your observation is that what the children are doing is wrong. In another sense, your observation is your thinking that thought. Moral observations might explain observations in the first sense but not in the second sense. Certain moral principles might help to explain why it was *wrong* of the children to set the cat on fire, but moral principles seem to be of no help in explaining *your thinking* that that is wrong. In the first sense of "observation," moral principles can be tested by observation—"That this act is wrong is evidence that causing unnecessary suffering is wrong." But in the second sense of "observation," moral principles cannot clearly be tested by observation, since they do not appear to help explain observations in this second sense of "observation." Moral principles do not seem to help explain your observing what you observe.

Of course, if you are already given the moral principle that it is wrong to cause unnecessary suffering, you can take your seeing the children setting the cat on fire as observational evidence that they are doing something wrong. Similarly, you can suppose that your seeing the vapor trail is observational evidence that a proton is going through the cloud chamber, if you are given the relevant physical theory. But there is an important apparent difference between the two cases. In the scientific case, your making that observation is itself evidence for the physical theory because the physical theory explains the proton, which explains the trail, which explains your observation. In the moral case, your making your observation does not seem to be evidence for the relevant moral principle because that principle does not seem to help explain your observation. The explanatory chain from principle to observation seems to be broken in morality. The moral principle may "explain" why it is wrong for the children to set the cat on fire. But the wrongness of that act does not appear to help explain the act, which you observe, itself. The explanatory chain appears to be broken in such a way that neither the moral principle nor the wrongness of the act can help explain why you observe what you observe.

A qualification may seem to be needed here. Perhaps the children perversely set the cat on fire simply "because it is wrong." Here it may seem at first that the actual wrongness of the act does help explain why they do it and therefore indirectly helps explain why you observe what you observe just as a physical theory, by explaining why the proton is producing a vapor trail, indirectly helps explain why the observer observes what he observes. But on reflection we must agree that this is probably an illusion. What explains the children's act is not clearly the actual wrongness of the act but, rather, their belief that the act is wrong. The actual rightness or wrongness of their act seems to have nothing to do with why they do it.

Observational evidence plays a part in science it does not appear to play in ethics, because scientific principles can be justified ultimately by their role in explaining observations, in the second sense of observation—by their explanatory role. Apparently, moral principles cannot be justified in the same way. It appears to be true that there can be no explanatory chain between moral principles and particular observings in

the way that there can be such a chain between scientific principles and particular observings. Conceived as an explanatory theory, morality, unlike science, seems to be cut off from observation.

Not that every legitimate scientific hypothesis is susceptible to direct observational testing. Certain hypotheses about "black holes" in space cannot be directly tested, for example, because no signal is emitted from within a black hole. The connection with observation in such a case is indirect. And there are many similar examples. Nevertheless, seen in the large, there is the apparent difference between science and ethics we have noted. The scientific realm is accessible to observation in a way the moral realm is not.

Ethics and mathematics

Perhaps ethics is to be compared, not with physics, but with mathematics. Perhaps such a moral principle as "You ought to keep your promises" is confirmed or disconfirmed in the way (whatever it is) in which such a mathematical principle as "$5 + 7 = 12$" is. Observation does not seem to play the role in mathematics it plays in physics. We do not and cannot perceive numbers, for example, since we cannot be in causal contact with them. We do not even understand what it would be like to be in causal contact with the number 12, say. Relations among numbers cannot have any more of an effect on our perceptual apparatus than moral facts can.

Observation, however, is relevant to mathematics. In explaining the observations that support a physical theory, scientists typically appeal to mathematical principles. On the other hand, one never seems to need to appeal in this way to moral principles. Since an observation is evidence for what best explains it, and since mathematics often figures in the explanations of scientific observations, there is indirect observational evidence for mathematics. There does not seem to be observational evidence, even indirectly, for basic moral principles. In explaining why certain observations have been made, we never seem to use purely moral assumptions. In this respect, then, ethics appears to differ not only from physics but also from mathematics.

Chapter 17

Nicholas Sturgeon

MORAL EXPLANATIONS

THERE IS one argument for moral skepticism that I respect even though I remain unconvinced. It has sometimes been called the argument from moral diversity or relativity, but that is somewhat misleading, for the problem arises not from the diversity of moral views, but from the apparent difficulty of *settling* moral disagreements, or even of knowing what would be required to settle them, a difficulty thought to be noticeably greater than any found in settling disagreements that arise in, for example, the sciences. This provides an argument for moral skepticism because one obviously possible explanation of our difficulty in settling moral disagreements is that they are really unsettleable, that there is no way of justifying one rather than another competing view on these issues; and a possible further explanation for the unsettleability of moral disagreements, in turn, is moral nihilism, the view that on these issue there just is no fact of the matter, that the impossibility of discovering and establishing moral truths is due to there not being any.

I am, as I say, unconvinced: partly because I think this argument exaggerates the difficulty we actually find in settling moral disagreements, partly because there are alternative explanations to be considered for the difficulty we do find. Under the latter heading, for example, it certainly matters to what extent moral disagreements depend on disagreements about other questions which, however disputed they may

be, are nevertheless regarded as having objective answers, questions such as which, if any, religion is true, which account of human psychology, which theory of human society. And it also matters to what extent consideration of moral questions is in practice skewed by distorting factors such as personal interest and social ideology. These are large issues. Although it is possible to say some useful things to put them in perspective,[1] it appears impossible to settle them quickly or in any a priori way. Consideration of them is likely to have to be piecemeal and, in the short run at least, frustratingly indecisive.

These large issues are not my topic here. But I mention them, and the difficulty of settling them, to show why it is natural that moral skeptics have hoped to find some quicker way of establishing their thesis. I doubt that any exist, but some have of course been proposed. Verificationist attacks on ethics should no doubt be seen in this light, and J. L. Mackie's recent "argument from queerness" is a clear instance.[2] The quicker response on which I shall concentrate, however, is neither of these, but instead an argument by Gilbert Harman designed to bring out the "basic problem" about morality, which in his view is "its apparent immunity from observational testing" and "the seeming irrelevance of observational evidence."[3] The argument is that reference to moral facts appears unnecessary for the *explanation* of our moral observations and beliefs.

Harman's view, I should say at once, is not in the end a skeptical one, and he does not view the argument I shall discuss as a decisive defense of moral skepticism or moral nihilism. Someone else might easily so regard it, however. For Harman himself regards it as creating a strong *prima facie* case for skepticism and nihilism, strong enough to justify calling it "the problem with ethics."[4] And he believes it shows that the only recourse for someone who wishes to avoid moral skepticism is to find defensible reductive definitions for ethical terms; so skepticism would be the obvious conclusion to draw for anyone who doubted the possibility of such definitions. I believe, however, that Harman is mistaken on both counts. I shall show that his argument for skepticism either rests on claims that most people would find quite implausible (and so cannot be what constitutes, for *them*, the problem with ethics); or else becomes just the application to ethics of a familiar *general* skeptical strategy, one which, if it works for ethics, will work equally well for unobservable theoretical entities, or for other minds, or for an external world (and so, again, can hardly be what constitutes the distinctive problem with *ethics*). I have argued elsewhere,[5] moreover, that one can in any case be a moral realist, and indeed an ethical naturalist, without believing that we are now or ever will be in possession of reductive naturalistic definitions for ethical terms.

I. The problem with ethics

Moral theories are often tested in thought experiments, against imagined examples; and, as Harman notes, trained researchers often test scientific theories in the same way. The problem, though, is that scientific theories can also be tested against the world, by observations or real experiments; and, Harman asks, "can moral principles be tested in the same way, out in the world?"

This would not be a very interesting or impressive challenge, of course, if it were merely

a resurrection of standard verificationist worries about whether moral assertions and theories have any testable empirical implications, implications statable in some relatively austere "observational" vocabulary. One problem with that form of the challenge, as Harman points out, is that there are no "pure" observations, and in consequence no purely observational vocabulary either. But there is also a deeper problem that Harman does not mention, one that remains even if we shelve worries about "pure" observations and, at least for the sake of argument, grant the verificationist his observational language, pretty much as it was usually conceived: that is, as lacking at the very least any obviously theoretical terminology from any recognized science, and of course as lacking any moral terminology. For then the difficulty is that moral principles fare just as well (or just as badly) against the verificationist challenge as do typical scientific principles. For it is by now a familiar point about scientific principles—principles such as Newton's law of universal gravitation or Darwin's theory of evolution—that they are entirely devoid of empirical implications when considered in isolation.[6] We do of course base observational predictions on such theories and so test them against experience, but that is because we do *not* consider them in isolation. For we can derive these predictions only by relying at the same time on a large background of additional assumptions, many of which are equally theoretical and equally incapable of being tested in isolation.

A less familiar point, because less often spelled out, is that the relation of moral principles to observation is similar in *both* these respects. Candidate moral principles—for example, that an action is wrong just in case there is something else the agent could have done that would have produced a greater balance of pleasure over pain—lack empirical implications when considered in isolation. But it is easy to derive empirical consequences from them, and thus to test them against experience, if we

allow ourselves, as we do in the scientific case, to rely on a background of other assumptions of comparable status. Thus, if we conjoin the act-utilitarian principle I just cited with the further view, also untestable in isolation, that it is always wrong deliberately to kill a human being, we can deduce from these two premises together the consequence that deliberately killing a human being always produces a lesser balance of pleasure over pain than some available alternative act; and this claim is one any positivist would have conceded we know, in principle at least, how to test. If we found it to be false, moreover, then we would be forced by this empirical test to abandon at least one of the moral claims from which we derived it.

It might be thought a worrisome feature of this example, however, and a further opening for skepticism, that there could be controversy about which moral premise to abandon, and that we have not explained how our empirical test can provide an answer to this question. And this may be a problem. It should be a familiar problem, however, because the Duhemian commentary includes a precisely corresponding point about the scientific case: that if we are at all cautious in characterizing what we observe, then the requirement that our theories merely be *consistent* with observation is a very weak one. There are always many, perhaps indefinitely many, different mutually inconsistent ways to adjust our views to meet this constraint. Of course, in practice we are often confident of how to do it: if you are a freshman chemistry student, you do not conclude from your failure to obtain the predicted value in an experiment that it is all over for the atomic theory of gases. And the decision can be equally easy, one should note, in a moral case. Consider two examples. From the surprising moral thesis that Adolf Hitler was a morally admirable person, together with a modest piece of moral theory to the effect that no morally admirable person would, for example, instigate and oversee the degradation and death of millions of persons, one can derive

the testable consequence that Hitler did not do this. But he did, so we must give up one of our premises; and the choice of which to abandon is neither difficult nor controversial.

Or, to take a less monumental example, contrived around one of Harman's own, suppose you have been thinking yourself lucky enough to live in a neighborhood in which no one would do anything wrong, at least not in public; and that the modest piece of theory you accept, this time, is that malicious cruelty, just for the hell of it, is wrong. Then, as in Harman's example, "you round a corner and see a group of young hoodlums pour gasoline on a cat and ignite it." At this point, either your confidence in the neighborhood or your principle about cruelty has got to give way. But the choice is easy, if dispiriting, so easy as hardly to require thought. As Harman says, "You do not need to *conclude* that what they are doing is wrong; you do not need to figure anything out; you can *see* that it is wrong" (p. 4). But a skeptic can still wonder whether this practical confidence, or this "seeing," rests in either sort of case on anything more than deeply ingrained conventions of thought—respect for scientific experts, say, and for certain moral traditions—as opposed to anything answerable to the facts of the matter, any reliable strategy for getting it right about the world.

Now, Harman's challenge is interesting partly because it does not rest on these verificationist doubts about whether moral beliefs have observational implications, but even more because what it does rest on is a partial answer to the kind of general skepticism to which, as we have seen, reflection on the verificationist picture can lead. Many of our beliefs are justified, in Harman's view, by their providing or helping to provide a reasonable *explanation* of our observing what we do. It would be consistent with your failure, as a beginning student, to obtain the experimental result predicted by the gas laws, that the laws are mistaken. But a better explanation, in light of your inexperience and the

general success experts have had in confirming and applying these laws, is that you made some mistake in running the experiment. So our scientific beliefs can be justified by their explanatory role; and so too, in Harman's view, can mathematical beliefs and many commonsense beliefs about the world.

Not so, however, moral beliefs: they appear to have no such explanatory role. That is "the problem with ethics." Harman spells out his version of this contrast:

> You need to make assumptions about certain physical facts to explain the occurrence of the observations that support a scientific theory, but you do not seem to need to make assumptions about any moral facts to explain the occurrence of the so-called moral observations I have been talking about. In the moral case, it would seem that you need only make assumptions about the psychology or moral sensibility of the person making the moral observation. (p. 6)

More precisely, and applied to his own example, it might be reasonable, in order to explain your judging that the hoodlums are wrong to set the cat on fire, to assume "that the children really are pouring gasoline on a cat and you are seeing them do it." But there is no

> obvious reason to assume anything about "moral facts," such as that it is really wrong to set the cat on fire. . . . Indeed, an assumption about moral facts would seem to be totally irrelevant to the explanation of your making the judgment you make. It would seem that all we need assume is that you have certain more or less well articulated moral principles that are reflected in the judgments you make, based on your moral sensibility. (p. 7)

And Harman thinks that if we accept this conclusion, suitably generalized, then, subject to one possible qualification concerning reduction that

I have discussed elsewhere,[7] we must conclude that moral theories cannot be tested against the world as scientific theories can, and that we have no reason to believe that moral facts are part of the order of nature or that there is any moral knowledge (pp. 23, 35).

My own view is that Harman is quite wrong, not in thinking that the explanatory role of our beliefs is important to their justification, but in thinking that moral beliefs play no such role.[8] I shall have to say something about the initial plausibility of Harman's thesis as applied to his own example, but part of my reason for dissenting should be apparent from the other example I just gave. We find it easy (and so does Harman [p. 108]) to conclude from the evidence not just that Hitler was not morally admirable, but that he was morally depraved. But isn't it plausible that Hitler's moral depravity—the fact of his really having been morally depraved—forms part of a reasonable explanation of why we believe he was depraved? I think so, and I shall argue concerning this and other examples that moral beliefs very commonly play the explanatory role Harman denies them. Before I can press my case, however, I need to clear up several preliminary points about just what Harman is claiming and just how his argument is intended to work.

II. Observation and explanation

(1) For there are several ways in which Harman's argument invites misunderstanding. One results from his focusing at the start on the question of whether there can be moral *observations*.[9] But this question turns out to be a side issue, in no way central to his argument that moral principles cannot be tested against the world. There are a couple of reasons for this, of which the more important[10] by far is that Harman does not really require of moral facts, if belief in them is to be justified, that they figure in the explanation of moral observations. It would be enough, on the one hand, if they were needed for the

explanation of moral beliefs that are not in any interesting sense observations. For example, Harman thinks belief in moral facts would be vindicated if they were needed to explain our drawing the moral conclusions we do when we reflect on hypothetical cases, but I think there is no illumination in calling these conclusions observations.[11] It would also be enough, on the other hand, if moral facts were needed for the explanation of what were clearly observations, but not moral observations. Harman thinks mathematical beliefs are justified, but he does not suggest that there are mathematical observations; it is rather that appeal to mathematical truths helps to explain why we make the physical observations we do (p. 10). Moral beliefs would surely be justified, too, if they played such a role, whether or not there are any moral observations.

So the claim is that moral facts are not needed to explain our having any of the moral beliefs we do, whether or not those beliefs are observations, and are equally unneeded to explain any of the observations we make, whether or not those observations are moral. In fact, Harman's view appears to be that moral facts aren't needed to explain anything at all: though it would perhaps be question-begging for him to begin with this strong a claim, since he grants that if there were any moral facts, then appeal to other moral facts—more general ones, for example— might be needed to explain them (p. 8). But he is certainly claiming, at the very least, that moral facts aren't needed to explain any nonmoral facts we have any reason to believe in.

(2)   Other possible misunderstandings concern what is meant in asking whether reference to moral facts is *needed* to explain moral beliefs. One warning about this question I have dealt with in my discussion of reduction elsewhere;[12] but another, about what Harman is clearly *not* asking, and about what sort of answer I can attempt to defend to the question he is asking, I can spell out here. For Harman's question is clearly not just whether there is *an*

explanation of our moral beliefs that does not mention moral facts. Almost surely there is. Equally surely, however, there is *an* explanation of our commonsense nonmoral beliefs that does not mention an external world: one which cites only our sensory experience, for example, together with whatever needs to be said about our psychology to explain why with that history of experience we would form just the beliefs we do. Harman means to be asking a question that will lead to skepticism about moral facts, but not to skepticism about the existence of material bodies or about well-established scientific theories of the world.

Harman illustrates the kind of question he is asking, and the kind of answer he is seeking, with an example from physics that it will be useful to keep in mind. A physicist sees a vapor trail in a cloud chamber and thinks, "There goes a proton." What explains his thinking this? Partly, of course, his psychological set, which largely depends on his beliefs about the apparatus and all the theory he has learned; but partly also, perhaps, the hypothesis that "there really was a proton going through the cloud chamber, causing the vapor trail, which he saw as a proton." We will not need this latter assumption, however, "if his having made that observation could have been equally well explained by his psychological set alone, without the need for any assumption about a proton" (p. 6).[13] So for reference to moral facts to be *needed* in the explanation of our beliefs and observations, is for this reference to be required for an explanation that is somehow *better* than competing explanations. Correspondingly, reference to moral facts will be unnecessary to an explanation, in Harman's view, not just because we can find some explanation that does not appeal to them, but because *no* explanation that appeals to them is any better than some competing explanation that does not.

Now, fine discriminations among competing explanations of almost anything are likely to be difficult, controversial, and provisional. Fortunately, however, my discussion of Harman's

argument will not require any fine discriminations. This is because Harman's thesis, as we have
seen, is *not* that moral explanations lose out by a
small margin; nor is it that moral explanations,
though sometimes initially promising, always
turn out on further examination to be inferior
to nonmoral ones. It is, rather, that reference to
moral facts always looks, right from the start, to
be "completely irrelevant" to the explanation of
any of our observations and beliefs. And my
argument will be that this is mistaken: that many
moral explanations appear to be good explanations, or components in good explanations, that
are not obviously undermined by anything else
that we know. My suspicion, in fact, is that moral
facts are needed in the sense explained, that they
will turn out to belong in our best overall
explanatory picture of the world, even in the
long run, but I shall not attempt to establish that
here. Indeed, it should be clear why I could not
pretend to do so. For I have explicitly put to one
side the issue (which I regard as incapable in any
case of quick resolution) of whether and to
what extent actual moral disagreements can be
settled satisfactorily; but I assume it would count
as a defect in any sort of explanation to rely on
claims about which rational agreement proved
unattainable. So I concede that it *could* turn out,
for anything I say here, that moral explanations
are all defective and should be discarded. What
I shall try to show is merely that many moral
explanations look reasonable enough to be in
the running; and, more specifically, that nothing
Harman says provides any reason for thinking
they are not. This claim is surely strong enough
(and controversial enough) to be worth
defending.

(3) It is implicit in this statement of my
project, but worth noting separately, that I take
Harman to be proposing an *independent* skeptical
argument—independent not merely of the
argument from the difficulty of settling disputed
moral questions, but also of other standard
arguments for moral skepticism. Otherwise his
argument is not worth separate discussion. For

any of these more familiar skeptical arguments
will of course imply that moral explanations are
defective, on the reasonable assumption that it
would be a defect in any explanation to rely on
claims as doubtful as these arguments attempt to
show all moral claims to be. But if *that* is why
there is a problem with moral explanations, one
should surely just cite the relevant skeptical
argument, rather than this derivative difficulty
about moral explanations, as the basic "problem
with ethics," and it is that argument we
should discuss. So I take Harman's interesting
suggestion to be that there is a *different* difficulty
that remains even if we put other arguments
for moral skepticism aside and *assume*, for
the sake of argument, that there are moral facts
(for example, that what the children in his
example are doing is really wrong): namely,
that these assumed facts *still* seem to play no
explanatory role.

This understanding of Harman's thesis
crucially affects my argumentative strategy in a
way to which I should alert the reader in
advance. For it should be clear that assessment of
this thesis not merely permits, but *requires*, that
we provisionally assume the existence of moral
facts. I can see no way of evaluating the claim
that *even* if we assumed the existence of moral
facts they would still appear explanatorily irrelevant, without assuming the existence of some,
to see how they would look. So I do freely
assume this in each of the examples I discuss in
the next section. (I have tried to choose plausible examples, moreover, moral facts most of us
would be inclined to believe in if we did believe
in moral facts, since those are the easiest to think
about; but the precise examples don't matter,
and anyone who would prefer others should feel
free to substitute her own.) I grant, furthermore,
that if Harman were right about the outcome of
this thought experiment—that even after we
assumed these facts they still looked irrelevant to
the explanation of our moral beliefs and other
nonmoral facts—then we might conclude with
him that there were, after all, no such facts. But I

claim he is wrong: that once we have provisionally assumed the existence of moral facts they *do* appear relevant, by perfectly ordinary standards, to the explanation of moral beliefs and of a good deal else besides. Does this prove that there *are* such facts? Well of course it helps support that view, but here I carefully make no claim to have shown so much. What I *show* is that any remaining reservations about the existence of moral facts must be based on those *other* skeptical arguments, of which Harman's argument is independent. In short, there may still be a "problem with ethics," but it has *nothing* special to do with moral explanations.

III. Moral explanations

Now that I have explained how I understand Harman's thesis, I turn to my arguments against it. I shall first add to my example of Hitler's moral character several more in which it seems plausible to cite moral facts as part of an explanation of nonmoral facts, and in particular of people's forming the moral opinions they do. I shall then argue that Harman gives us no plausible reason to reject or ignore these explanations; I shall claim, in fact, that the same is true for his own example of the children igniting the cat. I shall conclude, finally, by attempting to diagnose the source of the disagreement between Harman and me on these issues.

My Hitler example suggests a whole range of extremely common cases that appear not to have occurred to Harman, cases in which we cite someone's moral character as part of an explanation of his or her deeds, and in which that whole story is then available as a plausible further explanation of someone's arriving at a correct assessment of that moral character. Take just one other example. Bernard DeVoto, in *The Year of Decision: 1846*, describes the efforts of American emigrants already in California to rescue another party of emigrants, the Donner Party, trapped by snows in the High Sierras, once their plight became known. At a meeting in Yerba Buena (now San Francisco), the relief efforts were put under the direction of a recent arrival, Passed Midshipman Selim Woodworth, described by a previous acquaintance as "a great busybody and ambitious of taking a command among the emigrants."[14] But Woodworth not only failed to lead rescue parties into the mountains himself, where other rescuers were counting on him (leaving children to be picked up by him, for example), but had to be "shamed, threatened and bullied" even into organizing the efforts of others willing to take the risk; he spent time arranging comforts for himself in camp, preening himself on the importance of his position; and as a predictable result of his cowardice and his exercises in vainglory, many died who might have been saved, including four known still to be alive when he turned back for the last time in mid-March.

DeVoto concludes: "Passed Midshipman Woodworth was just no damned good" (1942, p. 442). I cite this case partly because it has so clearly the structure of an inference to a reasonable explanation. One can think of competing explanations, but the evidence points against them. It isn't, for example, that Woodworth was a basically decent person who simply proved too weak when thrust into a situation that placed heroic demands on him. He volunteered, he put no serious effort even into tasks that required no heroism, and it seems clear that concern for his own position and reputation played a much larger role in his motivation than did any concern for the people he was expected to save. If DeVoto is right about this evidence, moreover, it seems reasonable that part of the explanation of his believing that Woodworth was no damned good is just that Woodworth *was* no damned good.

DeVoto writes of course with more moral intensity (and with more of a flourish) than academic historians usually permit themselves, but it would be difficult to find a serious work of biography, for example, in which actions are not

explained by appeal to moral character: some-times by appeal to specific virtues and vices, but often enough also by appeal to a more general assessment. A different question, and perhaps a more difficult one, concerns the sort of example on which Harman concentrates, the explanation of judgments of right and wrong. Here again he appears just to have overlooked explanations in terms of moral character: a judge's thinking that it would be wrong to sentence a particular offender to the maximum prison term the law allows, for example, may be due in part to her decency and fairmindedness, which I take to be moral properties if any are. But do moral features of the action or institution being judged ever play an explanatory role? Here is an example in which they appear to. An interesting historical question is why vigorous and reasonably wide-spread moral opposition to slavery arose for the first time in the eighteenth and nineteenth centuries, even though slavery was a very old institution; and why this opposition arose primarily in Britain, France, and in French- and English-speaking North America, even though slavery existed throughout the New World.[15] There is a standard answer to this question. It is that chattel slavery in British and French America, and then in the United States, was much *worse* than previous forms of slavery, and much worse than slavery in Latin America. This is, I should add, a controversial explanation. But as is often the case with historical explanations, its propo-nents do not claim it is the whole story, and many of its opponents grant that there may be some truth in these comparisons, and that they may after all form a small part of a larger expla-nation.[16] This latter concession is all I require for my example. Equally good for my purpose would be the more limited thesis which explains the growth of antislavery sentiment in the United States, between the Revolution and the Civil War, in part by saying that slavery in the United States became a more oppressive institution during that time. The appeal in these standard explana-tions is straightforwardly to moral facts.

What is supposed to be wrong with all these explanations? Harman says that assumptions about moral facts seem "completely irrelevant" in explaining moral observations and moral beliefs (p. 7), but on its more natural reading that claim seems pretty obviously mistaken about these examples. For it is natural to think that if a particular assumption is completely irrelevant to the explanation of a certain fact, then that fact would have obtained, and we could have explained it just as well, even if the assumption had been false.[17] But I do not believe that Hitler would have done all he did if he had not been morally depraved, nor, on the assump-tion that he was not depraved, can I think of any plausible explanation for his doing those things. Nor is it plausible that we would all have believed he was morally depraved even if he hadn't been. Granted, there is a tendency for writers who do not attach much weight to fascism as a social movement to want to blame its evils on a single maniacal leader, so perhaps some of them would have painted Hitler as a moral monster even if he had not been one. But this is only a tendency, and one for which many people know how to discount, so I doubt that our moral belief really is overdetermined in this way. Nor, similarly, do I believe that Woodworth's actions were over-determined, so that he would have done just as he did even if he had been a more admirable person. I suppose one could have doubts about DeVoto's objectivity and reliability; it is obvious he dislikes Woodworth, so perhaps he would have thought him a moral loss and convinced his readers of this no matter what the man was really like. But it is more plausible that the dislike is mostly based on the same evidence that supports DeVoto's moral view of him, and that very different evidence, at any rate, would have produced a different verdict. If so, then Woodworth's moral character is part of the explanation of DeVoto's belief about his moral character.

It is more plausible of course that serious moral opposition to slavery would have emerged

in Britain, France, and the United States even if slavery hadn't been worse in the modern period than before, and worse in the United States than in Latin America, and that the American anti-slavery movement would have grown even if slavery had not become more oppressive as the nineteenth century progressed. But that is because these moral facts are offered as at best a partial explanation of these developments in moral opinion. And if they really *are* part of the explanation, as seems plausible, then it is also plausible that whatever effect they produced was not entirely overdetermined; that, for example, the growth of the antislavery movement in the United States would at least have been somewhat slower if slavery had been and remained less bad an institution. Here again it hardly seems "completely irrelevant" to the explanation whether or not these moral facts obtained.

It is more puzzling, I grant, to consider Harman's own example in which you see the children igniting a cat and react immediately with the thought that this is wrong. Is it true, as Harman claims, that the assumption that the children are really doing something wrong is "totally irrelevant" to any reasonable explanation of your making that judgment? Would you, for example, have reacted in just the same way, with the thought that the action is wrong, even if what they were doing *hadn't* been wrong, and could we explain your reaction equally well on this assumption? Now, there is more than one way to understand this counterfactual question, and I shall return below to a reading of it that might appear favorable to Harman's view. What I wish to point out for now is merely that there is a natural way of taking it, parallel to the way in which I have been understanding similar counterfactual questions about my own examples, on which the answer to it has to be simply: it depends. For to answer the question, I take it,[18] we must consider a situation in which what the children are doing is not wrong, but which is otherwise as much like the actual situation as possible, and then decide what your reaction

would be in that situation. But since what makes their action wrong, what its wrongness *consists* in, is presumably something like its being an act of gratuitous cruelty (or, perhaps we should add, of intense cruelty, and to a helpless victim), to imagine them not doing something wrong we are going to have to imagine their action different in this respect. More cautiously and more generally, if what they are actually doing is wrong, and if moral properties are, as many writers have held, supervenient on natural ones,[19] then in order to imagine them not doing something wrong we are going to have to suppose their action different from the actual one in some of its natural features as well. So our question becomes: Even if the children had been doing something else, something just different enough not to be wrong, would you have taken them even so to be doing something wrong?

Surely there is no one answer to this question. It depends on a lot about you, including your moral views and how good you are at seeing at a glance what some children are doing. It probably depends also on a debatable moral issue; namely, just *how* different the children's action would have to be in order not to be wrong. (Is unkindness to animals, for example, also wrong?) I believe we can see how, in a case in which the answer was clearly affirmative, we might be tempted to agree with Harman that the wrongness of the action was no part of the explanation of your reaction. For suppose you are like this. You hate children. What you especially hate, moreover, is the sight of children enjoying themselves; so much so that whenever you see children having fun, you immediately assume they are up to no good. The more they seem to be enjoying themselves, furthermore, the readier you are to fasten on any pretext for thinking them engaged in real wickedness. Then it is true that even if the children had been engaged in some robust but innocent fun, you would have thought they were doing something wrong; and Harman is perhaps right[20] about you that the actual wrongness of the action you

see is irrelevant to your thinking it wrong. This is because your reaction is due to a feature of the action that coincides only very accidentally with the ones that make it wrong.[21] But, of course, and fortunately, many people aren't like this (nor does Harman argue that they are). It isn't true of them, in general, that if the children had been doing something similar, although different enough not to be wrong, they would still have thought the children were doing something wrong. And it isn't true either, therefore, that the wrongness of the action is irrelevant to the explanation of why they think it wrong.

Now, one might have the sense from my discussion of all these examples, but perhaps especially from my discussion of this last one, Harman's own, that I have perversely been refusing to understand his claim about the explanatory irrelevance of moral facts in the way he intends. And perhaps I have not been understanding it as he wishes. In any case, I agree, I have certainly not been understanding the crucial counterfactual question, of whether we would have drawn the same moral conclusion even if the moral facts had been different, in the way he must intend. But I am not being perverse. I believe, as I have said, that my way of taking the question is the more natural one. And, more importantly: although there is, I grant, a reading of that question on which it will always yield the answer Harman wants—namely, that a difference in the moral facts would *not* have made a difference in our judgment—I do not believe this reading can support his argument. I must now explain why.

It will help if I contrast my general approach with his. I am approaching questions about the justification of belief in the spirit of what Quine has called "epistemology naturalized."[22] I take this to mean that we have in general no a priori way of knowing which strategies for forming and refining our beliefs are likely to take us closer to the truth. The only way we have of proceeding is to assume the approximate truth of what seems to us the best overall theory we

already have of what we are like and what the world is like, and to decide in the light of *that* what strategies of research and reasoning are likely to be reliable in producing a more nearly true overall theory. One result of applying these procedures, in turn, is likely to be the refinement or perhaps even the abandonment of parts of the tentative theory with which we began.

I take Harman's approach, too, to be an instance of this one. He says we are justified in believing in those facts that we need to assume to explain why we observe what we do. But he does not think that our knowledge of this principle about justification is a priori. Furthermore, as he knows, we cannot decide whether one explanation is better than another without relying on beliefs we already have about the world. Is it really a better explanation of the vapor trail the physicist sees in the cloud chamber to suppose that a proton caused it, as Harman suggests in his example, rather than some other charged particle? Would there, for example, have been no vapor trail in the absence of that proton? There is obviously no hope of answering such questions without assuming at least the approximate truth of some quite far-reaching microphysical theory, and our knowledge of such theories is not a priori.

But my approach differs from Harman's in one crucial way. For among the beliefs in which I have enough confidence to rely on in evaluating explanations, at least at the outset, are some moral beliefs. And I have been relying on them in the following way.[23] Harman's thesis implies that the supposed moral fact of Hitler's being morally depraved is irrelevant to the explanation of Hitler's doing what he did. (For we may suppose that if it explains his doing what he did, it also helps explain, at greater remove, Harman's belief and mine in his moral depravity.) To assess this claim, we need to conceive a situation in which Hitler was *not* morally depraved and consider the question whether in that situation he would still have done what he did. My answer is that he would

not, and this answer relies on a (not very contro-versial) moral view: that in any world at all like the actual one, only a morally depraved person could have initiated a world war, ordered the "final solution," and done any number of other things Hitler did. That is why I believe that, if Hitler hadn't been morally depraved, he wouldn't have done those things, and hence that the fact of his moral depravity is relevant to an explanation of what he did.

Harman, however, cannot want us to rely on any such moral views in answering this counter-factual question. This comes out most clearly if we return to his example of the children igniting the cat. He claims that the wrongness of this act is irrelevant to an explanation of your thinking it wrong, that you would have *thought* it wrong even if it wasn't. My reply was that in order for the action not to be wrong it would have had to lack the feature of deliberate, intense, pointless cruelty, and that if it had differed in this way you might very well *not* have thought it wrong. I also suggested a more cautious version of this reply: that since the action is in fact wrong, and since moral properties supervene on more basic natural ones, it would have had to be different in *some* further natural respect in order not to be wrong; and that we do not know whether if it had so differed you would still have thought it wrong. Both of these replies, again, rely on moral views, the latter merely on the view that there is *something* about the natural features of the action in Harman's example that makes it wrong, the former on a more specific view as to which of these features do this.

But Harman, it is fairly clear, intends for us *not* to rely on any such moral views in evaluating his counterfactual claim. His claim is not that if the action had not been one of deliberate cruelty (or had otherwise differed in whatever way would be required to remove its wrongness), you would still have thought it wrong. It is, instead, that if the action were one of deliberate, point-less cruelty, but this *did not make it wrong*, you would still have thought it was wrong. And to

return to the example of Hitler's moral char-acter, the counterfactual claim that Harman will need in order to defend a comparable conclu-sion about that case is not that if Hitler had been, for example, humane and fairminded, free of nationalistic pride and racial hatred, he would still have done exactly as he did. It is, rather, that if Hitler's psychology, and anything else about his situation that could strike us as morally relevant, had been exactly as it in fact was, but this had *not constituted moral depravity*, he would still have done exactly what he did.

Now the antecedents of these two condi-tionals are puzzling. For one thing, both are, I believe, necessarily false. I am fairly confident, for example, that Hitler really was morally depraved;[24] and since I also accept the view that moral features supervene on more basic natural properties,[25] I take this to imply that there is no possible world in which Hitler has just the personality he in fact did, in just the situation he was in, but is not morally depraved. Any attempt to describe such a situation, moreover, will surely run up against the limits of our moral concepts—what Harman calls our "moral sensibility"—and this is no accident. For what Harman is asking us to do, in general, is to consider cases in which absolutely *everything* about the nonmoral facts that could seem morally relevant to us, in light of whatever moral theory we accept and of the concepts required for understanding that theory, is held fixed, but in which the moral judgment that our theory yields about the case is nevertheless mistaken. So it is hardly surprising that, using that theory and those concepts, we should find it difficult to conceive in any detail what such a situation would be like. It is especially not surprising when the cases in question are as paradigmatic in light of the moral outlook we in fact have as is Harman's example or is, even more so, mine of Hitler's moral character. The only way we could be wrong about this latter case (assuming we have the nonmoral facts right) would be for our whole theory to be hopelessly wrong, so

radically mistaken that there could be no hope of straightening it out through adjustments from within.

But I do not believe we should conclude, as we might be tempted to,[26] that we therefore know a priori that this is not so, or that we cannot understand these conditionals that are crucial to Harman's argument. Rather, now that we have seen how we have to understand them, we should grant that they are true: that if our moral theory were somehow hopelessly mistaken, but all the nonmoral facts remained exactly as they in fact are, then, since we do *accept* that moral theory, we would still draw exactly the moral conclusions we in fact do. But we should deny that any skeptical conclusion follows from this. In particular, we should deny that it follows that moral facts play no role in explaining our moral judgments.

For consider what follows from the parallel claim about microphysics, in particular about Harman's example in which a physicist concludes from his observation of a vapor trail in a cloud chamber, and from the microphysical theory he accepts, that a free proton has passed through the chamber. The parallel claim, notice, is *not* just that if the proton had not been there the physicist would still have thought it was. This claim is implausible, for we may assume that the physicist's theory is generally correct, and it follows from that theory that if there hadn't been a proton there, then there wouldn't have been a vapor trail. But in a perfectly similar way it is implausible that if Hitler hadn't been morally depraved we would still have thought he was: for we may assume that our moral theory also is at least roughly correct, and it follows from the most central features of that theory that if Hitler hadn't been morally depraved, he wouldn't have done what he did. The *parallel* claim about the microphysical example is, instead, that if there hadn't been a proton there, but there *had* been a vapor trail, the physicist would still have concluded that a proton was present. More precisely, to maintain

a perfect parallel with Harman's claims about the moral cases, the antecedent must specify that although no proton is present, absolutely *all* the non-microphysical facts that the physicist, in light of his theory, might take to be relevant to the question of whether or not a proton is present, are exactly as in the actual case. (These macrophysical facts, as we may for convenience call them, surely include everything one would normally think of as an observable fact.) Of course, we shall be unable to imagine this without imagining that the physicist's theory is pretty badly mistaken;[27] but I believe we should grant that, if the physicist's theory were somehow this badly mistaken, but all the macrophysical facts (including all the observable facts) were held fixed, then the physicist, since he does accept that theory, would still draw all the same conclusions that he actually does. That is, this conditional claim, like Harman's parallel claim about the moral cases, is true.

But no skeptical conclusions follow; nor can Harman, since he does not intend to be a skeptic about physics, think that they do. It does not follow, in the first place, that we have any reason to think the physicist's theory *is* generally mistaken. Nor does it follow, furthermore, that the hypothesis that a proton really did pass through the cloud chamber is not part of a good explanation of the vapor trail, and hence of the physicist's thinking this has happened. This looks like a reasonable explanation, of course, only on the assumption that the physicist's theory is at least roughly true, for it is this theory that tells us, for example, what happens when charged particles pass through a supersaturated atmosphere, what other causes (if any) there might be for a similar phenomenon, and so on. But, as I say, we have not been provided with any reason for not trusting the theory to this extent.

Similarly, I conclude, we should draw no skeptical conclusions from Harman's claims about the moral cases. It is true that if our moral theory were seriously mistaken, but we still believed it, and the nonmoral facts were held

fixed, we would still make just the moral judgments we do. But this fact by itself provides us with no reason for thinking that our moral theory is generally mistaken. Nor, again, does it imply that the fact of Hitler's really having been morally depraved forms no part of a good explanation of his doing what he did and hence, at greater remove, of our thinking him depraved. This explanation will appear reasonable, of course, only on the assumption that our accepted moral theory is at least roughly correct, for it is this theory that assures us that only a depraved person could have thought, felt, and acted as Hitler did. But, as I say, Harman's argument has provided us with no reason for not trusting our moral views to this extent, and hence with no reason for doubting that it is sometimes moral facts that explain our moral judgments.

I conclude with three comments about my argument.

(1) I have tried to show that Harman's claim—that we would have held the particular moral beliefs we do even if those beliefs were untrue—admits of two readings, one of which makes it implausible, and the other of which reduces it to an application of a general skeptical strategy, a strategy which could as easily be used to produce doubt about microphysical as about moral facts. The general strategy is this. Consider any conclusion C we arrive at by relying both on some distinguishable "theory" T and on some body of evidence not being challenged, and ask whether we would have believed C even if it had been false. The plausible answer, if we are allowed to rely on T, will often be no: for if C had been false, then (according to T) the evidence would have had to be different, and in that case we wouldn't have believed C. (I have illustrated the plausibility of this sort of reply for all my moral examples, as well as for the microphysical one.) But the skeptic of course intends us *not* to rely on T in this way, and so rephrases the question: Would we have believed C even if it were false but all the evidence had been exactly as it in fact was? Now the answer has to be yes; and the

skeptic concludes that C is doubtful. (It should be obvious how to extend this strategy to belief in other minds, or in an external world.) I am of course not convinced: I do not think answers to the rephrased question show anything interesting about what we know or justifiably believe. But it is enough for my purposes here that no such *general* skeptical strategy could pretend to reveal any problems peculiar to belief in *moral* facts.

(2) My conclusion about Harman's argument, although it is not exactly the same as, is nevertheless similar to and very much in the spirit of the Duhemian point I invoked earlier against verificationism. There the question was whether typical moral assertions have testable implications, and the answer was that they do, so long as you include additional moral assumptions of the right sort among the background theories on which you rely in evaluating these assertions. Harman's more important question is whether we should ever regard moral facts as relevant to the explanation of nonmoral facts, and in particular of our having the moral beliefs we do. But the answer, again, is that we should, so long as we are willing to hold the right sorts of *other* moral assumptions fixed in answering counterfactual questions. Neither answer shows morality to be on any shakier ground than, say, physics, for typical microphysical hypotheses, too, have testable implications, and appear relevant to explanations, only if we are willing to assume at least the approximate truth of an elaborate microphysical theory and to hold this assumption fixed in answering counterfactual questions.

(3) Of course, this picture of how explanations depend on background theories, and moral explanations in particular on moral background theories, does show why someone already tempted toward moral skepticism on other grounds (such as those I mentioned at the beginning of this essay) might find Harman's claim about moral explanations plausible. To the extent that you already have pervasive doubts

about moral theories, you will also find moral facts nonexplanatory. So I grant that Harman has located a natural symptom of moral skepticism; but I am sure he has neither traced this skepticism to its roots nor provided any independent argument for it. His claim (p. 22) that we do not in fact cite moral facts in explanation of moral beliefs and observations cannot provide such an argument, for that claim is false. So, too, is the claim that assumptions about moral facts seem irrelevant to such explanations, for many do not. The claim that we *should* not rely on such assumptions because they *are* irrelevant, on the other hand, unless it is supported by some independent argument for moral skepticism, will just be question-begging: for the principal test of whether they are relevant, in any situation in which it appears they might be, is a counterfactual question about what would have happened if the moral fact had not obtained, and how we answer that question depends precisely upon whether we *do* rely on moral assumptions in answering it.

My own view I stated at the outset: that the only argument for moral skepticism with any independent weight is the argument from the difficulty of settling disputed moral questions. I have shown that anyone who finds Harman's claim about moral explanations plausible must already have been tempted toward skepticism by some other considerations, and I suspect that the other considerations will typically be the ones I sketched. So that is where discussion should focus. I also suggested that those considerations may provide less support for moral skepticism than is sometimes supposed, but I must reserve a thorough defense of that thesis for another occasion.[28]

Notes

1 As, for example, in Alan Gewirth, "Positive 'Ethics' and Normative 'Science' ", *The Philosophical Review* 69 (1960), pp. 311–30, in which there are some useful remarks about the first of them.

2 J. L. Mackie, *Ethics: Inventing Right and Wrong* (Harmondsworth, England: Penguin, 1977), pp. 38–42.

3 Gilbert Harman, *The Nature of Morality: An Introduction to Ethics* (New York: Oxford University Press, 1977), pp. vii, viii. Parenthetical page references are to this work.

4 Harman's title for the entire first section of his book.

5 In the longer article of which this is an abridgement.

6 This point is generally credited to Pierre Duhem; see *The Aim and Structure of Physical Theory*, trans. Philip P. Wiener (Princeton, NJ: Princeton University Press, 1954). It is a prominent theme in the influential writings of W. V. O. Quine. For an especially clear application of it, see Hilary Putnam, "The 'Corroboration' of Theories," in *Mathematics, Matter and Method: Philosophical Papers, Volume I*, second ed. (Cambridge: Cambridge University Press, 1977), pp. 250–69.

7 See note 5.

8 Harman is careful always to say only that moral beliefs *appear* to play no such role, and since he eventually concludes that there *are* moral facts (p. 132), this caution may be more than stylistic. I shall argue that this more cautious claim, too, is mistaken (indeed, that is my central thesis). But to avoid issues about Harman's intent, I shall simply mean by "Harman's argument" the skeptical argument of his first two chapters, whether or not he means to endorse all of it. This argument surely deserves discussion in its own right in either case, especially since Harman never explains what is wrong with it.

9 He asks: "Can moral principles be tested in the same way [as scientific hypotheses can], out in the world? You can observe someone do something, but can you ever perceive the rightness or wrongness of what he does?" (p. 4).

10 The other is that Harman appears to use "observe" (and "perceive" and "see") in a surprising way. One would normally take observing (or perceiving, or seeing) something to involve knowing it was the case. But Harman apparently takes an observation to be *any* opinion arrived at as "a direct result of perception" (p. 5) or, at any rate (see next footnote), "immediately and without

conscious reasoning" (p. 7). This means that observations need not even be true, much less known to be true. A consequence is that the existence of moral observations, in Harman's sense, would not be sufficient to show that there is moral knowledge, although this *would* be sufficient if "observe" were being used in a more standard sense. What I argue in the text is that the existence of moral observations (in either Harman's or the standard sense) is not *necessary* for showing that there is moral knowledge, either.

11 This sort of case does not meet Harman's characterization of an observation as an opinion that is "a direct result of perception" (p. 5), but he is surely right that moral facts would be as well vindicated if they were needed to explain our drawing conclusions about hypothetical cases as they would be if they were needed to explain observations in the narrower sense. To be sure, Harman is still confining his attention to cases in which we draw the moral conclusion from our thought experiment "immediately and without conscious reasoning" (p. 7), and it is no doubt the existence of such cases that gives purchase to talk of a "moral sense." But this feature, again, can hardly matter to the argument: would belief in moral facts be less justified if they were needed only to explain the instances in which we draw the moral conclusion *slowly*? Nor can it make any difference for that matter whether the case we are reflecting on is hypothetical: so my example in which we, quickly or slowly, draw a moral conclusion about Hitler from what we know of him, is surely relevant.

12 In the longer paper from which this one is abridged. The salient point is that there are two very *different* reasons one might have for thinking that no reference to moral facts is needed in the explanation of moral beliefs. One—Harman's reason, and my target in this essay—is that no moral explanations even *seem* plausible, that reference to moral facts always strikes us as "completely irrelevant" to the explanation of moral beliefs. This claim, if true, would tend to support moral skepticism. The other, which might appeal to a "reductive" naturalist in ethics, is that any moral explanations that *do* seem plausible can be paraphrased without explanatory loss in entirely

nonmoral terms. I doubt this view, too, and I argue in the longer version of this paper that no ethical naturalist need hold it. But anyone tempted by it should note that it is anyway no version of moral skepticism: for what it says is that we know so *much* about ethics that we are always able to say, in entirely nonmoral terms, exactly which natural properties the moral terms in any plausible moral explanations refer to—that's why the moral expressions are dispensable. These two reasons should not be confused with one another.

13 It is surprising that Harman does not mention the obvious intermediate possibility, which would occur to any instrumentalist: to cite the physicist's psychological set *and* the vapor trail, but say nothing about protons or other unobservables. It is *this* explanation, as I emphasize below, that is most closely parallel to an explanation of beliefs about an external world in terms of sensory experience and psychological makeup, or of moral beliefs in terms of nonmoral facts together with our "moral sensibility."

14 Bernard DeVoto, *The Year of Decision: 1846* (Boston: Houghton Mifflin, 1942), p. 426; a quotation from the notebooks of Francis Parkman. The account of the entire rescue effort is on pp. 124–44.

15 What is being explained, of course, is not just why people came to think slavery wrong, but why people who were not themselves slaves or in danger of being enslaved came to think it so seriously wrong as to be intolerable. There is a much larger and longer history of people who thought it wrong but tolerable and an even longer one of people who appear not to have gotten past the thought that the world would be a better place without it. See David Brion Davis, *The Problem of Slavery in Western Culture* (Ithaca, NY: Cornell University Press, 1966).

16 For a version of what I am calling the standard view of slavery in the Americas, see Frank Tannenbaum, *Slave and Citizen* (New York: Alfred A. Knopf, 1947). For an argument against both halves of the standard view, see Davis, *The Problem of Slavery*, esp. pp. 60–61, 223–25, 262–63.

17 This counterfactual test requires qualification to be exactly right, but none of the plausible qualifications matters to my examples. See the longer version of this paper.

18 Following, informally, Stalnaker and Lewis on counterfactuals. See Robert Stalnaker, "A Theory of Conditionals," in Nicholas Rescher, ed., *Studies in Logical Theory*, APQ Monograph No. 2 (Oxford: Basil Blackwell, 1968); and David Lewis, *Counterfactuals* (Cambridge, MA: Harvard University Press, 1973).

19 What would be generally granted is just that if there are moral properties they supervene on natural properties. But, remember, we are assuming for the sake of argument that there are.

I think moral properties *are* natural properties; and from this view it of course follows trivially that they supervene on natural properties: that, necessarily, nothing could differ in its moral properties without differing in some natural respect. But I also accept the more interesting thesis usually intended by the claim about supervenience—that there are more basic natural features such that, necessarily, once they are fixed, so are the moral properties. (In supervening on more basic natural facts of some sort, moral facts are like most natural facts. Social facts like unemployment, for example, supervene on complex histories of many individuals and their relations; and facts about the existence and properties of macroscopic physical objects—colliding billiard balls, say—clearly supervene on the microphysical constitution of the situations that include them.)

20 Not *certainly* right, because there is still the possibility that your reaction is to some extent overdetermined, and is to be explained partly by your sympathy for the cat and your dislike of cruelty, as well as by your hatred for children (although this last alone would have been sufficient to produce it).

We could of course rule out this possibility by making you an even less attractive character, indifferent to the suffering of animals and not offended by cruelty. But it may then be hard to imagine that such a person (whom I shall cease calling "you") could retain enough of a grip on moral thought for us to be willing to say he thought the action *wrong*, as opposed to saying that he merely pretended to do so. This difficulty is perhaps not insuperable, but it is revealing. Harman says that the actual wrongness of the action is "completely irrelevant" to the explanation of the observer's reaction. Notice that what is in fact true, however, is that it is *very hard* to imagine someone who reacts in the way Harman describes, but whose reaction is not due, at least in part, to the actual wrongness of the action.

21 Perhaps deliberate cruelty is worse the more one enjoys it (a standard counterexample to hedonism). If so, the fact that the children are enjoying themselves makes their action worse, but presumably isn't what makes it wrong to begin with.

22 W. V. O. Quine, "Epistemology Naturalized," in *Ontological Relativity and Other Essays* (New York: Columbia University Press, 1969), pp. 69–90. In the same volume, see also "Natural Kinds," pp. 114–38.

23 Harman of course allows us to assume the moral facts whose explanatory relevance is being assessed: that Hitler was depraved, or that what the children in his example are doing is wrong. But I have been assuming something more—something about what depravity *is*, and about what *makes* the children's action wrong. (At a minimum, in the more cautious version of my argument, I have been assuming that *something* about its more basic features makes it wrong, so that it could not have differed in its moral quality without differing in those other features as well.)

24 And anyway, remember, this is the sort of fact Harman allows us to assume in order to see whether, if we assume it, it will look explanatory.

25 It is about here that I have several times encountered the objection: but surely *supervenient* properties aren't needed to explain anything. It is a little hard, however, to see just what this objection is supposed to come to. If it includes endorsement of the conditional I here attribute to Harman, then I believe the remainder of my discussion is an adequate reply to it. If it is the claim that, because moral properties are supervenient, we can always exploit the insights in any moral explanations, however plausible, without resort to moral *language*, then I have already dealt with it in my discussion of reductionism (see note 10, above): the claim is probably false, but even if it is true it is no support for Harman's view, which is not that moral explanations are plausible but reducible, but that they are totally implausible. And doubts about the causal efficacy of supervenient facts seem misplaced in any case, as attention to my earlier examples (note 17) illustrates. High

unemployment causes widespread hardship, and can also bring down the rate of inflation. The masses and velocities and two colliding billiard balls causally influence the subsequent trajectories of the two balls. There is no doubt some sense in which these facts are causally efficacious *in virtue of* the way they supervene on—that is, are constituted out of, or causally realized by—more basic facts, but this hardly shows them inefficacious. (Nor does Harman appear to think it does: for his *favored* explanation of your moral belief about the burning cat, recall, appeals to psychological facts [about your moral sensibility], a biological fact [that it's a cat], and macrophysical facts [that it's on fire]—supervenient facts all, on his physicalist view and mine.) If anyone does hold to a general suspicion of causation by supervenient facts and properties, however, as Jaegwon Kim appears to (see "Causality, Identity, and Supervenience in the Mind-Body Problem," *Midwest Studies in Philosophy* 4 [1979], pp. 31–49), it is enough to note that this suspicion cannot diagnose any special difficulty with *moral* explanations, any distinctive "problem with ethics." The "problem," arguably, will be with every discipline but fundamental physics.

26 And as I take it Philippa Foot, for example, is still prepared to do, at least about paradigmatic cases. See her *Moral Relativism* (Lawrence: The University of Kansas, 1978).

27 If we imagine the physicist *regularly* mistaken in this way, moreover, we will have to imagine his theory not just mistaken but hopelessly so. And we can easily reproduce the other notable feature of Harman's claims about the moral cases, that what we are imagining is *necessarily* false, if we suppose that one of the physicist's (or better, chemist's) conclusions is about the microstructure of some common substance, such as water. For I agree with Saul Kripke that whatever microstructure water has is essential to it, that it has this structure in every possible world in which it exists (Saul Kripke, *Naming and Necessity* [Cambridge, MA: Harvard

University Press, 1980]). If we are right (as we have every reason to suppose) in thinking that water is actually H_2O, therefore, the conditional, "If water were not H_2O, but all the observable, macrophysical facts were just as they actually are, chemists would still have come to *think* it was H_2O," has a necessarily false antecedent; just as, if we are right (as we also have good reason to suppose) in thinking that Hitler was actually morally depraved, the conditional, "If Hitler were just as he was in all natural respects, but not morally depraved, we would still have *thought* he was depraved," has a necessarily false antecedent. Of course, I am not suggesting that in either case our knowledge that the antecedent is false is a priori.

These counterfactuals, because of their impossible antecedents, will have to be interpreted over worlds that are (at best) only "epistemically" possible; and, as Richard Boyd has pointed out to me, this helps to explain why anyone who accepts a causal theory of knowledge (or any theory according to which the justification of our belief depends on what explains our holding them) will find their truth irrelevant to the question of how much we know, either in chemistry or in morals. For although there certainly are counterfactuals that are relevant to questions about what causes what (and, hence, about what explains what), these have to be counterfactuals about real possibilities, not merely epistemic ones.

28 This essay has benefited from helpful discussion of earlier versions read at the University of Virginia, Cornell University, Franklin and Marshall College, Wayne State University, and the University of Michigan. I have been aided by a useful correspondence with Gilbert Harman; and I am grateful also for specific comments from Richard Boyd, David Brink, David Copp, Stephen Darwall, Terence Irwin, Norman Kretzmann, Ronald Nash, Peter Railton, Bruce Russell, Sydney Shoemaker, and Judith Slein.

Chapter 18

J. L. Mackie

THE SUBJECTIVITY OF VALUES

1. Moral scepticism

THERE ARE no objective values. This is a bald statement of the thesis of this chapter, but before arguing for it I shall try to clarify and restrict it in ways that may meet some objections and prevent some misunderstanding.

The statement of this thesis is liable to provoke one of three very different reactions. Some will think it not merely false but pernicious; they will see it as a threat to morality and to everything else that is worthwhile, and they will find the presenting of such a thesis in what purports to be a book on ethics paradoxical or even outrageous. Others will regard it as a trivial truth, almost too obvious to be worth mentioning, and certainly too plain to be worth much argument. Others again will say that it is meaningless or empty, that no real issue is raised by the question whether values are or are not part of the fabric of the world. But, precisely because there can be these three different reactions, much more needs to be said.

The claim that values are not objective, are not part of the fabric of the world, is meant to include not only moral goodness, which might be most naturally equated with moral value, but also other things that could be more loosely called moral values or disvalues—rightness or wrongness, duty, obligation, an action's being rotten and contemptible, and so on. It also includes non-moral values, notably aesthetic ones, beauty and various kinds of artistic merit. I shall not discuss these explicitly, but clearly much the same considerations apply to aesthetic and to moral values, and there would be at least some initial implausibility in a view that gave the one a different status from the other.

Since it is with moral values that I am primarily concerned, the view I am adopting may be called moral scepticism. But this name is likely to be misunderstood: 'moral scepticism' might also be used as a name for either of two first order views, or perhaps for an incoherent mixture of the two. A moral sceptic might be the sort of person who says 'All this talk of morality is tripe,' who rejects morality and will take no notice of it. Such a person may be literally rejecting all moral judgements; he is more likely to be making moral judgements of his own, expressing a positive moral condemnation of all that conventionally passes for morality; or he may be confusing these two logically incompatible views, and saying that he rejects all morality, while he is in fact rejecting only a particular morality that is current in the society in which he has grown up. But I am not at present concerned with the merits or faults of such a position. These are first order moral views, positive or negative: the person who adopts either of them is taking a certain practical, normative, stand. By contrast, what I am discussing is a second order view, a view about the status of moral values and the nature of moral valuing,

about where and how they fit into the world. These first and second order views are not merely distinct but completely independent: one could be a second order moral sceptic without being a first order one, or again the other way round. A man could hold strong moral views, and indeed ones whose content was thoroughly conventional, while believing that they were simply attitudes and policies with regard to conduct that he and other people held. Conversely, a man could reject all established morality while believing it to be an objective truth that it was evil or corrupt.

With another sort of misunderstanding moral scepticism would seem not so much pernicious as absurd. How could anyone deny that there is a difference between a kind action and a cruel one, or that a coward and a brave man behave differently in the face of danger? Of course, this is undeniable; but it is not to the point. The kinds of behaviour to which moral values and disvalues are ascribed are indeed part of the furniture of the world, and so are the natural, descriptive, differences between them; but not, perhaps, their differences in value. It is a hard fact that cruel actions differ from kind ones, and hence that we can learn, as in fact we all do, to distinguish them fairly well in practice, and to use the words 'cruel' and 'kind' with fairly clear descriptive meanings; but is it an equally hard fact that actions which are cruel in such a descriptive sense are to be condemned? The present issue is with regard to the objectivity specifically of value, not with regard to the objectivity of those natural, factual, differences on the basis of which differing values are assigned.

2. Subjectivism

Another name often used, as an alternative to 'moral scepticism', for the view I am discussing is 'subjectivism'. But this too has more than one meaning. Moral subjectivism too could be a first order, normative, view, namely that everyone

really ought to do whatever he thinks he should. This plainly is a (systematic) first order view; on examination it soon ceases to be plausible but that is beside the point, for it is quite independent of the second order thesis at present under consideration. What is more confusing is that different second order views compete for the name 'subjectivism'. Several of these are doctrines about the meaning of moral terms and moral statements. What is often called moral subjectivism is the doctrine that, for example, 'This action is right' *means* 'I approve of this action', or more generally that moral judgements are equivalent to reports of the speaker's own feelings or attitudes. But the view I am now discussing is to be distinguished in two vital respects from any such doctrine as this. First, what I have called moral scepticism is a negative doctrine, not a positive one: it says what there isn't, not what there is. It says that there do not exist entities or relations of a certain kind, objective values or requirements, which many people have believed to exist. Of course, the moral sceptic cannot leave it at that. If his position is to be at all plausible, he must give some account of how other people have fallen into what he regards as an error, and this account will have to include some positive suggestions about how values fail to be objective, about what has been mistaken for, or has led to false beliefs about, objective values. But this will be a development of his theory, not its core: its core is the negation. Secondly, what I have called moral scepticism is an ontological thesis, not a linguistic or conceptual one. It is not, like the other doctrine often called moral subjectivism, a view about the meanings of moral statements. . . .

It is true that those who have accepted the moral subjectivism which is the doctrine that moral judgements are equivalent to reports of the speaker's own feelings or attitudes have usually presupposed what I am calling moral scepticism. It is because they have assumed that there are no objective values, that they have looked elsewhere for an analysis of what moral

statements might mean, and have settled upon subjective reports. Indeed, if all our moral statements were such subjective reports, it would follow that, at least so far as we are aware, there are no objective moral values. If we were aware of them, we would say something about them. In this sense this sort of subjectivism entails moral scepticism. But the converse entailment does not hold. The denial that there are objective values does not commit one to any particular view about what moral statements mean, and certainly not to the view that they are equivalent to subjective reports. No doubt if moral values are not objective they are in some very broad sense subjective, and for this reason I would accept 'moral subjectivism' as an alternative name to 'moral scepticism'. But subjectivism in this broad sense must be distinguished from the specific doctrine about meaning referred to above. Neither name is altogether satisfactory: we simply have to guard against the (different) misinterpretations which each may suggest.

3. The multiplicity of second order questions

The distinctions drawn in the last two sections rest not only on the well-known and generally recognized difference between first and second order questions, but also on the more controversial claim that there are several kinds of second order moral questions. Those most often mentioned are questions about the meaning and use of ethical terms, or the analysis of ethical concepts. With these go questions about the logic of moral statements: there may be special patterns of moral argument, licensed, perhaps, by aspects of the meanings of moral terms—for example, it may be part of the meaning of moral statements that they are universalizable. But there are also ontological, as contrasted with linguistic or conceptual, questions about the nature and status of goodness or rightness or whatever it is that first order moral statements are distinctively about. These are questions of

factual rather than conceptual analysis: the problem of what goodness is cannot be settled conclusively or exhaustively by finding out what the word 'good' means, or what it is conventionally used to say or to do.

Recent philosophy, biased as it has been towards various kinds of linguistic inquiry, has tended to doubt this, but the distinction between conceptual and factual analysis in ethics can be supported by analogies with other areas. The question of what perception is, what goes on when someone perceives something, is not adequately answered by finding out what words like 'see' and 'hear' mean, or what someone is doing in saying 'I perceive . . .', by analysing, however fully and accurately, any established concept of perception. There is a still closer analogy with colours. Robert Boyle and John Locke called colours 'secondary qualities', meaning that colours as they occur in material things consist simply in patterns of arrangement and movement of minute particles on the surfaces of objects, which make them, as we would now say, reflect light of some frequencies better than others, and so enable these objects to produce colour sensations in us, but that colours as we see them do not literally belong to the surfaces of material things. Whether Boyle and Locke were right about this cannot be settled by finding out how we use colour words and what we mean in using them. Naive realism about colours might be a correct analysis not only of our pre-scientific colour concepts but also of the conventional meanings of colour words; and even of the meanings with which scientifically sophisticated people use them when they are off their guard, and yet it might not be a correct account of the status of colours.

Error could well result, then, from a failure to distinguish factual from conceptual analysis with regard to colours, from taking an account of the meanings of statements as a full account of what there is. There is a similar and in practice even greater risk of error in moral philosophy. There is another reason, too, why it would be a

mistake to concentrate second order ethical discussions on questions of meaning. The more work philosophers have done on meaning, both in ethics and elsewhere, the more complications have come to light. It is by now pretty plain that no simple account of the meanings of first order moral statements will be correct, will cover adequately even the standard, conventional, senses of the main moral terms; I think, none the less, that there is a relatively clear-cut issue about the objectivity of moral values which is in danger of being lost among the complications of meaning.

· · ·

5. Standards of evaluation

One way of stating the thesis that there are no objective values is to say that value statements cannot be either true or false. But this formulation, too, lends itself to misinterpretation. For there are certain kinds of value statements which undoubtedly can be true or false, even if, in the sense I intend, there are no objective values. Evaluations of many sorts are commonly made in relation to agreed and assumed standards. The classing of wool, the grading of apples, the awarding of prizes at sheepdog trials, flower shows, skating and diving championships, and even the marking of examination papers are carried out in relation to standards of quality or merit which are peculiar to each particular subject-matter or type of contest, which may be explicitly laid down but which, even if they are nowhere explicitly stated, are fairly well understood and agreed by those who are recognized as judges or experts in each particular field. Given any sufficiently determinate standards, it will be an objective issue, a matter of truth and falsehood, how well any particular specimen measures up to those standards. Comparative judgements in particular will be capable of truth and falsehood: it will be a factual question whether this sheepdog has performed better than that one.

The subjectivist about values, then, is not denying that there can be objective evaluations relative to standards, and these are as possible in the aesthetic and moral fields as in any of those just mentioned. More than this, there is an objective distinction which applies in many such fields, and yet would itself be regarded as a peculiarly moral one: the distinction between justice and injustice. In one important sense of the word it is a paradigm case of injustice if a court declares someone to be guilty of an offence of which it knows him to be innocent. More generally, a finding is unjust if it is at variance with what the relevant law and the facts together require, and particularly if it is known by the court to be so. More generally still, any award of marks, prizes, or the like is unjust if it is at variance with the agreed standards for the contest in question: if one diver's performance in fact measures up better to the accepted standards for diving than another's, it will be unjust if the latter is awarded higher marks or the prize. In this way the justice or injustice of decisions relative to standards can be a thoroughly objective matter, though there may still be a subjective element in the interpretation or application of standards. But the statement that a certain decision is thus just or unjust will not be objectively prescriptive: in so far as it can be simply true it leaves open the question whether there is an objective requirement to do what is just and to refrain from what is unjust, and equally leaves open the practical decision to act in either way.

Recognizing the objectivity of justice in relation to standards, and of evaluative judgements relative to standards, then, merely shifts the question of the objectivity of values back to the standards themselves. The subjectivist may try to make his point by insisting that there is no objective validity about the choice of standards. Yet he would clearly be wrong if he said that the choice of even the most basic standards in any field was completely arbitrary. The standards used in sheepdog trials clearly bear some relation to the work that sheepdogs are kept to do,

the standards for grading apples bear some relation to what people generally want in or like about apples, and so on. On the other hand, standards are not as a rule strictly validated by such purposes. The appropriateness of standards is neither fully determinate nor totally indeterminate in relation to independently specifiable aims or desires. But however determinate it is, the objective appropriateness of standards in relation to aims or desires is no more of a threat to the denial of objective values than is the objectivity of evaluation relative to standards. In fact it is logically no different from the objectivity of goodness relative to desires. Something may be called good simply in so far as it satisfies or is such as to satisfy a certain desire; but the objectivity of such relations of satisfaction does not constitute in our sense an objective value.

6. Hypothetical and categorical imperatives

We may make this issue clearer by referring to Kant's distinction between hypothetical and categorical imperatives, though what he called imperatives are more naturally expressed as 'ought'-statements than in the imperative mood. 'If you want X, do Y' (or 'You ought to do Y') will be a hypothetical imperative if it is based on the supposed fact that Y is, in the circumstances, the only (or the best) available means to X, that is, on a causal relation between Y and X. The reason for doing Y lies in its causal connection with the desired end, X; the oughtness is contingent upon the desire. But 'You ought to do Y' will be a categorical imperative if you ought to do Y irrespective of any such desire for any end to which Y would contribute, if the oughtness is not thus contingent upon any desire. But this distinction needs to be handled with some care. An 'ought'-statement is not in this sense hypothetical merely because it incorporates a conditional clause. 'If you promised to do Y, you ought to do Y' is not a hypothetical imperative merely on account of the stated if-clause; what is

meant may be either a hypothetical or a categorical imperative, depending upon the implied reason for keeping the supposed promise. If this rests upon some such further unstated conditional as 'If you want to be trusted another time', then it is a hypothetical imperative; if not, it is categorical. Even a desire of the agent's can figure in the antecedent of what, though conditional in grammatical form, is still in Kant's sense of a categorical imperative. 'If you are strongly attracted sexually to young children you ought not to go in for school teaching' is not, in virtue of what it explicitly says, a hypothetical imperative: the avoidance of school teaching is not being offered as a means to the satisfaction of the desires in question. Of course, it could still be a hypothetical imperative, if the implied reason were a prudential one; but it could also be a categorical imperative, a moral requirement where the reason for the recommended action (strictly, avoidance) does not rest upon that action's being a means to the satisfaction of any desire that the agent is supposed to have. Not every conditional ought-statement or command, then, is a hypothetical imperative; equally, not every non-conditional one is a categorical imperative. An appropriate if-clause may be left unstated. Indeed, a simple command in the imperative mood, say a parade-ground order, which might seem most literally to qualify for the title of a categorical imperative, will hardly ever be one in the sense we need here. The implied reason for complying with such an order will almost always be some desire of the person addressed, perhaps simply the desire to keep out of trouble. If so, such an apparently categorical order will be in our sense a hypothetical imperative. Again, an imperative remains hypothetical even if we change the 'if' to 'since': the fact that the desire for X is actually present does not alter the fact that the reason for doing Y is contingent upon the desire for X by way of Y's being a means to X. In Kant's own treatment, while imperatives of skill relate to desires which an agent may or may not have,

imperatives of prudence relate to the desire for happiness which, Kant assumes, everyone has. So construed, imperatives of prudence are no less hypothetical than imperatives of skill, no less contingent upon desires that the agent has at the time the imperatives are addressed to him. But if we think rather of a counsel of prudence as being related to the agent's future welfare, to the satisfaction of desires that he does not yet have—not even to a present desire that his future desires should be satisfied—then a counsel of prudence is a categorical imperative, different indeed from a moral one, but analogous to it.

A categorical imperative, then, would express a reason for acting which was unconditional in the sense of not being contingent upon any present desire of the agent to whose satisfaction the recommended action would contribute as a means—or more directly: 'You ought to dance', if the implied reason is just that you want to dance or like dancing, is still a hypothetical imperative. Now Kant himself held that moral judgements are categorical imperatives, or perhaps are all applications of one categorical imperative, and it can plausibly be maintained at least that many moral judgements contain a categorically imperative element. So far as ethics is concerned, my thesis that there are no objective values is specifically the denial that any such categorically imperative element is objectively valid. The objective values which I am denying would be action-directing absolutely, not contingently (in the way indicated) upon the agent's desires and inclinations.

Another way of trying to clarify this issue is to refer to moral reasoning or moral arguments. In practice, of course, such reasoning is seldom fully explicit: but let us suppose that we could make explicit the reasoning that supports some evaluative conclusion, where this conclusion has some action-guiding force that is not contingent upon desires or purposes or chosen ends. Then what I am saying is that somewhere in the input to this argument—perhaps in one or more of the premisses, perhaps in some part of the form of the argument—there will be something which cannot be objectively validated—some premiss which is not capable of being simply true, or some form of argument which is not valid as a matter of general logic, whose authority or cogency is not objective, but is constituted by our choosing or deciding to think in a certain way.

7. The claim to objectivity

If I have succeeded in specifying precisely enough the moral values whose objectivity I am denying, my thesis may now seem to be trivially true. Of course, some will say, valuing, preferring, choosing, recommending, rejecting, condemning, and so on, are human activities, and there is no need to look for values that are prior to and logically independent of all such activities. There may be widespread agreement in valuing, and particular value-judgements are not in general arbitrary or isolated: they typically cohere with others, or can be criticized if they do not, reasons can be given for them, and so on: but if all that the subjectivist is maintaining is that desires, ends, purposes, and the like figure somewhere in the system of reasons, and that no ends or purposes are objective as opposed to being merely intersubjective, then this may be conceded without much fuss.

But I do not think that this should be conceded so easily. As I have said, the main tradition of European moral philosophy includes the contrary claim, that there are objective values of just the sort I have denied. I have referred already to Plato, Kant, and Sidgwick [see original reading]. Kant in particular holds that the categorical imperative is not only categorical and imperative but objectively so: though a rational being gives the moral law to himself, the law that he thus makes is determinate and necessary. Aristotle begins the *Nicomachean Ethics* by saying that the good is that at which all things aim, and that ethics is part of a science which he calls 'politics', whose goal is not knowledge but

practice; yet he does not doubt that there can be *knowledge* of what is the good for man, nor, once he has identified this as well-being or happiness, *eudaimonia*, that it can be known, rationally determined, in what happiness consists; and it is plain that he thinks that this happiness is intrinsically desirable, not good simply because it is desired. The rationalist Samuel Clarke holds that

> these eternal and necessary differences of things make it *fit and reasonable* for creatures so to act ... even separate from the consideration of these rules being the *positive will or command of God*; and also antecedent to any respect or regard, expectation, or apprehension, of any *particular private and personal advantage or disadvantage, reward or punishment*, either present or future ...

Even the sentimentalist Hutcheson defines moral goodness as 'some quality apprehended in actions, which procures approbation ...', while saying that the moral sense by which we perceive virtue and vice has been given to us (by the Author of nature) to direct our actions. Hume indeed was on the other side, but he is still a witness to the dominance of the objectivist tradition, since he claims that when we 'see that the distinction of vice and virtue is not founded merely on the relations of objects, nor is perceiv'd by reason', this 'wou'd subvert all the vulgar systems of morality'. And Richard Price insists that right and wrong are 'real characters of actions', not 'qualities of our minds', and are perceived by the understanding; he criticizes the notion of moral sense on the ground that it would make virtue an affair of taste, and moral right and wrong 'nothing in the objects themselves'; he rejects Hutcheson's view because (perhaps mistakenly) he sees it as collapsing into Hume's.

But this objectivism about values is not only a feature of the philosophical tradition. It has also a firm basis in ordinary thought, and even in the meanings of moral terms. . . . The ordinary user

of moral language means to say something about whatever it is that he characterizes morally, for example a possible action, as it is in itself, or would be if it were realized, and not about, or even simply expressive of, his, or anyone else's, attitude or relation to it. But the something he wants to say is not purely descriptive, certainly not inert, but something that involves a call for action or for the refraining from action, and one that is absolute, not contingent upon any desire or preference or policy or choice, his own or anyone else's. Someone in a state of moral perplexity, wondering whether it would be wrong for him to engage, say, in research related to bacteriological warfare, wants to arrive at some judgement about this concrete case, his doing this work at this time in these actual circumstances; his relevant characteristics will be part of the subject of the judgement, but no relation between him and the proposed action will be part of the predicate. The question is not, for example, whether he really wants to do this work, whether it will satisfy or dissatisfy him, whether he will in the long run have a pro-attitude towards it, or even whether this is an action of a sort that he can happily and sincerely recommend in all relevantly similar cases. Nor is he even wondering just whether to recommend such action in all relevantly similar cases. He wants to know whether this course of action would be wrong in itself. Something like this is the everyday objectivist concept of which talk about non-natural qualities is a philosopher's reconstruction.

The prevalence of this tendency to objectify values—and not only moral ones—is confirmed by a pattern of thinking that we find in existentialists and those influenced by them. The denial of objective values can carry with it an extreme emotional reaction, a feeling that nothing matters at all, that life has lost its purpose. Of course this does not follow; the lack of objective values is not a good reason for abandoning subjective concern or for ceasing to want anything. But the abandonment of a belief in

objective values can cause, at least temporarily, a decay of subjective concern and sense of purpose. That it does so is evidence that the people in whom this reaction occurs have been tending to objectify their concerns and purposes, have been giving them a fictitious external authority. A claim to objectivity has been so strongly associated with their subjective concerns and purposes that the collapse of the former seems to undermine the latter as well.

This view, that conceptual analysis would reveal a claim to objectivity, is sometimes dramatically confirmed by philosophers who are officially on the other side. Bertrand Russell, for example, says that 'ethical propositions should be expressed in the optative mood, not in the indicative'; he defends himself effectively against the charge of inconsistency in both holding ultimate ethical valuations to be subjective and expressing emphatic opinions on ethical questions. Yet at the end he admits:

> Certainly there *seems* to be something more. Suppose, for example, that some one were to advocate the introduction of bull-fighting in this country. In opposing the proposal, I should *feel*, not only that I was expressing my desires, but that my desires in the matter are *right*, whatever that may mean. As a matter of argument, I can, I think, show that I am not guilty of any logical inconsistency in holding to the above interpretation of ethics and at the same time expressing strong ethical preferences. But in feeling I am not satisfied.

But he concludes, reasonably enough, with the remark: 'I can only say that, while my own opinions as to ethics do not satisfy me, other people's satisfy me still less.'

I conclude, then, that ordinary moral judgements include a claim to objectivity, an assumption that there are objective values in just the sense in which I am concerned to deny this. And I do not think it is going too far to say that this assumption has been incorporated in the basic,

conventional, meanings of moral terms. Any analysis of the meanings of moral terms which omits this claim to objective, intrinsic, prescriptivity is to that extent incomplete and this is true of any non-cognitive analysis, any naturalist one, and any combination of the two.

If second order ethics were confined, then, to linguistic and conceptual analysis, it ought to conclude that moral values at least are objective: that they are so is part of what our ordinary moral statements mean: the traditional moral concepts of the ordinary man as well as of the main line of western philosophers are concepts of objective value. But it is precisely for this reason that linguistic and conceptual analysis is not enough. The claim to objectivity, however ingrained in our language and thought, is not self-validating. It can and should be questioned. But the denial of objective values will have to be put forward not as the result of an analytic approach, but as an 'error theory', a theory that although most people in making moral judgements implicitly claim, among other things, to be pointing to something objectively prescriptive, these claims are all false. It is this that makes the name 'moral scepticism' appropriate.

But since this is an error theory, since it goes against assumptions ingrained in our thought and built into some of the ways in which language is used, since it conflicts with what is sometimes called common sense, it needs very solid support. It is not something we can accept lightly or casually and then quietly pass on. If we are to adopt this view, we must argue explicitly for it. Traditionally it has been supported by arguments of two main kinds, which I shall call the argument from relativity and the argument from queerness, but these can, as I shall show, be supplemented in several ways.

8. The argument from relativity

The argument from relativity has at its premiss the well-known variation in moral codes from one society to another and from one period to

another, and also the differences in moral beliefs between different groups and classes within a complex community. Such variation is in itself merely a truth of descriptive morality, a fact of anthropology which entails neither first order nor second order ethical views. Yet it may indirectly support second order subjectivism: radical differences between first order moral judgements make it difficult to treat those judgements as apprehensions of objective truths. But it is not the mere occurrence of disagreements that tells against the objectivity of values. Disagreement on questions in history or biology or cosmology does not show that there are no objective issues in these fields for investigators to disagree about. But such scientific disagreement results from speculative inferences or explanatory hypotheses based on inadequate evidence, and it is hardly plausible to interpret moral disagreement in the same way. Disagreement about moral codes seems to reflect people's adherence to and participation in different ways of life. The causal connection seems to be mainly that way round: it is that people approve of monogamy because they participate in a monogamous way of life rather than that they participate in a monogamous way of life because they approve of monogamy. Of course, the standards may be an idealization of the way of life from which they arise: the monogamy in which people participate may be less complete, less rigid, than that of which it leads them to approve. This is not to say that moral judgements are purely conventional. Of course there have been and are moral heretics and moral reformers, people who have turned against the established rules and practices of their own communities for moral reasons, and often for moral reasons that we would endorse. But this can usually be understood as the extension, in ways which, though new and unconventional, seemed to them to be required for consistency, of rules to which they already adhered as arising out of an existing way of life. In short, the argument from relativity has some force simply because the actual variations in the

moral codes are more readily explained by the hypothesis that they reflect ways of life than by the hypothesis that they express perceptions, most of them seriously inadequate and badly distorted, of objective values.

But there is a well-known counter to this argument from relativity, namely to say that the items for which objective validity is in the first place to be claimed are not specific moral rules or codes but very general basic principles which are recognized at least implicitly to some extent in all society—such principles as provide the foundations of what Sidgwick has called different methods of ethics: the principle of universalizability, perhaps, or the rule that one ought to conform to the specific rules of any way of life in which one takes part, from which one profits, and on which one relies, or some utilitarian principle of doing what tends, or seems likely, to promote the general happiness. It is easy to show that such general principles, married with differing concrete circumstances, different existing social patterns or different preferences, will beget different specific moral rules; and there is some plausibility in the claim that the specific rules thus generated will vary from community to community or from group to group in close agreement with the actual variations in accepted codes.

The argument from relativity can be only partly countered in this way. To take this line the moral objectivist has to say that it is only in these principles that the objective moral character attaches immediately to its descriptively specified ground or subject: other moral judgements are objectively valid or true, but only derivatively and contingently—if things had been otherwise, quite different sorts of actions would have been right. And despite the prominence in recent philosophical ethics of universalization, utilitarian principles, and the like, these are very far from constituting the whole of what is actually affirmed as basic in ordinary moral thought. Much of this is concerned rather with what Hare calls 'ideals' or, less kindly, 'fanaticism'. That is,

people judge that some things are good or right, and others are bad or wrong, not because—or at any rate not only because—they exemplify some general principle for which widespread implicit acceptance could be claimed, but because something about those things arouses certain responses immediately in them, though they would arouse radically and irresolvably different responses in others. 'Moral sense' or 'intuition' is an initially more plausible description of what supplies many of our basic moral judgements than 'reason'. With regard to all these starting points of moral thinking the argument from relativity remains in full force.

9. The argument from queerness

Even more important, however, and certainly more generally applicable, is the argument from queerness. This has two parts, one metaphysical, the other epistemological. If there were objective values, then they would be entities or qualities or relations of a very strange sort, utterly different from anything else in the universe. Correspondingly, if we were aware of them, it would have to be by some special faculty of moral perception, or intuition, utterly different from our ordinary ways of knowing everything else. These points were recognized by Moore when he spoke of non-natural qualities, and by the intuitionists in their talk about a 'faculty of moral intuition'. Intuitionism has long been out of favour, and it is indeed easy to point out its implausibilities. What is not so often stressed, but is more important, is that the central thesis of intuitionism is one to which any objectivist view of values is in the end committed: intuitionism merely makes unpalatably plain what other forms of objectivism wrap up. Of course the suggestion that moral judgements are made or moral problems solved by just sitting down and having an ethical intuition is a travesty of actual moral thinking. But, however complex the real process, it will require (if it is to yield authoritatively prescriptive conclusions) some

input of this distinctive sort, either premisses or forms of argument or both. When we ask the awkward question, how we can be aware of this authoritative prescriptivity, of the truth of these distinctively ethical premisses or of the cogency of this distinctively ethical pattern of reasoning, none of our ordinary accounts of sensory perception or introspection or the framing and confirming of explanatory hypotheses or inference or logical construction or conceptual analysis, or any combination of these, will provide a satisfactory answer; 'a special sort of intuition' is a lame answer, but it is the one to which the clearheaded objectivist is compelled to resort.

Indeed, the best move for the moral objectivist is not to evade this issue, but to look for companions in guilt. For example, Richard Price argues that it is not moral knowledge alone that such an empiricism as those of Locke and Hume is unable to account for, but also our knowledge and even our ideas of essence, number, identity, diversity, solidity, inertia, substance, the necessary existence and infinite extension of time and space, necessity and possibility in general, power, and causation. If the understanding, which Price defines as the faculty within us that discerns truth, is also a source of new simple ideas of so many other sorts, may it not also be a power of immediately perceiving right and wrong, which yet are real characters of action?

This is an important counter to the argument from queerness. The only adequate reply to it would be to show how, on empiricist foundations, we can construct an account of the ideas and beliefs and knowledge that we have of all these matters. I cannot even begin to do that here, though I have undertaken some parts of the task elsewhere. I can only state my belief that satisfactory accounts of most of these can be given in empirical terms. If some supposed metaphysical necessities or essences resist such treatment, then they too should be included, along with objective values, among the targets of the argument from queerness.

This queerness does not consist simply in the fact that ethical statements are 'unverifiable'. Although logical positivism with its verifiability theory of descriptive meaning gave an impetus to non-cognitive accounts of ethics, it is not only logical positivists but also empiricists of a much more liberal sort who should find objective values hard to accommodate. Indeed, I would not only reject the verifiability principle but also deny the conclusion commonly drawn from it, that moral judgements lack descriptive meaning. The assertion that there are objective values or intrinsically prescriptive entities or features of some kind, which ordinary moral judgements presuppose, is, I hold, not meaningless but false.

Plato's Forms give a dramatic picture of what objective values would have to be. The Form of the Good is such that knowledge of it provides the knower with both a direction and an overriding motive; something's being good both tells the person who knows this to pursue it and makes him pursue it. An objective good would be sought by anyone who was acquainted with it, not because of any contingent fact that this person, or every person, is so constituted that he desires this end, but just because the end has to-be-pursuedness somehow built into it. Similarly, if there were objective principles of right and wrong, any wrong (possible) course of action would have not-to-be-doneness somehow built into it. Or we should have something like Clarke's necessary relations of fitness between situations and actions, so that a situation would have a demand for such-and-such and action somehow built into it.

The need for an argument of this sort can be brought out by reflection on Hume's argument that 'reason'—in which at this stage he includes all sorts of knowing as well as reasoning—can never be an 'influencing motive of the will'. Someone might object that Hume has argued unfairly from the lack of influencing power (not contingent upon desires) in ordinary objects of knowledge and ordinary reasoning, and might maintain that values differ from natural objects precisely in their power, when known, automatically to influence the will. To this Hume could, and would need to, reply that this objection involves the postulating of value-entities or value-features of quite a different order from anything else with which we are acquainted, and of a corresponding faculty with which to detect them. That is, he would have to supplement his explicit argument with what I have called the argument from queerness.

Another way of bringing out this queerness is to ask, about anything that is supposed to have some objective moral quality, how this is linked with its natural features. What is the connection between the natural fact that an action is a piece of deliberate cruelty—say, causing pain just for fun—and the moral fact that it is wrong? It cannot be an entailment, a logical or semantic necessity. Yet it is not merely that the two features occur together. The wrongness must somehow be 'consequential' or 'supervenient'; it is wrong because it is a piece of deliberate cruelty. But just what *in the world* is signified by this 'because'? And how do we know the relation that it signifies, if this is something more than such actions being socially condemned, and condemned by us too, perhaps through our having absorbed attitudes from our social environment? It is not even sufficient to postulate a faculty which 'sees' the wrongness: something must be postulated which can see at once the natural features that constitute the cruelty, and the wrongness, and the mysterious consequential link between the two. Alternatively, the intuition required might be the perception that wrongness is a higher order property belonging to certain natural properties; but what is this belonging of properties to other properties, and how can we discern it? How much simpler and more comprehensible the situation would be if we could replace the moral quality with some sort of subjective response which could be causally related to the detection of the natural features on which the supposed quality is said to be consequential.

It may be thought that the argument from queerness is given an unfair start if we thus relate it to what are admittedly among the wilder products of philosophical fancy—Platonic Forms, non-natural qualities, self-evident relations of fitness, faculties of intuition, and the like. Is it equally forceful if applied to the terms in which everyday moral judgements are more likely to be expressed—though still, as has been argued in Section 7, with a claim to objectivity—'you must do this', 'you can't do that', 'obligation', 'unjust', 'rotten', 'disgraceful', 'mean', or talk about good reasons for or against possible actions? Admittedly not; but that is because the objective prescriptivity, the element a claim for whose authoritativeness is embedded in ordinary moral thought and language, is not yet isolated in these forms of speech, but is presented along with relations to desires and feelings, reasoning about the means to desired ends, interpersonal demands, the injustice which consists in the violation of what are in the context the accepted standards of merit, the psychological constituents of meanness, and so on. There is nothing queer about any of these, and under cover of them the claim for moral authority may pass unnoticed. But if I am right in arguing that it is ordinarily there, and is therefore very likely to be incorporated almost automatically in philosophical accounts of ethics which systematize our ordinary thought even in such apparently innocent terms as these, it needs to be examined, and for this purpose it needs to be isolated and exposed as it is by the less cautious philosophical reconstructions.

10. Patterns of objectification

Considerations of these kinds suggest that it is in the end less paradoxical to reject than to retain the common-sense belief in the objectivity of moral values, provided that we can explain how this belief, if it is false, has become established and is so resistant to criticisms. This proviso is not difficult to satisfy.

On a subjectivist view, the supposedly objective values will be based in fact upon attitudes which the person has who takes himself to be recognizing and responding to those values. If we admit what Hume calls the mind's 'propensity to spread itself on external objects', we can understand the supposed objectivity of moral qualities as arising from what we can call the projection or objectification of moral attitudes. This would be analogous to what is called the 'pathetic fallacy', the tendency to read our feelings into their objects. If a fungus, say, fills us with disgust, we may be inclined to ascribe to the fungus itself a non-natural quality of foulness. But in moral contexts there is more than this propensity at work. Moral attitudes themselves are at least partly social in origin: socially established—and socially necessary—patterns of behaviour put pressure on individuals, and each individual tends to internalize these pressures and to join in requiring these patterns of behaviour of himself and of others. The attitudes that are objectified into moral values have indeed an external source, though not the one assigned to them by the belief in their absolute authority. Moreover, there are motives that would support objectification. We need morality to regulate interpersonal relations, to control some of the ways in which people behave towards one another, often in opposition to contrary inclinations. We therefore want our moral judgements to be authoritative for other agents as well as for ourselves: objective validity would give them the authority required. Aesthetic values are logically in the same position as moral ones; much the same metaphysical and epistemological considerations apply to them. But aesthetic values are less strongly objectified than moral ones; their subjective status, and an 'error theory' with regard to such claims to objectivity as are incorporated in aesthetic judgements, will be more readily accepted, just because the motives for their objectification are less compelling.

But it would be misleading to think of the objectification of moral values as primarily the

projection of feelings, as in the pathetic fallacy. More important are wants and demands. As Hobbes says, 'whatsoever is the object of any man's Appetite or Desire, that is it, which he for his part called *Good*'; and certainly both the adjective 'good' and the noun 'goods' are used in non-moral contexts of things because they are such as to satisfy desires. We get the notion of something's being objectively good, or having intrinsic value, by reversing the direction of dependence here, by making the desire depend upon the goodness, instead of the goodness on the desire. And this is aided by the fact that the desired thing will indeed have features that make it desired, that enable it to arouse a desire or that make it such as to satisfy some desire that is already there. It is fairly easy to confuse the way in which a thing's desirability is indeed objective with its having in our sense objective value. The fact that the word 'good' serves as one of our main moral terms is a trace of this pattern of objectification.

Similarly related uses of words are covered by the distinction between hypothetical and categorical imperatives. The statement that someone 'ought to' or, more strongly, 'must' do such-and-such may be backed up explicitly or implicitly by reference to what he wants or to what his purposes and objects are. Again, there may be a reference to the purposes of someone else, perhaps the speaker: 'You must do this'— 'Why?'—'Because I want such-and-such'. The moral categorical imperative which could be expressed in the same words can be seen as resulting from the suppression of the conditional clause in a hypothetical imperative without its being replaced by any such reference to the speaker's wants. The action in question is still required in something like the way in which it would be if it were appropriately related to a want, but it is no longer admitted that there is any contingent want upon which is being required depends. Again this move can be understood when we remember that at least our central and basic moral judgements represent

social demands, where the source of the demand is indeterminate and diffuse. Whose demands or wants are in question, the agent's, or the speaker's, or those of an indefinite multitude of other people? All of these in a way, but there are advantages in not specifying them precisely. The speaker is expressing demands which he makes as a member of a community, which he has developed in and by participation in a joint way of life; also, what is required of this particular agent would be required of any other in a relevantly similar situation; but the agent too is expected to have internalized the relevant demands, to act as if the ends for which the action is required were his own. By suppressing any explicit reference to demands and making the imperatives categorical we facilitate conceptual moves from one such demand relation to another. The moral uses of such words as 'must' and 'ought' and 'should', all of which are used also to express hypothetical imperatives, are traces of this pattern of objectification.

It may be objected that this explanation links normative ethics too closely with descriptive morality, with the mores or socially enforced patterns of behaviour that anthropologists record. But it can hardly be denied that moral thinking starts from the enforcement of social codes. Of course it is not confined to that. But even when moral judgements are detached from the mores of any actual society they are liable to be framed with reference to an ideal community of moral agents, such as Kant's kingdom of ends, which but for the need to give God a special place in it would have been better called a commonwealth of ends.

Another way of explaining the objectification of moral values is to say that ethics is a system of law from which the legislator has been removed. This might have been derived either from the positive law of a state or from a supposed system of divine law. There can be no doubt that some features of modern European moral concepts are traceable to the theological ethics of Christianity. The stress on quasi-imperative notions, on what

ought to be done or on what is wrong in a sense that is close to that of 'forbidden', are surely relics of divine commands. Admittedly, the central ethical concepts for Plato and Aristotle also are in a broad sense prescriptive or intrinsically action-guiding, but in concentrating rather on 'good' than on 'ought' they show that their moral thought is an objectification of the desired and the satisfying rather than of the commanded. Elizabeth Anscombe has argued that modern, non-Aristotelian, concepts of *moral* obligation, *moral* duty, of what is *morally* right and wrong, and of the *moral* sense of 'ought' are survivals outside the framework of thought that made them really intelligible, namely the belief in divine law. She infers that 'ought' has 'become a word of mere mesmeric force', with only a 'delusive appearance of content', and that we would do better to discard such terms and concepts altogether, and go back to Aristotelian ones.

There is much to be said for this view. But while we can explain some distinctive features of modern moral philosophy in this way, it would be a mistake to see the whole problem of the claim to objective prescriptivity as merely local

and unnecessary, as a post-operative complication of a society from which a dominant system of theistic belief has recently been rather hastily excised. As Cudworth and Clarke and Price, for example, show, even those who still admit divine commands, or the positive law of God, may believe moral values to have an independent objective but still action-guiding authority.

Responding to Plato's *Euthyphro* dilemma, they believe that God commands what he commands because it is in itself good or right, not that it is good or right merely because and in that he commands it. Otherwise God himself could not be called good. Price asks, 'What can be more preposterous, than to make the Deity nothing but will; and to exalt this on the ruins of all his attributes?' The apparent objectivity of moral value is a widespread phenomenon which has more than one source: the persistence of a belief in something like divine law when the belief in the divine legislator has faded out is only one factor among others. There are several different patterns of objectification, all of which have left characteristic traces in our actual moral concepts and moral language.

Chapter 19

Thomas Nagel

THE OBJECTIVITY OF ETHICS

1. Realism and objectivity

OBJECTIVITY is the central problem of ethics. Not just in theory, but in life. The problem is to decide in what way, if at all, the idea of objectivity can be applied to practical questions, questions of what to do or want. To what extent can they be dealt with from a detached point of view toward ourselves and the world? I have already indicated, in the discussion of free will [see original reading], a connection between ethics and the objective standpoint. I want now to defend the objectivity of ethics by showing how that standpoint alters and constrains our motives. The possibility of ethics and many of its problems can be best understood in terms of the impact of objectivity on the will. If we can make judgments about how we should live even after stepping outside of ourselves, they will provide the material for moral theory.

In theoretical reasoning objectivity is advanced when we form a new conception of reality that includes ourselves as components. This involves an alteration or at least an extension of our beliefs. In the sphere of values or practical reasoning, the problem is different. As in the theoretical case, we must take up a new, comprehensive viewpoint after stepping back and including our former perspective in what is to be understood. But here the new viewpoint will be not a new set of beliefs, but a new or extended set of values. We try to arrive at normative judgments, with motivational content, from an impersonal standpoint. We cannot use a nonnormative criterion of objectivity, for if values are objective, they must be so in their own right and not through reducibility to some other kind of objective fact. They have to be objective *values*, not objective anything else.

Here as elsewhere there is a connection between objectivity and realism, though realism about values is different from realism about empirical facts. Normative realism is the view that propositions about what gives us reasons for action can be true or false independently of how things appear to us, and that we can hope to discover the truth by transcending the appearances and subjecting them to critical assessment. What we aim to discover by this method is not a new aspect of the external world, called value, but rather just the truth about what we and others should do and want.

It is important not to associate this form of realism with an inappropriate metaphysical picture: it is not a form of Platonism. The claim is that there are reasons for action, that we have to discover them instead of deriving them from our preexisting motives—and that in this way we can acquire new motives superior to the old. We simply aim to reorder our motives in a direction that will make them more acceptable from an external standpoint. Instead of bringing our thoughts into accord with an external reality, we try to bring an external view into the determination of our conduct.

The connection between objectivity and truth is therefore closer in ethics than it is in science. I do not believe that the truth about how we should live could extend radically beyond any capacity we might have to discover it (apart from its dependence on nonevaluative facts we might be unable to discover). The subject matter of ethics is how to engage in practical reasoning and the justification of action once we expand our consciousness by occupying the objective standpoint—not something else about action which the objective standpoint enables us to understand better. Ethical thought is the process of bringing objectivity to bear on the will, and the only thing I can think of to say about ethical truth in general is that it must be a possible result of this process, correctly carried out. I recognize that this is empty. If we wish to be more specific, all we can do is to refer to the arguments that persuade us of the objective validity of a reason or the correctness of a normative principle (and a given principle may be established in more than one way—got at from different starting points and by different argumentative routes).

Perhaps a richer metaphysic of morals could be devised, but I don't know what it would be. The picture I associate with normative realism is not that of an extra set of properties of things and events in the world, but of a series of possible steps in the development of human motivation which would improve the way we lead our lives, whether or not we will actually take them. We begin with a partial and inaccurate view, but by stepping outside of ourselves and constructing and comparing alternatives we can reach a new motivational condition at a higher level of objectivity. Though the aim is normative rather than descriptive, the method of investigation is analogous in certain respects to that of seeking an objective conception of what there is. We first form a conception of the world as centerless—as containing ourselves and other beings with particular points of view. But the question we then try to answer is not

"What can we see that the world contains, considered from this. impersonal standpoint?" but "What is there reason to do or want, considered from this impersonal standpoint?"

The answer will be complex. As in metaphysics, so in the realm of practical reason the truth is sometimes best understood from a detached standpoint; but sometimes it will be fully comprehensible only from a particular perspective within the world. If there are such subjective values, then an objective conception of what people have reasons to do must leave room for them. (I said something about this in the last chapter, under the heading of objective tolerance.) [see original reading] But once the objective step is taken, the possibility is also open for the recognition of values and reasons that are independent of one's personal perspective and have force for anyone who can view the world impersonally, as a place that contains him. If objectivity means anything here, it will mean that when we detach from our individual perspective and the values and reasons that seem acceptable from within it, we can sometimes arrive at a new conception which may endorse some of the original reasons but will reject some as false subjective appearances and add others.

So without prejudging the outcome—that is, how much of the domain of practical reasons can be objectively understood—we can see what the objectifying impulse depends on. The most basic idea of practical objectivity is arrived at by a practical analogue of the rejection of solipsism in the theoretical domain. Realism about the facts leads us to seek a detached point of view from which reality can be discerned and appearance corrected, and realism about values leads us to seek a detached point of view from which it will be possible to correct inclination and to discern what we really should do. Practical objectivity means that practical reason can be understood and even engaged in by the objective self.

This assumption, though powerful, is not yet an ethical position. It merely marks the place

which an ethical position will occupy if we can make sense of the subject. It says that the world of reasons, including my reasons, does not exist only from my own point of view. I am in a world whose character is to a certain extent independent of what I think, and if I have reasons to act it is because the person who I am has those reasons, in virtue of his condition and circumstances. The basic question of practical reason from which ethics begins is not "What shall I do?" but "What should this person do?"

This sets a problem and indicates a method of attacking it. The problem is to discover the form which reasons for action take, and whether it can be described from no particular point of view. The method is to begin with the reasons that appear to obtain from my own point of view and those of other individuals; and ask what the best perspectiveless account of those reasons is. As in other domains, we begin from our position inside the world and try to transcend it by regarding what we find here as a sample of the whole.

That is the hope. But the claim that there are objective values is permanently controversial, because of the ease with which values and reasons seem to disappear when we transcend the subjective standpoint of our own desires. It can seem, when one looks at life from outside, that there is no room for values in the world at all. So to say: "There are just people with various motives and inclinations, some of which they may express in evaluative language; but when we regard all this from outside, all we see are psychological facts. The ascent to an objective view, far from revealing new values that modify the subjective appearances, reveals that appearances are all there is: it enables us to observe and describe our subjective motives but does not produce any new ones. Objectivity has no place in this domain except what is inherited from the objectivity of theoretical and factual elements that play a role in practical reasoning. Beyond that it applies here with a nihilistic result: nothing is objectively right or wrong because objectively nothing matters; if there are such things as right and wrong, they must rest on a subjective foundation."

I believe this conclusion is the result of a mistake comparable to the one that leads to physicalism, with its attendant reductionist elaborations. An epistemological criterion of reality is being assumed which pretends to be comprehensive but which in fact excludes large domains in advance without argument.

The assumption is surreptitious, but natural. Values can seem really to disappear when we step outside of our skins, so that it strikes us as a philosophical *perception* that they are illusory. This is a characteristic Humean step: we observe the phenomenon of people acting for what they take to be reasons, and *all we see* (compare Hume's treatment of causality) are certain natural facts: that people are influenced by certain motives, or would be if they knew certain things.

We are continually tempted to reoccupy Hume's position by the difficulties we encounter when we try to leave it. Skepticism, Platonism, reductionism, and other familiar philosophical excesses all make their appearance in ethical theory. Particularly attractive is the reaction to skepticism which reinterprets the whole field, ethics included, in completely subjective terms. Like phenomenalism in epistemology, this conceals the retreat from realism by substituting a set of judgments that in some way resemble the originals.

The only way to resist Humean subjectivism about desires and reasons for action is to seek a form of objectivity appropriate to the subject. This will not be the objectivity of naturalistic psychology. It must be argued that an objective view limited to such observations is not correct. Or rather, not necessarily correct, for the point is that an objective view of ourselves should leave room for the apprehension of reasons—should not exclude them in advance.

They seem to be excluded in advance if the objective, standpoint is assumed to be one of pure observation and description.[1] When we

direct this sort of attention to what appears subjectively as a case of acting for reasons and responding to good and evil, we get a naturalistic account that seems to give the complete objective description of what is going on. Instead of normative reasons, we see only a psychological explanation.

But I believe it is a mistake to give these phenomena a purely psychological reading when we look at them from outside. What we see, unless we are artificially blind, is not just people being moved to act by their desires, but people acting and forming intentions and desires for reasons, good or bad. That is, we recognize their reasons *as reasons*—or perhaps we think they are bad reasons—but in any case we do not drop out of the evaluative mode as soon as we leave the subjective standpoint. The recognition of reasons as reasons is to be contrasted with their use purely as a form of psychological explanation (see Davidson (1)) [see original reading]. The latter merely connects action with the agent's desires and beliefs, without touching the normative question whether he *had* an adequate reason for acting—whether he should have acted as he did. If this is all that can be said once we leave the point of view of the agent behind, then I think it would follow that we don't really act for reasons at all. Rather, we are caused to act by desires and beliefs, and the terminology of reasons can be used only in a diminished, nonnormative sense to express this kind of explanation.

The substitution of an account in which values or normative reasons play no part is not something that simply falls out of the objective view. It depends on a particular objective claim that can be accepted only if it is more plausible than its denial: the claim that our sense that the world presents us with reasons for action is a subjective illusion, produced by the projection of our preexisting motives onto the world, and that there aren't objectively any reasons for us to do anything—though of course there are motives, some of which mimic normative reasons in form.

But this would have to be established: it does not follow from the idea of objectivity alone. When we take the objective step, we don't leave the evaluative capacity behind automatically, since that capacity does not depend on antecedently present desires. We may find that it continues to operate from an external standpoint, and we may conclude that this is not just a case of subjective desires popping up again in objective disguise. I acknowledge the dangers of false objectification, which elevates personal tastes and prejudices into cosmic values. But it isn't the only possibility.

2. Antirealism

Where does the burden of proof lie with respect to the possibility of objective values? Does their possibility have to be demonstrated before we can begin to think more specifically about which values are revealed or obliterated by the objective standpoint? Or is such an inquiry legitimate so long as objective values haven't been shown to be impossible?

I think the burden of proof has been often misplaced in this debate, and that a defeasible presumption that values need not be illusory is entirely reasonable until it is shown not to be. Like the presumption that things exist in an external world, the presumption that there are real values and reasons can be defeated in individual cases, if a purely subjective account of the appearances is more plausible. And like the presumption of an external world, its complete falsity is not self-contradictory. The reality of values, impersonal or otherwise, is not entailed by the totality of appearances any more than the reality of a physical universe is. But if either of them is recognized as a possibility, then its reality in detail can be confirmed by appearances, at least to the extent of being rendered more plausible than the alternatives. So a lot depends on whether the possibility of realism is admitted in the first place.

It is very difficult to argue for such a possibility, except by refuting arguments against it.

(Berkeley's argument against the conceivability of a world independent of experience is an impossibility argument in the domain of metaphysics.) What is the result when such an argument is refuted? Is the contrary possibility in a stronger position? I believe so: in general, there is no way to prove the possibility of realism; one can only refute impossibility arguments, and the more often one does this the more confidence one may have in the realist alternative. So to consider the merits of an admission of realism about value, we have to consider the reasons against it—against its possibility or against its truth. I shall discuss three. They have been picked for their apparent capacity to convince.

The first type of argument depends on the unwarranted assumption that if values are real, they must be real objects of some other kind. John Mackie, in his book *Ethics*, denies the objectivity of values by saying that they are "not part of the fabric of the world," and that if they were, they would have to be "entities or qualities or relations of a very strange sort, utterly different from anything else in the universe" (Mackie (2), p. 38) [see original reading]. He clearly has a definite picture of what the universe is like, and assumes that realism about value would require crowding it with extra entities, qualities, or relations, things like Platonic Forms or Moore's nonnatural qualities. But this assumption is not correct. The objective badness of pain, for example, is not some mysterious further property that all pains have, but just the fact that there is reason for anyone capable of viewing the world objectively to want it to stop. The view that values are real is not the view that they are real occult entities or properties, but that they are real values: that our claims about value and about what people have reason to do may be true or false independently of our beliefs and inclinations. No other kinds of truths are involved. Indeed, no other kinds of truths *could* imply the reality of values. This applies not only to moral values but also to prudential ones, and even to the simple reasons people have to do what will achieve their present aims.

In discussion, Mackie objected that his disbelief in the reality of values and reasons did not depend on the assumption that to be real they must be strange entities or properties. As he says in his book, the point applies directly to reasons themselves. For whatever they are they are not needed to explain anything that happens, and there is consequently no reason to believe in their existence.

But this raises the same issue. Mackie meant that reasons play no role in causal explanations. But it begs the question to assume that this sort of explanatory necessity is the test of reality for values. The claim that certain reasons exist is a normative claim, not a claim about the best causal explanation of anything. To assume that only what has to be included in the best causal theory of the world is real is to assume that there are no irreducibly normative truths.

However, there is another difficulty here which I'm not sure how to deal with. If there are normative truths, they enter into normative rather than causal explanations of the existence of particular reasons or the rightness or wrongness of particular actions. But our apprehension of these truths also explains our acquisition of new motives, and ultimately it can influence our conduct. Even if we set aside the issues about free will and the intentional explanation of action discussed in the previous chapter, there is a problem here about the relation between normative and causal explanation. It is not clear whether normative realism is compatible with the hypothesis that all our normative beliefs can be accounted for by some kind of naturalistic psychology.

Gilbert Harman formulates the problem thus:

Observation plays a role in science that it does not seem to play in ethics. The difference is that you need to make assumptions about certain physical facts to explain the occurrence of the observations that support a scientific theory, but you do not seem to need to make assumptions about any moral facts to

explain the occurrence of . . . so-called moral observations . . . In the moral case, it would seem that you need only make assumptions about the psychology or moral sensibility of the person making the moral observation.[2]

Any defender of realism about values must claim that the purely psychological account is incomplete, either because normative explanations are an additional element or because they are somehow present in certain types of psychological explanations—perhaps in a way like that in which explanations of belief by logical reasoning can be simultaneously causal and justificatory (if in fact they can be). So when, for example, we become convinced by argument that a distinction is morally relevant, the explanation of our conviction can be given by the content and validity of the argument.

While we cannot prove the purely psychological, antirealist account to be false—so that it remains literally true that you don't *need* to explain normative judgments in terms of normative truths—I believe the most plausible account will refer to such truths, even at the most elementary level. To dispense with them is too radical a denial of the appearances. If I have a severe headache, the headache seems to me to be not merely unpleasant, but a bad thing. Not only do I dislike it, but I think I have a reason to try to get rid of it. It is barely conceivable that this might be an illusion, but if the idea of a bad thing makes sense at all, it need not be an illusion, and the true explanation of my impression may be the simplest one, namely that headaches are bad, and not just unwelcome to the people who have them.

Everything depends on whether the idea makes sense. If the possibility of real values is admitted, specific values become susceptible to a kind of observational testing, but it operates through the kind of explanation appropriate to the subject: normative explanation. In physics, one infers from factual appearances to their most plausible explanation in a theory of how the world is. In ethics, one infers from appearances of value to their most plausible explanation in a theory of what there is reason to do or want. All the inferences will rely on general ideas of reality that do not derive from appearance—the most important being the general idea of objective reality itself. And in both science and ethics some of the appearances will turn out to be mistaken and to have psychological explanations of a kind that do not confirm their truth.

My belief that the distinction between appearance and reality applies here is based not on a metaphysical picture, but on the capacity of a realistic approach to make sense of our thoughts. If we start by regarding appearances of value as appearances of something, and then step back to form hypotheses about the broader system of motivational possibilities of which we have had a glimpse, the result is a gradual opening out of a complex domain which we apparently discover. The method of discovery is to seek the best normative explanation of the normative appearances. I believe that the actual results of this method tend to confirm the realistic assumption behind it—though I recognize that a skeptic may object that the results are contaminated by the assumption itself and cannot therefore supply independent confirmation.

Let me now turn to the second argument against realism. Unlike the first, it is not based on a misinterpretation of moral objectivity. Instead, it tries to represent the unreality of values as an objective discovery. The argument is that if claims of value have to be objectively correct, and if they are not reducible to any other kind of objective claim, then we can just see that all positive value claims must be false. Nothing has any objective value, because objectively nothing matters at all. If we push the claims of objective detachment to their logical conclusion, and survey the world from a standpoint completely detached from all interests, we discover that there is nothing—no values left of any kind: things can be said to matter at all only

to individuals within the world. The result is objective nihilism.

I don't deny that the objective standpoint tempts one in this direction, and I'll say more about it later, when discussing the meaning of life. But I believe this can seem like the required conclusion only if one makes the mistake of assuming that objective judgments of value must emerge from the detached standpoint alone. It is true that with nothing to go on but a conception of the world from nowhere, one would have no way of telling whether anything had value. But an objective view has more to go on, for its data include the appearance of value to individuals with particular perspectives, including oneself. In this respect practical reason is no different from anything else. Starting from a pure idea of a possible reality and a very impure set of appearances, we try to fill in the idea of reality so as to make some partial sense of the appearances, using objectivity as a method. To find out what the world is like from outside we have to approach it from within: it is no wonder that the same is true for ethics.

And indeed, when we take up the objective standpoint, the problem is not that values seem to disappear but that there seem to be too many of them, coming from every life and drowning out those that arise from our own. It is just as easy to form desires from an objective standpoint as it is to form beliefs. Probably easier. Like beliefs, these desires and evaluations must be criticized and justified partly in terms of the appearances. But they are not just further appearances, any more than the beliefs about the world which arise from an impersonal standpoint are just further appearances.

The third type of argument against the objective reality of values is an empirical argument. It is also perhaps the most common. It is intended not to rule out the possibility of real values from the start, but rather to demonstrate that even if their possibility is admitted, we have no reason to believe that there are any. The claim is that if we consider the wide cultural variation in normative beliefs, the importance of social pressure and other psychological influences to their formation, and the difficulty of settling moral disagreements, it becomes highly implausible that they are anything but pure appearances.

Anyone offering this argument must admit that not every psychological factor in the explanation of an appearance shows that the appearance corresponds to nothing real. Visual capacities and elaborate training play a part in explaining the physicist's perception of a cloud-chamber track, or a student's coming to believe a proposition of geometry, but the nature of the particle and the truth of the proposition also play an essential part in these explanations. No one has produced a general account of the kinds of psychological explanation that discredit an appearance. But some skeptics about ethics feel that because of the way we acquire moral beliefs and other impressions of value, there are grounds for confidence that here, nothing real is being talked about.

I find the popularity of this argument surprising. The fact that morality is socially inculcated and that there is radical disagreement about it across cultures, over time, and even within cultures at a time is a poor reason to conclude that values have no objective reality. Even where there is truth, it is not always easy to discover. Other areas of knowledge are taught by social pressure, many truths as well as falsehoods are believed without rational grounds, and there is wide disagreement about scientific and social facts, especially where strong interests are involved which will be affected by different answers to a disputed question. This last factor is present throughout ethics to a uniquely high degree: it is an area in which one would expect extreme variation of belief and radical disagreement however objectively real the subject actually was. For comparably motivated disagreements about matters of fact, one has to go to the heliocentric theory, the theory of evolution, the Dreyfus case, the Hiss case, and the genetic contribution to racial differences in I.Q.

Although the methods of ethical reasoning are rather primitive, the degree to which agreement can be achieved and social prejudices transcended in the face of strong pressures suggests that something real is being investigated, and that part of the explanation of the appearances, both at simple and at complex levels, is that we perceive, often inaccurately, that there are certain reasons for action, and go on to infer, often erroneously, the general form of the principles that best account for those reasons.

Again let me stress that this is not to be understood on the model of perception of features of the external world. The subject matter of our investigations is how to live, and the process of ethical thought is one of motivational discovery. The fact that people can to some extent reach agreement on answers which they regard as objective suggests that when they step outside of their particular individual perspectives, they call into operation a common evaluative faculty whose correct functioning provides the answers, even though it can also malfunction and be distorted by other influences. It is not a question of bringing the mind into correspondence with an external reality which acts causally on it, but of reordering the mind itself in accordance with the demands of its own external view of itself.

I have not discussed all the possible arguments against realism about values, but I have tried to give general reasons for skepticism about such arguments. It seems to me that they tend to be supported by a narrow preconception of what sorts of truths there are, and that this is essentially question-begging. Nothing said here will force a reductionist to give up his denial of normative realism, but perhaps it has been shown to be a reasonable position. I should add that the search for objective principles makes sense even if we do not assume that all of ethics or human value is equally objective. Objectivity need not be all or nothing. So long as realism is true in some of these areas, we can reasonably pursue the method of objective reflection as far as it will take us.

3. Desires and reasons

There is no preset method of carrying out a normative investigation, though the aim of achieving integration between the subjective and objective standpoints gives the process direction and sets conditions of success and failure. We look at human life from within and without simultaneously, and try to arrive at a reasonable set of attitudes. The process of development can go on indefinitely, as is true in the pursuit of any other type of knowledge. Some aspects of practical reason may prove to be irreducibly subjective, so that while their existence must be acknowledged from an objective standpoint their content cannot be understood except from a more particular perspective. But other reasons will irresistibly engage the objective will.

The initial data are reasons that appear from one's own point of view in acting. They usually present themselves with some pretensions of objectivity to begin with, just as perceptual appearances do. When two things look the same size to me, they look at least initially as if they *are* the same size. And when I want to take aspirin because it will cure my headache, I believe at least initially that this is a reason for me to take aspirin.

The ordinary process of deliberation, aimed at finding out what I should do, assumes the existence of an answer to this question. And in difficult cases especially it is often accompanied by the belief that I may not arrive at the correct answer. I do not assume that the correct answer is just whatever will result from consistent application of deliberative methods—even assuming perfect information about the facts. In deliberation we are trying to arrive at conclusions that are correct in virtue of something independent of our arriving at them. So although some of the starting points will be abandoned on the way, the pursuit of an objective account has its basis in the claims of ordinary practical reasoning.

It is important to recognize that the objectivity of reasons may be implied by a great

variety of substantive views about what reasons there are, including some that have little or no ethical content. By way of illustration, consider a minimal position that some find plausible and that I shall call, following Parfit, the Instrumental theory: that basic general reasons depend exclusively on the desires of the agent, whatever their objects (Parfit, p.117). Roughly, the position is that each person has a reason to do what will satisfy his desires or preferences at the time of action, where these can to some extent be identified independently of what he does, so that it is not a tautology that he is always rational relative to his beliefs. The desires need not have experiences as objects, and their satisfaction need not be experienced, for it can consist simply in the occurrence of the thing desired, which may be something not involving the agent at all, or something he will not live to see.

This position is reached by a fairly minimal generalization from one's own case. (I believe it errs in being both too minimal and in another sense too broad, but let me leave that aside for now.) One translates one's own reasons into a form that can be accepted by people with different preferences, so that it can be used by anyone to account generally for his own reasons and those of others. Nothing but the need for an account that can be understood from no particular perspective would require the adoption of such general principles.

The point is that even this minimal form of generalization is produced by a requirement of objectivity. The Instrumental theory makes general claims about the conditions under which people have reasons, which provide a basis for regarding some of their acts as irrational. If one were concerned only to decide what to do oneself, it would be sufficient to reason practically in terms of the preferences and desires one actually has. It would not be necessary to ascend to this level of generality.

We wish to formulate our reasons in general terms that relativize them to interests and desires so that they can be recognized and *accepted* from

outside, either by someone else or by us when we regard the situation objectively, independent of the preferences and desires we actually have. From such a point of view we still want to be able to see what reasons we have, and this is made possible by a general, relativized formulation which enables us to say what others have reasons to do, and also what we would ourselves have reasons to do if our desires were different. We can still apply it after stepping back. It is not enough that our actions be motivationally explainable by others, and that we should likewise be able to explain theirs. We assume the justifications are also objectively correct, and this means they must be based on impersonally acceptable principles that allow for more particular variation in desires.

If this is right, then even the apparently subjective Instrumental theory is the thin end of an objective wedge. Even though the reasons it identifies are based on desires, they will not necessarily be recognized and acted upon by the subject of those desires. The reasons are real, they are not just appearances. To be sure, they will be attributed only to a being that has, in addition to desires, a general capacity to develop an objective view of what it should do. Thus, if cockroaches cannot think about what they should do, there is nothing they should do. But this capacity is open-ended. We cannot replace practical reasoning by the psychology of our practical reasoning capacity, any more than we can replace mathematical reasoning by the psychology of our mathematical capacity. The pursuit of objective practical principles is not to be conceived of as a psychological exploration of our moral sense, but as an employment of it. We must engage in reasoning to discover what reasons we have, and exercise of the capacity will not always yield the right answer.

The quest for objectivity is responsible for even the limited form of generality found in the Instrumental theory. But once this principle is seen as the solution to a problem, and the problem is described, alternative solutions can

also be considered, and some of them may prove superior. Perhaps not all reasons are based on desires, and not all desires generate reasons. More than one hypothesis can account from an objective standpoint for a large range of individual cases. The task of ethical theory is to develop and compare conceptions of how to live, which can be understood and considered from no particular perspective, and therefore from many perspectives insofar as we can abstract from their particularity. All these conceptions will attempt to reconcile the apparent requirement of generality that objectivity imposes with the richness, variety, and reality of the reasons that appear subjectively.

The Instrumental view is conservative because it imposes the minimum generalization compatible with preserving certain premoral subjective reasons that individuals appear to have. It adds essentially nothing to these, but merely subsumes them under an account general enough to be applicable to any person A by any other person B who knows what A's preferences, desires, beliefs, and circumstances are. One is not forced by the formal condition of generality to go any further than this. But that does not mean that the view is correct. One is not forced to stay wherever one cannot be forced to leave. There are too many such places.

In an earlier discussion I argued that motivation by reasons does not always depend on antecedently existing desires (Nagel (1), ch. 5) [see original reading]. Sometimes a desire appears only because I recognize that there is reason to do or want something. This is true of prudential motivation, which stems from the expectation of future desires or interests and requires none in the present. It is even more clearly true of altruistic motivation, which stems from recognition of the desires and interests of others, and requires no desires in the agent except those that are motivated by that recognition.[3] But even when a present desire of the agent is among the grounds for rational action, a purely descriptive causal account of what

happens is incomplete. I want my headache to go away—but this doesn't directly cause me to take aspirin. I take aspirin because I recognize that my desire to be rid of the headache gives me a reason to take it, justifies my wanting to take it. That's *why* I take it, and from inside I can't think that it would be no less rational to bang my head against a fire hydrant instead.

If we suppose, then, that I have a reason in this particular case, the question becomes, what kind of reason is it, when we look at the matter objectively? How does it fit into a more general conception of the kinds of reasons there are—a conception that applies not just to me?

4. Types of generality

The search for generality is one of the main impulses in the construction of an objective view—in normative as in theoretical matters. One takes the particular case as an example, and forms hypotheses about what general truth it is an example of. There is more than one type of generality, and no reason to assume that a single form will apply to every type of value. Since the choice among types of generality defines some of the central issues of moral theory, let me describe the options.

One respect in which reasons may vary is in their breadth. A principle may be general in the sense that it applies to everyone but be quite narrow in content; and it is an open question to what extent narrower principles of practical reason (don't lie; develop your talents) can be subsumed under broader ones (don't hurt others; consider your long-term interests), or even at the limit under a single widest principle from which all the rest derive. Reasons may be universal, in other words, without forming a unified system that always provides a method for arriving at determinate conclusions about what one should do.

A second respect in which reasons vary is in their *relativity to the agent*, the person for whom they are reasons. The distinction between reasons

that are relative to the agent and reasons that are not is an extremely important one.[4] If a reason can be given a general form which does not include an essential reference to the person who has it, it is an *agent-neutral* reason. For example, if it is a reason for anyone to do or want something that it would reduce the amount of wretchedness in the world, then that is a neutral reason. If on the other hand the general form of a reason does include an essential reference to the person who has it, it is an *agent-relative* reason. For example, if it is a reason for anyone to do or want something that it would be in *his* interest, then that is a relative reason. In such a case, if something were in Jones's interest but contrary to Smith's, Jones would have reason to want it to happen and Smith would have the same reason to want it not to happen. (Both agent-relative and agent-neutral reasons are objective, if they can be understood and affirmed from outside the viewpoint of the individual who has them.)

A third way in which reasons may vary is in their degree of externality, or independence of the concerns of sentient beings. Most of the apparent reasons that initially present themselves to us are intimately connected with interests and desires, our own or those of others, and often with experiential satisfaction. But it seems that some of these interests give evidence that their objects have an intrinsic value which is not merely a function of the satisfaction that people may derive from them or of the fact that anyone wants them—a value which is not reducible to their value for anyone. I don't know how to establish whether there are any such values, but the objectifying tendency produces a strong impulse to believe that there are—especially in aesthetics, where the object of interest is external and the interest seems perpetually capable of criticism in light of further attention to the object. The problem is to account for external values in a way which avoids the implausible consequence that they retain their practical importance even if no one will *ever* be able to

respond to them. (So that if all sentient life is destroyed, it will still be a good thing if the Frick Collection survives.)

There may be other significant dimensions of variation. I want to concentrate on these because they locate the main controversies about what ethics is. Reasons and values that can be described in these terms provide the material for objective judgments. If one looks at human action and its conditions from outside and considers whether some normative principles are plausible, these are the forms they will take.

The actual acceptance of a general normative judgment will have motivational implications, for it will commit you under some circumstances to the acceptance of reasons to want and do things yourself.

This is most clear when the objective judgment is that something has agent-neutral or impersonal value. That means anyone has reason to want it to happen—and that includes someone considering the world in detachment from the perspective of any particular person within it. Such a judgment has motivational content even before it is brought back down to the particular perspective of the individual who has accepted it objectively.

Relative reasons are different. An objective judgment that some kind of thing has agent-relative value commits us only to believing that someone has reason to want and pursue it if it is related to him in the right way (being in his interest, for example). Someone who accepts this judgment is not even committed to wanting it to be the case that people in general are influenced by such reasons. The judgment commits him to wanting something only when its implications are drawn for the individual person he happens to be. With regard to others, the content of the objective judgment concerns only what *they* should do or want.

Judgments of both these kinds, as well as others, are evoked from us when we take up an objective standpoint, and the pressure to combine intelligibly the two standpoints toward

action can lead to the refinement and extension of such judgments.

The choice among normative hypotheses is difficult and there is no general method of making it, any more than there is a general method of selecting the most plausible objective account of the facts on the basis of the appearances. The only "method," here or elsewhere, is to try to generate hypotheses and then to consider which of them seems most reasonable, in light of everything else one is fairly confident of. Since we may assume that not every alternative has been thought of, the best we can hope for is a comparison among those available, not a firm solution.

This is not quite empty, for it means at least that logic alone can settle nothing. We do not have to be shown that the denial of some kind of objective value is self-contradictory in order to be reasonably led to accept its existence. There is no constraint to pick the weakest or narrowest or most economical principle consistent with the initial data that arise from individual perspectives. Our admission of reasons beyond these is determined not by logical entailment, but by the relative plausibility of those normative hypotheses—including the null hypothesis—that are consistent with the evidence.

In this respect ethics is no different from anything else: theoretical knowledge does not arise by deductive inference from the appearances either. The main difference is that our objective thinking about practical reasons is very primitive and has difficulty taking even the first step. Philosophical skepticism and idealism about values are much more popular than their metaphysical counterparts. Nevertheless, I believe they are no more correct. Although no single objective principle of practical reason like egoism or utilitarianism covers everything, the acceptance of some objective values is unavoidable—not because the alternative is inconsistent but because it is not *credible*. Someone who, as in Hume's example (*Treatise*, bk. 2, pt. 3, sec. 3), prefers the destruction of the whole world to the scratching of his finger may not be involved in a contradiction or in any false expectations, but there is something the matter with him nonetheless, and anyone else not in the grip of an overnarrow conception of what reasoning is would regard his preference as objectively wrong.

But even if it is unreasonable to deny that anyone ever objectively has a reason to do anything, it is not easy to find positive objective principles that *are* reasonable. In particular it is not easy to follow the objectifying impulse without distorting individual life and personal relations. We want to be able to understand and accept the way we live from outside, but it may not always follow that we should control our lives from inside by the terms of that external understanding. Often the objective viewpoint will not be suitable as a replacement for the subjective, but will coexist with it, setting a standard with which the subjective is constrained not to clash. In deciding what to do, for example, we should not reach a result different from what we could decide objectively that that *person* should do—but we need not arrive at the result in the same way from the two standpoints.

Sometimes, also, the objective standpoint will allow us to judge how people should be or should live, without permitting us to translate this into a judgment about what they have reasons to do. For in some respects it is better to live and act not for reasons, but because it does not occur to us to do anything else. This is especially true of close personal relations. Here the objective standpoint cannot be brought into the perspective of action without diminishing precisely what it affirms the value of. Nevertheless, the possibility of objective affirmation is important. We should be *able* to view our lives from outside without extreme dissociation or distaste, and the extent to which we should live without considering the objective point of view or even any reasons at all is itself determined largely from that point of view.

It is also possible that some idiosyncratic individual grounds of action, or the values of

strange communities, will prove objectively inaccessible. To take an example in our midst: people who want to be able to run twenty-six miles without stopping are not exactly irrational, but their reasons can be understood only from the perspective of a value system that some find alien to the point of unintelligibility.[5] A correct objective view will have to allow for such pockets of unassimilable subjectivity, which need not clash with objective principles but won't be affirmed by them either. Many aspects of personal taste will come in this category if, as I think, they cannot all be brought under a general hedonistic principle.

But the most difficult and interesting problems of accommodation appear where objectivity can be employed as a standard, and we have to decide how. Some of the problems are these: To what extent should an objective view admit external values? To what extent should it admit agent-neutral values? To what extent should reasons to respect the interests of others take an agent-relative form? To what extent is it legitimate for each person to give priority to his own interests or to the interests of those close to him? These are all questions about the proper form of generality for different kinds of practical reasoning, and the proper relation between objective principles and the deliberations of individual agents.

• • •

6. Overobjectification

It will be obvious from the way the argument has gone so far that I don't believe all objective reasons have the same form. The interaction between objectivity and the will yields complex results which cannot necessarily be formed into a unified system. This means that the natural ambition of a comprehensive system of ethics may be unrealizable.

I have argued against skepticism, and in favor of realism and the pursuit of objectivity in the domain of practical reason. But if realism is admitted as a possibility, one is quickly faced with the opposite of the problem of skepticism, namely the problem of overobjectification: the temptation to interpret the objectivity of reasons in too strong a way.

In ethics, as in metaphysics, the allure of objectivity is very great: there is a persistent tendency in both areas to seek a single complete objective account of reality. In the area of value that means a search for the most objective possible account of all reasons for action: the account which engages us from a maximally detached standpoint.

This idea underlies the fairly common moral assumption that the only real values are impersonal values, and that someone can really have a reason to do something only if there is an agent-neutral reason for it to happen. That is the essence of traditional forms of consequentialism: the only reason for anyone to do anything is that it would be better in itself, considering the world as a whole, if he did it.

• • •

We can no more assume that all values are impersonal than that all reality is physical. I argued earlier that not everything there is can be gathered into a uniform conception of the universe from nowhere within it. If certain perspectives evidently exist which cannot be analyzed in physical terms, we must modify our idea of objective reality to include them. If that is not enough, we must admit to reality some things that cannot be objectively understood. Similarly, if certain reasons for action which appear to exist cannot be accommodated within a purely neutral system—or even perhaps within a general but relative system—then we may have to modify our realist idea of value and practical reason accordingly. I don't mean to suggest that there is no conflict here. The opposition between objective reasons and subjective inclinations may be severe, and may require us to change our lives. I mean only that the truth, if there is any,

will be arrived at by the exploration of this conflict rather than by the automatic victory of the most transcendent standpoint. In the conduct of life, of all places, the rivalry between the view from within and the view from without must be taken seriously.

Notes

1   Cf. Anscombe, p. 137: "This often happens in philosophy; it is argued that 'all we find' is such-and-such, and it turns out that the arguer has excluded from his idea of 'finding' the sort of thing he says we don't 'find.' "

2   G. Harman, p. 6; this is his formulation of the problem, not his proposed solution.

3   The distinction I am making between unmotivated desires that originate motivation and desires that are themselves rationally motivated has a good deal in common with Kant's distinction between inclination (*Neigung*) and interest (*Interesse*) (Kant, p. 413n.)—though Kant believes that a purely rational interest appears only in morality.

4   In Nagel I marked it by speaking of "subjective" and "objective" reasons, but since those terms are being put to different use here, I shall adopt Parfit's terms, "agent-relative" and "agent-neutral" (Parfit, p. 143). Often I shall shorten these to "relative" and "neutral"; and sometimes I shall refer to the corresponding values as "personal" and "impersonal."

5   Though one never knows where it will strike next: it's like *Invasion of the Body-Snatchers*.

References

Anscombe, G. E. M. "Causality and Determination," Inaugural lecture, Cambridge University, 1971, in *Metaphysics and the Philosophy of Mind: Collected Philosophical Papers vol. III*, University of Minnesota Press, 1981.

Harman, G. *The Nature of Morality*, Oxford University Press, 1977.

Kant, I. *Foundations of the Metaphysics of Morals*, 1785; Prussian Academy ed., vol. IV.

Nagel, T. *The Possibility of Altruism*, Oxford University Press, 1970; rpt. Princeton University Press, 1978.

Parfit, D. *Reasons and Persons*, Oxford University Press, 1984.

Chapter 20

Walter Sinnott-Armstrong

MORAL SKEPTICISM

1.2. Epistemology applied to morality

THE CENTRAL topic here is moral epistemology, which is just epistemology applied to substantive moral beliefs. Epistemology is the study of knowledge and justified belief in general. It asks whether, when, and how people can know or be justified in believing anything. Moral epistemology asks these questions about moral beliefs in particular. Answers to such questions make second-order claims about the epistemic status of first-order moral beliefs.

Of course, we cannot determine whether any claim is justified or known if we have no idea what that claim means, so moral epistemology depends in some ways on moral semantics. Moreover, some philosophers (including Hare 1965, 1981; and Habermas 1990) try to justify moral beliefs by appealing primarily to a theory of moral language, so moral epistemology might be based on moral semantics. The same might be said for moral ontology, the definition of morality, deontic logic, and moral psychology. Nonetheless, moral epistemology differs from other areas of meta-ethics in that it focuses directly on knowledge and justified belief in morality and brings in other issues only when relevant to these central concerns.

Moral epistemology is also distinct from substantive ethics. Both fields ask whether something is justified, but they ask this question about different kinds of things. Moral epistemology asks whether *beliefs* are justified, whereas substantive ethics asks whether *actions* (or policies, institutions, etc.) are justified. For example, the question of whether I am justified in breaking the speed limit to get to class on time is a question of substantive ethics, but the question of whether I am justified in believing that I am justified in breaking the speed limit to get to class on time is a question of moral epistemology. People can be epistemically unjustified in believing that an act is morally justified, such as when they believe that capital punishment is morally justified, and they believe this only because they read it in a book that they are not epistemically justified in trusting. (This can happen whether or not capital punishment really is morally justified.) People can also be epistemically justified in believing that an act is morally unjustified, such as when they have a trustworthy basis for believing that capital punishment is unjustified. (Again, this can happen whether or not capital punishment is morally justified.) All of this shows that being epistemically justified is separate from being morally justified.

Similarly, people can have epistemic reasons for moral beliefs without moral reasons for action, and vice versa. Some philosophers do seem to assume that nobody can have a reason to do an act without having any reason to believe that he has a reason to do that act. Others assume

that, if an agent has a reason to believe that there is a reason for that agent to do a certain action, then that agent does have a reason to do that action. I find both assumptions dubious. Moreover, even if reasons for action did follow from reasons for belief and vice versa, a reason for an action would still be distinguishable from a reason to believe in that reason for action, since the reasons have different objects. One is about actions. The other is about beliefs. That is enough to separate the fields of substantive ethics and moral epistemology.

These distinctions, admittedly, get confusing. Suppose a critic claims that it is morally wrong for colleges to use racial quotas in admissions. A defender of affirmative action quotas asks, "Why?" This question asks for some kind of reason or justification, but it is not clear whether it asks for a reason against the racial quotas themselves or, instead, for a reason for the belief that the racial quotas are morally wrong. In response to the former question, the critic might point to features of the racial quotas that make them morally wrong in his opinion, such as that some applicants will be affected adversely although they personally did nothing wrong. Then he is offering a reason not to use the racial quotas, which is a reason for action. In contrast, if the question "Why?" is interpreted differently, a critic of the racial quotas might say that he has studied racial quotas long and hard, consulting with many students and experts, and this long process has made it obvious to him that these racial quotas are immoral. This is not directly a reason for action. Instead, he is offering a reason for his belief, that is, a list of sources or factors that make him justified in believing that the racial quotas are immoral. These reasons for belief are facts about him (including his beliefs), whereas the reasons for action were facts about racial quotas. Other kinds of reasons for belief might seem closer to reasons for action. Sometimes a reason to believe that an action is morally right (or wrong) is a *belief* that the action has certain properties, and the *fact* that the action

has those properties is a reason for (or against) doing the action. Since to state the fact is to express the belief, it is then hard to tell whether a speaker is referring to the reason for belief or, instead, to the reason for action. That explains why so many people conflate these distinct kinds of reasons. It is often not clear which kind of reason is being sought when someone asks "Why?" or which kind of reason is being given when someone answers that question. But here we need to avoid such confusions and unclarity. If we do, then moral epistemology can be distinguished from substantive ethics.

These fields are still related, insofar as an adequate moral epistemology must cohere with the best substantive ethics. Nonetheless, theories in moral epistemology are supposed to be neutral among competing substantive moral views, just as logic, semantics, and general epistemology need to be neutral among competing views in history or biology. When people disagree about the morality of abortion, they often want a method to resolve their dispute or a test of whether either view is justified. Moral epistemologists study and sometimes propose such methods and tests. To avoid begging the question, these methods and tests must be neutral among the views under dispute. Of course, some theories in moral epistemology are not really so neutral. Maybe no theory in moral epistemology can be completely neutral among all possible substantive moral views. Even so, some theories in moral epistemology can still be neutral among the competitors in a particular dispute. Then they might be useful in choosing among those particular alternatives. That would help a lot, but it remains to be seen whether even that much can be accomplished. If so, then moral epistemology is distinct from substantive ethics at least in such contexts.

Whether or not its questions can be answered independent of substantive ethics, moral epistemology at least asks distinctive questions. Indeed, several different questions that are not directly about substantive ethics are asked and

answered within moral epistemology. A first question concerns *conditions* for justified belief and knowledge in morality. Some moral epistemologists attempt to spell out necessary or sufficient conditions for a person to be justified in believing a moral claim or to know that a certain moral claim is true. A second question concerns practical *procedures* or *methods*. Some moral epistemologists propose steps that a person can or must go through in order to gain justified moral belief or knowledge. A third question asks how we can *show* that moral claims or beliefs are true or justified or known. A fourth question asks about *degrees* to which moral beliefs can be justified—which are justified better or best—while admitting that different beliefs are justified also but not as well. Still other moral epistemologists ask parallel questions about justifications or arguments or epistemic virtues or reliability regarding moral beliefs, each of which is different from the question of when moral beliefs are justified.

All of these questions are important and lie within moral epistemology, but we cannot discuss all of them at once. In this book, I will focus on the questions of which conditions are necessary or sufficient for moral knowledge and for a person to be justified in believing a substantive moral claim.

1.3. Varieties of moral skepticism

The primary challenge in moral epistemology is posed by moral skepticism. However, many very different views have been described as moral skepticism. The best way to explain the particular kind of moral skepticism that will concern us here is to contrast it with the other views that sometimes go by the same name.

In general, what makes moral skepticism *moral* is that it concerns morality rather than other topics. Moral skeptics might go on to be skeptics about the external world or about other minds or about induction or about all beliefs, but these other skepticisms are not entailed by

moral skepticism alone. What makes moral skeptics *skeptics* is that they raise doubts about common beliefs. Moral skeptics then differ in the kinds of doubts they raise and the targets of those doubts.

The most central versions of moral skepticism correspond to two varieties of general epistemological skepticism. These views are often conflated and confused, but the distinction between them is crucial to my project. One tradition descends from Plato's Academy, so it is called *Academic* skepticism.[1] This position is sometimes known as *Cartesian* skepticism, but that is misleading, because Descartes (1641) argued against it. Whatever you call it, this kind of skepticism is defined by the claim that nobody knows or is justified in believing anything.[2]

In contrast, this claim is neither asserted nor believed by skeptics in the other tradition. They also neither deny nor disbelieve it. They have so much doubt that they do not make any claim about whether or not anyone has any knowledge or justified belief. They suspend belief about Academic skepticism. This other variety of skepticism descends from the ancient philosopher Pyrrho, so it is often called *Pyrrhonian* skepticism.[3] Those who prefer descriptive names can think of Academic skepticism as dogmatic, doctrinaire, assertive, or committed skepticism, and Pyrrhonian skepticism as non-dogmatic, non-doctrinaire, non-assertive, and non-committed, since Pyrrhonians do not assert or commit themselves to any dogma, doctrine, or claim (positive or negative) about whether anyone knows or is justified in believing anything.

Moral skepticism comes in two corresponding varieties. *Pyrrhonian skeptics about moral knowledge* do not believe that anyone knows that any substantive moral belief is true. They doubt that anyone has moral knowledge. Still, they also do not believe the opposite, that nobody has moral knowledge. They doubt that too. Their doubts are so extreme that they do not adopt any position one way or the other about whether anyone has moral knowledge. In other words:

Pyrrhonian skeptics about moral knowledge suspend belief about whether or not anyone knows that any substantive moral belief is true.

Similarly:

Pyrrhonian skeptics about justified moral belief suspend belief about whether or not anyone is justified in holding any moral belief.

Pyrrhonian moral skeptics still might hold some substantive moral beliefs, but they do not endorse any higher-order epistemic claim about whether their own moral beliefs are justified or known.

In contrast, *Academic moral skeptics* make definite claims about the epistemic status of moral beliefs:

Academic skepticism about moral knowledge is the claim that nobody ever knows that any substantive moral belief is true.

Academic skepticism about justified moral belief is the claim that nobody is ever justified in holding any substantive moral belief.

The relation between these two versions of Academic moral skepticism depends on the nature of knowledge. If knowledge implies justified belief, as is traditionally supposed, then Academic skepticism about justified moral belief implies Academic skepticism about moral knowledge. However, even if knowledge does require justified belief, it does not require *only* justified belief, so Academic skepticism about moral knowledge does not imply Academic skepticism about justified moral belief. There might be no moral knowledge but plenty of justified moral beliefs.

In any case, both of these versions of epistemological skepticism need to be distinguished from yet another form of moral skepticism:

Skepticism about moral truth is the claim that no substantive moral belief is true.

This claim implies Academic skepticism about moral knowledge, since knowledge implies truth. However, skepticism about moral truth cannot be based on skepticism about moral knowledge, since lack of knowledge does not imply lack of truth. For similar reasons, skepticism about moral truth also cannot be based on skepticism about justified moral belief. Instead, skepticism about moral truth is usually based on views of moral language or metaphysics.

Some philosophers of language argue that sentences like "Cheating is morally wrong" cannot be either true or false because of how they resemble pure expressions of emotion (such as "Boo, Knicks!") or imperatives (such as "Go, Celtics!"). These kinds of expressions and imperatives cannot be either true or false. Thus, if these analogies hold in this respect, then, because of their nature, substantive moral beliefs also cannot be either true or false. In other words, they are not apt for evaluation in terms of truth, so:

Skepticism about moral truth-aptness is the claim that no substantive moral belief is truth-apt (that is, the right kind of thing to be either true or false).

This claim is often described as *non-cognitivism*. That label would be misleading here, however, since etymology suggests that cognitivism is about cognition, which is tied to knowledge both etymologically and in common use. Although skepticism about moral truth-aptness has implications for moral knowledge, it is directly about truth-aptness and not about moral knowledge.

Whatever you call it, skepticism about moral truth-aptness is often denied. [. . .] Opponents of such views claim that moral assertions express *beliefs*. In particular, they express beliefs that certain acts, institutions, or people have certain moral properties (such as moral rightness or wrongness) or beliefs in moral facts (such as the

fact that a certain act is morally right or wrong). This non-skeptical linguistic analysis presents moral beliefs as the right kind of thing to be true in the right conditions, but it still does not show that any moral claims are or even can be true, since assertions can express beliefs that are false or, at least, not true. Truth-*aptness* does not ensure *truth*. Thus, opponents of skepticism about truth-aptness still may endorse another version of moral skepticism, which claims that all moral beliefs must be erroneous:

> *Skepticism with moral error* (or a moral error theory) is the claim that some substantive moral beliefs are truth-apt, but none is true.[4]

This claim follows from the combination of the linguistic view that moral assertions express beliefs, a view of truth in which a belief cannot be true unless it corresponds to a fact, and a metaphysical thesis:

> *Skepticism about moral reality* is the claim that no moral facts or properties exist.[5]

• • •

Moral error theorists and skeptics about moral truth-aptness disagree about the content of moral assertions, but they still agree that no moral claim or belief is true, so both are skeptics about moral truth. None of these skeptical theses is implied by either skepticism about moral knowledge or skepticism about justified moral belief. Some moral claims might be true, even if we cannot know or have justified beliefs about which ones are true. In contrast, a converse implication seems to hold: if knowledge implies truth, and if moral claims are never true, then there cannot be any knowledge of what is moral or immoral (assuming that skeptics deny the same kind of truth that knowledge requires). Nonetheless, since the implication holds in only one direction, skepticism about moral truth is still distinct from all kinds of epistemological moral skepticism.

Yet another non-epistemological form of moral skepticism answers the question "Why be moral?" This question is used to raise many different issues. Almost everyone admits that there is sometimes some kind of reason to do some moral acts. However, many philosophers deny various universal claims, including the claims that there is always *some* reason to be moral, that there is always a distinctively *moral* (as opposed to self-interested) reason to be moral, and/or that there is always an *adequate* reason that makes it irrational not to be moral or at least not irrational to be moral. These distinct denials can be seen as separate forms of *practical moral skepticism*.

Practical moral skepticism resembles epistemological moral skepticism insofar as both kinds of skepticism deny a role to reasons in morality. However, epistemological moral skepticism is about reasons for *belief*, whereas practical moral skepticism is about reasons for *action*. Moreover, practical moral skeptics usually deny that there is *always* enough reason for moral action, whereas epistemological moral skeptics deny or doubt that there is *ever* an adequate reason for moral belief. Consequently, practical moral skepticism does not imply epistemological moral skepticism. Some moral theorists do assume that a reason to believe that an act is immoral cannot be adequate unless it also provides a reason not to do that act. However, even if the two kinds of reasons are related in this way, they are still distinct, so practical moral skepticism must not be confused with epistemological moral skepticism.

Altogether, these forms of moral skepticism are diagrammed in [Figure 20.1]. Epistemological moral skepticism will be the main topic in most of this book [see original reading], so that group of views is what I will mean henceforth whenever I refer to moral skepticism without qualification. When the context does not already make it clear, I will specify whether I have in mind Pyrrhonian or Academic skepticism and whether this skepticism is about knowledge or justified belief.

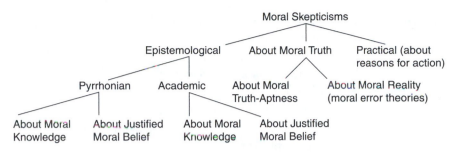

Figure 20.1

1.4. Presumptions against moral skepticism

All of these moral skepticisms come in for heavy criticism. Some opponents of moral skepticism are on a mission to save the world from horrible acts that are supposed to result when people become moral skeptics of any variety. However, skeptics about moral knowledge and justified moral belief can act well and be nice people. They need not be any less motivated to be moral, nor need they have or believe in any less reason to be moral than non-skeptics. Moral skeptics can hold substantive moral beliefs just as strongly as non-skeptics. Their substantive moral beliefs can be common and plausible ones. Moral skeptics can even believe that their moral beliefs are true by virtue of corresponding to an independent moral reality. All that moral skeptics deny is that their or anyone's moral beliefs are justified or known (and Pyrrhonian moral skeptics don't even deny that). This meta-ethical position about the epistemic status of moral beliefs need not trickle down and infect anyone's substantive moral beliefs or actions.[6]

Anti-skeptics might respond that moral skepticism does in fact often have detrimental effects on moral beliefs and actions. Nice moral skeptics might ascribe such effects to misunderstanding, but, if such misunderstandings are common, then moral skepticism might be dangerous. This fear is natural. Roy Sorensen, for example, reports that he loaned a book that defends moral skepticism to a student. As the student left, Roy wondered whether he would ever see his book again. He didn't. Still, this does not show that moral skepticism weakens moral beliefs. Maybe students with antecedently weak moral beliefs are drawn to moral skepticism.

Besides, overly strong moral beliefs can create other problems. Some busy-bodies might be less likely to interfere with other people's choices if they were moral skeptics. Moral skepticism might prevent bombastic moralists from being overbearing in ways that often thwart negotiation and sometimes ignite wars. When all such considerations are weighed, it is not at all clear that moral skepticism has bad consequences overall.

In any case, the main question here is whether moral skepticism is true. Even if adopting moral skepticism does have bad consequences, that cannot show that it is not true. Maybe belief in evolution or certain economic views also leads to bad consequences, but that would be no argument against evolution or the economic views. Similarly, even if opponents could show that it is dangerous to believe in moral skepticism, that could not show that moral skepticism is not true. So I will not spend any more time defending moral skepticism against such charges.

Critics still argue that moral skepticism conflicts with common sense. Most people think that they are justified in holding many moral beliefs, such as that it is morally wrong for parents to spank their children too hard. People also claim moral knowledge, such as when a

neighbor says, "I know that it is wrong for him to spank his daughter so hard, but I don't know what I should do about it." Moral skepticism conflicts with these common ways of talking and thinking, so moral skeptics seem to owe us some argument for their claims.

Academic moral skepticism is, moreover, a universal and abstruse claim. It is the claim that all moral beliefs have a certain epistemic status. Normally one should not make such a strong claim without some reason. One should not, for example, claim that all astronomical beliefs are unjustified unless one has some reason for this claim. Analogously, it seems that one should not claim that all moral beliefs are unjustified unless one has some positive argument. Thus, its form, like its conflict with common sense, seems to create a presumption against moral skepticism.

Moral skeptics, in response, sometimes try to shift the burden of proof to their opponents. Anyone who makes the positive moral claim that homosexual sodomy (or abortion or adultery or arson) is morally wrong seems to need some reason for that claim, just as someone who claims that there is life on Mars seems to need evidence for that claim. If the presumption is always against those who make positive moral claims, then it is opponents of moral skepticism who must carry the burden of proof. Or, at least, moral skeptics can deny that the burden of proof is on moral skeptics. Then moral skeptics may criticize any moral belief or theory without needing to offer any positive argument for moral skepticism, and their opponents need to take moral skepticism seriously enough to argue against it (see Copp 1991).

This controversy about burden of proof can be resolved by distinguishing Academic moral skepticism from Pyrrhonian moral skepticism. Academic moral skeptics (about either moral knowledge or justified moral belief) make an abstruse universal claim that conflicts with common sense, so they seem to have the burden of arguing for their claim. In contrast, Pyrrhonian moral skeptics neither assert nor deny any claim

about the epistemic status of any moral belief. They simply raise doubts about whether moral beliefs are ever known or justified. This difference suggests that Pyrrhonian moral skeptics do not take on as much burden of proof as do Academic moral skeptics.

Pyrrhonians also thereby avoid the infamous problem of the criterion (Chisholm 1982, Nelson 2003). Academic skeptics seem to assume that we can discover general criteria or conditions of knowledge before we decide which particular beliefs, if any, count as knowledge. Non-skeptics often respond that we need to determine which particular beliefs count as knowledge before we can figure out which general conditions need to be met in order for knowledge to occur. Pyrrhonians stand back from this whole debate and ask whether there is any adequate reason to begin either with general criteria or with particular cases. Since Pyrrhonians do not favor either starting point, they do not seem to need an argument for picking one starting point as opposed to the other.[7]

• • •

4.3. Arguments against justified moral belief

Epistemological moral skeptics offer a variety of arguments for their position. Here I will focus on two arguments for Academic skepticism about justified moral belief, but these arguments could be reformulated to support skepticism about moral knowledge. [. . .] In the current section, 4.3, whenever I refer to moral skepticism, I will have in mind Academic skepticism about justified moral belief.

The arguments to be discussed here are versions of well-known arguments for Academic skepticism about all beliefs of any kind, but Academic moral skeptics apply these arguments to morality in particular. Although these arguments can also be used outside morality, they should not be dismissed simply because they are

general. If the problems raised by these arguments cannot be solved at least in morality, then we cannot be justified in believing any moral claims, so Academic moral skepticism is true.

Moreover, I will argue below that these skeptical arguments have special force within morality. One reason is that special problems with moral beliefs create a greater need for inferential confirmation. [...] Also, many smart people actually do believe and have some reason to believe in the skeptical hypothesis of moral nihilism. [...] The role of these differences between moral beliefs and other beliefs will come out as we outline the skeptical arguments.

4.3.1. A regress argument

The first featured argument is a regress argument, which derives from Sextus Empiricus (1996, book I, chap. XV). Arguments of this kind sometimes concern knowledge, but the version here will focus on justified belief. Its goal is to lay out all of the ways in which a person might be justified in believing something and then to argue that none of them works.

The first premise denies that any moral belief can be justified non-inferentially (that is, independently of the believer's ability to infer that belief):

> (1) If any person S is ever justified in believing any moral claim that p, then S must be able to infer p from some other beliefs of S.

In short, any justified moral belief must be justified by some inference.[8]

Premise (1) is often supported by examples of moral disagreements and of moral beliefs that are distorted by cultural and psychological forces. [...] When moral believers disagree, both believers might be permissively or instrumentally or somewhat or personally justified, but it is hard to see how both conflicting moral beliefs could be positively, epistemically, adequately, and impersonally justified apart from any inference at all. To claim to be so justified in the face of disagreement without being able to give any reason that could be expressed in any inference would seem dogmatic, arrogant, and disrespectful of those with whom one disagrees. Even if some moral beliefs are not subject to disagreement, moral disagreements and distortions are widespread enough to make all of morality an area where inferential justification is needed, according to moral skeptics. [...] This need is registered in premise (1).

Once inference is required, there are only three options:

> (2) Any inference must have either (a) no normative premises or (b) some normative premises but no moral premises or (c) some moral premises.

Option (a) might seem to have advantages if non-normative premises are easier to justify than normative premises. This is why some naturalists try to derive morality from science.

However, moral skeptics deny that non-normative premises alone could ever be enough to justify conclusions that are moral and, hence, normative:

> (3) No person S is ever justified in believing any moral claim that p by an inference with no normative premises.

If an inference has no normative premises at all, but its conclusion is that an act is morally wrong, then the inference seems to depend on a suppressed premise that all acts with certain non-normative features are morally wrong. Such suppressed premises seem moral and, hence, normative. But then the crucial inference does not really work without any normative premises. So premise (3) seems safe.

The next possibility is to justify a moral conclusion with an inference whose premises are not moral but still are normative in some

other way. The most popular variety within this approach is contractarianism. Such contractarians start with supposedly non-moral premises about who is rational and sometimes also about who is impartial. Then they argue that rational impartial people would agree to certain moral rules (or norms or standards), so the corresponding moral beliefs are true or justified. A basic problem with this approach is that inferences like these assume that an act is morally wrong if it violates a rule that would be accepted by all people who are rational and impartial in the specified ways. This bridge principle might seem innocuous at first, because it has little content until "rational" and "impartial" are defined. Once these terms are defined, however, the bridge principle ceases to be morally neutral. This becomes clear when different contractarians use different notions of rationality and impartiality to reach conflicting moral conclusions.

There are other arguments from non-moral norms to moral conclusions, but they run into similar problems.[9] Moral skeptics generalize to the conclusion that:

(4) No person S is ever justified in believing any moral claim that p by an inference with some normative premises but no moral premises.

Premises (1)–(4) together imply that moral beliefs must be justified by actual or potential inferences from moral beliefs.

This creates a problem. Although the justifying premises must include some moral beliefs, not just any moral beliefs will do:

(5) No person S is ever justified in believing a moral claim that p by an inference with a moral premise unless S is also justified in believing that moral premise itself.

Premise (5) is denied by some contextualists (Wellman 1971; Annis 1978; Timmons 1998), who claim that, even if a moral belief is not itself justified, if it is shared within a certain social context without being questioned, then it can be used to justify other moral beliefs. However, the fact that a moral belief happens to be held without question by everyone in a social group is not sufficient to make anyone justified in believing it or what follows from it. To see this, suppose that everyone in a small town believes without question that it is immoral for a black person to marry a white person. They infer that it is immoral for Ray, who is black, to marry Terry, who is white. This conclusion is not justified, because the general belief is not justified (since it should be questioned, even if it isn't). Indeed, every belief would be justified if a belief could be justified simply by inferring it from an unjustified belief, since every belief can be validly inferred from itself. The only way to avoid such absurd results, according to moral skeptics, is to accept (5).

But then how can the needed moral premises be justified? The only remaining alternative is to infer the moral premises from still other moral beliefs which must also be justified by inferring them from still other moral beliefs, and so on. To justify a moral belief thus requires a chain (or branching tree) of justifying beliefs or premises. This justifying chain can take only two forms, so:

(6) No person S is justified in believing any moral claim that p by an inference from moral premises unless S is justified by a chain of inferences that either goes on infinitely or includes p itself as an essential premise.

The latter kind of chain is usually described as circular, although its structure is more complex than a simple circle.

Moral skeptics deny that either kind of chain can justify any moral belief. First:

(7) No person S is ever justified in believing any moral claim that p by a chain of inferences that includes p as an essential premise.

Any argument that includes its conclusion as a premise will be valid and will remain valid if other premises are added. However, anyone who doubts the conclusion will have just as much reason to doubt the premise. So, skeptics claim that nothing is gained when a premise just restates the belief to be justified.

Premise (7) is opposed by moral coherentists. Recent coherentists have emphasized that they are not inferring a belief from itself in a linear way. Instead, a moral belief is supposed to be justified because it coheres in some way with a body of beliefs that is coherent in some way. Still, moral skeptics deny that coherence is enough for justification. One reason is that the internal coherence of a set of beliefs is not evidence of any relation to anything outside of the beliefs. Moreover, every belief—no matter how ridiculous—can cohere with some body of beliefs that is internally coherent. Such possibilities are supposed to show why coherence is not enough to justify moral beliefs and why premise (7) holds.

The final possible form of justification is an infinite chain. Moral skeptics, of course, claim that:

> (8) No person S is ever justified in believing any moral claim that p by a chain of inferences that goes on infinitely.

Someone who denied this premise could be called a moral infinitist, but nobody clearly develops this approach (though suggestions can be found in Peirce 1934, 154–55, 158, and 186; Brink 1989, appendix 1; and Sanford 1984).

Now moral skeptics can draw a final conclusion. (1)–(8) together imply:

> (9) No person is ever justified in believing any moral claim.

This is Academic skepticism about justified moral belief. It might seem implausible, but the regress argument is valid, so its conclusion can be escaped only by denying one or more of its premises.

Different premises are denied by different opponents of moral skepticism. Moral intuitionists deny premise (1). Moral naturalists deny premise (3). Moral normativists deny premise (4). Moral contextualists deny premise (5). Moral coherentists deny premise (7). And moral infinitists would deny premise (8). The regress argument, thus, provides a useful way to classify theories in moral epistemology, regardless of whether it establishes moral skepticism.

The most important question, however, is whether the regress argument shows that Academic moral skepticism is true. I have tried to say enough to give some initial plausibility to the premises of the regress argument, but each premise deserves much more careful attention. [. . .] There is much to be said on both sides of this regress argument for Academic moral skepticism. That is one reason why Pyrrhonian moral skeptics end up suspending belief about its conclusion.

4.3.2. *A skeptical hypothesis argument*

The second featured argument, which derives from René Descartes (1641), starts from the common experience of being deceived. For example, yesterday I was driving down a strange road. I thought I saw a lake in the distance. My wife thought and said that it was really a river, not a lake. We were in a hurry, so we did not check it out, but I still believe that it was a lake. Is my belief justified? Not if my experience was compatible with its being either a lake or a river and I have no other ground for believing that my wife was incorrect. My belief that it is a lake also cannot be justified if I cannot rule out the possibility that it was a bay or a bayou, even if I can rule out the possibility of a river. Such everyday examples suggest the general principle that I am not justified in believing something if there is any contrary hypothesis that I cannot rule out.

This does not mean that I must self-consciously think about every other possibility and run through an argument to rule out each one. If I don't think about the possibility of an inlet off the ocean, I still can rule out that possibility if I possess the background information that we are in Kansas, which is nowhere near any ocean, assuming that I have the minimal intelligence needed to use this information. As long as I possess that information and intelligence, I am able to rule out the hypothesis of an inlet off the ocean, even if I never actually bother to use that information to rule out that possibility. However, if I have no information from any source that could be used to rule out the possibility of an inlet, then I cannot rule out that possibility. The same goes for the possibilities of a bay and a bayou. If I cannot rule out any one of the contrary hypotheses, then I am not justified in believing that what I see is a lake. This is supposed to be a common standard for justified belief.

When this supposedly common sense principle is applied thoroughly, it leads to skepticism. All that skeptics need to show is that, for each belief, there is some contrary hypothesis that cannot be ruled out. It need not be the same hypothesis contrary to every belief. However, skeptics usually buy wholesale instead of retail, so they seek a single hypothesis that is contrary to all or very many common beliefs and which cannot be ruled out in any way.

The famous Cartesian hypothesis is of a demon who deceives me in all of my beliefs about the external world while also ensuring that my beliefs are completely coherent. If there is such a deceiving demon, then there really is no lake when I think that I see one. Nobody claims that such a deceiving demon actually exists, but that is not needed for the argument. All the argument needs is that a deceiving demon is possible. Descartes' deceiving demon does seem possible.[10] In addition, this possibility cannot be ruled out by any experiences or beliefs of any kind, because of how the deceiving

demon is defined. Whatever I seem to see, feel, hear, smell, or taste, my sensations might all be caused by a deceiving demon. The deceiving demon hypothesis is contrary to many of my beliefs, but that is just what one would expect if there were a deceiving demon. Since there is no way to rule out this skeptical hypothesis, my beliefs about the lake are not justified, according to the above principle. Moreover, there is nothing special about my beliefs about the lake. Everything I believe about the external world (or even mathematics) is incompatible with the deceiving demon hypothesis. Skeptics conclude that no such belief is justified.

This kind of argument can be applied to moral beliefs in several ways. First, another demon might deceive us about morality (either alone or in addition to other topics). Almost everyone believes that it is morally wrong to torture babies just for fun, but we might be deceived in our beliefs that babies feel pain or that they have moral rights. A demon might make us believe that some creatures have moral rights when really they do not, although other things do; or a demon might make us believe that some creatures have moral rights when really nothing does (just as a demon might deceive us into believing that some women are witches when really none are). Such a deceiving demon seems possible and cannot be ruled out by the fact that it seems obvious that babies have moral rights, any more than Descartes' deceiving demon could be ruled out by the fact that it seems obvious to me when I am swimming in water. Such responses would beg the question.

Some philosophers (e.g., Peirce 1934) object to such deception scenarios on the grounds that nobody really does believe in such deceiving demons and nobody could have any reason to believe in them, so skeptical hypotheses like these are idle and do not express real doubts. I do not see why this matters, so this response strikes me as inadequate. However, I do not want my argument to depend on this assumption, so

I will avoid this objection by discussing a different skeptical scenario.

The same kind of argument can be constructed with a skeptical hypothesis that people really do believe and give reasons to believe.[11] We already discussed this one:

> Moral Nihilism = Nothing is morally wrong, required, bad, good, etc.[12]

This hypothesis is constructed so as to leave no way to rule it out. Since moral nihilists question all of our beliefs that anything is morally wrong, and so on, they leave us with no moral starting points on which to base arguments against them without begging the question at issue. If we cannot start from moral premises, then the only way to refute moral nihilism is to derive moral conclusions from morally neutral premises, but all such attempts are subject to strong criticisms from many philosophers, not only moral skeptics. So there seems to be no way to rule out moral nihilism. (See part II.) [see original reading] Thus, this hypothesis fits perfectly into a skeptical argument.

The skeptical hypothesis argument is clearest when applied to an example. Moral nihilism implies that it is not morally wrong to torture babies just for fun. So, according to the general principle above, one must be able to rule out moral nihilism in order to be justified in believing that torturing babies just for fun is morally wrong. Moral skeptics conclude that this moral belief is not justified. More precisely:

(i)   I am not justified in believing that moral nihilism is false.

(ii) I am justified in believing that (p) "It is morally wrong to torture babies just for fun" entails (q) "Moral nihilism is false."

(iii) If I am justified in believing that p, and I am justified in believing that p entails q,[13] then I am justified in believing that q.

(iv) Therefore, I am not justified in believing that (p) it is morally wrong to torture babies just for fun.

This moral belief (p) is not especially problematic in any way. Indeed, it seems as obvious as any definite moral belief.[14] Hence, the argument can be generalized to cover any moral belief. Moral skeptics conclude that no moral belief is justified.[15]

There are two main ways to respond to such skeptical arguments. First, some anti-skeptics deny (i) and claim that skeptical hypotheses can be ruled out somehow. They might argue that moral nihilism can be ruled out by logic and semantics alone, because it is inconsistent or meaningless or semantically incoherent. [. . .] Other attempts to rule out moral nihilism are made by naturalists, normativists, intuitionists, and coherentists. These attempts mirror the stages of the regress argument in the preceding Section (4.3.1) [. . .] The basic dilemma is clear: moral nihilism cannot be ruled out without at least some moral assumptions, but any moral assumptions beg the question against moral nihilism, no matter how obvious they might seem to us. If there is no way around or out of this dilemma, then there is no way to rule out moral nihilism, as premise (i) claims.

Another response, which has gained popularity recently (DeRose and Warfield 1999, part two), is to deny premise (iii). This is often described as a principle of closure. Since a belief entails the denial of every contrary hypothesis, this closure principle in effect says that I cannot be justified in believing p unless I am justified in denying every hypothesis contrary to p, that is, unless I can rule out all contrary hypotheses. This principle has been denied by relevant alternative theorists, who claim instead that only relevant hypotheses need to be ruled out. On this theory, if skeptical hypotheses are not relevant, then a belief that it is morally wrong to torture babies just for fun can be justified, even if the believer cannot rule out moral nihilism.

For this response to have force, however, opponents of moral skepticism need to say why

moral nihilism is irrelevant. It certainly seems relevant, for the simple reason that it is coherent, believed, supported by arguments, and directly contrary to the moral belief that is supposed to be justified. Compare Curly, who gets a sealed letter from Larry. Curly believes that the letter is a dinner invitation, but Moe thinks that the letter is a request for a favor. Each has some reason for his belief, each tells the other, and their reasons are equally strong. In these circumstances, before reading the letter, Curly does not seem epistemically justified in believing that the letter is a dinner invitation unless he can rule out Moe's contrary hypothesis that it is a request for a favor. That hypothesis cannot be dismissed as irrelevant as long as it is coherent and believed for some reason. The same standards suggest that the hypothesis of moral nihilism also cannot be dismissed as irrelevant as long as it is coherent and believed for some reason. Just as Curly needs to open the letter to rule out Moe's hypothesis before he can be justified in believing his contrary hypothesis, so opponents of moral nihilism need to find some way to rule out moral nihilism before they can be epistemically justified in their positive moral beliefs.

This point holds even if it is legitimate to dismiss skeptical hypotheses that nobody believes or has any reason to believe. The hypothesis of moral nihilism is coherent, some intelligent people believe it, and they give reasons to believe it. In addition to those already discussed [. . .] some people are led to moral nihilism because they cannot find any defensible moral theory. If consequentialism is indefensible (as its critics argue), and if deontological restrictions and permissions are mysterious and unfounded (as their critics argue), then some people might believe moral nihilism because they rule out the alternatives. The point is not that such reasons for moral nihilism are adequate. The point here is only that there is enough reason to believe moral nihilism that it cannot baldly be dismissed as irrelevant on this basis.

Notes

1 My stipulated usage should not be confused with the different meaning of "academical" skepticism in Hume ([1748] 1888).

2 Most skeptics in this tradition make the stronger modal claim that nobody *can* know or be justified in believing anything. I define Academic skepticism by the weaker non-modal claim about what people *do* know rather than what they *can* know, because I will criticize Academic skepticism, and I do not want to be accused of being unfair to this opponent by making its claim too strong. For various views on Academic skepticism, see DeRose and Warfield 1999.

3 For more on Pyrrho and recent Pyrrhonians, see Sinnott-Armstrong 2004.

4 Examples include Mackie (1946, 1977), who claims that positive moral beliefs are false; and Joyce (2001), who claims that positive moral beliefs are neither true nor false, despite being truth-apt. See also Robinson (1948), J. P. Burgess (1979), Hinckfuss (1987), Garner (1994), J. A. Burgess (1998), and Greene (2002).

5 Compare Nietzsche [1888] 1954: "There are altogether no moral facts." The nature of moral facts will be discussed in sections 2.2.4 and 3.1 [see original reading].

6 Even if some moral skeptics did give up the belief that harming others is morally wrong, for example, they still might have enough non-moral reason not to harm other people if they care about other people. Thus, even the lack of moral belief need not lead to immoral action.

7 Pyrrhonian moral skepticism thereby avoids problems pointed out by Nelson (2003), who argued that my earlier Academic moral skepticism begs the question as much as its denial, which he endorses. I am very grateful to Nelson for his criticisms, which were part of what convinced me to become a Pyrrhonian moral skeptic instead of an Academic moral skeptic.

8 To be justified by an inference is to be justified by either an actual inference or a potential inference that the believer could but does not draw. Thus, believers are justified by an inference when an ability to infer is required for them to be justified.

9 Premises (3) and (4) are also often supported by the general doctrine that logic is conservative in

the sense that all of the content of a valid argument must be contained somewhere in the premises, so you can't get out what you didn't put in. See, for example, Pigden 1991, 423.

10   Despite arguments often attributed to Putnam (1981, chap. 1). For responses to Putnam, see DeRose and Warfield 1999, part one.

11   Defenders of something like moral nihilism include Mackie (1946, 1977), Robinson (1948), J. P. Burgess (1979), Hinckfuss (1987), Garner (1994), J. A. Burgess (1998), Joyce (2001), and Greene (2002). Parallel arguments could be constructed with other coherent but extreme hypotheses, such as moral egoism (see Rachels 1971), relativism (Harman 1977), and so on, which people really do believe and give reasons to believe. However, I will focus on moral nihilism.

12   This hypothesis is normally embedded in a larger theory that explains why most people deny it. I will focus on the hypothesis alone when its logical relations are what matter, but it should be remembered that moral nihilists also try to explain away contrary appearances and beliefs, so their overall theory is more complex than this central claim in isolation.

13   Some might want to add that it must also be true that p entails q, or that I am justified in believing the conjunction of p and (p entails q), but these additions would not affect the main points here.

14   Disjunctions might seem more obvious, such as: it is morally wrong either to torture babies just for fun or to commit genocide or to cheat just to win a game against a friend or. . . . The disjunction could go on; and the longer it is, the more chance that at least one of its disjuncts is true. Long disjunctions could be avoided by existential quantifiers. It might seem even more obvious that *some* act is morally wrong. However, to use that claim against moral nihilists is like saying "Surely, something is a sin" to those who deny (the religious notion of) sins or "Surely, someone is a witch" to refute those who deny witches.

15   The argument could also be run against moral knowledge: I do not know that moral nihilism is not true; but I do know that "It is morally wrong to torture babies just for fun" entails "Moral nihilism is not true"; and, if I know that p, and I know that p entails q, then I know that q; so I do not know that

it is morally wrong to torture babies just for fun. However, I will focus on justified moral belief.

References

Annis, David B. 1978. "A Contextualist Theory of Epistemic Justification." *American Philosophical Quarterly* 15:213–19.

Brink, David. 1989. *Moral Realism and the Foundations of Ethics.* New York: Cambridge University Press.

Burgess, J. A. 1998. "Error Theories and Values." *Australasian Journal of Philosophy* 76(4):534–52.

Burgess, J. P. 1979. "Against Ethics." Unpublished manuscript, Department of Philosophy, Princeton University.

Chisholm, Roderick M. 1982. "The Problem of the Criterion." In *The Foundations of Knowing.* Minneapolis: University of Minnesota Press.

Copp, David. 1991. "Moral Skepticism." *Philosophical Studies* 62:203–33.

DeRose, Keith, and Warfield, Ted, eds. 1999. *Skepticism: A Contemporary Reader.* New York: Oxford University Press.

Descartes, René. 1641. *Meditations.*

Garner, Richard. 1994. *Beyond Morality.* Philadelphia: Temple University Press.

Greene, Joshua. 2002. *The Terrible, Horrible, No Good, Very Bad Truth about Morality and What to Do About It.*

Habermas, Jürgen. 1990. *Moral Consciousness and Communicative Action.* Trans. C. Lenhart and S. Weber. Cambridge: MIT Press.

Hare, R.M. 1965. *Freedom and Reason.* Oxford: Clarendon Press.

———. 1981. *Moral Thinking.* Oxford: Clarendon Press.

Harman, Gilbert. 1977. *Morality.* New York: Oxford University Press.

Hinckfuss, Ian. 1987. "The Moral Society: Its Structures and Effects." Preprint Series in Environmental Philosophy, Department of Philosophy, 16, Australian National University.

Hume, David. 1748. *Enquiries Concerning Human Understanding and Concerning the Principles of Morals,* ed. L. A. Selby-Bigge. Oxford: Clarendon Press, 1888.

Joyce, Richard. 2001. *The Myth of Morality.* New York: Cambridge University Press.

Mackie, J. L. 1946. "A Refutation of Morals." *Australasian Journal of Philosophy* 24:77–90.

——. 1977. *Ethics: Inventing Right and Wrong.* Harmondsworth, Middlesex, UK: Penguin.

Nelson, Mark. 2003. "Sinnott-Armstrong's Moral Scepticism." *Ratio* 16:63–82.

Nietzsche, Friedrich. 1888. *Twilight of the Idols.* In *The Portable Nietzsche,* trans. Walter Kaufmann. New York: Viking Press, 1954.

Peirce, Charles Saunders. 1934. *Collected Papers,* Vol. 5. Cambridge: Harvard University Press.

Pigden, Charles. 1991. "Naturalism." In *A Companion to Ethics,* ed. Peter Singer. Oxford: Blackwell.

Putnam, Hilary. 1981. *Reason, Truth, and History.* New York: Cambridge University Press.

Rachels, James. 1971. "Egoism and Moral Skepticism." In *A New Introduction to Philosophy,* ed. Steven M. Cahn. New York: Harper and Row.

Robinson, R. 1948. "The Emotive Theory of Ethics." *Proceedings of the Aristotelian Society, Supplementary Volume.*

Sanford, David. 1984. "Infinite Regress Arguments." In *Principles of Philosophical Reasoning,* ed. James H. Fetzer. Totowa, NJ: Rowman and Allanheld.

Sextus Empiricus. 1996. *Outlines of Pyrrhonism.* In *The Skeptic Way,* trans. Benson Mates. New York: Oxford University Press.

Sinnott-Armstrong, Walter. ed. 2004. *Pyrrhonian Skepticism.* New York: Oxford University Press.

Timmons, Mark. 1998. *Morality without Foundations: A Defense of Ethical Contextualism.* New York: Oxford University Press.

Wellman, Carl. 1971. *Challenge and Response: Justification in Ethics.* Carbondale: Southern Illinois University Press.

Chapter 21

George Sher

BUT I COULD BE WRONG

I. Introduction

MY AIM in this essay is to explore the implications of the fact that even our most deeply held moral beliefs have been profoundly affected by our upbringing and experience—that if any of us had had a sufficiently different upbringing and set of experiences, he almost certainly would now have a very different set of moral beliefs and very different habits of moral judgment. This fact, together with the associated proliferation of incompatible moral doctrines, is sometimes invoked in support of liberal policies of toleration and restraint, but the relevance of these considerations to individual moral deliberation has received less attention.[1] In Sections II through V, I shall argue that this combination of contingency and controversy poses a serious challenge to the authority of our moral judgments. In Section VI, I shall explore a promising way of responding to this challenge.

II. The challenge to my moral judgments

In Chapter II of *On Liberty*, John Stuart Mill observes that the person who uncritically accepts the opinion of "the world"

> devolves upon his own world the responsibility of being in the right against the dissentient worlds of other people; and it never

troubles him that mere accident has decided which of these numerous worlds is the object of his reliance, and that the same causes which made him a churchman in London would have made him a Buddhist or a Confucian in Peking.[2]

Along similar lines, John Rawls observes in *Political Liberalism* that the "burdens of judgment" that make moral disagreement inevitable include the fact that

> to some extent (how great we cannot tell) the way we assess evidence and weight moral and political values is shaped by our total experience, our whole course of life up to now; and our total experiences must always differ.[3]

Despite their sketchiness, both passages appear to contain much truth. Moreover, the two passages are complementary in that Mill emphasizes the influence of contingent factors on the content of a person's most basic religious (and, by extension, moral and philosophical) convictions, while Rawls focuses more on the influence that contingent factors have on the inferences and judgments that a person makes *within* his basic frame-work. Thus, taken together, the two passages suggest that the influence of contingent factors on moral judgment is certainly extensive and may well be pervasive.

The principles that Mill and Rawls are defending in these passages are not the same: the passage from Mill appears in his famous defense of freedom of speech, while Rawls's point is that in a pluralistic society, a conception of justice must be defensible in terms accessible to all. However, each of these principles purports to provide a reason not to act in all the ways that initially appear to be called for by one's moral beliefs. This is why Mill and Rawls are both comfortable invoking a consideration—the influence of contingent factors on our moral beliefs—which, if taken seriously, is bound to undermine our confidence in the truth or rational defensibility of these moral beliefs.

But the same consideration that is so congenial to liberal principles that require us to distance ourselves from our moral beliefs in political contexts is decidedly uncongenial to our efforts to marshal these moral beliefs when we deliberate as individuals. My awareness that I would now have different moral convictions if I had had a different upbringing or different experiences may make it easier for me to put my moral beliefs out of play in the interest of allowing competing beliefs a fair hearing, or for the sake of arriving at terms of social cooperation acceptable to all. This same awareness, however, makes it correspondingly *harder* for me to act on my moral convictions when these conflict with the moral convictions of others. There is an obvious tension between my belief that my moral assessment of a situation is right while yours is wrong and my further belief that it is only an accident of fate that I assess the situation in my way rather than yours.

This tension raises questions about what I have reason to do in various practical interpersonal contexts. Perhaps most obviously, it raises such questions when I take myself to be morally justified in treating you in a way that you find morally objectionable—when, for example, I think I am not obligated to finance your dubious business venture despite our long friendship, or when you demand attention that I feel I do not

owe. The tension also muddies the waters when you and I disagree about something we must do together—when, for example, I want to give our failing student a retest but you worry about fairness to other students, or when we disagree about how much of our joint income we should donate to charity. It even raises doubts when I am contemplating taking some action that will not affect you at all, but of which you morally disapprove—when, for example, I am considering joining the Marines, contributing to a pro-choice candidate, or taking spectacular revenge on a hated rival, but you offer dissenting counsel.[4] In all of the aforementioned contexts, my awareness that I might well have taken a position like yours if my history had been sufficiently different will not sit well with my belief that I have more reason to act on my moral beliefs than I have to act on yours.[5]

Why, exactly, do these beliefs not sit well together? The answer, I think, is that my belief that I have more reason to act on my own moral beliefs than on yours appears to rest on a further belief that my own moral beliefs are somehow *better*—that they are truer, more defensible, more reasonable, or something similar. However, if I believe that it is only an accident of history that I hold my own moral beliefs rather than yours, then I must also believe that which of us has the better moral beliefs is also an accident of history. This of course does not mean that my belief that my own moral beliefs are better is wrong or baseless, but it does mean that I would have that same belief even if it *were* wrong or baseless. However, once I realize that I would have this belief whether or not it were true, I no longer seem entitled to use it in my practical deliberations.

III. The challenge not a form of skepticism

As just presented, the problems raised by the contingent origins of our moral beliefs bear a striking similarity to certain familiar skeptical

worries. There is, in particular, an obvious affinity between the claim advanced at the end of the preceding section—that we are not in a position to tell whether we hold our moral beliefs because they are defensible or true or merely because of our upbringing—and the standard skeptical claim that we are not in a position to tell whether we hold our empirical beliefs because they represent reality accurately or merely because they have been instilled in us by an evil demon or a mad scientist stimulating a brain in a vat. Thus, isn't the current problem merely a special case of a far more general skeptical challenge—a challenge whose force we all acknowledge, but with which we long ago learned to coexist?

There is both something right and something wrong about this suggestion. What is right is its premise that the current problem has the same abstract structure as a very common form of skepticism; what is wrong is its conclusion that we can therefore live with the current problem as easily as we can live with skepticism. In fact, for three reasons, the current problem is far more vexing and urgent.

First, unlike the standard skeptical hypotheses, the claim that each person's moral beliefs were shaped by his upbringing and life experiences has an obvious basis in fact. We have no evidence at all that any of our empirical beliefs were caused by an evil demon or a mad scientist; and even the hypothesis that I am now dreaming, though somewhat more realistic, is improbable in light of the low frequency with which experiences with all the marks of wakefulness—vividness, continuity, coherence, self-consciousness, and the rest—have in the past turned out to be dreams. Thus, the most that any skeptical hypothesis can show is that all of our beliefs about the world *might* have had causes that operate independently of the truth of what we believe. In stark contrast, however, the fact that people's moral beliefs vary systematically with their backgrounds and life experiences shows considerably more, for in becoming aware of this, I acquire a

positive reason to suspect that when you and I disagree about what morality demands, my taking the position I do has less to do with the superiority of my moral insight than with the nature of the causes that have operated on me.

The second reason that the current problem is harder to live with than is general skepticism is that we have significant second-order reason to be confident in our shared empirical beliefs, but no corresponding second-order reason to be confident in our controversial moral beliefs. In the case of our shared empirical beliefs, the second-order reason for confidence is provided by the various background theories that imply the reliability, within broad limits, of the processes through which these beliefs were formed—physiological theories about the mechanisms through which our sensory receptors put us in contact with the world, biological theories that imply that reliable belief-forming mechanisms have survival value, and so on. Even if appealing to these theories begs the question against global skepticism, our acceptance of them still makes such skepticism easier to ignore by reinforcing the confidence that we feel in our empirical beliefs when we are not contemplating the skeptical challenge. By contrast, my acceptance of the same background theories does not similarly reinforce my confidence that my own moral beliefs are better than yours, for because the theories imply the reliability of belief-forming mechanisms that are common to all members of our species, they provide no basis for any distinctions *among* individuals. Indeed, if anything, my awareness that a different upbringing and set of experiences would have caused me to acquire a different set of moral beliefs provides evidence that the processes through which I acquired my actual moral beliefs are probably *not* reliable.

Even by themselves, these two reasons would suggest that the current problem is much harder to live with than is general skepticism. However, a third reason makes the case even more strongly.

Simply put, the most serious obstacle to our bracketing the current problem in the same way we routinely bracket skepticism is that unlike the fabrications of the skeptic, the current challenge to our moral beliefs is directly relevant to action.

For, as is often remarked, the hypotheses that all of my beliefs are being orchestrated by an evil demon or a master neuromanipulator, or that I am now dreaming, have no obvious impact either on what I *ought* to do or on what I am *inclined* to do. Even if I were able to suspend my commonsense beliefs, my awareness that various types of experience have been regularly connected in the past might well justify my "acting" as if the world were exactly as it seemed;[6] and, in any case, suspending my commonsense beliefs in practical contexts is not a live option. As Hume famously observed, even if I find skepticism convincing in the isolation of my study, I will, as soon as I emerge, "find myself absolutely and necessarily determined to live, and talk, and act like other people in the common affairs of life."[7] When it comes time to act, our robust animal realism will always dominate.

But not so our corresponding tendency to *moral* realism, for although we standardly do proceed as though our moral convictions are in some sense true, our confidence in their truth is neither anchored in our animal nature (since nonhuman animals evidently do not share it) nor invulnerable to reflective challenge. Because this confidence is relatively superficial, we cannot assume that it would survive a compelling demonstration that it cannot be defended. There is, to be sure, a real question about what it would be rational for me to do if I did lose confidence in my own moral beliefs—I would, after all, have exactly the same grounds for doubt about your moral beliefs as I would about mine—but at a minimum, this loss of confidence would reopen many questions that my own moral beliefs were previously thought to settle. Because of this, the challenge to the authority of my moral judgments seems capable of destabilizing my practical deliberation in a way that general skepticism cannot.

IV. The interplay of controversy and contingency

As just presented, the challenge to the authority of my moral judgments has a dual focus, for it appears to rest both on a premise about moral disagreement and on a premise about the contingent origins of my moral beliefs and ways of assessing evidence and weighting competing values. (For brevity, I shall henceforth refer to the combination of a person's moral beliefs and his ways of assessing evidence and weighting values as his *moral outlook*.) Respectively, these premises are as follows:

(1) I often disagree with others about what I morally ought to do.

(2) The moral outlook that supports my current judgment about what I ought to do has been shaped by my upbringing and experiences; for (just about) any alternative judgment, there is some different upbringing and set of experiences that would have caused me to acquire a moral outlook that would in turn have supported this alternative judgment.

Because these premises are logically distinct—because it could be true that you and I disagree about what one of us ought to do but false that our backgrounds have shaped our moral outlooks, or true that our backgrounds have shaped our moral outlooks but false that we disagree—it is not entirely obvious how (1) and (2) fit together. Are they both doing real work in the argument challenging the authority of my moral judgments? If so, why are they both needed? If not, which is necessary and which superfluous?

One possible answer is that the argument does not require both (1) and (2), but that each provides an independent route to the argument's

conclusion. On this account, the version of the argument that relies exclusively on (1) is simply that

> (A1) Because I am just another member of the human species (and because I am far from the smartest, the most clearheaded, or the best-informed member of that species), I have no special reason to regard my own moral judgments as being any better grounded, or any more likely to be true, than the moral judgments of any number of others who see things differently.[8]

By contrast, the version that relies exclusively on (2) asserts that

> (A2) Because a different upbringing and set of experiences would have caused me to have a very different moral outlook, my having the moral outlook that informs my specific moral judgments is unlikely to have much to do with that outlook's justifiability or truth.

Because these two versions of the argument have such different structures—because (A1) turns on the fact that there is nothing special about me while (A2) turns on the very different fact that the process through which I acquired my moral outlook is unlikely to be reliable—we may be tempted to conclude that each version must be evaluated separately and hence that the original combined appeal to (1) and (2) is a misbegotten hybrid.

But that temptation should be resisted; for by thus separating the appeals to (1) and (2), we would gravely weaken the case for the conclusion that they both seek to establish. The reason that separating them would have this effect is that (A1)'s appeal to (1) is vulnerable to an obvious objection that is best blocked by introducing (2), while (A2)'s appeal to (2) is similarly vulnerable to an obvious objection that is best blocked by introducing (1). To bring out the underlying synergy between (1) and (2),

and thus to reconstruct the challenge to the authority of our moral judgments in its strongest form, we must look more closely at each of these simpler arguments.

To argument (A1), which asserts that I have no special reason to favor my own moral judgments over those of others who are no less intelligent and well-informed, the obvious rejoinder is that the grounds for favoring one moral judgment over another typically consist not of facts about the persons who make the judgments, but rather of evidence or arguments for and against the judgments themselves. There are, to be sure, some obvious counterexamples to this claim—we may indeed be justified in discounting someone's moral judgments if we have independent evidence that he is misinformed, confused, biased, or very stupid—but such cases are the exception rather than the rule. In the far more standard case, our reasoning runs just the other way: we infer that our interlocutor's thought processes must somehow have gone awry because we believe there are independent grounds for rejecting his conclusion. Thus, as long as the challenge to my own moral judgments extends no further than (1)'s claim that many others do not share them, I can resist it through the simple expedient of reminding myself of whichever considerations I take to make my own judgments more plausible than those of my interlocutors.

This rejoinder becomes problematic, however, as soon as we factor in (2)'s claim that my having the moral outlook that informs my moral judgment is itself an accident of my history; for the import of this claim is to cast doubt not only on my judgment itself, but also on whatever evidence or arguments I take to support it. If my upbringing and experiences had been sufficiently different, I would now share not only my interlocutor's conviction that I ought to abandon my grand plan to humiliate the rival who has tormented me for years, but also my interlocutor's disdain for the moral arguments that I currently take to underwrite

that plan. However, once I agree that I have been caused to accept these arguments by factors independent of their force, I can no longer confidently base my decision on my conviction that they *have* force.

Thus, argument (A1), which appeals to (1) alone, seems unlikely to succeed unless it is supplemented by (2). Conversely, argument (A2), which appeals to (2) alone, requires supplementation by (1). Argument (A2), it will be recalled, attempts to move from (2)'s claim that a different upbringing and set of experiences would have caused me to acquire a different moral outlook to the conclusion that my having the moral outlook I do (and, by extension, my reaching the moral judgments I do) probably has little to do with its (and their) justifiability or truth. However, as it stands, this argument is a non sequitur, since even if the upbringing and experiences that caused me to acquire my current moral outlook would have had this effect on me whether or not my current moral outlook was justifiable or true, it hardly follows that the social conditions that caused me to have that upbringing and those experiences would also have existed regardless of whether or not my current moral outlook was justifiable or true. For all that has yet been said, it may have been precisely the truth or justifiability of the various elements of my current moral outlook that caused them to work their way into the culture that in turn caused me to acquire that outlook.[9] Because this possibility remains open, it does not follow from the fact that a different upbringing and set of experiences would have caused me to acquire a different moral outlook that it is unreasonable for me to continue acting on the judgments that my actual moral outlook supports.

But whatever force this rejoinder has against (A2)'s appeal to (2) alone, the rejoinder becomes problematic as soon as we factor in (1)'s claim that people's moral judgments often differ; for if my socially inculcated moral outlook has led me to reach one conclusion about what I ought to do while yours has led you to reach another, then the social determinants of at least one of our moral outlooks *cannot* be indirectly traceable to the justifiability or truth of all of its operative elements. Even if I can reasonably believe that I was caused to acquire all the operative elements of my own moral outlook by social factors that owed their existence to the justifiability or truth of those elements as long as you and I agree that I may not torture or murder my hated rival, I can no longer reasonably believe this when you go on to condemn even the less extreme plan to humiliate my rival that I consider entirely appropriate. As soon as we disagree, I am forced to conclude that at least one of us must have been caused to acquire some operative element of his moral outlook by some aspect of his upbringing or experience that did *not* owe its existence to that element's truth or justifiability; and the problem, once again, is that I have no special reason to believe that that someone is you rather than me.

Thus, to give the challenge to the authority of my moral judgments the strongest possible run for its money, we cannot represent it as resting exclusively on either (1) or (2). Just as the version of the challenge that begins by appealing to (1) is unlikely to succeed without supplementation by (2), the version that begins by appealing to (2) is unlikely to succeed without supplementation by (1). Hence, no matter where we start, we will end by concluding that (1) and (2) work best when they work together.[10]

V. The role of reflection

How well, though, *does* the combined appeal to (1) and (2) work? Must I really accept its corrosive implication that I often have no better reason to rely on my own moral judgments than on the judgments of those with whom I strongly disagree? Are (1) and (2) both firmly enough grounded to support this disturbing conclusion?

There is, I think, little point in contesting (1), for its claim that I often disagree with others about what I morally ought to do is all too

obviously true. However, when we turn to (2)'s claim that I would now view my moral obligations differently if my upbringing and experiences had been sufficiently different, the issue becomes more complicated. Briefly put, the complication is that although a person's upbringing and experiences clearly do cause him to acquire various moral beliefs and habits of judgment, these cannot be assumed to persist unaltered over time. No less than any other beliefs and habits, our moral beliefs and habits of moral judgment can be expected to evolve in response to various intellectual pressures.

We may not fully register this if we focus too exclusively on Mill's claim that "the same causes that made [someone] a churchman in London would have made him a Buddhist or a Confucian in Peking," for this claim draws attention to a single aspect of what a person believes—the particular religion he accepts—that often *is* a direct result of his background. It is obviously impossible for someone who has only been exposed to one religion to become devout in another. However, the more pertinent question is whether a person who has only been exposed to a single religion may nevertheless come to reject some or all of its teachings; and to this further question, the answer is clearly "Yes."

For because any set of claims about religion (or, by extension, morality) can be subjected to rational scrutiny, people can and often do reject even the religious and moral doctrines to which they have been most relentlessly exposed. Even when someone has at first been nonrationally caused to acquire a certain religious or moral belief, it is open to him rationally to evaluate that belief at any later point. Of course, in so doing, he will rely on various ways of assessing evidence and weighting values, and it is likely that the ways he uses will themselves have been shaped by his experiences (and, we may add, by his culture). Still, no matter how far these influences extend—and, as Rawls notes about the influence of experience, this is something we cannot know—their introduction does not alter the basic point

because any resulting ways of assessing evidence and weighting values can be rationally scrutinized in turn. Thus, properly understood, the moral outlook that we have been nonrationally caused to acquire is best viewed not as a permanent fixture of our thought, but rather as a starting point that we may hope successively to improve through ongoing critical reflection.

There is, of course, no guarantee that this hope will be realized. Despite my best efforts, it remains possible that my moral outlook has from the start been hopelessly compromised by some massive error, and that my lack of access to the source of error has systematically subverted all my ameliorative endeavors. However, this hypothesis, if backed by no positive argument, is no less speculative than is the hypothesis that all my experiences are caused by a scientist stimulating a brain in a vat. Thus, as long as I have no concrete reason to believe otherwise, it may well be reasonable for me to assume that my efforts to think through the arguments for and against my fundamental moral convictions, and to correct for the distortions, biases, and false beliefs that my upbringing and earlier experiences have inevitably introduced, have on the whole made things better rather than worse.[11]

How, exactly, would the truth of this meliorist assumption bear on (2)'s claim that if I had had a sufficiently different upbringing and set of experiences, I would now judge my moral obligations differently? The answer, I think, is complicated. The truth of the meliorist assumption would not show that (2)'s claim is false, but would indeed lessen (2)'s sting. However, it would also leave intact the challenge to the authority of my moral judgments that (2) poses in conjunction with (1). Let me argue briefly for each of these three points in turn.

At first glance, the assumption that reflecting on one's moral outlook tends to improve it may indeed seem to tell against (2), for if this assumption is correct, then even two radically different moral outlooks can be expected eventually to converge if subjected to enough

reflection. However, for at least two reasons, this way of arguing against (2) does not seem promising. First, even if we grant both that I would have reflected seriously on the alternative moral outlook that a given alternative history would have caused me to acquire and that I did reflect seriously on the moral outlook that my actual history caused me to acquire, there is no guarantee that the two starting points are close enough to allow anything approaching full convergence within my lifetime (or, *a fortiori*, now). In addition, at least some of the alternative histories that would have caused me to acquire a different moral outlook would also have caused me to be disinclined to engage in the kind of reflection that would be necessary to secure *any* degree of convergence. For both reasons, the assumption that reflecting on one's moral outlook generally improves it does not seem capable of supporting a refutation of (2).

Even if this is so, however, the assumption does make (2) more palatable, for as long as I can even partially overcome the nonrational origins of my moral outlook by critically reflecting on it, the fact that my moral outlook would now be different if my history had been different will not entirely undermine its credibility. Given the validating effects of critical reflection, I will, by virtue of engaging in it, at least partly transcend my moral outlook's merely contingent origins.

Yet even if this is so, it will hardly follow that I have any more reason to rely on my own moral judgments than on the judgments of others with whom I strongly disagree; for because these disagreements take place within a society that prizes reflection (and because, as an academic, I tend to interact with the more reflective segment of my society), I cannot assume that those with whom I disagree have been any less reflective than I. Given that they, too, may well have sought to transcend the merely historical origins of their moral outlooks, an appeal to the validating effects of my reflections will not resolve my problem, but will only reraise it at a higher level. When you and I disagree about what I ought to do—when, for example, my own conscientious reflection leaves me convinced that the revenge I am planning falls well within tolerable moral limits, while yours leaves you no less convinced that I really ought to resist my ugly, vengeful urges—I cannot reasonably assume that it is I rather than you who has successfully thought his way out of his causally induced errors.

And if I am tempted to think otherwise, I need only remind myself of how often such situations arise. If I am entitled to assume that you have been less successful than me in purging your thinking of causally induced error, then I must be entitled to make the same assumption about the great majority of others with whom I disagree—about vast numbers of intelligent and sophisticated vegetarians, pacifists, postmodernists, deconstructionists, gender feminists, prolifers, proponents of partial-birth abortion, neutralists, advocates of hate-speech codes, fundamentalists, libertines, rigorists, and egoists, to name just a few. But although it is certainly possible that I have been more successful in avoiding error than some of these others—this is likely on statistical grounds alone—it strains credulity to suppose that I have been more successful than all, or even most, of them. It would be something of a miracle if, out of all the disputants, it was just me who got it all right.

VI. Practical solution to these doubts?

So what should I do? More precisely, how should I respond to the challenge to my ability to decide on rational grounds what I should do? I can see three main possibilities: first, to renew my quest for a convincing reason to believe that my own moral judgments are more likely to be true or justified than are those of the innumerable others with whom I disagree; second, to concede both that no such reason is likely to be forthcoming and that I therefore cannot rationally base my actions on my own moral judgments; and third, to acknowledge that no such reason is

forthcoming but deny that this makes it irrational to base my actions on my own moral judgments. Unfortunately, of these three strategies, the first is pretty clearly doomed, while the second would commit me to a wholesale rejection of the moral point of view. Thus, if I am to avoid the twin pitfalls of futility and moral skepticism, I will probably have to implement some variant of the third strategy.

To do this, I will have to block the inference from "I have no good reason to believe that my own moral judgments are more likely to be justified or true than those of innumerable others who disagree with me" to "I cannot rationally base my actions on my own moral judgments." This in turn requires a demonstration that what makes it rational for me to base my actions on my own moral judgments is not simply the strength of my reasons for believing that these judgments are justified or true. More specifically, what I must show is that even when I realize that my own moral judgments are no more likely to be true or justified than are yours, it nevertheless remains rational for me to act on my own judgments simply because they are my own.

Can anything like this be shown? If so, it seems the argument would likely have to turn on certain features of practical reason itself. In particular, its pivotal premise seems likely to be that because no one can act rationally without basing his decisions on his own assessment of the reasons for and against the actions available to him, practical reason itself requires that I give pride of place to my own judgments. Although I can of course rationally discount any particular judgment that I take to be false or unjustified, the reason I can do this is that to discount a particular judgment is not to abdicate the task of judging; rather, it is only to allow one of my own judgments to trump another. Because acting rationally necessarily involves basing my decisions on the way I see things, I cannot entirely transcend my own outlook without moving decisively beyond the bounds of practical reason.

This much, I think, is clear enough. However, because not all reasons for acting are moral reasons—because, for example, I can also have reasons that are prudential, hedonistic, or aesthetic—the mere fact that practical reason requires that I base my actions on my own judgments about what I have reason to do is not sufficient to vindicate the rationality of acting on my own best moral judgments. To show that practical reason requires this, I must take the further step of arguing that even an attempt to transcend my own moral outlook would take me beyond the bounds of practical reason; and unlike the previous step, this one may seem problematic indeed.

For because my moral outlook encompasses only a small fraction of what I believe, want, and aim at, simply disregarding it would hardly leave me with nothing, or too little, upon which to base my practical decisions. Even if I were to set aside every one of my moral beliefs, I could still choose one action over another on any number of further grounds—for example, because the chosen action would be fun, because it would advance the aims of some person I care about, or because it is required for the completion of some project I have undertaken. Thus, given my awareness that my own moral judgments are no more likely to be true or justified than are the moral judgments of any number of others, isn't it indeed rational for me to set moral considerations aside and make my decisions exclusively on other grounds?

The answer, I think, is that this is not rational, for if I were to do it, I would merely be discounting one set of practical judgments in favor of another whose members are no less compromised by the now-familiar combination of controversy and contingency. Although a full defense of this final claim is beyond my scope, I shall end this section with a brief sketch of the argument for it.

The first thing that needs to be said is that just as the great majority of my moral judgments would be contested by various persons who are no less reflective than I, so too would the great

majority of my *nonmoral* practical judgments. Indeed, the latter disagreements seem if anything to be even more wide-ranging, since they encompass both disagreements about which *sorts* of nonmoral considerations are relevant to the decision at hand—for example, disagreements about whether I should make the decision mainly on hedonistic, prudential, aesthetic, or affectional grounds—and disagreements about what each type of consideration gives me reason to do. Although some such disagreements obviously turn on different understandings of the facts of a given situation, many others do not. Also, while many endorse the metaprinciple that what I ought to do depends on my *own* weighting of the competing nonmoral considerations, there are also many who reject this metaprinciple. Thus, all in all, my nonmoral practical judgments are sure to be every bit as controversial as my moral judgments.

Moreover, second, my having the beliefs and habits of thought that combine to support the relevant practical judgments seems equally contingent in both the moral and nonmoral cases. Just as it is true that if I had had a sufficiently different upbringing and set of experiences, I would now hold your view rather than mine about what I *morally* ought to do, so too is it true that if I had had a sufficiently different upbringing and set of experiences, I would now hold your view rather than mine about what I have *nonmoral* reason to do. Our attitudes about the value of culture, work, friendship, planning, and much else are no less accidents of our upbringing and experiences, and are no less influential in shaping our judgments about how to live, than are our beliefs about virtue and vice and what we owe to each other.

Thus, in the end, my moral and nonmoral judgments about what I ought to do—or, better, the moral and nonmoral components of my integrated judgments about what, all things considered, I ought to do—seem likely to stand or fall together. Either it is rational for me to set both components of my own practical judgments aside or it is not rational for me to set either of them aside. If I were to set both components aside, I would indeed lack any basis upon which to make reasoned decisions about what to do. Hence, given the inescapability of my commitment to acting for reasons, my tentative conclusion is that practical rationality precludes my setting either of the components aside.

VII. Conclusion

My main contention in this essay has been that given the degree to which merely contingent factors appear to have shaped our moral outlooks, there is a serious question about whether I ever have good grounds for believing that I am right and you are wrong when you and I disagree about what I ought to do. However, I have also suggested that even if I never *do* have good grounds for believing this, it may nevertheless often remain rational for me to base my actions on my own moral judgments rather than yours. When they are combined, these claims have the paradoxical implication that it is often rational for me to act on the basis of moral judgments the objective likelihood of whose truth or justifiability I have good reason to regard as quite low. This implication casts (fresh) doubt on our ability to integrate our reasons for believing and for acting—that is, on our ability to square the demands of theoretical and practical reason. It also suggests that the price we pay for being clear-eyed moral agents may be a disconcerting awareness of a certain inescapable form of bad faith. Whether these are the only conclusions that the paradoxical implication warrants, or whether, in addition, it provides a platform for some further thrust by the moral skeptic, is a question I will not attempt to answer here.

Notes

1 One work in which the issue is discussed did not come to my attention until after this essay was

written; see Gerald Cohen, *If You're an Egalitarian, How Come You're So Rich?* (Cambridge, MA: Harvard University Press, 2000), chap. 1.

2 John Stuart Mill, *On Liberty* (Indianapolis, IN: Hackett, 1978), 17.

3 John Rawls, *Political Liberalism* (New York: Columbia University Press, 1993), 56–57.

4 As these examples suggest, I take morality to encompass only a set of duties that we owe to others and, by extension, a set of virtues and vices connected to these duties. As so construed, the realm of the moral excludes many forms of value.

5 Although the cases just mentioned all involve actual disagreement, essentially the same problem appears to arise in cases in which no one actually disagrees with me, but I know there is (or could be?) someone who *would* disagree if given the chance.

6 The point I am making here applies only to the form of skepticism that asserts that our current experiences (or beliefs about them) might have causes that have nothing to do with their truth. Only this form of skepticism has the same abstract structure as our current problem.

7 David Hume, *A Treatise of Human Nature*, ed. L. A. Selby-Bigge (Oxford: Clarendon Press, 1960), bk. I, sec. 7, p. 269.

8 Although this reasoning is seldom couched in singular terms, its collective counterpart appears to play a substantial role in supporting the cultural relativist's refusal to take sides when his own society's values conflict with those of other societies.

9 The parallel is not exact, but something roughly akin to this appears to happen whenever children are taught history or arithmetic by rote. Although the children are not given any reasons for believing what they are taught (and although they would form different beliefs if given different material to memorize), the reason they are asked to memorize precisely this material is that there in fact *are* good reasons for accepting it.

10 As was pointed out by several contributors to this volume, the authority of my empirical beliefs faces a challenge analogous to that faced by my moral judgments. As is the case with moral judgments, I disagree with others about various empirical matters, and for (just about) any empirical belief that I reject but someone else accepts, there is some different upbringing and set of experiences that would have caused me to accept that empirical belief.

Because I have taken the fact that a different background would have caused me to weigh the evidence in a way that supports your moral judgment rather than mine to undermine the authority of my own moral judgment, I can hardly deny that the fact that a different background would have caused me to weigh the evidence in a way that supports your empirical belief rather than mine is similarly subversive of the authority of my own empirical belief. However, there are several things worth noting here. First, very few of my actual empirical beliefs *are* disputed by thoughtful, conscientious people who have simply weighed the evidence differently. Second, when an empirical disagreement is of this nature—when, for example, you and I disagree about what to make of the evidence about the causes of a phenomenon such as intergenerational poverty—considerable diffidence on both sides is indeed in order. It is worth noting, too, that if those with whom I disagree have not merely assessed the shared evidence differently but either lack or are unresponsive to evidence I have—if, for example, they are members of a prescientific society that attributes diseases to spirits rather than microorganisms, or are creationists—then the fact that I would have their beliefs if I had their background does *not* undermine the authority of my own beliefs. Here I can see that, and why, my own background is the more favored. Taken together, these considerations suggest that the combination of controversy and contingency poses far less of a threat to the authority of my empirical beliefs than it does to the authority of my moral judgments.

11 Race/class/gender theory can be read as an attempt to show that all past reflection on our moral beliefs and habits of judgment *has* been subverted by a massive error—namely, our ignorance of the fact that those beliefs and habits merely rationalize the power of the privileged. However, even if this claim were true, it would not show that reflection cannot improve matters, since the aim of advancing the claim is precisely to unmask what has previously been hidden.

Normative ethics: consequentialism

INTRODUCTION TO SECTION IV

WHEN PHILOSOPHERS ADVANCE theories about moral reasons, the meaning of moral language, or the objectivity of morality, they take no position about *what* is right or good. Such theories do not make claims about what morality requires, but instead make claims *about* claims about what morality requires. The branch of ethics which deals with these higher-order claims is known as *metaethics*, while the branch which advances ground-level claims about what is right and good, and which thus discusses actual norms of conduct, is known as *normative ethics*.

Within normative ethics, some theories take an act's rightness to depend entirely on the goodness of its consequences, while others take this to depend wholly or partly on facts of other sorts. Theories of the first sort are known as *consequentialist*, and they are the focus of the current section. Because there is no consensus about what makes something good – for discussion, see the chapters in Section VII – there is also no consensus about the best version of consequentialism. However, many consequentialists believe, first, that the good consists of pleasure, happiness, or the satisfaction of desire, and, second, what is right is whatever will maximize one of these goods. This combination of views is called *utilitarianism*, and it is given classic formulation by John Stuart Mill in Chapter 22.

As Mill emphasizes, the happiness that a utilitarian seeks to maximize is not just his own, but that of everyone his acts will affect. Because there must always be one act, out of those an agent can perform, that would bring more happiness than any other (we may set aside the possibility of a tie), there is always a clear theoretical answer to the question of what a utilitarian should do. Of course, in practice, what would maximize utility is often unclear, but Mill argues that this is not a serious problem. When we don't know which act would have the best consequences, we can rely on experience to tell us what sorts of actions *usually* have the best consequences. Moreover, according to Mill, the lessons learned from experience are codified in such precepts of common morality as "tell the truth" and "do not kill." Although the principle of utility looks very different from these rules, Mill argues that it both explains why we accept them and captures what is correct about them. The relation between utilitarianism and common morality is discussed further by R. M. Hare in Chapter 64.

Utilitarianism has had many critics, and one of the most prominent is Bernard Williams. As Williams points out in Chapter 23, the claim that an act's rightness depends exclusively on its outcomes implies that we act just as wrongly when we allow others to inflict harm as when we inflict harm ourselves. Thus, Williams argues that utilitarians must reject the commonly held view that "each of us is specially responsible for what *he* does, rather than what other people do." Williams argues, as well, that because utilitarianism does not allow us to assign a special status to our own projects – because it compels us to view them only as one potential cause of

happiness among innumerable others – it alienates us from our deepest commitments and in so doing undermines our integrity. Because a utilitarian cannot favor a friend or spouse over a stranger unless his doing so would maximize utility, Williams adds in Chapter 41 that utilitarianism belongs to a class of theories whose acceptance alienates people from those who matter to them. In Chapter 24, John Rawls offers what many view as a general diagnosis of what is wrong with utilitarianism – namely, that because it determines what is right by aggregating the satisfactions and frustrations of many different individuals, it "does not take seriously the distinction between persons."

Can an adherent of utilitarianism (or of some other form of consequentialism) avoid being alienated from others and losing his integrity? At least where alienation from other people is concerned, Peter Railton argues that the answer is "yes." In Chapter 25, Railton distinguishes between *objective consequentialism*, which says that what determines whether an act is right is whether it produces the most good, and *subjective consequentialism*, which says that given a choice of what to do, we should always *try* to produce the most good. As Railton points out, it is possible to accept objective but not subjective consequentialism: a person might believe that what is right is always what maximizes the good, yet also believe that the best *way* to maximize the good is not to try to do so on every occasion. Instead, what maximize the good may be traits that sometimes manifest themselves in acts that do *not* seek to maximize the good. If those traits include habits of concern and loving behavior, as Railton suggests they will, then an objective consequentialist need not be alienated from other people. Even if he would try to change his habits if he came to believe that they do not maximize the good, he will, because he now has those habits, be a concerned friend and a loving spouse.

Although Railton's sophisticated version of consequentialism goes well beyond the simple idea that we should always try to maximize the good, he does not deny that an act's rightness depends exclusively on its consequences. But other consequentialists do deny this. One who does so is Brad Hooker, who argues in Chapter 26 that what makes an act right is not the goodness of *its* consequences, but rather, roughly, its being permitted by a set of rules whose internalization by most of the population would have better consequences than the internalization of any other set. For obvious reasons, this view is called *rule-consequentialism* while its rival is known as *act-consequentialism*. In his resourceful discussion, Hooker clarifies various aspects of rule-consequentialism and defends it on several grounds, among them that it is more consistent than act-consequentialism with our ordinary moral beliefs. He argues, for example, that whereas an act-consequentialist must allow that it is right to lie as long as this will bring even slightly more good than telling the truth, a rule-consequentialist can explain why lying under these conditions is wrong by pointing out that a system of rules that permitted it would be worse than one that did not.

Another consequentialist who denies that an act's rightness depends exclusively on the goodness of its consequences is Alastair Norcross. However, unlike Hooker, who accepts the distinction between right and wrong acts, Norcross argues in Chapter 27 that we should not think in these terms at all. According to Norcross, a consequentialist should not ask which acts are right (or which acts we ought, or are obligated,

to perform), but instead should restrict himself to asking which acts are better than which others. For a utilitarian such as Norcross, this means asking which acts produce more happiness than which others. This "scalar" version of consequentialism is preferable, Norcross argues, because rightness is an all-or-nothing notion – because each act must either be right or not right – while the goodness of an act's consequences is always a matter of degree. By substituting the notion of comparative goodness for that of rightness, we can avoid this mismatch. In addition, by adopting the scalar view, we can avoid the common objection that utilitarianism demands too much of us by pointing out that scalar utilitarianism imposes no demands at all. However, at the same time, scalar utilitarianism remains action-guiding because it still implies that we have stronger reasons to perform some acts than to perform others.

Although consequentialism is controversial, even those who reject it generally agree that an act's consequences sometimes do matter. For example, most would agree that if we must choose between saving a greater or a smaller number of people, and if none have any special claims on us, then we should save the greater number. However, in Chapter 28, John Taurek denies this. He advances the provocative view that if we have a limited supply of a drug that can be used to save either one seriously ill person or five who are less ill, the difference in numbers should not count at all. In defense of this view, Taurek argues that although each person's death would be a great loss for him, it does not follow that five deaths are five times worse than one. Rather, because death would be equally bad for each person, each should be given an equal chance to avoid it. Relatedly, he rejects "the apparent tendency of some people to react to the thought of each of fifty individuals suffering a pain of a given intensity in the same way as they might to the thought of some individual suffering a pain many or fifty times more intense." By arguing against this way of thinking, Taurek challenges an assumption that is central to consequentialism.

Chapter 22

John Stuart Mill

UTILITARIANISM

What utilitarianism is

THE CREED which accepts as the foundation of morals "utility" or the "greatest happiness principle" holds that actions are right in proportion as they tend to promote happiness; wrong as they tend to produce the reverse of happiness. By happiness is intended pleasure and the absence of pain; by unhappiness, pain and the privation of pleasure. To give a clear view of the moral standard set up by the theory, much more requires to be said; in particular, what things it includes in the ideas of pain and pleasure, and to what extent this is left an open question. But these supplementary explanations do not affect the theory of life on which this theory of morality is grounded—namely, that pleasure and freedom from pain are the only things desirable as ends; and that all desirable things (which are as numerous in the utilitarian as in any other scheme) are desirable either for pleasure inherent in themselves or as means to the promotion of pleasure and the prevention of pain.

Now such a theory of life excites in many minds, and among them in some of the most estimable in feeling and purpose, inveterate dislike. To suppose that life has (as they express it) no higher end than pleasure—no better and nobler object of desire and pursuit—they designate as utterly mean and groveling, as a doctrine worthy only of swine, to whom the followers of Epicurus were, at a very early period, contemptuously likened; and modern holders of the doctrine are occasionally made the subject of equally polite comparisons by its German, French, and English assailants.

When thus attacked, the Epicureans have always answered that it is not they, but their accusers, who represent human nature in a degrading light, since the accusation supposes human beings to be capable of no pleasures except those of which swine are capable. If this supposition were true, the charge could not be gainsaid, but would then be no longer an imputation; for if the sources of pleasure were precisely the same to human beings and to swine, the rule of life which is good enough for the one would be good enough for the other. The comparison of the Epicurean life to that of beasts is felt as degrading, precisely because a beast's pleasures do not satisfy a human being's conceptions of happiness. Human beings have faculties more elevated than the animal appetites and, when once made conscious of them, do not regard anything as happiness which does not include their gratification. I do not indeed, consider the Epicureans to have been by any means faultless in drawing out their scheme of consequences from the utilitarian principle. To do this in any sufficient manner, many Stoic, as well as Christian, elements require to be included. But there is no known Epicurean theory of life which does not assign to the

pleasures of the intellect, of the feelings and imagination, and of the moral sentiments a much higher value as pleasures than to those of mere sensation. It must be admitted, however, that utilitarian writers in general have placed the superiority of mental over bodily pleasures chiefly in the greater permanency, safety, uncost-liness, etc., of the former—that is, in their circumstantial advantages rather than in their intrinsic nature. And on all these points utilitar-ians have fully proved their case; but they might have taken the other and, as it may be called, higher ground with entire consistency. It is quite compatible with the principle of utility to recog-nize the fact that some kinds of pleasure are more desirable and more valuable than others. It would be absurd that, while in estimating all other things quality is considered as well as quantity, the estimation of pleasure should be supposed to depend on quantity alone.

If I am asked what I mean by difference of quality in pleasures, or what makes one pleasure more valuable than another, merely as a pleasure, except its being greater in amount, there is but one possible answer. Of two pleasures, if there be one to which all or almost all who have experience of both give a decided preference, irrespective of any feeling of moral obligation to prefer it, that is the most desirable pleasure. If one of the two is, by those who are competently acquainted with both, placed so far above the other that they prefer it, even though knowing it to be attended with a greater amount of discon-tent, and would not resign it for any quantity of the other pleasure which their nature is capable of, we are justified in ascribing to the preferred enjoyment a superiority in quality so far outweighing quantity as to render it, in compar-ison, of small account.

Now it is an unquestionable fact that those who are equally acquainted with and equally capable of appreciating and enjoying both do give a most marked preference to the manner of existence which employs their higher faculties. Few human creatures would consent to be changed into any of the lower animals for a promise of the fullest allowance of a beast's pleasures; no intelligent human being would consent to be a fool, no instructed person would be an ignoramus, no person of feeling and conscience would be selfish and base, even though they should be persuaded that the fool, the dunce, or the rascal is better satisfied with his lot than they are with theirs. They would not resign what they possess more than he for the most complete satisfaction of all the desires which they have in common with him. If they ever fancy they would, it is only in cases of unhappiness so extreme that to escape from it they would exchange their lot for almost any other, however undesirable in their own eyes. A being of higher faculties requires more to make him happy, is capable probably of more acute suffering, and certainly accessible to it at more points, than one of an inferior type; but in spite of these liabilities, he can never really wish to sink into what he feels to be a lower grade of existence. We may give what explanation we please of this unwillingness; we may attribute it to pride, a name which is given indiscriminately to some of the most and to some of the least estimable feelings of which mankind are capable; we may refer it to the love of liberty and personal independence, an appeal to which was with the Stoics one of the most effective means for the inculcation of it; to the love of power or to the love of excitement, both of which do really enter into and contribute to it; but its most appropriate appellation is a sense of dignity, which all human beings possess in one form or other, and in some, though by no means in exact, proportion to their higher faculties, and which is so essential a part of the happiness of those in whom it is strong that nothing which conflicts with it could be otherwise than momentarily an object of desire to them. Who-ever supposes that this preference takes place at a sacrifice of happiness—that the superior being, in anything like equal circumstances, is not happier than the inferior—confounds the

two very different ideas of happiness and content. It is indisputable that the being whose capacities of enjoyment are low has the greatest chance of having them fully satisfied; and a highly endowed being will always feel that any happiness which he can look for, as the world is constituted, is imperfect. But he can learn to bear its imperfections, if they are at all bearable; and they will not make him envy the being who is indeed unconscious of the imperfections, but only because he feels not at all the good which those imperfections qualify. It is better to be a human being dissatisfied than a pig satisfied; better to be Socrates dissatisfied than a fool satisfied. And if the fool, or the pig, are of a different opinion, it is because they only know their own side of the question. The other party to the comparison knows both sides.

It may be objected that many who are capable of the higher pleasures occasionally, under the influence of temptation, postpone them to the lower. But this is quite compatible with a full appreciation of the intrinsic superiority of the higher. Men often, from infirmity of character, make their election for the nearer good, though they know it to be the less valuable; and this no less when the choice is between two bodily pleasures than when it is between bodily and mental. They pursue sensual indulgences to the injury of health, though perfectly aware that health is the greater good. It may be further objected that many who begin with youthful enthusiasm for everything noble, as they advance in years, sink into indolence and selfishness. But I do not believe that those who undergo this very common change voluntarily choose the lower description of pleasures in preference to the higher. I believe that, before they devote themselves exclusively to the one, they have already become incapable of the other. Capacity for the nobler feelings is in most natures a very tender plant, easily killed, not only by hostile influences, but by mere want of sustenance; and in the majority of young persons it speedily dies away if the occupations to which their position in life has devoted them, and the society into which it has thrown them, are not favorable to keeping that higher capacity in exercise. Men lose their high aspirations as they lose their intellectual tastes, because they have not time or opportunity for indulging them; and they addict themselves to inferior pleasures, not because they deliberately prefer them, but because they are either the only ones to which they have access or the only ones which they are any longer capable of enjoying. It may be questioned whether anyone who has remained equally susceptible to both classes of pleasures ever knowingly and calmly preferred the lower, though many, in all ages, have broken down in an ineffectual attempt to combine both.

From this verdict of the only competent judges, I apprehend there can be no appeal. On a question which is the best worth having of two pleasures, or which of two modes of existence is the most grateful to the feelings, apart from its moral attributes and from its consequences, the judgment of these who are qualified by knowledge of both, or, if they differ, that of the majority among them, must be admitted as final. And there needs be the less hesitation to accept this judgment respecting the quality of pleasures, since there is no other tribunal to be referred to even on the question of quantity. What means are there of determining which is the acutest of two pains, or the interest of two pleasurable sensations, except the general suffrage of those who are familiar with both? Neither pains nor pleasures are homogeneous, and pain is always heterogeneous with pleasure. What is there to decide whether a particular pleasure is worth purchasing at the cost of a particular pain, except the feelings and judgment of the experienced? When, therefore, those feelings and judgment declare the pleasures derived from the higher faculties to be preferable in kind, apart from the question of intensity, to those of which the animal nature, disjoined from the higher faculties, is susceptible, they are entitled on this subject to the same regard.

• • •

I must again repeat what the assailants of utilitarianism seldom have the justice to acknowledge, that the happiness which forms the utilitarian standard of what is right in conduct is not the agent's own happiness but that of all concerned. As between his own happiness and that of others, utilitarianism requires him to be as strictly impartial as a disinterested and benevolent spectator. In the golden rule of Jesus of Nazareth, we read the complete spirit of the ethics of utility. "To do as you would be done by," and "to love your neighbor as yourself," constitute the ideal perfection of utilitarian morality. As the means of making the nearest approach to this ideal, utility would enjoin, first, that laws and social arrangements should place the happiness or (as, speaking practically, it may be called) the interest of every individual as nearly as possible in harmony with the interest of the whole; and, secondly, that education and opinion, which have so vast a power over human character, should so use that power as to establish in the mind of every individual an indissoluble association between his own happiness and the good of the whole, especially between his own happiness and the practice of such modes of conduct, negative and positive, as regard for the universal happiness prescribes; so that not only he may be unable to conceive the possibility of happiness to himself, consistently with conduct opposed to the general good, but also that a direct impulse to promote the general good may be in every individual one of the habitual motives of action, and the sentiments connected therewith may fill a large and prominent place in every human being's sentient existence. If the impugners of the utilitarian morality represented it to their own minds in this its true character, I know not what recommendation possessed by any other morality they could possibly affirm to be wanting to it; what more beautiful or more exalted developments of human nature any other ethical system can be supposed to foster, or what springs of action, not accessible to the utilitarian, such systems rely on for giving effect to their mandates.

The objectors to utilitarianism cannot always be charged with representing it in a discreditable light. On the contrary, those among them who entertain anything like a just idea of its disinterested character sometimes find fault with its standard as being too high for humanity. They say it is exacting too much to require that people shall always act from the inducement of promoting the general interest of society. But this is to mistake the very meaning of a standard of morals and confound the rule of action with the motive of it. It is the business of ethics to tell us what are our duties, or by what test we may know them; but no system of ethics requires that the sole motive of all we do shall be a feeling of duty; on the contrary, ninety-nine hundredths of all our actions are done from other motives, and rightly so done if the rule of duty does not condemn them. It is the more unjust to utilitarianism that this particular misapprehension should be made a ground of objection to it, inasmuch as utilitarian moralists have gone beyond almost all others in affirming that the motive has nothing to do with the morality of the action, though much with the worth of the agent. He who saves a fellow creature from drowning does what is morally right, whether his motive be duty or the hope of being paid for his trouble; he who betrays the friend that trusts him is guilty of a crime, even if his object be to serve another friend to whom he is under greater obligation.[1] But to speak only of actions done from the motive or duty, and in direct obedience to principle: it is a misapprehension of the utilitarian mode of thought to conceive it as implying that people should fix their minds upon so wide a generality as the world, or society at large. The great majority of good actions are intended not for the benefit of the world, but for that of individuals, of which the good of the world is made up; and the thoughts of the most virtuous man need not on these occasions travel beyond the particular persons concerned, except so far as is necessary to assure himself that in benefiting them he is not

violating the rights, that is, the legitimate and authorized expectations, of anyone else. The multiplication of happiness is, according to the utilitarian ethics, the object of virtue: the occasions on which any person (except one in a thousand) has it in his power to do this on an extended scale—in other words, to be a public benefactor—are but exceptional; and on these occasions alone is he called on to consider public utility; in every other case, private utility, the interest or happiness of some few persons, is all he has to attend to. Those alone the influence of whose actions extends to society in general need concern themselves habitually about so large an object. In the case of abstinences indeed—of things which people forbear to do from moral considerations, though the consequences in the particular case might be beneficial—it would be unworthy of an intelligent agent not to be consciously aware that the action is of a class which, if practiced generally, would be generally injurious, and that this is the ground of the obligation to abstain from it. The amount of regard for the public interest implied in this recognition is no greater than is demanded by every system of morals, for they all enjoin to abstain from whatever is manifestly pernicious to society.

The same considerations dispose of another reproach against the doctrine of utility, founded on a still grosser misconception of the purpose of a standard of morality and of the very meaning of the words "right" and "wrong." It is often affirmed that utilitarianism renders men cold and unsympathizing; that it chills their moral feelings toward individuals; that it makes them regard only the dry and hard consideration of the consequences of actions, not taking into their moral estimate the qualities from which those actions emanate. If the assertion means that they do not allow their judgment respecting the rightness or wrongness of an action to be influenced by their opinion of the qualities of the person who does it, this is a complaint not against utilitarianism, but against

any standard or morality at all; for certainly no known ethical standard decides an action to be good or bad because it is done by a good or bad man, still less because done by an amiable, a brave, or a benevolent man, or the contrary. These considerations are relevant, not to the estimation of actions, but of persons; and there is nothing in the utilitarian theory inconsistent with the fact that there are other things which interest us in persons besides the rightness and wrongness of their actions. The Stoics, indeed, with the paradoxical misuse of language which was part of their system, and by which they strove to raise themselves above all concern about anything but virtue, were fond of saying that he who has that has everything; that he, and only he, is rich, is beautiful, is a king. But no claim of this description is made for the virtuous man by the utilitarian doctrine. Utilitarians are quite aware that there are other desirable possessions and qualities besides virtue, and are perfectly willing to allow to all of them their full worth. They are also aware that a right action does not necessarily indicate a virtuous character, and that actions which are blamable often proceed from qualities entitled to praise. When this is apparent in any particular case, it modifies their estimation, not certainly of the act, but of the agent. I grant that they are, notwithstanding, of opinion that in the long run the best proof of a good character is good actions; and resolutely refuse to consider any mental disposition as good of which the predominant tendency is to produce bad conduct. This makes them unpopular with many people, but it is an unpopularity which they must share with everyone who regards the distinction between right and wrong in a serious light; and the reproach is not one which a conscientious utilitarian need be anxious to repel.

• • •

Again, utility is often summarily stigmatized as an immoral doctrine by giving it the name of "expediency," and taking advantage of the

popular use of that term to contrast it with principle. But the expedient, in the sense in which it is opposed to the right, generally means that which is expedient for the particular interest of the agent himself; as when a minister sacrifices the interests of his country to keep himself in place. When it means anything better than this, it means that which is expedient for some immediate object, some temporary purpose, but which violates a rule whose observance is expedient in a much higher degree. The expedient, in this sense, instead of being the same thing with the useful, is a branch of the hurtful. Thus it would often be expedient, for the purpose of getting over some momentary embarrassment or attaining some object immediately useful to ourselves or others, to tell a lie. But inasmuch as the cultivation in ourselves of a sensitive feeling on the subject of veracity is one of the most useful, and the enfeeblement of that feeling one of the most hurtful, things to which our conduct can be instrumental; and inasmuch as any, even unintentional, deviation from truth does that much toward weakening the trustworthiness of human assertion, which is not only the principal support of all present social well-being, but the insufficiency of which does more than any one thing that can be named to keep back civilization, virtue, everything on which human happiness on the largest scale depends—we feel that the violation, for a present advantage, of a rule of such transcendent expediency is not expedient, and that he who, for the sake of convenience to himself or to some other individual, does what depends on him to deprive mankind of the good, and inflict upon them the evil, involved in the greater or less reliance which they can place in each other's words, acts the part of one of their worst enemies. Yet that even this rule, sacred as it is, admits of possible exceptions is acknowledged by all moralists; the chief of which is when the withholding of some fact (as of information from a malefactor, or of bad news from a person dangerously ill) would save an individual (especially an individual other than oneself) from great and unmerited evil, and when the withholding can only be effected by denial. But in order that the exception may not extend itself beyond the need, and may have the least possible effect in weakening reliance on veracity, it ought to be recognized and, if possible, its limits defined; and, if the principle of utility is good for anything, it must be good for weighing these conflicting utilities against one another and marking out the region within which one or the other preponderates.

Again, defenders of utility often find themselves called upon to reply to such objections as this—that there is not time, previous to action, for calculating and weighing the effects of any line of conduct on the general happiness. This is exactly as if anyone were to say that it is impossible to guide our conduct by Christianity because there is not time, on every occasion on which anything has to be done, to read through the Old and New Testaments. The answer to the objection is that there has been ample time, namely, the whole past duration of the human species. During all that time mankind have been learning by experience the tendencies of actions; on which experience all the prudence as well as all the morality of life are dependent. People talk as if the commencement of this course of experience had hitherto been put off, and as if, at the moment when some man feels tempted to meddle with the property or life of another, he had to begin considering for the first time whether murder and theft are injurious to human happiness. Even then I do not think that he would find the question very puzzling; but, at all events, the matter is now done to his hand. It is truly a whimsical supposition that, if mankind were agreed in considering utility to be the test of morality, they would remain without any agreement as to what is useful, and would take no measures for having their notions on the subject taught to the young and enforced by law and opinion. There is no difficulty in proving any ethical standard whatever to work ill if we suppose universal idiocy to be conjoined with

it; but on any hypothesis short of that, mankind must by this time have acquired positive beliefs as to the effects of some actions on their happiness; and the beliefs which have thus come down are the rules of morality for the multitude, and for the philosopher until he has succeeded in finding better. That philosophers might easily do this, even now, on many subjects; that the received code of ethics is by no means of divine right; and that mankind have still much to learn as to the effects of actions on the general happiness, I admit or rather earnestly maintain. The corollaries from the principle of utility, like the precepts of every practical art, admit of indefinite improvement, and, in a progressive state of the human mind, their improvement is perpetually going on. But to consider the rules of morality as improvable is one thing; to pass over the intermediate generalization entirely and endeavor to test each individual action directly by the first principle is another. It is a strange notion that the acknowledgment of a first principle is inconsistent with the admission of secondary ones. To inform a traveler respecting the place of his ultimate destination, is not to forbid the use of landmarks and direction-posts on the way. The proposition that happiness is the end and aim of morality does not mean that no road ought to be laid down to that goal, or that persons going thither should not be advised to take one direction rather than another. Men really ought to leave off talking a kind of nonsense on this subject, which they would neither talk nor listen to on other matters of practical concernment. Nobody argues that the art of navigation is not founded on astronomy because sailors cannot wait to calculate the Nautical Almanac. Being rational creatures, they go to sea with it ready calculated; and all rational creatures go out upon the sea of life with their minds made up on the common questions of right and wrong, as well as on many of the far more difficult questions of wise and foolish. And this, as long as foresight is a human quality, it is to be presumed they will

continue to do. Whatever we adopt as the fundamental principle of morality, we require subordinate principles to apply it by; the impossibility of doing without them, being common to all systems, can afford no argument against any one in particular; but gravely to argue as if no such secondary principles could be had, and as if mankind had remained till now, and always must remain, without drawing any general conclusions from the experience of human life is as high a pitch, I think, as absurdity has ever reached in philosophical controversy.

The remainder of the stock arguments against utilitarianism mostly consist in laying to its charge the common infirmities of human nature, and the general difficulties which embarrass conscientious persons in shaping their course through life. We are told that a utilitarian will be apt to make his own particular case an exception to moral rules, and, when under temptation, will see a utility in the breach of a rule, greater than he will see in its observance. But is utility the only creed which is able to furnish us with excuses for evil-doing and means of cheating our own conscience? They are afforded in abundance by all doctrines which recognize as a fact in morals the existence of conflicting considerations, which all doctrines do that have been believed by sane persons. It is not the fault of any creed, but of the complicated nature of human affairs, that rules of conduct cannot be so framed as to require no exceptions, and that hardly any kind of action can safely be laid down as either always obligatory or always condemnable. There is no ethical creed which does not temper the rigidity of its laws by giving a certain latitude, under the moral responsibility of the agent, for accommodation to peculiarities of circumstances; and under every creed, at the opening thus made, self-deception and dishonest casuistry get in. There exists no moral system under which there do not arise unequivocal cases of conflicting obligation. These are the real difficulties, the knotty points both in the theory of ethics and in the conscientious guidance of

personal conduct. They are overcome practically, with greater or with less success, according to the intellect and virtue of the individual; but it can hardly be pretended that anyone will be the less qualified for dealing with them, from possessing an ultimate standard to which conflicting rights and duties can be referred. If utility is the ultimate source of moral obligations, utility may be invoked to decide between them when their demands are incompatible. Though the application of the standard may be difficult, it is better than none at all; while in other systems, the moral laws all claiming independent authority, there is no common umpire entitled to interfere between them; their claims to precedence one over another rest on little better than sophistry, and, unless determined, as they generally are, by the unacknowledged influence of consideration of utility, afford a free scope for the action of personal desires and partialities. We must remember that only in these cases of conflict between secondary principles is it requisite that first principles should be appealed to. There is no case of moral obligation in which some secondary principle is not involved; and if only one, there can seldom be any real doubt which one it is, in the mind of any person by whom the principle itself is recognized.

Of what sort of proof the principle of utility is susceptible

It has already been remarked that questions of ultimate ends do not admit of proof, in the ordinary acceptation of the term. To be incapable of proof by reasoning is common to all first principles, to the first premises of our knowledge, as well as to those of our conduct. But the former, being matters of fact, may be the subject of a direct appeal to the faculties which judge of fact—namely, our senses and our internal consciousness. Can an appeal be made to the same faculties on questions of practical ends? Or by what other faculty is cognizance taken of them?

Questions about ends are, in other words, questions of what things are desirable. The utilitarian doctrine is that happiness is desirable, and the only thing desirable, as an end; all other things being only desirable as means to that end. What ought to be required of this doctrine, what conditions is it requisite that the doctrine should fulfill—to make good its claim to be believed?

The only proof capable of being given that an object is visible is that people actually see it. The only proof that a sound is audible is that people hear it; and so of the other sources of our experience. In like manner, I apprehend, the sole evidence it is possible to produce that anything is desirable is that people do actually desire it. If the end which the utilitarian doctrine proposes to itself were not, in theory and in practice, acknowledged to be an end, nothing could ever convince any person that it was so. No reason can be given why the general happiness is desirable, except that each person, so far as he believes it to be attainable, desires his own happiness. This, however, being a fact, we have not only all the proof which the case admits of, but all which it is possible to require, that happiness is a good, that each person's happiness is a good to that person, and the general happiness, therefore, a good to the aggregate of all persons. Happiness has made out its title as *one* of the ends of conduct and, consequently, one of the criteria of morality.

But it has not, by this alone, proved itself to be the sole criterion. To do that, it would seem, by the same rule, necessary to show, not only that people desire happiness, but that they never desire anything else. Now it is palpable that they do desire things which, in common language, are decidedly distinguished from happiness. They desire, for example, virtue and the absence of vice no less really than pleasure and the absence of pain. The desire of virtue is not as universal, but it is as authentic a fact as the desire of happiness. And hence the opponents of the utilitarian standard deem that they have a right to infer that there are other ends of human action

besides happiness, and that happiness is not the standard of approbation and disapprobation.

But does the utilitarian doctrine deny that people desire virtue, or maintain that virtue is not a thing to be desired? The very reverse. It maintains not only that virtue is to be desired, but that it is to be desired disinterestedly, for itself. Whatever may be the opinion of utilitarian moralists as to the original conditions by which virtue is made virtue, however they may believe (as they do) that actions and dispositions are only virtuous because they promote another end than virtue, yet this being granted, and it having been decided, from considerations of this description, what is virtuous, they not only place virtue at the very head of the things which are good as means to the ultimate end, but they also recognize as a psychological fact the possibility of its being, to the individual, a good in itself, without looking to any end beyond it; and hold that the mind is not in a right state, not in a state conformable to utility, not in the state most conducive to the general happiness, unless it does love virtue in this manner—as a thing desirable in itself, even although, in the individual instance, it should not produce those other desirable consequences which it tends to produce, and on account of which it is held to be virtue. This opinion is not, in the smallest degree, a departure from the happiness principle. The ingredients of happiness are very various, and each of them is desirable in itself, and not merely when considered as swelling an aggregate. The principle of utility does not mean that any given pleasure, as music, for instance, or any given exemption from pain, as for example health, is to be looked upon as means to a collective something termed happiness, and to be desired on that account. They are desired and desirable in and for themselves; besides being means, they are a part of the end. Virtue, according to the utilitarian doctrine, is not naturally and originally part of the end, but it is capable of becoming so; and in those who live it disinterestedly it has become so, and is desired and cherished, not as a means to happiness, but as part of their happiness.

To illustrate this further, we may remember that virtue is not the only thing originally a means, and which if it were not a means to anything else would be and remain indifferent, but which by association with what it is a means to comes to be desired for itself, and that too with the utmost intensity. What, for example, shall we say of the love of money? There is nothing originally more desirable about money than about any heap of glittering pebbles. Its worth is solely that of the things which it will buy; the desires for other things than itself, which it is a means of gratifying. Yet the love of money is not only one of the strongest moving forces of human life, but money is, in many cases, desired in and for itself; the desire to possess it is often stronger than the desire to use it, and goes on increasing when all the desires which point to ends beyond it, to be compassed by it, are falling off. It may, then, be said truly that money is desired not for the sake of an end, but as part of the end. From being a means to happiness, it has come to be itself a principal ingredient of the individual's conception of happiness. The same may be said of the majority of the great objects of human life: power, for example, or fame, except that to each of these there is a certain amount of immediate pleasure annexed, which has at least the semblance of being naturally inherent in them—a thing which cannot be said of money. Still, however, the strongest natural attraction, both of power and of fame, is the immense aid they give to the attainment of our other wishes; and it is the strong association thus generated between them and all our objects of desire which gives to the direct desire of them the intensity it often assumes, so as in some characters to surpass in strength all other desires. In these cases the means have become a part of the end, and a more important part of it than any of the things which they are means to. What was once desired as an instrument for the attainment of happiness

has come to be desired for its own sake. In being desired for its own sake it is, however, desired as *part* of happiness. The person is made, or thinks he would be made, happy by its mere possession; and is made unhappy by failure to obtain it. The desire of it is not a different thing from the desire of happiness any more than the love of music or the desire of health. They are included in happiness. They are some of the elements of which the desire of happiness is made up. Happiness is not an abstract idea but a concrete whole; and these are some of its parts. And the utilitarian standard sanctions and approves their being so. Life, would be a poor thing, very ill provided with sources of happiness, if there were not this provision of nature by which things originally indifferent, but conducive to, or otherwise associated with, the satisfaction of our primitive desires, become in themselves sources of pleasure more valuable than the primitive pleasures, both in permanency, in the space of human existence that they are capable of covering, and even in intensity.

Virtue, according to the utilitarian conception is a good of this description. There was no original desire of it, or motive to it, save its conduciveness to pleasure, and especially to protection from pain. But through the association thus formed it may be felt a good in itself, and desired as such with as great intensity as any other good; and with this difference between it and the love of money, of power, or of fame—that all of these may, and often do, render the individual noxious to the other members of the society to which he belongs, whereas there is nothing which makes him so much a blessing to them as the cultivation of the disinterested love of virtue. And consequently, the utilitarian standard, while it tolerates and approves those other acquired desires, up to the point beyond which they would be more injurious to the general happiness than promotive of it, enjoins and requires the cultivation of the love of virtue up to the greatest strength possible, as being above all things important to the general happiness.

It results from the preceding considerations that there is in reality nothing desired except happiness. Whatever is desired otherwise than as a means to some end beyond itself, and ultimately to happiness, is desired as itself a part of happiness, and is not desired, for itself until it has become so. Those who desire virtue for its own sake desire it either because the consciousness of it is a pleasure, or because the consciousness of being without it is a pain, or for both reasons united; as in truth the pleasure and pain seldom exist separately, but almost always together—the same person feeling pleasure in the degree of virtue attained, and pain in not having attained more. If one of these gave him no pleasure, and the other no pain, he would not love or desire virtue, or would desire it only for the other benefits which it might produce to himself or to persons whom he cared for.

We have now, then, an answer to the question, of what sort of proof the principle of utility is susceptible. If the opinion which I have now stated is psychologically true—if human nature is so constituted as to desire nothing which is not either a part of happiness or a means of happiness—we can have no other proof, and we require no other, that these are the only things desirable. If so, happiness is the sole end of human action, and the promotion of it the test by which to judge of all human conduct; from whence it necessarily follows that it must be the criterion of morality, since a part is included in the whole.

And now to decide whether this is really so, whether mankind do desire nothing for itself but that which is a pleasure to them, or of which the absence is a pain, we have evidently arrived at a question of fact and experience, dependent, like all similar questions, upon evidence. It can only be determined by practiced self-consciousness and self-observation, assisted by observation of others. I believe that these sources of evidence, impartially consulted, will declare that desiring a thing and finding it pleasant, aversion to it and thinking of it as painful, are phenomena entirely

inseparable or, rather, two parts of the same phenomenon—in strictness of language, two different modes of naming the same psychological fact; that to think of an object as desirable (unless for the sake of its consequences) and to think of it as pleasant are one and the same thing; and that to desire anything except in proportion as the idea of it is pleasant is a physical and metaphysical impossibility.

So obvious does this appear to me that I expect it will hardly be disputed; and the objection made will be, not that desire can possibly be directed to anything ultimately except pleasure and exemption from pain, but that the will is a different thing from desire; that a person of confirmed virtue or any other person whose purposes are fixed carries out his purposes without any thought of the pleasure he has in contemplating them or expects to derive from their fulfillment, and persists in acting on them, even though these pleasures are much diminished by changes in his character or decay of his passive sensibilities, or are outweighed by the pains which the pursuit of the purposes may bring upon him. All this I fully admit and have stated it elsewhere as positively and emphatically as anyone. Will, the active phenomenon, is a different thing from desire, the state of passive sensibility, and, though originally an offshoot from it, may in time take root and detach itself from the parent stock, so much so that in the case of a habitual purpose, instead of willing the thing because we desire it, we often desire it only because we will it. This, however, is but an instance of that familiar fact, the power of habit, and is nowise confined to the case of virtuous actions. Many indifferent things which men originally did from a motive of some sort they continue to do from habit. Sometimes this is done unconsciously, the consciousness coming only after the action; at other times with conscious volition, but volition which has become habitual and is put in operation by the force of habit, in opposition perhaps to the deliberate preference, as often happens with those who have contracted habits of vicious or hurtful indulgence. Third and last comes the case in which the habitual act of will in the individual instance is not in contradiction to the general intention prevailing as other times, but in fulfillment of it, as in the case of the person of confirmed virtue and of all who pursue deliberately and consistently any determinate end. The distinction between will and desire thus understood is an authentic and highly important psychological fact; but the fact consists solely in this—that will, like all other parts of our constitution, is amenable to habit, and that we may will from habit what we no longer desire for itself, or desire only because we will it. It is not the less true that will, in the beginning, is entirely produced by desire, including in that term the repelling influence of pain as well as the attractive one of pleasure. Let us take into consideration no longer the person who has a confirmed will to do right, but him in whom that virtuous will is still feeble, conquerable by temptation, and not to be fully relied on; by what means can it be strengthened? How can the will to be virtuous, where it does not exist in sufficient force, be implanted or awakened? Only by making the person *desire* virtue—by making him think of it in a pleasurable light, or of its absence in a painful one. It is by associating the doing right with pleasure, or the wrong with pain, or by eliciting and impressing and bringing home to the person's experience the pleasure naturally involved in the one or the pain in the other, that it is possible to call forth that will to be virtuous which, when confirmed, acts without any thought of either pleasure or pain. Will is the child of desire, and passes out of the dominion of its parent only to come under that of habit. That which is the result of habit affords no presumption of being intrinsically good; and there would be no reason for wishing that the purpose of virtue should become independent of pleasure and pain were it not that the influence of the pleasurable and painful associations which prompt to virtue is not sufficiently

to be depended on for unerring constancy of action until it has acquired the support of habit. Both in feeling and in conduct, habit is the only thing which imparts certainty; and it is because of the importance to others of being able to rely absolutely on one's feelings and conduct, and to oneself of being able to rely on one's own, that the will to do right ought to be cultivated into this habitual independence. In other words, this state of the will is a means to good, not intrinsically a good; and does not contradict the doctrine that nothing is a good to human beings but in so far as it is either itself pleasurable or a means of attaining pleasure or averting pain.

But if this doctrine be true, the principle of utility is proved. Whether it is so or not must now be left to the consideration of the thoughtful reader.

Note

1   An opponent, whose intellectual and moral fairness it is a pleasure to acknowledge (the Rev. J. Llewellyn Davies), has objected to this passage, saying, "Surely the rightness or wrongness of saving a man from drowning does depend very much upon the motive with which it is done. Suppose that a tyrant, when his enemy jumped into the sea to escape from him, saved him from drowning simply in order that he might inflict upon him more exquisite tortures, would it tend to clearness to speak of that rescue as 'a morally right action'? Or suppose again, according to one of the stock illustrations of ethical inquiries, that a man betrayed a trust received from a friend, because the discharge of it would fatally injure that friend himself or someone belonging to him, would utilitarianism compel one to call the betrayal 'a crime' as much as if it had been done from the meanest motive?"

I submit that he who saves another from drowning in order to kill him by torture afterwards does not differ only in motive from him who does the same thing from duty or benevolence; the act itself is different. The rescue of the man is, in the case supposed, only the necessary first step of an act far more atrocious than leaving him to drown would have been. Had Mr. Davies said, "The rightness or wrongness of saving a man from drowning does depend very much"—not upon the motive, but—"upon the *intention*," no utilitarian would have differed from him. Mr. Davies, by an oversight too common not to be quite venial, has in this case confounded the very different ideas of Motive and Intention. There is no point which utilitarian thinkers (and Bentham pre-eminently) have taken more pains to illustrate than this. The morality of the action depends entirely upon the intention—that is, upon what the agent *wills to do*. But the motive, that is, the feeling which makes him will so to do, if it makes no difference in the act, makes none in the morality: though it makes a great difference in our moral estimation of the agent, especially if it indicates a good or a bad habitual *disposition*—a bent of character from which useful, or from which hurtful actions are likely to arise.

Chapter 23

Bernard Williams

A CRITIQUE OF UTILITARIANISM

CONSEQUENTIALISM IS basically indifferent to whether a state of affairs consists in what I do, or is produced by what I do, where that notion is itself wide enough to include, for instance, situations in which other people do things which I have made them do, or allowed them to do, or encouraged them to do, or given them a chance to do. All that consequentialism is interested in is the idea of these doings being *consequences* of what I do, and that is a relation broad enough to include the relations just mentioned, and many others.

Just what the relation is, is a different question, and at least as obscure as the nature of its relative, cause and effect. It is not a question I shall try to pursue; I will rely on cases where I suppose that any consequentialist would be bound to regard the situations in question as consequences of what the agent does. There are cases where the supposed consequences stand in a rather remote relation to the action, which are sometimes difficult to assess from a practical point of view, but which raise no very interesting question for the present enquiry. The more interesting points about consequentialism lie rather elsewhere. There are certain situations in which the causation of the situation, the relation it has to what I do, is in no way remote or problematic in itself, and entirely justifies the claim that the situation is a consequence of what I do: for instance, it is quite clear, or reasonably clear, that if I do a certain thing, this situation

will come about, and if I do not, it will not. So from a consequentialist point of view it goes into the calculation of consequences along with any other state of affairs accessible to me. Yet from some, at least, non-consequentialist points of view, there is a vital difference between some such situations and others: namely, that in some a vital link in the production of the eventual outcome is provided by *someone else's* doing something. But for consequentialism, all causal connexions are on the same level, and it makes no difference, so far as that goes, whether the causation of a given state of affairs lies through another agent, or not.

Correspondingly, there is no relevant difference which consists just in one state of affairs being brought about by me, without intervention of other agents, and another being brought about through the intervention of other agents; although some genuinely causal differences involving a difference of value may correspond to that (as when, for instance, the other agents derive pleasure or pain from the transaction), that kind of difference will already be included in the specification of the state of affairs to be produced. Granted that the states of affairs have been adequately described in causally and evaluatively relevant terms, it makes no further comprehensible difference who produces them. It is because consequentialism attaches value ultimately to states of affairs, and its concern is with what states of affairs the world contains,

that it essentially involves the notion of *negative responsibility*: that if I am ever responsible for anything, then I must be just as much responsible for things that I allow or fail to prevent, as I am for things that I myself, in the more everyday restricted sense, bring about. Those things also must enter my deliberations, as a responsible moral agent, on the same footing. What matters is what states of affairs the world contains, and so what matters with respect to a given action is what comes about if it is done, and what comes about if it is not done, and those are questions not intrinsically affected by the nature of the causal linkage, in particular by whether the outcome is partly produced by other agents.

The strong doctrine of negative responsibility flows directly from consequentialism's assignment of ultimate value to states of affairs. Looked at from another point of view, it can be seen also as a special application of something that is favoured in many moral outlooks not themselves consequentialist—something which, indeed, some thinkers have been disposed to regard as the essence of morality itself: a principle of impartiality. Such a principle will claim that there can be no relevant difference from a moral point of view which consists just in the fact, not further explicable in general terms, that benefits or harms accrue to one person rather than to another—'it's me' can never in itself be a morally comprehensible reason.[1] This principle, familiar with regard to the reception of harms and benefits, we can see consequentialism as extending to their production: from the moral point of view, there is no comprehensible difference which consists just in my bringing about a certain outcome rather than someone else's producing it. That the doctrine of negative responsibility represents in this way the extreme of impartiality, and abstracts from the identity of the agent, leaving just a locus of causal intervention in the world—that fact is not merely a surface paradox. It helps to explain why consequentialism can seem to some to express a more

serious attitude than non-consequentialist views, why part of its appeal is to a certain kind of high-mindedness. Indeed, that is part of what is wrong with it.

For a lot of the time so far we have been operating at an exceedingly abstract level. This has been necessary in order to get clearer in general terms about the differences between consequentialist and other outlooks, an aim which is important if we want to know what features of them lead to what results for our thought. Now, however, let us look more concretely at two examples, to see what utilitarianism might say about them, what we might say about utilitarianism and, most importantly of all, what would be implied by certain ways of thinking about the situations. The examples are inevitably schematized, and they are open to the objection that they beg as many questions as they illuminate. There are two ways in particular in which examples in moral philosophy tend to beg important questions. One is that, as presented, they arbitrarily cut off and restrict the range of alternative courses of action—this objection might particularly be made against the first of my two examples. The second is that they inevitably present one with the situation as a going concern, and cut off questions about how the agent got into it, and correspondingly about moral considerations which might flow from that: this objection might perhaps specially arise with regard to the second of my two situations. These difficulties, however, just have to be accepted, and if anyone finds these examples cripplingly defective in this sort of respect, then he must in his own thought rework them in richer and less question-begging form. If he feels that no presentation of any imagined situation can ever be other than misleading in morality, and that there can never be any substitute for the concrete experienced complexity of actual moral situations, then this discussion, with him, must certainly grind to a halt: but then one may legitimately wonder whether every discussion with him about conduct will

not grind to a halt, including any discussion about the actual situations, since discussion about how one would think and feel about situations somewhat different from the actual (that is to say, situations to that extent imaginary) plays an important role in discussion of the actual.

(1) George, who has just taken his Ph.D. in chemistry, finds it extremely difficult to get a job. He is not very robust in health, which cuts down the number of jobs he might be able to do satisfactorily. His wife has to go out to work to keep them, which itself causes a great deal of strain, since they have small children and there are severe problems about looking after them. The results of all this, especially on the children, are damaging. An older chemist, who knows about this situation, says that he can get George a decently paid job in a certain laboratory, which pursues research into chemical and biological warfare. George says that he cannot accept this, since he is opposed to chemical and biological warfare. The older man replies that he is not too keen on it himself, come to that, but after all George's refusal is not going to make the job or the laboratory go away; what is more, he happens to know that if George refuses the job, it will certainly go to a contemporary of George's who is not inhibited by any such scruples and is likely if appointed to push along the research with greater zeal than George would. Indeed, it is not merely concern for George and his family, but (to speak frankly and in confidence) some alarm about this other man's excess of zeal, which has led the older man to offer to use his influence to get George the job. . . . George's wife, to whom he is deeply attached, has views (the details of which need not concern us) from which it follows that at least there is nothing particularly wrong with research into CBW. What should he do?

(2) Jim finds himself in the central square of a small South American town. Tied up against the wall are a row of twenty Indians, most terrified, a few defiant, in front of them several armed men in uniform. A heavy man in a sweat-stained khaki shirt turns out to be the captain in charge and, after a good deal of questioning of Jim which establishes that he got there by accident while on a botanical expedition, explains that the Indians are a random group of the inhabitants who, after recent acts of protest against the government, are just about to be killed to remind other possible protestors of the advantages of not protesting. However, since Jim is an honoured visitor from another land, the captain is happy to offer him a guest's privilege of killing one of the Indians himself. If Jim accepts, then as a special mark of the occasion, the other Indians will be let off. Of course, if Jim refuses, then there is no special occasion, and Pedro here will do what he was about to do when Jim arrived, and kill them all. Jim, with some desperate recollection of schoolboy fiction, wonders whether if he got hold of a gun, he could hold the captain, Pedro and the rest of the soldiers to threat, but it is quite clear from the set-up that nothing of that kind is going to work: any attempt at that sort of thing will mean that all the Indians will be killed, and himself. The men against the wall, and the other villagers, understand the situation, and are obviously begging him to accept. What should he do?

To these dilemmas, it seems to me that utilitarianism replies, in the first case, that George should accept the job, and in the second, that Jim should kill the Indian. Not only does utilitarianism give these answers but, if the situations are essentially as described and there are no further special factors, it regards them, it seems to me, as *obviously* the right answers. But many of us would certainly wonder whether, in (1), that could possibly be the right answer at all; and in the case of (2), even one who came to think that perhaps that was the answer, might well wonder whether it was obviously the answer. Nor is it just a question of the rightness or obviousness of these answers. It is also a question of what sort of considerations come into

finding the answer. A feature of utilitarianism is that it cuts out a kind of consideration which for some others makes a difference to what they feel about such cases: a consideration involving the idea, as we might first and very simply put it, that each of us is specially responsible for what *he* does, rather than for what other people do. This is an idea closely connected with the value of integrity. It is often suspected that utilitarianism, at least in its direct forms, makes integrity as a value more or less unintelligible. I shall try to show that this suspicion is correct. Of course, even if that is correct, it would not necessarily follow that we should reject utilitarianism; perhaps, as utilitarians sometimes suggest, we should just forget about integrity, in favour of such things as a concern for the general good. However, if I am right, we cannot merely do that, since the reason why utilitarianism cannot understand integrity is that it cannot coherently describe the relations between a man's projects and his actions.

Two kinds of remoter effects

A lot of what we have to say about this question will be about the relations between my projects and other people's projects. But before we get on to that, we should first ask whether we are assuming too hastily what the utilitarian answers to the dilemmas will be. In terms of more direct effects of the possible decisions, there does not indeed seem much doubt about the answer in either case; but it might be said that in terms of more remote or less evident effects counterweights might be found to enter the utilitarian scales. Thus the effect on George of a decision to take the job might be invoked, or its effect on others who might know of his decision. The possibility of there being more beneficent labours in the future from which he might be barred or disqualified, might be mentioned; and so forth. Such effects—in particular, possible effects on the agent's character, and effects on the public at large—are often invoked by

utilitarian writers dealing with problems about lying or promise-breaking, and some similar considerations might be invoked here.

There is one very general remark that is worth making about arguments of this sort. The certainty that attaches to these hypotheses about possible effects is usually pretty low; in some cases, indeed, the hypothesis invoked is so implausible that it would scarcely pass if it were not being used to deliver the respectable moral answer, as in the standard fantasy that one of the effects of one's telling a particular lie is to weaken the disposition of the world at large to tell the truth. The demands on the certainty or probability of these beliefs as beliefs about particular actions are much milder than they would be on beliefs favouring the unconventional course. It may be said that this is as it should be, since the presumption must be in favour of the conventional course: but that scarcely seems a *utilitarian* answer, unless utilitarianism has already taken off in the direction of not applying the consequences to the particular act at all.

Leaving aside that very general point, I want to consider now two types of effect that are often invoked by utilitarians, and which might be invoked in connexion with these imaginary cases. The attitude or tone involved in invoking these effects may sometimes seem peculiar; but that sort of peculiarity soon becomes familiar in utilitarian discussions, and indeed it can be something of an achievement to retain a sense of it.

First, there is the psychological effect on the agent. Our descriptions of these situations have not so far taken account of how George or Jim will be after they have taken the one course or the other; and it might be said that if they take the course which seemed at first the utilitarian one, the effects on them will be in fact bad enough and extensive enough to cancel out the initial utilitarian advantages of that course. Now there is one version of this effect in which, for a utilitarian, some confusion must be involved,

namely that in which the agent feels bad, his subsequent conduct and relations are crippled and so on, *because he thinks that he has done the wrong thing*—for if the balance of outcomes was as it appeared to be *before* invoking this effect, then he has not (from the utilitarian point of view) done the wrong thing. So that version of the effect, for a rational and utilitarian agent, could not possibly make any difference, to the assessment of right and wrong. However, perhaps he is not a thoroughly rational agent, and is disposed to have bad feelings, whichever he decided to do. Now such feelings, which are from a strictly utilitarian point of view irrational—nothing, a utilitarian can point out, is advanced by having them—cannot, consistently, have any great weight in a utilitarian calculation. I shall consider in a moment an argument to suggest that they should have no weight at all in it. But short of that, the utilitarian could reasonably say that such feelings should not be encouraged, even if we accept their existence, and that to give them a lot of weight is to encourage them. Or, at the very best, even if they are straightforwardly and without any discount to be put into the calculation, their weight must be small: they are after all (and at best) one man's feelings.

• • •

If, then, one is really going to regard one's feelings from a strictly utilitarian point of view, Jim should give very little weight at all to his; it seems almost indecent, in fact, once one has taken that point of view, to suppose that he should give any at all. In George's case one might feel that things were slightly different. It is interesting, though, that one reason why one might think that—namely that one person principally affected is his wife—is very dubiously available to a utilitarian. George's wife has some reason to be interested in George's integrity and his sense of it; the Indians, quite properly, have no interest in Jim's. But it is not at all clear how utilitarianism would describe that difference.

There is an argument, and a strong one, that a strict utilitarian should give not merely small extra weight, in calculations of right and wrong, to feelings of this kind, but that he should give absolutely no weight to them at all. This is based on the point, which we have already seen, that if a course of action is, before taking these sorts of feelings into account, utilitarianly preferable, then bad feelings about that kind of action will be from a utilitarian point of view irrational. Now it might be thought that even if that is so, it would not mean that in a utilitarian calculation such feelings should not be taken into account; it is after all a well-known boast of utilitarianism that it is a realistic outlook which seeks the best in the world as it is, and takes any form of happiness or unhappiness into account. While a utilitarian will no doubt seek to diminish the incidence of feelings which are utilitarianly irrational—or at least of disagreeable feelings which are so—he might be expected to take them into account while they exist. This is without doubt classical utilitarian doctrine, but there is good reason to think that utilitarianism cannot stick to it without embracing results which are startlingly unacceptable and perhaps self-defeating.

Suppose that there is in a certain society a racial minority. Considering merely the ordinary interests of the other citizens, as opposed to their sentiments, this minority does no particular harm; we may suppose that it does not confer any very great benefits either. Its presence is in those terms neutral or mildly beneficial. However, the other citizens have such prejudices that they find the sight of this group, even the knowledge of its presence, very disagreeable. Proposals are made for removing in some way this minority. If we assume various quite plausible things (as that programmes to change the majority sentiment are likely to be protracted and ineffective) then even if the removal would be unpleasant for the minority, a utilitarian calculation might well end up favouring this step, especially if the minority were a rather small minority and the majority were very severely prejudiced, that is to say, were made

very severely uncomfortable by the presence of the minority.

A utilitarian might find that conclusion embarrassing; and not merely because of its nature, but because of the grounds on which it is reached. While a utilitarian might be expected to take into account certain other sorts of consequences of the prejudice, as that a majority prejudice is likely to be displayed in conduct disagreeable to the minority, and so forth, he might be made to wonder whether the unpleasant experiences of the prejudiced people should be allowed, *merely as such*, to count. If he does count them, merely as such, then he has once more separated himself from a body of ordinary moral thought which he might have hoped to accommodate; he may also have started on the path of defeating his own view of things. For one feature of these sentiments is that they are from the utilitarian point of view itself irrational, and a thoroughly utilitarian person would either not have them, or if he found that he did tend to have them, would himself seek to discount them. Since the sentiments in question are such that a rational utilitarian would discount them in himself, it is reasonable to suppose that he should discount them in his calculations about society; it does seem quite unreasonable for him to give just as much weight to feelings—considered just in themselves, one must recall, as experiences of those that have them—which are essentially based on views which are from a utilitarian point of view irrational, as to those which accord with utilitarian principles. Granted this idea, it seems reasonable for him to rejoin a body of moral thought in other respects congenial to him, and discount those sentiments, just considered in themselves, totally, on the principle that no pains or discomforts are to count in the utilitarian sum which their subjects have just because they hold views which are by utilitarian standards irrational. But if he accepts that, then in the cases we are at present considering no extra weight at all can be put in for bad feelings of George or Jim about their choices, if those choices are, leaving

out those feelings, on the first round utilitarianly rational.

The psychological effect on the agent was the first of two general effects considered by utilitarians, which had to be discussed. The second is in general a more substantial item, but it need not take so long, since it is both clearer and has little application to the present cases. This is the *precedent effect*. As Burke rightly emphasized, this effect can be important: that one morally *can* do what someone has actually done, is a psychologically effective principle, if not a deontically valid one. For the effect to operate, obviously some conditions must hold, on the publicity of the act and on such things as the status of the agent (such considerations weighed importantly with Sir Thomas More); what these may be will vary evidently with circumstances.

In order for the precedent effect to make a difference to a utilitarian calculation, it must be based upon a confusion. For suppose that there is an act which would be the best in the circumstances, except that doing it will encourage by precedent other people to do things which will not be the best things to do. Then the situation of those other people must be relevantly different from that of the original agent; if it were not, then in doing the same as what would be the best course for the original agent, they would necessarily do the best thing themselves. But if the situations are in this way relevantly different, it must be a confused perception which takes the first situation, and the agent's course in it, as an adequate precedent for the second.

However, the fact that the precedent effect, if it really makes a difference, is in this sense based on a confusion, does not mean that it is not perfectly real, or that it is to be discounted: social effects are by their nature confused in this sort of way. What it does emphasize is that calculations of the precedent effect have got to be realistic, involving considerations of how people are actually likely to be influenced. In the present examples, however, it is very implausible to think that the precedent effect could be invoked

to make any difference to the calculation. Jim's case is extraordinary enough, and it is hard to imagine who the recipients of the effect might be supposed to be; while George is not in a sufficiently public situation or role for the question to arise in that form, and in any case one might suppose that the motivations of others on such an issue were quite likely to be fixed one way or another already.

No appeal, then, to these other effects is going to make a difference to what the utilitarian will decide about our examples. Let us now look more closely at the structure of those decisions.

Integrity

The situations have in common that if the agent does not do a certain disagreeable thing, someone else will, and in Jim's situation at least the result, the state of affairs after the other man has acted, if he does, will be worse than after Jim has acted, if Jim does. The same, on a smaller scale, is true of George's case. I have already suggested that it is inherent in consequentialism that it offers a strong doctrine of negative responsibility: if I know that if I do X, O_1 will eventuate, and if I refrain from doing X, O_2 will, and that O_2 is worse than O_1, then I am responsible for O_2 if I refrain voluntarily from doing X. 'You could have prevented it', as will be said, and truly, to Jim, if he refuses, by the relatives of the other Indians. (I shall leave the important question, which is to the side of the present issue, of the obligations, if any, that nest around the word 'know': how far does one, under utilitarianism, have to research into the possibilities of maximally beneficent action, including prevention?)

In the present cases, the situation of O_2 includes another agent bringing about results worse than O_1. So far as O_2 has been identified up to this point—merely as the worse outcome which will eventuate if I refrain from doing X—we might equally have said that what that other brings about is O_2; but that would be to under-describe the situation. For what occurs if Jim refrains from action is not solely twenty Indians dead, but *Pedro's killing twenty Indians*, and that is not a result which Pedro brings about, though the death of the Indians is. We can say: what one does is not included in the outcome of what one does, while what another does can be included in the outcome of what one does. For that to be so, as the terms are now being used, only a very weak condition has to be satisfied: for Pedro's killing the Indians to be the outcome of Jim's refusal, it only has to be causally true that if Jim had not refused, Pedro would not have done it.

That may be enough for us to speak, in some sense, of Jim's responsibility for that outcome, if it occurs; but it is certainly not enough, it is worth noticing, for us to speak of Jim's *making* those things happen. For granted this way of their coming about, he could have made them happen only by making Pedro shoot, and there is no acceptable sense in which his refusal makes Pedro shoot. If the captain had said on Jim's refusal, 'you leave me with no alternative', he would have been lying, like most who use that phrase. While the deaths, and the killing, may be the outcome of Jim's refusal, it is misleading to think in such a case, of Jim having an *effect* on the world through the medium (as it happens) of Pedro's acts; for this is to leave Pedro out of the picture in his essential role of one who has intentions and projects, projects for realizing which Jim's refusal would leave an opportunity. Instead of thinking in terms of supposed effects of Jim's projects on Pedro, it is more revealing to think in terms of the effects of Pedro's projects on Jim's decision.

• • •

Let us now go back to the agent as utilitarian, and his higher-order project of maximizing desirable outcomes. At this level, he is committed only to that: what the outcome will actually consist of will depend entirely on the facts, on what persons with what projects and what

potential satisfactions there are within calculable reach of the causal levers near which he finds himself. His own substantial projects and commitments come into it, but only as one lot among others—they potentially provide one set of satisfactions among those which he may be able to assist from where he happens to be. He is the agent of the satisfaction system who happens to be at a particular point at a particular time: in Jim's case, our man in South America. His own decisions as a utilitarian agent are a function of all the satisfactions which he can affect from where he is: and this means that the projects of others, to an indeterminately great extent, determine his decision.

This may be so either positively or negatively. It will be so positively if agents within the causal field of his decision have projects which are at any rate harmless, and so should be assisted. It will equally be so, but negatively, if there is an agent within the causal field whose projects are harmful, and have to be frustrated to maximize desirable outcomes. So it is with Jim and the soldier Pedro. On the utilitarian view, the undesirable projects of other people as much determine, in this negative way, one's decisions as the desirable ones do positively: if those people were not there, or had different projects, the causal nexus would be different, and it is the actual state of the causal nexus which determines the decision. The determination to an indefinite degree of my decisions by other people's projects is just another aspect of my unlimited responsibility to act for the best in a causal framework formed to a considerable extent by their projects.

The decision so determined is, for utilitarianism, the right decision. But what if it conflicts with some project of mine? This, the utilitarian will say, has already been dealt with: the satisfaction to you of fulfilling your project, and any satisfactions to others of your so doing, have already been through the calculating device and have been found inadequate. Now in the case of many sorts of projects, that is a perfectly reasonable sort of answer. But in the case of projects of the sort I have called 'commitments', those with which one is more deeply and extensively involved and identified, this cannot just by itself be an adequate answer, and there may be no adequate answer at all. For, to take the extreme sort of case, how can a man, as a utilitarian agent, come to regard as one satisfaction among others, and a dispensable one, a project or attitude round which he has built his life, just because someone else's projects have so structured the causal scene that that is how the utilitarian sum comes out?

The point here is not, as utilitarians may hasten to say, that if the project or attitude is that central to his life, then to abandon it will be very disagreeable to him and great loss of utility will be involved. I have already argued . . . that it is not like that; on the contrary, once he is prepared to look at it like that, the argument in any serious case is over anyway. The point is that he is identified with his actions as flowing from projects and attitudes which in some cases he takes seriously at the deepest level, as what his life is about (or, in some cases, this section of his life—seriously is not necessarily the same as persistence). It is absurd to demand of such a man, when the sums come in from the utility network which the projects of others have in part determined, that he should just step aside from his own project and decision and acknowledge the decision which utilitarian calculation requires. It is to alienate him in a real sense from his actions and the source of his action in his own convictions. It is to make him into a channel between the input of everyone's projects, including his own, and an output of optimific decision; but this is to neglect the extent to which *his* actions and *his* decisions have to be seen as the actions and decisions which flow from the projects and attitudes with which he is most closely identified. It is thus, in the most literal sense, an attack on his integrity.[2]

These sorts of considerations do not in themselves give solutions to practical dilemmas such

as those provided by our examples; but I hope they help to provide other ways of thinking about them. In fact, it is not hard to see that in George's case, viewed from this perspective, the utilitarian solution would be wrong. Jim's case is different, and harder. But if (as I suppose) the utilitarian is probably right in this case, that is not to be found out just by asking the utilitarian's questions. Discussions of it—and I am not going to try to carry it further here—will have to take seriously the distinction between my killing someone, and its coming about because of what I do that someone else kills them: a distinction based, not so much on the distinction between action and inaction, as on the distinction between my projects and someone else's projects. At least it will have to start by taking that seriously, as utilitarianism does not; but then it will have to build out from there by asking why that distinction seems to have less, or a different, force in this case than it has in George's. One question here would be how far one's powerful objection to killing people just is, in fact, an application of a powerful objection to their being killed. Another dimension of that is the issue of how much it matters that the people at risk are actual, and there, as opposed to hypothetical, or future, or merely elsewhere.[3]

There are many other considerations that could come into such a question, but the immediate point of all this is to draw one particular contrast with utilitarianism: that to reach a grounded decision in such a case should not be regarded as a matter of just discounting one's reactions, impulses and deeply held projects in the face of the pattern of utilities, nor yet merely adding them in—but in the first instance of trying to understand them.

Notes

1 There is a tendency in some writers to suggest that it is not a comprehensible reason at all. But this, I suspect, is due to the overwhelming importance those writers ascribe to the moral point of view.

2 Interestingly related to these notions is the Socratic idea that courage is a virtue particularly connected with keeping a clear sense of what one regards as most important. They also centrally raise questions about the value of pride. Humility, as something beyond the real demand of correct self-appraisal, was specially a Christian virtue because it involved subservience to God. In a secular context it can only represent subservience to other men and their projects.

3 For a more general discussion of this issue see Charles Fried, *An Anatomy of Values* (Cambridge, MA: Harvard University Press, 1970), Part Three.

Chapter 24

John Rawls

CLASSICAL UTILITARIANISM

THERE ARE many forms of utilitarianism, and the development of the theory has continued in recent years. I shall not survey these forms here, nor take account of the numerous refinements found in contemporary discussions. My aim is to work out a theory of justice that represents an alternative to utilitarian thought generally and so to all of these different versions of it. I believe that the contrast between the contract view and utilitarianism remains essentially the same in all these cases. Therefore I shall compare justice as fairness with familiar variants of intuitionism, perfectionism, and utilitarianism in order to bring out the underlying differences in the simplest way. With this end in mind, the kind of utilitarianism I shall describe here is the strict classical doctrine which receives perhaps its clearest and most accessible formulation in Sidgwick. The main idea is that society is rightly ordered, and therefore just, when its major institutions are arranged so as to achieve the greatest net balance of satisfaction summed over all the individuals belonging to it.[1]

We may note first that there is, indeed, a way of thinking of society which makes it easy to suppose that the most radical conception of justice is utilitarian. For consider: each man in realizing his own interests is certainly free to balance his own losses against his own gains. We may impose a sacrifice on ourselves now for the sake of a greater advantage later. A person quite properly acts, at least when others are not affected, to achieve his own greatest good, to advance his rational ends as far as possible. Now why should not a society act on precisely the same principle applied to the group and therefore regard that which is rational for one man as right for an association of men? Just as the well-being of a person is constructed from the series of satisfactions that are experienced at different moments in the course of his life, so in very much the same way the well-being of society is to be constructed from the fulfillment of the systems of desires of the many individuals who belong to it. Since the principle for an individual is to advance as far as possible his own welfare, his own system of desires, the principle for society is to advance as far as possible the welfare of the group, to realize to the greatest extent the comprehensive system of desire arrived at from the desire of its members. Just as an individual balances present and future gains against present and future losses, so a society may balance satisfactions and dissatisfactions between different individuals. And so by these reflections one reaches the principle of utility in a natural way: a society is properly arranged when its institutions maximize the net balance of satisfaction. The principle of choice for an association of men is interpreted as an extension of the principle of choice for one man. Social justice is the principle of rational prudence applied to an aggregative conception of the welfare of the group (§30).[2]

This idea is made all the more attractive by a further consideration. The two main concepts of ethics are those of the right and the good; the concept of a morally worthy person is, I believe, derived from them. The structure of an ethical theory is, then, largely determined by how it defines and connects these two basic notions. Now it seems that the simplest way of relating them is taken by teleological theories: the good is defined independently from the right, and then the right is defined as that which maximizes the good.[3] More precisely, those institutions and acts are right which of the available alternatives produce the most good, or at least as much good as any of the other institutions and acts open as real possibilities (a rider needed when the maximal class is not a singleton). Teleological theories have a deep intuitive appeal since they seem to embody the idea of rationality. It is natural to think that rationality is maximizing something and that in morals it must be maximizing the good. Indeed, it is tempting to suppose that it is self-evident that things should be arranged so as to lead to the most good.

It is essential to keep in mind that in a teleological theory the good is defined independently from the right. This means two things. First, the theory accounts for our considered judgments as to which things are good (our judgments of value) as a separate class of judgments intuitively distinguishable by common sense, and then proposes the hypothesis that the right is maximizing the good as already specified. Second, the theory enables one to judge the goodness of things without referring to what is right. For example, if pleasure is said to be the sole good, then presumably pleasures can be recognized and ranked in value by criteria that do not presuppose any standards of right, or what we would normally think of as such. Whereas if the distribution of goods is also counted as a good, perhaps a higher order one, and the theory directs us to produce the most good (including the good of distribution among

others), we no longer have a teleological view in the classical sense. The problem of distribution falls under the concept of right as one intuitively understands it, and so the theory lacks an independent definition of the good. The clarity and simplicity of classical teleological theories derives largely from the fact that they factor our moral judgments into two classes, the one being characterized separately while the other is then connected with it by a maximizing principle.

Teleological doctrines differ, pretty clearly, according to how the conception of the good is specified. If it is taken as the realization of human excellence in the various forms of culture, we have what may be called perfectionism. This notion is found in Aristotle and Nietzsche, among others. If the good is defined as pleasure, we have hedonism; if as happiness, eudaimonism, and so on. I shall understand the principle of utility in its classical form as defining the good as the satisfaction of desire, or perhaps better, as the satisfaction of rational desire. This accords with the view in all essentials and provides, I believe, a fair interpretation of it. The appropriate terms of social cooperation are settled by whatever in the circumstances will achieve the greatest sum of satisfaction of the rational desires of individuals. It is impossible to deny the initial plausibility and attractiveness of this conception.

The striking feature of the utilitarian view of justice is that it does not matter, except indirectly, how this sum of satisfactions is distributed among individuals any more than it matters, except indirectly, how one man distributes his satisfactions over time. The correct distribution in either case is that which yields the maximum fulfillment. Society must allocate its means of satisfaction whatever these are, rights and duties, opportunities and privileges, and various forms of wealth, so as to achieve this maximum if it can. But in itself no distribution of satisfaction is better than another except that the more equal distribution is to be preferred to break ties.[4] It is true that certain common sense

precepts of justice, particularly those which concern the protection of liberties and rights, or which express the claims of desert, seem to contradict this contention. But from a utilitarian standpoint the explanation of these precepts and of their seemingly stringent character is that they are those precepts which experience shows should be strictly respected and departed from only under exceptional circumstances if the sum of advantages is to be maximized.[5] Yet, as with all other precepts, those of justice are derivative from the one end of attaining the greatest balance of satisfaction. Thus there is no reason in principle why the greater gains of some should not compensate for the lesser losses of others; or more importantly, why the violation of the liberty of a few might not be made right by the greater good shared by many. It simply happens that under most conditions, at least in a reasonably advanced stage of civilization, the greatest sum of advantages is not attained in this way. No doubt the strictness of common sense precepts of justice has a certain usefulness in limiting men's propensities to injustice and to socially injurious actions, but the utilitarian believes that to affirm this strictness as a first principle of morals is a mistake. For just as it is rational for one man to maximize the fulfillment of his system of desires, it is right for a society to maximize the net balance of satisfaction taken over all of its members.

The most natural way, then, of arriving at utilitarianism (although not, of course, the only way of doing so) is to adopt for society as a whole the principle of rational choice for one man. Once this is recognized, the place of the impartial spectator and the emphasis on sympathy in the history of utilitarian thought is readily understood. For it is by the conception of the impartial spectator and the use of sympathetic identification in guiding our imagination that the principle for one man is applied to society. It is this spectator who is conceived as carrying out the required organization of the desires of all persons into one coherent system of desire; it is by this construction that many persons are fused into one. Endowed with ideal powers of sympathy and imagination, the impartial spectator is the perfectly rational individual who identifies with and experiences the desires of others as if these desires were his own. In this way he ascertains the intensity of these desires and assigns them their appropriate weight in the one system of desire the satisfaction of which the ideal legislator then tries to maximize by adjusting the rules of the social system. On this conception of society separate individuals are thought of as so many different lines along which rights and duties are to be assigned and scarce means of satisfaction allocated in accordance with rules so as to give the greatest fulfillment of wants. The nature of the decision made by the ideal legislator is not, therefore, materially different from that of an entrepreneur deciding how to maximize his profits by producing this or that commodity, or that of a consumer deciding how to maximize his satisfaction by the purchase of this or that collection of goods. In each case there is a single person whose system of desires determines the best allocation of limited means. The correct decision is essentially a question of efficient administration. This view of social cooperation is the consequence of extending to society the principle of choice for one man, and then, to make this extension work, conflating all persons into one through the imaginative acts of the impartial sympathetic spectator. Utilitarianism does not take seriously the distinction between persons.

Notes

1 I shall take Henry Sidgwick's *The Methods of Ethics*, 7th ed. (London, 1907), as summarizing the development of utilitarian moral theory. Book III of his *Principles of Political Economy* (London, 1883) applies this doctrine to questions of economic and social justice, and is a precursor of A. C. Pigou, *The Economics of Welfare* (London, Macmillan, 1920). Sidgwick's

Outlines of the History of Ethics, 5th ed. (London, 1902), contains a brief history of the utilitarian tradition. We may follow him in assuming, somewhat arbitrarily, that it begins with Shaftesbury's *An Inquiry Concerning Virtue and Merit* (1711) and Hutcheson's *An Inquiry Concerning Moral Good and Evil* (1725). Hutcheson seems to have been the first to state clearly the principle of utility. He says in *Inquiry*, sec. III, §8, that "that action is best, which procures the greatest happiness for the greatest numbers; and that, worst, which, in like manner, occasions misery." Other major eighteenth-century works are Hume's *A Treatise of Human Nature* (1739), and *An Enquiry Concerning the Principles of Morals* (1751); Adam Smith's *A Theory of the Moral Sentiments* (1759); and Bentham's *The Principles of Morals and Legislation* (1789). To these we must add the writings of J. S. Mill represented by *Utilitarianism* (1863) and F. Y. Edgeworth's *Mathematical Psychics* (London, 1888).

The discussion of utilitarianism has taken a different turn in recent years by focusing on what we may call the coordination problem and related questions of publicity. This development stems from the essays of R. F. Harrod, "Utilitarianism Revised," *Mind*, vol. 45 (1936); J. D. Mabbott, "Punishment," *Mind*, vol. 48 (1939); Jonathan Harrison, "Utilitarianism, Universalisation, and Our Duty to Be Just," *Proceedings of the Aristotelian Society*, vol. 53 (1952–53); and J. O. Urmson, "The Interpretation of the Philosophy of J. S. Mill," *Philosophical Quarterly*, vol. 3 (1953). See also J. J. C. Smart, "Extreme and Restricted Utilitarianism," *Philosophical Quarterly*, vol. 6 (1956), and his *An Outline of a System of Utilitarian Ethics* (Cambridge, The University Press, 1961). For an account of these matters, see David Lyons, *Forms and Limits of Utilitarianism* (Oxford, The Clarendon Press, 1965); and Allan Gibbard, "Utilitarianisms and Coordination" (dissertation, Harvard University, 1971). The problems raised by these works, as important as they are, I shall leave aside as not bearing directly on the more elementary question of distribution which I wish to discuss.

Finally, we should note here the essays of J. C. Harsanyi, in particular, "Cardinal Utility in Welfare Economics and in the Theory of Risk-Taking," *Journal of Political Economy*, 1953, and "Cardinal Welfare, Individualistic Ethics, and Interpersonal Comparisons of Utility," *Journal of Political Economy*, 1955; and R. B. Brandt, "Some Merits of One Form of Rule-Utilitarianism," *University of Colorado Studies* (Boulder, Colorado, 1967).

2   On this point see also D. P. Gauthier, *Practical Reasoning* (Oxford, Clarendon Press, 1963), pp. 126f. The text elaborates the suggestion found in "Constitutional Liberty and the Concept of Justice," *Nomos VI: Justice*, ed. C. J. Friedrich and J. W. Chapman (New York, Atherton Press, 1963), pp. 124f, which in turn is related to the idea of justice as a higher-order administrative decision. See "Justice As Fairness," *Philosophical Review*, 1958, pp. 185–87.... That the principle of social integration is distinct from the principle of personal integration is stated by R. B. Perry, *General Theory of Value* (New York, Longmans, Green, and Company, 1926), pp. 674–77. He attributes the error of overlooking this fact to Émile Durkheim and others with similar views. His conception of social integration is that brought about by a shared and dominant benevolent purpose.

3   Here I adopt W. K. Frankena's definition of teleological theories in *Ethics* (Englewood Cliffs, NJ: Prentice Hall, Inc., 1963), p. 13.

4   On this point see Sidgwick, *The Methods of Ethics*, pp. 416f.

5   See J. S. Mill, *Utilitarianism*, ch. V, last two pars.

Peter Railton

ALIENATION, CONSEQUENTIALISM, AND THE DEMANDS OF MORALITY

Introduction

LIVING UP to the demands of morality may bring with it alienation—from one's personal commitments, from one's feelings or sentiments, from other people, or even from morality itself. In this article I will discuss several apparent instances of such alienation, and attempt a preliminary assessment of their bearing on questions about the acceptability of certain moral theories. Of special concern will be the question whether problems about alienation show consequentialist moral theories to be self-defeating.

I will not attempt a full or general characterization of alienation. Indeed, at a perfectly general level alienation can be characterized only very roughly as a kind of estrangement, distancing, or separateness (not necessarily consciously attended to) resulting in some sort of loss (not necessarily consciously noticed).[1] Rather than seek a general analysis I will rely upon examples to convey a sense of what is involved in the sorts of alienation with which I am concerned. There is nothing in a word, and the phenomena to be discussed below could all be considered while avoiding the controversial term 'alienation.' My sense, however, is that there is some point in using this formidable term, if only to draw attention to commonalities among problems not always noticed. . .

I. John and Anne and Lisa and Helen

To many, John has always seemed a model husband. He almost invariably shows great sensitivity to his wife's needs, and he willingly goes out of his way to meet them. He plainly feels great affection for her. When a friend remarks upon the extraordinary quality of John's concern for his wife, John responds without any self-indulgence or self-congratulation. "I've always thought that people should help each other when they're in a specially good position to do so. I know Anne better than anyone else does, so I know better what she wants and needs. Besides, I have such affection for her that it's no great burden—instead, I get a lot of satisfaction out of it. Just think how awful marriage would be, or life itself, if people didn't take special care of the ones they love." His friend accuses John of being unduly modest, but John's manner convinces him that he is telling the truth: this is really how he feels.

Lisa has gone through a series of disappointments over a short period, and has been profoundly depressed. In the end, however, with the help of others she has emerged from the long night of anxiety and melancholy. Only now is she able to talk openly with friends about her state of mind, and she turns to her oldest friend, Helen, who was a mainstay throughout. She'd like to find a way to thank Helen, since she's only too aware of how much of a burden she's

been over these months, how much of a drag and a bore, as she puts it. "You don't have to thank me, Lisa," Helen replies, "you deserved it. It was the least I could do after all you've done for me. We're friends, remember? And we said a long time ago that we'd stick together no matter what. Some day I'll probably ask the same thing of you, and I know you'll come through. What else are friends for?" Lisa wonders whether Helen is saying this simply to avoid creating feelings of guilt, but Helen replies that she means every word—she couldn't bring. herself to lie to Lisa if she tried.

II. What's missing?

What is troubling about the words of John and Helen? Both show stout character and moral awareness. John's remarks have a benevolent, consequentialist cast, while Helen reasons in a deontological language of duties, reciprocity, and respect. They are not self-centered or without feeling. Yet something seems wrong.

The place to look is not so much at what they say as what they don't say. Think, for example, of how John's remarks might sound to his wife. Anne might have hoped that it was, in some ultimate sense, in part for *her* sake and the sake of their love as such that John pays such special attention to her. That he devotes himself to her because of the characteristically good consequences of doing so seems to leave her, and their relationship as such, too far out of the picture— this despite the fact that these characteristically good consequences depend in important ways on his special relation to her. She is being taken into account by John, but it might seem she is justified in being hurt by the way she is being taken into account. It is as if John viewed her, their relationship, and even his own affection for her from a distant, objective point of view—a moral point of view where reasons must be reasons for any rational agent and so must have an impersonal character even when they deal with personal matters. His wife might think a

more personal point of view would also be appropriate, a point of view from which "It's my wife" or "It's Anne" would have direct and special relevance, and play an unmediated role in his answer to the question *Why do you attend to her so?*"

Something similar is missing from Helen's account of why she stood by Lisa. While we understand that the specific duties she feels toward Lisa depend upon particular features of their relationship, still we would not be surprised if Lisa finds Helen's response to her expression of gratitude quite distant, even chilling. We need not question whether she has strong feeling for Lisa, but we may wonder at how that feeling finds expression in Helen's thinking.[2]

John and Helen both show alienation: there would seem to be an estrangement between their affections and their rational, deliberative selves; an abstract and universalizing point of view mediates their reponses to others and to their own sentiments. We should not assume that they have been caught in an uncharacteristic moment of moral reflection or after-the-fact rationalization; it is a settled part of their characters to think and act from a moral point of view. It is as if the world were for them a fabric of obligations and permissions in which personal considerations deserve recognition only to the extent that, and in the way that, such considerations find a place in this fabric.

To call John and Helen alienated from their affections or their intimates is not of itself to condemn them, nor is it to say that they are experiencing any sort of distress. One may be alienated from something without recognizing this as such or suffering in any conscious way from it, much as one may simply be uninterested in something without awareness or conscious suffering. But alienation is not mere lack of interest: John and Helen are not *uninterested* in their affections or in their intimates; rather, their interest takes a certain alienated form. While this alienation may not itself be a

psychological affliction, it may be the basis of such afflictions—such as a sense of loneliness or emptiness—or of the loss of certain things of value—such as a sense of belonging or the pleasures of spontaneity. Moreover, their alienation may cause psychological distress in others, and make certain valuable sorts of relationships impossible.

However, we must be on guard lest oversimple categories distort our diagnosis. It seems to me wrong to picture the self as ordinarily divided into cognitive and affective halves, with deliberation and rationality belonging to the first, and sentiments belonging to the second. John's alienation is not a problem on the boundary of naturally given cognitive and affective selves, but a problem partially constituted by the bifurcation of his psyche into these separate spheres. John's deliberative self seems remarkably divorced from his affections, but not all psyches need be so divided. That there is a cognitive element in affection—that affection is not a mere "feeling" that is a given for the deliberative self but rather involves as well certain characteristic modes of thought and perception—is suggested by the difficulty some may have in believing that John really does love Anne if he persistently thinks about her in the way suggested by his remarks. Indeed, his affection for Anne does seem to have been demoted to a mere "feeling." For this reason among others, we should not think of John's alienation from his affections and his alienation from Anne as wholly independent phenomena, the one the cause of the other.[3] Of course, similar remarks apply to Helen.

III. The moral point of view

Perhaps the lives of John and Anne or Helen and Lisa would be happier or fuller if none of the alienation mentioned were present. But is this a problem for *morality*? If, as some have contended, to have a morality is to make normative judgments from a moral point of view and be guided by them, and if by its nature a moral point of view must exclude considerations that lack universality, then any genuinely moral way of going about life would seem liable to produce the sorts of alienation mentioned above.[4] Thus it would be a conceptual confusion to ask that we never be required by morality to go beyond a personal point of view, since to fail ever to look at things from an impersonal (or nonpersonal) point of view would be to fail ever to *be* distinctively moral—not immoralism, perhaps, but amoralism. This would not be to say that there are not other points of view on life worthy of our attention,[5] or that taking a moral point of view is always appropriate—one could say that John and Helen show no moral defect in thinking so impersonally, although they do moralize to excess. But the fact that a particular morality requires us to take an impersonal point of view could not sensibly be held against it, for that would be what makes it a morality at all.

This sort of position strikes me as entirely too complacent. First, we must somehow give an account of practical reasoning that does not merely multiply points of view and divide the self—a more unified account is needed. Second, we must recognize that loving relationships, friendships, group loyalties, and spontaneous actions are among the most important contributors to whatever it is that makes life worthwhile; any moral theory deserving serious consideration must itself give them serious consideration. As William K. Frankena has written, "Morality is made for man, not man for morality."[6] Moral considerations are often supposed to be overriding in practical reasoning. If we were to find that adopting a particular morality led to irreconcilable conflict with central types of human well-being—as cases akin to John's and Helen's have led some to suspect—then this surely would give us good reason to doubt its claims.[7]

For example, in the closing sentences of A *Theory of Justice* John Rawls considers the "perspective of eternity," which is impartial across all individuals and times, and writes that this is a "form of *thought and feeling* that rational persons

can adopt in the world." "Purity of heart," he concludes, "would be to see clearly and act with grace and self-command from this point of view."[8] This may or may not be purity of heart, but it could not be the standpoint of actual life without radically detaching the individual from a range of personal concerns and commitments. Presumably we should not read Rawls as recommending that we adopt this point of view in the bulk of our actions in daily life, but the fact that so purely abstracted a perspective is portrayed as a kind of moral ideal should at least start us wondering.[9] If to be more perfectly moral is to ascend ever higher toward *sub specie aeternitatis* abstraction, perhaps we made a mistake in boarding the moral escalator in the first place. Some of the very "weaknesses" that prevent us from achieving this moral ideal—strong attachments to persons or projects—seem to be part of a considerably more compelling human ideal.

Should we say at this point that the lesson is that we should give a more prominent role to the value of non-alienation in our moral reasoning? That would be too little too late: the problem seems to be the way in which morality asks us to look at things, not just the things it asks us to look at.

IV. The "paradox of hedonism"

Rather than enter directly into the question whether being moral is a matter of taking a moral point of view and whether there is thus some sort of necessary connection between being moral and being alienated in a way detrimental to human flourishing, I will consider a related problem the solution to which may suggest a way of steering around obstacles to a more direct approach.

One version of the so-called "paradox of hedonism" is that adopting as one's exclusive ultimate end in life the pursuit of maximum happiness may well prevent one from having certain experiences or engaging in certain sorts of relationships or commitments that are among the greatest sources of happiness.[10] The hedonist, looking around him, may discover that some of those who are less concerned with their own happiness than he is, and who view people and projects less instrumentally than he does, actually manage to live happier lives than he despite his dogged pursuit of happiness. The "paradox" is pragmatic, not logical, but it looks deep nonetheless: the hedonist, it would appear, ought not to be a hedonist. It seems, then, as if we have come across a second case in which mediating one's relations to people or projects by a particular point of view—in this case, a hedonistic point of view—may prevent one from attaining the fullest possible realization of sought-after values.

However, it is important to notice that even though adopting a hedonistic life project may tend to interfere with realizing that very project, there is no such natural exclusion between acting for the sake of another or a cause as such and recognizing how important this is to one's happiness. A spouse who acts for the sake of his mate may know full well that this is a source of deep satisfaction for him—in addition to providing him with reasons for acting internal to it, the relationship may also promote the external goal of achieving happiness. Moreover, while the pursuit of happiness may not be the reason he entered or sustains the relationship, he may also recognize that if it had not seemed likely to make him happy he would not have entered it, and that if it proved over time to be inconsistent with his happiness he would consider ending it.

It might be objected that one cannot really regard a person or a project as an end as such if one's commitment is in this way contingent or overridable. But were this so, we would be able to have very few commitments to ends as such. For example, one could not be committed to both one's spouse and one's child as ends as such, since at most one of these commitments could be overriding in cases of conflict. It is easy to confuse the notion of a commitment to an

end *as such* (or *for its own sake*) with that of an *overriding* commitment, but strength is not the same as structure. To be committed to an end as such is a matter of (among other things) whether it furnishes one with reasons for acting that are not mediated by other concerns. It does not follow that these reasons must always outweigh whatever opposing reasons one may have, or that one may not at the same time have other, mediating reasons that also incline one to act on behalf of that end.

Actual commitments to ends as such, even when very strong, are subject to various qualifications and contingencies.[11] If a friend grows too predictable or moves off to a different part of the world, or if a planned life project proves less engaging or practical than one had imagined, commitments and affections naturally change. If a relationship were highly vulnerable to the least change, it would be strained to speak of genuine affection rather than, say, infatuation. But if members of a relationship came to believe that they would be better off without it, this ordinarily would be a non-trivial change, and it is not difficult to imagine that their commitment to the relationship might be contingent in this way but nonetheless real. Of course, a relationship involves a shared history and shared expectations as well as momentary experiences, and it is unusual that affection or concern can be changed overnight, or relationships begun or ended at will. Moreover, the sorts of affections and commitments that can play a decisive role in shaping one's life and in making possible the deeper sorts of satisfactions are not those that are easily overridden or subject to constant reassessment or second-guessing. Thus a sensible hedonist would not forever be subjecting his affections or commitments to egoistic calculation, nor would he attempt to break off a relationship or commitment merely because it might seem to him at a given moment that some other arrangement would make him happier. Commitments to others or to causes as such may be very closely linked to the self, and a hedonist who knows what he's about will not be one who turns on his self at the slightest provocation. Contingency is not expendability, and while some commitments are remarkably non-contingent—such as those of parent to child or patriot to country—it cannot be said that commitments of a more contingent sort are never genuine, or never conduce to the profounder sorts of happiness.[12]

Following these observations, we may reduce the force of the "paradox of hedonism" if we distinguish two forms of hedonism. *Subjective hedonism* is the view that one should adopt the hedonistic point of view in action, that is, that one should whenever possible attempt to determine which act seems most likely to contribute optimally to one's happiness, and behave accordingly. *Objective hedonism* is the view that one should follow that course of action which would in fact most contribute to one's happiness, even when this would involve not adopting the hedonistic point of view in action. An act will be called *subjectively hedonistic* if it is done from a hedonistic point of view; an act is *objectively hedonistic* if it is that act, of those available to the agent, which would most contribute to his happiness.[13] Let us call someone a *sophisticated hedonist* if he aims to lead an objectively hedonistic life (that is, the happiest life available to him in the circumstances) and yet is not committed to subjective hedonism. Thus, within the limits of what is psychologically possible, a sophisticated hedonist is prepared to eschew the hedonistic point of view whenever taking this point of view conflicts with following an objectively hedonistic course of action. The so-called paradox of hedonism shows that there will be such conflicts: certain acts or courses of action may be objectively hedonistic only if not subjectively hedonistic. When things are put this way, it seems that the sophisticated hedonist faces a problem rather than a paradox: how to act in order to achieve maximum possible happiness if this is at times—or even often—not a matter of carrying out hedonistic deliberations.

The answer in any particular case will be complex and contextual—it seems unlikely that any one method of decision making would always promote thought and action most conducive to one's happiness. A sophisticated hedonist might proceed precisely by looking at the complex and contextual: observing the actual modes of thought and action of those people who are in some ways like himself and who seem most happy. If our assumptions are right, he will find that few such individuals are subjective hedonists; instead, they act for the sake of a variety of ends as such. He may then set out to develop in himself the traits of character, ways of thought, types of commitment, and so on, that seem common in happy lives. For example, if he notes that the happiest people often have strong loyalties to friends, he must ask how he can become a more loyal friend—not merely how he can seem to be a loyal friend (since those he has observed are not happy because they merely seem loyal)—but how he can in fact be one.

Could one really make such changes if one had as a goal leading an optimally happy life? The answer seems to me a qualified *yes*, but let us first look at a simpler case. A highly competitive tennis player comes to realize that his obsession with winning is keeping him from playing his best. A pro tells him that if he wants to win he must devote himself more to the game and its play as such and think less about his performance. In the commitment and concentration made possible by this devotion, he is told, lies the secret of successful tennis. So he spends a good deal of time developing an enduring devotion to many aspects of the activity, and finds it peculiarly satisfying to become so absorbed in it. He plays better, and would have given up the program of change if he did not, but he now finds that he plays tennis more for its own sake, enjoying greater internal as well as external rewards from the sport. Such a person would not keep thinking—on or off the court—"No matter how I play, the only thing I really care about is whether I win!" He would recognize

such thoughts as self-defeating, as evidence that his old, unhelpful way of looking at things was returning. Nor would such a person be self-deceiving. He need not hide from himself his goal of winning, for this goal is consistent with his increased devotion to the game. His commitment to the activity is not eclipsed by, but made more vivid by, his desire to succeed at it.

The same sort of story might be told about a sophisticated hedonist and friendship. An individual could realize that his instrumental attitude toward his friends prevents him from achieving the fullest happiness friendship affords. He could then attempt to focus more on his friends as such, doing this somewhat deliberately, perhaps, until it comes more naturally. He might then find his friendships improved and himself happier. If he found instead that his relationships were deteriorating or his happiness declining, he would reconsider the idea. None of this need be hidden from himself: the external goal of happiness reinforces the internal goals of his relationships. The sophisticated hedonist's motivational structure should therefore meet a *counterfactual condition*: he need not always act for the sake of happiness, since he may do various things for their own sake or for the sake of others, but he would not act as he does if it were not compatible with his leading an objectively hedonistic life. Of course, a sophisticated hedonist cannot guarantee that he will meet this counterfactual condition, but only attempt to meet it as fully as possible.

• • •

It still seems possible that the happiest sorts of lives ordinarily attainable are those led by people who would reject even sophisticated hedonism, people whose character is such that if they were presented with a choice between two entire lives, one of which contains less total happiness but nonetheless realizes some other values more fully, they might well knowingly choose against maximal happiness. If this were so, it would show that a sophisticated hedonist might have reason for changing his beliefs so

that he no longer accepts hedonism in any form. This still would not refute objective hedonism as an account of the (rational, prudential, or moral) *criterion* one's acts should meet, for it would be precisely in order to meet this criterion that the sophisticated hedonist would change his beliefs.[14]

V. The place of non-alienation among human values

Before discussing the applicability of what has been said about hedonism to morality, we should notice that alienation is not always a bad thing, that we may not want to overcome all forms of alienation, and that other values, which may conflict with non-alienation in particular cases, may at times have a greater claim on us. Let us look at a few such cases.

It has often been argued that a morality of duties and obligations may appropriately come into play in familial or friendly relationships when the relevant sentiments have given out, for instance, when one is exasperated with a friend, when love is tried, and so on.[15] 'Ought' implies 'can' (or, at least, 'could'), and while it may be better in human terms when we do what we ought to do at least in part out of feelings of love, friendship, or sympathy, there are times when we simply cannot muster these sentiments, and the right thing to do is to act as love or friendship or sympathy would have directed rather than refuse to perform any act done merely from a sense of duty.

But we should add a further role for unspontaneous, morally motivated action: even when love or concern is strong, it is often desirable that people achieve some distance from their sentiments or one another. A spouse may act toward his mate in a grossly overprotective way; a friend may indulge another's ultimately destructive tendencies; a parent may favor one child inordinately. Strong and immediate affection may overwhelm one's ability to see what another person actually needs or deserves. In

such cases a certain distance between people or between an individual and his sentiments, and an intrusion of moral considerations into the gap thus created, may be a good thing, and part of genuine affection or commitment. The opposite view, that no such mediation is desirable as long as affection is strong, seems to me a piece of romanticism. Concern over alienation therefore ought not to take the form of a cult of "authenticity at any price."

Moreover, there will occur regular conflicts between avoiding alienation and achieving other important individual goals. One such goal is autonomy. Bernard Williams has emphasized that many of us have developed certain "ground projects" that give shape and meaning to our lives, and has drawn attention to the damage an individual may suffer if he is alienated from his ground projects by being forced to look at them as potentially overridable by moral considerations.[16] But against this it may be urged that it is crucial for autonomy that one hold one's commitments up for inspection—even one's ground projects. Our ground projects are often formed in our youth, in a particular family, class, or cultural background. It may be alienating and even disorienting to call these into question, but to fail to do so is to lose autonomy. Of course, autonomy could not sensibly require that we question all of our values and commitments at once, nor need it require us to be forever detached from what we are doing. It is quite possible to submit basic aspects of one's life to scrutiny and arrive at a set of autonomously chosen commitments that form the basis of an integrated life. Indeed, psychological conflicts and practical obstacles give us occasion for reexamining our basic commitments rather more often than we'd like.

At the same time, the tension between autonomy and non-alienation should not be exaggerated. Part of avoiding exaggeration is giving up the Kantian notion that autonomy is a matter of escaping determination by any contingency whatsoever. Part, too, is refusing to

conflate autonomy with sheer independence from others. Both Rousseau and Marx emphasized that achieving control over one's own life requires participation in certain sorts of social relations—in fact, relations in which various kinds of alienation have been minimized.

Autonomy is but one value that may enter into complex trade-offs with non-alienation. Alienation and inauthenticity do have their uses. The alienation of some individuals or groups from their milieu may at times be necessary for fundamental social criticism or cultural innovation. And without some degree of inauthenticity, it is doubtful whether civil relations among people could long be maintained. It would take little ingenuity, but too much of the reader's patience, to construct here examples involving troubling conflicts between non-alienation and virtually any other worthy goal.

VI. Reducing alienation in morality

Let us now move to morality proper. To do this with any definiteness, we must have a particular morality in mind. For various reasons, I think that the most plausible sort of morality is consequentialist in form, assessing rightness in terms of contribution to the good. In attempting to sketch how we might reduce alienation in moral theory and practice, therefore, I will work within a consequentialist framework (although a number of the arguments I will make could be made, *mutatis mutandis*, by a deontologist).

Of course, one has adopted no morality in particular even in adopting consequentialism unless one says what the good is. Let us, then, dwell briefly on axiology. One mistake of dominant consequentialist theories, I believe, is their failure to see that things other than subjective states can have intrinsic value. Allied to this is a tendency to reduce all intrinsic values to one—happiness. Both of these features of classical utilitarianism reflect forms of alienation. First, in divorcing subjective states from their objective counterparts, and claiming that we seek the latter exclusively for the sake of the former, utilitarianism cuts us off from the world in a way made graphic by examples such as that of the experience machine, a hypothetical device that can be programmed to provide one with whatever subjective states he may desire. The experience machine affords us decisive subjective advantages over actual life: few, if any, in actual life think they have achieved all that they could want, but the machine makes possible for each an existence that he cannot distinguish from such a happy state of affairs.[17] Despite this striking advantage, most rebel at the notion of the experience machine. As Robert Nozick and others have pointed out, it seems to matter to us what we actually *do* and *are* as well as how life *appears* to us.[18] We see the point of our lives as bound up with the world and other people in ways not captured by subjectivism, and our sense of loss in contemplating a life tied to an experience machine, quite literally alienated from the surrounding world, suggests where subjectivism has gone astray. Second, the reduction of all goals to the purely abstract goal of happiness or pleasure, as in hedonistic utilitarianism, treats all other goals instrumentally. Knowledge or friendship may promote happiness, but is it a fair characterization of our commitment to these goals to say that this is the only sense in which they are ultimately valuable? Doesn't the insistence that there is an abstract and uniform goal lying behind all of our ends bespeak an alienation from these particular ends?

Rather than pursue these questions further here, let me suggest an approach to the good that seems to me less hopeless as a way of capturing human value: a pluralistic approach in which several goods are viewed as intrinsically, non-morally valuable—such as happiness, knowledge, purposeful activity, autonomy, solidarity, respect, and beauty.[19] These goods need not be ranked lexically, but may be attributed weights, and the criterion of rightness for an act would be that it most contribute to the weighted

sum of these values in the long run. This creates the possibility of trade-offs among values of the kinds discussed in the previous section. However, I will not stop here to develop or defend such an account of the good and the right, since our task is to show how certain problems of alienation that arise in moral contexts might be dealt with if morality is assumed to have such a basis.

Consider, then, Juan, who, like John, has always seemed a model husband. When a friend remarks on the extraordinary concern he shows for his wife, Juan characteristically responds: "I love Linda. I even *like* her. So it means a lot to me to do things for her. After all we've been through, it's almost a part of me to do it." But his friend knows that Juan is a principled individual, and asks Juan how his marriage fits into that larger scheme. After all, he asks, it's fine for Juan and his wife to have such a close relationship, but what about all the other, needier people Juan could help if he broadened his horizon still further? Juan replies, "Look, it's a better world when people can have a relationship like ours—and nobody could if everyone were always asking themselves who's got the most need. It's not easy to make things work in this world, and one of the best things that happens to people is to have a close relationship like ours. You'd make things worse in a hurry if you broke up those close relationships for the sake of some higher goal. Anyhow, I know that you can't always put family first. The world isn't such a wonderful place that it's OK just to retreat into your own little circle. But still, you need that little circle. People get burned out, or lose touch, if they try to save the world by themselves. The ones who can stick with it and do a good job of making things better are usually the ones who can make that fit into a life that does not make them miserable. I haven't met any real saints lately, and I don't trust people who think they *are* saints."

If we contrast Juan with John, we do not find that the one allows moral considerations to enter his personal life while the other does not. Nor do we find that one is less serious in his moral concern. Rather, what Juan recognizes to be morally required is not by its nature incompatible with acting directly for the sake of another. It is important to Juan to subject his life to moral scrutiny—he is not merely stumped when asked for a defense of his acts above a personal level, he does not just say "Of course I take care of her, she's my wife!" or "It's Linda" and refuse to listen to the more impersonal considerations raised by his friend. It is consistent with what he says to imagine that his motivational structure has a form akin to that of the sophisticated hedonist, that is, his motivational structure meets a counterfactual condition: while he ordinarily does not do what he does simply for the sake of doing what's right, he would seek to lead a different sort of life if he did not think his were morally defensible. His love is not a romantic submersion in the other to the exclusion of worldly responsibilities, and to that extent it may be said to involve a degree of alienation from Linda. But this does not seem to drain human value from their relationship. Nor need one imagine that Linda would be saddened to hear Juan's words the way Anne might have been saddened to overhear the remarks of John.[20]

Moreover, because of his very willingness to question his life morally, Juan avoids a sort of alienation not sufficiently discussed—alienation from others, beyond one's intimate ties. Individuals who will not or cannot allow questions to arise about what they are doing from a broader perspective are in an important way cut off from their society and the larger world. They may not be troubled by this in any very direct way, but even so they may fail to experience that powerful sense of purpose and meaning that comes from seeing oneself as part of something larger and more enduring than oneself or one's intimate circle. The search for such a sense of purpose and meaning seems to me ubiquitous—surely much of the impulse to religion, to ethnic or regional identification (most strikingly, in the "rediscovery" of such

identities), or to institutional loyalty stems from this desire to see ourselves as part of a more general, lasting, and worthwhile scheme of things.[21] This presumably is part of what is meant by saying that secularization has led to a sense of meaninglessness, or that the decline of traditional communities and societies has meant an increase in anomie. (The sophisticated hedonist, too, should take note: one way to gain a firmer sense that one's life is worthwhile, a sense that may be important to realizing various values in one's own life, is to overcome alienation from others.)

Drawing upon our earlier discussion of two kinds of hedonism, let us now distinguish two kinds of consequentialism. *Subjective consequentialism* is the view that whenever one faces a choice of actions, one should attempt to determine which act of those available would most promote the good, and should then try to act accordingly. One is behaving as subjective consequentialism requires—that is, leading a *subjectively consequentialist life*—to the extent that one uses and follows a distinctively consequentialist mode of decision making, consciously aiming at the overall good and conscientiously using the best available information with the greatest possible rigor. *Objective consequentialism* is the view that the criterion of the rightness of an act or course of action is whether it in fact would most promote the good of those acts available to the agent. Subjective consequentialism, like subjective hedonism, is a view that prescribes following a particular mode of deliberation in action; objective consequentialism, like objective hedonism, concerns the outcomes actually brought about, and thus deals with the question of deliberation only in terms of the tendencies of certain forms of decision making to promote appropriate outcomes. Let us reserve the expression *objectively consequentialist act* (or *life*) for those acts (or that life) of those available to the agent that would bring about the best outcomes.[22] To complete the parallel, let us say that a *sophisticated consequentialist* is someone who has a standing

commitment to leading an objectively consequentialist life, but who need not set special stock in any particular form of decision making and therefore does not necessarily seek to lead a subjectively consequentialist life. Juan, it might be argued (if the details were filled in), is a sophisticated consequentialist, since he seems to believe he should act for the best but does not seem to feel it appropriate to bring a consequentialist calculus to bear on his every act.

Is it bizarre, or contradictory, that being a sophisticated consequentialist may involve rejecting subjective consequentialism? After all, doesn't an adherent of subjective consequentialism also seek to lead an objectively consequentialist life? He may, but then he is mistaken in thinking that this means he should always undertake a distinctively consequentialist deliberation when faced with a choice. To see his mistake, we need only consider some examples.

It is well known that in certain emergencies, the best outcome requires action so swift as to preclude consequentialist deliberation. Thus a sophisticated consequentialist has reason to inculcate in himself certain dispositions to act rapidly in obvious emergencies. The disposition is not a mere reflex, but a developed pattern of action deliberately acquired. A simple example, but it should dispel the air of paradox.

Many decisions are too insignificant to warrant consequentialist deliberation ("Which shoelace should I do up first?") or too predictable in outcome ("Should I meet my morning class today as scheduled or should I linger over the newspaper?"). A famous old conundrum for consequentialism falls into a similar category: before I deliberate about an act, it seems I must decide how much time would be optimal to allocate for this deliberation; but then I must first decide how much time would be optimal to allocate for this time-allocation decision; but before that I must decide how much time would be optimal to allocate for *that* decision; and so on. The sophisticated consequentialist can block

this paralyzing regress by noting that often the best thing to do is not to ask questions about time allocation at all; instead, he may develop standing dispositions to give more or less time to decisions depending upon their perceived importance, the amount of information available, the predictability of his choice, and so on. I think we all have dispositions of this sort, which account for our patience with some prolonged deliberations but not others.

There are somewhat more intriguing examples that have more to do with psychological interference than mere time efficiency: the timid, put-upon employee who knows that if he deliberates about whether to ask for a raise he will succumb to his timidity and fail to demand what he actually deserves; the self-conscious man who knows that if, at social gatherings, he is forever wondering how he should act, his behavior will be awkward and unnatural, contrary to his goal of acting naturally and appropriately; the tightrope walker who knows he must not reflect on the value of keeping his concentration; and so on. People can learn to avoid certain characteristically self-defeating lines of thought—just as the tennis player in an earlier example learned to avoid thinking constantly about winning—and the sophisticated consequentialist may learn that consequentialist deliberation is in a variety of cases self-defeating, so that other habits of thought should be cultivated.

The sophisticated consequentialist need not be deceiving himself or acting in bad faith when he avoids consequentialist reasoning. He can fully recognize that he is developing the dispositions he does because they are necessary for promoting the good. Of course, he cannot be preoccupied with this fact all the while, but then one cannot be *preoccupied* with anything without this interfering with normal or appropriate patterns of thought and action.

To the list of cases of interference we may add John, whose all-purpose willingness to

look at things by subjective consequentialist lights prevents the realization in him and in his relationships with others of values that he would recognize to be crucially important.

Bernard Williams has said that it shows consequentialism to be in grave trouble that it may have to usher itself from the scene as a mode of decision making in a number of important areas of life.[23] Though I think he has exaggerated the extent to which we would have to exclude consequentialist considerations from our lives in order to avoid disastrous results, it is fair to ask: If maximizing the good were in fact to require that consequentialist reasoning be *wholly* excluded, would this refute consequentialism? Imagine an all-knowing demon who controls the fate of the world and who visits unspeakable punishment upon man to the extent that he does not employ a Kantian morality. (Obviously, the demon is not himself a Kantian.) If such a demon existed, sophisticated consequentialists would have reason to convert to Kantianism, perhaps even to make whatever provisions could be made to erase consequentialism from the human memory and prevent any resurgence of it.

Does this possibility show that objective consequentialism is self-defeating? On the contrary, it shows that objective consequentialism has the virtue of not blurring the distinction between the truth-conditions of an ethical theory and its acceptance-conditions in particular contexts, a distinction philosophers have generally recognized for theories concerning other subject matters. It might be objected that, unlike other theories, ethical theories must meet a condition of publicity, roughly to the effect that it must be possible under all circumstances for us to recognize a true ethical theory as such and to promulgate it publicly without thereby violating that theory itself.[24] Such a condition might be thought to follow from the social nature of morality. But any such condition would be question-begging against consequentialist theories, since it would require that one

class of actions—acts of adopting or promulgating an ethical theory—not be assessed in terms of their consequences. Moreover, I fail to see how such a condition could emanate from the social character of morality. To prescribe the adoption and promulgation of a mode of decision making regardless of its consequences seems to me radically detached from human concerns, social or otherwise. If it is argued that an ethical theory that fails to meet the publicity requirement could under certain conditions endorse a course of action leading to the abuse and manipulation of man by man, we need only reflect that no psychologically possible decision procedure can guarantee that its widespread adoption could never have such a result. A "consequentialist demon" might increase the amount of abuse and manipulation in the world in direct proportion to the extent that people act according to the categorical imperative. Objective consequentialism (unlike certain deontological theories) has valuable flexibility in permitting us to take consequences into account in assessing the appropriateness of certain modes of decision making, thereby avoiding any sort of self-defeating decision procedure worship.

A further objection is that the lack of any direct link between objective consequentialism and a particular mode of decision making leaves the view too vague to provide adequate guidance in practice. On the contrary, objective consequentialism sets a definite and distinctive criterion of right action, and it becomes an empirical question (though not an easy one) which modes of decision making should be employed and when. It would be a mistake for an objective consequentialist to attempt to tighten the connection between his criterion of rightness and any particular mode of decision making: someone who recommended a particular mode of decision making regardless of consequences would not be a hard-nosed, non-evasive objective consequentialist, but a self-contradicting one.

Notes

1 The loss in question need not be a loss of something of value, and *a fortiori* need not be a bad thing overall; there are some people, institutions, or cultures alienation from which would be a boon. Alienation is a more or less troubling phenomenon depending upon what is lost; and in the cases to be considered, what is lost is for the most part of substantial value. It does not follow, as we will see in Section V, that in all such cases alienation is a bad thing on balance. Moreover, I do not assume that the loss in question represents an actual *decline* in some value as the result of a separation coming into being where once there was none. It seems reasonable to say that an individual can experience a loss in being alienated from nature, for example, without assuming that he was ever in communion with it, much as we say it is a loss for someone never to receive an education or never to appreciate music. Regrettably, various relevant kinds and sources of alienation cannot be discussed here. A general, historical discussion of alienation may be found in Richard Schacht, *Alienation* (Garden City, NY: Doubleday, 1971).

2 This is not to say that no questions arise about whether Helen's (or John's) feelings and attitudes constitute the fullest sort of affection, as will be seen shortly.

3 Moreover, there is a sense in which someone whose responses to his affections or feelings are characteristically mediated by a calculating point of view may fail to know himself fully, or may seem in a way unknowable to others, and this "cognitive distance" may itself be part of his alienation. I am indebted here to Allan Gibbard.

4 There is a wide range of views about the nature of the moral point of view and its proper role in moral life. Is it necessary that one actually act on universal principles, or merely that one be willing to universalize the principles upon which one acts? Does the moral point of view by its nature require us to consider everyone alike? Here I am using a rather strong reading of the moral point of view, according to which taking the moral point of view involves universalization and the equal consideration of all.

5 A moral point of view theorist might make use of the three points of view distinguished by Mill: the

moral, the aesthetic, and the sympathetic. "The first addresses itself to our reason and conscience; the second to our imagination; the third to our human fellow-feeling," from "Bentham," reprinted in *John Stuart Mill: Utilitarianism and Other Writings*, ed. Mary Warnock (New York: New American Library, 1962), p. 121. What is morally right, in his view, may fail to be "loveable" (e.g., a parent strictly disciplining a child) or "beautiful" (e.g., an inauthentic gesture). Thus, the three points of view need not concur in their positive or negative assessments. Notice, however, that Mill has divided the self into three realms, of "reason and conscience," of "imagination," and of "human fellow-feeling"; notice, too, that he has chosen the word 'feeling' to characterize human affections.

6 William K. Frankena, *Ethics*, 2d ed. (Englewood Cliffs, NJ: Prentice-Hall, 1973), p. 116. Moralities that do not accord with this dictum—or a modi-fied version of it that includes all sentient beings— might be deemed alienated in a Feuerbachian sense.

7 Mill, for instance, calls the moral point of view "unquestionably the first and most important," and while he thinks it the error of the moralizer (such as Bentham) to elevate the moral point of view and "sink the [aesthetic and sympathetic] entirely," he does not explain how to avoid such a result if the moral point of view is to be, as he says it ought, "paramount." See his "Bentham," pp. 121f.

Philosophers who have recently raised doubts about moralities for such reasons include Bernard Williams, in "A Critique of Utilitarianism," in J.J.C. Smart and B. Williams, *Utilitarianism: For and Against* (Cambridge: Cambridge University Press, 1973), and Michael Stacker, in "The Schizophrenia of Modern Ethical Theories," *Journal of Philosophy* 73 (1976): 453–66.

8 John Rawls, *A Theory of Justice* (Cambridge: Harvard University Press, 1971), p. 587, emphasis added.

9 I am not claiming that we should interpret all of Rawls' intricate moral theory in light of these few remarks. They are cited here merely to illustrate a certain tendency in moral thought, especially that of a Kantian inspiration.

10 This is a "paradox" for individual, egoistic hedon-ists. Other forms the "paradox of hedonism" may

take are social in character: a society of egoistic hedonists might arguably achieve less total happi-ness than a society of more benevolent beings; or, taking happiness as the sole social goal might lead to a less happy society overall than could exist if a wider range of goals were pursued.

11 This is not to deny that there are indexical com-ponents to commitments.

12 It does seem likely to matter just what the commit-ment is contingent upon as well as just how contingent it is. I think it is an open question whether commitments contingent upon the satis-faction of egoistic hedonist criteria are of the sort that might figure in the happiest sorts of lives ordinarily available. We will return to this problem presently.

Those who have had close relationships often develop a sense of duty to one another that may outlast affection or emotional commitment, that is, they may have a sense of obligation to one another that is less contingent than affection or emotional commitment, and that should not simply be confused with them. If such a sense of obligation is in conflict with self-interest, and if it is a normal part of the most satisfying sorts of close relationships, then this may pose a problem for the egoistic hedonist.

13 A few remarks are needed. First, I will say that an act is available to an agent if he would succeed in performing it if he tried. Second, here and else-where in this article I mean to include quite "thick" descriptions of actions, so that it may be part of an action that one perform it with a certain intention or goal. In the short run (but not so much the long run) intentions, goals, motives, and the like are usually less subject to our delib-erate control than overt behavior—it is easier to say "I'm sorry" than to say it and mean it. This, however, is a fact about the relative availability of acts to the agent at a given time, and should not dictate what is to count as an act. Third, here and elsewhere I ignore for simplicity's sake the possi-bility that more than one course of action may be maximally valuable. And fourth, for reasons I will not enter into here, I have formulated objective hedonism in terms of actual outcomes rather than expected values (relative to the information available to the agent). One could make virtually

the same argument using an expected value formulation.

14 An important objection to the claim that objective hedonism may serve as the *moral* criterion one's acts should meet, even if this means not believing in hedonism, is that moral principles must meet a *publicity* condition. I will discuss this objection in Section VI.

15 See, for example, Stocker, "The Schizophrenia of Modern Ethical Theories."

16 Williams, "Critique."

17 At least one qualification is needed: the subjective states must be psychologically possible. Perhaps some of us desire what are, in effect, psychologically impossible states.

18 Robert Nozick, *Anarchy, State, and Utopia* (New York: Basic Books, 1974), pp. 42ff.

19 To my knowledge, the best-developed method for justifying claims about intrinsic value involves thought-experiments of a familiar sort, in which, for example, we imagine two lives, or two worlds, alike in all but one respect, and then attempt to determine whether rational, well-informed, widely-experienced individuals would (when vividly aware of both alternatives) be indifferent between the two or have a settled preference for one over the other. Since no one is ideally rational, fully informed, or infinitely experienced, the best we can do is to take more seriously the judgments of those who come nearer to approximating these conditions. Worse yet: the best we can do is to take more seriously the judgments of those we think better approximate these conditions. (I am not supposing that facts or experience somehow entail values, but that in rational agents, beliefs and values show a marked mutual influence and coherence.) We may overcome some narrowness if we look at behavior and preferences in other societies and other epochs, but even here we must rely upon interpretations colored by our own beliefs and values. Within the confines of this article I must leave unanswered a host of deep and troubling questions about the nature of values and value judgments. Suffice it to say that there is no reason to think that we are in a position to give anything but a tentative list of intrinsic goods.

It becomes a complex matter to describe the psychology of intrinsic value. For example, should

we say that one values a relationship of solidarity, say, a friendship, *because* it *is* a friendship? That makes it sound as if it were somehow instrumental to the realization of some abstract value, friendship. Surely this is a misdescription. We may be able to get a clearer idea of what is involved by considering the case of happiness. We certainly do not value a particular bit of experienced happiness because it is instrumental in the realization of the abstract goal, happiness—we value the experience for its own sake because it is a happy experience. Similarly, a friendship is itself the valued thing, the thing of a valued kind. Of course, one can say that one values friendship and therefore seeks friends, just as one can say one values happiness and therefore seeks happy experiences. But this locution must be contrasted with what is being said when, for example, one talks of seeking *things that make one happy*. Friends are not "things that make one achieve friendship"—they partially constitute friendships, just as particular happy experiences partially constitute happiness for an individual. Thus taking friendship as an intrinsic value does not entail viewing particular friendships instrumentally.

20 If one objects that Juan's commitment to Linda is lacking because it is contingent in some ways, the objector must show that the *kinds* of contingencies involved would destroy his relationship with Linda, especially since moral character often figures in commitments—the character of the other, or the compatibility of a commitment with one's having the sort of character one values—and the contingencies in Juan's case are due to his moral character.

21 I do not mean to suggest that such identities are always matters of choice for individuals. Quite the reverse, identities often arise through socialization, prejudice, and similar influences. The point rather is that there is a very general phenomenon of identification, badly in need of explanation, that to an important extent underlies such phenomena as socialization and prejudice, and that suggests the existence of certain needs in virtually all members of society—needs to which identification with entities beyond the self answers.

Many of us who resist raising questions about our lives from broader perspectives do so, I fear,

not out of a sense that it would be difficult or impossible to lead a meaningful life if one entertained such perspectives, but rather out of a sense that our lives would not stand up to much scrutiny therefrom, so that leading a life that *would* seem meaningful from such perspectives would require us to change in some significant way.

22 Although the language here is causal—'promoting' and 'bringing about'—it should be said that the relation of an act to the good need not always be causal. An act of learning may non-causally involve coming to have knowledge (an intrinsic good by my reckoning) as well as contributing causally to later realizations of intrinsic value. Causal consequences as such do not have a privileged status. As in the case of objective hedonism, I have formulated objective consequentialism in terms of actual outcomes (so-called "objective duty") rather than expected values relative to what is rational for the agent to believe ("subjective duty"). The main arguments of this article could be made using expected value, since the course of action with highest expected value need not in general be the subjectively consequentialist one. See also notes 13 and 19.

Are there any subjective consequentialists? Well, various theorists have claimed that a consequentialist must be a subjective consequentialist in order to be genuine—see Williams, "Critique," p. 135, and Rawls, *Theory of Justice*, p. 182.

23 Williams, "Critique," p. 135.

24 For discussion of a publicity condition, see Rawls, *Theory of Justice*, pp. 133, 177–82, 582. The question whether a publicity condition can be justified is a difficult one, deserving fuller discussion than I am able to give it here.

Chapter 26

Brad Hooker

RULE-CONSEQUENTIALISM

1 Introduction

JUST WHAT is the connection between moral rightness and consequences? For nearly half a century now, consequentialists have divided themselves into different camps with respect to this question. Act-consequentialists believe that the moral rightness of an act depends entirely on whether the act's consequences are at least as good as that of any alternative act. Rule-consequentialists believe that the rightness of an act depends not on its own consequences, but rather on the consequences of a code of rules. [...] This essay explores the prospects for rule-consequentialism.

2 What constitutes benefit?

Rule-consequentialism holds that any code of rules is to be evaluated in terms of how much *good* could reasonably be expected to result from the code. By 'good' here I mean whatever has non-instrumental value. What has non-instrumental value?

Utilitarians, who have been the most prominent kind of consequentialists, believe that the only thing with non-instrumental value is utility. All utilitarians have held that pleasure and the absence of pain are at least a large part of utility. Indeed, utilitarianism is often said to maintain that pleasure and the absence of pain are the *only* things that matter non-instrumentally. Certainly,

this was the official view of the classic utilitarians Jeremy Bentham, J. S. Mill, and Henry Sidgwick – though in Sidgwick's case, equality seems to have independent weight as a tie breaker [...]

Perhaps more common over the last thirty years has been the view that utility is constituted by the fulfillment of people's desires, even if these desires are for things other than pleasure. Many people, even when fully informed and thinking carefully, persistently want things in addition to pleasure. They care, for example, about knowing important truths, about achieving valuable goals, about having deep personal relationships, about living their lives in broad accordance with their own choices rather than always in accordance with someone else's [...]. The pleasure these things can bring is of course important. Still, human beings can care about these things in themselves, i.e., in addition to whatever pleasure they bring.

This view, however, can be challenged. Some desires seem to be about things too unconnected with you for them to play a direct role in determining your good. Would your desiring that a stranger recovers fully from her illness make her recovery good for you, even if you never see or hear from her again? [...] Naturally, the fulfillment of such a desire would *indirectly* benefit you if it brought you pleasure or peace of mind. But this is not to say that the fulfillment of your desire that the stranger recovers herself

constitutes a benefit to you. Rather if you get pleasure or peace of mind from the fulfillment of this desire, this pleasure or peace of mind constitutes a benefit to you (since you doubtless also desire pleasure and peace of mind for yourself).

The view that the fulfillment of your desires itself *constitutes* a benefit to you – if this view is to be at all plausible – will have to limit the desires in question. The only desires the fulfillment of which constitutes a benefit to you are your desires for states of affairs in which you are an essential constituent [. . .]. You are not an essential constituent of the state of affairs in which this stranger recovers. So her recovery doesn't itself constitute a benefit to you.

There seem to be reasons for further restrictions on the desires directly relevant to personal good. Think how bizarre desires can be. When we encounter particularly bizarre ones, we might begin to wonder whether the things are good simply because they are desired. Would my desiring to count all the blades of grass in the lawns on the street make this good for me? [. . .] Whatever *pleasure* I get from the activity would be good for me. But it seem that the *desire-fulfillment as such* is worthless in this case. Intuitively, the fulfillment of my desires constitutes a benefit to me only if these desires are for the right things [. . .] Indeed, some things seem to be desired because they are perceived as valuable, not valuable merely because desired or pleasant. [. . .]

Views holding that something benefits a person if and only if it increases the person's pleasure or desire-fulfillment are in a sense "subjectivist" theories of personal good. For these theories make something's status as a benefit depend always on the person's subjective mental states. "Objectivist" theories claim that the contribution to personal good made by such things as important knowledge, important achievement, friendship, and autonomy is not exhausted by the extent to which these things bring people pleasure or fulfil their desires. These things can constitute benefits even when they don't increase pleasure. Likewise, they can

constitute benefits even when they are not the objects of desire. Objectivist theories will typically add that pleasure is of course an objective good. These theories will also hold that ignorance, failure, friendlessness, servitude, and pain constitute harms.

For the most part, I will be neutral in this essay about which theory of personal good is best. Usually what gives people pleasure or enjoyment is also what satisfies their desires and involves the objective goods that could plausibly be listed. So usually we don't need to decide as among these theories of personal good.

But not always. Suppose the ruling elite believed that quantity of pleasure were all that matters. Then (to take a familiar leaf from *Nineteen Eighty-Four*) they might feel justified in manipulating the people and even giving them drugs that induce contentment but drain ambition and curiosity, if they thought such practices would maximize aggregate pleasure. Or suppose the ruling elite believed that the fulfillment of desire were all that matters. Again, the ruling elite might feel justified in manipulating the formation of preferences and development of desires such that these are easily satisfied. Now we can accept that – to some extent – our desires should be modified so that there is some reasonable hope of fulfilling them. But this could be pushed too far either in the name of maximizing pleasure or in the name of maximizing desire-fulfillment. A life could be maximally pleasurable, have maximum desire-fulfillment, and still be empty – if it lacked desires for friendship, achievement, knowledge, and autonomy.

3   Distribution

The term "rule-utilitarianism" is usually used to refer to theories that evaluate acts in terms of rules selected for their utility – i.e., for their effects on social well-being. The term "rule-consequentialism" is usually used to refer to a broader class of theories of which rule-utilitarian theories are a subclass. Rule-consequentialist

theories evaluate acts in terms of rules selected for their good consequences. Non-utilitarian versions of rule-consequentialism say the consequences that matter are not limited to net effects on overall well-being. Most prominently, some versions of rule-consequentialism say that what matters are not only how much well-being results but also how it is distributed, in particular the fairness of alternative distributions. Table 26.1 might prove helpful.

Which version of rule-consequentialism is best? The problem with rule-utilitarianism is that it has the potential to be unfairly inegalitarian. [. . .] Consider a set of rules which leaves each member of a smaller group very badly off, and each member of a much larger group very well off (Table 26.2).

Now if no alternative rule would provide greater net aggregate benefit, then utilitarians would endorse this code. Yet suppose the next best rule from the point of view of utility would be one with the results set out in Table 26.3.

Let us assume that the first code leaves the people in group A less well off for some reason other than that these people opted to work less hard or imprudently took bad risks. In that case, the second code seems morally superior to, because fairer than, the first code. This is why we should reject rule-utilitarianism in favor of a distribution-sensitive rule-consequentialism that considers fairness as well as well-being.

What are the relative weights given to well-being and fairness by this distribution-sensitive rule-consequentialism? Clearly, well-being does not have overriding weight. For there can be cases in which the amount of aggregate net benefit produced would not justify rules that were unfair to some group. That was what my schematic example above was meant to show.

Does fairness have overriding weight? This is particularly unsettled territory, since even what constitutes fairness is unclear. Nevertheless, we cannot rule out the possibility that some unfair practice so greatly increases overall well-being

Table 26.1

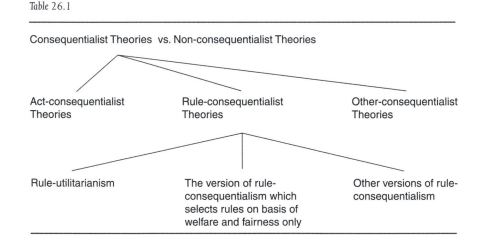

Table 26.2 Well-being

First Code:	per person	per group	for both groups
10,000 people in group A	1	10,000	
100,000 people in group B	10	1,000,000	
			1,010,000

Table 26.3 Well-being

Second Code:	per person	per group	for both groups
10,000 people in group A	8	80,000	
100,000 people in group B	9	900,000	
			980,000

that the practice is justified. But it is certainly unclear where the threshold is for fairness to trump well-being. Perhaps the best we can say is that, in the choice between codes, judgment will be needed in balancing fairness against well-being. By evaluating rules in terms of two values (well-being and fairness) instead of one (well-being), distribution-sensitive rule-consequentialism is messier than rule-utilitarianism. Still, this seems to be a case where the more plausible theory is the messier one.

4 Criteria of rightness versus decision procedures

Rule-consequentialism is often portrayed as merely part of a broader consequentialist theory. This broader theory evaluates *all things* by their consequences. So it evaluates the desirability of acts by their consequences, the desirability of rules by their consequences, etc. The standard point to make along these lines is that, even if the rightness of an act depends on its consequences, better consequences will result if people do *not* try always to decide what to do by calculating consequences than if they try always to decide in this way. In other words, consequentialists can and should deny that

> On every occasion, an agent should decide which act to do by ascertaining which act has the greatest expected good.

Consequentialists agree that our *decision procedure* for day-to-day moral thinking should instead be as follows:

> At least normally, an agent should decide how to act by referring to tried and true rules, such as "Don't harm others", "Don't steal", "Keep your promises", "Tell the truth", etc.

Why? First, we frequently lack information about the probable consequences of various acts we might do. Where we cannot even estimate

the consequences, we can hardly choose on the basis of maximizing the good. Second, we often do not have the time to collect this information. Third, human limitations and biases are such that we are not accurate calculators of the expected overall consequences of our alternatives. For example, most of us are biased in such a way that we tend to underestimate the harm to others of acts that would benefit us.

Now if there will be greater overall good where people are largely disposed to focus and act on non-consequentialist considerations, then consequentialism itself endorses such dispositions. So consequentialists advocate firm dispositions to follow certain rules, including firm dispositions not to harm others, not to steal, not to break promises, etc. Different consequentialists thus by and large agree about how people should do their day-to-day moral thinking.

What different kinds of consequentialists disagree about is what makes an act morally permissible, i.e., about the criterion for moral rightness.

> *Act-consequentialism* claims that an act is morally right (both permissible and required) if and only if the actual (or expected) good produced by *that particular act* would be at least as great as that of any other act open to the agent.

In contrast,

> *Rule-consequentialism* claims that an act is permissible if and only if it is allowed by a code that could reasonably be expected to result in as much good as could reasonably be expected to result from any other identifiable code.

The distinction between act-consequentialism's criterion of rightness and the dispositions it favors is important in many ways. It is important if we want to know what act-consequentialism wants from us. It is also important if act-consequentialism had better not conflict too sharply with our intuitive moral reactions. For if

act-consequentialism claimed that we should always be focused on and motivated by calculations of what would maximize the good impartially conceived, many philosophers have thought it would be ridiculous. But the idea that act-consequentialism must make this ridiculous prescription is undermined by the distinction between act-consequentialism's criterion of rightness and the decision procedures it favors.

Nevertheless, the distinction is powerless to protect act-consequentialism from other objections. True, act-consequentialism's implications *about focus and motivation* are not as counter-intuitive as might initially be thought. But this is irrelevant to objections about act-consequentialism's criterion of rightness.

5 Formulations of rule-consequentialism

We need to augment our formulation of rule-consequentialism. All recognizable forms of rule-consequentialism make moral rightness depend on rules which are evaluated in terms of their consequences. But different forms of rule-consequentialism disagree about the conditions under which rules are to be evaluated. For instance, one version of rule-consequentialism is formulated in terms of the rules the *compliance with which* would be optimific. Another version is formulated in terms of rules the *acceptance of which* would produce the most good. Should rule-consequentialism be formulated in terms of compliance or in terms of acceptance?

Although compliance with the right rules is the first priority, it isn't the only thing of importance. We also care about people's having *moral concerns*. So we had better consider the costs of securing not only compliance but also adequate moral motivation. From a rule-consequentialist point of view, "moral motivation" means acceptance of moral rules. By "acceptance of moral rules", I mean a disposition to comply with them, dispositions to feel guilt when one breaks them and to resent others' breaking them, and a

belief that the rules and these dispositions are justified. [. . .]

The focus on *acceptance of rules*, i.e., *dispositions*, is crucial because the acceptance of a rule – or perhaps at this point it would be better to say the internalization of a rule – can have consequences over and above compliance with the rule. [. . .]

The most obvious example of this involves rules that deter perfectly. Suppose you accept a rule prescribing that you retaliate against attackers. Suppose also that you are totally transparent, in the sense that people can see exactly what your dispositions are. So everyone knows about your disposition to retaliate, and therefore *never* attacks you. Thus, your accepting the rule is so successful at deterring attack that you *never* have an opportunity to comply with the rule. Your accepting the rule thus obviously has important consequences that simply *cannot* come from your acting on the rule, since you in fact never do. [. . .]

Now suppose everyone internalized rules such as "Don't kill except when killing will maximize the aggregate good," "Don't steal except when stealing will maximize the aggregate good," "Don't break your promises except when breaking them will maximize the good," etc. Presumably, if everyone had internalized these rules, sooner or later awareness of this would become widespread. And people's becoming aware of this would undermine their ability to rely confidently on others to behave in agreed-upon ways. Trust would break down. The consequences would be terrible. And these terrible consequences would result, not from individual acts of complying with these rules, but from public awareness that the rules' exception clauses – the ones prescribing killing, stealing, and so on when such acts would maximize the good – were too available. [. . .]

I am aware that there has been some controversy over the argument just outlined. But there is another way in which a cost-benefit analysis of *internalization* is richer than a cost-benefit analysis of compliance. Getting one code of rules internalized might involve greater costs

than getting another code internalized. These costs are immensely important. For example, one possible objection to a code might be that it is so complicated or calls for so much self-sacrifice that too much of humanity's resources would have to be devoted to getting it widely internalized. The internalization costs would be so high that internalizing this code would not, on balance, be optimal. When this is the case, rule-consequentialists hold that the code isn't justified, and complying with it isn't required.

These points about internalization costs beg to be deployed at a number of places in the discussion of rule-consequentialism. One such place I explore in the next section.

6 Collapse

If we formulate rule-consequentialism in terms of *compliance*, we risk having rule-consequentialism collapse into act-consequentialism. The objection that rule-consequentialism collapses into extensional equivalence with act-consequentialism assumes rules are to be evaluated in terms of only the effects of compliance. While compliance can be one effect of internalizing rules, we have seen that there are also other effects. We must consider not only the benefits of compliance but also the other effects of rule internalization. With these effects factored into the evaluation of rules, the cost-benefit analysis will not favor rules extensionally equivalent to act-consequentialism.

One version of the objection that rule-consequentialism collapses into act-consequentialism claims that rule-consequentialism must favor just the one simple rule that one must always do what will maximize the good. [. . .] The objection assumes that, if each person successfully complies with a rule requiring the maximization of the good, then the good would be maximized. That the good would be maximized under these conditions has been challenged. [. . .] But whether or not everyone's

complying with the act-consequentialist principle would maximize the good, we should again consider the wider costs and benefits of rule *internalization*. The impartial good would not in fact be maximized by the internalization of just this one act-consequentialist rule. To internalize just the one act-consequentialist rule is to have just one moral disposition, the disposition to try to comply with act-consequentialism. To have just this one moral disposition is to have act-consequentialism as one's moral decision procedure. But we've already seen why act-consequentialism is not a good decision procedure.

In addition, the costs of getting a disposition to try to comply with act-consequentialism internalized would be extremely high. For getting that one rule internalized amounts to getting people to be disposed always to do what would be impartially best. Such a disposition would have to overcome people's immensely powerful natural biases towards themselves and their loved ones. To be sure, there are great benefits to be gained from getting people to care about others, and to be willing to make sacrifices for strangers. But think how much time, energy, attention, and psychological conflict that would be required to get people to internalize an overriding completely impartial altruism (if this is even possible at all). The costs of trying to make humans into saints would be too great.

That may seem like a paradoxical thing to assert. Wouldn't a world full of people each with an overriding disposition to maximize the impartial good be so ideal as to be worth any costs of getting from here to there? I think not. Bear in mind that the costs would hardly be a once-and-for-all-time sacrifice. Rather, getting this overriding impartiality internalized would have to be done for every new generation. We are contemplating here a radical reshaping of something deep in human nature. It is not as if the impartiality internalized by one generation will be reflected in the genes of their children.

Rather, there will be the high cost of getting the overriding impartiality internalized in their children, just as there was when the parents were children themselves. (I am ignoring here the possibility of genetic engineering to create more altruistic humans.) The internalization costs will be incurred for each new generation of humans.

I have been arguing as if getting overriding impartiality internalized by the vast majority is a serious possibility, though one with prohibitive transition costs. It may not, however, be a serious possibility. In any case, the only *realistic* way to make humans totally and always impartial would be to reduce their special concern for themselves and those with whom they have special attachments. What would be left might be merely a life of insipid impartiality, devoid of deep personal attachments and inimical to great enthusiasm and joy. Strong concern and commitment focused on particular projects and individuals play an ineliminable role in a rewarding human life. But these features would have to be eliminated if human beings are to internalize an overriding motivation to maximize the impartial good. [. . .]

So in the light of the transition and permanent costs of getting internalized an overriding impartiality, I hold that there must be some point short of this where the costs of going further outweigh the benefits. Remember why this matters here. Getting internalized an overriding impartiality would be part of getting internalized an overriding disposition to do what will maximize the impartial good. So if there is a compelling rule-consequentialist reason against getting internalized an overriding impartiality, there is a compelling rule-consequentialist reason against getting internalized an overriding disposition to do what will maximize the impartial good. I have just argued that there is a compelling rule-consequentialist reason against getting internalized an overriding impartiality. Such a disposition would *not* find favor with rule-consequentialism. So there is a compelling rule-consequentialist reason against getting internalized an overriding disposition to do what will maximize the impartial good. This kills the first way of developing the collapse objection.

The other way of developing the collapse objection starts by admitting that internalization of just the one act-consequentialist rule would lead to bad consequences. But this way of developing the collapse objection maintains that utility could be gained from the provision of specific exception clauses to moral rules against harming others, breaking promises, etc. If this is right, then rule-consequentialists are forced by their own criterion for rule selection to embrace rules with these exception clauses. The same sort of reasoning will militate in favor of adding specific exceptions aimed at each situation in which following some rule would not bring about the best consequences. Once all the exception clauses are added, rule-consequentialism will have the same implications for action that act-consequentialism has. This would be a fatal collapse.

To this way of developing the collapse objection, rule-consequentialists will reply by returning to the points about trust and expectations that I alluded to earlier. How much confidence would you have in others if you knew they accepted such highly qualified rules? How much mutual trust would there be in a society of agents who accepted endless exceptions to rules against harming others breaking promises, lying, etc.?

Furthermore, the point about internalization costs is again relevant. The more plentiful and more complicated the rules to be learned, the higher the costs of learning them would be. At some point the costs of having to learn more rules, or more complications, would outweigh the benefits. Hence, the rules whose teaching and internalization would have the best results are limited in number and complexity. These limitations will keep the code from being extensionally equivalent with act-consequentialism.

So this kind of rule-consequentialism does *not* collapse into act-consequentialism.

7 Rule-consequentialism and the distribution of acceptance

A relatively simple form of rule-consequentialism selects rules by their consequences given internalization of them by 100 percent of the population. But I think the theory should be formulated in terms of internalization by less than 100 percent of the population. Rule-consequentialism needs to be formulated this way in order to make room for rules about what to do when others have no moral conscience at all. Let us refer to such people as unmitigated amoralists.

Suppose we assume internalization of the rules by 100 percent of the population. We might still need rules for dealing with non-compliance, since *internalization* by 100 percent of the people does not guarantee 100 percent *compliance*. Some people might fully accept the best rules and yet sometimes, seduced by temptation, act wrongly. Thus there is need for rules dealing with non-compliance. These rules might specify, for example, what penalties apply for what crimes. They might also specify what to do when those around you accept that they should be helping to save others but aren't.

Contrast what is needed to deter or rehabilitate someone with a moral conscience too weak to ensure good behavior in some circumstances, with what is needed to deal with unmitigated amoralists (people who have no moral conscience at all). If we imagine a world with acceptance of the best code by 100 percent of the population, we have simply imagined unmitigated amoralists out of existence. Hence, we have imagined out of existence any rule-consequentialist rationale for having rules for deterring and dealing with unmitigated amoralists.

Here is why. On the rule-consequentialist view, there is always at least some cost associated with every additional rule added to the code. Every additional rule takes at least a little time to learn and at least a little memory to store. Then the question is whether there is some benefit from internalization of the rule that outweighs the cost. We can of course frame rules applying to non-existent situations. For example, "be kind to any rational non-humans living on the moon." But, if the situation envisaged really is non-existent, where is the benefit of including such a rule in the code to be internalized? Presumably there are no benefits from such never-to-be-applied rules. These rules, which have *some* costs and *no* benefits, fail a cost-benefit analysis.

The reasoning seems to me to generate the following important conclusion. Rule-consequentialism cannot generate or justify rules about how to deter murder, rape, robbery, fraud, etc., *by unmitigated amoralists*, unless rule-consequentialism picks its rules with reference to an imagined world where there is internalization of the envisaged rules by less than 100 percent of the population. So rule-consequentialism should evaluate rules in terms of internalization by less than 100 percent of the population.

But should we assume internalization by 99, or 90, or 80 percent, or even less? Any precise number will of course be somewhat arbitrary, but we do have some relevant factors to consider. On one hand, we want a percentage close enough to 100 percent to hold on to the idea that moral rules are for acceptance *by the whole society of human beings*. On the other hand, we want a percentage far enough short of 100 percent to *make salient the problems about non-compliance* — such problems should not be thought of as incidental. Acknowledging that any one percentage will nevertheless be somewhat arbitrary, I propose we take internalization by 90 percent of people in each future generation as the condition under which rules have to be optimal. Let me just add that this distinction between the 90 percent who are moral and the 10 percent who are amoral is

supposed to cut across all other distinctions, such as distinctions in nationality and financial status.

8 Arguments for rule-consequentialism

One argument for rule-consequentialism is that general internalization of rule-consequentialism would actually maximize the impartial good. The idea is that *from a purely consequentialist point of view* rule-consequentialism seems better than act-consequentialism and all other theories.

Many act-consequentialists reply by invoking their distinction between their criterion of rightness and the decision procedure for day-to-day moral decisions. They admit act-consequentialism is not a good procedure for agents to use when deciding what to do. But they think this does not invalidate act-consequentialism's criterion of rightness. They would add that, even if rule-consequentialism is an optimal decision procedure, this would not entail that rule-consequentialism correctly identifies what makes right acts right and wrong acts wrong.

Let us turn, then, to arguments for rule-consequentialism other than the one that internalizing rule-consequentialism would maximize the good. Consider the moral code whose acceptance by society would be best, i.e., would maximize net good, impartially calculated. Shouldn't we try to follow that code? Isn't the code best for general adoption by the group of which we are members the one we should try to follow? These general thoughts about morality seem intuitively attractive and broadly rule-consequentialist.

And consider the related question "What if everyone felt free to do what you're doing?" This question may in the end prove to be an inadequate test of moral rightness. But there is no denying its initial appeal. And there is no denying that rule-consequentialism is an (at least initially) appealing interpretation of the test.

Rule-consequentialism thus taps into and develops familiar and intuitively plausible ideas about morality. Morality is to be understood as a social code, a collective enterprise, something people are to pursue together. And the elements of this code are to be evaluated in terms of both fairness and the overall effects on the well-being of individuals, impartially considered.

But rule-consequentialism's leading rivals all likewise emerge from attractive general ideas about morality. For example, act-utilitarianism can be seen as emerging from the idea that all that ultimately matters from the moral point of view is whether individuals are benefitted or harmed, that everything else is only instrumentally important. [. . .] And act-consequentialism, the broader theory than act-utilitarianism, can be seen as emerging from the intuition that it can't be wrong to do what produces the most good. [. . .]

Now consider moral contractualism, the theory that an act is right if and only if allowed by rules which could not be reasonably rejected by anyone motivated to find rules that no one with this same motivation could reject. Contractualism develops from the idea that morality consists of rules to which everyone would consent under appropriate conditions. This seems a very appealing general idea – moral rules grounded in reasonable agreement.

Consider yet another theory. The moral particularism of Jonathan Dancy (1993) builds on the idea that moral truth is found not in cold inflexible principles but rather through a finely tuned sensitivity to particular cases in all their rich complexity. Actually, to be distinct, moral particularism must go beyond the claim that there are some conflicts between competing moral considerations which are so difficult that agents would have to have fine moral sensitivity and judgement to resolve them correctly. To be distinct, moral particularism must be the view that what counts as a consideration at all can be decided only on a case by case basis. This is just how Dancy frames his theory: the very same

consideration can count morally in favor of doing an action in one case, and against in another, and there are few if any considerations that must always count on the same side morally. (Dancy points out that such properties as moral rightness itself do *always* count morally in favor of an act.)

Finally, as I understand what has come to be called virtue ethics, this approach grows from the thought that right and wrong actions can be understood only in terms of choices that a fully virtuous person would make. This thought then suggests that we take the nature of and rationale for the virtues as the primary focal points for our moral philosophy.

Thus all these moral theories – rule consequentialism, act-utilitarianism, act-consequentialism, contractualism, particularism, virtue ethics – tap into familiar and intuitively attractive general ideas about morality, though different ones. So no one could claim that any one theory is the only one with this feature. The conclusion to draw from this is simple. The fact that a theory arises from and develops attractive general ideas about morality is hardly enough to show that it is superior to all its rivals.

Now among the questions we can go on to ask about competing moral theories are (1) whether they are coherent and develop from initially attractive ideas about morality, and (2) whether the claims they end up making about right and wrong in various circumstances are intuitively plausible. I have already argued that rule-consequentialism develops from attractive ideas about morality. But I shall not fully discuss here the objection that rule-consequentialism *incoherently* claims that maximizing the good is the good overarching goal and then that following certain rules can be right even when breaking them would produce more good. I admit that if we start from an overarching commitment to maximize overall good, then our rule-consequentialism might be an incoherent account of moral rightness. But I propose our route to rule-consequentialism starts elsewhere: we don't start from, and indeed don't have, an overarching commitment to maximize overall good. If I am right about that, then this objection falls apart. [. . .]

What other route to rule-consequentialism might there be? In the next few sections, I will show that rule-consequentialism's implications about what is right or wrong in particular circumstances match our confident moral convictions quite well. But let me immediately address the familiar challenge to the idea that moral theories are to be tested by their match with intuitions. The familiar challenge is that moral convictions are merely inherited prejudices, and as such cannot provide good reason for anything.

In reply to this challenge, let me say I of course recognize that people from different cultures have different moral intuitions, as do people even from the same culture. We must always be willing to reconsider our moral intuitions. They are scarcely infallible.

But, while they are not infallible, they can be crucial. Suppose we have two moral theories which are each coherent developments of appealing general ideas about morality. Suppose one of these theories has implications that match our convictions quite closely, and the other has implications that conflict with many of our most confidently held moral convictions. In this case, I cannot see what could reasonably keep us from thinking better of the theory with the more intuitively plausible implications. Indeed, it seems to me that we are at least as confident about what is right in *some* specific kinds of situation as we are about any of the general ideas about morality that get developed into different moral theories such as Aristotelianism, Kantianism, contractualism, and act-consequentialism. This is why almost all moral philosophers are unable to resist "testing" these theories by comparing the judgments that follow from them with our confident convictions about right and wrong in various kinds of situations.

Let me take stock. I've suggested three different ways of arguing for rule-consequentialism.

One is that rule-consequentialism is, from a purely consequentialist point of view, best. I myself am not relying on this argument.

The second is that rule-consequentialism develops from some very attractive general ideas about morality. Though this is an important feature of rule-consequentialism, I acknowledge rule-consequentialism is hardly the only theory that plugs into or develops from attractive general ideas about morality. So the fact that a theory is a coherent development of some initially very attractive ideas is not enough to make it superior to all its rivals.

The third argument for rule-consequentialism is that we can reach a reflective equilibrium between rule-consequentialism and our confident moral convictions. At least *some* moral convictions seem more secure than any theory that could oppose them. If this is right, then appeal to reflective equilibrium between abstract theory and moral conviction must be part of the defense of rule-consequentialism.

9 Rule-consequentialism on prohibitions

Whatever act-consequentialism says about day-to-day moral thinking, act-consequentialism's criterion of moral rightness entails that *whenever* killing an innocent person, or stealing, or breaking a promise, etc., would maximize the good, such acts would be morally right. W. D. Ross put forward the following example (Table 26.4) to illustrate that keeping one's promises can be right even when this would produce *slightly* less good (Ross 1930: 34–35):

Table 26.4 Numbers below represent units of good

	Effect on person A	Effect on person B	Total good
Keeping promise to A	1000	0	1000
Keeping promise to A	0	1001	1001

Most of us would agree with Ross that keeping the promise would be morally right in this case. Act-consequentialism, of course, favors breaking the promise in this case, since that is the alternative with the most good. So, if we agree with Ross about this case, we must reject act-consequentialism.

Most of us also believe (as Ross went on to observe) that, if breaking the promise would produce *much greater* good than keeping it, breaking the promise could be right. We believe parallel things about inflicting harm on innocent people, stealing, lying, etc. Thus most of us reject what is sometimes called "absolutism" in ethics. Absolutists hold that certain acts (e.g., physical attack on the innocent, promise-breaking, stealing, lying) are *always* wrong, even when they would prevent the most extreme *disasters*.

Absolutism and act-consequentialism are, we might say, two ends of a spectrum. Whereas absolutism never permits certain kinds of act, even when necessary to prevent extreme disaster, act-consequentialism insists such acts are right not only when a great disaster is at stake but also when a *marginal* gain in net good is in the offing. Act-consequentialists seem mistaken about these cases of marginal gain, just as absolutists seem mistaken about the disaster cases. Thus, absolutism seems to go too far in one direction, act-consequentialism in the other.

Rule-consequentialism, on the other hand, concurs with our beliefs both about when we can, and when we cannot, do normally forbidden acts for the sake of the overall good. It claims that individual acts of murder, torture, promise-breaking, and so on, can be wrong even when they result in somewhat more good than not doing them would. The rule-consequentialist reason for this is that the general internalization of a code prohibiting murder, torture, promise-breaking, and so on would clearly result in more good than general internalization of a code with no prohibitions on such acts.

Another rule whose general internalization would be optimal is a rule telling us to do what is necessary to prevent disasters. This rule is relevant when the only way to prevent a disaster is to break a promise or do some other normally prohibited act. In such cases, rule-consequentialism holds that the normally prohibited act should be done. I mention this rule about preventing disaster because its existence undermines the objection that rule-consequentialism would, in a counterintuitive way, prescribe sticking to rules even when this would result in disaster.

10 Doing good for others

Morality paradigmatically requires us to be willing to make sacrifices for others. Yet act-consequentialism is widely accused of going too far here too. Utility, impartially calculated, would be maximized if I gave away most of my material goods to the appropriate charities. Giving away most of my material goods is therefore required of me by (most versions of) act-consequentialism. I should probably even change to some more lucrative employment so that I would then have more money to give to charity. [. . .] I could make much more money as a corporate lawyer, banker, stockbroker, accountant, gossip-columnist, or bounty-hunter than as an employee of a philosophy department. If people should be willing to make any sacrifices that are smaller than the benefits thereby secured for others, then I should move to the better paying job so that I will have a bigger salary to contribute to the needy. With a bigger salary, I would then have to give an even larger percentage of my earnings to aid agencies. The result would be a life of devoted money-making – only then to deny myself virtually all the rewards I could buy for myself with the money. After all, from an act-consequentialist perspective, my own enjoyment is insignificant compared to the very lives of those who would be saved by my additional contributions.

Such reflections give special poignancy to Shelly Kagan's remark: "Given the parameters of the actual world, there is no question that [maximally] promoting the good would require a life of hardship, self-denial, and austerity" (1989: 360).

But many of us may on reflection think that it would be *morally unreasonable* to demand this level of self-sacrifice for the sake of others. However praiseworthy such self-sacrifice may be, most of us are quite confident that perpetual self-impoverishment for the sake of strangers is above and beyond what morality *requires* of us.

I have been discussing the objection that act-consequentialism requires us to make *huge* sacrifices in order to maximize our contribution to famine relief. Act-consequentialism also requires self-sacrifice even when the benefit to the other person is only *slightly* larger than the cost to the agent. Consider, for example, the corner office in our building. Offices are allotted on the basis of seniority. Suppose you are the most senior person who might want this corner office. But if you do not take it, it will go to an acquaintance who spends ten percent more time in her office than you do in yours. Suppose we therefore reasonably guess that she would benefit a bit more from moving into this office than you would. This is not a life and death matter. Nor will she be so depressed by not getting the corner office that her work or domestic life will be seriously compromised. Nevertheless, she would get a bit more enjoyment out of the better office than you would. But you still take it for yourself. No one would think you unreasonable or immoral for doing so. Except in special circumstances, morality does not, we think, really *require* you to sacrifice your own good for the sake of slightly larger gains to others.

I have offered two objections about the demands of act-consequentialism. (1) Act-consequentialism requires *huge* sacrifices from you. (2) Act-consequentialism requires

you to sacrifice your own good even when the aggregate good will be only *slightly* increased by your sacrifice. In both ways, act-consequentialism is *unreasonably demanding*.

In contrast, rule-consequentialism would not require you to pass up the corner office and let your colleague have it. You are certainly permitted to do that if you want, but rule-consequentialism would not *require* such impartiality in your decisions about what to do with your own time, energy, money, or place in line. The rules the internalization of which could reasonably be thought to produce the most good would *allow* each person considerable partiality towards self (and even *require* partiality towards friends and family). [. . .] For, as I noted earlier, the costs of getting a complete impartiality internalized by each new generation would be prohibitive.

Likewise, whereas act-consequentialism requires huge sacrifices for the sake of maximizing the good, rule-consequentialism seems not to require more than a reasonable amount of sacrifice for this purpose. Why? A rule-consequentialist might point out that, if everyone relatively well off in the world were to contribute quite modest amounts to the best aid agencies, the worst elements of poverty could be overcome.

The World Bank has been calling for contributions from the rich countries of 0.7 percent of GDP, the current average being less than half that. Much of this aid does not go to the most needy, but instead to countries that offer business for, or military alliances with, the donor country. The UN estimates that if merely 60 percent of the aid that the rich countries now give (i.e., 60 percent of about $57 billion) were intelligently spent on providing basic health services and clean water and on eliminating illiteracy, these problems could be fixed (*The Economist*, June 22, 1996: 64).

A rule-consequentialist will be interested in redistribution beyond what is required to secure the very basic necessities. But even after including these other potential benefits in the cost-benefit analysis, we might well conclude that the amount the world's relatively well off would each be required to give would not be unreasonably severe. [. . .]

Consider the following example. Walking along a deserted road on your way to the airport for a flight to the other side of the world, you see a child drowning in a shallow pool beside the road. You could easily save the child, at no risk to yourself. But if you do save the child, you will miss your flight and lose the cost of the nonrefundable ticket.

Everyone agrees you are obligated to save the child. This is true even if you are not terribly rich. Suppose the ticket costs as much as a tenth of your annual income. You would still be morally wrong not to make the sacrifice and save the child. And even if the probability of the child's drowning without your rescue is less than 100 percent – suppose, for example, it is 80 percent – you are obligated to sacrifice your ticket to save the child.

Now consider a variant of the example. [. . .] You and I are walking to the airport when we see two small children drowning in a lake. You and I could each easily save the children, at no risk to ourselves. The two children are positioned in the lake in such a way that you and I could each save one and still get to our flights. But if one of us saves both children, he will miss his flight. Suppose you save one child, but I do nothing. Surely, you should now save the other.

Yet, were rule-consequentialism framed in terms of 100 percent compliance, how could it tell you to save the other? With 100 percent compliance, there would be no need for you to save the second child. With 100 percent compliance, once you'd done your share, you'd have done all that was needed. The rule that would be best given 100 percent compliance would presumably not require you to sacrifice more than you would have to sacrifice if everyone did their part. But if this rule is applied to our case, where I am in fact not coming to the rescue, you

are *not* obligated to save this child. This is clearly an implausible implication.

But I argued that rule-consequentialism should be framed in terms of less than 100 percent compliance. If rule-consequentialism is framed in terms of 90 percent compliance, we can envisage that there is a need for rules about how to act when others around you aren't doing their part. The rule might be, "When you happen to be surrounded by others who are not helping, then prevent disaster even if this involves doing more than you would have to do if the others helped." This rule *would* require you to save the second child from the shallow pond.

But if the world we live in – the real world – is one where partial compliance is ubiquitous, then a rule requiring you to make up for the non-compliance of others could become unreasonably demanding. Just how much would rule-consequentialism require you to make up for non-compliance by other people in a position to help? In earlier work, I assumed that rule-consequentialism would formulate a rule about aiding the needy in terms of a *fairly precise* level of contribution or sacrifice to the reduction of world poverty.

I now think this approach is hopeless. Consider a concrete moral code that could reasonably be expected to produce at least as much good as any other we can identify. It would contain rules requiring us not to injure others physically, not to steal, not to break promises, not to lie, etc. These rules might have *some* exceptions built into them (though not a general break-the-rule-whenever-you-could-thereby-produce-more-good exception, nor an unlimited set of much more specific exceptions). Nonetheless, there is pressure to have *fairly general* rules that can be applied to a wide array of situations. Oxfam's petitioning the rich to help the very poor is hardly the only situation where some people have an opportunity to help others at relatively little cost to themselves. There will be situations where the rich can help other rich, situations where poor can help other poor, even situations where the poor can help the rich. And there will be situations where the help needs to be in the form of physical effort, other situations where the help needs to be in the form of money or time.

Given all this, perhaps the optimific rule for such a world would not be "the rich should give the very needy at least precisely n percent of their annual income", but rather "people should help others in great need when they can do so at modest to themselves, cost being assessed aggregatively, not iteratively" (Cullity 1995: 293–95). Such a rule would apply in a wide array of situations – indeed, whenever some person can help another in great need. It is not limited to what the rich should do nor to what should be done concerning world poverty.

But because cost to the agent is to be assessed aggregatively rather than iteratively, the rule does not require one to help another in great need whenever the cost of helping *on that particular occasion* is modest. Having to help others whenever doing so *on that occasion* involves modest cost could easily be very costly. For each of us faces an indefinitely long string of such occasions, because any day on which we could give money to UNICEF or Oxfam counts as such an occasion. But many small sacrifices added together can amount to a huge sacrifice. The end of that road is self-impoverishment. If I am right, rule-consequentialism instead endorses a rule requiring sacrifices over the course of your life that add up to something significant. It allows but does not require personal sacrifice beyond this point.

I propose that this rule *would* have good consequences even in possible worlds that are either much poorer or much richer than ours. I don't have space here to argue either that rule-consequentialism would indeed end up with this rule in *all* possible worlds, or that this rule *always* has intuitively acceptable consequences. I mention this rule only in order

to sketch one way in which a defense of rule-consequentialism might go. [. . .]

11 Conclusion

Rule-consequentialism has an uncertain future. It needs to be carefully formulated if it is to avoid being a sitting target. In this essay, I have tried to improve its defenses by fine-tuning its formulation. I have also argued here that the theory develops from appealing general beliefs about morality, that it does not collapse into act-consequentialism, and that it coheres well with our intuitions about moral prohibitions and permissible partiality. As I see things, the theory is healthy now. But it is hardly invulnerable. Like someone walking through a dangerous city who has so far managed to fight off muggers emerging from behind every corner, the theory might meet an attack it cannot survive. I am curious to see whether that happens.

References

Cullity Garrett: "Moral Character and the Iteration Problem," *Utilitas*, 7 (1995): 289–99.

Dancy, Jonathan: *Moral Reasons* (Oxford: Blackwell, 1993).

Kagan, Shelly: *The Limits of Morality* (Oxford: Clarendon Press, 1989).

Quinn, Warren: *Morality and Action* (New York: Cambridge University Press, 1993).

Ross, W. D.: *The Right and the Good* (Oxford: Clarendon Press, 1930).

Singer, Peter: "Famine, Affluence, and Morality," *Philosophy and Public Affairs*, 1 (1972): 229–43.

Chapter 27

Alastair Norcross

SCALAR MORALITY

Introduction

MY CONCERN in this paper is to argue that consequentialist theories such as utilitarianism are best understood purely as theories of the comparative value of alternative actions, not as theories of right and wrong that demand, forbid, or permit the performance of certain actions. Consequentialist morality, I will argue, provides reasons for actions, without issuing demands (or permissions). Such an approach can answer the three related criticisms of consequentialism that it requires too much sacrifice of agents, leaves inadequate room for moral freedom, and does not allow for supererogation.[1] These criticisms focus on the maximizing feature of the most common forms of consequentialism, pointing out that maximization leaves little room for options. I will also argue that these criticisms have very little force against more traditional versions of consequentialism, on any reasonable understanding of what rightness amounts to. The rejection of rightness, though, does not address a different type of criticism of consequentialism. According to some, consequentialist theories are unacceptable, because they fail to account for constraints on permissible behavior. I will briefly discuss Peter Vallentyne's version of this criticism, which claims that such constraints are required to recognize what he (and others) calls the "normative separateness of persons." I will argue

that, despite the undoubted rhetorical appeal of this phrase, it does not provide the basis for a convincing criticism of consequentialism. Either 'the normative separateness of persons' signifies a feature fully accounted for by consequentialism (and probably not by rival theories), or it refers simply to the claims that (a) persons have certain rights, and (b) usually (or even always) rights not to be harmed are more stringent than rights to be aided. I shall conduct most of my discussion in terms of utilitarianism, since this is the most popular form of consequentialism. None of my points, however, will rely on the utilitarian value theory.[2] I will also not devote much time to explaining the basic structure of utilitarianism, since both William Shaw and Peter Vallentyne do an excellent job in that regard.

The demands of utilitarianism

The three criticisms of utilitarianism, that it requires too much sacrifice of agents, leaves inadequate room for moral freedom, and does not allow for supererogation, can be seen as applications of the more general criticism that utilitarianism is *too demanding*. But how, exactly, are we to take this criticism? Utilitarianism is too demanding *for what*? If I take up a hobby, say mountain climbing, I may well decide that it is too demanding *for me*. By that, I mean that I am simply not willing to accept the demands of this

hobby. I may, therefore, decide to adopt the less demanding hobby of reading about mountain climbing instead. However, unless we adopt a radically subjectivist view of the nature of morality, according to which I am free simply to pick whichever moral theory pleases me, this approach will not work for the claim that utilitarianism is too demanding. When critics object to what they see as utilitarianism's demands, they are not simply declaring themselves unwilling to accept these demands, but are claiming that morality doesn't, in fact, make such demands. We are not, they claim, actually required to sacrifice our own interests for the good of others, at least not as much as utilitarianism tells us. Furthermore, we really do have a (fairly) wide range of moral freedom, and there really are times when we can go above and beyond the call of duty. Since utilitarianism seems to deny these claims, it must be rejected.

How should a utilitarian respond to this line of criticism? One perfectly respectable response is simply to deny the claims at the heart of it. We might insist that morality really is very demanding, in precisely the way utilitarianism says it is. But doesn't this fly in the face of common sense? Well, perhaps it does, but so what? Until relatively recently, moral "common sense" viewed women as having an inferior moral status to men, and some races as having an inferior status to others. These judgments were not restricted to the philosophically unsophisticated. Such illustrious philosophers as Aristotle and Hume accepted positions of this nature. Many utilitarians (myself included) believe that the interests of sentient non-human animals should be given equal consideration in moral decisions with the interests of humans. This claim certainly conflicts with the "common sense" of many (probably most) humans, and many (perhaps most) philosophers. It should not, on that account alone, be rejected. Indeed, very few philosophers base their rejection of a principle of equal consideration for non-human animals merely on its conflict with "common

sense." Furthermore, it is worth noting that the main contemporary alternative to a (roughly) consequentialist approach to morality is often referred to as 'common-sense morality'.[3] Those who employ this phrase do not intend the label itself to constitute an argument against consequentialism.

As I said, a perfectly respectable utilitarian response to the criticism that utilitarianism is too demanding is simply to insist that morality really is very demanding. However, there are powerful reasons to take a different approach altogether. Instead of either maintaining the demands of maximizing utilitarianism or altering the theory to modify its demands, we should reject the notion that morality issues demands at all. In order to see why this might be an attractive option, I will briefly examine the alleged category of supererogatory actions, and an attempted modification of utilitarianism to accommodate it.

Maximizing utilitarianism, since it classifies as wrong all acts that fail to maximize, leaves no room for supererogation. A supererogatory act is generally characterized as an act which is not required, but which is in some way better than the alternatives. For example, a doctor, who hears of an epidemic in another town may choose to go to the assistance of the people who are suffering there, although in doing so he will be putting himself at great risk.[4] Such an action is not morally required of the doctor, but it produces more utility than the morally permissible alternative of remaining in his home town. The category of the supererogatory embodies two connected intuitions that are at odds with maximizing utilitarianism. First, it seems that people sometimes go beyond the call of duty. Maximizing utilitarianism would not allow that. To do your duty is to do the best thing you can possibly do. And second, people who fail to make certain extreme sacrifices for the greater good are usually not wrong. It seems harsh to demand or expect that the doctor sacrifice his life for the villagers.

The utilitarian can avoid these consequences by retreating to a form of satisficing utilitarianism.[5] For example, one can allow that the boundary between right and wrong can in some cases be located on the scale at some point short of the best. This would allow that an agent can do her duty without performing the best action available to her, and it would make it possible for her to go beyond the call of duty. The position of the boundary between right and wrong may be affected by such factors as how much self-sacrifice is required of the agent by the various options, and how much utility or disutility they will produce. For example, it may be perfectly permissible for the doctor to stay at home, even though the best option would have been to go and help with the epidemic. On the other hand, if all the doctor could do and needed to do to save the villagers were to send a box of tablets or a textbook on diseases, then he would be required to do all he could to save them.

Satisficing versions of utilitarianism, no less than the traditional ones, assume that the rightness of an action is an all-or-nothing property. If an action does not produce at least the required amount of good, then it is wrong; otherwise it is right. On a maximizing theory the required amount is the most good available. On a non-maximizing theory what is required may be less than the best. Both forms of utilitarianism share the view that a moral miss is as good as a mile. If you don't produce as much good as is required, then you do something wrong, and that's all there is to it.

Utilitarianism has traditionally been viewed as a theory of right action. Utilitarians have employed theories of value, theories that tell us what things are good and bad, in functions that tell us what actions are right and wrong. The most common function from the good to the right is the maximizing one: an act is right if and only if it produces at least as much good as any alternative available to the agent; otherwise it is wrong. According to this maximizing function, rightness and wrongness are not matters of

degree. Utilitarians are not alone on this score. Deontologists concur that rightness and wrongness are not matters of degree. There is an important difference, though. In typical deontological theories, properties that make an action right and wrong – e.g., being a keeping of a binding promise, a killing of an innocent person, or a telling of a lie – are not naturally thought of as matters of degree. So one wouldn't expect the rightness or wrongness of an act to be a matter of degree for deontology.[6] But this is not the case with utilitarianism. Goodness and badness are clearly matters of degree. So the property of an act that makes it right or wrong – how much good it produces relative to available alternatives – is naturally thought of as a matter of degree. Why, then, is rightness and wrongness not a matter of degree?

Scalar utilitarianism

Here's an argument for the view that rightness and wrongness isn't an all-or-nothing affair.[7] Suppose that we have some obligations of beneficence, e.g. the wealthy are required to give up a minimal proportion of their incomes for the support of the poor and hungry. (Most people, including deontologists such as Kant and Ross, would accept this.) Suppose Jones is obligated to give 10 percent of his income to charity. The difference between giving 8 percent and 9 percent is the same, in some obvious physical sense, as the difference between giving 9 percent and 10 percent, or between giving 11 percent and 12 percent. Such similarities should be reflected in moral similarities. A moral theory which says that there is a *really significant* moral difference between giving 9 percent and 10 percent, but *not* between giving 11 percent and 12 percent, looks misguided. At least, no utilitarian should accept this. She will be equally concerned about the difference between giving 11 percent and 12 percent as the difference between giving 9 percent and 10 percent. To see this, suppose that Jones were torn between

giving 11 percent and 12 percent and that Smith were torn between giving 9 percent and 10 percent. The utilitarian will tell you to spend the same amount of time persuading each to give the larger sum, assuming that other things are equal. This is because she is concerned with certain sorts of consequences, in this case, with getting money to people who need it. An extra $5,000 from Jones (who has already given 11 percent) would satisfy this goal as well as an extra $5,000 from Smith (who has given 9 percent). It does not matter whether the $5,000 comes from one who has already given 11 percent or from one who has given a mere 9 percent.

An all-or-nothing theory of right and wrong would have to say that there was a *threshold*, e.g., at 10 percent, such that if one chose to give 9 percent one would be wrong, whereas if one chose to give 10 percent one would be right. If this distinction is to be interesting, it must say that there is a *big* difference between right and wrong, between giving 9 percent and giving 10 percent, and a small difference between pairs of right actions, or pairs of wrong actions. The difference between giving 9 percent and 8 percent is just the difference between a wrong action and a slightly worse one; and the difference between giving 11 percent and 12 percent is just the difference between one supererogatory act and a slightly better one. Given the argument I just rehearsed, the utilitarian should not accept this.[8]

A related reason to reject an all-or-nothing line between right and wrong is that the choice of any point on the scale of possible options as a threshold for rightness will be *arbitrary*. Even maximization is subject to this criticism. One might think that the difference between the best and the next best option constitutes a really significant moral difference, quite apart from the difference in goodness between the options. We do, after all, attach great significance to the difference between winning a race and coming second, even if the two runners are separated by

only a fraction of a second. We certainly don't attach anything like the same significance to the difference between finishing, say, seventh and eighth, even when a much larger interval separates the runners. True enough, but I don't think that it shows that there really is a greater significance in the difference between first and second than in any other difference. We do, after all, also attach great significance to finishing in the top three. We give medals to the top three and to no others. We could just as easily honor the top three equally and not distinguish between them. When we draw these lines – between the first and the rest, or between the top three and the rest, or between the final four and the others – we seem be laying down arbitrary conventions. And saying that giving 10 percent is right and giving only 9 percent is wrong seems analogously conventional and arbitrary.

By contrast, good and bad are scalar concepts, but as with many other scalar concepts, such as rich and tall, we speak of a state of affairs as good or bad (*simpliciter*). This distinction is not arbitrary or conventional. The utilitarian can give a fairly natural account of the distinction between good and bad states of affairs. For example: consider each morally significant being included in the state of affairs. Determine whether her conscious experience is better than no experience. Assign it a positive number if it is, and a negative one if it isn't. Then add together the numbers of all morally significant beings in the state of affairs. If the sum is positive, the state of affairs is good. If it is negative, the state of affairs is bad.

Note that although this gives an account of a real distinction between good and bad, it doesn't give us reason to attach much significance to the distinction. It doesn't make the difference between a minimally good state of affairs and a minimally bad state of affairs more significant than the difference between pairs of good states of affairs or between bad states of affairs. To see this, imagine that you are consulted by two highly powerful amoral gods, Bart and

Lisa. Bart is trying to decide whether to create a world that is ever so slightly good overall or one that is ever so slightly bad overall. Lisa is trying to decide whether to create a world that is clearly, but not spectacularly, good, or one that is clearly spectacularly good. They each intend to flip a coin, unless you convince them one way or the other in the next five minutes. You can only talk to one of them at a time. It is clearly more important to convince Lisa to opt for the better of her two choices than to convince Bart to opt for the better of his two choices.

However, if utilitarianism only gives an account of goodness, how do we go about determining our moral obligations and duties? It's all very well to know how good my different options are, but this doesn't tell me what morality requires of me. Traditional maximizing versions of utilitarianism, though harsh, are perfectly clear on the question of moral obligation. My obligation is to do the best I can. Even a satisficing version can be clear about how much good it is my duty to produce. How could a utilitarian, or other consequentialist, theory count as a moral theory, if it didn't give an account of duty and obligation? After all, isn't the central task of a moral theory to give an account of moral duty and obligation?

Utilitarians, and consequentialists in general, seem to have agreed with deontologists that their central task was to give an account of moral obligation. They have disagreed, of course, sometimes vehemently, over what actually is morally required. Armed with an account of the good, utilitarians have proceeded to give an account of the right by means of a simple algorithm from the good to the right. In addition to telling us what is good and bad, they have told us that morality requires us to produce a certain amount of good, usually as much as possible, that we have a moral obligation to produce a certain amount of good, that any act that produces that much good is right, and any act that produces less good is wrong. And in doing so they have played into the hands of their deontological opponents.

A deontologist, as I said earlier, is typically concerned with such properties of an action as whether it is a killing of an innocent person, or a telling of a lie, or a keeping of a promise. Such properties do not usually come in degrees. (A notable exception is raised by the so-called duty of beneficence.) It is hard, therefore, to construct an argument against particular deontological duties along the lines of my argument against particular utility thresholds. If a utilitarian claims that one has an obligation to produce x amount of utility, it is hard to see how there can be a significant utilitarian distinction between an act that produces x utility and one that produces slightly less. If a deontologist claims that one has an obligation to keep one's promises, a similar problem does not arise. Between an act of promise-keeping and an alternative act that does not involve promise-keeping, there is clearly a significant deontological distinction, no matter how similar in other respects the latter act may be to the former. A utilitarian may, of course, claim that he is concerned not simply with utility, but with maximal utility. Whether an act produces at least as much utility as any alternative is not a matter of degree. But why should a utilitarian be concerned with maximal utility, or any other specific amount?

To be sure, a utilitarian cannot produce an account of duty and obligation to rival the deontologist's, unless he claims that there are morally significant utility thresholds. But why does he want to give a rival account of duty and obligation at all? Why not instead regard utilitarianism as a far more radical alternative to deontology, and simply reject the claim that duties or obligations constitute any part of fundamental morality, let alone the central part? My suggestion is that utilitarianism should be treated simply as a theory of the goodness of states of affairs and of the comparative value of actions, which rates alternative possible actions in comparison with each other. This system of evaluation yields information about which alternatives are better than which and by how much.

In the example of the doctor, this account will say that the best thing to do is to go and help with the epidemic, but it will say neither that he is required to do so, nor that he is completely unstained morally if he fails to do so.

If a utilitarian has an account of goodness and badness, according to which they are scalar phenomena, why not say something similar about right and wrong: that they are scalar phenomena but that there is a point (perhaps a fuzzy point) at which wrong shades into right? Well, what would that point be? I said earlier that differences in goodness should be reflected by differences in rightness. Perhaps the dividing line between right and wrong is just the dividing line between good and bad. There are two reasons to reject this suggestion. The first is that it seems to collapse the concepts of right and wrong into those of good and bad respectively, and, hence, to make the former pair redundant. The second is that, on the account of good and bad states of affairs I offered the utilitarian, it is not clear that there is any satisfactory account of the difference between good and bad *actions* (as opposed to *states of affairs*) with which to equate the difference between right and wrong actions. I do not here have the space to defend this claim, though I have done so extensively elsewhere.[9]

If utilitarianism is interpreted as a scalar theory, that doesn't issue any demands at all, it clearly can't be criticized for being too demanding. Does this mean that the scalar utilitarian must agree with the critic who claims (i) we are not frequently required to sacrifice our own interests for the good of others, (ii) we really do have a (fairly) wide range of moral freedom, and (iii) there really are times when we can go above and beyond the call of duty? Strictly speaking, the answers are 'yes' to (i), 'no' to (iii), and 'it depends' to (ii). (i) It may frequently be better to sacrifice our interests for the good of others than to perform any action that preserves our interests. Sometimes it may be much better to do so. However, these facts don't entail any further facts to the effect that we are *required* to do so. (ii) If the claim that we have a wide range of moral freedom is simply the claim that morality doesn't demand only one course of action in most situations, then scalar utilitarians can agree with this. If, on the other hand, moral freedom is supposed to entail not only that morality doesn't narrow down our options with demands, but that we are frequently faced with a wide array of equally choiceworthy alternatives, scalar utilitarians will quite rightly deny this. (iii) As for supererogation, the scalar utilitarian will deny the existence of duty as a fundamental moral category, and so will deny the possibility of actions that go "beyond" our duty, in the sense of being better than whatever duty demands. The intuition that drives the belief in supererogation can, however, be explained in terms of actions that are considerably better than what would be expected of a reasonably decent person in the circumstances.

At this point, someone might object that I have thrown out the baby with the bath water. To be sure, scalar utilitarianism isn't too demanding: it's not nearly demanding enough! How can a theory that makes no demands fulfill the central function of morality, which is to guide our actions? I turn to this question in the next section.

Rightness and goodness as guides to action

Utilitarianism should not be seen as giving an account of right action, in the sense of an action *demanded* by morality, but only as giving an account of what states of affairs are good and which actions are better than which other possible alternatives and by how much. The fundamental moral fact about an action is how good it is relative to other available alternatives. Once a range of options has been evaluated in terms of goodness, all the morally relevant facts about those options have been discovered. There is no further fact of the form 'x is right', 'x is to-be-done', or 'x is demanded by morality'.

This is not to say that it is a bad thing for people to use the phrases such as 'right', 'wrong', 'ought to be done', or 'demanded by morality', in their moral decision-making, and even to set up systems of punishment and blame which assume that there is a clear and significant line between right and wrong. It may well be that societies that believe in such a line are happier than societies that don't. It might still be useful to employ the notions of rightness and wrongness for the purposes of everyday decision-making. If it is practically desirable that people should think that rightness is an all-or-nothing property, my proposed treatment of utilitarianism suggests an approach to the question of what function to employ to move from the good to the right. In different societies the results of employing different functions may well be different. These different results will themselves be comparable in terms of goodness. And so different functions can be assessed as better or worse depending on the results of employing them.

It is clear that the notions of right and wrong play a central role in the moral thinking of many. It will be instructive to see why this so. There are two main reasons for the concentration on rightness as an all-or-nothing property of actions: (i) a diet of examples which present a choice between options which differ greatly in goodness; (ii) the imperatival model of morality. Let's consider (i). When faced with a choice between helping a little old lady across the road, and mugging her, it is usually much better to help her across the road. If these are the only two options presented, it is easy to classify helping the old lady as the 'right' thing to do, and mugging her as 'wrong'. Even when there are other bad options, such as kidnapping her or killing and eating her, the gap between the best of these and helping her across the road is so great that there is no question as to what to do. When we move from considering choices such as these to considering choices between options which are much closer in value, such as helping

the old lady or giving blood, it is easy to assume that one choice must be wrong and the other right.

Let us move now to (ii). Morality is commonly thought of as some sort of guide to life. People look to morality to tell them what to do in various circumstances, and so they see it as issuing commands. When they obey these, they do the right thing, and when they disobey, they do a wrong thing. This is the form of some simple versions of divine command ethics and some other forms of deontology. Part of the motivation for accepting such a theory is that it seems to give one a simple, easily applicable practical guide. Problems arise, of course, when someone finds herself in a situation in which she is subject to two different commands, either of which can be obeyed, but not both. In these cases we could say that there is a higher-order command for one rather than the other to be done, or that the agent cannot help doing wrong. The effect of allowing higher-order commands is to complicate the basic commands, so "Do not kill" becomes "Do not kill, unless. . . ." The effect of allowing that there could be situations in which an agent cannot help doing wrong is to admit that morality may not always help to make difficult choices. In either case, one of the motivations for accepting an imperatival model of morality – simplicity, and thus ease of application – is undermined.

Unless one does espouse a simple form of divine command theory, according to which the deity's commands should be obeyed just because they are the deity's commands, it seems that the main justification for the imperatival model of morality is pragmatic. After all, if we don't have the justification that the commands issue from a deity, it is always legitimate to ask what grounds them. That certain states of affairs are good or bad, and therefore should or should not be brought about, seems like a far more plausible candidate to be a fundamental moral fact than that someone should act in a certain way. However, it is generally easier to make choices if

one sees oneself as following instructions. It may well be, then, that the imperatival model of morality, with the attendant prominence of the notions of right and wrong, has a part to play at the level of application. It may in fact be highly desirable that most people's moral thinking is conducted in terms of right and wrong. On the other hand, it may be desirable that everyone abandon the notions of right and wrong. I do not wish to argue for either option here, since the issue could probably only be settled by extensive empirical research.

The approach of the last few paragraphs might seem merely to relocate a problem to a different level. I have been claiming that, although morality doesn't actually tell us what we ought to do, there may be pragmatic benefits in adopting moral practices that include demands. Societies that adopt such practices may be better (happier, more flourishing, etc.) than those that don't. But surely this doesn't solve anything. We want to know whether we *ought* to adopt such practices. Scalar utilitarianism seems to be silent on that question. Since scalar utilitarianism doesn't tell us what we ought to do, it can't guide our actions (including our choices of what moral practices to adopt and/or encourage in society). But any adequate moral theory must guide our actions. Therefore the theory should be rejected. This argument has three premises:

1   If a theory doesn't guide our action, it is no good.
2   If a theory doesn't tell us what we ought to do, it doesn't guide our action.
3   Utilitarianism, as I have described it, does not tell us what we ought to do.

To assess this argument, we need to disambiguate its first premise. The expression 'guide our action' can mean several things. If it means 'tell us what we ought to do' then premise (1) is question-begging. I shall construe it to mean something more like, 'provide us with reasons

for acting'. On that reading, I shall concede (1), and shall argue that (2) is false. Here is Sidgwick in defense of something like (2):

> Further, when I speak of the cognition or judgement that 'X ought to be done' – in the stricter ethical sense of the term ought – as a 'dictate' or 'precept' of reason to the persons to whom it relates, I imply that in rational beings as such this cognition gives an impulse or motive to action: though in human beings, of course, this is only one motive among others which are liable to conflict with it, and is not always – perhaps not usually – a predominant motive. (1981: 34)

As Sidgwick acknowledges, this reason can be overridden by other reasons, but when it is, it still exerts its pull in the form of guilt or uneasiness.

Sidgwick's point rests on internalism, the view that moral beliefs are essentially motivating. Internalism is controversial. Instead of coming down on one side or the other of this controversy, I shall argue that, whether one accepts internalism or externalism, the fact that a state of affairs is bad gives reason to avoid producing it as much as would the fact that producing it is wrong.

Suppose internalism is correct. In that case the belief that an act is wrong gives one a reason not to do it. Furthermore, such a reason is necessarily a motivating reason.[10] It seems that the utilitarian internalist should take the position that the belief that a state of affairs is *bad* is also a motivating reason to avoid producing it, and the belief that one state of affairs is *better than the other* may well give the believer a stronger reason to produce the first than the second. If the fact that an act is wrong gives us reason to avoid it, then the fact that it involves the production of a bad state of affairs, by itself, gives us reason to avoid it.

Now let's suppose externalism is true. In that case the fact that an act is wrong gives one a

motivating reason to avoid doing it *if one cares about avoiding wrong-doing*. If this is what wrongness amounts to, then it seems no defect in a theory that it lacks a concept of wrongness. For it may be true that one cannot consistently want to avoid doing wrong, believe that an act is wrong, and do the act without feeling guilt. But this doesn't provide a distinctive account of wrongness, because we can replace each occurrence of the word 'wrong' and its cognates in the above sentence with other moral terms such as 'an action which produces less than the best possible consequences' or 'much worse than readily available alternatives' and the principle remains true. If the agent cares about doing the best he can, then he will be motivated to do so, feel guilt if he doesn't, and so on. It is true that few of us care about doing the best we can. But then, many of us do not care about doing what we ought either.[11]

Whether internalism is correct or not, it looks as if premise (2) in the above argument is false. Abolishing the notion of 'ought' will not seriously undermine the action-guiding nature of morality. The fact that one action is better than another gives us a moral reason to prefer the first to the second. Morality thus guides action in a scalar fashion. This should come as no surprise. Other action-guiding reasons also come in degrees. Prudential reasons certainly seem to function in this way. My judgment that pizza is better for me than cauliflower will guide my action differently depending on how much better I judge pizza to be than cauliflower. Whether moral facts are reasons for all who recognize them (the debate over internalism) is an issue beyond the scope of this paper, but whether they are or not, the significance each of us gives to such moral reasons relative to other reasons, such as prudential and aesthetic reasons, is not something which can be settled by a moral theory.

There are two other reasons I have encountered for requiring utilitarianism to provide an account of the right. The first might be expressed like this: "If utilitarianism is not a theory of the right, it must only be a theory of the good. Likewise, different consequentialist theories will be different theories of the good. But then how do we explain the difference between consequentialist and non-consequentialist theories in general? Since there are no restrictions on the kind of good that any particular version of consequentialism may be a theory of, we are left with nothing that is distinctive about consequentialism."[12]

This is not correct. I can still claim this distinctive feature for consequentialism: it includes the view that the relative value of an action depends entirely on the goodness of its consequences. Of the acts available to the agent, the best action will be the one that produces the best consequences, the next best will be the one that produces the next best consequences, and so on. I can also claim that the better the action, the stronger the moral reason to perform it. This is not to concede the point to my opponents. The fact that there is a moral reason to perform some action, even that there is more moral reason to perform it than any other action, doesn't mean that one ought to perform it. (Most of us would acknowledge that one has more moral reason to behave in a supererogatory fashion than simply to do one's duty.) This distinguishes consequentialism from deontology, which allows that one may have a stronger moral reason to perform an action which produces worse consequences. For example, if faced with a choice between killing one and letting five die, the deontologist may acknowledge that five deaths are worse than one, but insist that the better behavior is to allow the five to die. According to that view, morality provides stronger reasons for allowing five deaths than for killing one.[13] One advantage of the suggestion I offer here over, say, the view that it is of the essence of consequentialism to insist that the agent ought always to do whatever will produce the best consequences, is that it allows satisficing consequentialists and scalar consequentialists to count as consequentialists.

I have also encountered the following reason for requiring utilitarianism to provide an account of the right as well as the good: The utilitarian will have to provide a function from the good to the right in order to compare her theory with various deontological alternatives. Our chief method for comparing moral theories, according to this suggestion, consists in comparing their judgments about which acts are right or wrong. It is true that contemporary discussions of the relative merits of utilitarianism and deontology have often focused on particular examples, asking of the different theories what options are right or wrong. However, to assume that a moral theory must provide an account of the right in order to be subjected to critical scrutiny begs the question against my proposed treatment of utilitarianism. That utilitarians have felt the need to provide accounts of rightness is testimony to the pervasion of deontological approaches to ethics. Part of what makes utilitarianism such a radical alternative to deontology, in my view, is its claim that right and wrong are not fundamental ethical concepts.

Rightness as an ideal

In this paper, I have argued that utilitarianism is best conceived as a theory of the good, that judges actions to be better or worse than possible alternatives, and thus provides reasons for actions. I have argued that the traditional utilitarian account of rightness as an all-or-nothing property, whether the maximizing or satisficing version, should be abandoned. However, there may be an alternative account of rightness that is particularly congenial to a utilitarian approach. If, instead of conceiving of rightness as a standard that *must* be met (perhaps to avoid censure), we conceive of it as an ideal to which we aspire, we may be able to accommodate it within a scalar framework. The suggestion is that the ideally right action is the maximizing action, and alternatives are more or less right, depending

on how close they come to maximizing. Although the ideal itself is often difficult to attain, the theory cannot be charged with being too demanding, since it doesn't include the demand that one attain the ideal. Nonetheless, the ideal functions as a guide. This would be similar to the approach taken by many Christians, who view Christ as a moral exemplar. A common articulation of this view is the question "What would Jesus do?" – often abbreviated on bracelets, bumper stickers, handguns, and the like as "WWJD." Inasmuch as the extant accounts of Christ's life provide a basis for answering this question, the answer is clearly supposed to function as an ideal towards which we are supposed to aspire, and not as a demand that must be met in order to avoid wrongdoing. The closer we come to emulating the life or the actions of Christ, the better our lives or our actions are.

The utilitarian version (WWJSMD?) might be easier to apply, both epistemically and practically. There are, of course, well-known epistemic problems with even a subjective expected-utility version of utilitarianism, but these pale into insignificance compared with the difficulty of figuring out what Jesus would do, whether the (presumably) actual historical figure, or the literary composite portrayed in the biblical (and other) sources. As for the practical problems with viewing Christ as an exemplar, it may turn out that the ideal is not simply difficult to attain, but in some cases impossible. On the assumption that Christ had divine powers, an assumption that is undoubtedly accepted by most adherents of the Christ-as-exemplar moral theory, we may sometimes be literally unable to do what Jesus would have done. For example, suppose I am attending a wedding in Lubbock (TX), and the wine runs out. Amid the wailing and the gnashing of teeth I glance at the "WWJD" engraved on my cowboy boots. Well, it's clear what Jesus would do in this case (John: 2, 1–10), but I simply can't turn water into wine. However, the utilitarian ideal is, by definition, possible. In this case it might involve driving outside the city limits (Lubbock is dry in

more than one sense) to one of the drive-through liquor stores, loading up on the surprisingly good local wines, and returning to spread cheer and much-needed intoxication to the wedding festivities. Or perhaps, more plausibly, it might involve sending the money to famine relief.

Prohibitions and the "separateness of persons"

For those who are inclined to think that traditional maximizing utilitarianism is seriously threatened by the objection that it is too demanding, the suggestion that we interpret the theory in scalar fashion, either abandoning the notion of rightness altogether or interpreting it as an ideal, may be particularly attractive. There are also, as I have argued, independent reasons for adopting a scalar version of utilitarianism.[14] However, adopting a scalar version of utilitarianism does not, as far as I can see, have any bearing on Peter Vallentyne's second line of criticism of consequentialist theories, that they don't include constraints required to recognize the "normative separateness of persons." I will, therefore, close with a brief discussion of why I don't think a utilitarian (any version) should be worried by this line of attack on the theory.

The criticism that utilitarianism does not recognize or account for the "separateness of persons" has become commonplace since Rawls (1971), but what exactly does it mean? Peter Vallentyne's explanation is fairly representative:

> [I]ndividuals have certain rights that may not be infringed simply because the consequences are better. Unlike prudential rationality, morality involves many distinct centers of will (choice) or interests, and these cannot simply be lumped together and traded off against each other.

The basic problem with standard versions of core consequentialism is that they fail to recognize adequately the *normative separateness of persons.*

Psychological autonomous beings (as well, perhaps, as other beings with moral standing) are not merely means for the promotion of value. They must be *respected* and *honored*, and this means that at least sometimes certain things may not be done to them, even though this promotes value overall. An innocent person may not be killed against her will, for example, in order to make a million happy people significantly happier. This would be sacrificing her for the benefit of others.

There seem to be several distinct ideas here. (1) Individuals have rights, that at least sometimes trump utility calculations. (2) Individuals' interests can't simply be traded off against each other. (3) Individuals must be *respected* or *honored*. Consider these claims in reverse order. A utilitarian may claim, with some justification, that the demand for equal consideration of interests embodied in her theory (and other consequentialist theories) is precisely what it means to respect or honor individuals. It is only when I weigh your interests equally with the interests of all others whom I can affect that I adequately respect or honor you. Deontological constraints function to disallow the consideration of certain interests in certain circumstances. Thus they, at least sometimes, prevent us from respecting or honoring certain individuals.

At this point, the critic of utilitarianism will no doubt claim that I have (perhaps willfully) misunderstood (3). In fact, he might claim that (1) and (2) explain *what it means* to honor or respect individuals. (2) denies the aggregative feature of utilitarianism. The problem with the denial of tradeoffs or aggregation is that even committed anti-consequentialists accept them in many circumstances. For example, suppose that Homer is faced with the painful choice between saving Barney from a burning building, or saving both Moe and Apu from the building. Clearly it is better for Homer to save the larger number, *precisely because it is a larger number.* The proponent of (ii) might try to accommodate this intuition by limiting the scope of tradeoffs. For example, perhaps we are allowed to trade lives for lives (or

similarly serious harms), but we are not allowed to trade lives for convenience.[15] Homer can save the lives of Moe and Apu rather than Barney, but he can't leave Barney to die in order to provide all the inhabitants of Springfield with a few minutes extra free time every day.[16] However, any such attempt to limit the scope for tradeoffs faces at least two serious problems. First, such a move almost certainly entails denying the transitivity of 'all-things-considered better than'. Second, we commonly accept tradeoffs between lives and much lesser values, such as convenience. For example, we allow public projects such as building a bridge in order to make travel between two places more convenient, even when we know that several people will die in the course of the construction. Likewise, even most anti-consequentialists don't demand that highway speed limits be lowered to the optimal point for saving lives, even though the advantages of higher speed limits are increased convenience for many.[17]

We are left with (1), the claim that individuals have rights that sometimes trump utilities. Utilitarianism is criticized for failing to distinguish between the following pair of cases (adapted from Foot 1984): (a) Homer must choose whether to save Barney, who is trapped on one side of Springfield, or both Moe and Apu, who are trapped on the other side. He can't save all three, and no one else can save any of them, (b) Homer, and no one else, can save both Moe and Apu, who are trapped on the edge of Springfield Gorge. However, in order to reach them in time to save them, he must run over and kill Barney, who is trapped on a narrow segment of the only road leading to the gorge. We are supposed to agree that Homer may choose to save Moe and Apu in (a), but not in (b). If he saves Moe and Apu in (b), he will violate Barney's right not to be killed. But don't Moe and Apu have the right to be saved? Perhaps, but, if so, it is not as important (strict, stringent, etc.) as Barney's right not to be killed. In general, if the rights view is to present a genuine alternative to consequentialism, negative rights not to

be harmed in some way must be stronger than the corresponding positive rights, if any, to be aided in avoiding such harm. More specifically, the duty not to harm in a certain way must be stricter than the corresponding duty to prevent such harm. Claims that negative rights and duties are (at least usually) stronger than positive rights and duties will have to be grounded in an account of the alleged moral significance of the general distinction between doing and allowing, of which the distinction between killing and letting die is a specific example. This topic is the subject of much debate, which I don't have the space here to recapitulate.[18] It is, however, no surprise that consequentialists deny the moral significance of the doing/allowing distinction.[19] If, as I have only briefly suggested here, the criticism that consequentialism does not recognize the "normative separateness of persons" really amounts to the claim that consequentialism does not endow the doing/allowing distinction with intrinsic moral significance, no consequentialist should be troubled by it.

Notes

1 Given certain ways of stating the second and third objections, my theory doesn't answer them. Peter Vallentyne's statements of these criticisms of utilitarianism are "(2) it leaves agents inadequate moral freedom (judges too few actions morally permissible), and (3) it leaves no room for permissible actions that are morally better than other permitted actions." On my approach, *no* actions are permissible. However, since no actions are impermissible either, the spirit of the criticisms clearly doesn't apply.

2 I am concerned only with theories which are agent-neutral, and whose value theories are relatively fine-grained.

3 My apologies to the proponents of virtue ethics, the third-party candidate of ethical theories.

4 See, for example, Feinberg (1961).

5 Slote (1985: ch. 3) discusses this suggestion.

6 Though the approach of W. D. Ross might plausibly be interpreted in a scalar fashion.

7   I take the term 'scalar' from Slote (1985), who discusses scalar morality in his chapter 5.

8   It might be objected that maximizing utilitarianism does in fact give a scalar account of wrongness, if not of rightness. Some actions are closer to being right than are others, and so are less wrong. However, the claim that an action is closer to the best action than is another is quite consistent with the claim that it is no less wrong than the latter.

9   Norcross (1997a).

10 There can be reasons that are not necessarily motivating, e.g. prudential reasons. You may have a prudential reason to act in a certain way, be aware of the reason, and yet be not in the least motivated so to act. I am not here thinking of cases in which other motivations – moral, aesthetic, self-indulgent, and the like – simply overwhelm prudential motivations. In such cases you would still be motivated to act prudentially, but more motivated to act in other ways. If you simply didn't care about your own well-being, prudential reasons would not be in the least motivating. But someone who didn't care about her own well-being could still have, and even be aware of, prudential reasons. Similarly, if you are asked what is the sum of five and seven, you have a reason to reply 'twelve', but you may be not in the least motivated to do so, for you may not care about arithmetic truth, or any other truth. There may be reasons other than moral reasons that are necessarily motivating. For example, the belief that a particular action is the best way to satisfy one of your desires may provide a necessarily motivating reason to perform that action. The motivation may be outweighed by other motivations.

11 Slote (1985) points this out.

12 I have heard this objection from Daniel Howard-Snyder and Shelly Kagan.

13 The full story about what distinguishes consequentialism from deontology will have to be more complicated than this. It may, for example, incorporate the claim that the consequentialist ranking of states of affairs is not agent-centered. See Scheffler (1982) for a discussion of this notion. On the other hand, we may wish to maintain (as Peter Vallentyne does in his contribution to this volume) [see original reading] that an agent-relative value theory may be incorporated into a consequentialist structure to give a form of consequentialism. Whether we classify, for example, ethical egoism as a form of consequentialism or as an entirely different form of moral theory (or not as a moral theory at all) seems to me to be of very little interest.

14 For more discussion of these and other reasons see, for example, Howard-Snyder and Norcross (1993), Norcross (1997a; 2004).

15 Scanlon (1998) tries such a move. I critique it in Norcross (2002).

16 I leave the reader to fill in the details of this and other examples involving the endlessly fascinating inhabitants of Springfield.

17 For detailed discussion of both these points, see Norcross (1997b).

18 See, for example, Bennett (1995), Norcross (2003), Steinbock and Norcross (1994).

19 It may be possible to construct a consequentialist theory that is sensitive to this distinction (see Norcross 1995), but I know of no one who embraces such a theory.

References

Bennett, J. (1995). *The Act Itself*. Oxford: Oxford University Press.

Feinberg, J. (1961). "Supererogation and rules." *Ethics*, 71: 276–88.

Foot, P. (1984). "Killing and letting die." Repr. in Steinbock and Norcross (eds.), 280–89.

Howard-Snyder, F. and Norcross, A. (1993). "A consequentialist case for rejecting the right." *The Journal of Philosophical Research*, 18: 109–25.

Norcross, A. (1995). "Should utilitarianism accommodate moral dilemmas?" *Philosophical Studies*, 79(1): 59–85.

Norcross, A. (1997a). "Good and bad actions." *The Philosophical Review*, 106(1): 1–34.

Norcross, A. (1997b). "Comparing harms: headaches and human lives." *Philosophy and Public Affairs*, 26(2): 135–67.

Norcross, A. (2002). "Contractualism and aggregation." *Social Theory and Practice*, 28(2): 303–14.

Norcross, A. (2003). "Killing and letting die." In R. G. Frey and C. H. Wellman (eds.), *The Blackwell Companion to Applied Ethics*. Oxford: Blackwell.

Norcross, A. (2004). "Scalar act-utilitarianism." In H. West (ed.), *Blackwell Guide to Mill's Utilitarianism*. Oxford: Blackwell.

Rawls, J. (1971). *A Theory of Justice*. Cambridge, Mass.: Belknap Press of Harvard University Press.

Scanlon, T. M. (1998). *What We Owe to Each Other*. Cambridge, Mass.: Belknap Press of Harvard University Press.

Scheffler, S. (1982). *The Rejection of Consequentialism*. Oxford: Clarendon Press.

Sidgwick, H. (1981). *The Methods of Ethics*. 7th edn. Indianapolis, Ind.: Hackett.

Slote, M. (1985). *Common-sense Morality and Consequentialism*. Boston; Routledge and Kegan Paul.

Steinbock, B. and Norcross, A. (eds.) (1994). *Killing and Letting Die*. 2nd edn. New York: Fordham University Press.

Chapter 28

John M. Taurek

SHOULD THE NUMBERS COUNT?

WE HAVE resources for bestowing benefits and for preventing harms. But there are limitations. There are many people we are not in a position to help at all. That is one kind of limitation. But there is another kind of limitation we encounter. Often we must choose between bestowing benefits on certain people, or preventing certain harms from befalling them, and bestowing benefits on or preventing harms from befalling certain others. We cannot do both. The general question discussed here is whether we should, in such trade-off situations, consider the relative numbers of people involved as something in itself of significance in determining our course of action.[1] The conclusion I reach is that we should not. I approach this general question by focusing on a particular hypothetical case in which we find ourselves in a position of being able to prevent a certain harm from befalling one person or to prevent a like harm from befalling each of five others, but unable to spare all six from harm.

The situation is that I have a supply of some life-saving drug.[2] Six people will all certainly die if they are not treated with the drug. But one of the six requires all of the drug if he is to survive. Each of the other five requires only one-fifth of the drug. What ought I to do?

To many it seems obvious that in such cases, special considerations apart, one ought to save the greater number. I cannot accept this view. I believe that at least some of those who do accept it fail to appreciate the difficulty of reconciling their thinking here with other convictions they are inclined to hold with even greater tenacity. First, I want to delineate some of these difficulties. I hope that, in view of them, others might be brought to reflect more critically on the intuitions that underlie this position. I shall then present what seems to me a more appropriate and appealing way of viewing trade-off situations of the kind in question.

Those who think that I ought to distribute my drug in fifths to the five people usually qualify their position. They maintain that "other things being equal, or special considerations apart, one ought to save the greater number." What sort of special considerations to the contrary do they have in mind? What is being ruled out by the "other things being equal" clause?

One thing they have in mind, I think, is the possibility of special facts about the one person that would, in their view, make his death a far worse thing than one might otherwise have supposed. Perhaps he is close to discovering some wonder drug or is on the verge of negotiating a lasting peace in the world's perennial trouble spot. The idea is that it could happen that this one person's continued existence is in some way crucial to the welfare of an unusually large number of people. This would make his death a far worse thing in the minds of some than it would otherwise be. Of course, they also have in

mind the possibility that special facts about these five persons could make their deaths not nearly so bad a thing after all. They might be five driveling old people or five idiot infants, loved by no one. In light of such facts as these it may well be permissible, perhaps even obligatory in the view of some, to save the one wholesome person instead of the five others. So when people say, "other things being equal, one ought to save the greater number," they mean to rule out such special considerations as these. The thinking here is that, apart from some such considerations, the death of five innocent persons is a worse thing, a greater evil, a greater loss, than the death of one innocent person. Since I am in a position to prevent either of these bad things from happening, but not both, I am morally required to prevent the worst.

Such reasoning seems appealing to many. I find it difficult to understand and even more difficult to see how it is to be reconciled with certain other convictions widely shared by these same people. Suppose this one person, call him David, is someone I know and like, and the others are strangers to me. I might well give all of my drug to him. And I am inclined to think that were I to do so, I would not be acting immorally. I suspect that many share this view with me.

• • •

On the view in question, one is morally required to save the five instead of the one, other things being equal, because, other things being equal, it is a very much worse thing that these five innocent people should die than it is that this one should. But if this fact constitutes a compelling ground for a moral obligation to give the drug to these five rather than to this one, then I too shall have to acknowledge its moral force. The problem, then, is to explain, especially perhaps to these five people, how it is that merely because I know and like David and am unacquainted with them I can so easily escape the moral requirement to save their lives that would fall on most anyone else in my position. The only relevant consideration here is that I happen to like David more than I like any of them. Imagine my saying to them, "Admittedly, the facts are such that I would be morally obligated to give you this drug, if it didn't happen that I prefer to give it to him." The moral force of such facts must be feeble indeed to be overridden by an appeal as feeble as this.

Contrast this situation with almost any other in which we would be prepared to acknowledge the existence of grounds for a moral requirement to give the drug to these five people. Suppose, for example, that these five had contracted with me in advance to deliver this drug to them at this time and place. It would not seem likely that anyone would think that the fact that I would prefer to give it to someone else instead would alter in any way what I was morally required to do. But of course it might make it harder, psychologically, for me to do what I ought to do. Again, suppose that these five are American soldiers and I am an army doctor with what little is left of the issue of this drug. And let us suppose that this other person is someone I know and like but is a citizen of some other country. Would anyone imagine that the fact that I would prefer to use the drug to save this one person could somehow nullify or lift my obligation to distribute the drug to the five soldiers?

The point is this. Generally, when the facts are such that any impartial person would recognize a moral obligation to do something as important to people as giving this drug to these five would be to them, then an appeal to the fact that one happens to be partial to the interests of some others would do nothing to override the moral obligation. Yet this is the position of those who maintain that in this situation any impartial person would be *morally required* to distribute his drug in fifths to the five. But because I, personally, would prefer to give it to someone else, it is permissible for me to do so.[3]

I am inclined to think, then, that we should either agree that it would be wrong for me to save David in this situation or admit that there

are no grounds for a moral requirement on anyone, special obligations apart, to save the five instead of David. Now as I said earlier there are those who will take the view that I do wrong when I give preference to David in this situation. They may feel that what has been said so far only proves the point. So now I would like to say something in support of the opinion that it would be morally permissible for a person in such circumstances to save a friend rather than the five strangers.

Suppose the drug belongs to your friend David. It is his drug, his required dosage. Now there are these five strangers, strangers to David as well as to you. Would you try to persuade David to give his drug to these five people? Do you think you should? Suppose you were to try. How would you begin? You are asking him to give up his life so that each of the five others, all strangers to him, might continue to live.

Imagine trying to reason with David as you would, presumably, have reasoned with yourself were the drug yours. "David, to be sure it is a bad thing, a very bad thing, that you should die. But don't you see it is a far worse thing that these five people should die? Now you are in a position to prevent either of these bad things from happening. Unfortunately you cannot prevent them both. So you ought to insure that the worst thing doesn't happen."

Don't you think that David might demur? Isn't he likely to ask: "Worse for whom?" And it seems natural and relevant that he should continue to put his case in some such way as this: "It is a far worse thing for me that I should die than that they should. I allow that for each of them it would be a worse thing were they all to die while I continue to live than it would be were I to die and they to continue to live. Indeed I wouldn't ask, nor would I expect, any one of them to give up his life so that I, a perfect stranger, might continue to live mine. But why should you, or any one of them, expect me to give up my life so that each of them might continue to live his?"

I think David's question deserves an answer. What could there be about these strangers that might induce David to think it worth giving up his life so that they might continue to live theirs? The usual sort of utilitarian reasoning would be comical if it were not so outrageous. Imagine any one of these five entreating David, "Look here David. Here I am but one person. If you give me one-fifth of your drug I will continue to live. I am confident that I will garner over the long haul a net balance of pleasure over pain, happiness over misery. Admittedly, if this were all that would be realized by your death I should not expect that you would give up your life for it. I mean, it may not be unreasonable to think that you yourself, were you to continue to live, might succeed in realizing at least as favorable a balance of happiness. But here, don't you see, is a second person. If he continues to live he too will accumulate a nice balance of pleasure over pain. And here is yet a third, a fourth, and finally a fifth person. Now, we would not ask you to die to make possible the net happiness realized in the life of any one of us five. For you might well suppose that you could realize as much in your own lifetime. But it would be most unreasonable for you to think that you could realize in your one lifetime anything like as much happiness as we get when we add together our five distinct favorable balances."

Such reasoning coming from some disinterested outside party might be a little less contemptible, but surely not a bit less foolish. But if we recognize the absurdity of trying to sell David on the idea that it would be a worse thing were these five persons to die than it would be were he to die by suggesting he focus on the large sum of their added happinesses as compared to his own, just what kind of reasoning would sound less absurd? Is it less absurd to ask him to focus on the large sum of intrinsic value possessed by five human beings, quite apart from considerations of their happiness, as compared to the value of himself alone?

I cannot imagine that I could give David any reason why *he* should think it better that these five strangers should continue to live than that he should. In using his drug to preserve his own life he acts to preserve what is, understandably, more important to him. He values his own life more than he values any of theirs. This is, of course, not to say that he thinks he is more valuable, period, than any one of them, or than all of them taken together. (Whatever could such a remark mean?) Moreover, and this I would like to stress, in not giving his drug to these five people he does not wrong any of them. He violates no one's rights. None of these five has a legitimate claim on David's drug in this situation, and so the five together have no such claim. Were they to attack David and to take his drug, they would be murderers. Both you and David would be wholly within your rights to defend against any such attempt to deprive him of his drug.

Such, in any case, is my view. I hope that most people would agree with me. But if it is morally permissible for David in this situation to give himself all of his drug, why should it be morally impermissible for me to do the same? It is my drug. It is more important to me that David should continue to live than it is that these five strangers should. I value his life more than I value theirs. None of these five has any special claim to my drug in this situation. None of them can legitimately demand of me that I give him the drug instead of giving it to David. And so the five together have no such special claim. I violate no one's rights when I use my drug to save David's life. Were these five, realizing that I was about to give my drug to David, to attempt to take it from me, I would think myself wholly justified in resisting.

Thus far I have argued that, since it would not be morally impermissible for the one person, David, to use all of his drug to save himself instead of these five others, it cannot be morally impermissible for me, were the drug mine and given that I am under no special obligations to

any of these five, to use it all to save David instead of these other five. In so arguing I have committed myself to a view that may strike some as counterintuitive. On my view, if one party, A, must decide whether to spare another party, B, some loss or harm H, or to spare a third party, C, some loss or harm H′, it cannot be A's moral duty, special obligations apart, to spare C harm H′ unless it would be B's duty, in the absence of special obligations to the contrary, to spare C harm H′ if he could, even at the expense of suffering H himself. To put it another way, my thinking here is simply this. If it would be morally permissible for B to choose to spare himself a certain loss, H, instead of sparing another person, C, a loss, H′, in a situation where he cannot spare C and himself as well, then it must be permissible for someone else, not under any relevant special obligations to the contrary, to take B's perspective, that is, to choose to secure the outcome most favorable to B instead of the outcome most favorable to C, if he cannot secure what would be best for each.

The following kind of case might be raised as a counterexample. Many of us, perhaps most of us, might agree that were B somehow situated so that he could spare C the loss of his life, or spare himself the loss of an arm, but could not do both, it would not be morally required, special obligations apart, that he choose to spare C the loss of his life. "But," it will be asked, "suppose you are the one who must choose? You can either spare this person, C, the loss of his life, or spare B the loss of his arm. Even apart from any special obligations to C, wouldn't you acknowledge that you ought to spare C the loss of his life? Wouldn't it be wrong for you to spare B his loss and let C die?"

Well, I do not think it would be morally impermissible for me to spare B the loss of his arm in such a situation. What exactly would be the ground for such a moral requirement? I am to choose which of two possible outcomes is to be realized: in the one, B retains his arm intact and C dies; in the other, B loses his arm and C

does not die. If the choice were B's it would be permissible for him to choose the first outcome. But it is not permissible for me to make this same choice? Why exactly is this? By hypothesis, I am under no relevant special obligations in this situation. So what is the difference between B and me in virtue of which I am morally required to secure the outcome most favored by C, though B would not be? Unless it is for some reason morally impermissible for one person to take the same interest in another's welfare as he himself takes in it, it must be permissible for me, in the absence of special obligations to the contrary, to choose the outcome that is in B's best interest. And, of course, this is what I would do if B's welfare were more important to me than C's.

There may well come a point, however, at which the difference between what B stands to lose and C stands to lose is such that I would spare C his loss. But in just these situations I am inclined to think that even if the choice were B's he too should prefer that C be spared his loss. For some people such a point of difference may already have been reached in the case where B stands to lose an arm, while C stands to lose his life. There are profoundly important differences in attitude among people here that I do not know how to reconcile. I personally do not think that anyone should be moved, in the absence of special considerations, to spare me the loss of my life rather than sparing themselves the loss of an arm. Others seem to think that they should.

I suspect that many of those who see in the purported counterexample a forceful objection to my view are people who more than half believe that (ideally) they really should be prepared to spare me the loss of my life even at the expense of losing their arms. Yet they are doubtful that they could bring themselves to make such a choice were it actually to come to that. Sensing this about themselves they are understandably reluctant to openly place such a demand on another. However when they imagine themselves in the role of a third party,

who is not especially concerned about B, they feel less conflict about sparing C the loss of his life. They, after all, will not have to lose their arms. But if this is their thinking, then they are not raising a serious objection to the view I have taken.

Let me return now to a further discussion of the original trade-off situation. It is my conviction that were the drug David's to use, he would do nothing wrong, special obligations apart, were he to use it to save himself instead of giving it up to the five strangers. For the same reasons, I believe that were the drug mine and David someone I know and like, it would not be wrong of me, special obligations apart, to save him rather than the five strangers. And so I feel compelled to deny that any third party, relevant special obligations apart, would be *morally required* to save the five persons and let David die. So what do I think one should do in such a situation in the absence of any special concern for any of the parties involved?

First, let me suggest what I would do in many such cases. Here are six human beings. I can empathize with each of them. I would not like to see any of them die. But I cannot save everyone. Why not give each person an equal chance to survive? Perhaps I could flip a coin. Heads, I give my drug to these five. Tails, I give it to this one. In this way I give each of the six persons a fifty-fifty chance of surviving. Where such an option is open to me it would seem to best express my equal concern and respect for each person. Who among them could complain that I have done wrong? And on what grounds?[4]

The claim that one ought to save the many instead of the few was made to rest on the claim that, other things being equal, it is a worse thing that these five persons should die than that this one should. It is this evaluative judgment that I cannot accept. I do not wish to say in this situation that it is or would be a worse thing were these five persons to die and David to live than it is or would be were David to die and these five to continue to live. I do not wish to say this

unless I am prepared to qualify it by explaining to whom or for whom or relative to what purpose it is or would be a worse thing.

I grant that for each one of the five persons, it would be worse were David to survive and they to die than it would be if David were to die and the five to survive. But, of course, from David's perspective the matter is otherwise. For him it would be a worse thing were he to die. From my perspective, I am supposing in this situation that it does not really matter who lives and who dies. My situation is not worsened or bettered by either outcome. No doubt others will be affected differently by what happens. For those who love or need David it would be a better thing were the others to die. But for those especially attached to or dependent on one or the other of these five, it would be better were David to die and these five to live.

Some will be impatient with all this. They will say it is true, no doubt, but irrelevant. They will insist that I say what would be a worse (or a better) thing, period. It seems obvious to them that from the moral point of view, since there is nothing special about any of these six persons, it is a worse thing that these five should die while this one continues to live than for this one to die while these five continue to live. It is a worse thing, not necessarily for anyone in particular, or relative to anyone's particular ends, but just a worse thing in itself.

I cannot give a satisfactory account of the meaning of judgments of this kind. But there are important differences between them and those judgments which relativize the value ascribed to some particular person or group, purpose or end. When I judge of two possible outcomes that the one would be worse (or better) for this person or this group, I do not, typically, thereby express a preference between these outcomes. Typically, I do not feel constrained to admit that I or anyone *should* prefer the one outcome to the other. But when I evaluate outcomes from an impersonal perspective (perhaps we may say from a moral perspective), matters are importantly different. When I judge that it would be a worse thing, period, were this to happen than were that to happen, then I do, typically, thereby express a preference between these outcomes. Moreover, at the very least, I feel constrained to admit that I *should* have such a preference, even if I do not. It is a moral shortcoming not to prefer what is admittedly in itself a better thing to what is in itself a worse thing.

Hence, I cannot give such an impersonal evaluative judgment as the ground for a decision to give the drug to the five instead of to the one. I could not bring myself to say to this one person, "I give my drug to these five and let you die because, don't you see, it is a worse thing, a far worse thing, that they should die than that you should." I do not expect that David, or anyone in his position, should think it a better thing were he to die and these five others to survive than it would be were he to survive and they to die. I do not think him morally deficient in any way because he prefers the outcome in which he survives and the others die to the outcome in which they survive and he dies.

In a situation where the one person, David, is a friend of mine and the others strangers to me, I do have a preference for the one outcome as against the other, to me a natural and acceptable preference. But since I do not expect everyone to share such a preference I will not elevate its expression to the status of a universally binding evaluation. I do not say to the five strangers that I give all of my drug to my friend because it is a better thing in itself that he should survive than that they should. I do not believe any such thing. Rather, I simply explain that David is my friend. His survival is more important to me than theirs. I would expect them to understand this, provided they were members of a moral community acceptable to me, just as I would were our roles reversed. Further, in securing David's survival I violate no one's rights. No further justification of my action is needed, just as no further justification is needed in a situation where the drug belongs to the one person.

He need not, and plainly should not, give as the ground for his decision to use his drug to secure his own survival the judgment that it is better in itself that he should survive than that they should. Who could expect any of them to accept that? He need only point out, as if this really needed remarking, that it is more important to him that he survive than it is to him that they should. Furthermore, in thus securing his own survival he violates none of their rights. What more need be said?

In the trade-off situation as presently conceived, all six persons are strangers to me. I have no special affection for any one of them, no greater concern for one than for any of the others. Further, by hypothesis, my situation will be made neither worse nor better by either outcome. Any preference I might show, therefore, if it is not to be thought arbitrary, would require grounding. Of course this is precisely what an impersonal evaluative judgment of the kind discussed would do. It would provide a reason for the preference I show should I give the drug to the five. But for the reasons given, I cannot subscribe to such an evaluation of these outcomes. Hence, in this situation I have absolutely no reason for showing preference to them as against him, and no reason for showing preference to him as against them. Thus I am inclined to treat each person equally by giving each an equal chance to survive.

Yet I can imagine it will still be said, despite everything, "But surely the numbers must count for something." I can hear the incredulous tones: "Would you flip a coin were it a question of saving fifty persons or saving one? Surely in situations where the numbers are this disproportionate you must admit that one ought to save the many rather than the few or the one."

I would flip a coin even in such a case, special considerations apart. I cannot see how or why the mere addition of numbers should change anything. It seems to me that those who, in situations of the kind in question, would have me count the relative numbers of people involved as

something in itself of significance, would have me attach importance to human beings and what happens to them in merely the way I would to objects which I valued. If six objects are threatened by fire and I am in a position to retrieve the five in this room or the one in that room, but unable to get out all six, I would decide what to do in just the way I am told I should when it is human beings who are threatened. Each object will have a certain value in my eyes. If it happens that all six are of equal value, I will naturally preserve the many rather than the one. Why? Because the five objects are together five times more valuable in my eyes than the one.

But when I am moved to rescue human beings from harm in situations of the kind described, I cannot bring myself to think of them in just this way. I empathize with them. My concern for what happens to them is grounded chiefly in the realization that each of them is, as I would be in his place, terribly concerned about what happens to him. It is not my way to think of them as each having a certain *objective* value, determined however it is we determine the objective value of things, and then to make some estimate of the combined value of the five as against the one. If it were not for the fact that these objects were creatures much like me, for whom what happens to them is of great importance, I doubt that I would take much interest in their preservation. As merely intact objects they would mean very little to me, being, as such, nearly as common as toadstools. The loss of an arm of the *Pietà* means something to me not because the *Pietà* will miss it. But the loss of an arm of a creature like me means something to me only because I know he will miss it, just as I would miss mine. It is the loss *to this person* that I focus on. I lose nothing of value to me should he lose his arm. But if I have a concern for him, I shall wish he might be spared his loss.

And so it is in the original situation. I cannot but think of the situation in this way. For each of these six persons it is no doubt a terrible thing

to die. Each faces the loss of something among the things he values most. His loss means something to me only, or chiefly, because of what it means to him. It is the loss to the individual that matters to me, not the loss of the individual. But should any one of these five lose his life, his loss is no greater a loss to him because, as it happens, four others (or forty-nine others) lose theirs as well. And neither he nor anyone else loses anything of greater value to him than does David, should David lose his life. Five individuals each losing his life does not add up to anyone's experiencing a loss five times greater than the loss suffered by any one of the five.

If I gave my drug to the five persons and let David die I cannot see that I would thereby have preserved anyone from suffering a loss greater than that I let David suffer. And, similarly, were I to give my drug to David and let the five die I cannot see that I would thereby have allowed anyone to suffer a loss greater than the loss I spared David. Each person's potential loss has the same significance to me, only as a loss to that person alone. Because, by hypothesis, I have an equal concern for each person involved, I am moved to give each of them an equal chance to be spared his loss.

My way of thinking about these trade-off situations consists, essentially, in seriously considering what will be lost or suffered by this one person if I do not prevent it, and in comparing the significance of that *for him* with what would be lost or suffered by anyone else if I do not prevent it. This reflects a refusal to take seriously in these situations any notion of the sum of two persons' separate losses. To me this appears a quite natural extension of the way in which most would view analogous trade-off situations involving differential losses to those involved, indeed even most of those who find my treatment of the cases thus far described paradoxical. Perhaps then, in one last effort to persuade them, it may be helpful to think about a trade-off situation of this kind.

Suppose I am told that if you, a stranger to me, agree to submit to some pain of significant intensity I will be spared a lesser one. Special circumstances apart, I can see no reason whatever why you should be willing to make such a sacrifice. It would be cowardly of me to ask it of you. Now add a second person, also a stranger to you. Again we are told that if you volunteer to undergo this same considerable pain each of us will be spared a lesser one. I feel it would be no less contemptible of me to ask you to make such a sacrifice in this situation. There is no reason you should be willing to undergo such a pain to spare me mine. There is no reason you should be willing to undergo such a pain to spare this other person his. And that is all there is to it.

Now, adding still others to our number, not one of whom will suffer as much as you are asked to bear, will not change things for me. It ought not to change things for any of us. If not one of us can give you a good reason why you should be willing to undergo a greater suffering so that he might be spared a lesser one, then there is simply no good reason why you should be asked to suffer so that the group may be spared. Suffering is not additive in this way. The discomfort of each of a large number of individuals experiencing a minor headache does not add up to anyone's experiencing a migraine. In such a trade-off situation as this we are to compare your pain or your loss, not to our collective or total pain, whatever exactly that is supposed to be, but to what will be suffered or lost by *any given single one of us*.

Perhaps it would not be unseemly for a stranger who will suffer some great agony or terrible loss unless you willingly submit to some relatively minor pain to ask you to consider this carefully, to ask you to empathize with him in what he will have to go through. But to my way of thinking it would be contemptible for any one of us in this crowd to ask you to consider carefully, "not, of course, what I personally will have to suffer. None of us is thinking of himself here! But contemplate, if you will, what *we the*

group, will suffer. Think of the awful sum of pain that is in the balance here! There are so very many more of us." At best such thinking seems confused. Typically, I think, it is outrageous.

Yet, just such thinking is engaged in by those who, in situations of the kind described earlier, would be moved to a course of action by a *mere consideration* of the relative numbers of people involved. If the numbers should not be given any significance by those involved in these trade-off situations, why should they count for anyone? Suppose that I am in a position either to spare you your pain or to spare this large number of individuals each his lesser pain, but unable to spare both you and them. Why should I attach any significance to their numbers if none of those involved should? I cannot understand how I am supposed to add up their separate pains and attach significance to that alleged sum in a way that would be inappropriate were any of those involved to do it. If, by allowing you to suffer your pain, I do not see that I can thereby spare a single person any greater pain or, in this case, even as much pain, I do not see why calling my attention to the numbers should move me to spare them instead of you, any more than focusing on the numbers should move you to sacrifice for them collectively when you have no reason to sacrifice for them individually.

It is not my intention to argue that in this situation I ought to spare you rather than them just because your pain is "greater" than would be the pain of any one of them. Rather, I want to make it clear that in reaching a decision in such a case it is natural to focus on a comparison of the pain you will suffer, if I do not prevent it, with the pain that would be suffered by any given individual in this group, if I do not prevent it. I want to stress that it does not seem natural in such a case to attempt to add up their separate pains. I would like to combat the apparent tendency of some people to react to the thought of each of fifty individuals suffering a pain of some given intensity in the same way as they might to the thought of some individual suffering a pain many or fifty times more intense. I cannot but think that some such tendency is at work in the minds of those who attribute significance to the numbers in these trade-off situations.

In the original situation we were to imagine that I must choose between sparing David the loss of his life and sparing five others the loss of their lives. In making my decision I am not to compare his loss, on the one hand, to the collective or total loss to these five, on the other, whatever exactly that is supposed to be. Rather, I should compare what David stands to suffer or lose, if I do not prevent it, to what will be suffered or lost by any other person, if I do not prevent that. Calling my attention to the numbers should not move me to spare them instead of him, any more than focusing on the numbers should move him to sacrifice his life for the group when he has no reason to sacrifice for any individual in the group. The numbers, in themselves, simply do not count for me. I think they should not count for any of us.

Notes

I owe a large debt to Rita V. Lewis, whose views on the issues dealt with in this paper have had a pervasive influence on both its content and style. I should also like to thank Herbert Morris for helpful comments made on an earlier version of this essay.

1   The trade-off situations I am focusing on have relatively simple structures. They present us with three relevant options: (1) We may aid a certain person or group of persons. (2) We may aid an entirely different group of persons. (3) We may do nothing at all to aid anyone. (I exclude from consideration this last option, though I do not argue that doing nothing for anyone is impermissible. Whether, why or in what sense it is, are questions best left to another occasion.) Robert Schwartz has caused me some worries about trade-off situations that are as aptly styled as these simpler ones, and that involve different but overlapping groups of possible beneficiaries. For example, perhaps the exercise of one

option would bring aid to *A* but none to either *B* or *C*. A second option might bring aid to both *A* and *B* but none to *C*. Yet a third option might be available that would bring aid to *C* but none to either *A* or *B*. It will be seen that it is not completely obvious how one holding the views I present on the simpler trade-off situations would deal with this case and with cases of still greater complexity. After having caused me the worries, Schwartz had the decency to think out an approach to these decision problems that would appear compatible with my thinking about the simpler ones. But I fear that a discussion of these complications would obscure my main argument here, so I have avoided it.

2 This is the case described by Philippa Foot in her paper on "Abortion and the Doctrine of Double Effect," in *Moral Problems*, ed. James Rachels (New York, 1971).

3 There are a number of possible contortions that one might go through in an attempt to reconcile these views. I cannot consider them all here. What I am chiefly interested in stressing is that there are serious difficulties involved in any attempt to reconcile these positions. My hope is that, in view of these difficulties, those who would maintain the original position might be brought to reconsider with an open mind the alleged grounds for the moral requirement to save the greater number in cases where one is in fact impartial in one's concern for those involved.

4 After I had written this paper, my attention was called to Miss Anscombe's note of some years back on this case as put originally by Mrs. Foot. She too was impressed by the fact that in the event a person gave his drug to the one, none of the five others could complain that he had been wronged. Her note is entitled, "Who is Wronged?" *The Oxford Review*, no. 5, 1967.

Normative ethics: deontology

INTRODUCTION TO SECTION V

ALTHOUGH MANY PHILOSOPHERS take an act's rightness to depend entirely on its consequences, many others take this to depend, largely or entirely, on other factors. The term *deontological* (from the Greek, *deon*, for duty) will here be used to designate all such non-consequentialist theories, though it can also be used more narrowly.

The most influential deontological theory is Immanuel Kant's (Chapter 29). According to Kant, morality must be binding on everyone and must have an authority that is independent of anyone's desires. Kant believes that only one principle satisfies this requirement – he calls it *the categorical imperative* – but that that principle can be expressed in several ways. In one formulation, the categorical imperative tells us to "[a]ct only according to that maxim [i.e. that rule of conduct] by which you can at the same time will that it should become a universal law"; in another, it says "[a]ct so that you treat humanity, whether in your own person or in that of another, always as an end and never as a means only." Although they look very different, these formulas are connected at a deep level, and they require and forbid all the same acts. So, for example, when we make a deceptive promise to get what we want, we treat the person to whom we make it as a mere means. Also, and not coincidentally, we act on a maxim that cannot be a universal law; for if everyone made deceptive promises, then "no one would believe what was promised to him but would only laugh at any such assertion as vain pretense." According to Kant, it is only by adopting the categorical imperative, and by resisting any inclinations that conflict with it, that we express our nature as free and autonomous beings.

Kant's views are rich and complex, and his theory can be understood in more than one way. In Chapter 30, David Velleman develops an interpretation that is structured around Kant's claim that we can come to understand the contents of our obligations simply by coming to understand what being obligated *is*. Through a series of careful steps, Velleman unpacks the presuppositions that underlie the notion of duty – for example, that having a duty requires an ability to resist one's inclinations, and that we can have that ability only if we have principles saying that we have good reason to resist – and in so doing illuminates the connections between duty and universality. Velleman's essay can be read either as an unorthodox interpretation of Kant or as an original contribution to moral philosophy.

One common criticism of Kant is that his theory is overly rigid. Moreover, one important variant of this criticism is that if we may never lie or use coercion, then we cannot defend ourselves against others who *are* willing to lie, coerce, or otherwise act unjustly. This criticism is discussed, from very different points of view, both by Christine Korsgaard in Chapter 31 and by Rae Langton in Chapter 32.

Drawing on Kant's different formulations of the categorical imperative, Korsgaard argues that his theory has the resources to answer the criticism. In her view, the

formula of humanity, which states that we should treat all rational agents as ends in themselves, provides an ideal of conduct to which we should always aspire, but the formula of universality, which tells us to act only on maxims we can will to be universal, allows us to relax certain requirements in the actual imperfect world. She argues, for example, that although the maxim "lie when it serves your purposes" cannot be a universal law, the maxim "lie to those who wrongly think they have deceived you" *can* be a universal law. She reasons that even if everyone acted on that maxim, the unsuccessful deceiver would not know that you have seen through his deception, and so would not "laugh at your assertion as vain pretense." Thus, properly understood, Kant's theory does not leave us defenseless against evil.

Rae Langton reaches a related conclusion via a very different route. Quoting from an actual correspondence between Kant and one of his disciples, Maria Von Herbert, Langton tests Kant's theory against a dilemma that has its roots in social injustice. Von Herbert, despondent because her suitor rejected her after she confessed to lying about a previous involvement, had sought Kant's advice about whether to end her life. Kant's reply, in effect, was that she had done her duty and should take comfort in that. Langton argues that Kant wrongly elevates duty over a happy, fulfilling life. She argues, as well, that von Herbert only faced this choice because of an unjust social system in which "women, as things, as items in the sexual marketplace, have a market value that depends in part on whether they have been used." Although Kant himself thought it would be wrong for von Herbert to continue the lie, Langton maintains that his theory, which dictates respect for oneself, actually implies that "she may have had a duty to lie." A question for the reader to consider is what Korsgaard might say about this case.

Although Kantianism is the most prominent alternative to consequentialism, it is far from the only one. Two other broadly deontological approaches are, first, one which holds that the correct moral principles are (roughly) those to which reasonable persons would agree, and, second, one which denies that our moral obligations can be straightforwardly derived from any principles at all. The remaining essays in the current section include two representatives of each approach.

Because the first approach grounds our obligations in a certain sort of agreement or contract, it is known as *contractualism*. Importantly, the agreement is not one that anyone has made, but one that a reasonable person *would* make if asked to choose under fair conditions. In Chapter 33, John Rawls uses this strategy to justify principles to govern the structure of a society's basic institutions, while in Chapter 34, Thomas Scanlon employs it to justify principles to govern the conduct of individuals. According to Rawls, the appropriate choice situation is one in which the parties want to do as well as possible for themselves, but are ignorant of all facts – for example, about their levels of wealth, talents, race, or gender – that might enable them to tailor the principles to their advantage. Under these conditions, Rawls argues, the parties would choose principles dictating maximal equal liberty for all and allowing economic inequality only when it will benefit those who have least. Scanlon, by contrast, does not imagine the parties as choosing behind Rawls's "veil of ignorance," but simply asks, for each candidate principle, whether anyone who was affected by it could reasonably reject it in light of the burdens it imposes on him compared with the

benefits it provides to others. To be morally permissible, according to Scanlon, an act must be permitted by at least one system of principles that no one could reasonably reject. Moreover, because various classes of activities (for example, keeping agreements and providing aid) could be governed by more than one non-rejectable set of principles, an action that falls in one of these categories is only permissible if the sets of non-rejectable principles that allow it include one that the agent's society actually accepts.

One question that any deontological theory must face is how to handle conflicts of duty. If we have both a duty to keep our agreements and a duty to help others, then what should we do when helping someone means breaking a promise? One obvious possibility is to appeal to a higher-order principle which tells us which duty takes precedence. In Chapters 35 and 36, however, W. D. Ross and Jonathan Dancy both reject this approach. According to Ross, we have a number of irreducibly different basic duties, including not only fidelity and mutual aid, but also duties not to harm and duties of self-improvement, justice, and gratitude, but these are duties only in the sense that each one tells in favor of any act that satisfies it. Each is what Ross calls a *prima facie* duty − that is, a factor that "would be a duty proper if [the act] were not at the same time of another kind which is morally significant" − and each may have a different weight on different occasions. Because we have no principled way of establishing an ordering among these duties, Ross argues that our decisions about what, on balance, we ought to do, must be based on judgment rather than any kind of mechanical procedure.

Dancy takes Ross's position further in a number of ways. For one thing, whereas Ross speaks only of six prima facie duties, Dancy maintains that any number of considerations can tell for and against any action. For another, Dancy points out that such considerations can vary not only in strength but also in polarity: what is a reason for performing a given action in some contexts may actually be a reason against performing it in others. Most importantly, Dancy presents a number of subtle arguments in favor of what he calls *particularism*, the view that "the possibility of moral thought does not depend on the provision of a suitable supply of moral principles." In advancing these arguments, Dancy mounts a powerful challenge to one dominant aspect of contemporary moral thought.

Chapter 29

Immanuel Kant

MORALITY AND RATIONALITY

A. The good will

NOTHING in the world—indeed nothing even beyond the world—can possibly be conceived which could be called good without qualification except a *good will*. Intelligence, wit, judgment, and the other talents of the mind, however they may be named, or courage, resoluteness, and perseverance as qualities of temperament, are doubtless in many respects good and desirable. But they can become extremely bad and harmful if the will, which is to make use of these gifts of nature and which in its special constitution is called character, is not good. It is the same with the gifts of fortune, power, riches, honor, even health, general well-being, and the contentment with one's condition which is called happiness, make for pride and even arrogance if there is not a good will to correct their influence on the mind and on its principles of action so as to make it universally conformable to its end. It need hardly be mentioned that the sight of a being adorned with no feature of a pure and good will, yet enjoying uninterrupted prosperity, can never give pleasure to a rational impartial observer. Thus the good will seems to constitute the indispensable condition even of worthiness to be happy.

Some qualities seem to be conducive to this good will and can facilitate its action, but, in spite of that, they have no intrinsic unconditional worth. They rather presuppose a good will, which limits the high esteem which one otherwise rightly has for them and prevents their being held to be absolutely good. Moderation in emotions and passions, self-control, and calm deliberation not only are good in many respects but even seem to constitute a part of the inner worth of the person. But however unconditionally they were esteemed by the ancients, they are far from being good without qualification. For without the principle of a good will they can become extremely bad, and the coolness of a villain makes him not only far more dangerous but also more directly abominable in our eyes than he would have seemed without it.

The good will is not good because of what it effects or accomplishes or because of its adequacy to achieve some proposed end; it is good only because of its willing, i.e., it is good of itself. And, regarded for itself, it is to be esteemed incomparably higher than anything which could be brought about by it in favor of any inclination or even of the sum total of all inclinations. Even if it should happen that, by a particularly unfortunate fate or by the niggardly provision of a stepmotherly nature, this will should be wholly lacking in power to accomplish its purpose, and if even the greatest effort should not avail it to achieve anything of its end, and if there remained only the good will (not as a mere wish but as the summoning of all the means in our power), it would sparkle like a

jewel in its own right, as something that had its full worth in itself. Usefulness or fruitlessness can neither diminish nor augment this worth. Its usefulness would be only its setting, as it were, so as to enable us to handle it more conveniently in commerce or to attract the attention of those who are not yet connoisseurs, but not to recommend it to those who are experts or to determine its worth.

But there is something so strange in this idea of the absolute worth of the will alone, in which no account is taken of any use, that, notwithstanding the agreement even of common sense, the suspicion must arise that perhaps only high-flown fancy is its hidden basis, and that we may have misunderstood the purpose of nature in its appointment of reason as the ruler of our will. We shall therefore examine this idea from this point of view.

In the natural constitution of an organized being, i.e., one suitably adapted to life, we assume as an axiom that no organ will be found for any purpose which is not the fittest and best adapted to that purpose. Now if its preservation, its welfare—in a word, its happiness—were the real end of nature in a being having reason and will, then nature would have hit upon a very poor arrangement in appointing the reason of the creature to be the executor of this purpose. For all the actions which the creature has to perform with this intention, and the entire rule of its conduct, would be dictated much more exactly by instinct, and that end would be far more certainly attained by instinct than it ever could be by reason. And if, over and above this, reason should have been granted to the favored creature, it would have served only to let it contemplate the happy constitution of its nature, to admire it, to rejoice in it, and to be grateful for it to its beneficent cause. But reason would not have been given in order that the being should subject its faculty of desire to that weak and delusive guidance and to meddle with the purpose of nature. In a word, nature would have taken care that reason did not break forth into

practical use nor have the presumption, with its weak insight, to think out for itself the plan of happiness and the means of attaining it. Nature would have taken over not only the choice of ends but also that of the means, and with wise foresight she would have entrusted both to instinct alone.

And, in fact, we find that the more a cultivated reason deliberately devotes itself to the enjoyment of life and happiness, the more the man falls short of true contentment. From this fact there arises in many persons, if only they are candid enough to admit it, a certain degree of misology, hatred of reason. This is particularly the case with those who are most experienced in its use. After counting all the advantages which they draw—I will not say from the invention of the arts of common luxury—from the sciences (which in the end seem to them to be also a luxury of the understanding), they nevertheless find that they have actually brought more trouble on their shoulders instead of gaining in happiness; they finally envy, rather than despise, the common run of men who are better guided by mere natural instinct and who do not permit their reason much influence on their conduct. And we must at least admit that a morose attitude or ingratitude to the goodness with which the world is governed is by no means found always among those who temper or refute the boasting eulogies which are given of the advantages of happiness and contentment with which reason is supposed to supply us. Rather their judgment is based on the idea of another and far more worthy purpose of their existence for which, instead of happiness, their reason is properly intended, this purpose, therefore, being the supreme condition to which the private purposes of men must for the most part defer.

Reason is not, however, competent to guide the will safely with regard to its objects and the satisfaction of all our needs (which it in part multiplies), and to this end an innate instinct would have led with far more certainty. But

reason is given to us as a practical faculty, i.e., one which is meant to have an influence on the will. As nature has elsewhere distributed capacities suitable to the functions they are to perform, reason's proper function must be to produce a will good in itself and not one good merely as a means, for to the former reason is absolutely essential. This will must indeed not be the sole and complete good but the highest good and the condition of all others, even of the desire for happiness. In this case it is entirely compatible with the wisdom of nature that the cultivation of reason, which is required for the former unconditional purpose, at least in this life restricts in many ways—indeed can reduce to less than nothing—the achievement of the latter conditional purpose, happiness. For one perceives that nature here does not proceed unsuitably to its purpose, because reason, which recognizes its highest practical vocation in the establishment of a good will, is capable only of a contentment of its own kind, i.e., one that springs from the attainment of a purpose which is determined by reason, even though this injures the ends of inclination.

We have, then, to develop the concept of a will which is to be esteemed as good of itself without regard to anything else. It dwells already in the natural sound understanding and does not need so much to be taught as only to be brought to light. In the estimation of the total worth of our actions it always takes first place and is the condition of everything else. In order to show this, we shall take the concept of duty. It contains that of a good will, though with certain subjective restrictions and hindrances; but these are far from concealing it and making it unrecognizable, for they rather bring it out by contrast and make it shine forth all the brighter.

B. Acting from the motive of duty

I here omit all actions which are recognized as opposed to duty, even though they may be useful in one respect or another, for with these the question does not arise at all as to whether they may be carried out from duty, since they conflict with it. I also pass over the actions which are really in accordance with duty and to which one has no direct inclination, rather executing them because impelled to do so by another inclination. For it is easily decided whether an action in accord with duty is performed from duty or for some selfish purpose. It is far more difficult to note this difference when the action is in accordance with duty and, in addition, the subject has a direct inclination to do it. For example, it is in fact in accordance with duty that a dealer should not overcharge an inexperienced customer, and wherever there is much business the prudent merchant does not do so, having a fixed price for everyone, so that a child may buy of him as cheaply as any other. Thus the customer is honestly served. But this is far from sufficient to justify the belief that the merchant has behaved in this way from duty and principles of honesty. His own advantage required this behavior; but it cannot be assumed that over and above that he had a direct inclination to the purchaser and that, out of love, as it were, he gave none an advantage in price over another. Therefore the action was done neither from duty nor from direct inclination but only for a selfish purpose.

On the other hand, it is a duty to preserve one's life, and moreover everyone has a direct inclination to do so. But for that reason the often anxious care which most men take of it has no intrinsic worth, and the maxim of doing so has no moral import. They preserve their lives according to duty, but not from duty. But if adversities and hopeless sorrow completely take away the relish for life, if an unfortunate man, strong in soul, is indignant rather than despondent or dejected over his fate and wishes for death, and yet preserves his life without loving it and from neither inclination nor fear but from duty—then his maxim has a moral import.

To be kind where one can is duty, and there are, moreover, many persons so sympathetically

constituted that without any motive of vanity or selfishness they find an inner satisfaction in spreading joy, and rejoice in the contentment of others which they have made possible. But I say that, however dutiful and amiable it may be, that kind of action has no true moral worth. It is on a level with [actions arising from] other inclinations, such as the inclination to honor, which, if fortunately directed to what in fact accords with duty and is generally useful and thus honorable, deserve praise and encouragement but no esteem. For the maxim lacks the moral import of an action done not from inclination but from duty. But assume that the mind of that friend to mankind was clouded by a sorrow of his own which extinguished all sympathy with the lot of others and that he still had the power to benefit others in distress, but that their need left him untouched because he was preoccupied with his own need. And now supposed him to tear himself, unsolicited by inclination, out of this dead insensibility and to perform this action only from duty and without any inclination— then for the first time his action has genuine moral worth. Furthermore, if nature has put little sympathy in the heart of a man, and if he, though an honest man, is by temperament cold and indifferent to the sufferings of others, perhaps because he is provided with special gifts of patience and fortitude and expects or even requires that others should have the same—and such a man would certainly not be the meanest product of nature—would not he find in himself a source from which to give himself a far higher worth than he could have got by having a good-natured temperament? This is unquestionably true even though nature did not make him philanthropic, for it is just here that the worth of the character is brought out, which is morally and incomparably the highest of all: he is beneficent not from inclination but from duty.

To secure one's own happiness is at least indirectly a duty, for discontent with one's condition under pressure from many cares and amid unsatisfied wants could easily become a great temptation to transgress duties. But without any view to duty all men have the strongest and deepest inclination to happiness, because in this idea all inclinations are summed up. But the precept of happiness is often so formulated that it definitely thwarts some inclinations, and men can make no definite and certain concept of the sum of satisfaction of all inclinations which goes under the name of happiness. It is not to be wondered at, therefore, that a single inclination, definite as to what it promises and as to the time at which it can be satisfied, can outweigh a fluctuating idea, and that, for example, a man with the gout can choose to enjoy what he likes and to suffer what he may, because according to his calculations at least on this occasion he has not sacrificed the enjoyment of the present moment to a perhaps groundless expectation of a happiness supposed to lie in health. But even in this case, if the universal inclination to happiness did not determine his will, and if health were not at least for him a necessary factor in these calculations, there yet would remain, as in all other cases, a law that he ought to promote his happiness, not from inclination but from duty. Only from this law would his conduct have true moral worth.

It is in this way, undoubtedly, that we should understand those passages of Scripture which command us to love our neighbor and even our enemy, for love as an inclination cannot be commanded. But beneficence from duty, when no inclination impels it and even when it is opposed by a natural and unconquerable aversion, is practical love, not pathological love; it resides in the will and not in the propensities of feeling, in principles of action and not in tender sympathy; and it alone can be commanded.

[Thus the first proposition of morality is that to have moral worth an action must be done from duty.] The second proposition is: An action performed from duty does not have its moral worth in the purpose which is to be achieved through it but in the maxim by which it is

determined. Its moral value, therefore, does not depend on the realization of the object of the action but merely on the principle of volition by which the action is done, without any regard to the objects of the faculty of desire. From the preceding discussion it is clear that the purposes we may have for our actions and their effects as ends and incentives of the will cannot give the actions any unconditional and moral worth. Wherein, then, can this worth lie, if it is not in the will in relation to its hoped-for effect? It can lie nowhere else than in the principle of the will, irrespective of the ends which can lie realized by such action. For the will stands, as it were, at the crossroads halfway between its a priori principle which is formal and its a posteriori incentive which is material. Since it must be determined by something, if it is done from duty it must be determined by the formal principle of volition as such since every material principle has been withdrawn from it.

The third principle, as a consequence of the two preceding, I would express as follows: Duty is the necessity of an action executed from respect for law. I can certainly have an inclination to the object as an effect of the proposed action, but I can never have respect for it precisely because it is a mere effect and not an activity of a will. Similarly, I can have no respect for any inclination whatsoever, whether my own or that of another; in the former case I can at most approve of it and in the latter I can even love it, i.e., see it as favorable to my own advantage. But that which is connected with my will merely as ground and not as consequence, that which does not serve my inclination but overpowers it or at least excludes it from being considered in making a choice—in a word, law itself—can be an object of respect and thus a command. Now as an act from duty wholly excludes the influence of inclination and therewith every object of the will, nothing remains which can determine the will objectively except the law, and nothing subjectively except pure respect for this practical law. This subjective element is the maxim[1] that I

ought to follow such a law even if it thwarts all my inclinations.

Thus the moral worth of an action does not lie in the effect which is expected from it or in any principle of action which has to borrow its motive from this expected effect. For all these effects (agreeableness of my own condition, indeed even the promotion of the happiness of others) could be brought about through other causes and would not require the will of a rational being, while the highest and unconditional good can be found only in such a will. Therefore, the preeminent good can consist only in the conception of the law in itself (which can be present only in a rational being) so far as this conception and not the hoped-for effect is the determining ground of the will. This preeminent good, which we call moral, is already present in the person who acts according to this conception, and we do not have to look for it first in the result.[2]

C. The moral law

But what kind of a law can that be, the conception of which must determine the will without reference to the expected result? Under this condition alone the will can be called absolutely good without qualification. Since I have robbed the will of all impulses which could come to it from obedience to any law, nothing remains to serve as a principle of the will except universal conformity of its action to law as such. That is, I should never act in such a way that I could not also will that my maxim should be a universal law. Mere conformity to law as such (without assuming any particular law applicable to certain actions) serves as the principle of the will, and it must serve as such a principle if duty is not to be a vain delusion and chimerical concept. The common reason of mankind in its practical judgments is in perfect agreement with this and has this principle constantly in view.

Let the question, for example, be: May I, when in distress, make a promise with the

intention not to keep it? I easily distinguish the two meanings which the question can have, viz., whether it is prudent to make a false promise, or whether it conforms to my duty. Undoubtedly the former can often be the case, though I do see clearly that it is not sufficient merely to escape from the present difficulty by this expedient, but that I must consider whether inconveniences much greater than the present one may not later spring from this lie. Even with all my supposed cunning, the consequences cannot be so easily foreseen. Loss of credit might be far more disadvantageous than the misfortune I now seek to avoid, and it is hard to tell whether it might not be more prudent to act according to a universal maxim and to make it a habit not to promise anything without intending to fulfill it. But it is soon clear to me that such a maxim is based only on an apprehensive concern with consequences.

To be truthful from duty, however, is an entirely different thing from being truthful out of fear of disadvantageous consequences, for in the former case the concept of the action itself contains a law for me, while in the latter I must first look about to see what results for me may be connected with it. For to deviate from the principle of duty is certainly bad, but to be unfaithful to my maxim of prudence can sometimes be very advantageous to me, though it is certainly safe to abide by it. The shortest but most infallible way to find the answer to the question as to whether a deceitful promise is consistent with duty is to ask myself: Would I be content that my maxim (of extricating myself from difficulty by a false promise) should hold as a universal law for myself as well as for others? And could I say to myself that everyone may make a false promise when he is in a difficulty from which he otherwise cannot escape? I immediately see that I could will the lie but not a universal law to lie. For with such a law there would be no promises at all, inasmuch as it would be futile to make a pretense of my intention in regard to future actions to those who would not believe this pretense or—if they overhastily did so—who would pay me back in my own coin. Thus my maxim would necessarily destroy itself as soon as it was made a universal law.

D. Common morality and the need for philosophy

I do not, therefore, need any penetrating acuteness in order to discern what I have to do in order that my volition may be morally good. Inexperienced in the course of the world, incapable of being prepared for all its contingencies, I ask myself only: Can I will that my maxim become a universal law? If not, it must be rejected, not because of any disadvantage accruing to myself or even to others, but because it cannot enter as a principle into a possible universal legislation, and reason extorts from me an immediate respect for such legislation. I do not as yet discern on what it is grounded (a question the philosopher may investigate), but I at least understand that it is an estimation of the worth which far outweighs all the worth of whatever is recommended by the inclinations, and that the necessity of my actions from pure respect for the practical law constitutes duty. To duty every other motive must give place, because duty is the condition of a will good in itself, whose worth transcends everything.

Thus within the moral knowledge of common human reason we have attained its principle. To be sure, common human reason does not think of it abstractly in such a universal form, but it always has it in view and uses it as the standard of its judgments. It would be easy to show how common human reason, with this compass, knows well how to distinguish what is good, what is bad, and what is consistent or inconsistent with duty. Without in the least teaching common reason anything new, we need only to draw its attention to its own principle, in the manner of Socrates, thus showing that neither science nor philosophy is

needed in order to know what one has to do in order to be honest and good, and even wise and virtuous. We might have conjectured beforehand that the knowledge of what everyone is obliged to do and thus also to know would be within the reach of everyone, even the most ordinary man. Here we cannot but admire the great advantages which the practical faculty of judgment has over the theoretical in ordinary human understanding. In the theoretical, if ordinary reason ventures to go beyond the laws of experience and perceptions of the senses, it falls into sheer inconceivabilities and self-contradictions, or at least into a chaos of uncertainty, obscurity, and instability. In the practical, on the other hand, the power of judgment first shows itself to advantage when common understanding excludes all sensuous incentives from practical laws. It then becomes even subtle, quibbling with its own conscience or with other claims to what should be called right, or wishing to determine correctly for its own instruction the worth of certain actions. But the most remarkable thing about ordinary reason in its practical concern is that it may have as much hope as any philosopher of hitting the mark. In fact, it is almost more certain to do so than the philosopher, because he has no principle which the common understanding lacks, while his judgment is easily confused by a mass of irrelevant considerations, so that it easily turns aside from the correct way. Would it not, therefore, be wiser in moral matters to acquiesce in the common rational judgment, or at most to call in philosophy in order to make the system of morals more complete and comprehensible and its rules more convenient for use (especially in disputation) than to steer the common understanding from its happy simplicity in practical matters and to lead it through philosophy into a new path of inquiry and instruction?

Innocence is indeed a glorious thing, but, on the other hand, it is very sad that it cannot well maintain itself, being easily led astray. For this reason, even wisdom—which consists more in acting than in knowing—needs science, not to learn from it but to secure admission and permanence to its precepts. Man feels in himself a powerful counterpoise against all commands of duty which reason presents to him as so deserving of respect; this counterpoise is his needs and inclinations, the complete satisfaction of which he sums up under the name of happiness. Now reason issues inexorable commands without promising anything to the inclinations. It disregards, as it were, and holds in contempt those claims which are so impetuous and yet so plausible, and which will not allow themselves to be abolished by any command. From this a natural dialectic arises, i.e., a propensity to argue against the stern laws of duty and their validity, or at least to place their purity and strictness in doubt and, where possible, to make them more accordant with our wishes and inclinations. This is equivalent to corrupting them in their very foundations and destroying their dignity—a thing which even common practical reason cannot ultimately call good.

In this way common human reason is impelled to go outside its sphere and to take a step into the field of practical philosophy. But it is forced to do so not by any speculative need, which never occurs to it so long as it is satisfied to remain merely healthy reason; rather, it is so impelled on practical grounds in order to obtain information and clear instruction respecting the source of its principle and the correct determination of this principle in its opposition to the maxims which are based on need and inclination. It seeks this information in order to escape from the perplexity of opposing claims and to avoid the danger of losing all genuine moral principles through the equivocation in which it is easily involved. Thus, when practical common reason cultivates itself, a dialectic surreptitiously ensues which forces it to seek aid in philosophy, just as the same thing happens in the theoretical use of reason. In this case, as in the theoretical, it will find rest only in a thorough critical examination of our reason.

E. Acting according to the concept of law

In this study we do not advance merely from the common moral judgment (which here is very worthy of respect) to the philosophical, as this has already been done, but we advance by natural stages from a popular philosophy (which goes no further than it can grope by means of examples) to metaphysics (which is not held back by anything empirical and which, as it must measure out the entire scope of rational knowledge of this kind, reaches even Ideas, where examples fail us). In order to make this advance, we must follow and clearly present the practical faculty of reason from its universal rules of determination to the point where the concept of duty arises from it.

Everything in nature works according to laws. Only a rational being has the capacity of acting according to the conception of laws, i.e., according to principles. This capacity is will. Since reason is required for the derivation of actions from laws, will is nothing else than practical reason. If reason infallibly determines the will, the actions which such a being recognizes as objectively necessary are also subjectively necessary. That is, the will is a faculty of choosing only that which reason, independently of inclination, recognizes as practically necessary, i.e., as good. But if reason of itself does not sufficiently determine the will, and if the will is subjugated to subjective conditions (certain incentives) which do not always agree with objective conditions; in a word, if the will is not of itself in complete accord with reason (the actual case of men), then the actions which are recognized as objectively necessary are subjectively contingent, and the determination of such a will according to objective laws is constraint. That is, the relation of objective laws to a will which is not completely good is conceived as the determination of the will of a rational being by principles of reason to which this will is not by nature necessarily obedient.

The conception of an objective principle, so far as it constrains a will, is a command (of reason), and the formula of this command is called an *imperative*.

All imperatives are expressed by an "ought" and thereby indicate the relation of an objective law of reason to a will which is not in its subjective constitution necessarily determined by this law. This relation is that of constraint. Imperatives say that it would be good to do or to refrain from doing something, but they say it to a will which does not always do something simply because it is presented as a good thing to do. Practical good is what determines the will by means of the conception of reason and hence not by subjective causes but, rather, objectively, i.e., on grounds which are valid for every rational being as such. It is distinguished from the pleasant as that which has an influence on the will only by means of a sensation from merely subjective causes, which hold only for the senses of this or that person and not as a principle of reason which holds for everyone.

A perfectly good will, therefore, would be equally subject to objective laws (of the good), but it could not be conceived as constrained by them to act in accord with them, because, according to its own subjective constitution, it can be determined to act only through the conception of the good. Thus no imperatives hold for the divine will or, more generally, for a holy will. The "ought" is here out of place, for the volition of itself is necessarily in unison with the law. Therefore imperatives are only formulas expressing the relation of objective laws of volition in general to the subjective imperfection of the will of this or that rational being, e.g., the human will.

All imperatives command either hypothetically or categorically. The former present the practical necessity of a possible action as a means to achieving something else which one desires (or which one may possibly desire). The categorical imperative would be one which

presented an action as of itself objectively necessary, without regard to any other end.

Since every practical law presents a possible action as good and thus as necessary for a subject practically determinable by reason, all imperatives are formulas of the determination of action which is necessary by the principle of a will which is in any way good. If the action is good only as a means to something else, the imperative is hypothetical; but if it is thought of as good in itself, and hence as necessary in a will which of itself conforms to reason as the principle of this will, the imperative is categorical.

The imperative thus says what action possible to me would be good, and it presents the practical rule in relation to a will which does not forthwith perform an action simply because it is good, in part because the subject does not always know that the action is good and in part (when he does know it) because his maxims can still be opposed to the objective principles of practical reason.

The hypothetical imperative, therefore, says only that the action is good to some purpose, possible or actual. In the former case it is a problematical, in the latter an assertorical, practical principle. The categorical imperative, which declares the action to be of itself objectively necessary without making any reference to a purpose, i.e., without having any other end, holds as an apodictical (practical) principle.

• • •

F. How is the categorical imperative possible?

In attacking this problem, we will first inquire whether the mere concept of a categorical imperative does not also furnish the formula containing the proposition which alone can be a categorical imperative. For even when we know the formula of the imperative, to learn how such an absolute law is possible will require difficult and special labors which we shall postpone to the last section.

If I think of a hypothetical imperative as such, I do not know what it will contain until the condition is stated [under which it is an imperative]. But if I think of a categorical imperative, I know immediately what it contains. For since the imperative contains besides the law only the necessity that the maxim should accord with this law, while the law contains no condition to which it is restricted, there is nothing remaining in it except the universality of law as such to which the maxim of the action should conform; and in effect this conformity alone is represented as necessary by the imperative.

There is, therefore, only one categorical imperative. It is: Act only according to that maxim by which you can at the same time will that it should become a universal law.

Now if all imperatives of duty can be derived from this one imperative as a principle, we can at least show what we understand by the concept of duty and what it means, even though it remain undecided whether that which is called duty is an empty concept or not.

The universality of law according to which effects are produced constitutes what is properly called nature in the most general sense (as to form), i.e., the existence of things so far as it is determined by universal laws. [By analogy], then, the universal imperative of duty can be expressed as follows: Act as though the maxim of your action were by your will to become a universal law of nature.

We shall now enumerate some duties, adopting the usual division of them into duties to ourselves and to others and into perfect and imperfect duties.

1. A man who is reduced to despair by a series of evils feels a weariness with life but is still in possession of his reason sufficiently to ask whether it would not be contrary to his duty to himself to take his own life. Now he asks whether the maxim of his action could become a universal law of nature. His maxim, however, is: For love of myself, I make it my principle to shorten my life when by a longer duration it

threatens more evil than satisfaction. But it is questionable whether this principle of self-love could become a universal law of nature. One immediately sees a contradiction in a system of nature whose law would be to destroy life by the feeling whose special office is to impel the improvement of life. In this case it would not exist as nature; hence that maxim cannot obtain as a law of nature, and thus it wholly contradicts the supreme principle of all duty.

2. Another man finds himself forced by need to borrow money. He well knows that he will not be able to repay it, but he also sees that nothing will be loaned him if he does not firmly promise to repay it at a certain time. He desires to make such a promise, but he has enough conscience to ask himself whether it is not improper and opposed to duty to relieve his distress in such a way. Now, assuming he does decide to do so, the maxim of his action would be as follows: When I believe myself to be in need of money, I will borrow money and promise to repay it, although I know I shall never do so. Now this principle of self-love or of his own benefit may very well be compatible with his whole future welfare, but the question is whether it is right. He changes the pretension of self-love into a universal law and then puts the question: How would it be if my maxim became a universal law? He immediately sees that it could never hold as a universal law of nature and be consistent with itself; rather it must necessarily contradict itself. For the universality of a law which says that anyone who believes himself to be in need could promise what he pleased with the intention of not fulfilling it would make the promise itself and the end to be accomplished by it impossible; no one would believe what was promised to him but would only laugh at any such assertion as vain pretense.

3. A third finds in himself a talent which could, by means of some cultivation, make him in many respects a useful man. But he finds himself in comfortable circumstances and prefers indulgence in pleasure to troubling himself with broadening and improving his fortunate natural gifts. Now, however, let him ask whether his maxim of neglecting his gifts, besides agreeing with his propensity to idle amusement, agrees also with what is called duty. He sees that a system of nature could indeed exist in accordance with such a law, even though man (like the inhabitants of the South Sea Islands) should let his talents rust and resolve to devote his life merely to idleness, indulgence, and propagation—in a word, to pleasure. But he cannot possibly will that this should become a universal law of nature or that it should be implanted in us by a natural instinct. For, as a rational being, he necessarily wills that all his faculties should be developed, inasmuch as they are given to him for all sorts of possible purposes.

4. A fourth man, for whom things are going well, sees that others (whom he could help) have to struggle with great hardships, and he asks, "What concern of mine is it? Let each one be as happy as heaven wills, or as he can make himself; I will not take anything from him or even envy him; but to his welfare or to his assistance in time of need I have no desire to contribute." If such a way of thinking were a universal law of nature, certainly the human race could exist, and without doubt even better than in a state where everyone talks of sympathy and good will, or even exerts himself occasionally to practice them while, on the other hand, he cheats when he can and betrays or otherwise violates the rights of man. Now although it is possible that a universal law of nature according to that maxim could exist, it is nevertheless impossible to will that such a principle should hold everywhere as a law of nature. For a will which resolved this would conflict with itself, since instances can often arise in which he would need the love and sympathy of others, and in which he would have robbed himself, by such a law of nature springing from his own will, of all hope of the aid he desires.

The foregoing are a few of the many actual duties, or at least of duties we hold to be actual, whose derivation from the one stated principle is clear. We must be able to will that a maxim of our action become a universal law; this is the canon of the moral estimation of our action generally. Some actions are of such a nature that their maxim cannot even be thought as a universal law of nature without contradiction, far from it being possible that one could will that it should be such. In others this internal impossibility is not found, though it is still impossible to will that their maxim should be raised to the universality of a law of nature, because such a will would contradict itself. We easily see that the former maxim conflicts with the stricter or narrower (imprescriptible) duty, the latter with broader (meritorious) duty. Thus all duties, so far as the kind of obligation (not the object of their action) is concerned, have been completely exhibited by these examples in their dependence on the one principle.

When we observe ourselves in any transgression of a duty, we find that we do not actually will that our maxim should become a universal law. That is impossible for us; rather, the contrary of this maxim should remain as a law generally, and we only take the liberty of making an exception to it for ourselves or for the sake of our inclination, and for this one occasion. Consequently, if we weighed everything from one and the same standpoint, namely, reason, we would come upon a contradiction in our own will, viz., that a certain principle is objectively necessary as a universal law and yet subjectively does not hold universally but rather admits exceptions. However, since we regard our action at one time from the point of view of a will wholly conformable to reason and then from that of a will affected by inclinations, there is actually no contradiction, but rather an opposition of inclination to the precept of reason (*antagonismus*). In this the universality of the principle (*universalitas*) is changed into mere generality (*generalitas*), whereby the practical principle of reason meets the maxim halfway. Although this cannot be justified in our own impartial judgment, it does show that we actually acknowledge the validity of the categorical imperative and allow ourselves (with all respect to it) only a few exceptions which seem to us to be unimportant and forced upon us.

We have thus at least established that if duty is a concept which is to have significance and actual legislation for our actions, it can be expressed only in categorical imperatives and not at all in hypothetical ones. For every application of it we have also clearly exhibited the content of the categorical imperative which must contain the principle of all duty (if there is such). This is itself very much. But we are not yet advanced far enough to prove a priori that that kind of imperative really exists, that there is a practical law which of itself commands absolutely and without any incentives, and that obedience to this law is duty.

G. The ultimate worth of persons

[*We must now inquire how such a categorical imperative is possible.*]

With a view to attaining this, it is extremely important to remember that we must not let ourselves think that the reality of this principle can be derived from the particular constitution of human nature. For duty is practical unconditional necessity of action; it must, therefore, hold for all rational beings (to which alone an imperative can apply), and only for that reason can it be a law for all human wills. Whatever is derived from the particular natural situation of man as such, or from certain feelings and propensities, or even from a particular tendency of the human, reason which might not hold necessarily for the will of every rational being (if such a tendency is possible), can give a maxim valid for us but not a law; that is, it can give a subjective principle by which we might act only if we have the propensity and inclination, but not an objective principle by

which we would be directed to act even if all our propensity, inclination, and natural tendency were opposed to it. This is so far the case that the sublimity and intrinsic worth of the command is the better shown in a duty the fewer subjective causes there are for it and the more there are against it; the latter do not weaken the constraint of the law or diminish its validity.

Here we see philosophy brought to what is, in fact, a precarious position, which should be made fast even though it is supported by nothing in either heaven or earth. Here philosophy must show its purity as the absolute sustainer of its laws, and not as the herald of those which an implanted sense or who knows what tutelary nature whispers to it. Those may be better than no laws at all, but they can never afford fundamental principles, which reason alone dictates. These fundamental principles must originate entirely a priori and thereby obtain their commanding authority; they can expect nothing from the inclination of men but everything from the supremacy of the law and due respect for it. Otherwise they condemn man to self-contempt and inner abhorrence.

Thus everything empirical is not only wholly unworthy to be an ingredient in the principle of morality but is even highly prejudicial to the purity of moral practices themselves. For, in morals, the proper and inestimable worth of an absolutely good will consists precisely in the freedom of the principle of action from all influences from contingent grounds which only experience can furnish. We cannot too much or too often warn against the lax or even base manner of thought which seeks principles among empirical motives and laws, for human reason in its weariness is glad to rest on this pillow. In a dream of sweet illusions (in which it embraces not Juno but a cloud), it substitutes for morality a bastard patched up from limbs of very different parentage, which looks like anything one wishes to see in it, but not like virtue to anyone who has ever beheld her in her true form.

The question then is: Is it a necessary law for all rational beings that they should always judge their actions by such maxims as they themselves could will to serve as universal laws? If it is such a law, it must be connected (wholly a priori) with the concept of the will of a rational being as such. But in order to discover this connection we must, however reluctantly, take a step into metaphysics, although into a region of it different from speculative philosophy, i.e., into metaphysics of morals. In a practical philosophy it is not a question of assuming grounds for what happens but of assuming laws of what ought to happen even though it may never happen—that is to say, objective, practical laws. Hence in practical philosophy we need not inquire into the reasons why something pleases or displeases, how the pleasure of mere feeling differs from taste, and whether this is distinct from a general satisfaction of reason. Nor need we ask on what the feeling of pleasure or displeasure rests, how desires and inclinations arise, and how, finally, maxims arise from desires and inclination under the co-operation of reason. For all these matters belong to an empirical psychology, which would be the second part of physics if we consider it as philosophy of nature so far as it rests on empirical laws. But here it is a question of objectively practical laws and thus of the relation of a will to itself so far as it determines itself only by reason; for everything which has a relation to the empirical automatically falls away, because if reason of itself alone determines conduct it must necessarily do so a priori. The possibility of reason thus determining conduct must now be investigated.

The will is thought of as a faculty of determining itself to action in accordance with the conception of certain laws. Such a faculty can be found only in rational beings. That which serves the will as the objective ground of its self-determination is an end, and, if it is given by reason alone, it must hold alike for all rational beings. On the other hand, that which contains

the ground of the possibility of the action, whose result is an end, is called the means. The subjective ground of desire is the incentive, while the objective ground of volition is the motive. Thus arises the distinction between subjective ends, which rest on incentives, and objective ends, which depend on motives valid for every rational being. Practical principles are formal when they disregard all subjective ends; they are material when they have subjective ends, and thus certain incentives, as their basis. The ends which a rational being arbitrarily proposes to himself as consequences of his action are material ends and are without exception only relative, for only their relation to a particularly constituted faculty of desire in the subject gives them their worth. And this worth cannot, therefore, afford any universal principles for all rational beings or valid and necessary principles for every volition. That is, they cannot give rise to any practical laws. All these relative ends, therefore, are grounds for hypothetical imperatives only.

But suppose that there were something the existence of which in itself had absolute worth, something which, as an end in itself, could be a ground of definite laws. In it and only in it could lie the ground of a possible categorical imperative, i.e., of a practical law.

Now, I say, man and, in general, every rational being exists as an end in himself and not merely as a means to be arbitrarily used by this or that will. In all his actions, whether they are directed to himself or to other rational beings, he must always be regarded at the same time as an end. All objects of inclinations have only a conditional worth, for if the inclinations and the needs founded on them did not exist, their object would be without worth. The inclinations themselves as the sources of needs, however, are so lacking in absolute worth that the universal wish of every rational being must be indeed to free himself completely from them. Therefore, the worth of any objects to be obtained by our actions is at all times conditional. Beings whose existence does not depend on our will but on

nature, if they are not rational beings, have only a relative worth as means and are therefore called "things"; on the other hand, rational beings are designated "persons" because their nature indicates that they are ends in themselves, i.e., things which may not be used merely as means. Such a being is thus an object of respect and, so far, restricts all [arbitrary] choice. Such beings are not merely subjective ends whose existence as a result of our action has a worth for us, but are objective ends, i.e., beings whose existence in itself is an end. Such an end is one for which no other end can be substituted, to which these beings should serve merely as means. For, without them, nothing of absolute worth could be found, and if all worth is conditional and thus contingent, no supreme practical principle for reason could be found anywhere.

Thus if there is to be a supreme practical principle and a categorical imperative for the human will, it must be one that forms an objective principle of the will from the conception of that which is necessarily an end for everyone because it is an end in itself. Hence this objective principle can serve as a universal practical law. The ground of this principle is: rational nature exists as an end in itself. Man necessarily thinks of his own existence in this way; thus far it is a subjective principle of human actions. Also every other rational being thinks of his existence by means of the same rational ground which holds also for myself; thus it is at the same time an objective principle from which, as a supreme practical ground, it must be possible to derive all laws of the will. The practical imperative, therefore, is the following: Act so that you treat humanity, whether in your own person or in that of another, always as an end and never as a means only.

• • •

H. Moral agents as law-givers to themselves

If we now look back upon all previous attempts which have ever been undertaken to discover the

principle of morality, it is not to be wondered at that they all had to fail. Man was seen to be bound to laws by his duty, but it was not seen that he is subject only to his own, yet universal, legislation, and that he is only bound to act in accordance with his own will, which is, however, designed by nature to be a will giving universal laws. For if one thought of him as subject only to a law (whatever it may be), this necessarily implied some interest as a stimulus or compulsion to obedience because the law did not arise from his will. Rather, his will was constrained by something else according to a law to act in a certain way. By this strictly necessary consequence, however, all the labor of finding a supreme ground for duty was irrevocably lost, and one never arrived at duty but only at the necessity of action from a certain interest. This might be his own interest or that of another, but in either case the imperative always had to be conditional and could not at all serve as a moral command. This principle I will call the principle of *autonomy* of the will in contrast to all other principles which I accordingly count under heteronomy.

The concept of each rational being as a being that must regard itself as giving universal law through all the maxims of its will, so that it may judge itself and its actions from this standpoint, leads to a very fruitful concept, namely, that of a *realm of ends*.

By "realm" I understand the systematic union of different rational beings through common laws. Because laws determine ends with regard to their universal validity, if we abstract from the personal difference of rational beings and thus from all content of their private ends, we can think of a whole of all ends in systematic connection, a whole of rational beings as ends in themselves as well as of the particular ends which each may set for himself. This is a realm of ends, which is possible on the aforesaid principles. For all rational beings stand under the law that each of them should treat himself and all others never merely as means but in every case

also as an end in himself. Thus there arises a systematic union of rational beings through common objective laws. This is a realm which may be called a realm of ends (certainly only an ideal), because what these laws have in view is just the relation of these beings to each other as ends and means.

A rational being belongs to the realm of ends as a member when he gives universal laws in it while also himself subject to these laws. He belongs to it as sovereign when he, as legislating, is subject to the will of no other. The rational being must regard himself always as legislative in a realm of ends possible through the freedom of the will, whether he belongs to it as member or as sovereign. He cannot maintain the latter position merely through the maxims of his will but only when he is a completely independent being without need and with power adequate to his will.

Morality, therefore, consists in the relation of every action to that legislation through which alone a realm of ends is possible. This legislation, however, must be found in every rational being. It must be able to arise from his will, whose principle then is to take no action according to any maxim which would be inconsistent with its being a universal law and thus to act only so that the will through its maxims could regard itself at the same time as universally lawgiving. If now the maxims do not by their nature already necessarily conform to this objective principle of rational beings as universally lawgiving, the necessity of acting according to that principle is called practical constraint, i.e., duty. Duty pertains not to the sovereign in the realm of ends, but rather to each member, and to each in the same degree.

The practical necessity of acting according to this principle, i.e., duty, does not rest at all on feelings, impulses, and inclinations; it rests merely on the relation of rational beings to one another, in which the will of a rational being must always be regarded as legislative, for otherwise it could not be thought of as an

end in itself. Reason, therefore, relates every maxim of the will as giving universal laws to every other will and also to every action toward itself; it does so not for the sake of any other practical motive or future advantage but rather from the idea of the dignity of a rational being who obeys no law except that which he himself also gives.

In the realm of ends everything has either a *price* or a *dignity*. Whatever has a price can be replaced by something else as its equivalent; on the other hand, whatever is above all price, and therefore admits of no equivalent, has a dignity.

That which is related to general human inclinations and needs has a *market price*. That which, without presupposing any need, accords with a certain taste, i.e., with pleasure in the mere purposeless play of our faculties, has an *affective price*. But that which constituted the condition under which alone something can be an end in itself does not have mere relative worth, i.e., a price, but an intrinsic worth, i.e., *dignity*.

Now morality is the condition under which alone a rational being can be an end in itself, because only through it is it possible to be a legislative member in the realm of ends. Thus morality and humanity, so far as it is capable of morality, alone have dignity. Skill and diligence in work have a market value; wit, lively imagination, and humor have an affective price; but fidelity in promises and benevolence on principle (not from instinct) have intrinsic worth. Nature and likewise art contain nothing which could replace their lack, for their worth consists not in effects which flow from them, nor in advantage and utility which they procure; it consists only in intentions, i.e., maxims of the will which are ready to reveal themselves in this manner through actions even though success does not favor them. These actions need no recommendation from any subjective disposition or taste in order that they may be looked upon with immediate favor and satisfaction, nor do they have need of any immediate propensity or feeling directed to them. They exhibit the will

which performs them as the object of an immediate respect, since nothing but reason is required in order to impose them on the will. The will is not to be cajoled into them, for this, in the case of duties, would be a contradiction. This esteem lets the worth of such a turn of mind be recognized as dignity and puts it infinitely beyond any price, with which it cannot in the least be brought into competition or comparison without, as it were, violating its holiness.

And what is it that justifies the morally good disposition or virtue in making such lofty claims? Is it nothing less than the participation it affords the rational being in giving universal laws. He is thus fitted to be a member in a possible realm of ends to which his own nature already destined him. For, as an end in himself, he is destined to be legislative in the realm of ends, free from all laws of nature and obedient only to those which he himself gives. Accordingly, his maxims can belong to a universal legislation to which he is at the same time also subject. A thing has no worth other than that determined for it by the law. The legislation which determines all worth must therefore have a dignity, i.e., unconditional and incomparable worth. For the esteem which a rational being must have for it, only the word "respect" is a suitable expression. Autonomy is thus the basis of the dignity of both human nature and every rational nature.

The three aforementioned ways of presenting the principle of morality are fundamentally only so many formulas of the very same law, and each of them unites the others in itself.

• • •

Notes

1 A maxim is the subjective principle of volition. The objective principle (i.e., that which would serve all rational beings also subjectively as a practical principle if reason had full power over the faculty of desire) is the practical law.

2   It might be objected that I seek to take refuge in an obscure feeling behind the word "respect," instead of clearly resolving the question with a concept of reason. But though respect is a feeling, it is not one received through any [outer] influence but is self-wrought by a rational concept; thus it differs specifically from all feelings of the former kind which may be referred to inclination or fear. What I recognize directly as a law for myself I recognize with respect, which means merely the consciousness of the submission of my will to a law without the intervention of other influences on my mind. The direct determination of the will by the law and the consciousness of this determination is respect; thus respect can be regarded as the effect of the law on the subject and not as the cause of the law. Respect is properly the conception of a worth which thwarts my self-love. Thus it is regarded as an object neither of inclination nor of fear, though it has something analogous to both. The only object of respect is the law, and indeed only the law which we impose on ourselves and yet recognize as necessary in itself. As a law, we are subject to it without consulting self-love; as imposed on us by ourselves, it is a consequence of our will. In the former respect it is analogous to fear and in the latter to inclination. All respect for a person is only respect for the law (of righteousness, etc.) of which the person provides an example. Because we see the improvement of our talents as a duty, we think of a person of talents as the example of a law, as it were (the law that we should by practice become like him in his talents), and that constitutes our respect. All so-called moral interest consists solely in respect for the law.

Chapter 30

J. David Velleman

READING KANT'S *GROUNDWORK*[1]

The doctrine of moral worth

THE OVERALL strategy of Kant's moral theory is to derive the content of moral obligations from the very concept of an obligation. Kant thinks that we can figure out what morality requires by analyzing the very idea of being morally required to do something. Where I am using the word 'obligation' or 'requirement', Kant uses the German word *Pflicht*, which is usually translated into English as "duty" – an unfortunately antiquated term for what he has in mind. Sticking to Kant's terminology, however, we can say that the strategy is to figure out *what duty requires* by analyzing *what duty is*.

Kant says, "[W]e shall set before ourselves the concept of **duty**, which contains that of a good will though under certain subjective limitations and hindrances" (397, 10).[2] What he means is that the concept of duty is the concept of a requirement to do something whether or not we want to, indeed even if we want not to. When Kant speaks of "a good will . . . under certain subjective limitations and hindrances", he means a will that does something just because of being required to and despite wanting not to. Kant reasons that if we couldn't act that way, then we couldn't be required to act that way, and so we wouldn't have any duties at all. He concludes that if we have duties, then we must be capable of acting on them in opposition to our desires. (Where we speak of desires, Kant speaks of **inclinations**.)

Note that this conception of a good will is not what we ordinarily have in mind when using the term. In our minds, the term 'good will' connotes benevolence, as in the charitable organization of that name. For Kant, however, a good will is not a will that does good;[3] it's a will that does *right*. A will that does right by overcoming its inclinations is what Kant means by "a good will ... under certain subjective limitations and hindrances".

One of the most puzzling claims in Kant's *Groundwork* is that there is a special value in doing one's duty when one doesn't want to, a value that doesn't attach to doing one's duty when it's something one wants to do anyway. He draws a contrast between two shopkeepers, one of whom gives correct change because he wants to attract more customers, and the other of whom would prefer to shortchange his customers but doesn't solely because it's forbidden. The latter shopkeeper acts solely **from duty**, whereas the former acts **in accordance with duty** but from inclination. For this reason, according to Kant, the act of the latter shopkeeper has "moral worth", whereas the action of the former does not (397, 11).

Kant says that the moral worth of actions in which duty overcomes inclination is a value "higher" than that of actions in which duty and inclination coincide. Many readers take this statement to mean that acts of moral worth are better than or preferable to acts that satisfy both

duty and inclination – as if it would be better if we were averse to doing our duty. This interpretation cannot be right. In what sense, then, can the value of moral worth be "higher" than other values?

The answer begins with the fact that although Kant denies moral worth to acts that merely accord with duty, he does credit such acts with other modes of value. Speaking of a case in which someone satisfies his inclinations in doing his duty, Kant says that "an action of this kind . . . deserves praise and encouragement but not esteem" (398, 11).[4] In other words, the difference between acts done in accordance with duty but from inclination, on the one hand, and acts done from duty alone, on the other, is that they merit different kinds of appreciation – praise and encouragement in the former case, esteem in the latter. A clue to how these modes of appreciation differ can be found in Kant's statement that moral worth is not just the highest value but "incomparably the highest". Thus, esteem must regard its object as higher in value without regarding it as better, since 'better' is a term of evaluative comparison and so cannot apply to what is incomparable. The question is how a value can be higher than other values without being better.

Think of the value that siblings have in the eyes of their parents. The parents do not cherish any one of their children more than the others, but not because they compare the children to one another and find them equally valuable; rather, they value each child as special and hence as not to be rated or ranked against the others. Indeed, to rank their children in value would already be to devalue them, by disregarding their "specialness", which bars such comparisons. In other words, the parents regard each child as incomparably valuable. When Kant says that moral worth is incomparably higher than other values, he is saying that it is special, precisely in the sense that it must not be ranked against other values, not even as better. Kant uses the term 'esteem' for a mode of appreciation

that doesn't rank its objects but regards them as special; by contrast, praise and encouragement are comparative modes of appreciation.

The structure of the will

Kant says next that an action performed solely from duty "has its moral worth *not in the purpose* to be attained by it but in the maxim in accordance with which it is decided upon"; he also says that its worth "can lie nowhere else *than in the principle of the will*" (400, 130). As if to explain these statements, he continues: "For, the will stands between its *a priori* principle, which is formal, and its *a posteriori* incentive, which is material, as at a crossroads; and since it must still be determined by something, it must be determined by the formal principle of volition as such when an action is done from duty, where every material principle has been withdrawn from it" (*ibid.*). Unfortunately, this explanation seems to cast only shadow on the subject, not light.

Let's start with the concepts of an **incentive** and a **principle of volition**. An incentive is just something that we want, and our wanting it is what Kant calls an inclination. Kant describes incentives as *a posteriori* because they arise in experience. We learn by experience that something is attainable, and then we experience an inclination to attain it.

Kant says that the will stands between its *a posteriori* incentive and an *a priori* principle of volition. What is that? Kant never really explains, but here is a plausible hypothesis. When we find ourselves with an inclination, we consider whether it gives us a reason for acting. Suppose we know that in order to attain the object of our inclination – our incentive – we would have to take certain steps. We may then consider whether our inclination gives us sufficient reason to take those steps. What we are considering is whether there is a valid principle endorsing the inclination as a good enough reason for the action.[5]

Recall Kant's example. A shopkeeper wants to increase his profits without working any harder.

The only way to do so is to start shortchanging his customers. He asks himself whether a desire for easy gain is a good enough reason for shortchanging his customers. In asking this question, he is formulating a principle of reasoning, like this: "A desire for easy gain is a good enough reason to shortchange customers." Having formulated the principle, he is considering whether to base his decision on it – whether, that is, to make it the principle of his volition.

Kant says that a principle of volition is *a priori*. He means that it is not derived from experience. In that respect, it is like all other principles of reasoning. The principle of non-contradiction, for example, is not gleaned from experience. No observation or experiment tells us that the conjunction of a statement and its negation (*p and not-p*) must always be false: we know it without having to investigate. Similarly, it is *a priori* that a desire for an end is a reason for taking the means required for attaining it.[6] If the only means to easy gain is to shortchange one's customers, then it is *a priori* that a desire for the one is a reason for the other.

But is it also *a priori* that the desire is a *good enough* reason? That's the crucial question, to which we as yet don't know the answer. We'll come back to it shortly.

The passages quoted above contain one more concept that calls for explanation – the concept of a **maxim**. A maxim is the content of a possible or actual decision. The shopkeeper in our example is wondering whether to shortchange his customers in the interest of easy gain. "To shortchange my customers for easy gain" is the content of a decision that he is wondering whether to make, and the content of a possible decision is what Kant calls a maxim. If the shopkeeper decides to shortchange his customers for easy gain, then he will have "adopted" that maxim. Adopting a maxim is how the will decides to act.

Here, then, is a diagram of the "crossroads" at which the will of the shopkeeper stands:

A priori	THE WILL	A posteriori
Principle: "A desire for easy gain is good enough reason to shortchange customers."	Maxim: "to shortchange my customers in the interest of easy gain."	Inclination: desire for easy gain (an incentive).

The inclination on the right-hand side is presented to the will in experience. The will considers a maxim citing that inclination as a reason ("in the interest of easy gain") for taking an action ("to shortchange my customers"). Adopting the maxim would be rational only if the inclination was in fact a good enough reason for taking the action. And if it was, the agent would have an *a priori principle* to that effect, as shown on the left-hand side. In considering whether to adopt the maxim, then, the will is considering whether there is such a principle on the basis of which to adopt the maxim, as the will is inclined to do.

Assume for the sake of simplicity that a desire for easy gain is the shopkeeper's one and only inclination: it's all he wants in life, at least for the moment. Giving correct change to his customers will therefore entail acting contrary to every inclination he has. If he does give correct change, in that case, he will be performing an act of moral worth. (We are assuming that giving correct change is the right thing to do. It is the right thing, of course, but we don't yet know why it is, and so we can only assume so.)[7] But what reason can the shopkeeper have for giving correct change? The only inclination he has is a reason for giving *incorrect* change. He has no inclination that can be cited as a reason for doing the opposite. His reason, and the principle endorsing it, must therefore come from somewhere else. But from where?

The formula of universal law

In reply to this question, Kant says that in an act of moral worth, "there is left for the will nothing

that could determine it except objectively the *law* and subjectively *pure respect* for this practical law" (400–401, 13–14). The sudden appearance of law at this point is puzzling, but in order to solve the puzzle, we must press ahead to an even greater puzzle. Here it is:[8]

> But what kind of law can that be, the representation of which must determine the will, even without regard for the effect expected from it, in order for the will to be called good absolutely and without limitation? Since I have deprived the will of every impulse that could arise for it from obeying some law, nothing is left but the conformity of actions as such with universal law, which alone is to serve the will as its principle, that is *I ought never to act except in such a way that I could also will that my maxim should become a universal law.* (402, 14–15)

Read this passage as many times as you like, and it still won't make any sense. The only way to make sense of it is to think through the prior puzzle that it is meant to solve.

Let's revisit the shopkeeper as he considers shortchanging his customers. He considers this option by considering whether to adopt the maxim "to shortchange my customers in the interest of easy gain". Now, since we are assuming that it would be wrong to shortchange his customers, we must also assume that his inclination is not good enough reason for doing so. We must therefore assume that the agent is somehow blocked from finding an *a priori* principle endorsing his inclination as a sufficient reason. Why he is blocked remains to be explained. For the moment, however, the question is what principle of volition he can have instead, and what reason it can endorse. The principle we're looking for will be the one that determines him to perform an act of moral worth by giving correct change, out of duty and contrary to his one and only inclination. We're looking for a principle that endorses a reason for such an act. What reason can that be?

The answer is hiding in plain sight. The will stands at a crossroads between principle and inclination in the sense that the former indicates how to reason about the latter – how to reason, that is, about following the inclination on the opposite side of the crossroads. In most cases, the principle tells the agent that his inclination gives him good enough reason to act on it. But the agent in the present case has no such principle, and so he doesn't have sufficient reason for following his inclination. If he is to perform an act of moral worth – as must be possible if he is to have any duties at all – he will have to find a reason to resist his inclination instead. And what reason can the agent have to resist his inclination? He has no *inclination* to resist his inclination to give short change, since the latter is by hypothesis the only inclination he has. All he has in addition to that inclination, which doesn't provide sufficient reason, is an empty space where there could have been a principle saying that it does – the space where he seeks but doesn't find a principle endorsing his inclination as a good enough reason to act. So that empty space must be what gives him sufficient reason to resist. The only reason there can be for the agent to go against all of his inclinations is his very lack of a principle endorsing them as good enough reason to go along. The agent must therefore have a principle saying that he has a good enough reason to resist his inclination, consisting in the fact that he lacks a principle endorsing it as a good enough reason to follow it. In other words, the lack of a principle under which to follow his inclination must be a good enough reason to resist it.

Thus, when the shopkeeper lacks a principle endorsing his inclination as a good enough reason to give short change, he must gain access to a principle endorsing that very lack as a good enough reason not to give short change. And how can he *not* give short change, except by giving *correct* change? His principle must consequently say that the lack of a principle on which to go along with his inclination to shortchange

customers is a good enough reason to go against it, by giving them correct change instead.

This principle bears a resemblance to Kant's statement that "*I ought never to act except in such a way that I could also will that my maxim should become a universal law*". When the shopkeeper looks for a principle on the basis of which to adopt a maxim, he might be described as trying to turn the maxim into a law – for example, by turning the maxim "to shortchange my customers for easy gain" into the principle "A desire for easy gain is a good enough reason to shortchange customers." We don't yet see why he might fail in his attempt to turn his maxim into a law, but we have seen that if he fails, he will have found good enough reason not to adopt the maxim. Thus, he ought not to act on the maxim if he cannot turn it into a law, exactly as Kant says.[9] Kant thinks of himself at this point as having established a string of conditional conclusions:

i. If we have any duties, then we must be able to do what goes against our inclinations, just because it's required. (*Why? Because whatever duty requires, is required even if it goes against our inclinations, and going against our inclinations wouldn't be required if we were unable to do so.*)

ii. If we act in opposition to our inclinations, then we must have a principle saying that we have good enough reason to oppose them. (*Why? Because the will must operate on the basis of a principle about the inclinations on the opposite side of the crossroads.*)

iii. If we have a principle saying that we have good enough reason to go against our inclinations, then the reason must consist in the following fact: that we have no principle saying that we have good enough reason to go along with them. (*Why? Because the lack of the latter principle is all we have in addition to the inclinations themselves, which by hypothesis do not provide us with good enough reason to act.*)

Stringing these conditionals together, we get the conclusion that if we have any duties, then in some cases we must act on a principle of volition endorsing a good enough reason not to act on our inclinations, and that reason must consist in the fact that, in those cases, we have no principle endorsing our inclinations as good enough reason to act on them. This principle of volition must be the one on which we proceed when we go against all of our inclinations, as we do when our action has moral worth.

You may not have realized it, but we have now derived the content of our duty from the very concept of a duty. For we have discovered the one and only principle on which we can act against our inclinations, as duty sometimes requires us and must then enable us to do. When we act against our inclinations, what requires and enables us to do so is the principle that we have sufficient reason to resist inclinations for which we have no principle saying that they provide sufficient reason to act. So we have one and only one duty – that is, if we have any duties at all. Our duty is to act on a maxim only if we also have a principle endorsing the reason specified in that maxim as sufficient for the specified action.

Looking back on the argument thus far, we can see why Kant was so interested in acts of moral worth, in which duty must overcome all inclination. These acts are the ones in which duty must be the sole determinant of our will, with inclination playing no part. But if inclination plays no part in determining our will, then all there is to determine it is a principle of volition, which must therefore be the embodiment of our duty. And there turns out to be only one principle of volition that can determine our will to oppose all of our inclinations – namely, the principle of not acting on inclinations without a principle of volition endorsing them as good enough reason to act. That principle must therefore embody our one and only duty. I will therefore call it the *principle of duty* (though that's not Kant's term).

Many questions remain. Why does Kant say that we must be able to will that our maxim become universal law? And what does he mean in calling the presumptive law *universal*? Most importantly, why can't the shopkeeper will his easy-money maxim to become a universal law? Let's start with this last question.

Contradictions in conception

Earlier we considered the law of non-contradiction as a principle of reasoning. We said that it is *a priori* in the sense that it isn't gleaned from observation or experimentation or any other kind of experience. Its validity is obvious to us simply upon reflection.

What's more, the validity of this principle is obvious to any creature[10] that is capable of reasoning. A creature cannot reason unless it regards the law of non-contradiction as valid. A creature that had to learn the validity of this law from experience wouldn't be able to learn it at all, because learning it from experience would require reasoning that already treated the law as valid.

The fact that the validity of this principle is obvious to any reasoning creature is also obvious to any such creature. In short, everyone knows that the principle is valid, everyone knows that everyone knows it, and so on. The principle's validity is, as we say, *common knowledge* among creatures capable of reasoning. That's the sense in which the principle is universal.

Being universal in this sense is essential to the authority of principles and essential to their being *a priori*. Imagine that when you reflected on the law of non-contradiction, you saw it as valid for your reasoning but you weren't sure whether others would see it as valid for theirs. You would have to wonder whether you shouldn't be looking at the matter from their point-of-view instead of your own. For all you knew, your point-of-view on the validity of this principle might be like a literal, physical point-of-view, from which some things aren't visible

that are visible from other points-of-view, and vice versa. You would have to think: Maybe other people can see a problem with the principle that I can't see. The principle would lack authority over your reasoning, since you could always hope to get around it by resorting to a different point-of-view.

In reality, the principle of non-contradiction has authority in your eyes because you can see that there is no getting around it − no vantage point from which it doesn't hold, or from which there appears to be a vantage point from which it doesn't hold, and so on. It has authority, in short, because it is common knowledge among reasoners, yourself included.

Note that the universality of this principle is not represented in the principle's content. The principle of non-contradiction doesn't say that contradictions are false *for everyone*, or that *no one* should accept a contradiction, or that *anyone* who considers a contradiction should reject it. The principle is universal because everyone finds it valid for his own reasoning, and knows that everyone likewise finds it valid. It's universal, in other words, because its validity is common knowledge.

Principles of practical reasoning can be universal in the same sense. One example is the principle of instrumental reasoning, which says that having an end is a reason for adopting means to its attainment.[11] Everyone knows, and everyone knows that everyone knows, that the shopkeeper's end of easy gain is a reason for him to shortchange his customers, given that doing so is a necessary means to his end.

But the instrumental principle says only that having an end is *a* reason for adopting the means. The question remains, in any particular case, whether having the end is a *good enough* reason − good enough to act on, that is. What the shopkeeper needs is a principle to the effect that his end provides, not just a reason for giving short change, but a reason that's good enough.

Suppose that the latter were a universal principle whose validity was common knowledge

– evident to all, as was evident to all, and so on. In that case, it would be obvious to any profit-seeking shopkeeper that his desire for easy gain was a good enough reason for shortchanging his customers; and its being obvious to him would be obvious to all of his customers. But then all his customers would find it obvious that their own financial interests were good enough reason to count their change carefully – in which case, shortchanging them would be impossible. So if the end of easy gain were a good enough reason for the shopkeeper to shortchange his customers, then he would not be able to shortchange them, after all. Shortchanging customers and having good enough reason for doing so are incompatible.

We have now discovered why the easy-money maxim cannot become a principle of reasoning, or, in Kant's terms, a universal law. If there were such a principle, then the maxim would be a proposal to do something that was obviously impossible, and so the principle would be self-defeating. The shopkeeper who considers the easy-money maxim therefore finds himself without a viable principle, and he must fall back on the principle of duty, which tells him that not having a principle endorsing his inclination as a good enough reason *for* acting is itself a good enough reason *against*. Suppose I want you to think that I am the author of the leading text-book on Kantian ethics. Since there is no evidence of my having written any such book, I will just have to tell you that I have, in the hope that you will believe me. My maxim will then be as follows: "to tell people that I authored a book in order to get them to believe it". If my maxim became a universal law, it would read as follows: "A desire to get people to believe something is good enough reason for telling it to them."

If there were such a law, then everyone would know, and would know that everyone knew, that wanting to be credited with authorship of a book was good enough reason for claiming it. Yet if I claim something, and you understand what I say, then you will already know that I

want you to believe it. And if you also knew that this end, by itself, was good enough reason for making the claim, and that I knew it too, then you would know that I would still make the claim even if I didn't think it was true. In that case, you wouldn't believe me, and so making the claim wouldn't be a means of convincing you, after all. Thus, if the reason stated in my maxim were endorsed by a universal law, then it wouldn't *be* a reason for the proposed action. Wanting people to believe something would not really be a reason for claiming it if it were endorsed as a good enough reason by an *a priori* principle of reasoning.[12] Such a principle would therefore be self-defeating, and so there cannot be one. Lacking a viable principle on which to tell you this lie, I must fall back on the principle of duty, according to which I have good enough reason not to tell it.

Next suppose that a friend asks me to keep his valuables safe while he goes off to climb Mount Everest.[13] And suppose that he is killed in an avalanche, leaving no record of what he had deposited with me for safekeeping. Suppose, finally, that I would like to keep his valuables for myself, despite his having heirs to whom I could return them. My maxim would go like this: "to conceal the fact of a deposit in the interest of keeping it for myself". A universal law fashioned from this maxim would go like this: "Wanting to keep a deposit is good enough reason for concealing it."

If there were such a law, then everyone would know, and would know that everyone knew, that wanting to keep a deposit was good enough reason for concealing it. But then prospective depositors would know that their prospective trustees would have good enough reason for concealing their deposits, and so they would either make no deposits or leave a record of them with reliable proxies. If wanting to keep a deposit were good enough reason for concealing it, then concealing a deposit would be impossible, since no deposit would be made without being recorded. Again, a principle endorsing the

inclination as a sufficient reason would be self-defeating; hence there can be no such principle; and so I am left with the principle of duty, which tells me not to act without a principle.

When I find that I cannot fashion a maxim into a principle of reasoning, I am thrown back upon a principle of last resort, which says that not being able to fashion a principle on which to act is a good enough reason *not* to act.[14] As we have seen, this last-ditch principle embodies the one and only duty I have, if I have any duties at all. Oddly enough, my duty turns out to be a principle on which I act as a last resort, when I can find no other principle to act on.

That's why Kant draws such a sharp distinction between acting from duty alone and acting in accordance with duty but out of inclination. In the latter sort of action, my duty is out of sight, even out of mind. I have a principle endorsing my inclinations as good enough reasons, and I act on that principle, by acting for those reasons, without a second thought. Only when I cannot fashion a principle endorsing my inclinations do I fall back on duty as my principle of volition. Only then does my action have **moral content**, as Kant puts it (398, 11), for only then is my action informed by duty as its principle.[15] Otherwise, my action is not *about* morality at all.

You might think that even when I act on a principle endorsing my inclinations as providing sufficient reason, I am also acting partly from duty, which enjoins me never to act without such a principle. Not so. I am indeed acting in accordance with duty, because I have a principle that endorses my inclinations, and such a principle is just what duty requires me to have. But I do not act on the basis of duty's requirement until I find myself without a principle to endorse my inclinations, at which point the command of duty becomes my principle, on the basis of which I resist my inclinations. Provided that I have a principle endorsing those inclinations, however, I can follow them on the basis of that principle, without a thought for my duty.[16]

Of course, there must be something that induces me to make duty my principle when all else fails, but it cannot be duty itself. I don't have a duty to make duty my principle when all else fails, since I couldn't act from such a duty unless I had already made duty my principle. Why, then, do I make duty my principle when all else fails? We are not yet in a position to answer this question.

Note, in any case, that acts with moral content are always acts of omission, acts of not doing something because I cannot frame a principle endorsing my inclinations as providing good enough reason to do it. If a shopkeeper reluctantly gives correct change out of duty, he is, strictly speaking, not giving short change, as he is inclined to do; if I reluctantly inform my friend's heirs of his deposit, I am, strictly speaking, not following my inclination to conceal it. Acting from duty is always a matter of not acting from inclination, on the grounds that my inclinations do not give me good enough reason to act.

Willing the law

In each of these cases, the defeated reason really is a reason for acting. Wanting easy gain really is a reason for shortchanging customers; wanting people to believe something really is a reason for telling it to them; wanting to keep a deposit really is a reason for concealing it. Liars and crooks are not mistaken to treat these ends as reasons for lying and stealing. Their mistake is in treating these reasons as good enough.[17] Wanting people to believe something isn't a good enough reason for asserting it unless one believes it to be true. Wanting money or valuables isn't a good enough reason for holding on to them unless they don't belong to anyone else.

These extra conditions – that valuables don't belong to others, or that an assertion is believed to be true – are needed for the sufficiency of reasons based on the inclinations of these agents. Thus, an agent's deliberations are not complete

if he has merely surveyed his inclinations and balanced up the reasons they provide; he must also consider whether there are any additional conditions required for the sufficiency of those reasons.

How, then, can an agent tell when the reasons he has found are sufficient under the circumstances? Reasons for acting carry no seal of sufficiency guaranteeing that they're good enough. Nor do they carry on their face any indication of which further conditions, if any, would be needed to make them sufficient. It seems as if the agent must simply call a halt to his deliberations at some point and declare "Good enough!"

The necessity of calling a halt to deliberation also arises in the context of consequentialist theories, such as Utilitarianism, where the agent could in principle go on forever imagining alternative actions and their possible consequences. What's more, continuing this process or stopping it are themselves alternative actions whose consequences the agent could go on imagining forever. And the process of deliberating whether to stop deliberating about whether to stop deliberating — that process could go on forever, too. At some point, the agent must simply stop deliberating and act.

The problem is that whether to terminate deliberation appears to be arbitrary, because it cannot be based on deliberation. Consequentialists have no satisfactory solution to the problem. Kant thinks that he has one. We have already seen a part of Kant's solution. When one declares that reasons are good enough, one purports to state a principle of reasoning, which must be common knowledge among all reasoners. And some purported principles could not be common knowledge, since their being so would undermine them, by making the specified action impossible or canceling the specified reasons. If an agent proposes to perform that action for those reasons, he will encounter an obstacle to declaring them good enough, namely, that his declaration cannot embody a principle of reasoning, because such a principle would be self-defeating.

What about the remaining reasons for acting – the ones for which a declaration of their sufficiency *could* embody a principle of reasoning? It's not enough that there could be such a principle. The mere possibility of an *a priori* principle declaring these reasons to be good enough cannot make them so; there must actually be such a principle that is common knowledge among reasoners. As we have seen, however, reasons do not bear any obvious mark of sufficiency. How can there be common knowledge about something that isn't obvious?

Intractable as this problem may seem, it belongs to a class of problems that can in fact be solved.[18] Here is an analogous case. Suppose it's common knowledge that everyone in town wants to hold a demonstration, but no demonstration has been organized. Everyone wants to gather with the others in one place, but there has been no public announcement about where to gather. Each person in town will go wherever he thinks the others will go, but he knows that each of the others will be guided likewise, by where he thinks that others will go. How can anyone figure out where to go? What's needed is common knowledge of a gathering place, where everyone can go with confidence that everyone will go there.

Now suppose that there is a square in the middle of town. Obviously, that's where everyone will gather, but not because it has been publicly designated as the gathering place. Everyone will gather in the square simply because there is common knowledge that everyone wants to gather in one place and the square is the most salient place for a gathering. It doesn't have a "Gather Here" sign that everyone can see, but everyone can see that it sticks out, in the eyes of those wanting to gather, as if suggesting itself as site for their demonstration. Thus, common knowledge of a universal desire to converge, plus a uniquely salient point of convergence, can produce common knowledge that convergence will occur at that point.

In this example there is an ultimate, physical convergence, as demonstrators flock to the town

square. But there is also a prior, intellectual convergence consisting in common knowledge about where the physical convergence will occur. Demonstrators converge physically because they know that the square is where everyone will converge, that everyone knows it, and so on. So before they meet in the square, they have already reached a meeting of the minds about where they will meet.

Practical reasoners are in a somewhat similar situation – except that the ultimate convergence they seek is just a meeting of minds. Each reasoner aims to stop deliberating at a point where his reasons are endorsed as sufficient by a principle that is common knowledge. Like the townspeople who need a gathering point that's common knowledge, practical reasoners need principles of reasoning that are common knowledge; and like the townspeople, they need to arrive at common knowledge without any obvious signpost or signal.

Practical reasoners aren't hoping to converge on a single principle; rather, they are hoping that, with respect to any proposed principle, they will converge on either accepting or rejecting it. They must therefore hope that for any proposed principle, either acceptance or rejection will be the uniquely salient point of convergence. If either acceptance or rejection is the salient point of convergence for a given principle, then their converging on that point will already be common knowledge, given common knowledge of their need to converge, just as the salience of the town square already produces common knowledge that the square is where people will gather. And if it is common knowledge that reasoners will converge on accepting a principle, then the principle itself will be common knowledge, and so it will qualify as a genuine principle of reasoning; whereas if their converging on its rejection is common knowledge, then it won't qualify as a principle of reasoning.

How could acceptance or rejection of a principle achieve salience as a point of convergence

among reasoners? Well, rejection of a principle can be salient if convergence on acceptance would obviously be undesirable.[19]

Here is an analogy. Suppose that our imaginary town has both a courthouse square and a market square, equally salient as places for people to gather. And imagine that the market square is obviously too small for a demonstration: convergence on that square would cause a riot and a stampede. The market's obvious undesirability as a place for demonstrators to converge produces common knowledge that it won't be the site of the demonstration. In the same way, there can be principles of reasoning whose acceptance would be obviously undesirable as point for practical reasoners to converge.

An example will help.

Contradictions in the will

Suppose that you and I find ourselves in circumstances where each would lose something by cooperating with the other, no matter what the other does, but would lose even more from the other's failure to cooperate. The cooperation at issue might be helping to harvest one another's fields or (to invoke the relevant cliché) merely scratching one another's backs. In these circumstances, neither of us has anything to gain from helping the other, whether or not the other helps us, and both of us therefore face the prospect of the other's refusing to help. We might wish that we could escape the dilemma through an exchange of mutually dependent offers of the form "I will cooperate if you will." Unfortunately, the resulting agreement would generate a second-order dilemma, since each of us would lose by following through on the agreement, though he would lose even more from the other's refusal to follow through.

It is common knowledge between us that self-interest gives both of us reasons against cooperating. But are reasons of self-interest sufficient? Might self-interest be trumped by other considerations? We aren't sure, and each is

fairly sure that the other isn't sure, either, since self-interest doesn't bear a mark of sufficiency on its face. Hence neither of us is sure whether his reasons of self-interest are sufficient, not only because of his own doubts but also because of the doubts that he suspects are entertained by the other, which prevent the necessary principle from becoming common knowledge. Yet in order to find good enough reason for choosing one way or the other, we must have common knowledge as to what those reasons are; otherwise, nothing will count as good enough reason either way, given that what counts as good enough reason must be common knowledge.

Now, it is common knowledge between us that, in order to have sufficient reasons for choosing one way or the other, we need to arrive at common knowledge about what such reasons might be in circumstances like ours. And where there is common knowledge of a need to coordinate, coordination can occur, provided that there is a salient point of convergence whose salience as such is common knowledge. What is the salient point of convergence as to the reasons whether to cooperate in this case?

Well, self-interest gives each of us reason to prefer that, if we are to converge somewhere, then we converge on cooperating, since each will gain more from the other's cooperation than he will lose by his own. Refusing to cooperate is like the market square that would be an undesirable meeting place on which to converge, and whose undesirability as such is common knowledge. So cooperation is like the courthouse square – the most salient point of convergence as to what there is good enough reason to do in such a dilemma. Starting from a lack of common knowledge as to whether reasons of self-interest are trumped by other considerations, we arrive at common knowledge that they are, because it is common knowledge between us that we need to arrive at common knowledge on the question, and answering in the affirmative is the salient point of convergence.

Here is another example. As you walk down the street, you pass a beggar who asks for a dollar. You believe that he is genuinely in need, but you are saving up for a vacation and decide not to help him. Do you have a principle on which to make this decision?

Your maxim in this case is "to withhold help from a needy person in the interest of saving money". The corresponding principle would be "Wanting to save money is good enough reason for withholding help from someone in need." Is that principle common knowledge?

Well, it certainly could be common knowledge.[20] Refusing to help someone in need would still be possible if there were common knowledge that the desire to save was a good enough reason for such a refusal; and the desire would still be a reason for refusing even if its being a good enough reason were common knowledge. So the proposed principle wouldn't be self-defeating.

But whether it is a principle of reasoning isn't obvious. The desire to save money is obviously *a* reason for refusing to help someone in need, but it may or may not be good enough: there is nothing on the face of the desire to produce common knowledge that it is or is not a sufficient reason. You and your fellow practical reasoners are therefore on your own, as it were, when it comes to arriving at common knowledge on the subject. But like the townspeople who want to gather for a demonstration, you can reach a meeting of the minds on your own.

You and other reasoners need to have common knowledge as to whether a desire to save is good enough reason for refusing to help others in need. You therefore need to converge either on accepting or on rejecting a principle to that effect. So you must consider whether the salient point of convergence is to accept the principle or to reject it. But everyone would find it undesirable for there to be convergence on the principle that a desire to save was a good enough reason for refusing to help the needy. For everyone would see that such convergence

would entail that he himself would suffer in case of need.[21] No one would want everyone to converge on refusing to help him because of a desire to save.

The universal undesirability of converging on acceptance of this principle is obvious. Rejecting the principle is therefore salient as the point of convergence for agents who seek a meeting of the minds, just as avoiding the market square is salient for the townspeople who seek to gather for a demonstration. There is consequently common knowledge that the principle of stinginess fails to qualify as a principle of reasoning, and hence that the reason proposed in your maxim of stinginess is not a good enough reason, after all.[22]

There is one important difference between these Kantian examples and the example of converging on the town square. In that case, knowledge of the salient point of convergence depended on empirical information. In order to know that the town had a square, and that it was the obvious place to gather, you would need to have seen the town, or read about it, or learned about it in some other way. So what was common knowledge among the townspeople couldn't be common knowledge among all reasoners wherever they might live.

But a principle of reasoning that specifies what counts as a sufficient reason for acting must be common knowledge among all creatures capable of acting for reasons – that is, among all agents – just as the principle of logic must be common knowledge among all thinkers. That's why the Kantian cases rely only on concepts such as 'self-interest' and 'need', which any rational agent must have.

Thus, although you may be asking yourself whether to scratch the back of someone who has just scratched yours, or whether to put money into a beggar's cup, you needn't know anything about backs or cups in order to find the answer; indeed, if you do know anything about them, you mustn't rely on it. You must think about your situation in terms that any rational agent could understand. In the first case, the relevant description of your situation is simply that each of two people could gain something by refusing to act but would lose even more if the other refuses; in the second case, it's that an agent has needs that others could alleviate. The specific, real-world details are irrelevant.

The last few sections have offered an interpretation of Kant's notion that we must be able to will the principle of reasoning that corresponds to our maxim – or, as he puts it, that we must be able to will our maxim as a universal law. When Kant expresses this notion, he seems to be suggesting that an agent can will a principle of reasoning into existence – that an agent can conjure up such a principle by an act of will. This suggestion would be absurd. A principle of reasoning must be common knowledge among all reasoners, and no individual agent can create common knowledge just by willing it to exist.

But Kant doesn't mean to suggest otherwise. When he says that we must be able to will our maxim as a universal law, he means that practical reasoners must be willing and able to converge on the relevant principle, given the aim of common knowledge about the sufficiency of reasons. If convergence on the principle is neither impossible nor obviously undesirable, then the principle is salient as a point of convergence, agents therefore converge on it, and so it really is common knowledge. And we must act on principles that are common knowledge and that consequently qualify as genuine principles of reasoning.

Thus, we don't create common knowledge of a principle by an act of will; rather, a principle is common knowledge because we and other agents would be willing to converge on it in our search for common knowledge about reasons for acting. The will enters into creating principles of practical reasoning indirectly, by making them salient as points of spontaneous convergence among practical reasoners.

Freedom and autonomy

Let us now return to a question that we have three times postponed, namely, why we act on principles of reasoning in the first place, including, as a last resort, the principle of duty. In order to answer this question, we have to delve into Kant's theory of freedom and autonomy.

We are concrete beings whose behavior is governed by laws of physics, chemistry, biology, and psychology. Yet if we were no more than such beings, we wouldn't be agents. We would still move around, but the wind and waves move around, too. What distinguishes agents from the wind and waves, we think, is that agents choose how to act, and choosing how to act requires **freedom** from the laws governing concrete cause-and-effect.

Escaping the grip of cause-and-effect would not be enough for agency, however. Our behavior could escape from cause-and-effect simply by being random, but such chaotic behavior would not amount to action. In order to constitute action, our behavior has to be governed by *something*, though not by cause-and-effect; what it has to be governed by, in particular, is ourselves. In order to be agents, we have to be self-governing, or in Kant's term, **autonomous**.

Kant thinks that the only way for us to govern ourselves is literally to lay down laws for ourselves, as we do when we conform our behavior to principles, just as Kant describes in his account of the will. So in Kant's view, to be autonomous just is to have a will, and to have a will is to be autonomous. The wind and waves are not autonomous because they have no wills. We might say that they "have no wills of their own", but the last three words would be superfluous, since any will they had would *ipso facto* be their own, by virtue of constituting self-governance on their part.

Kant thinks that we can never know whether we really are free from concrete cause-and-effect. Even when we seem to be governing ourselves, we might still be under the control of causes beyond our ken. But Kant also thinks that

we aspire to be free, because we see freedom as a way of rising above the mundane empirical world. This aspiration is not a *desire* to be free but rather a form of *respect* for ourselves imagined *as* free. Freedom is not something that we want and pursue; it's something that we emulate, out of respect for the free selves that we might just be capable of being.

If freedom were something that we desired and pursued, then it would be just another incentive, and we would be back in the grip of empirical inclination. Under the sway of an external incentive, we would be **heteronomous**, in Kant's terminology. When we aspire to be free, however, there is nothing but, on the one hand, our actual aspiring selves and, on the other, the ideal selves that we aspire to be. We are the object of our own motive, and so from our perspective, at least, we are governed by nothing but ourselves.

Respect for our ideal selves is our motive for acting on principles of volition, including the principle of duty, when all others fail. We insist on having a principle before acting on our inclinations because we respect the free selves that we might become by doing so. We can't be sure that we will thereby succeed in being free, but we set our sights on freedom by doing what we can to embody it. That's why we act on principles – including, as a last resort, the principle of not acting without a principle.

In sum. The principle of duty tells us not to act on inclinations without a principle endorsing them as sufficient reasons for acting. That principle becomes the principle on which we act (or, as the case may be, refrain from acting) when we can find no principle endorsing our inclinations as reasons. We then act on that principle – as on other principles, when we can find them – out of respect for our own autonomy

An end in itself

Respect for myself cannot stop at my own freedom and autonomy. I can perhaps desire

autonomy just for myself, or like my own autonomy alone. But respect is an attitude toward a person as embodying some ideal; it is therefore an attitude ultimately toward the ideal, which other persons can embody as well. I cannot truly respect myself as autonomous unless I respect autonomy wherever the capacity for it appears, in others as well as myself; otherwise, I am merely desiring or liking my autonomy.

Thus, my motive for acting on principles, including the principle of duty, is an attitude toward autonomy as an ideal that can be embodied by anyone. Acting without respect for autonomy wherever it appears is therefore incompatible with the motive out of which I become autonomous myself and, when all else fails, give myself the principle of duty.

On the basis of such reasoning, or something like it, Kant concludes that I have a duty to respect autonomy wherever it appears.[23] Kant even claims that the duty to respect autonomy is just another form of the duty not to follow inclinations without a principle for doing so. Here I think that Kant cannot be right about the implications of his own theory. For if my reconstruction of the theory is correct, then respecting autonomy is not really a duty; it is rather the motive from which I act on principles, including the principle of duty.[24] Not to respect autonomy wherever it appears is thus to lack the only motive for doing our duty – a lack that constitutes a vice rather than a violation. According to the present interpretation, then, Kant's theory specifies both a rule, of not acting without a principle, and a virtue, of respecting autonomy, which requires not acting without a principle.

There are various cases in which the requirements of morality are better explained in terms of the virtue than in terms of the rule. These are cases in which there is no obvious point of convergence on the relevant principle of volition.

Consider paternalism, in which one agent is inclined to pre-empt another's choices for the latter's good. One agent may be inclined, for example, to deprive another of tempting but potentially harmful opportunities, or to withhold information about them. ("Don't tell her that he called: he's no good for her." "Don't offer to sell it to him: he can't afford it.") Is there an obvious point at which agents would converge on adopting or rejecting the principle of paternalism? Maybe not: some people would prefer to be deprived of dangerous opportunities, others would prefer to decide for themselves. So the principle of paternalism appears to be one for which there would be no convergence on the question of its validity.

Here the virtue of respecting autonomy can fill the gap. Respecting the person's autonomy entails allowing him/her to choose for herself, without paternalistic interference. Since creatures who act on principles do so out of respect for autonomy, there is after all a point of convergence among them on the principle of paternalism; for there is common knowledge that creatures who act on principles do so out of respect for autonomy, and will therefore converge on rejecting this one.

Conclusion

One last step and we'll be done.

You may recall that in deriving the content of our duties from the very concept of duty, we discovered what our duties would be *if we had any*. If there is anything to which the concept of duty applies, then we know what it must say. But is there such a thing?

Kant's answer is so remarkable that it's almost funny. His answer is, "It doesn't matter". Because we truly act only when we act on principles, and because acting on principles entails acting on the principle of duty when no other principle is available, we can only act *as* if that principle stands in the wings. So whether or not we have duties, we cannot but act as if we do. I would add: And so we do, after all.

This completes my reconstruction of Kant's moral theory as it is laid out in the *Groundwork*. It

is an absolutely audacious theory, aiming as it does to derive the content of our duties from the mere concept of a duty. In my view, the theory accounts for many of our deepest moral convictions. Whether it is true, or perhaps even the whole truth about morality, is a controversial question.

Notes

1 This essay supersedes my "Brief Introduction to Kantian Ethics", which appeared in my book *Self to Self: Selected Essays* (New York: Cambridge University Press, 2006), pp. 16–44. I hope that it is more faithful to both the letter and the spirit of the text – which is not to say that it is especially faithful to either one. My understanding of the *Groundwork* has profited from discussion with many graduate students who have attended my undergraduate Ethics course as teaching assistants or auditors, including: Jonny Cottrell, Mihailis Diamantis, Grace Helton, Shieva Kleinschmidt, Colin Marshall, Nick Riggle, Ang Tong; and especially Nandi Theunissen, who provided detailed written comments on an earlier draft, and Melis Erdur, who provided a key element of the interpretation (see note 14, below). Finally, I'm indebted to Kyla Ebels Duggan for comments on the penultimate draft.

2 References are, first, to the standard Academy Edition of the Groundwork and then to the Cambridge Texts edition, edited and translated by Mary Gregor (Cambridge: Cambridge University Press, 1977). Central Kantian terms are set in bold at their first appearance.

3 "A good will is not good because of what it effects or accomplishes, because of its fitness to attain some proposed end . . ." (394, 8).

4 The notion of esteem also appears here: "We have, then, to explicate the concept of a will that is to be esteemed in itself and that is good apart from any further purpose . . ." (397, 10). The notion that we have other attitudes of approval toward inclinations appears here: "I cannot have respect for an inclination as such, whether it is mine or that of another; I can at most in the first case approve it and in the second even love it . . ." (400, 13).

5 Kant himself does not use the concept of a reason for acting. Nevertheless, many contemporary interpreters regard the concept as essential to an understanding of Kant's view.

6 Some philosophers argue that desiring an end is not a reason for adopting the means to it. (See, for example, John Broome, "Wide or Narrow Scope?", *Mind* 116 [2007]: 359–70.) Rather, they argue, there is a rational requirement *either* to adopt the means *or* to give up the end. I disagree, although I must of course allow for cases in which giving up the end rationally dominates adopting the means. In my view, a desire for the end is indeed *a* reason for adopting the means, but it is not necessarily a *good enough* reason. There may be better reasons against adopting the means, and reasons against adopting the means for an end are also reasons for giving up the end. The difference between these views is that, in mine, there is a presumption in favor of adopting the means to a desired end, although that presumption can be overridden.

7 In making this assumption, we are following Kant's own method of proceeding from ordinary moral consciousness to moral philosophy. (See the title of Part I of the *Groundwork*.)

8 420–21, 31: "When I think of a *hypothetical* imperative in general I do not know beforehand what it will contain; I do not know this until I am given the condition. But when I think of a *categorical* imperative I know at once what it contains. For, since the imperative contains, beyond the law, only the necessity that the maxim be in conformity with this law, while the law contains no condition to which it would be limited, nothing is left with which the maxim of action is to conform but the universality of a law as such; and this conformity alone is what the imperative properly represents as necessary."

9 The formula "Act only on that maxim which you can at the same time will to be universal law" is called the Categorical Imperative. Kant and his interpreters spend much time explaining why it is an imperative and in what sense it is categorical. My interpretation skips over those issues, thus departing from both the text and its standard interpretations.

10 I find the word 'creature' less awkward than the word 'being'. Strictly speaking, however, a creature

is a *created* being, and Kant's theory applies also to beings that aren't created – for example, to God.

11 This principle roughly corresponds to Kant's Hypothetical Imperative. But it is not in imperatival form, and it uses the concept of a reason for acting – two respects in which it departs from the text and from standard interpretations. It is also controversial among contemporary theorists of practical reasoning. See note 6, above.

12 Having discovered that my maxim cannot be fashioned into a universal principle, I might try to revise it. I might say, "Oh, I don't care whether you *believe* what I'm saying; I just like the sound of it, and you happen to be nearby." I now have a maxim that can be universalized. But I have taken a clearly illegitimate step. I have revised my maxim in order to get around the fact that it can't be universalized; and I have done so by trying to believe something that I know to be untrue. This step has a maxim of its own, which cannot be universalized.

13 This example is adapted from one that appears, not in the *Groundwork*, but in Kant's *Critique of Practical Reason* (27, 27). See also Kant's essay "On the Proverb: That May be True in Theory, But Is of No Practical Use", in *Perpetual Peace and Other Essays*, trans. Ted Humphrey (Indianapolis: Hackett Publishing, 1983, 61–92, pp. 69–70). It is significant in that the example cannot be interpreted as relying on the consequences of a universal practice, since the practice in this case would be one of concealment that would never be discovered.

14 The main idea of this section is due to Melis Erdur. It constitutes a significant departure from standard interpretations of Kant, according to which the Categorical Imperative is always present, at least implicitly, in a moral agent's practical reasoning. According to Erdur's interpretation, the Imperative comes into play only when the agent's inclinations must be resisted for the sake of duty – hence only when it provides the basis for an action of moral worth. In the present interpretation, the Imperative then comes into play as a principle of volition, here described as the "principle of last resort". What is always present in an agent's practical reasoning, rather than the Categorical Imperative, is the agent's respect for his own autonomy, which

moves him to act on principles of reasoning rather than merely on inclinations. (See the sections titled "Autonomy" and "An End in Itself", below.)

15 Note that the German phrase *Moralischer Wert* can be translated "moral significance": actions performed on the principle of duty have moral significance, precisely because they have moral content.

16 This element of the interpretation begins to answer an objection that some commentators have raised to Kant's theory. Their objection is that the theory requires an agent always to have at least one eye on his duty, thereby entertaining "one thought too many". (The phrase comes from Bernard Williams, "Persons, Character and Morality", in *Moral Luck: Philosophical Papers 1973–1980* [Cambridge: Cambridge University Press 1981], p. 119.) Under the present interpretation, duty does not come into view until it is needed to restrain the agent from following his inclinations. Of course, it remains to be explained why the principle of duty, or any ordinary principle, enters into the agent's thinking, to begin with. That explanation will be provided in the sections titled "Autonomy" and "An End in Itself", below.

17 In the following sections, Kant's notion that agents "will the law" is interpreted in terms of what might be called the "sufficiency clause" in principles of volition. According to this interpretation, agents do not decide what counts as a reason, but they do decide whether their proposed reasons are "good enough" for their proposed action: they decide that their reasons are good enough by terminating deliberation, which is something that they must simply do. This interpretation of "willing the law" is non-standard, and there is no direct evidence for it in the text.

18 In what follows, "willing the law" is interpreted as a matter of terminating deliberation by declaring one's reasons to be good enough, where that declaration qualifies as a principle of reasoning – hence a law – because it is common knowledge among reasoners. How such a declaration can be common knowledge is then explained in terms of a co-ordination problem among reasoners who seek common knowledge about when reasons are good enough. And the *willing* involved in willing the law is taken to consist in the *willingness* of reasoners to converge on some coordination

points rather than others. This interpretation has virtually no support in the text, but it does manage to reconstruct many features of Kant's view – for example, his notion of a Kingdom of Ends.

19 If the principle would be self-defeating, then all of this reasoning about convergence is unecessary, since there cannot be a self-defeating principle.

20 424, 33: "Some actions are so constituted that their maxim cannot even be *thought* without contradiction as a universal law of nature, far less could one *will* that it *should* become such. In the case of others that inner impossibility is indeed not to be found, but it is still impossible to *will* that their maxim be raised to the universality of a law of nature because such a will would contradict itself."

21 See also 415, 26: "There is . . . *one* end that can be presupposed as actual in the case of all rational beings . . . and therefore one purpose that they not merely *could* have but that we can safely presuppose that they all actually *do have* by a natural necessity, and that purpose is *happiness*."

22 You might have a somewhat weaker maxim of stinginess, for which the corresponding principle would not be undesirable as a point of convergence. It's the maxim "in the interest of saving money, to do only my fair share of charity". If the corresponding principle were common knowledge, then everyone would judge himself to have sufficient reason for refusing to give, but only after he had given his fair share. And if everyone thought he had reason to stop giving only at that point, then no one would be left in need. (Leave aside for present purposes what counts as a "fair share".)

So is it common knowledge that a desire to save money is a good enough reason to do no more than one's fair share of charity? That principle could be common knowledge without undermining itself; and its being common knowledge would not be undesirable. Hence rejecting the

principle isn't salient as a point of convergence. But what about accepting it? Surely, there are cases in which a universal desire to converge is frustrated by the lack of a salient point. (What if the town had no central square?)

Practical reasoning is not such a case. Principles of reasoning are proposed for the sake of endorsing inclinations as providing good enough reason to act. Everyone wants to follow his inclinations, conditionally on their providing sufficient reason for doing so. Accepting principles that endorse inclinations is therefore the salient point of convergence, by default, barring conditions that shift salience to rejecting them. When practical reasoners seek common knowledge about the sufficiency of reasons, accepting them as sufficient is the salient point on which to converge.

23 428–29, 37–38. See also 431, 39: "[T]he ground of all practical lawgiving lies (in accordance with the first principle) *objectively in the rule* and the form of universality which makes it fit to be a law . . .; *subjectively*, however, it lies in the *end*; but the subject of all ends is every rational being as an end in itself (in accordance with the second principle)". . . . And 437–38, 45: "The principle, so act with reference to every rational being (yourself and others) that in your maxim it holds at the same time as an end in itself, is thus at bottom the same as the basic principle, act on a maxim that at the same time contains in itself its own universal validity for every rational being."

24 436, 43–44: "All maxims have, namely, (1) a *form*, which consists in universality; and in this respect the formula of the moral imperative is expressed thus: that maxims must be chosen as if they were to hold as universal laws of nature; (2) a *matter*, namely an end, and in this respect the formula says that a rational being, as an end by its nature and hence as an end in itself, must in every maxim serve as the limiting condition of all merely relative and arbitrary ends."

Chapter 31

Christine M. Korsgaard

THE RIGHT TO LIE: KANT ON DEALING WITH EVIL

ONE OF THE great difficulties with Kant's moral philosophy is that it seems to imply that our moral obligations leave us powerless in the face of evil. Kant's theory sets a high ideal of conduct and tells us to live up to that ideal regardless of what other persons are doing. The results may be very bad. But Kant says that the law "remains in full force, because it commands categorically" (G, 438–39/57).[1] The most well-known example of this "rigorism," as it is sometimes called, concerns Kant's views on our duty to tell the truth.

In two passages in his ethical writings, Kant seems to endorse the following pair of claims about this duty: first, one must never under any circumstances or for any purpose tell a lie; second, if one does tell a lie one is responsible for all the consequences that ensue, even if they were completely unforeseeable.

One of the two passages appears in the *Metaphysical Principles of Virtue*. There Kant classifies lying as a violation of a perfect duty to oneself. In one of the casuistical questions, a servant, under instructions, tells a visitor the lie that his master is not at home. His master, meanwhile, sneaks off and commits a crime, which would have been prevented by the watchman sent to arrest him. Kant says:

> Upon whom ... does the blame fall? To be sure, also upon the servant, who here violated a duty to himself by lying, the consequence

of which will now be imputed to him by his own conscience. (*MMV*, 431/93)

The other passage is the infamous one about the murderer at the door from the essay, "On a Supposed Right to Lie from Altruistic Motives." Here Kant's claims are more extreme, for he says that the liar may be held legally as well as ethically responsible for the consequences, and the series of coincidences he imagines is even more fantastic:

> After you have honestly answered the murderer's question as to whether his intended victim is at home, it may be that he has slipped out so that he does not come in the way of the murderer, and thus that the murder may not be committed. But if you had lied and said he was not at home when he had really gone out without your knowing it, and if the murderer had then met him as he went away and murdered him, you might justly be accused as the cause of his death. For if you had told the truth as far as you knew it, perhaps the murderer might have been apprehended by the neighbors while he searched the house and thus the deed might have been prevented. (*SRL*, 427/348)

Kant's readers differ about whether Kant's moral philosophy commits him to the claims he makes in these passages. Unsympathetic readers are

The right to lie: Kant on dealing with evil 361

inclined to take them as evidence of the horrifying conclusions to which Kant was led by his notion that the necessity in duty is rational necessity—as if Kant were clinging to a logical point in the teeth of moral decency. Such readers take these conclusions as a defeat for Kant's ethics, or for ethical rationalism generally; or they take Kant to have confused principles which are merely general in their application and *prima facie* in their truth with absolute and universal laws. Sympathetic readers are likely to argue that Kant here mistook the implications of his own theory, and to try to show that, by careful construction and accurate testing of the maxim on which this liar acts, Kant's conclusions can be blocked by his own procedures.

Sympathetic and unsympathetic readers alike have focused their attention on the implications of the first formulation of the categorical imperative, the Formula of Universal Law. The *Foundations of the Metaphysics of Morals* contains two other sets of terms in which the categorical imperative is formulated: the treatment of humanity as an end in itself, and autonomy, or legislative membership in a Kingdom of Ends. My treatment of the issue falls into three parts. First, I want to argue that Kant's defenders are right in thinking that, when the case is treated under the Formula of Universal Law, this particular lie can be shown to be permissible. Second, I want to argue that when the case is treated from the perspective provided by the Formulas of Humanity and the Kingdom of Ends, it becomes clear why Kant is committed to the view that lying is wrong in every case. But from this perspective we see that Kant's rigorism about lying is not the result of a misplaced love of consistency or legalistic thinking. Instead, it comes from an attractive ideal of human relations which is the basis of his ethical system. If Kant is wrong in his conclusion about lying to the murderer at the door, it is for the interesting and important reason that morality itself sometimes allows or even requires us to do something that from an ideal perspective is wrong.

The case does not impugn Kant's ethics as an *ideal* system. Instead, it shows that we need special principles for dealing with evil. My third aim is to discuss the structure that an ethical system must have in order to accommodate such special principles.

Universal law

The Formula of Universal Law tells us never to act on a maxim that we could not at the same time will to be a universal law. A maxim which cannot even be conceived as a universal law without contradiction is in violation of a strict and perfect duty, one which assigns us a particular action or omission. A maxim which cannot be willed as universal law without contradicting the will is in violation of a broad and imperfect duty, one which assigns us an end, but does not tell us what or how much we should do toward it. Maxims of lying are violations of perfect duty, and so are supposed to be the kind that cannot be conceived without contradiction when universalized.

The sense in which the universalization of an immoral maxim is supposed to "contradict" itself is a matter of controversy. On my reading, which I will not defend here, the contradiction in question is a "practical" one: the universalized maxim contradicts itself when the efficacy of the action as a method of achieving its purpose would be undermined by its universal practice.[2] So, to use Kant's example, the point against false promising as a method of getting ready cash is that if everyone attempted to use false promising as a method of getting ready cash, false promising would no longer *work* as a method of getting ready cash, since, as Kant says, "no one would believe what was promised to him but would only laugh at any such assertion as vain pretense" (G, 422/40).

Thus the test question will be: could this action be the universal method of achieving this purpose? Now when we consider lying in general, it looks as if it could not be the universal

method of doing anything. For lies are usually efficacious in achieving their purposes because they deceive, but if they were universally practiced they would not deceive. We believe what is said to us in a given context because most of the time people in that context say what they really think or intend. In contexts in which people usually say false things—for example, when telling stories that are jokes—we are not deceived. If a story that is a joke and is false counts as a lie, we can say that a lie in this case is not wrong, because the universal practice of lying in the context of jokes does not interfere with the *purpose* of jokes, which is to amuse and does not depend on deception. But in most cases lying falls squarely into the category of the sort of action Kant considers wrong: actions whose efficacy depends upon the fact that most people do not engage in them, and which therefore can only be performed by someone who makes an exception of himself (G, 424/42).

When we try to apply this test to the case of the murderer at the door, however, we run into a difficulty. The difficulty derives from the fact that there is probably already deception in the case. If murderers standardly came to the door and said: "I wish to murder your friend—is he here in your house?" then perhaps the universal practice of lying in order to keep a murderer from his victim would not work. If everyone lied in these circumstances the murderer would be aware of that fact and would not be deceived by your answer. But the murderer is not likely to do this, or, in any event, this is not how I shall imagine the case. A murderer who expects to conduct his business by asking questions must suppose that you do not know who he is and what he has in mind.[3] If these are the circumstances, and we try to ascertain whether there could be a universal practice of lying in these circumstances, the answer appears to be yes. The lie will be efficacious even if universally practiced. But the reason it will be efficacious is rather odd: it is because the murderer supposes you do not know what circumstances you are

in—that is, that you do not know you are addressing a murderer—and so does not conclude from the fact that people in those circumstances always lie that *you* will lie.

The same point can be made readily using Kant's publicity criterion (PP, 381–83/129–31). Can we announce in advance our intention of lying to murderers without, as Kant says, vitiating our own purposes by publishing our maxims (PP, 383/131)? Again the answer is yes. It does not matter if you say publicly that you will lie in such a situation, for the murderer supposes that you do not know you are in that situation.[4]

These reflections might lead us to believe, then, that Kant was wrong in thinking that it is never all right to lie. It is permissible to lie to deceivers in order to counteract the intended results of their deceptions, for the maxim of lying to a deceiver is universalizable. The deceiver has, so to speak, placed himself in a morally unprotected position by his own deception. He has created a situation which universalization cannot reach,

Humanity

When we apply the Formula of Humanity, however, the argument against lying that results applies to any lie whatever. The formula runs:

> Act so that you treat humanity, whether in your own person or in that of another, always as an end and never as a means only. (G, 429/47)

In order to use this formula for casuistical purposes, we need to specify what counts as treating humanity as an end. "Humanity" is used by Kant specifically to refer to the capacity to determine ends through rational choice (G, 437/56; MMV, 392/50). Imperfect duties arise from the obligation to make the exercise, preservation, and development of this capacity itself an end. The perfect duties—that is, the duties of

justice, and, in the realm of ethics, the duties of respect—arise from the obligation to make each human being's capacity for autonomous choice the condition of the value of every other end.

In his treatment of the lying promise case under the Formula of Humanity, Kant makes the following comments:

> For he whom I want to use for my own purposes by means of such a promise cannot possibly assent to my mode of acting against him and cannot contain the end of this action in himself . . . he who transgresses the rights of men intends to make use of the persons of others merely as means, without considering that as rational beings, they must always be esteemed at the same time as ends, i.e., only as beings who must be able to contain in themselves the end of the very same action. (G, 429–30/48)

In these passages, Kant uses two expressions that are the key to understanding the derivation of perfect duties to others from the Formula of Humanity. One is that the other person "cannot possibly assent to my mode of acting toward him" and the second is that the other person cannot "contain the end of this action in himself." These phrases provide us with a test for perfect duties to others: an action is contrary to perfect duty if it is not possible for the other to assent to it or to hold its end.

It is important to see that these phrases do not mean simply that the other person *does not* or *would not* assent to the transaction or that she does not happen to have the same end I do, but strictly that she *cannot* do so: that something makes it impossible. If what we cannot assent to means merely what we are likely to be annoyed by, the test will be subjective and the claim that the person does not assent to being used as a means will sometimes be false. The object you steal from me may be the gift I intended for you, and we may both have been motivated by the desire that you should have it. And I may care about

you too much or too little to be annoyed by the theft. For all that, this must be a clear case of your using me as a mere means.[5]

So it must not be merely that your victim will not like the way you propose to act, that this is psychologically unlikely, but that something makes it impossible for her to assent to it. Similarly, it must be argued that something makes it impossible for her to hold the end of the very same action. Kant never spells out why it is impossible, but it is not difficult to see what he has in mind.

People cannot *assent* to a way of acting when they are given no chance to do so. The most obvious instance of this is when coercion is used. But it is also true of deception: the victim of the false promise cannot assent to it because he doesn't know it is what he is being offered. But even when the victim of such conduct does happen to know what is going on, there is a sense in which he cannot assent to it. Suppose, for example, that you come to me and ask to borrow some money, falsely promising to pay it back next week, and suppose that by some chance I know perfectly well that your promise is a lie. Suppose also that I have the same end you do, in the sense that I want you to have the money, so that I turn the money over to you anyway. Now here I have the same end that you do, and I tolerate your attempts to deceive me to the extent that they do not prevent my giving you the money. Even in this case I cannot really assent to the transaction *you* propose. We can imagine the case in a number of different ways. If I call your bluff openly and say "never mind that nonsense, just take this money" then what I am doing is not accepting a false promise, but giving you a handout, and scorning your promise. The nature of the transaction is changed: now it is not a promise but a handout. If I don't call you on it, but keep my own counsel, it is still the same. I am not accepting a false promise. In this case what I am doing is *pretending* to accept your false promise. But there is all the difference in the world between

actually doing something and pretending to do it. In neither of these cases can I be described as accepting a false promise, for in both cases I fix it so that it is something else that is happening. My knowledge of what is going on makes it *impossible* for me to accept the deceitful promise in the ordinary way.

The question whether another can assent to your way of acting can serve as a criterion for judging whether you are treating her as a mere means. We will say that knowledge of what is going on and some power over the proceedings are the conditions of possible assent; without these, the concept of assent does not apply. This gives us another way to formulate the test for treating someone as a mere means: suppose it is the case that if the other person knows what you are trying to do and has the power to stop you, then what you are trying to do cannot be what is really happening. If this is the case, the action is one that by its very nature is impossible for the other to assent to. You cannot wrest from me what I freely give to you; and if I have the power to stop you from wresting something from me and do not use it, I am in a sense freely giving it to you. This is of course not intended as a legal point: the point is that any action which depends for its nature and efficacy on the other's ignorance or powerlessness fails this test. Lying clearly falls into this category of action: it only deceives when the other does not know that it is a lie.[6]

A similar analysis can be given of the possibility of holding the end of the very same action. In cases of violation of perfect duty, lying included, the other person is unable to hold the end of the very same action because the way that you act prevents her from *choosing* whether to contribute to the realization of that end or not. Again, this is obviously true when someone is forced to contribute to an end, but it is also true in cases of deception. If you give a lying promise to get some money, the other person is invited to think that the end she is contributing to is your temporary possession of the money: in fact, it is your permanent possession of it. It doesn't matter whether that would be all right with her if she knew about it. What matters is that she never gets a chance to choose the end, not knowing that it is to be the consequence of her action.[7]

According to the Formula of Humanity, coercion and deception are the most fundamental forms of wrongdoing to others—the roots of all evil. Coercion and deception violate the conditions of possible assent, and all actions which depend for their nature and efficacy on their coercive or deceptive character are ones that others cannot assent to. Coercion and deception also make it impossible for others to choose to contribute to our ends. This in turn makes it impossible, according to Kant's value theory, for the ends of such actions to be good. For on Kant's view "what we call good must be, in the judgment of every reasonable man, an object of the faculty of desire" (C_2, 60/62–63). If your end is one that others cannot choose—not because of what they want, but because they are not in a position to choose—it cannot, as the end of that action, be good. This means that in any cooperative project— whenever you need the decisions and actions of others in order to bring about your end—everyone who is to contribute must be in a position to *choose* to contribute to the end.

The sense in which a good end is an object for everyone is that a good end is in effect one that everyone, in principle, and especially everyone who contributes to it, gets to cast a vote on. This voting, or legislation, is the prerogative of rational beings; and the ideal of a world in which this prerogative is realized is the Kingdom of Ends.

The Kingdom of Ends

The Kingdom of Ends is represented by the kingdom of nature; we determine moral laws by considering their viability as natural laws. On Kant's view, the will is a kind of causality

(G, 446/64). A person, an end in itself, is a free cause, which is to say a first cause. By contrast, a thing, a means, is a merely mediate cause, a link in the chain. A first cause is, obviously, the initiator of a causal chain, hence a real determiner of what will happen. The idea of deciding for yourself whether you will contribute to a given end can be represented as a decision whether to initiate that causal chain which constitutes your contribution. Any action which prevents or diverts you from making this initiating decision is one that treats you as a mediate rather than a first cause; hence as a mere means, a thing, a tool. Coercion and deception both do this. And deception treats you as a mediate cause in a specific way: it treats your reason as a mediate cause. The false promiser thinks: if I tell her I will pay her back next week, then she will choose to give me the money. Your reason is worked, like a machine: the deceiver tries to determine what levers to pull to get the desired results from you. Physical coercion treats someone's person as a tool; lying treats someone's *reason* as a tool. This is why Kant finds it so horrifying; it is a direct violation of autonomy.

We may say that a tool has two essential characteristics: it is there to be used, and it does not control itself—its nature is to be directed by something else. To treat someone as a mere means is to treat her as if these things were true of her. Kant's treatment of our duties to others in the *Metaphysical Principles of Virtue* is sensitive to both characteristics. We are not only forbidden to use another as a mere means to our private purposes. We are also forbidden to take attitudes toward her which involve regarding her as not in control of herself, which is to say, as not using her reason.

This latter is the basis of the duties of respect. Respect is violated by the vices of calumny and mockery (*MMV*, 466–68/131–33): we owe to others not only a practical generosity toward their plans and projects—a duty of aid—but also a generosity of attitude toward their thoughts and motives. To treat another with

respect is to treat him as if he were using his reason and as far as possible as if he were using it well. Even in a case where someone evidently is wrong or mistaken, we ought to suppose he must have what he takes to be good reasons for what he believes or what he does. This is not because, as a matter of fact, he probably does have good reasons. Rather, this attitude is something that we *owe* to him, something that is his right. And he cannot forfeit it. Kant is explicit about this:

> Hereupon is founded a duty to respect man even in the logical use of his reason: not to censure someone's errors under the name of absurdity, inept judgment, and the like, but rather to suppose that in such an inept judgment there must be something true, and to seek it out.... Thus it is also with the reproach of vice, which must never burst out in complete contempt or deny the wrongdoer all moral worth, because on that hypothesis he could never be improved either—and this latter is incompatible with the idea of man, who as such (as a moral being) can never lose all predisposition to good. (*MMV*, 463–64/128–29)

To treat others as ends in themselves is always to address and deal with them as rational beings. Every rational being gets to reason out, for herself, what she is to think, choose, or do. So if you need someone's contribution to your end, you must put the facts before her and ask for her contribution. If you think she is doing something wrong, you may try to convince her by argument but you may not resort to tricks or force. The Kingdom of Ends is a democratic ideal, and poor judgment does not disqualify anyone for citizenship. In the *Critique of Pure Reason*, Kant says:

> Reason depends on this freedom for its very existence. For reason has no dictatorial authority; its verdict is always simply the

agreement of free citizens, of whom each one must be permitted to express, without let or hindrance, his objections or even his veto.[8]

This means that there cannot be a good reason for taking a decision out of someone else's hands. It is a rational being's prerogative, as a first cause, to have a share in determining the destiny of things.

This shows us in another way why lying is for Kant a paradigm case of treating someone as a mere means. Any attempt to control the actions and reactions of another by any means except an appeal to reason treats her as a mere means, because it attempts to reduce her to a mediate cause. This includes much more than the utterance of falsehoods. In the *Lectures on Ethics*, Kant says "whatever militates against frankness lowers the dignity of man" (LE, 231).[9] It is an everyday temptation, even (or perhaps especially) in our dealings with those close to us, to withhold something, or to tidy up an anecdote, or to embellish a story, or even just to place a certain emphasis, in order to be sure of getting the reaction we want.[10] Kant holds the Socratic view that any sort of persuasion that is aimed at distracting its listener's attention from either the reasons that she ought to use or the reasons the speaker thinks she will use is wrong.[11]

In light of this account it is possible to explain why Kant says what he does about the liar's responsibility. In a Kantian theory our responsibility has definite boundaries: each person as a first cause exerts some influence on what happens, and it is your part that is up to you. If you make a straightforward appeal to the reason of another person, your responsibility ends there and the other's responsibility begins. But the liar tries to take the consequences out of the hands of others; he, and not they, will determine what form their contribution to destiny will take. By refusing to share with others the determination of events, the liar takes the world into his own hands, and makes the events his own. The results, good or bad, are imputable to him,

at least in his own conscience. It does not follow from *this*, of course, that this is a risk one will never want to take.

Humanity and universal law

If the foregoing casuistical analyses are correct, then applying the Formula of Universal Law and the Formula of Humanity lead to different answers in the case of lying to the murderer at the door. The former seems to say that this lie is permissible, but the latter says that coercion and deception are the most fundamental forms of wrongdoing. In a Kingdom of Ends coercive and deceptive methods can never be used.

This result impugns Kant's belief that the formulas are equivalent. But it is not necessary to conclude that the formulas flatly say different things, and are unrelated except for a wide range of coincidence in their results. For one thing, lying to the murderer at the door was not shown to be permissible in a straightforward manner: the maxim did not so much pass as evade universalization. For another, the two formulas can be shown to be expressions of the same basic theory of justification. Suppose that your maxim is in violation of the Formula of Universal Law. You are making an exception of yourself, doing something that everyone in your circumstances could not do. What this means is that you are treating the reason *you* have for the action as if it were stronger, had more justifying force, than anyone else's exactly similar reason. You are then acting as if the fact that it was in particular *your* reason, and not just the reason of a human being, gave it special weight and force. This is an obvious violation of the idea that it is your humanity—your power of rational choice— which is the condition of all value and which therefore gives your needs and desires the justifying force of *reasons*. Thus, any violation of the Formula of Universal Law is also a violation of the Formula of Humanity. This argument, of course, only goes in one direction: it does not show that the two formulas are equivalent. The

Formula of Humanity is stricter than the Formula of Universal Law—but both are expressions of the same basic theory of value: that your rational nature is the source of justifying power of your reasons, and so of the goodness of your ends.

And although the Formula of Humanity gives us reason to think that all lies are wrong, we can still give an account in the terms it provides of what vindicates lying to a liar. The liar tries to use your reason as a means—your honesty as a tool. You do not have to passively submit to being used as a means. In the *Lectures on Ethics*, this is the line that Kant takes. He says:

> If we were to be at all times punctiliously truthful we might often become victims of the wickedness of others who were ready to abuse our truthfulness. If all men were well-intentioned it would not only be a duty not to lie, but no one would do so because there would be no point in it. But as men are malicious, it cannot be denied that to be punctiliously truthful is often dangerous. . . . if I cannot save myself by maintaining silence, then my lie is a weapon of defence. (LE, 228)

The common thought that lying to a liar is a form of self-defense, that you can resist lies with lies as you can resist force with force, is according to this analysis correct.[12] This should not be surprising, for we have seen that deception and coercion are parallel. Lying and the use of force are attempts to undercut the two conditions of possible assent to actions and of autonomous choice of ends, namely, knowledge and power. So, although the Formula of Universal Law and the Formula of Humanity give us different results, this does not show that they simply express different moral outlooks. The relation between them is more complex than that.

Two casuistical problems

Before I discuss this relation, however, I must take up two casuistical problems arising from the view I have presented so far. First, I have argued that we *may* lie to the murderer at the door. But most people think something stronger: that we ought to lie to the murderer—that we will have done something wrong if we do not. Second, I have argued that it is permissible to lie to a deceiver in order to counter the deception. But what if someone lies to you for a good end, and, as it happens, you know about it? The fact that the murderer's *end* is evil has played no direct role in the arguments I have given so far. We have a right to resist liars and those who try to use force because of their methods, not because of their purposes. In one respect this is a virtue of my argument. It does not license us to lie or to use violence against persons just because we think their purposes are bad. But it looks as if it may license us to lie to liars whose purposes are good. Here is a case: suppose someone comes to your door and pretends to be taking a survey of some sort.[13] In fact, this person is a philanthropist who wants to give his money to people who meet certain criteria, and this is his way of discovering appropriate objects for his beneficence. As it happens, you know what is up. By lying, you could get some money, although you do not in fact meet his criteria. The argument that I derived from the Formula of Universal Law about lying to the murderer applies here. Universalizing the lie to the philanthropist will not destroy its efficacy. Even if it is a universal law that everyone will lie in these circumstances, the philanthropist thinks you do not know you are in these circumstances. By my argument, it is permissible to lie in this case. The philanthropist, like the murderer, has placed himself in a morally unprotected position by his own deception.

Start with the first casuistical problem. There are two reasons to lie to the murderer at the door. First, we have a duty of mutual aid. This is an imperfect duty of virtue, since the law does not say exactly what or how much we must do along these lines. This duty gives us *a* reason to tell the lie. Whether it makes the lie imperative

depends on how one understands the duty of mutual aid, on how one understands the "wideness" of imperfect duties.[14] It may be that on such an urgent occasion, the lie is imperative. Notice that if the lie were impermissible, this duty would have no force. Imperfect duties are always secondary to perfect ones. But if the lie is permissible, this duty will provide a reason, whether or not an imperative one, to tell the lie.

The second reason is one of self-respect. The murderer wants to make you a tool of evil; he regards your integrity as a useful sort of predictability. He is trying to use you, and your good will, as a means to an evil end. You owe it to humanity in your own person not to allow your honesty to be used as a resource for evil. I think this would be a perfect duty of virtue; Kant does not say this specifically, but in his discussion of servility (the avoidance of which is a perfect duty of virtue) he says "Do not suffer your rights to be trampled underfoot by others with impunity" (MMV, 436/99).

Both of these reasons spring from duties of virtue. A person with a good character will tell the lie. Not to tell it is morally bad. But there is no duty of justice to tell the lie. If we do not tell it, we cannot be punished, or, say, treated as an accessory to the murder. Kant would insist that even if the lie ought to be told this does not mean that the punctiliously truthful person who does not tell it is somehow implicated in the murder. It is the murderer, not the truthful person, who commits this crime. Telling the truth cannot be part of the crime. On Kant's view, persons are not supposed to be responsible for managing each other's conduct. If the lie were a duty of justice, we would be responsible for that.

These reflections will help us to think about the second casuistical problem, the lie to the philanthropist. I think it does follow from the line of argument I have taken that the lie cannot be shown to be impermissible. Although the philanthropist can hardly be called evil, he is doing something tricky and underhanded, which on Kant's view is wrong. He should not use this method of getting the information he wants. This is especially true if the reason he does not use a more straightforward method is that he assumes that if he does, people will lie to him. We are not supposed to base our actions on the assumption that other people will behave badly. Assuming this does not occur in an institutional context, and you have not sworn that your remarks were true, the philanthropist will have no recourse to justice if you lie to him.[15] But the reasons that favor telling the lie that exist in the first case do not exist here. According to Kant, you do not have a duty to promote your own happiness. Nor would anyone perform such an action out of self-respect. This is, in a very trivial way, a case of dealing with evil. But you can best deal with it by telling the philanthropist that you know what he is up to, perhaps even that you find it sneaky. This is *because* the ideal that makes his action a bad one is an ideal of straightforwardness in human relations. This would also be the best way to deal with the murderer, if it *were* a way to deal with a murderer. But of course it is not.

Ideal and nonideal theory

I now turn to the question of what structure an ethical theory must have in order to accommodate this way of thinking. In *A Theory of Justice*, John Rawls proposes a division of moral philosophy into ideal and nonideal theory.[16] In that work, the task of ideal theory is to determine "what a perfectly just society would be like," while nonideal theory deals with punishment, war, opposition to unjust regimes, and compensatory justice (Sec. 2, pp. 8–9). Since I wish to use this feature of Rawls's theory for a model, I am going to sketch his strategy for what I will call a double-level theory.

Rawls identifies two conceptions of justice, which he calls the general conception and the special conception (Secs. 11, 26, 39, 46). The general conception tells us that all goods

distributed by society, including liberty and opportunity, are to be distributed equally unless an unequal distribution is to the advantage of everyone, and especially those who fall on the low side of the inequality (Sec. 13). Injustice, according to the general conception, occurs whenever there are inequalities that are not to the benefit of everyone (Sec. 11, p. 62). The special conception in its most developed form removes liberty and opportunity from the scope of this principle and says they must be distributed equally, forbidding tradeoffs of these goods for economic gains. It also introduces a number of priority rules, for example, the priority of liberty over all other considerations, and the priority of equal opportunity over economic considerations (Secs. 11, 46, 82).

Ideal theory is worked out under certain assumptions. One is strict compliance: it is assumed that everyone will act justly. The other, a little harder to specify, is that historical, economic, and natural conditions are such that realization of the ideal is feasible. Our conduct toward those who do not comply, or in circumstances which make the immediate realization of a just state of affairs impossible, is governed by the principles of nonideal theory. Certain ongoing natural conditions which may always prevent the full realization of the ideal state of affairs also belong to nonideal theory: the problems of dealing with the seriously ill or mentally disturbed, for instance, belong in this category. For purposes of constructing ideal theory, we assume that everyone is "rational and able to manage their own affairs" (Sec. 39, p. 248). We also assume in ideal theory that there are no massive historic injustices, such as the oppression of blacks and women, to be corrected. The point is to work out our ideal view of justice on the assumption that people, nature, and history will behave themselves so that the ideal can be realized, and then to determine—in light of that ideal—what is to be done in actual circumstances when they do not. The special conception is not applied without regard to circumstances. Special principles will be used in nonideal conditions.

Nonideal conditions exist when, or to the extent that, the special conception of justice cannot be realized effectively. In these circumstances our conduct is to be determined in the following way: the special conception becomes a goal, rather than an ideal to live up to; we are to work toward the conditions in which it is feasible. For instance, suppose there is a case like this: widespread poverty or ignorance due to the level of economic development is such that the legal establishment of equal liberties makes no real difference to the lot of the disadvantaged members of society. It is an empty formality. On the other hand, some inequality, temporarily instituted, would actually tend to foster conditions in which equal liberty could become a reality for everyone. In these circumstances, Rawls's double-level theory allows for the temporary inequality (Secs. 11, 39). The priority rules give us guidance as to which features of the special conception are most urgent. These are the ones that we should be striving to achieve as soon as possible. For example, if formal equal opportunity for blacks and women is ineffective, affirmative action measures may be in order. If some people claim that this causes inefficiency at first, it is neither here nor there, since equality of opportunity has priority over efficiency. The special conception may also tell us which of our nonideal options is least bad, closest to ideal conduct. For instance, civil disobedience is better than resorting to violence not only because violence is bad in itself, but because of the way in which civil disobedience expresses the democratic principles of the just society it aspires to bring about (Sec. 59). Finally, the general conception of justice commands categorically. In sufficiently bad circumstances none of the characteristic features of the special conception may be realizable. But there is no excuse *ever* for violation of the general conception. If inequalities are not benefiting those on the lower end of them in some way, they are

simply oppression. The general conception, then, represents the point at which justice becomes uncompromising.[17]

A double-level theory can be contrasted to two types of single-level theory, both of which in a sense fail to distinguish the way we should behave in ideal and nonideal conditions, but which are at opposite extremes. A consequentialist theory such as utilitarianism does not really distinguish ideal from nonideal conditions. Of course, the utilitarian can see the difference between a state of affairs in which everyone can be made reasonably happy and a state of affairs in which the utilitarian choice must be for the "lesser of evils," but it is still really a matter of degree. In principle we do not know what counts as a state in which everyone is "as happy as possible" absolutely. Instead, the utilitarian wants to make everyone as happy as possible relative to the circumstances, and pursues this goal regardless of how friendly the circumstances are to human happiness. The difference is not between ideal and nonideal states of affairs but simply between better and worse states of affairs.

Kant's theory as he understood it represents the other extreme of single-level theory. The standard of conduct he sets for us is designed for an ideal state of affairs: we are always to act as if we were living in a Kingdom of Ends, regardless of possible disastrous results. Kant is by no means dismissive toward the distressing problems caused by the evil conduct of other human beings and the unfriendliness of nature to human ideals, but his solution to these problems is different. He finds in them grounds for a morally motivated religious faith in God.[18] Our rational motive for belief in a moral author of the world derives from our rational need for grounds for hope that these problems will be resolved. Such an author would have designed the laws of nature so that, in ways that are not apparent to us, our moral actions and efforts do tend to further the realization of an actual Kingdom of Ends. With faith in God, we can trust that a Kingdom of Ends will be the consequence of our actions as well as the ideal that guides them.

In his *Critique of Utilitarianism*, Bernard Williams spells out some of the unfortunate consequences of what I am calling single-level theories.[19] According to Williams, the consequentialist's commitment to doing whatever is necessary to secure the best outcome may lead to violations of what we would ordinarily think of as integrity. There is no kind of action that is so mean or so savage that it can *never* lead to a better outcome than the alternatives. A commitment to always securing the best outcome never allows you to say "bad consequences or not, this is not the sort of thing I do; I am not that sort of person." And no matter how mean or how savage the act required to secure the best outcome is, the utilitarian thinks that you will be irrational to regret that you did it, for you will have done what is in the straightforward sense the right thing.[20] A Kantian approach, by defining a determinate *ideal* of conduct to live up to rather than setting a *goal* of action to strive for, solves the problem about integrity, but with a high price. The advantage of the Kantian approach is the definite sphere of responsibility. Your share of the responsibility for the way the world is is well-defined and limited, and if you act as you ought, bad outcomes are not your responsibility. The trouble is that in cases such as that of the murderer at the door it seems grotesque simply to say that I have done my part by telling the truth and the bad results are not my responsibility.

The point of a double-level theory is to give us both a definite and well-defined sphere of responsibility for everyday life and some guidance, at least, about when we may or must take the responsibility of violating ideal standards. The common-sense approach to this problem uses an intuitive quantitative measure: we depart from our ordinary rules and standards of conduct when the consequences of following them would be "very bad." This is unhelpful for

two reasons. First, it leaves us on our own about determining *how* bad. Second, the attempt to justify it leads down a familiar consequentialist slippery slope: if very bad consequences justify a departure from ordinary norms, why do not slightly bad consequences justify such a departure? A double-level theory substitutes something better than this rough quantitative measure. In Rawls's theory, for example, a departure from equal liberty cannot be justified by the fact that the consequences of liberty are "very bad" in terms of mere efficiency. This does not mean that an endless amount of inefficiency will be tolerated, because presumably at some point the inefficiency may interfere with the effectiveness of liberty. One might put the point this way: the measure of "very bad" is not entirely intuitive but rather, bad enough to interfere with the reality of liberty. Of course this is not an algorithmic criterion and cannot be applied without judgment, but it is not as inexact as a wholly intuitive quantitative measure, and, importantly, does not lead to a consequentialist slippery slope.

Another advantage of a double-level theory is the explanation it offers of the other phenomenon Williams is concerned about: that of regret for doing a certain kind of action even if in the circumstances it was the "right" thing. A double-level theory offers an account of at least some of the occasions for this kind of regret. We will regret having to depart from the ideal standard of conduct, for we identify with this standard and think of our autonomy in terms of it. Regret for an action we would not do under ideal circumstances seems appropriate even if we have done what is clearly the right thing.[21]

Kantian nonideal theory

Rawls's special conception of justice is a stricter version of the egalitarian ideal embodied in his general conception. In the same way, it can be argued that the Formula of Universal Law and the Formula of Humanity are expressions of the same idea—that humanity is the source of value, and of the justifying force of reason. But the Formula of Humanity is stricter, and gives implausible answers when we are dealing with the misconduct of others and the recalcitrance of nature. This comparison gives rise to the idea of using the two formulas and the relation between them to construct a Kantian double-level theory of individual morality, with the advantages of that sort of account. The Formulas of Humanity and the Kingdom of Ends will provide the ideal which governs our daily conduct. When dealing with evil circumstances we may depart from this ideal. In such cases, we can say that the Formula of Humanity is inapplicable because it is not designed for use when dealing with evil. But it can still guide our conduct. It defines the goal toward which we are working, and if we can generate priority rules we will know which features of it are most important. It gives us guidance about which of the measures we may take is the least objectionable.

Lying to deceivers is not the only case in which the Formula of Humanity seems to set a more ideal standard than the Formula of Universal Law. The arguments made about lying can all be made about the use of coercion to deal with evildoers. Another very difficult case in which the two formulas give different results, as I think, is suicide. Kant gives an argument against suicide under the Formula of Universal Law, but that argument does not work.[22] Yet under the Formula of Humanity we can give a clear and compelling argument against suicide: nothing is of any value unless the human person is so, and it is a great crime, as well as a kind of incoherence, to act in a way that denies and eradicates the source of all values. Thus it might be possible to say that suicide is wrong from an ideal point of view, though justifiable in circumstances of very great natural or moral evil.

There is also another, rather different sense of "rigorism" in which the Formula of Humanity seems to be more rigorous than that of Universal

Law. It concerns the question whether Kant's theory allows for the category of merely permissible ends and actions, or whether we must always be doing something that is morally worthy: that is, whether we should *always* pursue the obligatory ends of our own perfection and the happiness of others, when no other duty is in the case.

The Formula of Universal Law clearly allows for the category of the permissible. Indeed, the first contradiction test is a test for permissibility. But in the *Metaphysical Principles of Virtue*, there are passages which have sometimes been taken to imply that Kant holds the view that our conduct should always be informed by morally worthy ends (MMV, 390/48). The textual evidence is not decisive. But the tendency in Kant's thought is certainly there. For complete moral worth is only realized when our actions are not merely in accordance with duty but from duty, or, to say the same thing a different way, perfect autonomy is only realized when our actions and ends are completely determined by reason, and this seems to be the case only when our ends are chosen as instantiations of the obligatory ends.

Using the Formula of Humanity it is possible to argue for the more "rigorous" interpretation. First, the obligatory ends can be derived more straightforwardly from Humanity than from Universal Law. Kant does derive the obligatory ends from the Formula of Universal Law, but he does it by a curiously roundabout procedure in which someone is imagined formulating a maxim of rejecting them and then finding it to be impermissible. This argument does not show that there would be a moral failing if the agent merely unthinkingly neglected rather than rejected these ends. The point about the pervasiveness of these ends in the moral life is a more complicated one, one that follows from their adoption by this route: among the obligatory ends is our own moral perfection. Pursuing ends that are determined by reason, rather than merely acceptable to it, cultivates one's moral perfection in the required way (MMV, 380–81/37–38; 444–47/108–11).

It is important to point out that even if this is the correct way to understand Kant's ideal theory, it does not imply that Kantian ethics commands a life of conventional moral "good deeds." The obligatory ends are one's own perfection and the happiness of others; to be governed by them is to choose instantiations of these larger categories as the aim of your vocation and other everyday activities. It is worth keeping in mind that natural perfection is a large category, including all the activities that cultivate body and mind. Kant's point is not to introduce a strenuous moralism but to find a place for the values of perfectionism in his theory. But this perfectionism will be a part of ideal theory if the argument for it is based on the Formula of Humanity and cannot be derived from that of Universal Law. This seems to me a desirable outcome. People in stultifying economic or educational conditions cannot really be expected to devote all their spare time to the cultivation of perfectionist values. But they can be expected not to do what is impermissible, not to violate the Formula of Universal Law. Here again, the Formula of Humanity sheds light on the situation even if it is not directly applied: it tells us why it is morally as well as in other ways regrettable that people should be in such conditions.

Conclusion

If the account I have given is correct, the resources of a double-level theory may be available to the Kantian. The Formula of Humanity and its corollary, the vision of a Kingdom of Ends, provide an ideal to live up to in daily life as well as a long-term political and moral goal for humanity. But it is not feasible always to live up to this ideal, and where the attempt to live up to it would make you a tool of evil, you should not do so. In evil circumstances, but only then, the Kingdom of Ends can become a goal to seek rather than an ideal to live up to, and this will

provide us with some guidance. The Kantian priorities—of justice over the pursuit of obligatory ends, and of respect over benevolence—still help us to see what matters most. And even in the worst circumstances, there is always the Formula of Universal Law, telling us what we must not in any case do. For whatever bad circumstances may drive us to do, we cannot possibly be justified in doing something which others in those same circumstances could not also do. The Formula of Universal Law provides the point at which morality becomes uncompromising.

Let me close with some reflections about the extent to which Kant himself might have agreed with this modification of his views. Throughout this essay, I have portrayed Kant as an uncompromising idealist, and there is much to support this view. But in the historical and political writings, as well as in the *Lectures on Ethics*, we find a somewhat different attitude. This seems to me to be especially important. Kant believes that the Kingdom of Ends on earth, the highest political good, can only be realized in a condition of peace (MMJ, 354–55/127–29). But he does not think that this commits a nation to a simple pacifism that would make it the easy victim of its enemies. Instead, he draws up laws of war in which peace functions not as an uncompromising ideal to be lived up to in the present, but as a long-range goal which guides our conduct even when war is necessary (PP, 343–48/85–91; MMJ, 343–51/114–25). If a Kantian can hold such a view for the conduct of nations, why not for that of individuals? If this is right, the task of Kantian moral philosophy is to draw up for individuals something analogous to Kant's laws of war: special principles to use when dealing with evil.

Notes

This paper was delivered as the Randall Harris Lecture at Harvard University in October, 1985. Versions of the paper have been presented at the University of Illinois at Urbana–Champaign, the University of Wisconsin at Milwaukee, the University of Michigan, and to the Seminar on Contemporary Social and Political Theory in Chicago. I owe a great deal to the discussions on these occasions. I want to thank the following people for their comments: Margaret Atherton, Charles Chastain, David Copp, Stephen Darwall, Michael Davis, Gerald Dworkin, Alan Gewirth, David Greenstone, John Koethe, Richard Kraut, Richard Strier, and Manley Thompson. And I owe special thanks to Peter Hylton and Andrews Reath for extensive and useful comments on the early versions of the paper.

1   Where I cite or refer to any of Kant's works more than once, I have inserted the reference into the text. The following abbreviations are used:

G: *Foundations of the Metaphysics of Morals* (1785). The first page number is that of the Prussian Academy Edition Volume IV; the second is that of the translation by Lewis White Beck (Indianapolis: Bobbs-Merrill Library of Liberal Arts, 1959).

C_2: *Critique of Practical Reason* (1788). Prussian Academy Volume V; Lewis White Beck's translation (Indianapolis: Bobbs-Merrill Library of Liberal Arts, 1956).

MMV: *The Metaphysical Principles of Virtue* (1797). Prussian Academy Volume VI; James Ellington's translation in *Immanuel Kant: Ethical Philosophy* (Indianapolis: Hackett, 1983).

MMJ: *The Metaphysical Elements of Justice* (1797). Prussian Academy Volume VI; John Ladd's translation (Indianapolis: Bobbs-Merrill Library of Liberal Arts, 1965).

PP: *Perpetual Peace* (1795). Prussian Academy Volume VIII, translation by Lewis White Beck in *On History*, edited by Lewis White Beck (Indianapolis: Bobbs-Merrill Library of Liberal Arts, 1963).

SRL: "On a Supposed Right to Lie from Altruistic Motives" (1797). Prussian Academy Volume VIII; translation by Lewis White Beck in *Immanuel Kant: Critique of Practical Reason and Other Writings in Moral Philosophy* (Chicago: University of Chicago Press, 1949; reprint, New York: Garland Publishing Company, 1976).

LE: *Lectures on Ethics* (1775–80). Edited by Paul Menzer from the notes of Theodor Friedrich Brauer, using the notes of Gottlieb Kutzner and

Christian Mrongovius; translated by Louis Infield (London: Methuen & Co., Ltd., 1930; reprint, New York: Harper Torchbooks, 1963; current reprint, Indianapolis: Hackett Publishing Co., 1980).

2   I defend it in "Kant's Formula of Universal Law," *Pacific Philosophical Quarterly* 66, nos. 1 & 2 (January/April 1986): 24–47.

3   I am relying here on the assumption that when people ask us questions, they give us some account of themselves and of the context in which the questions are asked. Or, if they don't, it is because they are relying on a context that is assumed. If someone comes to your door looking for someone, you assume that there is a family emergency or some such thing. I am prepared to count such reliance as deception if the questioner knows about it and uses it, thinking that we would refuse to answer his questions if we knew the real context to be otherwise. Sometimes people ask me, "Suppose the murderer just asks whether his friend is in your house, without saying anything about why he wants to know?" I think that, in our culture anyway, people do not *just ask* questions of each other about anything except the time of day and directions for getting places. After all, the reason why refusal to answer is an unsatisfactory way of dealing with this case is that it will almost inevitably give rise to suspicion of the truth, and this is because people normally answer such questions. Perhaps if we did live in a culture in which people regularly *just asked* questions in the way suggested, refusal to answer would be commonplace and would not give rise to suspicion; it would not even be considered odd or rude. Otherwise there would be no way to maintain privacy.

4   In fact, it will now be the case that if the murderer supposes that you suspect him, he is not going to ask you, knowing that you will answer so as to deceive him. Since we must avoid the silly problem about the murderer being able to deduce the truth from his knowledge that you will speak falsely, what you announce is that you will say whatever is necessary in order to conceal the truth. There is no reason to suppose that you will be mechanical about this. You are not going to be a reliable source of information. The murderer will therefore seek some other way to locate his victim.

On the other hand, suppose that the murderer does, contrary to my supposition, announce his real intentions. Then the arguments that I have given do not apply. In this case, I believe your only recourse is refusal to answer (whether or not the victim is in your house, or you know his whereabouts). If an answer is extorted from you by force you may lie, according to the argument I will give later in this article.

5   Kant himself takes notice of this sort of problem in a footnote to this passage in which he criticizes Golden-Rule type principles for, among other things, the sort of subjectivity in question: such principles cannot establish the duty of beneficence, for instance, because "many a man would gladly consent that others should not benefit him, provided only that he might be excused from showing benevolence to them" (G, 430n./48n.).

6   Sometimes it is objected that someone could assent to being lied to in advance of the actual occasion of the lie, and that in such a case the deception might still succeed. One can therefore agree to be deceived. I think it depends what circumstances are envisioned. I can certainly agree to remain uninformed about something, but this is not the same as agreeing to be deceived. For example, I could say to my doctor: "Don't tell me if I am fatally ill, even if I ask." But if I then do ask the doctor whether I am fatally ill, I cannot be certain whether she will answer me truthfully. Perhaps what's being envisioned is that I simply agree to be lied to, but not about anything in particular. Will I then trust the person with whom I have made this odd agreement?

7   A similar conclusion about the way in which the Formula of Humanity makes coercion and deception wrong is reached by Onora O'Neill in "Between Consenting Adults," *Philosophy & Public Affairs* 14, no. 3 (Summer 1985): 252–77.

8   *Immanuel Kant's "Critique of Pure Reason,"* translated by Norman Kemp Smith (New York: St. Martin's Press, 1965) A738–39/B766–67, p. 593.

9   It is perhaps also relevant that in Kant's discussion of perfect moral friendship the emphasis is not on good will toward one another, but on complete confidence and openness. See *MMV*, 471–72/138–39.

10 Some evidence that Kant is concerned with this sort of thing may be found in the fact that he identifies two meanings of the word "prudence" (*Klugheit*); "The former sense means the skill of a man in having an influence on others so as to use them for his own purposes. The latter is the ability to unite all these purposes to his own lasting advantage" (*G*, 416n./33n.). A similar remark is found in *Anthropology from a Pragmatic Point of View* (1798). See the translation by Mary J. Gregor (The Hague: Martinus Nijhoff, 1974), p. 183; Prussian Academy Edition Volume VII, p. 322.

11 I call this view Socratic because of Socrates' concern with the differences between reason and persuasion and, in particular, because in the *Apology*, he makes a case for the categorical duty of straightforwardness. Socrates and Plato are also concerned with a troublesome feature of this moral view that Kant neglects. An argument must come packaged in some sort of presentation, and one may well object that it is impossible to make a straightforward presentation of a case to someone who is close to or admires you, without emphasis, without style, without taking some sort of advantage of whatever it is about you that has your listener's attention in the first place. So how can we avoid the nonrational influence of others? I take it that most obviously in the *Symposium*, but also in other dialogues concerned with the relation of love and teaching such as the *Phaedrus*, Plato is at work on the question whether you can use your sex appeal to draw another's attention to the reasons he has for believing or doing things, rather than as a distraction that aids your case illicitly.

12 Of course you may also resist force with lies, if resisting it with force is not an option for you. This gives rise to a question about whether these options are on a footing with each other. In many cases, lying will be the better option. This is because when you use coercion you risk doing injury to the person you coerce. Injuring people unnecessarily is wrong, a wrong that should be distinguished from the use of coercion. When you lie you do not risk doing this extra wrong. But Kant thinks that lying is in itself worse than coercion, because of the peculiarly direct way in which it violates autonomy. So it should follow that if you can deal with the murderer by coercion, this is a *better* option than lying. Others seem to share this intuition. Cardinal John Henry Newman, responding to Samuel Johnson's claim that he would lie to a murderer who asked which way his victim had gone, suggests that the appropriate thing to do is "to knock the man down, and to call out for the police" (*Apologia Pro Vita Sua: Being a History of His Religious Opinions* [London: Longmans, Green & Co., 1880], p. 361. I am quoting from Sissela Bok, *Lying* [New York: Vintage Books, 1979], p. 42). If you can do it without seriously hurting the murderer, it is, so to speak, cleaner just to kick him off the front porch than to lie. This treats the *murderer himself* more like a human being than lying to him does.

13 I owe this example to John Koethe.

14 For a discussion of this question see Barbara Herman, "Mutual Aid and Respect for Persons," *Ethics* 94 (July 1984): 577–602.

15 In the *Lectures on Ethics*, Kant takes the position that you may lie to someone who lies to or bullies you as long as you don't say specifically that your words will be true. He claims this is not lying, because such a person should not expect you to tell the truth. (*LE*, 227, 229).

16 John Rawls, *A Theory of Justice* (Cambridge, MA: Harvard University Press, 1971). Section and page numbers referring to this work will appear in the text.

17 In a nonideal case, one's actions may be guided by a more instrumental style of reasoning than in ideal theory. But nonideal theory is not a form of consequentialism. There are two reasons for this. One is that the goal set by the ideal is not just one of good consequences, but of a just state of affairs. If a consequentialist view is one that defines right action entirely in terms of good consequences (which are not themselves defined in terms of considerations of rightness or justice), then nonideal theory is not consequentialist. The second reason is that the ideal will also guide our choice among nonideal alternatives, importing criteria for this choice other than effectiveness. I would like to thank Alan Gewirth for prompting me to clarify my thoughts on this matter, and David Greenstone for helping me to do so.

18 See the "Dialectic of Pure Practical Reason" of the *Critique of Practical Reason*, and the *Critique of Teleological Judgment*, sec. 87.

19 Bernard Williams, in *Utilitarianism For and Against*, by J. J. C. Smart and Bernard Williams (Cambridge: Cambridge University Press, 1973), pp. 75–150.

20 Williams also takes this issue up in "Ethical Consistency," originally published in the Supplementary Volumes to the *Proceedings of the Aristotelian Society* XXXIX, 1965, and reprinted in his collection, *Problems of the Self* (Cambridge: Cambridge University Press, 1973), pp. 166–86.

21 It is important here to distinguish two kinds of exceptions. As Rawls points out in "Two Conceptions of Rules" (*The Philosophical Review* 64 [January 1965]), a practice such as promising may have certain exceptions built into it. Everyone who has learned the practice understands that the obligation to keep the promise is cancelled if one of these obtains. When one breaks a promise because this sort of exception obtains, regret would be inappropriate and obsessive. And these sorts of exceptions may occur even in "ideal" circumstances. The kind of exception one makes when dealing with evil should be distinguished from exceptions built into practices.

22 Kant's argument depends on a teleological claim: that the instinct whose office is to impel the improvement of life cannot universally be used to destroy life without contradiction (G, 422/40). But as I understand the contradiction in conception test, teleological claims have no real place in it. What matters is not whether nature assigns a certain purpose to a certain motive or instinct, but whether everyone with the same motive or instinct could act in the way proposed and still achieve their purpose. There is simply no argument to show that everyone suffering from acute misery could not commit suicide and still achieve their purpose: ending that misery.

Chapter 32

Rae Langton

MARIA VON HERBERT'S CHALLENGE TO KANT

THIS IS a paper about two philosophers who wrote to each other. One is famous; the other is not. It is about two practical standpoints, the strategic and the human, and what the famous philosopher said of them. And it is about friendship and deception, duty and despair. That is enough by way of preamble.

I. Friendship

In 1791 Kant received a letter from an Austrian lady whom he had never met. She was Maria von Herbert, a keen and able student of Kant's philosophy, and sister to Baron Franz Paul von Herbert, another zealous Kantian disciple. The zeal of her brother the Baron was indeed so great that he had left his lead factory, and his wife, for two years in order to study Kant's philosophy in Weimar and Jena. Upon his return, the von Herbert household had become a centre, a kind of salon, where the critical philosophy was intensely debated, against the backdrop of vehement opposition to Kant in Austria as in many German states. The household was, in the words of a student of Fichte's, 'a new Athens', an oasis of Enlightenment spirit, devoted to preaching and propagating the Kantian gospel, reforming religion, and replacing dull unthinking piety with a morality based on reason. Here is the letter.

1. To Kant, from Maria von Herbert, August 1791

Great Kant,

As a believer calls to his God, I call to you for help, for comfort, or for counsel to prepare me for death. Your writings prove that there is a future life. But as for this life, I have found nothing, nothing at all that could replace the good I have lost, for I loved someone who, in my eyes, encompassed within himself all that is worthwhile, so that I lived only for him, everything else was in comparison just rubbish, cheap trinkets. Well, I have offended this person, because of a long drawn out lie, which I have now disclosed to him, though there was nothing unfavourable to my character in it, I had no vice in my life that needed hiding. The lie was enough though, and his love vanished. As an honourable man, he doesn't refuse me friendship. But that inner feeling that once, unbidden, led us to each other, is no more – oh my heart splinters into a thousand pieces! If I hadn't read so much of your work I would certainly have put an end to my life. But the conclusion I had to draw from your theory stops me – it is wrong for me to die because my life is tormented, instead I'm supposed to live because of my being. Now put yourself in my place, and either damn me or comfort me. I've read the

metaphysic of morals, and the categorical imperative, and it doesn't help a bit. My reason abandons me just when I need it. Answer me, I implore you – or you won't be acting in accordance with your own imperative.

My address is Maria Herbert of Klagenfurt, Carinthia, care of the white lead factory, or perhaps you would rather send it via Reinhold because the mail is more reliable there.

Kant, much impressed by this letter, sought advice from a friend as to what he should do. The friend advised him strongly to reply, and to do his best to distract his correspondent from 'the object to which she [was] enfettered'.[1] We have the carefully prepared draft of Kant's response.

2. To Maria von Herbert, Spring 1792 (Kant's rough draft)

Your deeply felt letter comes from a heart that must have been created for the sake of virtue and honesty, since it is so receptive to instruction in those qualities. I must do as you ask, namely, put myself in your place, and prescribe for you a pure moral sedative. I do not know whether your relationship is one of marriage or friendship, but it makes no significant difference. For love, be it for one's spouse or for a friend, presupposes the same mutual esteem for the other's character, without which it is no more than perishable, sensual delusion.

A love like that wants to communicate itself completely, and it expects of its respondent a similar sharing of heart, unweakened by distrustful reticence. That is what the ideal of friendship demands. But there is something in us which puts limits on such frankness, some obstacle to this mutual outpouring of the heart, which makes one keep some part of one's thoughts locked within oneself, even when one is most intimate. The sages of old complained of this secret distrust – 'My dear friends, there is no such thing as a friend!'

We can't expect frankness of people, since everyone fears that to reveal himself completely would be to make himself despised by others. But this lack of frankness, this reticence, is still very different from dishonesty. What the honest but reticent man says is true, but not the whole truth. What the dishonest man says is something he knows to be false. Such an assertion is called, in the theory of virtue, a lie. It may be harmless, but it is not on that account innocent. It is a serious violation of a duty to oneself; it subverts the dignity of humanity in our own person, and attacks the roots of our thinking. As you see, you have sought counsel from a physician who is no flatterer. I speak for your beloved and present him with arguments that justify his having wavered in his affection for you.

Ask yourself whether you reproach yourself for the imprudence of confessing, or for the immorality intrinsic to the lie. If the former, then you regret having done your duty. And why? Because it has resulted in the loss of your friend's confidence. This regret is not motivated by anything moral, since it is produced by an awareness not of the act itself, but of its consequences. But if your reproach is grounded in a moral judgment of your behaviour, it would be a poor moral physician who would advise you to cast it from your mind.

When your change in attitude has been revealed to your beloved, only time will be needed to quench, little by little, the traces of his justified indignation, and to transform his coldness into a more firmly grounded love. If this doesn't happen, then the earlier warmth of his affection was more physical than moral, and would have disappeared anyway – a misfortune which we often encounter in life, and when we do, must meet with composure. For the value of life, insofar as it consists of the enjoyment we get from people, is vastly overrated.

Here then, my dear friend, you find the customary divisions of a sermon: instruction, penalty and comfort. Devote yourself to the

first two; when they have had their effect, comfort will be found by itself.

Kant's letter has an enormously interesting and sensitive discussion of friendship and secrecy, much of which turns up word for word in *The Doctrine of Virtue*, published some six years later.[2] But what Kant's letter fails to say is as at least as interesting as what it says. Herbert writes that she has lost her love, that her heart is shattered, that there is nothing left to make life worth living, and that Kant's moral philosophy hasn't helped a bit. Kant's reply is to suggest that the love is deservedly lost, that misery is an appropriate response to one's own moral failure, and that the really interesting moral question here is the one that hinges on a subtle but necessary scope distinction: the distinction between telling a lie and failing to tell the truth, between saying 'not-p', and not saying 'p'. Conspicuously absent is an acknowledgement of Herbert's more than theoretical interest in the question: is suicide compatible with the moral law? And perhaps this is just as well from a practical point of view. The sooner she gives up those morbid thoughts the better; the less said on the morbid subject, the less likely the morbid thoughts will arise. Perhaps it is also just as well, for Kant, from a theoretical point of view. Kant's conviction that suicide is incompatible with the moral law is not nearly as well founded as he liked to think; so here too, the less said, the better. Having posted his moral sedative off to Austria, and receiving no reply from the patient in more than a year, Kant enquired of a mutual friend who often saw her about the effect his letter had had. Herbert then wrote back, with apologies for her delay. This is her second letter.

3. To Kant, from Maria von Herbert, January 1793

Dear and revered sir,

Your kindness, and your exact understanding of the human heart, encourage me to describe to you, unshrinkingly, the further progress of my soul. The lie was no cloaking of a vice, but a sin of keeping something back out of consideration for the friendship (still veiled by love) that existed then. There was a struggle, I was aware of the honesty friendship demands, and at the same time I could foresee the terribly wounding consequences. Finally I had the strength and revealed the truth to my friend, but so late – and when I told him, the stone in my heart was gone, but his love was torn away in exchange. My friend hardened in his coldness, just as you said in your letter. But then afterwards he changed towards me, and offered me again the most intimate friendship. I'm glad enough about it, for his sake – but I'm not really content, because it's just amusement, it doesn't have any point.

My vision is clear now. I feel that a vast emptiness extends inside me, and all around me – so that I almost find my self to be superfluous, unnecessary. Nothing attracts me. I'm tormented by a boredom that makes life intolerable. Don't think me arrogant for saying this, but the demands of morality are too easy for me. I would eagerly do twice as much as they command. They only get their prestige from the attractiveness of sin, and it costs me almost no effort to resist that.

I comfort myself with the thought that, since the practice of morality is so bound up with sensuality, it can only count for this world. I can hope that the afterlife won't be yet another life ruled by these few, easy demands of morality, another empty and vegetating life. Experience wants to take me to task for this bad temper I have against life by showing me that nearly everyone finds his life ending much too soon, everyone is so glad to be alive. So as not to be a queer exception to the rule, I shall tell you of a remote cause of my deviation, namely my chronic poor health, which dates from the time I first wrote to you. I don't study the natural sciences or the arts any more, since I don't feel that I'm genius enough to

extend them; and for myself, there's no need to know them. I'm indifferent to everything that doesn't bear on the categorical imperative, and my transcendental consciousness – although I'm all done with those thoughts too.

You can see, perhaps, why I only want one thing, namely to shorten this pointless life, a life which I am convinced will get neither better nor worse. If you consider that I am still young and that each day interests me only to the extent that it brings me closer to death, you can judge what a great benefactor you would be if you were to examine this question closely. I ask you, because my conception of morality is silent here, whereas it speaks decisively on all other matters. And if you cannot give me the answer I seek, I beg you to give me something that will get this intolerable emptiness out of my soul. Then I might become a useful part of nature, and, if my health permits, would make a trip to Königsberg in a few years. I want to ask permission, in advance, to visit you. You must tell me your story then, because I would like to know what kind of life your philosophy has led you to – whether it never seemed to you to be worth the bother to marry, or to give your whole heart to anyone, or to reproduce your likeness. I have an engraved portrait of you by Bause, from Leipzig. I see a profound calm there, and moral depth – but not the astuteness of which the *Critique of Pure Reason* is proof. And I'm dissatisfied not to be able to look you right in the face.

Please fulfill my wish, if it's not too inconvenient. And I need to remind you: if you do me this great favour and take the trouble to answer, please focus on specific details, not on the general points, which I understand, and already understood back when I happily studied your works at the side of my friend. You would like him, I'm sure. He is honest, goodhearted, and intelligent – and besides that, fortunate enough to fit this world.

I am with deepest respect and truth, Maria Herbert.

Herbert's letter speaks for itself. The passion, the turbulence, has vanished. Desolation has taken its place, a 'vast emptiness', a vision of the world and the self that is chilling in its clarity, chilling in its nihilism. Apathy reigns. Desire is dead. Nothing attracts. Bereft of inclination, the self is 'superfluous', as Herbert so starkly puts it. Nothing has any point – except of course the categorical imperative. But morality itself has become a torment, not because it is too difficult, but because it is too easy. Without the counterweight of opposing inclination, what course could there be but to obey? The moral life is the empty, vegetating life, where one sees at a glance what the moral law requires and simply does it, unhampered by the competing attractions of sin. Herbert concludes that morality must be bound up with sensuality, that moral credit depends on the battle of the will with the sensual passions, a battle which, when there are no passions, is won merely, and tediously, by default – and where can be the credit in that? The imperative requires us never to treat persons merely as means to one's own ends. But if one has no ends, if one is simply empty, what could be easier than to obey? Herbert draws hope from her conclusion: if morality is bound to sensuality, with luck the next life will not be thus accursed.

This sounds like heresy. Is it? If so, Kant is blind to it. But perhaps it is not heresy at all. What Kant fails to see – what Herbert herself fails to see – is that her life constitutes a profound challenge to his philosophy, at least construed one way. Consider Kant's views on duty and inclination.

An action has moral worth when it is done for the sake of duty; it is not sufficient that the action conforms with duty.[3] Now, inclinations are often sufficient to make us perform actions that conform with our duty. To preserve one's life is a duty; and most of us have strong inclinations to preserve our lives. To help others where one can is a duty; and most of us are sympathetic enough and amiable enough to be inclined

to help others, at least some of the time. But – if we take Kant at his word here – actions thus motivated have no moral worth. The action of moral worth is that of 'the wretched man . . . [for whom] disappointments and hopeless misery have quite taken away the taste for life, who longs for death' but who, notwithstanding, preserves his life. The action that has moral worth is that of the misanthropist, 'the man cold in temperament and indifferent to the sufferings of others' who nonetheless helps others 'not from inclination but from duty'.[4]

This looks as though moral credit depends on both the absence of coinciding inclinations, such as sympathy; and the presence of opposing inclinations, like misanthropy. If so, Herbert is right: morality depends on there being inclinations to defeat. It is important to see though that even here, what Kant says is not motivated by a kind of blind rule worship, but by a sense of the gulf between the two standpoints from which we must view ourselves. We are at once cogs in the grand machine of nature, and free agents in the Kingdom of Ends. We are persons, members of an intelligible world, authors of our actions; and at the same time animals, puppets of our genes and hormones, buffeted about by our lusts and loathings. Inclinations are passions in the sense that they just happen to us. And insofar as we let our actions be driven by them we allow ourselves to be puppets, not persons. We allow ourselves, to use Kant's own metaphors, to become marionettes or automatons, which may appear to be initiators of action, but whose freedom is illusory, 'no better than the freedom of a turnspit, which, when once wound up also carries out its motions by itself'.[5] The inclinations are effects on us, they are pathe, and for that reason pathological. If we let them be causes of our behaviour, we abandon our personhood.

Whether they lead us towards the action of duty or away from it, inclinations are among virtue's chief obstacles. When inclination opposes duty, it is an obstacle to duty's performance. When inclination coincides with duty, it is

an obstacle at least to knowledge of the action's worth. 'Inclination, be it good-natured or otherwise, is blind and slavish . . . The feeling of sympathy and warmhearted fellow-feeling . . . is burdensome even to right-thinking persons, confusing their considered maxims and creating the wish to be free from them and subject only to law-giving reason.'[6] In the battle against the inclinations we can enlist the aid of that strange thing, respect, or reverence for the moral law. Reverence for the law serves to 'weaken the hindering influence of the inclinations'.[7] Reverence is a kind of feeling, but it is not something we 'passively feel', something inflicted upon us from outside. It is the sensible correlate of our own moral activity, the 'consciousness of the direct constraint of the will through law'.[8] Its function is not to motivate our moral actions, for that would still be motivation by feeling. Rather, its function is to remove the obstacles, to silence inclinations, something we should all look forward to. For inclinations are 'so far from having an absolute value . . . that it must . . . be the universal wish of every rational being to be wholly free from them'.[9]

Kant goes so far as to say we have a duty of apathy, a duty he is less than famous for. 'Virtue necessarily presupposes apathy', he says in *The Doctrine of Virtue*. 'The word "apathy" has fallen into disrepute', he continues, 'as if it meant lack of feeling and so subjective indifference regarding objects of choice: it has been taken for weakness. We can prevent this misunderstanding by giving the name "moral apathy" to that freedom from agitation which is to be distinguished from indifference, for in it the feelings arising from sensuous impressions lose their influence on moral feeling only because reverence for the law prevails over all such feelings'.[10] Something rather similar to apathy is described in the *Critique of Practical Reason*, but this time it is called not apathy, but 'bliss' (*Seligkeit*). Bliss is the state of 'complete independence from inclinations and desires'.[11] While it must be the universal wish of every rational being to achieve

bliss, can we in fact achieve it? Apparently not, or not here. Bliss is 'the self-sufficiency which can be ascribed only to the Supreme Being'.[12] The Supreme Being has no passions and inclinations. His intuition is intellectual, and not sensible. He can be affected by nothing, not even our prayers. He can have no pathe. God is the being more apathetic than which cannot be conceived.

What of Kant's moral patient? She is well beyond the virtue of apathy that goes with mastery of the inclinations. She has no inclinations left to master. She respects the moral law, and obeys it. But she needn't battle her passions to do so. She has no passions. She is empty – but for the clear vision of the moral law and unshrinking obedience to it. She is well on the way to bliss, lucky woman, and, if Kant is right about bliss, well on the way to Godhead. No wonder she feels that she – unlike her unnamed friend – does not quite 'fit the world'. She obeys the moral law in her day to day dealings with people from the motive of duty alone. She has no other motives. She is no heretic. She is a Kantian saint. Oh brave new world, that has such moral saints in it.[13]

What should Kant have said about inclinations? I have no clear view about this, but some brief remarks may be in order. A saner view is arguably to be found in Kant's own writings. In the Doctrine of Virtue[14] Kant apparently advocates the cultivation of natural sentiment to back up the motive of duty. It is hard, though, to reconcile this with his other teachings, which tell us that inclinations, all inclinations, are to be abjured, as 'blind and slavish', in the graphic phrase from the Critique of Practical Reason. 'Blind' is an evocative word in the Kantian context, associated as it is with the blind workings of nature, with the sensual as opposed to the intellectual. It calls to mind the famous slogan of the first Critique: thoughts without content are empty, intuitions without concepts are blind. That slogan famously captures the synthesis of rationalism and empiricism Kant thought necessary for knowledge. It acknowledges the twin aspects of

human creatures, as Kant sees us: we have a sensible intuition, a passive intuition, through which we are affected by the world; and an active intellect. We need both. If only Kant had effected a similar synthesis in the moral sphere: for if it is true, as he says, that inclinations without reasons are blind, it seems equally true that reasons without inclinations are empty. The moral life without inclinations is a life of 'intolerable emptiness', as Herbert found. We need both.

I said that Herbert has no inclinations: but there are two exceptions. She wants to die. And she wants to visit Kant. She is, it seems, like the would-be suicide Kant describes in The Groundwork: her persistence with life has moral worth, because it is so opposed to her inclinations. But is she really like him? Not quite. For she is not even sure that duty points to persistence with life. Notice the change here. In her first letter she believed that self-respect, respect for 'her own being', required her to persist with life. But as her 'being' has begun to contract, as the self has withered, sloughed off, become superfluous – as the emptiness has grown – so too has her doubt. Now her conception of morality is 'silent' on the question of suicide. She wants to die. She has almost no opposing inclinations. And morality is silent. It takes no expert to wonder if she is in danger.

Why does she want to visit Kant? She says (letter 3) 'I would like to know what kind of life your philosophy has led you to'. In the Critique of Practical Reason Kant cites approvingly what he took to be the practice of the ancients: no one was justified in calling himself a philosopher – a lover of wisdom – 'unless he could show [philosophy's] infallible effect on his own person as an example'.[15] Kant thinks we are justified in inquiring after the effect of philosophy on the philosopher, daunting as the prospect seems today. But what does Herbert have in mind? She wonders, perhaps, whether Kant's life is as empty as her own, and for the same reason. She discovered that love is 'pointless' when inclinations have withered, when you have no passions of

your own and therefore no passions to share. And she wonders whether Kant's life reflects this discovery. She wonders whether Kant's philosophy has led him to think that it was simply 'not worth the bother' to marry, or to 'give his whole heart' to anyone. Perhaps she is right to wonder.

II. Shipwreck

In reply to an enquiry, Kant received this explanatory letter from a mutual friend, Erhard.

4. To Kant, from J.B. Erhard, January 17, 1793

I can say little of Miss Herbert. She has capsized on the reef of romantic love. In order to realize an idealistic love, she gave herself to a man who misused her trust. And then, trying to achieve such love with another, she told her new lover about the previous one. That is the key to her letter. If my friend Herbert had more delicacy, I think she could still be saved.

Yours, Erhard.

Kant writes again, not to Herbert, but to someone about whom we know little:

5. From Kant, to Elisabeth Motherby, February 11, 1793

I have numbered the letters[16] which I have the honour of passing on to you, my dear mademoiselle, according to the dates I received them. The ecstatical little lady didn't think to date them. The third letter, from another source, provides an explanation of the lady's curious mental derangement. A number of expressions refer to writings of mine that she read, and are difficult to understand without an interpreter.

You have been so fortunate in your upbringing that I do not need to commend these letters to you as an example of warning, to guard you against the wanderings of a sublimated fantasy. But they may serve nonetheless to make your perception of that good fortune all the more lively.

I am, with the greatest respect, my honoured lady's most obedient servant,

I. Kant.

Kant is unaware that he has received a letter from a Kantian saint. Indeed, it is hard to believe that he has read her second letter. He relies on the opinion of his friend, whose diagnosis of the patient resorts to that traditional and convenient malady of feminine hysteria. Herbert 'has capsized on the reef of romantic love'. The diagnosis is exactly wrong. Herbert has no passions. Her vision is clear. Her life is empty. But it is easier not to take this in, easier to suppose a simpler illness. She is at the mercy (aren't all women?) of irrational passions. She is evidently beyond the reach of instruction, beyond the reach of his moral sedatives; so Kant abandons her. It is hard to imagine a more dramatic shift from the interactive stance to the objective.[17] In Kant's first letter, Herbert is 'my dear friend', she is the subject for moral instruction, and reprimand. She is responsible for some immoral actions, but she has a 'heart created for the sake of virtue', capable of seeing the good and doing it. Kant is doing his best to communicate, instruct, and console. He is not very good at it, hardly surprising if he believes – as I think he does – that he should master rather than cultivate his moral sentiments. But there is little doubt that the good will is there. He treats her as a human being, as an end, as a person. This is the standpoint of interaction.

But now? Herbert is *die kleine Schwärmerin*, the little dreamer, the ecstatical girl, suffering a 'curious mental derangement', lost in the 'wanderings of a sublimated fantasy', who doesn't think, especially about important things like dating letters. Kant is here forgetting an important aspect of the duty of respect, which requires something like a Davidsonian principle of charity. We have 'a duty of respect for man even in the logical use of his reason: a duty not

to censure his error by calling it absurdity . . . but rather to suppose that his error must yet contain some truth and to seek this out.'[18] Herbert, now deranged, is no longer guilty. She is merely unfortunate. She is not responsible for what she does. She is the pitiful product of a poor upbringing. She is an item in the natural order, a ship wrecked on a reef. She is a thing.

And, true to Kant's picture, it now becomes appropriate to use her as a means to his own ends. He bundles up her letters, private communications from a 'dear friend', letters that express thoughts, philosophical and personal, some of them profound. He bundles them up and sends them to an acquaintance under the title, 'Example of Warning'. The end is obscure and contradictory: it seems it is to warn somebody who, on Kant's own view, needs no warning. Is it gossip? Ingratiation? But the striking thing is that the letters are no longer seen as human communications. Far from it: Kant's presumption is that they will not be understood by their new recipient. For the letters 'refer to writings of mine that she read, that are difficult to understand without an interpreter'. This is not the speech of persons, to be understood and debated; this is derangement, to be feared and avoided. These are not thoughts, but symptoms. Kant is doing something with her as one does something with a tool: Herbert cannot share the end of the action. She cannot be co-author. Kant's deceiving of her – neatly achieved by reticence – has made sure of that. Her action of pleading for help, asking advice, arguing philosophy, her action of writing to a well-loved philosopher and then to a friend – these have become the action of warning of the perils of romantic love. She did not choose to do that. Well may Kant have warned 'My dear friends, there is no such thing as a friend'.

III. Strategy for the kingdom's sake

Enough. This is not a cautionary tale of the inability of philosophers to live by their philosophy. What interests me is what interested Kant at the outset: friendship and deception. What interests me is the very first problem: the 'long drawn out lie; disclosed'. Was it wrong for Herbert to deceive? Is it always wrong to deceive? Apparently, yes, from the Kantian perspective. In deceiving we treat our hearers as less than human. We act from the objective standpoint. We force others to perform actions they don't choose to perform. We make them things. If I reply to the murderer, 'No, my friend is not here', I deceive a human being, use his reasoning ability as a tool, do something that has a goal (saving my friend) that I make impossible for him to share, make him do something (abandon his prey) that he did not choose to do. I have made him, in this respect, a thing.

But this is too simple. Recall that Herbert puts her dilemma like this: 'I was aware of the honesty friendship demands and at the same time I could see the terribly wounding consequences . . . The lie . . . was a . . . keeping something back out of consideration for the friendship.'[19] She is torn. Friendship demands honesty; and friendship demands dishonesty. Is she confused? Is she in contradiction? Not at all. It is an old dilemma: having an ideal you want to live by, and an ideal you want to seek and preserve. You owe honesty to your friend; but the friendship will vanish if you are honest.

Friendship is a very great good: it is the Kingdom of Ends made real and local. Kant says that the man who is without a friend is the man who 'must shut himself up in himself', who must remain 'completely alone with his thoughts, as in a prison'.[20] One of the goods of friendship is that it makes possible the kind of relationship where one can unlock the prison of the self, reveal oneself to the compassionate and understanding eye of the other. But Kant sees true friendship to be a very rare thing, rare, he says, as a black swan.[21] And what threatens friendship most is asymmetry, inequality with regard to love or respect, which can result in the partial breakdown of the interactive stance. This asymmetry can be brought about by the very act

of self revelation: if one person 'reveals his failings while the other person concealed his own, he would lose something of the other's respect by presenting himself so candidly'.[22] What Kant is pointing to is the very problem encountered, far more acutely, by Herbert: in being a friend, in acting in the way that friendship demands, one can sometimes threaten friendship. To act as a member of the Kingdom can make the Kingdom more, and not less, remote.

How should we think of Kant's ideal: is the Kingdom an ideal to be lived by, or a goal to be sought? If it is ever the latter, then sometimes – in evil circumstances – it will be permissible, and even required, to act strategically for the Kingdom's sake.[23] There is a question about what evil is. But for Kant it must, above all, be this: the reduction of persons to things. Now consider Herbert's position. There is something we have been leaving out. Herbert is a *woman* in a society in which women start out on an unequal footing and then live out their lives that way, where women – especially women – must perpetually walk a tightrope between being treated as things and treated as persons. She must make her choices against a backdrop of social institutions and habits that strip her of the dignity due to persons, where what she does and what she says will always be interpreted in the light of that backdrop, so that even if she says 'my vision is clear', and speaks in a manner consistent with that claim, her speech will be read as the speech of the deranged, a mere plaything of the passions. Central among the institutions she must encounter in her life is that of the sexual marketplace, where human beings are viewed as having a price, and not a dignity, and where the price of women is fixed in a particular way. Women, as things, as items in the sexual marketplace, have a market value that depends in part on whether they have been used. Virgins fetch a higher price than second hand goods. Such are the background circumstances in which Herbert finds herself. They are, I suggest, evil circumstances, evil by Kantian lights (though Kant himself never saw it).

Despite these handicaps, Herbert has achieved a great thing: she has achieved something like a friendship of mutual love and respect, found someone with whom she can share her activities and goals, become a partner in a relationship where ends are chosen in such a way that the ends of both agents coincide (prominent among which was, it seems, the happy study of Kant's works!). She has achieved a relationship where frankness and honesty prevail – with one exception. Her lie is the lie of 'keeping something back for the sake of the friendship'. If she tells the truth, evil circumstance will see to it that her action will not be taken as the honest self-revelation of a person, but the revelation of her thing-hood, her hitherto unrecognised status as used merchandise, as item with a price that is lower than the usual. If she tells the truth, she becomes a thing, and the friendship – that small neighbourhood of the Kingdom – will vanish. Should she lie? Perhaps. If her circumstances are evil, she is permitted to have friendship as her goal, to be sought and preserved, rather than a law to be lived by. So she is permitted to lie. Then other considerations come in. She has a duty to 'humanity in her own person', of which Kant says: 'By virtue of this worth we are not for sale at any price; we possess an inalienable dignity which instils in us reverence for ourselves'. She has a duty of self esteem: she must respect her own person and demand such respect of others, abjuring the vice of servility.[24] I think she may have a duty to lie.

This is strategy, for the Kingdom's sake. Kant would not allow it. He thinks we should act as if the Kingdom of Ends is with us now. He thinks we should rely on God to make it all right in the end. But God will not make it all right in the end. And the Kingdom of Ends is not with us now. Perhaps we should do what we can to bring it about.

IV. Coda

Kant never replied, and his correspondent, as far as I know, did not leave Austria.[25] In 1803 Maria

von Herbert killed herself, having worked out at last an answer to that persistent and troubling question – the question to which Kant, and her own moral sense, had responded with silence. Was that a vicious thing to do? Not entirely. As Kant himself concedes, 'Self murder requires courage, and in this attitude there is always room for reverence for humanity in one's own person.'[26]

Notes

This paper is a shortened version of 'Duty and Desolation', which first appeared in *Philosophy 67 1992*, and appears in this form in Singer (ed.), *Oxford Reader: Ethics* (Oxford University Press, 1994). Letters are my adaptations and abridgements of those in Arnulf Zweig, *Kant: Philosophical Correspondence*, 1759–99 (University of Chicago Press, 1967), used with kind permission of Prof. Zweig and the publishers; original language versions in Vol. XI of the Prussian Academy of Sciences edition of Kant's *Works* (Walter de Gruyter, 1922). My interpretation of Kant owes a great debt to the work of P.F. Strawson ('Freedom and Resentment', in *Freedom and Resentment* (Methuen, 1974), 1–25), and Christine Korsgaard, whose views on Kant and lying are developed in 'The Right to Lie: Kant on Dealing with Evil', *Philosophy and Public Affairs* 15, No. 4 (1986), 325–49; and, on Kant and friendship, in 'Creating the Kingdom of Ends: Responsibility and Reciprocity in Personal Relations', *Philosophical Perspectives 6: Ethics*, James Tomberlin (ed.) (Atascadero, California: The Ridgeview Publishing Company, 1992).

1   Letter to Kant from Ludwig Ernst Borowski, probably August 1791.
2   Immanuel Kant, *The Doctrine of Virtue*, Part II of *The Metaphysic of Morals*, Mary Gregor (trans) (Harper and Row, 1964). One wonders whether these parts of *The Doctrine of Virtue* may have been influenced by Kant's thoughts about Herbert's predicament. An alternative explanation might be that *The Doctrine of Virtue* and Kant's letter to Herbert are both drawing on Kant's lecture notes.
3   *Groundwork of the Metaphysic of Morals*, Paton (trans.) (Harper and Row, 1964), 397.
4   Ibid., 398.
5   Immanuel Kant, *Critique of Practical Reason*, L.W. Beck (trans) (Macmillan, 1956), 97, 101.
6   Ibid., 119.
7   Ibid., 80.
8   Ibid., 117.
9   Op. cit. note 5, 428.
10   Op. cit. note 4, 407.
11   Op. cit. note 7, 118.
12   Ibid.
13   See Susan Wolf, 'Moral Saints', *The Journal of Philosophy* 79 (1982), 419–39, on the perils of sainthood.
14   See for example op. cit. note 4, 456.
15   Op. cit. note 7, 109.
16   Letters 1, 3 and 4 above. Elisabeth Motherby was the daughter of Kant's friend Robert Motherby, an English merchant in Königsberg.
17   This is Strawson's way of characterizing the two standpoints in Kant's moral philosophy (op. cit. note 1).
18   Op. cit. note 4, 462.
19   Letter 3.
20   Op. cit. note 4, 471. This is a remarkable metaphor for a philosopher who finds in the autonomous human self, and its self-legislating activity, the only source of intrinsic value.
21   Ibid., 471. Kant's ignorance of Antipodean bird life is (just) forgivable.
22   Ibid., 471.
23   This development of Kant's philosophy is proposed by Korsgaard as a way of addressing the problem of lying to the murderer at the door, in Korsgaard (1986), op. cit., note 1. I discuss it in more detail in the original version of this paper.
24   Op. cit. note 4, 434, 435.
25   There is one final letter from her on the record, dated early 1794, in which she expresses again a wish to visit Kant, and reflects upon her own desire for death.
26   Ibid., 424.

Chapter 33

John Rawls

A THEORY OF JUSTICE

The main idea of the theory of justice

MY AIM IS to present a conception of justice which generalizes and carries to a higher level of abstraction the familiar theory of the social contract as found, say, in Locke, Rousseau, and Kant.[1] In order to do this we are not to think of the original contract as one to enter a particular society or to set up a particular form of government. Rather, the guiding idea is that the principles of justice for the basic structure of society are the object of the original agreement. They are the principles that free and rational persons concerned to further their own interests would accept in an initial position of equality as defining the fundamental terms of their association. These principles are to regulate all further agreements; they specify the kinds of social cooperation that can be entered into and the forms of government that can be established. This way of regarding the principles of justice I shall call justice as fairness.

Thus we are to imagine that those who engage in social cooperation choose together, in one joint act, the principles which are to assign basic rights and duties and to determine the division of social benefits. Men are to decide in advance how they are to regulate their claims against one another and what is to be the foundation charter of their society. Just as each person must decide by rational reflection what constitutes his good, that is, the system of ends which it is rational for him to pursue, so a group of persons must decide once and for all what is to count among them as just and unjust. The choice which rational men would make in this hypothetical situation of equal liberty, assuming for the present that this choice problem has a solution, determines the principles of justice.

In justice as fairness the original position of equality corresponds to the state of nature in the traditional theory of the social contract. This original position is not, of course, thought of as an actual historical state of affairs, much less as a primitive condition of culture. It is understood as a purely hypothetical situation characterized so as to lead to a certain conception of justice.[2] Among the essential features of this situation is that no one knows his place in society, his class position or social status, nor does any one know his fortune in the distribution of natural assets and abilities, his intelligence, strength, and the like. I shall even assume that the parties do not know their conceptions of the good or their special psychological propensities. The principles of justice are chosen behind a veil of ignorance. This ensures that no one is advantaged or disadvantaged in the choice of principles by the outcome of natural chance or the contingency of social circumstances. Since all are similarly situated and no one is able to design principles to favor his particular condition, the principles of justice are the result of a fair agreement or bargain. For given the circumstances of the

original position, the symmetry of everyone's relations to each other, this initial situation is fair between individuals as moral persons, that is, as rational beings with their own ends and capable, I shall assume, of a sense of justice. The original position is, one might say, the appropriate initial status quo, and thus the fundamental agreements reached in it are fair. This explains the propriety of the name "justice as fairness": it conveys the idea that the principles of justice are agreed to in an initial situation that is fair. The name does not mean that the concepts of justice and fairness are the same, any more than the phrase "poetry as metaphor" means that the concepts of poetry and metaphor are the same.

Justice as fairness begins, as I have said, with one of the most general of all choices which persons might make together, namely, with the choice of the first principles of a conception of justice which is to regulate all subsequent criticism and reform of institutions. Then, having chosen a conception of justice, we can suppose that they are to choose a constitution and a legislature to enact laws, and so on, all in accordance with the principles of justice initially agreed upon. Our social situation is just if it is such that by this sequence of hypothetical agreements we would have contracted into the general system of rules which defines it. Moreover, assuming that the original position does determine a set of principles (that is, that a particular conception of justice would be chosen), it will then be true that whenever social institutions satisfy these principles those engaged in them can say to one another that they are cooperating on terms on which they would agree if they were free and equal persons whose relations with respect to one another were fair. They could all view their arrangements as meeting the stipulations which they would acknowledge in an initial situation that embodies widely accepted and reasonable constraints on the choice of principles. The general recognition of this fact would provide the basis for a public acceptance

of the corresponding principles of justice. No society can, of course, be a scheme of cooperation which men enter voluntarily in a literal sense; each person finds himself placed at birth in some particular position in some particular society, and the nature of this position materially affects his life prospects. Yet a society satisfying the principles of justice as fairness comes as close as a society can to being a voluntary scheme, for it meets the principles which free and equal persons would assent to under circumstances that are fair. In this sense its members are autonomous and the obligations they recognize self-imposed.

One feature of justice as fairness is to think of the parties in the initial situation as rational and mutually disinterested. This does not mean that the parties are egoists, that is, individuals with only certain kinds of interests, say in wealth, prestige, and domination. But they are conceived as not taking an interest in one another's interests. They are to presume that even their spiritual aims may be opposed, in the way that the aims of those of different religions may be opposed. Moreover, the concept of rationality must be interpreted as far as possible in the narrow sense, standard in economic theory, of taking the most effective means to given ends. I shall modify this concept to some extent, as explained later, but one must try to avoid introducing into it any controversial ethical elements. The initial situation must be characterized by stipulations that are widely accepted.

In working out the conception of justice as fairness one main task clearly is to determine which principles of justice would be chosen in the original position. To do this we must describe this situation in some detail and formulate with care the problem of choice which it presents. These matters I shall take up in the immediately succeeding chapters. It may be observed, however, that once the principles of justice are thought of as arising from an original agreement in a situation of equality, it is an open question whether the principle of utility would

be acknowledged. Offhand it hardly seems likely that persons who view themselves as equals, entitled to press their claims upon one another, would agree to a principle which may require lesser life prospects for some simply for the sake of a greater sum of advantages enjoyed by others. Since each desires to protect his interests, his capacity to advance his conception of the good, no one has a reason to acquiesce in an enduring loss for himself in order to bring about a greater net balance of satisfaction. In the absence of strong and lasting benevolent impulses, a rational man would not accept a basic structure merely because it maximized the algebraic sum of advantages irrespective of its permanent effects on his own basic rights and interests. Thus it seems that the principle of utility is incompatible with the conception of social cooperation among equals for mutual advantage. It appears to be inconsistent with the idea of reciprocity implicit in the notion of a well-ordered society. Or, at any rate, so I shall argue.

I shall maintain instead that the persons in the initial situation would choose two rather different principles: the first requires equality in the assignment of basic rights and duties, while the second holds that social and economic inequalities, for example, inequalities of wealth and authority, are just only if they result in compensating benefits for everyone, and in particular for the least advantaged members of society. These principles rule out justifying institutions on the grounds that the hardships of some are offset by a greater good in the aggregate. It may be expedient but it is not just that some should have less in order that others may prosper. But there is no injustice in the greater benefits earned by a few provided that the situation of persons not so fortunate is thereby improved. The intuitive idea is that since everyone's well-being depends upon a scheme of cooperation without which no one could have a satisfactory life, the division of advantages should be such as to draw forth the willing cooperation of everyone taking part in it, including those less well situated. Yet this can be expected only if reasonable terms are proposed. The two principles mentioned seem to be a fair agreement on the basis of which those better endowed, or more fortunate in their social position, neither of which we can be said to deserve, could expect the willing cooperation of others when some workable scheme is a necessary condition of the welfare of all.[3] Once we decide to look for a conception of justice that nullifies the accidents of natural endowment and the contingencies of social circumstance as counters in quest for political and economic advantage, we are led to these principles. They express the result of leaving aside those aspects of the social world that seem arbitrary from a moral point of view.

The problem of the choice of principles, however, is extremely difficult. I do not expect the answer I shall suggest to be convincing to everyone. It is, therefore, worth noting from the outset that justice as fairness, like other contract views, consists of two parts: (1) an interpretation of the initial situation and of the problem of choice posed there, and (2) a set of principles which, it is argued, would be agreed to. One may accept the first part of the theory (or some variant thereof), but not the other, and conversely. The concept of the initial contractual situation may seem reasonable although the particular principles proposed are rejected. To be sure, I want to maintain that the most appropriate conception of this situation does lead to principles of justice contrary to utilitarianism and perfectionism, and therefore that the contract doctrine provides an alternative to these views. Still, one may dispute this contention even though one grants that the contractarian method is a useful way of studying ethical theories and of setting forth their underlying assumptions.

• • •

A final remark. Justice as fairness is not a complete contract theory. For it is clear that the

contractarian idea can be extended to the choice of more or less an entire ethical system, that is, to a system including principles for all the virtues and not only for justice. Now for the most part I shall consider only principles of justice and others closely related to them; I make no attempt to discuss the virtues in a systematic way. Obviously if justice as fairness succeeds reasonably well, a next step would be to study the more general view suggested by the name "rightness as fairness." But even this wider theory fails to embrace all moral relationships, since it would seem to include only our relations with other persons and to leave out of account how we are to conduct ourselves toward animals and the rest of nature. I do not contend that the contract notion offers a way to approach these questions which are certainly of the first importance; and I shall have to put them aside. We must recognize the limited scope of justice as fairness and of the general type of view that it exemplifies. How far its conclusions must be revised once these other matters are understood cannot be decided in advance.

The original position and justification

I have said that the original position is the appropriate initial status quo which ensures that the fundamental agreements reached in it are fair. This fact yields the name "justice as fairness." It is clear, then, that I want to say that one conception of justice is more reasonable than another, or justifiable with respect to it, if rational persons in the initial situation would choose its principles over those of the other for the role of justice. Conceptions of justice are to be ranked by their acceptability to persons so circumstanced. Understood in this way the question of justification is settled by working out a problem of deliberation: we have to ascertain which principles it would be rational to adopt given the contractual situation. This connects the theory of justice with the theory of rational choice.

If this view of the problem of justification is to succeed, we must, of course, describe in some detail the nature of this choice problem. A problem of rational decision has a definite answer only if we know the beliefs and interests of the parties, their relations with respect to one another, the alternatives between which they are to choose, the procedure whereby they make up their minds, and so on. As the circumstances are presented in different ways, correspondingly different principles are accepted. The concept of the original position, as I shall refer to it, is that of the most philosophically favored interpretation of this initial choice situation for the purposes of a theory of justice.

But how are we to decide what is the most favored interpretation? I assume, for one thing, that there is a broad measure of agreement that principles of justice should be chosen under certain conditions. To justify a particular description of the initial situation one shows that it incorporates these commonly shared presumptions. One argues from widely accepted but weak premises to more specific conclusions. Each of the presumptions should by itself be natural and plausible; some of them may seem innocuous or even trivial. The aim of the contract approach is to establish that taken together they impose significant bounds on acceptable principles of justice. The ideal outcome would be that these conditions determine a unique set of principles; but I shall be satisfied if they suffice to rank the main traditional conceptions of social justice.

One should not be misled, then, by the somewhat unusual conditions which characterize the original position. The idea here is simply to make vivid to ourselves the restrictions that it seems reasonable to impose on arguments for principles of justice, and therefore on these principles themselves. Thus it seems reasonable and generally acceptable that no one should be advantaged or disadvantaged by natural fortune or social circumstances in the choice of principles. It also seems widely agreed that it should

be impossible to tailor principles to the circumstances of one's own case. We should ensure further that particular inclinations and aspirations and persons' conceptions of their good do not affect the principles adopted. The aim is to rule out those principles that it would be rational to propose for acceptance, however little the chance of success, only if one knew certain things that are irrelevant from the standpoint of justice. For example, if a man knew that he was wealthy, he might find it rational to advance the principle that various taxes for welfare measures be counted unjust; if he knew that he was poor, he would most likely propose the contrary principle. To represent the desired restrictions one imagines a situation in which everyone is deprived of this sort of information. One excludes the knowledge of those contingencies which sets men at odds and allows them to be guided by their prejudices. In this manner the veil of ignorance is arrived at in a natural way. This concept should cause no difficulty if we keep in mind the constraints on arguments that it is meant to express. At any time we can enter the original position, so to speak, simply by following a certain procedure, namely, by arguing for principles of justice in accordance with these restrictions.

It seems reasonable to suppose that the parties in the original position are equal. That is, all have the same rights in the procedure for choosing principles; each can make proposals, submit reasons for their acceptance, and so on. Obviously the purpose of these conditions is to represent equality between human beings as moral persons, as creatures having a conception of their good and capable of a sense of justice. The basis of equality is taken to be similarity in these two respects. Systems of ends are not ranked in value; and each man is presumed to have the requisite ability to understand and to act upon whatever principles are adopted. Together with the veil of ignorance, these conditions define the principles of justice as those which rational persons concerned to advance their interests would consent to as equals when none are known to be advantaged or disadvantaged by social and natural contingencies.

There is, however, another side to justifying a particular description of the original position. This is to see if the principles which would be chosen match our considered convictions of justice or extend them in an acceptable way. We can note whether applying these principles would lead us to make the same judgments about the basic structure of society which we now make intuitively and in which we have the greatest confidence; or whether, in cases where our present judgments are in doubt and given with hesitation, these principles offer a resolution which we can affirm on reflection. There are questions which we feel sure must be answered in a certain way. For example, we are confident that religious intolerance and racial discrimination are unjust. We think that we have examined these things with care and have reached what we believe is an impartial judgment not likely to be distorted by an excessive attention to our own interests. These convictions are provisional fixed points which we presume any conception of justice must fit. But we have much less assurance as to what is the correct distribution of wealth and authority. Here we may be looking for a way to remove our doubts. We can check an interpretation of the initial situation, then, by the capacity of its principles to accommodate our firmest convictions and to provide guidance where guidance is needed.

In searching for the most favored description of this situation we work from both ends. We begin by describing it so that it represents generally shared and preferably weak conditions. We then see if these conditions are strong enough to yield a significant set of principles. If not, we look for further premises equally reasonable. But if so, and these principles match our considered convictions of justice, then so far well and good. But presumably there will be discrepancies. In this case we have a choice. We can either modify the account of the initial situation or we can

revise our existing judgments, for even the judgments we take provisionally as fixed points are liable to revision. By going back and forth, sometimes altering the conditions of the contractual circumstances, at others withdrawing our judgments and conforming them to principle, I assume that eventually we shall find a description of the initial situation that both expresses reasonable conditions and yields principles which match our considered judgments duly pruned and adjusted. This state of affairs I refer to as reflective equilibrium.[4] It is an equilibrium because at last our principles and judgments coincide; and it is reflective since we know to what principles our judgments conform and the premises of their derivation. At the moment everything is in order. But this equilibrium is not necessarily stable. It is liable to be upset by further examination of the conditions which should be imposed on the contractual situation and by particular cases which may lead us to revise our judgments. Yet for the time being we have done what we can to render coherent and to justify our convictions of social justice. We have reached a conception of the original position.

• • •

Two principles of justice

I shall now state in a provisional form the two principles of justice that I believe would be chosen in the original position. In this section I wish to make only the most general comments, and therefore the first formulation of these principles is tentative. As we go on I shall run through several formulations and approximate step by step the final statement to be given much later. I believe that doing this allows the exposition to proceed in a natural way.

The first statement of the two principles reads as follows.

First: each person is to have an equal right to the most extensive basic liberty compatible with a similar liberty for others.

Second: social and economic inequalities are to be arranged so that they are both (a) reasonably expected to be to everyone's advantage, and (b) attached to positions and offices open to all.

There are two ambiguous phrases in the second principle, namely "everyone's advantage" and "open to all." . . .

By way of general comment, these principles primarily apply, as I have said, to the basic structure of society. They are to govern the assignment of rights and duties and to regulate the distribution of social and economic advantages. As their formulation suggests, these principles presuppose that the social structure can be divided into two more or less distinct parts, the first principle applying to the one, the second to the other. They distinguish between those aspects of the social system that define and secure the equal liberties of citizenship and those that specify and establish social and economic inequalities. The basic liberties of citizens are, roughly speaking, political liberty (the right to vote and to be eligible for public office) together with freedom of speech and assembly; liberty of conscience and freedom of thought; freedom of the person along with the right to hold (personal) property; and freedom from arbitrary arrest and seizure as defined by the concept of the rule of law. These liberties are all required to be equal by the first principle, since citizens of a just society are to have the same basic rights.

The second principle applies, in the first approximation, to the distribution of income and wealth and to the design of organizations that make use of differences in authority and responsibility, or chains of command. While the distribution of wealth and income need not be equal, it must be to everyone's advantage, and at the same time, positions of authority and offices of command must be accessible to all. One applies the second principle by holding positions open, and then, subject to this constraint,

arranges social and economic inequalities so that everyone benefits.

These principles are to be arranged in a serial order with the first principle prior to the second. This ordering means that a departure from the institutions of equal liberty required by the first principle cannot be justified by, or compensated for, by greater social and economic advantages. The distribution of wealth and income, and the hierarchies of authority, must be consistent with both the liberties of equal citizenship and equality of opportunity.

It is clear that these principles are rather specific in their content, and their acceptance rests on certain assumptions that I must eventually try to explain and justify. A theory of justice depends upon a theory of society in ways that will become evident as we proceed. For the present, it should be observed that the two principles (and this holds for all formulations) are a special case of a more general conception of justice that can be expressed as follows.

All social values—liberty and opportunity, income and wealth, and the bases of self-respect—are to be distributed equally unless an unequal distribution of any, or all, of these values is to everyone's advantage.

Injustice, then, is simply inequalities that are not to the benefit of all. Of course, this conception is extremely vague and requires interpretation.

As a first step, suppose that the basic structure of society distributes certain primary goods, that is, things that every rational man is presumed to want. These goods normally have a use whatever a person's rational plan of life. For simplicity, assume that the chief primary goods at the disposition of society are rights and liberties, powers and opportunities, income and wealth. (Later on in Part Three [see original reading] the primary good of self-respect has a central place.) These are the social primary goods. Other primary goods such as health and vigor, intelligence and imagination, are natural goods; although their possession is influenced by the basic structure, they are not so directly under its control. Imagine, then, a hypothetical initial arrangement in which all the social primary goods are equally distributed: everyone has similar rights and duties, and income and wealth are evenly shared. This state of affairs provides a benchmark for judging improvements. If certain inequalities of wealth and organizational powers would make everyone better off than in this hypothetical starting situation, then they accord with the general conception.

Now it is possible, at least theoretically, that by giving up some of their fundamental liberties men are sufficiently compensated by the resulting social and economic gains. The general conception of justice imposes no restrictions on what sort of inequalities are permissible; it only requires that everyone's position be improved. We need not suppose anything so drastic as consenting to a condition of slavery. Imagine instead that men forgo certain political rights when the economic returns are significant and their capacity to influence the course of policy by the exercise of these rights would be marginal in any case. It is this kind of exchange which the two principles as stated rule out; being arranged in serial order they do not permit exchanges between basic liberties and economic and social gains. The serial ordering of principles expresses an underlying preference among primary social goods. When this preference is rational so likewise is the choice of these principles in this order.

In developing justice as fairness I shall, for the most part, leave aside the general conception of justice and examine instead the special case of the two principles in serial order. The advantage of this procedure is that from the first the matter of priorities is recognized and an effort made to find principles to deal with it. One is led to attend throughout to the conditions under which the acknowledgment of the absolute weight of liberty with respect to social and economic advantages, as defined by the lexical order of the

two principles, would be reasonable. Offhand, this ranking appears extreme and too special a case to be of much interest; but there is more justification for it than would appear at first sight. Or at any rate, so I shall maintain. Furthermore, the distinction between fundamental rights and liberties and economic and social benefits marks a difference among primary social goods that one should try to exploit. It suggests an important division in the social system. Of course, the distinctions drawn and the ordering proposed are bound to be at best only approximations. There are surely circumstances in which they fail. But it is essential to depict clearly the main lines of a reasonable conception of justice; and under many conditions anyway, the two principles in serial order may serve well enough. When necessary we can fall back on the more general conception.

The fact that the two principles apply to institutions has certain consequences. Several points illustrate this. First of all, the rights and liberties referred to by these principles are those which are defined by the public rules of the basic structure. Whether men are free is determined by the rights and duties established by the major institutions of society. Liberty is a certain pattern of social forms. The first principle simply requires that certain sorts of rules, those defining basic liberties, apply to everyone equally and that they allow the most extensive liberty compatible with a like liberty for all. The only reason for circumscribing the rights defining liberty and making men's freedom less extensive than it might otherwise be is that these equal rights as institutionally defined would interfere with one another.

Another thing to bear in mind is that when principles mention persons, or require that everyone gains from an inequality, the reference is to representative persons holding the various social positions, or offices, or whatever, established by the basic structure. Thus in applying the second principle I assume that it is possible to assign an expectation of well-being

to representative individuals holding these positions. This expectation indicates their life prospects as viewed from their social station. In general, the expectations of representative persons depend on the distribution of rights and duties throughout the basic structure. When this changes, expectations change. I assume, then, that expectations are connected: by raising the prospects of the representative man in one position we presumably increase or decrease the prospects of representative men in other positions. Since it applies to institutional forms, the second principle (or rather the first part of it) refers to the expectations of representative individuals, As I shall discuss below, neither principle applies to distributions of particular goods to particular individuals who may be identified by their proper names. The situation where someone is considering how to allocate certain commodities to needy persons who are known to him is not within the scope of the principles. They are meant to regulate basic institutional arrangements. We must not assume that there is much similarity from the standpoint of justice between an administrative allotment of goods to specific persons and the appropriate design of society. Our common sense intuitions for the former may be a poor guide to the latter.

Now the second principle insists that each person benefit from permissible inequalities in the basic structure. This means that it must be reasonable for each relevant representative man defined by this structure, when he views it as a going concern, to prefer his prospects with the inequality to his prospects without it. One is not allowed to justify differences in income or organizational powers on the ground that the disadvantages of those in one position are outweighed by the greater advantages of those in another. Much less can infringements of liberty be counterbalanced in this way. Applied to the basic structure, the principle of utility would have us maximize the sum of expectations of representative men (weighed by the number of persons they represent, on the

classical view); and this would permit us to compensate for the losses of some by the gains of others. Instead, the two principles require that everyone benefit from economic and social inequalities.

• • •

Principles for individuals: the principle of fairness

In the discussion so far I have considered the principles which apply to institutions or, more exactly, to the basic structure of society. It is clear, however, that principles of another kind must also be chosen, since a complete theory of right includes principles for individuals as well.

• • •

Now the order in which principles are chosen raises a number of questions which I shall skip over. The important thing is that the various principles are to be adopted in a definite sequence and the reasons for this ordering are connected with the more difficult parts of the theory of justice. To illustrate: while it would be possible to choose many of the natural duties before those for the basic structure without changing the principles in any substantial way, the sequence in either case reflects the fact that obligations presuppose principles for social forms. And some natural duties also presuppose such principles, for example, the duty to support just institutions. For this reason it seems simpler to adopt all principles for individuals after those for the basic structure. That principles for institutions are chosen first shows the social nature of the virtue of justice, its intimate connection with social practices so often noted by idealists. When Bradley says that the individual is a bare abstraction, he can be interpreted to say, without too much distortion, that a person's obligations and duties presuppose a moral conception of institutions and therefore that the content of just institutions must be defined before the requirements for individuals can be set out.[5] And this is to say that, in most cases, the principles for

obligations and duties should be settled upon after those for the basic structure.

Therefore, to establish a complete conception of right, the parties in the original position are to choose in a definite order not only a conception of justice but also principles to go with each major concept falling under the concept of right. These concepts are I assume relatively few in number and have a determinate relation to each other. Thus, in addition to principles for institutions there must be an agreement on principles for such notions as fairness and fidelity, mutual respect and beneficence as these apply to individuals, as well as on principles for the conduct of states. The intuitive idea is this: the concept of something's being right is the same as, or better, may be replaced by, the concept of its being in accordance with the principles that in the original position would be acknowledged to apply to things of its kind. I do not interpret this concept of right as providing an analysis of the meaning of the term "right" as normally used in moral contexts. It is not meant as an analysis of the concept of right in the traditional sense. Rather, the broader notion of rightness as fairness is to be understood as a replacement for existing conceptions. There is no necessity to say that sameness of meaning holds between the word "right" (and its relatives) in its ordinary use and the more elaborate locutions needed to express this ideal contractarian concept of right. For our purposes here I accept the view that a sound analysis is best understood as providing a satisfactory substitute, one that meets certain desiderata while avoiding certain obscurities and confusions. In other words, explication is elimination: we start with a concept the expression for which is somehow troublesome; but it serves certain ends that cannot be given up. An explication achieves these ends in other ways that are relatively free of difficulty.[6] Thus if the theory of justice as fairness, or more generally of rightness as fairness, fits our considered judgments in reflective equilibrium, and if it enables us to say all that on due examination we want to say, then

it provides a way of eliminating customary phrases in favor of other expressions. So understood one may think of justice as fairness and rightness as fairness as providing a definition or explication of the concepts of justice and right.

• • •

The reasoning leading to the two principles of justice

• • •

It seems clear . . . that the two principles are at least a plausible conception of justice. The question, though, is how one is to argue for them more systematically. Now there are several things to do. One can work out their consequences for institutions and note their implications for fundamental social policy. In this way they are tested by a comparison with our considered judgments of justice. Part II [see original reading] is devoted to this. But one can also try to find arguments in their favor that are decisive from the standpoint of the original position. In order to see how this might be done, it is useful as a heuristic device to think of the two principles as the maximin solution to the problem of social justice. There is an analogy between the two principles and the maximin rule for choice under uncertainty.[7] This is evident from the fact that the two principles are those a person would choose for the design of a society in which his enemy is to assign him his place. The maximin rule tells us to rank alternatives by their worst possible outcomes: we are to adopt the alternative the worst outcome of which is superior to the worst outcomes of the others. The persons in the original position do not, of course, assume that their initial place in society is decided by a malevolent opponent. As I note below, they should not reason from false premises. The veil of ignorance does not violate this idea, since an absence of information is not misinformation. But that the two principles of justice would be chosen if the parties were forced to protect themselves against such a contingency explains the sense in which

this conception is the maximin solution. And this analogy suggests that if the original position has been described so that it is rational for the parties to adopt the conservative attitude expressed by this rule, a conclusive argument can indeed be constructed for these principles. Clearly the maximin rule is not, in general, a suitable guide for choices under uncertainty. But it is attractive in situations marked by certain special features. My aim, then, is to show that a good case can be made for the two principles based on the fact that the original position manifests these features to the fullest possible degree, carrying them to the limit, so to speak.

• • •

Now there appear to be three chief features of situations that give plausibility to this unusual rule.[8] First, since the rule takes no account of the likelihoods of the possible circumstances, there must be some reason for sharply discounting estimates of these probabilities. Offhand, the most natural rule of choice would seem to be to compute the expectation of monetary gain for each decision and then to adopt the course of action with the highest prospect. (This expectation is defined as follows: let us suppose that g_{ij} represent the numbers in the gain-and-loss table, where i is the row index and j is the column index; and let p_j, j = 1, 2, 3, be the likelihoods of the circumstances, with $\Sigma_{pj} = 1$. Then the expectation for the ith decision is equal to $\Sigma p_j g_{ij}$.) Thus it must be, for example, that the situation is one in which a knowledge of likelihoods is impossible, or at best extremely insecure. In this case it is unreasonable not to be skeptical of probabilistic calculations unless there is no other way out, particularly if the decision is a fundamental one that needs to be justified to others.

The second feature that suggests the maximin rule is the following: the person choosing has a conception of the good such that he cares very little, if anything, for what he might gain above the minimum stipend that he can, in fact, be sure of by following the maximin rule. It is not

worthwhile for him to take a chance for the sake of a further advantage, especially when it may turn out that he loses much that is important to him. This last provision brings in the third feature, namely, that the rejected alternatives have outcomes that one can hardly accept. The situation involves grave risks. Of course these features work most effectively in combination. The paradigm situation for following the maximin rule is when all three features are realized to the highest degree. This rule does not, then, generally apply, nor of course is it self-evident. Rather, it is a maxim, a rule of thumb, that comes into its own in special circumstances. Its application depends upon the qualitative structure of the possible gains and losses in relation to one's conception of the good, all this against a background in which it is reasonable to discount conjectural estimates of likelihoods.

• • •

Now, as I have suggested, the original position has been defined so that it is a situation in which the maximin rule applies. In order to see this, let us review briefly the nature of this situation with these three special features in mind. To begin with, the veil of ignorance excludes all but the vaguest knowledge of likelihoods. The parties have no basis for determining the probable nature of their society, or their place in it. Thus they have strong reasons for being wary of probability calculations if any other course is open to them. They must also take in account the fact that their choice of principles should seem reasonable to others, in particular their descendants, whose rights will be deeply affected by it. There are further grounds for discounting that I shall mention as we go along. For the present it suffices to note that these considerations are strengthened by the fact that the parties know very little about the gain-and-loss table. Not only are they unable to conjecture the likelihood of the various possible circumstances, they cannot say much about what the possible circumstances are, much less enumerate them and foresee the outcome of each

alternative available. Those deciding are much more in the dark than the illustration by a numerical table suggests. It is for this reason that I have spoken of an analogy with the maximin rule.

Several kinds of arguments for the two principles of justice illustrate the second feature. Thus, if we can maintain that these principles provide a workable theory of social justice, and that they are compatible with reasonable demands of efficiency, then this conception guarantees a satisfactory minimum. There may be, on reflection, little reason for trying to do better. Thus much of the argument . . . is to show, by their application to the main questions of social justice, that the two principles are a satisfactory conception. These details have a philosophical purpose. Moreover, this line of thought is practically decisive if we can establish the priority of liberty, the lexical ordering of the two principles. For this priority implies that the persons in the original position have no desire to try for greater gains at the expense of the equal liberties. The minimum assured by the two principles in lexical order is not one that the parties wish to jeopardize for the sake of greater economic and social advantages . . . .

Finally, the third feature holds if we can assume that other conceptions of justice may lead to institutions that the parties would find intolerable. For example, it has sometimes been held that under some conditions the utility principle (in either form) justifies, if not slavery or serfdom, at any rate serious infractions of liberty for the sake of greater social benefits. We need not consider here the truth of this claim, or the likelihood that the requisite conditions obtain. For the moment, this contention is only to illustrate the way in which conceptions of justice may allow for outcomes which the parties may not be able to accept. And having the ready alternative of the two principles of justice which secure a satisfactory minimum, it seems unwise, if not irrational, for them to take a chance that these outcomes are not realized.

• • •

The Kantian interpretation of justice as fairness

For the most part I have considered the content of the principle of equal liberty and the meaning of the priority of the rights that it defines. It seems appropriate at this point to note that there is a Kantian interpretation of the conception of justice from which this principle derives. This interpretation is based upon Kant's notion of autonomy. It is a mistake, I believe, to emphasize the place of generality and universality in Kant's ethics. That moral principles are general and universal is hardly new with him; and as we have seen these conditions do not in any case take us very far. It is impossible to construct a moral theory on so slender a basis, and therefore to limit the discussion of Kant's doctrine to these notions is to reduce it to triviality. The real force of his view lies elsewhere.[9]

For one thing, he begins with the idea that moral principles are the object of rational choice. They define the moral law that men can rationally will to govern their conduct in an ethical commonwealth. Moral philosophy becomes the study of the conception and outcome of a suitably defined rational decision. This idea has immediate consequences. For once we think of moral principles as legislation for a kingdom of ends, it is clear that these principles must not only be acceptable to all but public as well. Finally Kant supposes that this moral legislation is to be agreed to under conditions that characterize men as free and equal rational beings. The description of the original position is an attempt to interpret this conception. I do not wish to argue here for this interpretation on the basis of Kant's text. Certainly some will want to read him differently. Perhaps the remarks to follow are best taken as suggestions for relating justice as fairness to the high point of the contractarian tradition in Kant and Rousseau.

Kant held, I believe, that a person is acting autonomously when the principles of his action are chosen by him as the most adequate possible expression of his nature as a free and equal rational being. The principles he acts upon are not adopted because of his social position or natural endowments, or in view of the particular kind of society in which he lives or the specific things that he happens to want. To act on such principles is to act heteronomously. Now the veil of ignorance deprives the persons in the original position of the knowledge that would enable them to choose heteronomous principles. The parties arrive at their choice together as free and equal rational persons knowing only that those circumstances obtain which give rise to the need for principles of justice.

To be sure, the argument for these principles does add in various ways to Kant's conception. For example, it adds the feature that the principles chosen are to apply to the basic structure of society; and premises characterizing this structure are used in deriving the principles of justice. But I believe that this and other additions are natural enough and remain fairly close to Kant's doctrine, at least when all of his ethical writings are viewed together. Assuming, then, that the reasoning in favor of the principles of justice is correct, we can say that when persons act on these principles they are acting in accordance with principles that they would choose as rational and independent persons in an original position of equality. The principles of their actions do not depend upon social or natural contingencies, nor do they reflect the bias of the particulars of their plan of life or the aspirations that motivate them. By acting from these principles persons express their nature as free and equal rational beings subject to the general conditions of human life. For to express one's nature as a being of a particular kind is to act on the principles that would be chosen if this nature were the decisive determining element. Of course, the choice of the parties in the original position is subject to the restrictions of that situation. But when we knowingly act on the principles of justice in the ordinary course of events, we deliberately assume the limitations of the

original position. One reason for doing this, for persons who can do so and want to, is to give expression to one's nature.

The principles of justice are also categorical imperatives in Kant's sense. For by a categorical imperative Kant understands a principle of conduct that applies to a person in virtue of his nature as a free and equal rational being. The validity of the principle does not presuppose that one has a particular desire or aim. Whereas a hypothetical imperative by contrast does assume this: it directs us to take certain steps as effective means to achieve a specific end. Whether the desire is for a particular thing, or whether it is for something more general, such as certain kinds of agreeable feelings or pleasures, the corresponding imperative is hypothetical. Its applicability depends upon one's having an aim which one need not have as a condition of being a rational human individual. The argument for the two principles of justice does not assume that the parties have particular ends, but only that they desire certain primary goods. These are things that it is rational to want whatever else one wants. Thus given human nature, wanting them is part of being rational; and while each is presumed to have some conception of the good, nothing is known about his final ends. The preference for primary goods is derived, then, from only the most general assumptions about rationality and the conditions of human life. To act from the principles of justice is to act from categorical imperatives in the sense that they apply to us whatever in particular our aims are. This simply reflects the fact that no such contingencies appear as premises in their derivation.

We may note also that the motivational assumption of mutual disinterest accords with Kant's notion of autonomy, and gives another reason for this condition. So far this assumption has been used to characterize the circumstances of justice and to provide a clear conception to guide the reasoning of the parties. We have also seen that the concept of benevolence, being a second-order notion, would not work out well. Now we can add that the assumption of mutual disinterest is to allow for freedom in the choice of a system of final ends.[10] Liberty in adopting a conception of the good is limited only by principles that are deduced from a doctrine which imposes no prior constraints on these conceptions. Presuming mutual disinterest in the original position carries out this idea. We postulate that the parties have opposing claims in a suitably general sense. If their ends were restricted in some specific way, this would appear at the outset as an arbitrary restriction on freedom. Moreover, if the parties were conceived as altruists, or as pursuing certain kinds of pleasures, then the principles chosen would apply, as far as the argument would have shown, only to persons whose freedom was restricted to choices compatible with altruism or hedonism. As the argument now runs, the principles of justice cover all persons with rational plans of life, whatever their content, and these principles represent the appropriate restrictions on freedom. Thus it is possible to say that the constraints on conceptions of the good are the result of an interpretation of the contractual situation that puts no prior limitations on what men may desire. There are a variety of reasons, then, for the motivational premise of mutual disinterest. This premise is not only a matter of realism about the circumstances of justice or a way to make the theory manageable. It also connects up with the Kantian idea of autonomy.

There is, however, a difficulty that should be clarified. It is well expressed by Sidgwick.[11] He remarks that nothing in Kant's ethics is more striking than the idea that a man realizes his true self, when he acts from the moral law, whereas if he permits his actions to be determined by sensuous desires or contingent aims, he becomes subject to the law of nature. Yet in Sidgwick's opinion this idea comes to naught. It seems to him that on Kant's view the lives of the saint and the scoundrel are equally the outcome of a free choice (on the part of the noumenal self) and

equally the subject of causal laws (as a phenomenal self). Kant never explains why the scoundrel does not express in a bad life his characteristic and freely chosen selfhood in the same way that a saint expresses his characteristic and freely chosen selfhood in a good one. Sidgwick's objection is decisive, I think, as long as one assumes, as Kant's exposition may seem to allow, both that the noumenal self can choose any consistent set of principles and that acting from such principles, whatever they are, is sufficient to express one's choice as that of a free and equal rational being. Kant's reply must be that though acting on any consistent set of principles could be the outcome of a decision on the part of the noumenal self, not all such action by the phenomenal self expresses this decision as that of a free and equal rational being. Thus if a person realizes his true self by expressing it in his actions, and if he desires above all else to realize this self, then he will choose to act from principles that manifest his nature as a free and equal rational being. The missing part of the argument concerns the concept of expression. Kant did not show that acting from the moral law expresses our nature in identifiable ways that acting from contrary principles does not.

This defect is made good, I believe, by the conception of the original position. The essential point is that we need an argument showing which principles, if any, free and equal rational persons would choose and these principles must be applicable in practice. A definite answer to this question is required to meet Sidgwick's objection. My suggestion is that we think of the original position as the point of view from which noumenal selves see the world. The parties qua noumenal selves have complete freedom to choose whatever principles they wish; but they also have a desire to express their nature as rational and equal members of the intelligible realm with precisely this liberty to choose, that is, as beings who can look at the world in this way and express this perspective in their life as members of society. They must

decide, then, which principles when consciously followed and acted upon in everyday life will best manifest this freedom in their community, most fully reveal their independence from natural contingencies and social accident. Now if the argument of the contract doctrine is correct, these principles are indeed those defining the moral law, or more exactly, the principles of justice for institutions and individuals. The description of the original position interprets the point of view of noumenal selves, of what it means to be a free and equal rational being. Our nature as such beings is displayed when we act from the principles we would choose when this nature is reflected in the conditions determining the choice. Thus men exhibit their freedom, their independence from the contingencies of nature and society, by acting in ways they would acknowledge in the original position.

Properly understood, then, the desire to act justly derives in part from the desire to express most fully what we are or can be, namely free and equal rational beings with a liberty to choose. It is for this reason, I believe, that Kant speaks of the failure to act on the moral law as giving rise to shame and not to feelings of guilt. And this is appropriate, since for him acting unjustly is acting in a manner that fails to express our nature as a free and equal rational being. Such actions therefore strike at our self-respect, our sense of our own worth, and the experience of this loss is shame. We have acted as though we belonged to a lower order, as though we were a creature whose first principles are decided by natural contingencies. Those who think of Kant's moral doctrine as one of law and guilt badly misunderstand him. Kant's main aim is to deepen and to justify Rousseau's idea that liberty is acting in accordance with a law that we give to ourselves. And this leads not to a morality of austere command but to an ethic of mutual respect and self-esteem.[12]

The original position may be viewed, then, as a procedural interpretation of Kant's conception

of autonomy and the categorical imperative. The principles regulative of the kingdom of ends are those that would be chosen in this position, and the description of this situation enables us to explain the sense in which acting from these principles expresses our nature as free and equal rational persons. No longer are these notions purely transcendent and lacking explicable connections with human conduct, for the procedural conception of the original position allows us to make these ties. It is true that I have departed from Kant's views in several respects. I shall not discuss these matters here; but two points should be noted. The person's choice as a noumenal self I have assumed to be a collective one. The force of the self's being equal is that the principles chosen must be acceptable to other selves. Since all are similarly free and rational, each must have an equal say in adopting the public principles of the ethical commonwealth. This means that as noumenal selves, everyone is to consent to these principles. Unless the scoundrel's principles would be chosen, they cannot express this free choice, however much a single self might be of a mind to opt for them. Later I shall try to define a clear sense in which this unanimous agreement is best expressive of the nature of even a single self. It in no way overrides a person's interests as the collective nature of the choice might seem to imply. But I leave this aside for the present.

Secondly, I have assumed all along that the parties know that they are subject to the conditions of human life. Being in the circumstances of justice, they are situated in the world with other men who likewise face limitations of moderate scarcity and competing claims. Human freedom is to be regulated by principles chosen in the light of these natural restrictions. Thus justice as fairness is a theory of human justice and among its premises are the elementary facts about persons and their place in nature. The freedom of pure intelligences not subject to these constraints, and the freedom of God, is outside the scope of the theory. It might appear that Kant meant his doctrine to apply to all rational beings as such and therefore to God and the angels as well. Men's social situation in the world may seem to have no role in his theory in determining the first principles of justice. I do not believe that Kant held this view, but I cannot discuss this question here. It suffices to say that if I am mistaken, the Kantian interpretation of justice as fairness is less faithful to Kant's intentions than I am presently inclined to suppose.

Notes

1 As the text suggests, I shall regard Locke's *Second Treatise of Government*, Rousseau's *The Social Contract*, and Kant's ethical works beginning with *The Foundations of the Metaphysics of Morals* as definitive of the contract tradition. For all of its greatness, Hobbes's *Leviathan* raises special problems. A general historical survey is provided by J. W. Gough, *The Social Contract*, 2nd ed. (Oxford, The Clarendon Press, 1957), and Otto Gierke, *Natural Law and the Theory of Society*, trans. with an introduction by Ernest Barker (Cambridge, The University Press, 1934). A presentation of the contract view as primarily an ethical theory is to be found in G. R. Grice, *The Grounds of Moral Judgment* (Cambridge, The University Press, 1967). See also §19, note 30 [see original reading].

2 Kant is clear that the original agreement is hypothetical. See *The Metaphysics of Morals*, pt. I (*Rechtslehre*), especially §§47, 52; and pt. II of the essay "Concerning the Common Saying: This May Be True in Theory but It Does Not Apply in Practice," in *Kant's Political Writings*, ed. Hans Reiss and trans. by H. B. Nisber (Cambridge, The University Press, 1970), pp. 73–87. See Georges Vlachos, *La Pensée politique de Kant* (Paris, Presses Universitaires de France, 1962), pp. 326–35; and J. G. Murphy, *Kant: The Philosophy of Right* (London, Macmillan, 1970), pp. 109–12, 133–36, for a further discussion.

3 For the formulation of this intuitive idea I am indebted to Allan Gibbard.

4 The process of mutual adjustment of principles and considered judgments is not peculiar to moral philosophy. See Nelson Goodman, *Fact, Fiction, and Forecast* (Cambridge, MA, Harvard University Press,

1955), pp. 65–68, for parallel remarks concerning the justification of the principles of deductive and inductive inference.

5   See F. H. Bradley, *Ethical Studies*, 2nd ed. (Oxford, The Clarendon Press, 1927), pp. 163–89.

6   See W. V. Quine, *Word and Object* (Cambridge, MA, M.I.T. Press, 1960), pp. 257–62, whom I follow here.

7   An accessible discussion of this and other rules of choice under uncertainty can be found in W. J. Baumol, *Economic Theory and Operations Analysis*, 2nd ed. (Englewood Cliffs, NJ, Prentice-Hall, Inc., 1965), ch. 24. Baumol gives a geometric interpretation of these rules, including the diagram used in §13 to illustrate the difference principle. See pp. 558–62. See also R. D. Luce and Howard Raiffa, *Games and Decisions* (New York, John Wiley and Sons, Inc., 1957), ch. XIII, for a fuller account.

8   Here I borrow from William Fellner, *Probability and Profit* (Homewood, IL, R. D. Irwin, Inc., 1965), pp. 140–42, where these features are noted.

9   To be avoided at all costs is the idea that Kant's doctrine simply provides the general, or formal, elements for a utilitarian (or indeed for any other) theory. See, for example, R. M. Hare, *Freedom and Reason* (Oxford, The Clarendon Press, 1963), pp. 123f. One must not lose sight of the full scope of his view, one must take the later works into consideration. Unfortunately, there is no commentary on Kant's moral theory as a whole; perhaps it would prove impossible to write. But the standard works of H. J. Paron, *The Categorical Imperative* (Chicago, University of Chicago Press, 1948), and L. W. Beck, *A Commentary on Kant's Critique of Practical Reason* (Chicago, University of Chicago Press, 1960), and others need to be further complemented by studies of the other writings. See here M. J. Gregor's *Laws of Freedom* (Oxford, Basil Blackwell, 1963), an account of *The Metaphysics of Morals*, and j. G. Murphy's brief *Kant: The Philosophy of Right* (London, Macmillan, 1970). Beyond this, *The Critique of Judgment, Religion Within the Limits of Reason*, and the political writings cannot be neglected without distorting his doctrine. For the last, see *Kant's Political Writings*, ed. Hans Reiss and trans. H. B. Nisbet (Cambridge, The University Press, 1970).

10   For this point I am indebted to Charles Fried.

11   See *The Methods of Ethics*, 7th ed. (London, Macmillan, 1907), Appendix, "The Kantian Conception of Free Will" (reprinted from *Mind*, vol. 13, 1888), pp. 511–16, esp. p. 516.

12   See B. A. O. Williams, "The Idea of Equality," in *Philosophy, Politics and Society*, Second Series, ed. Peter Laslett and W. G. Runciman (Oxford, Basil Blackwell, 1962), pp. 115f. For confirmation of this interpretation, see Kant's remarks on moral education in *The Critique of Practical Reason*, pt. II. See also Beck, *Commentary on Kant's Critique of Practical Reason*, pp. 233–36.

Thomas Scanlon

CONTRACTUALISM AND UTILITARIANISM

To give an example of what I mean by contractualism, a contractualist account of the nature of moral wrongness might be stated as follows.

> An act is wrong if its performance under the circumstances would be disallowed by any system of rules for the general regulation of behaviour which no one could reasonably reject as a basis for informed, unforced general agreement.

This is intended as a characterisation of the kind of property which moral wrongness is. Like philosophical utilitarianism, it will have normative consequences, but it is not my present purpose to explore these in detail.

As a contractualist account of one moral notion, what I have set out here is only an approximation, which may need to be modified considerably. Here I can offer a few remarks by way of clarification.

The idea of 'informed agreement' is meant to exclude agreement based on superstition or false belief about the consequences of actions, even if these beliefs are ones which it would be reasonable for the person in question to have. The intended force of the qualification 'reasonably', on the other hand, is to exclude rejections that would be unreasonable *given* the aim of finding principles which could be the basis of informed, unforced general agreement. Given this aim, it would be unreasonable, for example, to reject a principle because it imposed a burden on you when every alternative principle would impose much greater burdens on others. I will have more to say about grounds for rejection later in the paper.

The requirement that the hypothetical agreement which is the subject of moral argument be unforced is meant not only to rule out coercion, but also to exclude being forced to accept an agreement by being in a weak bargaining position, for example because others are able to hold out longer and hence to insist on better terms. Moral argument abstracts from such considerations. The only relevant pressure for agreement comes from the desire to find and agree on principles which no one who had this desire could reasonably reject. According to contractualism, moral argument concerns the possibility of agreement among persons who are all moved by this desire, and moved by it to the same degree. But this counter-factual assumption characterises only the agreement with which morality is concerned, not the world to which moral principles are to apply. Those who are concerned with morality look for principles for application to their imperfect world which they could not reasonably reject, and which others in this world, who are not now moved by the desire for agreement, could not reasonably reject should they come to be so moved.[1]

The contractualist account of moral wrongness refers to principles 'which no one could reasonably reject' rather than to principles 'which everyone could reasonably accept' for the following reason.[2] Consider a principle under which some people will suffer severe hardships, and suppose that these hardships are avoidable. That is, there are alternative principles under which no one would have to bear comparable burdens. It might happen, however, that the people on whom these hardships fall are particularly self-sacrificing, and are willing to accept these burdens for the sake of what they see as the greater good of all. We would not say, I think, that it would be unreasonable of them to do this. On the other hand, it might not be unreasonable for them to refuse these burdens, and, hence, not unreasonable for someone to reject a principle requiring him to bear them. If this rejection would be reasonable, then the principle imposing these burdens is put in doubt, despite the fact that some particularly self-sacrificing people could (reasonably) accept it. Thus it is the reasonableness of rejecting a principle, rather than the reasonableness of accepting it, on which moral argument turns.

It seems likely that many non-equivalent sets of principles will pass the test of non-rejectability. This is suggested, for example, by the fact that there are many different ways of defining important duties, no one of which is more or less 'rejectable' than the others. There are, for example, many different systems of agreement-making and many different ways of assigning responsibility to care for others. It does not follow, however, that any action allowed by at least one of these sets of principles cannot be morally wrong according to contractualism. If it is important for us to have *some* duty of a given kind (some duty of fidelity to agreements, or some duty of mutual aid) of which there are many morally acceptable forms, then one of these forms needs to be established by convention. In a setting in which one of these forms *is* conventionally established, acts disallowed by it

will be wrong in the sense of the definition given. For, given the need for such conventions, one thing that could not be generally agreed to would be a set of principles allowing one to disregard conventionally established (and morally acceptable) definitions of important duties. This dependence on convention introduces a degree of cultural relativity into contractualist morality. In addition, what a person can reasonably reject will depend on the aims and conditions that are important in his life, and these will also depend on the society in which he lives. The definition given above allows for variation of both of these kinds by making the wrongness of an action depend on the circumstances in which it is performed.

The partial statement of contractualism which I have given has the abstract character appropriate in an account of the subject matter of morality. On its face, it involves no specific claim as to which principles could be agreed to or even whether there is a unique set of principles which could be the basis of agreement. One way, though not the only way, for a contractualist to arrive at substantive moral claims would be to give a technical definition of the relevant notion of agreement, e.g. by specifying the conditions under which agreement is to be reached, the parties to this agreement and the criteria of reasonableness to be employed. Different contractualists have done this in different ways. What must be claimed for such a definition is that (under the circumstances in which it is to apply) what it describes is indeed the kind of unforced, reasonable agreement at which moral argument aims. But contractualism can also be understood as an informal description of the subject matter of morality on the basis of which ordinary forms of moral reasoning can be understood and appraised without proceeding via a technical notion of agreement.

Who is to be included in the general agreement to which contractualism refers? The scope of morality is a difficult question of substantive

morality, but a philosophical theory of the nature of morality should provide some basis for answering it. What an adequate theory should do is to provide a framework within which what seem to be relevant arguments for and against particular interpretations of the moral boundary can be carried out. It is often thought that contractualism can provide no plausible basis for an answer to this question. Critics charge either that contractualism provides no answer at all, because it must begin with some set of contracting parties taken as given, or that contractualism suggests an answer which is obviously too restrictive, since a contract requires parties who are able to make and keep agreements and who are each able to offer the others some benefit in return for their cooperation. Neither of these objections applies to the version of contractualism that I am defending. The general specification of the scope of morality which it implies seems to me to be this: morality applies to a being if the notion of justification to a being of that kind makes sense. What is required in order for this to be the case? Here I can only suggest some necessary conditions. The first is that the being have a good, that is, that there be a clear sense in which things can be said to go better or worse for that being. This gives partial sense to the idea of what it would be reasonable for a trustee to accept on the being's behalf. It would be reasonable for a trustee to accept at least those things that are good, or not bad, for the being in question. Using this idea of trusteeship we can extend the notion of acceptance to apply to beings that are incapable of literally agreeing to anything. But this minimal notion of trusteeship is too weak to provide a basis for morality, according to contractualism. Contractualist morality relies on notions of what it would be reasonable to accept, or reasonable to reject, which are essentially comparative. Whether it would be unreasonable for me to reject a certain principle, given the aim of finding principles which no one with this aim could reasonably reject, depends not only on how much actions allowed by that principle might hurt me in absolute terms but also on how that potential loss compares with other potential losses to others under this principle and alternatives to it. Thus, in order for a being to stand in moral relations with us it is not enough that it have a good, it is also necessary that its good be sufficiently similar to our own to provide a basis for some system of comparability. Only on the basis of such a system can we give the proper kind of sense to the notion of what a trustee could reasonably reject on a being's behalf.

But the range of possible trusteeship is broader than that of morality. One could act as a trustee for a tomato plant, a forest or an ant colony, and such entities are not included in morality. Perhaps this can be explained by appeal to the requirement of comparability: while these entities have a good, it is not comparable to our own in a way that provides a basis for moral argument. Beyond this, however, there is in these cases insufficient foothold for the notion of justification to a being. One further minimum requirement for this notion is that the being constitute a point of view; that is, that there be such a thing as what it is like to be that being, such a thing as what the world seems like to it. Without this, we do not stand in a relation to the being that makes even hypothetical justification to it appropriate.

On the basis of what I have said so far contractualism can explain why the capacity to feel pain should have seemed to many to count in favour of moral status: a being which has this capacity seems also to satisfy the three conditions I have just mentioned as necessary for the idea of justification to it to make sense. If a being can feel pain, then it constitutes a centre of consciousness to which justification can be addressed. Feeling pain is a clear way in which the being can be worse off; having its pain alleviated a way in which it can be benefited; and these are forms of weal and woe which seem directly comparable to our own.

It is not clear that the three conditions I have listed as necessary are also sufficient for the idea of justification to a being to make sense. Whether they are, and, if they are not, what more may be required, are difficult and disputed questions. Some would restrict the moral sphere to those to whom justifications could in principle be communicated, or to those who can actually agree to something, or to those who have the capacity to understand moral argument. Contractualism as I have stated it does not settle these issues at once. All I claim is that it provides a basis for argument about them which is at least as plausible as that offered by rival accounts of the nature of morality. These proposed restrictions on the scope of morality are naturally understood as debatable claims about the conditions under which the relevant notion of justification makes sense, and the arguments commonly offered for and against them can also be plausibly understood on this basis.

Some other possible restrictions on the scope of morality are more evidently rejectable. Morality might be restricted to those who have the capacity to observe its constraints, or to those who are able to confer some reciprocal benefit on other participants. But it is extremely implausible to suppose that the beings excluded by these requirements fall entirely outside the protection of morality. Contractualism as I have formulated it[3] can explain why this is so: the absence of these capacities alone does nothing to undermine the possibility of justification to a being. What it may do in some cases, however, is to alter the justifications which are relevant. I suggest that whatever importance the capacities for deliberative control and reciprocal benefit may have is as factors altering the duties which beings have and the duties others have towards them, not as conditions whose absence suspends the moral framework altogether.

III

I have so far said little about the normative content of contractualism. For all I have said, the act utilitarian formula might turn out to be a theorem of contractualism. I do not think that this is the case, but my main thesis is that whatever the normative implications of contractualism may be it still has distinctive content as a philosophical thesis about the nature of morality. This content – the difference, for example, between being a utilitarian because the utilitarian formula is the basis of general agreement and being a utilitarian on other grounds – is shown most clearly in the answer that a contractualist gives to the first motivational question.

Philosophical utilitarianism is a plausible view partly because the facts which it identifies as fundamental to morality – facts about individual well-being – have obvious motivational force. Moral facts can motivate us, on this view, because of our sympathetic identification with the good of others. But as we move from philosophical utilitarianism to a specific utilitarian formula as the standard of right action, the form of motivation that utilitarianism appeals to becomes more abstract. If classical utilitarianism is the correct normative doctrine then the natural source of moral motivation will be a tendency to be moved by changes in aggregate well-being, however these may be composed. We must be moved in the same way by an aggregate gain of the same magnitude whether it is obtained by relieving the acute suffering of a few people or by bringing tiny benefits to a vast number, perhaps at the expense of moderate discomfort for a few. This is very different from sympathy of the familiar kind toward particular individuals, but a utilitarian may argue that this more abstract desire is what natural sympathy becomes when it is corrected by rational reflection. This desire has the same content as sympathy – it is a concern for the good of others – but it is not partial or selective in its choice of objects.

Leaving aside the psychological plausibility of this even-handed sympathy, how good a candidate is it for the role of moral motivation? Certainly sympathy of the usual kind is one of

the many motives that can sometimes impel one to do the right thing. It may be the dominant motive, for example, when I run to the aid of a suffering child. But when I feel convinced by Peter Singer's article[4] on famine, and find myself crushed by the recognition of what seems a clear moral requirement, there is something else at work. In addition to the thought of how much good I could do for people in drought-stricken lands, I am overwhelmed by the further, seemingly distinct thought that it would be wrong for me to fail to aid them when I could do so at so little cost to myself. A utilitarian may respond that his account of moral motivation cannot be faulted for not capturing this aspect of moral experience, since it is just a reflection of our non-utilitarian moral upbringing. Moreover, it must be groundless. For what kind of fact could this supposed further fact of moral wrongness be, and how could it give us a further, special reason for acting? The question for contractualism, then, is whether it can provide a satisfactory answer to this challenge.

According to contractualism, the source of motivation that is directly triggered by the belief that an action is wrong is the desire to be able to justify one's actions to others on grounds they could not reasonably[5] reject. I find this an extremely plausible account of moral motivation – a better account of at least my moral experience than the natural utilitarian alternative – and it seems to me to constitute a strong point for the contractualist view. We all might like to be in actual agreement with the people around us, but the desire which contractualism identifies as basic to morality does not lead us simply to conform to the standards accepted by others whatever these may be. The desire to be able to justify one's actions to others on grounds they could not reasonably reject will be satisfied when we know that there is adequate justification for our action even though others in fact refuse to accept it (perhaps because they have no interest in finding principles which we and others could not reasonably reject). Similarly, a person moved by this desire will not be satisfied by the fact that others accept a justification for his action if he regards this justification as spurious.

One rough test of whether you regard a justification as sufficient is whether you would accept that justification if you were in another person's position. This connection between the idea of 'changing places' and the motivation which underlies morality explains the frequent occurrence of 'Golden Rule' arguments within different systems of morality and in the teachings of various religions. But the thought experiment of changing places is only a rough guide; the fundamental question is what would it be unreasonable to reject as a basis for informed, unforced, general agreement. As Kant observed[6] our different individual points of view, taken as they are, may in general be simply irreconcilable. 'Judgemental harmony' requires the construction of a genuinely interpersonal form of justification which is nonetheless something that each individual could agree to. From this interpersonal standpoint, a certain amount of how things look from another person's point of view, like a certain amount of how they look from my own, will be counted as bias.

I am not claiming that the desire to be able to justify one's actions to others on grounds they could not reasonably reject is universal or 'natural'. 'Moral education' seems to me plausibly understood as a process of cultivating this desire and shaping it, largely by learning what justifications others are in fact willing to accept, by finding which ones you yourself find acceptable as you confront them from a variety of perspectives, and by appraising your own and others' acceptance or rejection of these justifications in the light of greater experience.

In fact it seems to me that the desire to be able to justify one's actions (and institutions) on grounds one takes to be acceptable is quite strong in most people. People are willing to go to considerable lengths, involving quite heavy sacrifices, in order to avoid admitting the

unjustifiability of their actions and institutions. The notorious insufficiency of moral motivation as a way of getting people to do the right thing is not due to simple weakness of the underlying motive, but rather to the fact that it is easily deflected by self-interest and self-deception.

It could reasonably be objected here that the source of motivation I have described is not tied exclusively to the contractualist notion of moral truth. The account of moral motivation which I have offered refers to the idea of a justification which it would be unreasonable to reject, and this idea is potentially broader than the contractualist notion of agreement. For let M be some non-contractualist account of moral truth. According to M, we may suppose, the wrongness of an action is simply a moral characteristic of that action in virtue of which it ought not to be done. An act which has this characteristic, according to M, has it quite independently of any tendency of informed persons to come to agreement about it. However, since informed persons are presumably in a position to recognise the wrongness of a type of action, it would seem to follow that if an action is wrong then such persons would agree that it is not to be performed. Similarly, if an act is not morally wrong, and there is adequate moral justification to perform it, then there will presumably be a moral justification for it which an informed person would be unreasonable to reject. Thus, even if M, and not contractualism, is the correct account of moral truth, the desire to be able to justify my actions to others on grounds they could not reasonably reject could still serve as a basis for moral motivation.

What this shows is that the appeal of contractualism, like that of utilitarianism, rests in part on a qualified scepticism. A non-contractualist theory of morality can make use of the source of motivation to which contractualism appeals. But a moral argument will trigger this source of motivation only in virtue of being a good justification for acting in a certain way, a justification which others would be unreasonable not to accept. So a non-contractualist theory must claim that there are moral properties which have justificatory force quite independent of their recognition in any ideal agreement. These would represent what John Mackie has called instances of intrinsic 'to-be-doneness' and 'not-to-be-doneness'.[7] Part of contractualism's appeal rests on the view that, as Mackie puts it, it is puzzling how there could be such properties 'in the world'. By contrast, contractualism seeks to explain the justificatory status of moral properties, as well as their motivational force, in terms of the notion of reasonable agreement. In some cases the moral properties are themselves to be understood in terms of this notion. This is so, for example, in the case of the property of moral wrongness, considered above. But there are also right- and wrong-making properties which are themselves independent of the contractualist notion of agreement. I take the property of being an act of killing for the pleasure of doing so to be a wrong-making property of this kind. Such properties are wrong-making because it would be reasonable to reject any set of principles which permitted the acts they characterise. Thus, while there are morally relevant properties 'in the world' which are independent of the contractualist notion of agreement, these do not constitute instances of intrinsic 'to-be-doneness' and 'not-to-be-doneness': their moral relevance – their force in justifications as well as their link with motivation – is to be explained on contractualist grounds.

In particular, contractualism can account for the apparent moral significance of facts about individual well-being, which utilitarianism takes to be fundamental. Individual well-being will be morally significant, according to contractualism, not because it is intrinsically valuable or because promoting it is self-evidently a right-making characteristic, but simply because an individual could reasonably reject a form of argument that gave his well-being no weight. This claim of moral significance is, however, only approximate, since it is a further difficult question exactly how 'well-being' is to be understood and

in what ways we are required to take account of the well-being of others in deciding what to do. It does not follow from this claim, for example, that a given desire will always and everywhere have the same weight in determining the rightness of an action that would promote its satisfaction, a weight proportional to its strength or 'intensity'. The right-making force of a person's desires is specified by what might be called a conception of morally legitimate interests. Such a conception is a product of moral argument; it is not given, as the notion of individual well-being may be, simply by the idea of what it is rational for an individual to desire. Not everything for which I have a rational desire will be something in which others need concede me to have a legitimate interest which they undertake to weigh in deciding what to do. The range of things which may be objects of my rational desires is very wide indeed, and the range of claims which others could not reasonably refuse to recognise will almost certainly be narrower than this. There will be a tendency for interests to conform to rational desire – for those conditions making it rational to desire something also to establish a legitimate interest in it – but the two will not always coincide.

One effect of contractualism, then, is to break down the sharp distinction, which arguments for utilitarianism appeal to, between the status of individual well-being and that of other moral notions. A framework of moral argument is required to define our legitimate interests and to account for their moral force. This same contractualist framework can also account for the force of other moral notions such as rights, individual responsibility and procedural fairness.

Notes

1 Here I am indebted to Gilbert Harman for comments which have helped me to clarify my statement of contractualism.

2 A point I owe to Derek Parfit.

3 On this view (as contrasted with some others in which the notion of a contract is employed) what is fundamental to morality is the desire for reasonable agreement, not the pursuit of mutual advantage. See section V below [see original reading]. It should be clear that this version of contractualism can account for the moral standing of future persons who will be better or worse off as a result of what we do now. It is less clear how it can deal with the problem presented by future people who would not have been born but for actions of ours which also made the conditions in which they live worse. Do such people have reason to reject principles, allowing these actions to be performed? This difficult problem, which I cannot explore here, is raised by Derek Parfit in Parfit 1976.

4 Singer 1972

5 Reasonably, that is, given the desire to find principles which others similarly motivated could not reasonably reject.

6 Kant 1785, section 2, footnote 14.

7 Mackie 1977, p. 42.

References

Kant, Immanuel, 1785, *Grundlegung zur Metaphysik der Sitten*, translated by H. J. Paton as *The Moral Law*, London: Hutchinson, 1948.

—— 1803, *Pädogogik*, translated as *On Education*, Ann Arbor, Michigan, 1960.

Mackie, J. L., 1977, *Ethics: Inventing Right and Wrong*, Harmondsworth: Pelican.

—— 1978, 'Can there be a Right-based Moral Theory?', *Midwest Studies in Philosophy*, 3.

Parfit, D., 1973, 'Later Selves and Moral Principles', in *Philosophy and Personal Relations*, edited by A. Montefiore, London: Routledge & Kegan Paul.

—— 1976, 'On Doing the Best for Our-Children', in *Ethics and Population*, edited by M. Bayles, Cambridge, Mass.: Schenkman Publishing Company Inc., pp. 100–115.

Singer, Peter, 1972, 'Famine, Affluence and Morality', *Philosophy and Public Affairs*, 1, pp. 229–43.

—— 1974, 'Sidgwick and Reflective Equilibrium', *The Monist*, 58, pp. 490–517.

Chapter 35

W. D. Ross

WHAT MAKES RIGHT ACTS RIGHT?

THE REAL point at issue between hedonism and utilitarianism on the one hand and their opponents on the other is not whether 'right' means 'productive of so and so'; for it cannot with any plausibility be maintained that it does. The point at issue is that to which we now pass, viz. whether there is any general character which makes right acts right, and if so, what it is. Among the main historical attempts to state a single characteristic of all right actions which is the foundation of their rightness are those made by egoism and utilitarianism. But I do not propose to discuss these, not because the subject is unimportant, but because it has been dealt with so often and so well already, and because there has come to be so much agreement among moral philosophers that neither of these theories is satisfactory. A much more attractive theory has been put forward by Professor Moore: that what makes actions right is that they are productive of more *good* than could have been produced by any other action open to the agent.

This theory is in fact the culmination of all the attempts to base rightness on productivity of some sort of result. The first form this attempt takes is the attempt to base rightness on conduciveness to the advantage or pleasure of the agent. This theory comes to grief over the fact, which stares us in the face, that a great part of duty consists in an observance of the rights and a furtherance of the interests of others, whatever the cost to ourselves may be. Plato and others

may be right in holding that a regard for the rights of others never in the long run involves a loss of happiness for the agent, that 'the just life profits a man'. But this, even if true, is irrelevant to the rightness of the act. As soon as a man does an action *because* he thinks he will promote his own interests thereby, he is acting not from a sense of its rightness but from self-interest.

To the egoistic theory hedonistic utilitarianism supplies a much-needed amendment. It points out correctly that the fact that a certain pleasure will be enjoyed by the agent is no reason why he *ought* to bring it into being rather than an equal or greater pleasure to be enjoyed by another, though, human nature being what it is, it makes it not unlikely that he will try to bring it into being. But hedonistic utilitarianism in its turn needs a correction. On reflection it seems clear that pleasure is not the only thing in life that we think good in itself, that for instance we think the possession of a good character, or an intelligent understanding of the world, as good or better. A great advance is made by the substitution of 'productive of the greatest good' for 'productive of the greater pleasure'.

Not only is this theory more attractive than hedonistic utilitarianism, but its logical relation to that theory is such that the latter could not be true unless it were true, while it might be true though hedonistic utilitarianism were not. It is in fact one of the logical bases of hedonistic utilitarianism. For the view that what produces

the maximum pleasure is right has for its bases the views (1) that what produces the maximum good is right, and (2) that pleasure is the only thing good in itself. If they were not assuming that what produces the maximum *good* is right, the utilitarians' attempt to show that pleasure is the only thing good in itself, which is in fact the point they take most pains to establish, would have been quite irrelevant to their attempt to prove that only what produces the maximum *pleasure* is right. If, therefore, it can be shown that productivity of the maximum good is not what makes all right actions right, we shall *a fortiori* have refuted hedonistic utilitarianism.

When a plain man fulfills a promise because he thinks he ought to do so, it seems clear that he does so with no thought of its total consequences, still less with any opinion that these are likely to be the best possible. He thinks in fact much more of the past than of the future. What makes him think it right to act in a certain way is the fact that he has promised to do so—that and, usually, nothing more. That his act will produce the best possible consequences is not his reason for calling it right. What lends colour to the theory we are examining, then, is not the actions (which form probably a great majority of our actions) in which some reflection as 'I have promised' is the only reason we give ourselves for thinking a certain action right, but the exceptional cases in which the consequences of fulfilling a promise (for instance) would be so disastrous to others that we judge it right not to do so. It must of course be admitted that such cases exist. If I have promised to meet a friend at a particular time for some trivial purpose, I should certainly think myself justified in breaking my engagement if by doing so I could prevent a serious accident or bring relief to the victims of one. And the supporters of the view we are examining hold that my thinking so is due to my thinking that I shall bring more good into existence by the one action than by the other. A different account may, however, be given of the matter, an account which will, I believe, show itself to be the true one. It may be said that

besides the duty of fulfilling promises I have and recognize a duty of relieving distress, and that when I think it right to do the latter at the cost of not doing the former, it is not because I think I shall produce more good thereby but because I think it the duty which is in the circumstances more of a duty. This account surely corresponds much more closely with what we really think in such a situation. If, so far as I can see, I could bring equal amounts of good into being by fulfilling my promise and by helping some one to whom I had made no promise, I should not hesitate to regard the former as my duty. Yet on the view that what is right is right because it is productive of the most good I should not so regard it.

There are two theories, each in its way simple, that offer a solution of such cases of conscience. One is the view of Kant, that there are certain duties of perfect obligation, such as those of fulfilling promises, of paying debts, of telling the truth, which admit of no exception whatever in favour of duties of imperfect obligation, such as that of relieving distress. The other is the view of, for instance, Professor Moore and Dr. Rashdall, that there is only the duty of producing good, and that all 'conflicts of duties' should be resolved by asking 'by which action will most good be produced?' But it is more important that our theory fit the facts than that it be simple, and the account we have given above corresponds (it seems to me) better than either of the simpler theories with what we really think, viz. that normally promise-keeping, for example, should come before benevolence, but that when and only when the good to be produced by the benevolent act is very great and the promise comparatively trivial, the act of benevolence becomes our duty.

In fact the theory of 'ideal utilitarianism', if I may for brevity refer so to the theory of Professor Moore, seems to simplify unduly our relations to our fellows. It says, in effect, that the only morally significant relation in which my neighbours stand to me is that of being possible beneficiaries by my action. They do stand in this relation to me, and this relation is morally significant. But they

may also stand to me in the relation of promisee to promiser, of creditor to debtor, of wife to husband, of child to parent, of friend to friend, of fellow countryman to fellow countryman, and the like; and each of these relations is the foundation of a *prima facie* duty, which is more or less incumbent on me according to the circumstances of the case. When I am in a situation, as perhaps I always am, in which more than one of these *prima facie* duties is incumbent on me, what I have to do is to study the situations as fully as I can until I form the considered opinion (it is never more) that in the circumstances one of them is more incumbent than any other; then I am bound to think that to do this *prima facie* duty is my duty *sans phrase* in the situation.

I suggest 'prima facie duty' or 'conditional duty' as a brief way of referring to the characteristic (quite distinct from that of being a duty proper) which an act has, in virtue of being of a certain kind (e.g., the keeping of a promise), of being an act which would be a duty proper if it were not at the same time of another kind which is morally significant. Whether an act is a duty proper or actual duty depends on *all* the morally significant kinds it is an instance of. The phrase 'prima facie duty' must be apologized for, since (1) it suggests that what we are speaking of is a certain kind of duty, whereas it is in fact not a duty, but something related in a special way to duty. Strictly speaking, we want not a phrase in which duty is qualified by an adjective, but a separate noun. (2) 'Prima' facie suggests that one is speaking only of an appearance which a moral situation presents at first sight, and which may turn out to be illusory; whereas what I am speaking of is an objective fact involved in the nature of the situation, or more strictly in an element of its nature, though not, as duty proper does, arising from its *whole* nature . . . .

There is nothing arbitrary about these *prima facie* duties. Each rests on a definite circumstance which cannot seriously be held to be without moral significance. Of *prima facie* duties I suggest, without claiming completeness or finality for it, the following division.

(1) Some duties rest on previous acts of my own. These duties seem to include two kinds, (a) those resting on a promise or what may fairly be called an implicit promise, such as the implicit undertaking not to tell lies which seems to be implied in the act of entering into conversation (at any rate by civilized men), or of writing books that purport to be history and not fiction. These may be called the duties of fidelity, (b) Those resting on a previous wrongful act. These may be called the duties of reparation. (2) Some rest on previous acts of other men, i.e., services done by them to me. These may be loosely described as the duties of gratitude. (3) Some rest on the fact or possibility of a distribution of pleasure or happiness (or of the means thereto) which is not in accordance with the merit of the persons concerned; in such cases there arises a duty to upset or prevent such a distribution. These are the duties of justice. (4) Some rest on the mere fact that there are other beings in the world whose conditions we can make better in respect of virtue, or of intelligence, or of pleasure. These are the duties of beneficence. (5) Some rest on the fact that we can improve our own condition in respect of virtue or of intelligence. These are the duties of self-improvement. (6) I think that we should distinguish from (4) the duties that may be summed up under the title of 'not injuring others'. No doubt to injure others is incidentally to fail to do them good; but it seems to me clear that nonmaleficence is apprehended as a duty distinct from that of beneficence, and as a duty of a more stringent character. . . . We should not in general consider it justifiable to kill one person in order to keep another alive, or to steal from one in order to give alms to another.

The essential defect of the 'ideal utilitarian' theory is that it ignores, or at least does not do full justice to, the highly personal character of duty. If the only duty is to produce the maximum of good, the question who is to have the good—whether it is myself, or my benefactor, or a person to whom I have made a promise to

confer that good on him, or a mere fellow man to whom I stand in no such special relation—should make no difference to my having a duty to produce that good. But we are all in fact sure that it makes a vast difference.

•   •   •

If the objection be made, that this catalogue of the main types of duty is an unsystematic one resting on no logical principle, it may be replied, first, that it makes no claim to being ultimate. It is a *prima facie* classification of the duties which reflection on our moral convictions seems actually to reveal. And if these convictions are, as I would claim that they are, of the nature of knowledge, and if I have not misstated them, the list will be a list of authentic conditional duties, correct as far as it goes though not necessarily complete. The list of *goods* put forward by the rival theory is reached by exactly the same method—the only sound one in the circumstances—viz. that of direct reflection on what we really think. Loyalty to the facts is worth more than a symmetrical architectonic or a hastily reached simplicity. If further reflection discovers a perfect logical basis for this or for a better classification, so much the better.

It may, again, be objected that our theory that there are these various and often conflicting types of *prima facie* duty leaves us with no principle upon which to discern what is our actual duty in particular circumstances. But this objection is not one which the rival theory is in a position to bring forward. For when we have to choose between the production of two heterogeneous goods, say knowledge and pleasure, the 'ideal utilitarian' theory can only fall back on an opinion, for which no logical basis can be offered, that one of the goods is the greater; and this is no better than a similar opinion that one of two duties is the more urgent. And again, when we consider the infinite variety of the effects of our actions in the way of pleasure, it must surely be admitted that the claim which *hedonism* sometimes makes, that it offers a readily applicable criterion of right conduct, is quite illusory.

I am unwilling, however, to content myself with an *argumentum ad hominem*, and I would contend that in principle there is no reason to anticipate that every act that is our duty is so for one and the same reason. Why should two sets of circumstances, or one set of circumstances, not possess different characteristics, any one of which makes a certain act our *prima facie* duty? When I ask what it is that makes me in certain cases sure that I have a *prima facie* duty to do so and so, I find that it lies in the fact that I have made a promise; when I ask the same question in another case, I find the answer lies in the fact that I have done a wrong. And if on reflection I find (as I think I do) that neither of these reasons is reducible to the other, I must not on any *a priori* ground assume that such a reduction is possible.

•   •   •

The duty of justice is particularly complicated, and the word is used to cover things which are really very different—things such as the payment of debts, the reparation of injuries done by oneself to another, and the bringing about of a distribution of happiness between other people in proportion to merit. I use the word to denote only the last of these three. [Elsewhere] I shall try to show that besides the three (comparatively) simple goods, virtue, knowledge, and pleasure, there is a more complex good, not reducible to these, consisting in the proportionment of happiness to virtue. The bringing of this about is a duty which we owe to all men alike, though it may be reinforced by special responsibilities that we have undertaken to particular men. This, therefore, with beneficence and self-improvement, comes under the general principle that we should produce as much good as possible, though the good here involved is different in kind from any other.

But besides this general obligation, there are special obligations. These may arise, in the first place, incidentally, from acts which were not essentially meant to create such an obligation, but which nevertheless create it. From the nature of the case such acts may be of two kinds—the

infliction of injuries on others, and the acceptance of benefits from them. It seems clear that these put us under a special obligation to other men, and that only these acts can do so incidentally. From these arise the twin duties of reparation and gratitude.

And finally there are special obligations arising from acts the very intention of which, when they were done, was to put us under such an obligation. The name for such acts is 'promises'; the name is wide enough if we are willing to include under it implicit promises, i.e., modes of behaviour in which without explicit verbal promise we intentionally create an expectation that we can be counted on to behave in a certain way in the interest of another person.

These seem to be, in principle, all the ways in which *prima facie* duties arise. In actual experience they are compounded together in highly complex ways. Thus, for example, the duty of obeying the laws of one's country arises partly (as Socrates contends in the *Crito*) from the duty of gratitude for the benefits one has received from it; partly from the implicit promise to obey which seems to be involved in permanent residence in a country whose laws we know we are *expected* to obey, and still more clearly involved when we ourselves invoke the protection of its laws (this is the truth underlying the doctrine of the social contract); and partly (if we are fortunate in our country) from the fact that its laws are potent instruments for the general good.

Or again, the sense of a general obligation to bring about (so far as we can) a just apportionment of happiness to merit is often greatly reinforced by the fact that many of the existing injustices are due to a social and economic system which we have, not indeed created, but taken part in and assented to; the duty of justice is then reinforced by the duty of reparation.

It is necessary to say something by way of clearing up the relation between *prima facie* duties and the actual or absolute duty to do one particular act in particular circumstances. If, as almost all moralists except Kant are agreed, and as most plain men think, it is sometimes right to tell a lie or to break a promise, it must be maintained that there is a difference between *prima facie* duty and actual or absolute duty. When we think ourselves justified in breaking, and indeed morally obliged to break, a promise in order to relieve some one's distress, we do not for a moment cease to recognize a *prima facie* duty to keep our promise, and this leads us to feel, not indeed shame or repentance, but certainly compunction, for behaving as we do; we recognize, further, that it is our duty to make up somehow to the promisee for the breaking of the promise. We have to distinguish from the characteristic of being our duty that of tending to our duty. Any act that we do contains various elements in virtue of which it falls under various categories. In virtue of being the breaking of a promise, for instance, it tends to be wrong; in virtue of being an instance of relieving distress it tends to be right . . . .

Another instance of the same distinction may be found in the operation of natural laws. *Qua* subject to the force of gravitation towards some other body, each body tends to move in a particular direction with a particular velocity; but its actual movement depends on *all* the forces to which it is subject. It is only by recognizing this distinction that we can preserve the absoluteness of laws of nature, and only by recognizing a corresponding distinction that we can preserve the absoluteness of the general principles of morality. But an important difference between the two cases must be pointed out. When we say that in virtue of gravitation a body tends to move in a certain way, we are referring to a causal influence actually exercised on it by another body or other bodies. When we say that in virtue of being deliberately untrue a certain remark tends to be wrong, we are referring to no causal relation, to no relation that involves succession in time, but to such a relation as connects the various attributes of a mathematical figure. And if the word 'tendency' is thought to suggest too much a causal relation, it is better to talk of certain types of act as being *prima facie* right or

wrong (or of different persons as having different and possibly conflicting claims upon us), than of their tending to be right or wrong.

Something should be said of the relation between our apprehension of the *prima facie* rightness of certain types of act and our mental attitude towards particular acts. It is proper to use the word 'apprehension' in the former case and not in the latter. That an act, *qua* fulfilling a promise, or *qua* effecting a just distribution of good, or *qua* returning services rendered, or *qua* promoting the good of others, or *qua* promoting the virtue or insight of the agent, is *prima facie* right, is self-evident; not in the sense that it is evident from the beginning of our lives, or as soon as we attend to the proposition for the first time, but in the sense that when we have reached sufficient mental maturity and have given sufficient attention to the proposition it is evident without any need of proof, or of evidence beyond itself. It is self-evident just as a mathematical axiom, or the validity of a form of inference, is evident. The moral order expressed in these propositions is just as much part of the fundamental nature of the universe (and, we may add, of any possible universe in which there were moral agents at all) as is the spatial or numerical structure expressed in the axioms of geometry or arithmetic. In our confidence that these propositions are true there is involved the same trust in our reason that is involved in our confidence in mathematics; and we should have no justification for trusting it in the latter sphere and distrusting it in the former. In both cases we are dealing with propositions that cannot be proved, but that just as certainly need no proof.

• • •

Our judgements about our actual duty in concrete situations have none of the certainty that attaches to our recognition of the general principles of duty. A statement is certain, i.e., is an expression of knowledge, only in one or other of two cases: when it is either self-evident, or a valid conclusion from self-evident premisses. And our judgements about our particular

duties have neither of these characters. (1) They are not self-evident. Where a possible act is seen to have two characteristics, in virtue of one of which it is *prima facie* right, and in virtue of the other *prima facie* wrong, we are (I think) well aware that we are not certain whether we ought or ought not to do it; that whether we do it or not, we are taking a moral risk. We come in the long run, after consideration, to think one duty more pressing than the other, but we do not feel certain that it is so. And though we do not always recognize that a possible act has two such characteristics, and though there may be cases in which it has not, we are never certain that any particular possible act has not, and therefore never certain that it is right, nor certain that it is wrong. For, to go no further in the analysis, it is enough to point out that any particular act will in all probability in the course of time contribute to the bringing about of good or of evil for many human beings, and thus have a *prima facie* rightness or wrongness of which we know nothing. (2) Again, our judgements about our particular duties are not logical conclusions from self-evident premisses. The only possible premisses would be the general principles stating their *prima facie* rightness or wrongness *qua* having the different characteristics they do have; and even if we could (as we cannot) apprehend the extent to which an act will tend on the one hand, for example, to bring out advantages for our benefactors, and on the other hand to bring about disadvantages for fellow men who are not our benefactors, there is no principle by which we can draw the conclusion that it is on the whole right or on the whole wrong. In this respect the judgement as to the rightness of a particular act is just like the judgement as to the beauty of a particular natural object or work of art. A poem is, for instance, in respect of certain qualities beautiful and in respect of certain others not beautiful; and our judgement as to the degree of beauty it possesses on the whole is never reached by logical reasoning from the apprehension of its particular beauties or particular defects. Both

in this and in the moral case we have more or less probable opinions which are not logically justified conclusions from the general principles that are recognized as self-evident.

There is therefore much truth in the description of the right act as a fortunate act. If we cannot be certain that it is right, it is our good fortune if the act we do is the right act. This consideration does not, however, make the doing of our duty a mere matter of chance. There is a parallel here between the doing of duty and the doing of what will be to our personal advantage. We never *know* what act will in the long run be to our advantage. Yet it is certain that we are more likely in general to secure our advantage if we estimate to the best of our ability the probable tendencies of our actions in this respect, than if we act on caprice. And similarly we are more likely to do our duty if we reflect to the best of our ability on the *prima facie* rightness or wrongness of various possible acts in virtue of the characteristics we perceive them to have, than if we act without reflection. With this greater likelihood we must be content.

Many people would be inclined to say that the right act for me is not that whose general nature I have been describing, viz. that which if I were omniscient I should see to be my duty, but that which on all the evidence available to me I should think to be my duty. But suppose that from the state of partial knowledge in which I think act A to be my duty, I could pass to a state of perfect knowledge in which I saw act B to be my duty, should I not say 'act B was the right act for me to do'? I should no doubt add 'though I am not to be blamed for doing act A' . . . .

It might seem absurd to suggest that it could be right for any one to do an act which would produce consequences less good than those which would be produced by some other act in his power. Yet a little thought will convince us that this is not absurd. The type of case in which it is easiest to see that this is so is, perhaps, that in which one has made a promise. In such a case we all think that *prima facie* it is our duty to fulfil

the promise irrespective of the precise goodness of the total consequences. And though we do not think it is necessarily our actual or absolute duty to do so, we are far from thinking that any, even the slightest, gain in the value of the total consequences will necessarily justify us in doing something else instead. Suppose, to simplify the case by abstraction, that the fulfillment of a promise to A would produce 1,000 units of good for him, but that by doing some other act I would produce 1,001 units of good for B, to whom I have made no promise, the other consequences of the two acts being of equal value; should we really think it self-evident that it was our duty to do the second act and not the first? I think not. We should, I fancy, hold that only a much greater disparity of value between the total consequences would justify us in failing to discharge our *prima facie* duty to A. After all, a promise is a promise, and is not to be treated so lightly as the theory we are examining would imply. What, exactly, a promise is, is not so easy to determine, but we are surely agreed that it constitutes a serious moral limitation to our freedom of action. To produce the 1,001 units of goods for B rather than fulfill our promise to A would be to take, not perhaps our duty as philanthropists too seriously, but certainly our duty as makers of promises too lightly.

• • •

I conclude that the attributes 'right' and 'optimific'* are not identical, and that we do not know either by intuition, by deduction, or by induction that they coincide in their application, still less that the latter is the foundation of the former. It must be added, however, that if we are ever under no special obligation such as that of fidelity to a promisee or of gratitude to a benefactor, we ought to do what will produce most good; and that even when we are under a special obligation the tendency of acts to promote general good is one of the main factors in determining whether they are right.

---

*   Productive of the most possible good.

In what has preceded, a good deal of use has been made of 'what we really think' about moral questions; a certain theory has been rejected because it does not agree with what we really think. It might be said that this is in principle wrong; that we should not be content to expound what our present moral consciousness tells us but should aim at a criticism of our existing moral consciousness in the light of theory. Now I do not doubt that the moral consciousness of men has in detail undergone a good deal of modification as regards the things we think right, at the hands of moral theory. But if we are told, for instance, that we should give up our view that there is a special obligatoriness attaching to the keeping of promises because it is self-evident that the only duty is to produce as much good as possible, we have to ask ourselves whether we really, when we reflect, *are* convinced that this is self-evident, and whether we really *can* get rid of our view that promise-keeping has a bindingness independent of productiveness of maximum good. In my own experience I find that I cannot, in spite of a very genuine attempt to do so; and I venture to think that most people will find the same, and that just because they cannot lose the sense of special obligation, they cannot accept as self-evident, or even as true, the theory which would require them to do so. In fact it seems, on reflection, self-evident that a promise, simply as such, is something that *prima facie* ought to be kept, and it does *not*, on reflection, seem self-evident that production of maximum good is the only thing that makes an act obligatory. And to ask us to give up at the bidding of a theory our actual apprehension of what is right and what is wrong seems like asking people to repudiate their actual experience of beauty, at the bidding of a theory which says 'only that which satisfies such and such conditions can be beautiful'. If what I have called our actual apprehension is (as I would maintain that it is) truly an apprehension, i.e., an instance of knowledge, the request is nothing less than absurd.

I would maintain, in fact, that what we are apt to describe as 'what we think' about moral questions contains a considerable amount that we do not think but know, and that this forms the standard by reference to which the truth of any moral theory has to be tested, instead of having itself to be tested by reference to any theory. I hope that I have in what precedes indicated what in my view these elements of knowledge are that are involved in our ordinary moral consciousness.

It would be a mistake to found a natural science on 'what we really think', i.e., on what reasonably thoughtful and well-educated people think about the subjects of the science before they have studied them scientifically. For such opinions are interpretations, and often misinterpretations, of sense-experience; and the man of science must appeal from these to sense-experience itself, which furnishes his real data. In ethics no such appeal is possible. We have no more direct way of access to the facts about rightness and goodness and about what things are right or good, than by thinking about them; the moral convictions of thoughtful and well-educated people are the data of ethics just as sense-perceptions are the data of a natural science. Just as some of the latter have to be rejected as illusory, so have some of the former; but as the latter are rejected only when they are in conflict with other more accurate sense-perceptions, the former are rejected only when they are in conflict with convictions which stand better the test of reflection. The existing body of moral convictions of the best people is the cumulative product of the moral reflection of many generations, which has developed an extremely delicate power of appreciation of moral distinctions; and this the theorist cannot afford to treat with anything other than the greatest respect. The verdicts of the moral consciousness of the best people are the foundation on which we must build; though he must first compare them with one another and eliminate any contradictions they may contain.

Chapter 36

Jonathan Dancy

PARTICULARISM

1. Holism in the theory of reasons

So I now plunge into the main theme. In the present chapter I lay out what I see as the main argument for particularism in ethics, which is based on holism in the theory of reasons. I start by repeating two distinctions introduced in Chapter 1 [see original reading], particularism vs. generalism and holism vs. atomism:

Particularism: the possibility of moral thought and judgement does not depend on the provision of a suitable supply of moral principles.
Generalism: the very possibility of moral thought and judgement depends on the provision of a suitable supply of moral principles.
Holism in the theory of reasons: a feature that is a reason in one case may be no reason at all, or an opposite reason, in another.
Atomism in the theory of reasons: a feature that is a reason in one case must remain a reason, and retain the same polarity, in any other.

I am going to work with a distinction between theoretical reasons and practical reasons, reasons for belief and reasons for action.[1] It doesn't matter for my purposes whether this distinction is exhaustive or not. The holism that I am talking about is intended to hold on both sides of it, and in the middle too, if there is anything in between. I start by trying to establish that theoretical reasons are holistic. We will quickly find that theoretical reasons are perfectly capable of changing their polarity according to context, without anyone making the slightest fuss about the matter. For instance, suppose that it currently seems to me that something before me is red. Normally, one might say, that is a reason (*some* reason, that is, not necessarily sufficient reason) for me to believe that there is something red before me. But in a case where I also believe that I have recently taken a drug that makes blue things look red and red things look blue, the appearance of a red-looking thing before me is reason for me to believe that there is a blue, not a red, thing before me. It is not as if it is some reason for me to believe that there is something red before me, though that reason is overwhelmed by contrary reasons. It is no longer *any reason at all* to believe that there is something red before me; indeed, it is a reason for believing the opposite.

As I say, it seems to me that nobody ever thought of denying what I am claiming here. I know of nobody who has nailed themselves to an atomistic conception of how theoretical reasons function. If generalism is taken to be the view that all reasons are general reasons, i.e. that if a feature is a reason in one case, it is the same reason in any other case, generalism is uncontentiously false of theoretical reasons.

Let us now turn to ordinary practical reasons. We will find just the same thing there. There are plenty of examples to persuade us that such reasons are holistic. For instance, that there will be nobody much else around is sometimes a

good reason for going there, and sometimes a very good reason for staying away. That one of the candidates wants the job very much indeed is sometimes a reason for giving it to her and sometimes a reason for doing the opposite. And so on. Now examples of this sort would be of little use if there were some theoretical obstacle to taking them at face value. But again we should remind ourselves that nobody has ever really debated the question whether ordinary practical reasons are holistic or not. There should be no *parti pris* on this issue; so the examples, which are legion, should be allowed to carry the day without resistance.

Perhaps this is too quick. There is a theory-based reason for doubting my claim that practical reasons are holistic, a reason that derives from the common thought that practical reasons are grounded in desires of the agent in a way that theoretical reasons are not. What one wants should not affect what one judges to be the case, on pain of charges of bias or prejudice. But what one wants can perfectly well affect what one has reason to do. Indeed, many find it hard to conceive of our having any practical reasons at all if we had no desires. My own view on this matter, however, is that even if a desireless creature could not have any reasons at all, it is not our desires that give us or ground our reasons. Reasons stem from the prospect of some good. If we have no other reason to do a certain action, wanting to do it will give us no reason at all; nor can wanting to do a silly action make it marginally less silly. (These are only the first moves in a long debate.[2] I mention them here only to show the sort of way in which I find myself denying the possibility of grounding practical reasons in desires of the agent.) This view of mine is, of course, an independent input in the present debate. I mention it only to show that a certain motive for doubting the analogy I have been drawing between theoretical and practical reason is itself contentious.

It may be that here we come across the real motivation for atomism in the theory of practical reason – an adherence to the view that reasons for action are partly grounded in desires. For if we accept that view, and if we then think of desires as giving the desirer the same reason wherever the desire occurs, the result looks atomistic. The right response to this, however, is to claim that even if all practical reasons are grounded in desires, the same desire need not always function as the same reason. Consider first the third-person case. That she wants power and he does not may be a reason to give the power to him rather than to her, as I have already said. But it may at the same time be a reason to give it to her, since according to me one feature can be a reason on both sides at once. Now consider the first-person case. Suppose that I am trying to train myself into indifference towards a woman. I want very much to spend time with her. But I also want not to have this want, since she is permanently indifferent to me. It is better for me not to think of her at all. If I spend time with her, this will make things worse for me rather than better—so long as I have not yet succeeded in training myself into indifference towards her. Once I am indifferent towards her, I can spend time with her without loss. In this situation, it seems, my desire to spend time with her may be a reason for me not to do so.[3]

So far we have it that theoretical reasons are holistic, and so are ordinary practical ones. Beyond the ordinary practical ones, what remain? There are two categories of reasons that have often been thought special: the aesthetic and the moral. Aesthetic reasons are difficult to categorize. They may not even be practical, but theoretical; that is, they may be reasons for judgement rather than for action. Luckily, I don't have to decide about that here. Whatever they are, they are largely holistic. It is undisputed that a feature that in one place adds something of aesthetic value may in another make things worse; a given metaphor may be telling in one context and trite in another. Converted into talk about reasons, there are reasons to introduce that

metaphor in the one case and reasons not to do so in the other. We might think that *some* features behave atomistically, that is, always provide the same reason wherever they occur. Most of these will be picked out using thick concepts. Perhaps imaginativeness is always for the better; I don't know. Painterliness seems to me a quality that can sometimes be out of place; symmetry too. And the same goes for most of the concepts with which aesthetic appreciation deals. Perhaps then there are some invariant aesthetic reasons, but I know of nobody who has ever suggested that one could erect a principle-based structure for aesthetic judgement in the sort of way that almost everybody thinks one can do for moral judgement. This, despite the many respects in which judgments of the two sorts are similar.

Now could it be the case that moral reasons are quite different from all the others in this respect, being the only atomistic ones? This is what many have supposed, in taking it that moral rationality is necessarily based on the existence of a suitable supply of moral principles. Moral reasons, they have held, necessarily behave in regular (or rule-bound) ways, though other reasons see no need to behave in that way at all. About this, I want to say that straight off it just seems incredible that the very logic of moral reasons should be so different from that of others in this sort of way. Consider here the sad fact that nobody knows how to distinguish moral from other reasons; every attempt has failed. How does that fit the suggestion that there is this deep difference between them? Not very well at all. Then of course there are examples to be considered, examples of apparently moral reasons functioning in a holistic way. I forbear to bore you with these. It just seems inevitable that moral reasons should function holistically in the way that other reasons do.

This certainly makes it hard to hold, as many do, that the very possibility of moral distinctions, of moral thought and judgement, is predicated on the existence of a range of moral principles. Moral principles, however we conceive of them, seem all to be in the business of specifying features as *general* reasons. The principle that it is wrong to lie, for instance, presumably claims that mendacity is always a wrong-making feature wherever it occurs (that is, it always makes the same negative contribution, though it often does not succeed in making the action wrong overall). The principle that it is wrong to lie cannot be merely a generalization, a claim that lies are mostly the worse for being lies, for if all moral principles were of this sort, the argument that moral thought and judgement depend on the possibility of moral principles would simply be the argument that such thought is impossible unless there is a considerable preponderance of normal cases over abnormal ones. I have never seen this argument made, and I doubt, what is more, whether it would be persuasive if restricted to ethics.

If moral reasons, like others, function holistically, it cannot be the case that the possibility of such reasons rests on the existence of principles that specify morally relevant features as functioning atomistically. A principle-based approach to ethics is inconsistent with the holism of reasons.

All the same, it might be argued, we have to admit that there are some invariant reasons— some features whose practical relevance is invariant. And surely I should allow this, because holism, as I expressed it, concerns only what may happen, not what must. It could be true that every reason may alter or lose its polarity from case to case, even though there are some reasons that do not do this. If they don't do it, this will be because of the particular reasons they are. Invariant reasons, should there be any, will be invariant not because they are reasons but because of their specific content. And this is something that the particularist, it seems, should admit. It is like the claims that a man can run a mile in four minutes, that Sam Smith is a man, and that Sam Smith cannot run a mile in four minutes. These claims are compatible, and so are the claims that reasons are variable *qua reasons*

though some reasons are (necessarily, given their content) invariant. The invariance, where it occurs, derives not from the fact that we are dealing here with a reason, but from the particular content of that reason.

So can the particularist admit the existence of *some* invariant reasons? The obvious examples are things like the causing of gratuitous pain on unwilling victims. Surely, it is commonly urged, this is always for the worse, even if overall we might in some case be morally forced to do it. Well, the first thing to say is that admitting the possibility of some invariant reasons is a far cry from admitting that the very possibility of moral thought and judgement is dependent on our being able to find some such reasons. To support any such suggestion, we would somehow need to be able to locate a sufficient range of invariant reasons, ones that together somehow cover the moral ground entirely and themselves explain the nature and role of the variant reasons. This is quite a different matter from simply trying to refute particularism by producing one counter-example of an invariant reason, which is normally what happens.

Further, we should remember that the question whether reasons are atomistic or holistic is a very basic question about the nature of rationality, of how reasons function from case to case. It is, I suppose, conceivable that though the vast bulk of reasons function according to a holistic logic, there are a few whose logic is atomistic. But if this were true we would have a hybrid conception of rationality. There would just be two sorts of reasons, each with their own logic, and moral thought would be the uncomfortable attempt to rub such reasons together. It is *much* more attractive, if at all possible, to think of our reasons as sharing a basic logic, so that all are atomistic, or all holistic.

Let us consider, then, how the supposed invariant reasons function as reasons in the particular case. Take the well-known example of the fat man stuck in the only outlet from a cave that is rapidly filling with water from below. We

and our families are caught in between the fat man and the rising water. But we have some dynamite. We could blow the fat man up and get out to safety. But the fat man is unwilling to be blown up (he, at least, is safe from drowning, being head up); and, let us immediately admit, he is blameless in being where he is, and in being fatter than the rest of us. So what we propose to do involves the destruction of an unwilling and blameless victim. As such, we might say, this is *some* reason against lighting the fuse and standing back. The question I want to raise is whether the fact that this feature (that we are causing the death of an unwilling and blameless victim) is functioning as the reason it here is, is in any way to be explained by appeal to the (supposed) fact that it functions in the same way in every case in which it occurs. It seems to me that this feature is the reason it is here quite independently of how it functions elsewhere.

Of course, if the feature is genuinely an invariant reason, this fact, should we discern it, will be of use to us in any case where we might be in doubt as to the contribution it is making. We can say, 'This is an invariant reason, it makes such-and-such a difference there, and so it must be making that difference here.' But suppose that we were to treat one of these supposedly invariant reasons as potentially variant, so as to deny ourselves the use of that inference. What sort of mistake would we have made? Would it be a failure of *rationality* to treat an invariant reason as potentially variant, or just a mistake of fact? I suggest that the invariance of the reason is an epistemic matter rather than what one might call a constitutive one. If we know or even merely suspect that the reason functions invariantly, this tells us, or at least gives us some idea, how it is functioning here, but in no way constitutes the sort of contribution it makes to the store of reasons here present. In that sense, the invariance of its contributions is not a matter of the logic of such a reason.

I conclude, then, that we should accept the possibility of invariant reasons, so long as the invariance is not a matter of the logic of such

reasons, but more the rather peculiar fact that some reasons happen to contribute in ways that are not affected by other features. We can admit this without adopting a hybrid theory of rationality, so long as we treat the invariance of any invariant reason as an epistemic matter rather than as a constitutive one.

2. From holism to particularism

This concludes the argument. So I now turn to ask what exactly it establishes. There are two reasons for thinking that any such simple attempt to present particularism as a direct consequence of holism will not work. The first reason is that particularism is about the ways in which actions are made right or wrong, and the argument in the previous section doesn't even address that topic. It is simply silent on the question whether the ways in which features can combine to make actions right or wrong are holistic or not. To think otherwise is to forget the distinction between two normative relations. The first is the favouring relation, the relation in which features of the situation stand to action or to belief when they are reasons for doing one thing rather than another or for believing one thing rather than another. The second is the right-making relation, the relation in which features of the situation stand to an action when they make it right or wrong. I seem to be suggesting that a feature can make an action right, or stand in the right-making relation to it, in one case, but not in another. But the argument for this, if it is contained in the previous section, seems to establish only the holism of the favouring relation. The holism of the right-making relation is something else, and it is not at all obvious, one might say, how this second holism is supposed to follow from the first. Of course it is not nothing to have established that the favouring relation is holistic. But particularists surely want both holisms, not just one. How are they going to get the second holism out of the first?[4]

• • •

[A] principled ethic can accept and indeed stress the truth of holism. The simplest way to see this is by looking at a candidate principled ethic that is explicitly holistic. Consider the following 'principle':

P1. If you have promised, that is some reason to do the promised act, unless your promise was given under duress.

This principle specifies a contributory moral reason, but explicitly says that the feature that gives the reason does not always do so. (One can even imagine a principle of this sort which ends up, 'in which case it is a reason not to do the act', if one wanted a principle which allowed for reversed polarity.) Now suppose that we have a set of such principles, all of them explicitly allowing for cases in which the normally reason-giving feature would fail to perform that role. And suppose that our set is wide or large enough to cover the ground, in the sense that it specifies all the moral reasons that there are. (There is nothing in the holism argument to show that such a thing is impossible.) The result is a principled but holistic ethic.[4]

To be sure, this result only emerges if we were lucky enough to be dealing with a set of morally relevant features whose defeasibility conditions, if we can use that phrase, are finitely specifiable. Nothing can guarantee that this will be so; nor does the suggestion at issue suppose otherwise. The point is only that one cannot argue from holism directly to the conclusion that moral principles are impossible.

What this shows is that the argument (if there is one at all) from holism to particularism is at best indirect. I suspect, indeed, that particularists will not agree among themselves about how best to proceed at this stage. I know some who will not be swayed by the point at all. I have in mind those who don't much care about what sort of moral outlook is officially possible or impossible, since their main interest is in showing that the morality we actually have is not grounded in

any principles. I certainly accept that our actual morality is unprincipled, but I was hoping to cast the net rather wider than that.

I think the best way to put the particularist conclusion is that, given the holism of reasons, it would be a sort of cosmic accident if it were to turn out that a morality could be captured in a set of holistic contributory principles of the sort that is here suggested. Most importantly, of course, it would be a cosmic accident if *our* morality could be expressed in this way, but the same would apply to any workable moral scheme. It would be an accident because, given the holism of reasons, there is no discernible need for a complete set of reasons to be like this. If our (or any other) morality turned out to be that way, there could be no possible explanation of that fact. It would be pure serendipity. There is no need for things to be so, and therefore there is nothing for the moral principles to do.

It was because of this issue that I characterized particularism as I did above, as the claim that the possibility of moral thought and judgement (and in general, one might say, of moral distinctions) in no way depends on the provision of a suitable set of moral principles. So characterized, it seems to me that particularism does follow from holism. What does not follow is a straight denial of the possibility of a moral principle, or at least of an invariant moral reason. But the loss of those conclusions is no real damage to the particularists' assault on the standard principle-based conception of morality. Their picture of what is required for there to be moral reasons, duties, obligations, and so on, remains in place.

The thought that the existence of a suitable provision of principles would be a cosmic accident depends on the claim that there is no discernible need for such a provision. In a sense, this claim is a challenge to the opposition to come up with a picture of moral thought and judgement which, though it respects the truth of reasons-holism, still *requires* (rather than merely makes possible) a provision of principles

that cover the ground. Some subject matters are such that we can expect such principles. In arithmetic, for instance, dividing one number by another will not always yield a smaller number; sometimes it will, and sometimes it won't. So the situation is holistic, in a sense. But nonetheless we can expect to find specifiable laws or principles that govern these operations. If morality were relevantly similar to arithmetic, a similar expectation would be appropriate.

•   •   •

What we are looking for is some positive suggestion as to why the behaviour of moral reasons might *need* to be capturable in some principled way, even though we continue to respect the truth of holism.[...] One is that morality is essentially a system of social constraints, and as such it must meet certain conditions. It must be reasonably simple, so as to be operable by the populace at large. It must be explicit, so as to give clear guidance so far as possible. And it must be regular, so that we can tell in advance what effects this or that feature will have on how we and others should behave. My own view about this is that it is a description of something like a set of traffic regulations. But morality was not invented by a group of experts sitting in council to serve the purposes of social control. It may be that it does serve those purposes, but even if so, it does not follow that one can derive from that fact a set of requirements on the nature of any effective moral system. The particularist claim would be that people are quite capable of judging how to behave case by case, in a way that would enable us to predict what they will in fact do, and which shows no need of the sort of explicit guidance that a set of principles (of a certain sort) would provide.

•   •   •

3. Supervenience and resultance

I now turn to a quite different way of showing that holism and principles are compatible. Remember that our question at the moment is

whether, despite the truth of holism, the enterprise of morality necessarily brings with it a suitable array of principles. The new answer to the question is that holism is not incompatible with the supervenience of the moral on the non-moral, and supervenience alone generates a vast array of general principles linking natural descriptions of the world to moral evaluations, in the sort of way that moral principles purport to do.

To see what is going on here we have to start by distinguishing two relations, supervenience and resultance. These two relations are often confused, but it is absolutely vital for present purposes to keep them apart. Resultance is a relation between a property of an object and the features that 'give' it that property. Not all properties are resultant; that is, not all properties depend on others in the appropriate way. But everyone agrees that moral properties are resultant.[5] A resultant property is one which 'depends' on other properties in a certain way. As we might say, nothing is just wrong; a wrong action is wrong because of other features that it has. The obscure 'because of' in this claim is sometimes expressed using the equally obscure phrase 'in virtue of'; a wrong action is wrong in virtue of other features than its wrongness. None of the phrases that are used to express the relation I am calling resultance is at all helpful, really, in trying to get a good intuitive grasp on the nature of that relation. But it is still of the utmost importance to get such a grasp, and in particular to distinguish it from other relations with which it is very easily confused. The 'resultance base' for the wrongness of a particular action consists in those features that make it wrong, the wrong-making features. There is, however, no such thing as the resultance base for a property (wrongness, say) in *general*. This is because a property that is resultant may be one that there are very many different ways of acquiring, and there need be no way of capturing all those ways at once. I would say this is how it is with wrongness: there are many different ways in which an action can get to be wrong.

So the resultance base for the wrongness of an act will consist in the properties that make that act wrong, which are sometimes called the 'ground' for its wrongness. At this point a crucial question arises: should we say that the properties in the resultance base for this act's wrongness are the same as those which disfavour the act (in the sense of 'disfavour' that I developed in Chapter 3 [see original reading], which is roughly equivalent to 'count against'), or should we take the resultance base to range rather more widely? For the moment, and for the sake of a clear initial contrast between resultance and supervenience, I am going to take it that we should say they are the same. So the resultance base for this act's wrongness consists in those features that make the act wrong in the sense of being the ones that count against doing it, that disfavour it.

There is a vast difference between resultance, so conceived, and supervenience. Moral properties supervene on others in the sense that if an action has a moral property, then any other action exactly similar to the first in non-moral respects will have that moral property too. Here the base we are talking about—the supervenience base—consists in *all the non-moral features of the action*, not just those that make it wrong. The supervenience base is far larger than the resultance base, then, and it includes crucially all the features that count in favour of the wrong action (defeated reasons for doing it) as well as those that count against, all enablers and the absence of all disablers, quite apart from all the other non-moral features as well. So the relation between the wrongness and the resultance base is going to be quite different from that between the wrongness and the supervenience base. Most obviously, if the action is made wrong by the features in the resultance base it cannot also be made wrong by the features in the supervenience base (unless we are dealing with a quite different sense of 'made wrong'—the sort of sense that people must have in mind when they talk of 'fixing the wrongness', a horrible expression).

There is an issue here about whether it even makes sense to talk of the supervenience base of this action's wrongness. Wrongness, like other moral properties, supervenes on non-moral properties. As I expressed things above, those properties are still properties of the action concerned. But I will suggest later that we should cast the supervenience net wider, so as to include features other than those of the relevant action. (We can do this by thinking of features of other things as 'Cambridge features' of this thing.) If so, there is no obvious point in thinking of supervenience as a relation between this action's moral properties and a supervenience base that consists in all the non-moral properties of anything whatever. It is better just to think of supervenience as a syncategorematic relation between moral and non-moral properties in general, expressed in the fully general claim that if we start from a wrong action and move out to the entire non-moral nature of the world in which it is situated, and then replicate that in a new world, we are certain to have a wrong action in the replicating world. There is nothing more to supervenience than this.

The point of the distinction between resultance and supervenience, for present purposes, is as follows. It is extremely plausible to suggest that if an action is wrong, every other action that is exactly similar in non-moral respects must be wrong also.[6] (Though the immediate attractiveness of this maxim is somewhat vitiated by the way in which we broadened our conception of supervenience in the previous paragraph.) It is nothing like so plausible to suggest that if an action is wrong, every other action that shares the features that make the first one wrong must also be wrong. Two actions may be similar to each other in a limited way, that is, in the respects that disfavour the first one wrong and thereby make it wrong, but differ in other respects so that the second is not wrong; the features that manage to make the first wrong are prevented from doing so in the second case because of variations that lie beyond the common

resultance base. I take this point to be established by appeal to the distinction between favourers and enablers.

Suppose that a moral principle says things of the following form: where things are in non-moral way N, there will be an action with moral property M. Supervenience generates things of that form, whose distinguishing feature is that they have an enormous left-hand side. Can we announce that this at least (*pace* the renegades who reject the supervenience of the moral on the non-moral) guarantees that there is a complete set of principles, even though they are much longer than the ones we are used to? Not really, I fear. First, these principles specify complexes of such a size and in such detail that there is effectively no chance that they should be capable of recurring. A principle that has only one instance is worse than useless, for no such principle could ever be a guide for judgement. Second, these things do not really have the form of a principle either. For they contain all sorts of irrelevancies. Principles are in the business of telling us which actions are wrong and why they are wrong. But the vast propositions generated by supervenience fail utterly to do this; they don't select in the right sort of way. They do no doubt contain the relevant information, but they do not reveal it; as far as supervenience is concerned, all features of the present case, including those that count in favour of the actually wrong act, are equally relevant. Supervenience, as a relation, is incapable of picking out the features that make the action wrong; it is too indiscriminate to be able to achieve such an interesting and important task. Finally, it is surely not irrelevant to point out that nobody could ever come to know the sort of supposed 'principle' generated by supervenience. So even if such 'principles' could have more than one instance, nobody could ever be guided by them.

Matters are quite different with the principles supposed to be generated by resultance. These principles are short, usable, and restrict themselves to specification of right-making and

wrong-making features. It is sad that, despite these advantages, they rest on sand, since resultance, as we are currently characterizing it, is not a generalizable relation. The resultance base, in a given case, is too narrowly delimited to ensure that where it recurs it will have the same effect.

This means that while supervenience has the advantage of generating truths, what it generates cannot serve as a moral principle, while resultance, though what it generates could serve as a moral principle, only manages to 'generate' such things by appeal to a fallacy.

Notes

1 Nothing hangs on my identification here of reasons for belief as theoretical reasons and reasons for action as practical ones. All that I am doing is introducing a little convenient terminology.

2 For the remainder of the debate, see my *Practical Reality*, ch. 2; or, perhaps better, Quinn (1993a), Raz (1986, 1998), and Scanlon (1998).

3 In this connection I cannot resist reporting an advertisement I saw in a bus in Washington, DC, which said 'Do you always want to look at pornography? If so, ring this number'. The number was that of a clinic which was offering to help one get rid of this intrusive and socially awkward desire.

4 I am very much in Michael Ridge's debt at this point. It is worth saying that the same point is made at the end of Jackson et al. (2000), but in that instance the point is associated with such a contentious example (as I tried to show in Chapter 4 [see original reading]) that it is impossible to know what, if anything, it can hope to establish. The Ridge approach, which is the one I have laid out in the text, is far more direct and forceful.

5 Moore (1942), p. 588; Ross (1930: 121–23). Ross sometimes talks in terms of the 'resultant' (1939: 168) and sometimes in terms of the 'consequential' (1939: 280).

6 I don't mean to suggest that the claim that moral properties supervene on others is not in any way controversial. Joseph Raz, for instance, denies it (2000c), and I at least have seen some reason to dispute it (1995: 278–79). But I will assume that it is true here, so as not to make life more difficult than it is already.

References

Dancy, J. (1995) 'In Defense of Thick Concepts', in P. French, T. E. Uehling, Jr., and H. K. Wettstein (eds.), *Midwest Studies in Philosophy*, vol. 20: *Moral Concepts*, 263–79.

—— (2000b) *Practical Reality* (Oxford: Clarendon Press).

Jackson, F., Pettit, P., and Smith, M. (2000) 'Ethical Particularism and Patterns', in Hooker and Little (2000: 79–99).

Moore, G. E. (1942) 'A Reply to my Critics', in P. A. Schilpp (ed.), *The Philosophy of G. E. Moore* (New York: Tudor Publishing Co.), 535–687.

Quinn, W. (1993a) 'Putting Rationality in Its Place', in R. Frey and C. Morris (eds.), *Value, Welfare and Morality* (Cambridge: Cambridge University Press); reprinted in Quinn (1993b: 228–55) and in Hursthouse et al. (1995: 181–208).

Raz, J. (1986) *The Morality of Freedom* (Oxford: Clarendon Press).

—— (1998) 'Incommensurability and Agency', in Chang (1998: 110–28).

—— (2000a) *Engaging Reason* (Oxford: Oxford University Press, 2000).

—— (2000c) 'The Truth in Particularism', in Raz (2000a: 218–46); reprinted in Hooker and Little (2000: 48–78). In the text, page references are given to both printings of this paper.

Ross, W.D. (1930) *The Right and the Good* (Oxford: Clarendon Press).

—— (1939) *Foundations of Ethics* (Oxford: Clarendon Press).

Scanlon, T. M. (1998) *What We Owe to Each Other* (Cambridge, Mass.: Harvard University Press).

SECTION VI

Virtue and character

INTRODUCTION TO SECTION VI

A S WE HAVE seen, many debates within normative ethics are organized around the question "Which acts are morally right?" However, an older tradition, which in recent decades has experienced a revival, begins with the different question "What sort of person should I be?" Of course, any complete theory must answer both questions, but there is room for disagreement about which is primary. To many who begin with rightness, the virtuous person is someone who is disposed to do the right thing; to many who begin with character, right acts are those that exemplify the virtues.

The view that ethics should be concerned with character goes back to Aristotle (Chapter 37), who advances both a theory about which traits are virtues and an account of how we acquire those traits. The virtues, he argues, are habits of conduct that strike a proper balance between extremes. So, for example, the courageous person is neither foolhardy nor cowardly, while the temperate person neither altogether ignores his appetites nor indulges them to excess. To act virtuously, one needs both the practical wisdom to recognize which actions are called for by one's situation and settled dispositions to perform such actions. These habits are not acquired through study alone, but are developed through practice and habituation: "we must perform just actions if we are to become just, and temperate actions if we are to be temperate." In this selection, too, Aristotle discusses the weak-willed person, who knows he should resist his impulses but is unable to do so. While Aristotle rejects the straightforward Socratic view that all wrong acts are done in ignorance, he offers a subtle account of the ways in which the weak-willed person can fail to have full knowledge.

Are the same traits virtues at all times and places, or was Aristotle merely recording the attitudes that prevailed in ancient Greece? This is the familiar challenge of cultural relativism (Chapter 15), applied now to theories of virtue rather than theories of the right, and in Chapter 38 Martha Nussbaum takes up the challenge on Aristotle's behalf. Nussbaum argues that each virtue that Aristotle discusses represents a response to an important and fixed feature of human life. Because all humans are vulnerable, are mortal, have various appetites, and must interact with others, every society must come to terms with these facts. Thus, for each sphere of activity, every society must recognize as a virtue "whatever it is that being disposed to choose and respond well consists in, in that sphere." Nussbaum acknowledges that different societies flesh out these abstract characterizations in different ways, and that there is much room for debate about which specifications are best. She acknowledges, as well, that a society's approach is bound to be influenced by the concepts it uses to describe and interpret our shared situation. Nevertheless, despite these concessions, Nussbaum maintains that "in life as it is lived, we do find a family of experiences, clustering around certain foci, which can provide reasonable starting points for cross-cultural reflection."

Thomas Hurka (Chapter 39) offers a very different account of virtue. Unlike Nussbaum, who views the virtues as dispositions that enable us to meet the important challenges of human life, Hurka views them as attitudes characterized by a certain structure. Hurka begins by suggesting that certain aspects of our lives – for example, pleasure, knowledge, and achievement – are intrinsically good, while others, such as pain, false belief, and failure in the pursuit of achievement, are intrinsically evil. He goes on to note that our orientation toward each entry on each list can be either positive (if we want, seek, and enjoy it) or negative (if we want and seek its nonexistence and are pained by its existence). Observing that loving the good and hating evil are themselves goods while loving evil and hating the good are themselves evils, Hurka then identifies virtue with the first sort of higher-order attitude and vice with the second. Because this proposal implies that the virtuous person will, among other things, want others to succeed, seek the truth, and be pained by the suffering of others, Hurka's account makes contact with many of our common judgments about virtue.

By contrast, Friedrich Nietzsche (Chapter 40) has nothing but contempt for those judgments. In a powerfully written selection, Nietzsche decries our familiar moral beliefs as manifestations of "herd-animal morality" – that is, a code that the weak have instituted to protect themselves from the strong. In his view, humanity in its highest form is not altruistic or self-sacrificing, but rather is proud, self-assertive, strong-willed, and unfettered by the restraints of convention. In taking this position, Nietzsche completely rejects the ideal of character that informs our ordinary moral outlook.

The tension between morality and more individualized imperatives is also discussed, albeit in a very different spirit, by Bernard Williams. In Chapter 41, Williams argues that morality, at least as reconstructed by utilitarians and Kantians, cannot do full justice either to the fact that each of us *has* a character or to the differences *between* our characters. In particular, Williams argues that utilitarianism cannot accommodate a person's continued existence as his character changes, that Kantians cannot accommodate the role that our basic commitments, which define our characters, play in our practical thought, and that both approaches distort the relationships that the differences in people's characters make possible. Analogously but more generally, Susan Wolf argues in Chapter 42 that the life of a perfectly moral person – a "moral saint" – would be lacking in a number of important dimensions. In addition to not being much fun to be around, such a person could not have deep interests in art, music, sports, or any of the other activities that make life interesting and worthwhile. According to Wolf, this does not mean that ideals of personal perfection should dominate those of morality, but it does compel us to "raise normative questions from a perspective that is unattached to a commitment to any particular well-ordered system of values."

Can a theory of the virtues support an account of rightness that is a genuine competitor to consequentialism and deontology? According to Rosalind Hursthouse (Chapter 43), the answer to this question is "yes." Instead of identifying right acts with acts that bring the best consequences or that conform to correct moral rules, a virtue ethicist will identify them with acts that a virtuous person would perform. As long as this formula is backed by an independent account of what makes a trait a

virtue, Hursthouse argues, it will convey genuine information. Moreover, although we will not be able to apply the formula without specifying which traits *are* virtues, this will not distinguish it from consequentialism, which requires that we specify which consequences are good, or deontology, which requires that we specify which rules are correct. Although applying the formula will indeed require practical judgment, Hursthouse suggests that this too is no less true of any other approach. For more discussion of these issues, the reader may wish to consult the selections by Aristotle, Ross, and Dancy in Chapters 37, 35 and 36.

Attributions of virtue presuppose that people consistently behave in certain ways. This presupposition – that some people regularly act honestly and kindly while others regularly act dishonestly and cruelly – may seem too obvious to question. However, in Chapter 44, John Doris draws on empirical data from the social sciences to raise important doubts about it. Doris cites many studies which suggest that how people behave depends far less on facts about them, and far more on facts about their situations, than is traditionally believed. For example, when we encounter others who need help, the degree of compassion that we are disposed to display is strongly influenced by factors such as mood, trust in authority, and the presence or absence of others. According to Doris, this does not mean that our behavioral tendencies are not stable over time, but it does mean that what are stable are not broad dispositions to act honestly or kindly, but narrower dispositions to act honestly and kindly in some situations and dishonestly and cruelly in others. A question for the reader to consider is to what degree Doris's conclusions about character are consistent with what Hursthouse and others in this section say about it.

Chapter 37

Aristotle

THE NATURE OF MORAL VIRTUE

From Nicomachean Ethics, Book Two

Chapter I

Virtue, then, is of two kinds, intellectual and moral. Of these the intellectual is in the main indebted to teaching for its production and growth, and this calls for time and experience. Moral goodness, on the other hand, is the child of habit, from which it has got its very name, ethics being derived from *ethos*, 'habit,' by a slight alteration in the quantity of the *e*. This is an indication that none of the moral virtues is implanted in us by nature, since nothing that nature creates can be taught by habit to change the direction of its development. For instance a stone, the natural tendency of which is to fall down, could never, however often you threw it up in the air, be trained to go in that direction. No more can you train fire to burn downwards. Nothing in fact, if the law of its being is to behave in one way, can be habituated to behave in another. The moral virtues, then, are produced in us neither by Nature nor *against* Nature. Nature, indeed, prepares in us the ground for their reception, but their complete formation is the product of habit.

Consider again these powers or faculties with which Nature endows us. We acquire the ability to use them before we do use them. The senses provide us with a good illustration of this truth. We have not acquired the sense of sight from repeated acts of seeing, or the sense of hearing from repeated acts of hearing. It is the other way round. We had these senses before we used them, we did not acquire them as a result of using them. But the moral virtues we do acquire by first exercising them. The same is true of the arts and crafts in general. The craftsman has to learn how to make things, but he learns in the process of making them. So men become builders by building, harp players by playing the harp. By a similar process we become just by performing just actions, temperate by performing temperate actions, brave by performing brave actions. Look at what happens in political societies—it confirms our view. We find legislators seeking to make good men of their fellows by making good behaviour habitual with them. That is the aim of every lawgiver, and when he is unable to carry it out effectively, he is a failure; nay, success or failure in this is what makes the difference between a good constitution and a bad.

Again, the creation and the destruction of any virtue are effected by identical causes and identical means; and this may be said, too, of every art. It is as a result of playing the harp that harpers become good or bad in their art. The same is true of builders and all other craftsmen. Men will become good builders as a result of building well, and bad builders as a result of building badly. Otherwise what would be the use of having anyone to teach a trade? Craftsmen would all be born either good or bad. Now this

holds also of the virtues. It is in the course of our dealings with our fellow-men that we become just or unjust. It is our behaviour in a crisis and our habitual reactions to danger that make us brave or cowardly, as it may be. So with our desires and passions. Some men are made temperate and gentle, others profligate and passionate, the former by conducting them selves in one way, the latter by conducting themselves in another, in situations in which their feelings are involved. We may sum it all up in the generalization, 'Like activities produce like dispositions.' This makes it our duty to see that our activities have the right character, since the differences of quality in them are repeated in the dispositions that follow in their train. So it is a matter of real importance whether our early education confirms us in one set of habits or another. It would be nearer the truth to say that it makes a very great difference indeed, in fact all the difference in the world.

Chapter II

Since the branch of philosophy on which we are at present engaged differs from the others in not being a subject of merely intellectual interest—I mean we are not concerned to know what goodness essentially is, but how we are to become good men, for this alone gives the study its practical value—we must apply our minds to the solution of the problems of conduct. For, as I remarked, it is our actions that determine our dispositions.

Now that when we act we should do so according to the right principle, is common ground and I propose to take it as a basis, of discussion.[1] But we must begin with the admission that any theory of conduct must be content with an outline without much precision in details. We noted this when I said at the beginning of our discussion of this part of our subject that the measure of exactness of statement in any field of study must be determined by the nature of the matter studied. Now matters of conduct and considerations of what is to our advantage have no fixity about them any more than matters affecting our health. And if this be true of moral philosophy as a whole, it is still more true that the discussion of particular problems in ethics admits of no exactitude. For they do not fall under any science or professional tradition, but those who are following some line of conduct are forced in every collocation of circumstances to think out for themselves what is suited to these circumstances, just as doctors and navigators have to do in their different *métiers*. We can do no more than give our arguments, inexact as they necessarily are, such support as is available.

Let us begin with the following observation. It is in the nature of moral qualities that they can be destroyed by deficiency on the one hand and excess on the other. We can see this in the instances of bodily health and strength.[2] Physical strength is destroyed by too much and also by too little exercise. Similarly health is ruined by eating and drinking either too much or too little, while it is produced, increased and preserved by taking the right quantity of drink and victuals. Well, it is the same with temperance, courage, and the other virtues. The man who shuns and fears everything and can stand up to nothing becomes a coward. The man who is afraid of nothing at all, but marches up to every danger, becomes foolhardy. In the same way the man who indulges in every pleasure without refraining from a single one becomes incontinent. If, on the other hand, a man behaves like the Boor in comedy and turns his back on every pleasure, he will find his sensibilities becoming blunted. So also temperance and courage are destroyed both by excess and deficiency, and they are kept alive by observance of the mean.

Let us go back to our statement that the virtues are produced and fostered as a result, and by the agency, of actions of the same quality as effect their destruction. It is also true that after the virtues have been formed they find expression in actions of that kind. We may see this in a

concrete instance—bodily strength. It results from taking plenty of nourishment and going in for hard training, and it is the strong man who is best fitted to cope with such conditions. So with the virtues. It is by refraining from pleasures that we become temperate, and it is when we have become temperate that we are most able to abstain from pleasures. Or take courage. It is by habituating ourselves to make light of alarming situations and to confront them that we become brave, and it is when we have become brave that we shall be most able to face an alarming situation.

Chapter III

We may use the pleasure (or pain) that accompanies the exercise of our dispositions as an index of how far they have established themselves. A man is temperate who abstaining from bodily pleasures finds this abstinence pleasant; if he finds it irksome, he is intemperate. Again, it is the man who encounters danger gladly, or at least without painful sensations, who is brave; the man who has these sensations is a coward. In a word, moral virtue has to do with pains and pleasures. There are a number of reasons for believing this. (1) Pleasure has a way of making us do what is disgraceful; pain deters us from doing what is right and fine. Hence the importance—I quote Plato—of having been brought up to find pleasure and pain in the right things. True education is just such a training. (2) The virtues operate with actions and emotions, each of which is accompanied by pleasure or pain. This is only another way of saying that virtue has to do with pleasures and pains. (3) Pain is used as an instrument of punishment. For in her remedies Nature works by opposites, and pain can be remedial. (4) When any disposition finds its complete expression it is, as we noted, in dealing with just those things by which it is its nature to be made better or worse, and which constitute the sphere of its operations. Now when men become bad it is under the influence

of pleasures and pains when they seek the wrong ones among them, or seek them at the wrong time, or in the wrong manner, or in any of the wrong forms which such offences may take; and in seeking the wrong pleasures and pains they shun the right. This has led some thinkers to identify the moral virtues with conditions of the soul in which passion is eliminated or reduced to a minimum. But this is to make too absolute a statement—it needs to be qualified by adding that such a condition must be attained 'in the right manner and at the right time' together with the other modifying circumstances.

So far, then, we have got this result. Moral goodness is a quality disposing us to act in the best way when we are dealing with pleasures and pains, while vice is one which leads us to act in the worst way when we deal with them.

The point may be brought out more clearly by some other considerations. There are three kinds of things that determine our choice in all our actions—the morally fine, the expedient, the pleasant; and three that we shun—the base, the harmful, the painful. Now in his dealings with all of these it is the good man who is most likely to go right, and the bad man who tends to go wrong, and that most notably in the matter of pleasure. The sensation of pleasure is felt by us in common with all animals, accompanying everything we choose, for even the fine and the expedient have a pleasurable effect upon us. (6) The capacity for experiencing pleasure has grown in us from infancy as part of our general development, and human life, being dyed in grain with it, receives therefrom a colour hard to scrape off. (7) Pleasure and pain are also the standards by which with greater or less strictness we regulate our considered actions. Since to feel pleasure and pain rightly or wrongly is an important factor in human behaviour, it follows that we are primarily concerned with these sensations. (8) Heraclitus says it is hard to fight against anger, but it is harder still to fight against pleasure. Yet to grapple with the harder has always been the business, as of art, so of

goodness, success in a task being proportionate to its difficulty. This gives us another reason for believing that morality and statesmanship must concentrate on pleasures and pains, seeing it is the man who deals rightly with them who will be good, and the man who deals with them wrongly who will be bad.

Here, then, are our conclusions. (*a*) Virtue is concerned with pains and pleasures. (*b*) The actions which produce virtue are identical in character with those which increase it. (*c*) These actions differently performed destroy it. (*d*) The actions which produced it are identical with those in which it finds expression.

Chapter IV

A difficulty, however, may be raised as to what we mean when we say that we must perform just actions if we are to become just, and temperate actions if we are to be temperate. It may be argued that, if I do what is just and temperate, I am just and temperate already, exactly as, if I spell words or play music correctly, I must already be literate or musical. This I take to be a false analogy, even in the arts. It is possible to spell a word right by accident or because somebody tips you the answer. But you will be a scholar only if your spelling is done as a scholar does it, that is thanks to the scholarship in your own mind. Nor will the suggested analogy with the arts bear scrutiny. A work of art is good or bad in itself—let it possess a certain quality, and that is all we ask of it. But virtuous actions are not done in a virtuous—a just or temperate—way merely because they have the appropriate quality. The *doer* must be in a certain frame of mind when he does them. Three conditions are involved. (1) The agent must act in full consciousness of what he is doing. (2) He must 'will' his action, and will it for its own sake. (3) The act must proceed from a fixed and unchangeable disposition. Now these requirements, if we expect mere knowledge, are not counted among the necessary qualifications of an artist. For the

acquisition of virtue, on the other hand, knowledge is of little or no value, but the other requirements are of immense, of sovran, importance, since it is the repeated performance of just and temperate actions that produces virtue. Actions, to be sure, are *called* just and temperate when they are such as a just or temperate man would do. But the doer is just or temperate not because he does such things but when he does them in the way of just and temperate persons. It is therefore quite fair to say that a man becomes just by the performance of just, and temperate by the performance of temperate, actions; nor is there the smallest likelihood of a man's becoming good by any other course of conduct. It is not, however, a popular line to take, most men preferring theory to practice under the impression that arguing about morals proves them to be philosophers, and that in this way they will turn out to be fine characters. Herein they resemble invalids, who listen carefully to all the doctor says but do not carry out a single one of his orders. The bodies of such people will never respond to treatment—nor will the souls of such 'philosophers.'

Chapter V

We now come to the formal definition of virtue. Note first, however, that the human soul is conditioned in three ways. It may have (1) feelings, (2) capacities, (3) dispositions; so virtue must be one of these three. By 'feelings' I mean a desire, anger, fear, daring, envy, gratification, friendliness, hatred, longing, jealousy, pity and in general all states of mind that are attended by pleasure or pain. By 'capacities' I mean those faculties in virtue of which we may be described as capable of the feelings in question—anger, for instance, or pain, or pity. By 'dispositions' I mean states of mind in virtue of which we are well or ill disposed in respect of the feelings concerned. We have, for instance, a bad disposition where angry feelings are concerned if we are disposed to become excessively or

insufficiently angry, and a good disposition in this respect if we consistently feel the due amount of anger, which comes between these extremes. So with the other feelings.

Now, neither the virtues nor the vices are feelings. We are not spoken of as good or bad in respect of our feelings but of our virtues and vices. Neither are we praised or blamed for the way we feel. A man is not praised for being frightened or angry, nor is he blamed just for being angry; it is for being angry in a particular way. But we *are* praised and blamed for our virtues and vices. Again, feeling angry or frightened is something we can't help, but our virtues are in a manner expressions of our will; at any rate there is an element of will in their formation. Finally, we are said to be 'moved' when our feelings are affected, but when it is a question of moral goodness or badness we are not said to be 'moved' but to be 'disposed' in a particular way. A similar line of reasoning will prove that the virtues and vices are not capacities either. We are not spoken of as good or bad, nor are we praised or blamed, merely because we are *capable* of feeling. Again, what capacities we have, we have by nature; but it is not nature that makes us good or bad. . . . So, if the virtues are neither feelings nor capacities, it remains that they must be dispositions . . . .

Chapter VI

It is not, however, enough to give this account of the *genus* of virtue—that it is a disposition; we must describe its *species*. Let us begin, then, with this proposition. Excellence of whatever kind affects that of which it is the excellence in two ways. (1) It produces a good state in it. (2) It enables it to perform its function well. Take eyesight. The goodness of your eye is not only that which makes your eye good, it is also that which makes it function well. Or take the case of a horse. The goodness of a horse makes him a good horse, but it also makes him good at running, carrying a rider and facing the enemy.

Our proposition, then, seems to be true, and it enables us to say that virtue in a man will be the disposition which (*a*) makes him a good man, (*b*) enables him to perform his function well. We have already touched on this point, but more light will be thrown upon it if we consider what is the specific nature of virtue.

In anything continuous and divisible it is possible to take the half, or more than the half, or less than the half. Now these parts may be larger, smaller and equal either in relation to the thing divided or in relation to us. The equal part may be described as a mean between too much and too little. By the mean of the thing I understand a point equidistant from the extremes; and this is one and the same for everybody. Let me give an illustration. Ten, let us say, is 'many' and two is 'few' of something. We get the mean of the thing if we take six;[3] that is, six exceeds and is exceeded by an equal number. This is the rule which gives us the arithmetical mean. But such a method will not give us the mean in relation to ourselves. Let ten pounds of food be a large, and two pounds a small, allowance for an athlete. It does not follow that the trainer will prescribe six pounds. That might be a large or it might be a small allowance for the particular athlete who is to get it. It would be little for Milo but a lot for a man who has just begun his training.[4] It is the same in all walks of life. The man who knows his business avoids both too much and too little. It is the mean he seeks and adopts—not the mean of the thing but the relative mean.

Every form, then, of applied knowledge, when it performs its function well, looks to the mean and works to the standard set by that. It is because people feel this that they apply the *cliché*, 'You couldn't add anything to it or take anything from it' to an artistic masterpiece, the implication being that too much and too little alike destroy perfection, while the mean preserves it. Now if this be so, and if it be true, as we say, that good craftsmen work to the standard of the mean, then, since goodness like nature is more exact and of a higher character than any art, it

follows that goodness is the quality that hits the mean. By 'goodness' I mean goodness of moral character, since it is moral goodness that deals with feelings and actions, and it is in them that we find excess, deficiency and a mean. It is possible, for example, to experience fear, boldness, desire, anger, pity, and pleasures and pains generally, too much or too little or to the right amount. If we feel them too much or too little, we are wrong. But to have these feelings at the right times on the right occasions towards the right people for the right motive and in the right way is to have them in the right measure, that is somewhere between the extremes; and this is what characterizes goodness. The same may be said of the mean and extremes in actions. Now it is in the field of actions and feelings that goodness operates; in them we find excess, deficiency and, between them, the mean, the first two being wrong, the mean right and praised as such.[5] Goodness, then, is a mean condition in the sense that it aims at and hits the mean.

Consider, too, that it is possible to go wrong in more ways than one. (In Pythagorean terminology evil is a form of the Unlimited, good of the Limited.) But there is only one way of being right. That is why going wrong is easy, and going right difficult; it is easy to miss the bull's-eye and difficult to hit it. Here, then, is another explanation of why the too much and the too little are connected with evil and the mean with good. As the poet says,

Goodness is one, evil is multiform.

We may now define virtue as a disposition of the soul in which, when it has to choose among actions and feelings, it observes the mean relative to us, this being determined by such a rule or principle as would take shape in the mind of a man of sense or practical wisdom. We call it a mean condition as lying between two forms of badness, one being excess and the other deficiency; and also for this reason, that, whereas badness either falls short of or exceeds the right

measure in feelings and actions, virtue discovers the mean and deliberately chooses it. Thus, looked at from the point of view of its essence as embodied in its definition, virtue no doubt is a mean; judged by the standard of what is right and best, it is an extreme.

But choice of a mean is not possible in every action or every feeling. The very names of some have an immediate connotation of evil. Such are malice, shamelessness, envy among feelings, and among actions adultery, theft, murder. All these and more like them have a bad name as being evil in themselves; it is not merely the excess or deficiency of them that we censure. In their case, then, it is impossible to act rightly; whatever we do is wrong. Nor do circumstances make any difference in the rightness or wrongness of them. When a man commits adultery there is no point in asking whether it is with the right woman or at the right time or in the right way, for to do anything like that is simply wrong. It would amount to claiming that there is a mean and excess and defect in unjust or cowardly or intemperate actions. If such a thing were possible, we should find ourselves with a mean quantity of excess, a mean of deficiency, an excess of excess and a deficiency of deficiency. But just as in temperance and justice there can be no mean or excess or deficiency, because the mean in a sense is an extreme, so there can be no mean or excess or deficiency in those vicious actions—however done, they are wrong. Putting the matter into general language, we may say that there is no mean in the extremes, and no extreme in the mean, to be observed by anybody.

Chapter VII

But a generalization of this kind is not enough; we must show that our definition fits particular cases. When we are discussing actions particular statements come nearer the heart of the matter, though general statements cover a wider field. The reason is that human behaviour consists in

the performance of particular acts, and our theories must be brought into harmony with them.

You see here a diagram of the virtues. Let us take our particular instances from that.

In the section confined to the feelings inspired by danger you will observe that the mean state is 'courage.' Of those who go to extremes in one direction or the other the man who shows an excess of fearlessness has no name to describe him, the man who exceeds in confidence or daring is called 'rash' or 'fool-hardy,' the man who shows an excess of fear and a deficiency of confidence is called a 'coward.' In the pleasures and pains—though not all pleasures and pains, especially pains—the virtue which observes the mean is 'temperance,' the excess is the vice of 'intemperance.' Persons defective in the power to enjoy pleasures are a somewhat rare class, and so have not had a name assigned to them: suppose we call them 'unimpressionable.' Coming to the giving and acquiring of money, we find that the mean is 'liberality,' the excess 'prodigality,' the deficiency 'meanness.' But here we meet a complication. The prodigal man and the mean man exceed and fall short in opposite ways. The prodigal exceeds in giving and falls short in getting money, whereas the mean man exceeds in getting and falls short in giving it away. Of course this is but a summary account of the matter—a bare outline. But it meets our immediate requirements. Later on these types of character will be more accurately delineated.

• • •

Chapter IX

I have said enough to show that moral excellence is a mean, and I have shown in what sense it is so. It is, namely, a mean between two forms of badness, one of excess and the other of defect, and is so described because it aims at hitting the mean point in feelings and in actions. This makes virtue hard of achievement, because finding the middle point is never easy. It is not everybody, for instance, who can find the centre of a circle—that calls for a geometrician. Thus, too, it is easy to fly into a passion—anybody can do that—but to be angry with the right person and to the right extent and at the right time and with the right object and in the right way—that is not easy, and it is not everyone who can do it. This is equally true of giving or spending money. Hence we infer that to do these things properly is rare, laudable and fine.

In view of this we shall find it useful when aiming at the mean to observe these rules (1) *Keep away from that extreme which is the more opposed to the mean.* It is Calypso's advice:

'Swing round the ship clear of this surf and surge.'

For one of the extremes is always a more dangerous error than the other; and—since it is hard to hit the bull's-eye—we must take the next best course and choose the least of the evils. And it will be easiest for us to do this if we follow the rule I have suggested. (2) *Note the errors into which we personally are most liable to fall.* (Each of us has his natural bias in one direction or another.) We shall find out what ours are by noting what gives us pleasure and pain. After that we must drag ourselves in the opposite direction. For our best way of reaching the middle is by giving a wide berth to our darling sin. It is the method used by a carpenter when he is straightening a warped board. (3) *Always be particularly on your guard against pleasure and pleasant things.* When Pleasure is at the bar the jury is not impartial. So it will be best for us if we feel towards her as the Trojan elders felt towards Helen, and regularly apply their words to her. If we are for packing her off, as they were with Helen, we shall be the less likely to go wrong.

To sum up. These are the rules by observation of which we have the best chance of hitting the mean. But of course difficulties spring up, especially when we are confronted with an exceptional case. For example, it is not easy to say precisely what is the right way to be angry and

with whom and on what grounds and for how long. In fact we are inconsistent on this point, sometimes praising people who are deficient in the capacity for anger and calling them 'gentle,' sometimes praising the choleric and calling them 'stout fellows.' To be sure we are not hard on a man who goes off the straight path in the direction of too much or too little, if he goes off only a little way. We reserve our censure for the man who swerves widely from the course, because then we are bound to notice it. Yet it is not easy to find a formula by which we may determine how far and up to what point a man may go wrong before he incurs blame. But this difficulty of definition is inherent in every object of perception; such questions of degree are bound up with the circumstances of the individual case, where our only criterion is the perception.

So much, then, has become clear. In all our conduct it is the mean state that is to be praised. But one should lean sometimes in the direction of the more, sometimes in that of the less, because that is the readiest way of attaining to goodness and the mean.

From Nicomachean Ethics, Book Seven

Chapter I

• • •

I cannot, however, omit here some account of incontinence and softness of luxuriousness, as well as of continence and fortitude or endurance. We should not think of either of these dispositions—the good and the bad—as identical with virtue and vice respectively. Neither must we think of them as different in kind.

The true method for us to follow, here and elsewhere, is to set forth the views which are held on the subject and then, after discussing the problems involved in these, to indicate what truth lies in all or—if that proves impossible—in the greatest in number and importance of the beliefs generally entertained about these states of mind. I am convinced that, if the difficulties

can be resolved and we are left with certain of these beliefs—those, namely, which have stood our test—we shall have reached as satisfactory a conclusion as is possible in cases of the kind. In the present case the general beliefs are these. (a) Continence and endurance are good and commendable qualities, whereas their opposites, incontinence and softness, are bad and blameworthy. (b) The continent man has the characteristic of sticking by the conclusions he has been led to draw, whereas the incontinent man tends to give his up. (c) The incontinent or morally weak man does wrong, knowing it to be wrong, because he cannot control his passions, whereas the continent man, knowing that his lusts are evil, refuses to follow them, because his principles forbid it. (d) The temperate man is always continent and enduring, though whether the continent man is always temperate is an open question, some asserting and others denying that it is so, the former distinguishing between the intemperate and the incontinent man, the latter confounding all distinction between them. (e) It is sometimes maintained that it is impossible for the prudent man to be incontinent, sometimes that *some* prudent and clever men are guilty of incontinence. (f) Some men are described as 'incontinent' in their anger and in their pursuit of honour or gain.—Such are the views that have found expression.

Chapter II

Now for the difficulties that may be raised. To take the third (c) of our opinions first, how can a man be said to show incontinence, if he has a correct apprehension of the fact that he is acting wrongly? Some thinkers maintain that he cannot, if he has full knowledge that the action is wrong. It is, as Socrates thought, hard to believe that, if a man really *knows*, and has this knowledge in his soul, it should be mastered by something else which, in Plato's phrase, 'hauls it about like a slave.' Socrates to be sure was out and out opposed to the view we are now

criticizing, on the ground that there is no such thing as this moral weakness we call 'incontinence.' For, said he, nobody acts in opposition to what is best—and the best is the goal of all our endeavours—if he has a clear idea of what he is doing. He can only go wrong out of ignorance. This reasoning, however, is in glaring contrast with notorious facts; and that obliges us to look more closely into the frame of mind on which it is based. Conceding that ignorance is the cause of moral weakness, let us consider what form of ignorance. For it is clear that the man who succumbs to temptation is not ignorant of the wrongness of his action *before* he is involved in the temptation.

• • •

Chapter III

We have then to consider these points. (1) When men show moral weakness (or incontinence) do they or do they not know the wrongness of their actions? If they know it, in what sense do they know it? (2) What are we to posit as the objects to which continence and incontinence are directed? I mean, are they concerned with every kind of pleasures and pains or only with a special division of them? (3) Is continence the same or not the same as endurance? (4) Other questions germane to the subject.

We may begin our enquiry by asking whether it is the objects or the dispositions of the continent and incontinent man that enter into the definition of these types as their differentiating qualities. Put it this way. Is a man to be described as incontinent merely because he cannot restrain his desires for certain things, or is it because he has a certain disposition, or do both causes operate? Here is a second question. Can incontinence and continence be exercised towards everything? Yes or no? One is aware that when a man is described as "incontinent" without further qualification it is not implied that he is incontinent in everything, but only in those things in which a man can show intemperance;

nor is it implied merely that he is concerned with those things,[6] but that he is concerned with them in a certain way. The intemperate man deliberately chooses to follow in the train of his lusts from a belief that he ought always to pursue the pleasure of the moment. The incontinent man pursues it too, but has no such belief.

(1) The theory that when men behave incontinently they are not acting against knowledge but against true opinion contributes nothing of value to our discussion. It never occurs to some people to question the truth of their opinions; indeed, they do not regard them as opinions but as ascertained truths. Consequently, if we base an argument on lack of conviction in some men, and say that this is the reason why those who shall be found to act against their conception of what is right must be said to have an opinion rather than knowledge, the difference between opinion and knowledge will vanish. For some men are just as sure of the truth of their opinions as are others of what they know. Heraclitus alone proves that. And if we say a man 'knows' something, we may be using the word in one of two senses. We may mean that he has the knowledge and acts upon it, or that he has the knowledge but makes no use of it. This being so, it will make a difference whether a man who is doing wrong knows that what he is doing is wrong but has this knowledge only in a latent or subconscious form, or whether, having the knowledge, he has it in an active form. If the latter, his doing wrong may well surprise us; but it will not, if his knowledge is not fully realized.

(2) When logical reasoning is applied to actions, the premises will assume two forms.[7] Now a man who is acting against knowledge may very well know both premises, yet put into practice only his knowledge of the universal or imajor premise and not his knowledge of the particular or minor premise. Yet it is this minor premise that is decisive for action, because acts are particulars. We have also to note that in reasoning about actions there are two universals

involved. One is predicated of the *man*, the other of the *thing*. For example, he may know, and be in a position to act on the knowledge, that (*a*) dry food is good for all men,[8] and (*b*) he is himself a man. But he may not know, or may not be prepared to act on his knowledge, whether the particular food before him is that sort of food. It will be found then that there is an immeasurable distance between these two ways of knowing, so that we cannot think it odd that the incontinent man should know in one and not the other. The truly strange thing would be if he *did* know in the other.

(3) Moreover, it is possible for men to have knowledge—I use the word without prejudice—in another way besides those described. We have noted the distinction between actual and potential knowledge. But even in the second case, which is a condition of having knowledge without allowing it to operate, we can see a distinction. For there is a sense in which a man can both have and not have knowledge—he might, for instance, be asleep or out of his mind, or drunk. And what better are people when their feelings are too much for them? Doesn't everybody know that rage and lust and some other passions actually produce physiological changes, in some cases even insanity? It is evident then that, if we must say that the incontinent have knowledge, it can only be like that possessed by the persons, to whom I have referred. The moral weakling may *say* he has knowledge, but that is no proof that he has it. People suffering from the disabilities I have mentioned will repeat to you the proof of some problem in geometry or a passage from Empedocles. In the same way people who have begun the study of a subject reel off a string of propositions which they do not as yet understand. For knowledge must be worked into the living texture of the mind, and this takes time. So we should think of incontinent men as like actors—mouthpieces of the sentiments of other people.

(4) It is also possible to study the cause of incontinence from the point of view of the scientist. This involves what we call the practical syllogism. In this the major premise is an opinion, while the minor premise is a statement about particulars, the objects of sense-perception. When the two premises are combined to form the syllogism, we have a result analogous to what we have in pure ratiocination. As in the latter the mind is forced to *affirm* the conclusion, so in the practical syllogism we are forced straight-way to *do* it. Suppose you have these premises: 'All sweet things ought to be tasted,' and 'That thing is sweet.'[9] When these premises are brought into relation you are bound, if nothing prevents you and you can do it, to go and taste the thing. Now there may be simultaneously present in the mind two universal judgments, one saying, 'You must not taste,' the other, 'Every sweet thing is pleasant.' When this happens, and then the minor premise, 'That thing is sweet,' presents itself,[10] while at the same time desire is present, then in spite of the fact that the first universal bids you avoid the thing in question, the desire leads you to it.[11] It is therefore, we conclude, to some extent an intellectual principle or opinion which influences the incontinent man to behave as he does—an opinion not in itself contradictory of the right principle but only opposed to it by an accidental conjunction of circumstances.[12] This is the reason why the lower animals are not incontinent. They are incapable of understanding a generalization; all they have is mental images and the memory of particular objects.

We may ask how the ignorance of the incontinent man is overcome and knowledge restored to him. The explanation which accounts for the so-called knowledge of the drunk or sleeping man will serve in this case also; it applies to more than continence. But on this point it is for the physiologist to instruct us.

There are then these points to be considered. (*a*) The last—that is the minor—premise, that which can influence action, is an opinion which is related to some object of sense-perception. (*b*) This opinion the incontinent man, when he

abandons himself to his emotions, does not possess or possesses only in such a way as does not entitle it to be regarded as knowledge, but only enables him to quote its tenor as a drunk man quotes Empedocles. (c) The ultimate term—that is the particular proposition which forms the minor premise—is not a universal and is not regarded as an object of knowledge in the way that a universal judgment is. Since these three statements are evidently true, it does appear that our conclusions must be that which Socrates directed his questions to prove. For the knowledge which accompanies the collapse of moral resistance is not what is thought to be knowledge properly speaking. Neither is it true knowledge that is dragged about by passion, but only such as can be supplied by the senses . . . .

Chapter VII

• • •

Opposed to incontinence is continence, opposed to softness is hardness or endurance. The difference between endurance and continence is this. Endurance consists in holding out, continence in preserving mastery. They are two very different things, as different as the avoidance of defeat from victory. We are bound therefore to prefer continence. A man who fails to withstand such pains as most people can and do support is soft or luxury-loving; for luxury is a kind of softness. He is the sort of man to let his cloak trail on the ground rather than have the bother of lifting it, or to affect the languor of sickness without reflecting that an assumed distress is a real distress. It is much the same with continence and incontinence. If a man gives way to violent or excessive pleasure or pain, that can surprise nobody. Indeed, he may be forgiven for succumbing, if he does not do it without a struggle. One thinks of Philoctetes when he is bitten by the viper in the play of Theodectes, or of Cercyon in the *Alope* of Carcinus. Or—to take an example of resistance to pleasure—think of a man trying his best to

hold in a laugh who bursts out at last into a stentorian guffaw.[13] But it does surprise us to see a man give way to pleasures and pains which most of us are capable of withstanding. It is different of course if his weakness is due to disease or some hereditary taint, such as the congenital impotence of the Scythian royal family, or the less hardy constitution of the female, as compared with the male, sex.

It is a popular notion that a love of amusement is a sign of intemperance. In reality it is a sign of softness. For amusement is a way of enjoying one's leisure by relaxation. You may say, then, that the devotee of amusement indulges too much in relaxation. But relaxation is not pleasure, and it is the man who is insatiable in his pursuit of pleasure that is intemperate.

Incontinence is found in two forms, which we may call (a) impulsiveness and (b) weakness. The weak do form a resolution, but they are prevented by their sensibilities from keeping to it. The impulsive or headstrong are carried away by their feelings, because they have not thought about the matter that excites them at all. If they had, their behaviour might be different. For some people can hold out against strong emotion, whether painful or pleasurable, if they feel or see it coming and have time to rouse themselves—by which I mean their reasoning faculty—beforehand, just as a man can't tickle you if you have tickled him first. It is high-strung and excitable people who are most prone to the impulsive form of incontinence. The high-strung are too hasty, and the excitable too vehement, to wait for reason, since they instinctively follow the suggestions of their own imaginations.

Chapter VIII

It is different with the intemperate man, who, as I said, does not repent or feel remorse, since he abides by his choice. The incontinent man on the other hand is always capable of remorse. Consequently the objection we mentioned—that

the intemperate man might be cured—is refuted by the fact. It is just the intemperate man who is incurable; the incontinent man is not. Vice such as is shown by the intemperate man is like dropsy or tuberculosis, whereas incontinence is like epilepsy. For vice is a chronic, incontinence an intermittent, ill. More than that, vice and incontinence are totally different in kind. The vicious man does not realize that he is vicious, but the incontinent man is aware of his incontinence.

With regard to the incontinent themselves, the impulsive among them are morally superior to the weak, who are in possession of the right principle but do not hold fast to it. These are worse, because they yield to a feebler impulse and after deliberation. Such men resemble dipsomaniacs, who get drunk quickly and on a small amount of wine or less than most people. It is obvious in fact that incontinence is not a vice, at least in the strict sense of that word. For vice is deliberate, and incontinence is not. Yet there is a similarity in the actions which result from them. Something of the kind is noted in the epigram of Demodocus upon the citizens of Miletus.

Milesians are no fools, you'd swear,
And yet they act as if they were.

To parody Demodocus: The incontinent are not bad, but they act badly.

To resume. While pursuing bodily pleasures of an excessive kind and contrary to right principle, the incontinent man is so constituted that he pursues them without the conviction that he is right, whereas the intemperate man has this conviction, which he has come to feel because it is now second nature with him to seek these gratifications. Hence the incontinent man can readily be persuaded to change his mode of behaviour—but not the other. For virtue preserves, while vice destroys, that intuitive perception of the true end of life which is the starting point in conduct. We may compare the propositions which the geometer sets out to prove and which are his starting-point. In moral as in mathematical science the knowledge of its first principles is not reached by a process of reasoning. The good man has it in virtue of his goodness, whether innate or acquired by the habit of thinking rightly about the first principle. Such a man is temperate, while the man who does not know the primary assumptions of all ethics is intemperate. But there is another type—the man who is driven from his considered course of action by a flood of emotion contrary to right principle. He is prevented by overmastering passion from acting in accordance with that principle, yet not so completely as to make him the kind of man to believe that it is right to abandon himself to such pleasures as he seeks. Such is the incontinent man. He is morally superior to the intemperate man and is not to be called bad without qualification, for he preserves his noblest element—that conviction on which all morality is founded. Different and at the opposite pole from him is the man who having made his choice holds fast by that, unshaken by the storms of passion. These considerations prove that continence is a good, and incontinence a bad, quality.

Notes

1 There will be an opportunity later of considering what is meant by this formula, in particular what is meant by 'the right principle' and how, in its ethical aspect, it is related to the moral virtues.
2 If we are to illustrate the material, it must be by concrete images.
3 $6-2 = 10-16$.
4 What applies to gymnastics applies also to running and wrestling.
5 Being right or successful and being praised are both indicative of excellence.
6 For if that were so, incontinence would be identical with intemperance.
7 In other words the application of a 'practical syllogism' involves two syllogisms.

8 We may even know that such and such a food is dry.

9 Here the minor premise is a particular instance of the class of things about which the major premise makes a general statement.

10 Remember that it is the minor premise that introduces the possibility of action.

11 This is because only desire can set the various limbs in motion—the body corresponding to the potential major premise, and the desire to the active minor.

12 It is the desire, not the opinion, that is the true opposite.

13 This actually happened to Xenophantus.

Martha Nussbaum

NON-RELATIVE VIRTUES: AN ARISTOTELIAN APPROACH

"ALL GREEKS used to go around armed with swords."

Thucydides, *History of the Peloponnesian War*

"The customs of former times might be said to be too simple and barbaric. For Greeks used to go around armed with swords; and they used to buy wives from one another, and there are surely other ancient customs that are extremely stupid. (For example, in Cyme there is a law about homicide, that if a man prosecuting a charge can produce a certain number of witnesses from among his own relations, the defendant will automatically be convicted of murder.) In general, all human beings seek not the way of their ancestors, but the good."

Aristotle, *Politics* 1268a39 ff.

"One may also observe in one's travels to distant countries the feelings of recognition and affiliation that link every human being to every other human being."

Aristotle, *Nicomachean Ethics* 1155a21–22

I

The virtues are attracting increasing interest in contemporary philosophical debate. From many different sides one hears of a dissatisfaction with ethical theories that are remote from concrete human experience. Whether this remoteness results from the utilitarian's interest in arriving at a universal calculus of satisfactions or from a Kantian concern with universal principles of broad generality, in which the names of particular contexts, histories, and persons do not occur, remoteness is now being seen by an increasing number of moral philosophers as a defect in an approach to ethical questions. In the search for an alternative approach, the concept of virtue is playing a prominent role. So, too, is the work of Aristotle, the greatest defender of an ethical approach based on the concept of virtue. For Aristotle's work seems, appealingly, to combine rigor with concreteness, theoretical power with sensitivity to the actual circumstances of human life and choice in all their multiplicity, variety, and mutability.

But on one central point there is a striking divergence between Aristotle and contemporary virtue theory. To many current defenders of an ethical approach based on the virtues, the return to the virtues is connected with a turn toward relativism—toward, that is, the view that the only appropriate criteria of ethical goodness are local ones, internal to the traditions and practices of each local society or group that asks itself questions about the good. The rejection of general algorithms and abstract rules in favor of an account of the good life based on specific modes of virtuous action is taken, by writers as otherwise diverse

as Alasdair MacIntyre, Bernard Williams, and Philippa Foot,[1] to be connected with the abandonment of the project of rationally justifying a single norm of flourishing life for and to all human beings and with a reliance, instead, on norms that are local both in origin and in application.

The positions of all of these writers, where relativism is concerned, are complex; none unequivocally endorses a relativist view. But all connect virtue ethics with a relativist denial that ethics, correctly understood, offers any trans-cultural norms, justifiable with reference to reasons of universal human validity, with reference to which we may appropriately criticize different local conceptions of the good. And all suggest that the insights we gain by pursuing ethical questions in the Aristotelian virtue-based way lend support to relativism.

For this reason it is easy for those who are interested in supporting the rational criticism of local traditions and in articulating an idea of ethical progress to feel that the ethics of virtue can give them little help. If the position of women, as established by local traditions in many parts of the world, is to be improved, if traditions of slave holding and racial inequality, if religious intolerance, if aggressive and warlike conceptions of manliness, if unequal norms of material distribution are to be criticized in the name of practical reason, this criticizing (one might easily suppose) will have to be done from a Kantian or utilitarian viewpoint, not through the Aristotelian approach.

This is an odd result, where Aristotle is concerned. For it is obvious that he was not only the defender of an ethical theory based on the virtues, but also the defender of a single objective account of the human good, or human flourishing. This account is supposed to be objective in the sense that it is justifiable with reference to reasons that do not derive merely from local traditions and practices, but rather from features of humanness that lie beneath all local traditions and are there to be seen whether or not they are in fact recognized in local traditions. And one of Aristotle's most obvious concerns is the criticism of existing moral traditions, in his own city and in others, as unjust or repressive, or in other ways incompatible with human flourishing. He uses his account of the virtues as a basis for this criticism of local traditions: prominently, for example, in Book II of the *Politics*, where he frequently argues against existing social forms by pointing to ways in which they neglect or hinder the development of some important human virtue.[2] Aristotle evidently believes that there is no incompatibility between basing an ethical theory on the virtues and defending the singleness and objectivity of the human good. Indeed, he seems to believe that these two aims are mutually supportive.

Now the fact that Aristotle believes something does not make it true. (Though I have sometimes been accused of holding that position!) But it does, on the whole, make that something a plausible *candidate* for the truth, one deserving our most serious scrutiny. In this case, it would be odd indeed if he had connected two elements in ethical thought that are self-evidently incompatible, or in favor of whose connectedness and compatibility there is nothing interesting to be said. The purpose of this paper is to establish that Aristotle does indeed have an interesting way of connecting the virtues with a search for ethical objectivity and with the criticism of existing local norms, a way that deserves our serious consideration as we work on these questions. Having described the general shape of the Aristotelian approach, we can then begin to understand some of the objections that might be brought against such a non-relative account of the virtues, and to imagine how the Aristotelian could respond to those objections.

II

The relativist, looking at different societies, is impressed by the variety and the apparent non-comparability in the lists of virtues she encounters. Examining the different lists, and observing the complex connections between each list and a concrete form of life and a concrete history, she may well feel that any list of virtues must be simply a reflection of local traditions and values, and that, virtues being (unlike Kantian principles or utilitarian algorithms) concrete and closely tied to forms of life, there can in fact be no list of virtues that will serve as normative for all these varied societies. It is not only that the specific forms of behavior recommended in connection with the virtues differ greatly over time and place, it is also that the very areas that are singled out as spheres of virtue, and the manner in which they are individuated from other areas, vary so greatly. For someone who thinks this way, it is easy to feel that Aristotle's own list, despite its pretensions to universality and objectivity, must be similarly restricted, merely a reflection of one particular society's perceptions of salience and ways of distinguishing. At this point, relativist writers are likely to quote Aristotle's description of the "great-souled" person, the *megalopsuchos*, which certainly contains many concrete local features and sounds very much like the portrait of a certain sort of Greek gentleman, in order to show that Aristotle's list is just as culture-bound as any other.[3]

But if we probe further into the way in which Aristotle in fact enumerates and individuates the virtues, we begin to notice things that cast doubt upon the suggestion that he has simply described what is admired in his own society. First of all, we notice that a rather large number of virtues and vices (vices especially) are nameless, and that, among the ones that are not nameless, a good many are given, by Aristotle's own account, names that are somewhat arbitrarily chosen by Aristotle,

and do not perfectly fit the behavior he is trying to describe.[4] Of such modes of conduct he writes, "Most of these are nameless, but we must try . . . to give them names in order to make our account clear and easy to follow" (NE 1108a16–19). This does not sound like the procedure of someone who is simply studying local traditions and singling out the virtue names that figure most prominently in those traditions.

What is going on becomes clearer when we examine the way in which he does, in fact, introduce his list. For he does so, in the *Nicomachean Ethics*,[5] by a device whose very straightforwardness and simplicity has caused it to escape the notice of most writers on this topic. What he does, in each case, is to isolate a sphere of human experience that figures in more or less any human life, and in which more or less any human being will have to make *some* choices rather than others, and act in *some* way rather than some other. The introductory chapter enumerating the virtues and vices begins from an enumeration of these spheres (NE 2.7); and each chapter on a virtue in the more detailed account that follows begins with "Concerning X . . ." or words to this effect, where "X" names a sphere of life with which all human beings regularly and more or less necessarily have dealings.[6] Aristotle then asks: What is it to choose and respond well within that sphere? What is it, on the other hand, to choose defectively? The "thin account" of each virtue is that it is whatever it is to be stably disposed to act appropriately in that sphere. There may be, and usually are, various competing specifications of what acting well, in each case, in fact comes to. Aristotle goes on to defend in each case some concrete specifications, producing, at the end, a full or "thick" definition of the virtue.

Here are the most important spheres of experience recognized by Aristotle, along with the names of their corresponding virtues:[7]

Sphere	Virtue
1. Fear of important damages, esp. death	courage
2. Bodily appetites and their pleasures	moderation
3. Distribution of limited resources	justice
4. Management of one's personal property, where others are concerned	generosity
5. Management of personal property, where hospitality is concerned	expansive hospitality
6. Attitudes and actions with respect to one's own worth	greatness of soul
7. Attitude to slights and damages	mildness of temper
8. "Association and living together and the fellowship of words and actions"	
a. truthfulness in speech	truthfulness
b. social association of a playful kind	easy grace (contrasted with coarseness, rudeness, insensitivity)
c. social association more generally	nameless, but a kind of friendliness (contrasted with irritability and grumpiness)
9. Attitude to the good and ill fortune of others	proper judgment (contrasted with enviousness, spitefulness, etc.)
10. Intellectual life	the various intellectual virtues (such as perceptiveness, knowledge, etc.)
11. The planning of one's life and conduct	practical wisdom

There is, of course, much more to be said about this list, its specific members, and the names Aristotle chooses for the virtue in each case, some of which are indeed culture bound. What I want, however, to insist is the care with which Aristotle articulates his general approach, beginning from a characterization of a sphere of universal experience and choice, and introducing the virtue name as the name (as yet undefined) of whatever it is to choose appropriately in that area of experience. On this approach, it does not seem possible to say, as the relativist wishes to, that a given society does not contain anything that corresponds to a given virtue. Nor does it seem to be an open question, in the case of a particular agent, whether a certain virtue should or should not be included in his or her life—except in the sense that she can always choose to pursue the corresponding deficiency instead. The point is that everyone makes some choices and acts somehow or other in these spheres: if not properly, then improperly. Everyone has *some* attitude and behavior toward her own death; toward her bodily appetites and their management; toward her property and its use; toward the distribution of social goods; toward telling the truth; toward being kindly or not kindly to others; toward cultivating or not cultivating a sense of play and delight; and so on. No matter where one lives one cannot escape these questions, so long as one is living a human life. But then this means that one's behavior falls, willy nilly, within the sphere of the Aristotelian virtue, in each case. If it is not appropriate, it is inappropriate; it cannot be off the map altogether. People will of course disagree about what the appropriate ways of acting and reacting in fact *are*. But in that case, as Aristotle has set

things up, they are arguing about the same thing, and advancing competing specifications of the same virtue. The reference of the virtue term in each case is fixed by the sphere of experience—by what we shall from now on call the "grounding experiences." The thin or "nominal definition" of the virtue will be, in each case, that it is whatever it is that being disposed to choose and respond well consists in, in that sphere. The job of ethical theory will be to search for the best further specification corresponding to this nominal definition, and to produce a full definition.

III

We have begun to introduce considerations from the philosophy of language. We can now make the direction of the Aristotelian account clearer by considering his own account of linguistic indicating (referring) and defining, which guides his treatment of both scientific and ethical terms, and of the idea of progress in both areas.[8]

Aristotle's general picture is as follows. We begin with some experiences—not necessarily our own, but those of members of our linguistic community, broadly construed.[9] On the basis of these experiences, a word enters the language of the group, indicating (referring to) whatever it is that is the content of those experiences. Aristotle gives the example of thunder.[10] People hear a noise in the clouds, and they then refer to it, using the word "thunder." At this point, it may be that nobody has any concrete account of the noise or any idea about what it really is. But the experience fixes a subject for further inquiry. From now on, we can refer to thunder, ask "What is thunder?" and advance and assess competing theories. The thin or, we might say, "nominal definition" of thunder is "That noise in the clouds, whatever it is." The competing explanatory theories are rival candidates for correct full or thick definition. So the explanation story citing Zeus' activities in the clouds is

a false account of the very same thing of which the best scientific explanation is a true account. There is just one debate here, with a single subject.

So too, Aristotle suggests, with our ethical terms. Heraclitus, long before him, already had the essential idea, saying, "They would not have known the name of justice, if these things did not take place."[11] "These things," our source for the fragment informs us, are experiences of injustice—presumably of harm, deprivation, inequality. These experiences fix the reference of the corresponding virtue word. Aristotle proceeds along similar lines. In the *Politics* he insists that only human beings, and not either animals or gods, will have our basic ethical terms and concepts (such as just and unjust, noble and base, good and bad), because the beasts are unable to form the concepts, and gods lack the experiences of limit and finitude that give a concept such as justice its point.[12] In the *Nicomachean Ethics* enumeration of the virtues, he carries the line of thought further, suggesting that the reference of the virtue terms is fixed by spheres of choice, frequently connected with our finitude and limitation, that we encounter in virtue of shared conditions of human existence.[13] The question about virtue usually arises in areas in which human choice is both non-optional and somewhat problematic. (Thus, he stresses, there is no virtue involving the regulation of listening to attractive sounds or seeing pleasing sights.) Each family of virtue and vice or deficiency words attaches to some such sphere. And we can understand progress in ethics, like progress in scientific understanding, to be progress in finding the correct fuller specification of a virtue, isolated by its thin or "nominal" definition. This progress is aided by a perspicuous mapping of the sphere of the grounding experiences. When we understand more precisely what problems human beings encounter in their lives with one another, what circumstances they face in which choice of some sort is required, we will have a way of assessing

competing responses to those problems, and we will begin to understand what it might be to act well in the face of them.

Aristotle's ethical and political writings provide many examples of how such progress (or, more generally, such a rational debate) might go. We find argument against Platonic asceticism, as the proper specification of moderation (appropriate choice and response vis-à-vis the bodily appetites) and the consequent proneness to anger over slights, that was prevalent in Greek ideals of maleness and in Greek behavior, together with a defense of a more limited and controlled expression of anger, as the proper specification of the virtue that Aristotle calls "mildness of temper." (Here Aristotle evinces some discomfort with the virtue term he has chosen, and he is right to do so, since it certainly loads the dice heavily in favor of his concrete specification and against the traditional one.)[14] And so on for all the virtues.

In an important section of *Politics* II, part of which forms one of the epigraphs to this paper, Aristotle defends the proposition that laws should be revisable and not fixed by pointing to evidence that there is progress toward greater correctness in our ethical conceptions, as also in the arts and sciences. Greeks used to think that courage was a matter of waving swords around; now they have (the *Ethics* informs us) a more inward and a more civic and communally attuned understanding of proper behavior toward the possibility of death. Women used to be regarded as property, bought and sold; now this would be thought barbaric. And in the case of justice as well we have, the *Politics* passage claims, advanced toward a more adequate understanding of what is fair and appropriate. Aristotle gives the example of an existing homicide law that convicts the defendant automatically on the evidence of the prosecutor's relatives (whether they actually witnessed anything or not, apparently). This, Aristotle says, is clearly a stupid and unjust law; and yet it once seemed appropriate—and, to a tradition-bound

community, must still be so. To hold tradition fixed is then to prevent ethical progress. What human beings want and seek is not conformity with the past, it is the good. So our systems of law should make it possible for them to progress beyond the past, when they have agreed that a change is good. (They should not, however, make change too easy, since it is no easy matter to see one's way to the good, and tradition is frequently a sounder guide than current fashion.)

In keeping with these ideas, the *Politics* as a whole presents the beliefs of the many different societies it investigates not as unrelated local norms, but as competing answers to questions of justice and courage (and so on) with which all the societies (being human) are concerned, and in response to which they are all trying to find what is good. Aristotle's analysis of the virtues gives him an appropriate framework for these comparisons, which seem perfectly appropriate inquiries into the ways in which different societies have solved common human problems.

In the Aristotelian approach it is obviously of the first importance to distinguish two stages of the inquiry: the initial demarcation of the sphere of choice, of the "grounding experiences" that fix the reference of the virtue term; and the ensuing more concrete inquiry into what appropriate choice, in that sphere, *is*. Aristotle does not always do this carefully, and the language he has to work with is often not helpful to him. We do not have much difficulty with terms like "moderation" and "justice" and even "courage," which seem vaguely normative but relatively empty, so far, of concrete moral content. As the approach requires, they can serve as extension-fixing labels under which many competing specifications may be investigated. But we have already noticed the problem with "mildness of temper," which seems to rule out by fiat a prominent contender for the appropriate disposition concerning anger. And much the same thing certainly seems to be true of the relativists'

favorite target, *megalopsuchia*, which implies in its very name an attitude to one's own worth that is more Greek than universal. (For example, a Christian will feel that the proper attitude to one's own worth requires understanding one's lowness, frailty, and sinfulness. The virtue of humility requires considering oneself *small*, not great.) What we ought to get at this point in the inquiry is a word for the proper behavior toward anger and offense and a word for the proper behavior toward one's worth that are more truly neutral among the competing specifications, referring only to the sphere of experience within which we wish to determine what is appropriate. Then we could regard the competing conceptions as rival accounts of one and the same thing, so that, for example, Christian humility would be a rival specification, of the same virtue whose Greek specification is given in Aristotle's account of *megalopsuchia*, namely, the proper way to behave toward the question of one's own worth.

And in fact, oddly enough, if one examines the evolution in the use of this word from Aristotle through the Stoics to the Christian fathers, one can see that this is more or less what happened, as "greatness of soul" became associated, first, with Stoic emphasis on the supremacy of virtue and the worthlessness of externals, including the body, and, through this, with the Christian denial of the body and of the worth of earthly life.[15] So even in this apparently unpromising case, history shows that the Aristotelian approach not only provided the materials for a single debate but actually succeeded in organizing such a debate, across enormous differences of both place and time.

Here, then, is a sketch for an objective human morality based upon the idea of virtuous action—that is, of appropriate functioning in each human sphere. The Aristotelian claim is that, further developed, it will retain virtue morality's immersed attention to actual human experiences, while gaining the ability to criticize local and traditional moralities in the name of a more inclusive account of the circumstances of human life, and of the needs for human functioning that these circumstances call forth.

IV

The proposal will encounter many objections. The concluding sections of this paper will present three of the most serious and will sketch the lines along which the Aristotelian conception might proceed in formulating a reply. To a great extent these objections are not imagined or confronted by Aristotle himself, but his position seems capable of confronting them.

• • •

The second objection goes deeper. For it questions the notion of spheres of shared human experience that lies at the heart of the Aristotelian approach. The approach, says this objector, seems to treat the experiences that ground the virtues as in some way primitive, given, and free from the cultural variation that we find in the plurality of normative conceptions of virtue. Ideas of proper courage may vary, but the fear of death is shared by all human beings. Ideas of moderation may vary, but the experiences of hunger, thirst, and sexual desire are (so the Aristotelian seems to claim) invariant. Normative conceptions introduce an element of cultural interpretation that is not present in the grounding experiences, which are, for that very reason, the Aristotelian's starting point.

But, the objector continues, such assumptions are naive. They will not stand up either to our best account of experience or to a close examination of the ways in which these so-called grounding experiences have in fact been differently constructed by different cultures. In general, first of all, our best accounts of the nature of experience, even perceptual experience, inform us that there is no such thing as an "innocent eye" that receives an uninterpreted "given." Even sense-perception is interpretive, heavily influenced by belief, teaching, language, and in general by social and contextual features.

There is a very real sense in which members of different societies do not see the same sun and stars, encounter the same plants and animals, hear the same thunder.

But if this seems to be true of human experience of nature, which was the allegedly unproblematic starting point for Aristotle's account of naming, it is all the more plainly true, the objector claims, in the area of the human good. Here it is only a very naive and historically insensitive moral philosopher who would say that the experience of the fear of death or the experience of bodily appetites is a human constant. Recent anthropological work on the social construction of the emotions,[16] for example, has shown to what extent the experience of fear has learned and culturally variant elements. When we add that the object of the fear in which the Aristotelian takes an interest is death, which has been so variously interpreted and understood by human beings at different times and in different places, the conclusion that the "grounding experience" is an irreducible plurality of experiences, highly various and in each case deeply infused with cultural interpretation, becomes even more inescapable.

Nor is the case different with the apparently less complicated experience of the bodily appetites. Most philosophers who have written about the appetites have treated hunger, thirst, and sexual desire as human universals, stemming from our shared animal nature. Aristotle himself was already more sophisticated, since he insisted that the object of appetite is "the apparent good" and that appetite is therefore something interpretive and selective, a kind of intentional awareness.[17] But he does not seem to have reflected much about the ways in which historical and cultural differences could shape that awareness. The Hellenistic philosophers who immediately followed him did so reflect, arguing that the experience of sexual desire and of many forms of the desire for food and drink are, at least in part, social constructs, built up over time on the basis of a social teaching about value that is

external to start with, but that enters so deeply into the perceptions of the individual that it actually forms and transforms the experience of desire.[18] Let us take two Epicurean examples. People are taught that to be well fed they require luxurious fish and meat, that a simple vegetarian diet is not enough. Over time, the combination of teaching with habit produces an appetite for meat, shaping the individual's perceptions of the objects before him. Again, people are taught that what sexual relations are all about is a romantic union or fusion with an object who is seen as exalted in value, or even as perfect. Over time, this teaching shapes sexual behavior and the experience of desire, so that sexual arousal itself responds to this culturally learned scenario.[19]

This work of social criticism has recently been carried further by Michel Foucault in his History of Sexuality.[20] This work has certain gaps as a history of Greek thought on this topic, but it does succeed in establishing that the Greeks saw the problem of the appetites and their management in an extremely different way from the way of twentieth-century Westerners. To summarize two salient conclusions of his complex argument, the Greeks did not single out the sexual appetite for special treatment; they treated it alongside hunger and thirst, as a drive that needed to be mastered and kept within bounds. Their central concern was with self-mastery, and they saw the appetites in the light of this concern. Furthermore, where the sexual appetite is concerned, they did not regard the gender of the partner as particularly important in assessing the moral value of the act. Nor did they identify or treat as morally salient a stable disposition to prefer partners of one sex rather than the other. Instead, they focused on the general issue of activity and passivity, connecting it in complex ways with the issue of self-mastery.

Work like Foucault's—and there is a lot of it in various areas, some of it very good—shows very convincingly that the experience of bodily desire, and of the body itself, has elements that vary with cultural and historical change. The

names that people call their desires and themselves as subjects of desire, the fabric of belief and discourse into which they integrate their ideas of desiring, all this influences, it is clear, not only their reflection about desire, but also their experience of desire itself. Thus, for example, it is naive to treat our modern debates about homosexuality as continuations of the very same debate about sexual activity that went on in the Greek world.[21] In a very real sense there was no "homosexual experience" in a culture that did not contain our emphasis on the gender of the object, our emphasis on the subjectivity of inclination and the permanence of appetitive disposition, our particular ways of problematizing certain forms of behavior.

If we suppose that we can get underneath this variety and this constructive power of social discourse in at least one case—namely, with the universal experience of bodily pain as a bad thing—even here we find subtle arguments against us. For the experience of pain seems to be embedded in a cultural discourse as surely as the closely related experiences of the appetites; and significant variations can be alleged here as well. The Stoics already made this claim against the Aristotelian virtues. In order to establish that bodily pain is not bad by its very nature, but only by cultural tradition, the Stoics had to provide some explanation for the ubiquity of the belief that pain is bad and of the tendency to shun it. This explanation would have to show that the reaction was learned rather than natural, and to explain why, in the light of this fact, it is learned so widely. This they did by pointing to certain features in the very early treatment of infants. As soon as an infant is born, it cries. Adults, assuming that the crying is a response to its pain at the unaccustomed coldness and harshness of the place where it finds itself, hasten to comfort it. This behavior, often repeated, teaches the infant to regard its pain as a bad thing—or, better, teaches it the concept of pain, which includes the notion of badness, and teaches it the forms of life its society shares

concerning pain. It is all social teaching, they claim, though this usually escapes our notice because of the early and non-linguistic nature of the teaching.[22]

These and related arguments, the objector concludes, show that the Aristotelian idea that there is a single non-relative discourse about human experiences such as mortality or desire is a naive idea. There is no such bedrock of shared experience, and thus no single sphere of choice within which the virtue is the disposition to choose well. So the Aristotelian project cannot even get off the ground.

• • •

V

Each of these objections is profound. To answer any one of them adequately would require a treatise. But we can still do something at this point to map out an Aristotelian response to each one, pointing the direction in which a fuller reply might go.

• • •

VI

We must now turn to the second objection. Here, I believe, is the really serious threat to the Aristotelian position. Past writers on virtue, including Aristotle himself, have lacked sensitivity to the ways in which different traditions of discourse, different conceptual schemes, articulate the world, and also to the profound connections between the structure of discourse and the structure of experience itself. Any contemporary defense of the Aristotelian position must display this sensitivity, responding somehow to the data that the relativist historian or anthropologist brings forward.

The Aristotelian should begin, it seems to me, by granting that with respect to any complex matter of deep human importance there is no "innocent eye"—no way of seeing the world that is entirely neutral and free of cultural

shaping. The work of philosophers such as Putnam, Goodman, and Davidson[23]—following, one must point out, from the arguments of Kant and, I believe, from those of Aristotle himself[24]—have shown convincingly that even where sense-perception is concerned, the human mind is an active and interpretive instrument and that its interpretations are a function of its history and its concepts, as well as of its innate structure. The Aristotelian should also grant, it seems to me, that the nature of human world-interpretations is holistic and that the criticism of them must, equally well, be holistic. Conceptual schemes, like languages, hang together as whole structures, and we should realize, too, that a change in any single element is likely to have implications for the system as a whole.

But these two facts do not imply, as some relativists in literary theory and in anthropology tend to assume, that all world interpretations are equally valid and altogether non-comparable, that there are no good standards of assessment and "anything goes." The rejection of the idea of ethical truth as correspondence to an altogether uninterpreted reality does not imply that the whole idea of searching for the truth is an old-fashioned error. Certain ways in which people see the world can still be criticized exactly as Aristotle criticized them: as stupid, pernicious, and false. The standards used in such criticisms must come from inside human life. (Frequently they will come from the society in question itself, from its own rationalist and critical traditions.) And the inquirer must attempt, prior to criticism, to develop an inclusive understanding of the conceptual scheme being criticized, seeing what motivates each of its parts and how they hang together. But there is so far no reason to think that the critic will not be able to reject the institution of slavery or the homicide law of Cyme as out of line with the conception of virtue that emerges from reflection on the variety of different ways in which human cultures have had the experiences that ground the virtues.

The "grounding experiences" will not, the Aristotelian should concede, provide precisely a single language—neutral bedrock on which an account of virtue can be straightforwardly and unproblematically based. The description and assessment of the ways in which different cultures have constructed these experiences will become one of the central tasks of Aristotelian philosophical criticism. But the relativist has, so far, shown no reasons why we could not, at the end of the day, say that certain ways of conceptualizing death are more in keeping with the totality of our evidence and with the totality of our wishes for flourishing life than others; that certain ways of experiencing appetitive desire are for similar reasons more promising than others.

Relativists tend, furthermore, to understate the amount of attunement, recognition, and overlap that actually obtains across cultures, particularly in the areas of the grounding experiences. The Aristotelian in developing her conception in a culturally sensitive way, should insist, as Aristotle himself does, upon the evidence of such attunement and recognition. Despite the evident differences in the specific cultural shaping of the grounding experiences, we do recognize the experiences of people in other cultures as similar to our own. We do converse with them about matters of deep importance, understand them, allow ourselves to be moved by them. When we read Sophocles' *Antigone*, we see a good deal that seems strange to us; and we have not read the play well if we do not notice how far its conceptions of death, womanhood, and so on, differ from our own. But it is still possible for us to be moved by the drama, to care about its people, to regard their debates as reflections upon virtue that speak to our own experience, and their choices as choices in spheres of conduct in which we too must choose. Again, when one sits down at a table with people from other parts of the world and debates with them concerning hunger or just distribution or in general the quality of human

life, one does find, in spite of evident conceptual differences, that it is possible to proceed as if we are all talking about the same human problem; and it is usually only in a context in which one or more of the parties is intellectually committed to a theoretical relativist position that this discourse proves impossible to sustain. This sense of community and overlap seems to be especially strong in the areas that we have called the areas of the grounding experiences. And this, it seems, supports the Aristotelian claim that those experiences can be a good starting point for ethical debate.

Furthermore, it is necessary to stress that hardly any cultural group today is as focused upon its own internal traditions and as isolated from other cultures as the relativist argument presupposes. Cross-cultural communication and debate are ubiquitous facts of contemporary life. Our experience of cultural interaction indicates that in general the inhabitants of different conceptual schemes do tend to view their interaction in the Aristotelian and not the relativist way. A traditional society, confronted with new technologies and sciences, and the conceptions that go with them, does not, in fact, simply fail to understand them or regard them as totally alien incursions upon a hermetically sealed way of life. Instead, it assesses the new item as a possible contributor to flourishing life, making it comprehensible to itself and incorporating elements that promise to solve problems of flourishing. Examples of such assimilation, and the debate that surrounds it,[25] suggest that the parties do, in fact, recognize common problems and that the traditional society is perfectly capable of viewing an external innovation as a device to solve a problem that it shares with the innovating society. The parties do, in fact, search for the good, not the way of their ancestors; only traditionalist anthropologists insist, nostalgically, on the absolute preservation of the ancestral.

And this is so even when cross-cultural discourse reveals a difference at the level of the conceptualization of the grounding experiences. Frequently the effect of work like Foucault's, which reminds us of the non-necessary and non-universal character of one's own ways of seeing in some such area, is precisely to prompt a critical debate in search of the human good. It is difficult, for example, to read Foucault's observations about the history of our sexual ideas without coming to feel that certain ways in which the Western contemporary debate on these matters has been organized, as a result of some combination of Christian morality with nineteenth-century pseudo-science, are especially silly, arbitrary, and limiting, inimical to a human search for flourishing. Foucault's moving account of Greek culture, as he himself insists in a preface,[26] provides not only a sign that someone once thought differently, but also evidence that it is possible for us to think differently. Foucault announced that the purpose of his book was to "free thought" so that it could think differently, imagining new and more fruitful possibilities. And close analysis of spheres of cultural discourse, which stresses cultural differences in the spheres of the grounding experiences, is being combined, increasingly, in current debates about sexuality and related matters, with the critique of existing social arrangements and attitudes, and with the elaboration of a new norm of human flourishing. There is no reason to think this combination incoherent.[27]

As we pursue these possibilities, the basic spheres of experience identified in the Aristotelian approach will no longer, we have said, be seen as spheres of *uninterpreted* experience. But we have also insisted that there is much family relatedness and much overlap among societies. And certain areas of relatively greater universality can be specified here, on which we should insist as we proceed to areas that are more varied in their cultural expression. Not without a sensitive awareness that we are speaking of something that is experienced differently in different contexts, we can

nonetheless identify certain features of our common humanity, closely related to Aristotle's original list, from which our debate might proceed.

1.   *Mortality.* No matter how death is understood, all human beings face it and (after a certain age) know that they face it. This fact shapes every aspect of more or less every human life.

2.   *The Body.* Prior to any concrete-cultural shapings, we are born with human bodies, whose possibilities and vulnerabilities do not as such belong to one culture rather than any other. Any given human being might have belonged to any culture. The experience of the body is culturally influenced; but the body itself, prior to such experience, provides limits and parameters that ensure a great deal of overlap in what is going to be experienced, where hunger, thirst, desire, the five senses are concerned. It is all very well to point to the cultural component in these experiences. But when one spends time considering issues of hunger and scarcity, and in general of human misery, such differences appear relatively small and refined, and one cannot fail to acknowledge that "there are no known ethnic differences in human physiology with respect to metabolism of nutrients. Africans and Asians do not burn their dietary calories or use their dietary protein any differently from Europeans and Americans. It follows then that dietary requirements cannot vary widely as between different races."[28] This and similar facts should surely be focal points for debate about appropriate human behavior in this sphere. And by beginning with the body, rather than with the subjective experience of desire, we get, furthermore, an opportunity to criticize the situation of people who are so persistently deprived that their *desire* for good things has actually

decreased. This is a further advantage of the Aristotelian approach, when contrasted with approaches to choice that stop with subjective expressions of preference.

3.   *Pleasure and pain.* In every culture, there is a conception of pain; and these conceptions, which overlap very largely with one another, can be plausibly seen as grounded in universal and pre-cultural experience. The Stoic story of infant development is highly implausible; the negative response to bodily pain is surely primitive and universal, rather than learned and optional, however much its specific "grammar" may be shaped by later learning.

4.   *Cognitive capability.* Aristotle's famous claim that "all human beings by nature reach out for understanding"[29] seems to stand up to the most refined anthropological analysis. It points to an element in our common humanity that is plausibly seen, again, as grounded independently of particular acculturation, however much it is later shaped by acculturation.

5.   *Practical reason.* All human beings, whatever their culture, participate (or try to) in the planning and managing of their lives, asking and answering questions about how one should live and act. This capability expresses itself differently in different societies, but a being who altogether lacked it would not be likely to be acknowledged as a human being, in any culture.[30]

6.   *Early infant development.* Prior to the greatest part of specific cultural shaping, though perhaps not free from all shaping, are certain areas of human experiences and development that are broadly shared and of great importance for the Aristotelian virtues: experiences of desire, pleasure, loss, one's own finitude, perhaps also of envy, grief, gratitude. One may argue about the merits of one or another psychoanalytical account of infancy. But it seems

difficult to deny that the work of Freud on infant desire and of Klein on grief, loss, and other more complex emotional attitudes has identified spheres of human experience that are to a large extent common to all humans, regardless of their particular society. All humans begin as hungry babies, perceiving their own helplessness, their alternating closeness to and distance from those on whom they depend, and so forth. Melanie Klein records a conversation with an anthropologist in which an event that at first looked (to Western eyes) bizarre was interpreted by Klein as the expression of a universal pattern of mourning. The anthropologist accepted her interpretation.[31]

7. *Affiliation.* Aristotle's claim that human beings as such feel a sense of fellowship with other human beings, and that we are by nature social animals, is an empirical claim, but it seems to be a sound one. However varied our specific conceptions of friendship and love are, there is a great point in seeing them as overlapping expressions of the same family of shared human needs and desires.

8. *Humor.* There is nothing more culturally varied than humor, and yet, as Aristotle insists, some space for humor and play seems to be a need of any human life. The human being was not called the "laughing animal" for nothing; it is certainly one of our salient differences from almost all animals, and (in some form or other) a shared feature, I somewhat boldly assert, of any life that is going to be counted as fully human.

This is just a list of suggestions, closely related to Aristotle's list of common experiences. One could subtract some of these items and/or add others. But it seems plausible to claim that in all these areas we have a basis for further work on the human good. We do not have a bedrock of completely uninterpreted "given" data, but we do have nuclei of experience around which the construction of different societies proceed. There is no Archimedean point here, and no pure access to unsullied "nature"—even, here, human nature—as it is in and of itself. There is just human life as it is lived. But in life as it is lived, we do find a family of experiences, clustering around certain foci, which can provide reasonable starting points for cross-cultural reflection.

Notes

1　A. MacIntyre, *AfterVirtue* (Notre Dame, IN, 1981); P. Foot, *Virtues and Vices* (Los Angeles, 1978); B. Williams, *Ethics and the Limits of Philosophy* (Cambridge, MA, 1985) and Tanner Lectures, Harvard, 1983. See also M. Walzer, *Spheres of Justice* (New York, 1983) and Tanner Lectures, Harvard, 1985.

2　For examples of this, see Nussbaum, "Nature, Function, and Capability: Aristotle on Political Distribution," circulated as a WIDER working paper, and in *Oxford Studies in Ancient Philosophy*, 1988, and also, in an expanded version, in the Proceedings of the 12th Symposium Aristotelicum.

3　See, for example, Williams, *Ethics and the Limits*, 34–36; Stuart Hampshire, *Morality and Conflict* (Cambridge, MA, 1983), 150 ff.

4　For "nameless" virtues and vices, see NE 1107b1–2, 1107b8, 1107b30–31, 1108a17, 1119a10–11, 1126b20, 1127a12, 1127a14; for recognition of the unsatisfactoriness of names given, see 1107b8, 1108a5–6, 1108a20 ff. The two categories are largely overlapping, on account of the general principles enunciated at 1108a16–19, that where there is no name a name should be given, unsatisfactory or not.

5　It should be noted that this emphasis on spheres of experience is not present in the *Eudemian Ethics*, which begins with a list of virtues and vices. This seems to me a sign that that treatise expresses a more primitive stage of Aristotle's thought on the virtues—whether earlier or not.

6　For statements with *peri*, connecting virtues with spheres of life, see 1115a6–7, 1117a29–30, 1117b25, 27, 1119b23, 1122a19, 1122b34, 1125b26, 1126b13; and NE 2.7 throughout. See also the related usages at 1126b11, 1127b32.

7 My list here inserts justice in a place of prominence. (In the NE it is treated separately, after all the other virtues, and the introductory list defers it for that later examination.) I have also added at the end of the list categories corresponding to the various intellectual virtues discussed in NE 6, and also to *phronesis* or practical wisdom, discussed in 6 as well. Otherwise the order and wording of my list closely follows 2.7, which gives the program for the more detailed analyses of 3.5–4.

8 For a longer account of this, with references to the literature and to related philosophical discussions, see Nussbaum, *The Fragility of Goodness* (Cambridge, MA, 1986), chap. 8.

9 Aristotle does not worry about questions of translation in articulating this idea; for some worries about this, and an Aristotelian response, see below sections IV and VI.

10 *Posterior Analytics*, 2.8, 93a21 ff.; see *Fragility*, chap. 8.

11 Heraclitus, fragment DK B23; see Nussbaum, "*Psuche* in Heraclitus, II," *Phronesis* 17 (1972): 153–70.

12 See *Politics* 1.2. 1253a1–18; that discussion does not deny the virtues to gods explicitly, but this denial is explicit at NE 1145a25–27 and 1178b10 ff.

13 Aristotle does not make the connection with his account of language explicit, but his project is one of defining the virtues, and we would expect him to keep his general view of defining in mind in this context. A similar idea about the virtues, and experience of a certain sort as a possible basis for a non-relative account, is developed, without reference to Aristotle, in a review of P. Foot's *Virtues and Vices* by N. Sturgeon, *Journal of Philosophy* 81 (1984): 326–33.

14 1108a5, where Aristotle says that the virtues and the corresponding person are "pretty much nameless," and says "Let us call . . ." when he introduces the names. See also 1125b29, 1126a3–4.

15 See John Procope, *Magnanimity* (1987); also R.-A. Gauthier, *Magnanimité* (Paris, 1951).

16 See, for example, *The Social Construction of the Emotions*, edited by Rom Harré (Oxford, 1986).

17 See Nussbaum, *Aristotle's De Motu Animalium* (Princeton, NJ, 1976), notes on chap. 6, and *Fragility*, chap. 9.

18 A detailed study of the treatment of these ideas in the three major Hellenistic schools was presented in Nussbaum, *The Therapy of Desire: Theory and Practice in Hellenistic Ethics*, The Martin Classical Pectures 1986, and forthcoming.

19 The relevant texts are discussed in Nussbaum, *The Therapy*, chaps. 4–6. See also Nussbaum, "Therapeutic Arguments: Epicurus and Aristotle," in *The Norms of Nature*, edited by M. Schofield and G. Striker (Cambridge, 1986), 31–74.

20 M. Foucault, *Histoire de la sexualité*, vols. 2 and 3 (Paris, 1984).

21 See the papers by D. Halperin arid J. Winkler in *Before Sexuality*, edited by D. Halperin, J. Winkler, and F. Zeitlin, forthcoming (Princeton).

22 The evidence for this part of the Stoic view is discussed in Nussbaum, *The Therapy*.

23 See H. Putnam, *Reason, Truth, and History* (Cambridge, 1981); *The Many Faces of Realism*, The Carus Lectures, forthcoming; and *Meaning and the Moral Sciences* (London, 1979); N. Goodman, *Languages of Art* (Indianapolis, 1968) and *Ways of World-Making* (Indianapolis, 1978); D. Davidson, *Inquiries into Truth and Interpretation* (Oxford, 1984).

24 On his debt to Kant, see Putnam, *The Many Faces*; on Aristotle's "internal realism," see Nussbaum, *Fragility*, chap. 8.

25 C. Abeysekera, paper presented at Value and Technology Conference, WIDER 1986.

26 Foucault, *Histoire*, vol. 2, preface.

27 This paragraph expands remarks made in a commentary on papers by D. Halperin and J. Winkler at the conference on "Homosexuality in History and Culture" at Brown University, February 1987. The combination of historically sensitive analysis with cultural criticism was forcefully developed at the same conference in Henry Abelove's "Is Gay History Possible?," forthcoming.

28 C. Gopalan, "Undernutrition: Measurement and Implications," paper prepared for the WIDER Conference on Poverty, Undernutrition, and Living Standards, Helsinki, 27–31 July 1987, and forthcoming in the volume of Proceedings, edited by S. Osmani.

29 *Metaphysics* 1.1.

30 See Nussbaum, "Nature, Function, and Capability," where this Aristotelian view is compared with Marx's views on human functioning.

31 M. Klein, in Postscript to "Our Adult World and Its Roots in Infancy," in *Envy, Gratitude and Other Works 1946–1963* (London, 1984), 247–63.

Chapter 39

Thomas Hurka

VIRTUE AND VICE

ONE TASK of moral theory is to explore the relationships between the fundamental moral properties of goodness, rightness, and virtue. Different substantive theories understand these relationships in different ways. For example, consequentialist theories take goodness to be explanatorily prior to rightness, which they always characterize in terms of goodness, whereas deontological theories treat rightness as at least partly independent of goodness. And this difference has profound implications for many further claims these theories make.

In recent philosophy the third moral property, virtue, has mostly been understood in either of two extreme ways. One view defines virtue as a disposition to produce what is otherwise good or to do what is otherwise right, thereby giving it only derivative and instrumental significance. Virtue may be crucial practically, if inculcating it is the best means of ensuring that people fulfill their moral responsibilities. But theoretically it has no intrinsic importance. The contrary view makes virtue the central property in a distinctive moral theory called virtue ethics, which is proposed as a fundamental alternative to consequentialism and deontology. Far from defining virtue as a means to goodness or rightness, this view treats it as primary, so that what is right and even what is good are identified by some relation to virtue. Virtue has sufficient importance to generate a comprehensive approach to ethics, one where it plays the foundational role.

The aim of this book is to develop an account of virtue intermediate between these extremes. The account treats virtue as intrinsically good, or good apart from its consequences, and it likewise treats vice as intrinsically evil. A person's having virtuous desires, motives, and feelings by itself makes her life better, and her having vicious attitudes makes it worse. But the account does not call for any new theory such as virtue ethics. It can be accommodated within a more familiar theory and, more specifically, within a theory that many think excludes it, namely consequentialism. The account is not confined to consequentialism, and in a later chapter I will show how it can be extended in a deontological setting. But its central claims are consistent with consequentialism, so it gives a consequentialist account of the intrinsic values of virtue and vice. Virtue and vice are good and evil in themselves, but in a way that satisfies consequentialist assumptions.

As I have said, many philosophers think this kind of account is impossible. Before developing it, I need to determine whether, given what consequentialism is, it can indeed value virtue intrinsically.

1. Consequentialism and virtue?

Consequentialist moral theories are distinguished by the central role they give the properties of intrinsic goodness and evil. They take these

properties, as had by states of affairs, to be the primary moral properties, and they characterize all other moral properties in terms of goodness and evil. Thus, standard consequentialist theories identify right actions by the quantity of good and evil in their outcome, so that, for example, right actions are always those with the best outcomes, or whose outcomes contain the greatest surplus of good over evil. In the bulk of this book I will assume that consequentialism identifies rightness in this way. But the more general definition of this position says it characterizes all other moral properties by some relation to intrinsic goodness and evil.

Despite agreeing that goodness and evil are primary, different consequentialists understand these properties in slightly different ways. Some, such as G. E. Moore, take goodness to be a simple, unanalyzable property had by some states of affairs.[1] Others, notably Franz Brentano, analyze goodness in terms of the correctness or appropriateness of certain emotions, so "we call a thing *good* when the love relating to it is correct."[2] Yet others analyze goodness in terms of reasons or oughts, so the good is what people have reason or ought to desire or pursue. Henry Sidgwick says the good is what one would desire if one's desires "were in harmony with reason," where reason is a faculty that apprehends "oughts."[3] Similarly, Shelly Kagan writes, "to say that from the moral standpoint one outcome is objectively better than another, is to say that *everyone* has a reason to choose the better outcome."[4]

Despite their differences, these three views about goodness are closely connected. Those who, like Moore, understand goodness as an unanalyzable property usually agree with Brentano that loving what is good is correct. They merely deny that a state's goodness is reducible to this correctness; it is something separate and more fundamental that explains the correctness. Similarly, both Moore and Brentano agree that agents have reason to desire or pursue what is good, but they deny that a state's

goodness is reducible to the existence of this reason. The goodness is again something more fundamental that explains the reason. Most consequentialists, in short, accept Sidgwick's and Kagan's claims about the good. It is just that some, such as Brentano, add one and others, such as Moore, add two more foundational claims that explain them.

Given these connections, we can for the most part abstract from the differences between the three views when discussing the goodness of virtue. More specifically, we can assume those claims about goodness that are shared by all consequentialists while remaining agnostic about any further claims. We can assume that to call a state good is to say at least that agents have reason to desire or pursue it; it may also be to say that love of the state is correct or that the state has an unanalyzable property, but we can ignore these further possibilities. To say that virtue is intrinsically good, we can assume, is to give it the same status, whatever exactly that is, as any other good in a consequentialist theory.[5]

Consequentialists can also disagree about what makes goodness "intrinsic." A strict view, defended by Moore, says that a state's intrinsic goodness can depend only on its intrinsic properties, that is, properties it has independently of any relations to other states. When value is "intrinsic," Moore writes, "the question whether a thing possesses it, and in what degree it possesses it, depends solely on the intrinsic nature of the thing in question."[6] A looser view equates intrinsic goodness just with non-instrumental goodness, or with that portion of the overall goodness of the world that is located in or assignable to a particular state. It is the state's own goodness, whatever its basis, rather than some other's.[7] Unlike the strict view, this looser one allows a state's intrinsic goodness to be affected by its relational properties. For example, it allows the view that a state such as knowledge is intrinsically good only when accompanied by desire for or pleasure in it for itself.[8] But again, we need not choose between

these views when developing an account of virtue. On the few occasions when the difference between them is relevant to the account, this fact can be noted.

Many consequentialisms start from claims about the good that are agent-neutral, with the same force for all moral agents. They make certain states good from all persons' points of view, or good simply, so all persons have reason to pursue the same moral goals. But some consequentialists say their theory can equally well be agent-relative. It can make what is good from different persons' points of view different, so they are directed to different goals. For example, it can say that what is good from each person's point of view is just some state of himself, so he has reason to pursue only that state and no comparable states of others.[9] Whether such agent-relativity is possible depends on our choice among the three views of goodness distinguished above. If goodness is a simple, unanalyzable property, it is hard to see how it can be agent-relative. How can a state have such a property "from one point of view" but not "from" another? Surely it either has the property or not. For this reason, those who accept this view of goodness usually deny the coherence of agent-relative consequentialism.[10] But there is no such difficulty given either of the other two views. If goodness is analyzed in terms of reasons or of the correctness of emotions, a theory can say that each person has reason to desire and pursue only states of himself, or that only his loving states of himself is correct. Since we are assuming only what is common to the three views of goodness, we are free to consider agent-relative consequentialism. That said, I will develop the account of virtue initially in an agent-neutral setting. A later chapter will extend the account to include agent-relative values and, with them, agent-relative virtues. But the initial formulation will be agent-neutral [see original reading].

A final distinction concerns the content of a consequentialist theory. Subjective or welfarist theories make each person's good depend on certain of her subjective mental states, such as her pleasures or desires. Hedonism, which holds that only pleasure is good and pain evil, is a version of subjectivism, as are theories that equate the good with the fulfillment of desires. Objective or perfectionist theories, by contrast, hold that certain states are good independently of pleasures or desires. Knowledge and achievement, for example, make a person's life better regardless of how much she enjoys or wants them, and their absence impoverishes her life even if it does not cause her regret.

Given this general account of consequentialism, it may seem easy for this type of theory to treat virtue as intrinsically good. It simply adds virtue, or a set of individual virtues such as benevolence, courage, and so on, to its list of basic intrinsic goods, and it likewise adds vice or a set of vices to its list of basic evils. Assuming that we know independently what virtue and vice consist in, it treats them as underivative intrinsic values. Virtue and vice are perfectionist rather than welfarist values, since they make a person's life better or worse regardless of his attitude to them. But in this they are like knowledge, achievement, and other perfectionist values, and they play a standard role in the evaluation of actions. If an action will embody or lead to virtue, this counts in favour of its being right; if to vice, this counts against it.

But this approach—simply adding virtue and vice to a list of underivative values—is not fully or properly consequentialist. If consequentialism characterizes *all* other moral properties in terms of goodness and evil, it must characterize virtue and vice in terms of goodness and evil. These, too, are moral properties and require a consequentialist treatment. A fully consequentialist approach cannot assume that we know from elsewhere what virtue and vice consist in but must somehow identify them, as it identifies right actions, by reference to the intrinsic values of states of affairs.

It is this requirement that leads many philosophers to conclude that consequentialism

cannot treat virtue as intrinsically good. If it characterizes virtue in terms of goodness and evil, they argue, it must characterize virtue as a disposition to promote good and prevent evil. But this makes virtue in essence instrumentally good, or good because of its consequences. And if virtue is in essence instrumentally good, it cannot at the same time be intrinsically good.

The most careful presentation of this argument is in Sidgwick's *Methods of Ethics*. Sidgwick is defending hedonistic consequentialism against rival versions, including one that says virtue is intrinsically good. He considers both a strong version of this view, that virtue is the only intrinsic good, and a weaker version, that it is one intrinsic good among others.

Against the strong version Sidgwick argues as follows. Virtue, he says, is a disposition to perform morally right actions, where right actions are identified by the quantity of good in their outcome. (He takes himself to have justified this second, consequentialist premise earlier in *The Methods of Ethics*.) Virtue is therefore a disposition to perform actions that promote what is good. And this implies that treating virtue as the only intrinsic good involves a "logical circle": virtue is a disposition that promotes what is good, where what is good is itself just a disposition that promotes what is good.[11]

We may dispute Sidgwick's first premise—his definition of virtue as a disposition to perform right actions. This definition is on the one hand too narrow, because it restricts the expression of virtue to the sphere of action. Though a person can certainly act virtuously, she can also have virtuous desires and feelings that never issue in action—for example, compassion for someone whose pain she is unable to relieve. So the definition excludes some important forms of virtue. On the other hand, Sidgwick's definition is also too broad. It counts as virtuous any disposition that reliably produces right actions, whatever motives that disposition involves.[12] This, too, is counterintuitive. Imagine that a store owner reliably gives his customers accurate change, but

only because he believes that doing so is in his economic self-interest. If his motive is in this way selfish, his disposition, however reliably it produces right actions, does not on most views count as virtuous.

These flaws in his definition of virtue do not substantially affect Sidgwick's first argument, which can be generalized to avoid them. Within consequentialism virtue must be characterized, if not as a disposition that promotes what is good, then in some way by reference to the good. And this means that treating virtue as the only intrinsic good does involve a logical circle. If virtue consists in a relation to other goods, it cannot be the only such good.

As Hastings Rashdall notes in a commentary on Sidgwick, one can accept something close to the premises of this argument yet reject its conclusion, agreeing that virtue must be characterized by reference to some other states yet still holding that it is the only intrinsic good. One can do this if one denies that the other states are good.[13] This is the Stoic view: certain states are "preferred" and provide the criterion for right action but are not themselves intrinsically good. What is good is only a virtuous attitude or relation to these states. But Rashdall agrees that this Stoic view is "in a high degree paradoxical." How can it be right to promote certain states, he asks, and how can they be the defining objects of virtue, if they are not themselves intrinsically good? If states playing these roles must be good, as consequentialism assumes, Sidgwick's first conclusion follows and virtue cannot be the only intrinsic good.

Against the weaker view that virtue is just one intrinsic good among others, Sidgwick's argument is by his own lights less conclusive, but it starts from similar premises. If virtue is a disposition that promotes what is good, it is by definition something instrumentally good. And "it seems difficult to conceive any kind of activity or process as both means and end, from precisely the same point of view and in respect of precisely the same quality."[14] Sidgwick acknowledges that

a state can be at once intrinsically and instrumentally good. But he argues that in normal circumstances, different properties give it the two kinds of goodness. If a pleasure is both intrinsically and instrumentally good, its being pleasant is what makes it intrinsically good, while its promoting other pleasures makes it instrumentally good. What Sidgwick finds "difficult to conceive" is that the same property—promoting something good—should give a state at once instrumental and intrinsic value. Yet precisely this would be the case if virtue, defined as a disposition that promotes what is good, were as such intrinsically good.

What Sidgwick finds "difficult to conceive" is impossible given the strict view of intrinsic value, according to which such value must rest on a state's intrinsic properties. But it is not impossible given the looser view. If a state's intrinsic value can depend on its relational properties, it is in principle possible for the instrumentally good to be as such intrinsically good. And in a certain restricted context this view is attractive. Several philosophers argue that when a person pursues a worthwhile goal, his successfully achieving that goal makes his activity intrinsically better than if it had ended in failure. Imagine that someone spends many years working for the preservation of Venice.[15] If after his death Venice is in fact preserved, and in a way that depends on his efforts, this outcome, it is said, makes his labours intrinsically better than if, through no fault of his, Venice had ended in ruins.[16] Here an activity's goodness is enhanced by a causal relation to another good. Nonetheless, even given the looser view, Sidgwick's second argument remains persuasive against its intended target. What is plausible given this view is only the restricted claim that an activity that is already intrinsically good, because it is aimed at a worthwhile goal, will be intrinsically better if its goal is achieved. What Sidgwick challenges is the more radical claim that a disposition's being instrumentally good can be a complete source of intrinsic goodness,

or by itself make it intrinsically good. Sidgwick is surely right that this view is "difficult to conceive" in the sense of not being intuitively plausible. If virtue is defined as any disposition that promotes what is good, the view that it is as such an intrinsic good is not credible.

Given his definition of virtue, then, Sidgwick is right that virtue is not plausibly even one intrinsic good among others. But we have seen that this definition is at once too narrow and too broad. And when his second argument is generalized to assume only that virtue involves some relation to goodness and evil, its persuasiveness disappears. Given only a general consequentialist definition of virtue, the argument can no longer exclude virtue from the list of intrinsic goods. As Rashdall points out, there is an account of the intrinsic goodness of virtue that satisfies consequentialist assumptions, is logically possible, and is intuitively attractive as well. If it incorporates this account, consequentialism can treat virtue as intrinsically good. The account agrees with Sidgwick that virtue must be defined somehow by relation to goodness and evil; it therefore accepts his first conclusion, that virtue cannot be the only intrinsic value. But it maintains against his second conclusion that virtue is one intrinsic value among others. The account takes virtue to consist in a non-causal, and more specifically an intentional, relation to goodness and evil and holds that as this relation, virtue is a further intrinsic good. The account has two principal components: a *recursive characterization of good and evil* and a *definition of virtue and vice* that fits this characterization. Together these components comprise a *recursive account* of the intrinsic goodness of virtue and intrinsic evil of vice. I will now present this recursive account, starting with its first component, the recursive characterization of good and evil.

2. The recursive characterization of good and evil

The idea of a recursive characterization should be familiar to philosophers from the

characterization given in elementary logic of a well-formed formula. This characterization starts with a base-clause stating that certain atomic sentences, for example, *a*, *b*, *c*, and *d*, are well-formed formulas. It then adds a recursion-clause, one whose application iterates or recurs, for each logical operator. Thus, the recursion-clause for "or" says that if X and Y are well-formed formulas, then X or Y is a well-formed formula. This makes *a* or *b* a well-formed formula, and also (*a* or *b*) or *c*, ((*a* or *b*) or *c*) or *d*, and so on.

The recursive characterization of good and evil has a similar structure. It starts with a base-clause stating that certain states of affairs other than virtue are intrinsically good. For our purposes it is not crucial what these states are, but let us assume the characterization starts with the following *base-clause about goods*, (BG):

(BG) Pleasure, knowledge, and achievement are intrinsically good.

This clause, which combines the welfarist good of pleasure with the perfectionist goods of knowledge and achievement, is agent-neutral. It says that each person's pleasure is good not just from his point of view, but from that of all persons; this means they all have the same reason to pursue his pleasure, as he has a parallel reason to pursue theirs.

Though the specific goods in (BG) could be replaced by others, it will be useful to describe them briefly. The first good, pleasure, is a sensation or feeling distinguished by an introspectible quality of pleasantness.[17] This quality can vary in intensity, with more intense pleasures having more intrinsic value. The quality of pleasantness can never be experienced on its own; it is always accompanied by other introspectible qualities that vary among pleasure sensations and make, say, the pleasure of suntanning introspectively very different from that of eating ice cream. In this it is like the loudness of sounds.[18] Loudness is an introspectible quality of sounds and can be used to rank them, but it

cannot be experienced apart from other qualities of pitch, timbre, and so on. Among pleasures as so defined, there is an important division between the simple and the intentional. Simple pleasures, such as that of suntanning, are unstructured sensations with the quality of pleasantness and other introspectible qualities that distinguish them from each other. Intentional pleasures have the internal structure of directedness to an intentional object. One is pleased by some object or that something is the case—for example, that one's friend got a promotion. These intentional pleasures are more complex than unstructured pleasure sensations and, as we will see, raise more complex issues in the theory of value. But they share with simple pleasures the defining element of introspectible pleasantness.

(BG)'s remaining goods, knowledge and achievement, are parallel goods of theory and practice.[19] Both involve a relation of correspondence between a mind and the world, either of true belief or of the successful realization of a goal. Both require this relation not to be a matter of luck: a person's true belief must be justified, and his goal must have been pursued in a way that made its attainment likely in advance. Finally, for both goods the degree of value of an instance of them is determined by formal rather than substantive criteria. The best knowledge is not that of any particular subject matter but that whose content extends farthest across times and objects—think of scientific laws—and which has the most other knowledge subordinate to it in an explanatory hierarchy. Similarly, the best achievements are not those with any particular goals—hence the independence of achievement from virtue—but those whose goals extend most across times and objects and organize the most other goals in a means-end hierarchy. There is therefore high achievement value in complex, difficult activities such as chess, novel writing, and political leadership.

The recursive characterization, then, starts with a base-clause such as (BG) affirming a set

466 Thomas Hurka

of intrinsic goods other than virtue. It then adds a recursion-clause about the intrinsic goodness of a certain attitude to what is good, namely, loving it, or, more specifically, *loving for itself what is good*, (LG):

(LG) If x is intrinsically good, loving x (desiring, pursuing, or taking pleasure in x) for itself is also intrinsically good.

This recursion-clause does not follow from the base-clause (BG); it is an independent principle requiring independent justification. The recursion-clause (LG) is like (BG) in being agent-neutral, making any person's loving what is good intrinsically good not just from her point of view, but from that of all persons. But what does it mean to "love" a state x, and what does it mean to love x "for itself"?

To "love" x is to be positively oriented toward x in one's desires, actions, or feelings, or, more generally, in one's attitudes. This positive orientation has three main forms. One can love x by desiring or wishing for it when it does not obtain, by actively pursuing it to make it obtain, or by taking pleasure in it when it does obtain. In the first case, one believes that x does not exist and desires or wishes that it did. Given the requisite further beliefs, this desire can lead to action aimed at producing x, but the desire can also exist before any action is performed, or even when, because circumstances will never be appropriate, no action will be possible. Thus, one can desire or wish that x will obtain in the future, but one can also wish that it did obtain now or had obtained in the past, and these latter desires can never issue in action. The second form of loving x does involve action, aimed either at producing x or at preserving it into the future. Regardless of whether this action succeeds in its aim, its origin in a desire for x makes it a form of loving x. The third form of loving x involves no desire or action: one takes x's existence as given and feels pleasure that it does, did, or will obtain. Instead of a conative

orientation toward x, there is here an affective one, involving feeling. Despite these differences, the three forms of loving x all involve a positive attitude to x and are therefore variant forms of a single orientation toward x. Which particular form of love one can have for a given state x depends on facts about x (does it obtain or not?) and about oneself (can one effectively promote x or not?). But for any state x, some form of loving x is possible.

To love a state x "for itself" is to love x apart from its consequences or for its own sake—that is, to love instances of x because they are instances of x. Thus, one loves pleasure for itself if one loves instances of pleasure because they are pleasures or because of their pleasantness. Similarly, one loves knowledge for itself if one loves instances of knowledge because they are knowledge. One does not love knowledge in this way if one cares about its instances only for some other reason. There are two more specific ways of loving a state such as pleasure for itself. One can believe that pleasure is intrinsically good and love it as something good or because of its goodness; here one's love derives from a prior judgment of intrinsic value. Alternatively, without relying on any belief about goodness, one can just be directly emotionally inclined toward pleasure for its own sake, desiring, pursuing, and taking pleasure in pleasure just because it is pleasure. Here one's love does not derive from any evaluative judgment, but is purely emotional or unreflective. These two forms of loving a state are importantly different, and their respective merits will be discussed in chapter 6 [see original reading]. But in both forms one loves a state such as pleasure for itself rather than as a means to something beyond it, or loves particular pleasures for their pleasantness rather than for some other property.

Understood in this way, "loving for itself" is a morally appropriate response to intrinsic goodness. If an intrinsic good does not obtain, it is fitting or appropriate to desire it for its own sake and, if possible, to try to make it obtain. If

an intrinsic good does obtain, it is appropriate to be pleased by this fact. What the recursion-clause (LG) affirms is the intrinsic goodness of a fitting or appropriate response to intrinsic goods, where loving for itself is that fitting response.

To see more concretely what this involves, let us combine the implications of base-clause (BG) and recursion-clause (LG). (BG) says that a pleasure felt by a person A is intrinsically good. (LG) adds that if another person B loves A's pleasure for itself—if, for example, B desires or pursues A's pleasure as an end in itself—his doing so is also intrinsically good. Since (LG)'s application iterates or recurs, (LG) also says that if a third person C loves B's love of A's pleasure for itself—if, for example, C is pleased by B's desire for A's pleasure—this too is intrinsically good. To take another example, (BG) says that knowledge is intrinsically good. (LG) adds that pursuing knowledge for its own sake is intrinsically good, as is being pleased by the pursuit of knowledge. Loving the good of knowledge is intrinsically good, as is loving the love of that good. And it is likewise good to love achievement and the love of achievement.

In some cases, a person's loving a good for itself will lead to action that produces that good, in which case her love is instrumentally good. But this need not be so. In the first example above, B may desire A's pleasure for itself but be unable to pursue it; she may try to produce A's pleasure but fail to do so; or encountering A already experiencing pleasure, she may simply take pleasure in this fact. In each of these cases, B's love, though it does not have good consequences, is still by (LG)'s lights intrinsically good. And even when B's love does have good consequences and is therefore instrumentally good, it is not only instrumentally good. As an instance of loving for itself what is good, it is also good in itself.

The recursive characterization that starts with (BG) and (LG) can extend itself if it adds a second base-clause stating that certain states

other than vice are intrinsically evil, as in the following *base-clause about evils*, (BE):

> (BE) Pain, false belief, and failure in the pursuit of achievement are intrinsically evil.

As with the earlier base-clause (BG), (BE)'s specific contents are not crucial for our purposes, though its agent-neutrality is. But (BE) fits well with (BG), making intrinsically evil states that are the exact contraries of the goods affirmed in (BG). Thus, pain is a sensation with an introspectible quality contrary to that of pleasantness, namely painfulness. Similarly, false belief and failure to achieve a pursued end involve not just a lack of correspondence between a mind and the world—as when one has no beliefs about a subject or pursues no end at all—but a positive mismatch between them. Since each of (BE)'s evils is in this way the contrary of a good affirmed by (BG), the second base-clause is a natural complement to the first.[20]

Given (BE), the characterization can then add another independent recursion-clause about the intrinsic evil of *loving for itself what is evil*, (LE):

> (LE) If x is intrinsically evil, loving x for itself is also intrinsically evil.

Whereas loving for itself is an appropriate response to intrinsic goods, it is a positively inappropriate response to intrinsic evils, and (LE) makes this second kind of loving intrinsically evil. Together with (BE), it says that a person B's desiring or pursuing another person A's pain for itself is intrinsically evil, as is B's taking malicious pleasure in A's pain. And if a third person C loves B's love of A's pain for itself—for example, by taking pleasure in B's malicious pleasure as malicious—that too is intrinsically evil, as is loving another's false belief or failure or loving someone's love of false belief or failure.

There can be further recursion-clauses about hating what is good or evil, that is, about

desiring or pursuing its not obtaining or being pained by its obtaining. One such clause concerns the intrinsic evil of *hating for itself what is good*, (HG):

(HG) If x is intrinsically good, hating x (desiring or pursuing x's not obtaining or being pained by x's obtaining) for itself is intrinsically evil.

Since hating is an inappropriate response to intrinsic goods, (HG) makes it intrinsically evil. Thus, (HG) makes it intrinsically evil for person B to desire or seek for itself the destruction of A's pleasure or to be pained by A's pleasure. A parallel clause concerns the intrinsic goodness of *hating for itself what is evil*, (HE):

(HE) If x is intrinsically evil, hating x for itself is intrinsically good.

(HE) makes it intrinsically good for B to be sympathetically pained by A's pain—to feel compassion, for A's pain—or to desire or try to relieve it. Even if B's compassion has no further effects, it is something good in itself. So are B's wanting to remove or being pained by A's false belief and her hating for itself A's love of evil or hatred of good—for example, being pained by A's malicious love of another's pain.

Behind these four recursion-clauses (LG), (LE), (HG), and (HE) is a simple idea: that it is intrinsically good to be oriented positively toward good and negatively toward evil, and intrinsically evil to be oriented negatively toward good and positively toward evil. In each case, a morally appropriate response to good or evil is intrinsically good and a morally inappropriate response is evil. It is intrinsically good if one's desires, actions, and feelings are oriented fittingly and intrinsically evil if they are oriented unfittingly.

The recursive characterization can be extended further by some non-recursive clauses about attitudes to instrumental goods and evils.

Imagine that x is instrumentally good because it promotes intrinsic good y. One can love x as a means to y, or because it promotes y. A first instrumental clause about *loving as a means what promotes good* says that doing so is intrinsically good:

> If x is instrumentally good because it promotes intrinsic good y, loving x because it promotes y is intrinsically good.

Combined with (BG), this clause says that loving a cause of pleasure because it causes pleasure is intrinsically good, as is loving a cause of knowledge because it causes knowledge. The clause does not say that the love of instrumental goods as means is good instrumentally, though this is often the case. If x is instrumental to intrinsic good y, a desire for x as a means can lead one to produce x and thereby to produce intrinsic good y. But the instrumental goodness of this desire does not need to be affirmed by a separate evaluative principle. It already follows from the intrinsic goodness of y plus empirical facts about the effects of one's desire for x, namely, its helping to produce y. What the clause says, rather, is that loving the means to goods as means is *intrinsically* good; it is another appropriate response to a kind of good and therefore good in itself. The love of good means presupposes a love of good ends and can only be an addition to it: one can love x for promoting y only if one already loves y. But the clause says this is a morally appropriate addition: responding fully to what is good requires loving intrinsic goods intrinsically and instrumental goods as means.

There are further clauses about attitudes to instrumental goods and evils. A state x can also be instrumentally good if it prevents intrinsic evil z; a second instrumental clause says that loving what prevents evil because it prevents evil is intrinsically good. And further clauses make it intrinsically evil to love as a means what is instrumentally evil in either of the two possible

ways, intrinsically evil to hate as a means what is instrumentally good, and intrinsically good to hate as a means what is instrumentally evil.

There can also be clauses about attitudes to states non-instrumentally related to intrinsic goods and evils. For example, *x* can be a standard effect of intrinsic good *y* or, without being an effect, can be a reliable indicator of *y*, perhaps because *x* and *y* are joint effects of a common cause.[21] One can then love *x* because it is an indicator of *y*. For example, one can desire, pursue, and take pleasure in a person's smile because it indicates that she is experiencing pleasure. In general, our attitudes to states for themselves tend to spread themselves. When we care about one state for itself, we naturally care about other states related to it because of that relation. A series of further relational clauses says that those attitudes can be intrinsically good and evil.

If it includes the instrumental and other relational clauses, the recursive characterization implies that a single state can be the object of more than one intrinsically good attitude. Imagine that person B tries to promote *A*'s pleasure for itself and does so successfully. It is intrinsically good for a third person C to love B's action for itself, as involving the active pursuit of pleasure. But it is also good for C to love B's action as a cause of pleasure, that is, for its instrumental as well as its intrinsic properties. In some cases, contrary attitudes can be appropriate to the same state. Imagine that B tries to promote *A*'s pleasure but ends up through no fault of his causing *A* pain. Here it is intrinsically good for person C to love B's action for its intrinsic character but to hate or regret it for its effects. The best balance of attitudes for C to take to B's action depends on which response should be stronger, the love or the hatred, which in turn depends on the magnitude of the values at which they are directed. If the intrinsic value of B's action is greater than its instrumental disvalue, C's best overall attitude to B's action is positive, though with an element of regret for the action's bad effects. If the action's

instrumental disvalue is greater, C's best overall attitude is negative.

Multiple attitudes can also be appropriate to a state because of its intrinsic properties. Imagine that B takes pleasure in *A*'s knowledge. His pleasure is good as an instance of love of what is good, but it is also good as an instance of pleasure, or as involving the quality of pleasantness that (BG) makes a base-level good. It is therefore good for C to love B's pleasure both for its directedness to a good object and for its pleasantness, that is, for two intrinsic properties. Once again, contrary attitudes can be appropriate to the same state. If B takes pleasure in something evil such as *A*'s pain or false belief, his pleasure is intrinsically evil as a love of what is evil, but also intrinsically good as a pleasure. It should therefore be hated for itself for the one quality and loved for itself for the other, with the best overall attitude to it depending on which is greater: the evil B's pleasure involves as a love of evil or the good it involves as a pleasure. (On this issue see chapter 5.) Or, if B is pained by *A*'s pain, his attitude is intrinsically good as a hatred of evil and intrinsically evil as pain, with contrary attitudes again appropriate. A similar conflict is possible for another base-level good, achievement. Imagine that B has the goal of causing *A* pain and achieves it. If this goal organizes a great many others in a means-end hierarchy, B's realizing it has positive value as an achievement. But his pursuing this goal also has negative value as an instance of the active pursuit of evil. Here, the best overall attitude to B's activity depends on the relative magnitudes of its intrinsic goodness as an achievement, its intrinsic evil as a form of loving evil, and its instrumental evil as causing *A*'s pain.

These multiple attitudes are possible because the elements of the recursive characterization—the two base-clauses, the four recursion-clauses, and all the relational clauses—are stated in terms of universals. They say it is good or evil to have attitudes to certain universal properties, or, more precisely, to have attitudes to particular states as

instantiating these properties. If a state instantiates several relevant properties, either intrinsic or instrumental, it will be intrinsically good to have several (perhaps conflicting) attitudes to it. But each of these attitudes will be in some way appropriate to it.

3. The definition of virtue and vice

Even as fully assembled, the recursive characterization makes no mention of virtue or vice. It says that certain attitudes to goods and evils are intrinsically good and evil, but not that they are virtuous or vicious. This lack is easily remedied by adopting a *definition of virtue and vice* that fits the characterization:

> The moral virtues are those attitudes to goods and evils that are intrinsically good, and the moral vices are those attitudes to goods and evils that are intrinsically evil.

If this definition is combined only with the recursion-clauses (LG)–(HE), it equates the virtues with appropriate attitudes to intrinsic goods and evils, namely, loving the former and hating the latter for themselves. It likewise equates the vices with inappropriate attitudes to intrinsic goods and evils. If the recursion-clauses are supplemented by the eight instrumental clauses, the definition finds further forms of virtue in appropriate attitudes to instrumental goods and evils and of vice in inappropriate attitudes to them, with a similar extension following from the other relational clauses. And when the recursive characterization is elaborated in greater detail, as it will be in chapter 3 [see original reading], the definition yields yet further forms of virtue and, especially, of vice. On its own the definition has no determinate content. To identify any particular states as virtuous or vicious, it must be combined with independent claims to the effect that some attitudes to goods and evils are intrinsically good and others intrinsically evil. Since these are just

the claims we find in the recursive characterization of good and evil, that characterization gives the definition content. In its present form, it makes the definition equate virtue more specifically with loving what is good for the properties that make it good and hating on a similar basis what is evil. In return, the definition connects the recursive characterization to the concepts of virtue and vice, so that the latter's clauses identify forms of virtue and vice. Given their close mutual fit, the recursive characterization and the definition together comprise a recursive account of the intrinsic goodness of virtue and the intrinsic evil of vice, one claiming that certain attitudes to good and evil are intrinsically good and virtuous and others intrinsically evil and vicious.

More specifically, the recursive characterization and definition together equate the virtues and vices with subsets of the intrinsic goods and evils in a multilevel theory of good and evil. The recursive characterization starts by affirming certain base-level goods and evils, those identified by (BG) and (BE). It then adds to its base-level goods an infinite series of higher-level intrinsic goods, with the goods at each higher level consisting in appropriate attitudes to intrinsic goods or evils at the immediately lower level or to relational goods or evils defined in terms of them. The characterization likewise adds to its base-level evils an infinite series of higher-level evils consisting in inappropriate attitudes to lower-level goods or evils. The definition then identifies the moral virtues with all the higher-level goods in this multilevel theory and the moral vices with all the higher-level evils, so any intrinsic good above the base level is a virtue and any intrinsic evil above it a vice. We have already seen what some of these individual virtues and vices are. Combined with the recursive characterization, the definition implies that benevolence—that is, desiring, pursuing, or taking pleasure in another's pleasure for itself— is a virtue, as are desiring, pursuing, and taking pleasure in one's own or another's benevolence. Pursuing knowledge for its own sake is virtuous,

as is feeling compassion for or trying compassionately to relieve another's pain. It is vicious to maliciously desire, pursue, or take pleasure in another's pain or maliciously desire or seek to destroy his pleasure. But it is virtuous to be pained by malice, in oneself or others, and to try to eliminate it.

To some extent this definition of virtue and vice is stipulative and could be replaced by some other definition. The attitudes the recursive characterization makes intrinsically good and evil can also have instrumental qualities and on that basis be all things considered good or evil. Consider again the case where B tries benevolently to promote A's pleasure but through no fault of his causes A pain. B's benevolent action, though intrinsically good, is instrumentally evil, and if the pain it causes A is sufficiently great, it can be all things considered evil. Similarly, if a malicious attempt to cause A pain in fact gives A pleasure, it can be instrumentally and even all things considered good. An alternative definition of virtue and vice focuses on these judgments of all-things-considered rather than just intrinsic goodness and evil. It equates the moral virtues with those attitudes to good and evil that are good all things considered, or good counting both their intrinsic and instrumental qualities, and the moral vices with those that are evil all things considered. Like Sidgwick's definition, this one counts an attitude's instrumental qualities as relevant to its status as virtuous or vicious, though it also counts its intrinsic qualities. It can even be seen as lying behind Sidgwick's definition. If one assumes that attitudes cannot be intrinsically good or evil, as Sidgwick appears to, the all-things-considered definition collapses into a simpler one defining the virtues and vices just as instrumentally good and evil.

This alternative definition cannot be dismissed as utterly false to our everyday understanding of virtue and vice. That understanding sees the virtues as states that are in some way desirable, and the all-things-considered definition interprets this desirability in one intelligible way. Nonetheless, and though the issue to some extent calls for stipulation, I think there are several reasons to prefer our initial definition's focus on intrinsic rather than all-things-considered goodness and evil.[22]

First, this definition has what I find more attractive implications than the all-things-considered definition. The latter implies that intense malice with sufficiently good consequences can be a virtue, while benevolence with sufficiently bad consequences, as when B's attempt to give A pleasure causes A pain, can be a vice. But surely it is counterintuitive to say that malice can ever be a virtue or benevolence a vice. The alternative definition could try to avoid this implication by equating the virtues with attitudes that are normally, or in standard conditions, good all things considered.[23] This would allow that in an exceptional case like that of B above, a particular instance of benevolence can be all things considered evil yet still virtuous. But this proposal does not entirely remove the difficulty, since we can imagine a possible world where benevolence regularly has bad effects and malice good ones, and it still seems counterintuitive to say that in this world benevolence is a vice and malice a virtue. Our definition has what some may see as its own odd implication, namely that in a situation like the one just described, a virtue can be all things considered evil and a vice all things considered good. But this implication does not seem to me unacceptable; on the contrary, it seems correct. What we think on balance about the value of a virtue can depend on its effects, so that what remains a virtue can be all things considered unfortunate. And as we will see more fully in chapter 4 [see original reading], our definition has many other attractive implications about particular virtues and vices. Though the all-things-considered definition is not entirely false to our everyday understanding of virtue and vice, our initial definition, I think, fits that understanding better.

Second, our initial definition fits far better with the main aim of this book: to

give a consequentialist account of the intrinsic goodness of virtue and evil of vice. This kind of account is certainly possible given the all-things-considered definition. Assuming the recursive characterization of good and evil, the latter implies that many virtues are intrinsically good and many intrinsically good attitudes are virtues. But the overlap between the two categories is not perfect. Some virtues are not intrinsically good—for example, malice that has sufficiently good consequences—and some intrinsically good attitudes are not virtues. This lack of overlap is avoided by our definition, which makes virtue always intrinsically good and vice always intrinsically evil. In fact, this definition allows a simple, rhetorically effective statement of the recursive account of the intrinsic goodness of virtue and evil of vice. If this account includes the definition, it treats the virtues as intrinsically good because it identifies them with a subset of the intrinsic goods, namely, all those above the base level in a multi-level theory of good and evil. Given the definition, it is not just that some intrinsically good attitudes are virtues and some virtues are intrinsically good. All the virtues are intrinsically good because they are defined as a kind of intrinsic good, one consisting in appropriate attitudes to other, lower-level goods and evils.

Notes

1 Moore, *Principia Ethica*, chap. 1.
2 Brentano, *The Origin of Our Knowledge of Right and Wrong*, p. 18.
3 Sidgwick, *The Methods of Ethics*, p. 112; see also my *Perfectionism*, pp. 57–58.
4 Kagan, *The Limits of Morality*, p. 161. Note that Kagan's definition is of what I later call "agent-neutral" goodness.
5 In abstracting from these issues we can also abstract from issues about moral realism and anti-realism, issues about whether judgments ascribing moral properties such as goodness can be objectively true or, on the contrary, express only sentiments or feelings. All three views about goodness

are compatible with moral realism, but they are also compatible with anti-realism. On an anti-realist interpretation, the last two views take judgments ascribing goodness to have a distinctive subject matter: they express sentiments about emotions, actions, or desires rather than about other possible objects. On an anti-realist interpretation, the first view takes judgments ascribing goodness to express a qualitatively distinct sentiment, one that grounds other moral sentiments. Here the claim that goodness is a simple, unanalyzable property is read as the claim that it expresses a simple, unanalyzable sentiment. But all three views are compatible with both realism and anti-realism and can therefore be discussed independently of them.

6 Moore, "The Conception of Intrinsic Value," p. 260; see also *Principia Ethica*, pp. 93, 95, 187; and *Ethics*, pp. 24, 68. A similar view is defended in Korsgaard, "Two Distinctions in Goodness"; Chisholm, *Brentano and Intrinsic Value*, pp. 58–53; and Lemos, *Intrinsic Value*, pp. 8–11.
7 For discussion of this looser view, see Kagan, "Rethinking Intrinsic Value," and my "Two Kinds of Organic Unity."
8 See Frankena, *Ethics*, pp. 89–92; and Parfit, *Reasons and Persons*, pp. 501–2.
9 See, e.g., Sidgwick, *The Methods of Ethics*, pp. 420–21, 497–98; and Sen, "Rights and Agency."
10 See Moore, *Principia Ethica*, pp. 97–102; and Regan, "Against Evaluator Relativity."
11 Sidgwick, *The Methods of Ethics*, p. 392.
12 See Sidgwick, *The Methods of Ethics*, pp. 323–24.
13 Rashdall, "Professor Sidgwick's Utilitarianism," p. 207.
14 Sidgwick, *The Methods of Ethics*, p. 396; see also p. 393.
15 Parfit, *Reasons and Persons*, p. 151; there is a related topic discussed in my book *Perfectionism*, pp. 108–12.
16 A claim somewhat similar to this one is allowed by the strict view of intrinsic goodness. Given this view, we cannot say that the preservation of Venice makes the person's activity in pursuit of that goal intrinsically better, but we can say that it makes a whole consisting of his activity plus its outcome plus the causal relation between them intrinsically better. (This claim relies on Moore's "principle of organic unities"; see *Principia Ethica*, pp. 37–36,

92–96, 183–885.) But this latter claim does not seem intuitively right. Surely success in pursuit of a worthwhile goal makes one's pursuit itself, and not just some whole containing it, intrinsically better. See my "Two Kinds of Organic Unity," p. 306.

17 For this general view of pleasure, see, e.g., Bentham, *Introduction to the Principles of Morals and Legislation*; and Sidgwick, *The Methods of Ethics*, p. 94.

18 See Kagan, "The Limits of Well-Being," pp. 172–73. My account of pleasure in this paragraph is based on Kagan's, which he in turn says is influenced by work by Leonard Katz.

19 For a fuller account of knowledge and achievement see my *Perfectionism*, chaps. 8–10.

20 It is not clear that failure belongs on a list of intrinsic evils. It is plausible that pain is intrinsically evil and also plausible that false belief is intrinsically worse than ignorance, or than having no belief at all about a subject. But is failure in pursuit of a highly general end worse than no pursuit at all? May it not be "better to have sought and failed than never to have sought at all"? Despite this worry, I have included failure as an evil in (BE) for the sake of symmetry with (BG).

21 For this concept of "indicating" goodness, see Feldman, *Doing the Best We Can*, p. 26; and Thomson, "On Some Ways in Which a Thing Can Be Good," pp. 100–101.

22 A third alternative is a definition that equates the virtues with attitudes that are both intrinsically *and* all things considered good. But my arguments against the simpler all-things-considered definition tell for the most part also against this more complex alternative.

23 This version of the instrumental view is suggested in Driver, "The Virtues and Human Nature," pp. 122–25.

References

Bentham, Jeremy. *Introduction to the Principles of Morals and Legislation*. Edited by J. H. Burns and H. L. A. Hart. London: Methuen, 1970.

Brentano, Franz. *The Origin of Our Knowledge of Right and Wrong*. Translated by Roderick M. Chisholm and Elizabeth Schneewind. London: Routledge & Kegan Paul, 1969.

Chisholm, Roderick M. *Brentano and Intrinsic Value*. Cambridge: Cambridge University Press, 1986.

Driver, Julia. "The Virtues and Human Nature." In *How Should One Live? Essays on the Virtues*, edited by Roger Crisp. Oxford: Clarendon Press, 1996.

Feldman, Fred. *Doing the Best We Can*. Dordrecht: Reidel, 1986.

Frankena, William K. *Ethics*. 2d ed. Englewood Cliffs, N.J.: Prentice-Hall, 1973.

Hurka, Thomas. *Perfectionism*. New York: Oxford University Press, 1993.

——. "Two Kinds of Organic Unity." *Journal of Ethics* 2 (1998): 299–320.

Kagan, Shelly. *The Limits of Morality*. Oxford: Clarendon Press, 1980

——. "The Limits of Well-Being." *Social Philosophy and Policy* 9, no. 2 (1992): 169–89.

——. "Rethinking Intrinsic Value." *Journal of Ethics* 2 (1998): 277–97.

Korsgaard, Christine M. "Two Distinctions in Goodness." *Philosophical Review* 92 (1983): 169–95.

Lemos, Noah M. *Intrinsic Value: Concept and Warrant*. Cambridge: Cambridge University Press, 1994.

Moore, G. E. "The Conception of Intrinsic Value." In *Philosophical Studies*. London: Routledge & Kegan Paul, 1922.

——. *Ethics*. London: Oxford University Press, 1912.

——. *Principia Ethica*. Cambridge: Cambridge University Press, 1903.

Parfit, Derek. *Reasons and Persons*. Oxford: Clarendon Press, 1984.

Rashdall, Hastings. "Professor Sidgwick's Utilitarianism." *Mind*, o.s. 10 (1885): 200–226.

Regan, Donald H. "Against Evaluator Relativity: A Response to Sen." *Philosophy and Public Affairs* 12 (1983): 93–112.

Sen, Amartya. "Rights and Agency." *Philosophy and Public Affairs* 11 (1982): 93–112.

Sidgwick, Henry. *The Methods of Ethics*. 7th ed. London: Macmillan, 1907.

Slote, Michael. "Agent-Based Virtue Ethics." In *Virtue Ethics*, edited by Roger Crisp and Michael Slote. Oxford: Oxford University Press, 1997.

Thomson, Judith Jarvis. "On Some Ways in Which a Thing Can Be Good." *Social Philosophy and Policy* 9, no. 2 (1992): 96–117.

Chapter 40

Friedrich Nietzsche

BEYOND MORALITY

From *Beyond Good and Evil*

Part Five: *On the Natural History of Morals*

186

MORAL sensibility is as subtle, late, manifold, sensitive and refined in Europe today as the 'science of morals' pertaining to it is still young, inept, clumsy and coarse-fingered – an interesting contrast which sometimes even becomes visible and incarnate in the person of a moralist. Even the expression 'science of morals' is, considering what is designated by it, far too proud, and contrary to *good* taste: which is always accustomed to choose the more modest expressions. One should, in all strictness, admit *what* will be needful here for a long time to come, *what* alone is provisionally justified here: assembly of material, conceptual comprehension and arrangement of a vast domain, of delicate value-feelings and value-distinctions which live, grow, beget and perish – and perhaps attempts to display the more frequent and recurring forms of these living crystallizations – as preparation of a *typology* of morals. To be sure: one has not been so modest hitherto. Philosophers one and all have, with a strait-laced seriousness that provokes laughter, demanded something much higher, more pretentious, more solemn of themselves as soon as they have concerned themselves with morality as a science: they wanted to furnish the *rational ground* of morality – and every philosopher hitherto has believed he has furnished this rational ground; morality itself, however, was taken as 'given'. How far from their clumsy pride was that apparently insignificant task left in dust and mildew, the task of description, although the most delicate hands and senses could hardly be delicate enough for it! It was precisely because moral philosophers knew the facts of morality only somewhat vaguely in an arbitrary extract or as a chance abridgement, as morality of their environment, their class, their church, the spirit of their times, their climate and zone of the earth, for instance – it was precisely because they were ill informed and not even very inquisitive about other peoples, ages and former times, that they did not so much as catch sight of the real problems of morality – for these come into view only if we compare *many* moralities. Strange though it may sound, in all 'science of morals' hitherto the problem of morality itself has been *lacking*: the suspicion was lacking that there was anything problematic here. What philosophers called 'the rational ground of morality' and sought to furnish was, viewed in the proper light, only a scholarly form of *faith* in the prevailing morality, a new way of *expressing* it, and thus itself a fact within a certain morality, indeed even in the last resort a kind of denial that this morality *ought* to be conceived of as a problem – and in any event the opposite of a testing, analysis, doubting and vivisection of this faith. Hear, for example, with what almost venerable

innocence Schopenhauer still presented his task, and draw your own conclusions as to how scientific a 'science' is whose greatest masters still talk like children and old women: – 'The principle', he says (Fundamental Problems of Ethics),

> the fundamental proposition on whose content all philosophers of ethics are *actually* at one: *neminem laede, immo omnes, quantum potes, juva* – is *actually* the proposition of which all the teachers of morals endeavour to furnish the rational ground . . . the *actual* foundation of ethics which has been sought for centuries like the philosopher's stone.

– The difficulty of furnishing the rational ground for the above-quoted proposition may indeed be great – as is well known, Schopenhauer too failed to do it – ; and he who has ever been certain how insipidly false and sentimental this proposition is in a world whose essence is will to power – may like to recall that Schopenhauer, although a pessimist, *actually* – played the flute. . . . Every day, after dinner: read his biographers on this subject. And by the way: a pessimist, a world-denier and God-denier, who *comes to a halt* before morality – who affirms morality and plays the flute, affirms *laede neminem* morality: what? is that actually – a pessimist?

187

Quite apart: from the value of such assertions as 'there exists in us a categorical imperative' one can still ask: what does such an assertion say of the man who asserts it? There are moralities which are intended to justify their authors before others; other moralities are intended to calm him and make him content with himself; with others he wants to crucify and humiliate himself; with others he wants to wreak vengeance, with others hide himself, with others transfigure himself and set himself on high; this morality serves to make its author forget, that to make him or something about him forgotten; many moralists would like to exercise power

and their creative moods on mankind; others, Kant perhaps among them, give to understand with their morality: 'what is worthy of respect in me is that I know how to obey – and things *ought* to be no different with you!' – in short, moralities too are only a *sign-language of the emotions*.

188

Every morality is, as opposed to *laisser aller*, a piece of tyranny against 'nature', likewise against 'reason': but that can be no objection to it unless one is in possession of some other morality which decrees that any kind of tyranny and unreason is impermissible. The essential and invaluable element in every morality is that it is a protracted constraint: to understand Stoicism or Port-Royal or Puritanism one should recall the constraint under which every language has hitherto attained strength and freedom – the metrical constraint, the tyranny of rhyme and rhythm. How much trouble the poets and orators of every nation have given themselves! – not excluding a few present-day prose writers in whose ear there dwells an inexorable conscience – 'for the sake of foolishness', as the utilitarian fools say, thinking they are clever – 'from subjection to arbitrary laws', as the anarchists say, feeling themselves 'free', even free-spirited. But the strange fact is that all there is or has been on earth of freedom, subtlety, boldness, dance and masterly certainty, whether in thinking itself, or in ruling, or in speaking and persuasion, in the arts as in morals, has evolved only by virtue of the 'tyranny of such arbitrary laws'; and, in all seriousness, there is no small probability that precisely this is 'nature' and 'natural' – and *not* that *laisser aller*! Every artist knows how far from the feeling of letting himself go his 'natural' condition is, the free ordering, placing, disposing, forming in the moment of 'inspiration' – and how strictly and subtly he then obeys thousandfold laws which precisely on account of their severity and definiteness mock all formulation in concepts (even the firmest concept is by comparison

something fluctuating, manifold, ambiguous –). The essential thing 'in heaven and upon earth' seems, to say it again, to be a protracted *obedience* in *one* direction: from out of that there always emerges and has always emerged in the long run something for the sake of which it is worthwhile to live on earth, for example virtue, art, music, dance, reason, spirituality – something trans-figuring, refined, mad and divine. Protracted unfreedom of spirit, mistrustful constraint in the communicability of ideas, the discipline thinkers imposed on themselves to think within an ecclesiastical or courtly rule or under Aristotelian presuppositions, the protracted spiritual will to interpret all events according to a Christian scheme and to redis-cover and justify the Christian God in every chance occurrence – all these violent, arbitrary, severe, gruesome and antirational things have shown themselves to be the means by which the European spirit was disciplined in its strength, ruthless curiosity and subtle flexibility: though admittedly an irreplaceable quantity of force and spirit had at the same time to be suppressed, stifled and spoiled (for here as everywhere 'nature' shows itself as it is, in all its prodigal and *indifferent* magnificence, which is noble though it outrage our feelings). That for thou-sands of years European thinkers thought only so as to prove something – today, on the contrary, we suspect any thinker who 'wants to prove something' – that they always knew in advance that which was *supposed* to result from the most rigorous cogitation, as used to be the case with Asiatic astrology and is still the case with the innocuous Christian-moral interpretation of the most intimate personal experiences 'to the glory of God' and 'for the salvation of the soul' – this tyranny, this arbitrariness, this rigorous and grandiose stupidity has *educated* the spirit; it seems that slavery, in the cruder and in the more refined sense, is the indispensable means also for spiritual discipline and breeding. Regard any morality from this point of view: it is 'nature' in it which teaches hatred of *laisser aller*, of too great

freedom, and which implants the need for limited horizons and immediate tasks – which teaches the *narrowing of perspective*, and thus in a certain sense stupidity, as a condition of life and growth. 'Thou shalt obey someone and for a long time: *otherwise* thou shalt perish and lose all respect for thyself' – this seems to me to be nature's imperative, which is, to be sure, neither 'categorical' as old Kant demanded it should be (hence the 'otherwise' –), nor addressed to the individual (what do individuals matter to nature!), but to peoples, races, ages, classes, and above all to the entire animal 'man', to *mankind*.

189

The industrious races find leisure very hard to endure: it was a masterpiece of *English* instinct to make Sunday so extremely holy and boring that the English unconsciously long again for their week- and working-days – as a kind of cleverly devised and cleverly intercalated *fast*, such as is also to be seen very frequently in the ancient world (although, as one might expect in the case of southern peoples, not precisely in regard to work –). There have to be fasts of many kinds; and wherever powerful drives and habits prevail legislators have to see to it that there are interca-lary days on which such a drive is put in chains and learns to hunger again. Seen from a higher viewpoint, entire generations and ages, if they are infected with some moral fanaticism or other, appear to be such intercalated periods of constraint and fasting, during which a drive learns to stoop and submit, but also to *purify and intensify* itself; certain philosophical sects (for example the Stoa in the midst of the Hellenistic culture, with its air grown rank and overcharged with aphrodisiac vapours) likewise permit of a similar interpretation. – This also provides a hint towards the elucidation of that paradox why it was precisely during Europe's Christian period and only under the impress of Christian value judgements that the sexual drive sublimated itself into love (*amour-passion*).

190

There is something in Plato's morality which does not really belong to Plato but is only to be met with in his philosophy, one might say in spite of Plato: namely Socratism, for which he was really too noble. 'No one wants to do injury to himself, therefore all badness is involuntary. For the bad man does injury to himself: this he would not do if he knew that badness is bad. Thus the bad man is bad only in consequence of an error; if one cures him of his error, one necessarily makes him – good.' – This way of reasoning smells of the *mob*, which sees in bad behaviour only its disagreeable consequences and actually judges 'it is *stupid* to act badly'; while it takes 'good' without further ado to be identical with 'useful and pleasant'. In the case of every utilitarian morality one may conjecture in advance a similar origin and follow one's nose: one will seldom go astray. – Plato did all he could to interpret something refined and noble into his teacher's proposition, above all himself – he, the most intrepid of interpreters, who picked up the whole of Socrates only in the manner of a popular tune from the streets, so as to subject it to infinite and impossible variations: that is, to make it into all his own masks and multiplicities. One might ask in jest, and in Homeric jest at that: what is the Platonic Socrates if not *prosthe Platōn opithen te Platōn messē te chimaira?*

191

The old theological problem of 'faith' and 'knowledge' – or, more clearly, of instinct and reason – that is to say, the question whether in regard to the evaluation of things instinct deserves to have more authority than rationality, which wants to evaluate and act according to reasons, according to a 'why?', that is to say according to utility and fitness for a purpose – this is still that old moral problem which first appeared in the person of Socrates and was already dividing the minds of men long before Christianity. Socrates himself, to be sure, had, with the taste appropriate to his talent – that of

a superior dialectician – initially taken the side of reason; and what indeed did he do all his life long but laugh at the clumsy incapacity of his noble Athenians, who were men of instinct, like all noble men, and were never able to supply adequate information about the reasons for their actions? Ultimately, however, in silence and secrecy, he laughed at himself too: he found in himself, before his more refined conscience and self-interrogation, the same difficulty and incapacity. But why, he exhorted himself, should one therefore abandon the instincts! One must help both them *and* reason to receive their due – one must follow the instincts, but persuade reason to aid them with good arguments. This was the actual *falsity* of that great ironist, who had so many secrets; he induced his conscience to acquiesce in a sort of self-outwitting: fundamentally he had seen through the irrational aspect of moral judgement. – Plato, more innocent in such things and without the craftiness of the plebeian, wanted at the expenditure of all his strength – the greatest strength any philosopher has hitherto had to expend! – to prove to himself that reason and instinct move of themselves towards *one* goal, towards the good, towards 'God'; and since Plato all theologians and philosophers have followed the same path – that is to say, in moral matters instinct, or as the Christians call it 'faith', or as I call it 'the herd', has hitherto triumphed. One might have to exclude Descartes, the father of rationalism (and consequently the grandfather of the Revolution), who recognised only the authority of reason: but reason is only an instrument, and Descartes was superficial.

• • •

197

One altogether misunderstands the beast of prey and man of prey (Cesare Borgia for example), one misunderstands 'nature', so long as one looks for something 'sick' at the bottom of these healthiest of all tropical monsters and growths, or even for an inborn 'hell' in them – : as virtually all moralists have done hitherto. It seems,

does it not, that there exists in moralists a hatred for the jungle and the tropics? And that the 'tropical man' has to be discredited at any cost, whether as the sickness and degeneration of man or as his own hell and self-torment? But why? For the benefit of 'temperate zones'? The benefit of temperate men? Of the 'moral'? Of the mediocre? – This for the chapter 'Morality as Timidity'.

198

All these moralities which address themselves to the individual person, for the promotion, of his 'happiness' as they say – what are they but prescriptions for behaviour in relation to the degree of *perilousness* in which the individual person lives with himself; recipes to counter his passions, his good and bad inclinations in so far as they have will to power in them and would like to play the tyrant; great and little artifices and acts of prudence to which there clings the nook-and-cranny odour of ancient household remedies and old-woman wisdom; one and all baroque and unreasonable in form – because they address themselves to 'all', because they generalize where generalization is impermissible – speaking unconditionally one and all, taking themselves for unconditional, flavoured with more than *one* grain of salt, indeed tolerable only, and occasionally even tempting, when they learn to smell overspiced and dangerous, to smell above all of 'the other world': all this is, from an intellectual point of view, of little value and far from constituting 'science', not to speak of 'wisdom', but rather, to say it again and to say it thrice, prudence, prudence, prudence, mingled with stupidity, stupidity, stupidity – whether it be that indifference and statuesque coldness towards the passionate folly of the emotions which the Stoics advised and applied; or that no-more-laughing and no-more-weeping of Spinoza, that destruction of the emotions through analysis and vivisection which he advocated so naïvely; or that depression of the emotions to a harmless mean at which they may be satisfied, the Aristotelianism of morals; even morality as enjoyment of the emotions in a deliberate thinning down and spiritualization through the symbolism of art, as music for instance, or as love of God or love of man for the sake of God – for in religion the passions again acquire civic rights, assuming that . . .; finally, even that easygoing and roguish surrender to the emotions such as Hafiz and Goethe taught, that bold letting fall of the reins, that spiritual-physical *licentia morum* in the. exceptional case of wise old owls and drunkards for whom there is 'no longer much risk in it'. This too for the chapter 'Morality as Timidity'.

199

Inasmuch as ever since there have been human beings there have also been human herds (family groups, communities, tribes, nations, states, churches), and always very many who obey compared with the very small number of those who command – considering, that is to say, that hitherto nothing has been practised and cultivated among men better or longer than obedience, it is fair to suppose that as a rule a need for it is by now innate as a kind of *formal conscience* which commands: 'thou shalt unconditionally do this, unconditionally not do that', in short 'thou shalt'. This need seeks to be satisfied and to fill out its form with a content; in doing so it grasps about wildly, according to the degree of its strength, impatience and tension, with little discrimination, as a crude appetite, and accepts whatever any commander – parent, teacher, law, class prejudice, public opinion – shouts in its ears. The strange narrowness of human evolution, its hesitations, its delays, its frequent retrogressions and rotations, are due to the fact that the herd instinct of obedience has been inherited best and at the expense of the art of commanding. If we think of this instinct taken to its ultimate extravagance there would be no commanders or independent men at all; or, if they existed, they would suffer from a bad conscience and in order to be able to command would have to practise a deceit upon themselves:

the deceit, that is, that they too were only obeying. This state of things actually exists in Europe today: I call it the moral hypocrisy of the commanders. They know no way of defending themselves against their bad conscience other than to pose as executors of more ancient or higher commands (commands of ancestors, of the constitution, of justice, of the law or even of God), or even to borrow herd maxims from the herd's way of thinking and appear as 'the first servant of the people' for example, or as 'instruments of the common good'. On the other hand, the herd-man in Europe today makes himself out to be the only permissible kind of man and glorifies the qualities through which he is tame, peaceable and useful to the herd as the real human virtues: namely public spirit, benevolence, consideration, industriousness, moderation, modesty, forbearance, pity. In those cases, however, in which leaders and bellwethers are thought to be indispensable, there is attempt after attempt to substitute for them an adding-together of clever herd-men: this, for example, is the origin of all parliamentary constitutions. All this notwithstanding, what a blessing, what a release from a burden becoming intolerable, the appearance of an unconditional commander is for this herd-animal European, the effect produced by the appearance of Napoleon is the latest great witness – the history of the effect of Napoleon is almost the history of the higher happiness this entire century has attained in its most valuable men and moments.

200

The man of an era of dissolution which mixes the races together and who therefore contains within him the inheritance of a diversified descent, that is to say contrary and often not merely contrary drives and values which struggle with one another and rarely leave one another in peace – such a man of late cultures and broken lights will, on average, be a rather weak man: his fundamental desire is that the war which he *is* should come to an

end; happiness appears to him, in accord with a sedative (for example Epicurean or Christian) medicine and mode of thought, pre-eminently as the happiness of repose, of tranquillity, of satiety, of unity at last attained, as a 'Sabbath of Sabbaths', to quote the holy rhetorician Augustine, who was himself such a man. – If, however, the contrariety and war in such a nature should act as one *more* stimulus and enticement to life – and if, on the other hand, in addition to powerful and irreconcilable drives, there has also been inherited and cultivated a proper mastery and subtlety in conducting a war against oneself, that is to say self-control, self-outwitting: then there arise those marvellously incomprehensible and unfathomable men, those enigmatic men predestined for victory and the seduction of others, the fairest examples of which are Alcibiades and Caesar (– to whom I should like to add that first European agreeable to my taste, the Hohenstaufen Friedrich II), and among artists perhaps Leonardo da Vinci. They appear in precisely the same ages as those in which that rather weak type with his desire for rest comes to the fore: the two types belong together and originate in the same causes.

201

So long as the utility which dominates moral value-judgements is solely that which is useful to the herd, so long as the object is solely the preservation of the community and the immoral is sought precisely and exclusively in that which seems to imperil the existence of the community: so long as that is the case there can be no 'morality of love of one's neighbour'. Supposing that even there a constant little exercise of consideration, pity, fairness, mildness, mutual aid was practised, supposing that even at that stage of society all those drives are active which are later honourably designated 'virtues' and are finally practically equated with the concept 'morality': in that era they do not yet by any means belong to the domain of moral

valuations – they are still *extra-moral*. An act of pity, for example, was during the finest age of Rome considered neither good nor bad, neither moral nor immoral; and even if it was commended, this commendation was entirely compatible with a kind of involuntary disdain, as soon, that is, as it was set beside any action which served the welfare of the whole, of the *res publica*. Ultimately 'love of one's neighbour' is always something secondary, in part conventional and arbitrarily illusory, when compared with *fear of one's neighbour*. Once the structure of society seems to have been in general fixed and made safe from external dangers, it is this fear of one's neighbour which again creates new perspectives of moral valuation. There are certain strong and dangerous drives, such as enterprisingness, foolhardiness, revengefulness, craft, rapacity, ambition, which had hitherto had not only to be honoured from the point of view of their social utility – under different names, naturally, from those chosen here – but also mightily developed and cultivated (because they were constantly needed to protect the community as a whole against the enemies of the community as a whole); these drives are now felt to be doubly dangerous – now that the diversionary outlets for them are lacking – and are gradually branded as immoral and given over to calumny. The antithetical drives and inclinations now come into moral honour; step by step the herd instinct draws its conclusions. How much or how little that is dangerous to the community, dangerous to equality, resides in an opinion, in a condition or emotion, in a will, in a talent, that is now the moral perspective: here again fear is the mother of morality. When the highest and strongest drives, breaking passionately out, carry the individual far above and beyond the average and lowlands of the herd conscience, the self-confidence of the community goes to pieces, its faith in itself, its spine as it were, is broken: consequently it is precisely these drives which are most branded and calumniated. Lofty spiritual independence, the will to

stand alone, great intelligence even, are felt to be dangerous; everything that raises the individual above the herd and makes his neighbour quail is henceforth called *evil*; the fair, modest, obedient, self-effacing disposition, the *mean and average* in desires, acquires moral names and honours. Eventually, under very peaceful conditions, there is less and less occasion or need to educate one's feelings in severity and sternness; and now every kind of severity, even severity in justice, begins to trouble the conscience; a stern and lofty nobility and self-responsibility is received almost as an offence and awakens mistrust, 'the lamb', even more 'the sheep', is held in higher and higher respect. There comes a point of morbid mellowing and over-tenderness in the history of society at which it takes the side even of him who harms it, the *criminal*, and does so honestly and wholeheartedly. Punishment: that seems to it somehow unfair – certainly the idea of 'being punished' and 'having to punish' is unpleasant to it, makes it afraid. 'Is it not enough to render him *harmless*? why punish him as well? To administer punishment is itself dreadful!' – with this question herd morality, the morality of timidity, draws its ultimate conclusion. Supposing all danger, the cause of fear, could be abolished, this morality would therewith also be abolished: it would no longer be necessary, it would no longer *regard itself* as necessary! – He who examines the conscience of the present-day European will have to extract from a thousand moral recesses and hiding-places always the same imperative, the imperative of herd timidity: 'we wish that there will one day *no longer be anything to fear!*' One day – everywhere in Europe the will and way to *that* day is now called 'progress'.

202

Let us straight away say once more what we have already said a hundred times: for ears today offer such truths – *our* truths – no ready welcome. We know well enough how offensive it sounds when someone says plainly and without

metaphor that man is an animal; but it will be reckoned almost a *crime* in us that precisely in regard to men of 'modern ideas' we constantly employ the terms 'herd', 'herd instinct', and the like. But what of that! we can do no other: for it is precisely here that our new insight lies. We have found that in all principal moral judgements Europe has become unanimous, including the lands where Europe's influence predominates: one manifestly *knows* in Europe what Socrates thought he did not know, and what that celebrated old serpent once promised to teach – one 'knows' today what is good and evil. Now it is bound to make a harsh sound and one not easy for ears to hear when we insist again and again: that which here believes it knows, that which here glorifies itself with its praising and blaming and calls itself good, is the instinct of the herd-animal man: the instinct which has broken through and come to predominate and prevail over the other instincts and is coming to do so more and more in proportion to the increasing physiological approximation and assimilation of which it is the symptom. *Morality is in Europe today herd-animal morality* – that is to say, as we understand the thing, only *one* kind of human morality beside which, before which, after which many other, above all *higher*, moralities are possible or ought to be possible. But against such a 'possibility', against such an 'ought', this morality defends itself with all its might: it says, obstinately and stubbornly, 'I am morality itself, and nothing is morality besides me!' – indeed, with the aid of a religion which has gratified and flattered the sublimest herd-animal desires, it has got to the point where we discover even in political and social institutions an increasingly evident expression of this morality: the *democratic* movement inherits the Christian. But that the tempo of this movement is much too slow and somnolent for the more impatient, for the sick and suffering of the said instinct, is attested by the ever more frantic baying, the ever more undisguised fang-baring of the anarchist dogs which now rove the streets

of European culture: apparently the reverse of the placidly industrious democrats and revolutionary ideologists, and even more so of the stupid philosophasters and brotherhood fanatics who call themselves socialists and want a 'free society', they are in fact at one with them all in their total and instinctive hostility towards every form of society other than that of the *autonomous* herd (to the point of repudiating even the concepts 'master' and 'servant' – *ni dieu ni maître* says a socialist formula –); at one in their tenacious opposition to every special claim, every special right and privilege (that is to say, in the last resort to *every* right: for when everyone is equal no one will need any 'rights' –); at one in their mistrust of punitive justice (as if it were an assault on the weaker, an injustice against the necessary consequence of all previous society –); but equally at one in the religion of pity, in sympathy with whatever feels, lives, suffers (down as far as the animals, up as far as 'God' – the extravagance of 'pity for God' belongs in a democratic era –); at one, one and all, in the cry and impatience of pity, in mortal hatred for suffering in general, in their almost feminine incapacity to remain spectators of suffering, to *let* suffer; at one in their involuntary gloom and sensitivity, under whose spell Europe seems threatened with a new Buddhism; at one in their faith in the morality of *mutual* pity, as if it were morality in itself and the pinnacle, the *attained* pinnacle of man, the sole hope of the future, the consolation of the present and the great redemption from all the guilt of the past – at one, one and all, in their faith in the community as the *saviour*, that is to say in the herd, in 'themselves' . . .

203

We, who have a different faith – we, to whom the democratic movement is not merely a form assumed by political organization in decay but also a form assumed by man in decay, that is to say in diminishment, in process of becoming mediocre and losing his value: whither must *we*

direct our hopes? – Towards *new philosophers*, we have no other choice; towards spirits strong and original enough to make a start on antithetical evaluations and to revalue and reverse 'eternal values'; towards heralds and forerunners, towards men of the future who in the present knot together the constraint which compels the will of millennia on to *new* paths. To teach man the future of man as his *will*, as dependent on a human will, and to prepare for great enterprises and collective experiments in discipline and breeding so as to make an end of that gruesome dominion of chance and nonsense that has hitherto been called 'history' – the nonsense of the 'greatest number' is only its latest form–: for that a new kind of philosopher and commander will some time be needed, in face of whom whatever has existed on earth of hidden, dreadful and benevolent spirits may well look pale and dwarfed. It is the image of such leaders which hovers before *our* eyes – may I say that aloud, you free spirits? The circumstances one would have in part to create, in part to employ, to bring them into existence; the conjectural paths and tests by virtue of which a soul could grow to such height and power it would feel *compelled* to these tasks; a revaluation of values under whose novel pressure and hammer a conscience would be steeled, a heart transformed to brass, so that it might endure the weight of such a responsibility; on the other hand, the need for such leaders, the terrible danger they might not appear or might fail or might degenerate – these are *our* proper cares and concerns, do you know that, you free spirits? These are the heavy, remote thoughts and thunder clouds that pass across our life's sky. There are few more grievous pains than once to have beheld, divined, sensed, how an extraordinary man missed his way and degenerated: but he who has the rare eye for the collective danger that 'man' himself *may degenerate*, he who, like us, has recognized the tremendous fortuitousness which has hitherto played its game with the future of man – a game in which no hand, not

even a 'finger of God' took any part! – he who has divined the fatality that lies concealed in the idiotic guilelessness and blind confidence of 'modern ideas', even more in the whole of Christian-European morality: he suffers from a feeling of anxiety with which no other can be compared – for he comprehends in a *single* glance all that which, given a favourable accumulation and intensification of forces and tasks, could be *cultivated out of man*, he knows with all the knowledge of his conscience how the greatest possibilities in man are still unexhausted and how often before the type man has been faced with strange decisions and new paths – he knows even better from his most painful memories against what wretched things an evolving being of the highest rank has hitherto usually been shattered and has broken off, sunk and has itself become wretched. The *collective degeneration of man* down to that which the socialist dolts and blockheads today see as their 'man of the future' – as their ideal! – this degeneration and diminution of man to the perfect herd animal (or, as they say, to the man of the 'free society'), this animalization of man to the pygmy animal of equal rights and equal pretensions is *possible*, there is no doubt about that! He who has once thought this possibility through to the end knows one more kind of disgust than other men do – and perhaps also a new *task*! . . .

From *The Genealogy of Morals*

First essay: "good and evil," "good and bad"

I

The English psychologists to whom we owe the only attempts that have thus far been made to write a genealogy of morals are no mean posers of riddles, but the riddles they pose are themselves, and being incarnate have one advantage over their books—they are interesting. What are these English psychologists really after? One finds them always, whether intentionally or not, engaged in the same task of pushing into the

foreground the nasty part of the psyche, looking for the effective motive forces of human development in the very last place we would wish to have them found, e.g., in the inertia of habit, in forgetfulness, in the blind and fortuitous association of ideas: always in something that is purely passive, automatic, reflexive, molecular, and, moreover, profoundly stupid. What drives these psychologists forever in the same direction? A secret, malicious desire to belittle humanity, which they do not acknowledge even to themselves? A pessimistic distrust, the suspiciousness of the soured idealist? Some petty resentment of Christianity (and Plato) which does not rise above the threshold of consciousness? Or could it be a prurient taste for whatever is embarrassing, painfully paradoxical, dubious and absurd in existence? Or is it, perhaps, a kind of stew—a little meanness, a little bitterness, a bit of anti-Christianity, a touch of prurience and desire for condiments? . . . But, again, people tell me that these men are simply dull old frogs who hop and creep in and around man as in their own element—as though man were a bog. However, I am reluctant to listen to this, in fact I refuse to believe it; and if I may express a wish where I cannot express a conviction, I do wish wholeheartedly that things may be otherwise with these men—that these microscopic examiners of the soul may be really courageous, magnanimous, and proud animals, who know how to contain their emotions and have trained themselves to subordinate all wishful thinking to the truth—any truth, even a homespun, severe, ugly, obnoxious, un-Christian, unmoral truth. For such truths do exist.

II

All honor to the beneficent spirits that may motivate these historians of ethics! One thing is certain, however, they have been quite deserted by the true spirit of history. They all, to a man, think unhistorically, as is the age-old custom among philosophers. The amateurishness of their procedure is made plain from the very beginning, when it is a question of explaining the provenance of the concept and judgment *good*. "Originally," they decree, "altruistic actions were praised and approved by their recipients, that is, by those to whom they were useful. Later on, the origin of that praise having been forgotten, such actions were felt to be good simply because it was the habit to commend them." We notice at once that this first derivation has all the earmarks of the English psychologists' work. Here are the key ideas of utility, forgetfulness, habit, and, finally, error, seen as lying at the root of that value system which civilized man had hitherto regarded with pride as the prerogative of all men. This pride must now be humbled, these values devalued. Have the de-bunkers succeeded?

Now it is obvious to me, first of all, that their theory looks for the genesis of the concept *good* in the wrong place: the judgment *good* does not originate with those to whom the good has been done. Rather it was the "good" themselves, that is to say the noble, mighty, highly placed, and high-minded who decreed themselves and their actions to be good, i.e., belonging to the highest rank, in contradistinction to all that was base, low-minded and plebeian. It was only this *pathos of distance* that authorized them to create values and name them—what was utility to them? The notion of utility seems singularly inept to account for such a quick jetting forth of supreme value judgments. Here we come face to face with the exact opposite of that lukewarmness which every scheming prudence, every utilitarian calculus presupposes—and not for a time only, for the rare, exceptional hour, but permanently. The origin of the opposites *good* and *bad* is to be found in the pathos of nobility and distance, representing the dominant temper of a higher, ruling class in relation to a lower, dependent one. (The lordly right of bestowing names is such that one would almost be justified in seeing the origin of language itself as an expression of the rulers' power. They say, "This is that or that"; they seal off each thing and action

with a sound and thereby take symbolic possession of it.) Such an origin would suggest that there is no *a priori* necessity for associating the word *good* with altruistic deeds, as those moral psychologists are fond of claiming. In fact, it is only after aristocratic values have begun to decline that the egotism-altruism dichotomy takes possession of the human conscience; to use my own terms, it is the herd instinct that now asserts itself. Yet it takes quite a while for this instinct to assume such sway that it can reduce all moral valuations to that dichotomy— as is currently happening throughout Europe, where the prejudice equating the terms *moral*, *altruistic*, and *disinterested* has assumed the obsessive force of an *idée fixe*.

• • •

X

The slave revolt in morals begins by rancor turning creative and giving birth to values—the rancor of beings who, deprived of the direct outlet of action, compensate by an imaginary vengeance. All truly noble morality grows out of triumphant self-affirmation. Slave ethics, on the other hand, begins by saying *no* to an "outside," an "other," a non-self, and that *no* is its creative act. This reversal of direction of the evaluating look, this invariable looking outward instead of inward, is a fundamental feature of rancor. Slave ethics requires for its inception a sphere different from and hostile to its own. Physiologically speaking, it requires an outside stimulus in order to act at all; all its action is reaction. The opposite is true of aristocratic valuations: such values grow and act spontaneously, seeking out their contraries only in order to affirm themselves even more gratefully and delightedly. Here the negative concepts, *humble, base, bad*, are late, pallid counterparts of the positive, intense and passionate credo, "We noble, good, beautiful, happy ones." Aristocratic valuations may go amiss and do violence to reality, but this happens only with regard to spheres which they do not know well, or from the knowledge of which

they austerely guard themselves: the aristocrat will, on occasion, misjudge a sphere which he holds in contempt, the sphere of the common man, the people. On the other hand we should remember that the emotion of contempt, of looking down, provided that it falsifies at all, is as nothing compared with the falsification which suppressed hatred, impotent vindictiveness, effects upon its opponent, though only in effigy. There is in all contempt too much casualness and nonchalance, too much blinking of facts and impatience, and too much inborn gaiety for it ever to make of its object a downright caricature and monster. Hear the almost benevolent nuances the Greek aristocracy, for example, puts into all its terms for the commoner; how emotions of compassion, consideration, indulgence, sugar-coat these words until, in the end, almost all terms referring to the common man survive as expressions for "unhappy," "pitiable" (cf. *deilos, deilaios, poneros, mochtheros*, the last two of which properly characterize the common man as a drudge and beast of burden); how, on the other hand, the words *bad, base, unhappy* have continued to strike a similar note for the Greek ear, with the timbre "unhappy" preponderating. The "wellborn" really felt that they were also the "happy." They did not have to construct their happiness factitiously by looking at their enemies, as all rancorous men are wont to do, and being fully active, energetic people they were incapable of divorcing happiness from action. They accounted activity a necessary part of happiness (which explains the origin of the phrase *eu prattein*).

All this stands in utter contrast to what is called happiness among the impotent and oppressed, who are full of bottled-up aggressions. Their happiness is purely passive and takes the form of drugged tranquillity, stretching and yawning, peace, "sabbath," emotional slackness. Whereas the noble lives before his own conscience with confidence and frankness (*gennaîos* "nobly bred" emphasizes the nuance "truthful" and perhaps also "ingenuous"), the

rancorous person is neither truthful nor ingenuous nor honest and forthright with himself. His soul squints; his mind loves hide-outs, secret paths, and back doors; everything that is hidden seems to him his own world, his security, his comfort; he is expert in silence, in long memory, in waiting, in provisional self-depreciation, and in self-humiliation. A race of such men will, in the end, inevitably be cleverer than a race of aristocrats, and it will honor sharp-wittedness to a much greater degree, i.e., as an absolutely vital condition for its existence. Among the noble, mental acuteness always tends slightly to suggest luxury and overrefinement. The fact is that with them it is much less important than is the perfect functioning of the ruling, unconscious instincts or even a certain temerity to follow sudden impulses, court danger, or indulge spurts of violent rage, love, worship, gratitude, or vengeance. When a noble man feels resentment, it is absorbed in his instantaneous reaction and therefore does not poison him. Moreover, in countless cases where we might expect it, it never arises, while with weak and impotent people it occurs without fail. It is a sign of strong, rich temperaments that they cannot for long take seriously their enemies, their misfortunes, their misdeeds; for such characters have in them an excess of plastic curative power, and also a power of oblivion. (A good modern example of the latter is Mirabeau, who lacked all memory for insults and meannesses done him, and who was unable to forgive because he had forgotten.) Such a man simply shakes off vermin which would get beneath another's skin—and only here, if anywhere on earth, is it possible to speak of "loving one's enemy." The noble person will respect his enemy, and respect is already a bridge to love. . . . Indeed he requires his enemy for himself, as his mark of distinction, nor could he tolerate any other enemy than one in whom he finds nothing to despise and much to esteem. Imagine, on the other hand, the "enemy" as conceived by the rancorous man! For this is his true creative achievement: he has conceived the

"evil enemy," the Evil One, as a fundamental idea, and then as a pendant he has conceived a Good One—himself.

XI

The exact opposite is true of the noble-minded, who spontaneously creates the notion good, and later derives from it the conception of the bad. How ill-matched these two concepts look, placed side by side: the bad of noble origin, and the evil that has risen out of the cauldron of unquenched hatred! The first is a by-product, a complementary color, almost an afterthought; the second is the beginning, the original creative act of slave ethics. But neither is the conception of good the same in both cases, as we soon find out when we ask ourselves who it is that is really evil according to the code of rancor. The answer is: precisely the good one of the opposite code, that is the noble, the powerful—only colored, reinterpreted, re-envisaged by the poisonous eye of resentment. And we are the first to admit that anyone who knew these "good" ones only as enemies would find them evil enemies indeed. For these same men who, amongst themselves, are so strictly constrained by custom, worship, ritual, gratitude, and by mutual surveillance and jealousy, who are so resourceful in consideration, tenderness, loyalty, pride and friendship, when once they step outside their circle become little better than uncaged beasts of prey. Once abroad in the wilderness, they revel in the freedom from social constraint and compensate for their long confinement in the quietude of their own community. They revert to the innocence of wild animals: we can imagine them returning from an orgy of murder, arson, rape, and torture, jubilant and at peace with themselves as though they had committed a fraternity prank—convinced, moreover, that the poets for a long time to come will have something to sing about and to praise. Deep within all these noble races there lurks the beast of prey, bent on spoil and conquest. This hidden urge has to be satisfied from time to time, the beast let loose in

the wilderness. This goes as well for the Roman, Arabian, German, Japanese nobility as for the Homeric heroes and the Scandinavian vikings. The noble races have everywhere left in their wake the catchword "barbarian." And even their highest culture shows an awareness of this trait and a certain pride in it (as we see, for example, in Pericles' famous funeral oration, when he tells the Athenians: "Our boldness has gained us access to every land and sea, and erected monuments to itself *for both good and evil*"). This "boldness" of noble races, so headstrong, absurd, incalculable, sudden, improbable (Pericles commends the Athenians especially for their *rathumia*), their utter indifference to safety and comfort, their terrible pleasure in destruction, their taste for cruelty—all these traits are embodied by their victims in the image of the "barbarian," the "evil enemy," the Goth or the Vandal. The profound and icy suspicion which the German arouses as soon as he assumes power (we see it happening again today) harks back to the persistent horror with which Europe for many centuries witnessed the raging of the blond Teutonic beast (although all racial connection between the old Teutonic tribes and ourselves has been lost). I once drew attention to the embarrassment Hesiod must have felt when he tried to embody the cultural epochs of mankind in the gold, silver, and iron ages. He could cope with the contradictions inherent in Homer's world, so marvelous on the one hand, so ghastly and brutal on the other, only by making two ages out of one and presenting them in temporal sequence; first, the age of the heroes and demigods of Troy and Thebes, as that world was still remembered by the noble tribes who traced their ancestry to it; and second, the iron age, which presented the same world as seen by the descendants of those who had been crushed, despoiled, brutalized, sold into slavery. If it were true, as passes current nowadays, that the real meaning of culture resides in its power to domesticate man's savage instincts, then we might be justified in viewing all those rancorous machinations by which the noble tribes, and their ideals, have been laid low as the true instruments of culture. But this would still not amount to saying that the *organizers* themselves represent culture. Rather, the exact opposite would be true, as is vividly shown by the current state of affairs. These carriers of the leveling and retributive instincts, these descendants of every European and extra-European slavedom, and especially of the pre-Aryan populations, represent human retrogression most flagrantly. Such "instruments of culture" are a disgrace to man and might make one suspicious of culture altogether. One might be justified in fearing the wild beast lurking within all noble races and in being on one's guard against it, but who would not a thousand times prefer fear when it is accompanied with admiration to security accompanied by the loathsome sight of perversion, dwarfishness, degeneracy? And is not the latter our predicament today? What accounts for our repugnance to man—for there is no question that he makes us suffer? Certainly not our fear of him, rather the fact that there is no longer anything to be feared from him; that the vermin "man" occupies the entire stage; that, tame, hopelessly mediocre, and savorless, he considers himself the apex of historical evolution; and not entirely without justice, since he is still somewhat removed from the mass of sickly and effete creatures whom Europe is beginning to stink of today.

• • •

XVI

Let us conclude. The two sets of valuations, good/bad and good/evil, have waged a terrible battle on this earth, lasting many millennia; and just as surely as the second set has for a long time now been in the ascendant, so surely are there still places where the battle goes on and the issue remains in suspension. It might even be claimed that by being raised to a higher plane the battle has become much more profound. Perhaps there is today not a single intellectual

worth his salt who is not divided on that issue, a battleground for those opposites.

•   •   •

Second essay: "guilt," "bad conscience," and related matters

I

To breed an animal with the right to make promises—is not this the paradoxical problem nature has set itself with regard to man? and is it not man's true problem? That the problem has in fact been solved to a remarkable degree will seem all the more surprising if we do full justice to the strong opposing force, the faculty of oblivion. Oblivion is not merely a *vis inertiae*, as is often claimed, but an active screening device, responsible for the fact that what we experience and digest psychologically does not, in the stage of digestion, emerge into consciousness any more than what we ingest physically does. The role of this active oblivion is that of a concierge: to shut temporarily the doors and windows of consciousness; to protect us from the noise and agitation with which our lower organs work for or against one another; to introduce a little quiet into our consciousness so as to make room for the nobler functions and functionaries of our organism which do the governing and planning. This concierge maintains order and etiquette in the household of the psyche; which immediately suggests that there can be no happiness, no serenity, no hope, no pride, no *present*, without oblivion. A man in whom this screen is damaged and inoperative is like a dyspeptic (and not merely *like* one): he can't be done with anything. . . . Now this naturally forgetful animal, for whom oblivion represents a power, a form of strong health, has created for itself an opposite power, that of remembering, by whose aid, in certain cases, oblivion may be suspended—specifically in cases where it is a question of promises. By this I do not mean a purely passive succumbing to past impressions, the indigestion of being unable to be done with

a pledge once made, but rather an active not wishing to be done with it, a continuing to will what has once been willed, a veritable "memory of the will"; so that, between the original determination and the actual perform-ance of the thing willed, a whole world of new things, conditions, even volitional acts, can be interposed without snapping the long chain of the will. But how much all this pre-supposes! A man who wishes to dispose of his future in this manner must first have learned to separate necessary from accidental acts; to think causally; to see distant things as though they were near at hand; to distinguish means from ends. In short, he must have become not only calculating but himself calculable, regular even to his own perception, if he is to stand pledge for his own future as a guarantor does.

II

This brings us to the long story of the origin or genesis or responsibility. The task of breeding an animal entitled to make promises involves, as we have already seen, the preparatory task of rendering man up to a certain point regular, uniform, equal among equals, calculable. The tremendous achievement which I have referred to in *Daybreak* as "the custom character of morals," that labor man accomplished upon himself over a vast period of time, receives its meaning and justification here—even despite the brutality, tyranny, and stupidity associated with the process. With the help of custom and the social strait-jacket, man was, in fact, made calculable. However, if we place ourselves at the terminal point of this great process, where society and custom finally reveal their true aim, we shall find the ripest fruit of that tree to be the sovereign individual, equal only to himself, all moral custom left far behind. This autonomous, more than moral individual (the terms *autono-mous* and *moral* are mutually exclusive) has devel-oped his own, independent, long-range will, which dares to make promises; he has a proud

and vigorous consciousness of what he has achieved, a sense of power and freedom, of absolute accomplishment. This fully emancipated man, master of his will, who dares make promises—how should he not be aware of his superiority over those who are unable to stand security for themselves? Think how much trust, fear, reverence he inspires (all three fully *deserved*), and how, having that sovereign rule over himself, he has mastery too over all weaker-willed and less reliable creatures! Being truly free and possessor of a long-range, pertinacious will, he also possesses a scale of values. Viewing others from the center of his own being, he either honors or disdains them. It is natural to him to honor his strong and reliable peers, all those who promise like sovereigns: rarely and reluctantly; who are chary of their trust; whose trust is a mark of distinction; whose promises are binding because they know that they will make them good in spite of all accidents, in spite of destiny itself. Yet he will inevitably reserve a kick for those paltry windbags who promise irresponsibly and a rod for those liars who break their word even in uttering it. His proud awareness of the extraordinary privilege responsibility confers has penetrated deeply and become a dominant instinct. What shall he call that dominant instinct, provided he ever feels impelled to give it a name? Surely he will call it his *conscience*.

Bernard Williams

PERSONS, CHARACTER, AND MORALITY

I

MUCH OF the most interesting recent work in moral philosophy has been of basically Kantian inspiration; Rawls' own work[1] and those to varying degrees influenced by him such as Richards[2] and Nagel[3] are very evidently in the debt of Kant, while it is interesting that a writer such as Fried[4] who gives evident signs of being pulled away from some characteristic features of this way of looking at morality nevertheless, I shall suggest later, tends to get pulled back into it. This is not of course a very pure Kantianism; and still less is it an expository or subservient one. It differs from Kant among other things in making no demands on a theory of noumenal freedom, and also, importantly, in admitting considerations of a general empirical character in determining fundamental moral demands, which Kant at least supposed himself not to be doing. But allowing for those and many other important differences, the inspiration is there and the similarities both significant and acknowledged. They extend far beyond the evident point that both the extent and the nature of opposition to Utilitarianism resembles Kant's: though it is interesting that in this respect they are more Kantian than a philosophy which bears an obvious but superficial formal resemblance to Kantianism, namely Hare's. Indeed, Hare now supposes that when a substantial moral theory is elicited from his philosophical premises, it

turns out to be a version of Utilitarianism. This is not merely because the universal and prescriptive character of moral judgments lays on the agent, according to Hare, a requirement of hypothetical identification with each person affected by a given decision—so much is a purely Kantian element. It is rather that each identification is treated just as yielding 'acceptance' or 'rejection' of a certain prescription, and they in turn are construed solely in terms of satisfactions, so that the outputs of the various identifications can, under the usual Utilitarian assumptions, be regarded additively.

Among Kantian elements in these outlooks are, in particular, these: that the moral point of view is basically different from a non-moral, and in particular self-interested, point of view, and by a difference of kind; that the moral point of view is specially characterized by its impartiality and its indifference to any particular relations to particular persons, and that moral thought requires abstraction from particular circumstances and particular characteristics of the parties, including the agent, except in so far as these can be treated as universal features of any morally similar situation; and that the motivations of a moral agent, correspondingly, involve a rational application of impartial principle and are thus different in kind from the sorts of motivations that he might have for treating some particular persons (for instance, though not exclusively, himself) differently

because he happened to have some particular interest towards them. Of course, it is not intended that these demands should exclude other and more intimate relations nor prevent someone from acting in ways demanded by and appropriate to them: that is a matter of the relations of the moral point of view to other points of view. But I think it is fair to say that included among the similarities of these views to Kant's is the point that like his they do not make the question of the relations between those points of view at all easy to answer. The deeply disparate character of moral and of non-moral motivation, together with the special dignity or supremacy attached to the moral, make it very difficult to assign to those other relations and motivations the significance or structural importance in life which some of them are capable of processing.

It is worth remarking that this detachment of moral motivations and the moral point of view from the level of particular relations to particular persons, and more generally from the level of all motivations and perceptions other than those of an impartial character, obtains even when the moral point of view is itself explained in terms of the self-interest under conditions of ignorance of some abstractly conceived contracting parties, as it is by Rawls, and by Richards, who is particularly concerned with applying directly to the characterization of the moral interest, the structure used by Rawls chiefly to characterize social justice. For while the contracting parties are pictured as making some kind of self-interested or prudential choice of a set of rules, they are entirely abstract persons making this choice in ignorance of their own particular properties, tastes, and so forth; and the self-interested choice of an abstract agent is intended to model precisely the moral choice of a concrete agent, by representing what he would choose granted that he made just the kinds of abstraction from his actual personality, situation and relations which the Kantian picture of moral experience requires.

Some elements in this very general picture serve already to distinguish the outlook in question from Utilitarianism. Choices made in deliberate abstraction from empirical information which actually exists are necessarily from a Utilitarian point of view irrational, and to that extent the formal structure of the outlook, even allowing the admission of *general* empirical information, is counter-Utilitarian. There is a further point of difference with Utilitarianism, which comes out if one starts from the fact that there is one respect at least in which Utilitarianism itself requires a notable abstraction in moral thought, an abstraction which in this respect goes even further than the Kantians': if Kantianism abstracts in moral thought from the identity of persons, Utilitarianism strikingly abstracts from their separateness. This is true in more than one way. First, as the Kantian theories have themselves emphasized, persons lose their separateness as beneficiaries of the Utilitarian provisions, since in the form which maximizes total utility, and even in that which maximizes average utility, there is an agglomeration of satisfactions which is basically indifferent to the separateness of those who have the satisfactions; this is evidently so in the total maximization system, and it is only superficially not so in the average maximization system, where the agglomeration occurs before the division. Richards,[5] following Rawls, has suggested that the device of the ideal observer serves to model the agglomeration of these satisfactions: equivalent to the world could be one person, with an indefinite capacity for happiness and pain. The Kantian view stands opposed to this; the idea of the contractual element, even between these shadowy and abstract participants, is in part to make the point that there are limitations built in at the bottom to permissible trade-offs between the satisfactions of individuals.

A second aspect of the Utilitarian abstraction from separateness involves agency.[6] It turns on the point that the basic bearer of value for Utilitarianism is the *state of affairs*, and hence,

when the relevant causal differences have been allowed for, it cannot make any further difference who produces a given state of affairs: if S1 consists of my doing something, together with consequences, and S2 consists of someone else doing something, with consequences, and S2 comes about just in case S1 does not, and S1 is better than S2, then I should bring about S1, however *prima facie* nasty S1 is. Thus, unsurprisingly, the doctrine of negative responsibility has its roots at the foundation of Utilitarianism; and whatever projects, desires, ideals, or whatever I may have as a particular individual, as a Utilitarian agent my action has to be the output of *all* relevant causal items bearing on the situation, including all projects and desires within causal reach, my own and others'. As a Utilitarian agent, I am just the representative of the satisfaction system who happens to be near certain causal levers at a certain time. At this level, there is abstraction not merely from the identity of agents, but once more, from their separateness, since a conceivable extension or restriction of the causal powers of a given agent could always replace the activities of some other agent, so far as Utilitarian outcomes are concerned, and an outcome allocated to two agents as things are could equivalently be the product of one agent, or three, under a conceivable redistribution of causal powers.

In this latter respect also the Kantian outlook can be expected to disagree. For since we are concerned not just with outcomes, but at a basic level with actions and policies, *who* acts in a given situation makes a difference, and in particular I have a particular responsibility for *my* actions. Thus in more than one way the Kantian outlook emphasizes something like the separateness of agents, and in that sense makes less of an abstraction than Utilitarianism does (though, as we have seen, there are other respects, with regard to causally relevant empirical facts, in which its abstraction is greater). But now the question arises, of whether the honourable instincts of Kantianism to defend the individuality of individuals against the agglomerative indifference of Utilitarianism can in fact be effective granted the impoverished and abstract character of persons as moral agents which the Kantian view seems to impose. Findlay has said 'the separateness of persons . . . is . . . the basic fact for morals',[7] and Richards hopes to have respected that fact.[8] Similarly Rawls claims that impartiality does not mean impersonality.[9] But it is a real question, whether the conception of the individual provided by the Kantian theories is in fact enough to yield what is wanted, even by the Kantians; let alone enough for others who, while equally rejecting Utilitarianism, want to allow more room than Kantianism can allow for the importance of individual character and personal relations in moral experience.

II

I am going to take up two aspects of this large subject. They both involve the idea that an individual person has a set of desires, concerns or, as I shall often call them, projects, which help to constitute a *character*. The first issue concerns the connection between that fact and the man's having a reason for living at all. I approach this through a discussion of some work by Derek Parfit; though I touch on a variety of points in this, my overriding aim is to emphasize the basic importance for our thought of the ordinary idea of a self or person which undergoes changes of character, as opposed to an approach which, even if only metaphorically, would dissolve the person, under changes of character, into a series of 'selves'.

In this section I am concerned just with the point that each person has a character, not with the point that different people have different characters. That latter point comes more to the fore on the second issue, which I take up in part III, and which concerns personal relations. Both issues suggest that the Kantian view contains an important misrepresentation.

First, then, I should like to comment on some arguments of Parfit which explore connections between moral issues and a certain view of personal identity: a view which, he thinks, might offer, among other things, 'some defence'[10] of the Utilitarian neglect of the separateness of persons. This view Parfit calls the 'Complex View'. This view takes seriously the idea that relations of psychological connectedness (such as memory and persistence of character and motivation) are what really matter with regard to most questions which have been discussed in relation to personal identity. The suggestion is that morality should take this seriously as well, and that there is more than one way of its doing so. Psychological connectedness (unlike the surface logic of personal identity) admits of degrees. Let us call the relevant properties and relations which admit of degrees, *scalar* items. One of Parfit's aims is to make moral thought reflect more directly the scalar character of phenomena which underlie personal identity. In particular, in those cases in which the scalar relations hold in reduced degree, this fact should receive recognition in moral thought.

Another, and more general, consequence of taking the Complex View is that the matter of personal identity may appear altogether less deep, as Parfit puts it, than if one takes the Simple View, as he calls that alternative view which sees as basically significant the all-or-nothing logic of personal identity. If the master of personal identity appears less deep, the *separateness* of persons, also, may come to seem less an ultimate and specially significant consideration for morality. The connection between those two thoughts is not direct, but there is more than one indirect connection between them.[11]

So far as the problems of *agency* are concerned, Parfit's treatment is not going to help Utilitarianism. His loosening of identity is diachronic, by reference to the weakening of psychological connectedness over time: where there is such weakening to a sufficient degree, he is prepared to speak of 'successive selves', though this is intended only as a *façon de parler*.[12] But the problems that face Utilitarianism about agency can arise with any agent whose projects stretch over enough time, and are sufficiently grounded in character, to be in any substantial sense *his* projects, and that condition will be satisfied by something that is, for Parfit, even *one* self. Thus there is nothing in this degree of dissolution of the traditional self which can help over agency.

In discussing the issues involved in making moral thought reflect more directly the scalar nature of what underlies personal identity, it is important to keep in mind that the talk of 'past selves', 'future selves' and generally 'several selves' is only a convenient fiction. Neglect of this may make the transpositions in moral thought required by the Complex View seem simpler and perhaps more inviting than they are, since they may glide along on what seems to be a mere multiplication, in the case of these new 'selves', of familiar interpersonal relations. We must concentrate on the scalar facts. But many moral notions show a notable resistance to reflecting the scalar: or, rather, to reflecting it in the right way. We may take the case of promising, which Parfit has discussed.[13] Suppose that I promise to A that I will help him in certain ways in three years time. In three years time a person appears, let us say A*, whose memories, character etc., bear some, but a rather low, degree of connectedness to A's. How am I to mirror these scalar facts in my thought about whether, or how, I am to carry out my promise?

Something, first, should be said about the promise itself. 'You' was the expression it used: 'I will help you', and it used that expression in such a way that it covered both the recipient of these words and the potential recipient of the help. This was not a promise that could be carried out (or, more generally, honoured) by helping anyone else, or indeed by doing anything except helping that person I addressed when I said 'you'—thus the situation is not like that with

some promises to the dead (those where there is still something one can do about it).[14] If there is to be any action of mine which is to count as honouring the promise, it will have to be action which consists in now helping *A**. How am I to mirror, in my action and my thought about it, *A**'s scalar relations to *A*?

There seem to be only three ways in which they could be so mirrored, and none seems satisfactory. First, the action promised might itself have some significant scalar dimension, and it might be suggested that this should vary with my sense of the proximity or remoteness of *A** from *A*. But this will not do: it is clearly a lunatic idea that if I promised to pay *A* a sum of money, then my obligation is to pay *A** some money, but a smaller sum. A more serious suggestion would be that what varies with the degree of connectedness of *A** to *A* is the degree of stringency of the obligation to do what was promised. While less evidently dotty, it is still, on reflection, dotty; thus, to take a perhaps unfair example, it seems hard to believe that if someone had promised to marry *A*, they would have an obligation to marry *A**, only an obligation which came lower down the queue.

What, in contrast, is an entirely familiar sort of thought is, last of all, one that embodies degrees of doubt or obscurity whether a given obligation (of fixed stringency) applies or not. Thus a secret agent might think that he was obliged to kill the man in front of him if and only if that man was Martin Bormann; and be in doubt whether he should kill this man, because he was in doubt whether it was Bormann. (Contrast the two analogously dotty types of solution to this case: that, at any rate, he is obliged to wound him; or, that he is obliged to kill him, but it has a lower priority than it would have otherwise.) But this type of thought is familiar at the cost of not really embodying the scalar facts; it is a style of thought appropriate to uncertainty about a matter of all-or-nothing and so embodies in effect what Parfit calls the Simple View, that which does not take seriously the scalar facts to which the Complex View addresses itself.

These considerations do not, of course, show that there are no ways of mirroring the Complex View in these areas of moral thought, but they do suggest that the displacements required are fairly radical. It is significant that by far the easiest place to which to find the influence of the scalar considerations is in certain *sentiments*, which themselves have a scalar dimension— here we can see a place where the Complex View and Utilitarianism easily fit together. But the structure of such sentiments is not adequate to produce the structure of all moral thought. The rest of it will have to be more radically adapted, or abandoned, if the Complex View is really to have its effect.

One vitally important item which is in part (though only in part) scalar is a man's concern for (what commonsense would call) his own future. That a man should have some interest now in what he will do or undergo later, requires that he have some desires or projects or concerns now which relate to those doings or happenings later; or, as a special case of that, that some very general desire or project or concern of his now relate to desires or projects which he will have then. The limiting case, at the basic physical level, is that in which he is merely concerned with future pain, and it may be that that concern can properly reach through any degree of psychological disconti- nuity.[15] But even if so, it is not our present concern, since the mere desire to avoid physical pain is not adequate to constitute a character. We are here concerned with more distinctive and structured patterns of desire and project, and there are possible psychological changes in these which could be predicted for a person and which would put his future after such changes beyond his present interest. Such a future would be, so to speak, over the horizon of his interest, though of course if the future picture could be filled in as a *series* of changes

leading from here to there, he might recapture an interest in the outcome.

• • •

It might be wondered why, unless we believe in a possibly hostile after-life, or else are in a muddle which the Epicureans claimed to expose, we should regard death as an evil.[16] One answer to that is that we desire certain things: if one desires something, then to that extent one has reason to resist the happening of anything which prevents one getting it, and death certainly does that, for a large range of desires. Some desires are admittedly contingent on the prospect of one's being alive, but not all desires can be in that sense conditional, since it is possible to imagine a person rationally contemplating suicide, in the face of some predicted evil, and if he decides to go on in life, then he is propelled forward into it by some desire (however general or inchoate) which cannot operate conditionally on his being alive, since it settles the question of whether he is going to be alive. Such a desire we may call a categorical desire. Most people have many categorical desires, which do not depend on the assumption of the person's existence, since they serve to prevent that assumption's being questioned, or to answer the question if it is raised. Thus one's pattern of interests, desires and projects not only provide the reason for an interest in what happens within the horizon of one's future, but also constitute the conditions of there being such a future at all.

Here, once more, to deal in terms of later selves who were like descendants would be to misplace the heart of the problem. Whether to commit suicide, and whether to leave descendants, are two separate decisions: one can produce children before committing suicide. A person might even choose deliberately to do that, for comprehensible sorts of reasons; or again one could be deterred, as by the thought that one would not be there to look after them. Later selves, however, evade all these thoughts by having the strange property that while they

come into existence only with the death of their ancestor, the physical death of their ancestor will abort them entirely. The analogy seems unhelpfully strained, when we are forced to the conclusion that the failure of all my projects, and my consequent suicide, would take with me all my 'descendants', although they are in any case a kind of descendants who arise only with my ceasing to exist. More than unhelpfully, it runs together what are two quite different questions: whether my projects having failed, I should cease to exist, and whether I shall have descendants whose projects may be quite different from mine and are in any case largely unknown. The analogy makes every question of the first kind involve a question of the second kind, and thus obscures the peculiar significance of the first question to the theory of the self. If, on the other hand, a man's future self is not another self, but the future of his self, then it is unproblematic why it should be eliminated with the failure of that which might propel him into it. The primacy of one's ordinary self is given, once more, by the thought that it is precisely what will not be in the world if one commits suicide.

The language of 'later selves', too literally taken, could exaggerate in one direction the degree to which my relation to some of my own projects resembles my relation to the projects of others. The Kantian emphasis on moral impartiality exaggerates it in quite another, by providing ultimately too slim a sense in which any projects are mine at all. This point once more involves the idea that my present projects are the condition of my existence,[17] in the sense that unless I am propelled forward by the conatus of desire, project and interest, it is unclear why I should go on at all: the world, certainly, as a kingdom of moral agents, has no particular claim on my presence or, indeed, interest in it. (That kingdom, like others, has to respect the natural right to emigration.) Now the categorical desires which propel one on do not have to be even very evident to consciousness, let alone grand or large; one good testimony to one's existence

having a point is that the question of its point does not arise, and the propelling concerns may be of a relatively everyday kind such as certainly provide the ground of many sorts of happiness. Equally, while these projects may present some conflicts with the demands of morality, as Kantianly conceived, these conflicts may be fairly minor; after all—and I do not want to deny or forget it—these projects, in a normally socialized individual, have in good part been formed within, and formed by, dispositions which constitute a commitment to morality. But, on the other hand, the possibility of radical conflict is also there. A man may have, for a lot of his life or even just for some part of it, a *ground* project or set of projects which are closely related to his existence and which to a significant degree give a meaning to his life.

I do not mean by that they provide him with a life-plan, in Rawls' sense. On the contrary, Rawls' conception, and the conception of practical rationality, shared by Nagel, which goes with it, seems to me rather to imply an external view of one's own life, as something like a given rectangle that has to be optimally filled in.[18] This perspective omits the vital consideration already mentioned, that the continuation and size of this rectangle is up to me; so, slightly less drastically, is the question of how much of it I care to cultivate. The correct perspective on one's life is *from now*. The consequences of that for practical reasoning (particularly with regard to the relevance of proximity or remoteness in time of one's objective), is a large question which cannot be pursued here; here we need only the idea of a man's ground projects providing the motive force which propels him into the future, and gives him a reason for living.

For a project to play this ground role, it does not have to be true that if it were frustrated or in any of various ways he lost it, he would have to commit suicide, nor does he have to think that. Other things, or the mere hope of other things, may keep him going. But he may feel in those

circumstances that he might as well have died. Of course, in general a man does not have one separable project which plays this ground role: rather, there is a nexus of projects, related to his conditions of life, and it would be the loss of all or most of them that would remove meaning.

Ground projects do not have to be selfish, in the sense that they are just concerned with things for the agent. Nor do they have to be self-centred, in the sense that the creative projects of a Romantic artist could be considered self-centred (where it has to be him, but not for him). They may certainly be altruistic, and in a very evident sense moral, projects; thus he may be working for reform, or justice, or general improvement. There is no contradiction in the idea of a man's dying for a ground project— quite the reverse, since if death really is necessary for the project, then to live would be to live with it unsatisfied, something which, if it really is his ground project, he has no reason to do.

That a man's projects were altruistic or moral would not make them immune to conflict with impartial morality, any more than the artist's projects are immune. Admittedly *some* conflicts are ruled out by the projects sincerely being *those* projects; thus a man devoted to the cause of curing injustice in a certain place, cannot just insist on his plan for doing that over others', if convinced that theirs will be as effective as his (something it may be hard to convince him of). For if he does insist on that, then we learn that his concern is not merely that injustice be removed, but that *he* remove it—not necessarily a dishonourable concern, but a different one. Thus some conflicts are ruled out by the project being not self-centred. But not all conflicts: thus his selfless concern for justice may do havoc to quite other commitments.

A man who has such a ground project will be required by Utilitarianism to give up what it requires in a given case just if that conflicts with what he is required to do as an impersonal utility-maximizer when all the causally relevant considerations are in. That is a quite absurd

to actual and present sufferers over absent or future ones, he writes:[21]

> surely it would be absurd to insist that if a man could, at no risk or cost to himself, save one or two persons in equal peril, and one of those in peril was, say, his wife, he must treat both equally, perhaps by flipping a coin. One answer is that where the potential rescuer occupies no office such as that of captain of a ship, public health official or the like, the occurrence of the accident may itself stand as a sufficient randomizing event to meet the dictates of fairness, so he may prefer his friend, or loved one. Where the rescuer does occupy an official position, the argument that he must overlook personal ties is not unacceptable.

The most striking feature of this passage is the direction in which Fried implicitly places the onus of proof: the fact that coin-flipping would be inappropriate raises some question to which an 'answer' is required, while the resolution of the question by the rescuer's occupying an official position is met with what sounds like relief (though it remains unclear what that rescuer does when he 'overlooks personal ties'—does *he* flip a coin?). The thought here seems to be that it is unfair to the second victim that, the first being the rescuer's wife, they never even get a chance of being rescued; and the answer (as I read the reference to the 'sufficient randomizing event') is that at another level it is sufficiently fair—although in this disaster this rescuer has a special reason for saving the other person, it might have been another disaster in which another rescuer had a special reason for saving them. But, apart from anything else, that 'might have been' is far too slim to sustain a reintroduction of the notion of fairness. The 'random' element in such events, as in certain events of tragedy, should be seen not so much as affording a justification, in terms of an appropriate application of a lottery, as

being a reminder that some situations lie beyond justifications.

But has anything yet shown that? For even if we leave behind thoughts of higher-order randomization, surely *this* is a justification on behalf of the rescuer, that the person he chose to rescue was his wife? It depends on how much weight is carried by 'justification': the consideration that it was his wife is certainly, for instance, an explanation which should silence comment. But something more ambitious than this is usually intended, essentially involving the idea that moral principle can legitimate his preference, yielding the conclusion that in situations of this kind it is at least all right (morally permissible) to save one's wife. (This could be combined with a variety of higher-order thoughts to give it a rationale: rule-Utilitarians might favour the idea that in matters of this kind it is best for each to look after his own, like house insurance.) But this construction provides the agent with one thought too many: it might have been hoped by some (for instance, by his wife) that his motivating thought, fully spelled out, would be the thought that it was his wife, not that it was his wife and that in situations of this kind it is permissible to save one's wife.

Perhaps others will have other feelings about this case. But the point is that somewhere (and if not in this case, where?) one reaches the necessity that such things as deep attachments to other persons will express themselves in the world in ways which cannot at the same time embody the impartial view, and that they also run the risk of offending against it.

They run that risk if they exist at all; yet unless such things exist, there will not be enough substance or conviction in a man's life to compel his allegiance to life itself. Life has to have substance if anything is to have sense, including adherence to the impartial system; but if it has substance, then it cannot grant supreme importance to the impartial system, and that system's hold on it will be, at the limit, insecure.

It follows that moral philosophy's habit, particularly in its Kantian forms, of treating persons in abstraction from character is not so much a legitimate device for dealing with one aspect of thought, but is rather a misrepresentation, since it leaves out what both limits and helps to define that aspect of thought. Nor can it be judged solely as a theoretical device: this is one of the areas in which one's conception of the self, and of oneself, most importantly meet.

Notes

1 John Rawls, *A Theory of Justice* (Oxford, 1972).

2 D. A. J. Richards, *A Theory of Reasons for Action* (Oxford, 1971).

3 Thomas Nagel, *The Possibility of Altruism* (Oxford, 1970).

4 Charles Fried, *An Anatomy of Values* (Cambridge, MA, 1970).

5 Richards, op. cit., p. 87 al; cf. Rawls, op. cit., p. 27; also Nagel, op. cit., p. 134. This is not the only, nor perhaps historically the soundest, interpretation of the device: cf. Derek Parfit, 'Later Selves and Moral Principles', in A. Montefiore, ed., *Philosophy and Personal Relations* (London, 1973), pp. 149–50 and nn. 30–34.

6 For a more detailed account, see 'A Critique of Utilitarianism', in J. J. C. Smart and B. Williams, *Utilitarianism: For and Against* (Cambridge, 1973).

7 Findlay, *Values and Intentions* (London, 1961), pp. 235–36.

8 Richards, op. cit., p. 87.

9 Rawls, op. cit., p. 190.

10 Parfit, op. cit., p. 160, his emphasis. In what follows and elsewhere in this chapter I am grateful to Parfit for valuable criticisms of an earlier draft.

11 Parfit develops one such connection in the matter of distributive justice: pp. 148ff. In general it can be said that one very natural correlate of being impressed by the separateness of several persons' lives is being impressed by the particular unity of one person's life.

12 Ibid., n. 14, pp. 161–62.

13 Ibid., pp. 144ff.

14 Ibid., p. 144 fin.

15 Cf. 'The Self and the Future', in *Problems of the Self* (Cambridge, 1973).

16 The argument is developed in more detail in *Problems of the Self*, pp. 82 ff.

17 We can note the consequence that present projects are the condition of future ones. This view stands in opposition to Nagel's: as do the formulations used above, [see original reading, p. 10]. But while, as Nagel says, taking a rational interest in preparing for the realization of my later projects does not require that they be my present projects, it seems nevertheless true that it presupposes my having some present projects which directly or indirectly reach out to a time when those later projects will be my projects.

18 It is of course a separate question what the criteria of optimality are, but it is not surprising that a view which presupposes that no risks are taken with the useful area of the rectangle should also favour a very low risk strategy in filling it: cf. Rawls (on prudential rationality in general), op. cit., p. 422: 'we have the guiding principle that a rational individual is always to act so that he need never blame himself no matter how things finally transpire.' Cf. also the passages cited in Rawls' footnote . . . .

19 Cf. 'A Critique of Utilitarianism', sections 3–5.

20 Richards, op. cit, p. 94.

21 Fried, op. cit., p. 227 [Note 1981]. Fried has perhaps now modified the view criticized here. He has himself used the idea of friendship as creating special moral relations, but in a connexion where, it seems to me, it is out of place. . . .

Chapter 42

Susan Wolf

MORAL SAINTS

I DON'T KNOW whether there are any moral saints. But if there are, I am glad that neither I nor those about whom I care most are among them. By *moral saint* I mean a person whose every action is as morally good as possible, a person, that is, who is as morally worthy as can be. Though I shall in a moment acknowledge the variety of types of person that might be thought to satisfy this description, it seems to me that none of these types serve as unequivocally compelling personal ideals. In other words, I believe that moral perfection, in the sense of moral saintliness, does not constitute a model of personal well-being toward which it would be particularly rational or good or desirable for a human being to strive.

Outside the context of moral discussion, this will strike many as an obvious point. But, within that context, the point, if it be granted, will be granted with some discomfort. For within that context it is generally assumed that one ought to be as morally good as possible and that what limits there are to morality's hold on us are set by features of human nature of which we ought not to be proud. If, as I believe, the ideals that are derivable from common sense and philosophically popular moral theories do not support these assumptions, then something has to change. Either we must change our moral theories in ways that will make them yield more palatable ideals, or, as I shall argue, we must change our conception of what is involved in affirming a moral theory.

In this paper, I wish to examine the notion of a moral saint, first, to understand what a moral saint would be like and why such a being would be unattractive, and second, to raise some questions about the significance of this paradoxical figure for moral philosophy. I shall look first at the model(s) of moral sainthood that might be extrapolated from the morality or moralities of common sense. Then I shall consider what relations these have to conclusions that can be drawn from utilitarian and Kantian moral theories. Finally, I shall speculate on the implications of these considerations for moral philosophy.

Moral saints and common sense

Consider first what, pretheoretically, would count for us—contemporary members of Western culture—as a moral saint. A necessary condition of moral sainthood would be that one's life be dominated by a commitment to improving the welfare of others or of society as a whole. As to what role this commitment must play in the individual's motivational system, two contrasting accounts suggest themselves to me which might equally be thought to qualify a person for moral sainthood.

First, a moral saint might be someone whose concern for others plays the role that is played in most of our lives by more selfish, or, at any rate, less morally worthy concerns. For the moral saint, the promotion of the welfare of others

might play the role that is played for most of us by the enjoyment of material comforts, the opportunity to engage in the intellectual and physical activities of our choice, and the love, respect, and companionship of people whom we love, respect, and enjoy. The happiness of the moral saint, then, would truly lie in the happiness of others, and so he would devote himself to others gladly, and with a whole and open heart.

On the other hand, a moral saint might be someone for whom the basic ingredients of happiness are not unlike those of most of the rest of us. What makes him a moral saint is rather that he pays little or no attention to his own happiness in light of the overriding importance he gives to the wider concerns of morality. In other words, this person sacrifices his own interests to the interests of others, and feels the sacrifice as such.

Roughly, these two models may be distinguished according to whether one thinks of the moral saint as being a saint out of love or one thinks of the moral saint as being a saint out of duty (or some other intellectual appreciation and recognition of moral principles). We may refer to the first model as the model of the Loving Saint; to the second, as the model of the Rational Saint.

The two models differ considerably with respect to the qualities of the motives of the individuals who conform to them. But this difference would have limited effect on the saints' respective public personalities. The shared content of what these individuals are motivated to be—namely, as morally good as possible—would play the dominant role in the determination of their characters. Of course, just as a variety of large-scale projects, from tending the sick to political campaigning, may be equally and maximally morally worthy, so a variety of characters are compatible with the ideal of moral sainthood. One moral saint may be more or less jovial, more or less garrulous, more or less athletic than another. But above all, a moral

saint must have and cultivate those qualities which are apt to allow him to treat others as justly and kindly as possible. He will have the standard moral virtues to a nonstandard degree. He will be patient, considerate, even-tempered, hospitable, charitable in thought as well as in deed. He will be very reluctant to make negative judgments of other people. He will be careful not to favor some people over others on the basis of properties they could not help but have.

Perhaps what I have already said is enough to make some people begin to regard the absence of moral saints in their lives as a blessing. For there comes a point in the listing of virtues that a moral saint is likely to have where one might naturally begin to wonder whether the moral saint isn't, after all, too good—if not too good for his own good, at least too good for his own well-being. For the moral virtues, given that they are, by hypothesis, *all* present in the same individual, and to an extreme degree, are apt to crowd out the nonmoral virtues, as well as many of the interests and personal characteristics that we generally think contribute to a healthy, well-rounded, richly developed character.

In other words, if the moral saint is devoting all his time to feeding the hungry or healing the sick or raising money for Oxfam, then necessarily he is not reading Victorian novels, playing the oboe, or improving his backhand. Although no one of the interests or tastes in the category containing these latter activities could be claimed to be a necessary element in a life well lived, a life in which *none* of these possible aspects of character are developed may seem to be a life strangely barren.

The reasons why a moral saint cannot, in general, encourage the discovery and development of significant nonmoral interests and skills are not logical but practical reasons. There are, in addition, a class of nonmoral characteristics that a moral saint cannot encourage in himself for reasons that are not just practical. There is a more

substantial tension between having any of these qualities unashamedly and being a moral saint. These qualities might be described as going against the moral grain. For example, a cynical or sarcastic wit, or a sense of humor that appreciates this kind of wit in others, requires that one take an attitude of resignation and pessimism toward the flaws and vices to be found in the world. A moral saint, on the other hand, has reason to take an attitude in opposition to this— he should try to look for the best in people, give them the benefit of the doubt as long as possible, try to improve regrettable situations as long as there is any hope of success. This suggests that, although a moral saint might well enjoy a good episode of *Father Knows Best*, he may not in good conscience be able to laugh at a Marx Brothers movie or enjoy a play by George Bernard Shaw.

An interest in something like gourmet cooking will be, for different reasons, difficult for a moral saint to rest easy with. For it seems to me that no plausible argument can justify the use of human resources involved in producing a *pâté de canard en croute* against possible alternative beneficent ends to which these resources might be put. If there is a justification for the institution of haute cuisine, it is one which rests on the decision not to justify every activity against morally beneficial alternatives, and this is a decision a moral saint will never make. Presumably, an interest in high fashion or interior design will face much the same, as will, very possibly, a cultivation of the finer arts as well.

A moral saint will have to be very, very nice. It is important that he may not be offensive. The worry is that, as a result, he will have to be dull-witted or humorless or bland.

This worry is confirmed when we consider what sorts of characters, taken and refined both from life and from fiction, typically form our ideals. One would hope they would be figures who are morally good—and by this I mean more than just not morally bad—but one would hope, too, that they are not just morally good, but talented or accomplished or attractive in

nonmoral ways as well. We may make ideals out of athletes, scholars, artists—more frivolously, out of cowboys, private eyes, and rock stars. We may strive for Katharine Hepburn's grace, Paul Newman's "cool"; we are attracted to the high-spirited passionate nature of Natasha Rostov; we admire the keen perceptiveness of Lambert Strether. Though there is certainly nothing immoral about the ideal characters or traits I have in mind, they cannot be superimposed upon the ideal of a moral saint. For although it is a part of many of these ideals that the characters set high, and not merely acceptable, moral standards for themselves, it is also essential to their power and attractiveness that the moral strengths go, so to speak, alongside of specific independently admirable, non-moral ground projects and dominant personal traits.

When one does finally turn one's eyes toward lives that are dominated by explicitly moral commitments, moreover, one finds oneself relieved at the discovery of idiosyncrasies or eccentricities not quite in line with the picture of moral perfection. One prefers the blunt, tactless, and opinionated Betsy Trotwood to the unfailingly kind and patient Agnes Copperfield; one prefers the mischievousness and the sense of irony in Chesterton's Father Brown to the innocence and undiscriminating love of St. Francis.

It seems that, as we look in our ideals for people who achieve nonmoral varieties of personal excellence in conjunction with or colored by some version of high moral tone, we look in our paragons of moral excellence for people whose moral achievements occur in conjunction with or colored by some interests or traits that have low moral tone. In other words, there seems to be a limit on how much morality we can stand.

One might suspect that the essence of the problem is simply that there is a limit to how much of *any* single value, or any single type of value, we can stand. Our objection then would not be specific to a life in which one's dominant

concern is morality, but would apply to any life that can be so completely characterized by an extraordinarily dominant concern. The objection in that case would reduce to the recognition that such a life is incompatible with well-roundedness. If that were the objection, one could fairly reply that well-roundedness is no more supreme a virtue than the totality of moral virtues embodied by the ideal it is being used to criticize. But I think this misidentifies the objection. For the way in which a concern for morality may dominate a life, or, more to the point, the way in which it may dominate an ideal of life, is not easily imagined by analogy to the dominance an aspiration to become an Olympic swimmer or a concert pianist might have.

A person who is passionately committed to one of these latter concerns might decide that her attachment to it is strong enough to be worth the sacrifice of her ability to maintain and pursue a significant portion of what else life might offer which a proper devotion of her dominant passion would require. But a desire to be as morally good as possible is not likely to take the form of one desire among others which, because of its peculiar psychological strength, requires one to forgo the pursuit of other weaker and separately less demanding desires. Rather, the desire to be as morally good as possible is apt to have the character not just of a stronger, but of a higher desire, which does not merely successfully compete with one's other desires but which rather subsumes or demotes them. The sacrifice of other interests for the interest in morality, then, will have the character, not of a choice, but of an imperative.

Moreover, there is something odd about the idea of morality itself, or moral goodness, serving as the object of a dominant passion in the way that a more concrete and specific vision of a goal (even a concrete *moral* goal) might be imagined to serve. Morality itself does not seem to be a suitable object of passion. Thus, when one reflects, for example, on the Loving Saint easily and gladly giving up his fishing trip or his stereo or his hot fudge sundae at the drop of the moral hat, one is apt to wonder not at how much he loves morality, but at how little he loves these other things. One thinks that, if he can give these up so easily, he does not know what it is to truly love them. There seems, in other words, to be a kind of joy which the Loving Saint, either by nature or by practice, is incapable of experiencing. The Rational Saint, on the other hand, might retain strong nonmoral and concrete desires—he simply denies himself the opportunity to act on them. But this is no less troubling. The Loving Saint one might suspect of missing a piece of perceptual machinery, of being blind to some of what the world has to offer. The Rational Saint, who sees it but forgoes it, one suspects of having a different problem—a pathological fear of damnation, perhaps, or an extreme form of self-hatred that interferes with his ability to enjoy the enjoyable in life.

In other words, the ideal of a life of moral sainthood disturbs not simply because it is an ideal of a life in which morality unduly dominates. The normal person's direct and specific desires for objects, activities, and events that conflict with the attainment of moral perfection are not simply sacrificed but removed, suppressed, or subsumed. The way in which morality, unlike other possible goals, is apt to dominate is particularly disturbing, for it seems to require either the lack or the denial of the existence of an identifiable, personal self.

This distinctively troubling feature is not, I think, absolutely unique to the ideal of the moral saint, as I have been using that phrase. It is shared by the conception of the pure aesthete, by a certain kind of religious ideal, and, somewhat paradoxically, by the model of the thorough-going self-conscious egoist. It is not a coincidence that the ways of comprehending the world of which these ideals are the extreme embodiments are sometimes described as "moralities" themselves. At any rate, they compete with what we ordinarily mean by

'morality'. Nor is it a coincidence that these ideals are naturally described as fanatical. But it is easy to see that these other types of perfection cannot serve as satisfactory personal ideals; for the realization of these ideals would be straightforwardly immoral. It may come as a surprise to some that there may in addition be such a thing as a *moral* fanatic.

Some will object that I am being unfair to "common-sense morality"—that it does not really require a moral saint to be either a disgusting goody-goody or an obsessive ascetic. Admittedly, there is no logical inconsistency between having any of the personal characteristics I have mentioned and being a moral saint. It is not morally wrong to notice the faults and shortcomings of others or to recognize and appreciate nonmoral talents and skills. Nor is it immoral to be an avid Celtic fan or to have a passion for caviar or to be an excellent cellist. With enough imagination, we can always contrive a suitable history and set of circumstances that will embrace such characteristics in one or another specific fictional story of a perfect moral saint.

If one turned onto the path of moral sainthood relatively late in life, one may have already developed interests that can be turned to moral purposes. It may be that a good golf game is just what is needed to secure that big donation to Oxfam. Perhaps the cultivation of one's exceptional artistic talent will turn out to be the way one can make one's greatest contribution to society. Furthermore, one might stumble upon joys and skills in the very service of morality. If, because the children are short a ninth player for the team, one's generous offer to serve reveals a natural fielding arm or if one's part in the campaign against nuclear power requires accepting a lobbyist's invitation to lunch at Le Lion d'Or, there is no moral gain in denying the satisfaction one gets from these activities. The moral saint, then, may, by happy accident, find himself with nonmoral virtues on which he can capitalize morally or which make psychological

demands to which he has no choice but to attend. The point is that, for a moral saint, the existence of these interests and skills can be given at best the status of happy accidents—they cannot be encouraged for their own sakes as distinct, independent aspects of the realization of human good.

It must be remembered that from the fact that there is a tension between having any of these qualities and being a moral saint it does not follow that having any of these qualities is immoral. For it is not part of common-sense morality that one ought to be a moral saint. Still, if someone just happened to want to be a moral saint, he or she would not have or encourage these qualities, and, on the basis of our common-sense values, this counts as a reason *not* to want to be a moral saint.

One might still wonder what kind of reason this is, and what kind of conclusion this properly allows us to draw. For the fact that the models of moral saints are unattractive does not necessarily mean that they are unsuitable ideals. Perhaps they are unattractive because they make us feel uncomfortable—they highlight our own weaknesses, vices, and flaws. If so, the fault lies not in the characters of the saints, but in those of our unsaintly selves.

To be sure, some of the reasons behind the disaffection we feel for the model of moral sainthood have to do with a reluctance to criticize ourselves and a reluctance to committing ourselves to trying to give up activities and interests that we heartily enjoy. These considerations might provide an *excuse* for the fact that we are not moral saints, but they do not provide a basis for criticizing sainthood as a possible ideal. Since these considerations rely on an appeal to the egoistic, hedonistic side of our natures, to use them as a basis for criticizing the ideal of the moral saint would be at best to beg the question and at worst to glorify features of ourselves that ought to be condemned.

The fact that the moral saint would be without qualities which we have and which,

indeed, we like to have, does not in itself provide reason to condemn the ideal of the moral saint. The fact that some of these qualities are good qualities, however, and that they are qualities we *ought* to like, does provide reason to discourage this ideal and to offer other ideals in its place. In other words, some of the qualities the moral saint necessarily lacks are virtues, albeit nonmoral virtues, in the unsaintly characters who have them. The feats of Groucho Marx, Reggie Jackson, and the head chef at *Lutèce* are impressive accomplishments that it is not only permissible but positively appropriate to recognize as such. In general, the admiration of and striving toward achieving any of a great variety of forms of personal excellence are character traits it is valuable and desirable for people to have. In advocating the development of these varieties of excellence, we advocate nonmoral reasons for acting, and in thinking that it is good for a person to strive for an ideal that gives a substantial role to the interests and values that correspond to these virtues, we implicitly acknowledge the goodness of ideals incompatible with that of the moral saint. Finally, if we think that it is *as* good, or even better for a person to strive for one of these ideals than it is for him or her to strive for and realize the ideal of the moral saint, we express a conviction that it is good not to be a moral saint.

Moral saints and moral theories

I have tried so far to paint a picture—or rather, two pictures—of what a moral saint might be like, drawing on what I take to be the attitudes and beliefs about morality prevalent in contemporary, common-sense thought. To my suggestion that common-sense morality generates conceptions of moral saints that are unattractive or otherwise unacceptable, it is open to someone to reply, "so much the worse for common-sense morality." After all, it is often claimed that the goal of moral philosophy is to correct and improve upon common-sense morality, and I

have as yet given no attention to the question of what conceptions of moral sainthood, if any, are generated from the leading moral theories of our time.

A quick, breezy reading of utilitarian and Kantian writings will suggest the images, respectively, of the Loving Saint and the Rational Saint. A utilitarian, with his emphasis on happiness, will certainly prefer the Loving Saint to the Rational one, since the Loving Saint will himself be a happier person than the Rational Saint. A Kantian, with his emphasis on reason, on the other hand, will find at least as much to praise in the latter as in the former. Still, both models, drawn as they are from common sense, appeal to an impure mixture of utilitarian and Kantian intuitions. A more careful examination of these moral theories raises questions about whether either model of moral sainthood would really be advocated by a believer in the explicit doctrines associated with either of these views.

Certainly, the utilitarian in no way denies the value of self-realization. He in no way disparages the development of interests, talents, and other personally attractive traits that I have claimed the moral saint would be without. Indeed, since just these features enhance the happiness both of the individuals who possess them and of those with whom they associate, the ability to promote these features both in oneself and in others will have considerable positive weight in utilitarian calculations.

This implies that the utilitarian would not support moral sainthood as a universal ideal. A world in which everyone, or even a large number of people, achieved moral sainthood—even a world in which they *strove* to achieve it—would probably contain less happiness than a world in which people realized a diversity of ideals involving a variety of personal and perfectionist values. More pragmatic considerations also suggest that, if the utilitarian wants to influence more people to achieve more good, then he would do better to encourage them to pursue happiness-producing goals that are more

attractive and more within a normal person's reach.

These considerations still leave open, however, the question of what kind of an ideal the committed utilitarian should privately aspire to himself. Utilitarianism requires him to want to achieve the greatest general happiness, and this would seem to commit him to the ideal of the moral saint.

One might try to use the claims I made earlier as a basis for an argument that a utilitarian should choose to give up utilitarianism. If, as I have said, a moral saint would be a less happy person both to be and to be around than many other possible ideals, perhaps one could create more total happiness by not trying too hard to promote the total happiness. But this argument is simply unconvincing in light of the empirical circumstances of our world. The gain in happiness that would accrue to oneself and one's neighbors by a more well-rounded, richer life than that of the moral saint would be pathetically small in comparison to the amount by which one could increase the general happiness if one devoted oneself explicitly to the care of the sick, the downtrodden, the starving, and the homeless. Of course, there may be psychological limits to the extent to which a person can devote himself to such things without going crazy. But the utilitarian's individual limitations would not thereby become a positive feature of his personal ideals.

The unattractiveness of the moral saint, then, ought not rationally convince the utilitarian to abandon his utilitarianism. It may, however, convince him to take efforts not to wear his saintly moral aspirations on his sleeve. If it is not too difficult, the utilitarian will try not to make those around him uncomfortable. He will not want to appear "holier than thou"; he will not want to inhibit others' ability to enjoy themselves. In practice, this might make the perfect utilitarian a less nauseating companion than the moral saint I earlier portrayed. But insofar as this kind of reasoning produces a more bearable public personality, it is at the cost of giving him a personality that must be evaluated as hypocritical and condescending when his private thoughts and attitudes are taken into account.

Still, the criticisms I have raised against the saint of common-sense morality should make some difference to the utilitarian's conception of an ideal which neither requires him to abandon his utilitarian principles nor forces him to fake an interest he does not have or a judgment he does not make. For it may be that a limited and carefully monitored allotment of time and energy to be devoted to the pursuit of some nonmoral interests or to the development of some nonmoral talents would make a person a better contributor to the general welfare than he would be if he allowed himself no indulgences of this sort. The enjoyment of such activities in no way compromises a commitment to utilitarian principles as long as the involvement with these activities is conditioned by a willingness to give them up whenever it is recognized that they cease to be in the general interest.

This will go some way in mitigating the picture of the loving saint that an understanding of utilitarianism will on first impression suggest. But I think it will not go very far. For the limitations on time and energy will have to be rather severe, and the need to monitor will restrict not only the extent but also the quality of one's attachment to these interests and traits. They are only weak and somewhat peculiar sorts of passions to which one can consciously remain so conditionally committed. Moreover, the way in which the utilitarian can enjoy these "extra-curricular" aspects of his life is simply not the way in which these aspects are to be enjoyed insofar as they figure into our less saintly ideals.

The problem is not exactly that the utilitarian values these aspects of his life only as a means to an end, for the enjoyment he and others get from these aspects are not a means to, but a part of, the general happiness. Nonetheless, he values these things only because of and insofar as they

are a part of the general happiness. He values them, as it were, under the description 'a contribution to the general happiness'. This is to be contrasted with the various ways in which these aspects of life may be valued by nonutilitarians. A person might love literature because of the insights into human nature literature affords. Another might love the cultivation of roses because roses are things of great beauty and delicacy. It may be true that these features of the respective activities also explain why these activities are happiness-producing. But, to the nonutilitarian, this may not be to the point. For if one values these activities in these more direct ways, one may not be willing to exchange them for others that produce an equal, or even a greater amount of happiness. From that point of view, it is not because they produce happiness that these activities are valuable; it is because these activities are valuable in more direct and specific ways that they produce happiness.

To adopt a phrase of Bernard Williams', the utilitarian's manner of valuing the not explicitly moral aspects of his life "provides (him) with one thought too many".[1] The requirement that the utilitarian have this thought—periodically, at least—is indicative of not only a weakness but a shallowness in his appreciation of the aspects in question. Thus, the ideals toward which a utilitarian could acceptably strive would remain too close to the model of the common-sense moral saint to escape the criticisms of that model which I earlier suggested. Whether a Kantian would be similarly committed to so restrictive and unattractive a range of possible ideals is a somewhat more difficult question.

The Kantian believes that being morally worthy consists in always acting from maxims that one could will to be universal law, and doing this not out of any pathological desire but out of reverence for the moral law as such. Or, to take a different formulation of the categorical imperative, the Kantian believes that moral action consists in treating other persons always as ends and never as means only. Presumably,

and according to Kant himself, the Kantian thereby commits himself to some degree of benevolence as well as to the rules of fair play. But we surely would not will that *every* person become a moral saint, and treating others as ends hardly requires bending over backwards to protect and promote their interests. On one interpretation of Kantian doctrine, then, moral perfection would be achieved simply by unerring obedience to a limited set of side-constraints. On this interpretation, Kantian theory simply does not yield an ideal conception of a person of any fullness comparable to that of the moral saints I have so far been portraying.

On the other hand, Kant does say explicitly that we have a duty of benevolence, a duty not only to allow others to pursue their ends, but to take up their ends as our own. In addition, we have positive duties to ourselves, duties to increase our natural as well as our moral perfection. These duties are unlimited in the degree to which they *may* dominate a life. If action in accordance with and motivated by the thought of these duties is considered virtuous, it is natural to assume that the more one performs such actions, the more virtuous one is. Moreover, of virtue in general Kant says, "it is an ideal which is unattainable while yet our duty is constantly to approximate to it".[2] On this interpretation, then, the Kantian moral saint, like the other moral saints I have been considering, is dominated by the motivation to be moral.

Which of these interpretations of Kant one prefers will depend on the interpretation and the importance one gives to the role of the imperfect duties in Kant's over-all system. Rather than choose between them here, I shall consider each briefly in turn.

On the second interpretation of Kant, the Kantian moral saint is, not surprisingly, subject to many of the same objections I have been raising against other versions of moral sainthood. Though the Kantian saint may differ from the utilitarian saint as to *which* actions he is

bound to perform and which he is bound to refrain from performing, I suspect that the range of activities acceptable to the Kantian saint will remain objectionably restrictive. Moreover, the manner in which the Kantian saint must think about and justify the activities he pursues and the character traits he develops will strike us, as it did with the utilitarian saint, as containing "one thought too many." As the utilitarian could value his activities and character traits only insofar as they fell under the description of 'contributions to the general happiness', the Kantian would have to value his activities and character traits insofar as they were manifestations of respect for the moral law. If the development of our powers to achieve physical, intellectual, or artistic excellence, or the activities directed toward making others happy are to have any moral worth, they must arise from a reverence for the dignity that members of our species have as a result of being endowed with pure practical reason. This is a good and noble motivation, to be sure. But it is hardly what one expects to be dominantly behind a person's aspirations to dance as well as Fred Astaire, to paint as well as Picasso, or to solve some outstanding problem in abstract algebra, and it is hardly what one hopes to find lying dominantly behind a father's action on behalf of his son or a lover's on behalf of her beloved.

Since the basic problem with any of the models of moral sainthood we have been considering is that they are dominated by a single, all-important value under which all other possible values must be subsumed, it may seem that the alternative interpretation of Kant, as providing a stringent but finite set of obligations and constraints, might provide a more acceptable morality. According to this interpretation of Kant, one is as morally good as can be so long as one devotes some limited portion of one's energies toward altruism and the maintenance of one's physical and spiritual health, and otherwise pursues one's independently motivated interests and values in such a way as to avoid overstepping certain bounds. Certainly, if it be a requirement of an acceptable moral theory that perfect obedience to its laws and maximal devotion to its interests and concerns be something we can wholeheartedly strive for in ourselves and wish for in those around us, it will count in favor of this brand of Kantianism that its commands can be fulfilled without swallowing up the perfect moral agent's entire personality.

Even this more limited understanding of morality, if its connection to Kant's views is to be taken at all seriously, is not likely to give an unqualified seal of approval to the nonmorally directed ideals I have been advocating. For Kant is explicit about what he calls "duties of apathy and self-mastery" (69/70)—duties to ensure that our passions are never so strong as to interfere with calm, practical deliberation, or so deep as to wrest control from the more disinterested, rational part of ourselves. The tight and self-conscious rein we are thus obliged to keep on our commitments to specific individuals and causes will doubtless restrict our value in these things, assigning them a necessarily attenuated place.

A more interesting objection to this brand of Kantianism, however, comes when we consider the implications of placing the kind of upper bound on moral worthiness which seemed to count in favor of this conception of morality. For to put such a limit on one's capacity to be moral is effectively to deny, not just the moral necessity, but the moral goodness of a devotion to benevolence and the maintenance of justice that passes beyond a certain, required point. It is to deny the possibility of going morally above and beyond the call of a restricted set of duties. Despite my claim that all-consuming moral saintliness is not a particularly healthy and desirable ideal, it seems perverse to insist that, were moral saints to exist, they would not, in their way, be remarkably noble and admirable figures. Despite my conviction that it is as rational and as good for a person to take Katharine Hepburn or Jane Austen as her role model instead of Mother

Teresa, it would be absurd to deny that Mother Teresa is a morally better person.

I can think of two ways of viewing morality as having an upper bound. First, we can think that altruism and impartiality are indeed positive moral interests, but that they are moral only if the degree to which these interests are actively pursued remains within certain fixed limits. Second, we can think that these positive interests are only incidentally related to morality and that the essence of morality lies elsewhere, in, say, an implicit social contract or in the recognition of our own dignified rationality. According to the first conception of morality, there is a cut-off line to the amount of altruism or to the extent of devotion to justice and fairness that is worthy of moral praise. But to draw this line earlier than the line that brings the altruist in question to a worse-off position than all those to whom he devotes himself seems unacceptably artificial and gratuitous. According to the second conception, these positive interests are not essentially related to morality at all. But then we are unable to regard a more affectionate and generous expression of good will toward others as a natural and reasonable extension of morality, and we encourage a cold and unduly self-centered approach to the development and evaluation of our motivations and concerns.

A moral theory that does not contain the seeds of an all-consuming ideal of moral sainthood thus seems to place false and unnatural limits on our opportunity to do moral good and our potential to deserve moral praise. Yet the main thrust of the arguments of this paper has been leading to the conclusion that when such ideals are present, they are not ideals to which it is particularly reasonable or healthy or desirable for human beings to aspire. These claims, taken together, have the appearance of a dilemma from which there is no obvious escape. In a moment, I shall argue that, despite appearances, these claims should not be understood as constituting a dilemma. But, before I do, let me briefly describe another path which those who are

convinced by my above remarks may feel inclined to take.

If the above remarks are understood to be implicitly critical of the views on the content of morality which seem more popular today, an alternative that naturally suggests itself is that we revise our views about the content of morality. More specifically, my remarks may be taken to support a more Aristotelian, or even a more Nietzschean, approach to moral philosophy. Such a change in approach involves substantially broadening or replacing our contemporary intuitions about which character traits constitute moral virtues and vices and which interests constitute moral interests. If, for example, we include personal bearing, or creativity, or sense of style, as features that contribute to one's *moral* personality, then we can create moral ideals which are incompatible with and probably more attractive than the Kantian and utilitarian ideals I have discussed. Given such an alteration of our conception of morality, the figures with which I have been concerned above might, far from being considered to be moral saints, be seen as morally inferior to other more appealing or more interesting models of individuals.

This approach seems unlikely to succeed, if for no other reason, because it is doubtful that any single, or even any reasonably small number of substantial personal ideals could capture the full range of possible ways of realizing human potential or achieving human good which deserve encouragement and praise. Even if we could provide a sufficiently broad characterization of the range of positive ways for human beings to live, however, I think there are strong reasons not to want to incorporate such a characterization more centrally into the framework of morality itself. For, in claiming that a character trait or activity is morally good, one claims that there is a certain kind of reason for developing that trait or engaging in that activity. Yet, lying behind our criticism of more conventional conceptions of moral sainthood, there seems to be a recognition that among the immensely

valuable traits and activities that a human life might positively embrace are some of which we hope that, if a person does embrace them, he does so not for moral reasons. In other words, no matter how flexible we make the guide to conduct which we choose to label "morality," no matter how rich we make the life in which perfect obedience to this guide would result, we will have reason to hope that a person does not wholly rule and direct his life by the abstract and impersonal consideration that such a life would be morally good.

Once it is recognized that morality itself should not serve as a comprehensive guide to conduct, moreover, we can see reasons to retain the admittedly vague contemporary intuitions about what the classification of moral and nonmoral virtues, interests, and the like should be. That is, there seem to be important differences between the aspects of a person's life which are currently considered appropriate objects of moral evaluation and the aspects that might be included under the altered conception of morality we are now considering, which the latter approach would tend wrongly to blur or to neglect. Moral evaluation now is focused primarily on features of a person's life over which that person has control; it is largely restricted to aspects of his life which are likely to have considerable effect on other people. These restrictions seem as they should be. Even if responsible people could reach agreement as to what constituted good taste or a healthy degree of well-roundedness, for example, it seems wrong to insist that everyone try to achieve these things or to blame someone who fails or refuses to conform.

If we are not to respond to the unattractiveness of the moral ideals that contemporary theories yield either by offering alternative theories with more palatable ideals or by understanding these theories in such a way as to prevent them from yielding ideals at all, how, then, are we to respond? Simply, I think, by admitting that moral ideals do not, and need not, make the best

personal ideals. Earlier, I mentioned one of the consequences of regarding as a test of an adequate moral theory that perfect obedience to its laws and maximal devotion to its interests be something we can wholeheartedly strive for in ourselves and wish for in those around us. Drawing out the consequences somewhat further should, I think, make us more doubtful of the proposed test than of the theories which, on this test, would fail. Given the empirical circumstances of our world, it seems to be an ethical fact that we have unlimited potential to be morally good, and endless opportunity to promote moral interests. But this is not incompatible with the not-so-ethical fact that we have sound, compelling, and not particularly selfish reasons to choose not to devote ourselves univocally to realizing this potential or to taking up this opportunity.

Thus, in one sense at least, I am not really criticizing either Kantianism or utilitarianism. Insofar as the point of view I am offering bears directly on recent work in moral philosophy, in fact, it bears on critics of these theories who, in a spirit not unlike the spirit of most of this paper, point out that the perfect utilitarian would be flawed in this way or the perfect Kantian flawed in that.[3] The assumption lying behind these claims, implicitly or explicitly, has been that the recognition of these flaws shows us something wrong with utilitarianism, as opposed to Kantianism, or something wrong with Kantianism as opposed to utilitarianism, or something wrong with both of these theories as opposed to some nameless third alternative. The claims of this paper suggest, however, that this assumption is unwarranted. The flaws of a perfect master of a moral theory need not reflect flaws in the intramoral content of the theory itself.

Moral saints and moral philosophy

In pointing out the regrettable features and the necessary absence of some desirable features in a

moral saint, I have not meant to condemn the moral saint or the person who aspires to become one. Rather, I have meant to insist that the ideal of moral sainthood should not be held as a standard against which any other ideal must be judged or justified, and that the posture we take in response to the recognition that our lives are not as morally good as they might be need not be defensive.[4] It is misleading to insist that one is *permitted* to live a life in which the goals, relationships, activities, and interests that one pursues are not maximally morally good. For our lives are not so comprehensively subject to the requirement that we apply for permission, and our non-moral reasons for the goals we set ourselves are not excuses, but may rather be positive, good reasons which do not exist *despite* any reasons that might threaten to outweigh them. In other words, a person may be *perfectly wonderful* without being *perfectly moral*.

Recognizing this requires a perspective which contemporary moral philosophy has generally ignored. This perspective yields judgments of a type that is neither moral nor egoistic. Like moral judgments, judgments about what it would be good for a person to be are made from a point of view outside the limits set by the values, interests, and desires that the person might actually have. And, like moral judgments, these judgments claim for themselves a kind of objectivity or a grounding in a perspective which any rational and perceptive being can take up. Unlike moral judgments, however, the good with which these judgments are concerned is not the good of anyone or any group other than the individual himself.

Nonetheless, it would be equally misleading to say that these judgments are made for the sake of the individual himself. For these judgments are not concerned with what kind of life it is in a person's interest to lead, but with what kind of interests it would be good for a person to have, and it need not be in a person's interest that he acquire or maintain objectively good interests. Indeed, the model of the Loving Saint, whose interests are identified with the interests of morality, is a model of a person for whom the dictates of rational self-interest and the dictates of morality coincide. Yet, I have urged that we have reason not to aspire to this ideal and that some of us would have reason to be sorry if our children aspired to and achieved it.

The moral point of view, we might say, is the point of view one takes up insofar as one takes the recognition of the fact that one is just one person among others equally real and deserving of the good things in life as a fact with practical consequences, a fact the recognition of which demands expression in one's actions and in the form of one's practical deliberations. Competing moral theories offer alternative answers to the question of what the most correct or the best way to express this fact is. In doing so, they offer alternative ways to evaluate and to compare the variety of actions, states of affairs, and so on that appear good and bad to agents from other, nonmoral points of view. But it seems that alternative interpretations of the moral point of view do not exhaust the ways in which our actions, characters, and their consequences can be comprehensively and objectively evaluated. Let us call the point of view from which we consider what kinds of lives are good lives, and what kinds of persons it would be good for ourselves and others to be, the *point of view of individual perfection*.

Since either point of view provides a way of comprehensively evaluating a person's life, each point of view takes account of, and, in a sense, subsumes the other. From the moral point of view, the perfection of an individual life will have some, but limited, value—for each individual remains, after all, just one person among others. From the perfectionist point of view, the moral worth of an individual's relation to his world will likewise have some, but limited, value—for, as I have argued, the (perfectionist) goodness of an individual's life does not vary proportionally with the degree to which it exemplifies moral goodness.

It may not be the case that the perfectionist point of view is like the moral point of view in being a point of view we are ever *obliged* to take up and express in our actions. Nonetheless, it provides us with reasons that are independent of moral reasons for wanting ourselves and others to develop our characters and live our lives in certain ways. When we take up this point of view and ask how much it would be good for an individual to act from the moral point of view, we do not find an obvious answer.[5]

The considerations of this paper suggest, at any rate, that the answer is not "as much as possible." This has implications both for the continued development of moral theories and for the development of metamoral views and for our conception of moral philosophy more generally. From the moral point of view, we have reasons to want people to live lives that seem good from outside that point of view. If, as I have argued, this means that we have reason to want people to live lives that are not morally perfect, then any plausible moral theory must make use of some conception of supererogation.[6]

If moral philosophers are to address themselves at the most basic level to the question of how people should live, however, they must do more than adjust the content of their moral theories in ways that leave room for the affirmation of nonmoral values. They must examine explicitly the range and nature of these nonmoral values, and, in light of this examination, they must ask how the acceptance of a moral theory is to be understood and acted upon. For the claims of this paper do not so much conflict with the content of any particular currently popular moral theory as they call into question a metamoral assumption that implicitly surrounds discussions of moral theory more generally. Specifically, they call into question the assumption that it is always better to be morally better.

The role morality plays in the development of our characters and the shape of our practical deliberations need be neither that of a universal medium into which all other values must be translated nor that of an ever-present filter through which all other values must pass. This is not to say that moral value should not be an important, even the most important, kind of value we attend to in evaluating and improving ourselves and our world. It is to say that our values cannot be fully comprehended on the model of a hierarchical system with morality at the top.

The philosophical temperament will naturally incline, at this point, toward asking, "What, then, *is* at the top—or, if there is no top, how *are* we to decide when and how much to be moral?" In other words, there is a temptation to seek a metamoral—though not, in the standard sense, metaethical—theory that will give us principles, or, at least, informal directives on the basis of which we can develop and evaluate more comprehensive personal ideals. Perhaps a theory that distinguishes among the various roles a person is expected to play within a life—as professional, as citizen, as friend, and so on—might give us some rules that would offer us, if nothing else, a better framework in which to think about and discuss these questions. I am pessimistic, however, about the chances of such a theory to yield substantial and satisfying results. For I do not see how a metamoral theory could be constructed which would not be subject to considerations parallel to those which seem inherently to limit the appropriateness of regarding moral theories as ultimate comprehensive guides for action.

This suggests that, at some point, both in our philosophizing and in our lives, we must be willing to raise normative questions from a perspective that is unattached to a commitment to any particular well-ordered system of values. It must be admitted that, in doing so, we run the risk of finding normative answers that diverge from the answers given by whatever moral theory one accepts. This, I take it, is the grain of truth in G. E. Moore's "open question" argument. In the background of this paper, then,

there lurks a commitment to what seems to me to be a healthy form of intuitionism. It is a form of intuitionism which is not intended to take the place of more rigorous, systematically developed, moral theories—rather, it is intended to put these more rigorous and systematic moral theories in their place.

Notes

I have benefited from the comments of many people who have heard or read an earlier draft of this paper. I wish particularly to thank Douglas MacLean, Robert Nozick, Martha Nussbaum, and the Society for Ethics and Legal Philosophy.

1   "Persons, Character and Morality" in Amelie Rorty, ed., *The Identities of Persons* (Berkeley: Univ. of California Press, 1976), p. 214.

2   Immanuel Kant, *The Doctrine of Virtue*, Mary J. Gregor, trans. (New York: Harper & Row, 1964), p. 71.

3   See, e.g., Williams, op. cit. and J. J. C. Smart and Bernard Williams, *Utilitarianism: For and Against* (New York: Cambridge, 1973). Also, Michael Stocker, "The Schizophrenia of Modern Ethical Theories," *The Journal of Philosophy*, LXIII, 14 (Aug. 12, 1976): 453–66.

4   George Orwell makes a similar point in "Reflections on Gandhi," in *A Collection of Essays by George Orwell* (New York: Harcourt Brace Jovanovich, 1945), p. 176: "sainthood is . . . a thing that human beings must avoid. . . . It is too readily assumed that . . . the ordinary man only rejects it because it is too difficult; in other words, that the average human being is a failed saint. It is doubtful whether this is true. Many people genuinely do not wish to be saints, and it is probable that some who achieve or aspire to sainthood have never felt much temptation to be human beings."

5   A similar view, which has strongly influenced mine, is expressed by Thomas Nagel in "The Fragmentation of Value," in *Mortal Questions* (New York: Cambridge, 1979), pp. 128–41. Nagel focuses on the difficulties such apparently incommensurable points of view create for specific, isolable practical decisions that must be made both by individuals and by societies. In focusing on the way in which these points of view figure into the development of individual personal ideals, the questions with which I am concerned are more likely to lurk in the background of any individual's life.

6   The variety of forms that a conception of supererogation might take, however, has not generally been noticed. Moral theories that make use of this notion typically do so by identifying some specific set of principles as universal moral requirements and supplement this list with a further set of directives which it is morally praiseworthy but not required for an agent to follow. [See, e.g., Charles Fried, *Right and Wrong* (Cambridge, MA: Harvard, 1979).] But it is possible that the ability to live a morally blameless life cannot be so easily or definitely secured as this type of theory would suggest. The fact that there are some situations in which an agent is morally required to do something and other situations in which it would be good but not required for an agent to do something does not imply that there are specific principles such that, in any situation, an agent is required to act in accordance with these principles and other specific principles such that, in any situation, it would be good but not required for an agent to act in accordance with those principles.

Chapter 43

Rosalind Hursthouse

VIRTUE ETHICS

VIRTUE ETHICS has been characterized in a number of ways. It is described (1) as an ethics which is 'agent-centred' rather than 'act-centred'; (2) as concerned with Being rather than Doing; (3) as addressing itself to the question, 'What sort of person should I be?' rather than to the question, 'What sorts of action should I do?'; (4) as taking certain areteic concepts (*good, excellence, virtue*) as basic rather than deontic ones (*right, duty, obligation*); (5) as rejecting the idea that ethics is codifiable in rules or principles that can provide specific action guidance.

I give this list because these descriptions of virtue ethics are so commonly encountered, not because I think they are good ones. On the contrary, I think that all of them, in their crude brevity, are seriously misleading. Of course, there is some truth in each of them, which is why they are so common, and I shall return to them as we proceed, to note what truth, with what qualifications, they may be seen as containing. Readers familiar with the recent literature I mentioned in the Introduction [see original reading], which has blurred the lines of demarcation between the three approaches in normative ethics, will no doubt have discarded or qualified them long since. But here, at the outset, it seems best to begin at a simple level, with the descriptions most readers will recognize, and work our way through some of the complications and subtleties that are not so well known.

Right action

The descriptions, especially when encountered for the first time, can easily be read as all making roughly the same point, and one way in which they are all misleading is that they encourage the thought that virtue ethics cannot be a genuine rival to utilitarianism and deontology. The thought goes like this:

If virtue ethics is 'agent-centred rather than act-centred', concerned with 'What sort of person should I be?' rather than 'What sorts of action should I do?' (with 'Being rather than Doing'), if it concentrates on the *good* or *virtuous* agent rather than on *right* action and on what anyone, virtuous or not, has an *obligation* to do; how can it be a genuine rival to utilitarianism and deontology? Surely ethical theories are supposed to tell us about right action, i.e. about what sorts of act we should do. Utilitarianism and deontology certainly do that; if virtue ethics does not, it cannot be a genuine rival to them.

Now the descriptions do not actually say that virtue ethics does not concern itself at all with right action, or what we should do; it is in so far as it is easy to take them that way they are misleading. For virtue ethics can provide action guidance. The way it does this can most helpfully be shown by comparing it with the

guidance given by some versions of utilitarianism and deontology, all laid out in a similar way.

Suppose an act utilitarian began her account of right action as follows:

P.1.   An action is right iff it promotes the best consequences.

This premise provides a specification of right action, forging the familiar act-utilitarian link between the concepts of right action and *best consequences*, but gives one no guidance about how to act until one knows what to count as the best consequences. So these must be specified in a second premise, for example:

P. 2.   The best consequences are those in which happiness is maximized—which forges the familiar utilitarian link between the concepts of *best consequences* and *happiness*.

Many simple versions of deontology can be laid out in a way that displays the same basic structure. They begin with a premise providing a specification of right action:

P.1.   An action is right iff it is in accordance with a correct moral rule or principle.

Like the first premise of act utilitarianism, this gives one no guidance about how to act until, in this case, one knows what to count as a correct moral rule (or principle). So this must be specified in a second premise, which begins

P.2.   A correct moral rule (principle) is one that . . .

and this may be completed in a variety of ways, for example,

(1)   . . . is on the following list – (and then a list follows, perhaps completed with an 'etc.'), or

(2)   . . . is laid down for us by God, or

(3)   . . . is universalizable/a categorical imperative, or

(4)   . . , would be the object of choice of all rational beings,

and so on.

Although this way of laying out fairly familiar versions of utilitarianism and deontology is hardly controversial, it shows that there is something wrong with an over-used description of them, namely the slogan, 'Utilitarianism begins with' (or 'takes as its fundamental concept' etc.) 'the Good, whereas deontology begins with the Right.'[1] If the concept a normative ethics 'begins with' is the one it uses to specify right action, then utilitarianism might indeed be said to begin with the Good (taking this to be the same concept as that of the best), but we should surely hasten to add, 'but only in relation to consequences or states of affairs, not, for instance, in relation to *good* agents, or living *well*'. And even then, we shall not be able to go on to say that most versions of deontology 'begin with' the Right, for they use the concept of moral rule or principle to specify right action. The only versions which, in this sense, 'begin with' the Right would have to be versions of what Frankena calls 'extreme act-deontology'[2] which (I suppose) specify a right action as one which just is right.

And if the slogan is supposed to single out, rather vaguely, the concept which is 'most important', then the concepts of *consequences* or *happiness* seem as deserving of mention as the concept of the Good for utilitarianism, and what counts as most important for deontologists (if any one concept does) would surely vary from case to case. For some it would be God, for others universalizability, for others the Categorical Imperative, for others rational acceptance, and so on. (Should we say that for Kant it is the good will, or the Categorical Imperative, or both?)

It is possible that too slavish a reliance on this slogan contributes to the belief that virtue ethics

cannot provide its own specification of right action. For many who rely on it go on to say, 'Utilitarianism derives the concept of the Right from that of the Good, and deontology derives the Good from the Right; but how can virtue ethics possibly derive the Good and the Right from the concept of the Virtuous Agent, which it begins with?' Now indeed, with no answer forthcoming to the questions 'Good *what*? Right *what*?', I have no idea. But if the question is, 'How can virtue ethics give an account of right action in such a way as to provide action guidance?' the answer is easy. Here is its first premise.

P.1.   An action is right iff it is what a virtuous agent would characteristically (i.e. acting in character) do in the circumstances.

This specification rarely, if ever, silences those who maintain that virtue ethics cannot tell us what we should do. On the contrary, it tends to provoke irritable laughter and scorn. 'That's no use', the objectors say. 'It gives us no guidance whatsoever. Who are the virtuous agents?'

But if the failure of the first premise of an account of right action, the premise which forges a link between the concept of right action and a concept distinctive of a particular normative ethics, may provoke scorn because it provides no practical guidance, why not direct similar scorn at the first premises of act utilitarianism and deontology in the form in which I have given them? Of each of them I remarked, apparently in passing, but really with a view to this point, that they gave us no guidance. Act utilitarianism must specify what are to count as the best consequences, and deontology what is to count as a correct moral rule, producing a second premise, before any guidance is given. And, similarly, virtue ethics must specify who is to count as a virtuous agent. So far, the three are all in the same position.

Of course, if the virtuous agent can be specified only as an agent disposed to act in accordance with correct moral rules, as is sometimes assumed, then virtue ethics collapses back into deontology and is no rival to it. So let us add a subsidiary premise to this skeletal outline, intended to show that virtue ethics aims to provide a non-deontological specification of the virtuous agent *via* a specification of the virtues, which will be given in its second premise.

P.1a.   A virtuous agent is one who has, and exercises, certain character traits, namely, the virtues.

P.2.   A virtue is a character trait that . . .

This second premise of virtue ethics, like the second premise of some versions of deontology, might be completed simply by enumeration— 'is on the following list'—and then a list is given, perhaps completed with 'etc.'. Or we might interpret the Hume of the second *Enquiry* as espousing virtue ethics. According to Hume, we might say, a virtue is a character trait (of human beings) that is useful or agreeable to its possessor or to others (inclusive 'or' both times). Or we might give the standard neo-Aristotelian completion, which claims that a virtue is a character trait a human being needs for *eudaimonia*, to flourish or live well.

Here, then, we have a specification of right action, whose structure closely resembles those of act utilitarianism and many simple forms of deontology. Comparing the three, we see that we could say, 'Virtue ethics (in its account of right action) is agent-centred rather than consequences- or rules-centred. It is agent-centred in that it introduces the concept of the virtuous *agent* in the first premise of its account of right action, where utilitarianism and deontology introduce the concepts of *consequences* and *moral rule* respectively.' That's true; it does. But note that it is not thereby 'agent-centred *rather than* act-centred'. It has an aswer to 'How shall I decide what to do?'

So there is the first misunderstanding cleared away. Virtue ethics does have something to say about right action. But this is only a first step in

dealing with the misunderstanding, for many people find what it has to say unsatisfactory. The reasons for their dissatisfaction are so varied that they will occupy us for several chapters; in this one, I shall concentrate on some that are naturally expressed in the complaint that virtue ethics does not and cannot tell us what to do; the complaint that it does not and cannot provide moral guidance.

'Virtue ethics does not provide us with moral guidance'—how can it fail to, when it has provided a specification of right action? Sometimes people suspect that it has provided only a circular specification, not a specification that we could use to guide us. 'It has told us that the right action is what a virtuous agent would do. But that's a truism. Of course the virtuous agent "does what is right"; if she didn't, she wouldn't be virtuous; we are just going round in circles.'

Now it is true that the first premise of virtue ethics' account of right action has the air of being a truism. For although act utilitarians will want to deny the deontologists' first premise ('No! We should break the rule if the consequences of doing so would be better than those of keeping it'), and deontologists will deny the utilitarian one ('No! We must stick to the rules regardless of the consequences'), it is quite likely that both of them would accept what virtue ethics says: 'An action is right iff it is what a virtuous agent would do.' But, if they did, they would each be assuming that they had settled what right action was already, using their first and second premises, and were then using the truism to specify what, for them, counted as a virtuous agent: 'A virtuous agent is one who does what is right (in my sense of "right").'[3]

What I need to emphasize is that the apparent truism, 'An action is right iff it is what a virtuous agent would characteristically do in the circumstances', is not figuring as a truism in virtue ethics' account of right action. It is figuring as the first premise of that account, a premise that, like the first premises of the other two accounts,

awaits filling out in the second premise. Perhaps I could make this clearer by restating the first premise, and its supplement, in a way that made the necessity for filling them out glaringly obvious, thus:

P.1.   An action is right iff it is what an X agent would characteristically do in the circumstances, and

P.1a. An X agent is one who has and exercises certain character traits, namely the Xs.

And put that way, P.1 does not look at all like a truism.

Unfortunately, it now looks uninformative, once again, apparently, contrasting unfavourably with the first premises of act utilitarianism and deontology: 'We all have some idea about what best consequences might be and of what correct moral rules or principles are, but what on earth is an X agent?' But now I must repeat the point made earlier. The other first premises, taken strictly, are equally uninformative. We overlook this point because the utilitarian specifications of best consequences are so familiar, and all the deontologists we know cite familiar moral rules. But, for all that is said in the first premise of either, strange things might emerge in the second.

Someone might specify the 'best consequences' as those in which the number of Roman Catholics was maximized (and the number of non-Catholics minimized). It would be a very odd view to hold; no proper Catholic could hold it, but some madman brought up in the Catholic faith might. Or someone might specify the 'best consequences' as those in which certain moral rules were adhered to. 'We all have some idea of what best consequences might be', not because this is *given* in the first premise of the act utilitarian account, but because we are all familiar with the idea that, by and large, if an action has, as a consequence, that many people are made happy, or much suffering is relieved, this counts as a good consequence.

Similarly, when we read the deontologist's first premise, we suppose that 'we all have some idea of what correct moral rules or principles are'. We expect (something like) 'Do not kill' and 'Keep promises'. We do not expect 'Purify the Aryan race', 'Keep women in their proper place, subordinate to men', 'Kill the infidel'. But we know only too well that these not only might be specified, but have been specified, as correct moral rules. As far as the first premise of the deontological account of right action goes, we do not, in fact, have any idea, given by that premise, of what correct moral rules or principles are; we bring our own ideas to it.

So, understood as a first premise comparable to those of act utilitarianism and deontology, 'An action is right iff it is what a virtuous agent would, characteristically, do in the circumstances', far from being a truism, is, like the first premises of the others, uninformative. All three start to be informative only when the second premise is added.

Epistemological problems

At this stage we may notice an interesting division in the three accounts, a division which puts act utilitarianism on one side, and deontology and virtue ethics on the other. As soon as act utilitarianism produces its second premise, saying that the best consequences are those in which happiness is maximized, we seem to know where the act utilitarian stands. (I shall question below whether we really do, but we certainly seem to.) We can work out that the act utilitarian will say, for example, that it is right to tell a lie when telling the truth would make no one happy and someone very unhappy. But whether we know what a deontologist and a virtue ethicist will say about such a case after they have produced their second premises depends on the form they take.

If a list of correct moral rules or virtues is given, we have something fairly concrete. If one list contains 'Do not lie' and the other 'Honesty',

we can work out that the deontologist and virtue ethicist are probably not going to agree with the act utilitarian about the rightness of telling the lie. But what if the deontologist's second premise is one of the others I gave? We all know that there has been, and is, much dispute about what God has laid down, and about what it is rational to accept, and so on—in short, much dispute about which moral rules or principles are the correct ones. When a deontologist produces one of her abstract tests for the correctness of a moral rule, we may be sure that she will defend and justify the rules she believes are correct in terms of it—but what these will be we do not know. Will she defend rules prohibiting suicide or abortion or rules permitting them? Will she turn out to be a pacifist or a supporter of killing in self-defence? We do not know.

Virtue ethics is similarly non-committal. We all know, it is said, that there has been, and is, much dispute about which character traits are the virtues. When a virtue ethicist produces one of her abstract tests, we may be sure that she will defend the character traits she believes are the virtues in terms of it, and dismiss the ones she does not accept—but what these will be we do not know. Will she defend humility, modesty, and compassion or (like Hume, Aristotle, and Nietzsche, respectively) will she dismiss them? Will she defend impartiality or friendship? We do not know.

So here we have an interesting contrast between act utilitarianism on the one hand, and deontology and virtue ethics on the other. The latter look as though they are bound to land us with a huge problem about how we can know that a particular action is right, for whatever either says, we can ask 'But how do we know which moral rules or principles are the correct ones, which character traits are the virtues?' If they each just produce their list we can worry whether it is the right list. If they produce one of their abstract tests we can worry about the fact that, with sufficient ingenuity, or different

further premises, these can be got to yield different results. So both lay themselves open to the threat of moral cultural relativism or, even worse, moral scepticism. Maybe we can do no more than list the rules, or character traits, accepted by our own culture or society and just have to accept that all we can know is what is right according to us, which might be wrong according to some other culture. Or, even worse, when we remember how much moral disagreement there is between 'us', maybe we cannot even do that. Maybe we have to accept that there isn't anything that counts as knowing that a particular action is right; all there is, is feeling convinced that it is because it is in accordance with a certain rule one personally wants to adhere to, or because it is what would be done by the sort of person one personally wants to be.

Act utilitarianism is not, or not immediately, open to the same threat. True, it may be hard, on occasion, to predict the consequences of an action, but this is a practical problem in life which all three accounts have to take on board. Though it is sometimes said that deontologists 'take no account of consequences', this is manifestly false, for many actions we deliberate about only fall under rules or principles when we bring in their predicted consequences. A deontological surgeon wondering whether she should perform a particular operation on a patient may be in doubt, not because she has any doubts about the correctness of her principles, but because it is so hard for her to predict whether the consequences of the operation will be that the patient enjoys several more years of life or is finished off. A surgeon who subscribes to virtue ethics has the same problem: she may not doubt that charity, which is concerned with others' good, is a virtue; her doubt is over whether the consequences of the operation will be that her patient is benefited or harmed.

The difficulty of being able to predict the consequences of one's actions does not bring with it the threat of moral relativism or moral scepticism; it is just a general problem in life.

However, if the consequences concern *happiness*, as in the utilitarian account, doesn't the threat come in there? Different cultures, different individuals, have different ideas of happiness. How can we know that a particular action is right if we cannot define precisely and correctly that 'happiness' we are supposed to be maximizing?

I think that one might well press something along these lines as a problem for utilitarianism, and this is a point to which I shall return below. But it is hardly plausible to say it shows that act utilitarianism is *immediately* open to the threat of moral relativism and scepticism. Suppose people's ideas of happiness do vary; why should that matter, for practical purposes? This person will be happy if I give her a book on religious contemplation and upset if I give her a sexy novel, someone else will delight in the novel but be bored to tears by the other. If I can afford both books, act utilitarianism makes it perfectly clear what I should do, without having to define happiness or worry about the fact that these two people doubtless have very different ideas of it. As Jonathan Glover robustly remarks, 'most of us, whether utilitarians or not, take some account of the likely effects of our actions on people's happiness, and we should all be in a mess if there was no correspondence between trying to make someone happier and succeeding'.[4]

So let us say, for the moment, that act utilitarianism is not immediately threatened by the spectre of moral relativism or scepticism, but that virtue ethics, in company with deontology, is. And, having said it and acknowledged the problem, let us put it to one side for later chapters [see original reading].[5] For the moment I shall assume that both deontology and virtue ethics give an open-ended, and familiar, list in their second premises. Deontology, we may suppose, lists such familiar rules as 'Do not kill', 'Tell the truth', 'Keep promises', 'Do no evil or harm to others', 'Help others/promote their well-being', etc.; virtue ethics lists such familiar character traits as justice, honesty, charity, courage, practical

wisdom, generosity, loyalty, etc. And, having assumed that, we can return to the question of whether virtue ethics, even given such a list, somehow fails to provide guidance in the way that act utilitarianism and deontology do.

Moral rules

A common objection goes as follows.

> Deontology gives a set of clear prescriptions which are readily applicable. But virtue ethics yields only the prescription, 'Do what the virtuous agent—the one who is just, honest, charitable etc.—would do in these circumstances.' And this gives me no guidance unless I am (and know I am) a virtuous agent myself—in which case I am hardly in need of it. If I am less than fully virtuous, I shall have no idea what a virtuous agent would do, and hence cannot apply the only prescription virtue ethics has given me. True, act utilitarianism also yields only a single prescription ('Do what maximizes happiness'), but there are no parallel difficulties in applying that; it too is readily applicable. So there is the way in which virtue ethics' account of right action fails to be action guiding where deontology and utilitarianism succeed.

In response, it is worth pointing out that, if I know that I am far from perfect, and am quite unclear what a virtuous agent would do in the circumstances in which I find myself, the obvious thing to do is to go and ask one, should this be possible. This is far from being a trivial point, for it gives a straightforward explanation of an important aspect of our moral life, namely the fact that we do not always act as 'autonomous', utterly self-determining agents, but quite often seek moral guidance from people we think are morally better than ourselves. When I am looking for an excuse to do something I have a horrid suspicion is wrong, I ask my moral inferiors (or peers if I am bad enough), 'Wouldn't

you do such-and-such if you were in my shoes?' But when I am anxious to do what is right, and do not see my way clear, I go to people I respect and admire: people who I think are kinder, more honest, more just, wiser, than I am myself, and ask them what they would do in my circumstances. How, or indeed whether, utilitarianism and deontology can explain this fact, I do not know, but, as I said, the explanation within the terms of virtue ethics is straightforward. If you want to do what is right, and doing what is right is doing what the virtuous agent would do in the circumstances, then you should find out what she would do if you do not already know.

Moreover, seeking advice from virtuous people is not the only thing an imperfect agent trying to apply the 'single prescription' of virtue ethics can do. For it is simply false that, in general, 'if I am less than fully virtuous, then I shall have no idea what a virtuous agent would do', as the objection claims. Recall that we are assuming that the virtues have been enumerated as, say, honesty, charity, fidelity, etc. So, *ex hypothesi*, a virtuous agent is one who is honest, charitable, true to her word, etc. So what she characteristically does is what is honest, charitable, true to her word, etc. and not what would be dishonest, uncharitable, untrue to her word. So, given such an enumeration of the virtues, I may well have a perfectly good idea of what the virtuous person would do in my circumstances, despite my own imperfection. Would she lie in her teeth to acquire an unmerited advantage? No, for that would be both dishonest and unjust. Would she help the wounded stranger by the roadside even though he had no right to her help, or pass by on the other side? The former, for that is charitable and the latter callous. Might she keep a death-bed promise even though living people would benefit from its being broken? Yes, for she is true to her word. And so on.[6]

This second response to the objection that virtue ethics' account of right action fails to be action guiding amounts to a denial of the oft-repeated claim that 'virtue ethics does not come

up with any rules' (which is another version of the thought that it is concerned with Being rather than Doing), and needs to be supplemented with rules. We can now see that it comes up with a large number of rules. Not only does each virtue generate a prescription—do what is honest, charitable, generous—but each vice a prohibition—do not do what is dishonest, uncharitable, mean.[7]

Once this point about virtue ethics is grasped (and it is remarkable how often it is overlooked), can there remain any reason for thinking that virtue ethics cannot tell us what we should do? Yes, there is one. The reason given is, roughly, that rules such as 'Do what is honest, do not do what is uncharitable' are, like the rule 'Do what the virtuous agent would do', still the wrong sort of rule, still somehow doomed to fail to provide the action guidance supplied by the rules (or rule) of deontology and act utilitarianism.

But how so? It is true that these rules of virtue ethics (henceforth 'v-rules') are couched in terms, or concepts, that are certainly 'evaluative' in *some* sense, or senses, of that difficult word. Is it this which dooms them to failure? Surely not, unless many forms of utilitarianism and deontology fail for this reason too.

There are, indeed, some forms of utilitarianism which aim to be entirely 'value-free' or empirical, such as those which define happiness in terms of the satisfaction of actual desires or preferences, regardless of their content, or as a mental state whose presence is definitively established by introspection. Such forms run into well-known problems, and have always seemed to me the least plausible, but I accept that anyone who embraces them may consistently complain that v-rules give inferior action guidance in virtue of containing 'evaluative' terms. But a utilitarian who wishes to employ any distinction between the higher and lower pleasures, or pronounce on what rational preferences would be, or rely on some list of goods (such as autonomy, friendship, or knowledge of

important matters) in defining happiness, must grant that even her single rule is implicitly 'evaluative'. (This is why, briefly, I think that utilitarianism is not generally immune to the threat of moral relativism or scepticism, as I mentioned above.)

What about deontology? If we concentrate on the single example of lying, defining lying to be 'asserting what you believe to be untrue, with the intention of deceiving your hearer(s)', then we might, for a moment, preserve the illusion that a deontologist's rules do not contain 'evaluative' terms. But as soon as we remember that few deontologists will want to forgo principles of non-maleficence and (or) beneficence, the illusion vanishes. For these principles, and their corresponding rules (do no evil or harm to others, help others, promote their well-being), rely on terms or concepts which are at least as 'evaluative' as those employed in the v-rules.

We see revealed here a further inadequacy in the slogan 'Utilitarianism begins with the Good, deontology with the Right' when this is taken as committing deontology to making the concept of the Good (and, presumably, the Bad or Evil) somehow derivative from the concept of the Right (and Wrong). A 'utilitarian' who relied on the concept of right, or virtuous, action in specifying his concept of happiness would find it hard to shrug off the scare quotes, but no one expects a deontologist to be able to state each of her rules without ever employing a concept of good which is not simply the concept of *right action for its own sake*, or without any mention of *evil* or *harm*.

We might also note that few deontologists will rest content with the simple, quasibiological 'Do not kill', but more refined versions of that rule such as 'Do not murder', or 'Do not kill the innocent', once again employ 'evaluative' terms, and 'Do not kill unjustly' is itself a particular instantiation of a v-rule.

Supposing this point were granted, a deontologist might still claim that the v-rules are markedly inferior to deontological rules as far as

providing guidance for children is concerned. Granted, adult deontologists must think hard about what really constitutes harming someone, or promoting their well-being, or respecting their autonomy, or murder, but surely the simple rules we learnt at our mother's knee are indispensable. How could virtue ethics plausibly seek to dispense with these and expect toddlers to grasp 'act charitably, honestly, and kindly, don't act unjustly', and so on? Rightly are these concepts described as 'thick'! Far too thick for a child to grasp.

Strictly speaking, this objection is rather different from the *general* objection that v-rules fail to provide action guidance, but it arises naturally in the context of the general one and I am more than happy to address it. For it pinpoints a condition of adequacy that any normative ethics must meet, namely that such an ethics must not only come up with action guidance for a clever rational adult, but also generate some account of moral education, of how one generation teaches the next what they should do. But an ethics inspired by Aristotle is unlikely to have forgotten the question of moral education, and the objection fails to hit home. Firstly, the implicit empirical claim that toddlers are taught only the deontologist's rules, not the 'thick' concepts, is surely false. Sentences such as 'Don't do that, it hurts the cat, you mustn't be cruel', 'Be kind to your brother, he's only little', 'Don't be so mean, so greedy', are commonly addressed to toddlers. For some reason, we do not seem to teach 'just' and 'unjust' early on, but we certainly teach 'fair' and 'unfair'.

Secondly, why should a proponent of virtue ethics deny the significance of such mother's-knee rules as 'Don't lie', 'Keep promises', 'Help others'? Although it is a mistake (I have claimed) to define a virtuous agent simply as one disposed to act in accordance with deontologists' moral rules, it is a very understandable mistake, given the obvious connection between, for example, the exercise of the virtue of honesty and refraining from lying. Virtue ethicists want to emphasize the fact that, if children are to be taught to be honest, they must be taught to love and prize the truth, and that *merely* teaching them not to lie will not achieve this end. But they need not deny that, to achieve this end, teaching them not to lie is useful, or even indispensable.

So we can see that virtue ethics not only comes up with rules (the v-rules, couched in terms derived from the virtues and vices) but, further, does not exclude the more familiar deontologists' rules. The theoretical distinction between the two is that the familiar rules, and their applications in particular cases, are given entirely different backings. According to deontology, I must not tell this lie because, applying the (correct) rule 'Do not lie' to this case, I find that lying is prohibited. According to virtue ethics, I must not tell this lie because it would be dishonest to do so, and dishonesty is a vice.[8]

Uncodifiability

What then of the claim that virtue ethics, typically, rejects the idea that ethics is codifiable in rules or principles that can provide specific action guidance? It now stands revealed as a claim that invites the rather tiresome response, 'Well, it all depends on what you mean by "codifiable".'

It used to be quite commonly held that the task of normative ethics was to come up with a set (possibly one-membered, as in the case of act utilitarianism) of universal rules or principles which would have two significant features: (a) they would amount to a decision procedure for determining what the right action was in any particular case; (b) they would be stated in such terms that any non-virtuous person could understand and apply them correctly.[9] Call this the 'strong codifiability thesis'. And it was, and is, indeed typical of virtue ethicists to reject that thesis.[10] But, for at least two, no doubt related, reasons, the idea is now much less common.

One reason has been the increasing sense that

the enterprise of coming up with such a set of rules or principles has failed. In the early, heady days of applied ethics, it looked feasible, but as more philosophers relying on the same abstract principles applied them in such a way as to produce different conclusions, as different modifications or exclusion clauses were put on the general principles to yield different conclusions, as more philosophers trying to resolve real-life hard cases in medical ethics found themselves compelled to say that there were good arguments on both sides—as, quite generally, the gap between the abstract principles and the complex particularity of concrete moral situations became more obvious, so the idea that the rules should have both the features mentioned began to lose its appeal.

The concurrent emergence of virtue ethics articulated at least one way in which the original idea needed to be modified. It became increasingly obvious, when one considered whether doctors needed to be virtuous, that arrogant, uncaring, dishonest, and self-centred ones could not be guaranteed to do what they should merely by requiring that they acted in accordance with certain rules. The Devil, after all, can quote scripture to serve his own purposes; one can conform to the letter of a rule while violating its spirit. Hence it was recognized that a certain amount of virtue and corresponding moral or practical wisdom (*phronesis*) might be required both to interpret the rules and to determine which rule was most appropriately to be applied in a particular case.[11]

Of course, I am not claiming that this is now universally recognized, only that it is much more common than it used to be, particularly in books of applied ethics as opposed to books about what normative ethics is or should be. So should we say that those who have given up the original idea 'reject the idea that ethics is codifiable' as, it is said, virtue ethicists do? Clearly, they share with virtue ethicists the view that ethics is not *as* codifiable as used to be commonly supposed, but there is still, I think, a lingering view that it is, or ought to be, more codifiable than virtue ethics makes it out to be.

Sometimes this amounts to no more than the mistake I noted earlier, namely the view that virtue ethics does not come up with any rules or principles, combined, I suspect, with a gut unwillingness to join the virtue ethics camp. Beauchamp and Childress, whose *Principles of Medical Ethics*, from being initially dismissive, has become increasingly friendly to virtue ethics in its successive editions, are still to be found insisting that virtue ethics needs to be *supplemented* by a list of principles, which they give. They do not say, but they might well, that it doesn't *codify* enough. But the list looks like this:

Principles	Corresponding Virtues
Respect for autonomy	Respectfulness
Nonmaleficence	Nonmalevolence
Beneficence	Benevolence
Justice	Justice or fairness
Rules	
Veracity	Truthfulness
etc.[12]	

Now if this is all that is at issue, let us by all means say that virtue ethics does *not* reject the idea that ethics is codifiable. It does not need to be supplemented by such principles; it embodies them already—and many many more besides. (It is a noteworthy feature of our virtue and vice vocabulary that, although our list of generally recognized virtue terms is, I think, quite short, our list of vice terms is remarkably—and usefully— long, far exceeding anything that anyone who thinks in terms of standard deontological rules has ever come up with. Much invaluable action guidance comes from avoiding courses of action that are irresponsible, feckless, lazy, inconsiderate, uncooperative, harsh, intolerant, indiscreet, incautious, unenterprising, pusillanimous, feeble, hypocritical, self-indulgent, materialistic, grasping, short-sighted, . . . and on and on.)[13]

What else might still be at issue? A prevailing criticism of virtue ethics, related to the idea that it gives up on codifiability too soon, that it does not

codify enough, is that it fails to provide action guidance when we come to hard cases or dilemmas. So it is to a consideration of virtue ethics in relation to hard cases—a surprisingly large topic—that we now turn [see original reading].

Notes

1 For a particularly illuminating critique of Rawls's distinction, see G. Watson, 'On the Primacy of Character' (1990). See also Hudson, 'What is Morality all About?' (1990) and Herman, *The Practice of Moral Judgement*, ch. 10, who both challenge the slogan in relation to Kant's deontology.

2 W. Frankena, *Ethics* (1973).

3 Cf. Watson's opening paragraphs in 'On the Primacy of Character'.

4 J. Glover, *Causing Death and Saving Lives*, 3.

5 Indeed, given the size of the problem, one might say 'for a later book' . . . .

6 Cf. Anscombe: 'It would be a great improvement if, instead of "morally wrong" one always named a genus such as "untruthful", "unchaste", "unjust" . . . the answer would sometimes be clear at once.' 'Modern Moral Philosophy' (1958, repr. 1981), 33.

7 Making this point in earlier articles, I expressed the generated rules adverbially—act honestly, charitably, generously; do not act dishonestly, etc. But the adverbs connote not only doing what the virtuous agent would do, but also doing it 'in the way' she would do it, which includes 'for the same sort(s) of reason(s)', and it has seemed to me better here to separate out the issue of the virtuous agent's reasons for a later chapter.

8 This clear distinction (between deontology and virtue ethics) is just one of the many things that has been blurred by the recent happy convergence of Kantians and virtue ethicists.

9 E. Pincoffs, 'Quandary Ethics' (1971), identified this as the dominant view of the task of normative ethics at the time, beginning his article with a number of illustrative quotes from contemporary authors.

10 Most notably, J. McDowell in 'Virtue and Reason' (1979).

11 'It is true that principles underdetermine decisions. This is hardly news for those who have advocated ethical theories that makes principles or rules central. Kant, for example, insisted that we can have no algorithm for judgement, since every application of a rule would itself need supplementing by further rules.' O'Neill, 'Abstraction, Idealization and Ideology in Ethics' (1987), 58.

12 T. L. Beauchamp and J. F. Childress (eds.). *Principles of Biomedical Ethics*, 4th edn. (1994), 67.

13 Some virtue ethicists might want to insist on a strong correspondence between the virtues and the vices; not only that to each virtue there corresponds at least one particular vice but also that every vice is opposed to some particular virtue. Of course one can, formally, insist that to laziness there corresponds the virtue of being the opposite of lazy, which happens to lack a word in English ('industriousness' doesn't really work); more plausibly one could claim that describing someone as 'responsible' in a character reference describes them as having a particular virtue for which we have the adjective but not the noun. But I do not myself believe that things are that tidy.

References

Anscombe, G. E. M. 'Modern Moral Philosophy' (1958), repr. in *Collected Philosophical Papers*, iii. 26–42. Minneapolis: University of Minnesota Press, 1981.

Beauchamp, T. L. and Childress, J. F. *Principles of Biomedical Ethics*, 4th edn. New York: Oxford University Press, 1994.

Glover, J. *Causing Death and Saving Lives*. London: Penguin, 1977.

Herman, B. *The Practice of Moral Judgement*. Cambridge, Mass.: Harvard University Press, 1993.

Hudson, Stephen. 'What is Morality all About?', *Philosophia* 20 (1990), 3–13.

McDowell, J. 'Virtue and Reason', *Monist* 62 (1979), 331–50.

O'Neill, O. 'Abstraction, Idealization and Ideology in Ethics', in J. D. G. Evans (ed.), *Moral Philosophy and Contemporary Problems*, Royal Institute of Philosophy Lecture Series 22 (suppl. to *Philosophy*), 55–70. Cambridge: Cambridge University Press, 1987.

Pincoffs, E. 'Quandary Ethics', *Mind* 80 (1971), 551–71.

Watson, G. 'On the Primacy of Character', in O. Flanagan and A. O. Rorty (eds.), *Identity, Character and Morality* (q.v.), 449–83.

Chapter 44

John Doris

A SITUATIONIST THEORY OF CHARACTER

I. Character and consistency

THE MYTH THEY CHOSE was the constant lovers.
The theme was richness over time.
It is a difficult story and the wise never
    choose it
because it requires a long performance
and because there is nothing, by definition,
    between the acts.

Robert Hass

Character and personality traits are invoked to explain what people do and how they live: Peter didn't mingle at the party because he's shy, and Sandra succeeds in her work because she's diligent. Traits also figure in prediction: Peggy will join in because she's impulsive, and Brian will forget our meeting because he's absentminded. So too for those rarefied traits called virtues: James stood his ground because he's brave, and Katherine will not overindulge because she's temperate. Such talk would not much surprise Aristotle (1984: 1106a14–23); for him, a virtue is a state of character that makes its possessors behave in ethically appropriate ways. I'll now begin arguing that predictive and explanatory appeals to traits, however familiar, are very often empirically inadequate: They are confounded by the extraordinary situational sensitivity observed in human behavior. Discussion of the descriptive psychology occupies me for several chapters;

afterward, I'll be positioned to address related normative concerns.

Traits and consistency

Dispositions

As I understand it, to attribute a character or personality trait is to say, among other things, that someone is disposed to behave a certain way in certain eliciting conditions. In philosophy, this seems a standard interpretation: Character traits, and virtues in particular, are widely held to involve dispositions to behavior. So understood, trait attribution is associated with a, conditional: *If a person possesses a trait, that person will exhibit trait-relevant behavior in trait-relevant eliciting conditions.* This conditional reflects some natural locutions – "I thought Andrew was loyal, but if he really was, he would have taken my side at the meeting" – but it inhabits philosophically shaky ground.

Metaphysicians have devoted considerable ingenuity to examples where a dispositional attribution looks true while the associated conditional looks false; some take these examples to show that the conditional approach cannot serve as an analysis of the notion of a disposition. Consider "masking" problems, where a disposition is present together with a countervailing disposition, manifest in identical circumstances, that prevents the first disposition from being manifested. Imagine that my crippling shyness prevents my friendliness from being expressed

and assume, as seems plausible, the same class of eliciting conditions is relevant to each trait; I have the disposition to friendliness, but the conditional will be false, because my shyness always trumps my friendliness. This is not simply metaphysical delicacy; people do say things like "he's really a nice person, he's just a little shy" by way of excusing the socially uneasy.

Such examples seem to show that the conditional analysis fails. No bother: I'm doing moral psychology, not metaphysics; my interest is not in conceptual analysis but in the evidential standards governing trait attribution. In outline, the relevant standards are not far to seek. If observed behavior conforms to the expectations expressed in the conditional, attribution looks to be warranted; if the expectations expressed in the conditional are unmet, there is pressure to withhold attribution. Think again of the masking problem: Are attributions of friendliness warranted when friendly behavior is invariably blocked by shyness? Perhaps such questions are not easily settled, but it's pretty clear who needs to be doing most of the talking: The burden of proof lies with someone attributing friendliness in the face of repeated failures to act friendly, while someone asserting the opposite view occupies an enviable rhetorical position. There are certainly metaphysical obscurities plaguing the notion of a disposition, but the conditional neatly articulates a thought that seems plain enough: Attribution of character and personality traits is associated with behavioral expectations.

Virtues

Talk of traits as dispositions risks vacuity, if it provides explanations no more enlightening than "he acted in this manner because he has dispositions to behave in this manner." In particular, describing virtues as behavioral dispositions is only a very partial accounting; virtue is standardly thought to involve not only what occurs "on the outside" in the form of overt behavior but also what occurs "on the inside" in the form of motives, emotions, and cognitions. For example,

according to McDowell's (1978: 21–23; 1979: 332–33) influential account, virtue is characterized by a "perceptual capacity" or "reliable sensitivity" to ethically salient features of one's surroundings. Virtues are not mere dispositions but intelligent dispositions, characterized by distinctive patterns of emotional response, deliberation, and decision as well as by more overt behavior.

This is not to say that behavior is inconsequential: "His ethical perceptions were unfailingly admirable, although he behaved only averagely" is an uninspiring epitaph. In Fitzgerald's *Gatsby*, Carraway puts it pointedly: "Conduct may be founded on the hard rock or the wet marshes, but after a certain point I don't care what it's founded on." Carraway's exasperation seems a bit willful, but he's right to say that there's no getting around the question of behavior, whatever psychological story gets told. I doubt any writer on virtue is seriously inclined to deny this. As Aristotle (1984: 1098b30–1099a5) observes, the activity, not the possession, of virtue is paramount; possession without activity means a life where nothing virtuous gets done. Accounts of virtue emphasizing "internal" processes are best understood as compliments, not competitors, to characterizations emphasizing behavioral dispositions, inasmuch as they explicate the psychological processes subserving behavior. For example, McDowell (1979: 332–33, 343–46) maintains that virtue's characteristic perceptual capacity produces ethically appropriate conduct; he invokes virtues to explain the virtuous person's behavior. While overt behavior is only one facet of interest for a moral psychology of traits, it is certainly of central interest.

I should say something more about the behaviors or, rather, patterns of behavior at issue. According to Aristotle (1984: 1105a27–b1), genuinely virtuous action proceeds from "firm and unchangeable character" rather than from transient motives. The virtues are *hexeis* (1984: 1106a11–12), and a *hexis* is a state that is "permanent and hard to change" (1984: *Categories*,

8b25–29a9). Accordingly, while the good person may suffer misfortune that impairs his activities and diminishes happiness, he "will never [*oudepote*] do the acts that are hateful and mean" (1984: 1100b32–34; cf. 1128b29; cf. Cooper 1999: 299n14). The presence of virtue is supposed to provide assurance as to what will get done as well as what won't; for Aristotle (1984: 1101a1–8; 1140a26–b30), the paradigmatically virtuous *phronimos*, or practically wise man, is characterized by his ability to choose the course of action appropriate to whatever circumstance he is in, whether it be easy or excruciating. *Arete*, Aristotle says, is "always concerned with what is harder" (1984: 1105a8–10); standing firm in the most terrifying crises, not just in any frightening situation, is diagnostic of the brave person (1984: 1115a24–26; 1117a15–22).

These features of Aristotle's moral psychology are prominent in contemporary virtue ethics. McDowell (1978: 26–27) contends that considerations favoring behavior contrary to virtue are "silenced" in the virtuous person; although she may experience inducements to vice, she will not count them as reasons for action. Again, good character provides positive as well as negative assurance; according to Dent (1975: 328), virtue effects appropriate behavior in "ever-various and novel situations," while for McDowell (1979: 331–33), genuine virtue is expected to "produce nothing but right conduct." As I put it, virtues are supposed to be *robust* traits; if a person has a robust trait, they can be confidently expected to display trait-relevant behavior across a wide variety of trait-relevant situations, even where some or all of these situations are not optimally conducive to such behavior. I've already burdened the text with too many quotations, but let me emphasize that the above selections are quite representative: An emphasis on robust traits and behavioral consistency is entirely standard in the Aristotelian tradition of character ethics.

Consistency alone does not a virtue make, as can be seen with another notion that has had some ethical currency, integrity. The term is sometimes used as a highly general term of approbation: Saying that a person has integrity can mean something similar to saying that they are a good or admirable person. But integrity can figure in a life that is morally suspect or even morally reprehensible; the Nazi who cannot be bribed to spare Jews very arguably displays integrity. As the etymological origin of "integrity" in the Latin *integritas* or "wholeness" tempts one to put it, the incorruptible Nazi manifests a unity between his reprehensible principles and his loathsome deeds; rather than being swayed by financial inducements, he consistently acts in accordance with his values. Whatever one cares about, this unity is necessary for executing one's projects in the face of obstacles; without integrity, it is only by luck that one's values will come to pass in their life. A stiff spine alone is not enough for a good life, but it is difficult to imagine a good life without one. Relatedly, to say that someone "has character" is not necessarily to express wholehearted approbation, as attributions of virtue (when offered without irony) typically are, but the locution will, it seems to me, generally carry at least grudging admiration; a bad man who stands up for what he believes can in this respect display estimable character, while falling dismally short of virtue. For my purposes, the thing to note is that the ethical interest of notions like robustness and behavioral consistency extends well beyond their association with virtue.

Character and personality

A preoccupation with behavioral consistency is not limited to ethics; it is equally evident in personality psychology. According to Pervin (1994a: 108), a personality trait is "a disposition to behave expressing itself in consistent patterns of functioning across a range of situations," while Brody (1988: 31) understands personality traits as "personal dispositions to behave in comparable ways in many diverse situations [...]." Once again, talk of traits as

dispositions invites a conditional: *If a person possesses a trait, that person will exhibit trait-relevant behavior in trait-relevant eliciting conditions.* This initial formulation is inadequate; it seems to imply that traits will exceptionlessly issue in trait-relevant behavior, but sporadic failures of trait-relevant behavior probably shouldn't be taken to disconfirm attributions. Then the conditional should be formulated probabilistically: *If a person possesses a trait, that person will engage in trait-relevant behaviors in trait-relevant eliciting conditions* with probability p. Not just any probability will do; probabilities of slightly above chance do not underwrite confident attributions of a trait. The conditional should be amended once more: *If a person possesses a trait, that person will engage in trait-relevant behaviors in trait-relevant eliciting conditions* with markedly above chance *probability p.* Now "markedly above chance" is not a locution of admirable precision. In a general statement, this imprecision is unavoidable, because the degree of predictive confidence associated with a trait attribution may vary according to the trait and individual in question. Fruitful argument must attend to particular instances, but insofar as it is safe to say that a chance probability of trait-relevant behavior is no evidence for attribution, it is quite plausible to think that in the generality of cases, the probability must substantially exceed chance.

Not every consistent behavior pattern is telling evidence for trait attribution: If someone consistently behaves gregariously across a run of situations where most everyone would, their behavior is not decisive evidence for extraversion. Rather, it is *individuating* behavior – behavior that is outside the population norm for a situation – that counts as evidence for trait attribution. Actually, individuation per se is not the issue; in principle, every individual in a population could possess a trait. Individuation is evidentially significant because where trait-relevant behavior varies markedly in a situation, there is reason to think that the situation is less than optimally conducive to that behavior.

Situations of this sort are *diagnostic*, unfavorable enough to trait-relevant behavior that such behavior seems better explained by reference to individual dispositions than by reference to situational facilitators. Behavioral consistency across a run of situations, where at least some of the situations are diagnostic, is the evidence required for attribution of personality traits. Like virtues, personality traits are supposed to be robust.

It's clear that philosophers' talk of character and psychologists' talk of personality exhibit substantial affinities, as psychologists' not infrequent use of "character" in discussions of traits and personality might lead one to suspect. Still, I should take a bit of care over the differences. Character traits appear to have an evaluative dimension that personality traits need not; for example, the honest person presumably behaves as she does because she values forthrightness, while the introvert may not value, and may in fact disvalue, retiring behavior in social situations. This is not to say that acting according to a value requires a conscious belief, and it is still less to say that the virtuous person must act "in the name" of virtue [...]. But if a person maintains a value, she can be expected to voice at least recognizable variants of its characteristic considerations when asked to rationalize her behavior; if a person has a virtue, the relevant evaluative commitments can be expected to surface under "evaluative cross-examination."

The thought that virtues have this sort of evaluative dimension is respectably Aristotelian; Aristotle (1984: 1105a30–b1) maintains that genuinely virtuous activity is undertaken knowingly and for its own sake. It is less clear that this thought neatly applies to vices and other negatively valenced traits of character; is cowardly behavior necessarily the expression of the actor's values? This is a reasonable concern, but I'll insist that cowardice and other negatively valenced character traits do involve the relevant sort of evaluative dimension; perhaps the coward values safety more than honor, loyalty, and dignity. To get tolerably clear on this would take

rather more discussion of evaluation, and the evaluations associated with each trait of character, than I'm going to provide. For my interest is not so much what distinguishes character and personality traits as what they have in common: behavioral consistency as a primary criterion of attribution.

My approach may seem simplistic even with regard to behavioral consistency: It appears to be a "one size fits all" account, deaf to differences amongst individual traits, while different traits may have different attributive standards. For example, conceptions of traits like courage and loyalty appear to have high standards for behavioral reliability "built in," while predictive confidence regarding displays of compassion may be considerably lower; loyalty may require unfailing fealty to obligation, while compassion may require only engaging a certain percentage of opportunities for compassionate behavior [...]. Moreover, attribution of negatively valenced traits may require very little in the way of behavioral consistency; perhaps one doesn't have to reliably falter, but only sporadically falter, to be counted a coward As a rough and ready generalization, I'm inclined to say that "generic" character and personality traits are typically expected to be less robust than virtues; in the exalted realm of virtue, attributive standards may be substantially more demanding. But matters are best put to the test by consideration of particular traits and concrete cases, something I'll need to do a good bit of as we go along. At present, please note that the difficulty I wish to press does not involve violations of some absolute and general standard of consistency for trait attribution; I do not suppose that any such standard exists. Rather, the difficulty is that for important examples of personality and character traits, there is a marked disparity between the extent of behavioral consistency that familiar conceptions of the trait lead one to expect and the extent of behavioral consistency that systematic observation suggests one is justified in expecting.

The inseparability of the virtues

Aristotelian moral psychology involves not only a view about the nature of character traits, but also a view of character organization. Aristotle (1984: 1144b30–1145a2) maintains a reciprocity thesis, the view that "you have one of the virtues of character if and only if you have them all" (see Irwin 1988: 61), while contemporary writers like McDowell have endorsed a unity thesis, where the apparently discrete virtues turn out to be different manifestations of a "single complex sensitivity" (1979: 333 [...]). Such claims have struck many commentators as badly contrary to fact [...]. It is easy to imagine a person who is, say, courageous and intemperate; indeed, it is tempting to think that such a person is courageous in part *because* she is intemperate.

However, the seemingly implausible inseparability thesis is motivated by two quite plausible claims: first, that virtue reliably secures ethically appropriate conduct and, second, that evaluative considerations are interdependent [...]. For example, I cannot know whether I should now battle unto death if I do not know whether the cause I champion is a just one; courage untempered by justice may effect conduct that is stupid, brutal, or both. With a little thought, such possibilities multiply: Justice is constrained by compassion, compassion by justice, and similarly for the other virtues; it becomes tempting to think that the full realization of one virtue requires the full realization of them all.

Skepticism lingers – one might reject either of the motivating claims. Perhaps virtue can lead us to do wrongly, as when a good person loyally carries out the orders of a bad one. Or perhaps practical problems are in a sense atomistic; the simple hoplite can be genuinely courageous while knowing nothing of justice. A more modest relative of the inseparability thesis holds only that virtues and vices cannot coexist in a single personality, because genuine instances of virtues manifest evaluative commitments that preclude vices [...]. This exclusionary thesis

demands less than the inseparability thesis; while it insists that a courageous person will not be cruel, it allows that he may not be especially compassionate. But it is bold enough; although it may seem trivially true that the presence of courage rules out the corresponding vice of cowardice, why think it rules out an apparently unrelated vice like illiberality?

More sensitive to stubborn separatist intuitions is a "limited" inseparability thesis; this allows for separability of virtues across different domains of practical endeavor but asserts that virtues are inseparable within a given practical domain. Recognizing the domain-specificity of practical endeavor helps explain how the upstanding public servant can be a faithless husband; the marital and the political are different practical domains and may engage very different cognitive, motivational, and evaluative structures. We can also understand how there may be considerable integration within a practical domain; a scholar must be both diligent and honest in her research if she is to do commendable work, although this does not entail that she exhibit the same qualities in her teaching. Domain specificity is important, and it will inform my own view later on, but notice that as it stands the limited inseparability thesis involves a strong demand for integration: If the public servant is honest in the domain of her work, she will also be compassionate in that domain. Once again, this may strike us as contrary to fact: The Queen intoning "Let them eat cake" isn't prevaricating, but it ain't compassion, either. Indeed, I eventually argue that there is good empirical reason to think that conflicting traits are frequently manifested within limited practical domains.

I'll keep in mind, though, that claims of inseparability make an elusive target for empirical attacks. Defenders may claim that inseparability holds only for perfect virtue; they can thereby allow the abundant appearances of separability and simply insist that these cases involve something less than the full realization of virtue

[…]. This expedient apparently removes inseparability from empirical threat; since we can expect perfect virtue to be extremely rare, neither a paucity of cases suggesting inseparability nor a plethora of cases suggesting separability need give defenders of inseparability pause. However, I think that characterological moral psychology is very often rather more empirically ambitious than this suggests. Irwin (1997: 213) remarks that Aristotelian standards of inseparability seem "neither unrealistic nor unreasonable," while Badhwar (1996: 317) understands limited inseparability as "an empirical thesis, subject to revision by developments in psychology." Questions regarding the empirical commitments of characterological moral psychology are delicate and various, and I must postpone fuller discussion until much later in the day. For the moment, it suffices to say that the literature provides some encouragement for empirically evaluating notions of inseparability.

Globalism

The conception of character at issue, which I'll call *globalism*, can now be stated a bit more precisely. Globalism maintains the following three theses, two regarding the nature of traits and the third regarding personality organization:

(1) *Consistency.* Character and personality traits are reliably manifested in trait-relevant behavior, across a diversity of trait-relevant eliciting conditions that may vary widely in their conduciveness to the manifestation of the trait in question.

(2) *Stability.* Character and personality traits are reliably manifested in trait-relevant behaviors over iterated trials of similar trait-relevant eliciting conditions.

(3) *Evaluative integration.* In a given character or personality the occurrence of a trait with a particular evaluative valence is probabilistically related to the occurrence of other traits with similar evaluative valences.

Taken together, these theses construe personality as more or less coherent and integrated with reliable, relatively situation-resistant, behavioral implications. Or, more pithily: Globalism construes personality as an *evaluatively integrated association of robust traits*. We are justified in inferring globalist personality structures if behavior reliably exhibits the patterns expected on the postulation of such structures: In the first instance, runs of trait-relevant behavior should exhibit consistency across situations (intratrait consistency); in the second, these runs of consistent behavior will exhibit evaluative affinities with other such runs (intertrait consistency). The honest person, for example, will be consistently honest, and will also exhibit consistent behavior indicative of traits related to honesty, such as loyalty and courage.

As the preceding discussion suggests, both characterological moral psychology and personality psychology are typically committed to the first two theses, consistency and stability. The idea of evaluative integration is rather less prominent in personality psychology than in character ethics, and even in character ethics, the comprehensive integration required by the inseparability and unity theses has been the object of suspicion. Moreover, the theses are detachable: Neither consistency nor stability entails integration, and stability does not entail consistency. It also seems to me that they are differentially plausible; while I reject the consistency and evaluative integration theses, I myself will endorse a variant of stability. Then argument regarding the three globalist theses must to a certain extent proceed independently, but all three theses have been associated with Aristotelian approaches to moral psychology; at least initially, there is good reason for thinking of them together.

These qualifications made, I'll state my central contention in descriptive moral psychology. Systematic observation typically fails to reveal the behavioral patterns expected by globalism; *globalist conceptions of personality are empirically inade-* quate. This is not to repudiate every aspect, or all variants, of characterological moral psychology and personality psychology; I mean only to quarrel with commitments to the empirically inadequate aspects of globalism. Of course, since I think that many participants in these endeavors exhibit very substantial globalist commitments, the quarrel is not inconsequential. But there may well be people working in both areas who avoid doing so. To them, I apologize in advance, for I sometimes lapse into locutions like "characterological" and "personological" when I intend only approaches committed to globalism. But again, I think globalism runs far and wide through both characterological moral psychology and personality psychology; with my apology made, I may on occasion omit the qualification.

Situationism

While globalist conceptions of personality have not received much scrutiny in ethical theory, they have long been the subject of rancorous debate in social and personality psychology. The crisis came in 1968 with the publication of two critical assessments of personality psychology by Mischel and Peterson. While they expressed similar views, Mischel (1968: 146) garnered the lion's share of discussion – and criticism – with the frank assertion that globalist conceptions of personality traits are "untenable." Mischel's basic argument is simple: Globalist conceptions of personality are predicated on the existence of substantial behavioral consistency, but the requisite consistency has not been empirically demonstrated (Mischel 1968: 6–9, 146–48). Subsequent controversy notwithstanding, I think Mischel's argument is still a good one, and it should by now be clear that I endorse something like it. But if I'm to come by this endorsement honestly, I'll have to provide a fuller explication.

The story really began long before Mischel with Hartshorne and May's (1928) monumental

"Character Education Inquiry," a comprehensive empirical study of honest and deceptive behavior in schoolchildren. Hartshorne and May (1928: I, 385) found that even across quite similar situations, honest and dishonest behavior were displayed inconsistently; they concluded that honesty is not an "inner entity" but is instead "a function of the situation." Shortly thereafter, their contention was buttressed by Newcomb's (1929) study of introversion and extraversion in "problem boys," which found that trait-relevant behaviors were not organized into consistent patterns but instead were highly situation-specific and inconsistent. The difficulty and expense of extensive behavioral observation has generally prohibited exhaustive study in the vein of Hartshorne and May and Newcomb (see Ross and Nisbett 1991: 98), but where relevant behavioral research has been conducted, degrees of situational sensitivity in behavior that confound globalist constructions of personality are typical. More than twenty years after Mischel's 1968 study, Ross and Nisbett's (1991: 2–3, 97) review echoed his conclusion: Existing empirical evidence for globalist conceptions of traits is seriously deficient.

It is this research tradition that has come to be known as "situationism." Situationism's three central theoretical commitments, amounting to a qualified rejection of globalism, concern behavioral variation, the nature of traits, and personality organization.

(1) Behavioral variation across a population owes more to situational differences than dispositional differences among persons. Individual dispositional differences are not so behaviorally individuating as might have been supposed; to a surprising extent it is safest to predict, for a particular situation, that a person will behave in a fashion similar to the population norm (Ross and Nisbett 1991: 113).

(2) Systematic observation problematizes the attribution of robust traits. People will quite typically behave inconsistently with respect to the attributive standards associated with a trait, and whatever behavioral consistency is displayed may be readily disrupted by situational variation. This is not to deny the existence of stability; the situationist acknowledges that individuals may exhibit behavioral regularity over iterated trials of substantially similar situations [...].

(3) Personality is not often evaluatively integrated. For a given person, the dispositions operative in one situation may have an evaluative status very different from those manifested in another situation; evaluatively inconsistent dispositions may "cohabitate" in a single personality.

In sum, situationism rejects the first and third globalist theses, consistency and evaluative integration, while allowing a variant of the second, stability.

In my interpretation, situationism does not entail an unqualified skepticism about the personological determinants of behavior; it is not a Skinnerian behaviorism. Although reflection on situationism has caused me to reject an understanding of behavior as ordered by robust traits, I allow for the possibility of temporally stable, situation-particular, "local" traits that are associated with important individual differences in behavior. As I understand things, these local traits are likely to be extremely fine-grained; a person might be repeatedly helpful in iterated trials of the same situation and repeatedly unhelpful in trials of another, surprisingly similar, situation. The difficulty for globalism is that local traits are not likely to effect the patterns of behavior expected on broad trait categories like "introverted," "compassionate," or "honest." Even seemingly inconsequential situational variations may "tap" different dispositions, eventuating in inconsistent behavior. I argue that systematic observation of behavior, rather than suggesting evaluatively integrated personality structures, suggests instead *fragmented* personality structures – evaluatively disintegrated associations of multiple local traits [...].

Unfortunately, situationism is sometimes the victim of caricature. Situationists have been

accused of foul play in setting the standards for trait theory, allegedly "demanding consistency of behavior in every single situation [...]." This could hardly apply to the approach I've taken here, which proposes probabilistic standards for trait attribution. Critics have also charged situationists with making grandiose claims for the power of situations; Funder and Ozer (1983: 111) claim that the situationists often take their experiments to suggest that "correlations between measurable dimensions of situations and single behaviors typically approach 1.0." Neither I nor any situationist I know of maintains such an unlikely view, which is tantamount to saying that individual differences are in general very nearly irrelevant to behavioral outcomes. Indeed, I've just proposed an account of personality that acknowledges individual dispositional differences.

The situationist must acknowledge with Mischel (1968: 8) that "previous experience and genetic and constitutional characteristics affect behavior and result in vast individual differences among people," while the personality theorist must acknowledge with Allport (1966: 2) that situations have extraordinary effects on behavior. We must take care to avoid needlessly polarizing the debate; all parties should agree that behavioral outcomes are inevitably a function of a complex interaction between organism and environment.

It likewise courts misunderstanding to suppose that situationism is embarrassed by the considerable behavioral regularity that undoubtedly is observed; because the preponderance of people's life circumstances may involve a relatively structured range of situations, behavioral patterns are not, for the most part, radically disordered (see Mischel 1968: 281). Still, there is reason to doubt that behavioral regularity is as substantial as casual observation may suggest. Every person, in the course of his or her life, exhibits a multitude of behaviors; since social observation is usually piecemeal and unsystematic (even intimates may be observed on

occasions limited in both number and diversity), observers should be hesitant to take a limited sampling of behaviors as evidence for confident interpretations of personality. At bottom, the question is whether the behavioral regularity we observe is to be primarily explained by reference to robust dispositional structures or situational regularity. I insist that the striking variability of behavior with situational variation favors the latter hypothesis.

Personality, behavior, and evidence

One response personality psychologists have made, when comparing their theoretical models with the messy and multifarious quality of human behavior, is to deemphasize the importance of overt behavior in the measurement of personality. Allport argued (1966: 1; cf. 1931) that "[a]cts, and even habits, that are inconsistent with a trait are not proof of the nonexistence of the trait." It is certainly right to say, given the importance of psychological dynamics to thinking about personality, that behavior alone is not diagnostically decisive. But if one leans too hard on this observation, one may start to say things that sound rather dubious; if a *habit* that is contrary to a trait does not undermine the attribution, it is hard to see what possibly could. Personality theory too lenient in its behavioral criteria is, because of its lack of empirically testable hypotheses, "unfalsifiable [...]."

A central reason for the neglect of overt behavior in personality psychology has been the difficulty and expense of systematic behavioral observation. The standard and substantially cheaper alternative is "paper and pencil" personality assessment based on subjects' self-reports, where investigators have found regularities in test responses favorable to standard theoretical constructions of personality [...]. Then it is hardly surprising that personality psychologists might pursue self-report measures at the expense of behavioral measures and insist, with Allport, that behavioral measures are not a decisive factor

in trait attribution. Unfortunately, there is often "a minimal correlation, or none at all" between self-report and overt behavioral measures of traits (Holzman and Kagan 1995: 5), so that the competing approaches to personality are likely to generate conflicting conclusions. It sometimes appears as though two discrete disciplines have emerged, one of self-report taxonomies and one of overt behavioral measures, with very different standards of success and, accordingly, very different results.

Judiciously interpreted responses to well-designed paper and pencil instruments can tell us much about what people are like; not all significant differences among persons are neatly related to overt behavior. But psychologists, like the rest of us, are interested in the behavioral implications of personality. Allport (1966: 1; cf. 1931), despite the hedge we have just considered, conceives of traits as "determinative" in behavior, while Tellegen (1991: 12) insists that "the contribution of traits to behavior makes a difference in life." This difference, I think, is fairly understood as involving more than results on pencil and paper personality inventories. A viable psychology of personality must rely on behavioral observations as well as self-report data; if trait attributions are to help tell us how people will get on in the world, they must be shown to have behavioral implications.

Nevertheless, an emphasis on overt behavior should not be allowed to obscure conceptual difficulty especially regarding which behaviors and situations are relevant to a trait. Only when there are at least rough and ready answers to these questions can empirical investigation be profitably pursued, yet the problem of fully specifying the conditions relevant to manifestation of a disposition is notoriously complex [...]. Fortunately, useful empirical work does not require full specification; so long as it is possible to identify conditions of uncontroversial relevance to a trait, empirical investigation of behavior in these conditions can be more or less conceptually untroubled. In the next chapter

[see original reading], I'll proceed in this fashion with the ethical trait I take as my central test case, compassion. I'll identify conditions that are obviously relevant to compassion, and since these conditions have been the subject of empirical study, I'll be able to put globalist conceptions of compassion to empirical test. If I'm right about what they show, such tests are powerful motivation for skepticism about traditional notions of character.

II. Moral character, moral behavior

The trouble with Eichmann was precisely that so many were like him, and that the many were neither perverted nor sadistic, that they were, and still are, terribly and terrifyingly normal.

Hannah Arendt

Totalitarianism specializes in the dissolution of fortitude, whether by the extremes of physical torture [...] or by the psychological degradation of "thought reform" or "brainwashing [...]." These practices are repellent, but their effects are not-unexpected. Aristotle (1984: 1115b7–9) acknowledged that some things exceed human endurance, and Russell (1945: 267), with another 2,000-odd years of history to consider, remarked that the will withstands the tyrant only so long as the tyrant is unscientific. Situationism teaches something more surprising and, in a sense, more disturbing. The unsettling observation doesn't concern behavior in extremis, but behavior in situations that are rather less than extreme; the problem is not that substantial situational factors have substantial effects on what people do, but that seemingly insubstantial situational factors have substantial effects on what people do. The disproportionate impact of these "insubstantial" situational factors presses charges of empirical inadequacy against characterological moral psychology: If dispositional structures were typically so robust as familiar conceptions of character and personality lead one to believe,

insubstantial factors would not so frequently have such impressive effects. In the present chapter, I'll document the evidence for this contention.

Prelude: character and compassion

On a March night in 1963, Catherine Genovese was stabbed to death. Her killer attacked her three times over a period of 35 minutes. Despite Genovese's clearly audible screams, 37 of 38 witnesses in her middle-class Queens neighborhood did not so much as call the police; one, after first calling a friend for advice, notified authorities only when the attacks had ended and Genovese was mortally wounded [...]. While there is room for controversy over just what compassion consists in, I suspect few would deny that complete inaction when a screaming young woman is slowly butchered nearby problematizes its attribution. As opposed to compassion the emotional syndrome, which may be quite transitory, compassion the character trait is a stable and consistent disposition to perform beneficent actions [...]; failures to behave compassionately when doing so is appropriate and not unduly costly are evidence against attributing the trait.

The experimental and historical records reveal that such omissions, as well as similarly incompassionate actions, commonly occur where the obstacles to compassion and the pressures to incompassion seem remarkably slight: the failures are disproportionate to the pressures. In the first instance, this problematizes drinking about compassion in terms of a robust character trait. If I'm right, however, compassion exemplifies a general problem for characterological moral psychology. I'll treat compassion as a sort of test case.

In part, this strategy is opportunistic: There are quantities of empirical work on compassion-relevant behavior. I'm not merely an opportunist, however; as a core ethical concern on a variety of evaluative perspectives, compassion is a natural locus of discussion. Somewhat awkwardly for me, compassion does not appear

in Aristotle's discussion of virtues, but I think it would be a mistake to suppose that he had no interest in the sort of concerns associated with compassion. For example, while Aristotle's magnanimous man is decidedly not a compassionate saint, Aristotle (1984: 1123b30–34) insists such a person will not wrong others; it would be surprising if Aristotle expected him to brutalize innocents or stand by while others do so. Behaviors associated with compassion are of substantial interest for any ethical perspective that emphasizes other-regarding concern, that is, most any recognizably ethical perspective. There may be those who reject this characterization of ethics, but there's little doubt that they are in the minority.

My arguments are not contingent on any particular understanding of compassion; I could as easily couch discussion in terms of what psychologists rather colorlessly call "prosocial behavior," [...] inasmuch as ethical reflection is preoccupied with such conduct. Moreover, my arguments do not depend on assuming any especially demanding ethical standard. Unlike "heroic" virtues such as courage, compassion is the subject of quite commonplace ethical demands, demands that are customarily applied to ordinary people in ordinary circumstances. The problem that the empirical work presents is not widespread failure to meet heroic standards – perhaps this would come as no surprise – but widespread failure to meet quite modest standards. All things considered, my test case should resonate rather broadly.

With this backdrop in mind, it's time for the empirical evidence. I beg the reader's indulgence in a long-winded discussion; this is the only way to responsibly assess a vast experimental literature.

Helping behavior

Mood effects

Imagine a person making a call in a suburban shopping plaza. As the caller leaves the phone

booth, along comes Alice, who drops a folder full of papers that scatter in the caller's path. Will the caller stop and help before the only copy of Alice's magnum opus is trampled by the bargain-hungry throngs? Perhaps it depends on the person: Jeff, an entrepreneur incessantly stalking his next dollar, probably won't, while Nina, a political activist who takes in stray cats, probably will. Nina is the compassionate type; Jeff isn't. In these circumstances we expect their true colors to show. But this may be a mistake, as an experiment by Isen and Levin (1972) shows. There the paper-dropper was an experimental assistant, or "confederate." For one group of callers, a dime was planted in the phone's coin return slot; for the other, the slot was empty. Here are the results (after Isen and Levin 1972: 387):

	Helped	Did Not Help
Found dime	14	2
Did not find dime	1	24

If greedy Jeff finds the dime, he'll likely help, and if compassionate Nina doesn't, she very likely won't. The situation, more than the person, seems to be making the difference.

On Isen and Levin's (1972: 387) reading, the determinative impact of finding the dime proceeds by influencing affective states; apparently, this small bit of good fortune elevates mood, and "feeling good leads to helping." Numerous studies have shown that mood can have powerful impacts on a wide variety of human functioning: risk taking [...], memory [...], cooperative behavior [...] and problem solving [...]. Most relevantly, positive affect has repeatedly been shown to be related to prosocial behavior [...]. The crucial observation is not that mood influences behavior – no surprise there – but just how unobtrusive the stimuli that induce the determinative moods can be. Finding a bit of change is something one would hardly bother to remark on in describing one's day, yet it makes the difference between helping and not.

Related studies suggest that people are more likely to help when exposed to pleasant aromas [...]. Baron and Thomley (1994: 780) suspect that the mediating factor is positive affect: Good smells induce good moods, which facilitate prosocial behavior. Once again, a rather trivial situational factor may have a nontrivial impact on prosocial behavior; Baron (1997: 500–501) found subjects near a fragrant bakery or coffee shop more likely to change a dollar bill when asked than those near a neutral-smelling dry goods store. If one must have trouble, best to have it where homey scents abound!

Back to our troublesome dime. Are Isen and Levin's nonhelpers behaving incompassionately? Scattered papers are a less-than-dire predicament, so the omission is not serious. On the other hand, the cost of action is low: Help round up the papers and be on your way. And if you've endured the humiliation of scrabbling after scattered papers on a busy street, you may regard such a mishap as one where compassionate behavior is appropriate. In numerous instances Isen and Levin's nonhelping subjects literally trampled the fallen papers; while the footprints they left behind may not be evidence of viciousness, they do seem to tell against the attribution of compassion. Of course, the situation presents bystanders some difficulty in interpretation – would she like help, or would I embarrass her? In fact, evidence suggests that situational ambiguity is likely to impede helping behavior: for example, individuals who hear an emergency may be less likely to help than those who both see and hear it [...]. This does not undermine Isen and Levin's result, however. While a sensitive look at the circumstances may tell against judging the passive bystanders too harshly, it does not alter the facts: A mere dime strongly influenced compassion relevant behavior.

Unfortunately, the Isen and Levin subjects did not undergo personality evaluations, so there's no direct evidence regarding dispositional differences, or the lack of dispositional differences, between the helpers and the nonhelpers.

But think for a moment of the data: Only 13 percent of dime finders failed to help, whereas 96 percent of nonfinders were similarly passive. Given these numbers, doesn't "He found a dime" look like a plausible, if incomplete, explanation of why Jeff the entrepreneur managed to help? Or are we to suppose that, of a more or less random sample of public phone users in a shopping mall, those possessing robust compassionate dispositions happened to luck into the dime, while their callous brethren didn't […]?

Now one person did help, despite not finding a dime; perhaps the study shows only that compassionate people are few and far between. Virtue, Aristotle (1984: 1105a7–12) tells us, is difficult; the fact that compassion often fails to be manifested in behavior will not surprise any but the most starry-eyed romantic. But the cases I consider here, like the phone booth study, are ones where prosocial behavior looks to be "minimally decent samaritanism" […]; the deeds in question do not require heroic commitment or sacrifice. I am not establishing a heroic standard for good character and arguing from the rarity of this standard being achieved to a general skepticism about characterological moral psychology. Rather, there are problems for standards of character that are well short of heroic, and they are often found in very ordinary places, like the coin return of a public phone.

Group effects

Another unsettling series of findings, partly instigated by public dismay over the Genovese murder, concern the oft-demonstrated inhibition of helping in groups, or "group effect." In a representative experiment by Latané and Darley (1970: 44–54), puffs of artificial smoke were introduced through a wall vent into a room where undergraduate subjects were filling out forms. After several minutes there was enough smoke to "obscure vision, produce a mildly acrid odor, and interfere with breathing." When the subject was alone in the room, 75 percent

(18 of 34) reported the smoke to experimenters within four minutes; when the subject was with two passive confederates, only 10 percent of subjects (1 of 10) reported it. In a trial with three naive subjects per group, in only 38 percent of groups did someone report the smoke, as opposed to the 98 percent one would expect statistically based on the 75 percent response rate in the alone condition. Latané and Darley (1970: 48–52) speculate that in this instance the group effect proceeded by influencing interpretative processes: Seeing confederates acting unconcerned, subjects were more inclined to interpret the "ambiguous" stimulus of artificial smoke as "nondangerous" steam or air conditioning vapors, despite the fact that it moved them to cough, rub their eyes, and open windows.

A related study by Latané and Rodin (1969; cf. Latané and Darley 1970: 57–67) solicited Columbia University undergraduates for participation in a market research study. When they reported to the experimental site, an attractive young woman introduced herself as a "market research representative," provided the subjects with some questionnaires to fill out, and withdrew behind a curtain dividing the room. Subjects were subsequently interrupted by a loud crash, followed by the woman's cries of pain. Apparently, this constituted an arresting and realistic impression of a serious fall taking place behind the curtain: Less than 5 percent of subjects reported suspecting that the victim's cries were recorded, as they in fact were. Seventy percent of bystanders offered help when they waited alone, compared with 7 percent in the company of an unresponsive confederate. When two subjects not previously acquainted waited together, in only 40 percent of groups did one of the subjects intervene, compared with the 91 percent expected based on a 70 percent rate when subjects were alone. Here, too, the group effect appeared to operate through the interpretative process: Nonhelpers said they were unsure of what happened or decided it was not serious.

Accordingly, postexperimental interviews revealed that passive subjects did not feel as though they had acted callously: They typically claimed they would readily help in a "real" emergency [...].

Latané and Darley (1970: 95–100) also discovered a somewhat different effect. They asked students to participate in a group discussion of the problems faced by college students in an urban environment. The ostensible "discussion" proceeded by intercom with the experimenter absent and the subject isolated in a cubicle, ostensibly to preserve anonymity; in fact, the other "participants" were tape recordings, and the situation was designed to address a variant of the group effect. One tape-recorded participant described his difficulty with seizures; he later gave an arresting impression of someone suffering a seizure (1970: 97, 100). Again, the group effect: 100 percent of subjects believing themselves alone with the seizure victim intervened, while only 62 percent of subjects in a "group" consisting of subject, victim, and five more tape-recorded participants did so.

Apparently, in this case the inhibiting mechanism consisted at least partly in a "diffusion of responsibility" (Latané and Darley 1970: 101, 111): The presence of others meant that no individual was forced to bear full responsibility for intervention. When the experimenter terminated each trial after 6 minutes, unresponsive subjects in group conditions appeared aroused and conflicted. Isolated in their cubicle, they lacked the social cues necessary to facilitate an interpretation congenial to inaction, but knowing there were other bystanders, it was not clear that intervention was up to them. In contrast, the passive bystanders in the previous two experiments, where social influence rather than diffusion of responsibility was the inhibiting factor, seemed relaxed; the presence of other passive bystanders assured them that their inaction was appropriate despite the considerable evidence to the contrary (Latané and Darley

1970: 111–12). Then the group effect involves more than one sort of effect. It is not simply that numbers of bystanders influence intervention; different configurations of bystanders may influence intervention in different ways. The operative processes are doubtless complicated, but one general implication of the group effect studies seems fairly clear: Mild social pressures can result in neglect of apparently serious ethical demands.

Good Samaritans

In one of the most widely discussed situationist experiments, Darley and Batson (1973) invited students at the Princeton Theological Seminary to participate in a study of "religious education and vocations." Subjects began experimental procedures by filling out questionnaires in one building and then reported to a nearby building for the second part of the experiment, which consisted in the giving a short verbal presentation. Before leaving the first site, subjects were told either that they were running late ("high hurry" condition), were right on time ("medium hurry" condition), or were a little early ("low hurry" condition); thus the conditions exerted a different degree of time pressure on the subjects. The behavior of interest occurred on the walk between the two sites, when each seminarian passed an experimental confederate slumped in a doorway, apparently in some sort of distress.

One might expect that most individuals training for a "helping profession" like the ministry would be strongly disposed to assist the unfortunate victim or at the very least inquire as to his condition. Instead, helping varied markedly according to degree of hurry (Darley and Batson 1973:105).

	Degree of Hurry		
	Low	Medium	High
Percentage helping	63	45	10

It's no surprise that haste can have people paying less regard to others. But the apparent disproportion between the seriousness of the situational pressures and the seriousness of the omission is surprising: The thought of being a few minutes late was enough to make subjects not notice or disregard a person's suffering. The imagery recalls the most cynical caricatures of modern life: Darley and Batson (1973: 107) report that in some cases a hurried seminarian literally stepped over the stricken form of the victim as he hurried on his way!

It is difficult to resist situationist conclusions. Subjects were hurried but certainly not coerced. Nor was there special reason to think, in the green fields of 1970s Princeton, New Jersey, that the victim posed some threat, as might be supposed in more threatening urban climes. Similarly, the placid suburban environment should have worked to reduce situational ambiguity. While urbanites who are daily confronted with the homeless may find themselves wondering whether the unfortunate individual lying on the sidewalk is sick or dying as opposed to inebriated or sleeping, such sights were presumably uncommon enough in the Princeton of 1970 to strongly suggest that something was seriously amiss [...]. But hurried seminarians failed to help. What was at stake for them? Did they somehow decide that their obligation to the experimenter trumped a general imperative to help others in distress? In its generality, this looks like a plausible interpretation, but it's hard to believe such an obligation could be viewed as very weighty: Subjects were volunteers being paid a modest $2.50, and the experimenter was someone they had only just met. Once again, there is the appearance of disproportion; in this case the demands of punctuality seem rather slight compared with the ethical demand to at least check on the condition of the confederate.

References

Allport, G. W. 1966. "Traits Revisited." *American Psychologist* 21: 1–10.

Aristotle 1984. *The Complete Works of Aristotle.* Edited by J. Barnes. Princeton: Princeton University Press.

Badhwar, N. K. 1996. "The Limited Unity of Virtue." *Noûs* 30: 306–79.

Baron, R. A. 1997. "The Sweet Smell of . . . Helping: Effects of Pleasant Ambient Fragrance on Prosocial Behavior in Shopping Malls." *Personality and Social Psychology Bulletin* 23: 498–503.

Baron, R. A., and Thomley, J. 1994. "A Whiff of Reality: Positive Affect as a Potential Mediator of the Effects of Pleasant Fragrances on Task Performance and Helping." *Environment and Behavior* 26: 766–84.

Brody, N. 1988. *Personality: In Search of Individuality.* New York: Academic.

Darley, J. M., and Batson, C. D. 1973. "From Jerusalem to Jericho: A Study of Situational and Dispositional Variables in Helping Behavior." *Journal of Personality and Social Psychology* 27: 100–108.

Dent, N. J. H. 1975. "Virtues and Actions." *Philosophical Quarterly* 25: 318–35.

Funder, D. C., and Ozer, D. J. 1983. "Behavior as a Function of the Situation." *Journal of Personality and Social Psychology* 44: 107–12.

Hartshorne, H., and May, M. A. 1928. *Studies in the Nature of Character,* vol. I: *Studies in Deceit.* New York: Macmillan.

Holzman, P., and Kagan, J. 1995. "Whither or Wither Personality Research." In P. E. Shrout and S. T. Fiske (eds.), *Personality Research, Methods, and Theory: A Festschrift Honoring Donald W. Fiske.* Hillsdale, N.J.: Lawrence Erlbaum Associates.

Irwin, T. H. 1988. "Disunity in the Aristotelian Virtues." *Oxford Studies in Ancient Philosophy: Supplementary Volume,* 1988.

Irwin, T. H. 1997. "Practical Reason Divided: Aquinas and His Critics." In G. Cullity and B. Gaut (eds.), *Ethics and Practical Reason.* Oxford: Oxford University Press.

Isen, A. M., and Levin, P. F. 1972. "Effect of Feeling Good on Helping: Cookies and Kindness." *Journal of Personality and Social Psychology* 21: 384–88.

Latané, B., and Darley, J. M. 1970. *The Unresponsive Bystander: Why Doesn't He Help?* New York: Appleton-Century-Crofts.

Latané, B., and Rodin, J. 1969. "A Lady in Distress: Inhibiting Effects of Friends and Strangers on Bystander Intervention." *Journal of Experimental Social Psychology* 5: 189–202.

McDowell, J. 1978. "Are Moral Requirements Hypothetical Imperatives?" *Aristotelian Society Supplementary Volume* 52: 13–29.

McDowell, J. 1979. "Virtue and Reason." *Monist* 62: 331–50.

Mischel, W. 1968. *Personality and Assessment*. New York: John J. Wiley and Sons.

Newcomb, T. M. 1929. *The Consistency of Certain Extrovert-Introvert Behavior Patterns in 51 Problem Boys*. New York: Columbia University, Teachers College, Bureau of Publications.

Pervin, L. A. 1994a. "A Critical Analysis of Current Trait Theory." *Psychological Inquiry* 5: 103–13.

Ross, L., and Nisbett, R. E. 1991. *The Person and the Situation*. Philadelphia: Temple University Press.

Russell, B. 1945. *A History of Western Philosophy*. New York: Simon and Schuster.

Tellegen, A. 1991. "Personality Traits: Issues of Definition, Evidence, and Assessment." In W. M. Grove and D. Cicchetti (eds.), *Thinking Clearly about Psychology*, vol. II: *Personality and Psychopathology*. Minneapolis: University of Minnesota Press.

Value and well-being

INTRODUCTION TO SECTION VII

WE ALL BELIEVE that many things – for example, health, success, and friend-ship – are good and worth having. But are these things good in themselves, or are they good only because they lead to further goods? And, more generally, what is it that *makes* something good?

According to one theory, known as *hedonism,* the only things that are good or bad in themselves are pleasant and painful experiences. Although hedonists of course acknowledge the goodness of health, security, loving relationships, and much else, they insist that these things are only good because they promote happiness and pleasure and prevent unhappiness and pain. This view is defended by Jeremy Bentham in Chapter 45. Because Bentham is a consequentialist as well as a hedonist, he believes that the right acts to perform are those that would produce the most overall pleasure, and he methodically analyzes the factors that determine the overall value of each pleasure and pain that is associated with each act. Because hedonism is a view about what is valuable or worth seeking, it does not attempt to describe or predict anyone's actual behavior. It thus differs from *psychological* hedonism – that is, the view that people *want and seek* only pleasure – which Joel Feinberg discusses in Chapter 2.

Because hedonism implies that the best lives are those that contain the most pleasure, it naturally raises the question of which lives *are* most pleasurable. The ancient Greek philosopher Epicurus takes up this question in Chapter 47. According to Epicurus, the surest route to a pleasurable life is to take pleasure in simple things. Whereas luxuries are beyond the grasp of many, simple foods and good friends are available to all and are just as satisfying as elaborate fare and expensive pastimes. By training ourselves to want only what we can have, we lose nothing in the quality of our pleasures, but avoid the unhappiness of frustrated desire. Nor, Epicurus argues, should we fear death; for the only things to fear are pain and suffering, and those who are dead cannot experience them.

Despite its elegance and simplicity, hedonism has been criticized by many. In Chapter 46, Robert Nozick develops one line of criticism by introducing a clever science-fiction example. Nozick asks us to imagine an "experience machine" – that is, a device that could give us any experiences we chose – and asks whether we would choose to live our lives plugged into such a machine. If all that mattered to us were our experiences, we would have no qualms about plugging in. However, Nozick thinks many would reject this option, and so he concludes that experience is not the only thing that matters.

Even if pleasure is not the only good, it is surely among life's goods. Similarly, severe pain can surely make one's life worse. But why, exactly, is pleasure good and pain bad? To the hedonist, these are simply facts that admit of no further explanation. However, others explain them by pointing out that everyone *wants* to experience

pleasure and to avoid pain. If being desired is what makes pleasure good, then anything else we desire will presumably be good too. Hence, to accept this explanation is in effect to replace hedonism with a different theory of the good – one that has been called *the desire-satisfaction theory*.

In its simplest version, this theory raises many questions. Is a person's life really made better by getting what he wants if this will leave him in misery? Is it good to satisfy desires that are based on misinformation? To satisfy obsessive or trivial desires? Guided by these questions, many desire-satisfaction theorists have sought to restrict the relevant desires to those that we would have if we were adequately informed. This idea is developed in different ways by Richard Brandt and Peter Railton (Chapters 48 and 49). According to Brandt, the significance of information is that it can causally affect our desires. For example, if someone learns that his ambition to become a doctor is based on a desire to please his parents, or that he is afraid of dogs because he was bitten by one when he was young, then he may come to prefer a different career and may come to be less afraid of dogs. If a desire would be altered in this way by exposure to new information, then for Brandt its satisfaction is not really part of the person's good. By contrast, for Railton, the crucial question is what the person would want for himself if he knew more about his situation than he actually does. As Railton himself puts it, "an individual's good consists of what he would want himself to want, or to pursue, were he to contemplate his present situation from a standpoint fully and vividly informed about himself and his circumstances . . . ."

Despite their differences, hedonism and the various desire-satisfaction theories all take a person's good to depend on facts about his individual psychology or subjective states. However, another type of theory maintains that certain states or events – for example, knowledge, close relationships, and achievements – are valuable for reasons independent of all such factors. Of the theories of this sort, some maintain that the value of knowledge, achievement, and the rest admits of no further explanation – this echoes what hedonists say about pleasure – while others maintain that their value can be explained by certain facts about human nature. The view that a state or activity is valuable when it realizes some aspect of human nature is known as *perfectionism*, and Thomas Hurka defends a version of it in Chapter 50. Following Aristotle, Hurka maintains that humans have various essential properties, including their physical organization and their capacities for theoretical and practical reason. In Hurka's view, the best life for human beings is one which develops their physical powers and both rational capacities to a high degree.

The last two chapters in the section, by Derek Parfit and Thomas Scanlon, do not advance further theories of value, but rather shed further light on the ones we have already encountered. In Chapter 51, Parfit presents a useful overview of the terrain. Although his vocabulary differs from that employed here, he distinguishes a number of variants of each major approach and lucidly summarizes the strengths and weaknesses of each. The truth, Parfit suggests, may lie in a combination of objective and subjective elements: what is valuable may be "to have knowledge, to be engaged in rational activity, to experience mutual love, and to be aware of beauty, while strongly wanting just these things." However, according to Scanlon (Chapter 52), the usual

ways of thinking rest on a presupposition that we should reject. In Scanlon's view, the idea that a thing's value gives us reason to promote it gets things exactly backward – instead, the notion of reasons is primary. He argues, for example, that we have various reasons to care about our friends, to be loyal to them, and to promote their interests, and that "the claim that friendship is valuable is best understood as the claim that . . . the reasons recognized by someone who values friendship are in fact good reasons." Scanlon's account relocates the source of our reasons from the value of things to their natural properties – for example, from the value of friendship to a friend's needs and concerns. For this reason, he refers to it as "the buck-passing account."

Chapter 45

Jeremy Bentham

PLEASURE AS THE GOOD

Value of a lot of pleasure or pain, how to be measured

I. Pleasures then, and the avoidance of pains, are the *ends* which the legislator has in view: it behooves him therefore to understand their *value*. Pleasures and pains are the *instruments* he has to work with: it behooves him therefore to understand their force, which is again, in other words, their value.

II. To a person considered *by himself*, the value of a pleasure or pain considered *by itself*, will be greater or less, according to the four following circumstances.[1]

1. Its *intensity*.
2. Its *duration*.
3. Its *certainty or uncertainty*.
4. Its *propinquity or remoteness*.

III. These are the circumstances which are to be considered in estimating a pleasure or a pain considered each of them by itself. But when the value of any pleasure or pain is considered for the purpose of estimating the tendency of any *act* by which it is produced, there are two other circumstances to be taken into the account; these are,

5. Its *fecundity*, or the chance it has of being followed by sensations of the *same* kind: that is, pleasures, if it be a pleasure: pains, if it be a pain.

6. Its *purity*, or the chance it has of *not* being followed by sensations of the *opposite* kind: that is, pains, if it be a pleasure: pleasures, if it be a pain.

These two last, however, are in strictness scarcely to be deemed properties of the pleasures or the pain itself; they are not, therefore, in strictness to be taken into the account of the value of that pleasure or that pain. They are in strictness to be deemed properties only of the act, or other event, by which such pleasure or pain has been produced; and accordingly are only to be taken into the account of the tendency of such act or such event.

IV. To a *number* of persons, with reference to each of whom the value of a pleasure or a pain is considered, it will be greater or less, according to seven circumstances: to wit, the six preceding ones; viz.

1. Its *intensity*.
2. Its *duration*.
3. Its *certainty or uncertainty*.
4. Its *propinquity or remoteness*.
5. Its *fecundity*.
6. Its *purity*.

And one other; to wit:

7. Its *extent*; that is, the number of persons to whom it *extends*; or (in other words) who are affected by it.

V. To take an exact account then of the general tendency of any act, by which the interests of a community are affected, proceed as follows. Begin with any one person of those whose interests seem most immediately to be affected by it: and take an account.

1. Of the value of each distinguishable *pleasure* which appears to be produced by it in the *first* instance.

2. Of the value of each *pain* which appears to be produced by it in the *first* instance.

3. Of the value of each pleasure which appears to be produced by it *after the first.* This constitutes the *fecundity of the first pleasure* and the impurity of the first pain.

4. Of the value of each *pain* which appears to be produced by it after the first. This constitutes the *fecundity of the first pain*, and the impurity of the first pleasure.

5. Sum up all the values of all the *pleasures* on the one side, and those of all the pains on the other. The balance, if it be on the side of pleasure, will give the *good* tendency of the act upon the whole, with respect to the interests of that *individual* person; if on the side of pain, the *bad* tendency of it upon the whole.

6. Take an account of the *number* of persons whose interests appear to be concerned; and repeat the above process with respect to each. *Sum up* the numbers expressive of the degrees of *good* tendency, which the act has, with respect to each individual, in regard to whom the tendency of it is *good* upon the whole: do this again with respect to each individual, in regard to whom the tendency of it is *bad* upon the whole. Take the *balance*; which, if on the side of *pleasure,* will give the general *good* *tendency* of the act, with respect to the total number of community of individuals concerned; if on the side of pain the general *evil tendency,* with respect to the same community.

VI. It is not to be expected that this process should be strictly pursued previously to every moral judgment, or to every legislative or judicial operation. It may, however, be always kept in view, and as near as the process actually pursued on these occasions approached to it, so near will such process approach to the character of an exact one.

VII. The same process is alike applicable to pleasure and pain in whatever shape they appear: and by whatever denomination they are distinguished: to pleasure, whether it be called *good* (which is properly the cause or instrument of pleasure), or *profit* (which is distant pleasure, or the cause or instrument of distant pleasure), or *convenience,* or *advantage, benefit, emolument, happiness,* and so forth: to pain, whether it be called *evil* (which corresponds to *good*), or *mischief,* or *inconvenience,* or *disadvantage,* or *loss,* or *unhappiness,* and so forth.

VIII. Nor is this a novel and unwarranted, any more than it is a useless theory. In all this there is nothing but what the practice of mankind, wheresoever they have a clear view of their own interest, is perfectly comfortable to. An article of property, an estate in land, for instance, is valuable, on what account? On account of the pleasures of all kinds which it enables a man to produce, and what comes to the same thing, the pains of all kinds which it enables him to avert. But the value of such an article of property is universally understood to rise or fall according to the length or shortness of the time which a man has in it: the certainty or uncertainty of its coming into possession: and the nearness or remoteness of the time at which, if at all, it is to come into possession. As to the *intensity* of the pleasures which a man may derive from it, this is never thought of, because it depends upon the use which each particular person may come to make of it; which cannot be estimated till the particular pleasures he may come to derive from it, or the particular pains he may come to exclude by means of it, are brought to view. For the same reason, neither does he think of the *fecundity* or purity of those pleasures.

• • •

No motives either constantly good, or constantly bad

IX. In all this chain of motives, the principal or original link seems to be the last internal motive in prospect; it is to this that all the other motives in prospect owe their materiality; and the immediately acting motive its existence. This motive in prospect, we see, is always some pleasure, or some pain; some pleasure, which the act in question is expected to be a means of continuing or producing: some pain which it is expected to be a means of discontinuing or preventing. A motive is substantially nothing more than pleasure or pain, operating in a certain manner.

X. Now, pleasure is in *itself* a good: nay, even setting aside immunity from pain, the only good: pain is in itself an evil; and, indeed, without exception, the only evil; or else the words good and evil have no meaning. And this is alike true of every sort of pain, and of every sort of pleasure. It follows, therefore, immediately and incontestably, that *there is no such thing as any sort of motive that is in itself a bad one*.[2]

XI. It is common, however, to speak of actions as proceeding from *good* or *bad* motives: in which case the motives meant are such as are internal. The impression is far from being an accurate one; and as it is apt to occur in the consideration of almost every kind of offence, it will be requisite to settle the precise meaning of it, and observe how far it quadrates with the truth of things.

XII. With respect to goodness and badness, as it is with everything else that is not itself either pain or pleasure, so is it with motives. If they are good or bad, it is only on account of their effects: good, on account of their tendency to produce pleasure, or avert pain: bad, on account of their tendency to produce pain, or avert pleasure. Now the case is, that from one and the same motive, and from every kind of motive, may proceed actions that are good, others that are bad, and others that are indifferent. This we shall proceed to show with respect to all the different kinds of motives, as determined by the various kinds of pleasures and pains.

Notes

1 These circumstances have since been denominated *elements* or *dimensions of value* in a pleasure or a pain.

Not long after the publication of the first edition, the following memoriter verses were framed, in the view of lodging more effectually, in the memory, these points, on which the whole fabric of morals and legislation may be seen to rest:

> *Intense, long, certain, speedy, fruitful, pure—*
> Such marks in *pleasures* and in *pains* endure.
> Such pleasures seek, if *private* be thy end:
> If it be *public*, wide let them *extend*.
> Such *pains* avoid, whichever be thy view:
> If pains *must* come, let them *extend* to few.

2 Let a man's motive be ill-will; call it even malice, envy, cruelty; it is still a kind of pleasure that is his motive: the pleasure he takes at the thought of the pain which he sees, or expects to see, his adversary undergo. Now even this wretched pleasure, taken by itself, is good: it may be faint; it may be short: it must at any rate be impure: yet while it lasts, and before any bad consequences arrive, it is good as any other that is not more intense.

Chapter 46

Robert Nozick

THE EXPERIENCE MACHINE

THERE ARE also substantial puzzles when we ask what matters other than how *people's* experiences feel "from the inside." Suppose there were an experience machine that would give you any experience you desired. Super-duper neuropsychologists could stimulate your brain so that you would think and feel you were writing a great novel, or making a friend, or reading an interesting book. All the time you would be floating in a tank, with electrodes attached to your brain. Should you plug into this machine for life, preprogramming your life's experiences? If you are worried about missing out on desirable experiences, we can suppose that business enterprises have researched thoroughly the lives of many others. You can pick and choose from their large library or smorgasbord of such experiences, selecting your life's experiences for, say, the next two years. After two years have passed, you will have ten minutes or ten hours out of the tank, to select the experiences of your *next* two years. Of course, while in the tank you won't know that you're there; you'll think it's all actually happening. Others can also plug in to have the experiences they want, so there's no need to stay unplugged to serve them. (Ignore problems such as who will service the machines if everyone plugs in.) Would you plug in? *What else can matter to us, other than how our lives feel from the inside?* Nor should you refrain because of the few moments of distress between the moment you've decided and the

moment you're plugged. What's a few moments of distress compared to a lifetime of bliss (if that's what you choose), and why feel any distress at all if your decision is the best one?

What does matter to us in addition to our experiences? First, we want to *do* certain things, and not just have the experience of doing them. In the case of certain experiences, it is only because first we want to do the actions that we want the experiences of doing them or thinking we've done them. (But *why* do we want to do the activities rather than merely to experience them?) A second reason for not plugging in is that we want to *be* a certain way, to be a certain sort of person. Someone floating in a tank is an indeterminate blob. There is no answer to the question of what a person is like who has long been in the tank. Is he courageous, kind, intelligent, witty, loving? It's not merely that it's difficult to tell; there's no way he is. Plugging into the machine is a kind of suicide. It will seem to some, trapped by a picture, that nothing about what we are like can matter except as it gets reflected in our experiences. But should it be surprising that what *we are* is important to us? Why should we be concerned only with how our time is filled, but not with what we are?

Thirdly, plugging into an experience machine limits us to a man-made reality, to a world no deeper or more important than that which people can construct. There is no *actual* contact with any deeper reality, though the experience of it can be

simulated. Many persons desire to leave themselves open to such contact and to a plumbing of deeper significance.[1] This clarifies the intensity of the conflict over psychoactive drugs, which some view as mere local experience machines, and others view as avenues to a deeper reality; what some view as equivalent to surrender to the experience machine, others view as following one of the reasons *not* to surrender!

We learn that something matters to us in addition to experience by imagining an experience machine and then realizing that we would not use it. We can continue to imagine a sequence of machines each designed to fill lacks suggested for the earlier machines. For example, since the experience machine doesn't meet our desire to *be* a certain way, imagine a transformation machine which transforms us into whatever sort of person we'd like to be (compatible with our staying us). Surely one would not use the transformation machine to become as one would wish, and thereupon plug into the experience machine![2] So something matters in addition to one's experiences *and* what one is like. Nor is the reason merely that one's experiences are unconnected with what one is like. For the experience machine might be limited to provide only experiences possible to the sort of person plugged in. Is it that we want to make a difference in the world? Consider then the result machine, which produces in the world any result you would produce and injects your vector input into any joint activity. We shall not pursue here the fascinating details of these or other machines. What is most disturbing about them is their living of our lives for us. Is it misguided to search for *particular* additional functions beyond the competence of machines to do for us? Perhaps what we desire is to live (an active web) ourselves, in contact with reality. (And this, machines cannot do for us.) Without elaborating on the implications of this, which I believe connect surprisingly with issues about free will and causal accounts of knowledge, we need merely note the intricacy of the question of what matters *for people* other than their experiences. Until one finds a satisfactory answer, and determines that this answer does not *also* apply to animals, one cannot reasonably claim that only the felt experiences of animals limit what we may do to them.

Notes

1   Traditional religious views differ on the *point* of contact with a transcendent reality. Some say that contact yields eternal bliss or Nirvana, but they have not distinguished this sufficiently from merely a *very* long run on the experience machine. Others think it is intrinsically desirable to do the will of a higher being which created us all, though presumably no one would think this if we discovered we had been created as an object of amusement by some superpowerful child from another galaxy or dimension. Still others imagine an eventual merging with a higher reality, leaving unclear its desirability, or where that merging leaves *us*.

2   Some wouldn't use the transformation machine at all; it seems like *cheating*. But the one-time use of the transformation machine would not remove all challenges; there would still be obstacles for the new us to overcome, a new plateau from which to strive even higher. And is this plateau any the less earned or deserved than that provided by genetic endowment and early childhood environment? But if the transformation machine could be used indefinitely often, so that we could accomplish anything by pushing a button to transform ourselves into someone who could do it easily, there would remain no limits we *need* to strain against or try to transcend. Would there be anything left *to do*? Do some theological views place God outside of time because an omniscient omnipotent being couldn't fill up his days?

Chapter 47

Epicurus

THE GOOD LIFE

Letter to Menoeceus

LET NO ONE when young delay to study philosophy, nor when he is old grow weary of his study. For no one can come too early or too late to secure the health of his soul. And the man who says that the age for philosophy has either not yet come or has gone by is like the man who says that the age for happiness is not yet come to him, or has passed away. Wherefore both when young and old a man must study philosophy, that as he grows old he may be young in blessings through the grateful recollection of what has been, and that in youth he may be old as well, since he will know no fear of what is to come. We must then meditate on the things that make our happiness, seeing that when that is with us we have all, but when it is absent we do all to win it.

The things which I used unceasingly to commend to you, these do and practise, considering them to be the first principles of the good life. First of all believe that god is a being immortal and blessed, even as the common idea of a god is engraved on men's minds, and do not assign to him anything alien to his immortality or illsuited to his blessedness: but believe about him everything that can uphold his blessedness and immortality. For gods there are, since the knowledge of them is by clear vision. But there are not such as the many believe them to be: for indeed they do not consistently represent them

as they believe them to be. And the impious man is not he who denies the gods of the many, but he who attaches to the gods the beliefs of the many. For the statements of the many about the gods are not conceptions derived from sensation, but false suppositions, according to which the greatest misfortunes befall the wicked and the greatest blessings the good by the gift of the gods. For men being accustomed always to their own virtues welcome those like themselves, but regard all that is not of their nature as alien.

Become accustomed to the belief that death is nothing to us. For all good and evil consists in sensation, but death is deprivation of sensation. And therefore a right understanding that death is nothing to us makes the mortality of life enjoyable, not because it adds to it an infinite span of time, but because it takes away the craving for immortality. For there is nothing terrible in life for the man who has truly comprehended that there is nothing terrible in not living. So that the man speaks but idly who says that he fears death not because it will be painful when it comes, but because it is painful in anticipation. For that which gives no trouble when it comes, is but an empty pain in anticipation. So death, the most terrifying of ills, is nothing to us, since so long as we exist, death is not with us; but when death comes, then we do not exist. It does not then concern either the living or the dead, since for the former it is not, and the latter are no more.

But the many at one moment shun death as the greatest of evils, at another yearn for it as a respite from the evils in life. But the wise man neither seeks to escape life nor fears the cessation of life, for neither does life offend him nor does the absence of life seem to be any evil. And just as with food he does not seek simply the larger share and nothing else, but rather the most pleasant, so he seeks to enjoy not the longest period of time, but the most pleasant.

And he who counsels the young man to live well, but the old man to make a good end, is foolish, not merely because of the desirability of life, but also because it is the same training which teaches to live well and to die well. Yet much worse still is the man who says it is good not to be born, but

'once born make haste to pass the gates of Death'.

For if he says this from conviction why does he not pass away out of life? For it is open to him to do so, if he had firmly made up his mind to this. But if he speaks in jest, his words are idle among men who cannot receive them.

We must then bear in mind that the future is neither ours, nor yet wholly not ours, so that we may not altogether expect it as sure to come, nor abandon hope of it, as if it will certainly not come.

We must consider that of desires some are natural, others vain, and of the natural some are necessary and others merely natural; and of the necessary some are necessary for happiness, others for the repose of the body, and others for very life. The right understanding of these facts enables us to refer all choice and avoidance to the health of the body and the soul's freedom from disturbance, since this is the aim of the life of blessedness. For it is to obtain this end that we always act, namely, to avoid pain and fear. And when this is once secured for us, all the tempest of the soul is dispersed, since the living creature has not to wander as though in search of something that is missing, and to look for some other thing by which he can fulfil the good of the soul and the good of the body. For it is then that we have need of pleasure, when we feel pain owing to the absence of pleasure, but when we do not feel pain, we no longer need pleasure. And for this cause we call pleasure the beginning and end of the blessed life. For we recognize pleasure as the first good innate in us, and from pleasure we begin every act of choice and avoidance, and to pleasure we return again, using the feeling as the standard by which we judge every good.

And since pleasure is the first good and natural to us, for this very reason we do not choose every pleasure, but sometimes we pass over many pleasures, when greater discomfort accrues to us as the result of them: and similarly we think many pains better than pleasures, since a greater pleasure comes to us when we have endured pains for a long time. Every pleasure then because of its natural kinship to us is good, yet not every pleasure is to be chosen: even as every pain also is an evil, yet not all are always of a nature to be avoided. Yet by a scale of comparison and by the consideration of advantages and disadvantages we must form our judgement on all these matters. For the good on certain occasions we treat as bad, and conversely the bad as good.

And again independence of desire we think a great good—not that we may at all times enjoy but a few things, but that, if we do not possess many, we may enjoy the few in the genuine persuasion that those have the sweetest pleasure in luxury who least need it, and that all that is natural is easy to be obtained, but that which is superfluous is hard. And so plain savours bring us pleasure equal to a luxurious diet, when all the pain due to want is removed; and bread and water produce the highest pleasure, when one who needs them puts them to his lips. To grow accustomed therefore to simple and not luxurious diet gives us health to the full, and makes a man alert for the needful employments of life,

and when after long intervals we approach luxuries, disposes us better towards them, and fits us to be fearless of fortune.

When, therefore, we maintain that pleasure is the end, we do not mean the pleasures of profligates and those that consist in sensuality, as is supposed by some who are either ignorant or disagree with us or do not understand, but freedom from pain in the body and from trouble in the mind. For it is not continuous drinkings and revellings, nor the satisfaction of lusts, nor the enjoyment of fish and other luxuries of the wealthy table, which produce a pleasant life, but sober reasoning, searching out the motives for all choice and avoidance, and banishing mere opinions, to which are due the greatest disturbance of the spirit.

Of all this the beginning and the greatest good is prudence. Wherefore prudence is a more precious thing even than philosophy: for from prudence are sprung all the other virtues, and it teaches us that it is not possible to live pleasantly without living prudently and honourably and justly, nor, again, to live a life of prudence, honour, and justice without living pleasantly. For the virtues are by nature bound up with the pleasant life, and the pleasant life is inseparable from them. For indeed who, think you, is a better man than he who holds reverent opinions concerning the gods, and is at all times free from fear of death, and has reasoned out the end ordained by nature? He understands that the limit of good things is easy to fulfil and easy to attain, whereas the course of ills is either short in time or slight in pain: he laughs at destiny, whom some have introduced as the mistress of all things. He thinks that with us lies the chief power in determining events, some of which happen by necessity and some by chance, and some are within our control; for while necessity cannot be called to account, he sees that chance is inconstant, but that which is in our control is subject to no master, and to it are naturally attached praise and blame. For, indeed, it were better to follow the myths about the gods than

to become a slave to the destiny of the natural philosophers: for the former suggests a hope of placating the gods by worship, whereas the latter involves a necessity which knows no placation. As to chance, he does not regard it as a god as most men do (for in a god's acts there is no disorder), nor as an uncertain cause of all things: for he does not believe that good and evil are given by chance to man for the framing of a blessed life, but that opportunities for great good and great evil are afforded by it. He therefore thinks it better to be unfortunate in reasonable action than to prosper in unreason. For it is better in a man's actions that what is well chosen should fail, rather than that what is ill chosen should be successful owing to chance.

Meditate therefore on these things and things akin to them night and day by yourself, and with a companion like to yourself, and never shall you be disturbed waking or asleep, but you shall live like a god among men. For a man who lives among immortal blessings is not like to a mortal being.

Principal doctrines

I.   The blessed and immortal nature knows no trouble itself nor causes trouble to any other, so that it is never constrained by anger or favour. For all such things exist only in the weak.

II.   Death is nothing to us: for that which is dissolved is without sensation; and that which lacks sensation is nothing to us.

III.   The limit of quantity in pleasures is the removal of all that is painful. Wherever pleasure is present, as long as it is there, there is neither pain of body nor of mind, nor of both at once.

IV.   Pain does not last continuously in the flesh, but the acutest pain is there for a very short time, and even that which just exceeds the pleasure in the flesh does not continue for many days at once. But chronic illnesses permit a predominance of pleasure over pain in the flesh.

V. It is not possible to live pleasantly without living prudently and honourably and justly, nor again to live a life of prudence, honour, and justice without living pleasantly. And the man who does not possess the pleasant life, is not living prudently and honourably and justly, and the man who does not possess the virtuous life, cannot possibly live pleasantly.

VI. To secure protection from men anything is a natural good, by which you may be able to attain this end.

VII. Some men wished to become famous and conspicuous, thinking that they would thus win for themselves safety from other men. Wherefore if the life of such men is safe, they have obtained the good which nature craves; but if it is not safe, they do not possess that for which they strove at first by the instinct of nature.

VIII. No pleasure is a bad thing in itself: but the means which produce some pleasures bring with them disturbances many times greater than the pleasures.

IX. If every pleasure could be intensified so that it lasted and influenced the whole organism or the most essential parts of our nature, pleasures would never differ from one another.

X. If the things that produce the pleasures of profligates could dispel the fears of the mind about the phenomena of the sky and death and its pains, and also teach the limits of desires and of pains, we should never have cause to blame them: for they would be filling themselves full with pleasures from every source and never have pain of body or mind, which is the evil of life.

XI. If we were not troubled by our suspicions of the phenomena of the sky and about death, fearing that it concerns us, and also by our failure to grasp the limits of pains and desires, we should have no need of natural science.

XII. A man cannot dispel his fear about the most important matters if he does not know what is the nature of the universe but suspects the truth of some mythical story. So that without natural science it is not possible to attain our pleasures unalloyed.

XIII. There is no profit in securing protection in relation to men, if things above and things beneath the earth and indeed all in the boundless universe remain matters of suspicion.

XIV. The most unalloyed source of protection from men, which is secured to some extent by a certain force of expulsion, is in fact the immunity which results from a quiet life and the retirement from the world.

XV. The wealth demanded by nature is both limited and easily procured; that demanded by idle imaginings stretches on to infinity.

XVI. In but few things chance hinders a wise man, but the greatest and most important matters reason has ordained and throughout the whole period of life does and will ordain.

XVII. The just man is most free from trouble, the unjust most full of trouble.

XVIII. The pleasure in the flesh is not increased, when once the pain due to want is removed, but is only varied: and the limit as regards pleasure in the mind is begotten by the reasoned understanding of these very pleasures and of the emotions akin to them, which used to cause the greatest fear to the mind.

XIX. Infinite time contains no greater pleasure than limited time, if one measures by reason the limits of pleasure.

XX. The flesh perceives the limits of pleasure as unlimited and unlimited time is

required to supply it. But the mind, having attained a reasoned understanding of the ultimate good of the flesh and its limits and having dissipated the fears concerning the time to come, supplies us with the complete life, and we have no further need of infinite time: but neither does the mind shun pleasure, nor, when circumstances begin to bring about the departure from life, does it approach its end as though it fell short in any way of the best life.

XXI.   He who has learned the limits of life knows that that which removes the pain due to want and makes the whole of life complete is easy to obtain; so that there is no need of actions which involve competition.

XXII.   We must consider both the real purpose and all the evidence of direct perception, to which we always refer the conclusions of opinion; otherwise, all will be full of doubt and confusion.

XXIII. If you fight against all sensations, you will have no standard by which to judge even those of them which you say are false.

XXIV.   If you reject any single sensation and fail to distinguish between the conclusion of opinion as to the appearance awaiting confirmation and that which is actually given by the sensation or feeling, or each intuitive apprehension of the mind, you will confound all other sensations as well with the same groundless opinion, so that you will reject every standard of judgement. And if among the mental images created by your opinion you affirm both that which awaits confirmation and that which does not, you will not escape error, since you will have preserved the whole cause of doubt in every judgement between what is right and what is wrong.

XXV.   If on each occasion instead of referring your actions to the end of nature, you turn to some other nearer standard when you are making a choice or an avoidance, your actions will not be consistent with your principles.

XXVI.   Of desires, all that do not lead to a sense of pain, if they are not satisfied, are not necessary, but involve a craving which is easily dispelled, when the object is hard to procure or they seem likely to produce harm.

XXVII. Of all the things which wisdom acquires to produce the blessedness of the complete life, far the greatest is the possession of friendship.

XXVIII. The same conviction which has given us confidence that there is nothing terrible that lasts for ever or even for long, has also seen the protection of friendship most fully completed in the limited evils of this life.

XXIX.   Among desires some are natural and necessary, some natural but not necessary, and others neither natural nor necessary, but due to idle imagination.

XXX.   Wherever in the case of desires which are physical, but do not lead to a sense of pain, if they are not fulfilled, the effort is intense, such pleasures are due to idle imagination, and it is not owing to their own nature that they fail to be dispelled, but owing to the empty imaginings of the man.

XXXI.   The justice which arises from nature is a pledge of mutual advantage to restrain men from harming one another and save them from being harmed.

XXXII. For all living things which have not been able to make compacts not to harm one another or be harmed, nothing ever is either just or unjust; and likewise too for all tribes of men which have been unable or unwilling to make compacts not to harm or be harmed.

XXXIII. Justice never is anything in itself, but in the dealings of men with one another in any place whatever and at any time it is a kind of compact not to harm or be harmed.

XXXIV. Injustice is not an evil in itself, but only in consequence of the fear which attaches to the apprehension of being unable to escape those appointed to punish such actions.

XXXV. It is not possible for one who acts in secret contravention of the terms of the compact not to harm or be harmed, to be confident that he will escape detection, even if at present he escapes a thousand times. For up to the time of death it cannot be certain that he will indeed escape.

XXXVI. In its general aspect justice is the same for all, for it is a kind of mutual advantage in the dealings of men with one another: but with reference to the individual peculiarities of a country or any other circumstances the same thing does not turn out to be just for all.

XXXVII. Among actions which are sanctioned as just by law, that which is proved on examination to be of advantage in the requirements of men's dealings with one another, has the guarantee of justice, whether it is the same for all or not. But if a man makes a law and it does not turn out to lead to advantage in men's dealings with each other, then it no longer has the essential nature of justice. And even if the advantage in the matter of justice shifts from one side to the other, but for a while accords with the general concept, it is none the less just for that period in the eyes of those who do not confound themselves with empty sounds but look to the actual facts.

XXXVIII. Where, provided the circumstances have not been altered, actions which were considered just, have been shown not to accord with the general concept in actual practice, then they are not just. But where, when circumstances have changed, the same actions which were sanctioned as just no longer lead to advantage, there they were just at the time when they were of advantage for the dealings of fellow-citizens with one another; but subsequently they are no longer just, when no longer of advantage.

XXXIX. The man who has best ordered the element of disquiet arising from external circumstances has made those things that he could akin to himself and the rest at least not alien: but with all to which he could not do even this, he has refrained from mixing, and has expelled from his life all which it was of advantage to treat thus.

XL. As many as possess the power to procure complete immunity from their neighbours, these also live most pleasantly with one another, since they have the most certain pledge of security, and after they have enjoyed the fullest intimacy, they do not lament the previous departure of a dead friend, as though he were to be pitied.

Chapter 48

Richard Brandt

GOODNESS AS THE SATISFACTION OF INFORMED DESIRE

THE GENERAL project of the first part of this book has been to see how far logic and evidence can take us in criticizing actions, pleasures, and desires. We have already discussed how far they can take us in criticizing actions to a first approximation, that is, while ignoring the question whether the desires or aversions involved in action can themselves be criticized on the basis of information. We now consider how we can appraise actions to a second approximation by providing a critique of desires and aversions.

This critique, based on the theory of the genesis of pleasures and desires, will tell us which things a fully rational—roughly, a fully informed—person would want or enjoy. I shall show that certain and only certain kinds of things would be rationally desired by certain kinds of persons or in certain kinds of situation, and in some cases that a certain kind of thing would be enjoyed or desired by *every* rational person.

Most philosophers have supposed that such a critique of desires and pleasures is impossible; it is thought that facts and logic cannot show, say, that an intrinsic desire is mistaken. Hume, it is supposed, had the last word:

> . . . it is only in two senses that any affection can be called unreasonable. First, when a passion such as hope or fear, grief or joy, despair or security, is founded on the supposition of the existence of objects, which really

do not exist. Secondly, when in exerting any passion in action, we choose means insufficient for the designed end, and deceive ourselves in our judgment of causes and effects. Where a passion is neither founded on false suppositions, nor chooses means insufficient for the end, the understanding can neither justify nor condemn it. It is not contrary to reason to prefer the destruction of the whole world to the scratching of my finger. It is not contrary to reason for me to choose my total ruin, to prevent the least uneasiness of an Indian, or person wholly unknown to me. It is as little contrary to reason to prefer even my own acknowledged lesser good to my greater, and have a more ardent affection for the former than the latter. A trivial good may, from certain circumstances, produce a desire superior to what arises from the greatest and most valuable enjoyment . . . .[1]

Of course, we are here concerned only with at least partly intrinsic desires and aversions—desires for some outcome at least partly for *itself*, not just because it is in some way a means to something else that is desired.

Earlier conclusions have already shown that some desires or aversions are in a sense mistaken. For they show that a rational person, with his desires just as they are, had sometimes better undertake psychological treatment to *remove a*

certain desire. A member of Congress might find that the whole set of outcomes he most wants can be realized only if he gives up drinking excessive amounts of alcohol. So the drinking has to go. And, if that has to go, the desire had also better be changed; removal of the desire will make him more comfortable. So, if he is rational, he will see to the removal of the desire. Such reflections do not show, however, that there is anything wrong with a desire for alcohol itself. All that is shown is the relation between this desire and the satisfaction of a large set of other desires. In what follows, however, I shall show something very different from this: that there is something mistaken about certain desires or aversions, just in themselves, or at least in their occurring with an intensity beyond a certain point.

The critique to come will show that some desires, aversions, or pleasures would be present (or absent) in some persons if their total motivational machinery were fully suffused by available information; and will show how to identify such desires, aversions, or pleasures for a given person. Less metaphorically, the aim is to show that some intrinsic desires and aversions would be present in some persons if relevant available information registered fully, that is, if the persons repeatedly represented to themselves, in an ideally vivid way, and at an appropriate time, the available information which is relevant in the sense that it would make a difference to desires and aversions if they thought of it. By 'ideally vivid way' I mean that the person gets the information at the focus of attention, with maximal vividness and detail, and with no hesitation or doubt about its truth. I mean by 'available information' . . . relevant beliefs which are a part of the 'scientific knowledge' of the day, or which are justified on the basis of publicly available evidence in accordance with the canons of inductive or deductive logic, or justified on the basis of evidence which could now be obtained by procedures known to science.

We need to restrict further the kind of information that qualifies as 'relevant', in order to guarantee that the effectiveness of the information is a function of its content. If every time I thought of having a martini, I made myself go through multiplication tables for five minutes, the valence of a martini might well decline. But obviously the desire for a martini is not misdirected simply if it fails to survive confrontation with the multiplication table in this way. Any desire would be discouraged by this procedure. We want to say that a thought is functioning properly in the criticism of desires only if its effect is not one its occurrence would have on any desire, and only if its effect is a function of its content. It must be a thought in some fairly restricted way about the thing desired; for instance, a thought about the expectable effects of the thing, or about the kind of thing it is, or about how well one would like it if it happened, and so on.

The claim is that relevant available information, if confronted on repeated occasions, affects our desires. But how often is 'repeated'? We cannot be, and need not be, precise on this. If several representations have no effect, we can reasonably infer that more of them would do no better. But if several representations have some effect, the question arises what would happen if there were more? Presumably what we are after is the asymptote: what desires, aversions, and pleasures a person would have if the number of representations increased without limit, if the reflection had maximal impact by representation as often as you like.

Finally, I have said that the self-stimulation by representation of relevant information should come at 'an appropriate time'. When is that? Obviously, when the effect will maximize counterconditioning, inhibition, or relevant discrimination. For instance, the appropriate times for a smoker to reflect on the bad consequences of his habit are (1) just after inhaling, when the reflection may destroy any pleasure he ordinarily takes in the cigarette; (2) when he wants or is thinking about lighting a cigarette, when the reflection will tend (a) to set up an association

between the idea of the state of affairs and contrary motivation, or (b) to make it clear that the total outcome will in fact not be pleasant with the inhibiting effect of that reflection; and (3) when he is having thoughts or images which tend to make the idea of smoking exciting, so that the reflection will associate these mental occurrences with a less glamorous image. But it is not clear that such reflections will be fruitless on any occasion when one is thinking about an outcome.

This whole process of confronting desires with relevant information, by repeatedly representing it, in an ideally vivid way, and at an appropriate time, I call *cognitive psychotherapy*. I call it so because the process relies simply upon reflection on available information, without influence by prestige of someone, use of evaluative language, extrinsic reward or punishment, or use of artificially induced feeling-states like relaxation. It is *value-free reflection*.

I shall call a person's desire, aversion, or pleasure 'rational' if it would survive or be produced by careful 'cognitive psychotherapy' for that person. I shall call a desire 'irrational' if it cannot survive compatibly with clear and repeated judgements about established facts. What this means is that rational desire (etc.) can confront, or will even be produced by, awareness of the truth; irrational desire cannot. It is obvious, of course, that desires do not logically follow from the awareness which supports them; the relation is causal and sometimes involves other desires, aversions, or pleasures.[2]

One implication of our definitions may be surprising. It arises from the fact that some valences, or dispositions to enjoy something, may resist extinction by inhibition and anything else, since they have been so firmly learned at an early age. By my definition these qualify as rational. For I use 'rational' as the contradictory of 'irrational' and have defined an 'irrational' desire (etc.) as one that would extinguish after cognitive psychotherapy. If a desire will not extinguish, then it is not irrational. This result is

consistent with the general view that a desire (etc.) is rational if it has been influenced by facts and logic as much as possible. Unextinguishable desires meet this condition.

What reason do we have for thinking that optimal exposure to certain information, such as contemplated in cognitive psychotherapy, will affect desires/aversions in specified ways? First there is theoretical reason. In the examples to follow I shall in each case present first a theory of the genesis of the relevant desires/aversions. In some cases this will be obvious, hardly open to controversy; in other cases I shall cite evidence to show that certain desires in fact have developed in a certain way. Then I shall show that desires/aversions produced in these ways are bound to extinguish by repeated self-stimulation by information, given the facts about how desires (etc.) extinguish as described in the preceding chapter. The procedure will therefore be deductive; it will be like showing how a physical particle of a given description must move under specified conditions, given what we know of gravitational attraction, electro-magnetism, and the theory of motion under forces.

There is also empirical support from the clinical reports of psychotherapists for the view that exposure to relevant information will affect desires/aversions in the ways to be suggested. There is less of this kind of support than we would like and one reason for this is probably that psychotherapists aim primarily to help the patient, at least mostly in the direction in which the patient himself asks for help, and not to help the patient find his ideal value-system. Usually the therapist is more engaged in reducing anxieties than he is in changing desires, or finding rational desires; and he uses whatever devices, from cognitive self-stimulations to electric shocks, will reach the intended goal. Nevertheless, many therapists have had a good deal of success in changing desires through patient self-stimulation by true statements—for example, making excessive alcohol consumption aversive, reducing the craving for the approval of

other people, mitigating the aversiveness of being alone, reducing the aversiveness of being self-assertive in relation to one's spouse or employer, reducing the intensity of the desire to achieve in all situations, and reducing the desire to smoke. So we have fairly direct observational evidence that self-stimulation can change desires (etc.) in the anticipated way. In fact, we hardly need to turn to therapists to know that reflections can change intrinsic desires and pleasures. What woman does not know that repeating to herself the facts that a beloved male is inflexible, selfish, unloving, not very bright, and wholly concerned with success in business, will over time reduce her emotional commitment to him, and make her enjoy his company less?

1. Some types of 'mistaken' desires, aversions, or pleasures

Let us now look at some types of likes/dislikes, or desires/aversions and see how it is that we must view them as irrational. The various types are neither exhaustive nor mutually exclusive. They are to be viewed as collections of examples, and should be used as a guide in thinking about cases of particular concern.

i. First mistake: dependence on false beliefs

It is obvious that persons often desire outcomes now as a result of having (falsely) thought them means to ends already wanted or enjoyed: associating the means with the end or with the thought of the end, or associating the thought of the means with the liked end or the thought of the liked end. For instance, a student may have begun to work for a Ph.D. and an academic profession because he thought his parents (themselves professors) would be disappointed in him if he did not; and now he wants an academic life for itself (but not because he has found it satisfying). Or, a person may have developed an aversion to the taste of a certain food because he thought it made him ill. A person

may now feel uncomfortable about enjoying himself because he thought God (or his parents) wanted him to work hard and eschew indulgences; and he wanted to please God (or his parents).

Let us suppose (as often happens) that the relevant beliefs are false. Parents wish a child only to be happy, not to enter an academic life; certain foods do not make one ill; there may be no God, or if there is one, he may not disapprove of personal indulgence. Assuming that there are no other facts, not involved in the genesis, reflection upon which supports the desire, a desire with such a genesis will extinguish in cognitive psychotherapy. Why?

Extinction will occur primarily through inhibition. If the person repeats to himself the fact that he will not achieve the goals involved in instituting the desire by doing a certain thing, the intrinsic desire for doing that thing will diminish. Consider the parallel with the salivation of Pavlov's dogs. The thought of the instrumental outcome (the Ph.D.) is like the sound of the buzzer; the desire for it to occur is like the salivation; the pleasant thought that its occurrence would please parents is like being offered the food. Then, as the dogs stopped salivating at the sound of the buzzer when the food was regularly omitted, so the student will stop being motivated to go for the Ph.D. when he regularly reminds himself that doing so will not please his parents. (Of course, the desire to get the Ph.D. will not extinguish if by this time the student has other reasons—for instance, finds academic work inherently satisfying.) Counterconditioning can presumably also play some role: if the student reminds himself that a Ph.D. is for him very hard work, that he was not cut out to be an academic, and so on.

ii. Second mistake: artificial desire-arousal in culture-transmission

An important factor in the genesis of desires, aversions, likes, dislikes, is a child's observation

of the attitudes and values of other persons—parents, teachers, or peers, not to mention films and television—producing ambition perhaps to own a powerful sports car, aspiration (to belong to a prestige occupation) or aversion (to belonging to a low-prestige one).

How does the observation of the attitudes of others produce these likes and dislikes, desires and aversions? In part the process is one of direct conditioning: the child feels anxiety when another child is the target of the critical attitudes of others . . .; and this anxiety becomes attached by conditioning to the idea of the situation for which the other child is criticized. Alternatively, the process may be one of those roughly classified as 'desire acquisition by identification' . . . .

Still again, there may be beliefs essentially involved. For instance, the statements of parents may make the child believe there are unspecified unpleasant consequences of being in a certain situation, from which the child will infer that the situation itself must be unpleasant in some way. Given any of these cases, an *intrinsic* aversion (desire, etc.) is produced after conditioning has done its work.

The production of these intrinsic desires/aversions is artificial if they could not have been brought about by experience with actual situations which the desires are for and the aversions against. Take, for instance, a non-prestige occupation like garbage collection, or marriage to a person of another race, religion or nationality. Actual experience with these situations could be highly satisfying (and there is no reason to suppose it would be aversive), and would not produce an intrinsic aversion. So, naturally produced desires/aversions would not coincide with those produced in these artificial ways. I shall call a desire/aversion artificial if it could not have been produced naturally. (A desire/aversion which could be produced naturally may be called 'authentic'.)

These attitudes do derive from the realities of the situation in one sense, for the firm attitudes of others are real facts with which people have to deal. But intense concern with the attitudes of other people is itself founded on error—the false belief that the attitudes of others are crucially important for an adult, especially if the attitudes in question are those of one's own parents only. An independent adult need not fear the sanctions his parents might try to impose; for, realistically, a person will not lose the affection of his parents through doing some of the things of which they disapprove. Of course, if a person wishes not to upset his parents, then their reaction is a fact to be taken into account like any other; just as, if all one's friends strongly dislike someone one is considering for marriage, that fact is one to be taken into account too. The situation arising from favourable or unfavourable attitudes of others is complex, but on the whole the attitudes of others hardly serve by themselves to render a desire realistic.

All artificial desires are prime candidates for extinction or diminution, by cognitive psychotherapy, through inhibition or counterconditioning, or both. Why? Partly because the usually essential supporting beliefs are false; and in so far as they are, the attitude will tend to extinguish for reasons already explained. Partly also because any anxiety conditioned through the attitudes of others will tend to extinguish by inhibition after a review of the relative unimportance of such attitudes for the mature adult. And partly by counterconditioning: through reflection on the fact that one's aversion is preventing one from having some potentially very satisfying experiences or relationships, or that one's desire is leading one into experiences or relationships one simply does not like. For instance, a person might want, as a result of these artificial processes, to be in the academic profession; but he might have good reason also to believe—if he thought about it—that he would be bored by the scholarly work involved, that he would not be effective as a teacher and therefore would dislike teaching, and that he would not like the limited financial prospects of the academic life. If he did reflect on these

things, he would tend to establish an aversion which would be incompatible with his ambition to hold an academic post.

Since such 'artificial' desires/aversions would extinguish by this kind of reflection, in 'cognitive psychotherapy', they are irrational.

Let us pause and apply our results so far to a desire which has received more attention in the psychological literature than any other, except perhaps sex: the desire for achievement. Unfortunately, when we say that a person has a strong desire to achieve, it is not clear precisely what we mean. Psychologists seem to agree on a rather broad but vague definition. Desire to achieve is said to be desire for 'success in competition with some standards of excellence.'[3] But a comparative notion gives us a more interesting conception. On this conception, the desire to achieve is not just a desire to do difficult things well, or make some important contribution in life, or reach some long-term professional goal. It is a desire to be, and to appear, superior in many areas in which one is emotionally involved—such as tennis, argument, doing well professionally, and so on.

Where might this general desire come from? It could come from native satisfaction from doing difficult things. Children take pleasure in learning to stand or turn over; they enjoy exploring the environment, constructing things, solving puzzles. In summary, they enjoy learning skills which enable effective interaction with their environment. Insofar as a desire to achieve is a desire just to do difficult things well, it derives from native liking, and is not artificial; but some persons desire achievement in my explained sense because they think it brings respect if not affection—a belief which is partially false, since achievement is apt to produce irritation; or, they think that achievement will lead to satisfaction of various sorts. Empirical studies suggest that the desire comes from early experiences, especially from demands made by, and rewards given by, parents who are anxious about the performance of their children.

A middle-class family, concerned for the child's later success, is apt to welcome any sign of precocity with delight and praise, and to be uncomfortably rejecting if the child fails to do well. One study has shown that children high in achievement motivation had mothers who (1) made demands on them for mastery of various forms of behaviour at a relatively early age (going outside to play, knowing their way about the city, doing well in competition), (2) gave more physically expressed affection for success, and (3) set relatively fewer restrictions on behaviour (such as forbidding sloppiness at the table, leaving clothes about, or failing in school).

If the desire for achievement must be explained in this way—primarily by the congratulations, rejections, and training practices of concerned parents—is it authentic and rational? Consider motivation to be superior in tennis. Could it have been produced realistically by contact with the costs and satisfactions to which such motivation leads? The motivation to be superior may lead to a determination to win (which can put off partners or opponents who merely want to enjoy the game), or to a choice of partners and opponents who are at least one's equal in competence (to the irritation of the others). Hence, being so motivated may be a loss. On the other hand, a reputation for competence will bring invitations to play from able players and one will enjoy more exciting competition. This is a gain. Such losses and gains have their analogues in professional or business life. Only here there are further costs: of encompassing absorption in getting ahead, which diminishes other benefits of living; of disappointment, because of the difficulty of being superior to everyone. Achievement motivation in this sense is very different from the desire just to work well, or to make a contribution to social life. In reviewing his motivation, a person must ask himself in detail where the total activity is leading. If, when he does this, his fever diminishes, his desire is shown to be at too high a pitch. At that level it is irrational.

Some business firms have thought it worth-while to encourage achievement motivation (in some sense) among their executives, and they have employed psychologists to bring about that motivation, apparently with some success. The reported methods raise some doubts about the rationality of the heightened motivation. The new level of motivation is neither authentic nor rational if it can be reached only by a mixture of threats, misinformation, and good company.

iii. Third mistake: generalization, from untypical examples

Some further values which would extinguish in cognitive psychotherapy are neither artificial attitudes, nor based on mistaken beliefs. Rather, they are attitudes which have developed from familiarity with samples of liked/disliked situations but from *untypical* samples, or in an untypical context. For instance, I may dislike dogs because in childhood one attacked me; or I may feel uncomfortable inside public school buildings because in my childhood I was punished or wholly bored there; or, on a simpler level, as a small boy I may refuse a serving of any kind of fish because I have eaten a piece of cod (my first and only experience of fish) and disliked it heartily, saying now, 'I can't stand fish.'

How do such attitudes come about? All learning involves some generalization. Much to our advantage we do not learn a response only to stimuli exactly like those in the original learning situation, but to a *range* of stimuli more or less like the originals. Thus, if I acquire a conditioned like or dislike (etc.) because of one or more experiences, the attitude will be directed towards some *type* of object, and this type may be much broader than the kind of example which was the source of that attitude. If I am attacked by a dog, I could develop an attitude towards all dogs or all mammals, or at least all mammals outside my house.

It is obvious that attitudes which are the result of wild generalizations from a narrow set of experiences—say an aversion to all dogs as a result of being bitten by a terrier which I had provoked—will extinguish in cognitive psychotherapy. Why will they? Partly by countercondi-tioning because, say, interaction with a friendly well-behaved intelligent poodle will elicit warm attitudes towards dogs of this type, incompatible with my aversion towards *all* dogs. But partly it will diminish by inhibition, since the aversion to all dogs will receive little or no support from further experience with dogs. As we broaden the set of samples of interaction with dogs, the conditioned disliking response will rarely be given new support by another unfortunate experience. So much is clear.[4]

But not all attitudes resulting from generaliza-tion are irrational. Let us try to state more exactly which such attitudes would extinguish in psycho-therapy and which would not. It is plausible to suppose that an attitude towards something which has its genesis in an experience not likely to repeat itself would extinguish. This generaliza-tion can be more precisely formulated if we define the notion of a 'typical experience' as one producing an attitude which would not extin-guish if the agent reflected on the percentage of experiences which could rationally be expected with things of that sort over the course of his life-time. Take my aversion towards dogs because of being bitten by a terrier which I had provoked by tramping on its nose. Suppose the aversion would extinguish after repeated reflection on the fact that only .0001 per cent of terriers will attack me if I do not provoke them. Or suppose that only .0001 per cent of St. Bernards will attack me even if I do step on both nose and tail, and reflection on this would extinguish my terrier-based aver-sion to St. Bernards. Then my actual aversion to all dogs is based on untypical experiences.[5] If we adopt this definition, then we can say of the atti-tudes based on generalization, only those which are untypical will extinguish in cognitive psycho-therapy and hence are irrational.[6]

J. S. Mill stated in *Utilitarianism* that power, fame, and money come to be wanted for themselves and indeed come to be part of one's 'happiness' (one really does like them for themselves and would be unhappy in their absence), because of associations with the good things to which they lead. Let us suppose he is right in this. Are the valence and liking irrational? To answer, we must first determine as best we can (on the basis of available information) the frequency and consistency with which money will provide us with the things we already like. Then, we must see if a clear awareness of these facts will extinguish our desire for money. Money does buy a good many things, and absence of it can have unpleasant consequences. But how much can it buy, and how universally does a merely modest income have unpleasant consequences? When we get the answer to these questions firmly in mind we shall be well on the way to knowing whether a desire for money is irrational.

Some critics might say that any desire for money for itself is irrational. It is obviously irrational to want money for any other reason than for what it buys. Our theory need not lead to this consequence; at least it does not if it is just a fact of human nature that we learn to like (want) for themselves things which reliably lead to other things we already like (want). But this consequence need not be dismaying; for we can discriminate various situations involving money, and our theory certainly does not imply that it is rational to prefer money to various other goods in life with which it might be in competition—quite the contrary.

iv. Fourth mistake: exaggerated valences produced by early deprivation

Some people, especially children, appear to have a virtually insatiable craving for attention. And there are abnormally high desires for commendation or admiration from others, or for the company of others. Sometimes these desires seem similar to the condition of persons who literally do not know when they have had enough to eat or drink, although the physiology cannot be parallel.[7]

Similarly there are abnormal aversions, say to spending money except for necessities, like that noted in the following letter to a columnist:

> Dear Abby: My husband grew up fatherless during the depression. Now, at age 50, his net worth is around the half-million dollar mark. He is a professor with tenure, and has an excellent retirement and insurance program. Yet he buys second-hand clothes, day-old bread, and refuses to spend any money on a decent car, vacations or travel.
>
> The reason? He wants to be sure he has enough money for his old age. What could be the matter with him?
>
> HIS WIFE.

This case is extreme, but in milder forms the syndrome is not infrequent. It appears among rats. Rats which have been deprived of food, especially shortly after the time of weaning, respond to restriction of food intake for a week or more, by massive hoarding when food becomes abundant, acquiring and storing as many as several hundred pellets an hour as compared with the normal practice of storing half-a-dozen pellets.

There is testimony that the absence of affection and warm cuddling early in a child's life can lead to insatiable demands for attention.

These cases suggest a syndrome whereby an early and prolonged deprivation of something wanted—enough for discomfort and anxiety to be involved—results in an abnormally high development of desire for that thing in later years. It looks as if anxiety gets associated with its absence or with the expectation, even quite small, of its absence. The anxiety then drives the person to relieve it, by securing the object the absence of which arouses it. Thus a child who has been deprived of affection and esteem may,

even very shortly after a friendly compliment, become anxious about the attitudes of others and can be made unanxious only by a steady stream of attention or praise. Or, a man who has been economically deprived during childhood will experience conditioned anxiety with the thought of absence of economic means, so that expenditure of money is a threatening experience. We may recall McClelland's point that the experience of deprivation is apt to be very emotionally disturbing at an early age, when the child does not have any clear expectation about when the deprivation will end.

It is not suggested that all 'insatiable' desires derive from early deprivation.

It seems that such abnormally strong desires would extinguish in cognitive psychotherapy. Such traditional psychoanalysts would say that if a person brought to consciousness the connection of early deprivation with his intense desire (= insight), the abnormally strong desire would abate. On the theory of learning and conditioning adopted earlier, the question is whether cognitive procedures can extinguish the connection between anxiety and the thought of the absence, or possible absence, of something. The answer is that if a person repeatedly reminds himself when he feels rejected, that others warmly accept him and will continue to do so in the foreseeable future, his anxiety in the absence of an expression of affection will diminish by inhibition. (One might also say that the thoughts will produce pleasant relaxation, so that the anxiety tends to be extinguished by counterconditioning.) Of course, the extinction process may take time. So, in so far as the suggested theory about these abnormal desires is correct, vivid repeated representation of knowable facts should bring about a reduction in intensity. We must conclude that a desire of this abnormal sort is 'irrational'.

What sorts of desires might be related to anxiety in this way? It would seem that desire for any situation thought to help secure the presence of an object of which one was once deprived might be a result. So, if the deprivation was of affection or acceptance, the desire might be to conform with conventional proprieties (others dislike unconventionality), to work for financial security (money buys affection), or to achieve in professional work (achievement buys love).[8]

The whole issue whether some desires or pleasures can be identified as irrational may seem purely theoretical. It may be thought that important decisions are so complex that, even if we became convinced that some desire was irrational, the discovery could make no significant difference to the decision process. This view, however, is a profound mistake. Very often difficult decisions are difficult because, although a great many pros point in one direction, and almost all cons can be overmatched by pros, there is one consideration which remains a serious matter. For instance, suppose a Harvard professor is offered a position in Los Angeles, and is tempted to take it: his salary will be better, the research facilities equal, the graduate students and colleagues equal, the climate appealing, and he likes surfing. There is one difficulty: he is appalled by the thought of detaching himself from Harvard. Not that he thinks his stature in his profession would be diminished if he were to move; he knows that this is not the case. But he 'identifies' with Harvard; he feels himself part of a great tradition, the historically most important educational institution in the United States. Furthermore, his father would have wanted him to be at Harvard. Now undoubtedly most persons have very good reasons for hesitating to leave Harvard, but it could well be that his reason, his 'identification' with Harvard, is just irrational. However that may be, the point is that if he found that his basic reason for preferring to stay at Harvard is irrational, his practical problem would be resolved. For a decision to move had been blocked by one particular concern. And, when he identifies this concern as irrational, he will be clear that the rational thing is to make the move.

Thus the identification of a single desire as irrational may have profound importance for a large personal decision.

2. Rational desires and the concept of the intrinsically good

We now have before us the concept of an irrational desire or aversion: one that would not survive cognitive psychotherapy, at least with its present strength. And we have the concept of a rational desire or aversion: one that is not irrational. How nearly does the notion of the rationally desired approximate to the concept of the *good?*

One might say that it makes no difference how close it is. For, if we want to desire and act with reason, we want to know what is a rational desire—one that is maximally criticized by facts and logic. When we have identified a rational desire, we have that: a desire in which all the changes confrontation with available information will bring have been wrought. If we are dedicated to rational desiring and acting, we have what we want. If the term 'good' does not refer to what is rationally desired, so much the worse for the concept of the 'good'.

Even so, it is of interest whether the term 'rationally desired', or some longer phrase incorporating it, means the same as 'good', or if not, would be a useful replacement for that term. If so, it might be wise to conduct primary education so as to give a new meaning to 'good'—in terms of 'rationally desired'.

The word 'good', of course, appears in many different constructions, and the meaning or use of the term in these several constructions is not identical. Consider, for instance: 'a good car', 'a good father', 'good at swimming', 'good for making jelly'. Historically, philosophers have been most concerned with its use in such sentences as 'Knowledge is intrinsically good.'

Recently, some philosophers have thought that no expression in which no value word occurs is either exactly or even approximately synonymous with 'good', at least in its important uses. In contrast, many other philosophers, from Aristotle to Sidgwick and Rawls, have thought that there are expressions approximately synonymous with 'good' in its important uses, or at least functionally good replacements for it. In particular, some have thought that for something to be intrinsically good is just for somebody, or everybody, to like it or want it for itself. On this view, if fame were what someone or everyone wants, it would be good. Others have thought that for something to be intrinsically good is for it to be wanted or liked by persons (or perhaps some individual person) with certain qualifications, perhaps knowledge or virtue. Obviously the proposal I have been making belongs with this latter group. We should notice, however, that the altruistic or at least non-self-interested desires pose a problem, for while something may be a good thing if it is the object of a rational altruistic desire, we should clearly hesitate to say that the object of someone's rational altruistic desire is necessarily something good for him, something that is a part of the person's welfare or well-being. This problem will arise again later.

We need not deliberate whether 'rationally desired' in my sense is exactly or approximately synonymous with 'intrinsically good' in its ordinary meaning. I have not argued that it is: in fact I think it is not. Whether it is a useful replacement I shall not debate at this juncture . . . .

I wish now, however, to put forward two claims on behalf of the conception of rational desire and its utility.

The first is that there is no sentence in which the word 'good' appears, at least in that core complex of uses which have been important for philosophy, which makes an identifiable point which cannot be made by a sentence containing 'rationally desired', doubtless in some complex clause but in which no 'value-word' is present. The claim is a large one. I shall not try to support it further, but merely offer two examples to make clear what claim is being made. Take: 'The

of the big time. She wonders whether she has made an uncomfortable discovery about herself or whether she simply is so impressed by the thought of her byline on the front page of the *Planet* that she has lost sight of what fundamentally matters to her. She worries whether what she most desires really corresponds to what would be the best sort of life for her.

The connection between this normative concern and her desires – as required by internalism – is indirect. Her sense that she is being less attentive to the actual prospects of the options she faces than to their immediate impact upon her self-image does not by itself so weaken her attraction to the *Planet* job that this desire no longer predominates. Like the rest of us, Sheila is concerned with her future well-being, but for her, like the rest of us, this concern is sometimes dim in comparison to more vivid goods. Still, a plausible version of internalism should allow the normative worry to stand, for it clearly has an internal grip on Sheila – it is a worry of *hers*.

There are other important classes of cases in which we question whether our good coincides with what we most desire. Consider Beth, a successful and happy accountant, who nonetheless wants above all to quit and devote herself full time to writing. Beth's desire, let us suppose, does not depend upon any failure to envisage vividly her best-warranted expectations about the future, nor does it involve any failure to calculate accurately with the information she has at hand. Unfortunately, however, although she has no convincing evidence to show it – after all, some of the short stories she wrote as an undergraduate were admired by her friends and teachers – Beth does not have the skill or temperament to be a writer. So, when the accumulation from her earnings enables her to give up ledgerbooks for copybooks, things go badly. She finds it enormously difficult to bring herself to write with any regularity, and what work she does produce fails to gain acceptance. Another sort of person might return more or less quickly to accounting, closing the episode, and putting

it down to experience. But Beth has never been one who knew when to cut her losses. She feels she must keep at it and make a success of it, so year in and year out she putters around her house while trying to spend time at the desk, traipses off to writers' workshops, takes part-time jobs, and sends off unsolicited manuscripts. Yet success does not arrive, and she becomes increasingly bitter, unproductive, and indebted. Looking back, she concludes that she paid too high a price in lost well-being and self-confidence for the information that she is not suited to writing. Knowing what she now knows, she thinks it would have been better had she fended off her desire to be a writer and remained an accountant with a few shelves of good current fiction.

This judgment distinguishes her good at a time from what she most desired at that time. Moreover, it distinguishes her good at a time from what was, given her beliefs and desires, instrumentally rational at that time. It may even so be said to assert a connection between her good and her all-things-considered desires, namely, between the all-things-considered desires of the sadder-but-wiser Beth and the good of her earlier self. Should internalism allow this sort of internal connection to support a judgment recommending against the writer's life for Beth at the time of her decision? There is an internal grip: Beth herself feels all too poignantly the evaluative force of her later, better-informed views.

Yet it is the later Beth who feels this force, for it is she who has the information.[3] What force would the views of the later Beth have for the earlier Beth, were they somehow to become known to her? It might have the effect of quickly dulling the earlier Beth's desire to write. But we can also imagine that her earlier self's desire to become a writer would remain quite strong, perhaps stronger than any competing desire. Yet even in this latter case, it is natural to expect that her desire *that this desire be effective* will become more tentative, and that some contrary desires will emerge.

Why is this natural? Partly because it is natural to care about whether one is happy and whether one's desires are satisfied. The earlier Beth has every reason to believe that her later self takes these concerns to heart, since the later Beth is contemplating what she would want to pursue were she actually to relive the intervening years. Moreover, the earlier Beth also has reason to believe that her later self is better situated than she to know what would most satisfy Beth's desires during those years.

These observations tend in a certain direction. Presumably, the earlier Beth would find the views of the later Beth still more compelling had the later Beth knowledge not only of the outcome of attempting a career in writing, but of the outcome of alternative pursuits as well. What, for example, would it really have been like for Beth to have remained in accounting? To have a desire is, among other things, to care whether or not it is satisfied. Although fuller information about how one's actual desires will fare in the world may not always contribute to the satisfaction of those desires – one may know too much – the advice of someone who has this fuller information, and also has the deepest sort of identification with one's fate, is bound to have some commending force.

To learn of a reassessment that would arise from full information (and vividness, rationality, and so on) may have force for another reason as well. The ground for this force is also – as it must be on the present account – in the contingent concerns of the actual individual. In this case, however, the concerns are immediately directed not at the satisfaction of desires, but at their defense.

Let us say that one *embraces* a desire, or accepts it as *goal setting*, when one desires that it be effective in regulating one's life. This is not to say one desires that it be overriding; rather one desires that it influence the course of one's life – insofar as this is within one's power – in rough proportion to its strength. In the examples given, Sheila worries whether to embrace her desire to take the *Planet* job and the later Beth, reflecting upon the circumstances of her earlier self, no longer embraces the desire to be a writer. At least one of the features that distinguishes those among our desires that we call our goals is that we normally do not – at least, not without qualm – call a desire that we are not prepared upon reflection to embrace a goal. For an individual to deem something a goal or value of his own involves the idea on his part that it is an appropriate object of desire or pursuit.[4] The notion of appropriateness at work is internal, but may concern the desires he would want to be effective in his actual life were he to contemplate that life with full awareness of the facts and full rationality in deliberation.

These counterfactual circumstances concern the defensibility of the desires themselves against certain sorts of criticism, although 'criticism' here has a special meaning. There is no logical contradiction involved in embracing wholeheartedly a desire that one knows one would want not to be effective in one's actual life were one fully informed and rational. The sort of conflict that is basic to the criticism of desires is psychological rather than logical. One might call this conflict "cognitive dissonance" were it merely cognitive. But what perhaps is most striking about it is that it involves a linkage between the cognitive and the conative. We should expect this sort of linkage in the psychology of value, since valuing is an *attitude*, and an attitude is neither merely a desire nor merely a belief: it involves a collection of desires and an associated *outlook* or characteristic way of seeing things, an outlook that is partly constituted by characteristic beliefs about what one is seeing, and by a tendency to interpret or explain things in certain ways rather than others. That is why, when crucial beliefs are altered or challenged, the agent's outlook itself shifts, with the result that the landscape he previously perceived changes and his desires, which had felt at home in that terrain, become unsettled.

If taking an attitude or embracing a desire involves certain beliefs, it also involves an assumption that these beliefs are not merely false, that one's outlook is not largely a matter of, or psychologically dependent upon, error or ignorance. What is it about the possibility of error or ignorance that creates a potential threat to one's outlook itself? The beginning of an answer may be this. We call upon our basic goals, as distinct from our mere (though perhaps insistent) desires, to explain to ourselves and to others the *worthwhileness* and *point* of our choices – indeed, of our lives. The price we pay for using our values in this way is a commitment to their defensibility. If our values are to support us, we must support them. And we defend our attitudes by appeal to facts psychologically congenial to them. Hence, if someone raises convincing doubts about our understanding of the facts, he causes us unease in our values. We could, of course, always in such circumstances insist that the absence of a logical connection between beliefs and desires permits us to keep our values intact, no matter how wrong or uninformed we discover ourselves to have been on the facts. It is interesting that we so seldom do this. One reason might be that such a response seems to be a shrinking from the task of explaining the worthwhileness and point of what we do. That is, it seems to involve something akin to an admission of defeat – an admission to others and to ourselves that there is less to our lives than had seemed to be the case.

Unless the idea that we must support those values that support us is to involve a mere conjuring trick, we must find somewhere outside our ends, seen as personal desires, to gain a toehold. Historically, this has been done by appeal to such things as gods, ancestors, and the order of nature. The existentialists were quite right in saying that if, as moderns, we reject these props, and if we further conclude that valuation and choice are a mere matter of fixing on something by fiat, then values cannot confer meaning and life becomes absurd. But there *are*

fixed points beyond the self. When we defend our values by appeal to facts, facts whose truth-values do not fluctuate with our particular desires or decisions, we are seeking such a toehold. Importantly, too, these truth-values do not fluctuate with the decisions or desires of others, so that this toehold can support us even when we find ourselves in a world with people whose beliefs or ends differ from our own. If we discover that our values are psychologically dependent upon ignorance or error, we lose this source of support.

Of course, our first-order desires may press upon us willy-nilly, and may be remarkably insensitive to discovery that we were wrong on the facts. But for this very reason it does not do much to explain to myself or others the worth-whileness or point of what I have done with my life to say that I have simply acted upon whatever desire happened to be most urgent at the moment. Higher-order desires of the sort that are involved in embracing a desire are more responsive to changes in belief, and so not only do they become more closely tied to our identity, they become the basis of the idea of value.

The proposal I would make, then, is the following: an individual's good consists in what he would want himself to want, or to pursue, were he to contemplate his present situation from a standpoint fully and vividly informed about himself and his circumstances, and entirely free of cognitive error or lapses of instrumental rationality. The wants in question, then, are wants regarding what he would seek were he to assume the place of his actual, incompletely informed and imperfectly rational self, taking into account the changes that self is capable of, the costs of those changes, and so on.[5] A fully informed and rational individual would, for example, have no use or desire for psychological strategies suited to circumstances of limited knowledge and rationality; but he no doubt would want his incompletely informed and imperfectly rational actual self to develop and deploy such strategies.

My claim is that this notion of someone's good affords an explanation of the normative force of judgments of one's good, for it gives expression to an idea of appropriateness or *fitness* of an end for an agent. Fitness consists in a certain match between an agent's motivational system, on the one hand, and his capacities and circumstances, on the other, when all are accurately represented and adequately appreciated. Moreover, this notion of someone's good also satisfies an appropriate internalist constraint: we can see in the psychology of value, as discussed previously, the ways in which the views we would have were we to become free of present defects in knowledge or rationality would induce an internal resonance in us as we now are.

Let us then say that an individual's *intrinsic* good consists in attainment of what he would in idealized circumstances want to want for its own sake – or, more accurately, to pursue for its own sake (for wanting is only one way of pursuing) – were he to assume the place of his actual self.

Notes

1   Thomas Hobbes, *Leviathan*, C.B. MacPherson, ed. (Harmondsworth, Middlesex: Penguin, 1981) 120.

2   It may be worth saying again that my concern in this essay is with non-moral value. We, of course, also sometimes wish to raise questions about the moral worth of our ends, or, for that matter, about their aesthetic merit. While I believe that these other dimensions of assessment exhibit important relations to intrinsic value, I also believe that clarity is served by recognizing the differences as well as the similarities in their evaluative bases and normative roles.

3   In Brandt's account of "rational desire," that which is good for someone is tied to the best available information at the time. On such a view, it might turn out that writing *was* good for Beth at the time she chose it, since the best information at that time may not have presaged what Beth later, to her regret, discovered. I find it much more natural to say that writing merely *appeared* good at the time. See Richard C. Brandt, *A Theory of the Good and the Right* (Oxford: Clarendon, 1979) 111f.

4   Hypocrisy arises when an individual who says he values X nevertheless does not really want this value to be effective (whether or not he admits this to himself). (Sheila may be in the midst of asking herself whether her earlier – and not infrequent – pronouncements on the value of freedom of action, nature, and family were to a degree hypocritical.) Weakness of the will arises when the desire for X to be effective is present, but some other desire, a desire that one does not upon reflection want to be effective in proportion to its strength, prevails. (Sheila may in the end come to want that her desire to stay put be effective, but then discover that the allure of Metropolis is stronger.) Obviously, these descriptions are very gross. Cf. Harry Frankfurt, "Freedom of the Will and the Concept of a Person," *The Journal of Philosophy* 68 (January 1971), 5–20.

5   This notion is not the same as that of an individual's welfare, for it may turn out that an ideally informed and rational individual would want to seek as an end in itself (were he to step into the place of his present self) the well-being of others as well as himself.

Chapter 50

Thomas Hurka

PERFECTIONISM

1. Introduction

1.1

SOME MORAL theories have been carefully studied in recent moral philosophy, but one, as important as any, has been largely neglected.

This moral theory starts from an account of the good human life, or the intrinsically desirable life. And it characterizes this life in a distinctive way. Certain properties, it says, constitute human nature or are definitive of humanity—they make humans humans. The good life, it then says, develops these properties to a high degree or realizes what is central to human nature. Different versions of the theory may disagree about what the relevant properties are and so disagree about the content of the good life. But they share the foundational idea that what is good, ultimately, is the development of human nature.

This theory appears in the work of many great moralists. Aristotle and Aquinas think it is human nature to be rational, and that a good human exercises rationality to a high degree. Marx views humans as both productive, because we transform nature through our labour, and social, because we do so co-operatively. The best life, he concludes, develops both capacities maximally, as will happen under communism. For Idealists such as Hegal and Bradley, humans are but one manifestation of Absolute Spirit, and their best activities most fully realize identity with Spirit, as social life does in one realm, and art, religion, and philosophy do in another. Even Nietzsche reasons this way, saying that humans essentially exercise a will to power and are most admirable when their wills are most powerful.

These are just some adherents of the theory; others are Plato, Spinoza, Leibniz, Kant, Green, and Bosanquet. Despite differing in their more specific moral claims, they all offer variants on a single theory, one centred on an ideal of the good life defined in terms of human nature.

1.2

I call this moral theory *perfectionism* and its distinguishing ideal that of *human perfection*. Other terms are available: "naturalism," "humanism," and "eudaimonism" for the theory, "flourishing" and "self-realization" for the ideal. But they have other established uses in ethics and could prove confusing here.

"Perfectionism" has its own disadvantages. If human development admits of degrees, so must human perfection, which initially sounds odd. And some readers may be used to broader definitions of the term. Last century, Sir William Hamilton defined "perfection" as "the full and harmonious development of all our faculties, corporeal and mental, intellectual and moral."[1] More recently, John Rawls has said that perfectionism directs us to "maximize the achievement of human excellence in art, science, and

culture."[2] Neither of these definitions mentions human nature, yet each has been influential.

The theory I have identified is perfectionist in both the broader senses used by Hamilton and Rawls. In urging us to develop our natures, it tells us to develop some capacities and also defines an ideal of excellence. My reason for defining "perfection" more narrowly is historical: I think this best fits the usage of writers such as Aristotle, Aquinas, Spinoza, and Leibniz. For them "perfection" means not just excellence, but excellence defined by human nature. The definition also has antecedents in philosophical English. In *Prolegomena to Ethics*, T. H. Green calls his Idealist morality "The Theory of the Good as Human Perfection,"[3] and similar language appears in Sidgwick and Bradley. Sidgwick defines "perfection" as "Excellence of Human Nature,"[4] while Bradley uses "development of human nature," "general perfection," and "perfection of human nature" interchangeably to refer to one moral ideal.[5] My usage mirrors that of Green, Sidgwick, and Bradley: I use "perfectionism" (or "narrow perfectionism") to refer to a moral theory based on human nature, and "broad perfectionism" for the more inclusive view that values some development of capacities or some achievement of excellence.

• • •

2. The concept of human nature

• • •

When perfectionism tells us to develop our natures as humans, what exactly does it mean? In what kinds of property does it take our nature to consist? The idea cannot be to develop all our human properties. These are innumerable, and, in any case, many cannot figure in a plausible ideal of perfection. The concept of nature is clearly meant to pick out a subset of human properties, ones that are somehow specially important to being human. Which properties are these?

To develop the best or most defensible perfectionism, we need, most fundamentally, the best concept of human nature. Here there are two tests to apply. Our initial account of perfectionism has moral appeal, and a specification of its central concept must, first, retain this appeal. It must remain close to whatever motivates the idea that the human good rests somehow in human nature, and also reasonably close to the perfectionist tradition. Our nature as defined must seem in itself morally significant. Second, the specification must have intuitively plausible consequences. A perfectionist concept of nature assigns intrinsic value to certain properties, and these must on their own seem morally worth developing. A concept of nature may fail this test by not including some properties that do seem valuable. This flaw is less serious, showing at most that perfectionism needs to be supplemented by other moral ideas. It is more damaging if a concept of nature includes properties that on their own seem morally trivial—if it gives value to what, intuitively, lacks it. This is a telling objection to the concept. A morality based on the concept will be hard to accept because it flouts our particular judgements about value.

Let us give this last objection a name: the *wrong-properties objection*. Then we have a dual task in this chapter. We want to specify a concept of nature that picks out a subset of human properties by using a criterion that is intrinsically appealing and true to the perfectionist idea. We also want a concept that avoids the wrong-properties objection, by having fall under it only properties that seem in their own right worth developing. We can hope that these two desiderata will coincide. If the perfectionist idea is genuinely appealing, the concept of nature most faithful to it should also have the most plausible consequences. Conversely, if a concept of nature picks out wrong properties, it should somehow deviate from the perfectionist idea.

What if the perfectionist idea proves too indeterminate to pick out a single best concept

necessarily red if red, and necessarily occupiers of space. None of these properties seems intrinsically worth developing. However well it does on the first test, the essence view fails the second test by including in our nature some intuitively trivial properties.

It may be replied that these trivial properties do not admit of degrees, so including them in human nature cannot affect the important perfectionist judgements distinguishing different modes of living. There may be something to this reply, but I doubt that there is enough. Can we be certain that no trivial essential properties admit of degrees? If humans necessarily occupy space, may some not do so more by occupying more space? More importantly, a concept of nature that includes morally idle properties is, to put it mildly, inelegant. If narrow perfection is a serious moral ideal, it should be specifiable without such useless clutter.

The objections should not make us abandon the concept of essence; it does too well by the first test. We should instead try to narrow the concept of nature so it includes some essential properties and not others: ones that avoid the wrong-properties objection but not ones that are trivial.

• • •

2.2 Essence and life

Each individual human has six classes of essential properties, distinguished by the range of objects they are shared by. First are the essential properties shared by all objects, such as self-identity and being red if red and, following that, a narrower class found only in physical objects. These properties include being made of (or being) elementary particles and occupying space. Let us identify these two classes as, first, the properties essential to a human qua object and, second, those essential to her qua physical object. Third come essential properties found only in living things and, fourth, those found

only in animals. Both these classes contain structural properties. Inanimate matter is made of the same elementary particles as living flesh, obeying the same physical laws. What distinguishes the latter must thus be the particles' organization. To count as animate, matter must be organized for functions such as nutrition, growth, and movement, and what is essential to a human qua living thing or qua animal is that her body is structured for these organic functions. The fifth class contains the essential properties that distinguish humans from other animals, perhaps including rationality. Finally, there are the essential properties that distinguish one human from others. These last properties are essential to her, not qua member of a species, but qua individual, and at the deepest level they are unique to her. Based ultimately on her material origin, they include the particular sperm and egg from which she developed and any further properties deriving from that.

Of these six classes, only the last could not figure in an ideal of narrow perfection. Because this ideal involves a nature common to all humans, it cannot depend on essential differences among them. Nonetheless, individually essential properties may be thought morally significant and deserve some discussion.

• • •

2.2.2

Let us return to our main argument and the five classes of essential property relevant to human-nature perfectionism. Using only the second test, about consequences, which of these classes do we want in our concept of nature? It is easy to eliminate the first class, properties essential to humans qua objects. Shared by numbers and other abstract entities, they are, intuitively, of no moral significance. The same holds for the second class, properties essential to humans qua physical objects. But the remaining three classes—those essential to humans qua living things, qua animals, and (only) qua humans—do seem worth retaining. Considering only

consequences, the most promising perfectionism identifies human nature with the essential properties in these three classes. Its ideal is the development of whatever properties are *essential to humans and conditioned on their being living things*. These are essential properties that humans could not have if they were not living; they presuppose life, or are necessarily distinctive of living things

This essence-and-life view retains several virtues from the essence-and-distinctiveness view. It retains part of the answer to the wrong-properties objection because it excludes the trivial essential properties we share with inanimate matter, such as self-identity and occupying space. We do not yet know what properties the view positively selects, and work will be needed to identify these, but the view does exclude many trivial properties. It is also reasonably close to the perfectionist tradition. Unlike the earlier view, however, it does not require difficult decisions about distinctiveness or make our good depend on other species. If some previously inanimate matter acquires a property in our nature, our nature has not changed. Instead, the matter has come alive. Finally, the view recognizes that we are embodied. When fully elaborated, it may not give the development of our physical nature great moral weight—this is a subject for later— but it does make it one intrinsic good.

The view avoids certain objections, but does it have a positive rationale? Does our initial perfectionist idea point to just this concept of nature? If not, this is no disaster. The perfectionist idea has taken us a long way, to the equation of human nature with some essential properties. If consequences are then needed to decide exactly which essential properties, this is legitimate fine-tuning of an already substantive ideal. But I believe we can do better. By looking more closely at traditional formulations of the ideal, we can justify this particular specification.

In characterizing perfection, perfectionists speak often of the "good human life." They describe, not a momentary state or achievement,

but a whole mode of living. Aristotle, for example, says that perfection can be achieved only "in a complete life"[18] and in weighing the leading accounts of it, compares, not politics and contemplation as such, but whole political and contemplative lives.[19] This emphasis on the life is multiply important. It reflects assumptions about how perfectionist values are aggregated and combined, and it also bears on our present concern. The centrality of the "good life" in perfectionism suggests that, whatever properties define it, they must presuppose that we are living. They must contribute to a way of living by themselves being forms of life. Properties shared by inanimate matter are not only intuitively trivial but also irrelevant to an outlook that asks above all how we should live. This outlook can justify its account of nature as follows: We start with the plausible idea that nature is essence and then narrow essence to living essence. This approach keeps our nature within ourselves— there is no dependence on other species—and also fits our original ideal. If that ideal was of a certain human life, we ensure that its elaboration will have an appropriate content.

The justification is deepened in a generalized perfectionism. If we apply perfectionist concepts to non-humans, we do so only to living things. It is only to animate kinds that we attribute perfection or a nature worth developing. (We do not speak of the good or flourishing of a rock or chemical.) The essence-and-life view reflects this division between kinds in its demarcation of human essential properties. It counts as relevant to our perfection what could be relevant to some species's perfection, and excludes what could not.

The best perfectionism, then, equates human nature with the properties essential to humans and conditioned on their being living things. We cannot yet endorse this perfectionism. We do not yet know what properties *are* essential to humans as living, as we must if we are to decide finally how perfectionism fares against the wrong-properties objection and, more generally, how

attractive it is. But, given its account of nature, this perfectionism offers the best hope for a defensible morality. I will underscore this claim shortly by using the account to answer some common objections against perfectionism. But first a clarification is needed.

2.2.3

The perfectionist ideal is a moral ideal in the following sense: It is an ideal people ought to pursue regardless of whether they now want it or would want it in hypothetical circumstances, and apart from any pleasures it may bring. In Kant's terminology, the ideal supports categorical, not hypothetical, imperatives, ones that are not contingent on impulses or desires.

The ideal need not be moral in a narrower sense that is sometimes used. In this sense, moral evaluations concern only the choices people make or the traits and dispositions behind their choices. On all theories of human nature, a person's perfection depends partly on her choices, but on many it also depends on factors outside her choices, such as her natural abilities, supply of material resources, and treatment by others. Given such a theory, the perfectionist ideal is moral in the broader sense of supporting categorical imperatives, but not in the narrower sense concerned only with choice and character.

Once it is understood as moral, the ideal can be expressed in several ways. A common formulation is in terms of the "good human life," one in which living essential properties are developed to a high degree. One can also speak of the "good human" (who develops these properties to a high degree) or simply of what is "good" (that the properties are developed). As well, one can speak of what is "good for" a human, if this is defined in terms of the preceding expressions. If something is "good for" a person whenever it is, for example, (simply) good and a state of the person, then developing human nature is "good for" us all. (If I use "good for," and the related expressions "benefit" and "harm," my use will always be in this derivative sense.) But the ideal

is not about what is "good for" humans in a more common sense.

In this more common sense, "good for" is tied to the concepts of well-being or welfare and interests: Something is "good for" a person if it increases his well-being or furthers his interests. Well-being itself is often characterized subjectively, in terms of actual or hypothetical desires. Given this subjective characterization, perfectionism cannot concern well-being. Its ideal cannot define the "good for" a human because the ideal is one he ought to pursue regardless of his desires. In my view, perfectionism should never be expressed in terms of well-being.[20] It gives an account of the good human life, or of what is good in a human, but not of what is "good for" a human in the sense tied to well-being.

• • •

4. The human essence

We are now in a position to ask what properties *are* essential to humans as living things. Using the intuitive and explanatory methods, this chapter will defend what I call an *Aristotelian theory of human nature*. According to this theory, humans share with other animals certain bodily essential properties but are also essentially rational, in both the theoretical and practical senses of "rational." Together with the perfectionist ideal, this theory yields an *Aristotelian perfectionism*, one with three values: physical perfection, which develops our physical nature, and theoretical and practical perfection, which develop theoretical and practical rationality.

4.1 The Aristotelian theory: physical essence

4.1.1

A first deliverance of the intuitive method is that humans necessarily have bodies. We can imagine purely spiritual beings and, perhaps, understand their psychology. But if they have no physical form they are not, intuitively, of our species.

Beyond this, intuition tells us that humans necessarily have bodies with a fairly determinate structure. No human can remain alive without a functioning respiratory, muscular, digestive, circulatory, and nervous system, and, analogously, no possible being without these systems passes the intuitive test for humanity. Unless its body permits it somehow to breathe, move, process nutrients, and exercise central control, it is not a human.

These claims are confirmed by the explanatory method. One explanation of human behaviour is physical explanation, and it makes central the very systems picked out by intuition. To explain why a runner is panting, we say her circulatory system needs to carry more oxygen to her muscles, which causes her respiratory system to process air at a greater rate than usual. If she pushes off with her legs, we say her nervous system is sending messages to her thigh muscles, causing them to contract. These explanations supervene on and may reduce to the explanations of some more basic science such as chemistry or physics. But this reduction is irrelevant in our version of perfectionism. We have defined human nature to exclude any properties shared by inanimate matter (2.2.2), which means that the explanations we look to must likewise be restricted to living things. Chemical and physical explanations apply to rocks and gases as well as to humans, and we must therefore consider only explanations that presuppose some organic structure. In humans this structure is expressed in certain major physiological systems—in respiratory, muscular, digestive, circulatory, and nervous systems—and the relevant explanations cite their operation.

Both methods have difficulty making these initial claims more precise. If humans essentially have some respiratory system, must they have the specific arrangement of organs they have? If we imagine beings like us in all respects except that they have three lungs, are we imagining humans? What of beings whose respiratory systems operate on different chemical

principles? These questions are difficult, and I cannot answer them decisively, but they may not be important in a moral study of perfectionism. In our world, no human can grow a third lung or alter chemical laws; we are stuck with the physiological systems we have. Given this, our physical perfection can depend only on how our actual systems function, that is, on events in our actual bodies. If a general description of our physical essence—one saying only that we need some respiratory system—defines clear degrees of our physical perfection it may not matter whether more specific descriptions do or do not remain essential.

4.1.2

What, then, defines degrees of physical perfection? This is more a question for physiology than for philosophy, but a rough answer is as follows. Each system in our body has a characteristic activity. The respiratory system extracts oxygen from air, the circulatory system distributes nutrients, and so on. For a human to remain alive, each system must perform its activity to some minimal degree; for her to achieve reasonable physical perfection, it must do so to a reasonable degree. But a system does this when it is free from outside interference and operating healthily. So the basic level of physical perfection is good bodily health, when all our bodily systems function in an efficient, unrestricted way. Then essential physical processes occur to a reasonable degree, and we have reasonable physical perfection.

This first implication is attractive. Even apart from their effects on other values, illness and poor organic functioning are intrinsically regrettable. The loss of a limb or of full activity in an important organ detracts from the completeness of a human life, and robustness adds to it. It makes the life more fully human. Physical health may not be a major perfectionist good, and it may receive less moral weight than the development of rationality. But a perfectionism that gives it some value acknowledges that some of

our nature is bodily and that, like others, this part can be more or less developed.

This connection with health is no accident, but has evolutionary origins. Like other aspects of our nature, our bodily systems were selected as those most likely to make for our survival and reproduction. Their unimpeded operation is healthy because otherwise beings possessed of them would be adaptively disadvantaged. In their present form the systems are essential to humans, who cannot exist without them. But, like humankind itself, they emerged from natural selection and were favoured over alternatives precisely because of their connection with healthy, self-maintaining activity.

Higher physical perfection comes in vigorous bodily activity. Here our major physical systems perform to higher degrees, processing more air, carrying more nutrients, and moving greater weights longer distances. This activity occurs most notably in athletics, and Aristotelian perfectionism finds the highest physical good in great athletic feats. These feats often embody perfections other than physical perfection. They require skill and dexterity and can follow months of careful planning. In both these ways they realize practical rationality, and this can account for much of their value. But there is also a physical dimension. When a human runs 100 meters in 9.86 seconds or long-jumps 29 feet, something physically splendid occurs. His bodily powers are realized to the full in a way that is intrinsically admirable and of intrinsic perfectionist worth.

Most of us are not outstanding athletes and cannot achieve the highest physical perfection. Still, we can preserve our basic health and pursue whatever mild athletics are compatible with our main projects. We have instrumental reasons to do both these things. Physical activity keeps us alert and can be the medium for some exercise of rationality. If Aristotelian perfectionism is correct, however, this activity is also a modest intrinsic good, as the development of our physical nature.

4.2 The Aristotelian theory: rationality

4.2.1

The most important Aristotelian claim is that humans are essentially rational. Its elaboration requires an account of degrees of theoretical and practical rationality, which will be given later (chapter 8–10) [see original reading]. But its core is this: Humans are rational because they can form and act on beliefs and intentions. More specifically, they are rational because they can form and act on sophisticated beliefs and intentions, ones whose contents stretch across persons and times and that are arranged in complex hierarchies. These last features distinguish human rationality from that of lower animals. Animals have isolated perceptual beliefs, but only humans can achieve explanatory understanding. They can grasp generalizations that apply across objects and times and can use them to explain diverse phenomena. A similar point holds for practical rationality. Animals have just local aims, but humans can envisage patterns of action that stretch through time or include other agents and can perform particular acts as means to them. By constructing hierarchies of ends, they can engage in intelligent tool use and have complex interactions with others. Distinctive properties do not matter as such in our perfectionism (2.1), but the Aristotelian theory makes essential a kind of rationality that at present is found only in humans.

That humans are essentially rational is supported, first, by the intuitive method. We do not think there were humans in the world until primates developed with sufficient intelligence, and the same view colours our judgements about possibilities. If we imagine a species with no capacity for a mental life, or with none more sophisticated than other animals', we do not take ourselves to be imagining humans. Whatever their physical form, they are not of our species. The degree to which humans exercise rationality varies from time to time in their lives, being lower, for example, when they are asleep.

But beings who never envisage or plan for a future are not, intuitively, humans.

Again, this claim is confirmed by the explanatory method. Alongside the physical explanation of human behaviour is psychological explanation, which explains at least intentional human action by citing beliefs and aims that make it rational. This explanation presupposes theoretical and practical rationality and ascribes their current exercise in all its particular accounts. It deserves closer examination.

4.2.2

A psychological explanation of person A's act of φ-ing has the following form:

A intended to make it the case that p.
A believed that φ-ing was the most effective means to p.
A was acting as a rational agent.
A was physically able to φ.
Therefore, A φ-ed intentionally.

Two features of this schema deserve comment. One is that it begins with an intention that p, rather than going back to a desire or wish that p. This point highlights the central role of intentions in practical reasoning. We have many desires that we never act on, because their objects are unattainable or because we think satisfying them is on balance unwise. These desires never affect our behaviour. Only when a desire generates an intention do we think seriously about its satisfaction or set ourselves properly to pursue it. The second feature is the claim that A was acting as a rational agent. This claim is required for the success of any psychological explanation but, within that explanation, is always contingent. Even if humans are essentially rational, they do not exercise full rationality at every moment. On the contrary, they sometimes succumb to weakness of will, self-deception, and other lapses from full rational control. To be subjects of psychological explanation, they must be generally rational, and

generally do what their beliefs and aims make appropriate. But full rationality need not always be present, and, when it is not, full rational explanation is not possible.

In this general form, psychological explanation applies to some other animals who also act on beliefs and aims.[21] This is not so, however, when the ascribed mental states are sophisticated, with extended contents and hierarchical relations. Then the premises of the explanation—beliefs about scientific laws or intentions for the distant future— are beyond other animals, and the conclusion may be as well. It may involve intelligent tool use or willed co-operation with others. The scope of the explanation also alters given sophisticated mental states. Instead of taking A's intention that p as given, sophisticated psychology can say that she intends p as a means to q, which she in turn wills as a means to r. It can explain a particular end as a means to others that appear above it in a rational hierarchy. It can also explain many beliefs. If A believes that φ-ing is the most effective means to p, sophisticated psychology may say:

A has evidence that φ-ing is the most effective means to p.
A is forming beliefs as a rational agent.
Therefore, A believes that φ-ing is the most effective means to p.

The rationality ascribed here is no longer the practical rationality that derives acts from intentions and beliefs, but the theoretical rationality that grounds beliefs in evidence. It is the rationality exercised when sophisticated beings use general principles to move from initial evidential beliefs to other, more speculative beliefs. The explanation does not claim that A is perfectly rational or always forms beliefs on the basis of evidence. She may sometimes suffer from slips of reasoning, wishful thinking, or self-deception. For her beliefs to be generally explicable, however, she must generally derive them from evidence, and for this particular explanation to succeed she must be doing so now.

The content of sophisticated psychology, then, gives it a sophisticated form. Instead of treating items of behaviour one by one, it ascribes a system of connected beliefs and aims to explain, not just a person's acts, but many of the mental states behind them. It explains aims in terms of beliefs and other aims, and beliefs in terms of other beliefs. The central role in this psychology is clearly played by the properties of theoretical and practical rationality. These properties are, first, presupposed in every premise of a psychological explanation. No one can have a belief or intention about p, especially if p is sophisticated, without the mental capacity to grasp its content. In saying that she believes or intends p, we assume that she has that degree of rationality. Nor can she have a belief or aim about p unless she generally acts on her beliefs and aims as reason requires. Unless she generally does what she believes will promote her goals, no goals can be ascribed to her. Unless she generally derives beliefs from evidence, she cannot have beliefs. Finally, a premise ascribing the present exercise of rationality is a crucial part of every psychological explanation. Unless A is now acting or forming beliefs rationally, the premises of the explanation will not entail its conclusion. Unless her rational powers are now being exercised, her having certain mental states will not explain a thing.

That the two forms of rationality are central does not, however, imply any natural tendency doctrine. Sophisticated psychology does not say that humans have an overriding desire to develop rationality or a supreme tendency in that direction. On the contrary, it places no restriction on the content of their goals. What it does, rather, is use the one property of rationality to explain how humans' different goals all issue in action. Its structure is therefore like that of explanations of gold. It starts from one ascription of rationality and shows how, given this rationality, people with different initial aims, experiences, and evidence will end up believing, intending, and acting differently. It uses reason to explain

goal-directed behaviour without making reason itself a goal.

Psychology also makes rationality essential without supporting moralism, the view that developing one's own nature requires the other-regarding virtues. Because the rationality it ascribes is formal, defined only by the scope and interrelations of a person's beliefs and aims, it can be realized as much in conventional immorality as in morality. If the immorality is wrong, it cannot be because it reduces the agent's own perfection.

4.2.3

This first explanatory argument gives us good reason to conclude that humans are essentially rational, but it is not the only such argument available.

As described to this point, sophisticated psychology uses pairs of beliefs and aims to explain human acts. How does it decide which pairs to use? How does it know which specific mental states to ascribe? In the case where A φ's intentionally, we may say that she intended p and believed that φ-ing was a means to p. But it would also explain her act if she intended some different end q or r and believed that φ-ing was a means to that, or intended not-p and believed mistakenly that φ-ing would prevent p. To give a determinate explanation of her φ-ing, psychology must be able to select one of these intention-belief pairs above the others. How does it do so?

The only answer I know makes rationality even more central to sophisticated psychology. Several writers, among them Donald Davidson, argue that this psychology is governed by a "principle of charity" requiring us to make an agent's overall behaviour as rational as possible.[22] In explaining a particular act, we must ascribe those beliefs and aims that make the most sense of her conduct as a whole. Different intention-belief pairs may do equally well in rationalizing her present act, but they will differ in their capacity to fit into a larger scheme explaining her total conduct through time. One allows us to

find rational origins for most of her other beliefs and acts; another forces us to leave many ungrounded in reasons. The principle of charity exploits this difference and, by requiring us to prefer the first ascription, permits a determinate explanation of what she has done.

Without something like a principle of charity, it is hard to see how psychology could give determinate explanations. But again, some clarifications are needed.

The principle of charity does not imply that everyone's behaviour is highly rational. It tells us to interpret for maximum rationality, but it cannot say what result this effort will have. One person's conduct may be such that its most charitable interpretation makes him very rational, whereas another's leaves him, even on the kindest construal, much further down a scale of coherence. An ideal of charity guides psychological explanation, but it cannot determine its final content. That depends on empirical facts about a person's behaviour.

Second, a plausible principle of charity has two parts, one theoretical and one practical. It tells us to maximize both theoretical and practical rationality, or rationality in belief and rationality in action. These different maximands can sometimes conflict, as in cases that suggest self-deception. To say that someone has deceived himself is to explain an act of belief formation as a rational means to some goal, for example, avoiding distress, but it is also to ascribe an unjustified belief. In deciding whether to interpret someone as self-deceived, we decide whether to maximize his theoretical or practical rationality, where we cannot do both.

A final point concerns the substance of the ideal of charity. When sophisticated psychology tells us to maximize theoretical and practical rationality, what exactly does it intend? What is the precise content of its interpretive goal? According to a simple view, rationality involves just acting on some intentions and believing on some evidence, so a charitable interpretation maximizes just the number of a person's acts

and beliefs with some rational origin. But this view is not the only one possible. Davidson, for example, says that interpretations should make a person so far as possible "consistent, a believer of truths, and a lover of the good."[23] This proposal goes beyond the simple view because a belief based in evidence may still be false and an act aimed at an end far from laudable. In fact, Davidson's account of charity is just one of many possible. On the theoretical side, we can imagine a weak principle telling us to maximize just the number of a person's beliefs that are consistent; two stronger principles telling us to maximize either the number that are justified or the number that are true; and a still stronger one telling us to maximize the number that are both justified and true, or that constitute knowledge.

There are further possibilities. Charity can tell us to prefer ascribing beliefs that are more sophisticated. It can, and in my view should, say that, other things equal, we should prefer ascribing beliefs with more extended contents and more elaborate inter-relations. We make agents more rational, and explain them better, if we assign states with greater reach and explanatory coherence. Unfortunately, views like this last one are hard to defend. However plausible it is that psychology requires *some* concept of charity, it is difficult to argue that this concept must take one rather than another specific form. Can we show that one account of charity is truer than all others to our everyday explanatory practice? Or that it gives what by independent criteria are clearly better explanations? I do not see a decisive argument here, and it may be that there is none. It may be that, despite the general importance to psychology of using some principle of charity, there is no one content that principle must have.

If this is right, there may be some indeterminacy in the concept of charity, but the indeterminacy does not undermine the general conclusion we can draw from Davidson. Even without a specific principle of charity, we can know what range an acceptable principle must

fall within, and we can also know its importance. If sophisticated psychology tells us to maximize the rationality (in some sense) of all agents, then rationality (in that sense) is even more central than before. Rationality is presupposed in the premises of every psychological explanation, and its current exercise must also be explicitly ascribed. Now we see, beyond this, that it is a regulative ideal governing psychology and determining which of the many rationalizations consistent with its general structure are indeed explanations. If psychology uses charity constraints, rationality is doubly central to it, and we have doubly good reason to include rationality in the human essence.

Alongside physical perfection, then, Aristotelian perfectionism recognizes two further goods, which we can call *theoretical* and *practical perfection*. Although their full description will come later [see original reading], they already look promising, and a perfectionism containing them seems likely to have attractive consequences. This is impressive, because in deriving the goods from the human essence we did not use moralism or any moral arguments. The claim that humans are essentially rational first emerged from thought experiments and then was confirmed by psychological explanations.

When this is added to the intrinsic appeal of the perfectionist idea, the prospects for Aristotelian perfectionism look good.

Notes

1 Hamilton, *Lectures on Metaphysics*, p. 14.

2 Rawls, *A Theory of Justice*, p. 325.

3 Green, *Prolegomena to Ethics*, sec. 352.

4 Sidgwick, *The Methods of Ethics*, p. 9.

5 Bradley, "The Limits of Individual and National Self-Sacrifice," pp. 168, 173, 175.

6 Plato, *Republic*, 353a.

7 Aristotle, *Nicomachean Ethics*, 1097b33–1098a2.

8 Kant, *The Doctrine of Virtue*, p. 51.

9 Marx and Engels, *The German Ideology*, p. 160.

10 Marx, *Economic and Philosophical Manuscripts*, p. 82; and *Capital*, vol. 1, pp. 283–84.

11 Williams, *Morality: An Introduction to Ethics*, p. 64; see also Nielsen, "Alienation and Self-Realization," pp. 23–24. Williams intends some of his properties, especially the last ones, to be not just morally trivial but repugnant. The issue is tricky, however. If killing things for fun is repugnant, it is primarily because of its effect on the things killed. That the killing is intrinsically evil, or makes the killer's life worse, is a more contentious claim that, in my view, perfectionism need not affirm. In any case, it is sufficient for Williams's objection if his properties are valueless, that is, lack positive worth.

12 Nozick, *Philosophical Explanations*, pp. 515–17.

13 Kripke, *Naming and Necessity*.

14 Hegel, *The Phenomenology of Spirit*, p. 297; and *The Philosophy of Right*, sec. 153.

15 Marx, *Economic and Philosophical Manuscripts*, pp. 83, 89.

16 Nietzsche, *Beyond Good and Evil*, sec. 186; and *The Will to Power*, sec. 693.

17 Other claims that seem equivalent to ones about essence are: that perfection consists in the conformity of human existence with its "idea" or "concept" (Hegel, Marx, Bradley), that something is the "species-being" or "species-activity" of humans (Marx), that something constitutes "life" or humans' "life-activity" (Marx, Nietzsche), and that certain capacities belong to a human's "real" or "true self," as opposed to his "apparent self" (Kant, Bradley).

18 Aristotle, *Nicomachean Ethics*, 1098a18–20.

19 Aristotle, *Nicomachean Ethics*, 1095b14–1096a10, 1177a11–1179a33; *Eudemian Ethics*, 1215a26–b14; and *Politics*, 1324a24–b1. See also Aquinas, *Summa Theologica*, 2a2ae, q. 182.

20 Could there not be an objective or perfectionist account of well-being, which characterizes well-being not in terms of desires, but in terms of developing human nature? I do not believe there is conceptual room for such an account, for I do not believe "well-being" has any meaning independent both of particular accounts of well-being and of the moral predicate "good." I do not see that "developing human nature constitutes well-being and is therefore good" says anything over and above "developing human nature is good," and prefer to confine perfectionism to the second, simpler claim.

21 Some may deny that lower animals have intentions, as opposed to mere desires. If so,

distinctively human psychology begins earlier than I claim.

22 Davidson, *Essays on Actions and Events*.

23 Davidson, "Mental Events," p. 222.

References

Aquinas, St. Thomas. *Summa Theologica*. Translated by the Fathers of the English Dominican Province. 4 vols. Westminster, Md.: Christian Classics, 1981.

Aristotle. *Eudemian Ethics*. Translated by J. Solomon, in *The Complete Works of Aristotle* edited by Jonathan Barnes. 2 vols. Princeton: Princeton University Press, 1984.

——. *Nicomachean Ethics*. Translated by W. D. Ross. In *The Complete Works of Aristotle*, edited by Jonathan Barnes. 2 vols. Princeton: Princeton University Press, 1984.

——. *Politics*. Translated by B. Jowett, in *The Complete Works of Aristotle* edited by Jonathan Barnes. 2 vols. Princeton: Princeton University Press, 1984.

Bradley, F. H. "The Limits of Individual and National Self-Sacrifice." In *Collected Essays*. Vol. 1. Oxford: Clarendon Press, 1935.

Davidson, Donald. *Essays on Actions and Events*. Oxford: Clarendon Press, 1980.

——. "Mental Events." In *Essays on Actions and Events*. Oxford: Clarendon Press, 1980.

Green, Thomas Hill. *Prolegomena to Ethics*. 5th ed. Oxford: Clarendon Press, 1907.

Hamilton, William. *Lectures on Metaphysics*. Vol. 1 of *Lectures on Metaphysics and Logic*. 2 vols. Edited by H. L. Mansel and John Veitch. New York: Sheldon and Company, 1880.

Hegel, G. W. F. *The Phenomenology of Spirit*. Translated by A. V. Miller. Oxford: Oxford University Press, 1977.

——. *The Philosophy of Right*. Translated by T. M. Knox. Oxford: Oxford University Press, 1967.

Kant, Immanuel. *The Doctrine of Virtue: Part 2 of The Metaphysics of Morals*. Translated by Mary J. Gregor. Philadelphia: University of Pennsylvania Press, 1964.

Kripke, Saul A. *Naming and Necessity*. Cambridge, Mass.: Harvard University Press, 1980.

Marx, Karl. *Capital*. Vol. 1. Translated by Ben Fowkes. New York: Vintage, 1977.

——. *Economic and Philosophical Manuscripts* (excerpt). In *Karl Marx: Selected Writings*, edited by David McLellan. Oxford: Oxford University Press, 1977.

Marx, Karl and Friedrich Engels. *The German Ideology* (excerpt). In *Karl Marx: Selected Writings*, edited by David McLellan. Oxford: Oxford University Press, 1977.

Nielsen, Kai. "Alienation and Self-Realization." *Philosophy* 48 (1973): 21–33.

Nietzsche, Friedrich. *Beyond Good and Evil*. Translated by Walter Kaufmann. New York: Vintage, 1966.

——. *The Will to Power*. Translated by Walter Kaufmann and R. J. Hollingdale. New York: Vintage, 1968.

Nozick, Robert. *Philosophical Explanations*. Cambridge, Mass.: Harvard University Press, 1981.

Plato. *Republic*. Translated by G. M. A. Grube. Indianapolis: Hackett, 1974.

Prichard, H. A. "The Meaning of *Agathon* in the Ethics of Aristotle." *Philosophy* 10 (1935): 27–39.

Rawls, John. *A Theory of Justice*. Cambridge, Mass.: Harvard University Press, 1971.

Sidgwick, Henry. *The Methods of Ethics*. 7th ed. London: Macmillan, 1907.

Williams, Bernard. *Morality: An Introduction to Ethics*. New York: Harper & Row, 1972.

Chapter 51

Derek Parfit

WHAT MAKES SOMEONE'S LIFE GO BEST?

WHAT WOULD BE best for someone, or would be most in this person's interests, or would make this person's life go, for him, as well as possible? Answers to this question I call *theories about self-interest*. There are three kinds of theory. On *Hedonistic Theories*, what would be best for someone is what would make his life happiest. On *Desire-Fulfillment Theories*, what would be best for someone is what, throughout his life, would best fulfil his desires. On *Objective List Theories*, certain things are good or bad for us, whether or not we want to have the good things, or to avoid the bad things.

Narrow Hedonists assume, falsely, that pleasure and pain are two distinctive kinds of experience. Compare the pleasures of satisfying an intense thirst or lust, listening to music, solving an intellectual problem, reading a tragedy, and knowing that one's child is happy. These various experiences do not contain any distinctive common quality.

What pains and pleasures have in common are their relations to our desires. On the use of 'pain' which has rational and moral significance, all pains are when experienced unwanted, and a pain is worse or greater the more it is unwanted. Similarly, all pleasures are when experienced wanted, and they are better or greater the more they are wanted. These are the claims of *Preference-Hedonism*. On this view, one of two experiences is more pleasant if it is preferred.

This theory need not follow the ordinary uses of the words 'pain' and 'pleasure'. Suppose that I could go to a party to enjoy the various pleasures of eating, drinking, laughing, dancing, and talking to my friends. I could instead stay at home and read *King Lear*. Knowing what both alternatives would be like, I prefer to read *King Lear*. It extends the ordinary use to say that this would give me more pleasure. But on Preference-Hedonism, if we add some further assumptions given below, reading *King Lear* would give me a better evening. Griffin cites a more extreme case. Near the end of his life Freud refused pain-killing drugs, preferring to think in torment than to be confusedly euphoric. Of these two mental states, euphoria is more pleasant. But on Preference-Hedonism thinking in torment was, for Freud, a better mental state. It is clearer here not to stretch the meaning of the word 'pleasant'. A Preference-Hedonist should merely claim that, since Freud preferred to think clearly though in torment, his life went better if it went as he preferred.

Consider next Desire-Fulfillment Theories. The simplest is the *Unrestricted Theory*. This claims that what is best for someone is what would best fulfil *all* of his desires, throughout his life. Suppose that I meet a stranger who has what is believed to be a fatal disease. My sympathy is aroused, and I strongly want this stranger to be cured. Much later, when I have forgotten our meeting, the stranger is cured. On the Unrestricted Desire-Fulfillment Theory, this event is good for me, and makes my life go

better. This is not plausible. We should reject this theory.

Another theory appeals only to someone's desires about his own life. I call this the *Success Theory*. This theory differs from Preference-Hedonism in only one way. The Success Theory appeals to all of our preferences about our own lives. A Preference-Hedonist appeals only to preferences about those present features of our lives that are introspectively discernible. Suppose that I strongly want not to be deceived by other people. On Preference-Hedonism it would be better for me if I believe that I am not being deceived. It would be irrelevant if my belief is false, since this makes no difference to my state of mind. On the Success Theory, it would be worse for me if my belief is false. I have a strong desire about my own life—that I should not be deceived in this way. It is bad for me if this desire is not fulfilled, even if I falsely believe that it is.

When this theory appeals only to desires that are about our own lives, it may be unclear what this excludes. Suppose that I want my life to be such that all of my desires, whatever their objects, are fulfilled. This may seem to make the Success Theory, when applied to me, coincide with the Unrestricted Desire-Fulfillment Theory. But a Success Theorist should claim that this desire is not really about my own life. This is like the distinction between a real change in some object, and a so-called *Cambridge-change*. An object undergoes a Cambridge-change if there is any change in the true statements that can be made about this object. Suppose that I cut my cheek while shaving. This causes a real change in me. It also causes a change in Confucius. It becomes true, of Confucius, that he lived on a planet in which later one more cheek was cut. This is merely a Cambridge-change.

Suppose that I am an exile, and cannot communicate with my children. I want their lives to go well. I might claim that I want to live the life of someone whose children's lives go well. A Success Theorist should again claim that this is not really a desire about my own life. If

unknown to me one of my children is killed by an avalanche, this is not bad for me, and does not make my life go worse.

A Success Theorist *would* count some similar desires. Suppose that I try to give my children a good start in life. I try to give them the right education, good habits, and psychological strength. Once again, I am now an exile, and will never be able to learn what happens to my children. Suppose that, unknown to me, my children's lives go badly. One finds that the education that I gave him makes him unemployable, another has a mental breakdown, another becomes a petty thief. If my children's lives fail in these ways, and these failures are in part the result of mistakes I made as their parent, these failures in my children's lives would be judged to be bad for me on the Success Theory. One of my strongest desires was to be a successful parent. What is now happening to my children, though it is unknown to me, shows that this desire is not fulfilled. My life failed in one of the ways in which I most wanted it to succeed. Though I do not know this fact, it is bad for me, and makes it true that I have had a worse life. This is like the case where I strongly want not to be deceived. Even if I never know, it is bad for me both if I am deceived and if I turn out to be an unsuccessful parent. These are not introspectively discernible differences in my conscious life. On Preference-Hedonism, these events are not bad for me. On the Success Theory, they are.

Because they are thought by some to need special treatment, I mention next the desires that people have about what happens after they are dead. For a Preference-Hedonist, once I am dead, nothing bad can happen to me. A Success Theorist should deny this. Return to the case where all my children have wretched lives, because of the mistakes I made as their parent. Suppose that my children's lives all go badly only after I am dead. My life turns out to have been a failure, in one of the ways I cared about most. A Success Theorist should

claim that, here too, this makes it true that I had a worse life.

Some Success Theorists would reject this claim. Their theory ignores the desires of the dead. I believe this theory to be indefensible. Suppose that I was asked, 'Do you want it to be true that you were a successful parent even after you are dead?' I would answer 'Yes'. It is irrelevant to my desire whether it is fulfilled before or after I am dead. These Success Theorists count it as bad for me if my desire is not fulfilled, even if, because I am an exile, I never know this. How then can it matter whether, when my desire is not fulfilled, I am dead? All that my death does is to *ensure* that I will never know this. If we think it irrelevant that I never know about the nonfulfillment of my desire, we cannot defensibly claim that my death makes a difference.

I turn now to questions and objections which arise for both Preference-Hedonism and the Success Theory.

Should we appeal only to the desires and preferences that someone actually has? Return to my choice between going to a party or staying at home to read *King Lear*. Suppose that, knowing what both alternatives would be like, I choose to stay at home. And suppose that I never later regret this choice. On one theory, this shows that staying at home to read *King Lear* gave me a better evening. This is a mistake. It might be true that, if I had chosen to go to the party, I would never have regretted that choice. According to this theory, this would have shown that going to the party gave me a better evening. This theory thus implies that each alternative would have been better than the other. Since this theory implies such contradictions, it must be revised. The obvious revision is to appeal not only to my actual preferences, in the alternative I choose, but also to the preferences that I would have had if I had chosen otherwise.

In this example, whichever alternative I choose, I would never regret this choice. If this is true, can we still claim that one of the alternatives would give me a better evening? On some theories, when in two alternatives I would have such contrary preferences, neither alternative is better or worse for me. This is not plausible when one of my contrary preferences would have been much stronger. Suppose that, if I choose to go to the party, I shall be only mildly glad that I made this choice, but that, if I choose to stay and read *King Lear*, I shall be extremely glad. If this is true, reading *King Lear* gives me a better evening.

Whether we appeal to Preference-Hedonism or the Success Theory, we should not appeal only to the desires or preferences that I actually have. We should also appeal to the desires and preferences that I would have had, in the various alternatives that were, at different times, open to me. One of these alternatives would be best for me if it is the one in which I would have the strongest desires and preferences fulfilled. This allows us to claim that some alternative life would have been better for me, even if throughout my actual life I am glad that I chose this life rather than this alternative.

There is another distinction which applies both to Preference-Hedonism and to the Success Theory. These theories are *Summative* if they appeal to all of someone's desires, actual and hypothetical, about his own life. In deciding which alternative would produce the greatest total net sum of desire-fulfillment, we assign some positive number to each desire that is fulfilled, and some negative number to each desire that is not fulfilled. How great these numbers are depends on the intensity of the desires in question. (In the case of the Success Theory, which appeals to past desires, it may also depend on how long these desires were had. [. . .] this may be a weakness in this theory. The issue does not arise for Preference-Hedonism, which appeals only to desires about one's present state of mind.) The total net sum of desire-fulfillment is the sum of the positive numbers minus the negative numbers. Provided that we can compare the relative strength of

different desires, this calculation could in theory be performed. The choice of a unit for the numbers makes no difference to the result.

Another version of both theories does not appeal, in this way, to all of a person's desires and preferences about his own life. It appeals only to *global* rather than *local* desires and preferences. A preference is global if it is about some part of one's life considered as a whole, or is about one's whole life. The *Global* versions of these theories I believe to be more plausible.

Consider this example. Knowing that you accept a Summative theory, I tell you that I am about to make your life go better. I shall inject you with an addictive drug. From now on, you will wake each morning with an extremely strong desire to have another injection of this drug. Having this desire will be in itself neither pleasant nor painful, but if the desire is not fulfilled within an hour it would then become extremely painful. This is no cause for concern, since I shall give you ample supplies of this drug. Every morning, you will be able at once to fulfil this desire. The injection, and its after-effects, would also be neither pleasant nor painful. You will spend the rest of your days as you do now.

What would the Summative theories imply about this case? We can plausibly suppose that you would not welcome my proposal. You would prefer not to become addicted to this drug, even though I assure you that you will never lack supplies. We can also plausibly suppose that, if I go ahead, you will always regret that you became addicted to this drug. But it is likely that your initial desire not to become addicted, and your later regrets that you did, would not be as strong as the desires you have each morning for another injection. Given the facts as I described them, your reason to prefer not to become addicted would not be very strong. You might dislike the thought of being addicted to anything. And you would regret the minor inconvenience that would be involved in remembering always to carry with you, like a diabetic, sufficient supplies. But these desires

might be far weaker than the desires you would have each morning for a fresh injection.

On the Summative Theories, if I make you an addict, I would be increasing the sum-total of your desire-fulfillment. I would be causing one of your desires not to be fulfilled: your desire not to become an addict, which, after my act, becomes a desire to be cured. But I would also be giving you an indefinite series of extremely strong desires, one each morning, all of which you can fulfil. The fulfillment of all these desires would outweigh the non-fulfillment of your desires not to become an addict, and to be cured. On the Summative Theories, by making you an addict, I would be benefiting you—making your life go better.

This conclusion is not plausible. Having these desires, and having them fulfilled, are neither pleasant nor painful. We need not be Hedonists to believe, more plausibly, that it is in no way better for you to have and to fulfil this series of strong desires.

Could the Summative Theories be revised, so as to meet this objection? Is there some feature of the addictive desires which would justify the claim that we should ignore them when we calculate the sum total of your desire-fulfillment? We might claim that they can be ignored because they are desires that you would prefer not to have. But this is not an acceptable revision. Suppose that you are in great pain. You now have a very strong desire not to be in the state that you are in. On our revised theory, a desire does not count if you would prefer not to have this desire. This must apply to your intense desire not to be in the state you are in. You would prefer not to have this desire. If you did not dislike the state you are in, it would not be painful. Since our revised theory does not count desires that you would prefer not to have, it implies, absurdly, that it cannot be bad for you to be in great pain.

There may be other revisions which could meet these objections. But it is simpler to appeal to the Global versions of both Preference-Hedonism

and the Success Theory. These appeal only to someone's desires about some part of his life, considered as a whole, or about his whole life. The Global Theories give us the right answer in the case where I make you an addict. You would prefer not to become addicted, and you would later prefer to cease to be addicted. These are the only preferences to which the Global Theories appeal. They ignore your particular desires each morning for a fresh injection. This is because you have yourself taken these desires into account in forming your global preference.

This imagined case of addiction is in its essentials similar to countless other cases. There are countless cases in which it is true both (1) that, if someone's life goes in one of two ways, this would increase the sum total of his local desire-fulfillment, but (2) that the other alternative is what he would globally prefer, whichever way his actual life goes.

Rather than describing another of the countless actual cases, I shall mention an imaginary case. . . . Suppose that I could either have fifty of years of life of an extremely high quality, or an indefinite number of years that are barely worth living. In the first alternative, my fifty years would, on any theory, go extremely well. I would be very happy, would achieve great things, do much good, and love and be loved by many people. In the second alternative my life would always be, though not by much, worth living. There would be nothing bad about this life, and it would each day contain a few small pleasures.

On the Summative Theories, if the second life was long enough, it would be better for me. In each day within this life I have some desires about my life that are fulfilled. In the fifty years of the first alternative, there would be a very great sum of local desire-fulfillment. But this would be a finite sum, and in the end it would be outweighed by the sum of desire-fulfillment in my indefinitely long second alternative. A simpler way to put this point is this. The first alternative would be good. In the second

alternative, since my life is worth living, living each extra day is good for me. If we merely add together whatever is good for me, some number of these extra days would produce the greatest total sum.

I do not believe that the second alternative would give me a better life. I therefore reject the Summative Theories. It is likely that, in both alternatives, I would globally prefer the first. Since the Global Theories would then imply that the first alternative gives me a better life, these theories seem to me more plausible.

Turn now to the third kind of Theory that I mentioned: the Objective List Theory. According to this theory, certain things are good or bad for people, whether or not these people would want to have the good things, or to avoid the bad things. The good things might include moral goodness, rational activity, the development of one's abilities, having children and being a good parent, knowledge, and the awareness of true beauty. The bad things might include being betrayed, manipulated, slandered, deceived, being deprived of liberty or dignity, and enjoying either sadistic pleasure, or aesthetic pleasure in what is in fact ugly.

An Objective List Theorist might claim that his theory coincides with the Global version of the Success Theory. On this theory, what would make my life go best depends on what I would prefer, now and in the various alternatives, if I knew all of the relevant facts about these alternatives. An Objective List Theorist might say that the most relevant facts are what his theory claims—what would in fact be good or bad for me. And he might claim that anyone who knew these facts would want what is truly good for him, and want to avoid what would be bad for him.

If this was true, though the Objective List Theory would coincide with the Success Theory, the two theories would remain distinct. A Success Theorist would reject this description of the coincidence. On his theory, nothing is good or bad for people, whatever their preferences

are. Something is bad for someone only if, knowing the facts, he wants to avoid it. And the relevant facts do not include the alleged facts cited by the Objective List Theorist. On the Success Theory it is, for instance, bad for someone to be deceived if and because this is not what he wants. The Objective List Theorist makes the reverse claim. People want not to be deceived because this is bad for them.

As these remarks imply, there is one important difference between on the one hand Preference-Hedonism and the Success Theory, and on the other hand the Objective List Theory. The first two kinds of theory give an account of self-interest which is entirely factual, or which does not appeal to facts about value. The account appeals to what a person does and would prefer, given full knowledge of the purely non-evaluative facts about the alternatives. In contrast, the Objective List Theory appeals directly to facts about value.

In choosing between these theories, we must decide how much weight to give to imagined cases in which someone's fully informed preferences would be bizarre. If we can appeal to these cases, they cast doubt on both Preference-Hedonism and the Success Theory. Consider the man that Rawls imagined who wants to spend his life counting the numbers of blades of grass in different lawns. Suppose that this man knows that he could achieve great progress if instead he worked in some especially useful part of Applied Mathematics. Though he could achieve such significant results, he prefers to go on counting blades of grass. On the Success Theory, if we allow this theory to cover all imaginable cases, it could be better for this person if he counts his blades of grass rather than achieves great and beneficial results in Mathematics.

The counter-example might be more offensive. Suppose that what someone would most prefer, knowing the alternatives, is a life in which, without being detected, he causes as much pain as he can to other people. On the Success Theory, such a life would be what is best for this person.

We may be unable to accept these conclusions. Ought we therefore to abandon this theory? This is what Sidgwick did, though those who quote him seldom notice this. He suggests that 'a man's future good on the whole is what he would now desire and seek on the whole if all the consequences of all the different lines of conduct open to him were accurately foreseen and adequately realised in imagination at the present point of time'. As he comments: 'The notion of "Good" thus attained has an ideal element: it is something that is not always actually desired and aimed at by human beings: but the ideal element is entirely interpretable in terms of fact, actual or hypothetical, and does not introduce any judgement of value'. Sidgwick then rejects this account, claiming that what is ultimately good for someone is what this person *would* desire if his desires were in harmony with reason. This last phrase is needed, Sidgwick thought, to exclude the cases where someone's desires are irrational. He assumes that there are some things that we have good reason to desire, and others that we have good reason not to desire. These might be the things which are held to be good or bad for us by Objective List Theories.

Suppose we agree that, in some imagined cases, what someone would most want both now and later, fully knowing about the alternatives, would *not* be what would be best for him. If we accept this conclusion, it may seem that we must reject both Preference-Hedonism and the Success Theory. Perhaps, like Sidgwick, we must put constraints on what can be rationally desired.

It might be claimed instead that we can dismiss the appeal to such imagined cases. It might be claimed that what people would in fact prefer, if they knew the relevant facts, would always be something that we could accept as what is really good for them. Is this a good reply? If we agree that in the imagined cases what someone would prefer might be something that is bad for him, in these cases we have

abandoned our theory. If this is so, can we defend our theory by saying that, in the actual cases, it would not go astray? I believe that this is not an adequate defence. But I shall not pursue this question here.

This objection may apply with less force to Preference-Hedonism. On this theory, what can be good or bad for someone can only be discernible features of his conscious life. These are the features that, at the time, he either wants or does not want. I asked above whether it is bad for people to be deceived because they prefer not to be, or whether they prefer not to be deceived because this is bad for them. Consider the comparable question with respect to pain. Some have claimed that pain is intrinsically bad, and that this is why we dislike it. As I have suggested, I doubt this claim. After taking certain kinds of drug, people claim that the quality of their sensations has not altered, but they no longer dislike these sensations. We would regard such drugs as effective analgesics. This suggests that the badness of a pain consists in its being disliked, and that it is not disliked because it is bad. The disagreement between these views would need much more discussion. But, if the second view is better, it is more plausible to claim that whatever someone wants or does not want to experience—however bizarre we find his desires—should be counted as being for this person truly pleasant or painful, and as being for that reason good or bad for him. There may still be cases where it is plausible to claim that it would be bad for someone if he enjoys certain kinds of pleasure. This might be claimed, for instance, about sadistic pleasure. But there may be few such cases.

If instead we appeal to the Success Theory, we are not concerned only with the experienced quality of our conscious life. We are concerned with such things as whether we are achieving what we are trying to achieve, whether we are being deceived, and the like. When considering this theory, we can more often plausibly claim that, even if someone knew the facts, his

preferences might go astray, and fail to correspond to what would be good or bad for him.

Which of these different theories should we accept? I shall not attempt an answer here. But I shall end by mentioning another theory, which might be claimed to combine what is most plausible in these conflicting theories. It is a striking fact that those who have addressed this question have disagreed so fundamentally. Many philosophers have been convinced Hedonists; many others have been as much convinced that Hedonism is a gross mistake.

Some Hedonists have reached their view as follows. They consider an opposing view, such as that which claims that what is good for someone is to have knowledge, to engage in rational activity, and to be aware of true beauty. These Hedonists ask, 'Would these states of mind be good, if they brought no enjoyment, and if the person in these states of mind had not the slightest desire that they continue?' Since they answer No, they conclude that the value of these states of mind must lie in their being liked, and in their arousing a desire that they continue.

This reasoning assumes that the value of a whole is just the sum of the value of its parts. If we remove the part to which the Hedonist appeals, what is left seems to have no value, hence Hedonism is the truth.

Suppose instead that we claim that the value of a whole may not be a mere sum of the value of its parts. We might then claim that what is best for people is a composite. It is not just their being in the conscious states that they want to be in. Nor is it just their having knowledge, engaging in rational activity, being aware of true beauty, and the like. What is good for someone is neither just what Hedonists claim, nor just what is claimed by Objective List Theorists. We might believe that if we had *either* of these, *without the other*, what we had would have little or no value. We might claim, for example, that what is good or bad for someone is to have knowledge, to be engaged in rational activity, to experience

mutual love, and to be aware of beauty, while strongly wanting just these things. On this view, each side in this disagreement saw only half of the truth. Each put forward as sufficient something that was only necessary. Pleasure with many other kinds of object has no value. And, if they are entirely devoid of pleasure, there is no value in knowledge, rational activity, love, or the awareness of beauty. What is of value, or is good for someone, is to have both; to be engaged in these activities, and to be strongly wanting to be so engaged.

Chapter 52

Thomas Scanlon

THE BUCK-PASSING ACCOUNT OF VALUE

Values: some examples

THE THINGS that philosophers have generally listed as intrinsically valuable fall into a few categories: certain states of consciousness; personal relationships; intellectual, artistic, and moral excellence; knowledge; and human life itself. In claiming that these things are valuable, these philosophers seem to mean that it is good that they occur. G. E. Moore was quite explicit about this, saying that in order to decide whether a thing is intrinsically valuable or not we should imagine a world in which only that thing existed and ask ourselves whether we would judge its existence to be good.[1] W. D. Ross was slightly less explicit, but his discussion of "What things are good?" also concentrates on the question of what makes some "states of the universe" better than others.[2] When we consider the things that are generally held to be intrinsically valuable, however, it becomes apparent that in most cases taking them to be valuable is not simply, or even primarily, a matter of thinking that certain states of the universe are better than others and are therefore to be promoted.

Consider first the case of friendship. Moore listed "the pleasures of human intercourse" as "one of the most valuable things we know or can imagine."[3] By this he meant that a world that contains two people enjoying the pleasures of reciprocated affection is made better, other things being equal, by containing this occurrence. Now

it may be true that the existence of friendship and the pleasures it brings make a world better, but it strikes me as odd to suggest that this is what is central to the value of friendship. Surely we are right to value friendship (and presumably this is part of what Moore was affirming), so one way of looking for a more plausible account of the matter is to ask what this "valuing" involves.

A person who values friendship will take herself to have reasons, first and foremost, to do those things that are involved in being a good friend: to be loyal, to be concerned with her friends' interests, to try to stay in touch, to spend time with her friends, and so on. Someone who values friendship will also believe that she has reasons of a slightly different kind to cultivate new friendships and to keep the ones she already has, and will think that having friends is a good worth seeking. Consequently, a person who values friendship will also think it good for other people that they have friends, and will be moved to bring this about insofar as these people are of concern to her.[4] It seems overblown to say that what is important about friendship is that it increases the value of the state of the universe in which it occurs. But there is nothing odd about saying that it improves the quality of a life. So reasons of the last three kinds I mentioned (reasons to bring it about that one has friends, to keep the ones one has, and to help bring it about that others whom one cares about have friends) might be seen as restating Moore's

thesis in a more modest form. They are at least like his thesis in having a teleological form: accepting them as reasons involves holding that it is good (in this case, good for the individuals in question) that friendship should occur and that friendship is therefore "to be promoted."

But the reasons in the first category, the ones involved in being a good friend, do not have this form. Some of them, such as reasons to be loyal to one's friends and not to betray them, are not teleological in this way: the primary reason to be loyal to one's friends is not that this is necessary in order for the friendship to continue to exist. Other reasons in this category are reasons to bring about certain states of affairs: to promote the interests of one's friends, for example, and to try to make them happy. But what is "to be promoted" here is not the occurrence of friendship but other specific ends.

Moreover, while all the reasons I have mentioned are ones that would be recognized by a person who valued friendship, it is the reasons in this first category (those involved in being a good friend) that are most central to friendship, and when conflicts occur these reasons take priority over the reasons we have to promote friendship (for ourselves or others). We would not say that it showed how much a person valued friendship if he betrayed one friend in order to make several new ones, or in order to bring it about that other people had more friends.[5]

I shifted, near the beginning of this discussion of the value of friendship, from the question of what it is for friendship to be valuable to the question of what is involved in valuing friendship. These are different questions. People value many things that are not in fact valuable. What I want to suggest, however, is that the claim that friendship is valuable is best understood as the claim that it is properly valued, that is to say, that the reasons recognized by someone who values friendship are in fact good reasons. Consider, as a contrast with friendship, "fanship": the state of being a devoted admirer of some famous person, such as a movie star, a singer, or an athlete. Some people value fanship. That is, they think that being a fan makes life better, more enjoyable, and more interesting. They may also think that it is important to be a good fan: that there is good reason, say, to see all the movies in which their favorite star appears as soon as they come out, and to defend the star when others criticize her, and that it would be a great thing to see the star in person, even from a great distance. According to the account of value I am suggesting, to hold that fanship is not valuable is just to hold that these reasons are not good reasons, or at least that a person who gave them great weight in shaping his life would be making a mistake. On the other hand, to hold that fanship, or friendship, is valuable is to hold that the reasons involved in valuing it are good ones and that it is therefore appropriate to give this notion an important place in shaping one's life.

If this claim is accepted, and if my claims about the reasons involved in valuing friendship are correct, then the claim that friendship is valuable is not primarily a claim that it is "to be promoted" or that a world in which it exists is for that reason a better one, although it will be true that if friendship is valuable then there are reasons to seek it for oneself and to promote it for others whom one cares about. When we consider the question of value in the way that Moore recommended, by asking what makes a world better, it is only reasons of this latter kind—reasons to have friendship occur—that we notice. These reasons are teleological and, in many cases, impartial. But when we take into account the perspective of the people who are friends, a wider range of reasons comes into view. These reasons are not in general impartial; some are not teleological at all; and among those that are, only a few are, directly or indirectly, reasons to bring it about that more friendship occurs. To claim that friendship is valuable is, on the view I am offering, to claim that all these reasons are good reasons.

I believe that much the same thing could be said about the value of other relationships commonly, and plausibly, held to be good, such as family relations. This may not be surprising, since friendship and family ties may be seen as moral values and "agent-relative" ones. But I believe that a similar structure can be seen in the reasons involved in values of other kinds such as the value of intellectual inquiry and understanding. I will discuss the case of scientific inquiry, but I think that what I will say holds as well for other forms of intellectual activity, in history, for example, or philosophy or mathematics.

The claim that science and scientific knowledge are intrinsically valuable supports a number of different conclusions about the reasons people have. One is that people who have the relevant ability and opportunity have reason to take up scientific inquiry as a career and to devote their lives to it. Second, those who take up science as a career have reason to try to be good scientists: to work hard, to choose lines of inquiry that are significant rather than those that are easiest or will get the most attention, to report their results accurately and in a way that will be helpful to other inquirers, and to treat the results of others fairly, recognizing their merits rather than simply emphasizing their weaknesses and deficiencies. Someone who failed to see strong reason to do these things could be said not to understand or not to care about the value of science, and to be in it just for the sake of money or fame or the thrill of competition.

Third, if science is valuable then those of us who are not scientists have reason to support scientific work as taxpayers or benefactors. Fourth, we have reason to study science and try to understand it. If science is valuable, then this kind of study is worthwhile, even if our understanding will always be highly imperfect. Finally, we have reason to respect science as an undertaking and to admire its achievements and those who make them.

One might try to account for all these reasons on a strictly teleological basis. Such an account could hold that the value of science lies, fundamentally, in the value of certain states of affairs: a world in which fundamental truths about nature are understood or investigated is for that reason a better world. People have reason to take up science as a career if they would be able to contribute to bringing about these valuable results. They have reason to be "good scientists" because by doing this they are likely to make a greater contribution of this kind. Others have reason to promote and support scientific work because this also promotes these valuable results. It is a little more difficult to explain, on this basis, why nonscientists have reason to study it. Perhaps this might be explained by broadening the class of valuable states to include the spread of even imperfect understanding. But it is easy to see why scientific work should be admired, namely, because it produces valuable results.

Such a view has great simplicity and evident appeal. It is much more plausible than the analogous claim that all the reasons involved in valuing friendship flow from the goodness of having friendships occur. But I do not think that such a view offers the most plausible account of the intrinsic value of science and scientific knowledge. To see this, consider first what the valuable states of affairs on which such a view would be based might be taken to be.

First, through their applications in technology, scientific achievements contribute to enlarging the range of things we can do, and to making our lives longer, safer, and more comfortable. These effects are no doubt valuable, but since they are not what people have in mind in claiming that scientific knowledge is *intrinsically* valuable, I will set them aside.

Second, engaging in scientific study and inquiry can be challenging, exciting, and absorbing, and it therefore enriches the lives of those who engage in it. But other pursuits are also challenging, exciting, and absorbing: mountain climbing and yacht racing, for

example. Insofar as scientific inquiry is thought to make a greater contribution than these pursuits to the quality of the lives of those who engage in it, this is, I assume, because it is thought to be a more worthwhile way to use one's time and talents. Perhaps it is thought worthwhile because of the practical benefits I have just mentioned, but I do not believe that this is the only reason. If it is not, then the distinctive contribution that devoting one's life to scientific activity makes to the quality of that life depends on the fact that the activity is intrinsically worthwhile, rather than the value of the activity depending on its contribution to the well-being of those who engage in it.

This suggests that the distinctive intrinsic value of science must derive, on a purely teleological account, from the fact that states of affairs in which scientific knowledge has been attained (and perhaps also ones in which scientific inquiry is engaged in in the right way) are better states of affairs and therefore "to be promoted." This way of putting the matter leads to some puzzling questions. Suppose that what is intrinsically valuable is true belief about the world, particularly about its most fundamental features. There is the slight problem that at any given time much of what science holds to be true about the most fundamental features of nature is likely to be false. Perhaps, then, it is valuable because it is a step on the way to attaining true belief. Or perhaps what is valuable is not just the true belief that results from scientific inquiry, but the occurrence of that inquiry itself, at least when it is done well. This is in some ways more plausible, but we would then need an independent explanation of how the value of science gives even nonscientists reason to try to understand it, to the degree that they can.

The mere fact that there are problems about how this view should be formulated does not, of course, show that it is mistaken. In my view what is most implausible about such an account, however, is the basic idea that we should understand all the reasons we have to engage in,

support, and study science by first identifying some class of ways that it would be better for the world to be, and then explaining these reasons by considering how the activities they count in favor of help to make the world be like this. There are some cases in which this order of explanation seems very plausible, as in the case of pain. A state of affairs in which I am in pain is, for that reason, a worse state of affairs for me, and this fact gives rise to reasons to do what is necessary to prevent it. But it is not always possible to identify outcomes whose independent value can plausibly be seen as a source of the reasons we have. In particular, even though the actions involved in scientific inquiry and study are each aimed at some end, the best account of our reasons for those actions may not flow from the value of these results to our concern with them.

An alternative line of explanation would begin with the idea that we have good reason to be curious about the natural world and to try to understand how it works. A person who responds to nature in this way is right to do so, and someone who fails to have this response is missing something. Since science is by far the most successful attempt at such understanding, studying it and trying to contribute to it are things we have reason to do: both are rational responses to our justified curiosity about the world. It follows that I have reason to adopt the goal of reading good books about science for laymen, and that scientists have reason to adopt the goal of coming up with new and better theories (quite apart from the usefulness of the knowledge that may be so gained). So we each correctly regard the achievement of these goals as good (even intrinsically good). But this is a conclusion from the claims about reasons I have mentioned, not their source.

Things look slightly different in this respect when we consider the matter from the point of view of a patron or benefactor, someone who gives money to support scientific research, or to educate the public about science. Such a person

is properly moved by the thought that it is good that scientific research should occur and that more people should appreciate its results. The reasons that move such a person are like those that figure in the Moorean perspective I mentioned earlier, and like some reasons that could move a person to promote the friendships of others. I am not suggesting that they are not good reasons, but only that they are not as central as might be supposed to the idea of the value of science.

A similar divergence of perspectives shows up when we consider two other reasons for thinking that the pursuit of scientific knowledge is a good thing to have occur. For example, science is to be admired and promoted because it is a form of human excellence, involving highly developed intellectual skills devoted to questions that merit inquiry. But from the point of view of practitioners of science, the reason for striving and thinking in the ways that constitute this excellence is that this is the best way of inquiring into their subject, not simply that it produces instances of excellence. Science may also merit our respect and admiration as a complex cooperative endeavor, extending over time and yoking together the highly developed capacities of many individuals. Someone who failed to appreciate this human and social aspect of science, and valued it only for its results, would be missing something important. But from the point of view of a practitioner, understanding this aspect of the value of science involves seeing reasons to respect the norms of the scientific community, not just reasons to think it good that that community exists.

It might seem that there is small difference at best between this account of the value of science and a purely teleological one. If fundamental questions about the natural world are worth inquiring into, doesn't this mean that the results produced by this inquiry, if it succeeds, are good? Otherwise, why would they be worth striving for?

In one sense this is quite true: if a state of affairs is worth striving for, then it is good. But there remains an important question about the order of explanation. What I am suggesting is that if we want to understand why scientific inquiry is worth engaging in and its results worth studying, we do better to consider why the questions it addresses are important and why it offers an appropriate way of trying to answer them than to focus on any particular results that scientific investigation or the study of science might produce (by, say, imagining a world containing a great scientific discovery, or one containing someone with the very imperfect understanding of quantum mechanics that I could attain by studying it in my spare time). Such results are, I believe, worth striving for, but to see why this is so we need to look elsewhere. If we begin with the reasonableness and appropriateness of curiosity about the world, and with the merits of science as a way of responding to this curiosity, this leads next to the various more specific ways in which responses to this curiosity can be incorporated into our lives. We thus arrive at a unified explanation of the various reasons mentioned above: reasons to devote oneself to science if one has the ability and opportunity, reasons to support it as a patron, reasons for others to try to understand it to the degree that they can, and so on. These are reasons to adopt certain goals and to regard their attainment as good. But, as I suggested above [see original reading] in discussing Scheffler's remarks about rationality, from the fact that deciding how to pursue one's goals plays an important part in practical thinking we should not conclude that goals are where all explanations of value must begin.

An abstract account of value

The examples of friendship and science suggest the following general picture. We value many different kinds of things, including at least the following: objects and their properties (such as beauty), persons, skills and talents, states of

character, actions, accomplishments, activities and pursuits, relationships, and ideals. To value something is to take oneself to have reasons for holding certain positive attitudes toward it and for acting in certain ways in regard to it. Exactly what these reasons are, and what actions and attitudes they support, will be different in different cases. They generally include, as a common core, reasons for admiring the thing and for respecting it, although "respecting" can involve quite different things in different cases. Often, valuing something involves seeing reasons to preserve and protect it (as, for example, when I value a historic building); in other cases it involves reasons to be guided by the goals and standards that the value involves (as when I value loyalty); in some cases both may be involved (as when I value the U.S. Constitution).[6]

To claim that something is valuable (or that it is "of value") is to claim that others also have reason to value it, as you do. We can, quite properly, value some things more than others without claiming that they are more valuable. So, for example, it is natural to say, and would be odd to deny, that I value my children; but it would be odd for me to put this by saying that they are valuable (except in the sense that everyone is). The reason behind this oddness is the one just mentioned: claiming that something is valuable involves claiming that its attributes merit being valued generally, and valuing one's own children above others, in the sense in which we all do this, lacks this impersonal quality and this dependence on what is merited or called for by their attributes. The present discussion of value is about what it is to be valuable rather than about valuing. I have discussed the latter only because it provides a helpful stepping-stone.

It is helpful in part because it draws attention to the variety of things that can be valuable and the variety of reasons that are involved in their being valuable. Believing that something is valuable can involve believing that there is reason to promote its existence, but it does not always

involve this. Commonly, as we saw in the cases of friendship and scientific knowledge, the judgment that something is valuable depends on further judgments about what things there is reason to bring about. As we saw in those cases, however, these judgments do not exhaust the relevant ideas of value, and they need not all flow from a central judgment about what it would be good to have exist or occur.

What I have sketched here is an abstract description of the structure of the idea of value, which contrasts with the familiar teleological conception of this structure. It is not a "theory" of value: neither a systematic account of which things are valuable, nor an explanation of the "source" of value. My account contains two separate elements, which are independent and should be distinguished. One is the idea, emphasized in the preceding section, that value is not a purely teleological notion. The other is the claim that being valuable is not a property that provides us with reasons. Rather, to call something valuable is to say that it has other properties that provide reasons for behaving in certain ways with regard to it. I am led to this "buck-passing" account of value by the following reflections on Moore's open-question argument about 'good'.[7]

We judge things to be good or to be valuable because of other properties that they have. Often these are physical or psychological properties, as, for example, when we judge something to be good because it is pleasant, or judge a discovery to be valuable because it provides new understanding of how cancer cells develop. But being good or valuable cannot be identified with any such "natural" property or, more generally, with any non-normative property. This is the lesson of the open-question argument. The question "X is pleasant, but is it good?" has what Moore called an "open feel." That is to say, it seems clearly to be a real question, and Moore pointed out that the same will be true of any question of the form "X is P, but is it good?" where 'P' is a term for some natural or metaphysical property. This openness, which marks questions about value as

well as about good, can be explained in the following way.

Judgments about what is good or valuable generally express practical conclusions about what would, at least under the right conditions, be reasons for acting or responding in a certain way. Natural or "metaphysical" facts may provide the grounds for such practical conclusions, as the facts that a thing is pleasant, or casts light on the causes of cancer, do in the examples I just gave. Judging that these facts obtain need not involve explicitly drawing these conclusions, however. Questions such as "This is C, but is it valuable?" (where 'C' is a term for some natural or "metaphysical" property) therefore have an open feel, because they explicitly ask whether a certain practical conclusion is to be drawn. Even if one believes that the properties that 'C' refers to provide grounds for drawing this conclusion, just saying that something has these properties does not involve drawing it. So the question feels "open" even if one believes that the answer to it is "yes."

But even if being valuable cannot be identified with having any set of natural properties, it remains true that a thing's having these properties can be grounds for concluding that it is valuable. What, then, are the relations between these natural properties, the property of being valuable, and the reasons that we have for behaving in certain ways in regard to things that are valuable? There seem to be two possibilities. The first is that when something has the right natural properties it has the further property of being valuable, and that property gives us reason to behave or react in certain ways with regard to it. Moore seems to be taking this view about goodness when he says that it is a simple, unanalyzable, non-natural property. The alternative, which I believe to be correct, is to hold that being good, or valuable, is not a property that itself provides a reason to respond to a thing in certain ways. Rather, to be good or valuable is to have other properties that constitute such reasons.[8] Since the claim that some property

constitutes a reason is a normative claim, this account also takes goodness and value to be non-natural properties, namely the purely formal, higher-order properties of having some lower-order properties that provide reasons of the relevant kind. It differs from the first alternative simply in holding that it is not goodness or value itself that provides reasons but rather other properties that do so. For this reason I call it a buck-passing account.

Buck-passing accounts of goodness and of value are supported in two ways by intuitions about the reasons we have to choose, prefer, recommend, and admire things that are valuable. First, when I consider particular cases it seems that these reasons are provided by the natural properties that make a thing good or valuable. So, for example, the fact that a resort is pleasant is a reason to visit it or to recommend it to a friend, and the fact that a discovery casts light on the causes of cancer is a reason to applaud it and to support further research of that kind. These natural properties provide a complete explanation of the reasons we have for reacting in these ways to things that are good or valuable. It is not clear what further work could be done by special reason-providing properties of goodness and value, and even less clear how these properties could provide reasons.

A second source of support for a buck-passing account is the fact that many different things can be said to be good or to be valuable, and the grounds for these judgments vary widely. There does not seem to be a single, reason-providing property that is common to all these cases. The most likely candidate might be "being the object of desire." But, as I argued in Chapter 1 [see original reading], the fact that I desire something does not itself provide me with a reason to pursue it. Being an object of a rational or "informed" desire may be correlated with the presence of such reasons, but these reasons are provided not by this hypothetical desire, but by the considerations that would give rise to it, or make it "rational."

I therefore accept buck-passing accounts of both goodness and value. One could accept such an account while still holding a purely teleological conception of value, since nothing in the argument just given rules out the possibility that the reasons associated with something's being valuable are all reasons to promote it, or perhaps to promote states of affairs in which it figures in various ways.[9] My rejection of the latter view is based on the consideration of examples like those mentioned earlier, in which being valuable involves there being reasons to act or to respond in a wider variety of ways.

One natural objection to this very abstract account of value is that it represents an objectionable form of intuitionism, because it holds that judgments about value involve appeals to diverse intuitions about what is "fitting" or "appropriate." There are two ways of taking this objection: one methodological, the other substantive. As far as the first is concerned, it is true that my argument has proceeded by calling attention to what might be called "linguistic intuitions," that is, to the fact that much of what we say about values and what is valuable does not fit the model according to which value is a matter of being "to be promoted." Even if I am right in my claims about what we usually say, this of course does not settle the matter. We need to decide whether we have reason to go on making these claims or whether, on reflection, we think we should revise our practice, perhaps bringing it more into line with this familiar teleological model. This choice is not between "appeals to intuition" and some other form of argument. Rather, it is a matter of deciding which of our "intuitions" best stands the test of careful reflection. Here we must use the method I described in Chapter 1 [see original reading] as applying to any decision about what reasons we have. The charge of appealing to "intuition" does not favor one answer over the other.

It is also true, as the substantive version of the objection would charge, that if we accept a view of the kind I have described then our subsequent thinking about value may be messier (and involve more independent appeals to "intuitions" of appropriateness) than it would if we adopted some more regimented and unified account, such as one that identified value with certain specific quantities that are to be maximized. But if this is true it will be true only because we have decided, in accepting the account I describe, that these diverse questions of appropriateness are indeed relevant. It would be a mistake to ignore judgments that we in fact take to be relevant just for the sake of greater neatness in our thinking.[10]

The complexity that judgments of value have on the account I am offering is thus not, in my view, an objection to that account. Once one recognizes the variety of things that can be valuable and the variety of responses that their value calls for, it becomes highly implausible that there could be a systematic "theory of value." Understanding the value of something is not just a matter of knowing *how valuable* it is, but rather a matter of knowing how to value it— knowing what kinds of actions and attitudes are called for. It is an advantage of the present account that it calls attention to this aspect of our ideas of value, one that is easily concealed by the assumption that the primary question about the value of something is *how great* that value is.[11]

This distinction—between the question of how valuable something is, and the question of how it is to be valued—can be seen clearly in the case of the value of art and music. It might be tempting to trace the value of these pursuits to its being good that certain forms of experience or enjoyment should occur. There surely are good reasons to want these experiences to occur, and they provide good grounds for supporting museums, concerts, and public education in the arts. But these reasons do not constitute a complete account of the values in question. This can be brought out by considering the different ways in which people might disagree about these values. One kind of disagreement would be about *how valuable* this kind

of experience is, and whether it is worth the effort and resources that would be needed to produce it. This is an important kind of disagreement. But another kind of disagreement one might have about musical experience is not about how valuable it is, but rather about the attitude with which one should approach it: is it to be savored or contemplated in a serious and concentrated way, or taken more lightheartedly, even casually, as something diverting and amusing?[12]

These are only two among many possible answers, and different answers will be appropriate when different music is in question. A disagreement of this kind is not just a disagreement about the mood and outlook that are necessary in order to induce the kind of experience it is valuable to have but, rather, a disagreement about the attitudes one should have toward that experience itself. It would be very natural and appropriate for one person to say of someone else with whom he or she disagrees on this question that that person "does not understand the value of this kind of music." Having recordings of Beethoven's late quartets played in the elevators, hallways, and restrooms of an office building, for example, would show a failure to understand the value of music of this kind. What I am suggesting is not that this would show a lack of respect for this music, but rather that it shows a lack of understanding of what one should expect from it, and in what way it is worth attending to. The question of what music, if any, to play in such a setting may not be a weighty one. But it illustrates a point of more general importance: that understanding the value of something often involves not merely knowing that it is valuable or how valuable it is, but also how it is to be valued.

Notes

1 G. E. Moore, *Principia Ethica*, p. 187. Moore also allows that things which are not valuable in themselves, as indicated by this test, can nonetheless contribute to the value of complex wholes of which they are a part. In this case their value is revealed by considering a world in which just that complex whole existed, first with and then without the part.

2 Ross, *The Right and the Good*, pp. 134–41.

3 Moore, *Principia Ethica*, p. 188.

4 I am indebted here to Michael Stocker's discussion in "Values and Purposes: The Limits of Teleology and the Ends of Friendship." See esp. sec. III, pp. 754–58.

5 The fact that it is good that friendship should occur, but that in order for it to occur people have to be moved by reasons other than the reason of promoting the occurrence of friendship, is an instance of what might be called a "paradox of teleology." (Following Henry Sidgwick, who gave the name "the paradox of hedonism" to the fact that one often cannot promote pleasure very effectively by aiming directly at it, but must have other aims which are not seen simply as means to pleasure. See *Methods of Ethics*, pp. 48, 136.)

6 Similar accounts of value have been offered recently by Gerald F. Gaus in *Value and Justification* and by Elizabeth Anderson in *Value in Ethics and Economics*, esp. chap. 1. I have benefited from their discussions. On the relation between "valuing" and "valuable," in particular, see Gaus, pp. 111, 156, 167; and Anderson, p. 17.

7 Moore, *Principia Ethica*, sect. 13.

8 In this respect my account of value resembles John Rawls's account of "goodness": "A is a good X if and only if A has ... the properties which it is rational to want in an X, given what X's are used for, or expected to do and the like (whichever rider is appropriate)"; *A Theory of Justice*, p. 399. Shelly Kagan's remark about the good as a "placeholder" seems also to express what I am here calling a buck-passing account. See *The Limits of Morality*, p. 60.

9 This claim may be more plausible with respect to goodness, which is a more specific notion. I do not think that a strictly teleological account is correct in that case either, but I will not go into that question here, or into the question of exactly how goodness differs from the broader idea of value that is my main concern. For a discussion of some differences see Gaus, *Value and Justification*, pp. 118–24 and 235–41. See also Paul Ziff, *Semantic Analysis*, p. 221.

10 In his encyclopedia entry "Consequentialism," Philip Pettit observes that there are two kinds of claims one can make about any value: that it should be promoted and that it should be honored, where by honoring a value he seems to have in mind something like the range of responses I have described. Consequentialism, as he defines it, holds that "whatever values an individual or institutional agent adopts, the proper response to those values is to promote them. The agent should honour values only insofar as honouring them is part of promoting them, or is necessary in order to promote them" (p. 231). My thesis, in his terms, comes close to the reverse: that promoting a value, when it is appropriate, is properly seen as one aspect of honoring it. In addition to being in tension with "standard views. of rationality," non-consequentialism, as Pettit sees it, "is seriously defective in regard to the methodological virtue of simplicity" (p. 237). While consequentialists endorse only one way of responding to values, nonconsequentialists endorse two (p. 238). And, he might have added, the second one is extremely complex. But it is not clear why "simplicity" of this kind should be seen as a virtue. Pettit cites the general methodological practice of preferring the simpler of two hypotheses "when otherwise they are equally satisfactory." But consequentialism and nonconsequentialism are not "equally satisfactory" if, as I have argued, the former involves giving up claims about value that are at least as plausible as the ones that it retains. So the case must turn, as he later suggests, on reflection on the relative plausibility of these claims.

11 Anderson's pluralistic conception of value also emphasizes the variety of ways of valuing things. See *Value in Ethics and Economics*, esp. pp. 8–16. While I agree with Anderson's pluralism and have learned from it, I do not accept her expressive theory of rational action, according to which when we have reason to treat a valued thing a certain way this is because that mode of treatment is in accord with norms for expressing our attitude of valuing. When valuing a thing involves seeing reason to treat it a certain way—for example, to protect it from harm, treating it this way may "express" my attitude of valuing it, and failing to protect it may express an attitude of not valuing it. But in such cases the idea of expression is secondary to and dependent on a prior idea of the reasons that the value in question involves.

12 Anderson describes a disagreement of this kind about the value of music in ibid., pp. 12–14.

References

Anderson, Elizabeth. *Value in Ethics and Economics*. Cambridge, Mass.: Harvard University Press, 1993.

Gaus, Gerald F. *Value and Justification*. Cambridge: Cambridge University. Press, 1990.

Kagan, Shelly. *The Limits of Morality*. Oxford: Oxford University Press, 1989.

Moore, G. E. *Principia Ethica*. Cambridge: Cambridge University Press, 1903.

Pettit, Philip. "Consequentialism." In *Blackwell's Companion to Ethics*. Edited by Peter Singer. Oxford: Blackwell, 1992. Pp. 230–40.

Rawls, John. *A Theory of Justice*. Cambridge, Mass.: The Belknap Press of Harvard University Press, 1971.

Ross, W. D. *The Right and the Good*. Oxford: Clarendon Press, 1930.

Sidgwick, Henry. *The Methods of Ethics*. 7th ed. Chicago: University of Chicago Press. 1907.

Stocker, Michael. "Values and Purposes: The Limits of Teleology and the Ends of Friendship." *Journal of Philosophy* 78 (1981): 747–65.

Ziff, Paul. *Semantic Analysis*. Ithaca: Cornell University Press, 1960.

Responsibility and moral psychology

INTRODUCTION TO SECTION VIII

HUMANS, UNLIKE DOGS or guinea pigs, are capable of responding to moral reasons, and humans alone are thought to be responsible for what they do. Which features of our mental make-up account for these differences? What do moral agency and responsibility require?

According to Harry Frankfurt (Chapter 53), the crucial difference lies in the complexity of our wills. Frankfurt equates a person's will with the desires that actually move him to act, and he distinguishes between different levels, or "orders," of desires. At the lower level, a person may want to perform a certain action – for example, to smoke – while at a higher level, he may want to be rid of this desire. According to Frankfurt, what distinguishes humans from animals is that humans often (though not always) have such "higher-order" desires. An animal or human that lacks them, Frankfurt says, is a "wanton." Although a wanton might reason about how to maximize the satisfaction of his first-order desires, he could not reflect about which ones are worth satisfying. Also, although he might be free to act as he wanted, his lack of second-order desires would mean that he could not be free to have the *will* he wanted. According to Frankfurt, a wanton would lack the features that are essential to being a person.

Another feature that is often said to set humans apart is their ability to feel shame, and in Chapter 54, J. David Velleman presents an illuminating analysis of this phenomenon. Taking as his point of departure the biblical story of Adam and Eve, Velleman links shame to our need to shape the ways in which others see us. To interact socially, we must be intelligible to others, and to fashion an intelligible persona, we must control what others know about us. This sometimes means acting against our inclinations, as animals cannot, and shame is what we feel when others discover what we are seeking to keep private. Even when what is revealed is not discreditable, its revelation compromises our status as self-presenting individuals. According to Velleman, this explains not only our shame at being seen naked, but also, for example, why teenagers are ashamed to be seen with their parents and why we are often ashamed of our moral flaws. Because Velleman holds that shame requires both reflective self-awareness and the will to inhibit some of our impulses, his account displays a number of interesting connections with Frankfurt's.

When an animal attacks us, we may try to ward it off, but we don't blame it or hold it responsible. By contrast, when another person attacks us, we may well have just these reactions. But are we justified in having them? When philosophers raise this question, they are usually asking whether attributions of responsibility are compatible with determinism – that is, with the thesis that everything that happens, including every action anyone performs, is caused by some combination of previous occurrences. However, in Chapter 55, P. F. Strawson argues that this famous debate is

612 Introduction to *section VIII*

misconceived, and that by coming to understand what responsibility really involves, we can see that determinism is irrelevant to it.

According to Strawson, it is a mistake to say that blame and attributions of responsibility are grounded in judgments that people are responsible for their actions. Instead, the ordering goes the other way: to hold someone responsible *just is* to have certain "reactive attitudes" toward him. It is, in particular, either to react to his failure to display good will with attitudes such as resentment and indignation, or to react to his display *of* good will with attitudes such as gratitude and regard. These are not reactions we can avoid, so our tendency to hold others (and ourselves) responsible is not something we can change. It is a deep and fixed feature of human life. Because resentment and indignation are directed at a person's failure to respond to the demand that he display good will, we do not have these reactions when a person's harmful act does not show that he lacks good will. We also do not have them when an agent is deranged or otherwise "outside the reach of personal relationships." In Strawson's view, the truth of determinism would tell us nothing either about the quality of anyone's will or about anyone's fitness for interpersonal relations. This is why he sees determinism as irrelevant to responsibility.

But, as Gary Watson notes in Chapter 56, there is a problem here – namely, that those who are outside the reach of personal relationships include not only small children and the insane, but also some who are deeply evil. As an illustration, Watson recounts the case of Robert Harris, a criminal who committed a particularly callous double murder. Although Harris was a prime candidate for blame, and although his behavior certainly elicits it, he had placed himself outside the moral community in a way that made him impervious to its demands. In addition – a further problem – our reaction to Harris becomes more complicated when we learn about the horrible childhood that shaped him into a monster: "the sympathy toward the boy he was is at odds with outrage toward the man he is." When we reflect, we realize that we, too, might have turned out like Harris if we had had a childhood like his.

This last thought – that because we did not choose the factors that shaped us, the goodness or badness of our characters is a matter of "moral luck" – is developed further by Thomas Nagel in Chapter 57. As Nagel points out, we are drawn to the idea that people are responsible only for what they can control, but our actual moral practices do not consistently reflect this idea. For example, when someone recklessly drives through a red light, we blame him far more if he hits a pedestrian than if he does not; yet whether a pedestrian appears in the crosswalk is not within his control. As Nagel also points out, moral luck can take a variety of forms; for we lack control not only over the outcomes of our actions and the factors that have shaped our characters, but also over the situations in which we find ourselves and the causes of our decisions. In Nagel's view, the source of the problem is that our sense of our own agency is undermined by the realization that we are parts of the natural world: "the self which acts and is the object of moral judgment is threatened with dissolution by the absorption of its acts and impulses into the class of events."

In order to evaluate our beliefs about responsibility and agency, we must understand what those beliefs involve; and in Chapter 58, Shaun Nichols and Joshua Knobe approach this question from an empirical perspective. Drawing on various studies,

they argue that the philosophical debate about whether causation is compatible with responsibility is rooted in a genuine division within human thought. They point out that although most people favor incompatibilism when the question is posed theoretically, most react to emotionally charged examples like that of Robert Harris by maintaining that the agents in these cases are responsible even if their behavior *was* caused. Knobe and Nichols describe three possible psychological structures that might explain this split. According to one model, emotion distorts our judgments, according to another, it is integral to the process that gives rise to them, and according to a third, it plays a mixed and more complex role. Although they acknowledge that the first model favors incompatibilism more than the second, Nichols and Knobe argue that much more work will have to be done before any philosophical conclusions can be drawn.

The role that emotion plays in accounting for our moral judgments is also discussed by Joshua Greene in Chapter 59. Like Nichols and Knobe, Greene is making an empirical argument, and like them, too, he maintains that the positions in a certain philosophical debate – in this case, the one between consequentialists and deontologists – can be traced to different underlying psychological mechanisms. Drawing on data from neural imaging, Greene notes that consequentialist judgments are accompanied by activity in the parts of the brain that are associated with cognition and reasoning and that deontological judgments are accompanied by activity in areas associated with emotion. Taking his cue from this, Greene suggests that the arguments deontologists give for their positions are constructed after the fact to rationalize their emotion-based judgments. Thus, provocatively, Greene relies on empirical data to support the substantive normative thesis of consequentialism. Taken together, the selections by Greene, Nichols and Knobe, and John Doris (Chapter 44) provide a sampling of the rapidly growing field of experimental philosophy.

Harry Frankfurt

FREEDOM OF THE WILL AND THE CONCEPT OF A PERSON

WHAT PHILOSOPHERS have lately come to accept as analysis of the concept of a person is not actually analysis of *that* concept at all. Strawson, whose usage represents the current standard, identifies the concept of a person as "the concept of a type of entity such that *both* predicates ascribing states of consciousness *and* predicates ascribing corporeal characteristics . . . are equally applicable to a single individual of that single type."[1] But there are many entities besides persons that have both mental and physical properties. As it happens – though it seems extraordinary that this should be so – there is no common English word for the type of entity Strawson has in mind, a type that includes not only human beings but animals of various lesser species as well. Still, this hardly justifies the misappropriation of a valuable philosophical term.

Whether the members of some animal species are persons is surely not to be settled merely by determining whether it is correct to apply to them, in addition to predicates ascribing corporeal characteristics, predicates that ascribe states of consciousness. It does violence to our language to endorse the application of the term "person" to those numerous creatures which do have both psychological and material properties but which are manifestly not persons in any normal sense of the word. This misuse of language is doubtless innocent of any theoretical error. But although the offense is "merely verbal," it does significant harm. For it

gratuitously diminishes our philosophical vocabulary, and it increases the likelihood that we will overlook the important area of inquiry with which the term "person" is most naturally associated. It might have been expected that no problem would be of more central and persistent concern to philosophers than that of understanding what we ourselves essentially are. Yet this problem is so generally neglected that it has been possible to make off with its very name almost without being noticed and, evidently, without evoking any widespread feeling of loss.

There is a sense in which the word "person" is merely the singular form of "people" and in which both terms connote no more than membership in a certain biological species. In those senses of the word which are of greater philosophical interest, however, the criteria for being a person do not serve primarily to distinguish the members of our own species from the members of other species. Rather, they are designed to capture those attributes which are the subject of our most humane concern with ourselves and the source of what we regard as most important and most problematical in our lives. Now these attributes would be of equal significance to us even if they were not in fact peculiar and common to the members of our own species. What interests us most in the human condition would not interest us less if it were also a feature of the condition of other creatures as well.

Our concept of ourselves as persons is not to be understood, therefore, as a concept of attributes that are necessarily species-specific. It is conceptually possible that members of novel or even of familiar non-human species should be persons; and it is also conceptually possible that some members of the human species are not persons. We do in fact assume, on the other hand, that no member of another species is a person. Accordingly, there is a presumption that what is essential to persons is a set of characteristics that we generally suppose – whether rightly or wrongly – to be uniquely human.

It is my view that one essential difference between persons and other creatures is to be found in the structure of a person's will. Human beings are not alone in having desires and motives, or in making choices. They share these things with the members of certain other species, some of whom even appear to engage in deliberation and to make decisions based upon prior thought. It seems to be peculiarly characteristic of humans, however, that they are able to form what I shall call "second-order desires" or "desires of the second order."

Besides wanting and choosing and being moved to do this or that, men may also want to have (or not to have) certain desires and motives. They are capable of wanting to be different, in their preferences and purposes, from what they are. Many animals appear to have the capacity for what I shall call "first-order desires" or "desires of the first order," which are simply desires to do or not to do one thing or another. No animal other than man, however, appears to have the capacity for reflective self-evaluation that is manifested in the formation of second-order desires.[2]

I

The concept designated by the verb "to want" is extraordinarily elusive. A statement of the form "R wants to X" – taken by itself, apart from a context that serves to amplify or to specify its meaning – conveys remarkably little information. Such a statement may be consistent, for example, with each of the following statements: (a) the prospect of doing X elicits no sensation or introspectible emotional response in A; (b) A is unaware that he wants to X; (c) A believes that he does not want to X; (d) A wants to refrain from X-ing; (e) A wants to Y and believes that it is impossible for him both to Y and to X; (f) A does not "really" want to X; (g) A would rather die than X; and so on. It is therefore hardly sufficient to formulate the distinction between first-order and second-order desires, as I have done, by suggesting merely that someone has a first-order desire when he wants to do or not to do such-and-such, and that he has a second-order desire when he wants to have or not to have a certain desire of the first order.

As I shall understand them, statements of the form "A wants to X" cover a rather broad range of possibilities.[3] They may be true even when statements like (a) through (g) are true: when A is unaware of any feelings concerning X-ing, when he is unaware that he wants to X, when he deceives himself about what he wants and believes falsely that he does not want to X, when he also has other desires that conflict with his desire to X, or when he is ambivalent. The desires in question may be conscious or unconscious, they need not be univocal, and A may be mistaken about them. There is a further source of uncertainty with regard to statements that identify someone's desires, however, and here it is important for my purposes to be less permissive.

Consider first those statements of the form "A wants to X" which identify first-order desires – that is, statements in which the term "to X" refers to an action. A statement of this kind does not, by itself, indicate the relative strength of A's desire to X. It does not make it clear whether this desire is at all likely to play a decisive role in what A actually does or tries to do. For it may correctly be said that A wants to X even when his desire to X is only one among his desires and

when it is far from being paramount among them. Thus, it may be true that *A* wants to X when he strongly prefers to do something else instead; and it may be true that he wants to X despite the fact that, when he acts, it is not the desire to X that motivates him to do what he does. On the other hand, someone who states that *A* wants to X may mean to convey that it is this desire that is motivating or moving *A* to do what he is actually doing or that *A* will in fact be moved by this desire (unless he changes his mind) when he acts.

It is only when it is used in the second of these ways that, given the special usage of "will" that I propose to adopt, the statement identifies *A*'s will. To identify an agent's will is either to identify the desire (or desires) by which he is motivated in some action he performs or to identify the desire (or desires) by which he will or would be motivated when or if he acts. An agent's will, then, is identical with one or more of his first-order desires. But the notion of the will, as I am employing it, is not coextensive with the notion of first-order desires. It is not the notion of something that merely inclines an agent in some degree to act in a certain way. Rather, it is the notion of an *effective* desire – one that moves (or will or would move) a person all the way to action. Thus the notion of the will is not coextensive with the notion of what an agent intends to do. For even though someone may have a settled intention to do X, he may nonetheless do something else instead of doing X because, despite his intention, his desire to do X proves to be weaker or less effective than some conflicting desire.

Now consider those statements of the form "*A* wants to X" which identify second-order desires – that is, statements in which the term "to X" refers to a desire of the first order. There are also two kinds of situation in which it may be true that *A* wants to want to X. In the first place, it might be true of *A* that he wants to have a desire to X despite the fact that he has a univocal desire, altogether free of conflict and

ambivalence, to refrain from X-ing. Someone might want to have a certain desire, in other words, but univocally want that desire to be unsatisfied.

Suppose that a physician engaged in psycho therapy with narcotics addicts believes that his ability to help his patients would be enhanced if he understood better what it is like for them to desire the drug to which they are addicted. Suppose that he is led in this way to want to have a desire for the drug. If it is a genuine desire that he wants, then what he wants is not merely to feel the sensations that addicts characteristically feel when they are gripped by their desires for the drug. What the physician wants, insofar as he wants to have a desire, is to be inclined or moved to some extent to take the drug.

It is entirely possible, however, that, although he wants to be moved by a desire to take the drug, he does not want this desire to be effective. He may not want it to move him all the way to action. He need not be interested in finding out what it is like to take the drug. And insofar as he now wants only to *want* to take it, and not to *take* it, there is nothing in what he now wants that would be satisfied by the drug itself. He may now have, in fact, an altogether univocal desire *not* to take the drug; and he may prudently arrange to make it impossible for him to satisfy the desire he would have if his desire to want the drug should in time be satisfied.

It would thus be incorrect to infer, from the fact that the physician now wants to desire to take the drug, that he already does desire to take it. His second-order desire to be moved to take the drug does not entail that he has a first-order desire to take it. If the drug were now to be administered to him, this might satisfy no desire that is implicit in his desire to want to take it. While he wants to want to take the drug, he may have *no* desire to take it; it may be that *all* he wants is to taste the desire for it. That is, his desire to have a certain desire that he does not have may not be a desire that his will should be at all different than it is.

desire to do it. The unwilling addict identifies himself, however, through the formation of a second-order volition, with one rather than with the other of his conflicting first-order desires. He makes one of them more truly his own and, in so doing, he withdraws himself from the other. It is in virtue of this identification and withdrawal, accomplished through the formation of a second-order volition, that the unwilling addict may meaningfully make the analytically puzzling statements that the force moving him to take the drug is a force other than his own, and that it is not of his own free will but rather against his will that this force moves him to take it.

The wanton addict cannot or does not care which of his conflicting first-order desires wins out. His lack of concern is not due to his inability to find a convincing basis for preference. It is due either to his lack of the capacity for reflection or to his mindless indifference to the enterprise of evaluating his own desires and motives.[6] There is only one issue in the struggle to which his first-order conflict may lead: whether the one or the other of his conflicting desires is the stronger. Since he is moved by both desires, he will not be altogether satisfied by what he does no matter which of them is effective. But it makes no difference *to him* whether his craving or his aversion gets the upper hand. He has no stake in the conflict between them and so, unlike the unwilling addict, he can neither win nor lose the struggle in which he is engaged. When a *person* acts, the desire by which he is moved is either the will he wants or a will he wants to be without. When a *wanton* acts, it is neither.

III

There is a very close relationship between the capacity for forming second-order volitions and another capacity that is essential to persons – one that has often been considered a distinguishing mark of the human condition. It is only because a person has volitions of the second order that he is capable both of enjoying and of lacking freedom of the will. The concept of a person is not only, then, the concept of a type of entity that has both first-order desires and volitions of the second order. It can also be construed as the concept of a type of entity for whom the freedom of its will may be a problem. This concept excludes all wantons, both infrahuman and human, since they fail to satisfy an essential condition for the enjoyment of freedom of the will. And it excludes those suprahuman beings, if any, whose wills are necessarily free.

Just what kind of freedom is the freedom of the will? This question calls for an identification of the special area of human experience to which the concept of freedom of the will, as distinct from the concepts of other sorts of freedom, is particularly germane. In dealing with it, my aim will be primarily to locate the problem with which a person is most immediately concerned when he is concerned with freedom of his will.

According to one familiar philosophical tradition, being free is fundamentally a matter of doing what one wants to do. Now the notion of an agent who does what he wants to do is by no means an altogether clear one: both the doing and the wanting, and the appropriate relation between them as well, require elucidation. But although its focus needs to be sharpened and its formulation refined, I believe that this notion does capture at least part of what is implicit in the idea of an agent who *acts* freely. It misses entirely, however, the peculiar content of the quite different idea of an agent whose *will* is free.

We do not suppose that animals enjoy freedom of the will, although we recognize that an animal may be free to run in whatever direction it wants. Thus, having the freedom to do what one wants to do is not a sufficient condition of having a free will. It is not a necessary condition either. For to deprive someone of his freedom of action is not necessarily to undermine the freedom of his will. When an agent is

aware that there are certain things he is not free to do, this doubtless affects his desires and limits the range of choices he can make. But suppose that someone, without being aware of it, has in fact lost or been deprived of his freedom of action. Even though he is no longer free to do what he wants to do, his will may remain as free as it was before. Despite the fact that he is not free to translate his desires into actions or to act according to the determinations of his will, he may still form those desires and make those determinations as freely as if his freedom of action had not been impaired.

When we ask whether a person's will is free we are not asking whether he is in a position to translate his first-order desires into actions. That is the question of whether he is free to do as he pleases. The question of the freedom of his will does not concern the relation between what he does and what he wants to do. Rather, it concerns his desires themselves. But what question about them is it?

It seems to me both natural and useful to construe the question of whether a person's will is free in close analogy to the question of whether an agent enjoys freedom of action. Now freedom of action is (roughly, at least) the freedom to do what one wants to do. Analogously, then, the statement that a person enjoys freedom of the will means (also roughly) that he is free to want what he wants to want. More precisely, it means that he is free to will what he wants to will, or to have the will he wants. Just as the question about the freedom of an agent's action has to do with whether it is the action he wants to perform, so the question about the freedom of his will has to do with whether it is the will he wants to have.

It is in securing the conformity of his will to his second-order volitions, then, that a person exercises freedom of the will. And it is in the discrepancy between his will and his second-order volitions, or in his awareness that their coincidence is not his own doing but only a happy chance, that a person who does not have

this freedom feels its lack. The unwilling addict's will is not free. This is shown by the fact that it is not the will he wants. It is also true, though in a different way, that the will of the wanton addict is not free. The wanton addict neither has the will he wants nor has a will that differs from the will he wants. Since he has no volitions of the second order, the freedom of his will cannot be a problem for him. He lacks it, so to speak, by default.

People are generally far more complicated than my sketchy account of the structure of a person's will may suggest. There is as much opportunity for ambivalence, conflict, and self-deception with regard to desires of the second order, for example, as there is with regard to first-order desires. If there is an unresolved conflict among someone's second-order desires, then he is in danger of having no second-order volition; for unless this conflict is resolved, he has no preference concerning which of his first-order desires is to be his will. This condition, if it is so severe that it prevents him from identifying himself in a sufficiently decisive way with any of his conflicting first-order desires, destroys him as a person. For it either tends to paralyze his will and to keep him from acting at all, or it tends to remove him from his will so that his will operates without his participation. In both cases he becomes, like the unwilling addict though in a different way, a helpless bystander to the forces that move him.

Another complexity is that a person may have, especially if his second-order desires are in conflict, desires and volitions of a higher order than the second. There is no theoretical limit to the length of the series of desires of higher and higher orders; nothing except common sense and, perhaps, a saving fatigue prevents an individual from obsessively refusing to identify himself with any of his desires until he forms a desire of the next higher order. The tendency to generate such a series of acts of forming desires, which would be a case of humanization run wild, also leads toward the destruction of a person.

It is possible, however, to terminate such a series of acts without cutting it off arbitrarily. When a person identifies himself *decisively* with one of his first-order desires, this commitment "resounds" throughout the potentially endless array of higher orders. Consider a person who, without reservation or conflict, wants to be motivated by the desire to concentrate on his work. The fact that his second-order volition to be moved by this desire is a decisive one means that there is no room for questions concerning the pertinence of desires or volitions of higher orders. Suppose the person is asked whether he wants to want to want to concentrate on his work. He can properly insist that this question concerning a third-order desire does not arise. It would be a mistake to claim that, because he has not considered whether he wants the second-order volition he has formed, he is indifferent to the question of whether it is with this volition or with some other that he wants his will to accord. The decisiveness of the commitment he has made means that he has decided that no further question about his second-order volition, at any higher order, remains to be asked. It is relatively unimportant whether we explain this by saying that this commitment implicitly generates an endless series of confirming desires of higher orders, or by saying that the commitment is tantamount to a dissolution of the pointedness of all questions concerning higher orders of desire.

Examples such as the one concerning the unwilling addict may suggest that volitions of the second order, or of higher orders, must be formed deliberately and that a person characteristically struggles to ensure that they are satisfied. But the conformity of a person's will to his higher-order volitions may be far more thoughtless and spontaneous than this. Some people are naturally moved by kindness when they want to be kind, and by nastiness when they want to be nasty, without any explicit forethought and without any need for energetic self-control. Others are moved by nastiness when they want to be kind and by kindness when they intend to be nasty, equally without forethought and without active resistance to these violations of their higher-order desires. The enjoyment of freedom comes easily to some. Others must struggle to achieve it.

IV

My theory concerning the freedom of the will accounts easily for our disinclination to allow that this freedom is enjoyed by the members of any species inferior to our own. It also satisfies another condition that must be met by any such theory, by making it apparent why the freedom of the will should be regarded as desirable. The enjoyment of a free will means the satisfaction of certain desires – desires of the second or of higher orders – whereas its absence means their frustration. The satisfactions at stake are those which accrue to a person of whom it may be said that his will is his own. The corresponding frustrations are those suffered by a person of whom it may be said that he is estranged from himself, or that he finds himself a helpless or a passive bystander to the forces that move him.

A person who is free to do what he wants to do may yet not be in a position to have the will he wants. Suppose, however, that he enjoys both freedom of action and freedom of the will. Then he is not only free to do what he wants to do; he is also free to want what he wants to want. It seems to me that he has, in that case, all the freedom it is possible to desire or to conceive. There are other good things in life, and he may not possess some of them. But there is nothing in the way of freedom that he lacks.

It is far from clear that certain other theories of the freedom of the will meet these elementary but essential conditions: that it be understandable why we desire this freedom and why we refuse to ascribe it to animals. Consider, for example, Roderick Chisholm's quaint version of the doctrine that human freedom entails an absence of causal determination.[7] Whenever a

person performs a free action, according to Chisholm, it's a miracle. The motion of a person's hand, when the person moves it, is the outcome of a series of physical causes; but some event in this series, "and presumably one of those that took place within the brain, was caused by the agent and not by any other events" (18). A free agent has, therefore, "a prerogative which some would attribute only to God: each of us, when we act, is a prime mover unmoved" (23).

This account fails to provide any basis for doubting that animals of subhuman species enjoy the freedom it defines. Chisholm says nothing that makes it seem less likely that a rabbit performs a miracle when it moves its leg than that a man does so when he moves his hand. But why, in any case, should anyone *care* whether he can interrupt the natural order of causes in the way Chisholm describes? Chisholm offers no reason for believing that there is a discernible difference between the experience of a man who miraculously initiates a series of causes when he moves his hand and a man who moves his hand without any such breach of the normal causal sequence. There appears to be no concrete basis for preferring to be involved in the one state of affairs rather than in the other.[8]

It is generally supposed that, in addition to satisfying the two conditions I have mentioned, a satisfactory theory of the freedom of the will necessarily provides an analysis of one of the conditions of moral responsibility. The most common recent approach to the problem of understanding the freedom of the will has been, indeed, to inquire what is entailed by the assumption that someone is morally responsible for what he has done. In my view, however, the relation between moral responsibility and the freedom of the will has been very widely misunderstood. It is not true that a person is morally responsible for what he has done only if his will was free when he did it. He may be morally responsible for having done it even though his will was not free at all.

A person's will is free only if he is free to have the will he wants. This means that, with regard to any of his first-order desires, he is free either to make that desire his will or to make some other first-order desire his will instead. Whatever his will, then, the will of the person whose will is free could have been otherwise; he could have done otherwise than to constitute his will as he did. It is a vexed question just how "he could have done otherwise" is to be understood in contexts such as this one. But although this question is important to the theory of freedom, it has no bearing on the theory of moral responsibility. For the assumption that a person is morally responsible for what he has done does not entail that the person was in a position to have whatever will he wanted.

This assumption *does* entail that the person did what he did freely, or that he did it of his own free will. It is a mistake, however, to believe that someone acts freely only when he is free to do whatever he wants or that he acts of his own free will only if his will is free. Suppose that a person has done what he wanted to do, that he did it because he wanted to do it, and that the will by which he was moved when he did it was his will because it was the will he wanted. Then he did it freely and of his own free will. Even supposing that he could have done otherwise, he would not have done otherwise; and even supposing that he could have had a different will, he would not have wanted his will to differ from what it was. Moreover, since the will that moved him when he acted was his will because he wanted it to be, he cannot claim that his will was forced upon him or that he was a passive bystander to its constitution. Under these conditions, it is quite irrelevant to the evaluation of his moral responsibility to inquire whether the alternatives that he opted against were actually available to him.[9]

In illustration, consider a third kind of addict. Suppose that his addiction has the same physiological basis and the same irresistible thrust as the addictions of the unwilling and wanton

addicts, but that he is altogether delighted with his condition. He is a willing addict, who would not have things any other way. If the grip of his addiction should somehow weaken, he would do whatever he could to reinstate it; if his desire for the drug should begin to fade, he would take steps to renew its intensity.

The willing addict's will is not free, for his desire to take the drug will be effective regardless of whether or not he wants this desire to constitute his will. But when he takes the drug, he takes it freely and of his own free will. I am inclined to understand his situation as involving the overdetermination of his first-order desire to take the drug. This desire is his effective desire because he is physiologically addicted. But it is his effective desire also because he wants it to be. His will is outside his control, but, by his second-order desire that his desire for the drug should be effective, he has made this will his own. Given that it is therefore not only because of his addiction that his desire for the drug is effective, he may be morally responsible for taking the drug.

My conception of the freedom of the will appears to be neutral with regard to the problem of determinism. It seems conceivable that it should be causally determined that a person is free to want what he wants to want. If this is conceivable, then it might be causally determined that a person enjoys a free will. There is no more than an innocuous appearance of paradox in the proposition that it is determined, ineluctably and by forces beyond their control, that certain people have free wills and that others do not. There is no incoherence in the proposition that some agency other than a person's own is responsible (even *morally* responsible) for the fact that he enjoys or fails to enjoy freedom of the will. It is possible that a person should be morally responsible for what he does of his own free will and that some other person should also be morally responsible for his having done it.[10]

On the other hand, it seems conceivable that it should come about by chance that a person is free to have the will he wants. If this is conceivable, then it might be a matter of chance that certain people enjoy freedom of the will and that certain others do not. Perhaps it is also conceivable, as a number of philosophers believe, for states of affairs to come about in a way other than by chance or as the outcome of a sequence of natural causes. If it is indeed conceivable for the relevant states of affairs to come about in some third way, then it is also possible that a person should in that third way come to enjoy the freedom of the will.

Notes

1   P. F. Strawson, *Individuals* (London: Methuen, 1959), pp. 101–2. Ayer's usage of "person" is similar: "it is characteristic of persons in this sense that besides having various physical properties . . . they are also credited with various forms of consciousness" (A. J. Ayer, *The Concept of a Person* [New York: St. Martin's, 1963], p. 82). What concerns Strawson and Ayer is the problem of understanding the relation between mind and body, rather than the quite different problem of understanding what it is to be a creature that not only has a mind and a body but is also a person.

2   For the sake of simplicity, I shall deal only with what someone wants or desires, neglecting related phenomena such as choices and decisions. I propose to use the verbs "to want" and "to desire" interchangeably, although they are by no means perfect synonyms. My motive in forsaking the established nuances of these words arises from the fact that the verb "to want," which suits my purposes better so far as its meaning is concerned, does not lend itself so readily to the formation of nouns as does the verb "to desire." It is perhaps acceptable, albeit graceless, to speak in the plural of someone's "wants." But to speak in the singular of someone's "want" would be an abomination.

3   What I say in this paragraph applies not only to cases in which "to X" refers to a possible action or inaction. It also applies to cases in which "to X" refers to a first-order desire and in which the statement that "*A* wants to X" is therefore a shortened version of a

statement – "*A* wants to want to *X*" – that identifies a desire of the second order.

4 It is not so clear that the entailment relation described here holds in certain kinds of cases, which I think may fairly be regarded as nonstandard, where the essential difference between the standard and the nonstandard cases lies in the kind of description by which the first-order desire in question is identified. Thus, suppose that *A* admires B so fulsomely that, even though he does not know what B wants to do, he wants to be effectively moved by whatever desire effectively moves B; without knowing what B's will is, in other words, *A* wants his own will to be the same. It certainly does not follow that *A* already has, among his desires, a desire like the one that constitutes B's will. I shall not pursue here the questions of whether there are genuine counterexamples to the claim made in the text or of how, if there are, that claim should be altered.

5 Creatures with second-order desires but no second-order volitions differ significantly from brute animals, and, for some purposes, it would be desirable to regard them as persons. My usage, which withholds the designation "person" from them, is thus somewhat arbitrary. I adopt it largely because it facilitates the formulation of some of the points I wish to make. Hereafter, whenever I consider statements of the form "*A* wants to want to *X*," I shall have in mind statements identifying second-order volitions and not statements identifying second-order desires that are not second-order volitions.

6 In speaking of the evaluation of his own desires and motives as being characteristic of a person, I do not mean to suggest that a person's second-order volitions necessarily manifest a *moral* stance on his part toward his first-order desires. It may not be from the point of view of morality that the person evaluates his first-order desires. Moreover, a person may be capricious and irresponsible in forming his second-order volitions and give no serious consideration to what is at stake. Second-order volitions express evaluations only in the sense that they are preferences. There is no essential restriction on the kind of basis, if any, upon which they are formed.

7 "Freedom and Action," in K. Lehrer (ed.), *Freedom and Determinism* (New York: Random House, 1966), pp. 11–44.

8 I am not suggesting that the alleged difference between these two states of affairs is unverifiable. On the contrary, physiologists might well be able to show that Chisholm's conditions for a free action are not satisfied, by establishing that there is no relevant brain event for which a sufficient physical cause cannot be found.

9 For another discussion of the considerations that cast doubt on the principle that a person is morally responsible for what he has done only if he could have done otherwise, see my "Alternate Possibilities and Moral Responsibility," Chapter 1 in this volume [see original reading].

10 There is a difference between being *fully* responsible and being *solely* responsible. Suppose that the willing addict has been made an addict by the deliberate and calculated work of another. Then it may be that both the addict and this other person are fully responsible for the addict's taking the drug, while neither of them is solely responsible for it. That there is a distinction between full moral responsibility and sole moral responsibility is apparent in the following example. A certain light can be turned on or off by flicking either of two switches, and each of these switches is simultaneously flicked to the "on" position by a different person, neither of whom is aware of the other. Neither person is solely responsible for the light's going on, nor do they share the responsibility in the sense that each is partially responsible; rather, each of them is fully responsible.

Chapter 54

J. David Velleman

THE GENESIS OF SHAME

I

"AND THEY were both naked, the man and his wife, and were not ashamed." So ends Chapter 2 of Genesis. Chapter 3 narrates the Fall and its aftermath: "The eyes of them both were opened, and they knew that they were naked; and they sewed fig leaves together, and made themselves aprons." Presumably, they made themselves aprons to cover their nakedness, because they were now ashamed.

Why were Adam and Eve ashamed? And why hadn't they been ashamed before? The text of Genesis 3 suggests that they became ashamed because they realized that they were naked. But what realization was that? They were not created literally blind, and so they weren't seeing their own skin for the first time. The realization that they were naked must have been the realization that they were unclothed, which would have required them to envision the possibility of clothing. Yet the mere idea of clothing would have had no effect on Adam and Eve unless they also saw why clothing was necessary. And when they saw the necessity of clothing, they were seeing—what, exactly? There was no preexisting culture to disapprove of nakedness or to enforce norms of dress. What Genesis suggests is that the necessity of clothing was not a cultural invention but a natural fact, evident to the first people whose eyes were sufficiently open.

Or, rather, this fact was brought about by their eyes' being opened. For when we are told

at the end of Chapter 2 that Adam and Eve were naked but not ashamed, we are not meant to suppose that they had something to be ashamed of but didn't see it, like people who don't know that their fly is open or their slip is showing. The reason why Adam and Eve were not ashamed of their nakedness at first is that they had no reason to be ashamed; and so they must not have needed clothing at that point. But in that case, the opening of their eyes must have produced the very fact that it enabled them to see: their eyes must have been opened in a way that simultaneously made clothing necessary and enabled them to see its necessity. What sort of eye-opening was that?

According to the story, their eyes were opened when they acquired a knowledge of good and evil. But this description doesn't answer our question. Although a knowledge of good and evil prompted them to remedy their nakedness—as evil, we suppose—we are still not meant to suppose that their nakedness had been evil antecedently. So the knowledge of good and evil didn't just reveal some evil in their nakedness; it must also have put that evil there. The question remains, what item of knowledge could have had that effect?

I am going to propose an account of shame that explains why eating from the tree of knowledge would have made Adam and Eve ashamed of their nakedness. Ultimately, this account will yield implications for current debates about the

shamelessness of our culture. The way to recover our sense of shame is not, as some moralists propose, to recover our former intolerance for conditions previously thought to be shameful. I will propose an alternative prescription, derived from my diagnosis of how Adam and Eve acquired a sense of shame.

II

The story of Genesis makes little sense under the standard philosophical analysis of shame as an emotion of reflected self-assessment. According to this analysis, the subject of shame thinks less of himself at the thought of how he is seen by others.[1] The problem is to explain how the shame of Adam and Eve could have involved a negative assessment of themselves.

In modern society, of course, public nakedness violates social norms and consequently elicits social censure, which can be echoed by self-censure on the part of its object. But assessments of this kind would have been unknown in the pre-social conditions of Eden. Adam and Eve's shame might still have reflected an observer's assessment if they thought of themselves as being judged by a natural rather than social ideal, but what could that ideal have been? It couldn't have been, for example, an ideal of attractiveness: Adam and Eve didn't think of themselves as being unattractive to one another. In any case, shame is more likely to arise in someone who feels all too attractive to an observer, such as the artist's model who blushes upon catching a glint of lust in his eye.[2]

This famous example might be taken to suggest that the knowledge acquired by Adam and Eve was knowledge of sex. What they suddenly came to see, according to this interpretation, were the sexual possibilities of their situation, which put lust in their eyes and then shame on their cheeks at the sight of the other's lust. Unlike the artist's model, however, Adam and Eve had no pretensions to a professional or purely aesthetic role from which they might

have felt demoted by becoming sexual objects to one another. So the requisite assessment of the self remains elusive.

III

This last interpretation also requires the implausible assumption that what the Creator sought to conceal from Adam and Eve, in forbidding them to eat from the tree, was the idea of using the genitals that He had given them. And God would hardly have created anything so absurd as human genitals if He intended them to have no more use than the human appendix. I don't deny that the knowledge initially withheld from Adam and Eve was sexual knowledge in some sense. But it must have been a special kind of sexual knowledge, involving more than the very idea of getting it on. I suggest that what they didn't think of until the Fall was the idea of not getting it on—though I admit that this suggestion will take some getting used to.

Here I am imagining that the knowledge gained from the tree was not physically extracted from the fruit itself; rather, it was knowledge gained in the act of eating the fruit. And this knowledge was gained in practice only after having been suggested in theory, by the serpent. What the serpent put into Eve's ear as a theory, which she and Adam went on to prove in practice, was the idea of disobedience: "You don't have to obey."

One might wonder how this piece of knowledge could have qualified as sexual. What was there for Adam and Eve to disobey when it came to sex? The Lord had already enjoined them to "[b]e fruitful and multiply," further explaining that "a man . . . shall cleave to his wife: and they shall be one flesh." And since the Lord expected Adam and Eve to cleave to one another in the fleshly sense, he must have equipped them with the sexual instincts required to make the flesh, so to speak, cleavable. With everything urging them toward sex, they would hardly have associated sex with disobedience.

But that's just my point. Everything urged them toward sex, and so there was indeed something for them to disobey—namely, the divine and instinctual demand to indulge. The serpent's suggestion that Adam and Eve didn't have to obey the Lord implied, among other things, that they didn't have to obey His injunction to be fruitful, or the instincts with which He had reinforced that injunction. So the serpent's message of disobedience did convey a piece of sexual knowledge, after all.

I may sound as if I'm saying, paradoxically, that the sexual knowledge imparted by the serpent was the idea of chastity: "You don't have to obey" could just as well be phrased "Just Say No." But I would prefer to say that the sexual knowledge imparted by the serpent amounted to the idea of privacy. What Adam and Eve hastened to cover up after the Fall would in some languages be called their "shameful" parts: their *pudenda* (Latin), *aidoia* (Greek), *Schamteile* (German), *parties honteuses* (French). But in English, those parts of the body are called private parts.[3] The genitals became shameful, I suggest, when they became private. And the advent of privacy would have required, if not the idea of saying "no" to sex, then at least the idea of saying "not here" and "not now." So the idea of disobeying their sexual instincts could well have been instrumental in the development of shame, via the development of privacy.

I am not going to argue that shame is always concerned with matters of privacy: matters of privacy are merely the primal locus of shame. Similarly, the genitals are the primal locus of privacy—which is why our creation myth traces the origin of shame to the nakedness of our first ancestors. After I interpret the myth, however, I will explain how privacy extends beyond the body, and how shame extends beyond matters of privacy, to express a broader and more fundamental concern. My analysis will thus proceed in stages, from the natural shamefulness of the genitals, to the shamefulness of matters that are private by choice or convention, to the shamefulness of matters that do not involve privacy at all.

IV

The philosopher who comes closest to understanding shame, in my view, is St. Augustine. According to Augustine, man's insubordination to God was punished by a corresponding insubordination to man on the part of his own flesh, and this punishment is what made our sexual organs shameful:[4]

[T]hese members themselves, being moved and restrained not at our will, but by a certain independent autocracy, so to speak, are called "shameful." Their condition was different before sin. For as it is written, "They were naked and were not ashamed"—not that their nakedness was unknown to them, but because nakedness was not yet shameful, because not yet did lust move those members without the will's consent; not yet did the flesh by its disobedience testify against the disobedience of man. For they were not created blind, as the unenlightened vulgar fancy; for Adam saw the animals to whom he gave names, and of Eve we read, "The woman saw that the tree was good for food, and that it was pleasant to the eyes." Their eyes, therefore, were open, but were not open to this, that is to say, were not observant so as to recognise what was conferred upon them by the garment of grace, for they had no consciousness of their members warring against their will. But when they were stripped of this grace, that their disobedience might be punished by fit retribution, there began in the movement of their bodily members a shameless novelty which made nakedness indecent: it at once made them observant and made them ashamed.

This passage has provided many of the elements in my discussion thus far. For reasons that I'll

presently explain, however, I think that the passage puts these elements together backwards.

Augustine says that the genitals became pudenda when they produced the "shameless novelty" of moving against their owners' will—in other words, when Adam lost the ability to control his erections, and Eve her secretions. The idea of their ever having possessed these abilities may seem odd, but it has a certain logic from Augustine's point-of-view. Augustine thinks that Adam and Eve did not experience lust before the Fall.[5] Yet he also thinks that the Lord's injunction to be fruitful and multiply must be interpreted literally. The combination of these thoughts leaves Augustine with a sexual conundrum. How was copulation supposed to occur without lust, which serves nowadays to produce the necessary anatomical preparations? Augustine's answer is this: "The man, then, would have sown the seed, and the woman received it, as need required, the generative organs being moved by the will, not excited by lust."[6] And it was because of being governed by the will, according to Augustine, that the genitals of Adam and Eve were not initially shameful.[7] They subsequently became shameful because they were removed from their owners' voluntary control, in punishment for original sin.

Let me introduce my disagreement with Augustine by pointing out how we differ on the relation between shame and punishment in Genesis. According to Augustine, bodily insubordination to the will, and the resulting shame, were inflicted on Adam and Eve as retribution for their disobedience. In Genesis, however, the Lord discovered the disobedience of Adam and Eve only by discovering that they were hiding from Him in shame; and so their shame must have preceded their punishment. Their punishment consisted rather in being banished from the garden and condemned to a life of toil and sorrow.

What's more, Augustine does not attribute Adam and Eve's shame to the knowledge that they acquired from eating the forbidden fruit.

He attributes their shame to their loss of voluntary control over their bodies, which was inflicted on them as punishment for their disobedience, which involved the tree of knowledge only incidentally, because that tree happened to be the one whose fruit was forbidden to them. Thus, eating from the tree of knowledge led to their shame indirectly, by angering God, who then hobbled their wills in a way that made their nakedness shameful. According to the text of Genesis, however, Adam and Eve were told by the serpent that eating from the tree of knowledge would open their eyes by itself, and it really did open their eyes, whereupon they were instantly ashamed. That this progression was antecedently predictable is implicit in the Lord's detective work: seeing their shame, He knew that they must have disobeyed. The text thus suggests that their shame was a predictable result of their eating from the tree of knowledge, not the result of any subsequent reengineering of their constitutions.

Note that the constitutional alteration to which Augustine attributes the shame of Adam and Eve could not have been brought about by the mere acquisition of knowledge. Having their eyes opened would not in itself have caused Adam and Eve to lose voluntary control that they previously possessed. But a slightly different alteration could indeed have been brought about by the acquisition of knowledge—and, in particular, by that knowledge of good and evil which Adam and Eve acquired in eating from the tree. For suppose, as I have already suggested, that this episode taught them about good and evil by teaching them about the possibility of disobeying God and their God-given instincts.[8] In that case, they must previously have been unaware that disobeying God and Nature was a possibility, and so they must have been in no position to disobey. They would have slavishly done as God and their instincts demanded, because of being unaware that they might do otherwise. And if they slavishly obeyed these demands, without a thought of doing

otherwise, then their free will would have been no more than a dormant capacity, which they wouldn't exercise until they discovered the possibility of alternatives on which to exercise it. That discovery, imparted by the serpent, would thus have activated the hitherto dormant human will, thereby making it fully effective for the first time since the Creation.

On this interpretation, the reason why Adam and Eve weren't ashamed of their nakedness at first is not that their anatomy was perfectly subordinate to the will but rather that they didn't have an effective will to which their anatomy could be insubordinate. In acquiring the idea of making choices contrary to the demands of their instincts, however, they would have gained, not only the effective capacity to make those choices, but also the realization that their bodies might obey their instincts instead, thus proving insubordinate to their newly activated will. Hence the knowledge that would have activated their will could also have opened their eyes to the possibility of that bodily recalcitrance which Augustine identifies as the occasion of their shame.

V

What remains to be explained is why the insubordination of the body to the will should be an occasion for shame. The explanation, I believe, is that the structure of the will provides shame with its central concern, of which the central instance is a concern for privacy.

Privacy is made possible by the ability to choose in opposition to inclination. To a creature who does whatever its instincts demand, there is no space between impulse and action, and there is accordingly less space between inner and outer selves. Because a dog has relatively little control over its impulses, its impulses are legible in its behavior. Whatever itches, it scratches (or licks or nips or drags along the ground), and so its itches are always overt, always public.

By contrast, our capacity to resist desires enables us to choose which desires our behavior will express. And we tend to make these choices cumulatively and consistently over time.[9] That is, we gradually compile a profile of the tastes, interests, and commitments on which we are willing to act, and we tend to enact that motivational profile while also resisting inclinations and impulses incompatible with it. This recension of our motivational natures becomes our outward face, insofar as it defines the shape of our behavior.

Putting an outward face on our behavior sounds like an essentially social enterprise, but I think that this enterprise is inherent in the structure of the individual will. Even Robinson Crusoe chose which of his desires to act on, and his need to understand and coordinate his activities required him to make choices by which he could consistently abide. He therefore lived in accordance with a persona that he composed, even though there was no audience for whom he composed it. Or, rather, he composed this persona for an audience consisting only of himself, insofar as it was designed to help him keep track and make sense of his solitary life. So even Robinson Crusoe had distinct overt and covert selves—the personality that he acted out, and a personality that differed from it by virtue of including all of the inclinations and impulses on which he chose not to act.

VI

In order to make sense and keep track of his life, Robinson Crusoe had to engage in a solitary form of self-presentation—displaying, if only to himself, behavior that was predictable and intelligible as manifesting a stable and coherent set of motives. Self-presentation serves a similar function in the social realm, since others cannot engage you in social interaction unless they find your behavior predictable and intelligible. Insofar as you want to be eligible for social intercourse, you must offer a coherent public image.[10]

Thus, for example, you cannot converse with others unless your utterances can be interpreted as an attempt to convey a minimally consistent meaning. You can't cooperate with others, or elicit their cooperation, unless your movements can be interpreted as attempts to pursue minimally consistent goals. In sum, you can't interact socially unless you present others with an eligible target for interaction, by presenting noises and movements that can be interpreted as the coherent speech and action of a minimally rational agent.

Indeed, fully social interaction requires that your noises and movements be interpretable, not merely as coherent speech and action, but also as intended to be interpretable as such. Only when your utterances can be recognized as aiming to be recognized as meaningful do they count as fully successful contributions to conversation;[11] only when your movements are recognized as aiming to be recognized as helpful do they count as fully successful contributions to cooperation; and even a competition or a conflict is not full-blown until the parties are recognized by one another as trying to be recognized as opponents. Full-blown social intercourse thus requires each party to compose an overt persona for the purpose, not just of being interpretable, but of being interpretable as having been composed partly for that purpose.

Note, then, that self-presentation is not a dishonest activity, since your public image purports to be exactly what it is: the socially visible face of a being who is presenting it as a target for social interaction.[12] Even aspects of your image that aren't specifically meant to be recognized as such are not necessarily dishonest. There is nothing dishonest about choosing not to scratch wherever and whenever it itches. Although you don't make all of your itches overt, in the manner of a dog, you aren't falsely pretending to be less itchy than a dog; you aren't pretending, in other words, that the itches you scratch are the only ones you have. You know that the only possible audience for such a

pretense would never be taken in by it, since other free agents are perfectly familiar with the possibility of choosing not to scratch an itch. And insofar as your persona is a positive bid for social interaction, you positively want it to be recognized as such. Not being recognized as a self-presenter would entail not being acknowledged as a potential partner in conversation, cooperation, or even competition and conflict.

You thus have a fundamental interest in being recognized as a self-presenting creature, an interest that is more fundamental, in fact, than your interest in presenting any particular public image. Not to be seen as honest or intelligent or attractive would be socially disadvantageous, but not to be seen as a self-presenting creature would be socially disqualifying: it would place you beyond the reach of social intercourse altogether. Threats to your standing as a self-presenting creature are thus a source of deep anxiety, and anxiety about the threatened loss of that standing is, in my view, what constitutes the emotion of shame. The realm of privacy is the central arena for shame, I think, because it is the central arena for threats to your standing as a social agent. As Thomas Nagel has put it, "Naked exposure itself, whether or not it arouses disapproval, is disqualifying."[13]

VII

Because of your interest in being recognized as a social agent, failures of privacy can set off a sense of escalating exposure. When something private about you is showing, you have somehow failed to manage your public image, and so an inadequacy in your capacity for self-presentation is showing as well, potentially undermining your standing as a social agent. Stripped of some accustomed item of clothing, you may also feel stripped of your accustomed cloak of sociality, your standing as a competent self-presenter eligible to participate in conversation, cooperation, and other forms of interaction. This escalating exposure is implicit in Bernard Williams's

description of shame when he says that "[t]he root of shame lies in exposure . . . in being at a disadvantage: in . . . a loss of power."[14] Failures of privacy put you at a disadvantage by threatening the power inherent in your role as a participating member of the community, and the resulting anxiety constitutes the emotion of shame.

I say "failures of privacy," not "violations." When people forcibly violate your privacy, no doubt is cast on your capacity for self-presentation. But then, violations of privacy do not properly occasion shame. If you learn that someone has been peeping through your bedroom keyhole, you don't feel ashamed at the thought of what he might have seen; or, at least, you shouldn't feel ashamed: you should feel angry and defiant. Proper occasions for shame are your own failures to manage your privacy, as symbolized in childhood culture by open flies and showing slips. In the case of the bedroom keyhole, the one who should be ashamed is the peeping Tom, who lacks the self-possession to keep any of his curiosity covert.[15] His naked curiosity is what should occasion shame, not your properly closeted nakedness.

The same goes for your intentional violations of your own privacy, which do not qualify as failures, either. Deliberately exposing yourself in public would not cause you to feel shame if it represented an unqualified success at publicizing your privates rather than a failure at concealing them. (That's why people don't usually feel ashamed of having posed for *Playboy* magazine.) Deliberate self-exposure occasions shame only when it entails some unintentional self-exposure as well—when you take off more than you meant to, or your taking it off exposes impulses that you didn't mean to expose. For only then do you feel vulnerable to the loss of your standing as a self-presenting person.

Although deliberate self-exposure doesn't necessarily occasion shame, there remains a sense in which public nakedness is naturally suited to occasion it and can therefore be called naturally shameful. What makes nakedness naturally shameful, I think, is the phenomenon adduced by St. Augustine—namely, the body's insubordination to the will. And I'm now in a position to explain why I agree with this much of Augustine's analysis.

VIII

Why does our culture tolerate frontal nudity in women more than in men? The politically correct explanation is that the culture is dominated by men and consequently tends to cast women as sex objects. An alternative explanation, however, is that male nudity is naturally more shameful.

Male nudity is more shameful because it is more explicit, not only in the sense that the male body is, as Mr. Rogers used to sing, fancy on the outside, but also in the sense that a man's outside is liable to reveal his feelings in a particularly explicit way, whether he likes it or not. The unwanted erection is a glaring failure of privacy. The naked man is unable to choose which of his impulses are to be public; and so he is only partly an embodied will and partly also the embodiment of untrammeled instincts. In such a condition, sustaining the role of a social agent becomes especially difficult.

Equally explicit, I think, is the curiosity expressed in looking at the naked male body. Viewing the naked female can easily be, or at least purport to be, an aesthetic exercise; whereas it's fairly difficult to look at the male organ without the thought of its sexual role, and hence without experiencing an undeniably sexual curiosity.

Thus, our double standard about nakedness may confirm St. Augustine's hypothesis that what's shameful about nakedness is the body's insubordination to the will.[16] And my account of privacy may explain this hypothesis by explaining why the insubordinate body threatens to put its owner in a socially untenable position, by undermining his standing as a self-presenting person. What my explanation implies is that the impulse to cover one's nakedness out of shame

is not, in the first instance, the impulse to hide something whose exposure might occasion disapproval. It's rather the impulse to guard one's capacity for self-presentation and, with it, one's standing as a social agent.

This explanation makes sense of my earlier suggestion that the sexual knowledge imparted to Adam and Eve by the serpent was the idea of not indulging. Only after Adam and Eve recognized the possibility of saying "no"—or, at least, "not now"—to their sexual impulses did they attain a standing that could be undermined if their genitals proceeded to signal "yes" instead. Hence only after they recognized their freedom with regard to sex could they find their nakedness inherently shameful.

IX

The relation between shame and bodily insubordination is also illustrated by the physiological response to shame, which is blushing. A familiar feature of this response is that one blush can set off a cascade of ever deeper blushes. The reason is that the blush itself is insubordinate to the will: one's complexion foils any attempt to conceal one's impulse toward concealment, or to keep private one's inflamed sense of privacy. This response to failures of privacy is in itself a further failure of the same kind.[17]

Having blushed can therefore be an occasion for blushing again. Subsequent blushes don't express or reflect any disapproval of the previous ones: there's nothing wrong or bad about blushing. Subsequent blushes merely express the sense that the previous blushes have further compromised one's capacity for self-presentation.

Of course, the face often betrays many feelings, and the question therefore arises why a bare face isn't considered even more shameful than naked genitals. The answer is that the face is also the primary medium for deliberate self-presentation. The face is indeed shameful insofar as it defies the will and thereby foils self-presentation; but insofar as it is instrumental to

self-presentation, the face is essential to the avoidance of shame—which may be why a shameful turn of events is described metaphorically as a loss of face.[18] Some cultures use veils or fans to cover the face in situations conducive to shame. But face is to be saved only for the sake of being effectively displayed; and most cultures therefore favor facial disciplines other than concealment.

X

My account bears a complex relation to the standard account of shame as an emotion of reflected self-assessment.[19] Mine might be assimilated to the standard account as an instance thereof, since I say that to feel shame is to feel vulnerable to a particular negative assessment, as less than a self-presenting person. But this assimilation of the two accounts would obscure an important difference. In my account, the essential content of shame has no place for an assessment of the self in terms of ethics, honor, etiquette, or other specific dimensions of personal excellence. Of course, one can be ashamed of being greedy, cowardly, rude, ugly, and so on. But these specific value judgments cannot play the role of the self-assessment that is involved in the very content shame, according to my account. These judgments stand outside the content of the shame that may be associated with them; and so shame can also occur without them. Let me explain, then, how specific value judgments acquire their contingent association with shame.

These judgments are associated with shame because they often serve as grounds for relegating aspects of ourselves to the private realm. This connection has already made a brief appearance, in my description of the peeping Tom, who may feel shame at having exposed his sexual curiosity. Many of our moral failings consist in impulsive or compulsive behavior in which we fail to keep some untoward impulse to ourselves. To acknowledge such behavior is to

realize that some untoward impulse is showing, such as our greed or our cowardice, and this realization can induce the anxiety that amounts to shame, in my view. If our reason for wanting to keep these impulses private is that we perceive or imagine disapproval of them, then our shame at their exposure will also be associated with a reflected assessment of the sort posited by the standard account. But shame would not be associated with that assessment in the absence of any sense of compromised self-presentation—for example, if we acted on the same impulses with abject resignation or brazen defiance.

Once we acquire the idea of privacy by learning that we can refuse to manifest some of our impulses, or manifest them only in solitude, we can think about excluding other, non-motivational facts from our self-presentation. We can think about omitting our ancestry or our income or our physical blemishes. Again, we wouldn't try to leave out these features of ourselves if we didn't think of them as somehow discreditable, and so our shame at their exposure is indeed associated with reflected disapproval. But if their exposure did not somehow compromise our efforts at self-presentation, they wouldn't cause us shame. If we humbly admitted to our discreditable ancestry, then our response to real or imagined disapproval of it would amount to no more than a feeling of frank inferiority.

The possibility of responding to denigrating regard with humility shows that the perception of facing such regard is not sufficient for shame. That perception doesn't lead to shame unless it leads to a sense of being compromised in our self-presentation. Humility preempts this sense of being compromised by deflating our pretensions and thereby rendering our self-presentation consistent with the criticism that we face. Feeling humbled is thus an alternative to, and incompatible with, feeling humiliated or ashamed.

What isn't incompatible with shame, however, is pride—which goes to show that a perception of denigrating regard is not necessary for shame either. We keep some things

private not because we fear disapproval of them but rather because we fear approval of a sort that we would experience as vulgar or cheap.[20] Even if we think that others would admire our poetry, for example, we may not like the idea of exposing it to their undiscerning admiration. And then if we mistakenly leave it in view, we may feel shame and pride together—a mixture of feelings that is not at all incongruous, because we needn't feel denigrated in order to feel undermined in our self-presentation.

XI

As the foregoing examples have illustrated, we can feel shame at many kinds of exposure other than nakedness, because our natural sense of privacy can be extended by choice to cover many things other than our bodies. Conversely, we can go naked without shame, if our natural sense of privacy has been modified by social norms.

Although a free will necessarily draws a line between the public and the private, individuals have considerable latitude in drawing that line, and society may therefore lay down norms for how to draw it. Because norms of privacy dictate that particular things ought to be concealed, they are implicitly norms of competence at self-presentation. The awareness of being seen to violate such norms induces the sense of vulnerability constitutive of shame—a sense of vulnerability, that is, to being discounted as a self-presenting social agent. Hence norms of privacy are implicitly norms of shame as well.

Such norms can modify or even nullify the natural shamefulness of things like nakedness or blushing.[21] These phenomena are naturally shameful only in the sense that they involve bodily insubordination, which is naturally suited to undermine self-presentation and thereby to cause the relevant sense of vulnerability. But which failures of self-presentation actually cause a subject to have or to feel this vulnerability can be modified by social norms.

Just as a society may dictate privacy for things that aren't naturally shameful, so it may permit publicity for things that are. And if a society rules that particular bodily upheavals aren't incompatible with competent self-presentation, then they are unlikely to undermine the subject's status as a self-presenting person. So what naturally caused shame in Eden may not have caused shame at all in Sodom and Gomorrah.

XII

Moreover, failures of privacy are not the only occasion for shame, although I do believe that they are the central occasion. One's standing as a self-presenting agent can be threatened without the exposure of anything specific, or of anything that one had specifically hoped to keep private. The result may be that one feels shame about things that are quite public, or about nothing in particular at all.[22]

Why does my sixteen-year-old son feel shame whenever his peers see him in the company of his parents? I don't think that he is ashamed specifically of us, in the sense of finding us especially discreditable as parents: we're no dorkier than the average mom and dad. The explanation, I think, is that being seen in the company of his parents tends to undermine the self-presentation that he has worked so hard to establish among his peers. Within his teenage milieu, he has tried to present himself as an independent and autonomous individual, and being seen with his parents is a public reminder that he is still in many ways a dependent child. Yet I think it would be wrong to say that his continuing subordination to parents is something that he has tried to keep private; rather, he has tried to relegate this unavoidably public fact about him to the background of his public image, while promoting to the foreground various facts that are in tension with it—facts such as his having a driver's license and a telephone. His efforts at self-presentation include not only separating what is to be public about him from what is to

be private, but also, within the public realm, separating what is to be salient and what is to be inconspicuous. His self-presentation can therefore be undermined by failures of obscurity as well as by failures of privacy.

A person can be shamed even by aspects of himself that he accepts as conspicuous, if they are so glaring as to eclipse his efforts at self-presentation. Someone who is obviously deformed may experience shame if he senses that he is perceived solely in terms of his deformity, to the exclusion of any self-definition on his part. His shame doesn't depend on a sense that his deformity is unattractive, since he might similarly be shamed by any glaring feature, from bright red hair to unusual height or an extraordinary figure. Even great beauty can occasion shame in situations where it is felt to drown out rather than amplify self-presentation.

A similar effect can befall victims of social stereotyping. The target of racist remarks is displayed, not just as "the nigger" or "the hymie," but as one who has thus been captured in a socially defined image that leaves no room for self-presentation. When he responds by feeling shame, he may accuse himself of racial self-hatred, on the assumption that what he feels is shame about his race. Yet he needn't be ashamed of his race in order to feel shame in response to racism; he need only feel the genuine vulnerability of being displayed as less than the master of his self-definition and therefore less than a socially qualified agent.[23]

As my account would predict, one defense against the shame of being stereotyped is to play the part, at the price of self-esteem. When someone paints blackface on his black face, he is trying to make the role his own, by incorporating the stereotype into a deliberate self-presentation; and he is thus trying to strike a compromise with racism, surrendering any positive image of his race in order to retain some shred of his role as a self-presenting person. Of course, observers may feel that performing in blackface is itself shameful, but

their feeling rests on the belief that the performer is only deceiving himself about being left with any real scope for self-presentation.

A better defense against racist remarks is to muster a lively contempt for the speaker and hearers, since regarding others as beyond one's social pale is a way of excluding them from the notional audience required for the emotion of shame. If one doesn't care about interacting with particular people, then one will not feel anxiety about being disqualified in their eyes from presenting a target for interaction. Hence the victim of a racist remark can rise above any feelings of shame if he can disregard the present company as contemptible racists, so as not to feel vulnerable to their disregard. Unfortunately, this defense can be undermined by the presence of a sympathetic observer whose recognition the victim hopes to retain. A racist incident can therefore be rendered more shameful for the victim if a friend is present to see him stripped of his social agency.

No amount of racial pride can protect the target of racism from the shamefulness of his position. Pride would protect him from self-hatred, but it can't protect him from shame, which is anxiety about disqualification rather than disapprobation, an anxiety that cannot be allayed by a sense of personal excellence, and especially not by a sense of racial excellence, which tends to be formulated in further stereotypes. What the victim of shame needs to recover is, not his pride in being African-American or Jewish, but his social power of self-definition, which he can hardly recover by allowing himself to be typed, even by his friends.[24]

XIII

The shame induced by racism is a case of utterly inchoate shame, whose subject is successfully shamed without being ashamed of anything in particular. Inchoate shame typically results, as in this case, from deliberate acts of shaming.

Consider, for example, the shaming carried

out by the Puritans by means of the pillory. The standard account of shame would imply that the pillory shamed a wrongdoer by exposing him to his neighbors' disapproval of his wrongdoing. But he would have been exposed to that disapproval anyway, as he went about his daily business. And surely the pillory was designed to inflict shame on him even if—indeed, especially if—his neighbors' disapproval left him unashamed.[25] My account of shame suggests how the pillory could have had such an effect. The physical constraints of the pillory—applied to the head and hands, which are the primary instruments of self-presentation—ensured that the wrongdoer was simultaneously displayed to the public and disabled from presenting himself, so that he was publicly stripped of his social status as a self-presenting person. Forcibly displaying him in this position had the effect of shaming him whether or not he was ashamed of what he had done.[26]

This effect is illustrated by another practice, which survives today and may be the closest that any of us has come to the pillory. As children, many of us were forced to perform for household guests, and our shame on these occasions did not necessarily involve any negative assessment of our performance. Being exposed against our will, and hence displayed as less than self-presenting persons, was enough to make our position shameful. It never helped for our parents to say that we had nothing to be ashamed of, because we weren't ashamed of anything in particular: we were merely sensible of being shamed.[27]

Try to imagine a culture in which heroes and paragons are displayed to the public in a pillory, the better to receive their neighbors' admiration. I find such a culture impossible to imagine, because forcibly displaying someone cannot help but seem like a means of shaming him.[28] The only way to bear up under admiring attention is to receive it actively or at least voluntarily—preferably not by strutting and preening, of course, but at least by holding up a pleased or grateful or even a modest face. Those

who are afraid of actively presenting themselves to admiring attention may experience the attention as pinning them down, and so they may experience praise itself as a kind of pillory.[29] That's why praise alone can make some people blush with shame, even though they have nothing to be ashamed of.

With these examples, I have completed the promised progression, from the natural shamefulness of the naked body, to the shamefulness of matters considered private by choice or convention, to the shamefulness of circumstances not involving privacy at all. In all of these cases, I have argued, shame is the anxious sense of being compromised in one's self-presentation in a way that threatens one's social recognition as a self-presenting person.

XIV

My account of shame has a present-day moral. We often hear that our culture has lost its sense of shame—an observation that I think is largely true. Some moralists take this observation as grounds for trying to re-scandalize various conditions that used to be considered shameful, such as out-of-wedlock birth or homosexuality. These moralists reason that nothing is shameful to us because nothing is an object of social disapproval, and hence that reviving disapproval is the only way to reawaken shame.

In my view, however, nothing is shameful to us because nothing is private: our culture has become too confessional and exhibitionistic.[30] The way to reawaken shame is to revive our sense of privacy, which needn't require disapproval at all. To say that people should keep their sexual practices to themselves is not to imply that there is anything bad or wrong about those practices. "What!" exclaims St. Augustine, "does not even conjugal intercourse, sanctioned as it is by law for the propagation of children, legitimate and honorable though it be, does it not seek retirement from every eye?"[31]

What's responsible for the exhibitionism of our culture, I think, is a mistake that I warned against earlier, about the dishonesty of self-presentation.[32] People now think that not to express inclinations or impulses is in effect to claim that one doesn't have them, and that honesty therefore requires one to express whatever inclinations or impulses one has. What they forget is that the overt personas we compose are not interpreted as accurate representations of our inner lives. We have sex in private but—to quote again from St. Augustine—"Who does not know what passes between husband and wife that children may be born?"[33] No one believes that our public faces perfectly reflect our private selves, and so we shouldn't be tempted to pretend that they do, or to accuse ourselves of dishonesty when they don't.

XV

The moralists are wrong, in my view, not only about the means of reawakening shame, but also about its proper objects. Although sexual behavior calls for privacy, for example, the homosexual variety calls for no more privacy than the heterosexual and is therefore no more an occasion for shame.

That said, I should add that the moralist's view of homosexuality as inherently shameful strikes me as intelligible. The politically correct interpretation of this view is that it is a blatant prejudice if not in fact a mental illness diagnosable as a phobia. I do think that this view of homosexuality is a grievously harmful mistake, but I also think that it is an understandable mistake, given the nature of shame.

People who think that homosexuality is shameful tend to be people who don't know any homosexuals—or, more likely, don't realize that they do. For them, heterosexuality is very much the default condition, and homosexuality is therefore especially salient. The fact that someone is a homosexual, if it ever comes to their attention, tends to occupy their attention in connection with that person.[34] And this fact is,

after all, a very private fact about the person, involving the anatomy of his bedmates and what passes between them in bed. If someone's sexual orientation is especially salient to people, then his very presence will cause them to think about his private life in ways that will occasion shame—vicarious shame on his behalf, for the imagined exposure of his sexuality, and shame on their own behalf, for the sexual curiosity aroused.

If they conclude that the homosexual ought to be ashamed, then the moralists (as I've called them) are behaving like outraged peeping Toms, mistaking their invasion of someone's privacy for a failure of privacy on his part. The mistake in this case is both less and more understandable: less, because the moralists are seeing the homosexual behavior only in their imaginations; more, because they cannot control their imaginations, which makes them feel that they are being forced to see, as if they were the victims of an exhibitionist.

The remedy for all of this shame, of course, is to get used to the fact of the person's homosexual behavior, so that it can be put out of mind. Moralists are simply wrong in thinking that they should induce the homosexual to share the vicarious shame that they feel on his behalf. For the homosexual to flaunt his sexuality, however, can at most be a means of forcing this error into the open; it cannot be part of the ultimate resolution, since the moralists have got at least this much right, that sexuality requires a realm of privacy.

To say that the homosexual should not, in the end, be flaunting his sexuality is not at all to suggest a return to the closet, since privacy is not the same as secrecy or denial. Everyone knows that most adults have sex with their dates or domestic partners (among others), and no reasonable norm of privacy would rule out discussion or display of who is dating or living with whom. But allowing people to know something should not be confused with presenting it to their view. There's a difference between "out

of the closet" and "in your face," and what makes the difference is privacy.

In short, Adam and Eve were right to avail themselves of fig leaves. Although the term "fig leaf" is now a term of derision, I think that fig leaves are nothing to be ashamed of. They manifest our sense of privacy, which is an expression of our personhood.

Notes

1   My characterization of the standard analysis is intended to be vague, so as to encompass the views of several philosophers, including John Deigh, "Shame and Self-Esteem: A Critique," *Ethics* 93 (1983): 225–45; Gabrielle Taylor, *Pride, Shame, and Guilt; Emotions of Self-Assessment* (Oxford: Clarendon Press, 1985), Chapter 3; Roger Scruton, *Sexual Desire; A Moral Philosophy of the Erotic* (New York: The Free Press, 1986), pp. 140–49; Simon Blackburn, *Ruling Passions* (Oxford: Clarendon Press, 1998), pp. 17–19; and Richard Wollheim, *On the Emotions* (New Haven: Yale University Press, 1999), Chapter 3. Other authors include only some of these elements in their accounts of shame. For example, some analyze shame in terms of a negative self-assessment, without reference to any real or imagined observer (e.g., John Rawls, *A Theory of Justice* [Cambridge: Harvard University Press, 1971], pp. 442–46; Michael Stocker and Elizabeth Hegeman, *Valuing Emotions* [Cambridge: Cambridge University Press, 1996], pp. 217–30; Jon Elster, *Strong Feelings: Emotion, Addiction, and Human Behavior* [Cambridge: MIT Press, 1999], p. 21). Others analyze shame as a response to the denigrating regard of others, without requiring a negative assessment of the self (e.g., Bernard Williams, *Shame and Necessity* [Berkeley: University of California Press, 1993], Appendix 2).

2   This example is discussed by Gabrielle Taylor, *Pride, Shame, and Guilt*, pp. 60–61; and by Richard Wollheim, *On the Emotions*, pp. 159–63. Wollheim traces it to Max Scheler, "Über Scham und Schmagefühle," in *Schriften aus dem Nachlass* (Bern: Francke Verlag, 1957), Vol. 1.

3   A recent report on the BBC World Service described a criminal defendant who appeared on the witness stand stark naked, "with nothing but a plastic

clipboard to hide his shame." Here the reporter replaced the English "private parts" with a translation of the Latin, French, or German expressions.

4   *The City of God*, Book XIV, chapter 15, transl. Marcus Dods (New York: The Modern Library, 1950), p. 463: "[B]y the just retribution of the sovereign God whom we refused to be subject to and serve, our flesh, which was subjected to us, now torments us by insubordination." I am grateful to George Mavrodes for directing me to these passages discussed below.

5   Ibid., Chapter 21, p. 468: "Far be it, then, from us to suppose that our first parents in Paradise felt that lust which caused them afterwards to blush and hide their nakedness, or that by its means they should have fulfilled the benediction of God, 'Increase and multiply and replenish the earth;' for it was after sin that lust began."

6   Ibid., Chapter 24, p. 472.

7   Ibid., Chapter 19, p. 467: "[T]hese parts, I say, were not vicious in Paradise before sin, for they were never moved in opposition to a holy will towards any object from which it was necessary that they should be withheld by the restraining bridle of reason."

8   Presumably, good and evil corresponded to the will's obedience and disobedience, respectively. But how could the good have consisted in obedience to instinct? The answer, I assume, is that human instincts were adapted to the conditions of Paradise in such a way that their promptings were unfailingly good.

9   In this and the following paragraph, I draw on a conception of agency that I have developed elsewhere. See my *Practical Reflection* (Princeton: Princeton University Press, 1989, also available at http://www-personal.umich.edu/-velleman/); *The Possibility of Practical Reason* (Oxford: Oxford University Press, 2000), esp. Chs. 1, 7, and 9; and "The Self as Narrator," to appear in *Decentering Autonomy*, ed. Joel Anderson and John Christman.

10 See Georg Simmel, "The Secret and the Secret Society," Part IV of *The Sociology of Georg Simmel*, transl. Kurt H. Wolff (Glencoe, Ill.: The Free Press, 1950), pp. 311–12:

>   All we communicate to another individual by means of words or perhaps in another

fashion—even the most subjective, impulsive, intimate matters—is a selection from that psychological-real whole whose absolutely exact report (absolutely exact in terms of content and sequence) would drive everybody into the insane asylum—if a paradoxical expression is permissible. In a quantitative sense, it is not only fragments of our inner life which we alone reveal, even to our closest fellowmen. What is more, these fragments are not a representative selection, but one made from the standpoint of reason, value, and relation to the listener and his understanding. . . . We simply cannot imagine any interaction or social relation or society which are not based on this teleologically determined non-knowledge of one another.

11 Here I am simply making the familiar Gricean point about the content of communicative intentions; in the remainder of the sentence, I extend the point to other modes of social interaction.

12 See Thomas Nagel, "Concealment and Exposure," *Philosophy & Public Affairs* 27, no. 1 (Winter 1998): 3–30, p. 6: "The first and most obvious thing to note about many of the most important forms of reticence is that they are not dishonest, because the conventions that govern them are generally known."; "[O]ne has to keep a firm grip on the fact that the social self that others present to us is not the whole of their personality. . .and that this is not a form of deception because it is meant to be understood by everyone" (p. 7).

13 Ibid., p. 4.

14 Williams, *Shame and Necessity*, p. 220.

15 The example is Sartre's, *Being and Nothingness*, transl. Hazel E. Barnes (New York: Philosophical Library, 1956), pp. 261–62.

16 Here is a piece of ethnographic evidence. In some cultures, men wear almost nothing other than penis sheaths, which have the effect of making every penis look erect. This mode of dress represents an alternative solution to the problem of keeping male arousal private, since it entails that an erect-looking penis is no longer a sign of arousal (just as wearing a yellow star in occupied Denmark was not a sign of being Jewish). Of course, the sight of penis sheaths can be alarming to outsiders if they belong to a culture that favors outright

concealment over camouflage. Another piece of evidence, I think, is that the traditional focus for women's shame about their bodies is not the genitals as such but rather menstrual blood, which is unlike female sexual arousal, but like male arousal, in being visibly insubordinate to the will.

17 On this feature of blushing, and its relation to sexual arousal, see Scruton, *Sexual Desire*, pp. 63–68. Another aspect of the reflexive response to shame is a sudden sense of confusion and disorientation: one's head spins, one's ears ring, and the lights may seem to go dim. A way of describing this aspect of the shame-response would be to say that shame causes a loss of self-possession; but I would prefer to say that shame is the experience of self-possession already lost. The occasion for shame is a failure to compose oneself in the manner distinctive of persons, and this failure comes to be felt as a loss of composure.

18 Also relevant here are various terms for shamelessness, such, as 'barefaced', 'cheek', and 'effrontery'. The shameless person holds up his or her face in circumstances where self-presentation has been discredited and should therefore be withdrawn. (See also notes 25 and 27, below.)

19 Of the existing accounts of shame, Sartre's is the one with which I most agree. For Sartre, the thought involved in shame is that "I *am* as the Other sees me." And this thought is in fact the recognition that I am an *object*: "I am put in the position of passing judgment on myself as on an object, for it is as an object that I appear to the Other" (*Being and Nothingness*, p. 222). Hence the reflected self-assessment in Sartre's analysis of shame is an assessment of the self as less than a freely self-defining person: thus far, I agree. As I understand Sartre, however, he also thinks that this assessment includes the attribution of a specific flaw or failing, such as vulgarity, which is attributed to the self as to an object; and here I disagree, for reasons explained below.

20 Williams mentions this possibility: "people can be ashamed of being admired by the wrong audience in the wrong way" (*Shame and Necessity*, p. 82).

21 Here is an example, which arose in discussion with members of the Philosophy Department at the University of Manitoba. It was pointed out that whereas men's locker rooms have communal showers, women's locker rooms have private showers, because women are less willing to be seen naked, even by other women. How can this difference be reconciled with my claim that male nakedness is naturally more shameful? The answer may be that our greater toleration for images of female nudity has resulted in more specific and more demanding standards of beauty for the naked female body than for the male. Although female nakedness is naturally less shameful, then, women are more likely to regard their bodies as ugly and to keep them private for that reason—a reason that applies in the locker room no less than elsewhere. Men generally keep their bodies private on account of their natural shamefulness, which is based in sexuality, whose relevance to the locker room is vehemently denied by social fictions of sexual orientation.

22 The fact that one can feel shame without being ashamed of anything in particular entails that an analysis of the emotion cannot simultaneously be an analysis of the word and all of its cognates. Not every instance of shame can be described in terms of what the subject is ashamed of. By the same token, a subject need not feel shame in order to be described as ashamed of something, since it may be something that the subject tries and succeeds at keeping private, with the result that it never occasions the emotion of shame. The words 'shame' and 'ashamed' have many uses that are related only indirectly to the emotion. I have not offered an account of the words, only an account of the emotion itself, as a sense of being compromised in one's standing as a self-presenting social agent.

23 For a deeper discussion of this issue, with references to relevant literature, see Cheshire Calhoun, "An Apology for Moral Shame" (MS). Calhoun argues that shame experienced in the face of racism or sexism may be a perfectly legitimate response that does not betray self-hatred. But Calhoun reaches this conclusion from a rather different analysis of shame and its place in the practice of morality. Liz Anderson has directed me to an apt passage in Ralph Ellison's *Invisible Man*, where the narrator describes the shame he felt to find himself enjoying a yam: "What a group of people we were, I thought. Why, you could cause

us the greatest humiliation simply by confronting us with something we liked. . . . This is all very wild and childish, I thought, but hell with being ashamed of what you liked. No more of that for me. I am what I am!" [*Invisible Man* (New York: New American Library, 1952), pp. 230–31]. The thought behind this shame is not that liking yams is wrong or bad; it is that liking yams is part of a stereotype that a black man must escape in order to be self-defining. Enjoying his yam, the narrator feels "I am as the Other sees me"—which is Sartre's formulation of the thought involved in shame. For further discussion of this formulation, see note 19, above.

24 Of course, positive stereotypes offer roles that are easier to play with that sense of conviction which feels like authorship. Hence people often fail to experience the shame that they ought to feel in letting themselves be co-opted into positive stereotypes, including such current favorites as The Good Liberal or The Right-Thinking Multiculturalist. But these stereotypes are only a further form of self-compromise, which might be described as putting on whiteface.

25 Here I disagree with Nathaniel Hawthorne, who says: "There can be no outrage .. more flagrant than to forbid the culprit to hide his face for shame; as it was the essence of this punishment to do" (*The Scarlet Letter* [New York: Bantam Books, 1986], p. 53). According to Hawthorne, the essence of the pillory was to prevent culprits from alleviating shame that they already felt—presumably, for their wrongdoing. I believe that the pillory was designed to inflict shame even on wrongdoers who were not ashamed of what they had done: it was a device for teaching shame to the shameless. To be sure, the shamefaced culprit was prevented by the pillory from alleviating his shame, but only by being denied the means of self-presentation. Hiding one's face in shame is a symbolic act, since it neither hides one from view nor spares one the awareness of being viewed. It is rather a symbolic admission of having failed to manage one's public self: one withdraws one's botched self-presentation, symbolized by the face, as if to set it right before returning it to public view. The pillory prevented this gesture of withdrawal, thereby preventing the culprit from symbolically

reestablishing self-possession and, with it, his or her claim to socially recognized personhood. It was by preventing this restorative self-presentation that the pillory blocked the wrongdoer's recovery from shame. As I argue in the text, this was only one means of self-presentation that the pillory denied the wrongdoer.

26 Another cultural practice of shaming is described by Jon Elster in *Strong Feelings*, pp. 100–101:

In nineteenth-century Corsica, contempt for the person who failed to abide by the norms of vengeance was expressed by the *rimbecco*, "a deliberate reminder of the unfulfilled revenge. It could take the form of a song, a remark, a gesture or a look, and be delivered by relatives, neighbors or strangers, men or women. It was a direct accusation of cowardice and dereliction":

> [. . .] "In Corsica, the man who has not avenged his father, an assassinated relative or a deceived daughter can no longer appear in public. Nobody speaks to him; he has to remain silent. If he raises his voice to emit an opinion, people will say to him: avenge yourself first, and then you can state your point of view." The *rimbecco* can occur at any moment and under any guise. It does not even need to express itself in words: an ironical smile, a contemptuous turning away of the head, a certain condescending look—there are a thousand small insults which at all times of the day remind the unhappy victim of how much he has fallen in the esteem of his compatriots. [Quoted from S. Wilson, *Feuding, Conflict, and Banditry in Nineteenth-Century Corsica* (Cambridge: Cambridge University Press, 1988), p. 203]

Elster interprets this practice as inducing shame in its victim by expressing the community's contempt. The practice does express contempt, of course, but it also conveys the victim's loss of credentials as a self-presenter. His every attempt to present himself to others is met with a reminder that their knowledge of his situation has rendered them deaf and blind to anything else about him.

27 One might think that what is felt on these occasions is embarrassment rather than shame. Let me

respond by explaining how I distinguish between the two. Note that 'embarrassment' is not, in the first instance, the name of an emotion at all. The primary meaning of the verb 'to embarrass' is "to impede or encumber," and the noun 'embarrassment' refers either to the encumbrance or the state of being encumbered. (Hence the concept of "financial embarrassments," which are not so called because they tend to make one blush.)

Insofar as 'embarrassment' refers to a mental state, it refers to the state of being mentally encumbered or impeded—that is, baffled, confounded, or flustered. In this generic sense, embarrassment can be a component or concomitant of any disconcerting emotion, including shame. In recent times, 'embarrassment' has also come to denote a particular emotion distinct from shame. (This use of the term is little more than a hundred years old, according to the Oxford English Dictionary.) This emotion begins with the sense of being the focus of undue or unwelcome attention—typically, ridicule or derision—and it culminates in self-consciousness, the self-focused attention that hinders fluid speech and behavior (and that consequently counts as embarrassment in the generic sense). Being flustered in the face of laughter is the typical case of the emotion called embarrassment. This emotion differs from shame, first, because it involves self-consciousness rather than anxiety and, second, because it involves a sense of attracting unwelcome recognition rather than of losing social recognition altogether. Being ridiculed is an essentially social kind of treatment. Self-consciousness in the face of ridicule is therefore different from anxiety at the prospect of social disqualification. Whereas the subject of embarrassment feels that he has egg on his face, the subject of shame feels a loss of face—the

difference being precisely that between presenting a target for ridicule and not presenting a target for social interaction at all. Returning to the example under discussion in the text, I grant that some children may suffer no more than embarrassment when forced to perform for guests, if they feel merely self-conscious about being the center of attention. But other children experience their position more profoundly, as a threat to their social selves, undermining their prospects of being taken seriously as persons.

28 Several readers have pointed out that our culture has a pillory of just this kind: the tabloids. But then, celebrities feel shame about being displayed in the tabloids, insofar as they are displayed in ways that undermine rather than enable self-presentation on their part.

29 Of course, these people may be afraid of actively receiving admiration because they would be ashamed of the vanity or exhibitionism that such a self-presentation would reveal. They consequently find themselves in a bind, with nowhere to turn without shame. Others may feel no more than embarrassment in the same circumstances: see note 27, above.

30 This point is the main theme of Nagel's "Concealment and Exposure."

31 *The City of God*, Chapter 18, p. 466.

32 See the quotations from Nagel in note 12, above.

33 *The City of God*, Chapter 18, p. 467. See again the quotations from Nagel in note 12, above.

34 As Liz Anderson has pointed out to me, this effect is aggravated by the moralists' tendency to think that homosexual relationships are all about sex and not at all about love and friendship, so that the social appearance of homosexual partners seems as indecent as the appearance of a heterosexual man with his prostitute.

Chapter 55

P. F. Strawson

FREEDOM AND RESENTMENT

I

SOME PHILOSOPHERS say they do not know what the thesis of determinism is. Others say, or imply, that they do know what it is. Of these, some – the pessimists perhaps – hold that if the thesis is true, then the concepts of moral obligation and responsibility really have no application, and the practices of punishing and blaming, of expressing moral condemnation and approval, are really unjustified. Others – the optimists perhaps – hold that these concepts and practices in no way lose their *raison d'être* if the thesis of determinism is true. Some hold even that the justification of these concepts and practices requires the truth of the thesis. There is another opinion which is less frequently voiced: the opinion, it might be said, of the genuine moral sceptic. This is that the notions of moral guilt, of blame, of moral responsibility are inherently confused and that we can see this to be so if we consider the consequences either of the truth of determinism or of its falsity. The holders of this opinion agree with the pessimists that these notions lack application if determinism is true, and add simply that they also lack it if determinism is false. If I am asked which of these parties I belong to, I must say it is the first of all, the party of those who do not know what the thesis of determinism is. But this does not stop me from having some sympathy with the others, and a wish to reconcile them.

Should not ignorance, rationally, inhibit such sympathies? Well, of course, though darkling, one has some inkling – some notion of what sort of thing is being talked about. This lecture is intended as a move towards reconciliation; so is likely to seem wrongheaded to everyone.

But can there be any possibility of reconciliation between such clearly opposed positions as those of pessimists and optimists about determinism? Well, there might be a formal withdrawal on one side in return for a substantial concession on the other. Thus, suppose the optimist's position were put like this: (1) the facts as we know them do not show determinism to be false; (2) the facts as we know them supply an adequate basis for the concepts and practices which the pessimist feels to be imperilled by the possibility of determinism's truth. Now it might be that the optimist is right in this, but is apt to give an inadequate account of the facts as we know them, and of how they constitute an adequate basis for the problematic concepts and practices; that the reasons he gives for the adequacy of the basis are themselves inadequate and leave out something vital. It might be that the pessimist is rightly anxious to get this vital thing back and, in the grip of his anxiety, feels he has to go beyond the facts as we know them; feels that the vital thing can be secure only if, beyond the facts as we know them, there is the further fact that determinism is false. Might *he* not be brought to make a formal withdrawal in return for a vital concession?

II

Let me enlarge very briefly on this, by way of preliminary only. Some optimists about determinism point to the efficacy of the practices of punishment, and of moral condemnation and approval, in regulating behaviour in socially desirable ways.[1] In the fact of their efficacy, they suggest, is an adequate basis for these practices; and this fact certainly does not show determinism to be false. To this the pessimists reply, all in a rush, that *just* punishment and *moral* condemnation imply moral guilt and guilt implies moral responsibility and moral responsibility implies freedom and freedom implies the falsity of determinism. And to this the optimists are wont to reply in turn that it is true that these practices require freedom in a sense, and the existence of freedom in this sense is one of the facts as we know them. But what 'freedom' means here is nothing but the absence of certain conditions the presence of which would make moral condemnation or punishment inappropriate. They have in mind conditions like compulsion by another, or innate incapacity, or insanity, or other less extreme forms of psychological disorder, or the existence of circumstances in which the making of any other choice would be morally inadmissible or would be too much to expect of any man. To this list they are constrained to add other factors which, without exactly being limitations of freedom, may also make moral condemnation or punishment inappropriate or mitigate their force: as some forms of ignorance, mistake, or accident. And the general reason why moral condemnation or punishment are inappropriate when these factors or conditions are present is held to be that the practices in question will be generally efficacious means of regulating behaviour in desirable ways only in cases where these factors are *not* present. Now the pessimist admits that the facts as we know them include the existence of freedom, the occurrence of cases of free action, in the negative sense which the optimist concedes; and admits, or rather insists, that the existence of freedom in this sense is compatible with the truth of determinism. Then what does the pessimist find missing? When he tries to answer this question, his language is apt to alternate between the very familiar and the very unfamiliar.[2] Thus he may say, familiarly enough, that the man who is the subject of justified punishment, blame or moral condemnation must really *deserve* it; and then add, perhaps, that, in the case at least where he is blamed for a positive act rather than an omission, the condition of his really deserving blame is something that goes beyond the negative freedoms that the optimist concedes. It is, say, a genuinely free identification of the will with the act. And this is the condition that is incompatible with the truth of determinism.

The conventional, but conciliatory, optimist need not give up yet. He may say: Well, people often decide to do things, really intend to do what they do, know just what they're doing in doing it; the reasons they think they have for doing what they do, often really are their reasons and not their rationalizations. These facts, too, are included in the facts as we know them. If this is what you mean by freedom – by the identification of the will with the act – then freedom may again be conceded. But again the concession is compatible with the truth of the determinist thesis. For it would not follow from that thesis that nobody decides to do anything; that nobody ever does anything intentionally; that it is false that people sometimes know perfectly well what they are doing. I tried to define freedom negatively. You want to give it a more positive look. But it comes to the same thing. Nobody denies freedom in this sense, or these senses, and nobody claims that the existence of freedom in these senses shows determinism to be false.

But it is here that the lacuna in the optimistic story can be made to show. For the pessimist may be supposed to ask: But *why* does freedom in this sense justify blame, etc.? You turn towards me first the negative, and then the positive, faces

of a freedom which nobody challenges. But the only reason you have given for the practices of moral condemnation and punishment in cases where this freedom is present is the efficacy of these practices in regulating behaviour in socially desirable ways. But this is not a sufficient basis, it is not even the right *sort* of basis, for these practices as we understand them.

Now my optimist, being the sort of man he is, is not likely to invoke an intuition of fittingness at this point. So he really has no more to say. And my pessimist, being the sort of man he is, has only one more thing to say; and that is that the admissibility of these practices, as we understand them, demands another kind of freedom, the kind that in turn demands the falsity of the thesis of determinism. But might we not induce the pessimist to give up saying this by giving the optimist something more to say?

III

I have mentioned punishing and moral condemnation and approval; and it is in connection with these practices or attitudes that the issue between optimists and pessimists – or, if one is a pessimist, the issue between determinists and libertarians – is felt to be particularly important. But it is not of these practices and attitudes that I propose, at first, to speak. These practices or attitudes permit, where they do not imply, a certain detachment from the actions or agents which are their objects. I want to speak, at least at first, of something else: of the non-detached attitudes and reactions of people directly involved in transactions with each other; of the attitudes and reactions of offended parties and beneficiaries; of such things as gratitude, resentment, forgiveness, love, and hurt feelings. Perhaps something like the issue between optimists and pessimists arises in this neighbouring field too; and since this field is less crowded with disputants, the issue might here be easier to settle; and if it is settled here, then it might become easier to settle it in the disputant-crowded field.

What I have to say consists largely of commonplaces. So my language, like that of commonplaces generally, will be quite unscientific and imprecise. The central commonplace that I want to insist on is the very great importance that we attach to the attitudes and intentions towards us of other human beings, and the great, extent to which our personal feelings and reactions depend upon, or involve, our beliefs about these attitudes and intentions. I can give no simple description of the field of phenomena at the centre of which stands this commonplace truth; for the field is too complex. Much imaginative literature is devoted to exploring its complexities; and we have a large vocabulary for the purpose. There are simplifying styles of handling it in a general way. Thus we may, like La Rochefoucauld, put self-love or self-esteem or vanity at the centre of the picture and point out how it may be caressed by the esteem, or wounded by the indifference or contempt, of others. We might speak, in another jargon, of the need for love, and the loss of security which results from its withdrawal; or, in another, of human self-respect and its connection with the recognition of the individual's dignity. These simplifications are of use to me only if they help to emphasize how much we actually mind, how much it matters to us, whether the actions of other people – and particularly of *some* other people – reflect attitudes towards us of goodwill, affection, or esteem on the one hand or contempt, indifference, or malevolence on the other. If someone treads on my hand accidentally, while trying to help me, the pain may be no less acute than if he treads on it in contemptuous disregard of my existence or with a malevolent wish to injure me. But I shall generally feel in the second case a kind and degree of resentment that I shall not feel in the first. If someone's actions help me to some benefit I desire, then I am benefited in any case; but if he intended them so to benefit me because of his general goodwill towards me, I shall reasonably feel a gratitude which I should not feel at all if

the benefit was an incidental consequence, unintended or even regretted by him, of some plan of action with a different aim.

These examples are of actions which confer benefits or inflict injuries over and above any conferred or inflicted by the mere manifestation of attitude and intention themselves. We should consider also in how much of our behaviour the benefit or injury resides mainly or entirely in the manifestation of attitude itself. So it is with good manners, and much of what we call kindness, on the one hand; with deliberate rudeness, studied indifference, or insult on the other.

Besides resentment and gratitude, I mentioned just now forgiveness. This is a rather unfashionable subject in moral philosophy at present; but to be forgiven is something we sometimes ask, and forgiving is something we sometimes say we do. To ask to be forgiven is in part to acknowledge that the attitude displayed in our actions was such as might properly be resented and in part to repudiate that attitude for the future (or at least for the immediate future); and to forgive is to accept the repudiation and to forswear the resentment.

We should think of the many different kinds of relationship which we can have with other people – as sharers of a common interest; as members of the same family; as colleagues; as friends; as lovers; as chance parties to an enormous range of transactions and encounters. Then we should think, in each of these connections in turn, and in others, of the kind of importance we attach to the attitudes and intentions towards us of those who stand in these relationships to us, and of the kinds of *reactive* attitudes and feelings to which we ourselves are prone. In general, we demand some degree of goodwill or regard on the part of those who stand in these relationships to us, though the forms we require it to take vary widely in different connections. The range and intensity of our *reactive* attitudes towards goodwill, its absence or its opposite vary no less widely. I have mentioned, specifically, resentment and gratitude; and they are a usefully

opposed pair. But, of course, there is a whole continuum of reactive attitude and feeling stretching on both sides of these and – the most comfortable area – in between them.

The object of these commonplaces is to try to keep before our minds something it is easy to forget when we are engaged in philosophy, especially in our cool, contemporary style, viz. what it is actually like to be involved in ordinary inter-personal relationships, ranging from the most intimate to the most casual.

IV

It is one thing to ask about the general causes of these reactive attitudes I have alluded to; it is another to ask about the variations to which they are subject, the particular conditions in which they do or do not seem natural or reasonable or appropriate; and it is a third thing to ask what it would be like, what it is like, not to suffer them. I am not much concerned with the first question; but I am with the second; and perhaps even more with the third.

Let us consider, then, occasions for resentment: situations in which one person is offended or injured by the action of another and in which – in the absence of special considerations – the offended person might naturally or normally be expected to feel resentment. Then let us consider what sorts of special considerations might be expected to modify or mollify this feeling or remove it altogether. It needs no saying now how multifarious these considerations are. But, for my purpose, I think they can be roughly divided into two kinds. To the first group belong all those which might give occasion for the employment of such expressions as 'He didn't mean to', 'He hadn't realized', 'He didn't know'; and also all those which might give occasion for the use of the phrase 'He couldn't help it', when this is supported by such phrases as 'He was pushed', 'He had to do it', 'It was the only way', 'They left him no alternative', etc. Obviously these various pleas, and the kinds of situations

in which they would be appropriate, differ from each other in striking and important ways. But for my present purpose they have something still more important in common. None of them invites us to suspend towards the agent, either at the time of his action or in general, our ordinary reactive attitudes. They do not invite us to view the *agent* as one in respect of whom these attitudes are in any way inappropriate. They invite us to view the *injury* as one in respect of which a particular one of these attitudes is inappropriate. They do not invite us to see the *agent* as other than a fully responsible agent. They invite us to see the *injury* as one for which he was not fully, or at all, responsible. They do not suggest that the agent is in any way an inappropriate object of that kind of demand for goodwill or regard which is reflected in our ordinary reactive attitudes. They suggest instead that the fact of injury was not in this case incompatible with that demand's being fulfilled, that the fact of injury was quite consistent with the agent's attitude and intentions being just what we demand they should be.[3] The agent was just ignorant of the injury he was causing, or had lost his balance through being pushed or had reluctantly to cause the injury for reasons which acceptably override his reluctance. The offering of such pleas by the agent and their acceptance by the sufferer is something in no way opposed to, or outside the context of, ordinary inter-personal relationships and the manifestation of ordinary reactive attitudes. Since things go wrong and situations are complicated, it is an essential and integral element in the transactions which are the life of these relationships.

The second group of considerations is very different. I shall take them in two subgroups of which the first is far less important than the second. In connection with the first subgroup we may think of such statements as 'He wasn't himself', 'He has been under very great strain recently', 'He was acting under post-hypnotic suggestion'; in connection with the second, we may think of 'He's only a child', 'He's a hopeless

schizophrenic', 'His mind has been systematically perverted', 'That's purely compulsive behaviour on his part'. Such pleas as these do, as pleas of my first general group do not, invite us to suspend our ordinary reactive attitudes towards the agent, either at the time of his action or all the time. They do not invite us to see the agent's action in a way consistent with the full retention of ordinary inter-personal attitudes and merely inconsistent with one particular attitude. They invite us to view the agent himself in a different light from the light in which we should normally view one who has acted as he has acted. I shall not linger over the first subgroup of cases. Though they perhaps raise, in the short term, questions akin to those raised, in the long term, by the second subgroup, we may dismiss them without considering those questions by taking that admirably suggestive phrase, 'He wasn't himself', with the seriousness that – for all its being logically comic – it deserves. We shall not feel resentment against the man he is for the action done by the man he is not; or at least we shall feel less. We normally have to deal with him under normal stresses; so we shall not feel towards him, when he acts as he does under abnormal stresses, as we should have felt towards him had he acted as he did under normal stresses.

The second and more important subgroup of cases allows that the circumstances were normal, but presents the agent as psychologically abnormal – or as morally undeveloped. The agent was himself; but he is warped or deranged, neurotic or just a child. When we see someone in such a light as this, all our reactive attitudes tend to be profoundly modified. I must deal here in crude dichotomies and ignore the ever-interesting and ever-illuminating varieties of case. What I want to contrast is the attitude (or range of attitudes) of involvement or participation in a human relationship, on the one hand, and what might be called the objective attitude (or range of attitudes) to another human being, on the other. Even in the same situation, I must

add, they are not altogether *exclusive* of each other; but they are, profoundly, *opposed* to each other. To adopt the objective attitude to another human being is to see him, perhaps, as an object of social policy; as a subject for what, in a wide range of sense, might be called treatment; as something certainly to be taken account, perhaps precautionary account, of; to be managed or handled or cured or trained; perhaps simply to be avoided, though *this* gerundive is not peculiar to cases of objectivity of attitude. The objective attitude may be emotionally toned in many ways, but not in all ways: it may include repulsion or fear, it may include pity or even love, though not all kinds of love. But it cannot include the range of reactive feelings and attitudes which belong to involvement or participation with others in inter-personal human relationships; it cannot include resentment, gratitude, forgiveness, anger, or the sort of love which two adults can sometimes be said to feel reciprocally, for each other. If your attitude towards someone is wholly objective, then though you may fight him, you cannot quarrel with him, and though you may talk to him, even negotiate with him, you cannot reason with him. You can at most pretend to quarrel, or to reason, with him.

Seeing someone, then, as warped or deranged or compulsive in behaviour or peculiarly unfortunate in his formative circumstances – seeing someone so tends, at least to some extent, to set him apart from normal participant reactive attitudes on the part of one who so sees him, tends to promote, at least in the civilized, objective attitudes. But there is something curious to add to this. The objective attitude is not only something we naturally tend to fall into in cases like these, where participant attitudes are partially or wholly inhibited by abnormalities or by immaturity. It is also something which is available as a resource in other cases too. We look with an objective eye on the compulsive behaviour of the neurotic or the tiresome behaviour of a very young child, thinking in terms of treatment or training. But we can sometimes look with something like the same eye on the behaviour of the normal and the mature. We have this resource and can sometimes use it: as a refuge, say, from the strains of involvement; or as an aid to policy; or simply out of intellectual curiosity. Being human, we cannot, in the normal case, do this for long, or altogether. If the strains of involvement, say, continue to be too great, then we have to do something else – like severing a relationship. But what is above all interesting is the tension there is, in us, between the participant attitude and the objective attitude. One is tempted to say: between our humanity and our intelligence. But to say this would be to distort both notions.

What I have called the participant reactive attitudes are essentially natural human reactions to the good or ill will or indifference of others towards us, as displayed in their attitudes and actions. The question we have to ask is: What effect would, or should, the acceptance of the truth of a general thesis of determinism have upon these reactive attitudes? More specifically, would, or should, the acceptance of the truth of the thesis lead to the decay or the repudiation of all such attitudes? Would, or should, it mean the end of gratitude, resentment, and forgiveness; of all reciprocated adult loves; of all the essentially *personal* antagonisms?

But how can I answer, or even pose, this question without knowing *exactly* what the thesis of determinism is? Well, there is one thing we do know: that if there is a coherent thesis of determinism, then there must be a sense of 'determined' such that, if that thesis is true, then all behaviour whatever is determined in that sense. Remembering this, we can consider at least what possibilities lie formally open; and then perhaps we shall see that the question can be answered *without* knowing exactly what the thesis of determinism is. We can consider what possibilities lie open because we have already before us an account of the ways in which particular reactive attitudes, or reactive attitudes

in general, may be, and, sometimes, we judge, should be, inhibited. Thus I considered earlier a group of considerations which tend to inhibit, and, we judge, should inhibit, resentment, in particular cases of an agent causing an injury, without inhibiting reactive attitudes in general towards that agent. Obviously this group of considerations cannot strictly bear upon our question; for that question concerns reactive attitudes in general. But resentment has a particular interest; so it is worth adding that it has never been claimed as a consequence of the truth of determinism that one or another of these considerations was operative in every case of an injury being caused by an agent; that it would follow from the truth of determinism that anyone who caused an injury either was quite simply ignorant of causing it or had acceptably overriding reasons for acquiescing reluctantly in causing it or . . ., etc. The prevalence of this happy state of affairs would not be a consequence of the reign of universal determinism, but of the reign of universal goodwill. We cannot, then, find here the possibility of an affirmative answer to our question, even for the particular case of resentment.

Next, I remarked that the participant attitude, and the personal reactive attitudes in general, tend to give place, and it is judged by the civilized should give place, to objective attitudes, just in so far as the agent is seen as excluded from ordinary adult human relationships by deep-rooted psychological abnormality – or simply by being a child. But it cannot be a consequence of any thesis which is not itself self-contradictory that abnormality is the universal condition.

Now this dismissal might seem altogether too facile; and so, in a sense, it is. But whatever is too quickly dismissed in this dismissal is allowed for in the only possible form of affirmative answer that remains. We can sometimes, and in part, I have remarked, look on the normal (those we rate as 'normal') in the objective way in which we have learned to look on certain

classified cases of abnormality. And our question reduces to this: could, or should, the acceptance of the determinist thesis lead us always to look on everyone exclusively in this way? For this is the only condition worth considering under which the acceptance of determinism could lead to the decay or repudiation of participant reactive attitudes.

It does not seem to be self-contradictory to suppose that this might happen. So I suppose we must say that it is not absolutely inconceivable that it should happen. But I am strongly inclined to think that it is, for us as we are, practically inconceivable. The human commitment to participation in ordinary inter-personal relationships is, I think, too thoroughgoing and deeply rooted for us to take seriously the thought that a general theoretical conviction might so change our world that, in it, there were no longer any such things as inter-personal relationships as we normally understand them; and being involved in inter-personal relationships as we normally understand them precisely is being exposed to the range of reactive attitudes and feelings that is in question.

This, then, is a part of the reply to our question. A sustained objectivity of inter-personal attitude, and the human isolation which that would entail, does not seem to be something of which human beings would be capable, even if some general truth were a theoretical ground for it. But this is not all. There is a further point, implicit in the foregoing, which must be made explicit. Exceptionally, I have said, we can have direct dealings with human beings without any degree of personal involvement, treating them simply as creatures to be handled in our own interests, or our side's, or society's – or even theirs. In the extreme case of the mentally deranged, it is easy to see the connection between the possibility of a wholly objective attitude and the impossibility of what we understand by ordinary inter-personal relationships. Given this latter impossibility, no other civilized attitude is available than that of viewing the

deranged person simply as something to be understood and controlled in the most desirable fashion. To view him as outside the reach of personal relationships is already, for the civilized, to view him in this way. For reasons of policy or self-protection we may have occasion, perhaps temporary, to adopt a fundamentally similar attitude to a 'normal' human being; to concentrate, that is, on understanding 'how he works', with a view to determining our policy accordingly or to finding in that very understanding a relief from the strains of involvement. Now it is certainly true that in the case of the abnormal, though not in the case of the normal, our adoption of the objective attitude is a consequence of our viewing the agent as *incapacitated in* some or all respects for ordinary inter-personal relationships. He is thus incapacitated, perhaps, by the fact that his picture of reality is pure fantasy, that he does not, in a sense, live in the real world at all; or by the fact that his behaviour is, in part, an unrealistic acting out of unconscious purposes; or by the fact that he is an idiot, or a moral idiot. But there is something else which, *because* this is true, is equally certainly *not* true. And that is that there is a sense of 'determined' such that (1) if determinism is true, all behaviour is determined in this sense, and (2) determinism might be true, i.e. it is not inconsistent with the facts as we know them to suppose that all behaviour might be determined in this sense, and (3) our adoption of the objective attitude towards the abnormal is the result of a prior embracing of the belief that the behaviour, or the relevant stretch of behaviour, of the human being in question *is* determined in this sense. Neither in the case of the normal, then, nor in the case of the abnormal is it true that, when we adopt an objective attitude, we do so *because* we hold such a belief. So my answer has two parts. The first is that we cannot, as we are, seriously envisage ourselves adopting a thoroughgoing objectivity of attitude to others as a result of theoretical conviction of the truth of determinism; and the second is that when we do

in fact adopt such an attitude in a particular case, our doing so is not the consequence of a theoretical conviction which might be expressed as 'Determinism in this case', but is a consequence of our abandoning, for different reasons in different cases, the ordinary inter-personal attitudes.

It might be said that all this leaves the real question unanswered, and that we cannot hope to answer it without knowing exactly what the thesis of determinism is. For the real question is not a question about what we actually do, or why we do it. It is not even a question about what we would *in fact* do if a certain theoretical conviction gained general acceptance. It is a question about what it would be *rational* to do if determinism were true, a question about the rational justification of ordinary inter-personal attitudes in general. To this I shall reply, first, that such a question could seem real only to one who had utterly failed to grasp the purport of the preceding answer, the fact of our natural human commitment to ordinary inter-personal attitudes. This commitment is part of the general framework of human life, not something that can come up for review as particular cases can come up for review within this general framework. And I shall reply, second, that if we could imagine what we cannot have, viz. a choice in this matter, then we could choose rationally only in the light of an assessment of the gains and losses to human life, its enrichment or impoverishment; and the truth or falsity of a general thesis of determinism would not bear on the rationality of this choice.[4]

V

The point of this discussion of the reactive attitudes in their relation – or lack of it – to the thesis of determinism was to bring us, if possible, nearer to a position of compromise in a more usual area of debate. We are not now to discuss reactive attitudes which are essentially those of offended parties or beneficiaries. We are

to discuss reactive attitudes which are essentially not those, or only incidentally are those, of offended parties or beneficiaries, but are nevertheless, I shall claim, kindred attitudes to those I have discussed. I put resentment in the centre of the previous discussion. I shall put moral indignation – or, more weakly, moral disapprobation – in the centre of this one.

The reactive attitudes I have so far discussed are essentially reactions to the quality of others' wills towards us, as manifested in their behaviour: to their good or ill will or indifference or lack of concern. Thus resentment, or what I have called resentment, is a reaction to injury or indifference. The reactive attitudes I have now to discuss might be described as the sympathetic or vicarious or impersonal or disinterested or generalized analogues of the reactive attitudes I have already discussed. They are reactions to the qualities of others' wills, not towards ourselves, but towards others. Because of this impersonal or vicarious character, we give them different names. Thus one who experiences the vicarious analogue of resentment is said to be indignant or disapproving, or morally indignant or disapproving. What we have here is, as it were, resentment on behalf of another, where one's own interest and dignity are not involved; and it is this impersonal or vicarious character of the attitude, added to its others, which entitle it to the qualification 'moral'. Both my description of, and my name for, these attitudes are, in one important respect, a little misleading. It is not that these attitudes are essentially vicarious – one can feel indignation on one's own account – but that they are essentially capable of being vicarious. But I shall retain the name for the sake of its suggestiveness; and I hope that what is misleading about it will be corrected in what follows.

The personal reactive attitudes rest on, and reflect, an expectation of, and demand for, the manifestation of a certain degree of goodwill or regard on the part of other human beings towards ourselves; or at least on the expectation of, and demand for, an absence of the manifestation of active ill will or indifferent disregard. (What will, in particular cases, count as manifestations of good or ill will or disregard will vary in accordance with the particular relationship in which we stand to another human being.) The generalized or vicarious analogues of the personal reactive attitudes rest on, and reflect, exactly the same expectation or demand in a generalized form; they rest on, or reflect, that is, the demand for the manifestation of a reasonable degree of goodwill or regard, on the part of others, not simply towards oneself, but towards all those on whose behalf moral indignation may be felt, i.e., as we now think, towards all men. The generalized and non-generalized forms of demand, and the vicarious and personal reactive attitudes which rest upon, and reflect, them are connected not merely logically. They are connected humanly; and not merely with each other. They are connected also with yet another set of attitudes which I must mention now in order to complete the picture. I have considered from two points of view the demands we make on others and our reactions to their possibly injurious actions. These were the points of view of one whose interest was directly involved (who suffers, say, the injury) and of others whose interest was not directly involved (who do not themselves suffer the injury). Thus I have spoken of personal reactive attitudes in the first connection and of their vicarious analogues in the second. But the picture is not complete unless we consider also the correlates of these attitudes on the part of those on whom the demands are made, on the part of the agents. Just as there are personal and vicarious reactive attitudes associated with demands on others for oneself and demands on others for others, so there are self-reactive attitudes associated with demands on oneself for others. And here we have to mention such phenomena as feeling bound or obliged (the 'sense of obligation'); feeling compunction; feeling guilty or remorseful or at least responsible; and the more complicated phenomenon of shame.

All these three types of attitude are humanly connected. One who manifested the personal reactive attitudes in a high degree but showed no inclination at all to their vicarious analogues would appear as an abnormal case of moral egocentricity, as a kind of moral solipsist. Let him be supposed fully to acknowledge the claims to regard that others had on him, to be susceptible of the whole range of self-reactive attitudes. He would then see himself as unique both as one (*the* one) who had a general claim on human regard and as one (*the* one) on whom human beings in general had such a claim. This would be a kind of moral solipsism. But it is barely more than a conceptual possibility; if it is that. In general, though within varying limits, we demand of others for others, as well as of ourselves for others, something of the regard which we demand of others for ourselves. Can we imagine, besides that of the moral solipsist, any other case of one or two of these three types of attitude being fully developed, but quite unaccompanied by any trace, however slight, of the remaining two or one? If we can, then we imagine something far below or far above the level of our common humanity – a moral idiot or a saint. For all these types of attitude alike have common roots in our human nature and our membership of human communities.

Now, as of the personal reactive attitudes, so of their vicarious analogues, we must ask in what ways, and by what considerations, they tend to be inhibited. Both types of attitude involve, or express, a certain sort of demand for inter-personal regard. The fact of injury constitutes a prima facie appearance of this demand's being flouted or unfulfilled. We saw, in the case of resentment, how one class of considerations may show this appearance to be mere appearance, and hence inhibit resentment, *without* inhibiting, or displacing, the sort of demand of which resentment can be an expression, without in any way tending to make us suspend our ordinary inter-personal attitudes to the agent. Considerations of this class operate in just the same way, for just the same reasons, in connection with moral disapprobation or indignation; they inhibit indignation without in any way inhibiting the sort of demand on the agent of which indignation can be an expression, the range of attitudes towards him to which it belongs. But in this connection we may express the facts with a new emphasis. We may say, stressing the moral, the generalized aspect of the demand, considerations of this group have no tendency to make us see the agent as other than a morally responsible agent; they simply make us see the injury as one for which he was not morally responsible. The offering and acceptance of such exculpatory pleas as are here in question in no way detracts in our eyes from the agent's status as a term of moral relationships. On the contrary, since things go wrong and situations are complicated, it is an essential part of the life of such relationships.

But suppose we see the agent in a different light: as one whose picture of the world is an insane delusion; or as one whose behaviour, or a part of whose behaviour, is unintelligible to us, perhaps even to him, in terms of conscious purposes, and intelligible only in terms of unconscious purposes; or even, perhaps, as one wholly impervious to the self-reactive attitudes I spoke of, wholly lacking, as we say, in moral sense. Seeing an agent in such a light as this tends, I said, to inhibit resentment in a wholly different way. It tends to inhibit resentment because it tends to inhibit ordinary inter-personal attitudes in general, and the kind of demand and expectation which those attitudes involve; and tends to promote instead the purely objective view of the agent as one posing problems simply of intellectual understanding, management, treatment, and control. Again the parallel holds for those generalized or moral attitudes towards the agent which we are now concerned with. The same abnormal light which shows the agent to us as one in respect of whom the personal attitudes, the personal demand, are to be suspended, shows him to us also as one in

respect of whom the impersonal attitudes, the generalized demand, are to be suspended. Only, abstracting now from direct personal interest, we may express the facts with a new emphasis. We may say: to the extent to which the agent is seen in this light, he is not seen as one on whom demands and expectations lie in that particular way in which we think of them as lying when we speak of moral obligation; he is not, to that extent, seen as a morally responsible agent, as a term of moral relationships, as a member of the moral community.

I remarked also that the suspension of ordinary inter-personal attitudes and the cultivation of a purely objective view is sometimes possible even when we have no such reasons for it as I have just mentioned. Is this possible also in the case of the moral reactive attitudes? I think so; and perhaps it is easier. But the motives for a total suspension of moral reactive attitudes are fewer, and perhaps weaker: fewer, because only where there is antecedent personal involvement can there be the motive of seeking refuge from the strains of such involvement; perhaps weaker, because the tension between objectivity of view and the moral reactive attitudes is perhaps less than the tension between objectivity of view and the personal reactive attitudes, so that we can in the case of the moral reactive attitudes more easily secure the speculative or political gains of objectivity of view by a kind of setting on one side, rather than a total suspension, of those attitudes.

These last remarks are uncertain; but also, for the present purpose, unimportant. What concerns us now is to inquire, as previously in connection with the personal reactive attitudes, what relevance any general thesis of determinism might have to their vicarious analogues. The answers once more are parallel; though I shall take them in a slightly different order. First, we must note, as before, that when the suspension of such an attitude or such attitudes occurs in a particular case, it is *never* the consequence of the belief that the piece of behaviour in question

was determined in a sense such that all behaviour *might be*, and, if determinism is true, all behaviour *is*, determined in that sense. For it is not a consequence of any general thesis of determinism which might be true that nobody knows what he's doing or that everybody's behaviour is unintelligible in terms of conscious purposes or that everybody lives in a world of delusion or that nobody has a moral sense, i.e. is susceptible of self-reactive attitudes, etc. In fact no such sense of 'determined' as would be required for a general thesis of determinism is ever relevant to our actual suspensions of moral reactive attitudes. Second, suppose it granted, as I have already argued, that we cannot take seriously the thought that theoretical conviction of such a general thesis would lead to the total decay of the personal reactive attitudes. Can we then take seriously the thought that such a conviction – a conviction, after all, that many have held or said they held – would nevertheless lead to the total decay or repudiation of the vicarious analogues of these attitudes? I think that the change in our social world which would leave us exposed to the personal reactive attitudes but not at all to their vicarious analogues, the generalization of abnormal egocentricity which this would entail, is perhaps even harder for us to envisage as a real possibility than the decay of both kinds of attitude together. Though there are some necessary and some contingent differences between the ways and cases in which these two kinds of attitudes operate or are inhibited in their operation, yet, as general human capacities or pronenesses, they stand or lapse together. Finally, to the further question whether it would not be *rational*, given a general theoretical conviction of the truth of determinism, so to change our world that in it all these attitudes were wholly suspended, I must answer, as before, that one who presses this question has wholly failed to grasp the import of the preceding answer, the nature of the human commitment that is here involved: it is *useless* to ask whether it would not be rational for us to do what it is not in our

nature to (be able to) do. To this I must add, as before, that if there were, say, for a moment open to us the possibility of such a godlike choice, the rationality of making or refusing it would be determined by quite other considerations than the truth or falsity of the general theoretical doctrine in question. The latter would be simply irrelevant; and this becomes ironically clear when we remember that for those convinced that the truth of determinism nevertheless really would make the one choice rational, there has always been the insuperable difficulty of explaining in intelligible terms how its falsity would make the opposite choice rational.

I am aware that in presenting the argument as I have done, neglecting the ever-interesting varieties of case, I have presented nothing more than a schema, using sometimes a crude opposition of phrase where we have a great intricacy of phenomena. In particular the simple opposition of objective attitudes on the one hand and the various contrasted attitudes which I have opposed to them must seem as grossly crude as it is central. Let me pause to mitigate this crudity a little, and also to strengthen one of my central contentions, by mentioning some things which straddle these contrasted kinds of attitude. Thus parents and others concerned with the care and upbringing of young children cannot have to their charges either kind of attitude in a pure or unqualified form. They are dealing with creatures who are potentially and increasingly capable both of holding, and being objects of, the full range of human and moral attitudes, but are not yet truly capable of either. The treatment of such creatures must therefore represent a kind of compromise, constantly shifting in one direction, between objectivity of attitude and developed human attitudes. Rehearsals insensibly modulate towards true performances. The punishment of a child is both like and unlike the punishment of an adult. Suppose we try to relate this progressive emergence of the child as a responsible being, as an object of non-objective

attitudes, to that sense of 'determined' in which, if determinism is a possibly true thesis, all behaviour may be determined, and in which, if it is a true thesis, all behaviour is determined. What bearing could such a sense of 'determined' have upon the progressive modification of attitudes towards the child? Would it not be grotesque to think of the development of the child as a progressive or patchy emergence from an area in which its behaviour is in this sense determined into an area in which it isn't? Whatever sense of 'determined' is required for stating the thesis of determinism, it can scarcely be such as to allow of compromise, borderline-style answers to the question, 'Is this bit of behaviour determined or isn't it?' But in this matter of young children, it is essentially a borderline, penumbral area that we move in. Again, consider – a very different matter – the strain in the attitude of a psychoanalyst to his patient. His objectivity of attitude, his suspension of ordinary moral reactive attitudes, is profoundly modified by the fact that the aim of the enterprise is to make such suspension unnecessary or less necessary. Here we may and do naturally speak of restoring the agent's freedom. But here the restoring of freedom means bringing it about that the agent's behaviour shall be intelligible in terms of conscious purposes rather than in terms only of unconscious purposes. This is the object of the enterprise; and it is in so far as this object is attained that the suspension, or half-suspension, of ordinary moral attitudes is deemed no longer necessary or appropriate. And in this we see once again the irrelevance of that concept of 'being determined' which must be the central concept of determinism. For we cannot both agree that this object is attainable and that its attainment has this consequence and yet hold (1) that neurotic behaviour is determined in a sense in which, it may be, all behaviour is determined, and (2) that it is because neurotic behaviour is determined in this sense that objective attitudes are deemed appropriate to neurotic behaviour. Not, at least, without

accusing ourselves of incoherence in our attitude to psychoanalytic treatment.

VI

And now we can try to fill in the lacuna which the pessimist finds in the optimist's account of the concept of moral responsibility, and of the bases of moral condemnation and punishment; and to fill it in from the facts as we know them. For, as I have already remarked, when the pessimist himself seeks to fill it in, he rushes beyond the facts as we know them and proclaims that it cannot be filled in at all unless determinism is false.

Yet a partial sense of the facts as we know them is certainly present to the pessimist's mind. When his opponent, the optimist, undertakes to show that the truth of determinism would not shake the foundations of the concept of moral responsibility and of the practices of moral condemnation and punishment, he typically refers, in a more or less elaborated way, to the efficacy of these practices in regulating behaviour in socially desirable ways. These practices are represented solely as instruments of policy, as methods of individual treatment and social control. The pessimist recoils from this picture; and in his recoil there is, typically, an element of emotional shock. He is apt to say, among much else, that the humanity of the offender himself is offended by this picture of his condemnation and punishment.

The reasons for this recoil – the explanation of the sense of an emotional, as well as a conceptual, shock – we have already before us. The picture painted by the optimists is painted in a style appropriate to a situation envisaged as wholly dominated by objectivity of attitude. The only operative notions invoked in this picture are such as those of policy, treatment, control. But a thoroughgoing objectivity of attitude, excluding as it does the moral reactive attitudes, excludes at the same time essential elements in the concepts of *moral* condemnation and *moral* responsibility. This is the reason for the conceptual shock. The deeper emotional shock is a reaction, not simply to an inadequate conceptual analysis, but to the suggestion of a change in our world. I have remarked that it is possible to cultivate an exclusive objectivity of attitude in some cases, and for some reasons, where the object of the attitude is not set aside from developed inter-personal and moral attitudes by immaturity or abnormality. And the suggestion which seems to be contained in the optimist's account is that such an attitude should be universally adopted to all offenders. This is shocking enough in the pessimist's eyes. But, sharpened by shock, his eyes see further. It would be hard to make this division in our natures. If to all offenders, then to all mankind. Moreover, to whom could this recommendation be, in any real sense, addressed? Only to the powerful, the authorities. So abysses seem to open.[5]

But we will confine our attention to the case of the offenders. The concepts we are concerned with are those of responsibility and guilt, qualified as 'moral', on the one hand – together with that of membership of a moral community; of demand, indignation, disapprobation and condemnation, qualified as 'moral', on the other hand – together with that of punishment. Indignation, disapprobation, like resentment, tend to inhibit or at least to limit our goodwill towards the object of these attitudes, tend to promote an at least partial and temporary withdrawal of goodwill; they do so in proportion as they are strong; and their strength is in general proportioned to what is felt to be the magnitude of the injury and to the degree to which the agent's will is identified with, or indifferent to, it. (These, of course, are not contingent connections.) But these attitudes of disapprobation and indignation are precisely the correlates of the moral demand in the case where the demand is felt to be disregarded. The making of the demand is the proneness to such attitudes. The holding of them does not, as the holding of objective

attitudes does, involve as a part of itself viewing their object other than as a member of the moral community. The partial withdrawal of goodwill which *these* attitudes entail, the modification they entail of the general demand that another should, if possible, be spared suffering, is, rather, the consequence of *continuing* to view him as a member of the moral community; only as one who has offended against its demands. So the preparedness to acquiesce in that infliction of suffering on the offender which is an essential part of punishment is all of a piece with this whole range of attitudes of which I have been speaking. It is not only moral reactive attitudes towards the offender which are in question here. We must mention also the self-reactive attitudes of offenders themselves. Just as the other-reactive attitudes are associated with a readiness to acquiesce in the infliction of suffering on an offender, within the 'institution' of punishment, so the self-reactive attitudes are associated with a readiness on the part of the offender to acquiesce in such infliction *without* developing the reactions (e.g. of resentment) which he would normally develop to the infliction of injury upon him; i.e. with a readiness, as we say, to accept punishment[6] as 'his due' or as 'just'.

I am not in the least suggesting that these readinesses to acquiesce, either on the part of the offender himself or on the part of others, are always or commonly accompanied or preceded by indignant boilings or remorseful pangs; only that we have here a continuum of attitudes and feelings to which these readinesses to acquiesce themselves belong. Nor am I in the least suggesting that it belongs to this continuum of attitudes that we should be ready to acquiesce in the infliction of injury on offenders in a fashion which we saw to be quite indiscriminate or in accordance with procedures which we knew to be wholly useless. On the contrary, savage or civilized, we have some belief in the utility of practices of condemnation and punishment. But the social utility of these practices, on which the

optimist, lays such exclusive stress, is not what is now in question. What is in question is the pessimist's justified sense that to speak in terms of social utility alone is to leave out something vital in our conception of these practices. The vital thing can be restored by attending to that complicated web of attitudes and feelings which form an essential part of the moral life as we know it, and which are quite opposed to objectivity of attitude. Only by attending to this range of attitudes can we recover from the facts as we know them a sense of what we mean, i.e. of *all* we mean, when, speaking the language of morals, we speak of desert, responsibility, guilt, condemnation, and justice. But we *do* recover it from the facts as we know them. We do not have to go beyond them. Because the optimist neglects or misconstrues these attitudes, the pessimist rightly claims to find a lacuna in his account. We can fill the lacuna for him. But in return we must demand of the pessimist a surrender of his metaphysics.

Optimist and pessimist misconstrue the facts in very different styles. But in a profound sense there is something in common to their misunderstandings. Both seek, in different ways, to over-intellectualize the facts. Inside the general structure or web of human attitudes and feelings of which I have been speaking, there is endless room for modification, redirection, criticism, and justification. But questions of justification are internal to the structure or relate to modifications internal to it. The existence of the general framework of attitudes itself is something we are given with the fact of human society. As a whole, it neither calls for, nor permits, an external 'rational' justification. Pessimist and optimist alike show themselves, in different ways, unable to accept this.[7] The optimist's style of over-intellectualizing the facts is that of a characteristically incomplete empiricism, a one-eyed utilitarianism. He seeks to find an adequate basis for certain social practices in calculated consequences, and loses sight (perhaps wishes to lose sight) of the human attitudes of which

these practices are, in part, the expression. The pessimist does not lose sight of these attitudes, but is unable to accept the fact that it is just these attitudes themselves which fill the gap in the optimist's account. Because of this, he thinks the gap can be filled only if some general metaphysical proposition is repeatedly verified, verified in all cases where it is appropriate to attribute moral responsibility. This proposition he finds it as difficult to state coherently and with intelligible relevance as its determinist contradictory. Even when a formula has been found ('contracausal freedom' or something of the kind) there still seems to remain a gap between its applicability in particular cases and its supposed moral consequences. Sometimes he plugs this gap with an intuition of fittingness – a pitiful intellectualist trinket for a philosopher to wear as a charm against the recognition of his own humanity.

Even the moral sceptic is not immune from his own form of the wish to over-intellectualize such notions as those of moral responsibility, guilt, and blame. He sees that the optimist's account is inadequate and the pessimist's libertarian alternative inane; and finds no resource except to declare that the notions in question are inherently confused, that 'blame is metaphysical'. But the metaphysics was in the eye of the metaphysician. It is a pity that talk of the moral sentiments has fallen out of favour. The phrase would be quite a good name for that network of human attitudes in acknowledging the character and place of which we find, I suggest, the only possibility of reconciling these disputants to each other and the facts.

There are, at present, factors which add, in a slightly paradoxical way, to the difficulty of making this acknowledgement. These human attitudes themselves, in their development and in the variety of their manifestations, have to an increasing extent become objects of study in the social and psychological sciences; and this growth of human self-consciousness, which we might expect to reduce the difficulty of

acceptance, in fact increases it in several ways. One factor of comparatively minor importance is an increased historical and anthropological awareness of the great variety of forms which these human attitudes may take at different times and in different cultures. This makes one rightly chary of claiming as essential features of the concept of morality in general, forms of these attitudes which may have a local and temporary prominence. No doubt to some extent my own descriptions of human attitudes have reflected local and temporary features of our own culture. But an awareness of variety of forms should not prevent us from acknowledging also that in the absence of *any* forms of these attitudes it is doubtful whether we should have anything that *we* could find intelligible as a system of human relationships, as human society. A quite different factor of greater importance is that psychological studies have made us rightly mistrustful of many particular manifestations of the attitudes I have spoken of. They are a prime realm of self-deception, of the ambiguous and the shady, of guilt-transference, unconscious sadism and the rest. But it is an exaggerated horror, itself suspect, which would make us unable to acknowledge the facts because of the seamy side of the facts. Finally, perhaps the most important factor of all is the prestige of these theoretical studies themselves. That prestige is great, and is apt to make us forget that in philosophy, though it also is a theoretical study, we have to take account of the facts in *all* their bearings; we are not to suppose that we are required, or permitted, as philosophers, to regard ourselves, as human beings, as detached from the attitudes which, as scientists, we study with detachment. This is in no way to deny the possibility and desirability of redirection and modification of our human attitudes in the light of these studies. But we may reasonably think it unlikely that our progressively greater understanding of certain aspects of ourselves will lead to the total disappearance of those aspects. Perhaps it is not inconceivable that it

should; and perhaps, then, the dreams of some philosophers will be realized.

If we sufficiently, that is *radically*, modify the view of the optimist, his view is the right one. It is far from wrong to emphasize the efficacy of all those practices which express or manifest our moral attitudes, in regulating behaviour in ways considered desirable; or to add that when certain of our beliefs about the efficacy of some of these practices turn out to be false, then we may have good reason for dropping or modifying those practices. What *is* wrong is to forget that these practices, and their reception, the reactions to them, really *are* expressions of our moral attitudes and not merely devices we calculatingly employ for regulative purposes. Our practices do not merely exploit our natures, they express them. Indeed the very understanding of the kind of efficacy these expressions of our attitudes have turns on our remembering this. When we do remember this, and modify the optimist's position accordingly, we simultaneously correct its conceptual deficiencies and ward off the dangers it seems to entail, without recourse to the obscure and panicky metaphysics of libertarianism.

Notes

1 Cf. P. H. Nowell-Smith, 'Freewill and Moral Responsibility', Mind, vol. LVII, 1948.

2 As Nowell-Smith pointed out in a later article: 'Determinists and Libertarians', Mind, vol. LXIII, 1954.

3 Perhaps not in every case *just* what we demand they should be, but in any case *not* just what we demand they should not be. For my present purpose these differences do not matter.

4 The question, then, of the connection between rationality and the adoption of the objective attitude to others is misposed when it is made to seem dependent on the issue of determinism. But there is another question which should be raised, if only to distinguish it from the misposed question. Quite apart from the issue of determinism might it not be said that we should be nearer to being purely rational creatures in proportion as our relation to others was in fact dominated by the objective attitude? I think this might be said; only it would have to be added, once more, that if such a choice were possible, it would not necessarily be rational to choose to be more purely rational than we are.

5 See J. D. Mabbott's 'Freewill and Punishment', published in *Contemporary British Philosophy*, 3rd ser., London, Allen & Unwin, 1956.

6 Of course not *any* punishment for *anything* deemed an offence.

7 Compare the question of the justification of induction. The human commitment to inductive belief-formation is original, natural, non-rational (not irrational), in no way something we choose or could give up. Yet rational criticism and reflection can refine standards and their application, supply 'rules for judging of cause and effect'. Ever since the facts were made clear by Hume, people have been resisting acceptance of them.

Chapter 56

Gary Watson

RESPONSIBILITY AND THE LIMITS OF EVIL: VARIATIONS ON A STRAWSONIAN THEME

RESPONSIBILITY IS . . . one aspect of the identity of character and conduct. We are responsible for our conduct because that conduct is ourselves objectified in actions.

—John Dewey, *Outlines of a Critical Theory of Ethics*

There is nothing regrettable about finding oneself, in the last analysis, left with something which one cannot choose to accept or reject. What one is left with is probably just oneself, a core without which there could be no choice belonging to the person at all. Some unchosen restrictions on choice are among the conditions of its possibility.

—Thomas Nagel, *The Possibility of Altruism*

Our practices do not merely exploit our natures, they express them.

—Peter Strawson, "Freedom and Resentment"

Introduction

Regarding people as responsible agents is evidently not just a matter of belief. So regarding them means something in practice. It is shown in an embrace or a thank you, in an act of reprisal or obscene gesture, in a feeling of resentment or sense of obligation, in an apology or demand for an apology. To regard people as responsible agents is to be ready to treat them in certain ways.

In "Freedom and Resentment,"[1] Peter Strawson is concerned to describe these forms of treatment and their presuppositions. As his title suggests, Strawson's focus is on such attitudes and responses as gratitude and resentment, indignation, approbation, guilt, shame, (some kinds of) pride, hurt feeling, (asking and granting) forgiveness, and (some kinds of) love. All traditional theories of moral responsibility acknowledge connections between these attitudes and holding one another responsible. What is original to Strawson is the way in which they are linked. Whereas traditional views have taken these attitudes to be secondary to seeing others as responsible, to be practical corollaries or emotional side effects of some independently comprehensible belief in responsibility, Strawson's radical claim is that these "reactive attitudes" (as he calls them) are *constitutive* of moral responsibility; to regard oneself or another as responsible just is the proneness to react to them in these kinds of ways under certain conditions. There is no more basic belief which provides the justification or rationale for these reactions. The practice does not rest on a theory at all, but rather on certain needs and aversions that are basic to our conception of being human. The idea that there is or needs to be such an independent basis is where traditional views, in Strawson's opinion, have gone badly astray.

For a long time, I have found Strawson's approach salutary and appealing. Here my aim is

not to defend it as superior to its alternatives, but to do something more preliminary. A comparative assessment is not possible without a better grasp of what Strawson's theory (or a Strawsonian theory)[2] is. As Strawson presents it, the theory is incomplete in important respects. I will investigate whether and how the incompleteness can be remedied in Strawsonian ways. In the end, I find that certain features of our practice of holding responsible are rather resistant to such remedies, and that the practice is less philosophically innocent than Strawson supposes. I hope that the issues uncovered by this investigation will be of sufficient importance to interest even those who are not as initially sympathetic to Strawson's approach as I am.[3]

Strawson's theory

Strawson presents the rivals to his view as responses to a prima facie problem posed by determinism. One rival—consequentialism—holds that blaming and praising judgments and acts are to be understood, and justified, as forms of social regulation. Apart from the question of its extensional adequacy, consequentialism seems to many to leave out something vital to our practice. By emphasizing their instrumental efficacy, it distorts the fact that our responses are typically personal reactions to the individuals in question that we sometimes think of as eminently appropriate reactions quite aside from concern for effects. Rightly "recoiling" from the consequentialist picture, some philosophers have supposed that responsibility requires a libertarian foundation, that to bring the "vital thing" back in, we must embrace a certain metaphysics of human agency. This is the other rival.

What these otherwise very different views share is the assumption that our reactive attitudes commit us to the truth of some independently apprehensible proposition which gives the content of the belief in responsibility; and so

either the search is on for the formulation of this proposition, or we must rest content with an intuition of its content. For the social-regulation theorist, this is a proposition about the standard effects of having and expressing reactive attitudes. For the libertarian, it is a proposition concerning metaphysical freedom. Since the truth of the former is consistent with the thesis of determinism, the consequentialist is a compatibilist; since the truth of the latter is shown or seen not to be, the libertarian is an incompatibilist.

In Strawson's view, there is no such independent notion of responsibility that explains the propriety of the reactive attitudes. The explanatory priority is the other way around: It is not that we hold people responsible because they *are* responsible; rather, the idea (our idea) that we are responsible is to be understood by the practice, which itself is not a matter of holding some propositions to be true, but of expressing our concerns and demands about our treatment of one another. These stances and responses are expressions of certain rudimentary needs and aversions: "it matters to us . . . whether the actions of other people . . . reflect attitudes toward us of good will, affection, or esteem on the one hand or contempt, indifference, or malevolence on the other" (p. 76). Accordingly, the reactive attitudes are "natural human reactions to the good or ill will or indifference of others toward us [or toward those we care about] as displayed in *their* attitudes and actions" (p. 80). Taken together, they express "the demand for the manifestation of a reasonable degree of good will or regard, on the part of others, not simply towards oneself, but towards all those on whose behalf moral indignation may be felt . . ." (p. 84).

Hence, Strawson accuses rival conceptions of "overintellectualizing" our practices. In their emphasis on social regulation, consequentialists lose sight of sentiments these practices directly express, without which the notion of moral

responsibility cannot be understood. Libertarians see the gaping hole in the consequentialist account, but rather than acknowledging that "it is just these attitudes themselves which fill the gap" (p. 92), they seek to ground these attitudes in a metaphysical intuition—"a pitiful intellectualist trinket for a philosopher to wear as a charm against the recognition of his own humanity" (p. 92). Holding responsible is as natural and primitive in human life as friendship and animosity, sympathy and antipathy. It rests on needs and concerns that are not so much to be justified as acknowledged.

Excusing and exempting

To say that holding responsible is to be explained by the range of reactive attitudes, rather than by a commitment to some independently comprehensible proposition about responsibility, is not to deny that these reactions depend on a context of belief and perceptions in particular contexts. They are not mere effusions of feeling, unaffected by facts. In one way, Strawson is anxious to insist that these attitudes have no "rationale," that they neither require nor permit a "rational justification" of some general sort. Nevertheless, Strawson has a good deal to say about the particular perceptions that elicit and inhibit them. Reactive attitudes do have internal criteria, since they are reactions to the moral qualities exemplified by an individual's attitudes and conduct.[4]

Thus reactive attitudes depend upon an interpretation of conduct. If you are resentful when jostled in a crowd, you will see the other's behavior as rude, contemptuous, disrespectful, self-preoccupied, or heedless: in short, as manifesting attitudes contrary to the basic demand for reasonable regard. Your resentment might be inhibited if you are too tired, or busy, or fearful, or simply inured to life in the big city. These are causal inhibitors. In contrast, you might think the other was pushed, didn't realize, didn't mean to.... These thoughts would provide reasons for the inhibition of resentment. What makes them reasons is, roughly, that they cancel or qualify the appearance of noncompliance with the basic demand.'[5]

In this way, Strawson offers a plausible account of many of the "pleas" that in practice inhibit or modify negative reactive attitudes. One type of plea is exemplified by the aforementioned reasons for inhibited sentiments. This type of plea corresponds to standardly acknowledged *excusing* conditions. It works by denying the appearance that the other failed to fulfill the basic demand; when a valid excuse obtains, the internal criteria of the negative reactive attitudes are not satisfied. Of course, justification does this as well, but in a different way. "He realized what he was doing, but it was an emergency." In general, an excuse shows that *one* was not to blame, whereas a justification shows that one was not to *blame*.

Strawson distinguishes a second type of plea. These correspond roughly to standard *exempting* conditions. They show that the agent, temporarily or permanently, globally or locally, is appropriately exempted from the basic demand in the first place. Strawson's examples are being psychotic, being a child, being under great strain, being hypnotized, being a sociopath ("moral idiot"), and being "unfortunate in formative circumstances." His general characterization of pleas of type 2 is that they present the other either as acting uncharacteristically due to extraordinary circumstances, or as psychologically abnormal or morally undeveloped in such a way as to be incapacitated in some or all respects for "ordinary adult interpersonal relationships."

In sum, type-2 pleas bear upon the question of whether the agent is an appropriate "object of that kind of demand for goodwill or regard which is reflected in ordinary reactive attitudes" (p. 65). If so, he or she is seen as a responsible agent, as a potential term in moral relationships, as a member (albeit, perhaps, in less than good standing) of the moral community. Assuming

the absence of such exemptions, type-1 pleas bear upon the question of whether the basic demand has been met. These inhibit negative reactive attitudes because they give evidence that their internal criteria are not satisfied. In contrast, type-2 pleas inhibit reactive attitudes because they inhibit the demand those attitudes express (p. 73).

When reactive attitudes are suspended on type-2 grounds, we tend to take what Strawson calls an "objective view." We see individuals not as ones to be resented or esteemed but as ones to be controlled, managed, manipulated, trained.... The objective view does not preclude all emotions: "It may include repulsion and fear, it may include pity or even love," though not reciprocal adult love. We have the capacity to adopt an objective view toward capable agents as well; for certain kinds of therapeutic relationship, or simply to relieve the "strains of involvement," we sometimes call upon this resource.

As we have seen, one of Strawson's concerns is to deny the relevance of any theoretical issue about determinism to moral responsibility. In effect, incompatibilists insist that the truth of determinism would require us to take the objective attitude universally. But in Strawson's view, when we adopt the objective attitude, it is never a result of a theoretical conviction in determinism, but either because one of the exempting pleas is accepted, or for external reasons—fatigue, for example, or relief from the strain of involvement. No coherent thesis of determinism entails that one or more of the pleas is always valid, that disrespect is never meant, or that we are all abnormal or undeveloped in the relevant ways. Holding responsible is an expression of the basic concern and the basic demand, whose "legitimacy" requires neither metaphysical freedom nor efficacy. The practice does not involve a commitment to anything with which determinism could conflict, or which considerations of utility could challenge.

Blaming and finding fault

This is the basic view as Strawson presents it. For convenience, we may call it the expressive theory of responsibility.[6] With certain caveats,[6] the expressive theory may be called a nonconsequentialist form of compatibilism; but it is not the only such form. It can be clarified by contrasting it with another.

Consider the following common view of blame and praise: To blame someone morally for something is to attribute it to a moral fault, or "shortcoming," or defect of character, or vice,[7] and similarly for praise. Responsibility could be construed in terms of the propriety conditions of such judgments: that is, judgments to the effect that an action or attitude manifests a virtue or vice.[8]

As I understand the Strawsonian theory, such judgments are only part of the story. They indicate what reactive attitudes are reactions to (namely, to the quality of the other's moral self as exemplified in action and attitude), but they are not themselves such reactions. Merely to cite such judgments is to leave out something integral to the practice of holding responsible and to the concept of moral responsibility (of being one to whom it is appropriate to respond in certain ways). It is as though in blaming we were mainly moral clerks, recording moral faults, for whatever purposes (the Last Assizes?).[9] In a Strawsonian view, blaming is not merely a fault-finding appraisal—which could be made from a detached and austerely "objective" standpoint—but a range of responses to the agent on the basis of such appraisals.[10] These nonpropositional responses are constitutive of the practice of holding responsible.

I will have something to say later about the nature of these responses. Clearly they make up a wide spectrum. Negative reactions range from bombing Tripoli to thinking poorly of a person. But even those at the more covert and less retributive end of the spectrum involve more than attributions of defects or shortcomings of moral

character. Thinking poorly (less well) of a person is a way of regarding him or her in view of those faults. It has subtle implications for one's way of treating and interacting with the other. (Where the other is dead or otherwise out of reach, these implications will be only dispositional or potential.) It is the sort of attitude that is forsworn by forgiveness, which itself presupposes the attribution of (former) fault.

Some critical questions

I turn now to certain hard questions for the expressive theory. It accounts nicely for "excusing conditions," pleas of type 1; but exactly—or even roughly—what is its account of type-2 pleas? The "participant" reactive attitudes are said to be "natural human reactions to the good or ill-will or indifference of others as displayed in their attitudes and actions" (p. 80); but this characterization must be incomplete, for some agents who display such attitudes are nevertheless exempted. A child can be malicious, a psychotic can be hostile, a sociopath indifferent, a person under great strain can be rude, a woman or man "unfortunate in formative circumstances" can be cruel. Evidently reactive attitudes are sensitive not only to the quality of others' wills, but depend as well upon a background of beliefs about the objects of those attitudes. What are those beliefs, and can they be accommodated without appealing to the rival accounts of responsibility that Strawson sets out to avoid?

Strawson says that type-2 pleas inhibit reactive attitudes not by providing an interpretation which shows that the other does not display the pertinent attitudes, but by "inhibiting" the basic demand. It would seem that many of the exemption conditions involve *explanations* of why the individuals display qualities to which the reactive attitudes are otherwise sensitive. So on the face of it, the reactive attitudes are also affected by these explanations. Strawson's essay does not provide an account of how this works or what kinds of explanations exempt.

The problem is not just that the theory is incomplete, but that what will be necessary to complete it might undermine the theory. Strawsonian rivals will rush to fill the gap with their own notions. So it will be said that what makes some of these explanations exempting is that they are deterministic; or it will be said that these conditions are exempting because they indicate conditions in which making the basic demand is inefficacious. To the extent that some such account seems necessary, our enterprise is doomed.

In the following sections, I investigate a Strawsonian alternative. Following Strawson's idea that type-2 pleas inhibit reactive attitudes by inhibiting the basic demand, I propose to construe the exempting conditions as indications of the constraints on intelligible moral demand or, put another way, of the constraints on moral address.

I shall not attempt anything like a comprehensive treatment of the type-2 pleas mentioned by Strawson. I discuss, first and rather briefly, the cases of being a child and being under great strain. I then turn to a more extended discussion of "being unfortunate in formative circumstances," for this looks to be entirely beyond the resources of the expressive theory.

Demanding and understanding

As Strawson is fully aware, being a child is not simply exempting. Children "are potentially and increasingly capable both of holding, and being objects of, the full range of human and moral attitudes, but are not yet fully capable of either" (p. 88). Children are gradually becoming responsible agents; but in virtue of what are they potentially and increasingly these things? A plausible partial answer to this question is "moral understanding." They do not yet (fully) grasp the moral concepts in such a way that they can (fully) engage in moral communication, and so be unqualified members of the moral community.

The relevance of moral understanding to the expressive theory is this: The negative reactive attitudes express a *moral* demand, a demand for reasonable regard. Now a very young child does not even have a clear sense of the reality of others; but even with this cognitive capacity, children may lack an understanding of the effects of their behavior on others. Even when they understand what it is to hurt another physically, they may lack a sense of what it is to hurt another's feelings, or of the various subtle ways in which that may be done; and even when these things are more or less mastered, they may lack the notion of *reasonable* regard, or of justification. The basic demand is, once more, a moral demand, a demand for reasonable regard, a demand addressed to a moral agent, to one who is capable of understanding the demand. Since the negative reactive attitudes involve this demand, they are not (as fully) appropriately directed to those who do not fully grasp the terms of the demand.

To be intelligible, demanding presumes understanding on the part of the object of the demand. The reactive attitudes are incipiently forms of communication, which make sense only on the assumption that the other can comprehend the message.

No doubt common views about the moral capacities of children are open to challenge, and the appeal to the notion of understanding itself raises important issues.[11] However, what is important here is whether these views can be understood by the Strawsonian theory, and it seems the ordinary view that reactive attitudes make less sense in the case of children is intelligible in Strawsonian terms; this exemption condition reflects constraints arising from the notion of moral demand.

In a certain sense, blaming and praising those with diminished moral understanding loses its "point." This way of putting it smacks of consequentialism, but our discussion suggests a different construction. The reactive attitudes are incipient forms of communication, though not

in the sense that resentment et al. are usually communicated; very, often, in fact, they are not. Rather, the most appropriate and direct expression of resentment is to address the other with a complaint and a demand. Being a child exempts, when it does, not because expressing resentment has no desirable effects; in fact, it often does. Rather the reactive attitudes lose their point as forms of moral address.[12]

Not being oneself

Let's consider whether this kind of explanation can be extended to another of Strawson's type-2 pleas: "being under great strain." Strawson includes this plea in a subgroup of exemptions that include "he wasn't himself" and "he was acting under posthypnotic suggestion." His statement of the rationale in the case of stress is somewhat cryptic:

> We shall not feel resentment against the man he is for the action done by the man he is not; or at least we shall feel less. We normally have to deal with him under normal stresses; so we shall not feel towards him, when he acts under abnormal stresses, as we should have felt towards him had he acted as he did under normal stresses. (p. 78)

I take it that what leads Strawson to group these cases together is that in each case the agent, due to special circumstances, acts *uncharacteristically*.

When you learn that someone who has treated you extremely rudely has been under great strain lately, has lost a job, say, or is going through a divorce, you may reinterpret the behavior in such a way that your erstwhile resentment or hurt feelings are inhibited and now seem inappropriate. How does this reinterpretation work? Notice, again, that unlike type-1 pleas, the new interpretation does not contradict the *judgment* that the person treated you rudely; rather, it provides an explanation of the rudeness.

What Strawson says about this case seems plausible. What seems to affect your reactive attitudes is the thought that she's not herself, that the behavior does not reflect or fully reflect the person's moral "personality." The following remark indicates the same phenomenon: "He was drunk when he said that; I wouldn't hold it against him." (There is room here for disagreement about the bounds of the moral self. Some parts of folk wisdom have it that one's "true self" is revealed when drunk. To my knowledge, this has never been claimed about stress.) Again, what is the Strawsonian rationale?

Perhaps this type of case can also be understood in terms of the conditions of intelligible moral address. Insofar as resentment is a form of reproach addressed to an agent, such an attitude loses much of its point here—not, as before, because the other does not fully understand the reproach, but because *he* or *she* (the true self) repudiates such conduct as well. Unlike the case in which the agent acts rudely in the absence of "strain," here the target of your resentment is not one who "really" endorses the behavior you are opposing. You see the behavior as not issuing from that person's moral self, and yet it is the person, qua moral self, that your resentment would address.

The point can be put more generally in this way: Insofar as the negative reactive attitudes express demands (or in some cases appeals) addressed to another moral self, they are conceptually conditioned in various ways. One condition is that, to be fully a moral self, the other must possess sufficient (for what?) moral understanding; another is that the conduct in question be seen as reflecting the moral self. Insofar as the person is subject to great stress, his or her conduct and attitudes fail to meet this latter condition.

I am unsure to what extent these remarks accord with Strawson's own views. They are in any case exceedingly sketchy, and raise problems I am unable to take up here. For one thing, the notion of moral address seems essentially inter-

personal, and so would be unavailing in the self-reflexive case. We have negative reactive attitudes toward and make moral demands upon ourselves. To determine whether this is a fatal asymmetry, we would have to investigate the reflexive cases in detail. For another thing, the notion of moral self is certainly not altogether transparent. Why are our responses under stress not reflections of our moral selves—namely, reflections of the moral self under stress? Clearly then, the explanation requires development.

It will be recalled, however, that I am not trying to determine whether a Strawsonian account of the exemption conditions is the *best* account, but to indicate what such an account might be. It will be enough for my purposes here if we can be satisfied that a Strawsonian theory has the resources to provide *some* explanation.

To recapitulate, then, the thesis is this: First, type-2 pleas indicate in different ways limiting conditions on moral address. These are relevant to reactive attitudes because those attitudes are incipiently forms of moral address. This thesis makes sense of Strawson's remark that pleas of this type inhibit reactive attitudes by inhibiting moral demand. Second, given that those conditions are satisfied, type-1 pleas indicate that the basic demand has not been flouted, contrary to appearances (though here again, we must distinguish excuse from justification).

On this account, the practice of holding responsible does indeed seem metaphysically modest, in that it involves no commitments to which issues about determinism are relevant. In a subsequent section I will consider some more bothersome features of our practice; but first I want to call attention to some general issues raised by the account given so far.

Evil and the limits of moral community

To understand certain exempting and extenuating considerations, I have appealed to the notion of

the conditions in which it makes sense morally to address another. I suggested that in different ways these conditions are not (fully) satisfied by the child and the person under severe stress. In the case of children, it seemed plausible to speak of a lack of understanding. What is involved in such understanding is a complex question. Obviously we do not want to make compliance with the basic demand a condition of moral understanding. (After all, for the most part, children do "comply," but without full understanding.) For the negative reactive attitudes come into play only when the basic demand has been flouted or rejected and flouting and rejecting, strictly speaking, require understanding.

These remarks raise a very general issue about the limits of responsibility and the limits of evil. It is tempting to think that understanding requires a shared framework of values. At any rate, some of Strawson's remarks hint at such a requirement on moral address. He writes that the reactive attitudes essentially involve regarding the other as "a morally responsible agent, as a term of moral relationships, as a member of the moral community" (p. 73). This last phrase suggests shared ends, at some level, or a shared framework for practical reasoning. Thus, comembers of the moral community are potential interlocutors. In his discussion of Strawson's essay, Lawrence Stern suggests this point:

> . . . when one morally disapproves of another person, it is normal to believe that he is susceptible to the appeal of the principles from the standpoint of which one disapproves. He either shares these principles or can come to share them.[13]

Does morally addressing another make sense unless we suppose that the other can see some reason to take us seriously, to acknowledge our claims? Can we be in a moral community with those who reject the basic terms of moral community? Are the enemies of moral community themselves members? If we suppose that moral address requires moral community, then some forms of evil will be exempting conditions. If holding responsible requires the intelligibility of moral address, and if a condition of such address is that the other be seen as a potential moral interlocutor, then the paradox results that extreme evil disqualifies one for blame.

Consider the case of Robert Harris.

On the south tier of Death Row, in a section called "Peckerwood Flats" where the white inmates are housed, there will be a small celebration the day Robert Alton Harris dies.

A group of inmates on the row have pledged several dollars for candy, cookies and soda. At the moment they estimate that Harris has been executed, they will eat, drink and toast to his passing.

"The guy's a misery, a total scumbag; we're going to party when he goes," said Richard (Chic) Mroczko, who lived in the cell next to Harris on San Quentin Prison's Death Row for more than a year. "He doesn't care about life, he doesn't care about others, he doesn't care about himself.

"We're not a bunch of Boy Scouts around here, and you might think we're pretty cold-blooded about the whole thing. But then, you just don't know the dude."

San Diego County Assistant Dist. Atty. Richard Huffman, who prosecuted Harris, said, "If a person like Harris can't be executed under California law and federal procedure, then we should be honest and say we're incapable of handling capital punishment."

State Deputy Atty. Gen. Michael D. Wellington asked the court during an appeal hearing for Harris, "If this isn't the kind of defendant that justifies the death penalty, is there ever going to be one?"

What crime did Robert Harris commit to be considered the archetypal candidate for the death penalty? And what kind of man

provokes such enmity that even those on Death Row . . . call for his execution?

On July 5, 1978, John Mayeski and Michael Baker had just driven through [a] fast-food restaurant and were sitting in the parking lot eating lunch. Mayeski and Baker . . . lived on the same street and were best friends. They were on their way to a nearby lake for a day of fishing.

At the other end of the parking lot, Robert Harris, 25, and his brother Daniel, 18, were trying to hotwire a [car] when they spotted the two boys. The Harris brothers were planning to rob a bank that afternoon and did not want to use their own car. When Robert Harris could not start the car, he pointed to the [car] where the 16-year-olds were eating and said to Daniel, "We'll take this one."

He pointed a . . . Luger at Mayeski, crawled into the back seat, and told him to drive east . . .

Daniel Harris followed in the Harrises' car. When they reached a canyon area . . ., Robert Harris told the youths he was going to use their car in a bank robbery and assured them that they would not be hurt. Robert Harris yelled to Daniel to get the .22 caliber rifle out of the back seat of their car.

"When I caught up," Daniel said in a recent interview, Robert was telling them about the bank robbery we were going to do. He was telling them that he would leave them some money in the car and all, for us using it. Both of them said that they would wait on top of this little hill until we were gone, and then walk into town and report the car stolen. Robert Harris agreed.

"Michael turned and went through some bushes. John said, 'Good luck,' and turned to leave."

As the two boys walked away, Harris slowly raised the Luger and shot Mayeski in the back, Daniel said. Mayeski yelled: "Oh, God," and slumped to the ground. Harris chased Baker down a hill into a little valley and shot him four times.

Mayeski was still alive when Harris climbed back up the hill, Daniel said. Harris walked over to the boy, knelt down, put the Luger to his head and fired.

"God, everything started to spin," Daniel said. "It was like slow motion. I saw the gun, and then his head exploded like a balloon, . . . I just started running and running. . . . But I heard Robert and turned around.

"He was swinging the rifle and pistol in the air and laughing. God, that laugh made blood and bone freeze in me."

Harris drove [the] car to a friend's house where he and Daniel were staying. Harris walked into the house, carrying the weapons and the bag [containing] the remainder of the slain youths' lunch. Then, about 15 minutes after he had killed the two 16-year-old boys, Harris took the food out of the bag . . . and began eating a hamburger. He offered his brother an apple turnover, and Daniel became nauseated and ran to the bathroom.

"Robert laughed at me," Daniel said. "He said I was weak; he called me a sissy and said I didn't have the stomach for it."

Harris was in an almost lighthearted mood. He smiled and told Daniel that it would be amusing if the two of them were to pose as police officers and inform the parents that their sons were killed. Then, for the first time, he turned serious. He thought that somebody might have heard the shots and that police could be searching for the bodies. He told Daniel that they should begin cruising the street near the bodies, and possibly kill some police in the area.

[Later, as they prepared to rob the bank,] Harris pulled out the Luger, noticed blood stains and remnants of flesh on the barrel as a result of the point-blank shot, and said, "I really blew that guy's brains out." And then, again, he started laughing.

. . . Harris was given the death penalty. He has refused all requests for interviews since the conviction.

"He just doesn't see the point of talking," said a sister, . . . who has visited him three times since he has been on Death Row. "He told me he had his chance, he took the road to hell and there's nothing more to say."

. . . Few of Harris' friends or family were surprised that he ended up on Death Row. He had spent seven of the previous 10 years behind bars. Harris, who has an eighth-grade education, was convicted of car theft at 15 and was sentenced to a federal youth center. After being released, he was arrested twice for torturing animals and was convicted of manslaughter for beating a neighbor to death after a dispute.

Barbara Harris, another sister, talked to her brother at a family picnic on July 4, 1978. He had been out of prison less than six months, and his sister had not seen him in several years.

. . . Barbara Harris noticed his eyes, and she began to shudder. . . . "I thought, 'My God, what have they done to him?' He smiled, but his eyes were so cold, totally flat. It was like looking at a rattlesnake or a cobra ready to strike. They were hooded eyes, with nothing but meanness in them.

"He had the eyes of a killer. I told a friend that I knew someone else would die by his hand."

The next day, Robert Harris killed the two youths. Those familiar with the case were as mystified as they were outraged by Harris' actions. Most found it incomprehensible that a man could be so devoid of compassion and conscience that he could kill two youths, laugh about their deaths and then casually eat their hamburgers . . . .

. . . Harris is a dangerous man on the streets and a dangerous man behind bars, said Mroczko, who spent more than a year in the cell next to Harris'. . . .

"You don't want to deal with him out there," said Mroczko, ... "We don't want to deal with him in here."

During his first year on the row, Mroczko said, Harris was involved in several fights on the yard and was caught trying to supply a prisoner in an adjacent yard with a knife. During one fight, Harris was stabbed and the other prisoner was shot by a guard. He grated on people's nerves and one night he kept the whole cell block awake by banging his shoe on a steel water basin and laughing hysterically.

An encounter with Harris always resulted in a confrontation. If an inmate had cigarettes, or something else Harris wanted, and he did not think "you could hold your mud," Mroczko said, he would try to take them.

Harris was a man who just did not know "when to be cool," he said. He was an obnoxious presence in the yard and in his cell, and his behavior precipitated unwanted attention from the guards. . . .

He acted like a man who did not care about anything. His cell was filthy, Mroczko said, and clothes, trash, tobacco and magazines were scattered on the floor. He wore the same clothes every day and had little interest in showers. Harris spent his days watching television in his cell, occasionally reading a Western novel.[14]

On the face of it, Harris is an "archetypal candidate" for blame. We respond to his heartlessness and viciousness with moral outrage and loathing. Yet if reactive attitudes were implicitly "invitations to dialogue" (as Stern puts it), then Harris would be an inappropriate object of such attitudes. For he is hardly a potential moral interlocutor, "susceptible to the appeal of the principles from the standpoint of which one disapproves." In this instance, an invitation to dialogue would be met with icy silence (he has "nothing more to say") or murderous contempt.

However, not all communication is dialogue. Harris refuses dialogue, and this refusal is meant to make a point. It is in effect a repudiation of the moral community; he thereby declares himself a moral outlaw. Unlike the small child, or in a different way the psychopath, he exhibits an inversion of moral concern, not a lack of understanding. His ears are not deaf, but his heart is frozen. This characteristic, which makes him utterly unsuitable as a moral interlocutor, intensifies rather than inhibits the reactive attitudes. Harris's form of evil *consists* in part in being beyond the boundaries of moral community. Hence, if we are to appeal to the constraints on moral address to explain certain type-2 pleas, we must not include among these constraints comembership in the moral community or the significant possibility of dialogue—unless, that is, evil is to be its own exemption. At these outer limits, our reactive attitudes can be nothing more (or less) than a denunciation forlorn of the hope of an adequate reply.

The roots of evil

I said that Harris is an archetypal candidate for blame—so, at least, we react to him. Does it matter to our reactions how he came to be so? Strawson thinks so, for, among type-2 pleas, he includes "being unfortunate in formative circumstances." We must now investigate the relevance of such historical considerations to the reactive attitudes. As it happens, the case of Robert Harris is again a vivid illustration.

[During the interview] Barbara Harris put her palms over her eyes and said softly, "I saw every grain of sweetness, pity and goodness in him destroyed. . . . It was a long and ugly journey before he reached that point."

Robert Harris' 29 years . . . have been dominated by incessant cruelty and profound suffering that he has both experienced and provoked. Violence presaged his birth, and a violent act is expected to end his life.

Harris was born Jan. 15, 1953, several hours after his mother was kicked in the stomach. She was 6½ months pregnant and her husband, an insanely jealous man, . . . came home drunk and accused her of infidelity. He claimed that the child was not his, threw her down and kicked her. She began hemorrhaging, and he took her to the hospital.

Robert was born that night. His heartbeat stopped at one point . . . but labor was induced and he was saved. Because of the premature birth, he was a tiny baby; he was kept alive in an incubator and spent months at the hospital.

His father was an alcoholic who was twice convicted of sexually molesting his daughters. He frequently beat his children . . . and often caused serious injury. Their mother also became an alcoholic and was arrested several times, once for bank robbery.

All of the children had monstrous childhoods. But even in the Harris family, . . . the abuse Robert was subjected to was unusual.

Before their mother died last year, Barbara Harris said, she talked incessantly about Robert's early years. She felt guilty that she was never able to love him; she felt partly responsible that he ended up on Death Row.

When Robert's father visited his wife in the hospital and saw his son for the first time, . . . the first thing he said was, "Who is the father of that bastard?" When his mother picked him up from the hospital . . . she said it was like taking a stranger's baby home.

The pain and permanent injury Robert's mother suffered as a result of the birth, . . . and the constant abuse she was subjected to by her husband, turned her against her son. Money was tight, she was overworked and he was her fifth child in just a few years. She began to blame all of her problems on Robert, and she grew to hate the child.

"I remember one time we were in the car and Mother was in the back seat with Robbie

in her arms. He was crying and my father threw a glass bottle at him, but it hit my mother in the face. The glass shattered and Robbie started screaming. I'll never forget it," she said. . . .

"Her face was all pink, from the mixture of blood and milk. She ended up blaming Robbie for all the hurt, all the things like that. She felt helpless and he was someone to vent her anger on."

. . . Harris had a learning disability and a speech problem, but there was no money for therapy. When he was at school he felt stupid and classmates teased him, his sister said, and when he was at home he was abused.

"He was the most beautiful of all my mother's children; he was an angel," she said. "He would just break your heart. He wanted love so bad he would beg for any kind of physical contact.

"He'd come up to my mother and just try to rub his little hands on her leg or her arm. He just never got touched at all. She'd just push him away or kick him. One time she bloodied his nose when he was trying to get close to her."

Barbara Harris put her head in her hands and cried softly. "One killer out of nine kids. . . . The sad thing is he was the most sensitive of all of us. When he was 10 and we all saw 'Bambi,' he cried and cried when Bambi's mother was shot. Everything was pretty to him as a child; he loved animals. But all that changed; it all changed so much."

. . . All nine children are psychologically crippled as a result of their father, she said, but most have been able to lead useful lives. But Robert was too young, and the abuse lasted too long, she said, for him ever to have had a chance to recover.

[At age 14] Harris was sentenced to a federal youth detention center [for car theft]. He was one of the youngest inmates there, Barbara Harris said, and he grew up "hard and fast."

. . . Harris was raped several times, his sister said, and he slashed his wrists twice in suicide attempts. He spent more than four years behind bars as a result of an escape, an attempted escape and a parole violation.

The centers were "gladiator schools," Barbara Harris said, and Harris learned to fight and be mean. By the time he was released from federal prison at 19, all his problems were accentuated. Everyone in the family knew that he needed psychiatric help.

The child who had cried at the movies when Bambi's mother dies had evolved into a man who was arrested several times for abusing animals. He killed cats and dogs, Daniel said, and laughed while torturing them with mop handles, darts and pellet guns. Once he stabbed a prize pig more than 1,000 times.

"The only way he could vent his feelings was to break or kill something," Barbara Harris said. "He took out all the frustrations of his life on animals. He had no feeling for life, no sense of remorse. He reached the point where there wasn't that much left of him."

. . . Harris' family is ambivalent about his death sentence. [Another sister said that] if she did not know her brother's past so intimately, she would support his execution without hesitation. Barbara has a 16-year-old son; she often imagines the horror of the slain boys' parents.

"If anyone killed my son, I'd try my damnedest, no matter what it took, to have my child revenged," Barbara Harris said. "I know how those parents must suffer every day.

"But Robbie in the gas chamber. . . ." She broke off in mid-sentence and stared out a window. "Well, I still remember the little boy who used to beg for love, for just one pat or word of kindness. . . . No I can't say I want my brother to die."

. . . Since Harris has been on Death Row,

he has made no demands of time or money on his family. Harris has made only one request; he wants a dignified and serene ceremony after he dies—a ceremony in marked contrast to his life.

He has asked his oldest brother to take his ashes, to drive to the Sierra, hike to a secluded spot and scatter his remains in the trees.[15]

No doubt this history gives pause to the reactive attitudes. Why does it do so? "No wonder Harris is as he is!" we think. What is the relevance of this thought?

Note, to begin with, that the story in no way undermines the judgments that he is brutal, vicious, heartless, mean.[16] Rather, it provides a kind of explanation for his being so. Can the expressive theory explain why the reactive attitudes should be sensitive to such an explanation?

Strawson's general rubric for type-2 pleas (or the subgroup in which this plea is classified) is "being incapacitated for ordinary interpersonal relationships." Does Harris have some independently identifiable incapacity for which his biography provides evidence? Apparently, he *is* incapacitated for such relationships—for example, for friendship, for sympathy, for being affected by moral considerations. To be homicidally hateful and callous in Harris's way is to lack moral concern, and to lack moral concern is to be incapacitated for moral community. However, to exempt Harris on these grounds is problematic. For then everyone who is evil in Harris's way will be exempt, independently of facts about their background. But we had ample evidence about this incapacity before we learned of his childhood misfortunes, and that did not affect the reactive attitudes. Those misfortunes affect our responses in a special and nonevidential way. The question is why this should be so.

This would seem to be a hard question for compatibilist views generally. What matters is whether, in one version, the practice of holding responsible can be efficacious as a means of social regulation, or whether, using the expressive theory, the conditions of moral address are met. These questions would seem to be settled by how individuals *are*, not by how they came to be. Facts about background would be, at most, evidence that some other plea is satisfied. In themselves, they would not seem to matter.

A plea of this kind is, on the other hand, grist for the incompatibilists' mill. For they will insist on an essential historical dimension to the concept of responsibility. Harris's history reveals him to be an inevitable product of his formative circumstances. And seeing him as a product is inconsistent with seeing him as a responsible agent. If his cruel attitudes and conduct are the inevitable result of his circumstances, then he is not responsible for them, unless he was responsible for those circumstances. It is this principle that gives the historical dimension of responsibility and of course entails the incompatibility of determinism and responsibility.

In this instance, however, an incompatibilist diagnosis seems doubtful. In the first place, our response to the case is not the simple suspension of reactive attitudes that this diagnosis would lead one to expect, but ambivalence. In the second place, the force of the example does not depend on a belief in the *inevitability* of the upshot. Nothing in the story supports such a belief. The thought is not "It had to be!" but, again, "No wonder!"

Sympathy and antipathy

How and why, then, does this larger view of Harris's life in fact affect us? It is too simple to say that it leads us to suspend our reactive attitudes. Our response is too complicated and conflicted for that. What appears to happen is that we are unable to command an overall view of his life that permits the reactive attitudes to be sustained without ambivalence. That is because the biography forces us to see him as a *victim*, and so seeing him does not sit well with the reactive attitudes that are so strongly elicited by

Harris's character and conduct. Seeing him as a victim does not totally dispel those attitudes. Rather, in light of the "whole" story, conflicting responses are evoked. The sympathy toward the boy he was is at odds with outrage toward the man he is. These responses conflict not in the way that fear dispels anger, but in the way that sympathy is opposed to antipathy. In fact, each of these responses is appropriate, but taken together they do not enable us to respond overall in a coherent way.

Harris both satisfies and violates the criteria of victimhood. His childhood abuse was a misfortune inflicted upon him against his will. But at the same time (and this is part of his very misfortune) he unambivalently endorses suffering, death, and destruction, and that is what (one form of) evil is. With this in focus, we see him as a victimizer and respond to him accordingly. The ambivalence results from the fact that an overall view simultaneously demands and precludes regarding him as a victim.

What we have here is not exactly a clash between what Thomas Nagel has called the objective and subjective standpoints.[17] It is not that from the more comprehensive viewpoint that reveals Harris as a victim, his responsibility is indiscernible. Rather, the clash occurs within a single point of view that reveals Harris as evil (and hence calling for enmity and moral opposition) and as one who is a victim (calling for sympathy and understanding). Harris's misfortune is such that scarcely a vestige remains of his earlier sensibilities. Hence, unless one knew Harris as a child or keeps his earlier self vividly in mind, sympathy can scarcely find a purchase.

Moral luck and moral equality

However, what is arresting about the Harris case is not just the clash between sympathy and antipathy. The case is troubling in a more personal way. The fact that Harris's cruelty is an intelligible response to his circumstances gives a foothold not only for sympathy, but for the

thought that if I had been subjected to such circumstances, I might well have become as vile. What is unsettling is the thought that one's moral self is such a fragile thing. One tends to think of one's moral sensibilities as going deeper than that (though it is not clear what this means). This thought induces not only an onto-logical shudder, but a sense of equality with the other: I too am a potential sinner.[18]

This point is merely the obverse of the point about sympathy. Whereas the point about sympathy focuses on our empathetic response to the other, the thought about moral luck turns one's gaze inward. It makes one feel less in a position to cast blame. The fact that my potential for evil has not been nearly so fully actualized is, for all I know, something for which I cannot take credit. The awareness that, in this respect, the others are or may be like oneself clashes with the distancing effect of enmity.

Admittedly, it is hard to know what to do with this conclusion. Equality of moral potential does not, of course, mean that Harris is not actu-ally a vile man; on the contrary, it means that in similar circumstances I would have become vile as well. Since he is an evil man, we cannot and should not treat him as we would a rabid dog. The awareness of moral luck, however, taints one's own view of one's moral self as an achieve-ment, and infuses one's reactive attitudes with a sense of irony. Only those who have survived circumstances such as those that ravaged Harris are in a good position to know what they would have done. We lucky ones can only wonder. As a product of reflection, this attitude is, of course, easily lost when the knife is at one's own throat.

• • •

Postscript to 'Responsibility and the Limits of Evil' (Added 2004)

Robert Harris, often described in the media as the 'laughing killer', didn't get the last laugh. That went to some of the witnesses of his execu-tion at San Quentin Prison on 21 April, 1992.

Chapter 57

Thomas Nagel

MORAL LUCK

Kant believed that good or bad luck should influence neither our moral judgment of a person and his actions, nor his moral assessment of himself.

> The good will is not good because of what it effects or accomplishes or because of its adequacy to achieve some proposed end; it is good only because of its willing, i.e., it is good of itself. And, regarded for itself, it is to be esteemed incomparably higher than anything which could be brought about by it in favor of any inclination or even of the sum total of all inclinations. Even if it should happen that, by a particular unfortunate fate or by the niggardly provision of a step-motherly nature, this will should be wholly lacking in power to accomplish its purpose, and if even the greatest effort should not avail it to achieve anything of its end, and if there remained only the good will (not as a mere wish but as the summoning of all the means in our power), it would sparkle like a jewel in its own right, as something that had its full worth in itself. Usefulness or fruitlessness can neither diminish nor augment this worth.[1]

He would presumably have said the same about a bad will: whether it accomplishes its evil purposes is morally irrelevant. And a course of action that would be condemned if it had a bad outcome cannot be vindicated if by luck it turns out well. There cannot be moral risk. This view seems to be wrong, but it arises in response to a fundamental problem about moral responsibility to which we possess no satisfactory solution.

The problem develops out of the ordinary conditions of moral judgment. Prior to reflection it is intuitively plausible that people cannot be morally assessed for what is not their fault, or for what is due to factors beyond their control. Such judgment is different from the evaluation of something as a good or bad thing, or state of affairs. The latter may be present in addition to moral judgment, but when we blame someone for his actions we are not merely saying it is bad that they happened, or bad that he exists: we are judging him, saying he is bad, which is different from his being a bad thing. This kind of judgment takes only a certain kind of object. Without being able to explain exactly why, we feel that the appropriateness of moral assessment is easily undermined by the discovery that the act or attribute, no matter how good or bad, is not under the person's control. While other evaluations remain, this one seems to lose its footing. So a clear absence of control, produced by involuntary movement, physical force, or ignorance of the circumstances, excuses what is done from moral judgment. But what we do depends in many more ways than these on what is not under our control—what is not produced by a

good or a bad will, in Kant's phrase. And external influences in this broader range are not usually thought to excuse what is done from moral judgment, positive or negative.

Let me give a few examples, beginning with the type of case Kant has in mind. Whether we succeed or fail in what we try to do nearly always depends to some extent on factors beyond our control. This is true of murder, altruism, revolution, the sacrifice of certain interests for the sake of others—almost any morally important act. What has been done, and what is morally judged, is partly determined by external factors. However jewel-like the good will may be in its own right, there is a morally significant difference between rescuing someone from a burning building and dropping him from a twelfth-story window while trying to rescue him. Similarly, there is a morally significant difference between reckless driving and manslaughter. But whether a reckless driver hits a pedestrian depends on the presence of the pedestrian at the point where he recklessly passes a red light. What we do is also limited by the opportunities and choices with which we are faced, and these are largely determined by factors beyond our control. Someone who was an officer in a concentration camp might have led a quiet and harmless life if the Nazis had never come to power in Germany. And someone who led a quiet and harmless life in Argentina might have become an officer in a concentration camp if he had not left Germany for business reasons in 1930.

I shall say more later about these and other examples. I introduce them here to illustrate a general point. Where a significant aspect of what someone does depends on factors beyond his control, yet we continue to treat him in that respect as an object of moral judgment, it can be called moral luck. Such luck can be good or bad. And the problem posed by this phenomenon, which led Kant to deny its possibility, is that the broad range of external influences here identified seems on close examination to undermine moral assessment as surely as does the narrower range of familiar excusing conditions. If the condition of control is consistently applied, it threatens to erode most of the moral assessments we find it natural to make. The things for which people are morally judged are determined in more ways than we at first realize by what is beyond their control. And when the seemingly natural requirement of fault or responsibility is applied in light of these facts, it leaves few pre-reflective moral judgments intact. Ultimately, nothing or almost nothing about what a person does seems to be under his control.

Why not conclude, then, that the condition of control is false—that it is an initially plausible hypothesis refuted by clear counter-examples? One could in that case look instead for a more refined condition which picked out the *kinds of* lack of control that really undermine certain moral judgments, without yielding the unacceptable conclusion derived from the broader condition, that most or all ordinary moral judgments are illegitimate.

What rules out this escape is that we are dealing not with a theoretical conjecture but with a philosophical problem. The condition of control does not suggest itself merely as a generalization from certain clear cases. It seems *correct* in the further cases to which it is extended beyond the original set. When we undermine moral assessment by considering new ways in which control is absent, we are not just discovering what *would* follow given the general hypothesis, but are actually being persuaded that in itself the absence of control is relevant in these cases too. The erosion of moral judgment emerges not as the absurd consequence of an over-simple theory, but as a natural consequence of the ordinary idea of moral assessment, when it is applied in view of a more complete and precise account of the facts. It would therefore be a mistake to argue from the unacceptability of the conclusions to the need for a different account of the conditions of moral responsibility. The view that moral luck is

paradoxical is not a *mistake*, ethical or logical, but a perception of one of the ways in which the intuitively acceptable conditions of moral judgment threaten to undermine it all.

It resembles the situation in another area of philosophy, the theory of knowledge. There too conditions which seem perfectly natural, and which grow out of the ordinary procedures for challenging and defending claims to knowledge, threaten to undermine all such claims if consistently applied. Most skeptical arguments have this quality: they do not depend on the imposition of arbitrarily stringent standards of knowledge, arrived at by misunderstanding, but appear to grow inevitably from the consistent application of ordinary standards.[2] There is a substantive parallel as well, for epistemological skepticism arises from consideration of the respects in which our beliefs and their relation to reality depend on factors beyond our control. External and internal causes produce our beliefs. We may subject these processes to scrutiny in an effort to avoid error, but our conclusions at this next level also result, in part, from influences which we do not control directly. The same will be true no matter how far we carry the investigation. Our beliefs are always, ultimately, due to factors outside our control, and the impossibility of encompassing those factors without being at the mercy of others leads us to doubt whether we know anything. It looks as though, if any of our beliefs are true, it is pure biological luck rather than knowledge.

Moral luck is like this because while there are various respects in which the natural objects of moral assessment are out of our control or influenced by what is out of our control, we cannot reflect on these facts without losing our grip on the judgments.

There are roughly four ways in which the natural objects of moral assessment are disturbingly subject to luck. One is the phenomenon of constitutive luck—the kind of person you are, where this is not just a question of what you deliberately do, but of your inclinations,

capacities, and temperament. Another category is luck in one's circumstances—the kind of problems and situations one faces. The other two have to do with the causes and effects of action: luck is how one is determined by antecedent circumstances, and luck in the way one's actions and projects turn out. All of them present a common problem. They are all opposed by the idea that one cannot be more culpable or estimable for anything than one is for that fraction of it which is under one's control. It seems irrational to take or dispense credit or blame for matters over which a person has no control, or for their influence on results over which he has partial control. Such things may create the conditions for action, but action can be judged only to the extent that it goes beyond these conditions and does not just result from them.

Let us first consider luck, good and bad, in the way things turn out. Kant, in the above-quoted passage, has one example of this in mind, but the category covers a wide range. It includes the truck driver who accidentally runs over a child, the artist who abandons his wife and five children to devote himself to painting,[3] and other cases in which the possibilities of success and failure are even greater. The driver, if he is entirely without fault, will feel terrible about his role in the event, but will not have to reproach himself. Therefore this example of agent-regret[4] is not yet a case of *moral* bad luck. However, if the driver was guilty of even a minor degree of negligence—failing to have his brakes checked recently, for example—then if that negligence contributes to the death of the child, he will not merely feel terrible. He will blame himself for the death. And what makes this an example of moral luck is that he would have to blame himself only slightly for the negligence itself if no situation arose which required him to brake suddenly and violently to avoid hitting a child. Yet the *negligence* is the same in both cases, and the driver has no control over whether a child will run into his path.

The same is true at higher levels of negligence. If someone has had too much to drink

and his car swerves onto the sidewalk, he can count himself morally lucky if there are no pedestrians in its path. If there were, he would be to blame for their deaths, and would probably be prosecuted for manslaughter. But if he hurts no one, although his recklessness is exactly the same, he is guilty of a far less serious legal offense and will certainly reproach himself and be reproached by others much less severely. To take another legal example, the penalty for attempted murder is less than that for successful murder—however similar the intentions and motives of the assailant may be in the two cases. His degree of culpability can depend, it would seem, on whether the victim happened to be wearing a bullet-proof vest, or whether a bird flew into the path of the bullet—matters beyond his control.

Finally, there are cases of decision under uncertainty—common in public and in private life. Anna Karenina goes off with Vronsky, Gauguin leaves his family, Chamberlain signs the Munich agreement, the Decembrists persuade the troops under their command to revolt against the czar, the American colonies declare their independence from Britain, you introduce two people in an attempt at match-making. It is tempting in all such cases to feel that some decision must be possible, in the light of what is known at the time, which will make reproach unsuitable no matter how things turn out. But this is not true; when someone acts in such ways he takes his life, or his moral position, into his hands, because how things turn out determines what he has done. It is possible *also* to assess the decision from the point of view of what could be known at the time, but this is not the end of the story. If the Decembrists had succeeded in overthrowing Nicholas I in 1825 and establishing a constitutional regime, they would be heroes. As it is, not only did they fail and pay for it but they bore some responsibility for the terrible punishments meted out to the troops who had been persuaded to follow them. If the American Revolution had been a bloody failure resulting in greater repression, then Jefferson, Franklin and Washington would still have made a noble attempt, and might not even have regretted it on their way to the scaffold, but they would also have had to blame themselves for what they had helped to bring on their compatriots. (Perhaps peaceful efforts at reform would eventually have succeeded.) If Hitler had not overrun Europe and exterminated millions, but instead had died of a heart attack after occupying the Sudetenland, Chamberlain's action at Munich would still have utterly betrayed the Czechs, but it would not be the great moral disaster that has made his name a household word.[5]

In many cases of difficult choice the outcome cannot be foreseen with certainty. One kind of assessment of the choice is possible in advance, but another kind must await the outcome, because the outcome determines what has been done. The same degree of culpability or estimability in intention, motive, or concern is compatible with a wide range of judgments, positive or negative, depending on what happened beyond the point of decision. The *mens rea* which could have existed in the absence of any consequences does not exhaust the grounds of moral judgment. Actual results influence culpability or esteem in a large class of unquestionably ethical cases ranging from negligence through political choice.

That these are genuine moral judgments rather than expressions of temporary attitude is evident from the fact that one can say *in advance* how the moral verdict will depend on the results. If one negligently leaves the bath running with the baby in it, one will realize, as one bounds up the stairs toward the bathroom, that if the baby has drowned one has done something awful, whereas if it has not one has merely been careless. Someone who launches a violent revolution against an authoritarian regime knows that if he fails he will be responsible for much suffering that is in vain, but if he succeeds he will be justified by the outcome. I do not mean that *any* action can be retroactively justified by history. Certain things are so bad in

themselves, or so risky, that no results can make them all right. Nevertheless, when moral judgment does depend on the outcome, it is objective and timeless and not dependent on a change of standpoint produced by success or failure. The judgment after the fact follows from an hypothetical judgment that can be made beforehand, and it can be made as easily by someone else as by the agent.

From the point of view which makes responsibility dependent on control, all this seems absurd. How is it possible to be more or less culpable depending on whether a child gets into the path of one's car, or a bird into the path of one's bullet? Perhaps it is true that what is done depends on more than the agent's state of mind or intention. The problem then is, why is it not irrational to base moral assessment on what people do, in this broad sense? It amounts to holding them responsible for the contributions of fate as well as for their own—provided they have made some contributions to begin with. If we look at cases of negligence or attempt, the pattern seems to be that overall culpability corresponds to the product of mental or intentional fault and the seriousness of the outcome. Cases of decision under uncertainty are less easily explained in this way, for it seems that the overall judgment can even shift from positive to negative depending on the outcome. But here too it seems rational to subtract the effects of occurrences subsequent to the choice, that were merely possible at the time, and concentrate moral assessment on the actual decision in light of the probabilities. If the object of moral judgment is the *person*, then to hold him accountable for what he has done in the broader sense is akin to strict liability, which may have its legal uses but seems irrational as a moral position.

The result of such a line of thought is to pare down each act to its morally essential core, an inner act of pure will assessed by motive and intention. Adam Smith advocates such a position in *The Theory of Moral Sentiments*, but notes that it runs contrary to our actual judgments.

But how well soever we may seem to be persuaded of the truth of this equitable maxim, when we consider it after this manner, in abstract, yet when we come to particular cases, the actual consequences which happen to proceed from any action, have a very great effect upon our sentiments concerning its merit or demerit, and almost always either enhance or diminish our sense of both. Scarce, in any one instance, perhaps, will our sentiments be found, after examination, to be entirely regulated by this rule, which we all acknowledge ought entirely to regulate them.[6]

Joel Feinberg points out further that restricting the domain of moral responsibility to the inner world will not immunize it to luck. Factors beyond the agent's control, like a coughing fit, can interfere with his decisions as surely as they can with the path of a bullet from his gun.[7] Nevertheless the tendency to cut down the scope of moral assessment is pervasive, and does not limit itself to the influence of effects. It attempts to isolate the will from the other direction, so to speak, by separating out constitutive luck. Let us consider that next.

Kant was particularly insistent on the moral irrelevance of qualities of temperament and personality that are not under the control of the will. Such qualities as sympathy or coldness might provide the background against which obedience to moral requirements is more or less difficult, but they could not be objects of moral assessment themselves, and might well interfere with confident assessment of its proper object— the determination of the will by the motive of duty. This rules out moral judgment of many of the virtues and vices, which are states of character that influence choice but are certainly not exhausted by dispositions to act deliberately in certain ways. A person may be greedy, envious, cowardly, cold, ungenerous, unkind, vain, or conceited, but *behave* perfectly by a monumental effort of will. To possess these vices is to be

unable to help having certain feelings under certain circumstances, and to have strong spontaneous impulses to act badly. Even if one controls the impulses, one still has the vice. An envious person hates the greater success of others. He can be morally condemned as envious even if he congratulates them cordially and does nothing to denigrate or spoil their success. Conceit, likewise, need not be displayed. It is fully present in someone who cannot help dwelling with secret satisfaction on the superiority of his own achievements, talents, beauty, intelligence, or virtue. To some extent such a quality may be the product of earlier choices; to some extent it may be amenable to change by current actions. But it is largely a matter of constitutive bad fortune. Yet people are morally condemned for such qualities, and esteemed for others equally beyond control of the will: they are assessed for what they are like.

To Kant this seems incoherent because virtue is enjoined on everyone and therefore must in principle be possible for everyone. It may be easier for some than for others, but it must be possible to achieve it by making the right choices, against whatever temperamental background.[8] One may want to have a generous spirit, or regret not having one, but it makes no sense to condemn oneself or anyone else for a quality which is not within the control of the will. Condemnation implies that you should not be like that, not that it is unfortunate that you are.

Nevertheless, Kant's conclusion remains intuitively unacceptable. We may be persuaded that these moral judgments are irrational, but they reappear involuntarily as soon as the argument is over. This is the pattern throughout the subject.

The third category to consider is luck in one's circumstances, and I shall mention it briefly. The things we are called upon to do, the moral tests we face, are importantly determined by factors beyond our control. It may be true of someone that in a dangerous situation he would behave in a cowardly or heroic fashion, but if the situation never arises, he will never have the chance to distinguish or disgrace himself in this way, and his moral record will be different.[9]

A conspicuous example of this is political. Ordinary citizens of Nazi Germany had an opportunity to behave heroically by opposing the regime. They also had an opportunity to behave badly, and most of them are culpable for having failed this test. But it is a test to which the citizens of other countries were not subjected, with the result that even if they, or some of them, would have behaved as badly as the Germans in like circumstances, they simply did not and therefore are not similarly culpable. Here again one is morally at the mercy of fate, and it may seem irrational upon reflection, but our ordinary moral attitudes would be unrecognizable without it. We judge people for what they actually do or fail to do, not just for what they would have done if circumstances had been different.[10]

This form of moral determination by the actual is also paradoxical, but we can begin to see how deep in the concept of responsibility the paradox is embedded. A person can be morally responsible only for what he does; but what he does results from a great deal that he does not do; therefore he is not morally responsible for what he is and is not responsible for. (This is not a contradiction, but it is a paradox.)

It should be obvious that there is a connection between these problems about responsibility and control and an even more familiar problem, that of freedom of the will. That is the last type of moral luck I want to take up, though I can do no more within the scope of this essay than indicate its connection with the other types.

If one cannot be responsible for consequences of one's acts due to factors beyond one's control, or for antecedents of one's acts that are properties of temperament not subject to one's will, or for the circumstances that pose one's moral choices, then how can one be responsible

even for the stripped-down acts of the will itself, if they are the product of antecedent circumstances outside of the will's control?

The area of genuine agency, and therefore of legitimate moral judgment, seems to shrink under this scrutiny to an extensionless point. Everything seems to result from the combined influence of factors, antecedent and posterior to action, that are not within the agent's control. Since he cannot be responsible for them, he cannot be responsible for their results—though it may remain possible to take up the aesthetic or other evaluative analogues of the moral attitudes that are thus displaced.

It is also possible, of course, to brazen it out and refuse to accept the results, which indeed seem unacceptable as soon as we stop thinking about the arguments. Admittedly, if certain surrounding circumstances had been different, then no unfortunate consequences would have followed from a wicked intention, and no seriously culpable act would have been performed; but since the circumstances were not different, and the agent in fact succeeded in perpetrating a particularly cruel murder, that is what he did, and that is what he is responsible for. Similarly, we may admit that if certain antecedent circumstances had been different, the agent would never have developed into the sort of person who would do such a thing; but since he did develop (as the inevitable result of those antecedent circumstances) into the sort of swine he is, and into the person who committed such a murder, that is what he is blameable for. In both cases one is responsible for what one actually does—even if what one actually does depends in important ways on what is not within one's control. This compatibilist account of our moral judgments would leave room for the ordinary conditions of responsibility—the absence of coercion, ignorance, or involuntary movement—as part of the determination of what someone has done—but it is understood not to exclude the influence of a great deal that he has not done.[11]

The only thing wrong with this solution is its failure to explain how skeptical problems arise. For they arise not from the imposition of an arbitrary external requirement, but from the nature of moral judgment itself. Something in the ordinary idea of what someone does must explain how it can seem necessary to subtract from it anything that merely happens—even though the ultimate consequence of such subtraction is that nothing remains. And something in the ordinary idea of knowledge must explain why it seems to be undermined by any influences on belief not within the control of the subject—so that knowledge seems impossible without an impossible foundation in autonomous reason. But let us leave epistemology aside and concentrate on action, character, and moral assessment.

The problem arises, I believe, because the self which acts and is the object of moral judgment is threatened with dissolution by the absorption of its acts and impulses into the class of events. Moral judgment of a person is a judgment not of what happens to him, but of him. It does not say merely that a certain event or state of affairs is fortunate or unfortunate or even terrible. It is not an evaluation of a state of the world, or of an individual as part of the world. We are not thinking just that it would be better if he were different, or did not exist, or had not done some of the things he has done. We are judging him, rather than his existence or characteristics. The effect of concentrating on the influence of what is not under his control is to make this responsible self seem to disappear, swallowed up by the order of mere events.

What, however, do we have in mind that a person must be to be the object of these moral attitudes? While the concept of agency is easily undermined, it is very difficult to give it a positive characterization. That is familiar from the literature on Free Will.

I believe that in a sense the problem has no solution, because something in the idea of

agency is incompatible with actions being events, or people being things. But as the external determinants of what someone has done are gradually exposed, in their effect on consequences, character, and choice itself, it becomes gradually clear that actions are events and people things. Eventually nothing remains which can be ascribed to the responsible self, and we are left with nothing but a portion of the larger sequence of events, which can be deplored or celebrated, but not blamed or praised.

Though I cannot define the idea of the active self that is thus undermined, it is possible to say something about its sources. There is a close connection between our feelings about ourselves and our feelings about others. Guilt and indignation, shame and contempt, pride and admiration are internal and external sides of the same moral attitudes. We are unable to view ourselves simply as portions of the world, and from inside we have a rough idea of the boundary between what is us and what is not, what we do and what happens to us, what is our personality and what is an accidental handicap. We apply the same essentially internal conception of the self to others. About ourselves we feel pride, shame, guilt, remorse—and agent-regret. We do not regard our actions and our characters merely as fortunate or unfortunate episodes—though they may also be that. We cannot *simply* take an external evaluative view of ourselves—of what we most essentially are and what we do. And this remains true even when we have seen that we are not responsible for our own existence, or our nature, or the choices we have to make, or the circumstances that give our acts the consequences they have. Those acts remain ours and we remain ourselves, despite the persuasiveness of the reasons that seem to argue us out of existence.

It is this internal view that we extend to others in moral judgment—when we judge *them* rather than their desirability or utility. We extend to others the refusal to limit ourselves to

external evaluation, and we accord to them selves like our own. But in both cases this comes up against the brutal inclusion of humans and everything about them in a world from which they cannot be separated and of which they are nothing but contents. The external view forces itself on us at the same time that we resist it. One way this occurs is through the gradual erosion of what we do by the subtraction of what happens.[12]

The inclusion of consequences in the conception of what we have done is an acknowledgment that we are parts of the world, but the paradoxical character of moral luck which emerges from this acknowledgment shows that we are unable to operate with such a view, for it leaves us with no one to be. The same thing is revealed in the appearance that determinism obliterates responsibility. Once we see an aspect of what we or someone else does as something that happens, we lose our grip on the idea that it has been done and that we can judge the doer and not just the happening. This explains why the absence of determinism is no more hospitable to the concept of agency than is its presence—a point that has been noticed often. Either way the act is viewed externally, as part of the course of events.

The problem of moral luck cannot be understood without an account of the internal conception of agency and its special connection with the moral attitudes as opposed to other types of value. I do not have such an account. The degree to which the problem has a solution can be determined only by seeing whether in some degree the incompatibility between this conception and the various ways in which we do not control what we do is only apparent. I have nothing to offer on that topic either. But it is not enough to say merely that our basic moral attitudes toward ourselves and others are determined by what is actual; for they are also threatened by the sources of that actuality, and by the external view of action which forces itself on us when we see

how everything we do belongs to a world that we have not created.

Notes

1 *Foundations of the Metaphysics of Morals*, first section, third paragraph.

2 See Thompson Clark, 'The Legacy of Skepticism', *Journal of Philosophy*, LXIX, no. 20 (November 9, 1972), 754–69.

3 Such a case, modelled on the life of Gauguin, is discussed by Bernard Williams in 'Moral Luck,' *Proceedings of the Aristotelian Society*, supplementary vol. L (1976), 115–35 (to which the original version of this essay was a reply). He points out that though success or failure cannot be predicted in advance, Gauguin's most basic retrospective feelings about the decision will be determined by the development of his talent. My disagreement with Williams is that his account fails to explain why such retrospective attitudes can be called moral. If success does not permit Gauguin to justify himself to others, but still determines his most basic feelings, that shows only that his most basic feelings need not be moral. It does not show that morality is subject to luck. If the retrospective judgment were moral, it would imply the truth of a hypothetical judgment made in advance, of the form 'If I leave my family and become a great painter, I will be justified by success; if I don't become a great painter, the act will be unforgivable.'

4 Williams' term (*ibid.*).

5 For a fascinating but morally repellent discussion of the topic of justification by history, see Maurice Merleau-Ponty, *Humanisme et Terreur* (Paris: Gallimard, 1947), translated as *Humanism and Terror* (Boston: Beacon Press, 1969).

6 Pt II, sect. 3, Introduction, para. 5.

7 'Problematic Responsibility in Law and Morals', in Joel Feinberg, *Doing and Deserving* (Princeton, NJ: Princeton University Press, 1970).

8 'If nature has put little sympathy in the heart of a man, and if he, though an honest man, is by temperament cold and indifferent to the sufferings of others; perhaps because he is provided with special gifts of patience and fortitude and expects or even requires that others should have the same—and such a man would certainly not be the meanest product of nature—would not he find in himself a source from which to give himself a far higher worth than he could have got by having a good-natured temperament?' (*Foundations of the Metaphysics of Morals*, first section, eleventh paragraph).

9 Cf. Thomas Gray, 'Elegy Written in a Country Churchyard':

> Some mute inglorious Milton here may rest,
> Some Cromwell, guiltless of his country's blood.

An unusual example of circumstantial moral luck is provided by the kind of moral dilemma with which someone can be faced through no fault of his own, but which leaves him with nothing to do which is not wrong. . . . Bernard Williams, 'Ethical Consistency', *Proceedings of the Aristotelian Society*, supplementary vol. xxxix (1965), reprinted in *Problems of the Self* (Cambridge: Cambridge University Press, 1973), pp. 166–86.

10 Circumstantial luck can extend to aspects of the situation other than individual behavior. For example, during the Vietnam War even U.S. citizens who had opposed their country's actions vigorously from the start often felt compromised by its crimes. Here they were not even responsible; there was probably nothing they could do to stop what was happening, so the feeling of being implicated may seem unintelligible. But it is nearly impossible to view the crimes of one's own country in the same way that one views the crimes of another country, no matter how equal one's lack of power to stop them in the two cases. One is a citizen of one of them, and has a connection with its actions (even if only through taxes that cannot be withheld)—that one does not have with the other's. This makes it possible to be ashamed of one's country, and to feel a victim of moral bad luck that one was an American in the 1960s.

11 The corresponding position in epistemology would be that knowledge consists of true beliefs formed in certain ways, and that it does not require all aspects of the process to be under the knower's control, actually or potentially. Both the correctness of these beliefs and the process by which they are arrived at would therefore be importantly subject to luck. The Nobel Prize is not

awarded to people who turn out to be wrong, no matter how brilliant their reasoning.

12 See P. F. Strawson's discussion of the conflict between the objective attitude and personal reactive attitudes in 'Freedom and Resentment', *Proceedings of the British Academy*, 1962, reprinted in *Studies in the Philosophy of Thought and Action*, ed. P. F. Strawson (London: Oxford University Press, 1968), and in P. F. Strawson, *Freedom and Resentment and Other Essays* (London: Methuen, 1974).

Shaun Nichols and Joshua Knobe

MORAL RESPONSIBILITY AND DETERMINISM: THE COGNITIVE SCIENCE OF FOLK INTUITIONS

1. Introduction

THE DISPUTE between compatibilists and incompatibilists must be one of the most persistent and heated deadlocks in Western philosophy. Incompatibilists maintain that people are not fully morally responsible if determinism is true, that is, if every event is an inevitable consequence of the prior conditions and the natural laws. By contrast, compatibilists maintain that even if determinism is true, our moral responsibility is not undermined in the slightest, for determinism and moral responsibility are perfectly consistent.[1]

The debate between these two positions has invoked many different resources, including quantum mechanics, social psychology, and basic metaphysics. But recent discussions have relied heavily on arguments that draw on people's intuitions about particular cases. Some philosophers have claimed that people have incompatibilist intuitions (e.g., Kane 1999, 218; Strawson 1986, 30; Vargas 2006); others have challenged this claim and suggested that people's intuitions actually fit with compatibilism (Nahmias et al. 2005). But although philosophers have constructed increasingly sophisticated arguments about the implications of people's intuitions, there has been remarkably little discussion about *why* people have the intuitions they do. That is to say, relatively little has been said about the specific psychological processes that generate or sustain people's intuitions. And yet, it seems clear that

questions about the sources of people's intuitions could have a major impact on debates about the compatibility of responsibility and determinism. There is an obvious sense in which it is important to figure out whether people's intuitions are being produced by a process that is generally reliable or whether they are being distorted by a process that generally leads people astray.

Our aim here is to present and defend a hypothesis about the processes that generate people's intuitions concerning moral responsibility. Our hypothesis is that people have an incompatibilist theory of moral responsibility that is elicited in some contexts but that they also have psychological mechanisms that can lead them to arrive at compatibilist judgments in other contexts.[2] To support this hypothesis, we report new experimental data. These data show that people's responses to questions about moral responsibility can vary dramatically depending on the way in which the question is formulated. When asked questions that call for a more abstract, theoretical sort of cognition, people give overwhelmingly incompatibilist answers. But when asked questions that trigger emotions, their answers become far more compatibilist.

2. Affect, blame, and the attribution of responsibility

In their attempts to get a handle on folk concepts and folk theories, naturalistic philosophers have

proceeded by looking at people's intuitions about particular cases (e.g., Knobe 2003a, 2003b; Nahmias et al. 2005; Nichols 2004a; Weinberg et al. 2001; Woolfolk et al. 2006). The basic technique is simple. The philosopher constructs a hypothetical scenario and then asks people whether, for instance, the agent in the scenario is morally responsible. By varying the details of the case and checking to see how people's intuitions are affected, one can gradually get a sense for the contours of the folk theory. This method is a good one, but it must be practiced with care. One cannot simply assume that all of the relevant intuitions are generated by the same underlying folk theory. It is always possible that different intuitions will turn out to have been generated by different psychological processes.

Here we will focus especially on the role of *affect* in generating intuitions about moral responsibility. Our hypothesis is that when people are confronted with a story about an agent who performs a morally bad behavior, this can trigger an immediate emotional response, and this emotional response can play a crucial role in their intuitions about whether the agent was morally responsible. In fact, people may sometimes declare such an agent to be morally responsible despite the fact that they embrace a theory of responsibility on which the agent is not responsible.

Consider, for example, Watson's (1987) interesting discussion of the crimes of Robert Harris. Watson provides long quotations from a newspaper article about how Harris savagely murdered innocent people, showing no remorse for what he had done. Then he describes, in equally chilling detail, the horrible abuse Harris had to endure as he was growing up. After reading all of these vivid details, it would be almost impossible for a reader to respond by calmly working out the implications of his or her theory of moral responsibility. Any normal reader will have a rich array of reactions, including not only abstract theorizing but also feelings of horror and disgust. A reader's intuitions about such a case might be swayed by her emotions, leaving her with a conclusion that contravened her more abstract, theoretical beliefs about the nature of moral responsibility.

Still, it might be thought that this sort of effect would be unlikely to influence people's reactions to ordinary philosophical examples. Most philosophical examples are purely hypothetical and thinly described (often only a few sentences in length). To a first glance at least, it might seem that emotional reactions are unlikely to have any impact on people's intuitions about examples like these. But a growing body of experimental evidence indicates that this commonsense view is mistaken. This evidence suggests that affect plays an important role even in people's intuitions about thinly described, purely hypothetical cases (Blair 1995; Greene et al. 2001; Nichols 2002; Haidt et al. 1993).

It may seem puzzling that affect should play such a powerful role, and a number of different models of the role of emotion in evaluative thought have been proposed. We will discuss some of these models in further detail in sections 5, 6, and 7. In the meantime, we want to point to one factor that appears to influence people's affective reactions. A recent study by Smart and Loewenstein (2005) shows that when a transgressor is made more 'determinate' for subjects, subjects experience greater negative affect and are more punitive toward that agent as a result. In the study, subjects play a game in which they can privately cooperate or defect. Each subject is assigned an identifying number, but none of the subjects knows anyone else's number. The experimenter puts the numbers of the defectors into an envelope. The cooperators are subsequently allowed to decide whether to penalize a defector. The cooperator is informed that he will pick a number out of the envelope to determine which defector will be penalized (or not). The manipulation was unbelievably subtle. In the *indeterminate* condition, subjects decide how much to penalize *before* they draw the number; in the *determinate*

condition, subjects decide how much to penalize *after* they draw the number. Despite this tiny difference, Smart and Loewenstein found a significant effect—subjects in the determinate condition gave worse penalties than subjects in the indeterminate condition. Furthermore, subjects filled out a self-report questionnaire on how much anger, blame, and sympathy they felt, and subjects in the determinate condition felt more anger and blame than subjects in the indeterminate condition. Finally, using mediational statistical analysis, Smart and Loewenstein found that determinateness impacts punitiveness by virtue of provoking stronger emotions.

As we shall see, previous studies of people's moral responsibility intuitions all featured determinate agents and therefore were designed in a way that would tend to trigger affective reactions. Our own study provides an opportunity to see how people's intuitions are altered when the stimuli are designed in a way that keeps affective reactions to a minimum.

3. Intuitions about free will and responsibility

Incompatibilist philosophers have traditionally claimed both that ordinary people believe that human decisions are not governed by deterministic laws and that ordinary people believe that determinism is incompatible with moral responsibility (e.g., Kane 1999; Strawson 1986). These claims have been based, not on systematic empirical research, but rather on anecdote and informal observation. For example, Kane writes, "In my experience, most ordinary persons start out as natural incompatibilists" (1999, 217). (As will be clear below, we think Kane is actually getting at something deep about our intuitions here.) In recent years, philosophers have sought to put claims like this one to the test using experimental methods. The results have sometimes been surprising.

First, consider the claim that ordinary people believe that human decisions are not governed

by deterministic laws. In a set of experiments exploring the lay understanding of choice, both children and adults tended to treat moral choices as indeterminist (Nichols 2004a). Participants were presented with cases of moral choice events (e.g., a girl steals a candy bar) and physical events (e.g., a pot of water comes to a boil), and they were asked whether, if everything in the world was the same right up until the event occurred, the event *had to* occur. Both children and adults were more likely to say that the physical event had to occur than that the moral choice event had to occur. This result seems to vindicate the traditional claim that ordinary people in our culture believe that at least some human decisions are not determined.

Experimental study has not been so kind to the traditional claim that ordinary people are incompatibilists about responsibility. Woolfolk, Doris, and Darley (2006) gave participants a story about an agent who is captured by kidnappers and given a powerful 'compliance drug.' The drug makes it impossible for him to disobey orders. The kidnappers order him to perform an immoral action, and he cannot help but obey. Subjects in the 'low identification condition' were told that the agent did not want to perform the immoral action and was only performing it because he had been given the compliance drug. Subjects in the 'high identification condition' were told that the agent wanted to perform the immoral action all along and felt no reluctance about performing it. The results showed a clear effect of identification: subjects in the high identification condition gave higher ratings of responsibility for the agent than subjects in the low identification condition. This result fits beautifully with the compatibilist view that responsibility depends on identification (e.g., Frankfurt 1988). However, subjects in both conditions showed an overall tendency to give low ratings of responsibility for the agent. So these results don't pose a direct threat to the view that people are incompatibilists about responsibility.

The final set of studies we'll review poses a greater problem for the view that people are intuitive incompatibilists. Nahmias, Morris, Nadelhoffer, and Turner (2005) find that participants will hold an agent morally responsible even when they are told to assume that the agent is in a deterministic universe. For instance, they presented participants with the following scenario:

> Imagine that in the next century we discover all the laws of nature, and we build a supercomputer which can deduce from these laws of nature and from the current state of everything in the world exactly what will be happening in the world at any future time. It can look at everything about the way the world is and predict everything about how it will be with 100% accuracy. Suppose that such a supercomputer existed, and it looks at the state of the universe at a certain time on March 25th, 2150 A.D., twenty years before Jeremy Hall is born. The computer then deduces from this information and the laws of nature that Jeremy will definitely rob Fidelity Bank at 6:00 PM on January 26th, 2195. As always, the supercomputer's prediction is correct; Jeremy robs Fidelity Bank at 6:00 PM on January 26th, 2195.

Participants were subsequently asked whether Jeremy is morally blameworthy for robbing the bank. The results were striking: 83% of subjects said that Jeremy was morally blameworthy for robbing the bank. In two additional experiments with different scenarios, similar effects emerged, suggesting that lay people regard moral responsibility as compatible with determinism. These findings are fascinating, and we will try to build on them in our own experiments.

Of course, it is possible to challenge the experiments on methodological grounds. For instance, the scenarios use technical vocabulary (e.g., "laws of nature," "current state"), and one might wonder whether the subjects really understood the scenarios. Further, one might complain that determinism is not made sufficiently salient in the scenarios. The story of the supercomputer focuses on the predictability of events in the universe, and many philosophers have taken the predictability of the universe to be less threatening to free will than causal inevitability. Although one might use these methodological worries to dismiss the results, we are not inclined to do so. For we think that Nahmias and colleagues have tapped into something of genuine interest.[3] They report three quite different scenarios that produce much the same effect. In each of their experiments, most people (60–85%) say that the agent is morally responsible even under the assumption that determinism is true. Moreover, the results coincide with independent psychological work on the assignment of punishment. Viney and colleagues found that college students who were identified as determinists were no less punitive than indeterminists (Viney et al. 1982) and no less likely to offer retributivist justifications for punishments (Viney et al. 1988).[4] So, we will assume that Nahmias et al. are right that when faced with an agent intentionally doing a bad action in a deterministic setting, people tend to hold the agent morally responsible.

But if people so consistently give compatibilist responses on experimental questionnaires, why have some philosophers concluded that ordinary people are incompatibilists?[5] Have these philosophers simply been failing to listen to their own undergraduate students? We suspect that something more complex is going on. On our view, most people (at least in our culture) really do hold incompatibilist theories of moral responsibility, and these theories can easily be brought out in the kinds of philosophical discussions that arise, for example, in university seminars. It's just that, in addition to these theories of moral responsibility, people also have immediate affective reactions to stories about immoral behaviors. What we see in the results of the experiments by Nahmias and colleagues is, in

part, the effect of these affective reactions. To uncover people's underlying theories, we need to offer them questions that call for more abstract, theoretical cognition.

4. Experimental evidence: first phase

We conducted a series of experiments to explore whether participants will be more likely to report incompatibilist intuitions if the emotional and motivational factors are minimized. In each experiment, one condition, the *concrete* condition, was designed to elicit greater affective response; the other condition, the *abstract* condition, was designed to trigger abstract, theoretical cognition. We predicted that people would be more likely to respond as compatibilists in the concrete condition.

Before we present the details of the experiments, we should note that there are many ways to characterize determinism. The most precise characterizations involve technical language about, for example, the laws of nature. However, we think it's a mistake to use technical terminology for these sorts of experiments, and we therefore tried to present the issue in more accessible language.[6] Of course, any attempt to translate complex philosophical issues into simpler terms will raise difficult questions. It is certainly possible that the specific description of determinism used in our study biased people's intuitions in one direction or another. Perhaps the overall rate of incompatibilist responses would have been somewhat higher or lower if we had used a subtly different formulation.

One should keep in mind, however, that our main focus here is on the *difference* between people's responses in the concrete condition and their responses in the abstract condition. Even though we use exactly the same description of determinism in these two conditions, we predict that people will give compatibilist responses in the concrete condition and incompatibilist responses in the abstract condition. Such an effect could not be dismissed as an artifact of

our description of determinism. If a difference actually does emerge, we will therefore have good evidence for the view that affect is playing some role in people's compatibilist intuitions.

All of our studies were conducted on undergraduates at the University of Utah,[7] and all of the studies began with the same setup. Participants were given the following description of a determinist universe and an indeterminist universe:

Imagine a universe (Universe A) in which everything that happens is completely caused by whatever happened before it. This is true from the very beginning of the universe, so what happened in the beginning of the universe caused what happened next, and so on right up until the present. For example one day John decided to have French fries at lunch. Like everything else, this decision was completely caused by what happened before it. So, if everything in this universe was exactly the same up until John made his decision, then it *had to happen* that John would decide to have French fries.

Now imagine a universe (Universe B) in which *almost* everything that happens is completely caused by whatever happened before it. The one exception is human decision making. For example, one day Mary decided to have French fries at lunch. Since a person's decision in this universe is not completely caused by what happened before it, even if everything in the universe was exactly the same up until Mary made her decision, it *did **not** have to happen* that Mary would decide to have French fries. She could have decided to have something different.

The key difference, then, is that in Universe A every decision is completely caused by what happened before the decision—given the past, each decision *has to happen* the way that it does. By contrast, in Universe B, decisions are not completely caused by the past, and each human decision *does **not** have to happen* the way that it does.

1. Which of these universes do you think is most like ours? (circle one)

   UNIVERSE A   UNIVERSE B
   Please briefly explain your answer.

The purpose of this initial question was simply to see whether subjects believe that our own universe is deterministic or indeterministic. Across conditions, nearly all participants (over 90%) judged that the indeterministic universe is more similar to our own.

After answering the initial question, subjects received a question designed to test intuitions about compatibilism and incompatibilism. Subjects were randomly assigned either to the *concrete* condition or to the *abstract* condition. We ran several different versions, but we will focus on the most important ones. In one of our concrete conditions, subjects were given the following question:

> In Universe A, a man named Bill has become attracted to his secretary, and he decides that the only way to be with her is to kill his wife and three children. He knows that it is impossible to escape from his house in the event of a fire. Before he leaves on a business trip, he sets up a device in his basement that burns down the house and kills his family.
>
> Is Bill fully morally responsible for killing his wife and children?
>
>   YES   NO

In this condition, most subjects (72%) gave the compatibilist response that the agent was fully morally responsible. This is comparable to results obtained in experiments by Nahmias and colleagues. But now consider one of our abstract conditions:

> In Universe A, is it possible for a person to be fully morally responsible for their actions?
>
>   YES   NO

In this condition, most subjects (86%) gave the *incompatibilist* response!

In short, most people give the compatibilist response to the concrete case, but the vast majority give the *incompatibilist* response to the abstract case. What on earth could explain this dramatic difference? Let's first consider a deflationary possibility. Perhaps the concrete condition is so long and complex that subjects lose track of the fact that the agent is in a determinist universe. This is a perfectly sensible explanation. To see whether this accounts for the difference, we ran another concrete condition in which the scenario was short and simple. Subjects were given all the same initial descriptions and then given the following question:

> In Universe A, Bill stabs his wife and children to death so that he can be with his secretary. Is it possible that Bill is fully morally responsible for killing his family?
>
>   YES   NO

Even in this simple scenario, 50% of subjects gave the compatibilist response, which is still significantly different from the very low number of compatibilist responses in the abstract condition.[8]

As we noted above, there are many ways of describing determinism, and the overall rate of incompatibilist responses might have been higher or lower if we had used a somewhat different description. Still, one cannot plausibly dismiss the high rate of incompatibilist responses in the abstract condition as a product of some subtle bias in our description of determinism. After all, the concrete condition used precisely the same description, and yet subjects in that condition were significantly more likely to give compatibilist responses.[9]

These initial experiments replicated the finding (originally due to Nahmias et al.) that people have compatibilist intuitions when presented with vignettes that trigger affective responses. But they also yielded a new and

surprising result. When subjects were presented with an abstract vignette, they had predominantly *incompatibilist* intuitions. This pattern of results suggests that affect is playing a key role in generating people's compatibilist intuitions.

5. Psychological models

Thus far, we have been providing evidence for the claim that different folk intuitions about responsibility are produced by different kinds of psychological processes. But if it is indeed the case that one sort of process leads to compatibilist intuitions and another leads to incompatibilist intuitions, which sort of process should we regard as the best guide to the true relationship between moral responsibility and determinism?

Before we can address this question, we need to know a little bit more about the specific psychological processes that might underlie different types of folk intuitions. We therefore consider a series of possible models. We begin by looking at three extremely simple models and then go on to consider ways that elements of these simple models might be joined together to form more complex models.

The performance error model

Perhaps the most obvious way of explaining the data reported here would be to suggest that strong affective reactions can bias and distort people's judgments. On this view, people ordinarily make responsibility judgments by relying on a tacit theory, but when they are faced with a truly egregious violation of moral norms (as in our concrete cases), they experience a strong affective reaction that makes them unable to apply the theory correctly. In short, this hypothesis posits an *affective performance error*. That is, it draws a distinction between people's underlying representations of the criteria for moral responsibility and the performance systems that enable them to apply those criteria to particular cases. It then suggests that people's affective reactions are interfering with the normal operation of the performance systems.

The performance error model draws support from the vast literature in social psychology on the interaction between affect and theoretical cognition. This literature has unearthed numerous ways in which people's affective reactions can interfere with their ability to reason correctly. Under the influence of affective or motivational biases, people are less likely to recall certain kinds of relevant information, less likely to believe unwanted evidence, and less likely to use critical resources to attack conclusions that are motivationally neutral (see Kunda 1990 for a review). Given that we find these biases in so many other aspects of cognition, it is only natural to conclude that they can be found in moral responsibility judgments as well.

More pointedly, there is evidence that affect sometimes biases attributions of responsibility. Lerner and colleagues found that when subjects' negative emotions are aroused, they hold agents more responsible and more deserving of punishment, *even when the negative emotions are aroused by an unrelated event* (Lerner et al. 1998). In their study, subjects in the *anger* condition watched a video clip of a bully beating up a teenager, while subjects in the *emotion-neutral* condition watched a video clip of abstract figures (Lerner et al. 1998, 566). All subjects were then presented with what they were told was a different experiment designed to examine how people assess responsibility for negligent behaviors. Subjects in the anger condition (i.e., those who had seen the bully video) gave higher responsibility ratings than subjects in the emotion-neutral condition. So, although the subjects' emotions were induced by the film, these emotions impacted their responsibility judgments in unrelated scenarios. The most natural way to interpret this result is that the emotion served to bias the reasoning people used in making their assessments of responsibility.

Proponents of the performance error model might suggest that a similar phenomenon is at

work in the experiments we have reported here. They would concede that people give compatibilist responses under certain circumstances, but they would deny that there is any real sense in which people can be said to hold a compatibilist view of moral responsibility. Instead, they would claim that the compatibilist responses we find in our concrete conditions are to be understood in terms of performance errors brought about by affective reactions. In the abstract condition, people's underlying theory is revealed for what it is—incompatibilist.

The affective competence model

There is, however, another possible way of understanding the role of affect in the assessment of moral responsibility. Instead of supposing that affect serves only to bias or distort our theoretical judgments, one might suggest that people's affective reactions actually lie at the core of the process by which they ordinarily assign responsibility. Perhaps people normally make responsibility judgments by experiencing an affective reaction that, in combination with certain other processes, enables an assessment of moral responsibility. Of course, it can hardly be denied that some people also have elaborate theories of moral responsibility and that they use these theories in certain activities (e.g., in writing philosophy papers), but the proponents of this second view would deny that people's cold cognitive theories of responsibility play any real role in the process by means of which they normally make responsibility judgments. This process, they would claim, is governed primarily by affect.

This 'affective competence' view gains some support from recent studies of people with deficits in emotional processing due to psychological illnesses. When these people are given questions that require moral judgments, they sometimes offer bizarre patterns of responses (Blair 1995; Blair et al. 1997; Hauser et al. 2006). In other words, when we strip away the capacity for affective reactions, it seems that we are not left with a person who can apply the fundamental criteria of morality in an especially impartial or unbiased fashion. Instead, we seem to be left with someone who has trouble understanding what morality is all about. Results from studies like these have led some researchers to conclude that affect must be playing an important role in the fundamental competence underlying people's moral judgments (Blair 1995; Haidt 2001; Nichols 2004b; Prinz 2007).

Proponents of this view might suggest that the only way to really get a handle on people's capacity for moral judgment is to look at their responses in cases that provoke affective reactions. When we examine these cases, people seem to show a marked tendency to offer compatibilist responses, and it might therefore be suggested that the subjects in our studies should be regarded as compatibilists. Of course, we have also provided data indicating that these subjects provide incompatibilist answers when given theoretical questions, but it might be felt that studying people's theoretical beliefs tells us little or nothing about how they really go about making moral judgments. (Think of what would happen if we tried to study the human capacity for language by asking people theoretical questions about the principles of syntax!) Thus, affective competency theorists might maintain that the best way to describe our findings would be to say that people's fundamental moral competence is a compatibilist one but that some people happen to subscribe to a theory that contradicts this fundamental competence.

The concrete competence model

Finally, we need to consider the possibility that people's responses are not being influenced by affect in any way. Perhaps people's responses in the concrete conditions are actually generated by a purely cognitive process. Even if we assume that the process at work here can only be applied to concrete cases, we should not necessarily

conclude that it makes essential use of affect. It might turn out that we have an entirely cognitive, affect-free process that, for whatever reason, can be applied to concrete questions but not to abstract ones.

One particularly appealing version of this hypothesis would be that people's intuitions in the concrete conditions are generated by an innate 'moral responsibility module.'[10] This module could take as input information about an agent and his or her behavior and then produce as output an intuition as to whether or not that agent is morally responsible. Presumably, the module would not use the same kinds of processes that are used in conscious reasoning. Instead, it would use a process that is swift, automatic, and entirely unconscious.

Here, the key idea is that only limited communication is possible between the module and the rest of the mind. The module takes as input certain very specific kinds of information about the agent (the fact that the agent is a human being, the fact that he knows what he is doing, etc.), but the vast majority of the person's beliefs would be entirely inaccessible to processes taking place inside of the module. Thus, the module would not be able to make use of the person's theory about the relationship between determinism and moral responsibility. It might not even be able to make use of the person's belief that the agent is in a deterministic universe. Because these beliefs would be inaccessible inside of the module, the conclusions of the module could differ dramatically from the conclusions that the person would reach after a process of conscious consideration.

Hybrid models

Thus far, we have been considering three simple models of responsibility attribution. It would be possible, however, to construct more complex models by joining together elements of the three simple ones we have already presented. So,

for example, it might turn out that moral responsibility judgments are subserved by a module but that the workings of this module are sometimes plagued with affective performance errors, or that the fundamental competence underlying responsibility judgments makes essential use of affect but that this affect somehow serves as input to a module, and many other possible hybrids might be suggested here.

Since we are unable to consider all of the possible hybrid models, we will focus on one that we find especially plausible. On the hybrid model we will be discussing, affect plays two distinct roles in the assignment of moral responsibility. Specifically, affect serves *both* as part of the fundamental competence underlying responsibility judgments *and* as a factor that can sometimes lead to performance errors. To get a sense for what we mean here, imagine that you are trying to determine whether certain poems should be regarded as 'moving,' and now suppose you discover that one of the poems was actually written by your best friend. Here, it seems that the basic competence underlying your judgment would involve one sort of affect (your feelings about the poems) but the performance systems enabling your judgment could be derailed by another sort of affect (your feelings about the friend). The hybrid model in question would suggest that a similar sort of process takes place in judgments of moral responsibility. The competence underlying these judgments does make use of affect, but affect can also be implicated in processes that ultimately lead to performance errors.

Proponents of this model might suggest that affect does play an important role in the competence underlying moral responsibility judgments but that the effect obtained in the experiments reported here should still be treated as a performance error.[11] In other words, even if we suppose that affect has an important role to play in moral responsibility judgments, we can still conclude that the basic competence underlying these judgments is an incompatibilist one

and that the responses we find in our concrete conditions are the result of a failure to apply that competence correctly.

6. Experimental evidence: second phase

Now that we have described some of the psychological models that might explain our results, we can explore a bit more deeply whether experimental evidence counts against any of the models. One key question is whether or not the compatibilist responses in our experiments are really the product of affect. We compared concrete conditions with abstract conditions, and we suggested that the concrete descriptions triggered greater affective response, which in turn pushed subjects toward compatibilist responses. However, it's possible that what really mattered was concreteness itself, not any affect associated with concreteness. That is, it's possible that the compatibilist responses were not influenced by affect but were elicited simply because the scenario involved a particular act by a particular individual. Indeed, this is exactly the sort of explanation one would expect from the responsibility module account. Fortunately, there is a direct way to test this proposal.

To explore whether concreteness alone can explain the compatibilist responses, we ran another experiment in which the affective salience varied across the two questions, but concreteness was held constant. Again, all subjects were given the initial descriptions of the two universes, A and B, and all subjects were asked which universe they thought was most similar to ours. Subjects were randomly assigned either to the *high affect* or *low affect* condition. In the *high affect* condition, subjects were asked the following:

> As he has done many times in the past, Bill stalks and rapes a stranger. Is it possible that Bill is fully morally responsible for raping the stranger?

In the *low affect* condition, subjects were asked:

> As he has done many times in the past, Mark arranges to cheat on his taxes. Is it possible that Mark is fully morally responsible for cheating on his taxes?

In addition, in each condition, for half of the subjects, the question stipulated that the agent was in Universe A; for the other half, the agent was in Universe B. Thus, each subject was randomly assigned to one of the cells in Table 58.1.

What did we find? Even when we used these exclusively concrete scenarios, there was a clear difference between the high affect and low affect cases. Among subjects who were asked about agents in a *determinist* universe, people were much more likely to give the incompatibilist answer in the low affect case than in the high affect case. Indeed, most people said that it is *not* possible that the tax cheat is fully morally responsible, and a clear majority said that it is possible that the rapist is fully morally responsible. By contrast, for subjects who were asked about an agent in an indeterminist universe, most people said that it is possible for the agent to be fully morally responsible, regardless of whether he was a tax cheat or a rapist.[12] See Table 58.2.

Table 58.1

	Agent in indeterminist universe	Agent in determinist universe
High affect case		
Low affect case		

Table 58.2

	Agent in indeterminist universe	Agent in determinist universe
High affect case	95%	64%
Low affect case	89%	23%

These results help to clarify the role that affect plays in people's responsibility attributions. Even when we control for concreteness, we still find that affect impacts people's intuitions about responsibility under determinism. The overall pattern of results therefore suggests that affect is playing an important role in the process that generates people's compatibilist intuitions.

We now have good evidence that affect plays a role in compatibilist judgments. But there remains the difficult question of whether what we see in these responses is the result of an affective competence or an affective performance error. Let's consider whether one of these models provides a better explanation of the experiment we just reported.

We think that the affective performance error model provides quite a plausible explanation of our results. What we see in the tax cheat case is that, when affect is minimized, people give dramatically different answers depending on whether the agent is in a determinist or indeterminist universe. On the performance error hypothesis, these responses reveal the genuine competence with responsibility attribution, for in the low affect cases, the affective bias is minimized. When high affect is introduced, as in the serial rapist case, the normal competence with responsibility attribution is skewed by the emotions; that explains why there is such a large difference between the high and low affect cases in the determinist conditions.

Now let's turn to the affective competence account. It's much less clear that the affective competence theorist has a good explanation of the results. In particular, it seems difficult to see how the affective competence account can explain why responses to the low affect case drop precipitously in the determinist condition, since this doesn't hold for the high affect case. Perhaps the affective competence theorist could say that low affect cases like the tax cheat case fail to trigger our competence with responsibility attribution, and so we should not treat those responses as reflecting our normal competence. But obviously it would take significant work to show that such everyday cases of apparent responsibility attribution don't really count as cases in which we exercise our competence at responsibility attribution. Thus, at first glance, the performance error account provides a better explanation of these results than the affective competence account.

Of course, even if it is true that our results are best explained by the performance error account, this doesn't mean that affect is irrelevant to the normal competence. As noted in the previous section, one option that strikes us as quite plausible is a hybrid account on which (i) our normal competence with responsibility attribution does depend on affective systems, but (ii) affect also generates a bias leading to compatibilist responses in our experiments.

Although our experiment provides some reason to favor the performance error account of the compatibilist responses we found, it seems clear that deciding between the affective performance error and the affective competence models of compatibilist responses is not the sort of issue that will be resolved by a single crucial experiment. What we really need here is a deeper understanding of the role that affect plays in moral cognition more generally. (Presumably, if we had a deeper understanding of this more general issue, we would be able to do a better job of figuring out how empirical studies could address the specific question about the role of affect in judgments of moral responsibility.) But our inability to resolve all of the relevant questions immediately is no cause for pessimism. On the contrary, we see every reason to be optimistic about the prospects for research in this area. Recent years have seen a surge of interest in the ways in which affect can influence moral cognition—with new empirical studies and theoretical developments coming in all the time—and it seems likely that the next few years will yield important new insights into the question at hand.

7. Philosophical implications

Our findings help to explain why the debate between compatibilists and incompatibilists is so stubbornly persistent. It seems that certain psychological processes tend to generate compatibilist intuitions, while others tend to generate incompatibilist intuitions. Thus, each of the two major views appeals to an element of our psychological makeup.

But the experimental results do not serve merely to give us insight into the causal origins of certain philosophical positions; they also help us to evaluate some of the arguments that have been put forward in support of those positions. After all, many of these arguments rely on explicit appeals to intuition. If we find that different intuitions are produced by different psychological mechanisms, we might conclude that some of these intuitions should be given more weight than others. What we need to know now is which intuitions to take seriously and which to dismiss as products of mechanisms that are only leading us astray.

Clearly, the answer will depend partly on which, if any, of the three models described above turns out to be the right one, and since we don't yet have the data we need to decide between these competing models, we will not be able to offer a definite conclusion here. Our approach will therefore be to consider each of the models in turn and ask what implications it would have (if it turned out to be correct) for broader philosophical questions about the role of intuitions in the debate over moral responsibility.

The performance error model

If compatibilist intuitions are explained by the performance error model, then we shouldn't assign much weight to these intuitions. For on that model, as we have described it, compatibilist intuitions are a product of the distorting effects of emotion and motivation. If we could eliminate the performance errors, the compatibilist intuitions should disappear.

Note that the performance error model does not claim that people's compatibilist intuitions are actually *incorrect*. What it says is simply that the process that generates these intuitions involves a certain kind of error. It is certainly possible that, even though the process involves this error, it ends up yielding a correct conclusion. Still, we feel that the performance error model has important philosophical implications. At the very least, it suggests that the fact that people sometimes have compatibilist intuitions does not itself give us reason to suppose that compatibilism is correct.

The philosophical implications of the performance error model have a special significance because the experimental evidence gathered thus far seems to suggest that the basic idea behind this model is actually true. But the jury is still out. Further research might show that one of the other models is in fact more accurate, and we therefore consider their philosophical implications as well.

The affective competence model

On the affective competence model, people's responses in the concrete conditions of our original experiment are genuine expressions of their underlying competence. The suggestion is that the compatibilist responses people give in these conditions are not clouded by any kind of performance error. Rather, these responses reflect a successful implementation of the system we normally use for making responsibility judgments, and that system should therefore be regarded as a compatibilist one.

In many ways, this affective competence model is reminiscent of the view that P. F. Strawson (1962) puts forward in his classic paper "Freedom and Resentment." On that view, it would be a mistake to go about trying to understand the concept of moral responsibility by seeking to associate it with some sort of

metaphysical theory. Rather, the best place to start is with an examination of the 'reactive attitudes' (blame, remorse, gratitude, etc.) and the role they play in our ordinary practice of responsibility attribution.

Yet, despite the obvious affinities between the affective competence model and Strawson's theory, it is important to keep in mind certain respects in which the affective competence model is making substantially weaker claims. Most importantly, the model isn't specifically claiming that people proceed *correctly* in the concrete conditions. All it says is that people's responses in these conditions reflect a successful implementation of their own underlying system for making responsibility judgments. This claim then leaves it entirely open whether the criteria used in that underlying system are themselves correct or incorrect.

For an analogous case, consider the ways in which people ordinarily make probability judgments. It can be shown that people's probability judgments often involve incorrect inferences, and one might therefore be tempted to assume that people are not correctly applying their own underlying criteria for probabilistic inference. But many psychologists reject this view. They suggest that people actually are correctly applying their underlying criteria and that the mistaken probabilistic inferences only arise because people's underlying criteria are themselves faulty (see, e.g., Tversky and Kahneman 1981, 1983).

Clearly, a similar approach could be applied in the case of responsibility judgments. Even if people's compatibilist intuitions reflect a successful implementation of their underlying system for making responsibility judgments, one could still argue that this underlying system is itself flawed. Hence, the affective competence model would vindicate the idea that people's core views about responsibility are compatibilist, but it would be a mistake to regard the model as an outright vindication of those intuitions.

The concrete competence model

The implications of the concrete competence model depend in a crucial way on the precise details of the competence involved. Since it is not possible to say anything very general about all of the models in this basic category, we will focus specifically on the implications of the claim that people's responsibility attributions are subserved by an encapsulated module.

As a number of authors have noted, modularity involves a kind of trade-off. The key advantages of modules are that they usually operate automatically, unconsciously, and extremely quickly. But these advantages come at a price. The reason why modules are able to operate so quickly is that they simply ignore certain sources of potentially relevant information. Even when we know that the lines in the Müller-Lyer illusion are the same length, we still have the visual illusion. Perhaps in the assignment of moral responsibility, we are dealing with a similar sort of phenomenon—a 'moral illusion.' It might be that people have a complex and sophisticated theory about the relationship between determinism and moral responsibility but that the relevant module just isn't able to access this theory. It continues to spit out judgments that the agent is blameworthy even when these judgments go against a consciously held theory elsewhere in the mind.

Of course, defenders of compatibilism might point out that this argument can also be applied in the opposite direction. They might suggest that the module itself contains a complex and sophisticated theory to which the rest of the mind has no access. The conclusion would be that, unless we use the module to assess the relationship between determinism and moral responsibility, we will arrive at an impoverished and inadequate understanding. This type of argument definitely seems plausible in certain domains (e.g., in the domain of grammatical theory). It is unclear at this point whether

something analogous holds true for the domain of responsibility attribution.[13]

Reflective equilibrium

Our concern in this section has been with philosophical questions about whether knowledge of particular mental processes is likely to give us valuable insight into complex moral issues. Clearly, these philosophical questions should be carefully distinguished from the purely psychological question as to whether people *think* that particular mental processes give them insight into these issues. Even if people think that a given process is affording them valuable moral insight, it might turn out that this process is actually entirely unreliable and they would be better off approaching these issues in a radically different way.

Still, we thought it would be interesting to know how people themselves resolve the tension between their rival intuitions, and we therefore ran one final experiment. All subjects were given a brief description of the results from our earlier studies and then asked to adjudicate the conflict between the compatibilist and incompatibilist intuitions. Given that people's intuitions in the concrete conditions contradict their intuitions in the abstract conditions, would they choose to hold on to the concrete judgment that Bill is morally responsible or the abstract judgment that no one can be responsible in a deterministic universe?[14] The results showed no clear majority on either side. Approximately half of the subjects chose to hold onto the judgment that the particular agent was morally responsible, while the other half chose to hold onto the judgment that no one can be responsible in a deterministic universe.[15] Apparently, there is no more consensus about these issues among the folk than there is among philosophers.

8. Conclusion

As we noted at the outset, participants in the debate over moral responsibility have appealed to an enormous variety of arguments. Theories from metaphysics, moral philosophy, philosophy of mind, and even quantum mechanics have all been shown to be relevant in one way or another, and researchers are continually finding new ways in which seemingly unrelated considerations can be brought to bear on the issue. The present essay has not been concerned with the full scope of this debate. Instead, we have confined ourselves to just one type of evidence– evidence derived from people's intuitions.

Philosophers who have discussed lay intuitions in this area tend to say either that folk intuitions conform to compatibilism or that they conform to incompatibilism. Our actual findings were considerably more complex and perhaps more interesting. It appears that people have *both* compatibilist *and* incompatibilist intuitions. Moreover, it appears that these different kinds of intuitions are generated by different kinds of psychological processes. To assess the importance of this finding for the debate over moral responsibility, one would have to know precisely what sort of psychological process produced each type of intuition and how much weight to accord to the output of each sort of process. We have begun the task of addressing these issues here, but clearly far more remains to be done.

Notes

Several people gave us great feedback on an early draft of this essay. We'd like to thank John Doris, Chris Hitchcock, Bob Kane, Neil Levy, Al Mele, Stephen Morris, Thomas Nadelhoffer, Eddy Nahmias, Derk Pereboom, Lynne Rudder-Baker, Tamler Sommers, Jason Turner, and Manuel Vargas. Thanks also to John Fischer for posting a draft of this essay on the Garden of Forking Paths Weblog (http://gfp.typepad.com/). Versions of this essay were delivered at the UNC/Duke workshop on Naturalized Ethics, the Society for Empirical Ethics, the Society for Philosophy and Psychology, Yale University, the University of Arizona, and the Inland Northwest Philosophy Conference. We thank the participants for their helpful comments.

1   Actually, compatibilists and incompatibilists argue both (1) about whether determinism is compatible with moral responsibility and (2) about whether determinism is compatible with free will. As Fischer (1999) has emphasized, these two questions are logically independent. One might maintain that determinism is compatible with moral responsibility but not with free will. Here, however, our concern lies entirely with the first of the two questions—whether determinism is compatible with moral responsibility.

2   We use the term 'theory' here loosely to refer to an internally represented body of information. Also, when we claim that the folk have an incompatibilist theory, we are not suggesting that this theory has a privileged status over the psychological systems that generate compatibilist intuitions. As will be apparent, we think that it remains an open question whether the system that generates incompatibilist intuitions has a privileged status.

3   One virtue of Nahmias and colleagues' question about moral responsibility is that the notion of 'moral responsibility' is supposed to be common between philosophers and the folk. That is, philosophers tend to assume that the notion of moral responsibility deployed in philosophy closely tracks the notion that people express when they attribute moral responsibility. Furthermore, incompatibilists often specify that the relevant incompatibilist notion of free will is precisely the notion of free will that is required for moral responsibility (e.g., Campbell 1951). Nahmias and colleagues also ask questions about whether the agent in the deterministic scenario "acts of his own free will," and they find that people give answers consonant with compatibilism. We find these results less compelling. For the expression 'free will' has become a term of philosophical art, and it's unclear how to interpret lay responses concerning such technical terms. Moreover, incompatibilists typically grant that there are compatibilist notions of freedom that get exploited by the folk. Incompatibilists just maintain that there is also a commonsense notion of freedom that is not compatibilist.

4   Although these results from Viney and colleagues are suggestive, the measure used for identifying determinists is too liberal, and as a result, the group of subjects coded as 'determinists' might well include indeterminists. (See McIntyre et al. 1984 for a detailed description of the measure.) It remains to be seen whether this result will hold up using better measures for identifying determinists.

5   A related problem for the incompatibilist concerns the history of philosophy—if incompatibilism is intuitive, why has compatibilism been so popular among the great philosophers in history? An incompatibilist-friendly explanation is given in Nichols (2007).

6   In our deterministic scenario, we say that given the past, each decision *has to happen* the way that it does. This scenario allows us to test folk intuitions about the type of compatibilism most popular in contemporary philosophy. Most contemporary compatibilists argue, following Frankfurt (1969), that an agent can be morally responsible for her behavior even if she *had to* act the way she did. (As we shall see, most subjects in our concrete condition give responses that conform to this view.) However, it would also be possible for a compatibilist to maintain that (1) we can never be responsible for an event that had to occur the way it did but also that (2) even if a particular behavior is determined to occur by the laws of nature, the agent does not necessarily *have to* perform that behavior. Our experiment does not address the possibility that the folk subscribe to this type of compatibilism. With any luck, that possibility will be investigated in future research.

7   It will, of course, be important to investigate whether our results extend to other populations. However, as we will stress throughout, we are primarily looking at how subjects from the same population give different answers in the different conditions.

8   χ^2 (1, N = 41) = 6.034, p < .05, two-tailed.

9   We also ran an experiment that used a more real-world kind of case than the deterministic set up described in our main experiments. This was sparked by some perceptive comments from Daniel Batson, who also gave us extremely helpful suggestions in designing the study. Again, the idea was to test whether abstract conditions were more likely to generate incompatibilist responses than affect-laden concrete conditions. All subjects were told about a genetic condition that leads a person

to perform horrible actions, but they were also told that there is now an inexpensive pill that counteracts the condition and that now everyone with the condition gets this pill. In the abstract condition, subjects were then asked to indicate whether the people who had this condition before the pill was created could be held morally responsible for their actions. In the concrete condition, subjects were told that Bill had this condition before the pill was invented, and Bill killed his wife and children to be with his secretary. Subjects were then asked to indicate whether Bill was morally responsible for his action. The results were quite clear, and they were in concert with all of our earlier findings. Subjects given the abstract question gave significantly lower ratings of responsibility than subjects given the concrete question. Thus, the basic effect can be obtained using quite different materials.

10   As far as we know, no prior research has posited a moral responsibility module, but there has been considerable enthusiasm for the more general idea that many basic cognitive capacities are driven by modules (Fodor 1983; Leslie 1994), and a number of authors have suggested that certain aspects of moral judgment might be subserved by module-like mechanisms (Dwyer 1999; Harman 1999; Hauser 2006).

11   We are grateful to Jesse Prinz for suggesting this possibility.

12   As in our previous experiments, the vast majority of subjects said that our universe was most similar to the indeterminist universe. We suspect that being a determinist might actually lead people to have more compatibilist views (see Nichols 2006), and as a result, we antecedently decided to exclude the minority who gave the determinist response from our statistical analyses. The statistical details are as follows. The contrast between high and low affect for the determinist condition was significant (χ^2 (1, N = 44) = 8.066, p < .01). That is, people were more likely to say that it's possible for the rapist to be fully morally responsible. The contrast between the two high affect conditions was also significant (χ^2 (1, N = 45) = 7.204, p < .01); that is, people were more likely to say that it's possible that the rapist is fully morally responsible in the indeterminist universe. The contrast between the

two low affect conditions was very highly significant (χ^2 (1, N = 45) = 26.492, p < 0.0001). Subjects were dramatically more likely to say that it's possible for the tax cheat to be fully morally responsible in the indeterminist universe.

13   The distinction between modularity hypotheses and affective hypotheses first entered the philosophical literature in the context of the debate about the role of moral considerations in intentional action (Knobe 2006; Malle and Nelson 2003; Nadelhoffer 2004; Young et al. 2006). In that context, modularity hypotheses are usually regarded as vindicating folk intuitions. However, there is a key difference between that context and the present one. The difference is that information about the moral status of the action might be accessible in an intentional action module, but information about determinism is unlikely to be accessible in a moral responsibility module.

14   The design of the pilot study was modeled on the initial experiments described in section 3. Participants were asked both the high affect (Bill stabbing his wife) and the abstract questions (counterbalanced for order). They then answered the reflective equilibrium question:

Previous research indicates that when people are given question 3 above, they often say that Bill is fully morally responsible for killing his family. But when people are given question 2 above, most people say that it is not possible that people in Universe A are fully morally responsible for their actions. Clearly these claims are not consistent. Because if it is not possible to be fully morally responsible in Universe A, then Bill can't be fully morally responsible.

We are interested in how people will resolve this inconsistency. So, regardless of how you answered questions 2 and 3, please indicate which of the following you agree with most:

i. In Universe A, it is not possible for people to be morally responsible for their actions.
ii. Bill, who is in Universe A, is fully morally responsible for killing his family.

15   There were 19 subjects. Of these, 10 gave incompatibilist responses to the reflective equilibrium question; 9 gave compatibilist responses.

References

Blair, R. 1995. "A Cognitive Developmental Approach to Morality: Investigating the Psychopath." *Cognition* 57.

Blair, R., Jones, L., Clark, F., Smith, M., and Jones, L. 1997. "The Psychopathic Individual: A Lack of Responsiveness to Distress Cues?" *Psychophysiology* 34.

Campbell, C. A. 1951. "Is 'Free Will' a Pseudo-problem?" *Journal of Philosophy* 60.

Dwyer, S. 1999. "Moral Competence." In K. Murasugi and R. Stainton (eds.), *Philosophy and Linguistics*. Westview Press.

Fischer, J. 1999. "Recent Work on Moral Responsibility." *Ethics* 110.

Fodor, J. 1983. *Modularity of Mind*. MIT Press.

Frankfurt, H. 1969. "Alternate Possibilities and Moral Responsibility." *Journal of Philosophy* 66.

Frankfurt, H. 1988. *The Importance of What We Care About: Philosophical Essays*. Cambridge University Press.

Greene, J., Sommerville, R., Nystrom, L., Darley, J., and Cohen, J. 2001. "An fMRI Investigation of Emotional Engagement in Moral Judgment." *Science* 293.

Haidt, J. 2001. "The Emotional Dog and Its Rational Tail: A Social Intuitionist Approach to Moral Judgment." *Psychological Review* 108.

Haidt, J., Koller, S. H., and Dias, M. G. 1993. "Affect, Culture, and Morality, or Is It Wrong to Eat Your Dog?" *Journal of Personality and Social Psychology* 65.

Harman, G. 1999. "Moral Philosophy and Linguistics." In K. Brinkmann (ed.), *Proceedings of the 20th World Congress of Philosophy: Volume 1: Ethics*. Philosophy Documentation Center.

Hauser, M. 2006. *Moral Minds: The Unconscious Voice of Right and Wrong*. HarperCollins.

Hauser, M., Young, L., and Cushman, F. 2008. "Reviving Rawls' Linguistic Analogy: Operative Principles and the Causal Structure of Moral Actions." In W. Sinnott-Armstrong (ed.), *Moral Psychology*. MIT Press.

Hume, D. 1740/1978. *A Treatise of Human Nature*. Oxford University Press.

Kane, R. 1999. "Responsibility, Luck, and Chance: Reflections on Free Will and Indeterminism." *Journal of Philosophy* 96.

Knobe, J. 2003a. "Intentional Action and Side-Effects in Ordinary Language." *Analysis* 63.

Knobe, J. 2003b. "Intentional Action in Folk Psychology: An Experimental Investigation." *Philosophical Psychology* 16.

Knobe, J. 2006. "The Concept of Intentional Action: A Case Study in the Uses of Folk Psychology." *Philosophical Studies* 130.

Kunda, Z. 1990. "The Case for Motivated Reasoning." *Psychological Bulletin* 108.

Lerner, J., Goldberg, J., and Tetlock, P. 1998. "Sober Second Thought: The Effects of Accountability, Anger, and Authoritarianism on Attributions of Responsibility." *Personality and Social Psychology Bulletin* 24.

Leslie, A. 1994. "ToMM, ToBY and Agency: Core Architecture and Domain Specificity." In L. Hirschfeld and S. Gelman (eds.), *Mapping the Mind*. Cambridge University Press.

Malle, B., and Nelson, S. 2003. "Judging Mens Rea: The Tension between Folk Concepts and Legal Concepts of Intentionality." *Behavioral Sciences and the Law* 21.

McIntyre, R., Viney, D., and Viney, W. 1984. "Validity of a Scale Designed to Measure Beliefs in Free Will and Determinism." *Psychological Reports* 54.

Nadelhoffer, T. 2004. "Praise, Side Effects, and Folk Ascriptions of Intentional Action." *Journal of Theoretical and Philosophical Psychology* 24.

Nahmias, E., Morris, S., Nadelhoffer, T., and Turner, J. 2005. "Surveying Freedom: Folk Intuitions about Free Will and Moral Responsibility." *Philosophical Psychology* 18.

Nichols, S. 2002. "Norms with Feeling." *Cognition* 84.

Nichols, S. 2004a. "The Folk Psychology of Free Will: Fits and Starts." *Mind and Language* 19.

Nichols, S. 2004b. *Sentimental Rules: On the Natural Foundations of Moral Judgment*. Oxford University Press.

Nichols, S. 2006. "Folk Intuitions about Free Will." *Journal of Cognition and Culture* 6.

Nichols, S. 2007. "The Rise of Compatibilism: A Case Study in the Quantitative History of Philosophy." *Midwest Studies in Philosophy* 31.

Prinz, J. 2007. *The Emotional Construction of Morals*. Oxford University Press.

Pylyshyn, Z. 1999. "Is Vision Continuous with Cognition? The Case for Cognitive Impenetrability of Visual Perception." *Behavioral and Brain Sciences* 22.

Smart, D., and Loewenstein, G. 2005. "The Devil You Know: The Effect of Identifiability on Punitiveness." *Journal of Behavioral Decision Making* 18.

Strawson, G. 1986. *Freedom and Belief*. Oxford University Press.

Strawson, P. 1962. "Freedom and Resentment." *Proceedings of the British Academy* 48. Reprinted in G.

Watson (ed.), *Free Will*. Oxford University Press, 1980. Page references are to the reprinted version.

Tversky, A., and Kahneman, D. 1981. "The Framing of Decisions and the Psychology of Choice." *Science* 211.

Tversky, A., and Kahneman, D. 1983. "Extensional versus Intuitive Reasoning: The Conjunction Fallacy in Probabilistic Reasoning." *Psychological Review* 90.

Van Inwagen, P. 1983. *An Essay on Free Will*. Oxford University Press.

Vargas, M. 2006. "On the Importance of History for Responsible Agency." *Philosophical Studies* 127.

Viney, W., Waldman, D., and Barchilon, J. 1982. "Attitudes toward Punishment in Relation to Beliefs in Free Will and Determinism." *Human Relations* 35.

Viney, W., Parker-Martin, P., and Dotten, S. D. H. 1988. "Beliefs in Free Will and Determinism and Lack of Relation to Punishment Rationale and Magnitude." *Journal of General Psychology* 115.

Watson, G. 1987. "Responsibility and the Limits of Evil: Variations on a Strawsonian Theme." In F. Schoeman (ed.), *Responsibility, Character, and the Emotions: New Essays in Moral Psychology*. Cambridge University Press.

Weinberg, J., Nichols, S., and Stich, S. 2001. "Normativity and Epistemic Intuitions." *Philosophical Topics* 29.

Woolfolk, R., Doris, J., and Darley, J. 2006. "Identification, Situational Constraint, and Social Cognition." *Cognition* 100.

Young, L., Cushman, F., Adolphs, R., Tranel, D., and Hauser, M. 2006. "Does Emotion Mediate the Effect of an Action's Moral Status on Its Intentional Status? Neuropsychological Evidence." *Journal of Cognition and Culture* 6.

Chapter 59

Joshua D. Greene

THE SECRET JOKE OF KANT'S SOUL

Two things fill the mind with ever new and increasing wonder and awe, the oftener and more steadily we reflect on them: the starry heavens above me and the moral law within me.

—Immanuel Kant

That such an unnatural use (and so misuse) of one's sexual attributes is a violation of one's duty to himself and is certainly in the highest degree opposed to morality strikes everyone upon his thinking of it. . . . However, it is not so easy to produce a rational demonstration of the inadmissibility of that unnatural use, and even the mere unpurposive use, of one's sexual attributes as being a violation of one's duty to himself (and indeed in the highest degree where the unnatural use is concerned). The ground of proof surely lies in the fact that a man gives up his personality (throws it away) when he uses himself merely as a means for the gratification of an animal drive.

—Immanuel Kant, "Concerning Wanton Self-Abuse"

Kant's Joke—Kant wanted to prove, in a way that would dumbfound the common man, that the common man was right: that was the secret joke of this soul. He wrote against the scholars in support of popular prejudice, but for scholars and not for the people.

—Friedrich Nietzsche

There is a substantial and growing body of evidence suggesting that much of what we do, we do unconsciously, and for reasons that are inaccessible to us. In one experiment, for example, people were asked to choose one of several pairs of pantyhose displayed in a row. When asked to explain their preferences, people gave sensible enough answers, referring to the relevant features of the items chosen—superior knit, sheerness, elasticity, etc. However, their choices had nothing to do with such features because the items on display were in fact identical. People simply had a preference for items on the right-hand side of the display. What this experiment illustrates—and there are many, many such illustrations—is that people make choices for reasons unknown to them, and they make up reasonable-sounding justifications for their choices, all the while remaining unaware of their actual motives and subsequent rationalizations.

Jonathan Haidt applies these psychological lessons to the study of moral judgment in his influential paper, "The Emotional Dog and Its Rational Tail: A Social Intuitionist Approach to Moral Judgment" (Haidt, 2001). He argues that for the most part moral reasoning is a post hoc affair: We decide what's right or wrong on the basis of emotionally driven intuitions, and then, if necessary, we make up reasons to explain and justify our judgments. Haidt concedes that some people, some of the time, may actually reason

their way to moral conclusions, but he insists that this is not the norm. More important for the purposes of this essay, Haidt does not distinguish among the various approaches to ethics familiar to moral philosophers: consequentialism, deontology, virtue ethics, etc. Rather, his radical thesis is intended, if only implicitly, to apply equally to the adherents of all moral philosophies, though not necessarily well to moral philosophers as a group.

Jonathan Baron (1994), in contrast, draws a psychological distinction between consequentialist and nonconsequentialist judgments, arguing that the latter are especially likely to be made on the basis of heuristics, simple rules of thumb for decision making. Baron, however, does not regard emotion as essential to these heuristic judgments.

In this chapter, I draw on Haidt's and Baron's respective insights in the service of a bit of philosophical psychoanalysis. I will argue that deontological judgments tend to be driven by emotional responses and that deontological philosophy, rather than being grounded in moral *reasoning*, is to a large extent an exercise in moral *rationalization*. This is in contrast to consequentialism, which, I will argue, arises from rather different psychological processes, ones that are more "cognitive," and more likely to involve genuine moral reasoning. These claims are strictly empirical, and I will defend them on the basis of the available evidence. Needless to say, my argument will be speculative and will not be conclusive. Beyond this, I will argue that if these empirical claims are true, they may have normative implications, casting doubt on deontology as a school of normative moral thought.

• • •

Defining "cognition" and "emotion"

In what follows I will argue that deontological judgment tends to be driven by emotion, while consequentialist judgment tends to be driven by "cognitive" processes. What do we mean by

"emotion" and "cognition," and how do these things differ?

Sometimes "cognition" refers to information processing in general, as in "cognitive science," but often "cognition" is used in a narrower sense that contrasts with "emotion," despite the fact that emotions involve information processing. I know of no good off-the-shelf definition of "cognition" in this more restrictive sense, despite its widespread use. Elsewhere, my collaborators and I offered a tentative definition of our own (Greene, Nystrom, Engell, Darley, & Cohen, 2004), one that is based on the differences between the information-processing requirements of stereotyped versus flexible behavior.

The rough idea is that "cognitive" representations are inherently neutral representations, ones that do not automatically trigger particular behavioral responses or dispositions, while "emotional" representations do have such automatic effects, and are therefore behaviorally valenced. (To make things clear, I will use quotation marks to indicate the more restrictive sense of "cognitive" defined here, and I will drop the quotation marks when using this term to refer to information processing in general.) Highly flexible behavior requires "cognitive" representations that can be easily mixed around and recombined as situational demands vary, and without pulling the agent in sixteen different behavioral directions at once. For example, sometimes you need to avoid cars, and other times you need to approach them. It is useful, then, if you can represent CAR in a behaviorally neutral or "cognitive" way, one that doesn't automatically presuppose a particular behavioral response. Stereotyped behavior, in contrast, doesn't require this sort of flexibility and therefore doesn't require "cognitive" representations, at least not to the same extent.

While the whole brain is devoted to cognition, "cognitive" processes are especially important for reasoning, planning, manipulating information in working memory, controlling

impulses, and "higher executive functions" more generally. Moreover, these functions tend to be associated with certain parts of the brain, primarily the dorsolateral surfaces of the prefrontal cortex and parietal lobes. Emotion, in contrast, tends to be associated with other parts of the brain, such as the amygdala and the medial surfaces of the frontal and parietal lobes. And while the term "emotion" can refer to stable states such as moods, here we will primarily be concerned with emotions subserved by processes that in addition to being valenced, are quick and automatic, though not necessarily conscious.

Here we are concerned with two different kinds of moral judgment (deontological and consequentialist) and two different kinds of psychological process ("cognitive" and emotional). Crossing these, we get four basic empirical possibilities. First, it could be that both kinds of moral judgment are generally "cognitive," as Kohlberg's theories suggest (Kohlberg, 1971).[1] At the other extreme, it could be that both kinds of moral judgment are primarily emotional, as Haidt's view suggests (Haidt, 2001). Then there is the historical stereotype, according to which consequentialism is more emotional (emerging from the "sentimentalist" tradition of David Hume [1740/1978] and Adam Smith [1759/1976]) while deontology is more "cognitive" (encompassing the Kantian "rationalist" tradition [Kant, 1959]). Finally, there is the view for which I will argue, that deontology is more emotionally driven while consequentialism is more "cognitive." I hasten to add, however, that I don't believe that either approach is strictly emotional or "cognitive" (or even that there is a sharp distinction between "cognition" and emotion). More specifically, I am sympathetic to Hume's claim that all moral judgment (including consequentialist judgment) must have some emotional component (Hume, 1978). But I suspect that the kind of emotion that is essential to consequentialism is fundamentally different from the

kind that is essential to deontology, the former functioning more like a currency and the latter functioning more like an alarm. We will return to this issue later.

Scientific evidence

Evidence from neuroimaging

In recent decades, philosophers have devised a range of hypothetical moral dilemmas that capture the tension between the consequentialist and deontological viewpoints. A well-known handful of these dilemmas gives rise to what is known as the "trolley problem" which begins with the *trolley* dilemma.

A runaway trolley is headed for five people who will be killed if it proceeds on its present course. The only way to save these people is to hit a switch that will turn the trolley onto a side track, where it will run over and kill one person instead of five. Is it okay to turn the trolley in order to save five people at the expense of one? The consensus among philosophers as well as people who have been tested experimentally is that it is morally acceptable to save five lives at the expense of one in this case.

Next consider the *footbridge* dilemma . . .: As before, a runaway trolley threatens to kill five people, but this time you are standing next to a large stranger on a footbridge spanning the tracks, in between the oncoming trolley and the five people. The only way to save the five people is to push this stranger off the bridge and onto the tracks below. He will die as a result, but his body will stop the trolley from reaching the others. Is it okay to save the five people by pushing this stranger to his death? Here the consensus is that it is not okay to save five lives at the expense of one.

People exhibit a characteristically consequentialist response to the *trolley* case and a characteristically deontological response to the *footbridge* case. Why? Philosophers have generally offered a variety of *normative* explanations. That is, they

have assumed that our responses to these cases are correct, or at least reasonable, and have sought principles that justify treating these two cases differently. For example, one might suppose, following Kant (1785/1959) and Aquinas (1265–72/1988), that it is wrong to harm someone as a means to helping someone else. In the *footbridge* case, the proposed action involves literally using the person on the footbridge as a trolley stopper, whereas in the *trolley* case the victim is to be harmed merely as a side effect. (Were the single person on the alternative track to magically disappear, we would be very pleased.) In response to this proposal, Thomson devised the *loop* case (Thomson, 1986). Here the situation is similar to that of the *trolley* dilemma, but this time the single person is on a piece of track that branches off of the main track and then rejoins it at a point before the five people. In this case, if the person were not on the side track, the trolley would return to the main track and run over the five people. The consensus here is that it is morally acceptable to turn the trolley in this case, despite the fact that here, as in the *footbridge* case, a person will be used as a means.

There have been many such normative attempts to solve the trolley problem, but none of them has been terribly successful. My collaborators and I have proposed a partial and purely descriptive solution to this problem and have collected some scientific evidence in favor of it. We hypothesized that the thought of pushing someone to his death in an "up close and personal" manner (as in the *footbridge* dilemma) is more emotionally salient than the thought of bringing about similar consequences in a more impersonal way (e.g., by hitting a switch, as in the *trolley* dilemma). We proposed that this difference in emotional response explains why people respond so differently to these two cases. That is, people tend toward consequentialism in the case in which the emotional response is low and tend toward deontology in the case in which the emotional response is high.

The rationale for distinguishing between *personal* and *impersonal* forms of harm is largely evolutionary. "Up close and personal" violence has been around for a very long time, reaching far back into our primate lineage. Given that personal violence is evolutionarily ancient, predating our recently evolved human capacities for complex abstract reasoning, it should come as no surprise if we have innate responses to personal violence that are powerful but rather primitive. That is, we might expect humans to have negative emotional responses to certain basic forms of interpersonal violence, where these responses evolved as a means of regulating the behavior of creatures who are capable of intentionally harming one another, but whose survival depends on cooperation and individual restraint. In contrast, when a harm is *impersonal*, it should fail to trigger this alarmlike emotional response, allowing people to respond in a more "cognitive" way, perhaps employing a cost-benefit analysis. As Josef Stalin once said, "A single death is a tragedy; a million deaths is a statistic." His remarks suggest that when harmful actions are sufficiently impersonal, they fail to push our emotional buttons, despite their seriousness, and as a result we think about them in a more detached, actuarial fashion.

This hypothesis makes some strong predictions regarding what we should see going on in people's brains while they are responding to dilemmas involving personal versus impersonal harm (henceforth called "personal" and "impersonal" moral dilemmas). The contemplation of personal moral dilemmas like the *footbridge* case should produce increased neural activity in brain regions associated with emotional response and social cognition, while the contemplation of impersonal moral dilemmas like the *trolley* case should produce relatively greater activity in brain regions associated with "higher cognition."[2] This is exactly what was observed (Greene et al., 2004; Greene et al., 2001). Contemplation of personal moral dilemmas produced relatively greater activity in

three emotion-related areas: the posterior cingulate cortex, the medial prefrontal cortex, and the amygdala. This effect was also observed in the superior temporal sulcus, a region associated with various kinds of social cognition in humans and other primates. At the same time, contemplation of impersonal moral dilemmas produced relatively greater neural activity in two classically "cognitive" brain areas, the dorsolateral prefrontal cortex and inferior parietal lobe.

This hypothesis also makes a prediction regarding people's reaction times. According to the view I have sketched, people tend to have emotional responses to personal moral violations, responses that incline them to judge against performing those actions. That means that someone who judges a personal moral violation to be *appropriate* (e.g., someone who says it's okay to push the man off the bridge in the *footbridge* case) will most likely have to override an emotional response in order to do it. This overriding process will take time, and thus we would expect that "yes" answers will take longer than "no" answers in response to personal moral dilemmas like the *footbridge* case. At the same time, we have no reason to predict a difference in reaction time between "yes" and "no" answers in response to impersonal moral dilemmas like the *trolley* case because there is, according to this model, no emotional response (or much less of one) to override in such cases. Here, too, the prediction has held. Trials in which the subject judged in favor of personal moral violations took significantly longer than trials in which the subject judged against them, but there was no comparable reaction time effect observed in response to impersonal moral violations (Greene et al., 2004; Greene et al., 2001).

Further results support this model as well. Next we subdivided the personal moral dilemmas into two categories on the basis of difficulty (i.e., based on reaction time). Consider the following moral dilemma (the *crying baby* dilemma): It is wartime, and you and some of your fellow villagers are hiding from enemy soldiers in a basement. Your baby starts to cry, and you cover your baby's mouth to block the sound. If you remove your hand, your baby will cry loudly, the soldiers will hear, and they will find you and the others and kill everyone they find, including you and your baby. If you do not remove your hand, your baby will smother to death. Is it okay to smother your baby to death in order to save yourself and the other villagers?

This is a very difficult question. Different people give different answers, and nearly everyone takes a relatively long time. This is in contrast to other personal moral dilemmas, such as the *infanticide* dilemma, in which a teenage girl must decide whether to kill her unwanted newborn. In response to this case, people (at least the ones we tested) quickly and unanimously say that this action is wrong.

What's going on in these two cases? My colleagues and I hypothesized as follows. In both cases there is a prepotent, negative emotional response to the personal violation in question, killing one's own baby. In the *crying baby* case, however, a cost-benefit analysis strongly favors smothering the baby. After all, the baby is going to die no matter what, and so you have nothing to lose (in consequentialist terms) and much to gain by smothering it, awful as it is. In some people the emotional response dominates, and those people say "no." In other people, this "cognitive," cost-benefit analysis wins out, and these people say "yes."

What does this model predict that we will see going on in people's brains when we compare cases like *crying baby* and *infanticide*? First, this model supposes that cases like *crying baby* involve an increased level of "response conflict," that is, conflict between competing representations for behavioral response. Thus, we should expect that difficult moral dilemmas like *crying baby* will produce increased activity in a brain region that is associated with response conflict, the anterior cingulate cortex. Second, according to our model, the crucial difference between cases

like *crying baby* and those like *infanticide* is that the former evoke strong "cognitive" responses that can effectively compete with a prepotent, emotional response. Thus, we should expect to see increased activity in classically "cognitive" brain areas when we compare cases like *crying baby* with cases like *infanticide*, despite the fact that difficult dilemmas like *crying baby* are personal moral dilemmas, which were previously associated with emotional response (Greene et al., 2001).

These two predictions have held (Greene et al., 2004). Comparing high-reaction-time personal moral dilemmas like *crying baby* with low-reaction-time personal moral dilemmas like *infanticide* revealed increased activity in the anterior cingulate cortex (conflict) as well as the anterior dorsolateral prefrontal cortex and the inferior parietal lobes, both classically "cognitive" brain regions.

Cases like *crying baby* are especially interesting because they allow us to directly compare the neural activity associated with characteristically consequentialist and deontological responses. According to our model, when people say "yes" to such cases (the consequentialist answer), it is because the "cognitive" cost-benefit analysis has successfully dominated the prepotent emotional response that drives people to say "no" (the deontological answer). If that is correct, then we should expect to see increased activity in the previously identified "cognitive" brain regions (the dorsolateral prefrontal cortex and inferior parietal cortex) for the trials in which people say "yes" in response to cases like *crying baby*. This is exactly what we found. In other words, people exhibit more "cognitive" activity when they give the consequentialist answer.[3]

To summarize, people's moral judgments appear to be products of at least two different kinds of psychological processes. First, both brain imaging and reaction-time data suggest that there are prepotent negative emotional responses that drive people to disapprove of the personally harmful actions proposed in cases like the *footbridge* and *crying baby* dilemmas. These responses are characteristic of deontology, but not of consequentialism. Second, further brain imaging results suggest that "cognitive" psychological processes can compete with the aforementioned emotional processes, driving people to approve of personally harmful moral violations, primarily when there is a strong consequentialist rationale for doing so, as in the *crying baby* case. The parts of the brain that exhibit increased activity when people make characteristically consequentialist judgments are those that are most closely associated with higher cognitive functions such as executive control, complex planning, deductive and inductive reasoning, taking the long view in economic decision making, and so on. Moreover, these brain regions are among those most dramatically expanded in humans compared with other primates.

Emotion and the sense of moral obligation

In his classic article, "Famine, Affluence, and Morality," Peter Singer (1972) argues that we in the affluent world have an obligation to do much more than we do to improve the lives of needy people. He argues that if we can prevent something very bad from happening without incurring a comparable moral cost, then we ought to do it. For example, if one notices a small child drowning in a shallow pond, one is morally obliged to wade in and save that child, even if it means muddying one's clothes. As Singer points out, this seemingly innocuous principle has radical implications, implying that all of us who spend money on unnecessary luxuries should give up those luxuries in order to spend the money on saving and/or improving the lives of impoverished peoples. Why, Singer asks, do we have a strict obligation to save a nearby drowning child but no comparable obligation to save faraway sick and starving children through charitable donations to organizations like Oxfam?

Many normative explanations come to mind, but none is terribly compelling. Are we allowed to ignore the plight of faraway children because they are citizens of foreign nations? If so, then would it be acceptable to let the child drown, provided that the child was encountered while traveling abroad? Or in international waters? And what about the domestic poor? This argument does not relieve us of our obligations to them. Is it because of diffused responsibility—because many are in a position to help a starving child abroad, but only you are in a position to help this hypothetical drowning child? What if there were many people standing around the pond doing nothing? Would that make it okay for you to do nothing as well? Is it because international aid is ultimately ineffective, only serving to enrich corrupt politicians or create more poor people? In that case, our obligation would simply shift to more sophisticated relief efforts incorporating political reform, economic development, family planning education, and so on. Are all relief efforts doomed to ineffectiveness? That is a bold empirical claim that no one can honestly make with great confidence.

Here we find ourselves in a position similar to the one we faced with the trolley problem. We have a strong intuition that two moral dilemmas are importantly different, and yet we have a hard time explaining what that important difference is. It turns out that the same psychological theory that makes sense of the trolley problem can make sense of Singer's problem. Note that the interaction in the case of the drowning child is "up close and personal," the sort of situation that might have been encountered by our human and primate ancestors. Likewise, note that the donation case is not "up close and personal," and is not the sort of situation that our ancestors could have encountered. At no point were our ancestors able to save the lives of anonymous strangers through modest material sacrifices. In light of this, the psychological theory presented here suggests that we are likely to find the obligation to save the drowning child more pressing simply because that "up close and personal" case pushes our emotional buttons in a way that the more impersonal donation case does not (Greene, 2003). As it happens, these two cases were among those tested in the brain imaging study described earlier, with a variation on the drowning child case included in the *personal* condition and the donation case included in the *impersonal* condition (Greene et al., 2004; Greene et al., 2001).

Few people accept Singer's consequentialist conclusion. Rather, people tend to believe, in a characteristically deontological way, that they are within their moral rights in spending their money on luxuries for themselves, despite the fact that their money could be used to dramatically improve the lives of other people. This is exactly what one would expect if (1) the deontological sense of obligation is driven primarily by emotion, and (2) when it comes to obligations to aid, emotions are only sufficiently engaged when those to whom we might owe something are encountered (or conceived of) in a personal way.

Emotion and the pull of identifiable victims

One aspect of someone's being "up close and personal" is that such a person is always, in some sense, an identifiable, determinate individual and not a mere statistical someone (Greene and Haidt, 2002; Greene et al., 2001). The drowning child, for example, is presented as a particular person, while the children you might help through donations to Oxfam are anonymous and, as far as you know, indeterminate.[4] Many researchers have observed a tendency to respond with greater urgency to identifiable victims, compared with indeterminate, "statistical" victims. This is known as the "identifiable victim effect."

You may recall, for example, the case of Jessica McClure, a.k.a. "Baby Jessica," who in 1987 was trapped in a well in Texas. More than

$700,000 was sent to her family to support the rescue effort (Small & Loewenstein, 2003). As Small and Loewenstein point out, that amount of money, if it had been spent on preventive healthcare, could have been used to save the lives of many children. This observation raises a normative question that is essentially the same as Singer's. Do we have a greater obligation to help people like Baby Jessica than we do to help large numbers of others who could be saved for less? If all else is equal, a consequentialist would say "no," while most people apparently would say "yes." Furthermore, most people, if pressed to explain their position, would probably do so in deontological terms. That is, they would probably say that we have a duty to aid someone like Baby Jessica, even if doing so involves great effort and expense, while we have no comparable duty to the countless others who might be helped using the same resources.

The same "up close and personal" theory of emotional engagement can explain this pattern of judgment. Others have proposed what amounts to the same hypothesis, and others still have gathered independent evidence to support it. In Thomas Schelling's seminal article on this topic, he observes that the death of a particular person invokes "anxiety and sentiment, guilt and awe, responsibility and religion, [but] . . . most of this awesomeness disappears when we deal with statistical death" (Schelling, 1968). Inspired by Schelling's observation, Small and Loewenstein conducted two experiments aimed at testing the hypothesis that "identifiable victims stimulate a more powerful emotional response than do statistical victims."

Their crucial move was to design their experiments in such a way that their results could count against all normative explanations of the identifiable victim effect, i.e., explanations that credit decision makers with normatively respectable reasons for favoring identifiable victims. This is difficult because the process of identifying a victim inevitably provides information about that victim (name, age, gender, appearance, etc.) that could serve as a rational basis for favoring that person. To avoid this, they sought to document a weaker form of the identifiable victim effect, which one might call the "determinate victim effect." They examined people's willingness to benefit determined versus undetermined individuals under conditions in which all meaningful information about the victims was held constant.

Their first experiment worked as follows. Ten laboratory subjects were each given an "endowment" of $10. Some subjects randomly drew cards that said "KEEP" and were allowed to retain their endowments, while other subjects drew cards that said "LOSE" and subsequently had their endowments taken away, thus rendering them "victims." Each of the nonvictim subjects was anonymously paired with one of the victims as a result of drawing that victim's number. The nonvictim subjects were allowed to give a portion of their endowments to their respective victims, and each could choose how much to give. However—the crucial manipulation—some nonvictim subjects drew the victim's number *before* deciding how much to give, while others drew the victim's number *after* deciding, knowing in advance that they would do so later. In other words, some subjects had to answer the question, "How much do I want to give to person #4?" (determined victim), whereas other subjects had to answer the question, "How much do I want to give to the person whose number I will draw?" (undetermined victim). At no point did the nonvictim subjects ever know who would receive their money. The results: The mean donation for the group who gave to determined victims was 60 percent higher than that of the group giving to undetermined victims. The median donation for the determined victim group was more than twice as high.

It is worth emphasizing the absurdity of this pattern of behavior. There is no rational basis for giving more money to "randomly determined person #4" than to "person #? to be randomly

determined," and yet that is what these people did.[5] (Note that the experiment was designed so that none of the participants would ever know who chose what.) Why would people do this? Here, too, the answer implicates emotion. In a follow-up study replicating this effect, the subjects reported on the levels of sympathy and pity they felt for the determined and undetermined victims with whom they were paired. As expected, their reported levels of sympathy and pity tracked their donation levels.

One might wonder whether this pattern holds up outside the lab. To find out, Small and Loewenstein conducted a subsequent study in which people could donate money to Habitat for Humanity to provide a home for a needy family, where the family was either determined or to be determined. As predicted, the mean donation was 25 percent higher in the determined family condition, and the median donation in the determined family condition was double that of the undetermined family condition.

And then there is Baby Jessica. We can't say for sure that resources were directed to her instead of to causes that could use the money more effectively because of people's emotional responses (and not because of people's deontological reasoning about rights and duties), but what evidence there is suggests that that is the case. As Stalin might have said, "A determinate individual's death is a tragedy; a million indeterminate deaths is a statistic."

Anger and deontological approaches to punishment

While consequentialists and deontologists agree that punishment of wrongdoing is necessary and important, they disagree sharply over the proper justification for punishment. Consequentialists such as Jeremy Bentham (1789/1982) argue that punishment is justified solely by its future beneficial effects, primarily through deterrence and (in the case of criminal law) the containment of dangerous individuals. While few would deny that the prevention of future harm provides a legitimate justification for punishment, many believe that such pragmatic considerations are not the only legitimate reasons to punish, or even the main ones. Deontologists such as Kant (1796–97/2002), for example, argue that the primary justification for punishment is retribution, to give wrongdoers what they deserve based on what they have done, regardless of whether such retribution will prevent future wrongdoing.

One might wonder, then, about the psychology of the typical punisher. Do people punish, or endorse punishment, because of its beneficial effects, or do people punish because they are motivated to give people what they deserve, in proportion to their "internal wickedness," to use Kant's phrase. Several studies speak to this question, and the results are consistent. People endorse both consequentialist and retributivist justifications for punishment in the abstract, but in practice, or when faced with more concrete hypothetical choices, people's motives appear to be predominantly retributivist. Moreover, these retributivist inclinations appear to be emotionally driven. People punish in proportion to the extent that transgressions make them angry.

First, let us consider whether punitive judgments are predominantly consequentialist or deontological and retributivist.[6] Jonathan Baron and colleagues have conducted a series of experiments demonstrating that people's punitive judgments are, for the most part, retributivist rather than consequentialist. In one study, Baron and Ritov (1993) presented people with hypothetical corporate liability cases in which corporations could be required to pay fines. In one set of cases, a corporation that manufactures vaccines is being sued because a child died as a result of taking one of its flu vaccines. Subjects were given multiple versions of this case. In one version, it was stipulated that a fine would have a positive deterrent effect. That is, a fine would

make the company produce a safer vaccine. In a different version, it was stipulated that a fine would have a "perverse" effect. Instead of causing the firm to make a safer vaccine available, a fine would cause the company to stop making this kind of vaccine altogether, a bad result given that the vaccine in question does more good than harm and that no other firm is capable of making such a vaccine. Subjects indicated whether they thought a punitive fine was appropriate in either of these cases and whether the fine should differ between these two cases. A majority of subjects said that the fine should not differ at all. Baron and Ritov achieved similar results using a complementary manipulation concerning deterrent effects on the decisions of other firms. In a different set of studies, Baron and colleagues found a similar indifference to consequentialist factors in response to questions about the management of hazardous waste (Baron, Gowda, & Kunreuther, 1993).

The results of these studies are surprising in light of the fact that many people regard the deterrence of future harmful decisions as a major reason, if not the primary reason, for imposing such fines in the real world. The strength of these results is also worth emphasizing. The finding here is not simply that people's punitive judgments fail to accord with consequentialism, the view that consequences are ultimately the *only* things that should matter to decision makers. Much more than that, it seems that a majority of people give *no weight whatsoever* to factors that are of clear consequentialist importance, at least in the contexts under consideration.

If people do not punish for consequentialist reasons, what motivates them? In a study by Kahneman and colleagues (Kahneman, Schkade, & Sunstein, 1998), subjects responded to a number of similar hypothetical scenarios (e.g., a case of anemia due to benzene exposure at work). For each scenario subjects rated the extent to which the defendant's action was "outrageous." They also rated the extent to

which the defendant in each case should be punished. The correlation between the mean outrage ratings for these scenarios and their mean punishment ratings were nearly perfect, with a Pearson's correlation coefficient (r) of 0.98. (A value of 1 indicates a perfect correlation.) Kahneman and colleagues conclude that the extent to which people desire to see a corporation punished for its behavior is almost entirely a function of the extent to which they are emotionally outraged by that corporation's behavior.

Carlsmith and colleagues (Carlsmith et al., 2002) conducted a similar set of studies aimed explicitly at determining whether people punish for consequentialist or deontological reasons. Here, as earlier, subjects were presented with scenarios involving morally and legally culpable behavior, in this case perpetrated by individuals rather than corporations. As before, subjects were asked to indicate how severe each person's punishment should be, first in abstract terms ("not at all severe" to "extremely severe") and then in more concrete terms ("not guilty/no punishment" to "life sentence"). The experimenters varied the scenarios in ways that warranted different levels of punishment, depending on the rationale for punishment. For example, a consequentialist theory of punishment considers the detection rate associated with a given kind of crime and the publicity associated with a given kind of conviction to be relevant factors in assigning punishments. According to consequentialists, if a crime is difficult to detect, then the punishment for that crime ought to be made more severe in order to counterbalance the temptation created by the low risk of getting caught. Likewise, if a conviction is likely to get a lot of publicity, then a law enforcement system interested in deterrence should take advantage of this circumstance by "making an example" of the convict with a particularly severe punishment, thus getting a maximum of deterrence "bang" for its punishment "buck."

The results were clear. For the experimental group as a whole, there was no significant change in punishment recommendations when the detection rates and levels of publicity were manipulated. In other words, people were generally indifferent to factors that according to consequentialists should matter, at least to some extent. This is in spite of the fact that Carlsmith et al., as well as others, found that subjects readily expressed a general kind of support for deterrence-oriented penal systems and corporate policies.

In a follow-up study, subjects were explicitly instructed to adopt a consequentialist approach, with the consequentialist rationale explicitly laid out and with extra manipulation checks included to ensure that the subjects understood the relevant facts. Here, too, the results were striking. Subjects did modify their judgments when they were told to think like consequentialists, but not in a genuinely consequentialist way. Instead of becoming selectively sensitive to the factors that increase the consequentialist benefits of punishment, subjects indiscriminately ratcheted up the level of punishment in all cases, giving perpetrators the punishment that they thought the perpetrators deserved based on their actions, plus a bit more for the sake of deterrence.

What motivated these subjects' punitive judgments? Here, too, an important part of the answer appears to be "outrage." Subjects indicated the extent to which they were "morally outraged" by the offenses in question, and the extent of moral outrage in response to a given offense was a pretty good predictor of the severity of punishment assigned to the perpetrator, although the effect here was weaker than that observed in Kahneman et al.'s study.[7] Moreover, a structural equation model of these data suggests that the factors that had the greatest effect on people's judgments about punishment (severity of the crime, presence of mitigating circumstances) worked their effects through "moral outrage."

You will recall Small and Loewenstein's research on the "identifiable victim effect" discussed in the previous section. More recently they have documented a parallel effect in the domain of punishment. Subjects played an "investment game" in which individuals were given money that they could choose to put into a collective investment pool. The game allows individuals to choose the extent to which they will play cooperatively, benefiting the group at the chooser's expense. After the game, cooperators were given the opportunity to punish selfish players by causing them to lose money, but the punishing cooperators had to pay for the pleasure. As before, the crucial manipulation was between determined and undetermined individuals, in this case the selfish players. Some subjects were asked, "How much would you like to punish uncooperative subject #4?" while others were asked, "How much would you like to punish the uncooperative subject whose number you will draw?" Consistent with previous results, the average punishment was almost twice as high for the determined group, and once again the subjects' reports of their emotional responses (in this case a composite measure of anger and blame) tracked their behavior (Small & Loewenstein, 2005).

Recent neuroimaging studies also suggest that the desire to punish is emotionally driven. Alan Sanfey, Jim Rilling, and colleagues (Sanfey, Rilling, Aronson, Nystrom, & Cohen, 2003) conducted a brain imaging study of the ultimatum game to study the neural bases of people's sense of fairness. The ultimatum game works as follows. There is a sum of money, say $10, and the first player (the proposer) makes a proposal on how to divide it up between her or himself and the other player. The second player, the responder, can either accept the offer, in which case the money is divided as proposed, or reject the offer, in which case no one gets anything. Proposers usually make offers that are fair (i.e., a fifty-fifty split) or close to fair, and responders tend to reject offers that are more than a little unfair. In other words, responders will typically pay for the privilege of punishing

unfair proposers, even when the game is played only once. Why do people do this?

The answer, once again, implicates emotion. The experimenters found that unfair offers, compared with fair offers, produced increased activity in the anterior insula, a brain region associated with anger, disgust, and autonomic arousal. Moreover, individuals' average levels of insula activity correlated positively with the percentage of offers they rejected and was weaker for trials in which the subject believed that the unfair offer was made by a computer program rather than a real person. Of course, it is conceivable that people were punishing in an attempt to deter unfair proposers from being unfair to others in the future, but that seems unlikely given the consistent finding that people are insensitive to manipulations that modulate the deterrent effects of punishment. Instead, it seems much more likely that people inflicted punishment for its own sake. And once again, it seems that this retributivist tendency is emotionally driven. A more recent neuroimaging study of punishment in response to violations of trust yields a similar conclusion (de Quervain, Fischbacher, Treyer, Schellhammer, Schnyder, et al., 2004). In this study, the extent of punishment was correlated with the level of activity in the caudate nucleus, a brain region associated with emotion and related more specifically to motivation and reward.

When people are asked in a general and abstract way about why it makes sense to punish, consequentialist arguments are prominent. However, when people are presented with more concrete cases involving specific individuals carrying out specific offenses, people's judgments are largely, and in many cases completely, insensitive to factors affecting the consequences of punishment. This is so even when the consequentialist rationale for responding to these factors is highlighted and when people are explicitly instructed to think like consequentialists. It seems, then, that consequentialist thinking plays a negligible role in commonsense punitive judgment and that commonsense punitive judgment is almost entirely retributivist and deontological, as long as the matter is sufficiently concrete. Moreover, the available evidence, both from self-reports and neuroimaging data, suggests that people's deontological and retributivist punitive judgments are predominantly emotional, driven by feelings of anger or "outrage."

Emotion and the moral condemnation of harmless actions

According to consequentialists, actions are wrong because of their harmful consequences. In contrast, deontologists, along with many commonsense moralists, will condemn actions that do not cause harm in any ordinary sense. For example, a deontologist would likely say that it is wrong to break promises, regardless of whether doing so would have harmful consequences. Jonathan Haidt (Haidt, Koller, & Dias, 1993) has conducted a series of studies of moral judgments made in response to harmless actions. Two themes relevant to the present discussion emerge from this work. First, the moral condemnation of harmless action appears to be driven by emotion. Second, experience that encourages a more "cognitive" approach to moral decision making tends to make people less willing to condemn harmless actions.

Haidt and two Brazilian colleagues conducted a cross-cultural study of moral judgment using a large set of subjects varying in socioeconomic status (SES), nationality (Brazilian versus American), and age (children versus adults). The subjects were presented with a number of scenarios involving morally questionable, harmless actions:

1. A son promises his dying mother that he will visit her grave every week after she has died, but then doesn't because he is busy.
2. A woman uses an old American or Brazilian flag to clean the bathroom.

3. A family eats its dog after it has been killed accidentally by a car.
4. A brother and sister kiss on the lips.
5. A man masturbates using a dead chicken before cooking and eating it.

Subjects answered questions about each case: Is this action wrong? If so, why? Does this action hurt anyone? If you saw someone do this, would it bother you? Should someone who does this be stopped or punished? If doing this is the custom in some foreign country, is that custom wrong?

When people say that such actions are wrong, why do they say so? One hypothesis is that these actions are perceived as harmful, whether or not they really are. Kissing siblings could cause themselves psychological damage. Masturbating with a chicken could spread disease, etc. If this hypothesis is correct, then we would expect people's answers to the question "Does this action hurt anyone?" to correlate with their degree of moral condemnation, as indexed by affirmative answers to the questions: "Is this wrong?" "Should this person be stopped or punished?" "Is it wrong if it's the local custom?" Alternatively, if emotions drive moral condemnation in these cases, then we would expect people's answers to the question "If you saw this, would it bother you?" to better predict their answers to the moral questions posed. As expected, Haidt and colleagues found that an affirmative answer to the "Would it bother you?" question was a better predictor of moral condemnation than an affirmative answer to the harm question.[8]

Equally interesting were the between-group differences. First, the high-SES subjects in Philadelphia and Brazil were far less condemning than their low-SES counterparts, so much so that the high-SES groups in Philadelphia and Brazil resembled each other more than they resembled their low-SES neighbors. Second, people from less "westernized"[9] cities tended to be more condemning. Third, children in both places

tended to be more condemning than adults. In other words, education (SES), westernization, and growing up were associated with more consequentialist judgments in response to the scenarios used here. These three findings make sense in light of the model of moral judgment we have been developing, according to which intuitive emotional responses drive prepotent moral intuitions while "cognitive" control processes sometimes rein them in. Education is to a large extent the development of one's "cognitive" capacities, learning to think in ways that are abstract, effortful, and often either non-intuitive or counterintuitive. The westernization factor is closely related. While westerners may not be any more "cognitively" developed than members of other cultures, the western tradition takes what is, from an anthropological perspective, a peculiarly "cognitive" approach to morality. Westerners are more likely than members of other cultures to argue for and justify their moral beliefs and values in abstract terms. Moreover, western culture tends to be more pluralistic than other cultures, explicitly valuing multiple perspectives and an intellectual awareness that alternative perspectives exist. Finally, the capacity for "cognitive control" continues to develop through adolescence. Children, like adults, are very good at feeling emotions such as anger, sympathy, and disgust, but unlike adults they are not very good at controlling their behavior when experiencing such feelings. Thus, as before, there seems to be a link between "cognition" and consequentialist judgment.

In this study, the connection between a reluctance to condemn and consequentialism is fairly straightforward. Consequentialists do not condemn harmless actions.[10] The connection between the tendency to condemn harmless actions and deontology is, however, less straightforward and more questionable. It is not obvious, for example, that deontologists are any more likely than consequentialists to condemn flag desecration or eating the family dog. Similar

doubts apply to the case of kissing siblings and the man who masturbates with a dead chicken, although it's worth noting that Kant argued that incest, masturbation, bestiality, and pretty much every other form of sexual experimentation are against the moral law (Kant, 1930; Kant, 1785/1994). The broken promise case, however, is "downtown deontology." Of course, not all deontologists would condemn someone for harmlessly breaking a promise to one's deceased mother, but anyone who would condemn such behavior (without appealing in some way to consequences) is exhibiting characteristically deontological behavior.[11] In light of this, it is worth examining this case more closely, and it turns out that this case fits the pattern for the intergroup differences quite well. Among high SES adults, the percentage of subjects in each city who said that this action should be stopped or punished ranged from 3% to 7%, while the percentage of low SES adults who said the same ranged from 20% (Philadelphia) to 57% (Recife, Brazil). Likewise, among high SES adults, the percentage who said that this behavior would be wrong even if it were the local custom ranged from 20% to 28%, while the corresponding percentages for low SES subjects ranged from 40% to 87%. The tendency to condemn this behavior also decreased with westernization, and within every group children were more willing to condemn it than adults. (If you want someone to visit your grave when you're dead, you can't beat poor children from Recife, Brazil. Ninety-seven percent endorsed punishing or stopping people who renege on grave-visiting promises, and 100% condemn cultures in which doing so is the custom.) Thus, the argument made earlier connecting "cognition" and consequentialism applies specifically to the case in which moral condemnation is most characteristically deontological. Haidt et al. did not provide data regarding the "Would it bother you?" question for this case specifically, but the fact that this case was not an exception to the general "cognitive" pattern (less condemnation in the presence of "cognition"-boosting factors) suggests that it is unlikely to be an exception to the general emotion-related pattern (condemnation correlated with negative emotions).

More powerful and direct evidence for the role of emotion in condemning harmless moral violations comes from two more recent studies. In the first of these, Thalia Wheatley and Jonathan Haidt (2005) gave hypnotizable individuals a posthypnotic suggestion to feel a pang of disgust upon reading the word "often" (and to forget that they received this suggestion). The other subjects (also hypnotizable individuals) were given the same treatment, except that they were sensitized to the word "take." The subjects were then presented with scenarios, some of which involved no harm. In one scenario, for example, second cousins have a sexual relationship in which they "*take/often go* on weekend trips to romantic hotels in the mountains." The subjects who received the matching post-hypnotic suggestion (i.e., read the word to which they were hypnotically sensitized) judged this couple's actions to be more morally wrong than did the other subjects.

In a second experiment, Wheatley and Haidt used a scenario in which the person described did nothing wrong at all. It was the case of a student council representative who "*often picks*" (or "*tries to take up*") topics of broad interest for discussion. Many subjects who received matching posthypnotic suggestions indicated that his behavior was somewhat wrong, and two subjects gave it high wrongness ratings. Subjects said things like: "It just seems like he's up to something," "It just seems so weird and disgusting," and, "I don't know [why it's wrong], it just is." Again, we see emotions driving people to nonconsequentialist conclusions.

In a more recent study, Simone Schnall, Jonathan Haidt, and Gerald Clore (2004) manipulated feelings of disgust, not with hypnosis, but by seating subjects at a disgusting desk while they filled out their questionnaires. (The desk

was stained and sticky, located near an over-flowing trashcan containing used pizza boxes and dirty-looking tissues, etc.) These subjects responded to a number of moral judgment scenarios, including variations on the dog-eating and masturbation scenarios mentioned earlier. Here, as before, the disgust manipulation made people more likely to condemn these actions, though only for subjects who were rated as highly sensitive to their own bodily states.

Two patterns of moral judgment

The experiments conducted by Greene et al., Small and Loewenstein, Baron et al., Kahneman et al., Carlsmith et al., Sanfey et al., de Quervain et al., and Haidt et al. together provide multiple pieces of independent evidence that deontological patterns of moral judgment are driven by emotional responses while consequentialist judgments are driven by "cognitive" processes. Any one of the results and interpretations described here may be questioned, but the convergent evidence assembled here makes a decent case for the association between deontology and emotion, especially since there is, to my knowledge, no empirical evidence to the contrary. Of course, deontologists may regard themselves and their minds as exceptions to the statistically significant and multiply convergent psychological patterns identified in these studies, but in my opinion the burden is on them to demonstrate that they are psychologically exceptional in a way that preserves their self-conceptions.

Why should deontology and emotion go together? I believe the answer comes in two parts. First, moral emotion provides a natural solution to certain problems created by social life. Second, deontological philosophy provides a natural "cognitive" interpretation of moral emotion. Let us consider each of these claims in turn.

First, why moral emotions? In recent decades many plausible and complementary explanations have been put forth, and a general consensus seems to be emerging. The emotions most relevant to morality exist because they motivate behaviors that help individuals spread their genes *within a social context*. The theory of kin selection explains why individuals have a tendency to care about the welfare of those individuals to whom they are closely related. Because close relatives share a high proportion of their genes, one can spread one's own genes by helping close relatives spread theirs. The theory of reciprocal altruism explains the existence of a wider form of altruism: Genetically unrelated individuals can benefit from being nice to each other as long as they are capable of keeping track of who is willing to repay their kindness. More recent evolutionary theories of altruism attempt to explain the evolution of "strong reciprocity," a broader tendency to reward cooperative behavior and punish uncooperative behavior, even in contexts in which the necessary conditions for kin selection (detectable genetic relationships) and reciprocal altruism (detectable cooperative dispositions) are not met. These theories explain the widespread human tendency to engage in cooperative behaviors (e.g., helping others and speaking honestly) and to avoid uncooperative behaviors (e.g., hurting others and lying), even when relatives and close associates are not involved. Moreover, these theories explain "altruistic punishment," people's willingness to punish antisocial behavior even when they cannot expect to benefit from doing so. Other evolutionary theories make sense of other aspects of morality. For example, the incest taboo can be explained as a mechanism for avoiding birth defects, which are more likely to result from matings between close relatives. Finally, the emerging field of cultural evolution promises to explain how moral norms (and cultural practices more broadly) develop and spread.

Such evolutionary accounts of moral phenomena have received a great deal of attention in recent years and therefore I will not elaborate upon them here. I will simply assume that

the general thrust of these theories is correct: that our most basic moral dispositions are evolutionary adaptations that arose in response to the demands and opportunities created by social life. The pertinent question here concerns the psychological implementation of these dispositions. Why should our adaptive moral behavior be driven by moral emotions as opposed to something else, such as moral reasoning? The answer, I believe, is that emotions are very reliable, quick, and efficient responses to recurring situations, whereas reasoning is unreliable, slow, and inefficient in such contexts.

Nature doesn't leave it to our powers of reasoning to figure out that ingesting fat, sugar, and protein is conducive to our survival. Rather, it makes us hungry and gives us an intuitive sense that things like meat and fruit will satisfy our hunger. Nature doesn't leave it to us to figure out that fellow humans are more suitable mates than baboons. Instead, it endows us with a psychology that makes certain humans strike us as appealing sexual partners, and makes baboons seem frightfully unappealing in this regard. And, finally, Nature doesn't leave it to us to figure out that saving a drowning child is a good thing to do. Instead, it endows us with a powerful "moral sense" that compels us to engage in this sort of behavior (under the right circumstances). In short, when Nature needs to get a behavioral job done, it does it with intuition and emotion wherever it can. Thus, from an evolutionary point of view, it is no surprise that moral dispositions evolved, and it is no surprise that these dispositions are implemented emotionally.

Now, onto the second part of the explanation. Why should the existence of moral emotions give rise to the existence of deontological philosophy? To answer this question, we must appeal to the well-documented fact that humans are, in general, irrepressible explainers and justifiers of their own behavior. Psychologists have repeatedly found that when people don't know why they're doing what they're doing, they just make up a plausible-sounding story.

Recall, for example, the pantyhose experiment described earlier. The subjects didn't know that they were drawn to items on the right side of the display, but when they were asked to explain themselves, they made up perfectly rational, alternative explanations for their preferences (Nisbett & Wilson, 1977). In a similar experiment, Nisbett and Wilson (1977) induced subjects to prefer the laundry detergent Tide by priming them with word pairs like "ocean-moon" in a preceding memory test. When subjects explained their preferences, they said things like "Tide is the best-known detergent," or "My mother uses Tide," or "I like the Tide box." In an early experiment by Maier (Maier, 1931; Nisbett & Wilson, 1977), subjects had to figure out a way to tie together two cords hanging from the ceiling, a challenging task since the cords were too far apart to be reached simultaneously. The solution was to tie a heavy object to one of the cords so that it could swing like a pendulum. The subject could then hold onto one cord while waiting for the other one to swing into reach. Maier was able to help his subjects solve this problem by giving them a subtle clue. As he was walking around the room he would casually put one of the cords in motion. The subjects who were aided by this clue, however, were unaware of its influence. Instead, they readily attributed their insights to a different, more conspicuous cue (Maier's twirling a weight on a cord), despite the fact that this cue was demonstrated to be useless in other versions of the experiment.

In a similar experiment, Dutton and Aron (Dutton & Aron, 1974; Wilson, 2002) had male subjects cross a scary footbridge spanning a deep gorge, after which they were met by an attractive female experimenter. Control subjects rested on a bench before encountering the attractive experimenter. The subjects who had just braved the scary bridge, with their sweaty palms and hearts a'pounding, were more than twice as likely as the control subjects to call the experimenter later and ask her for a date. These

individuals (many of them, at any rate) interpreted their increased physiological arousal as increased attraction to the woman they had met.

The tendency toward post hoc rationalization is often revealed in studies of people with unusual mental conditions. Patients with Korsakoff's amnesia and related memory disorders are prone to "confabulation." That is, they attempt to paper over their memory deficits by constructing elaborate stories about their personal histories, typically delivered with great confidence and with no apparent awareness that they are making stuff up. For example, a confabulating patient seated near an air conditioner was asked if he knew where he was. He replied that he was in an air-conditioning plant. When it was pointed out that he was wearing pajamas, he said, "I keep them in my car and will soon change into my work clothes." Likewise, individuals acting under post-hypnotic suggestion will sometimes explain away their behaviors in elaborately rational terms. In one case, a hypnotized subject was instructed to place a lampshade on another person's head upon perceiving an arbitrary cue. He did as instructed, but when he was asked to explain why he did what he did, he made no reference to the posthypnotic suggestion or the cue: "Well, I'll tell you. It sounds queer but it's just a little experiment in psychology. I've been reading on the psychology of humor and I thought I'd see how you folks reacted to a joke that was in very bad taste."

Perhaps the most striking example of this kind of post hoc rationalization comes from studies of split-brain patients, people in whom there is no direct neuronal communication between the cerebral hemispheres. In one study, a patient's right hemisphere was shown a snow scene and instructed to select a matching picture. Using his left hand, the hand controlled by the right hemisphere, he selected a picture of a shovel. At the same time, the patient's left hemisphere, the hemisphere that is dominant for language, was shown a picture of a chicken claw. The patient was asked verbally why he chose the shovel with his left hand. He answered, "I saw a claw and picked a chicken, and you have to clean out the chicken shed with a shovel" (Gazzaniga & Le Doux, 1978). Gazzaniga and Lé Doux argue that these sorts of confabulations are not peculiar to spilt-brain patients, that this tendency was not created when these patients' intercerebral communication lines were cut. Rather, they argue, we are all confabulators of a sort. We respond to the conscious deliverances of our unconscious perceptual, mnemonic, and emotional processes by fashioning them into a rationally sensible narrative, and without any awareness that we are doing so. This widespread tendency for rationalization is only revealed in carefully controlled experiments in which the psychological inputs and behavioral outputs can be carefully monitored, or in studies of abnormal individuals who are forced to construct a plausible narrative out of meager raw material.

We are now ready to put two and two together. What should we expect from creatures who exhibit social and moral behavior that is driven largely by intuitive emotional responses and who are prone to rationalization of their behaviors? The answer, I believe, is deontological moral philosophy. What happens when we contemplate pushing the large man off the footbridge? If I'm right, we have an intuitive emotional response that says "no!" This nay-saying voice can be overridden, of course, but as far as the voice itself is concerned, there is no room for negotiation. Whether or not we can ultimately justify pushing the man off the footbridge, it will always *feel* wrong. And what better way to express that feeling of non-negotiable absolute wrongness than via the most central of deontological concepts, the concept of a *right*: You can't push him to his death because that would be a violation of his *rights*. Likewise, you can't let that baby drown because you have a *duty* to save it.

Deontology, then, is a kind of moral confabulation. We have strong feelings that tell us in clear and uncertain terms that some things *simply cannot*

be done and that other things *simply must be done.* But it is not obvious how to make sense of these feelings, and so we, with the help of some especially creative philosophers, make up a rationally appealing story: There are these things called "rights" which people have, and when someone has a right you can't do anything that would take it away. It doesn't matter if the guy on the footbridge is toward the end of his natural life, or if there are seven people on the tracks below instead of five. If the man has a right, then *the man has a right.* As John Rawls (1971, pp. 3–4) famously said, "Each person possesses an inviolability founded on justice that even the welfare of society as a whole cannot override" and, "In a just society the rights secured by justice are not subject to political bargaining or to the calculus of social interests." These are applause lines because they make emotional sense. Deontology, I believe, is a natural "cognitive" expression of our deepest moral emotions.

This hypothesis raises a further question. Why just deontology? Why not suppose that all moral philosophy, even all moral reasoning, is a rationalization of moral emotion? (This is the strong form of the view defended by Jonathan Haidt, 2001, whose argument is the model for the argument made here.)[12] The answer, I think, is that consequentialist moral judgment is not driven by emotion, or at least it is not driven by the sort of "alarm bell" emotion that drives deontological judgment. The evidence presented earlier supports this hypothesis, suggesting that consequentialist judgment is less emotional and more "cognitive," but it doesn't explain why this should be so. I argued earlier that there is a natural mapping between the content of deontological philosophy and the functional properties of alarmlike emotions. Likewise, I believe that there is a natural mapping between the content of consequentialist philosophy and the functional properties of "cognitive" processes. Indeed, I believe that consequentialism is inherently "cognitive," that it couldn't be implemented any other way.

Consequentialism is, by its very nature, systematic and aggregative. It aims to take nearly everything into account, and grants that nearly everything is negotiable. All consequentialist decision making is a matter of balancing competing concerns, taking into account as much information as is practically feasible. Only in hypothetical examples in which "all else is equal" does consequentialism give clear answers. For real-life consequentialism, everything is a complex guessing game, and all judgments are revisable in light of additional details. There is no moral clarity in consequentialist moral thought, with its approximations and simplifying assumptions. It is fundamentally actuarial.

Recall the definition of "cognitive" proposed earlier: "Cognitive" representations are inherently neutral representations, ones that, unlike emotional representations, do not automatically trigger particular behavioral responses or dispositions. Once again, the advantage of having such neutral representations is that they can be mixed and matched in a situation-specific way without pulling the agent in multiple behavioral directions at once, thus enabling highly flexible behavior. These are precisely the sorts of representations that a consequentialist needs in order to make a judgment based on aggregation, one that takes all of the relevant factors into account: "Is it okay to push the guy off the bridge if he's about to cure cancer?" "Is it okay to go out for sushi when the extra money could be used to promote health education in Africa?" And so on. Deontologists can dismiss these sorts of complicated, situation-specific questions, but consequentialists cannot, which is why, I argue, that consequentialism is inescapably "cognitive."

Some clarifications: First, I am not claiming that consequentialist judgment is emotionless. On the contrary, I am inclined to agree with Hume (1740/1978) that all moral judgment must have some affective component, and suspect that the consequentialist weighing of harms and benefits is an emotional process. But, if I am right, two things distinguish this sort of

process from those associated with deontology. First, this is, as I have said, a weighing process and not an "alarm" process. The sorts of emotions hypothesized to be involved here say, "Such-and-such matters this much. Factor it in." In contrast, the emotions hypothesized to drive deontological judgment are far less subtle. They are, as I have said, alarm signals that issue simple commands: "Don't do it!" or "Must do it!" While such commands can be overridden, they are designed to dominate the decision rather than merely influence it.

Second, I am not claiming that deontological judgment cannot be "cognitive." Indeed, I believe that sometimes it is. Rather, my hypothesis is that deontological judgment is affective at its core, while consequentialist judgment is inescapably "cognitive." One could, in principle, make a characteristically deontological judgment by thinking explicitly about the categorical imperative and whether the action in question is based on a maxim that could serve as a universal law. And if one were to do that, then the psychological process would be "cognitive." What I am proposing, however, is that this is not how characteristically deontological conclusions tend to be reached and that, instead, they tend to be reached on the basis of emotional responses. This contrasts with consequentialist judgments which, according to my hypothesis, cannot be implemented in an intuitive, emotional way. The only way to reach a distinctively consequentialist judgment (i.e., one that doesn't coincide with a deontological judgment) is to actually go through the consequentialist, cost-benefit reasoning using one's "cognitive" faculties, the ones based in the dorsolateral prefrontal cortex (Greene et al., 2004).

This psychological account of consequentialism and deontology makes sense of certain aspects of their associated phenomenologies. I have often observed that consequentialism strikes students as appealing, even as tautologically true, when presented in the abstract, but that its appeal is easily undermined by specific counterexamples. (See the earlier discussion contrasting people's real-world motives and abstract justifications for punishment.) When a first-year ethics student asks, "But isn't it obvious that one should do whatever will produce the most good?" all you have to do is whip out the *footbridge* case and you have made your point. Whatever initial "cognitive" appeal consequentialist principles may have is quickly neutralized by a jolt of emotion, and the student is a newly converted deontologist: "Why is it wrong to push the man off the footbridge? Because he has a *right*, an inviolability founded on justice that even the welfare of society as a whole cannot override!" Then it's time for a new counterexample: "What if the trolley is headed for a detonator that will set off a nuclear bomb that will kill half a million people?" Suddenly the welfare of society as a whole starts to sound important again. "Cognition" strikes back with a more compelling utilitarian rationale, and the student is appropriately puzzled. As this familiar dialectic illustrates, the hypothesis that deontology is emotionally based explains the "*NEVER!*—except sometimes" character of rights-based, deontological ethics. An alarmlike emotional response presents itself as unyielding and absolute, until an even more compelling emotional or "cognitive" rationale comes along to override it.

This hypothesis also makes sense of certain deontological anomalies, which I suspect will turn out to be the "exceptions that prove the rule." I have argued that deontology is driven by emotion, but I suspect this is not always the case. Consider, for example, Kant's infamous claim that it would be wrong to lie to a would-be murderer in order to protect a friend who has taken refuge in one's home (Kant, 1785/1983). Here, in a dramatic display of true intellectual integrity, Kant sticks to his theory and rejects the intuitive response. (He "bites the bullet," as philosophers say.) But what is interesting about this bit of Kantian ethics is that it's something of an embarrassment to contemporary Kantians,

who are very keen to explain how Kant somehow misapplied his own theory in this case (Korsgaard, 1996a). Presumably the same goes for Kant's views of sexual morality (Kant, 1930, pp. 169–71; Kant, 1994). Modern academics are no longer so squeamish about lust, masturbation, and homosexuality, and so Kant's old-fashioned views on these topics have to be explained away, which is not difficult, since his arguments were never terribly compelling to begin with (see the epigraph). If you want to know which bits of Kant contemporary Kantians will reject, follow the emotions.

Notes

Many thanks to Walter Sinnott-Armstrong, Jonathan Haidt, Shaun Nichols, and Andrea Heberlein for very helpful comments on this chapter.

1   Kohlberg was certainly partial to deontology and would likely say that it is more "cognitive" than consequentialism.

2   It turns out that determining what makes a moral dilemma "personal" and "like the footbridge case" versus "impersonal" and "like the trolley case" is no simple matter, and in many ways reintroduces the complexities associated with traditional attempts to solve the trolley problem. For the purposes of this discussion, however, I am happy to leave the personal-impersonal distinction as an intuitive one, in keeping with the evolutionary account given earlier. For the purposes of designing the brain imaging experiment discussed later, however, my collaborators and I developed a more rigid set of criteria for distinguishing personal from impersonal moral violations (Greene et al., 2001). I no longer believe that these criteria are adequate. Improving these is a goal of ongoing research.

3   It is worth noting that no brain regions, including those implicated in emotion, exhibited the opposite effect. First, it's not clear that one would expect to see such a result since the hypothesis is that everyone experiences the intuitive emotional response, while only some individuals override it. Second, it is difficult to draw conclusions from negative neuroimaging results because current neuroimaging techniques, which track changes in blood flow, are relatively crude instruments for detecting patterns in neural function.

4   Of course, some aid organizations deliberately pair individual donors with individual recipients to make the experience more personal.

5   First, when I say that this behavior cannot be rationally defended, I do not mean that it is logically or metaphysically impossible for a rational person to behave this way. Someone could, for example, have a basic preference for helping determined victims and only determined victims. I am assuming, however, that none of the subjects in this experiment have such bizarre preferences and that therefore their behavior is irrational. Second, I am not claiming that the general psychological tendency that produces this behavior has no "rationale" or that it is not adaptive. Rather, I am simply claiming that this particular behavior is irrational in this case. Few, if any, of the participants in this study would knowingly choose to respond to the experimental manipulation (determined versus undetermined victim) by giving more to the determined victim. In other words, this experimental effect would have been greatly diminished, if not completely eliminated, had this experiment employed a within-subject design instead of a between-subject design.

6   I am assuming that within the domain of punishment, "deontological" and "retributivist" are effectively interchangeable, even though they are conceptually distinct. (For example, one could favor punishment as an end in itself, but in unpredictable ways that defy all normative rules.) So far as I know, all well-developed alternatives to consequentialist theories of punishment are, in one way or another, retributivist. Moreover, retributivism is explicitly endorsed by many noteworthy deontologists, including Kant (2002).

7   Some complications arise in interpreting the results of these two studies of "outrage" and punishment. It is not clear whether the "outrage" scale used by Kahneman et al. elicits a subjective report of the subject's emotional state or a normative judgment concerning the defendant's behavior. A skeptic might say that the so-called "outrage" rating is really just a rating of the overall moral severity of the crime, which, not

surprisingly, correlates with the extent to which people think it warrants punishment.

The Carlsmith et al. study addresses this worry (though not intentionally), and suggests that it may have some validity. The outrage measure used in the Carlsmith et al. study asks explicitly for a subjective report: "How morally outraged were you by this offense?" And, perhaps as a result of this change in tactic, the connection between "outrage" and punitive judgment is weakened from near perfect to fairly strong. Note also that in choosing a strong word like "outrage" in a study of fairly mild, hypothetical crimes, the experimenters may have set the bar too high for subjective reports, thus weakening their results.

8 This result, however, only held for the subgroups that did the majority of the condemning. The subjects who were most reluctant to condemn harmless violations (chiefly high-SES, educated westerners) found harm where others did not and cited that as a reason for condemnation, an effect that Haidt has documented elsewhere and which he has dubbed "moral dumbfounding" (Haidt, Bjorklund, & Murphy, 2000).

9 "Westernization" refers to "the degree to which each of three cities [Philadelphia and two Brazilian cities, Porto Alegre and Recife] has a cultural and symbolic life based on European traditions, including a democratic political structure and an industrialized economy" (Haidt, Koller, & Dias, 1993, 615). Philadelphia is more westernized than Porto Alegre, which is more westernized than Recife.

10 A consequentialist might favor a prohibition against a class of actions, some of which are not harmful, if the prohibition produces the best available consequences. Likewise, a consequentialist might pretend to condemn (or publicly condemn, while privately refraining from condemning) an action if this public condemnation were deemed beneficial.

11 Subjects were asked to justify their answers, and typical justifications for condemning this action did not appeal to consequences, but rather simply stated that it's wrong to break a promise.

12 Haidt (2001), however, believes that philosophers may be exceptional in that they actually do reason their way to moral conclusions (Kuhn, 1991).

References

Aquinas, T. (1988). Of killing. In W. P. Baumgarth & R. J. Regan (Eds.), On law, morality, and politics (pp. 226–27). Indianapolis, IN: Hackett. (Original work written 1265–73)

Baron, J. (1994). Nonconsequentialist decisions. Behavioral and Brain Sciences, 17, 1–42.

Baron, J., & Ritov, I. (1993). Intuitions about penalties and compensation in the context of tort law. Journal of Risk and Uncertainty, 7, 17–33.

Baron, J., Gowda, R., & Kunreuther, H. (1993). Attitudes toward managing hazardous waste: What should be cleaned up and who should pay for it? Risk Analysis, 13(2), 183–92.

Bentham, J. (1982). An introduction to the principles of morals and legislation. London: Methuen. (Original work published 1789)

Carlsmith, K. M., Darley, J. M., & Robinson, P. H. (2002). Why do we punish? Deterrence and just deserts as motives for punishment. Journal of Personality and Social Psychology, 83, 284–99.

de Quervain, D. J.-F., Fischbacher, U., Treyer, V., Schellhammer, M., Schnyder, U., Buck, A., & Fehr, E. (2004). The neural basis of altruistic punishment. Science, 305, 1254–58.

Dutton, D. G., & Aron, A. P. (1974). Some evidence for heightened sexual attraction under conditions of high anxiety. Journal of Personality and Social Psychology, 30, 510–17.

Gazzaniga, M. S., & Le Doux, J. E. (1978). The integrated mind. New York: Plenum.

Goel, V., & Dolan, R. J. (2004). Differential involvement of left prefrontal cortex in inductive and deductive reasoning. Cognition, 93, B109–B121.

Greene, J. (2003). From neural "is" to moral "ought": What are the moral implications of neuroscientific moral psychology? Nature Reviews Neuroscience, 4, 846–49.

Greene, J., & Haidt, J. (2002). How (and where) does moral judgment work? Trends in Cognitive Sciences, 6(12), 517–23.

Greene, J. D., Nystrom, L. E., Engell, A. D., Darley, J. M., & Cohen, J. D. (2004). The neural bases of cognitive conflict and control in moral judgment. Neuron, 44, 389–400.

Greene, J. D., Sommerville, R. B., Nystrom, L. E., Darley, J. M., & Cohen, J. D. (2001), An fMRI investigation

of emotional engagement in moral judgment. *Science, 293*(5537), 2105–8.

Haidt, J. (2001). The emotional dog and its rational tail: A social intuitionist approach to moral judgment. *Psychological Review 108*(4), 814–34.

Haidt, J., Bjorklund, F., & Murphy, S. (2000). Moral dumbfounding: When intuition finds no reason. (Unpublished manuscript, University of Virginia, Charlottesville.)

Haidt, J., Koller, S. H., & Dias, M. G. (1993). Affect, culture and morality, or is it wrong to eat your dog? *Journal of Personality and Social Psychology 65*(4), 613–28.

Hamilton, W. D. (1964). The genetical evolution of social behavior. *Journal of Theoretical Biology, 7,* 1–52.

Hume, D. (1978). *A treatise of human nature* (L. A. Selby-Bigge & P. H. Nidditch, Eds.). Oxford: Oxford University Press. (Original work published 1740)

Kagan, S. (1989). *The limits of morality.* New York: Oxford University Press.

Kahneman, D., Schkade, D., & Sunstein, C. R. (1998). Shared outrage and erratic rewards: The psychology of punitive damages. *Journal of Risk and Uncertainty, 16,* 49–86.

Kant, I. (1930). *Lectures on ethics.* Indianapolis, IN: Hackett.

Kant, I. (1959). *Foundations of the metaphysics of morals.* Indianapolis, IN: Bobbs-Merrill. (Original work published 1785)

Kant, I. (1983). *On a supposed right to lie because of philanthropic concerns.* In Kant, *Grounding for the Metaphysics of Morals* (J. W. Ellington, Trans., M. 162–66). Indianapolis, IN: Hackett. (Original work published 1785)

Kant, I. (1994). The metaphysics of morals. In Kant, *Ethical philosophy.* Indianapolis, IN: Hackett. (Original work published 1785)

Kant, I. (2002). *The philosophy of law: An exposition of the fundamental principles of jurisprudence as the science of right.* Union, NJ: Lawbook Exchange. (Original work published 1796–97)

Kohlberg, L. (1971). From is to ought: How to commit the naturalistic fallacy and get away with it in the study of moral development. In T. Mischel (Ed.), *Cognitive development and epistemology* (pp. 151–235). New York: Academic Press.

Korsgaard, C. M. (1996a). *Creating the kingdom of ends.* New York: Cambridge University Press.

Kuhn, D. (1991). *The skills of argument.* Cambridge: Cambridge University Press.

Maier, N. R. F. (1931). Reasoning in humans: II. The solution of a problem and its appearance in consciousness. *Journal of Comparative Psychology, 12,* 181–94.

Nisbett, R. E., & Wilson, T. D. (1977). Telling more than we can know: Verbal reports on mental processes. *Psychological Review, 84,* 231–59.

Rawls, J. (1971). *A theory of justice.* Cambridge, MA: Harvard University Press.

Sanfey, A. G., Rilling, J. K., Aronson, J. A., Nystrom, L. E., & Cohen, J D. (2003). The neural basis of economic decision-making in the ultimatum game. *Science, 300,* 1755–58.

Schelling, T. C. (1968). The life you save may be your own. In S. B. Chase (Ed.), *Problems in public expenditure analysis* (pp. 127–76). Washington, DC: Brookings Institution.

Schnall, S., Haidt, J., & Clore, G. (2004). Irrelevant disgust makes moral judgment more severe, for those who listen to their bodies. Unpublished manuscript.

Singer, P. (1972). Famine, affluence and morality. *Philosophy & Public Affairs, 1,* 229–43.

Small, D. A., & Loewenstein, G. (2003). Helping a victim or helping the victim. *Journal of Risk and Uncertainty, 26,* 5–16.

Small, D. A., & Loewenstein, G. (2005). The devil you know: The effects of identifiability on punitiveness. *Journal of Behavioral Decision Making, 18,* 311–18.

Smith, A. (1976). *The theory of moral sentiments.* Oxford: Oxford University Press. (Original work published 1759)

Thomson, J. J. (1986). *Rights, restitution, and risk: Essays in moral theory,* (Ed.) W. Parent. Cambridge, Mass.: Harvard University Press.

Wheatley, T., & Haidt, J. (2005). Hypnotically induced disgust makes moral judgments more severe. *Psychological Science, 16*(10), 780–84.

Wilson, T. D. (2002). *Strangers to ourselves: Discovering the adaptive unconscious.* Cambridge, MA: Harvard University Press.

SECTION IX

Applications

INTRODUCTION TO SECTION IX

THE QUESTIONS OF ethics have their origins in practical concerns, so we may expect their answers to shed light on those concerns. The essays in the current section bear out this expectation. By bringing various theoretical perspectives to bear on controversial topics, the authors both deepen our understanding of their theories and bring clarity to urgent practical debates.

One such debate concerns abortion. When people discuss this topic, they usually focus on the moral status of the fetus. Those who support abortion argue that fetuses lack moral standing, while those who oppose abortion argue that they have such standing. However, in a now-classic article (Chapter 60), Judith Jarvis Thomson denies that this is the real issue. Thomson argues that even if fetuses have the same status as adult humans, and thus have a right to life, abortion remains permissible in many contexts. She argues that a right to life does not include a right to be provided with whatever one needs to remain alive, and that even adult humans lack the latter right when others own what they need. Thus, because a woman has a right to control her body, the developing fetus does not have a right not to be removed from it. To dramatize this point, Thomson asks us to imagine awakening to find that a famous violinist has been attached to our kidneys while we slept. Even if the violinist will die if he is removed within the next nine months, we will, she argues, surely insist that we have a right to remove him. In taking this position, we will invoke the very principle on which her argument rests.

Although the most important question about abortion concerns its permissibility, it also raises questions of other sorts. One such question is whether the state should subsidize abortions for women who want but cannot afford them. Another is what restraints, if any, should govern either the activities of those who view abortion as murder or the activities of those who resist their efforts. In Chapter 61, George Sher argues that these questions are connected. After arguing that there is no right to be provided with elective abortions, he suggests that an acceptable moral compromise may be one in which the state does not fund abortion while its opponents reciprocate by not resisting abortion with all the tactics they would otherwise deploy against what they view as mass murder. In evaluating this argument, the reader may wish to compare what Sher says about the right to be provided with an abortion with what Thomson says about the right to be provided with what one needs in order to live.

Another topic that raises questions about our obligations to provide others with what they need but cannot otherwise acquire is famine relief. In Chapters 62 and 63, Peter Singer and Richard Miller develop different approaches to this topic. According to Singer, the principle that determines how much we ought to contribute to alleviate starvation is "if it is in our power to prevent somthing bad from happening, without thereby sacrificing anything of comparable moral importance, we ought, morally, to

do it." Because this principle requires only the prevention of bad things, but not the promotion of good ones, it is not a variant of utilitarianism. However, like utilitarianism, it does take our obligations to depend entirely on the consequences of the acts we might perform. There is, according to Singer, no relevant difference between the suffering of those who live near us and that of persons half a world away. It also does not matter that other affluent individuals are just as able to prevent starvation as we are, given that they are in fact not going to do so. Thus, in Singer's view, we are obligated to give away much, if not all, of what we now spend on things we could do without.

Although Miller is in sympathy with much that Singer says, he does not accept either Singer's conclusion or the principle from which he derives it. In place of Singer's principle, which tells us how we should act toward those who are in need, Miller proposes a principle which tells us how we should be *disposed* to act toward persons who are in need. The dispositions that we should have, he suggests, need only be "sufficiently demanding that giving which would express greater underlying concern [for the needy] would impose a significant risk of worsening one's life, if one fulfilled all further responsibilities." Because our lives are enriched by activities such as eating in nice restaurants and wearing stylish clothes, anyone who acquired a disposition that entirely prevented him from doing these things would thereby come to live a significantly worse life. Thus, although acquiring a disposition that satisfies Miller's principle may well lead us to make substantial sacrifices, it will not lead us to give up everything that we find satisfying or meaningful.

Unlike abortion and famine relief, about which many disagree, slavery is universally deplored within our society. However, because utilitarianism evaluates all practices by their consequences, it seems to imply that slavery would be morally acceptable if it had better consequences than any other available practice. This implication is often said to tell heavily against utilitarianism, but R. M. Hare argues in Chapter 64 that it does not. According to Hare, the abhorrence that we feel toward slavery can itself be explained in utilitarian terms: it reflects our awareness, based on what we know of human psychology and other deep facts about the world, that any actual system of slavery would yield few benefits and much misery. Although Hare acknowledges that he shares this abhorrence, he suggests that when we describe an unrealistic situation in which slavery does have the best consequences, we find that we can no longer see exactly what is wrong with it. In Hare's view, such imaginary cases do not pose problems for utilitarianism because morality must deal with the world as it actually is.

Although Onora O'Neill does not mention slavery, her topic in Chapter 65 is a pair of Kantian requirements – that we must not use people and must treat them as ends in themselves – that it clearly violates. Thus, her discussion provides a natural alternative to Hare's account of what is wrong with slavery. But what, exactly, do these requirements come to? As O'Neill reconstructs it, Kant's view requires not only that we refrain from coercing and deceiving, practices which use others by treating them in ways to which they could not consent, but also that we treat others as ends by respecting, and helping them advance, their own ends. To illustrate these requirements, O'Neill looks in detail at two contexts – sexuality on the one hand and

employment on the other – in which they are easily violated. In this discussion, she elaborates both the many subtle opportunities that sexuality offers for manipulation, coercion, and failures of respect and love and the deep tensions between capitalism and the ideal of treating each individual as the full person he is.

The book's last selection is about death. Unlike Epicurus (Chapter 47), who maintains that death is not an evil because we cannot be harmed unless we are alive, Thomas Nagel argues in Chapter 66 that "a man's life includes much that does not take place within the boundaries of his body and his mind, and what happens to him can include much that does not take place within the boundaries of his life." Drawing on this idea, Nagel argues that the reason death is bad is that it deprives us of goods that we could enjoy if we remained alive. Because it is only possible to enjoy goods after we have come into existence, Nagel suggests that his view may explain why we are troubled by the eternity that will follow our life as we are not by the eternity that preceded it. Nagel also asks whether, on his account, it should matter whether we die when we are young or old, since we will be deprived of further goods in either case. By subtly exploring these issues, Nagel further illustrates the ways in which our understanding of the questions that concern us all is enriched by philosophical inquiry.

Chapter 60

Judith Jarvis Thomson

A DEFENSE OF ABORTION[1]

MOST OPPOSITION to abortion relies on the premise that the fetus is a human being, a person, from the moment of conception. The premise is argued for, but, as I think, not well. Take, for example, the most common argument. We are asked to notice that the development of a human being from conception through birth into childhood is continuous; then it is said that to draw a line, to choose a point in this development and say "before this point the thing is not a person, after this point it is a person" is to make an arbitrary choice, a choice for which in the nature of things no good reason can be given. It is concluded that the fetus is, or anyway that we had better say it is, a person from the moment of conception. But this conclusion does not follow. Similar things might be said about the development of an acorn into an oak tree, and it does not follow that acorns are oak trees, or that we had better say they are. Arguments of this form are sometimes called "slippery slope arguments"— the phrase is perhaps self-explanatory—and it is dismaying that opponents of abortion rely on them so heavily and uncritically.

I am inclined to agree, however, that the prospects for "drawing a line" in the development of the fetus look dim. I am inclined to think also that we shall probably have to agree that the fetus has already become a human person well before birth. Indeed, it comes as a surprise when one first learns how early in its life it begins to acquire human characteristics. By the tenth week, for example, it already has a face, arms and legs, fingers and toes; it has internal organs, and brain activity is detectable.[2] On the other hand, I think that the premise is false, that the fetus is not a person from the moment of conception. A newly fertilized ovum, a newly implanted clump of cells, is no more a person than an acorn is an oak tree. But I shall not discuss any of this. For it seems to me to be of great interest to ask what happens if, for the sake of argument, we allow the premise. How, precisely, are we supposed to get from there to the conclusion that abortion is morally impermissible? Opponents of abortion commonly spend most of their time establishing that the fetus is a person, and hardly any time explaining the step from there to the impermissibility of abortion. Perhaps they think the step too simple and obvious to require much comment. Or perhaps instead they are simply being economical in argument. Many of those who defend abortion rely on the premise that the fetus is not a person, but only a bit of tissue that will become a person at birth; and why pay out more arguments than you have to? Whatever the explanation, I suggest that the step they take is neither easy nor obvious, that it calls for closer examination than it is commonly given, and that when we do give it this closer examination we shall feel inclined to reject it.

I propose then, that we grant that the fetus is a person from the moment of conception. How

does the argument go from here? Something like this, I take it. Every person has a right to life. So the fetus has a right to life. No doubt the mother has a right to decide what shall happen in and to her body, everyone would grant that. But surely a person's right to life is stronger and more stringent than the mother's right to decide what happens in and to her body, and so outweighs it. So the fetus may not be killed; an abortion may not be performed.

It sounds plausible. But now let me ask you to imagine this. You wake up in the morning and find yourself back to back in bed with an unconscious violinist. A famous unconscious violinist. He has been found to have a fatal kidney ailment, and the Society of Music Lovers has canvassed all the available medical records and found that you alone have the right blood type to help. They have therefore kidnapped you, and last night the violinist's circulatory system was plugged into yours, so that your kidneys can be used to extract poisons from his blood as well as your own. The director of the hospital now tells you, "Look, we're sorry the Society of Music Lovers did this to you—we would never have permitted it if we had known. But still, they did it, and the violinist now is plugged into you. To unplug you would be to kill him. But never mind, it's only for nine months. By then he will have recovered from his ailment, and can safely be unplugged from you." Is it morally incumbent on you to accede to this situation? No doubt it would be very nice of you if you did, a great kindness. But do you *have* to accede to it? What if it were not nine months, but nine years? Or longer still? What if the director of the hospital says, "Tough luck, I agree, but you've now got to stay in bed, with the violinist plugged into you, for the rest of your life. Because remember this. All persons have a right to life, and violinists are persons. Granted you have a right to decide what happens in and to your body, but a person's right to life outweighs your right to decide what happens in and to your body. So you cannot ever be unplugged from him." I imagine you would

regard this as outrageous, which suggests that something really is wrong with that plausible-sounding argument I mentioned a moment ago.

In this case, of course, you were kidnapped; you didn't volunteer for the operation that plugged the violinist into your kidneys. Can those who oppose abortion on the ground I mentioned make an exception for a pregnancy due to rape? Certainly. They can say that persons have a right to life only if they didn't come into existence because of rape; or they can say that all persons have a right to life, but that some have less of a right to life than others, in particular, that those who came into existence because of rape have less. But these statements have a rather unpleasant sound. Surely the question of whether you have a right to life at all, or how much of it you have, shouldn't turn on the question of whether or not you are the product of a rape. And in fact the people who oppose abortion on the ground I mentioned do not make this distinction, and hence do not make an exception in case of rape.

Nor do they make an exception for a case in which the mother has to spend the nine months of her pregnancy in bed. They would agree that would be a great pity, and hard on the mother; but all the same, all persons have a right to life, the fetus is a person, and so on. I suspect, in fact, that they would not make an exception for a case in which, miraculously enough, the pregnancy went on for nine years, or even the rest of the mother's life.

Some won't even make an exception for a case in which continuation of the pregnancy is likely to shorten the mother's life; they regard abortion as impermissible even to save the mother's life. Such cases are nowadays very rare, and many opponents of abortion do not accept this extreme view. All the same, it is a good place to begin: a number of points of interest come out in respect to it.

1. Let us call the view that abortion is impermissible even to save the mother's life "the extreme view." I want to suggest first that it does

not issue from the argument I mentioned earlier without the addition of some fairly powerful premises. Suppose a woman has become pregnant, and now learns that she has a cardiac condition such that she will die if she carries the baby to term. What may be done for her? The fetus, being a person, has a right to life, but as the mother is a person too, so has she a right to life. Presumably they have an equal right to life. How is it supposed to come out that an abortion may not be performed? If mother and child have an equal right to life, shouldn't we perhaps flip a coin? Or should we add to the mother's right to life her right to decide what happens in and to her body, which everybody seems to be ready to grant—the sum of her rights now outweighing the fetus' right to life?

The most familiar argument here is the following. We are told that performing the abortion would be directly killing[3] the child, whereas doing nothing would not be killing the mother, but only letting her die. Moreover, in killing the child, one would be killing an innocent person, for the child has committed no crime, and is not aiming at his mother's death. And then there are a variety of ways in which this might be continued. (1) But as directly killing an innocent person is always and absolutely impermissible, an abortion may not be performed. Or, (2) as directly killing an innocent person is murder, and murder is always and absolutely impermissible, an abortion may not be performed.[4] Or, (3) as one's duty to refrain from directly killing an innocent person is more stringent than one's duty to keep a person from dying, an abortion may not be performed. Or, (4) if one's only options are directly killing an innocent person or letting a person die, one must prefer letting the person die, and thus an abortion may not be performed.[5]

Some people seem to have thought that these are not further premises which must be added if the conclusion is to be reached, but that they follow from the very fact that an innocent person has a right to life.[6] But this seems to me to be a mistake, and perhaps the simplest way to show this is to bring out that while we must certainly grant that innocent persons have a right to life, the theses in (1) through (4) are all false. Take (2), for example. If directly killing an innocent person is murder, and thus is impermissible, then the mother's directly killing the innocent person inside her is murder, and thus is impermissible. But it cannot seriously be thought to be murder if the mother performs an abortion on herself to save her life. It cannot seriously be said that she *must* refrain, that she *must* sit passively by and wait for her death. Let us look again at the case of you and the violinist. There you are, in bed with the violinist, and the director of the hospital says to you, "It's all most distressing, and I deeply sympathize, but you see this is putting an additional strain on your kidneys, and you'll be dead within the month. But you *have* to stay where you are all the same. Because unplugging you would be directly killing an innocent violinist, and that's murder, and that's impermissible." If anything in the world is true, it is that you do not commit murder, you do not do what is impermissible, if you reach around to your back and unplug yourself from that violinist to save your life.

The main focus of attention in writings on abortion has been on what a third party may or may not do in answer to a request from a woman for an abortion. This is in a way understandable. Things being as they are, there isn't much a woman can safely do to abort herself. So the question asked is what a third party may do, and what the mother may do, if it is mentioned at all, is deduced, almost as an afterthought, from what it is concluded that third parties may do. But it seems to me that to treat the matter in this way is to refuse to grant to the mother that very status of person which is so firmly insisted on for the fetus. For we cannot simply read off what a person may do from what the third party may do. Suppose you find yourself trapped in a tiny house with a growing child. I mean a very tiny house, and a rapidly growing child—you are

734 Judith Jarvis Thomson

already up against the wall of the house and in a few minutes you'll be crushed to death. The child on the other hand won't be crushed to death; if nothing is done to stop him from growing he'll be hurt, but in the end he'll simply burst open the house and walk out a free man. Now I could well understand it if a bystander were to say, "There's nothing we can do for you. We cannot choose between your life and his, we cannot be the ones to decide who is to live, we cannot intervene." But it cannot be concluded that you too can do nothing, that you cannot attack it to save your life. However innocent the child may be, you do not have to wait passively while it crushes you to death. Perhaps a pregnant woman is vaguely felt to have the status of house, to which we don't allow the right of self-defense. But if the woman houses the child, it should be remembered that she is a person who houses it.

I should perhaps stop to say explicitly that I am not claiming that people have a right to do anything whatever to save their lives. I think, rather, that there are drastic limits to the right of self-defense. If someone threatens you with death unless you torture someone else to death, I think you have not the right, even to save your life, to do so. But the case under consideration here is very different. In our case there are only two people involved, one whose life is threatened, and one who threatens it. Both are innocent: the one who is threatened is not threatened because of any fault, the one who threatens does not threaten because of any fault. For this reason we may feel that we bystanders cannot intervene. But the person threatened can.

In sum, a woman surely can defend her life against the threat to it posed by the unborn child, even if doing so involves its death. And this shows not merely that the theses in (1) through (4) are false; it shows also that the extreme view of abortion is false, and so we need not canvass any other possible ways of arriving at it from the argument I mentioned at the outset.

2. The extreme view could of course be weakened to say that while abortion is permissible to save the mother's life, it may not be performed by a third party, but only by the mother herself. But this cannot be right either. For what we have to keep in mind is that the mother and the unborn child are not like two tenants in a small house which has, by an unfortunate mistake, been rented to both: the mother owns the house. The fact that she does adds to the offensiveness of deducing that the mother can do nothing from the supposition that third parties can do nothing. But it does more than this: it casts a bright light on the supposition that third parties can do nothing. Certainly it lets us see that a third party who says "I cannot choose between you" is fooling himself if he thinks this is impartiality. If Jones has found and fastened on a certain coat, which he needs to keep him from freezing, but which Smith also needs to keep him from freezing, then it is not impartiality that says "I cannot choose between you" when Smith owns the coat. Women have said again and again "This body is my body!" and they have reason to feel angry, reason to feel that it has been like shouting into the wind. Smith, after all, is hardly likely to bless us if we say to him, "Of course it's your coat, anybody would grant that it is. But no one may choose between you and Jones who is to have it."

We should really ask what it is that says "no one may choose" in the face of the fact that the body that houses the child is the mother's body. It may be simply a failure to appreciate this fact. But it may be something more interesting, namely the sense that one has a right to refuse to lay hands on people, even where it would be just and fair to do so, even where justice seems to require that somebody do so. Thus justice might call for somebody to get Smith's coat back from Jones, and yet you have a right to refuse to be the one to lay hands on Jones, a right to refuse to do physical violence to him. This, I think, must be granted. But when what should be said is not "no one may choose," but only "I cannot

choose," and indeed not even this, but "I will not *act*," leaving it open that somebody else can or should, and in particular that anyone in a position of authority, with the job of securing people's rights, both can and should. So this is no difficulty. I have not been arguing that any given third party must accede to the mother's request that he perform an abortion to save her life, but only that he may.

I suppose that in some views of human life the mother's body is only on loan to her, the loan not being one which gives her any prior claim to it. One who held this view might well think it impartiality to say "I cannot choose." But I shall simply ignore this possibility. My own view is that if a human being has any just, prior claim to anything at all, he has a just, prior claim to his own body. And perhaps this needn't be argued for here anyway, since, as I mentioned, the arguments against abortion we are looking at do grant that the woman has a right to decide what happens in and to her body.

But although they do grant it, I have tried to show that they do not take seriously what is done in granting it. I suggest the same thing will reappear even more clearly when we turn away from cases in which the mother's life is at stake, and attend, as I propose we now do, to the vastly more common cases in which a woman wants an abortion for some less weighty reason than preserving her own life.

3. Where the mother's life is not at stake, the argument I mentioned at the outset seems to have a much stronger pull. "Everyone has a right to life, so the unborn person has a right to life." And isn't the child's right to life weightier than anything other than the mother's own right to life, which she might put forward as ground for an abortion?

This argument treats the right to life as if it were unproblematic. It is not, and this seems to me to be precisely the source of the mistake.

For we should now, at long last, ask what it comes to, to have a right to life. In some views having a right to life includes having a right to be given at least the bare minimum one needs for continued life. But suppose that what in fact is the bare minimum a man needs for continued life is something he has no right at all to be given? If I am sick unto death, and the only thing that will save my life is the touch of Henry Fonda's cool hand on my fevered brow, then all the same, I have no right to be given the touch of Henry Fonda's cool hand on my fevered brow. It would be frightfully nice of him to fly in from the West Coast to provide it. It would be less nice, no doubt well meant, if my friends flew out to the West Coast and carried Henry Fonda back with them. But I have no right at all against anybody that he should do this for me. Or again, to return to the story I told earlier, the fact that for continued life that violinist needs the continued use of your kidneys does not establish that he has a right to be given the continued use of your kidneys. He certainly has no right against you that *you* should give him continued use of your kidneys. For nobody has any right to use your kidneys unless you give him such a right; and nobody has the right against you that you shall give him this right—if you do allow him to go on using your kidneys, this is a kindness on your part, and not something he can claim from you as his due. Nor has he any right against anybody else that *they* should give him continued use of your kidneys. Certainly he has no right against the Society of Music Lovers that they should plug him into you in the first place. And if you now start to unplug yourself, having learned that you will otherwise have to spend nine years in bed with him, there is nobody in the world who must try to prevent you, in order to see to it that he is given something he has a right to be given.

Some people are rather stricter about the right to life. In their view, it does not include the right to be given anything, but amounts to, and only to, the right not to be killed by anybody. But here a related difficulty arises. If everybody is to refrain from killing that violinist, then everybody must refrain from doing a great many

different sorts of things. Everybody must refrain from slitting his throat, everybody must refrain from shooting him—and everybody must refrain from unplugging you from him. But does he have a right against everybody that they shall refrain from unplugging you from him? To refrain from doing this is to allow him to continue to use your kidneys. It could be argued that he has a right against us that we should allow him to continue to use your kidneys. That is, while he had no right against us that we should give him the use of your kidneys, it might be argued that he anyway has a right against us that we shall not now intervene and deprive him of the use of your kidneys. I shall come back to third-party interventions later. But certainly the violinist has no right against you that you shall allow him to continue to use your kidneys. As I said, if you do allow him to use them, it is a kindness on your part, and not something you owe him.

The difficulty I point to here is not peculiar to the right to life. It reappears in connection with all the other natural rights; and it is something which an adequate account of rights must deal with. For present purposes it is enough just to draw attention to it. But I would stress that I am not arguing that people do not have a right to life—quite to the contrary, it seems to me that the primary control we must place on the acceptability of an account of rights is that it should turn out in that account to be a truth that all persons have a right to life. I am arguing only that having a right to life does not guarantee having either a right to be given the use of or a right to be allowed continued use of another person's body—even if one needs it for life itself. So the right to life will not serve the opponents of abortion in the very simple and clear way in which they seem to have thought it would.

4. There is another way to bring out the difficulty. In the most ordinary sort of case, to deprive someone of what he has a right to is to treat him unjustly. Suppose a boy and his small brother are jointly given a box of chocolates for Christmas. If the older boy takes the box and refuses to give his brother any of the chocolates, he is unjust to him, for the brother has been given a right to half of them. But suppose that, having learned that otherwise it means nine years in bed with that violinist, you unplug yourself from him. You surely are not being unjust to him, for you gave him no right to use your kidneys, and no one else can have given him any such right. But we have to notice that in unplugging yourself, you are killing him; and violinists, like everybody else, have a right to life, and thus in the view we were considering just now, the right not to be killed. So here you do what he supposedly has a right you shall not do, but you do not act unjustly to him in doing it.

The emendation which may be made at this point is this: the right to life consists not in the right not to be killed, but rather in the right not to be killed unjustly. This runs a risk of circularity, but never mind: it would enable us to square the fact that the violinist has a right to life with the fact that you do not act unjustly toward him in unplugging yourself, thereby killing him. For if you do not kill him unjustly, you do not violate his right to life, and so it is no wonder you do him no injustice.

But if this emendation is accepted, the gap in the argument against abortions stares us plainly in the face: it is by no means enough to show that the fetus is a person, and to remind us that all persons have a right to life—we need to be shown also that killing the fetus violates its right to life, i.e., that abortion is unjust killing. And is it?

I suppose we may take it as a datum that in a case of pregnancy due to rape the mother has not given the unborn person a right to the use of her body for food and shelter. Indeed, in what pregnancy could it be supposed that the mother has given the unborn person such a right? It is not as if there were unborn persons drifting about the world, to whom a woman who wants a child says "I invite you in."

But it might be argued that there are other ways one can have acquired a right to the use of another person's body than by having been invited to use it by that person. Suppose a woman voluntarily indulges in intercourse, knowing of the chance it will issue in pregnancy, and then she does become pregnant; is she not in part responsible for the presence, in fact the very existence, of the unborn person inside her? No doubt she did not invite it in. But doesn't her partial responsibility for its being there itself give it a right to the use of her body?[7] If so, then her aborting it would be more like the boy's taking away the chocolates, and less like your unplugging yourself from the violinist—doing so would be depriving it of what it does have a right to, and thus would be doing it an injustice.

And then, too, it might be asked whether or not she can kill it even to save her own life: If she voluntarily called it into existence, how can she now kill it, even in self-defense?

The first thing to be said about this is that it is something new. Opponents of abortion have been so concerned to make out the independence of the fetus, in order to establish that it has a right to life, just as its mother does, that they have tended to overlook the possible support they might gain from making out that the fetus is *dependent* on the mother, in order to establish that she has a special kind of responsibility for it, a responsibility that gives it rights against her which are not possessed by any independent person—such as an ailing violinist who is a stranger to her.

On the other hand, this argument would give the unborn person a right to its mother's body only if her pregnancy resulted from a voluntary act, undertaken in full knowledge of the chance a pregnancy might result from it. It would leave out entirely the unborn person whose existence is due to rape. Pending the availability of some further argument, then, we would be left with the conclusion that unborn persons whose existence is due to rape have no right to the use of their mothers' bodies, and thus that aborting them is not depriving them of anything they have a right to and hence is not unjust killing.

And we should also notice that it is not at all plain that this argument really does go even as far as it purports to. For there are cases and cases, and the details make a difference. If the room is stuffy, and I therefore open a window to air it, and a burglar climbs in, it would be absurd to say, "Ah, now he can stay, she's given him a right to the use of her house—for she is partially responsible for his presence there, having voluntarily done what enabled him to get in, in full knowledge that there are such things as burglars, and that burglars burgle." It would be still more absurd to say this if I had had bars installed outside my windows, precisely to prevent burglars from getting in, and a burglar got in only because of a defect in the bars. It remains equally absurd if we imagine it is not a burglar who climbs in, but an innocent person who blunders or falls in. Again, suppose it were like this: people-seeds drift about in the air like pollen, and if you open your windows, one may drift in and take root in your carpets or upholstery. You don't want children, so you fix up your windows with fine mesh screens, the very best you can buy. As can happen, however, and on very, very rare occasions does happen, one of the screens is defective; and a seed drifts in and takes root. Does the person-plant who now develops have a right to the use of your house? Surely not—despite the fact that you voluntarily opened your windows, you knowingly kept carpets and upholstered furniture, and you knew that screens were sometimes defective. Someone may argue that you are responsible for its rooting, that it does have a right to your house, because after all you *could* have lived out your life with bare floors and furniture, or with sealed windows and doors. But this won't do— for by the same token anyone can avoid a pregnancy due to rape by having a hysterectomy, or anyway by never leaving home without a (reliable!) army.

It seems to me that the argument we are looking at can establish at most that there are *some* cases in which the unborn person has a right to the use of its mother's body, and therefore *some* cases in which abortion is unjust killing. There is room for much discussion and argument as to precisely which, if any. But I think we should sidestep this issue and leave it open, for at any rate the argument certainly does not establish that all abortion is unjust killing.

5. There is room for yet another argument here, however. We surely must all grant that there may be cases in which it would be morally indecent to detach a person from your body at the cost of his life. Suppose you learn that what the violinist needs is not nine years of your life, but only one hour: all you need do to save his life is to spend one hour in that bed with him. Suppose also that letting him use your kidneys for that one hour would not affect your health in the slightest. Admittedly you were kidnapped. Admittedly you did not give anyone permission to plug him into you. Nevertheless it seems to me plain you *ought* to allow him to use your kidneys for that hour—it would be indecent to refuse.

Again, suppose pregnancy lasted only an hour, and constituted no threat to life or health. And suppose that a woman becomes pregnant as a result of rape. Admittedly she did not voluntarily do anything to bring about the existence of a child. Admittedly she did nothing at all which would give the unborn person a right to the use of her body. All the same it might well be said, as in the newly emended violinist story, that she *ought* to allow it to remain for that hour—that it would be indecent in her to refuse.

Now some people are inclined to use the term "right" in such a way that it follows from the fact that you ought to allow a person to use your body for the hour he needs, that he has a right to use your body for the hour he needs, even though he has not been given that right by any person or act. They may say that it follows also that if you refuse, you act unjustly toward him. This use of the term is perhaps so common that it cannot be called wrong; nevertheless it seems to me to be an unfortunate loosening of what we would do better to keep a tight rein on. Suppose that box of chocolates I mentioned earlier had not been given to both boys jointly, but was given only to the older boy. There he sits, stolidly eating his way through the box, his small brother watching enviously. Here we are likely to say "You ought not to be so mean. You ought to give your brother some of those chocolates." My own view is that it just does not follow from the truth of this that the brother has any right to any of the chocolates. If the boy refuses to give his brother any, he is greedy, stingy, callous—but not unjust. I suppose that the people I have in mind will say it does follow that the brother has a right to some of the chocolates, and thus that the boy does act unjustly if he refuses to give his brother any. But the effect of saying this is to obscure what we should keep distinct, namely the difference between the boy's refusal in this case and the boy's refusal in the earlier case, in which the box was given to both boys jointly, and in which the small brother thus had what was from any point of view clear title to half.

A further objection to so using the term "right" from that the fact that A ought to do a thing for B, it follows that B has a right against A that A do it for him, is that it is going to make the question of whether or not a man has a right to a thing turn on how easy it is to provide him with it; and this seems not merely unfortunate, but morally unacceptable. Take the case of Henry Fonda again. I said earlier that I had no right to the touch of his cool hand on my fevered brow, even though I needed it to save my life. I said it would be frightfully nice of him to fly from the West Coast to provide me with it, but that I had no right against him that he should do so. But suppose he isn't on the West Coast. Suppose he has only to walk across the room, place a hand briefly on my brow—and lo, my life is saved. Then surely he ought to do it, it would be

indecent to refuse. Is it to be said "Ah, well, it follows that in this case she has a right to the touch of his hand on her brow, and so it would be an injustice in him to refuse"? So that I have a right to it when it is easy for him to provide it, though no right when it's hard? It's rather a shocking idea that anyone's rights should fade away and disappear as it gets harder and harder to accord them to him.

So my own view is that even though you ought to let the violinist use your kidneys for the one hour he needs, we should not conclude that he has a right to do so—we should say that if you refuse, you are, like the boy who owns all the chocolates and will give none away, self-centered and callous, indecent in fact, but not unjust. And similarly, that even supposing a case in which a woman pregnant due to rape ought to allow the unborn person to use her body for the hour he needs, we should not conclude that he has a right to do so; we should conclude that she is self-centered, callous, indecent, but not unjust, if she refuses. The complaints are no less grave; they are just different. However, there is no need to insist on this point. If anyone does wish to deduce "he has a right" from "you ought," then all the same he must surely grant that there are cases in which it is not morally required of you that you allow that violinist to use your kidneys, and in which he does not have a right to use them, and in which you do not do him an injustice if you refuse. And so also for mother and unborn child. Except in such cases as the unborn person has a right to demand it—and we were leaving open the possibility that there may be such cases— nobody is morally *required* to make large sacrifices, of health, of all other interests and concerns, of all other duties and commitments, for nine years, or even for nine months, in order to keep another person alive.

6. We have in fact to distinguish between two kinds of Samaritan: the Good Samaritan and what we might call the Minimally Decent Samaritan. The story of the Good Samaritan, you will remember, goes like this:

> A certain man went down from Jerusalem to Jericho, and fell among thieves, which stripped him of his raiment, and wounded him, and departed, leaving him half dead.
>
> And by chance there came down a certain priest that way; and when he saw him, he passed by on the other side.
>
> And likewise a Levite, when he was at the place, came and looked on him, and passed by on the other side.
>
> But a certain Samaritan, as he journeyed, came where he was; and when he saw him he had compassion on him.
>
> And went to him, and bound up his wounds, pouring in oil and wine, and set him on his own beast, and brought him to an inn, and took care of him.
>
> And on the morrow, when he departed, he took out two pence, and gave them to the host, and said unto him, "Take care of him; and whatsoever thou spendest more, when I come again, I will repay thee."
>
> (Luke 10:30–35)

The Good Samaritan went out of his way, at some cost to himself, to help one in need of it. We are not told what the options were, that is, whether or not the priest and the Levite could have helped by doing less than the Good Samaritan did, but assuming they could have, then the fact they did nothing at all shows they were not even Minimally Decent Samaritans, not because they were not Samaritans, but because they were not even minimally decent.

These things are a matter of degree, of course, but there is a difference, and it comes out perhaps most clearly in the story of Kitty Genovese, who, as you will remember, was murdered while thirty-eight people watched or listened, and did nothing at all to help her. A Good Samaritan would have rushed out to give direct assistance against the murderer. Or perhaps we had better allow that it would have been a Splendid Samaritan who did this, on the

ground that it would have involved a risk of death for himself. But the thirty-eight not only did not do this, they did not even trouble to pick up a phone to call the police. Minimally Decent Samaritanism would call for doing at least that, and their not having done it was monstrous.

After telling the story of the Good Samaritan, Jesus said "Go, and do thou likewise." Perhaps he meant that we are morally required to act as the Good Samaritan did. Perhaps he was urging people to do more than is morally required of them. At all events it seems plain that it was not morally required of any of the thirty-eight that he rush out to give direct assistance at the risk of his own life, and that it is not morally required of anyone that he give long stretches of his life—nine years or nine months—to sustaining the life of a person who has no special right (we were leaving open the possibility of this) to demand it.

Indeed, with one rather striking class of exceptions, no one in any country in the world is *legally* required to do anywhere near as much as this for anyone else. The class of exceptions is obvious. My main concern here is not the state of the law in respect to abortion, but it is worth drawing attention to the fact that in no state in this country is any man compelled by law to be even a Minimally Decent Samaritan to any person; there is no law under which charges could be brought against the thirty-eight who stood by while Kitty Genovese died. By contrast, in most states in this country women are compelled by law to be not merely Minimally Decent Samaritans, but Good Samaritans to unborn persons inside them. This doesn't by itself settle anything one way or the other, because it may well be argued that there should be laws in this country—as there are in many European countries—compelling at least Minimally Decent Samaritanism.[8] But it does show that there is a gross injustice in the existing state of the law. And it shows also that the groups currently working against liberalization of abortion laws, in fact working toward having it declared unconstitutional for a state to permit abortion, had better start working for the adoption of Good Samaritan laws generally, or earn the charge that they are acting in bad faith.

I should think, myself, that Minimally Decent Samaritan laws would be one thing, Good Samaritan laws quite another, and in fact highly improper. But we are not here concerned with the law. What we should ask is not whether anybody should be compelled by law to be a Good Samaritan, but whether we must accede to a situation in which somebody is being compelled—by nature, perhaps—to be a Good Samaritan. We have, in other words, to look now at third-party interventions. I have been arguing that no person is morally required to make large sacrifices to sustain the life of another who has no right to demand them, and this even where the sacrifices do not include life itself; we are not morally required to be Good Samaritans or anyway Very Good Samaritans to one another. But what if a man cannot extricate himself from such a situation? What if he appeals to us to extricate him? It seems to me plain that there are cases in which we can, cases in which a Good Samaritan would extricate him. There you are, you were kidnapped, and nine years in bed with that violinist lie ahead of you. You have your own life to lead. You are sorry, but you simply cannot see giving up so much of your life to the sustaining of his. You cannot extricate yourself, and ask us to do so. I should have thought that—in light of his having no right to the use of your body—it was obvious that we do not have to accede to your being forced to give up so much. We can do what you ask. There is no injustice to the violinist in our doing so.

7. Following the lead of the opponents of abortion, I have throughout been speaking of the fetus merely as a person, and what I have been asking is whether or not the argument we began with, which proceeds only from the fetus' being a person, really does establish its conclusion. I have argued that it does not.

But of course there are arguments and arguments, and it may be said that I have simply fastened on the wrong one. It may be said that what is important is not merely the fact that the fetus is a person, but that it is a person for whom the woman has a special kind of responsibility issuing from the fact that she is its mother. And it might be argued that all my analogies are therefore irrelevant—for you do not have that special kind of responsibility for that violinist, Henry Fonda does not have that special kind of responsibility for me. And our attention might be drawn to the fact that men and women both are compelled by law to provide support for their children.

I have in effect dealt (briefly) with this argument in section 4 [see original reading]; but a (still briefer) recapitulation now may be in order. Surely we do not have any such "special responsibility" for a person unless we have assumed it, explicitly or implicitly. If a set of parents do not try to prevent pregnancy, do not obtain an abortion, and then at the time of birth of the child do not put it out for adoption, but rather take it home with them, then they have assumed responsibility for it, they have given it rights, and they cannot now withdraw support from it at the cost of its life because they now find it difficult to go on providing for it. But if they have taken all reasonable precautions against having a child, they do not simply by virtue of their biological relationship to the child who comes into existence have a special responsibility for it. They may wish to assume responsibility for it, or they may not wish to. And I am suggesting that if assuming responsibility for it would require large sacrifices, then they may refuse. A Good Samaritan would not refuse—or anyway, a Splendid Samaritan, if the sacrifices that had to be made were enormous. But then so would a Good Samaritan assume responsibility for that violinist; so would Henry Fonda, if he is a Good Samaritan, fly in from the West Coast and assume responsibility for me.

8. My argument will be found unsatisfactory on two counts by many of those who want to regard abortion as morally permissible. First, while I do argue that abortion is not impermissible, I do not argue that it is always permissible. There may well be cases in which carrying the child to term requires only Minimally Decent Samaritanism of the mother, and this is a standard we must not fall below. I am inclined to think it a merit of my account precisely that it does *not* give a general yes or a general no. It allows for and supports our sense that, for example, a sick and desperately frightened fourteen-year-old schoolgirl, pregnant due to rape, may *of course* choose abortion, and that any law which rules this out is an insane law. And it also allows for and supports our sense that in other cases resort to abortion is even positively indecent. It would be indecent in the woman to request an abortion, and indecent in a doctor to perform it, if she is in her seventh month, and wants the abortion just to avoid the nuisance of postponing a trip abroad. The very fact that the arguments I have been drawing attention to treat all cases of abortion, or even all cases of abortion in which the mother's life is not at stake, as morally on a par ought to have made them suspect at the outset.

Secondly, while I am arguing for the permissibility of abortion in some cases, I am not arguing for the right to secure the death of the unborn child. It is easy to confuse these two things in that up to a certain point in the life of the fetus it is not able to survive outside the mother's body; hence removing it from her body guarantees its death. But they are importantly different. I have argued that you are not morally required to spend nine months in bed, sustaining the life of that violinist; but to say this is by no means to say that if, when you unplug yourself, there is a miracle and he survives, you then have a right to turn round and slit his throat. You may detach yourself even if this costs him his life; you have no right to be guaranteed his death, by some other means, if unplugging yourself does not kill him. There are some people who will feel dissatisfied by this feature

of my argum   ly devas-
tated by th   ild, a bit of herself,
put out f   never seen or heard
of again. S   ore want not merely
that the chi   from her, but more,
that it die.   its of abortion are
inclined to reg   beneath contempt—
thereby showin   vity to what is surely a
powerful source of   ir. All the same, I agree
that the desire for the child's death is not one
which anybody may gratify, should it turn out to
be possible to detach the child alive.

At this place, however, it should be remembered that we have only been pretending
throughout that the fetus is a human being from
the moment of conception. A very early abortion
is surely not the killing of a person, and so is not
dealt with by anything I have said here.

Notes

1 I am very much indebted to James Thomson for
discussion, criticism, and many helpful suggestions.

2 Daniel Callahan, *Abortion: Law, Choice and Morality* (New
York, 1970), p. 373. This book gives a fascinating
survey of the available information on abortion. The
Jewish tradition is surveyed in David M. Feldman,
Birth Control in Jewish Law (New York, 1968), Part 5;
the Catholic tradition in John T. Noonan, Jr., "An
Almost Absolute Value in History," in *The Morality of
Abortion*, ed. John T. Noonan, Jr. (Cambridge, MA,
1970).

3 The term "direct" in the arguments I refer to is a
technical one. Roughly, what is meant by "direct
killing" is either killing as an end in itself, or killing
as a means to some end, for example, the end of
saving someone else's life. See note 6, below, for an
example of its use.

4 Cf. Encyclical Letter of Pope Pius XI on *Christian Marriage*,
St. Paul Editions (Boston, n.d.), p. 32: "however much
we may pity the mother whose health and even life is
gravely imperiled in the performance of the duty
allotted to her by nature, nevertheless what could ever
be a sufficient reason for excusing in any way the
direct murder of the innocent? This is precisely what
we are dealing with here." Noonan (*The Morality of
Abortion*, p. 43) reads this as follows: "What cause can
ever avail to excuse in any way the direct killing of the
innocent? For it is a question of that."

5 The thesis in (4) is in an interesting way weaker
than those in (1), (2), and (3): they rule out abortion even in cases in which both mother *and* child
will die if the abortion is not performed. By
contrast, one who held the view expressed in
(4) could consistently say that one needn't prefer
letting two persons die to killing one.

6 Cf. the following passage from Pius XII, *Address to the
Italian Catholic Society of Midwives*: "The baby in the
maternal breast has the right to life immediately
from God.—Hence there is no man, no human
authority, no science, no medical, eugenic, social,
economic or moral 'indication' which can establish
or grant a valid juridical ground for a direct deliberate disposition of an innocent human life, that is
a disposition which looks to its destruction either
as an end or as a means to another end perhaps in
itself not illicit.—The baby, still not born, is a man
in the same degree and for the same reason as the
mother" (quoted in Noonan, *The Morality of Abortion*,
p. 45).

7 The need for a discussion of this argument was
brought home to me by members of the Society for
Ethical and Legal Philosophy, to whom this paper
was originally presented.

8 For a discussion of the difficulties involved, and a
survey of the European experience with such laws,
see *The Good Samaritan and the Law*, ed. James M.
Ratcliffe (New York, 1966).

George Sher

SUBSIDIZED ABORTION: MORAL RIGHTS AND MORAL COMPROMISE

Most philosophical discussions of abortion have addressed such issues as the personhood of the fetus, the omission-commission distinction, and the rights of women to control their bodies. But as central as these issues are, they do not exhaust the moral problems connected with abortion. Further problems, less noticed by philosophers, are raised by society's role in the affair, and specifically by the fact that the government may not only tolerate abortions, but also may fund them through programs such as Medicaid or welfare. Of the questions thus raised, one is whether women have a right to be provided with abortions that they want but cannot afford, while another is how society should respond to the deep moral disagreement about abortion that divides its constituent groups. In this essay, I shall discuss these questions and the connections between them. Although my main aim is to bring philosophical order to an often undisciplined public debate, I also hope to shed reflected light on some broader issues of rights and moral compromise.

I

The distinction between elective and therapeutic abortion is not exclusive. A woman may elect to have an abortion for purposes wholly or partly related to her health. Nevertheless, the issues that concern us here emerge most clearly when the aim is entirely nontherapeutic; and I shall consider only such polar cases here. For similar reasons, I shall adopt narrow definitions of health and therapy, so that, for example, poverty and a hard life are not themselves states of ill health that could be mitigated by abortion. While it may be tempting to say that abortions performed for these reasons are therapeutic, this tactic would gain us no real ground. If we adopted it, our distinction between therapy and non-therapy would merely reappear as a distinction between *types* of therapy.

Given the view of elective abortions outlined here, should we say that poor women have a moral right to be provided with them? Prima facie, it may seem impossible to answer this question without first ascertaining the moral status of abortion itself. If elective abortions are seriously wrong, then poor women cannot have a right to be provided with them. But on further inspection, this suggestion is not fully satisfactory. Whatever their ultimate moral status, elective abortions are now widely available in the United States, and their availability has been found by the Supreme Court to be constitutionally guaranteed. Because abortion is thus officially tolerated by our legal system, its permissibility for us as a society is no longer an open question. In condoning elective abortion for women who can afford it, we have in effect reached a societal judgment that the practice is not seriously wrong. Moreover, despite some continuing controversy, we also seem to be

moving toward a decision to provide basic medical care for those who cannot afford it. In view of this, a right to be provided with elective abortions may seem to follow from the more general right to consistent and nondiscriminatory treatment. Given our tolerance of elective abortions and our funding of other medical services, how can we refuse to provide funding for elective abortions? To be consistent, must we not either fund abortion as we do other medical procedures, or else reverse our judgment that abortion is permissible for those who can afford it? If we do otherwise, then are we not merely discriminating against the poor?

There is plainly something right about this argument. Given the societal judgment that abortion is morally permissible, we cannot consistently refuse to fund abortions for the poor on the grounds that they (alone) are morally wrong. To do this would be to indulge in the worst sort of hypocrisy. However, it is one thing to say that this sort of refusal to fund elective abortions is indefensibly inconsistent, and quite another to say the same for *any* refusal to fund such abortions. To say the latter would be to invoke an inappropriately rigid standard of consistency in policy making. It is true that society tolerates abortions and funds appendectomies, and true also that both are performed by medical personnel in a clinical setting. Still, as long as appendectomies differ from abortions in significant ways, it is no more inconsistent for government to fund the former but not the latter than it is for government to provide coupons for the purchase of food but not sweaters, or tax credits for insulation but not other home improvements. Moreover, whatever their moral status, abortions plainly do differ from appendectomies in many significant ways. Even if they are morally permissible, abortions remain distasteful in a way that appendectomies are not. Moreover, elective abortions are not aimed primarily at improving health, while appendectomies are. Given these and other differences, the case for government funding of elective abortions cannot be made on grounds of formal consistency alone. And neither, I think, can it be made on the related grounds that to permit abortions without funding them is to discriminate against the poor, for precisely the same is true in *every* instance where we permit the enjoyment of an amenity without subsidizing it for everyone.

The claim that it is consistent to fund appendectomies but not elective abortions establishes very little. A policy may be consistent and yet violate any number of other substantive rights. But which other rights, exactly, could ground the right to be provided with elective abortions? The right to be provided with medical care is inappropriate because of the fact, already noted, that elective abortions are not typically aimed at the maintenance or improvement of health. The right to privacy is another possibility; but despite what the Supreme Court has said about it, its connection with abortion seems too tenuous and indirect to be credible. In view of this, the most promising basis for a right to be provided with elective abortions may seem to be a kind of generalized welfare right: a right to have one's basic needs met by society if one cannot meet them oneself. Of course, since welfare rights are positive rights—rights not merely to be left alone, but rather to be provided with goods or services supplied by others—their very existence is a matter of controversy. But we cannot resolve this controversy here, and so I shall simply assume that some such rights exist. Granting this, how plausible is it to suppose that the right to be provided with elective abortions falls among them?

Since welfare rights are rights to be provided with what one needs but cannot afford, the question of whether they include the right to elective abortions depends on whether elective abortions satisfy basic needs, and this depends on our interpretation of basic needs. If basic needs encompass only the requirements for biological survival, then a general welfare right will dictate some therapeutic abortions, but no

purely elective ones. However, basic needs may also be construed more broadly, as encompassing all the requirements for effective functioning in contemporary society; and on this interpretation, the case for a right to elective abortions looks more promising. Given the limitations imposed by children one cannot afford, it seems reasonable to suppose that an abortion is often as necessary for a poor woman's effective functioning as access to transportation, education, or some discretionary income. Of course, while one cannot avoid the need for transportation, education, or money, one *can* avoid encumbrance by an unwanted child by simply giving it up for adoption. However, given the strength of parental feelings, the request that one give up a child already brought to term seems neither reasonable nor humane. Thus, the proper conclusion seems to be that elective abortion is lower than the most essential items, but higher than many others, on the overall scale of basic needs for the poor.

Given this conclusion, the right to be provided with elective abortions may seem to follow from a liberal, yet not implausible, interpretation of welfare rights. But on closer inspection, even this liberal interpretation does not secure the desired result. If the purpose of providing elective abortions is to enable poor women to function effectively within society, then that purpose will be equally well served by providing them with enough additional money and ancillary services to support their unaborted children. If such additional support is provided, then they will not be thrust into unmanageable poverty by those children. Hence, a right to the prerequisites for effective functioning does not automatically yield a right to elective abortions. Instead, it yields at best a disjunctive right to be provided with either additional support or abortion. Of course, the additional support is apt to be considerably more costly than abortion; but whether society can or should absorb this cost is a separate issue. The present point is only that if society does choose to absorb it, it violates nobody's rights.

This conclusion might be disputed. What we have missed, it may be argued, is that even if a woman is not thrust deeper into poverty by her unwanted child, that child can drastically restrict her freedom of movement. It can drastically reduce her vocational, geographic, and personal options, and so impose a real limitation on her liberty. In view of this, the right to be provided with elective abortions may seem to flow from a more general right to be provided with the prerequisites of liberty and self-determination. And this more general right may be defended either as being fundamental or as being an important corollary of the right to have one's basic needs satisfied.

If this argument were sound, it would indeed establish a categorical right to be provided with elective abortions. But even apart from any difficulties with the alleged general right to be supplied with the prerequisites of liberty,[1] the argument is highly problematical. On any reasonable interpretation, the proposed general right will not require the protection of liberties that are threatened by the prior exercise of liberty itself. If one's options are foreclosed by the foreseeable and easily avoidable consequences of one's own past choices, and not by uncontrollable externalities, then any right to the prerequisites of liberty has already been satisfied. But given the easy availability of reliable contraception, precisely this appears true of most unwanted adult pregnancies. Setting aside the young and uneducated, for whom special provision might be made, most women who become pregnant without wanting to appear to do so because they neglect to take rudimentary contraceptive precautions (or to see that such precautions are taken). But if so, then a right to be provided with elective abortions is not derivable in the standard case at all.

There is, moreover, a further difficulty with the attempt to ground a right to elective abortions in a more general right to the prerequisites of liberty. Even where pregnancy is due to the unavailability or ineffectiveness of contraception,

obvious that a woman's liberty will be drastically restricted if she is not provided with an abortion. Her liberty would be so restricted if women had to raise all the children they bore. However, as we noted above, it is always possible to give an unwanted child up for adoption. It is not humane to make a woman's material well-being depend on her willingness to give up her child. But where the issue is not her material well-being, but rather her preference for a life without the child, the case looks quite different. Here any right to liberty seems well enough served if she is allowed to choose between the child and the style of life she wishes to have after the child is born. Of course, the choice is apt to be considerably more difficult then; but difficult choices, far from impeding the exercise of liberty, are part and parcel of it. One might perhaps counter that complete liberty requires the ability to prevent the formation of desires (for example, maternal ones) that one believes will lead to the abandonment of one's present plans. However, while our relation to our future selves is puzzling and difficult,[2] it seems implausible to say that a person's freedom is seriously restricted by the inability to manipulate future desires. In view of this, it seems unlikely that a categorical right to be provided with elective abortions can be derived from a right to the prerequisites of liberty.

II

So far, we have focused entirely on the claim that the poor have a moral right to be provided with elective abortions. We have considered and rejected three distinct attempts to establish such a right. But even if all appeals to this right are mere inflated rhetoric, it hardly follows that the government has no reason to fund elective abortions. Given the enormous financial cost of providing adequate support for all unaborted children, given the manifest undesirability of further overpopulation, and given the carnage wrought by illegal abortions performed under

unsanitary conditions, there is obviously a strong utilitarian case for government funding. Of course, utilitarian arguments are often overridden by the fact that maximizing utility would violate someone's rights; but here, as before, the appeal to the fetus' right to life seems to be blocked by the prior societal decision that there is no such right. Thus, the utilitarian case for government funding may at first appear quite overwhelming.

But even if the utilities do strongly favor government funding, there is a further dimension to the problem. To bring this out, we need only recall that the decision to tolerate abortion is by no means unanimous. Even if society as a whole *has* accepted the permissibility of abortion, many members of it emphatically have not. To these individuals, the legalization of abortion represents a serious moral error, and a government policy of paying for it merely compounds the error. For them, any appeal to society's collective decision is vitiated by the conviction that that decision is badly mistaken. But what exactly does this mean? Given their own moral views, must these persons continue to oppose abortion with every tactic that they believe appropriate to its gravity? Or is there a more general and independently grounded moral principle that tells against this? If there is, does it require that those who tolerate abortion make any concession in return? To ask these questions is to raise the difficult issue of compromise among parties with radically divergent moral views; and it is to this issue that I now turn.

One argument against continuing opposition by anti-abortionists can be dismissed at the outset. It is often maintained that those who oppose abortion are acting properly when they themselves refuse to abort, but not when they attempt to prevent others from aborting as well. When they try to ban *all* abortions, the argument goes, they overstep the bounds of tolerance by imposing their own moral views upon others. But the principle that underlies this argument— that all morally controversial decisions should

be matters of individual conscience—is plainly untenable. Even the most ardent proponents of tolerance would deny that wife-beating, slavery, or murder are matters of individual conscience; and their position would hardly be affected by the discovery that some or most other persons consider such practices morally permissible. The abortion issue is clouded by the fact that some who oppose abortion do so on religious rather than purely moral grounds. However, as long as the conservative position on abortion can be articulated in purely secular terms—as I believe it can—the basic point remains. If an act is seriously wrong, we may well be obligated to prevent others from performing it. Hence, those who believe that abortion is murder are hardly overstepping the bounds of tolerance when they try to prevent others from aborting.

Given these considerations, the opponents of abortion appear to be doing exactly what they should be doing when they seek its total abolition. Indeed, given the enormity of the wrong that they believe abortion to involve, what is puzzling is why they are not doing even more. Where systematic murder is concerned, not only political pressure, but also relentless civil disobedience and other forms of extralegal resistance, seem called for.[3] Of course, such actions are not really justified unless abortion really is murder; but since we have no direct access to moral facts, this observation is not particularly helpful. What is important is that from their own perspective, conservatives seem obligated to wage a no-holds-barred campaign against abortion, while from their perspective liberals seem equally obligated to resist those tactics that they view as outside the bounds of political legitimacy. If each side acts consistently on principles conscientiously arrived at, the result will apparently be an unending, acrimonious, and lawless contest of wills.

Now there may be some disputes whose contending factions are committed by their principles to just this sort of strife. It may even be that the abortion dispute is among these. But

before we accept this pessimistic conclusion, we will do well to examine an alternative possibility. It seems possible to combine even a stern deontological code of ethics with a higher-order moral principle that moderates what one is required to do when one's efforts to act morally conflict with the similarly motivated efforts of others. By accepting a principle of this sort, we acknowledge both our own fallibility and the status of others besides ourselves as moral agents. But if some such principle is acceptable, then the parties to the abortion debate may not be locked into an endless and no-holds-barred struggle. Instead, even if the legal status of abortion continues to divide them, definite limits may be introduced into the conflict. Tactics that are permissible to prevent murder (or to defend against the unwarranted use of such tactics by others) may no longer be permitted. The conflict may be de-escalated.

It is not easy to specify precisely the conditions under which one can compromise one's moral convictions without compromising oneself.[4] However, one plainly relevant factor is the complexity and uncertainty of the subject. If one's convictions involve principles whose grounding is itself problematical, if the opposing view is also supported by plausible-sounding arguments, and if thoughtful and intelligent persons are unable to agree about the issues, then only a dogmatist will deny that he may well be mistaken, and his adversary correct. But once this acknowledgment is made, such considerations as respect for one's opponent and the value of mutual accommodation may permit (or even require) adjustments in behavior that would otherwise be inappropriate. Moreover, precisely these features are present in the abortion dispute. Such issues as the possibility of imaginative identification with the fetus and the moral significance of potential personhood are as obscure and difficult as any in the moral sphere; and neither liberals nor conservatives have produced a powerful general account of the moral personhood of normal adult humans.[5] In

view of this, the abortion dispute is quite unlike such apparently related questions as whether contraception is permissible. Concerning abortion, but not contraception, both liberals and conservatives must in candor admit that the opposition has a genuine chance of being right.

Given all of this, the case for moral compromise in the abortion dispute appears promising. But what form, exactly, might such a compromise take? Because abortion is now widely available and because a total ban on it would violate a strong presumption against unnecessary government interference with citizens' activities, it does not seem reasonable to ask liberals to accept a proposal to make all abortions illegal. However, what does seem reasonable is to ask them to accept measures whose effect is to diminish the number of abortions without undue government interference. Such measures might include expanded programs of contraception, expanded adoption facilities, and perhaps also laws limiting abortions to the stages of pregnancy at which personhood is least certain. On the other side, since conservatives consider abortion a form of murder, it seems unreasonable to ask them to relinquish their efforts to make it totally illegal. However, what we may reasonably ask of them, in return for measures limiting the number of abortions performed, is that they (continue to) abjure the more extreme responses that would normally be called for by an officially sanctioned policy of murder. It is one thing to apply political pressure, quite another to fire-bomb an abortion clinic. Even if the conservative forswears only the latter tactics—tactics that would have been quite appropriate if employed in Hitler's Germany—his concession will be a major one and the gain in civility substantial.

With this in mind, we may now return to our original topic of government funding of elective abortion. Because both sides of the abortion dispute may have good moral reasons to compromise their positions, the natural question to ask about such funding is what role it

might play in a reasonable compromise between them. Because an acceptable compromise will limit abortions without forbidding them entirely and because not subsidizing abortions seems to violate no one's rights, the obvious suggestion is that a proper compromise will include no government funding of elective abortions. This impression is confirmed, moreover, by two further considerations. First, any policy of government funding for abortions must draw upon tax monies collected from conservatives as well as liberals; and this must place conservatives in a position of actively supporting abortions rather than reluctantly tolerating their performance by others.[6] Second, such a policy must amount to an implicit government endorsement of abortion, and so must provide it with a symbolic legitimacy that conservatives wish to withhold. On both grounds, a compromise that includes government funding of elective abortions may not be one that conservatives can reasonably be asked to accept.

If this is so, then even a stalwart liberal may have a good (second-level) moral reason not to press for government funding of elective abortions. By relinquishing his claims in this area and attending to the needs of the poor in other ways, he may hope to reach an accommodation with the conservative that is not otherwise possible. This accommodation may indeed be more costly than providing abortions for all who want them; but if the accommodation is genuinely called for on moral grounds, its cost should not be prohibitive. And, of course, the liberal who accepts it may still contribute voluntarily to private organizations providing free abortions to the poor. The more difficult question is whether conservatives should accept even this type of compromise. We have presented some considerations in favor of it; but there are arguments on the other side as well. More specifically, it may be contended that (1) the propriety of a moral compromise should not depend on such morally irrelevant facts as the baseline determined by the current wide availability of abortions, that (2)

we can morally compromise our own interests but never our duty to protect the interests of others, or that (3) the greater concessions should be made by the side whose actions are potentially the more seriously wrong—in this case, the liberal side. If one of these replies is correct—and it would take a full-fledged theory of moral compromise to evaluate them all— then the liberal's restraint concerning government funding will warrant no answering concession by the conservative. However, in that case, the conservative will justifiably view his position as more nearly uncompromisable than the liberal's; and so the liberal's restraint may still be called for. Some conciliatory gestures are appropriate even though they will be neither acknowledged nor reciprocated.

Notes

1 One problem with the alleged right concerns its intelligibility. Because it treats liberty as a single item, and not as the absence of particular restraints on particular activities, the right as stated seems incompatible with Gerald MacCallum, Jr.'s widely accepted triadic analysis of freedom. For details, see Gerald MacCallum, Jr., "Negative and Positive Freedom," *Philosophical Review* 76, no. 3 (July 1967): 312–34.

2 For an interesting discussion of the way our relation to our future selves is connected to our moral obligations, see Derek Parfit, "Later Selves and Moral Principles," in *Philosophy and Personal Relations*, ed. Alan Montefiore (London: Routledge & Kegan Paul, 1973), 137–69.

3 Some extra-legal resistance to abortion has surfaced in the years since *Roe v. Wade*. As one magazine article reported, "Many ... women (have) had to cross picket lines to obtain abortions; some subsequently received telephone calls charging them with murder. Abortion clinics in every region of the country have been disrupted repeatedly and more than a dozen have been fire-bombed. In St. Paul, Minn., where Planned Parenthood has spent

$284,000 repairing fire damages, staffers continue to cope with arson, attempted bombings, bullets fired at the clinic, windows smashed with cement blocks, walls sprayed with graffiti (including swastikas and Ku Klux Klan initials), door locks sealed with glue, pickets, boycotts of businesses associated with Planned Parenthood's board of directors, prayer vigils, and kidnap threats." Helen Epstein, "Abortion: An Issue That Won't Go Away," *The New York Times Magazine*, March 30, 1980, 45. But as striking as such activities are, they hardly begin to approach what might be done to combat (what conservatives must consider) the many millions of murders of unborn persons committed since 1967.

4 This apt formulation is introduced by Arthur Kuflik in his article "Morality and Compromise," *Nomos XXI: Compromise in Ethics, Law, and Politics*, ed. J. Roland Pennock and John Chapman (New York: New York University Press, 1979), 38–65. Throughout this section, I have drawn heavily on Kuflik's illuminating discussion.

5 The recent literature on these issues is voluminous. Several of the more important articles are reprinted in *The Rights and Wrongs of Abortion*, ed. Marshall Cohen, Thomas Nagel, and Thomas Scanlon (Princeton, N.J.: Princeton University Press, 1974). Also worthwhile are Jane English, "Abortion and the Concept of a Person," *Canadian Journal of Philosophy* 5, no. 2 (October 1975): 233–43; and H. M. Hare, "Abortion and the Golden Rule," *Philosophy and Public Affairs* 4, no. 3 (Spring 1975): 201–22.

6 The point I am making here is not that tax monies should never be used to support policies with which some segments of the population disagree. Although this principle is sometimes invoked against subsidized abortion, it is implausible on its face. If government never funded policies that were unpopular or controversial, it would be unable to do much of anything. The point I am making is much narrower and applies only to cases in which public policy is contested on moral grounds. Furthermore, the principles underlying the disagreement must be both supported by reasonable arguments and serious enough to justify extra-legal activity.

Chapter 62

Peter Singer

FAMINE, AFFLUENCE, AND MORALITY

As I write this, in November 1971, people are dying in East Bengal from lack of food, shelter, and medical care. The suffering and death that are occurring there now are not inevitable, not unavoidable in any fatalistic sense of the term. Constant poverty, a cyclone, and a civil war have turned at least nine million people into destitute refugees; nevertheless, it is not beyond the capacity of the richer nations to give enough assistance to reduce any further suffering to very small proportions. The decisions and actions of human beings can prevent this kind of suffering. Unfortunately, human beings have not made the necessary decisions. At the individual level, people have, with very few exceptions, not responded to the situation in any significant way. Generally speaking, people have not given large sums to relief funds; they have not written to their parliamentary representatives demanding increased government assistance; they have not demonstrated in the streets, held symbolic fasts, or done anything else directed toward providing the refugees with the means to satisfy their essential needs. At the government level, no government has given the sort of massive aid that would enable the refugees to survive for more than a few days. Britain, for instance, has given rather more than most countries. It has, to date, given £14,750,000. For comparative purposes, Britain's share of the nonrecoverable development costs of the Anglo-French Concorde project is already in excess of £275,000,000, and on present estimates will reach £440,000,000. The implication is that the British government values a supersonic transport more than thirty times as highly as it values the lives of the nine million refugees. Australia is another country which, on a per capita basis, is well up in the "aid to Bengal" table. Australia's aid, however, amounts to less than one-twelfth of the cost of Sydney's new opera house. The total amount given, from all sources, now stands at about £65,000,000. The estimated cost of keeping the refugees alive for one year is £464,000,000. Most of the refugees have now been in the camps for more than six months. The World Bank has said that India needs a minimum of £300,000,000 in assistance from other countries before the end of the year. It seems obvious that assistance on this scale will not be forthcoming. India will be forced to choose between letting the refugees starve or diverting funds from her own development program, which will mean that more of her own people will starve in the future.[1]

These are the essential facts about the present situation in Bengal. So far as it concerns us here, there is nothing unique about this situation except its magnitude. The Bengal emergency is just the latest and most acute of a series of major emergencies in various parts of the world, arising both from natural and from man-made causes. There are also many parts of the world in

which people die from malnutrition and lack of food independent of any special emergency. I take Bengal as my example only because it is the present concern, and because the size of the problem has ensured that it has been given adequate publicity. Neither individuals nor governments can claim to be unaware of what is happening there.

What are the moral implications of a situation like this? In what follows, I shall argue that the way people in relatively affluent countries react to a situation like that in Bengal cannot be justified; indeed, the whole way we look at moral issues—our moral conceptual scheme—needs to be altered, and with it, the way of life that has come to be taken for granted in our society.

In arguing for this conclusion I will not, of course, claim to be morally neutral. I shall, however, try to argue for the moral position that I take, so that anyone who accepts certain assumptions, to be made explicit, will, I hope, accept my conclusion.

I begin with the assumption that suffering and death from lack of food, shelter, and medical care are bad. I think most people will agree about this, although one may reach the same view by different routes. I shall not argue for this view. People can hold all sorts of eccentric positions, and perhaps from some of them it would not follow that death by starvation is in itself bad. It is difficult, perhaps impossible, to refute such positions, and so for brevity I will henceforth take this assumption as accepted. Those who disagree need read no further.

My next point is this: if it is in our power to prevent something bad from happening, without thereby sacrificing anything of comparable moral importance, we ought, morally, to do it. By "without sacrificing anything of comparable moral importance" I mean without causing anything else comparably bad to happen, or doing something that is wrong in itself, or failing to promote some moral good, comparable in significance to the bad thing that we can prevent. This principle

seems almost as uncontroversial as the last one. It requires us only to prevent what is bad, and not to promote what is good, and it requires this of us only when we can do it without sacrificing anything that is, from the moral point of view, comparably important. I could even, as far as the application of my argument to the Bengal emergency is concerned, qualify the point so as to make it: if it is in our power to prevent something very bad from happening, without thereby sacrificing anything morally significant, we ought, morally, to do it. An application of this principle would be as follows: if I am walking past a shallow pond and see a child drowning in it, I ought to wade in and pull the child out. This will mean getting my clothes muddy, but this is insignificant, while the death of the child would presumably be a very bad thing.

The uncontroversial appearance of the principle just stated is deceptive. If it were acted upon, even in its qualified form, our lives, our society, and our world would be fundamentally changed. For the principle takes, firstly, no account of proximity or distance. It makes no moral difference whether the person I can help is a neighbor's child ten yards from me or a Bengali whose name I shall never know, ten thousand miles away. Secondly, the principle makes no distinction between cases in which I am the only person who could possibly do anything and cases in which I am just one among millions in the same position.

I do not think I need to say much in defense of the refusal to take proximity and distance into account. The fact that a person is physically near to us, so that we have personal contact with him, may make it more likely that we *shall* assist him, but this does not show that we *ought* to help him rather than another who happens to be further away. If we accept any principle of impartiality, universalizability, equality, or whatever, we cannot discriminate against someone merely because he is far away from us (or we are far away from him). Admittedly, it is possible that we are in a better position to judge what

needs to be done to help a person near to us than one far away, and perhaps also to provide the assistance we judge to be necessary. If this were the case, it would be a reason for helping those near to us first. This may once have been a justification for being more concerned with the poor in one's own town than with famine victims in India. Unfortunately for those who like to keep their moral responsibilities limited, instant communication and swift transportation have changed the situation. From the moral point of view, the development of the world into a "global village" has made an important, though still unrecognized, difference to our moral situation. Expert observers and supervisors, sent out by famine relief organizations or permanently stationed in famine-prone areas, can direct our aid to a refugee in Bengal almost as effectively as we could get it to someone in our own block. There would seem, therefore, to be no possible justification for discriminating on geographical grounds.

There may be a greater need to defend the second implication of my principle—that the fact that there are millions of other people in the same position, in respect to the Bengali refugees, as I am, does not make the situation significantly different from a situation in which I am the only person who can prevent something very bad from occurring. Again, of course, I admit that there is a psychological difference between the cases; one feels less guilty about doing nothing if one can point to others, similarly placed, who have also done nothing. Yet this can make no real difference to our moral obligations.[2] Should I consider that I am less obliged to pull the drowning child out of the pond if on looking around I see other people, no further away than I am, who have also noticed the child but are doing nothing? One has only to ask this question to see the absurdity of the view that numbers lessen obligation. It is a view that is an ideal excuse for inactivity; unfortunately most of the major evils—poverty, over-population, pollution—are problems in which everyone is almost equally involved.

The view that numbers do make a difference can be made plausible if stated in this way: if everyone in circumstances like mine gave £5 to the Bengal Relief Fund, there would be enough to provide food, shelter, and medical care for the refugees; there is no reason why I should give more than anyone else in the same circumstances as I am; therefore I have no obligation to give more than £5. Each premise in this argument is true, and the argument looks sound. It may convince us, unless we notice that it is based on a hypothetical premise, although the conclusion is not stated hypothetically. The argument would be sound if the conclusion were: if everyone in circumstances like mine were to give £5, I would have no obligation to give more than £5. If the conclusion were so stated, however, it would be obvious that the argument has no bearing on a situation in which it is not the case that everyone else gives £5. This, of course, is the actual situation. It is more or less certain that not everyone in circumstances like mine will give £5. So there will not be enough to provide the needed food, shelter, and medical care. Therefore by giving more than £5 I will prevent more suffering than I would if I gave just £5.

It might be thought that this argument has an absurd consequence. Since the situation appears to be that very few people are likely to give substantial amounts, it follows that I and everyone else in similar circumstances ought to give as much as possible, that is, at least up to the point at which by giving more one would begin to cause serious suffering for oneself and one's dependents—perhaps even beyond this point to the point of marginal utility, at which by giving more one would cause oneself and one's dependents as much suffering as one would prevent in Bengal. If everyone does this, however, there will be more than can be used for the benefit of the refugees, and some of the sacrifice will have been unnecessary. Thus, if everyone does what he ought to do, the result will not be as good as it would be if everyone

did a little less than he ought to do, or if only some do all that they ought to do.

The paradox here arises only if we assume that the actions in question—sending money to the relief funds—are performed more or less simultaneously, and are also unexpected. For if it is to be expected that everyone is going to contribute something, then clearly each is not obliged to give as much as he would have been obliged to had others not been giving too. And if everyone is not acting more or less simultaneously, then those giving later will know how much more is needed, and will have no obligation to give more than is necessary to reach this amount. To say this is not to deny the principle that people in the same circumstances have the same obligations, but to point out that the fact that others have given, or may be expected to give, is a relevant circumstance: those giving after it has become known that many others are giving and those giving before are not in the same circumstances. So the seemingly absurd consequence of the principle I have put forward can occur only if people are in error about the actual circumstances—that is, if they think they are giving when others are not, but in fact they are giving when others are. The result of everyone doing what he really ought to do cannot be worse than the result of everyone doing less than he ought to do, although the result of everyone doing what he reasonably believes he ought to do could be.

If my argument so far has been sound, neither our distance from a preventable evil nor the number of other people who, in respect to that evil, are in the same situation as we are, lessens our obligation to mitigate or prevent that evil. I shall therefore take as established the principle I asserted earlier. As I have already said, I need to assert it only in its qualified form: if it is in our power to prevent something very bad from happening, without thereby sacrificing anything else morally significant, we ought, morally, to do it.

The outcome of this argument is that our traditional moral categories are upset. The traditional distinction between duty and charity cannot be drawn, or at least, not in the place we normally draw it. Giving money to the Bengal Relief Fund is regarded as an act of charity in our society. The bodies which collect money are known as "charities." These organizations see themselves in this way—if you send them a check, you will be thanked for your "generosity." Because giving money is regarded as an act of charity, it is not thought that there is anything wrong with not giving. The charitable man may be praised, but the man who is not charitable is not condemned. People do not feel in any way ashamed or guilty about spending money on new clothes or a new car instead of giving it to famine relief. (Indeed, the alternative does not occur to them.) This way of looking at the matter cannot be justified. When we buy new clothes not to keep ourselves warm but to look "well-dressed" we are not providing for any important need. We would not be sacrificing anything significant if we were to continue to wear our old clothes, and give the money to famine relief. By doing so, we would be preventing another person from starving. It follows from what I have said earlier that we ought to give money away, rather than spend it on clothes which we do not need to keep us warm. To do so is not charitable, or generous. Nor is it the kind of act which philosophers and theologians have called "supererogatory"—an act which it would be good to do, but not wrong not to do. On the contrary, we ought to give the money away, and it is wrong not to do so.

I am not maintaining that there are no acts which are charitable, or that there are no acts which it would be good to do but not wrong not to do. It may be possible to redraw the distinction between duty and charity in some other place. All I am arguing here is that the present way of drawing the distinction, which makes it an act of charity for a man living at the level of affluence which most people in the "developed nations" enjoy to give money to save someone else from starvation, cannot be

supported. It is beyond the scope of my argument to consider whether the distinction should be redrawn or abolished altogether. There would be many other possible ways of drawing the distinction—for instance, one might decide that it is good to make other people as happy as possible but not wrong not to do so.

Despite the limited nature of the revision in our moral conceptual scheme which I am proposing, the revision would, given the extent of both affluence and famine in the world today, have radical implications. These implications may lead to further objections, distinct from those I have already considered. I shall discuss two of these.

One objection to the position I have taken might be simply that it is too drastic a revision of our moral scheme: People do not ordinarily judge in the way I have suggested they should. Most people reserve their moral condemnation for those who violate some moral norm, such as the norm against taking another person's property. They do not condemn those who indulge in luxury instead of giving to famine relief. But given that I did not set out to present a morally neutral description of the way people make moral judgments, the way people do in fact judge has nothing to do with the validity of my conclusion. My conclusion follows from the principle which I advanced earlier, and unless that principle is rejected, or the arguments shown to be unsound, I think the conclusion must stand, however strange it appears.

It might, nevertheless, be interesting to consider why our society, and most other societies, do judge differently from the way I have suggested they should. In a well-known article, J. O. Urmson suggests that the imperatives of duty, which tell us what we must do, as distinct from what it would be good to do but not wrong not to do, function so as to prohibit behavior that is intolerable if men are to live together in society.[3] This may explain the origin and continued existence of the present division between acts of duty and acts of charity. Moral attitudes are shaped by the needs of society, and no doubt society needs people who will observe the rules that make social existence tolerable. From the point of view of a particular society, it is essential to prevent violations of norms against killing, stealing, and so on. It is quite inessential, however, to help people outside one's own society.

If this is an explanation of our common distinction between duty and supererogation, however, it is not a justification of it. The moral point of view requires us to look beyond the interests of our own society. Previously, as I have already mentioned, this may hardly have been feasible, but it is quite feasible now. From the moral point of view, the prevention of the starvation of millions of people outside our society must be considered at least as pressing as the upholding of property norms within our society.

It has been argued by some writers, among them Sidgwick and Urmson, that we need to have a basic moral code which is not too far beyond the capacities of the ordinary man, for otherwise there will be a general breakdown of compliance with the moral code. Crudely stated, this argument suggests that if we tell people that they ought to refrain from murder and give everything they do not really need to famine relief, they will do neither, whereas if we tell them that they ought to refrain from murder and that it is good to give to famine relief but not wrong not to do so, they will at least refrain from murder. The issue here is: Where should we draw the line between conduct that is required and conduct that is good although not required, so as to get the best possible result? This would seem to be an empirical question, although a very difficult one. One objection to the Sidgwick-Urmson line of argument is that it takes insufficient account of the effect that moral standards can have on the decisions we make. Given a society in which a wealthy man who gives five percent of his income to famine-relief is regarded as most generous, it is not surprising that a proposal that we all ought to give away

half our incomes will be thought to be absurdly unrealistic. In a society which held that no man should have more than enough while others have less than they need, such a proposal might seem narrowminded. What it is possible for a man to do and what he is likely to do are both, I think, very greatly influenced by what people around him are doing and expecting him to do. In any case, the possibility that by spreading the idea that we ought to be doing very much more than we are to relieve famine we shall bring about a general breakdown of moral behavior seems remote. If the stakes are an end to widespread starvation, it is worth the risk. Finally, it should be emphasized that these considerations are relevant only to the issue of what we should require from others, and not to what we ourselves ought to do.

The second objection to my attack on the present distinction between duty and charity is one which has from time to time been made against utilitarianism. It follows from some forms of utilitarian theory that we all ought, morally, to be working full time to increase the balance of happiness over misery. The position I have taken here would not lead to this conclusion in all circumstances, for if there were no bad occurrences that we could prevent without sacrificing something of comparable moral importance, my argument would have no application. Given the present conditions in many parts of the world, however, it does follow from my argument that we ought, morally, to be working full time to relieve great suffering of the sort that occurs as a result of famine or other disasters. Of course, mitigating circumstances can be adduced—for instance, that if we wear ourselves out through overwork, we shall be less effective than we would otherwise have been. Nevertheless, when all considerations of this sort have been taken into account, the conclusion remains: we ought to be preventing as much suffering as we can without sacrificing something else of comparable moral importance. This conclusion is one which we may be

reluctant to face. I cannot see, though, why it should be regarded as a criticism of the position for which I have argued, rather than a criticism of our ordinary standards of behavior. Since most people are self-interested to some degree, very few of us are likely to do everything that we ought to do. It would, however, hardly be honest to take this as evidence that it is not the case that we ought to do it.

It may still be thought that my conclusions are so wildly out of line with what everyone else thinks and has always thought that there must be something wrong with the argument somewhere. In order to show that my conclusions, while certainly contrary to contemporary Western moral standards, would not have seemed so extraordinary at other times and in other places, I would like to quote a passage from a writer not normally thought of as a way-out radical, Thomas Aquinas.

> Now, according to the natural order instituted by divine providence, material goods are provided for the satisfaction of human needs. Therefore the division and appropriation of property, which proceeds from human law, must not hinder the satisfaction of man's necessity from such goods. Equally, whatever a man has in superabundance is owed, of natural right, to the poor for their sustenance. So Ambrosius says, and it is also to be found in the *Decretum Gratiani*: "The bread which you withhold belongs to the hungry; the clothing you shut away, to the naked; and the money you bury in the earth is the redemption and freedom of the penniless."[4]

I now want to consider a number of points, more practical than philosophical, which are relevant to the application of the moral conclusion we have reached. These points challenge not the idea that we ought to be doing all we can to prevent starvation, but the idea that giving away a great deal of money is the best means to this end.

It is sometimes said that overseas aid should be a government responsibility, and that therefore one ought not to give to privately run charities. Giving privately, it is said, allows the government and the noncontributing members of society to escape their responsibilities.

This argument seems to assume that the more people there are who give to privately organized famine relief funds, the less likely it is that the government will take over full responsibility for such aid. This assumption is unsupported, and does not strike me as at all plausible. The opposite view—that if no one gives voluntarily, a government will assume that its citizens are uninterested in famine relief and would not wish to be forced into giving aid—seems more plausible. In any case, unless there were a definite probability that by refusing to give one would be helping to bring about massive government assistance, people who do refuse to make voluntary contributions are refusing to prevent a certain amount of suffering without being able to point to any tangible beneficial consequence of their refusal. So the onus of showing how their refusal will bring about government action is on those who refuse to give.

I do not, of course, want to dispute the contention that governments of affluent nations should be giving many times the amount of genuine, no-strings-attached aid that they are giving now. I agree, too, that giving privately is not enough, and that we ought to be campaigning actively for entirely new standards for both public and private contributions to famine relief. Indeed, I would sympathize with someone who thought that campaigning was more important than giving oneself, although I doubt whether preaching what one does not practice would be very effective. Unfortunately, for many people the idea that "it's the government's responsibility" is a reason for not giving which does not appear to entail any political action either.

Another, more serious reason for not giving to famine relief funds is that until there is effective population control, relieving famine merely postpones starvation. If we save the Bengal refugees now, others, perhaps the children of these refugees, will face starvation in a few years' time. In support of this, one may cite the now well-known facts about the population explosion and the relatively limited scope for expanded production.

This point, like the previous one, is an argument against relieving suffering that is happening now, because of a belief about what might happen in the future; it is unlike the previous point in that very good evidence can be adduced in support of this belief about the future. I will not go into the evidence here. I accept that the earth cannot support indefinitely a population rising at the present rate. This certainly poses a problem for anyone who thinks it important to prevent famine. Again, however, one could accept the argument without drawing the conclusion that it absolves one from any obligation to do anything to prevent famine. The conclusion that should be drawn is that the best means of preventing famine, in the long run, is population control. It would then follow from the position reached earlier that one ought to be doing all one can to promote population control (unless one held that all forms of population control were wrong in themselves, or would have significantly bad consequences). Since there are organizations working specifically for population control, one would then support them rather than more orthodox methods of preventing famine.

A third point raised by the conclusion reached earlier relates to the question of just how much we all ought to be giving away. One possibility, which has already been mentioned, is that we ought to give until we reach the level of marginal utility—that is, the level at which, by giving more, I would cause as much suffering to myself or my dependents as I would relieve by my gift. This would mean, of course, that one would reduce oneself to very near the material circumstances of a Bengali refugee. It will be recalled

that earlier I put forward both a strong and a moderate version of the principle of preventing bad occurrences. The strong version, which required us to prevent bad things from happening unless in doing so we would be sacrificing something of comparable moral significance, does seem to require reducing ourselves to the level of marginal utility. I should also say that the strong version seems to me to be the correct one. I proposed the more moderate version—that we should prevent bad occurrences unless, to do so, we had to sacrifice something morally significant—only in order to show that even on this surely undeniable principle a great change in our way of life is required. On the more moderate principle, it may not follow that we ought to reduce ourselves to the level of marginal utility, for one might hold that to reduce oneself and one's family to this level is to cause something significantly bad to happen. Whether this is so I shall not discuss, since, as I have said, I can see no good reason for holding the moderate version of the principle rather than the strong version. Even if we accepted the principle only in its moderate form, however, it should be clear that we would have to give away enough to ensure that the consumer society, dependent as it is on people spending on trivia rather than giving to famine relief, would slow down and perhaps disappear entirely. There are several reasons why this would be desirable in itself. The value and necessity of economic growth are now being questioned not only by conservationists, but by economists as well.[5] There is no doubt, too, that the consumer society has had a distorting effect on the goals and purposes of its members. Yet looking at the matter purely from the point of view of overseas aid, there must be a limit to the extent to which we should deliberately slow down our economy; for it might be the case that if we gave away, say, forty percent of our Gross National Product, we would slow down the economy so much that in absolute terms we would be giving less than if we gave twenty-five percent of the much larger

GNP that we would have if we limited our contribution to this smaller percentage.

I mention this only as an indication of the sort of a factor that one would have to take into account in working out an ideal. Since Western societies generally consider one percent of the GNP an acceptable level for overseas aid, the matter is entirely academic. Nor does it affect the question of how much an individual should give in a society in which very few are giving substantial amounts.

It is sometimes said, though less often now than it used to be, that philosophers have no special role to play in public affairs, since most public issues depend primarily on an assessment of facts. On questions of fact, it is said, philosophers as such have no special expertise, and so it has been possible to engage in philosophy without committing oneself to any position on major public issues. No doubt there are some issues of social policy and foreign policy about which it can truly be said that a really expert assessment of the facts is required before taking sides or acting, but the issue of famine is surely not one of these. The facts about the existence of suffering are beyond dispute. Nor, I think, is it disputed that we can do something about it, either through orthodox methods of famine relief or through population control or both. This is therefore an issue on which philosophers are competent to take a position. The issue is one which faces everyone who has more money than he needs to support himself and his dependents, or who is in a position to take some sort of political action. These categories must include practically every teacher and student of philosophy in the universities of the Western world. If philosophy is to deal with matters that are relevant to both teachers and students, this is an issue that philosophers should discuss.

Discussion, though, is not enough. What is the point of relating philosophy to public (and personal) affairs if we do not take our conclusions seriously? In this instance, taking our

conclusion seriously means acting upon it. The philosopher will not find it any easier than anyone else to alter his attitudes and way of life to the extent that, if I am right, is involved in doing everything that we ought to be doing. At the very least, though, one can make a start. The philosopher who does so will have to sacrifice some of the benefits of the consumer society, but he can find compensation in the satisfaction of a way of life in which theory and practice, if not yet in harmony, are at least coming together.

Notes

1   There was also a third possibility: that India would go to war to enable the refugees to return to their land. Since I wrote this paper, India has taken this way out. The situation is no longer that described above, but this does not affect my argument, as the next paragraph indicates.

2   In view of the special sense philosophers often give to the term, I should say that I use "obligation" so that "I have an obligation to" means no more, and no less, than "I ought to." This usage is in accordance with the definition of "ought" given by the *Shorter Oxford English Dictionary*: "the general verb to express duty or obligation." I do not think any issue of substance hangs on the way the term is used; sentences in which I use "obligation" could all be rewritten, although somewhat clumsily, as sentences in which a clause containing "ought" replaces the term "obligation."

3   J. O. Urmson, "Saints and Heroes," in *Essays in Moral Philosophy*, ed. Abraham I. Melden (Seattle and London, 1958), p. 214. For a related but significantly different view see also Henry Sidgwick, *The Methods of Ethics*, 7th edn. (London, 1907), pp. 220–21, 492–93.

4   *Summa Theologica*, II–II, Question 66, Article 7, in *Aquinas, Selected Political Writings*, ed. A. P. d'Entreves, trans. J. G. Dawson (Oxford, 1948), p. 171.

5   See, for instance, John Kenneth Galbraith, *The New Industrial State* (Boston, 1967); and E. J. Mishan, *The Costs of Economic Growth* (London, 1967).

Chapter 63

Richard W. Miller

BENEFICENCE, DUTY AND DISTANCE

ACCORDING TO Peter Singer, virtually all of us would be forced by adequate reflection on our own convictions to embrace a radical conclusion about giving. The following principle, he says, is "surely undeniable," at least once we reflect on secure convictions concerning rescue, as in his famous case of the drowning toddler.

> *The Principle of Sacrifice.* If it is in our power to prevent something very bad from happening, without thereby sacrificing anything else morally significant, we ought, morally, to do so.[1]

Combined with further, uncontroversial premises, this principle leads to a demanding imperative to give which I will call *the radical conclusion*:

> Everyone has a duty not to spend money on luxuries or frills, and to use the savings due to abstinence to help those in dire need.

For example, Singer condemns buying clothes "not to keep ourselves warm but to look 'well-dressed'" (p. 235), and insists that everyone who is not needy has a duty to donate until donating more would impoverish her or a dependent.[2] The first of the two further, auxiliary premises needed to derive the radical conclusion is an uncontroversial assessment of importance: on any particular occasion, or small bunch of occasions, on which one has the opportunity to buy a luxury or frill, the choice, instead, to spend no more than what is needed to buy a plain, functional alternative is not a morally significant sacrifice. After all, no one outside of the inevitable minority of eccentrics would claim that I make a morally significant sacrifice if I buy a plain, warm department-store brand sweater for $22.95 instead of a stunning designer label sweater on sale for $49.95. The second auxiliary is an uncontroversial claim about current consequences of giving: because of the availability of international aid agencies, donating money saved by avoiding the purchase of a luxury or frill (perhaps combined with money saved on similar occasions in a small bunch) is always a way of preventing something very bad from happening. For example, I could buy the cheaper sweater and donate $27.00 to a UNICEF campaign in which it will be used to immunize a child in serious peril of death or crippling by readily preventable infection. If I buy the designer label sweater instead, I do wrong, violating the Principle of Sacrifice.

I believe that Singer's effort to derive the radical from the obvious misconstrues ordinary morality. Adequate reflection on our most secure convictions would lead most of us to embrace a less demanding principle of general beneficence, which permits many purchases that Singer would prohibit while condemning callous indifference. I will begin by describing this alternative moderate principle and its

implications for beneficence, defending it against some initial criticisms. Then, I will describe how ordinary secure convictions concerning special relationships and partiality lead to an interpretation of the demands of equal respect that justifies this principle. Finally, with these resources in hand, I will confront Singer's most powerful appeal to those who start within the circle of ordinary morality, his attempt to derive the Principle of Sacrifice from ordinary secure convictions concerning rescue, as in his famous case of an encounter with a drowning toddler.

The Principle of Sympathy

Like Singer's Principle of Sacrifice, the more moderate rival is meant to describe our duty to give to others apart from special relationships, circumstances, and shared histories. I will call it

> *The Principle of Sympathy.* One's underlying disposition to respond to neediness as such ought to be sufficiently demanding that giving which would express greater underlying concern would impose a significant risk of worsening one's life, if one fulfilled all further responsibilities; and it need not be any more demanding than this.

Someone's choices or a pattern of choices on his part violate this principle if he would not so act if he had the attitude it dictates and were relevantly well-informed.

The "neediness" in question is the sort of deprivation that Singer labels "very bad." By "a significant risk of worsening one's life," I mean a nontrivial chance that one's life as a whole will be worse than it would otherwise be. The untoward episodes that make a life worse than it would otherwise be need not extend through a long period of someone's life or impose grave burdens. Still, the mere fact that things could have gone better for me at a certain time or that a desire of mine is unfulfilled does not entail

that my life is worse than it would have been had things gone my way. When I eat in a restaurant and am not served as good a meal as might be served, I do not, by that token, have a worse life.[3] Admittedly, some would respond to this example with a judgment that my life is worse, but only insignificantly. There is no need to pursue the disagreement here. Rather, I ask such a reader to recalibrate the Principle of Sympathy and my subsequent discussion to fit this other appraisal: treat "significant risk of worsening one's life" as short for "significant risk of significantly worsening one's life."

By "underlying disposition to respond to others' neediness," I mean the responsiveness to others' neediness as a reason to help that would express the general importance one ascribes to relieving neediness, in other words, one's basic concern for others' neediness. This is the disposition that would figure in a judgment of one's character as kind or callous. Underlying dispositions, expressing basic concerns, need not, by themselves, entail any very definite association of specific conduct with specific circumstances. In their bearing on conduct our basic concerns are usually coarse-grained. Still, in processes that Harry Frankfurt and Michael Bratman have trenchantly described, basic concerns rationalize and are manifested in more specific determinations to act in certain ways.[4] In particular, basic concern for others' neediness rationalizes and is manifested in more specific inclinations to aid others in certain ways in certain kinds of circumstances. I will call such specific standing commitments *personal policies*, in contrast to the deeper and vaguer "underlying dispositions" which are the immediate subject of the Principle of Sympathy. Clearly, different people can express the same underlying responsiveness to neediness through different sets of personal policies. Thus, some are inclined to contribute to cancer research, while others, whose basic concern with human neediness is the same, are inclined to contribute to the relief of hunger.

A moderate duty

The Principle of Sacrifice only led to the radical conclusion in light of assessments of the moral significance of costs. Similarly, the impact of Sympathy on obligatory beneficence will depend on what counts as worsening someone's life. If these assessments are compatible with the judgments, on reflection, of most of us, as Singer's project requires, then the outcome is an intermediate position, in which it is typically wrong to fill vast closets with designer clothes in a world in which many must dress in rags, but not wrong occasionally to purchase a designer-label shirt that is especially stylish and, though not outlandishly expensive, more expensive than neat, plain alternatives.

Additional responsiveness to others' neediness worsens someone's life by depriving him of adequate resources to pursue, enjoyably and well, a worthwhile goal with which he is intelligently identified and from which he could not readily detach. By "a goal with which someone identifies," I mean a basic interest that gives point and value to specific choices and plans. Such a constituent of someone's personality might be part of her description of "the sort of person I am." Suppose her affirmation of a goal in such a self-portrayal would properly be unapologetic. Given her other goals and capacities, her attachment to this goal is an interest that enriches her life if she can pursue it well. Then it is, for that person, a worthwhile goal.

On certain puritanical conceptions of what goals are worthwhile, no goal requiring the occasional acquisition of a luxury or frill should be affirmed without apology; every such goal ought to be condemned as a source of corruption rather than enrichment. But these are minority doctrines, not elements of the ordinary moral thinking to which Singer appeals. In ordinary assessments, my worthwhile goals include the goal of presenting myself to others in a way that expresses my own aesthetic sense and engages in the fun of mutual aesthetic

recognition. I need not apologize for being the sort of person who exercises his aesthetic sense and social interest in these ways. My life is enriched, not stultified by this interest, given my other interests and capacities. And to pursue this goal enjoyably and well, I must occasionally purchase a luxury or frill, namely, some stylish clothing, rather than a less expensive, plain alternative. Similarly, I could not pursue, enjoyably and well, my worthwhile goal of eating in a way that explores a variety of interesting aesthetic and cultural possibilities if I never ate in nice restaurants; and I could not adequately fulfill my worthwhile goal of enjoying the capacity of great composers and performers to exploit nuances of timbre and texture to powerful aesthetic effect without buying more than minimal stereo equipment. So I do not violate Sympathy in occasionally purchasing these luxuries and frills.[5]

Granted, others' lives are illuminated, as least as brightly, by the pursuit of less expensive goals than my goals of sartorial expression, gustatory savoring, and music appreciation. Perhaps I could have identified with their less expensive goals, if helped to do so at an early age, so that these would have been the goals giving point and value to my choices. However, since the Principle of Sympathy regulates my duty of beneficence by what threatens to worsen my own life, the limits of my duty are set by the demands of the worthwhile goals with which I could now readily identify. For if someone cannot readily identify with less demanding goals, the possibility that they might have been his does not determine what would actually worsen his life. Many poor people in the United States would not be burdened by their poverty if, through some project of self-transformation, they made their life-goals similar enough to well-adjusted hermit monks' and nuns'. This does not entail that their lives are not worse because of their poverty.

In general, in order to respect others, one need not be prepared to do violence to who one

is, radically changing one's worthwhile goals in order to be a more productive satisfier of others' urgent needs. Just as parents have a prerogative, within limits, to try to pass on their way of life to their children, I can reasonably reject a rule that requires me to end the continuing presence of my current personality in my own life even though my goals are worthwhile. This prerogative of continuity does not just reflect costs of disruption, assessed, like moving expenses, apart from the personal discontinuity itself. I need not take a pill, with no side-effects, that will give me a new outlook that would lead me to join an ascetic monastic order after donating my savings to worthy causes, even if I have reached a point at which this change of course would be my most effective way of contributing to human well-being.

Even though Sympathy permits lots of non-altruistic spending that Sacrifice would forbid, it still requires significant giving from most of the nonpoor. The underlying goals to which most of us who are not poor are securely attached leave room for this giving: we could pursue these goals enjoyably and well and fulfill our other responsibilities, while giving significant amounts to the needy. This is, then, our duty, according to Sympathy. Indeed, this principle preserves some of the critical edge of the radical conclusion, since people are prone to exaggerate risks of self-worsening. It is hard to avoid overrating what merely frustrates, blowing it up into something that worsens one's life. It is extremely difficult to avoid excessive anxieties about the future that make insignificant risks of self-worsening seem significant. It is easy to convince oneself that one cannot readily detach from a goal that one could actually slough off with little effort, developing or strengthening cheaper interests instead. Because of these enduring pressures to misapply the Principle of Sympathy, it is a constant struggle to live up to its demands.

Admittedly, the demands of Sympathy are sometimes lower because someone cannot readily detach from an exorbitantly expensive goal that most of us live well enough without. Perhaps some people are like Louis, in Ronald Dworkin's parable of expensive tastes.[6] What they can ultimately care about is dominated by an extremely expensive, worthwhile goal of ultra-refined savoring of food and drink meriting such sensory discrimination. On account of a sufficiently strong attachment to such a goal, someone might need to retain much more than he otherwise would to avoid worsening his life. But although Sympathy reduces the demands of general beneficence in such cases, it does not coddle high-fliers in ways that violate ordinary moral convictions. For it does not make someone's secure attachment to a worthwhile exorbitant goal a reason why others should, if necessary, help this person pursue his exorbitant goal enjoyably and well. A middle-income Louis would need more than he has to pursue his underlying goals enjoyably and well, but this does not make him needy *simpliciter*, in the sphere of those with whom Sympathy is concerned.

Ultimate concerns and relevant limits

Because I am seeking a principle allowing consumption that Singer would forbid, I have emphasized the relevance of costly personal goals to obligatory beneficence, according to the Principle of Sympathy. But the incremental nature of this principle, its focus on worsening rather than some absolute threshold, might still seem to generate Singer's radical conclusion, in the end. After all, at any level of monthly giving above the level of material deprivation, if anyone asks herself, "Would giving a dollar more each month impose a significant risk of making my life worse than it would be if I did not give this little bit more?", the answer is "No." So her underlying responsiveness to neediness would seem to be less than the Principle of Sympathy demands, until she has brought herself to the margin of genuine material deprivation,

which is all that Singer's radical conclusion requires.[7]

On the face of it, this argument is an exasperating trick, like a child's recurrent objection, "You're being too strict. What difference will it make if I stay up ten minutes more?" The trick is the confusion of underlying dispositions with personal policies that might express them. In typical cases, how kind one is, how concerned one is for neediness as such, does not depend on whether one gives a dollar more or less a month. Underlying concern for neediness, at the level of what is ultimately important to a person, is not that fine-grained. By the same token, a situation in which greater underlying concern would impose a significant risk of worsening one's life will be a situation in which one could not have a policy of giving a *significantly* greater amount without imposing this risk.

What makes insistence on the coarse-grainedness of underlying attitudes seem, nonetheless, an inadequate response to the argument from the trivial burden of giving a little bit more is the naturalness of being drawn to more giving by the thought, "Giving even one more dollar a month would save innocent children from desperate peril," and the typical absurdity of reassuring oneself that one's unrevised practice is all right by the further thought, "But after all, underlying concern for neediness is not subject to such fine distinctions." This *is* an absurd response to nearly all actual nagging self-doubts, among affluent people, when they read appeals from Oxfam and other groups noting how much difference a small contribution would make. But nearly all of us affluent people are aware that substantially greater helping of the needy would not significantly risk worsening our lives—or, in any case, Oxfam appeals trigger such awareness. In this context, the thought based on the fact about a little bit more that ought to prompt more giving is: "I should be doing lots more, but temptations abound and worries about what I may need are hard to keep in perspective. Still, without struggle and anxiety,

I could do this little bit of all that I should be doing, and it would still do much good."

Suppose, in contrast, that someone can assure herself that her ongoing pattern of giving adequately expresses her underlying concern for neediness and that the significantly greater giving that would express greater underlying concern would impose a significant risk of worsening her life. After reading an Oxfam mailing describing the relief provided by a small donation beyond her pattern, she could, cogently, tell herself, "I could have arrived at a slightly larger aid budget, but this slight difference would not have made me someone with greater underlying concern for the needy. Underlying concern for the needy is not subject to such fine distinctions. Since I am sufficiently well-disposed in my underlying attitude toward the needy, I do not have to give a little bit more, through extra donations on this scale."[8]

In addition to evading the incremental argument for excessive sacrifice, emphasis on basic concern for neediness also avoids a rigidity in the setting of thresholds of sacrifice that could require too little, in the face of changed needs. Liam Murphy asks people who set a threshold on mandatory giving to "suppose that the amount of good there is to be done in the world increases dramatically. Catastrophe on an unprecedented scale hits some part of the world, and many millions will die unless *all* of us in the industrial West give up a great deal of money over a period of years. Are we content to say that once the upper limit to demands is set . . . no change in the circumstances, no amount of increase in the amount of good to be done, can increase the demands of beneficence?"[9]

This is an appropriate warning of the moral danger of any personal policy setting a moderate limit to costs of aid that is insensitive to changes in needs. However, the Principle of Sympathy is about the basic concern for neediness that characterizes a whole personality, regulating personal policies in the course of a life. Quite generally, the strength of a concern at this level involves a

commitment to sacrifice within a normally expected range in response to normally expected opportunities to protect from peril *and* a commitment to greater sacrifice in connection with circumstances of extreme peril that are not expected normally to occur. Someone's underlying concern that opera thrive in her community, which was previously expressed in a small donation, does not become greater when the local opera house burns down and she responds with a specially large donation. Perhaps I would not have become someone's friend if I thought that he would routinely be in need of support, and my inclination to help him, while he is doing fairly well, is not very demanding. Still, the same underlying concern for my friend could lead me to do a great deal more if he were struck by an unexpected catastrophe. A "fair-weather friend" is no friend at all. Similarly, a reasonably beneficent friend of humanity, no more disposed to aid than Sympathy requires, may have to do much more than usual to avoid being a fairweather friend of humanity in the face of Murphy's "catastrophe on an unprecedented scale."

• • •

Rejecting Singer's principle

If the Principle of Sympathy is compatible with equal respect, then Singer's Principle of Sacrifice should be rejected. Given ordinary judgments of what worsens a life, judgments that Singer's argument does not criticize, the crucial difference between the principles is what gets scrutinized: the impact, on particular occasions, of particular choices, or the impact of an underlying attitude on a life as a whole. On particular occasions on which donating the difference would prevent something very bad from happening, the Principle of Sacrifice only permits the more expensive purchase of a luxury or frill if choosing the cheaper, plain alternative would constitute a morally significant sacrifice. There is no occasion or small bunch of occasions on which my declining an opportunity to buy a more luxurious item, buying a plain, cheaper one instead, constitutes a morally significant loss. After all, such a choice never makes my life worse; at most, it involves mere frustration. So, because of the opportunity presented by aid agencies, Sacrifice dictates abstinence. And what prohibits luxurious purchases on all particular occasions prohibits them, period. This would make it impossible for a typical, relatively affluent person to pursue, enjoyably and well, worthwhile goals to which he is securely attached, such as the sartorial goal I described. So observance of Sacrifice would have an impact on someone's life as a whole in virtue of which it is to be rejected as too demanding, if Sympathy is right. No purchase prohibited by Singer's principle is morally significant, but the loss imposed by enduring commitment to the principle is, i.e., it is the sort of loss that can make it all right to embrace a less demanding commitment, which would otherwise be morally inadequate. (Although I lack the space to examine the general role of dispositions in morality, it is worth noting the good fit of a principle scrutinizing the impact of underlying concerns and enduring commitments on a person's life with a morality based on an enduring, underlying attitude of equal respect, governing a morally responsible person's life.)[10]

Of course, the thought that a donation could relieve desperate needs does, properly, lead people not to make a luxurious purchase on particular occasions, even when the purchase would advance a worthwhile goal. The Principle of Sympathy provides a basis for such reasoning, just as much as the Principle of Sacrifice. Recognizing both his inclination to purchase that stylish, somewhat more expensive shirt *and* the troubling possibility of relieving desperate needs by a donation, a conscientious shopper might ask himself whether his life would really be worse if his inclination to spend money on nice clothes were more tightly constrained by concern for neediness. His judgments of his

inclinations, under the guidance of Sympathy, might, then, support a decision not to buy that particular luxury on that occasion, for one of the following reasons. Perhaps he realizes that the luxurious purchase would violate a personal policy that is his way of conforming to the demands of Sympathy, say, a policy of only buying fancy clothes on sale and a considerable time after the last such purchase. Then, he ought to stay the course unless other considerations intrude. (An occasional "just this once" departure from his policy might be a means of pursuing the goal of avoiding rigid regimentation. But hasn't he been using this excuse rather often lately?) Or perhaps he realizes that the luxurious purchase would violate a personal policy that he should adopt, but hasn't yet, as a means of resisting departures from Sympathy; or he sees that he is simply spending more on nice clothes than he has to in order to avoid worsening his life. Then, in the absence of special considerations (say, a truly once-in-a-lifetime sale), he ought to implement such judgments of inadequate general sensitivity to others' needs through abstinence and donation now. The appalling ease with which one can submerge insight into one's deficient concern for neediness is a powerful reason to respond right away to the realization that one is moved by inclinations violating Sympathy.

Rescue and distance

Within the circle of ordinary morality, this case for Sympathy is threatened by Singer's most famous argument, which appeals to very widely shared secure convictions concerning rescue. Singer notes (p. 235) that it is a secure conviction of virtually everyone that if he walks past a shallow pond on his way to give a lecture and sees a toddler drowning, he must wade in and save the child so long as he only incurs a morally insignificant loss, for example, muddied clothes. It would be "grotesque" to deny this.[11] But by giving to international aid agencies, one can also rescue distant people from peril, for example, children in distant villages imperiled by lack of access to safe water and basic medical care. And someone's life is no less valuable because she is not near. So if we have a duty to prevent something very bad from happening to a nearby toddler at morally insignificant cost, it might seem that we have the same duty of aid to everyone in peril near or far, just as Sacrifice requires. Indeed, similar extrapolation to those near and far of plausible variants of Singer's example would impose even more serious demands than Sacrifice. Suppose Bob is rushing to catch the only flight that will enable him to give the job talk that provides his one remaining realistic prospect of a career in philosophy before he must abandon this life goal; it seems that he must take the time to extract a toddler whom he encounters sinking into quicksand, even if he knows he will miss the flight and may well have to lead a less satisfying life.[12]

Do these arguments succeed in exposing a conflict between Sympathy and secure convictions in ordinary morality, namely, convictions concerning duties of nearby rescue and the fundamental duty to display an equal appreciation of the value of everyone's life? This would certainly be the case if the commitment to moral equality required someone to be sensitive solely to the degree of neediness of others, the extent of her capacity to relieve it, and the cost of the relief, when she chooses whether and how much to help those in dire straits. However, the ordinary construal of equal respect does not impose this requirement: for example, while appreciating the equal worth of everyone's life, one can also be specially responsive to the needs of one's child, friend, or spouse. Of course, in the toddler examples, rescuer and victim are not bound by any special relationship. But even when no special relationship or past interaction is in play, the requirement of sensitivity to neediness, capability, and cost alone oversimplifies most people's conception of equal respect.

According to the argument for Sympathy, appreciation of the equal worth of everyone's life does entail a basic concern for neediness as such. For someone who is faithful to this concern, a commitment to aid that does the most to help those in direst need is, as it were, the default personal policy: in allocating the demands of Sympathy, he only departs from it for adequate reasons. However, adequate reasons for departure do not have to appeal to costs or to any especially weighty consideration. The only large charitable bequest in my step-father's will was to help the blind. He was aware that the same donation to the fight against infectious disease in developing countries (the leading worldwide cause of death before the age of five) would have more effectively helped those in direst peril. But he gave to help the blind because his own vision problems made their plight especially poignant to him. In ordinary moral thinking, my step-father's reason was good enough to reconcile his departure from the default policy with equal valuation of everyone's life. (In contrast, a rationale involving contempt for those whose needs he did not serve would have displayed unequal respect, even if the bequest helped those in need.) Similarly, someone who appreciates the equal worth of everyone's life could be specially responsive to urgent needs encountered close at hand because actual presence makes an urgent plight especially vivid and gripping to her. Her allocating aid on the basis of this reason no more expresses disvaluing of distant lives than my getting my car's brakes checked once a year expresses contempt for those whom my car approaches eleven months later.

However, appreciation of the diversity of reasons that make special responsiveness all right is only the first step in meeting the challenge of the toddler judgments. More must be done to explain the duties toward the toddlers in a way that fits the case for Sympathy. In ordinary moral thinking, specific, potentially demanding responsiveness to imminent peril encountered close at hand is not just a personal policy compatible with equal respect for all. It is a requirement of equal respect. Yet the case for Sympathy depended on an interpretation of equal respect that might seem too permissive for such a requirement. The concern for neediness as such that equal respect requires was supposed to be an underlying disposition, regulated by its impact on one's life as a whole; the fact that one could relieve a dire burden on a particular occasion at no morally significant cost was not supposed to dictate aid on this occasion. Why, then, does equal respect require responsiveness to urgent peril of those encountered close at hand on the occasion of encounter? Equal respect was supposed to be compatible with unwillingness to display basic concern for neediness that would impose a significant risk of worsening one's life. Why, then, is Bob required to pull the toddler from the quicksand? If ordinary morality cannot explain the toddler duties and Sympathy while answering these questions, then, given the appeal of the toddler judgments, Sympathy is threatened. For (as Shelly Kagan has emphasized in similar contexts) we want our moral principles "to hang together, to be mutually supportive, to be jointly illuminated by the moral concepts to which we appeal."[13] In the absence of an explanation that fits Sympathy, sterner principles of general beneficence, based on more demanding construals of equal respect, are waiting in the wings, to explain the toddler duties as specific consequences of their general demands.

To meet this challenge, I will begin by describing how reasons shared by everyone who equally respects all lead to a policy of special responsiveness to those encountered closeby in urgent peril, even though concern for neediness as such is governed by Sympathy's occasion-neutral requirement. Then, vindicating and extending assumptions in this rationale, I will consider how demanding a policy of nearby rescue a morally responsible person must adopt. Here, I will argue that appropriate deliberations

over the burdens of requirements of aid would lead everyone who equally respects all to adopt a policy of nearby rescue stringent enough to require rescue by Bob, even though such deliberations do not dictate basic concern for neediness as such beyond the demands of Sympathy. My goal in both parts of the argument is to show that an appropriate duty of rescue exists given a normal background of human interaction, which this duty, like virtually all definite duties, presupposes.

In the normal background of human interaction, at least three mutually reinforcing considerations, shared by all who appreciate the equal worth of everyone's life, are compelling grounds for adopting a policy of special responsiveness to those in urgent peril who are near. First, any human who is, in other ways, disposed to display equal respect for all finds in herself a strong impulse to come to the aid of those whom she encounters in urgent peril close at hand. Assuming that she has no adequate reason to rein in this impulse as too demanding (an assumption that I will make in this paragraph and argue for later on), she ought to embrace it as a personal policy. Equal respect for all requires responsiveness to neediness that does not impose a serious risk of worsening one's life, and it is very hard to live up to this demand. It would be the height of arrogance to restrain a powerful impulse that helps to fulfill this imperative, if there is no reason to reject the impulse as excessively demanding. In the second place, the prevalent special inclination to respond to nearby calamity with aid plays a distinctive coordinative role in advancing the general project of alleviating neediness that Sympathy imposes on us all: if people take on a special personal responsibility to aid someone in urgent peril encountered close at hand, then the probability of disastrous delay in meeting urgent needs is much less than it would be if no such specific allocation of responsibility were prevalent.[14] An otherwise responsible person who lacks this special tendency takes advantage of others' having it, in advancing a cause he shares, while lacking an adequate reason to abstain. Finally, the expectation that others who encounter us would help us if we needed to be rescued from imminent peril makes us much less alone, much more at home in our social world. Even if I were guaranteed not to need help in emergencies from mere passersby—say, because official emergency services were so wonderfully effective—I would be profoundly deprived of fellowship if those whom I encountered typically had no such inclination to help me if need be. (We find it chilling if someone "looks straight through us," even if we know this person is intensely active in relieving neediness worldwide.) So deep social interests of any self-respecting person are served by the prevalent inclination to help those encountered in distress; if she does not share it, she takes advantage of others' good will, not joining in a stance whose prevalence vitally concerns her, while lacking an adequate reason to abstain.

Of course, neediness would be relieved even more effectively if the inclination to nearby rescue were just one consequence of a demanding inclination to relieve dire burdens whenever one is in a good position to do so; and human fellowship would be even greater if the strong inclination to help an encountered victim were part of a strong inclination to help on any occasion on which one is aware of an opportunity to relieve distress. But these are not prevalent inclinations, actually benefiting all, and a proposal that we should all be so responsive could be rejected by some who have equal respect for all, as imposing a significant risk of worsening their lives.

(What if we lacked an inclination to help those in urgent peril encountered close at hand? If our capacities and interests were otherwise the same, each of us, if morally responsible, would have reasons to want all to share in such an inclination, in order to coordinate the advancement of Sympathy and satisfy the interest in fellowship. Such an aspiration provides a morally

model and act in accordance with the inclination so long as the costs of doing so when others do not are not excessive. This is a weaker reason than the avoidance of parasitism, and noncompliance by others would increase net expected costs. Still, at least some specific concern for those closeby would be a duty. As we shall see, an even more radically altered world, in which interests and capacities are changed, could break the tie between nearness and duty entirely.)

These reasons for responding to nearby perils on the occasion of encounter will only make a specific policy of special responsiveness compelling for all if no one who respects all can reject the policy as too demanding. It might seem that a view of equal respect requiring responsiveness so demanding that Bob must save the toddler is incompatible with the previous case for Sympathy. But there is no such conflict if burdens are appropriately assessed.

In asking whether a choice would be morally wrong, one faces a question of principles. In effect, one asks whether the choice would be permitted by a system of principles that no one, while equally respecting all, could reject as a moral code for everyone to follow. The choice is wrong just in case it would be ruled out by any such moral code.[15] If the toddler judgments are right, then no one who respects all could reject a principle along the following lines:

> The Principle of Nearby Rescue. One has a duty to rescue someone encountered closeby who is in imminent peril of severe harm and whom one can help to rescue with means at hand, if the sacrifice of rescue does not itself involve a grave risk of harm of similar seriousness or of serious physical harm, and does not involve wrongdoing.

The worry is that the arguments for Sympathy create a need to amend Nearby Rescue with the following proviso, which exempts Bob: "unless rescue imposes a significant risk of worsening life." However, this worry reflects a ought to guide the acceptance and rejection of a moral code. These deliberations involve individuals' reflections, ex ante, on expected costs to them of general observance of alternative codes.[16] Unfortunately for Bob, a moral principle that he could not reasonably reject in the relevant, ex ante deliberations has come due in circumstances that were not to be expected.

In negotiations over the terms of a particular joint project, each party's particular current circumstances determine what terms she could reject while showing equal respect for all (perhaps rejecting the terms "only for now, because of the fix I am in"). But we are trying to determine what personal concerns are an acceptable basis for rejecting or accepting a moral code that would be in the background of responses to particular current circumstances; this is the sort of enduring commitment that a person of moral integrity brings into interactions with others, as they arise. Here, greater abstraction from current particular circumstances is appropriate. The rejection of a proposed moral principle as too demanding should be tied to the assessment of likely costs and benefits in light of the background of resources and underlying goals with which the agent approaches particular circumstances and the ex ante probabilities of the various particular circumstances in which the sharing of the proposed commitment would affect her life. Decisions made behind a veil of ignorance blocking all awareness of personal resources and concerns would abstract even more strenuously from full knowledge of current circumstances. But the requirement of this much abstraction would impose principles of moral obligation that can, in fact, be rejected, without unequal respect, if previous arguments are right. The intermediate level of abstraction further specifies the morally decisive deliberations.

In the relevant ex ante reflections, Bob would note that the Principle of Nearby Rescue may

require him to give up a great deal. But the chance of his being called on, through encounter with someone in imminent severe peril, is quite small. The costs of his monitoring his circumstances and conduct to insure commitment to the Principle of Nearby Rescue are exceptionally small, adding nothing significant to his normal attention to his immediate environment. Moreover, from the appropriate ex ante perspective, Bob must consider the possible consequences for him of general acceptance or nonacceptance of the Principle of Nearby Rescue if he should be the one in dire straits: in such circumstances, he obviously has much to gain from a demanding general commitment that binds people closeby, the people who, in general, most readily notice such peril and initiate aid.

The result of these facts in the background of the relevant ex ante assessment will be a no more than trivial net risk that his life will be worsened by participation in general acceptance of the Principle of Nearby Rescue. Thus, in the relevant assessment of moral codes, Bob could not reject the principle as excessively burdensome while treating others' lives as no less valuable than his own.

Of course, Bob could be any of us. Facts about everyone's capacities and potential needs make the expected net costs of the Principle of Nearby Rescue no more than trivial, from everyone's relevant ex ante perspective.[17] So, given the reasons for special attentiveness to closeness that were previously rehearsed, someone who equally values everyone's life must adopt this principle, as a basis for responding to neediness close at hand. From the relevant perspective, it meets the same test of demandingness that made Sympathy the right principle to govern general beneficence: it does not impose a significant risk of worsening one's life.[18]

Like virtually any definite principle of obligation, Nearby Rescue presupposes normal background circumstances of human interaction. A radical change in this background could qualitatively change ex ante expectations of the costs and benefits of adherence to Nearby Rescue. These departures deprive Nearby Rescue of moral force in ways that confirm the crucial status of such expectations in ordinary moral thinking about rescue. If encounters with those in imminent peril were as common as encounters with those in severe financial need or those in nonimminent physical peril, the expected net burden of rescue could be substantial. Similarly, the monitoring of what is nearby would be burdensome and would not be very useful for nearby victims in a future society in which people lead their lives with eyes fixed on computer screens and keyboards grafted onto their bodies, with only the most awkward and peripheral awareness of their immediate noncomputer environments. Just as the explanation of Bob's duty would lead one to expect, potential rescuers in these background circumstances do not seem to be bound by the most demanding constraints of Nearby Rescue, even though they would still be bound by Sympathy. Nearby Rescue binds agents who are embodied, aware, capable, and emotionally sensitive in the actual human way, in environments in which the propensity to encounter dire emergencies lies in a normal range.

Beyond nearness

Arguing for a distance-neutral morality of aid, Peter Unger has described a case in which rescue seems to be obligatory even though the one in peril is not close by: you might be driving in the countryside in a CB-equipped car, and receive a plea for rescue from someone stranded ten miles away, who will lose his mangled, bleeding leg unless taken to a hospital. You would be wrong not to save the one in peril, Unger says, even if you foresee that his bleeding will cause five thousand dollars' worth of damage to your car's leather upholstery.[18] This judgment seems to undermine the moderate view of beneficence that I have defended. For all the morally relevant factors mentioned in the Principle of Nearby Rescue are present in Unger's example, except

for closeness, and no other factor seems, at first glance, to be in play. If the absence of closeness does not eliminate the traveler's obligation, shouldn't the Principle of Nearby Rescue be rejected in favor of a principle requiring costly aid to those in dire peril regardless of whether they are close?

Rejection of closeness as irrelevant to duties of rescue would be a misguided response to Unger's example. Rather, the example shows that in the absence of closeness other relevant special features of a circumstance of urgent need can also give rise to a definite, significantly demanding obligation to aid. A plea for help from someone who shares a sparsely inhabited territory is a circumstance of this kind, for reasons resembling those that establish the duty of nearby rescue.

Unger seems to have in mind a traveler in a sparsely settled countryside. A rule requiring people who are in a sparsely settled territory to respond to the discovery of someone's urgent peril elsewhere in this territory, even in a distant part, is not excessively demanding. The odds of being singled out as a source of rescue are low, while the probability that one's nearest potential rescuer will be distant, if one is oneself in peril, is high. So the net expected burden of adherence to a shared code including this rule is trivial, at most. In contrast, in a densely populated territory in which such distant pleas are frequent, a requirement of aid in response to a distant plea would be much more demanding. And there does not seem to be a similarly strong duty to respond to every such plea in this different sort of circumstance. Fortunately, fellow-residents of a densely populated place normally are provided with facilities including public employees responsible for rescue. But if such facilities are absent (say, because some strange calamity has befallen the public employees), someone is not morally obliged to respond to every overheard cross-town CB plea for rescue, even when rescue would not place her in serious physical jeopardy.

Granted, a form of responsiveness to need that is not excessively demanding can merely be

duty of Sympathy, for it to be obligatory, there must be reasons why this specific form of responsiveness should be in everyone's package of beneficent policies. In cases such as Unger's, considerations reminiscent of the rationale for Nearby Rescue provide such reasons. We are drawn to help when we become aware that someone is in urgent physical distress, that we are in a good position to relieve it, and that no one else is apt to respond. This inclination is a psychological resource for holding oneself to the demands of Sympathy; so one should not restrain this inclination in ways that are not necessary to avoid excessive demands. In addition, if the traveler were not responsive to urgent pleas in sparsely populated territories, he would fail to take part in a strategy for allocating responsibility that advances Sympathy's project of relieving suffering, and he would lack an adequate reason to abstain. Finally, just as his interest in fellowship leads him to value the normal inclination to nearby rescue, he should cherish normal dispositions to respond to urgent expressions of distress with aid, as valuable aspects of human relatedness, valuable apart from their pay-off in aid actually given. Regardless of how often people benefit from rescue, the capacity of communication to summon aid makes communication more valuable, an appropriate antidote to loneliness, not just a vehicle of information.

Of course, in the mail and from television, a person in a rich country might very well frequently receive a plea to help desperate people in poor countries, in a communication of a kind that could generate a duty to help if it linked the traveler and the victim in Unger's example. But relatively affluent people can reject a moral code requiring response to all such pleas, while showing equal respect for all. Given global inequality, poverty and communication, their acceptance of this code would impose a significant risk of worsening their lives, when assessed from the relevant ex ante perspective.

Beyond beneficence

In Singer's effort to derive the radical from the obvious, a principle of general beneficence, regardless of special relationships, circumstances or shared histories, is the immediate source of the radical demand. So, in response, I have concentrated on the defense of a rival principle of general beneficence, only defending further, special requirements as needed to cope with examples meant to undermine it. However, in ordinary morality, duties to give up advantages in the interests of others respond to a great variety of special relationships to them, not just intimate relationships, such as parenting or friendship, but relatively impersonal relationships, such as fellow-citizenship. Might it be that current relationships between relatively affluent people in developed countries and needy people in developing countries generate extensive obligations to transfer benefits, in addition to the demands of Sympathy? Poor people in developing countries seem to hold this view. Their most insistent plea seems to be "Stop taking advantage of us," not "Take pity on us." Might duties to repair defects in specific transnational relationships combine with Sympathy to create a demand for transfer that goes far beyond current aid, even if it falls short of prohibiting luxuries and frills? I think that this can be shown, through adequate reflection on secure moral convictions and empirically accurate descriptions of global interactions. If so, the critique of Singer's argument should be a preliminary to a better, more political argument in the interest of those he seeks to help. As an effort to base a fairly radical conclusion about giving on ordinary moral convictions, this further project pays homage to Singer's pathbreaking work.

Notes

I am indebted to the Editors of *Philosophy & Public Affairs* who provided extremely helpful criticisms and suggestions in response to earlier versions of this article. I have also benefited from the insightful comments of Harry Brighouse, Claudia Card, Carolina Sartorio, Peter Singer, and others in discussions under the auspices of the University of Wisconsin (Madison) Philosophy Department and the Cornell Center for the Study of Inequality.

1 See Peter Singer, "Famine, Affluence and Morality," *Philosophy & Public Affairs* 1 (1972): 241, 235. Unadorned page numbers will refer to this article. Singer quickly adds that "ought, morally" is meant to single out a dictate of moral duty, "not an act that it would be good to do, but not wrong not to do."

2 See p. 242, and Singer, "Reconsidering the Famine Relief Argument" in *Food Policy*, ed. Peter Brown and Henry Shue (New York: Free Press, 1977), p. 49. Singer would exempt purchases that are essential to someone's most effective strategy for helping the needy, say, the purchase of a fancy suit in order to maximize donations through use of income earned at a dressy Wall Street law firm. Similarly, the radical conclusion about spending money on luxuries or frills is only meant to prohibit purchases of luxuries or frills, at additional expense, for the sake of enjoyed consumption.

3 In *The Morality of Freedom* (Oxford: Oxford University Press, 1986), pp. 241–43, Joseph Raz presents similar examples as part of a case for the thesis, "When happiness is understood as a quality of a person's life or of periods of his life, the pursuit of happiness is . . . satiable [i.e., involves a goal that can be completely met]," p. 241.

4 See, for example, Harry Frankfurt, "The Importance of What We Care About" (1982) in his *The Importance of What We Care About* (Cambridge: Cambridge University Press, 1988); Michael Bratman, "Reflection, Planning, and Temporally Extended Agency," *Philosophical Review* 109 (2000): 35–61.

5 In these cases, a goal consists of doing well in certain activities. But in general, I intend "goal" broadly, to include the full range of ways of doing well, including doing well in relationships one values and in expressing traits one values. One worthwhile trait that virtually all of us value is relaxed openness to occasional harmless indulgences that do not promote the goals that structure our lives as a whole by focussing our strivings. So

sufficient success ...   ,
utes to our sufficiently successful pursuit of our goals in the relevant broad sense, even though it departs from a narrower goal-directedness. (I am indebted to a comment by an Editor of *Philosophy & Public Affairs*, which revealed the importance of this distinction.)

6 See Ronald Dworkin, "What Is Equality? Part I: Equality of Welfare," *Philosophy & Public Affairs* (1981): 228–40 (also in Dworkin, *Sovereign Virtue* [Cambridge, Mass.: Harvard University Press, 2000], pp. 48–59).

7 At the end of "International Aid and the Scope of Kindness," *Ethics* 105 (1994): 126f., Garrett Cullity offers a similar argument as the most powerful basis for insisting that a duty of kindness requires a "huge" sacrifice by the affluent in response to worldwide suffering. He says that this argument can be blocked, but not by any means as yet presented in the literature.

8 This is not to say that there can never be an obligation to do a little bit more to provide for others' needs even though one's basic concern for neediness meets the demands of Sympathy. For example (as an Editor of *Philosophy & Public Affairs* has pointed out), a scientist might be obliged to check a calculation one more time, even if her life is made worse by the scrupulousness that leads to such rechecking. However, this obligation will reflect the special responsibilities of her role, not her duty of general beneficence, regardless of special relationships.

9 Liam Murphy, *Moral Demands in Nonideal Theory* (New York: Oxford University Press, 2000), pp. 66ff.

10 Rule-utilitarianism provides an alternative way of avoiding excessive demands by giving priority to the whole impact of general constraints. But the rule-utilitarian project of basing moral obligation on the rules whose general inculcation would be optimific has further liabilities. The typical positive impact of personal attachments on the tendency to do good, which is the source of rule-utilitarian limits on duties of general beneficence, does not provide a plausible reason why someone such as the emergency-room doctor I described, whose attachments, atypically, reduce his tendency to do good, has, like the rest of us, a prerogative to

...ents. Even putting atypical peopl...
quences of implementing alternative norms does not determine the moral significance of actual people's actual attachments. Perhaps the needs of people in the least developed countries are so desperate that overall well-being would be increased if everyone took a pill transforming special attentiveness to the near and dear to impartial benevolence. A parent, child or friend in an affluent country would still be justified in rejecting this transformative project on account of his commitment to his actual relationships. In response, rule-utilitarianism could be mitigated by adding a personal prerogative. Indeed, my arguments for the permissive aspect of Sympathy could be seen as establishing such a prerogative. But if ordinary moral convictions include materials for reconciling this prerogative with equal respect, they also seem to include materials for prohibiting further measures, such as optimific but oppressive divisions of labor, that the hybrid doctrine allows.

11 Singer's apt comment in a recent presentation of the argument, *OneWorld*, p. 156.

12 In support of a radical conclusion about donations to lessen the serious suffering of others ("a typical well-off person, like you and me, must give away most of her financial assets, and much of her income"), Peter Unger has appealed to a duty to rescue in an analogous case, involving sacrificed resources for retirement, the Case of Bob's Bugatti. See Unger, *Living High and Letting Die* (New York: Oxford University Press, 1996), pp. 134–39.

13 See Kagan, *The Limits of Morality* (New York: Oxford University Press, 1989), p. 14.

14 In "The Possibility of Special Duties," *Canadian Journal of Philosophy* 16 (1986): 651–76, Philip Pettit and Robert Goodin. emphasize the coordinative benefits of widely shared norms allocating special responsibilities. However, they are not concerned with the moral status of closeness, and they deploy a rule-consequentialist framework that would yield Singer's radical conclusion in current global circumstances of neediness and inequality.

15 This formulation further develops the descriptions of moral wrongness on which I have already relied, making explicit some features that are especially salient in the judgment of Bob. As

I noted in the course of arguing for Sympathy as against Sacrifice, equal respect for all is most plausibly viewed as an enduring personality trait, specified by describing enduring commitments that guide particular choices and reasons as circumstances arise. Also, if one respects all, one will commit oneself to ultimate principles of moral obligation that are the same as those incumbent on others, despite different ramifications in different circumstances: the denial that one is on a par with others to this extent expresses contempt ("I don't have to observe the standards that bind the likes of you") or condescension ("I am made of finer moral stuff and do wrong unless I follow a higher standard").

16 If extensive noncompliance is actually expected, further deliberations may be needed, along the lines at which I briefly gestured in the parenthetic discussion of a world lacking the pervasive inclination to aid those encountered in dire peril. Even in these further deliberations, the relevant costs are ex ante expectations. In the case at hand, inclinations corresponding to Nearby Rescue are sufficiently prevalent that no such complication is needed.

17 "Nil," as opposed to "no more than trivial," would be an exaggeration. Some people, after all, are less vulnerable than most to catastrophes creating a need for rescue. So they have some net risk of serious loss, even from an appropriate ex ante perspective. The existence of such people seems an insuperable obstacle to grounding Nearby Rescue on a morality of mutual benefit. As Liam Murphy notes, in criticizing efforts to base restricted principles of obligatory rescue on "a mutually beneficial ex ante bargain," "a well-guarded billionaire who never . . . takes personal risks . . . might well be called on in emergencies . . . while his chances of needing a stranger's assistance are close to zero" (Murphy, *Moral Demands in Nonideal Theory*, p. 158). However, in the morality of equal respect, the role of reflection on the ex ante net expected costs of Nearby Rescue is not to establish universal mutual benefit, but to show that someone who regards others' lives as no less valuable than his own would not regard Nearby Rescue as too demanding, given the triviality of the ex ante risks it imposes.

18 There are, of course, people who respect all who would prefer that everyone had stronger commitments to rescue and beneficence than Nearby Rescue and Sympathy describe. These are people whose vulnerability is great and whose local sources of aid are meager. But they will hardly be opposed to the view that everyone should be at least as giving as Sympathy and Nearby Rescue require. Beyond this point, the relevant unanimity ends, and, with it, moral obligation. In the relevant moral reasoning, prohibitions are established and, then, permission follows according to the rule, "What is not prohibited is allowed." Indeed, someone does not respect all if he insists on a moral code with constraints that some could refuse to impose on themselves while respecting all.

19 See Unger, *Living High and Letting Die*, pp. 34f. Some previous stage-setting is on pp. 24f.

R. M. Hare

WHAT IS WRONG WITH SLAVERY

NEARLY EVERYBODY would agree that slavery is wrong; and I can say this perhaps with greater feeling than most, having in a manner of speaking *been* a slave. However, there are dangers in just taking for granted that something is wrong; for we may then assume that it is obvious that it is wrong and indeed obvious why it is wrong; and this leads to a prevalence of very bad arguments with quite silly conclusions, all based on the so-called absolute value of human freedom. If we could see more clearly what is valuable about freedom, and why it is valuable, then we might be protected against the rhetoric of those who, the moment anything happens that is disadvantageous or distasteful to them, start complaining loudly about some supposed infringement of their liberty, without telling us why it is wrong that they should be prevented from doing what they would like to do. It may well *be* wrong in many such cases; but until we have some way of judging when it is and when it is not, we shall be at the mercy of every kind of demagogy.

This is but one example of the widespread abuse of the appeal to human rights. We may even be tempted to think that our politics would be more healthy if rights had never been heard of; but that would be going too far. It is the unthinking appeal to ill-defined rights, unsupported by argument, that does the harm. There is no doubt that arguments justifying some of these appeals are possible; but since the forms of such arguments are seldom understood even by philosophers, it is not surprising that many quite unjustified claims of this sort go unquestioned, and thus in the end bring any sort of appeal to human rights into disrepute. It is a tragedy that this happens, because there really are rights that ought to be defended with all the devotion we can command. Things are being done the world over which can properly be condemned as infringements of human rights; but so long as rights are used so loosely as an all-purpose political weapon, often in support of very questionable causes, our protests against such infringements will be deprived of most of their force.

Another hazard of the appeal to rights is that it is seldom that such an appeal by one side cannot be countered with an appeal to some conflicting right by the opposite side. The controversies which led finally to the abolition of slavery provide an excellent example of this, with one side appealing to rights of liberty and the other to rights of property. But we do not have to go so far back in history to find examples of this sort of thing. We have only to think of the disputes about distributive justice between the defenders of equality and of individual liberty; or of similar arguments about education. I have written about both these disputes elsewhere, in the attempt to substitute for intuitions some more solid basis for argument.[1] I have the same general motive in raising

the topic of slavery, and also a more particular motive. Being a utilitarian, I need to be able to answer the following attack frequently advanced by opponents of utilitarianism. It is often said that utilitarianism must be an objectionable creed because it could in certain circumstances condone or even commend slavery, given that circumstances can be envisaged in which utility would be maximized by preserving a slave-owning society and not abolishing slavery. The objectors thus seek to smear utilitarians with the taint of all the atrocious things that were done by slave-traders and slave-owners. The objection, as I hope to show, does not stand up; but in order to see through this rhetoric we shall have to achieve a quite deep understanding of some rather difficult issues in moral philosophy; and this, too, adds to the importance and interest of the topic.

First, we have to ask what this thing, slavery, is, about whose wrongness we are arguing. As soon as we ask this question we see at once, if we have any knowledge of history, that it is, in common use, an extremely ill-defined concept. Even if we leave out of account such admittedly extended uses of 'wage-slave' in the writings of Marxists, it is clear that the word 'slave' and its near-equivalents such as 'servus' and 'doulos' have meant slightly different things in different cultures; for slavery is, primarily, a *legal* status, defined by the disabilities or the liabilities which are imposed by the law on those called slaves; and obviously these may vary from one jurisdiction to another. Familiar logical difficulties arise about how we are to decide, of a word in a foreign language, that it means the same as the English word 'slave'. Do the relevant laws in the country where the language is spoken have to be identical with those which held in English-speaking countries before slavery was abolished? Obviously not; because it would be impossible for them to be identical with the laws of all such countries at all periods, since these did not remain the same. Probably we have a rough idea of the kind of

laws which have to hold in a country before we can say that that country has an institution properly called 'slavery'; but it is pretty rough.

It would be possible to pursue at some length, with the aid of legal, historical and anthropological books on slavery in different cultures and jurisdictions, the different shades of meaning of the word 'slave'. But since my purpose is philosophical, I shall limit myself to asking what is essential to the notion of slavery in common use. The essential features are, I think, to be divided under two heads: slavery is, first, a *status* in society, and secondly, a *relation* to a master. The slave is so called first of all because he occupies a certain place in society, lacking certain rights and privileges secured by the law to others, and subject to certain liabilities from which others are free. And secondly, he is the slave of another person or body (which might be the state itself). The first head is not enough to distinguish slavery from other legal disabilities; for example the lower castes in some societies are as lacking in legal rights as slaves in some others, or more so, but are not called slaves because they are not the slaves of anybody.

The *status* of a slave was defined quite early by the Greeks in terms of four freedoms which the slave lacks. These are: a legally recognized position in the community, conferring a right of access to the courts; protection from illegal seizure and detention and other personal violence; the privilege of going where he wants to go; and that of working as he pleases. The first three of these features are present in a manumission document from Macedonia dated about 235 B.C.; the last is added in the series of manumission documents from Delphi which begins about thirty years later.[2] The state could to some extent regulate by law the treatment of slaves without making us want to stop calling them slaves, so that the last three features are a bit wobbly at the edges. But we are seeking only a rough characterization of slavery, and shall have to put up with this indefiniteness of the concept.

The reason... ... I shall invite the reader's judg-

some extent indefinite. It might seem that we could tie it up tight by saying that a slave has to be the *property* of an *owner*; but a moment's reflection will show what unsafe ground this is. So-called property-owners do not need to be reminded that legal restrictions upon the use and enjoyment of property can become so onerous as to make it almost a joke to call it property at all. I am referring not only to such recent inventions as zoning and other planning laws (though actually they are not so recent, having been anticipated even in ancient times), and to rent acts, building regulations, clean air acts and the like, but also to the ancient restrictions placed by the common law on uses of one's property which might be offensive to one's neighbours. In relation to slavery, it is also instructive to think of the cruelty-to-animals legislation which now rightly forbids one to do what one likes to one's own dog or cow which one has legally purchased. Legislation of just this kind was passed in the days before abolition, and was even to some extent enforced, though not always effectively. The laws forbidding the slave trade were, of course, the outstanding example of such legislation preventing people from doing what they wanted with their own property.

However, as before, we are seeking only a general and rough characterization of slavery, and shall therefore have to put up with the open texture of the concept of property. This, like slavery itself, is defined by the particular rights and obligations which are conferred or imposed by a particular legal system, and these may vary from one such system to another. It will be enough to have a general idea of what would stop us calling a person the slave of another— how far the law would have to go in assigning rights to slaves before we stopped using that word of them. I have gone into these difficulties in such detail as space has allowed only because I am now going on to describe, for the purposes of our moral discussion, certain conditions of

what I am describing is not really slavery. The case I shall sketch is admittedly to some extent fantastic; and this, as we shall later see, is very important when we come to assess the philosophical arguments that have been based on similar cases. But although it is extremely unlikely that what I describe should actually occur, I wish to maintain that if it occurred, we should still call it slavery, so that if imaginary cases are allowed to be brought into the arguments, this case will have to be admitted.

It may be helpful if, before leaving the question of what slavery is, I list a few conditions of life which have to be *distinguished* from slavery proper. The first of these is *serfdom* (a term which, like 'slavery' itself, has a wide range of meaning). A serf is normally tied, not directly to a master, but to a certain area of land; the rights to his services pass with the land if it changes hands. This very distinction, however, separates the English villein in gross, who approximates to a slave although enjoying certain legal rights, from the villein regardant, whose serfdom arises through his feudal tenure of land. Those who unsuccessfully tried to persuade Lord Mansfield in Sommersett's case that slavery could exist in England attempted to show that the defendant was a villein in gross.[3] Secondly, one is not a slave merely because one belongs to a *caste* which has an inferior legal status, even if it has pretty well no rights; as I have said, the slave has to be the slave of some owner. Thirdly, slavery has to be distinguished from *indenture*, which is a form of contract. Apprentices in former times, and football players even now, are bound by contract, entered into by themselves or, in the case of children, by their parents, to serve employers for a fixed term under fixed conditions, which were in some cases extremely harsh (so that the actual sufferings of indentured people could be as bad as those of slaves).[4] The difference lies in the voluntariness of the contract and in its fixed term. We must note however that in some

societies (Athens before Solon for example) one could *choose* to become a slave by selling one's person to escape debt;[5] and it might be possible to sell one's children as well, as the Greeks sometimes did, so that even the hereditability of the slave status does not serve to make definite the rather fuzzy boundary between slavery and indenture.

We ought perhaps to notice two other conditions which approximate to slavery but are not called slavery. The first is a compulsory *military* or *naval service* and, indeed, other forced labour. The impressed sailors of Nelson's navy no doubt endured conditions as bad as many slaves; Dr. Johnson remarked that nobody would choose to be a sailor if he had the alternative of being put in prison.[6] But they were not called slaves, because their status as free men was only in abeyance and returned to them on discharge. By contrast, the galley slaves of the Mediterranean powers in earlier times really were slaves. Secondly, although the term 'penal servitude' was once in use, *imprisonment* for crime is not usually called slavery. This is another fuzzy boundary, because in ancient times it was possible for a person to lose his rights as a citizen and become a slave by sentence of a court for some crime;[7] though when something very like this happened recently in South Africa, it was not *called* slavery, officially.[8] Again, prisoners of war and other captives and bondsmen are not always called slaves, however grim their conditions, although in ancient times capture in war was a way of becoming a slave, if one was not fortunate enough to be ransomed.[9] I have myself, as a prisoner of war, worked on the Burma railway in conditions not *at the time* distinguishable from slavery; but because my status was temporary I can claim to have been a slave only 'in a manner of speaking'.

I shall put my philosophical argument, to which we have now come, in terms of an imaginary example, to which I shall give as much verisimilitude as I can. It will be seen, however, that quite unreal assumptions have to be made in order to get the example going—and this is very important for the argument between the utilitarians and their opponents. It must also be noted that to play its role in the argument the example will have to meet certain requirements. It is intended as a fleshed-out substitute for the rather jejune examples often to be found in anti-utilitarian writers. To serve its purpose it will have to be a case in which to abolish slavery really and clearly would diminish utility. This means, first, that the slavery to be abolished must really be slavery, and, secondly, that it must have a total utility clearly, but not enormously, greater than the total utility of the kind of regime which would be, in that situation, a practical alternative to slavery.

If it were not *clearly* greater, utilitarians could argue that, since all judgements of this sort are only probable, caution would require them to stick to a well-tried principle favouring liberty, the principle itself being justified on utilitarian grounds (see below); and thus the example would cease to divide them from their opponents, and would become inapposite.

If, on the other hand, the utility of slavery were *enormously* greater, anti-utilitarians might complain that their own view was being made too strong; for many anti-utilitarians are pluralists and hold that among the principles of morality a principle requiring beneficence is to be included. Therefore, if the advantages of retaining slavery are made sufficiently great, a non-utilitarian with a principle of beneficence in his repertory could agree that it ought to be retained—that is, that *in this case* the principle of beneficence has greater weight than that favouring liberty. Thus there would again be no difference, in this case, between the verdicts of the utilitarians and their opponents, and the example would be inapposite.

There is also another dimension in which the example has to be carefully placed. An anti-utilitarian might claim that the example I shall give makes the difference between the conditions

society too small, and the number of slaves too great. If, he might claim, I had made the number of slaves small and the difference between the miseries of the slaves and the pleasures of the slave-owners much greater, then the society might have the same total utility as mine (that is, greater than that of the free society with which I compare it), but it would be less plausible for me to maintain that if such a comparison had to be made in real life, we ought to follow the utilitarians and prefer the slave society.[10]

I cannot yet answer this objection without anticipating my argument; I shall merely indicate briefly how I would answer it. The answer is that the objection rests on an appeal to our ordinary intuitions; but that these are designed to deal with ordinary cases. They give no reliable guide to what we ought to say in highly unusual cases. But, further, the case desiderated is never likely to occur. How could it come about that the existence of a small number of slaves was necessary in order to preserve the happiness of the rest? I find it impossible to think of any technological factors (say, in agriculture or in transport by land or sea) which would make the preservation of slavery for a small class necessary to satisfy the interests of the majority. It is quite true that in the past there have been *large* slave populations supporting the higher standard of living of *small* minorities. But in that case it is hard to argue that slavery has more utility than its abolition, if the difference in happiness between slaves and slave-owners is great. Yet if, in order to produce a case in which the retention of slavery really would be optimal, we reduce the number of slaves relative to slave-owners, it becomes hard to say how the existence of this relatively small number of slaves is necessary for the happiness of the large number of free men. What on earth are the slaves doing that could not be more efficiently done by paid labour? And is not the abolition (perhaps not too abrupt) of slavery likely to promote those very mechanical changes which

of the slaves ... ... able the society to do without ...

The crux of the matter, as we shall see, is that in order to use an appeal to our ordinary intuitions as an argument, the opponents of utilitarianism have to produce cases which are not too far removed from the sort of cases with which our intuitions are designed to deal, namely the ordinary run of cases. If the cases they use fall outside this class, then the fact that our common intuitions give a different verdict from utilitarianism has no bearing on the argument; our intuitions could well be wrong about such cases, and be none the worse for that, because they will never have to deal with them in practice.

We may also notice, while we are sifting possible examples, that cases of *individual* slave-owners who are kind to their slaves will not do. The issue is one of whether slavery is an institution protected by law should be preserved; and if it is preserved, though there may be individuals who do not take advantage of it to maltreat their slaves, there will no doubt be many others who do.

Let us imagine, then, that the battle of Waterloo, that 'damned nice thing, the nearest run thing you ever saw in your life',[11] as Wellington called it, went differently from the way it actually did go, in two respects. The first was that the British and Prussians lost the battle; the last attack of the French Guard proved too much for them, the Guard's morale having been restored by Napoleon who in person led the advance instead of handing it over to Ney. But secondly, having exposed himself to fire as Wellington habitually did, but lacking Wellington's amazing good fortune, Napoleon was struck by a cannon ball and killed instantly. This so disorganized the French, who had no other commanders of such ability, that Wellington was able to rally his forces and conduct one of those holding operations at which he was so adept, basing himself on the Channel ports and their intricate surrounding waterways; the result was a cross

between the Lines of Torres Vedras and the trench warfare of the first World War. After a year or two of this, with Napoleon out of the way and the war party discredited in England, liberal (that is, neither revolutionary nor reactionary) regimes came into power in both countries, and the Congress of Vienna reconvened in a very different spirit, with the French represented on equal terms.

We have to consider these events only as they affected two adjacent islands in the Caribbean which I am going to call Juba and Camaica. I need not relate what happened in the rest of the world, because the combined European powers could at that time command absolute supremacy at sea, and the Caribbean could therefore be effectively isolated from world politics by the agreement which they reached to take that area out of the imperial war game. All naval and other forces were withdrawn from it except for a couple of bases on small islands for the suppression of the slave trade, which, in keeping with their liberal principles, the parties agreed to prohibit (those that had not already done so). The islands were declared independent and their white inhabitants, very naturally, all departed in a hurry, leaving the government in the hands of local black leaders, some of whom were of the calibre of Toussaint l'Ouverture and others of whom were very much the reverse.

On Juba, a former Spanish colony, at the end of the colonial period there had been formed, under pressure of military need, a militia composed of slaves under white officers, with conditions of service much preferable to those of the plantation slaves, and forming a kind of elite. The senior serjeant-major of this force found himself, after the white officers fled, in a position of unassailable power, and, being a man of great political intelligence and ability, shaped the new regime in a way that made Juba the envy of its neighbours.

What he did was to retain the institution of slavery but to remedy its evils. The plantations were split up into smaller units, still under overseers, responsible to the state instead of to the former owners. The slaves were given rights to improved conditions of work; the wage they had already received as a concession in colonial times was secured to them and increased; all cruel punishments were prohibited. However, it is still right to call them slaves, because the state retained the power to direct their labour and their place of residence and to enforce these directions by sanctions no more severe than are customary in countries without slavery, such, as fines and imprisonment. The Juban government, influenced, by early communist ideas (though Marx had not yet come on the scene), kept the plantations in its own hands; but private persons were also allowed to own a limited number of slaves under conditions at least as protective to the slaves as on the state-owned plantations.

The island became very prosperous, and the slaves in it enjoyed a life far preferable in every way to that of the free inhabitants of the neighbouring island of Camaica. In Camaica there had been no such focus of power in the early days. The slaves threw off their bonds and each seized what land he could get hold of. Though law and order were restored after a fashion, and democracy of a sort prevailed, the economy was chaotic, and this, coupled with a population explosion, led to widespread starvation and misery. Camaica lacked what Juba had: a government with the will *and the instrument, in the shape of the institution of slavery*, to control the economy and the population, and so make its slave-citizens, as I said, the envy of their neighbours. The flood of people in fishing boats seeking to emigrate from free Camaica and insinuate themselves as slaves into the plantations of Juba became so great that the Juban government had to employ large numbers of coastguards (slaves of course) to stop it.

That, perhaps, will do for our imaginary example. Now for the philosophical argument. It is commonly alleged that utilitarianism could condone or commend slavery. In the situation

described, ~~utility~~,
not increased if the Juban government had abolished slavery and if as a result the economy of Juba had deteriorated to the level of that of Camaica. So, it might be argued, a utilitarian would have had to oppose the abolition. But everyone agrees, it might be held, that slavery is wrong; so the utilitarians are convicted of maintaining a thesis which has consequences repugnant to universally accepted moral convictions.

What could they reply to this attack? There are, basically, two lines they could take. These lines are not incompatible but complementary; indeed, the defence of utilitarianism could be put in the form of a dilemma. Either the defender of utilitarianism is allowed to question the imagined facts of the example, or he is not. First let us suppose that he is not. He might then try, as a first move, saying that in the situation *as portrayed* it would indeed be wrong to abolish slavery. If the argument descends to details, the anti-utilitarians may be permitted to insert any amount of extra details (barring the actual abolition of slavery itself) in order to make sure that its retention really does maximize utility. But then the utilitarian sticks to his guns and maintains that in that case it *would* be wrong to abolish slavery, and that, further, most ordinary people, if they could be got to consider the case on its merits and not allow their judgements to be confused by association with more detestable forms of slavery, would agree with this verdict. The principle of liberty which forbids slavery is a prima facie principle admitting of exceptions, and this imaginary case is one of the exceptions. If the utilitarians could sustain this line of defence, they would win the case; but perhaps not everyone would agree that it is sustainable.

So let us allow the utilitarian another slightly more sophisticated move, still staying, however, perched on the first horn of the dilemma. He might admit that not everyone would agree on the merits of this case, but explain this by pointing to the fantastic and unusual nature of the case, which, he might claim, would be

~~...~~ in real life. If he is not allowed to ~~question~~
that abolition would be wrong; but ordinary people, he might say, cannot see this because the principles of political and social morality which we have all of us *now* absorbed (as contrasted with our eighteenth-century ancestors), and with which we are deeply imbued, prevent us from considering the case on its merits. The principles are framed to cope with the cases of slavery which actually occur (all of which are to a greater or less degree harmful). Though they are the best principles for us to have when confronting the actual world, they give the wrong answer when presented with this fantastic case. But all the same, the world being as it is, we should be morally worse people if we did not have these principles; for then we might be tempted, whether through ignorance or by self-interest, to condone slavery in cases in which, though actually harmful, it could be colourably represented as being beneficial. Suppose, it might be argued, that an example of this sort had been used in anti-abolitionist writings in, say, 1830 or thereabouts. Might it not have persuaded many people that slavery *could* be an admirable thing, and thus have secured their votes against abolition; and would this not have been very harmful? For the miseries caused by the *actual* institution of slavery in the Caribbean and elsewhere were so great that it was desirable from a utilitarian point of view that people should hold and act on moral convictions which condemned slavery as such and without qualification, because this would lead them to vote for its abolition.

If utilitarians take this slightly more sophisticated line, they are left saying at one and the same time that it would have been wrong to abolish slavery in the imagined circumstances, *and* that it is a good thing that nearly everyone, if asked about it, would say that it was right. Is this paradoxical? Not, I think, to anybody who understands the realities of the human situation. What resolves the paradox is that the example is

imaginary and that therefore people are not going to have to pronounce, as a practical issue, on what the laws of Juba are to be. In deciding what principles it is good that people have, it is not necessary or even desirable to take into account such imaginary cases. It does not really matter, from a practical point of view, what judgements people reach about imaginary cases, provided that this does not have an adverse effect upon their judgements about real cases. From a practical point of view, the principles which it is best for them to have are those which will lead them to make the highest proportion of right decisions in actual cases where their decisions make a difference to what happens—weighted, of course, for the importance of the cases, that is, the amount of difference the decisions make to the resulting good or harm.

It is therefore perfectly acceptable that we should at one and the same time feel a strong moral conviction that even the Juban slave system, however beneficial, is wrong, *and* confess, when we reflect on the features of this imagined system, that we cannot see anything specifically wrong about it, but rather a great deal to commend. This is bound to be the experience of anybody who has acquired the sort of moral convictions that one ought to acquire, and at the same time is able to reflect rationally on the features of some unusual imagined situation. I have myself constantly had this experience when confronted with the sort of anti-utilitarian examples which are the stock-in-trade of philosophers like Bernard Williams. One is led to think, on reflection, that if such cases were to occur, one ought to do what is for the best in the circumstances (as even Williams himself appears to contemplate in one of his cases);[12] but one is bound also to find this conclusion repugnant to one's deepest convictions; if it is not, one's convictions are not the best convictions one could have.

Against this, it might be objected that if one's deep moral convictions yield the wrong answer even in imaginary or unusual cases, they are *not*

the best one could have. Could we not succeed, it might be asked, in inculcating into ourselves convictions of a more accommodating sort? Could we not, that is to say, absorb principles which had written into them either exceptions to deal with awkward cases like that in my example, or even provision for writing in exceptions ad hoc when the awkward cases arose? Up to a point this is a sensible suggestion; but beyond that point (a point which will vary with the temperament of the person whose principles they are to be) it becomes psychologically unsound. There are some simple souls, no doubt, who really cannot keep themselves in the straight and narrow way unless they cling fanatically and in the face of what most of us would call reason to extremely simple and narrow principles. And there are others who manage to have very complicated principles with many exceptions written into them (only 'written' is the wrong word, because the principles of such people defy formulation). Most of us come somewhere in between. It is also possible to have fairly simple principles but to attach to them a rubric which allows us to depart from them, either when one conflicts with another in a particular case, or where the case is such an unusual one that we find ourselves doubting whether the principles were designed to deal with it. In these cases we may apply utilitarian reasoning directly; but it is most unwise to do this in more normal cases, for those are precisely the cases (the great majority) which our principles *are* designed to deal with, since they were chosen to give the best results in the general run of cases. In normal cases, therefore, we are more likely to achieve the right decision (even from the utilitarian point of view) by sticking to these principles than by engaging in utilitarian reasoning about the particular case, with all its temptations to special pleading.

I have dealt with these issues at length elsewhere.[13] Here all I need to say is that there is a psychological limit to the complexity and to the flexibility of the moral principles that we can

tions, into our character; and the person who tries to go beyond this limit will end up as (what he will be called) an unprincipled person, and will not in fact do the best he could with his life, even by the test of utility. This may explain why I would always vote for the abolition of slavery, even though I can admit that cases could be *imagined* in which slavery would do more good than harm, and even though I am a utilitarian.

So much, then, for the first horn of the dilemma. Before we come to the second horn, on which the utilitarian is allowed to object to his opponents' argument on the ground that their example would not in the actual world be realized, I wish to make a methodological remark which may help us to find our bearings in this rather complex dispute. Utilitarianism, like any other theory of moral reasoning that gets anywhere near adequacy, consists of two parts, one formal and one substantial. The formal part is no more than a rephrasing of the requirement that moral prescriptions be universalizable: this has the consequence that equal interests of all are to be given equal weight in our reasoning: everybody to count for one and nobody for more than one. One should not expect such a formal requirement to generate, by itself, any substantial conclusions even about the actual world, let alone about all logically possible worlds. But there is also a substantial element in the theory. This is contributed by factual beliefs about what interests people in the real world actually have (which depends on what they actually want or like or dislike, and on what they would want or like or dislike under given conditions); and also about the actual effects on these interests of different actions in the real world. Given the truth of these beliefs, we can reason morally and shall come to certain moral conclusions. But the conclusions are not generated by the formal part of the theory alone.

Utilitarianism therefore, unlike some other theories, is *exposed* to the facts. The utilitarian

cannot reason a priori that whatever the facts about He has to show that it is wrong by showing, through a study of history and other factual observation, that slavery does have the effects (namely the production of misery) which make it wrong. This, though it may at first sight appear a weakness in the doctrine, is in fact its strength. A doctrine, like some kinds of intuitionism, according to which we can think up examples as fantastic as we please and the doctrine will still come up with the same old answers, is really showing that it has lost contact with the actual world with which the intuitions it relies on were designed to cope. Intuitionists think they can face the world armed with nothing but their inbred intuitions; utilitarians know that they have to look at what actually goes on in the world and see if the intuitions are really the best ones to have in that sort of world.

I come now to the second horn of the dilemma, on which the utilitarian is allowed to say, 'Your example won't do: it would never happen that way'. He may admit that Waterloo and the Congress of Vienna could have turned out differently—after all it was a damned nice thing, and high commanders were in those days often killed on the battlefield (it was really a miracle that Wellington was not), and there were liberal movements in both countries. But when we come to the Caribbean, things begin to look shakier. Is it really likely that there would have been such a contrast between the economies of Juba and Camaica? I do not believe that the influence of particular national leaders is ever so powerful, or that such perfectly wise leaders are ever forthcoming. And I do not believe that in the Caribbean or anywhere else a system of nationalized slavery could be made to run so smoothly. I should, rather, expect the system to deteriorate very rapidly. I base these expectations on general beliefs about human nature, and in particular upon the belief that people in the power of other people will be exploited,

whatever the good intentions of those who founded the system.

Alternatively, if there really had been leaders of such amazing statesmanship, could they not have done better by abolishing slavery and substituting a free but disciplined society? In the example, they gave the slaves some legal rights; what was to prevent them giving others, such as the right to change residences and jobs, subject of course to an overall system of land-use and economic planning such as exists in many free countries? Did the retention of *slavery* in particular contribute very much to the prosperity of Juba that could not have been achieved by other means? And likewise, need the government of Camaica have been so incompetent? Could it not without reintroducing slavery, have kept the economy on the rails by such controls as are compatible with a free society? In short, did not the optimum solution lie somewhere *between* the systems adopted in Juba and Camaica, but on the free side of the boundary between slavery and liberty?

These factual speculations, however, are rather more superficial than I can be content with. The facts that it is really important to draw attention to are rather deep facts about human nature which must always, or nearly always, make slavery an intolerable condition.[14] I have mentioned already a fact about slave ownership; that ordinary, even good, human beings will nearly always exploit those over whom they have absolute power. We have only to read the actual history of slavery in all centuries and cultures to see that. There is also the effect on the characters of the exploiters themselves. I had this brought home to me recently when, staying in Jamaica, I happened to pick up a history book[15] written there at the very beginning of the nineteenth century, before abolition, whose writer had added at the end an appendix giving his views on the abolition controversy, which was then at its height. Although obviously a kindly man with liberal leanings, he argues against abolition; and one of his arguments

struck me very forcibly. He argues that although slavery can be a cruel fate, things are much better in Jamaica now: there is actually a law that a slave on a plantation may not be given more than thirty-six lashes by the foreman without running him up in front of the overseer. The contrast between the niceness of the man and what he says here does perhaps more than any philosophical argument to make the point that our moral principles have to be designed for human nature as it is.

The most fundamental point is one about the human nature of the slave which makes ownership by another more intolerable for him than for, say, a horse (not that we should condone cruelty to horses). Men are different from other animals in that they can look a long way ahead, and therefore can become an object of deterrent punishment. Other animals, we may suppose, can only be the object of Skinnerian reinforcement and Pavlovian conditioning. These methods carry with them, no doubt, their own possibilities of cruelty; but they fall short of the peculiar cruelty of human slavery. One can utter to a man threats of punishment in the quite distant future which he can understand. A piece of human property, therefore, unlike a piece of inanimate property or even a brute animal in a man's possession, can be subjected to a sort of terror from which other kinds of property are immune; and, human owners being what they are, many will inevitably take advantage of this fact. That is the reason for the atrocious punishments that have usually be inflicted on slaves; there would have been no point in inflicting them on animals. A slave is the only being that is *both* able to be held responsible in this way, *and* has no escape from, or even redress against, the power that this ability to threaten confers upon his oppressor. If he were a free citizen, he would have rights which would restrain the exercise of the threat; if he were a horse or a piece of furniture, the threat would be valueless to his owner because it would not be understood. By being subjected to the threat of legal and other punishment, but

at the same time against its abuse (since he has no say in what the laws are to be, nor much ability to avail himself of such laws as there are), the slave becomes, or is likely to become if his master is an ordinary human, the most miserable of all creatures.

No doubt there are other facts I could have adduced. But I will end by reiterating the general point I have been trying to illustrate. The wrongness of slavery, like the wrongness of anything else, has to be shown in the world as it actually is. We can do this by first reaching an understanding of the meaning of this and the other moral words, which brings with it certain rules of moral reasoning, as I have tried to show in other places.[16] One of the most important of these rules is a formal requirement reflected in the Golden Rule: the requirement that what we say we ought to do to others we have to be able to say ought to be done to ourselves were we in precisely their situation with their interests. And this leads to a way of moral reasoning (utilitarianism) which treats the equal interests of all as having equal weight. Then we have to apply this reasoning to the world as it actually is, which will mean ascertaining what will actually be the result of adopting certain principles and policies, and how this will actually impinge upon the interests of ourselves and others. Only so can we achieve a morality suited for use in real life; and nobody who goes through this reasoning in real life will adopt principles which permit slavery, because of the miseries which in real life it causes. Utilitarianism can thus show what is wrong with slavery; and so far as I can see it is the kind of moral reasoning best able to show this, as opposed to merely protesting that slavery is wrong.

Notes

This is a revised version of a lecture given in 1978 in the Underwood Memorial Series, Wesleyan University, Middletown, Connecticut.

1 ... Equality', in J. Arthur and W. H. Shaw, Cliffs, NJ: Prentice-Hall, 1978); Opportunity ... What?: Some Remarks on Current Disputes About Equality in Education', Oxford Review of Education 3 (1977).

2 See W. L. Westermann, The Slave Systems of Greek and Roman Antiquity (Philadelphia: American Philosophical Society, 1955), p. 35.

3 Summing up for defence and judgement of Lord Mansfield in Sommersett's case, King's Bench, 12 George III, 1771–72, Howell's State Trials 20, pp. 1 ff.

4 See O. Patterson, The Sociology of Slavery (London: MacGibbon and Kee, 1967), p. 74; A. Sampson, Drum (London: Collins, 1956), chap. 3.

5 See Westermann, Slave Systems, p. 4.

6 Boswell, Life of Johnson, ed. G. B. Hill and L. F. Powell (Oxford: Oxford University Press, 1934), vol. 1, p. 348, 16 March 1759.

7 See Westermann, Slave Systems, p. 81. In pre-revolutionary France one could be sentenced to the galleys.

8 See Sampson, Drum, p. 241.

9 See Westermann, Slave Systems, pp. 2, 5–7, 29.

10 I am grateful to the Editors for pressing this objection. I deal with it only so far as it concerns slavery such as might occur in the world as we know it. Brave New World situations in which people are conditioned from birth to be obedient slaves and given disagreeable or dangerous tasks require separate treatment which is beyond the scope of this paper, though anti-utilitarian arguments based on them meet the same defence, namely the requirement to assess realistically what the consequences of such practices would actually be.

11 For references, see E. Longford, Wellington, The Years of the Sword (London: Weidenfeld and Nicolson, 1969), p. 489.

12 See Williams, 'A Critique of Utilitarianism', in J. J. C. Smart and B. Williams, Utilitarianism: For and Against (Cambridge: Cambridge University Press, 1973), p. 99.

13 See my 'Ethical Theory and Utilitarianism', in H. D. Lewis, ed., Contemporary British Philosophy 4 (London: Allen and Unwin, 1976), and the references given there.

14 For the effects of slavery on slaves and slave-owners, see O. Patterson, Sociology of Slavery; and

S. M. Elkins, *Slavery* (Chicago: University of Chicago Press, 1959).

15 R. C. Dallas, *The History of the Maroons* (London: Longman and Rees, 1803; reprinted by Frank Cass, 1968). I have not been able to obtain the book again to verify this reference.

16 See fn. 13 above, and my *Freedom and Reason* (Oxford: Oxford University Press, 1963), especially chap. 6.

Onora O'Neill

BETWEEN CONSENTING ADULTS

MUCH OF Kant's ethics is distant from the ordinary moral consciousness of our day. But one pair of Kantian notions is still widely current. Few moral criticisms strike deeper than the allegation that somebody has used another; and few ideals gain more praise than that of treating others as persons.

But this consensus is often shallow, since there is little agreement about what it takes to use others in morally problematic ways or to treat them as persons. I shall look here at three common conceptions of these ideals, which make little distinction between the two of them. I shall then outline interpretations of both which seem to me more convincing and richer than the commonly accepted ones. On the interpretations I offer the two ideals are distinct, though related. Merely not to be used is not enough for being treated as a person. Making another into a tool or instrument in my project is one way of failing to treat that other as a person: but only one way.

At a certain point I shall return to the Kantian texts to suggest that the sort of understanding of these ideals that I have outlined is at stake there. But the exegetical ambitions are limited. I shall say nothing about Kant's conception of a person and its metaphysical background. I shall not spell out all the textual considerations that lie behind this reading of the Formula of the End in Itself. I merely state and will not try to show that one of these reasons is that this interpretation can make sense of Kant's puzzling claims about the equivalence of the various formulations of the Categorical Imperative. I shall not explore Kant's thoughts about using oneself and treating oneself as a person. I shall try only to make plausible a certain understanding of what it is to use others and to treat them as persons. I shall therefore use illustrations from areas of life where we often fear that others are used or not treated as persons, and in particular from presumed sexual and economic uses of others. I shall argue that an adequate understanding of what it is to treat others as persons must view them not abstractly as possibly consenting adults, but as particular men and women with limited and determinate capacities to understand or to consent to proposals for action. Unless we take one another's limitations seriously we risk acting in ways which would be enough to treat "ideal" rational beings as persons, but are not enough for treating finitely rational, human beings as persons.

A second aim is to provide a reading of some central claims of Kant's ethics which does not depend on an inflated view of human cognitive and volitional capacities, does not generate implications which are rigorously insensitive to variations of circumstances, and is not tied to a strongly individualistic conception of agency.

The personal touch

One view of treating another as a person rather than using him or her is that it demands a certain

tone and manner. If we show indifference to others, we do not treat them as persons; if our interactions are personal in tone, whether sympathetic or hostile, we treat them as persons. On this view employers who are cold or distant with their employees do not treat them as persons, but involved employers do so. A prostitute who does her or his job with uninvolved perfunctoriness is using the clients, and if their manner is similar they use her or him; but if each had a personal manner, the relationship would be personal and neither would use the other.

If this is what it is to treat others as persons and not to use them, neither notion can be fundamental for moral or political thought. We are familiar with uses of others which are cloaked by an involved and concerned manner. A planned seduction of someone less experienced treats him or her as means even when charmingly done. Employers who take paternalistic interest in employees' lives may yet both use them and fail to treat them as persons. Yet relationships without a personal tone may neither use others nor fail to treat them as persons. An impersonal relationship with a sales assistant may not use him or her in any morally objectionable way, nor fail in treating him or her as other than a person. A personal touch may, we shall see, be an important aspect of treating others as persons. But the notion entirely fails to capture the requirements for avoiding using others and provides a scanty account of treating others as persons.

Actual consent

A deeper and historically more important understanding of the idea of treating others as persons sees their consent to actions which affect them as morally significant. On this view it is morally objectionable to treat others in ways to which they do not consent. To do so treats another as a thing or tool, which cannot, so does not, consent to the ways in which it is used; so

fails to treat others as persons, who can choose, so may withhold consent from actions which affect them.

On this understanding of treating others as persons, rape and seduction are decisively unacceptable. The rapist's victim is coerced rather than consenting; and the seducer's victim lacks insight into what is proposed, so neither can nor does consent to it. But many relationships between prostitutes and their clients are not, on this view, morally objectionable, since they are relationships between consenting adults. Similarly, slavery and forced labor and various forms of economic fraud use others and don't treat them as persons, but a contractual relationship like that between employer and employee does not use others or fail to treat them as persons.

This liberal understanding of avoiding using others and of treating them as persons encounters difficulties of various sorts when we consider what consent is.

An initial difficulty is that it is unclear what constitutes consent. In legal and institutional contexts the criteria are supposedly clearest. Here formal procedures supposedly show who consents to which actions by which others. But here too presumptions of consent are defeasible. Even the clearest formulas of consent, such as signatures and formal oaths, may not indicate consent when there is ignorance, duress, misrepresentation, pressure, or the like.[1] Such circumstances may void contracts and even nullify marriages. Formal procedures for consenting may reveal only spurious consent, so cannot guarantee that everyone is treated as a person in this second sense.

Where formal procedures are lacking, the problem of determining what has been consented to is greater. Various debates about express and tacit consent reflect these difficulties. But the real problem here is not that consent is sometimes given in ways that are implicit rather than explicit, but that it is unclear where consent—even the most explicit consent—stops.

price increased by a specified amount for a particular lot. At other times the boundaries of explicit consent are unclear. Like other propositional attitudes, consent is opaque. Consent may not extend to the logical implications, likely results, or the indispensable presuppositions of that which is explicitly consented to. A classical and instructive example of this range of difficulties occurs in liberal political debates over how far consent to a particular constitution (explicitly or implicitly given) signifies consent to particular governments formed under that constitution, and how far consent to a particular government or party constitutes consent to various components of government or party policy. The notion of loyal opposition is never more than contextually determinate.

A second range of difficulties arises when the consent given does not match the activities it supposedly legitimates. Marxist critics of capitalist economic forms suggest that workers do not consent to their employment despite its outwardly contractual form. For workers, unlike capitalists, cannot (at least in "ideal" capitalism) choose to be without work, on pain of starvation. Hence the outward contractual form masks an underlying coercion. Workers choose between employers (in boom times) and cannot choose or consent to nonemployment. Analogously, women in most societies hitherto have not really consented to their restricted life possibilities. A choice between marriage partners does not show that the married life has been chosen. The outward form of market economies and of unarranged marriages mask how trivial the range of dissent and consent is. In a Marxist view bourgeois freedom is not the real thing, and men and women in bourgeois societies are still often treated as things rather than as persons. Bourgeois ideologies offer a fiction of freedom. They structure a false consciousness which obscures the extent to which human beings are used and not treated as persons.

A third range of difficulties with taking actual ... emerges when abilities to consent ... are impaired. Discussions in medical ethics show how hard it is to ensure that the consent that patients provide to their treatment is genuine. It is not genuine whenever they don't understand what they are supposedly consenting to or lack the autonomy to do anything other than "consent" to what they think the doctor wants or requires. Patients cannot easily understand complex medical procedures; yet if they consent only to a simplified account, they may not consent to the treatment proposed. And their peculiar dependence makes it hard even for those who are informed to make autonomous decisions about proposed treatment. Paradoxically, the case of severely impaired patients may seem easiest to handle. Patients too impaired to give informed consent evidently cannot be treated as persons in this sense. Paternalism may then seem permissible, even required, for those who are, if temporarily, only patients. But with less impaired patients we are not so ready to set aside the ideal of treating others as persons. The difficult case is raised by those who are, as Mill would have put it, "in the maturity of their faculties." Even when we are mature we are seldom ideal rational patients. Here we confront the possibility that consent may be spurious even when based on average understanding and a standard ability to make decisions.

It is not only when we are subjects or employees or patients that we have a partial understanding of ways in which others propose to act toward us and an incomplete ability to make decisions for ourselves. Others' apparent consent, even their apparently informed consent, may standardly be insufficient to show that we treat them as persons when we interact with them. The problems of the defeasibility and indeterminacy of consent, of ideological distortions and self-deception, and of impaired capacities to consent, are all forms of one

underlying problem. The deeper problem in this area is simply a corollary of the opacity of intentionality. When we consent to another's proposals we consent, even when "fully" informed, only to some specific formulation of what the other has it in mind to do. We may remain ignorant of further, perhaps equally pertinent, accounts of what is proposed, including some to which we would not consent. ("I didn't know I was letting myself in for that!" we may protest.) Even when further descriptions are inferable from the one consented to, the inference may not be made; and often we cannot infer which determinate action will enact some proposal. If we want to give an account of genuine, morally significant, consent, we need to explain which aspects of actions must be consented to if nobody is to be used or treated as less than a person. An account of genuine consent must then show how the morally significant aspects of plans, proposals, and intentions are picked out as candidates for consent.

Hypothetical consent

Before considering how this might be done, I shall look at an account of treating others as persons which doesn't require us to know what they consent to. This strategy explains treating others as persons not in terms of the consent actually given, but in terms of the hypothetical consent fully rational beings would give to the same proposal. The strategy has obvious merits.

One merit is that it suggests that at least sometimes actual consent is not morally decisive, even if well informed. Hence it allows for our strong intuitions that even a consensus may be iniquitous or irrelevant (perhaps it reflects false consciousness), and that not everything done between consenting adults treats the other as a person. This approach also deals readily with cases of impaired capacities to consent. Since it appeals to capacities that are standardly lacking, there is, in a way, no difference in its approach to those in "the maturity of their faculties" and

to those more gravely impaired. By the standards of full rationality we are all impaired. But we can always ask whether the fully rational would consent.

But these merits are the acceptable face of a serious deficiency in this strategy. If treating others as persons requires only hypothetical rational consent, we may, as Berlin long ago pointed out, find ourselves overriding the actual dissent of others, coercing them in the name of higher and more rational selves who would consent to what is proposed. It seems implausible that treating others as persons should even sometimes be a matter of overriding what others as we know them actually choose.

Other difficulties with this strategy arise from the varied conceptions of rationality invoked. Many conceptions of rationality presuppose a given set of desires. If these are the actual desires of the consenter, appeal to hypothetical consent will not overcome the worry that a consensus may be iniquitous or reflect local ideology. Yet if there is no appeal to the consenter's actual desires, but only to some hypothetical set of rationally structured desires, then the theory may be too weak to determine what would rationally be consented to. Given that there are many rationally structured sets of hypothetical desires, rational structure alone cannot determine what would rationally be consented to. But there are difficulties in spelling out the content and grounds of a stronger (e.g., quasi-Platonic) account of rational desires that might determine hypothetical consent.

The appeal of hypothetical consent criteria of treating others as persons is to overcome the limitations of actual consent criteria by endowing hypothetical agents with cognitive capacities that extend their understanding of what is proposed. But it is just not clear how far the insight of even the ideally rational reaches. Do they, for example, have a more determinate insight into proposals addressed to them than do those who make the proposals? What do they make of internally incoherent proposals? Which

aspects

the consent or dissent of the fully rational. A convincing account of hypothetical rational consent has to explain which aspects of others' actions must be hypothetically consented to if those actions are not to use others or fail to treat them as persons. This approach cannot exempt us from the need to discover the morally significant aspects of plans, proposals, and intentions that are candidates for consent.

Significant and spurious consent

If the notion of consent is to help explicate what it is to treat others as persons, we need an account of genuine, morally significant consent, and to distinguish this from spurious or morally trivial consent. Three preliminary points seem to me significant.

First, morally significant consent cannot be consent to all aspects of another's proposals which may affect me. Any complicated action will be done under many descriptions; but most of these will be without moral significance. Morally significant consent will, I suggest, be consent to the deeper or more fundamental aspects of another's proposals. If I consent to be the subject for a medical experiment which drags on longer than expected, I may have been inconvenienced, but not gravely misled. But my consent will have been spurious, and I will not have been treated as a person, but indeed used, if I consented to a seriously misleading account of the experiment and its risks.

Second, if another's consent is to be morally significant, it must indeed be his or her consent. To treat others as persons we must allow them *the possibility either to consent to or to dissent from what is proposed.* The initiator of action can ensure this; but the consenting cannot be up to him or her. The morally significant aspect of treating others as persons may lie in making their consent or dissent *possible*, rather than in what they actually consent to or would hypothetically consent to if fully rational. A requirement that we ensure that

this possibility cuts deep whenever

There isn't much difficulty in ensuring that those who will in any case be no more than spectators have a genuine possibility of dissent from their minimal part in a project. They need only be allowed to absent themselves or to express disagreement, distaste, or the like. But those closely involved in or affected by a proposal have no genuine possibility of dissent unless they can avert or modify the action by withholding consent and collaboration. If those closely affected have the possibility of dissent, they will be able to require an initiator of action either to modify the action, or to desist or to override the dissent. But an initiator who presses on in the face of actively expressed dissent undercuts any genuine possibility of refusing the proposal and rather chooses to enforce it on others. Any "consent" the proposal then receives will be spurious, and will not show that others have not been used, let alone that they have been treated as persons.

Third, we need to understand what makes genuine consent to the more fundamental aspects of action possible. But there is no guarantee that any one set of requirements makes genuine consent possible in all circumstances. There may be some necessary conditions, whose absence always makes genuine consent or dissent impossible, and other conditions which are needed to make consent possible only in some circumstances. It is plausible to think that when we act in ways that would *always* preclude genuine consent or dissent, we will have used others. For example, if we coerce or deceive others, their dissent, and so their genuine consent, is in principle ruled out. Here we do indeed use others, treating them as mere props or tools in our own projects. Even the most autonomous cannot genuinely consent to proposals about which they are deceived or with which they are compelled to comply. Even if a proposal would have been welcomed, and coercion or deception is otiose, its enforcement or surreptitious imposition precludes consent.

In other cases a proposal for action may not in principle preclude consent and dissent, but the particular others affected may be unable to dissent from it, or genuinely to consent to it. A full understanding of treating others as persons should, I suggest, take some account of the particularities of persons. It must allow that we take seriously the possibility of dissent and consent for others who, far from being abstractly autonomous beings, have their particular cognitive limitations and partial autonomy, which affect their abilities to dissent and to consent variously in varying circumstances. We are concerned not only to be treated as a person—any person—but to some extent as the particular persons we are. We are not merely possibly consenting adults, but particular friends, colleagues, clients, rivals, relations, lovers, neighbors; we have each of us a particular history, character, set of abilities and weaknesses, interests and desires. Even when others do not deceive or coerce us, or treat us in any way as tools, we may yet feel that they do not treat us as persons either. There is some point to the thought that being treated as a person needs a personal touch. Not being used may be enough for being treated as a person when our particular identity and specific character are irrelevant, for example in commercial or other transactions with anonymous members of the public. (Even here we may think standards of courtesy must be met.) Still, in public contexts not being used may be the major part of being treated as a person: for if consent and dissent are in principle possible, we can refuse the opportunities, offers, or activities that do not suit us. But where we have specific relations with particular others, being treated as a person may require far more. It may demand that we treat others not impersonally, but to some extent as the persons they are.

Possible consent: a Kantian reading

A shift of focus to possible consent has deep implications. When we see morally required actions as those to which others either actually or hypothetically consent, we implicitly view morality as closely connected to desires. Another's actual consent will usually reflect his or her wants or preferences; and standard modern views of hypothetical consent construe it in terms of actual preferences on which a rational ordering is hypothetically imposed. Yet it seems implausible that treating others as persons can be of *prime* moral importance if it amounts only to avoiding what they don't want or wouldn't rationally want. In a moral theory in which wants are basic, the notion of treating others as persons carries no independent weight. In Kantian terms we might say that the notion of a person doesn't matter in a heteronomous moral theory. If wants or rationalized preferences are morally fundamental, consent is of derivative concern. It is only within moral theories for beings who can sometimes act independently of desires—who are to that extent autonomous—that the notion of consent carries independent weight. In such theories it is important that consent be possible for others, but of less concern whether what they consent to is what they want.

An account of using others and treating them as persons which starts from the notions of possible consent and dissent reveals the Kantian origins of these notions. The Kantian texts also provide suggestions for explicating, elaborating, and differentiating the two notions.[2]

Kant's theory of action sees each act as done on a *maxim*, an underlying principle (often, but not necessarily, an agent's fundamental intention) used to guide and orchestrate more specific, ancillary aspects of action.[3] The Formula of the End in Itself enjoins action on maxims that

treat humanity whether in your own person or in the person of any other never simply as a means, but always at the same time as an end (*Groundwork*, p. 429).

others as persons: the maxim must not use _____ (negatively) as mere means, but must also (positively) treat them as ends in themsleves (cf. ibid., p. 430).

Kant describes the first sort of failure as action on maxims to which no other could possibly consent, and the second as pursuit of ends another cannot share. He writes of such a case:

> The man whom I seek to use for my purposes by such a (false) promise cannot possibly agree with my way of behaving to him, and so cannot himself share the end of action (ibid., p. 429).

The failure is dual: the victim of deceit *cannot agree* to the initiator's maxim, so is used, and *a fortiori cannot share* the initiator's end, so is not treated as a person. Similarly with a maxim of coercion: victims cannot agree with a coercer's fundamental principle or maxim (which denies them the choice between consent and dissent), and further cannot share a coercer's ends. (Victims may *want* the same ends as their coercers; but that is not the same as sharing those ends, for one who is coerced, even if pointlessly, is not pursuing, nor therefore sharing, ends at all.) Those who are either deceived or coerced are then *both* used *and* not treated as persons.

It does not follow from this that nothing done in acting on a maxim of deception or coercion can be agreed to or shared by those deceived or coerced. On the contrary, deception standardly works by revealing subsidiary intentions or aspects of action, which misleadingly point to some underlying maxim to which consent can be given. Deception only works when the underlying intention or proposal is kept obscure. The deceiver's actual maxim therefore cannot be consented to. A maxim of coercion does not have to be obscure—it may be brutally plain—but clearly denies victims the choice between consent and dissent.

While the boundaries of coercive action are _____ involving physical force, _____ _____ threats and institutionalized forms of domination such as slavery. But here too victims can and do consent to many of the coercer's subsidiary intentions. It is always hard to know when "going along with" what is coercively proposed becomes collaboration with the coercer. (Rape trials are instructive.[4]) And it is hard to tell just when an ostensibly deceived party becomes a conniving party. But while such complexities make judgment of actual cases hard, they don't alter the point that a maxim of deception or coercion treats another as mere means and not as a person, even if the victim becomes so involved in the initiator's action that we judge that he or she has become a collaborator or accessory.

The second part of Kant's account of treating others as persons urges us not merely not to use them as means, but to treat them as "ends in themselves." By this he doesn't mean that others should be our goals or purposes. Only what we aim for, including what we desire, can be a goal or purpose. This sort of subjective end depends on us for its existence. Others who exist independently of our action can't be subjective ends, but only ends in themselves. Ends in themselves may provide us with grounds of action not by being the *aim* or *effect* of action, but by constituting limits to our actions (*Groundwork*, p. 428).[5] Others may limit my action by being autonomous beings whose maxims guide their projects and activities to their varied ends. To respect a limit of this sort cannot be thought of on a spatial analogy of avoiding certain areas, for the varying activities of others take place in the world that we share, and not in discrete spatial capsules (as libertarians might prefer). Not to treat others as mere means introduces minimal, but indispensable, requirements for coordinating action in a world shared by autonomous beings, namely that nobody act in ways others cannot possibly consent to, so in

principle precluding their autonomous action. To treat others as ends may also require action when dissent is in principle possible, but those who are actually involved have limited capacities to dissent.

The negative requirement of not using others can be stated in some (no doubt incomplete) abstraction from the particular features of other rational beings ("the problem of justice can be solved even for a 'nation of devils' " [Kant's Political Writings, p. 112]), but we can give only an indeterminate account of the "positive" requirements for treating others as ends in themselves. Whenever treating others as persons goes beyond not using them, we must take into account "humanity in their person," i.e., their *particular* capacities for rational and autonomous action.[6] This can be done with vacuous ease for abstractly rational beings. But human beings, while they are creatures of reason rather than instinct, are yet only limitedly rational beings, of whose capacities for autonomous action we can give no determinate account in the abstract. Hence the only abstract account we can give of the "positive" maxims on which we must act in treating other men and women as persons are very general policies. But these "wide" duties to share others' ends (and develop talents) can have determinate implications in particular contexts.

The "positive" aspects of treating others as ends in themselves require action on maxims of sharing others' ends. It is not enough when we deal with other human beings (as opposed to abstract rational beings) to act on maxims with which they can possibly agree, whatever their ends. It is also necessary to adopt maxims which "endeavour to further the ends of others" (Groundwork, p. 430). To treat human beings as persons, rather than as "ideal" rational beings, we must not only not use them, but must take their particular capacities for autonomy and rationality into account. Since other humans have varied ends, are precariously autonomous and rational, and far from self-sufficient in other ways, sharing even some of their ends may make

varied demands. Kant claims that these demands can be grouped under the headings of respect and love (or beneficence). He repeatedly uses physical metaphors to express the ways in which these two sorts of demands differ:

> The principle of *mutual love* admonishes men constantly to *come nearer* to each other; that of the *respect* which they owe each other to keep themselves at a *distance* from one another (The Doctrine of Virtue, p. 447).

Policies of respect must recognize that others' maxims and projects are *their* maxims and projects. They must avoid merely taking over or achieving the aims of these maxims and projects, and allow others the "space" in which to pursue them for themselves. Respect for others requires, Kant thinks, that we avoid contempt, mockery, disdain, detraction, and the like and that we show others recognition (ibid., pp. 461–68). Policies of practical love or beneficence require us to recognize the needs particular others have for assistance in acting on their maxims and achieving their ends. Love requires us to adopt maxims of "active practical benevolence (beneficence) which consists in making another's happiness my own" (ibid., p. 451). To do this is to make the other's ends, whose achievement would constitute his or her happiness, in part my own. Such beneficence includes assistance to others, generosity, active sympathy, and conciliatoriness and the avoidance of envy and malicious joy (ibid., pp. 451–60).

However, the Kantian conception of beneficence is from the start antipaternalistic. The duty to seek others' happiness is always a duty to promote and share others' ends *without* taking them over, rather than a duty to provide determinate goods and services or to meet others' needs, or to see that their ends are achieved. Beneficence of this sort presupposes others who are at least partly autonomous and have their own ends. The tension between beneficence and treating others as persons, which is central to

Kant's account.

> I cannot do good to anyone according to my conception of happiness (except to young children and the insane) but only according to that of the one I intend to benefit (ibid., p. 453).

What remains is, as Kant indicates, the unavoidable tension between love and respect. We experience it every time we try to work out how to share others' ends without taking them over.[7] It is a tension that has no general solution, but can be resolved in particular contexts. Kant's wide duties specify no rules of action for all rational beings, for the ways in which sharing others' ends can perhaps be exemplified would differ wholly for other sorts of rational beings (imagine beings who are psychologically impervious to one another, or less dependent on the physical world than we are), and will in any case differ greatly for human beings with varied ends.

The overall picture which this reading of the Formula of the End in Itself generates is that a morally worthy life must be based on maxims of justice (including noncoercion and nondeceit), of respect, and of love. Such a life neither uses others (by acting on maxims which preempt consent or dissent), nor fails to share others' ends (by acting on maxims which either disregard or take over those ends or lend them no support). In each case it is our *fundamental* proposals, principles, or basic intentions that must meet these conditions. We neither do nor can make it possible for others, even for others closely affected, to consent to or dissent from *every* aspect (or even every intentional aspect) of what we propose; nor can we lead lives in which we at all times help all others achieve all their ends. Justice and respect vary with circumstances, and beneficence is in addition unavoidably selective. Nevertheless there are occasions when action of a specific sort is required: there

are contexts and relationships to others in which the underlying maxim of principle lacking in respect or nonbeneficent. Although love and beneficence are unavoidably selective, this does not mean that when we act on these maxims we can neglect all the central projects of lives with which ours are closely involved.

Morally worthy maxims and consenting adults

If this reading of the Formula of the End in Itself is to be more than Kantian exegesis, it should help us to think about using others and failing to treat them as persons. The classical examples of presumed sexual and economic use of others, in particular, should be illuminated. But there is one further difficulty in pursuing this thought.

Kant's analysis of treating others as persons leads him, in the first instance, to claims about maxims of morally worthy action. His fundamental moral categories are those of moral worth and lack of moral worth rather than those of right and wrong. Right and wrong, the categories of "legality," are, in his eyes, derivative from those of morality.[8] Right action conforms in outward respects, but perhaps only in outward respects, with what is morally worthy. Specifically obligatory action not merely conforms outwardly to what moral worth requires, but is mandated (in those circumstances) by some maxim of moral worth.

Yet we have seen that no determinate outward performance either conforms to or is prescribed by maxims of sharing others' ends. "Wide" duties do not have determinate outward manifestations. Even "strict" duties may be performed in outwardly varying ways. For any underlying principle or maxim will have to be enacted or embodied in different ancillary aspects of action in differing situations. How then can we get from a Kantian account of not using others and sharing their ends—of morally worthy action—to a view of what is right or wrong to do? How,

in particular, can a Kantian account help us to think about particular sexual or economic problems? Isn't it likely that there is no timeless sexual or economic morality for abstractly autonomous beings? (And no sex and no economics.)

Yet we may have got a great deal of what we are likely to need. For we need to understand what would be right or wrong in actual, determinate situations. Kantian maxims do not entail rules or prescriptions for all possible contexts. Since a maxim is the *maxima propositio* or major premise of a piece of practical reasoning, it is not there that we should look for details about determinate situations. But when a maxim is supplemented by an account of a particular situation—the minor premise of practical reasonings[9]—we may discover which sorts of outward performance are required, compatible, or proscribed in that situation. We may, for example, find that in *these* circumstances there is no way in which *that* sort of action could be compatible with justice; or on the other hand, that in *this* situation we must, if fundamentally committed to a maxim of love or respect, include something of *that* sort. The conclusions of such reasoning will not be unrestricted; they will hold good not for rational beings as such, nor even for the human condition, but for quite specific human conditions. But when we act this is just what we need to know. We do not need to know what it would be to refrain from detraction or to be generous in all possible worlds, but only how to discern what would be respectful or generous in particular situations. Casuistry is indispensable in all movements from major premise to decision, and all claims about what is obligatory, permissible, and forbidden hold only for determinate contexts. Even when we have reasons for thinking that the maxim of some action was itself not morally worthy, judgments of what is obligatory (or merely permissible or forbidden) are made by reference to the outward aspects of action that would have been required (or compatible or

ruled out) by acting on a morally worthy maxim in that situation.

Treating others as persons in sexual relationships

If this account of using others and treating them as persons is plausible, it should throw light on areas of life where such failures are thought common. One such area is sexual relationships and encounters. We might also hope to gain some understanding of *why* sexual relationships are thought peculiarly vulnerable to these sorts of failure.

Some sexual coercion is relatively straightforward. It isn't hard to see why the victim of rape or of lesser sexual assault is used. However, rape differs from other forms of coercion in that, because of the implicit nature of much sexual communication and social traditions which encourage forms of sexual duplicity, it is unusually hard to be sure when there has been coercion. Also coercion of less straightforward sorts may occur in some sexual relationships and transactions, including in relationships between prostitutes and their clients. Here the outward transaction may be an agreement between consenting adults. But when we remember the institutional context of much (at least contemporary, western) prostitution, including the practices of pimping, brothel keeping, and various forms of social ostracism and consequent dependence on a harsh subculture, we may come to think that not all transactions between prostitutes and clients are uncoerced: but it may not be the client who coerces.

Deception is a pervasive possibility in sexual encounters and relationships. Not only are there well-known deceptions, such as seduction and breach of promise, but varied further possibilities. Many of these reflect the peculiarly implicit nature of sexual communication. Commercial and various distanced sexual encounters standardly use the very means of expression which deeper and longer lasting attachments use. But

are not used to convey what they standardly convey, miscommunication is peculiarly likely. Endearments standardly express not just momentary enthusiasm but affection; the contact of eyes, lips, skin conveys some openness, acceptance, and trust (often enough much more); embrace conveys a commitment which goes beyond a momentary clinging. These are potent gestures of human emotional life. If insufficient trust and commitment are present to warrant such expression, then those who use these endearments and gestures risk giving false messages about feelings, desires, and even commitments. But perhaps, we may think, at least in sexual relationships which are commercial or very casual or largely formal, it is well understood by all concerned that these expressions have been decontextualized and no longer express the underlying intentions or attitudes or principles that they might express in a more wholehearted relationship. But if such expressions are fully decontextualized, what part are they playing in an entirely casual or commercial or formalized encounter? If the expressions are taken at face value, yet what they would standardly express is lacking, each is likely to deceive the other. Relationship of prostitution, casual sexual encounters, and the sexual aspect of faded marriages are not invariably deceptive. Such sexual relations may be either too crudely mechanical to use or misuse expressions of intimacy, or sufficiently informed by trust and concern for the language of intimacy to be appropriate. But relationships and encounters which standardly combine superficial expression of commitment with its underlying absence are peculiarly vulnerable to deception. Where too much is unexpressed, or misleadingly expressed, each risks duping the other and using him or her as means.

Avoiding deceit and coercion are only the core of treating others as persons in sexual relationships. In avoiding these we avoid clear and obvious ways of using as (mere) means. But to treat another as a person in an intimate, and requires far more. These further requirements reflect the intimacy rather than the specifically sexual character of a relationship. However, if sexual relationships cannot easily be merely relationships between consenting adults, further requirements for treating another as a person are likely to arise in any sexual relationship. Intimate bodies cannot easily have separate lives.

Intimacy, sexual or not, alters relationships in two ways that are relevant here. First, those who are intimate acquire deep and detailed (but incomplete) knowledge of one another's life, character, and desires. Secondly, each forms some desires which incorporate or refer to the other's desires, and consequently finds his or her happiness in some ways contingent upon the fulfillment of the other's desires.[10] Intimacy is not a merely cognitive relationship, but one where special possibilities for respecting and sharing (alternatively for disrespecting and frustrating) another's ends and desires develop. It is in intimate relationships that we are most able to treat others as persons—and most able to fail to do so.

Intimacy makes failures of respect and of love more possible. Lack of respect in intimate relationships may, for example, take both manipulative and paternalistic forms. The manipulator trades on the fact that the other is not just a possibly consenting adult, but one whose particular desires are known and may depend in part on the manipulator's desires. One who succumbs to so-called "moral" blackmail could have refused without suffering coercion and was not deceived, but was confronted with the dilemma of sacrificing something central to his or her life—perhaps career or integrity or relationships with others, or perhaps mainly the desire to accommodate the manipulator's desires—unless willing to comply. In intimate relationships it is all too easy to make the other an offer he or she cannot refuse; when we are close to others we can undercut their pursuit of ends without

coercion or deceit. Modes of bargaining and negotiating with others which do not make dissent impossible for consenting adults in the abstract, and might be acceptable in public contexts, may yet undercut others' pursuit of their ends in intimate relationships. Here it is peculiarly demanding to leave the other "space" for his or her pursuit of ends. To do so, and so maintain respect for those with whom we are intimate, requires us to take account not only of the particular interlock of desires, dependencies, and vulnerabilities that have arisen in a given relationship, but also that we heed any wider social context whose modes of discourse and received opinions may systematically undermine or belittle the other's ends and capacities to pursue them. Respect for others—the most basic aspect of sharing their ends—requires the greatest tact and insight when we are most aware of ways in which others' capacities to pursue ends autonomously are vulnerable.

Contexts which make manipulation hard to avoid also offer opportunities for paternalistic failures of respect. Unlike the manipulator, the paternalist does not deploy knowledge of the other and the other's ends to reduce his or her "space" for pursuit of those ends. The paternalist rather begins from a failure to acknowledge either *what* the other's ends are, or that they are the *other's* ends. This failure of respect entails failures to share those ends, for to the paternalist they are either invisible or else not the other's ends but rather the ends to be sought for the other. The paternalist tries to express beneficence or love by imposing a conception of others' ends or interests. Lack of respect is then compounded by lack of love. Those who try to remake or control the lives of others with whom they are intimate do not merely fail in respect, however sincerely they may claim to seek the other's good. Paternalism towards those who have their own ends is not a form of love. However, since it is only fundamental principles of actions (whether plans, proposals, policies, or intentions) that must meet these standards,

superficial departure from them when acting on morally acceptable fundamental principles may be acceptable, or even required. The jokes and surprises in which friendship may be expressed do not count as deceptions; but if they were incident to action on other maxims might constitute fraud or serious disrespect or unacceptable paternalism.[11]

Even in intimate relationships not all failures of love are consequent upon failures of respect. It is not only in manipulative and paternalistic action, where others' ends are respectively used and overlooked, that we may fail to share the ends of those with whom we are intimate. Failures of love also occur when the other's ends are indeed respected, and he or she is left the "space" in which to pursue them, yet no positive encouragement, assistance, or support for their pursuit is given. Vulnerable, finite beings do not treat one another as ends *merely* by leaving each other an appropriate "space." Here again detailed knowledge of others and their desires, strengths, and weaknesses offers wider possibilities. The support, concern, and generosity we need from particular others if our pursuit of ends is to be not merely unprevented but sufficiently shared to be a genuine possibility are quite specific. If we are to treat others with whom we are intimate with love as well as respect, we must both see and (to some extent) support their ends.

Avoiding using others and treating them as persons both demand a lot in intimate relationships. Only the avoidance of coercion demands no more than usual here, perhaps because coercion tends to destroy intimacy. Deception remains a possibility in any relationship, and more so where much is conveyed elliptically or by gesture. In brief sexual encounters as well as in commercial and formalized sexual relations the discrepancy of expression and underlying attitude offers many footholds for deception; even in sustained intimate relationships underlying attitudes and outlook can become, as it were, decoupled from the expression and

the language of intimacy is used. Intimate relationships also provide appropriate settings for manipulative and paternalistic failures of respect and consequent and other failures of love. But the other side of these gloomy thoughts is that intimacy also offers the best chances for treating others as the persons they are.

Treating others as persons in work and employment

It is odd that working life is also often thought to involve uses of others and failures to treat them as persons. Here we do not find the features that open sexual and intimate relationships to these failures. In modern employment relations, communication is usually explicit; employers and employees must have some coinciding desires, but need and often have no desires whose content is determined by the other's desires, and may be quite ignorant of one another's specific desires and capacities. Yet there are reasons why this area of life too makes it hard to ensure that nobody is either used or treated as less than a person.

To begin with there are straightforward ways in which we can be used by those for whom we work. Coercion is as vivid a possibility here as in sexual contexts. Sporadic forms include press-ganging and underpayment of wages; institutionalized forms evidently include slavery and forced labor. Straightforward deception is also well entrenched in many forms of employment, and includes fraud and trickery of enormous variety. Hence some ways of being used in working contexts are obvious enough. But these are the working relationships that developed economic forms, including specifically capitalism, preclude. Yet it is widely claimed that capitalist and (perhaps) other modern economic forms not merely do not treat workers as persons, but use them.

This claim can be sustained only if there are unstraightforward ways in which workers are used, in which no maxims of coercion or deception are invoked. When individuals act on maxims of coercion we have straightforward failures, with which the legal system of capitalist or other developed economic forms can deal, and which the Kantian perspective, even in its standard interpretations, is well designed to detect. But unobvious forms of coercion or deception are harder to grasp.

A principal source of this problem is that the Kantian approach, like the legal frameworks with which it tallies, is standardly interpreted as individualistic. The interpretation of maxims adopted here is, however, too broad to entail individualism; it does not require that maxims be consciously entertained, nor therefore see only the fundamental intentions of individuals as maxims. On this account the guiding principle of any endeavor or practice or institution is its maxim. In many capitalist economic relations, including employment, all individual intentions may be morally acceptable. The capitalist employer may have fundamental conscious intentions to which his employees can indeed consent or dissent, so appears on this score not to treat them in any morally objectionable way. What could be more paradigmatic of an offer that can be refused than an offer of employment that is, as they say in wage negotiations, "on the table"? If we argue that such offers are either coercive or deceptive, we must take a broader view of maxims, and judge not the principles which particular would-be employers have in mind, but the principles which guide the institution of employment in a capitalist system. The underlying principle of capitalist employment, whatever that may be, may perhaps use some as means or to fail to treat them as persons, even where individuals' intentions fail in neither way.

The extension of ethical reasoning beyond individual concerns must then use the results of social inquiry. If, for example, we take an idealized Marxist account of capitalist employment, the Kantian approach would generate clear

ethical results. On that account capitalist employers, whatever their individual intentions, base their action on a maxim of extracting surplus value (if they did not, employing others would be pointless). Since capitalism aims at profit, it must pay workers less than the value they produce. But this essential feature of capitalism is obscured from workers, who accept deceptive accounts of the terms of their employment to which consent and dissent are possible. But if the principle to which consent is possible (and actually given) is not the underlying maxim of capitalist employment, then this consent cannot show that there has been no deception at a fundamental level. What it can, however, show is that if there has been such deception, then it is, as in the case of the institutionalized coercion of organized prostitution, a deception without an individual deceiver.

Whether the underlying principle of capitalist employment in fact has the structure Marxists claim and so makes consent impossible is a further question. Might there not be a nondeceptive form of capitalism, in which the possibility of dissent is ensured by framing offers of employment in terms of the principles which really underlie capitalist employment relations? On this hypothesis workers with fully raised consciousness would have a genuine possibility to dissent from or consent to a maxim of employment which was not ideologically masked, and so would not be used. They would understand that profits would be made off their labor, but could still accept the terms offered. If deceptive forms were all that is wrong with a capitalist maxim of employment, it might be remediable. But on a Marxist analysis coercion lurks behind the deception. When the underlying form of the capitalist maxim of employment is disclosed we supposedly discover that the deception served a purpose (or many purposes), and in particular that it makes an activity that workers (under "ideal" capitalism) cannot choose to avoid except on pain of the coercion of starvation, appear to them as one

which they could choose or refuse. Employees will then invariably be used, since they have the possibility of dissenting or consenting only to a principle that isn't really the underlying principle of their employment at all. Either they will be both deceived and coerced, if they do not see through this offer, or if they see through it, they will not be deceived, but only coerced. In either case they will be used. The underlying maxim of "ideal" capitalist employment requires workers to choose between unemployment without welfare benefit and a wage "bargain" which is backed by this threat.

This argument, of course, depends on accepting a Marxist account of the fundamental maxim of capitalist employment and rejecting ideologically opposed accounts, such as those which view all maxims as specific to individual agents and deny that the market itself can be thought of as grounded in maxims. The argument neither supposes nor shows that the claims made about employment relations in "ideal" capitalism apply accurately to employment relations in actual capitalist economies, where, for example, welfare payments may mitigate or remove the coercive character of threatened unemployment. For present purposes the interest of the sketch is to show *one* way in which workers may be used in the Kantian sense even under systems of employment that ostensibly enshrine the principle of free, hence of possible, consent, and more generally how Kantian ethical reasoning might be extended beyond the private sphere.

In employment, as in other activities, being used is only one way of being treated as less than a person. A great many complaints that workers are not being treated as persons can be traced not to the ways in which they may be straightforwardly or unstraightforwardly used, but to the degree to which contemporary employment practices make a point of treating workers uniformly, and so not as the particular persons that they are.[12] In this matter modern employment practices are wholly different from

...ism (not only capitalist) economies are treated... and uniform ways which take little account of differences in ends and capacities to seek them. Where work is "rationalized" and there is a "rate for the job," and hours and qualifications are standardized, there are few ways in which employees' particular ends and abilities to pursue them are taken into account on the job. If doing a job well amounts to doing it like the robot who may replace you, the maxim of such organization of work cannot go far to treat employees as the particular persons they are. In such employment it is not misuse of information about others' ends or capacities for autonomy, nor intentional failure to share ends, but rather systematic disregard of all particular characteristics that lies behind failure to respect or to share ends. Rationalized work practices treat all workers as persons (qualms about exploitation of employees apart), but take little account of their specific characteristics. This may be partly remedied in the practices of some workplaces, or eased by management or work practices which allow more worker involvement or self-management. But if such arrangements are only a matter of introducing "a personal touch," they impose outward forms of respect and beneficence without underlying changes that would treat workers as the particular persons they are, and may only introduce paternalistic and manipulative practices into working life.

A larger question in this area is whether working life should be like this. Shouldn't working life be impersonal? Isn't this our guarantee against nepotism, favoritism, and other types of personal bias and patronage? Is not justice the sole relevant standard in employment relations? The career open to talents has to be based on maxims of impersonal fairness. But the career open to talents is also the career closed to lack of talent and conducted without concern for the fact that we are not abstractly consenting adults. Perhaps the underlying issue is whether

and when the lives of those who work with or for... justice to be the only consideration... respect, solidarity, and assistance that go beyond what the job requires may not be dispensable whenever work is collaborative. Our working relations too are relations with determinate others and not with abstractly rational economic men and women.

Conclusions

The popular view that we can readily be used or treated as less than persons both in intimate relationships and at work can be sustained in a Kantian framework. In each context we may be faced with proposals to which we *cannot* (whether because deceived or because coerced) give our consent. But the characteristic ways in which we may be treated as less than persons even when not used are quite different in the two contexts. In intimate relationships everything is there which would make it possible to treat the other as the particular person he or she is, by respecting and sharing his or her pursuit of ends. Here if we fail to respect or to share the other's ends the failure is imputable to us. But contemporary employment relations are set up on principles that are impersonal. Employer and employee have only "relevant" information about one another, and need only slightly coinciding ends. Hence when employees are not treated as the particular persons they are, the failure does not standardly rest with a particular employer, who may correctly think that he or she has done all that an employer should. The demand that employees be treated as ends in themselves and shown respect and beneficence is a political demand for new economic structures, whose "maxim of employment" acknowledges our desire, and perhaps need, to be treated more as the persons we are, and less impersonally. It is a demand which we must take seriously if we doubt that we are, even in the maturity of our faculties, merely consenting adults.

Notes

Earlier versions of this article were helped by a number of discussions. I am particularly grateful to Thomas Hill, Sally Ruddick, Arnold Zweig, R. R. Rockingham Gill, Raaman Gillon, Adam Morton, Patricia Greenspan, Heinz Lubasz, David Krell, Diana Bell, Lenn Goodman, and William Ruddick.

1 Excessive reliance on formal indicators of "consent" suggests doubt whether the consent is genuine. Consider the widespread European use of "treaties" to "legitimize" acquisition of land or sovereignty by seeking the signatures of barely literate native peoples with no understanding of European moral and legal traditions. Cf. D. F. McKenzie's discussion of the treaty of Waitangi in "The Sociology of a Text: Orality, and Print Literacy in Early New Zealand," *The Library*, ser. VI, vol. 6, no. 4 (1984): 333–65.

2 References to Kantian texts will be parenthetical, using the following editions: *Groundwork*, trans. H. J. Paton, as *The Moral Law* (London: Hutchinson), 1953, Prussian Academy pagination; *The Doctrine of Virtue*, trans. M. Gregor (New York: Harper & Row), 1964, Prussian Academy pagination; "Perpetual Peace" in *Kant's Political Writings*, ed. Hans Reiss, trans. H. B. Nisbet (Cambridge: Cambridge University Press, 1971).

3 For more detailed discussion of Kant's maxims see also Otfried Höffe, "Kant's kategorischer Imperativ als Kriterium des Sittlichen," *Zeitschrift für Philosophische Forschung*, Vol. 31, 1977, pp. 254–84 and O. O'Neill, "Consistency in Action," in *Morality and Universality: Essays on Ethical Universalizability*, ed. N. Potter and M. Timmons (Reidel, forthcoming). The most basic consideration is that maxims are underlying principles, by which subsidiary aspects of action are governed and orchestrated. They must often be inferred from these subsidiary aspects. Even when they are the maxims of individual action, they are not always accessible to consciousness. And some maxims are not maxims of individual agents, but the maxims of institutions or practices. Hence not all maxims are intentions. Nor are all intentions maxims, since trivial and superficial aspects of action are often intended. The Categorical Imperative provides only a test of maxims; but it doesn't follow that anything is permissible provided it is a nonfundamental aspect of action. Since maxims guide subsidiary aspects of action, the latter will be morally required (or forbidden) when they are indispensable (or incompatible) with what is needed to enact and embody a morally worthy maxim in a particular context. Only in drastic conditions will what would otherwise be deeply wrong be legitimated because needed to enact a morally worthy maxim. In wartime Poland Schindler could act on a maxim of protecting some Jews only by enslaving them and collaborating with the Nazis. Cf. Thomas Keneally, *Schindler's Ark* (Hodder & Stoughton, 1982). In prerevolutionary St. Petersburg Sonya Marmeladovna could support and sustain her family only by prostitution. It does not follow that such actions would be either permissible or required to enact fundamental principles of justice or of love outside such very special circumstances.

4 In more than one way. In this area remarkably exacting, but varied, conceptions of what constitutes evidence of dissent are put forward. Cf. Carole Pateman, "Women and Consent," *Political Theory*, Vol. 8 (1980): 149–68. Cf. also her discussion of some inadequacies of "consenting adult" accounts of prostitution, in "Defending Prostitution: Charges Against Ericsson," *Ethics* 93 (1983): 561–65.

5 See Thomas Hill, "Humanity as an End in Itself," *Ethics* 91 (1980–81): 84–99. Hill's analysis of the Formula of the End in Itself is acute and instructive. However, he suggests that it has the advantage that it needs no interpretation of the notion of a maxim (p. 91). But the question of whether we are using others, or treating them as persons, is as sensitive to how we describe what we are doing as the question whether what we propose could be universally done.

6 Hill construes "humanity" as "including only those powers necessarily associated with rationality and the 'power to set ends,' " ibid., p. 86. The reading offered here takes this point of departure but also stresses, as we must for instructive consideration of "wide" duties, that human rationality and autonomy are quite limited. Only so can we understand why Kant thinks both that others are limits, ends which are to be "conceived only negatively—that is, as an end against which we should never act" (*Groundwork*, p. 437), and that there are

autonomy are patently ... them if we assume that they are not and fail to support them. Cf. O. O'Neill, "Paternalism and Partial Autonomy," *Journal of Medical Ethics* 10 (1984): 173–78.

7 But what will count as a good resolution? One guideline might be this: the underlying principle of action should be one that subordinates sharing ends to leaving another with ends that can be shared. Hence only nonfundamental failures of respect may be part of loving action (e.g., presuming to make a minor arrangement or commitment for another which he or she will likely want made; Sonya Marmeladovna's sacrifice of self-respect out of love for her brothers and sisters); but where lack of respect is fundamental the supposedly loving action will cease to be so.

8 Cf. *Groundwork*, 397ff.; *The Doctrine of Virtue*, 218–20 and O. O'Neill, "Kant After Virtue," *Inquiry* 26 (1984): 387–405.

9 Contrary to a whole tradition of Kant commentary, Kant has a lot to say about the minor premise in practical reasoning, especially in *The Critique of Judgement*. For recent discussions see Hannah Arendt, *Lectures on Kant's Political Philosophy*, ed. Ronald Beiner (Chicago: University of Chicago Press, 1982); Beiner's interpretive essay in the same volume and his *Political Judgment* (London: Methuen, 1983); O. O'Neill, "The Power of Example," *Philosophy*, forthcoming.

10 By this I don't mean merely that sexual desire may include desires that refer to the other's sexual desires, but more broadly that at least some desires in intimate relationships are altruistic in the strict sense that they can be specified only by reference ... macy where desire ... than the fulfillment of the other's desires.

11 A sensitive element of the pattern of casuistry outlined here is determining which principles are the maxim(s) of a given action, and which ancillary. Here counterfactual considerations must always be introduced. We can reject claims that some principle of action is the maxim of a given act when we have reason to believe that, without fundamental changes either in circumstance or in moral outlook, that principle would not have been acted on. A claim to be acting out of friendship rather than disrespect in throwing a surprise party would be rebutted if the party would be thrown even when friendship would require other implementations (the friend is exhausted or ill or bereaved or shy). A claim that demands on another are not coercive but benevolent could be rebutted only if there are good reasons for thinking the actual refusal wholly neurotic, as well as that disregard of the refusal would benefit the refuser. Imposition of, for example, medical treatment or sexual attentions in the face of refusal could be fundamentally respectful and benevolent only if the coercion would be dropped given some evidence that the refusal is not entirely neurotic.

12 For an account of the nature of working life under modern "scientific" management practices, see, for example, Harry Braverman, *Labor and Monopoly Capital* (New York: Monthly Review Press, 1974). The changes he chronicles are not unique to capitalism.

Chapter 66

Thomas Nagel

DEATH

IF DEATH IS the unequivocal and permanent end of our existence, the question arises whether it is a bad thing to die.

There is conspicuous disagreement about the matter: some people think death is dreadful; others have no objection to death *per se*, though they hope their own will be neither premature nor painful. Those in the former category tend to think those in the latter are blind to the obvious, while the latter suppose the former to be prey to some sort of confusion. On the one hand it can be said that life is all we have and the loss of it is the greatest loss we can sustain. On the other hand it may be objected that death deprives this supposed loss of its subject, and that if we realize that death is not an unimaginable condition of the persisting person, but a mere blank, we will see that it can have no value whatever, positive or negative.

Since I want to leave aside the question whether we are, or might be, immortal in some form, I shall simply use the word 'death' and its cognates in this discussion to mean *permanent* death, unsupplemented by any form of conscious survival. I want to ask whether death is in itself an evil; and how great an evil, and of what kind, it might be. The question should be of interest even to those who believe in some form of immortality, for one's attitude toward immortality must depend in part on one's attitude toward death.

If death is an evil at all, it cannot be because of its positive features, but only because of what it deprives us of. I shall try to deal with the difficulties surrounding the natural view that death is an evil because it brings to an end all the goods that life contains. We need not give an account of these goods here, except to observe that, some of them, like perception, desire, activity, and thought, are so general as to be constitutive of human life. They are widely regarded as formidable benefits in themselves, despite the fact that they are conditions of misery as well as of happiness, and that a sufficient quantity of more particular evils can perhaps outweigh them. That is what is meant, I think, by the allegation that it is good simply to be alive, even if one is undergoing terrible experiences. The situation is roughly this: There are elements which, if added to one's experience, make life better; there are other elements which, if added to one's experience, make life worse. But what remains when these are set aside is not merely *neutral*: it is emphatically positive. Therefore life is worth living even when the bad elements of experience are plentiful, and the good ones too meager to outweigh the bad ones on their own. The additional positive weight is supplied by experience itself, rather than by any of its contents.

I shall not discuss the value that one person's life or death may have for others, or its objective value, but only the value it has for the person who is its subject. That seems to me the primary case, and the case which presents the greatest

First, the value of life and its content does not attach to mere organic survival: almost everyone would be indifferent (other things equal) between immediate death and immediate coma followed by death twenty years later without reawakening. And second, like most goods, this can be multiplied by time: more is better than less. The added quantities need not be temporally continuous (though continuity has its social advantages). People are attracted to the possibility of long-term suspended animation or freezing, followed by the resumption of conscious life, because they can regard it from within simply as a *continuation* of their present life. If these techniques are ever perfected, what from outside appeared as a dormant interval of three hundred years could be experienced by the subject as nothing more than a sharp discontinuity in the character of his experiences. I do not deny, of course, that this has its own disadvantages. Family and friends may have died in the meantime; the language may have changed; the comforts of social, geographical, and cultural familiarity would be lacking. Nevertheless these inconveniences would not obliterate the basic advantage of continued, though discontinuous, existence.

If we turn from what is good about life to what is bad about death, the case is completely different. Essentially, though there may be problems about their specification, what we find desirable in life are certain states, conditions, or types of activity. It is *being* alive, *doing* certain things, having certain experiences, that we consider good. But if death is an evil, it is the *loss of life*, rather than the state of being dead, or nonexistent, or unconscious, that is objectionable.[1] This asymmetry is important. If it is good to be alive, that advantage can be attributed to a person at each point of his life. It is a good of which Bach had more than Schubert, simply because he lived longer. Death, however, is not an evil of which Shakespeare has so far received a larger portion than Proust. If death is a disadvantage, it is not easy to say when a man

There are two other indications that we do not object to death merely because it involves long periods of nonexistence. First, as has been mentioned, most of us would not regard the *temporary* suspension of life, even for substantial intervals, as in itself a misfortune. If it ever happens that people can be frozen without reduction of the conscious lifespan, it will be inappropriate to pity those who are temporarily out of circulation. Second, none of us existed before we were born (or conceived), but few regard that as a misfortune. I shall have more to say about this later.

The point that death is not regarded as an unfortunate *state* enables us to refute a curious but very common suggestion about the origin of the fear of death. It is often said that those who object to death have made the mistake of trying to imagine what it is like to *be* dead. It is alleged that the failure to realize that this task is logically impossible (for the banal reason that there is nothing to imagine) leads to the conviction that death is a mysterious and therefore terrifying prospective *state*. But this diagnosis is evidently false, for it is just as impossible to imagine being totally unconscious as to imagine being dead (though it is easy enough to imagine oneself, from the outside, in either of those conditions). Yet people who are averse to death are not usually averse to unconsciousness (so long as it does not entail a substantial cut in the total duration of waking life).

If we are to make sense of the view that to die is bad, it must be on the ground that life is a good and death is the corresponding deprivation or loss, bad not because of any positive features but because of the desirability of what it removes. We must now turn to the serious difficulties which this hypothesis raises, difficulties about loss and privation in general, and about death in particular.

Essentially, there are three types of problem. First, doubt may be raised whether *anything* can

be bad for a man without being positively unpleasant to him: specifically, it may be doubted that there are any evils which consist merely in the deprivation or absence of possible goods, and which do not depend on someone's *minding* that deprivation. Second, there are special difficulties, in the case of death, about how the supposed misfortune is to be assigned to a subject at all. There is doubt both as to *who* its subject is, and as to *when* he undergoes it. So long as a person exists, he has not yet died, and once he has died, he no longer exists; so there seems to be no time when death, if it is a misfortune, can be ascribed to its unfortunate subject. The third type of difficulty concerns the asymmetry, mentioned above, between our attitudes to posthumous and prenatal nonexistence. How can the former be bad if the latter is not?

It should be recognized that if these are valid objections to counting death as an evil, they will apply to many other supposed evils as well. The first type of objection is expressed in general form by the common remark that what you don't know can't hurt you. It means that even if a man is betrayed by his friends, ridiculed behind his back, and despised by people who treat him politely to his face, none of it can be counted as a misfortune for him so long as he does not suffer as a result. It means that a man is not injured if his wishes are ignored by the executor of his will, or if, after his death, the belief becomes current that all the literary works on which his fame rests were really written by his brother, who died in Mexico at the age of 28. It seems to me worth asking what assumptions about good and evil lead to these drastic restrictions.

All the questions have something to do with time. There certainly are goods and evils of a simple kind (including some pleasures and pains) which a person possesses at a given time simply in virtue of his condition at that time. But this is not true of all the things we regard as good or bad for a man. Often we need to know his history to tell whether something is a misfortune

or not; this applies to ills like deterioration, deprivation, and damage. Sometimes his experiential *state* is relatively unimportant – as in the case of a man who wastes his life in the cheerful pursuit of a method of communicating with asparagus plants. Someone who holds that all goods and evils must be temporally assignable states of the person may of course try to bring difficult cases into line by pointing to the pleasure or pain that more complicated goods and evils cause. Loss, betrayal, deception, and ridicule are on this view bad because people suffer when they learn of them. But it should be asked how our ideas of human value would have to be constituted to accommodate these cases directly instead. One advantage of such an account might be that it would enable us to explain *why* the discovery of these misfortunes causes suffering – in a way that makes it reasonable. For the natural view is that the discovery of betrayal makes us unhappy because it is bad to be betrayed – not that betrayal is bad because its discovery makes us unhappy.

It therefore seems to me worth exploring the position that most good and ill fortune has as its subject a person identified by his history and his possibilities, rather than merely by his categorical state of the moment – and that while this subject can be exactly located in a sequence of places and times, the same is not necessarily true of the goods and ills that befall him.[2]

These ideas can be illustrated by an example of deprivation whose severity approaches that of death. Suppose an intelligent person receives a brain injury that reduces him to the mental condition of a contented infant, and that such desires as remain to him can be satisfied by a custodian, so that he is free from care. Such a development would be widely regarded as a severe misfortune, not only for his friends and relations, or for society, but also, and primarily, for the person himself. This does not mean that a contented infant is unfortunate. The intelligent adult who has been *reduced* to this condition is the subject of the misfortune. He is the one we

condition – there is some doubt, in fact, where he can be said to exist any longer.

The view that such a man has suffered a misfortune is open to the same objections which have been raised in regard to death. He does not mind his condition. It is in fact the same condition he was in at the age of three months, except that he is bigger. If we did not pity him then, why pity him now; in any case, who is there to pity? The intelligent adult has disappeared, and for a creature like the one before us, happiness consists in a full stomach and a dry diaper.

If these objections are invalid, it must be because they rest on a mistaken assumption about the temporal relation between the subject of a misfortune and the circumstances which constitute it. If, instead of concentrating exclusively on the oversized baby before us, we consider the person he was, and the person he could be now, then his reduction to this state and the cancellation of his natural adult development constitute a perfectly intelligible catastrophe.

This case should convince us that it is arbitrary to restrict the goods and evils that can befall a man to nonrelational properties ascribable to him at particular times. As it stands, that restriction excludes not only such cases of gross degeneration, but also a good deal of what is important about success and failure, and other features of a life that have the character of processes. I believe we can go further, however. There are goods and evils which are irreducibly relational; they are features of the relations between a person, with spatial and temporal boundaries of the usual sort, and circumstances which may not coincide with him either in space or in time. A man's life includes much that does not take place within the boundaries of his body and his mind, and what happens to him can include much that does not take place within the boundaries of his life. These boundaries are commonly crossed by the misfortunes of being deceived, or despised, or betrayed. (If this is correct, there is a simple account of what is wrong with breaking a deathbed promise. It is it is possible to regard time as just another type of distance.). The case of mental degeneration shows us an evil that depends on a contrast between the reality and the possible alternatives. A man is the subject of good and evil as much because he has hopes which may or may not be fulfilled, or possibilities which may or may not be realized, as because of his capacity to suffer and enjoy. If death is an evil, it must be accounted for in these terms, and the impossibility of locating it within life should not trouble us.

When a man dies we are left with his corpse, and while a corpse can suffer the kind of mishap that may occur to an article of furniture, it is not a suitable object for pity. The man, however, is. He has lost his life, and if he had not died, he would have continued to live it, and to possess whatever good there is in living. If we apply to death the account suggested for the case of dementia, we shall say that although the spatial and temporal locations of the individual who suffered the loss are clear enough, the misfortune itself cannot be so easily located. One must be content just to state that his life is over and there will never be any more of it. That fact, rather than his past or present condition, constitutes his misfortune, if it is one. Nevertheless if there is a loss, someone must suffer it, and he must have existence and specific spatial and temporal location even if the loss itself does not. The fact that Beethoven had no children may have been a cause of regret to him, or a sad thing for the world, but it cannot be described as a misfortune for the children that he never had. All of us, I believe, are fortunate to have been born. But unless good and ill can be assigned to an embryo, or even to an unconnected pair of gametes, it cannot be said that not to be born is a misfortune. (That is a factor to be considered in deciding whether abortion and contraception are akin to murder.)

This approach also provides a solution to the problem of temporal asymmetry, pointed out by

Lucretius. He observed that no one finds it disturbing to contemplate the eternity preceding his own birth, and he took this to show that it must be irrational to fear death, since death is simply the mirror image of the prior abyss. That is not true, however, and the difference between the two explains why it is reasonable to regard them differently. It is true that both the time before a man's birth and the time after his death are times when he does not exist. But the time after his death is time of which his death deprives him. It is time in which, had he not died then, he would be alive. Therefore any death entails the loss of *some* life that its victim would have led had he not died at that or any earlier point. We know perfectly well what it would be for him to have had it instead of losing it, and there is no difficulty in identifying the loser.

But we cannot say that the time prior to a man's birth is time in which he would have lived had he been born not then but earlier. For aside from the brief margin permitted by premature labor, he *could* not have been born earlier: anyone born substantially earlier than he was would have been someone else. Therefore the time prior to his birth is not time in which his subsequent birth prevents him from living. His birth, when it occurs, does not entail the loss to him of any life whatever.

The direction of time is crucial in assigning possibilities to people or other individuals. Distinct possible lives of a single person can diverge from a common beginning, but they cannot converge to a common conclusion from diverse beginnings. (The latter would represent not a set of different possible lives of one individual, but a set of distinct possible individuals, whose lives have identical conclusions.) Given an identifiable individual, countless possibilities for his continued existence are imaginable, and we can clearly conceive of what it would be for him to go on existing indefinitely. However inevitable it is that this will not come about, its possibility is still that of the continuation of

a good for him, if life is the good we take it to be.[3]

We are left, therefore, with the question whether the nonrealization of this possibility is in every case a misfortune, or whether it depends on what can naturally be hoped for. This seems to me the most serious difficulty with the view that death is always an evil. Even if we can dispose of the objections against admitting misfortune that is not experienced, or cannot be assigned to a definite time in the person's life, we still have to set some limits on *how* possible a possibility must be for its nonrealization to be a misfortune (or good fortune, should the possibility be a bad one). The death of Keats at 24 is generally regarded as tragic; that of Tolstoy at 82 is not. Although they will both be dead for ever, Keats' death deprived him of many years of life which were allowed to Tolstoy; so in a clear sense Keats' loss was greater (though not in the sense standardly employed in mathematical comparison between infinite quantities). However, this does not prove that Tolstoy's loss was insignificant. Perhaps we record an objection only to evils which are gratuitously added to the inevitable; the fact that it is worse to die at 24 than at 82 does not imply that it is not a terrible thing to die at 82, or even at 806. The question is whether we can regard as a misfortune any limitation, like mortality, that is normal to the species. Blindness or near-blindness is not a misfortune for a mole, nor would it be for a man, if that were the natural condition of the human race.

The trouble is that life familiarizes us with the goods of which death deprives us. We are already able to appreciate them, as a mole is not able to appreciate vision. If we put aside doubts about their status as goods and grant that their quantity is in part a function of their duration, the question remains whether death, no matter when it occurs, can be said to deprive its victim, of what is in the relevant sense a possible continuation of life.

The situation is an ambiguous one. Observed from without, human beings obviously have a

a hundred years. A man's sense of his own existence, on the other hand, does not embody this idea of a natural limit. His existence defines for him an essentially open-ended possible future, containing the usual mixture of goods and evils that he has found so tolerable in the past. Having been gratuitously introduced to the world by a collection of natural, historical, and social accidents, he finds himself the subject of a life, with an indeterminate and not essentially limited future. Viewed in this way, death, no matter how inevitable, is an abrupt cancellation of indefinitely extensive possible goods. Normality seems to have nothing to do with it, for the fact that we will all inevitably die in a few score years cannot by itself imply that it would not be good to live longer. Suppose that we were all inevitably going to die in *agony* – physical agony lasting six months. Would inevitability make *that* prospect any less unpleasant? And why should it be different for a deprivation? If the normal lifespan were a thousand years, death at 80 would be a tragedy. As things are, it may just be a more widespread tragedy. If there is no limit to the amount of life that it would be good to have, then it may be that a bad end is in store for us all.

Notes

1   It is sometimes suggested that what we really mind is the process of *dying*. But I should not really object to dying if it were not followed by death.

2   It is certainly not true in general of the things that can be said of him. For example, Abraham Lincoln was taller than Louis XIV. But when?

3   I confess to being troubled by the above argument, for the same reason that makes it hard to explain the simple difference between prenatal and posthumous nonexistence. For this reason I suspect that something essential is omitted from the account of the badness of death by an analysis which treats it as a deprivation of possibilities. My suspicion is supported by the following suggestion of Robert Nozick. We could imagine discovering that people developed from individual spores that had existed indefinitely far in advance of their birth. In this fantasy, birth never occurs naturally more than a hundred years before the permanent end of the spore's existence. But then we discover a way to trigger the premature hatching of these spores, and people are born who have thousands of years of active life before them. Given such a situation, it would be possible to imagine *oneself* having come into existence thousands of years previously. If we put aside the question whether this would really be the same person, even given the identity of the spore, then the consequence appears to be that a person's birth at a given time *could* deprive *him* of many earlier years of possible life. Now while it would be cause for regret that one had been deprived of all those possible years of life by being born too late, the feeling would differ from that which many people have about death. I conclude that something about the future *prospect* of permanent nothingness is not captured by the analysis in terms of denied possibilities. If so, then Lucretius' argument still awaits an answer. I suspect that it requires a general treatment of the difference between past and future in our attitudes toward our own lives. Our attitudes toward past and future pain are very different, for example. Derek Parfit's unpublished writings on this topic have revealed its difficulty to me.

Index

Ethics: Essential Readings in Moral Theory

Ethics: Essential Readings in Moral Theory is an outstanding anthology of the most important topics, theories, and debates in ethics, compiled by one of the leading experts in the field. It includes 66 readings covering the central domains of ethics:

- why be moral?
- the meaning of moral language
- morality and objectivity
- consequentialism
- deontology
- virtue and character
- value and well-being
- moral psychology
- applications: including abortion, famine relief, and consent.

Included are both classical extracts from Plato, Aristotle, Hume, Kant, and Mill as well as contemporary classics from philosophers such as Thomas Nagel, Thomas Scanlon, Martha Nussbaum, Derek Parfit, and Peter Singer.

A key feature of the anthology is that it covers the perennial topics in ethics as well as very recent ones, such as moral psychology, responsibility, and experimental philosophy. Each section is introduced and placed in context by the editor, making this an ideal anthology for anyone studying ethics or ethical theory.

George Sher is Herbert S. Autrey Professor of Philosophy at Rice University. He is the author of five books: *Desert* (Princeton), *Beyond Neutrality: Perfectionism and Politics* (Cambridge), *Approximate Justice: Studies in Non-Ideal Theory* (Rowman and Littlefield), *In Praise of Blame* (Oxford), and *Who Knew? Responsibility Without Awareness* (Oxford). His current project is a book with the working title *Equality for Inegalitarians*.